lonely planet

# Zimbabwe, Botswana & Namibia

**Deanna Swaney**

**Zimbabwe, Botswana & Namibia**

**3rd edition**

**Published by**
   **Lonely Planet Publications**
   Head Office:    PO Box 617, Hawthorn, Vic 3122, Australia
   Branches:       150 Linden Street, Oakland, CA 94607, USA
                   10a Spring Place, London NW5 3BH, UK
                   1 rue du Dahomey, 75011 Paris, France

**Printed by**
   SNP Printing Pte Ltd, Singapore

**Photographs**
   Most of the images in this guide are available for licensing from Lonely Planet Images.
   email: lpi@lonelyplanet.com.au

   Safari Guide images supplied by Lonely Planet Images and ABPL Image Library.

   Front cover: Textile with traditional designs printed at Hands-On Zimbabwe Studio,
                Mutare, Zimbabwe (Jean-Bernard Carillet)

**First Published**
   February 1992

**This Edition**
   January 1999

**Although the authors and publisher have tried to make the information as
accurate as possible, they accept no responsibility for any loss, injury or
inconvenience sustained by any person using this book.**

National Library of Australia Cataloguing in Publication Data

Swaney, Deanna.
   Zimbabwe, Botswana & Namibia.

   3rd ed.
   Includes index.
   ISBN 0 86442 545 7.

   1. Zimbabwe – Guidebooks. 2. Botswana – Guidebooks.
   3. Namibia – Guidebooks. I. Title.

916.8

text & maps © Lonely Planet 1999
photos © photographers as indicated 1999

## Deanna Swaney

After completing university studies Deanna made a shoestring tour of Europe and has been addicted to travel ever since. Despite an erstwhile career in computer programming, she avoided encroaching yuppiedom in midtown Anchorage, Alaska, by making a break for South America, where she wrote Lonely Planet's *Bolivia* guide. Subsequent travels led through a circuit of island paradises – Arctic and tropical – and resulted in three more guides: *Tonga*, *Samoa* and *Iceland, Greenland & the Faroe Islands*.

She returned to dry land for the first edition of this book and has since worked on Lonely Planet's *Brazil*, *Mauritius, Réunion & Seychelles*, *Madagascar & Comoros* and *Africa – the South* guides, and contributed to shoestring guides to Africa, South America and Scandinavia.

She now divides her time between travelling and her home base in Alaska's Susitna Valley, and has most recently worked on the new guide to *Norway*.

## From the Author

I'd like to thank Annemarie Byrne of Hendon, UK, for her hospitality and enduring love of Africa. Mike & Anna Scott of Khangela Safaris, Bulawayo, provided the optimum possible perspective of their country. I'm also grateful to Laura Campbell, for her useful Zimbabwean history update, and to Margaret Moyo, for her linguistic expertise and help with both Shona and Ndebele. Jennifer McGaw, Ernst & Norbert Schürer and Jean-Marie Bayle were excellent and supportive travel companions, and Norbert Schürer also provided an enlightening and thoroughly researched rundown of Namibian literature and the politics of all three countries, and helped with the music section for Zimbabwe.

Thanks also to Irene Sharp for insight on Zimbabwean conservation issues; Russell & Colleen Pumfrey, for their boundless hospitality and a great day at Inanke Cave; Sue & Frans van der Merwe, for turning a vehicular crisis into one of the best experiences imaginable; Karen, Mike & Natalie Magee, Bulawayo, for continuing support; Colin McVey & Cecilia Mooketsi, Gaborone, for their down-to-earth views and language expertise; Alex at Travellers' Inn, Bulawayo, for ongoing encouragement; Aulden & Rachel Harlech-Jones, for lots of Windhoek Lager, mopane worm combat, invaluable assistance, Windhoek diversions and lots of new info; Fred Peterson, for updates on malaria and other horrible tropical ailments; Erwin, for spiritual inspiration; Chris Tragner for good company in the Tsodilo Hills; and Paul Quinn, for Livingstone updates.

Thanks also to Mike Godfrey of Crazy Kudu Safaris for organising the mother of all Namibian safaris; Steve Caballero of Phakawe Safaris for a long-anticipated return to the Tsodilo Hills; Brett Saunders and Dave Sandenberg, for creating Paradise on Earth at Katombora Rapids; Hans & Valerie van der Heiden, for their enduring friendship and commitment to budget travellers in upmarket Kariba; Dr Jennifer McGaw and Dr Fred Peterson, for researching and writing up way, way, way too much on veterinary and conservation issues; Marie Holstensen & Grant Burton, for their long-standing friendship and insights; John Berry at The Zambezi Safari & Travel Co, for an afternoon of the latest information on Kariba; Elaine and Shirley at the Manicaland Publicity Association, for Zimbabwe's best-organised tourist information office; Jane & Dee in Chimanimani, for invaluable local information and for making time for me at a most inopportune moment; John Egan in Harare for helpful last-minute updates; Joan Leaver at Audi Camp, Maun; and Karl Zdero (Australia) who had insightful suggestions on Harare and the Eastern Highlands.

I'm also grateful to Marisa Mowszowski of Melbourne, Australia and Paul Novitski of Dandemutande in Seattle, who contributed their expertise to the Zimbabwe music section.

Thanks also to David Else, UK, for input on Zambia; George Monbiot, UK, for direction on conservation issues; Val Bell in Bulawayo, for her continuing efforts; Bruce & Iris Brinson in Masvingo, for their faith in and commitment to backpackers; Wimpie & Marietjie Otto, Grootfontein, for introducing their creative spirit to the Namibian tourist scene; Dr Daniel Okeyo at the University of Namibia for his study of the proposed Kunene dam; Michelle at Penduka, near Windhoek, for updates on that worthwhile enterprise; and also to Tony Wheeler, Geoff Crowther and Charlotte Hindle for their useful suggestions, ideas and updates.

For their continuing tolerance and support, the best of my love and wishes go to Dave Dault (Anchorage); Earl, Dean, Kimberley and Jennifer Swaney (Fresno); and Keith & Holly Hawkings (Anchorage). I'd also like to convey love and best wishes to Robert Strauss, for his talent and commitment to publishing excellence.

### From the Publisher
This third edition of *Zimbabwe, Botswana & Namibia* was edited in Lonely Planet's London office by Tim Ryder and David Rathborne, with assistance from Rick Bouwman. Corinne Simcock, David Rathborne, Paul Bloomfield and Christine Stroyan did the proofing. Dale Buckton co-ordinated the mapping and design, and was assisted by David Wenk, Michelle Lewis, Tom Fawcett and Caro Sahanouk. Kylie Smerdon drew the illustrations, and most of the photographs were supplied by Lonely Planet Images.

Thanks to Isabelle Young for her help with the Health section, to Quentin Frayne for the language sections, and to Leonie Mugavin, Sacha Pearson, Sarah Mathers and Wendy Bashford for additional research. Thanks also to Sam Carew, Cathy Lanigan, Michelle Lewis, Katrina Browning and Charlotte Hindle for their advice and assistance.

### This Book
The first edition of *Zimbabwe, Botswana & Namibia* was written by Deanna Swaney and Myra Shackley. This new edition was thoroughly updated by Deanna Swaney. The Safari Guide was originally written by Hugh Finlay, Geoff Crowther, Deanna Swaney and Myra Shackley; the original bird section was written by David Andrew. For this edition the guide was revised and rewritten by Andrew MacColl.

### Thanks
Special thanks to all those readers who used the last edition of this guide and found the time and energy to write to us with their suggestions and comments. You'll find their names listed on page 814.

### Warning & Request
Things change – prices go up, schedules change, good places go bad and bad places go bankrupt – nothing stays the same. So, if you find things better or worse, recently opened or long since closed, please tell us and help make the next edition even more accurate and useful.

We value all of the feedback we receive from travellers. Julie Young co-ordinates a small team who read and acknowledge every letter, postcard and email, and ensure that every morsel of information finds its way to the appropriate authors, editors and publishers.

Everyone who writes to us will find their name in the next edition of the appropriate guide and will also receive a free subscription to our quarterly newsletter, *Planet Talk*. The very best contributions will be rewarded with a free Lonely Planet guide.

Excerpts from your correspondence may appear in new editions of this guide; in our newsletter, *Planet Talk*; or in updates on our Web site – so please let us know if you don't want your letter published or your name acknowledged.

# Contents

# Map Indexes

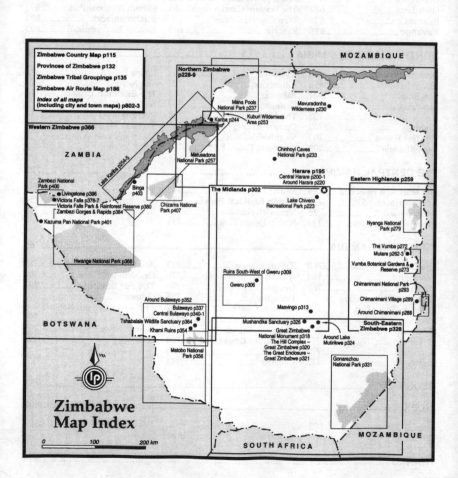

Zimbabwe Country Map p115
Provinces of Zimbabwe p132
Zimbabwe Tribal Groupings p135
Zimbabwe Air Route Map p186
*Index of all maps
(including city and town maps) p802-3*

MOZAMBIQUE

Northern Zimbabwe p228-9

Western Zimbabwe p366

Mana Pools National Park p237

Mavuradonha Wilderness p230

Kuburi Wilderness Area p253

Kariba p244

ZAMBIA

Matusadona National Park p257

Chinhoyi Caves National Park p233

Zambezi National Park p400

Livingstone p396
Victoria Falls p376-7
Victoria Falls Park & Rainforest Reserve p380
Zambezi Gorges & Rapids p384

Kazuma Pan National Park p401

Binga p403

Chizarira National Park p407

Harare p195
Central Harare p200-1
Around Harare p220

The Midlands p302

Lake Chivero Recreational Park p223

Eastern Highlands p259

Nyanga National Park p279

Hwange National Park p368

Ruins South-West of Gweru p309

Gweru p306

Masvingo p313

The Vumba p272
Mutare p262-3
Vumba Botanical Gardens & Reserve p273

Chimanimani National Park p293

Chimanimani Village p289

Around Chimanimani p288

Around Bulawayo p352
Bulawayo p337
Central Bulawayo p340-1
Tshabalala Wildlife Sanctuary p364
Khami Ruins p354

Mushandika Sanctuary p326

South-Eastern Zimbabwe p328

Great Zimbabwe National Monument p318
The Hill Complex – Great Zimbabwe p320
The Great Enclosure – Great Zimbabwe p321

Around Lake Mutirikwe p324

BOTSWANA

Matobo National Park p356

Gonarezhou National Park p331

Zimbabwe Map Index

0      100      200 km

BOTSWANA

SOUTH AFRICA

MOZAMBIQUE

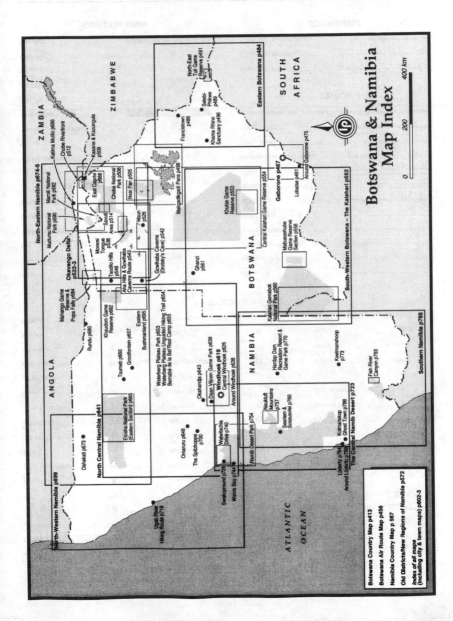

# Botswana & Namibia Map Index

**ZAMBIA**

**ZIMBABWE**

Katima Mulilo p686
Chobe Riverfront p512
Kasane & Kazungula p509
North-Eastern Namibia p674-5
East Caprivi p688
Chobe National Park p508
North-East Tuli Game Reserve p491
Mamili National Park p692
Nxai Pan p505
Mudumu National Park p690
Francistown p486
Savuti Area p514
Selebi-Phikwe p489
Makgadikgadi Pans p498
Khama Rhino Sanctuary p496
Moremi Tongue p538
Maun p526
Okavango Delta p532-3
Tsodilo Hills p548
Aba Hills & Gcwihaba Caverns Route p543
Gcwihaba Caverns (Drotsky's Cave) p542
Mahango Game Reserve & Popa Falls p664
Gaborone p467
Lobatse p481
Around Gaborone p475
Rundu p680
Ghanzi p561
Khutse Game Reserve p553
Central Kalahari Game Reserve p554
Khaudom Game Reserve p682
Groetfontein p657
Tsumeb p660
**ANGOLA**
Waterberg Plateau Park p653
Waterberg Plateau Unguided Hiking Trail p654
Bernabe de la Bat Rest Camp p655
Eastern Bushmanland p695
**BOTSWANA**
Mabuasehube Game Reserve Section p558
Oshakati p673
Etosha National Park (Eastern Section) p665
**North Central Namibia p641**
Kalahari Gemsbok National Park p560
South-Western Botswana – The Kalahari p552
Eastern Botswana p484
**SOUTH AFRICA**
Okahandja p643
Daan Viljoen Game Park p639
Windhoek p619
Central Windhoek p626
Around Windhoek p638
Omaruru p648
The Spitzkoppe p700
Hardap Dam Recreation Resort & Game Park p770
**NAMIBIA**
Keetmanshoop p773
Welwitschia Drive p740
Naukluft Mountains p757
Fish River Canyon p793
Sesriem & Sossusvlei p760
Namib Desert Park p754
**North-Western Namibia p699**
Ugab River Hiking Route p719
Swakopmund p728
Walvis Bay p744
Kolmanskop p784
Lüderitz p784
Around Lüderitz p788
Ghost Town p788
**The Central Namib Desert p723**
**Southern Namibia p766**
Fish River Canyon p793

**ATLANTIC OCEAN**

0    200    400 km

Botswana Country Map p413
Botswana Air Route Map p456
Namibia Country Map p 567
Old Districts/New Regions of Namibia p572
Index of all maps
(including city and town maps) p802-3

# Map Legend

## BOUNDARIES

............... International Boundary
................. Provincial Boundary
................. Regional Boundary

## ROUTES

A25 ..... Freeway, with Route Number
............................ Major Road
............................ Minor Road
............ Minor Road – Unsealed
................................. City Road
................................ City Street
.................................. City Lane
.................................. 4WD Track
.......................... Walking Track
..............Railway, with Station
................................ Ferry Route
...................................... Fence

## AREA FEATURES

...................................Building
...................................Cemetery
.........................................Park
.......................................Market
...........................Pedestrian Mall
.............................. Urban Area
............. Desert or Sand Dunes
......................................Rocks
..........................Mountain Range

## HYDROGRAPHIC FEATURES

....................................Coastline
...............................Creek, River
......................... Rapids, Waterfalls
.........Lake, Intermittent Lake
......................Salt Lake or Pan
...................................... Swamp

## SYMBOLS

| | | | | | |
|---|---|---|---|---|---|
| ✪ **CAPITAL** | ......... National Capital | ⚲ | ...... Border Crossing | 🄿 | .................... Parking |
| ● **CITY** | ........................ City | ♜ | .................... Castle | )( | .................... Pass |
| ● **Town** | ........................ Town | ⌒ | .................... Cave | ⓟ | ........... Petrol Station |
| ● Village | ........................ Village | ⛪ | ..... Church or Chapel | ▣ | .............. Picnic Area |
| ■ | ............... Place to Stay | ⌣⌣⌣ | .... Cliff or Escarpment | ★ | .......... Police Station |
| Å | ...... Camping Ground | ⬭ | ................. Depression | ✉ | .............. Post Office |
| ⌂ | ....................... Hut | ○ | .................. Embassy | ☀ | ........ Scenic Lookout |
| ▼ | ............... Place to Eat | ✿ | .................. Garden | ☒ | .............. Shipwreck |
| ☗ | ............... Pub or Bar | ⚑ | .............. Golf Course | ❖ | ....... Shopping Centre |
| ✈ ✛ | .......... Airport, Airfield | ⊕ | .................. Hospital | ◎ | .................... Spring |
| ⌒ | ... Ancient or City Wall | ⊛ | .................. Kraal | ▭ | ....... Swimming Pool |
| ∴ | ... Archaeological Site | 🗼 | ............... Lighthouse | ☎ | .............. Telephone |
| ⊖ | ...................... Bank | ✕ | .................. Mine | ☉ | ...................... Toilet |
| ⸖ | ............... Bird Sanctuary | ⚑ | ............ Monument | ⓘ | ....Tourist Information |
| | | ▲ | ......... Mountain or Hill | ⊝ | ................. Transport |
| | | 🏛 | .................. Museum | 🄿 | ........ Wildlife Lookout |
| | | ⚓ | ............ National Park | 🗙 | .................... Windmill |

*Note: not all symbols displayed above appear in this book*

# Introduction

Forming an east-west band across southern Africa, Zimbabwe, Botswana and Namibia are three distinctly different countries, each with its own unique topography, government and people. Some of today's visitors may have first known them as Rhodesia, Bechuanaland and South West Africa, but over the past four decades all have emerged as independent nations and in shedding their colonial governments they've also assumed new identities.

Zimbabwe is the most populated and perhaps best known of the three. The name is still associated with the violent war and subsequent uprisings that resulted in its break from the racially unethical Rhodesian regime and the establishment of majority government. Nevertheless, it has now been

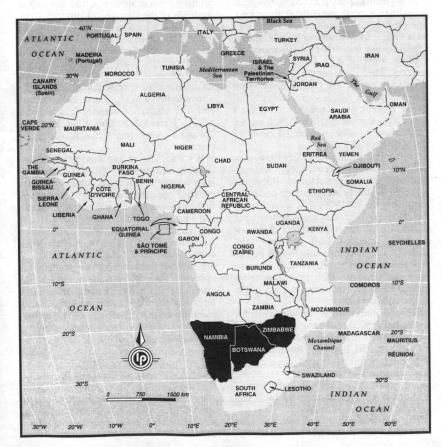

independent for nearly two decades and has enjoyed a stable peace for nearly as long.

While it's not without problems, friendly and easy-going Zimbabwe is a beautiful and relatively safe country that caters to all budgets from shoestring to Sheraton. Zimbabweans have accomplished wonders with their world-famous music, sculpture and traditional crafts and their bright cities of Harare and Bulawayo boast a range of museums, parks, markets, restaurants and nightclubs and provide havens from the uncertainties of African travel.

Away from the cities, Zimbabwe presents a wealth of natural and cultural attractions. The greatest crowd puller is of course Victoria Falls, but Zimbabwe also has equally appealing but less visited destinations, including some of Africa's finest wildlife reserves. Then there are the lovely Eastern Highlands – more like Canada or Scotland than archetypal Africa – and the ruins of Great Zimbabwe, sub-Saharan Africa's greatest ancient capital. In the south are the extraordinary rocks and painted caves of Matobo National Park.

To the west of Zimbabwe lies Botswana, truly an African success story. A long-neglected British protectorate, Botswana achieved its timely independence under democratic rule in 1966, and immediately thereafter discovered in the Kalahari three of the world's most productive diamond-bearing formations. Both politically and ideologically, it enjoys enlightened nonracial policies and health, educational and economic standards that, apart from those in South Africa, are unequalled anywhere on the continent.

Beyond the narrow eastern corridor where the capital, Gaborone, and most of the population, transport and development are concentrated, Botswana is a country for the more intrepid traveller. A largely roadless wilderness of vast spaces – savannas, desert, wetlands and saltpans – and myriad traditional villages, it requires time and effort to enjoy to the fullest.

All its economic success has put Botswana – also rich in wildlife, artistic tradition and natural appeal – in a unique situation. In response to the need to preserve the country's natural assets and still derive the benefits of tourism, the government has embraced a policy of courting only high-cost, low-impact tourism. As a result, the best of Botswana is inaccessible to shoestring travellers. Mid-range budgets are accommodated in places by relatively inexpensive camp sites, but there are no concessions to the impecunious. Having said that, you'll still find some reasonably priced options for visiting the country's primary tourist attraction, the anomalous wetlands of the Okavango Delta.

Namibia, which gained its independence in 1990, lies wedged between the Kalahari and the chilly South Atlantic, and is a country of practically unlimited potential and promise. Rich in natural resources and unquestionably spectacular beauty, it has also inherited a solid, modern infrastructure and a diversity of cultures and national origins: Herero, San, Khoi-Khoi, Kavango, Owambo, Afrikaner, German, Asian and others.

It's also safe to say that Namibia's attractions are unparalleled anywhere. Well known only in southern Africa, its bush-walking opportunities, rugged seascapes, European and African cities and villages – and nearly unlimited elbow room – have only recently been discovered by outsiders. Along the coast stretches the Namib Desert with its brilliant red dunes and the surprising oasis of Sossusvlei. In the south is the immense Fish River Canyon, and in the north are the wild Skeleton Coast, the forests of the Caprivi, the mysterious rock paintings of the Brandberg and the colourful desert ranges and traditional cultures of Damaraland and Kaokoland.

Beyond Etosha National Park, Africa's largest wildlife reserve, Namibia also hosts a whimsical array of floral and faunal oddities – where else, for example, would you come across a 'dead' plant that has lived for around 1200 years, or beaches shared by antelope, flamingoes, penguins, sea lions and ostrich!

# Facts about the Region

## HISTORY
### Prehistory

Southern Africa's human history extends back through the millennia to the first rumblings of humanity on the planet, and the countries covered in this book contain an archaeological record dating back to the world's earliest human inhabitants. In geological time, the last two million years or so comprise the Pleistocene era – the last ice age – and, although no ice reached southern Africa, its effects were apparent in a series of climatic shifts which set the stage for human evolution.

Continuing controversy among scholars makes it difficult to state categorically who evolved into whom, but most accept that the earliest human-like creatures were a group of upright-walking hominids, who became established nearly four million years ago in the savannas of southern and eastern Africa. At least one advanced variety of these small creatures eventually developed rudimentary tool-making abilities around 1.3 million years ago, allowing them to hunt rather than just scavenge for food. This, combined with a series of climatic changes in the region (alternating wet or dry trends lasting thousands of years each) preceded an increase in brain size, changes in body form and a growing population.

The next clearly identifiable stage is an early form of human called *Homo erectus* or 'man who stands upright', whose camps and stone tools are found scattered throughout the region. One archaeological site in the Namib Desert provides evidence that these early people were hunting the ancestors of present-day elephants and butchering their remains with stone hand-axes as early as 750,000 years ago. The tools of the era were large and clumsy, but by 150,000 years ago, people were using lighter stone points, projectile heads, knives, saws and other finer tools useful for various hunting and gathering activities.

By the southern African middle Stone Age, which lasted until 20,000 years ago, the Boskop people, the primary human group in southern Africa, had progressed into an organised hunting and gathering society. These people are the presumed ancestors of the present-day San (traditionally known as Bushmen, although there is some controversy over the use of this name nowadays). Use of fire was universal, tools – made from wood and animal products as well as stone – had become more sophisticated, and natural pigments were being used for personal adornment. Artefacts from middle Stone Age sites in the Namib Desert suggest that certain nomadic groups hunted only particular species.

Between 20,000 and 30,000 years ago, southern Africans made sudden and significant progress in their standard of tool manufacture. Tools became smaller and better designed and this greatly increased hunting efficiency and allowed time for further innovation and artistic pursuits. This stage is known as the microlithic revolution because it was characterised by small-flake working of microliths, or small stones. In some caves and rock shelters, particularly in Namibia's Brandberg mountains, several metres of archaeological deposits from this period have been discovered revealing clear evidence of food gathering, consumption of shellfish and working of wood, bone and ostrich eggshell beads.

Not all late Stone Age people used microliths, however, and although some believe they were ancestors of the modern Khoisan groups – San (Bushmen) and Khoi-Khoi (Hottentot or Nama) – this isn't certain. What is well substantiated is that from around 8000 BC, the hunting and gathering people of the late Stone Age began producing pottery and occupied rock shelters and caves throughout the southern African region.

The artistic traditions and material crafts

## Ancient Rock Art

Many visitors to southern Africa have the privilege to see examples of ancient rock paintings. There's a lot of speculation about the origins of these paintings, but no way of dating them reliably without destroying them. Thanks to deposits left in painted caves and scenes depicted in the paintings themselves, it's surmised that the artists were nomadic hunter-gatherers, without knowledge of agriculture or pottery. For that reason, it's assumed that these wilderness art galleries are the work of early San people.

As one would expect, most rock painting reflected people's relationship with nature. Some were stylised representations but the majority faithfully and skilfully portray the people and animals of the region: hunters, giraffe, elephant, rhino, lion, antelope and so on in red, yellow, brown and ochre.

Common themes include the roles of men and women, hunting scenes and natural medicine. This last includes examples of trance dancing and spiritual healing using the San life force, known as *nxum*, which was invoked to control aspects of the natural world, including climate and disease. All these things still feature in San tradition.

It has been speculated that, as with similar cave art found in various places in Europe, the animal paintings were intended to ensure an abundance of those animals. However, this concept hasn't been noted in any present-day African culture, and there's no evidence of ancient ties with Europe. Furthermore, few of the animals portrayed served as food for the ancient San.

Although the earliest works have long faded, flaked and eroded into oblivion, the dry climate and their normal location in sheltered granite overhangs have preserved many of the more recent ones. Anthropological studies have used the content, skill level and superposition of the paintings to identify three distinct stages.

The earliest paintings seem to reflect a period of gentle nomadism during which people were occupied primarily with the hunt. Later works suggest peaceful incursions by outside groups, perhaps Bantu or Khoisan (from whom the San and Khoi-Khoi/Nama are descended). During this stage, many significant paintings were produced, revealing great artistic improvement.

The final stage indicates a decline in the standard of the paintings; either a loss of interest in, and facility with, the genre or imitation of earlier works by newly arrived peoples. For the archaeologist, there are considerable difficulties in relating the paintings to the cultural sequences preserved in soil layers of caves and rock shelters, but recent advances in radiocarbon dating are beginning to shed some light.

The red pigments were ground mainly from iron oxides, which were powdered and mixed with animal fat to form an adhesive paste. The whites came from silica, powdered quartz and white clays and were by nature less adhesive than the red pigments. For that reason, white paintings survive only in sheltered locations, such as well protected caves. Both pigments were applied to the rock using sticks, the artist's fingers and brushes made from animal hair.

The most poignant thing about rock art is that it remains in the spot where it was created. Unlike in a museum, sensitive viewers may catch a glimpse of the inspiration that went into the paintings. The best place to see rock art in Zimbabwe is undoubtedly Matobo National Park. Almost as good are Domboshawa and Ngomakurira, both north of Harare. There are also several sites around Mutoko, Lake Mutirikwe and Lake Chivero, as well as scattered in rock overhangs all around the country. Botswana also has numerous examples, the most renowned of which are found at the Tsodilo Hills.

Many of the detailed animal engravings at Twyfelfontein date from the early Stone Age (Nam).

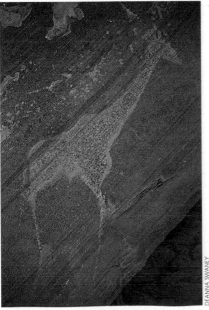
Detail of giraffe, Twyfelfontein (Nam).

Running zebra painting, Ngomakurira (Zim).

Ancient San rock paintings, Matobo NP (Zim).

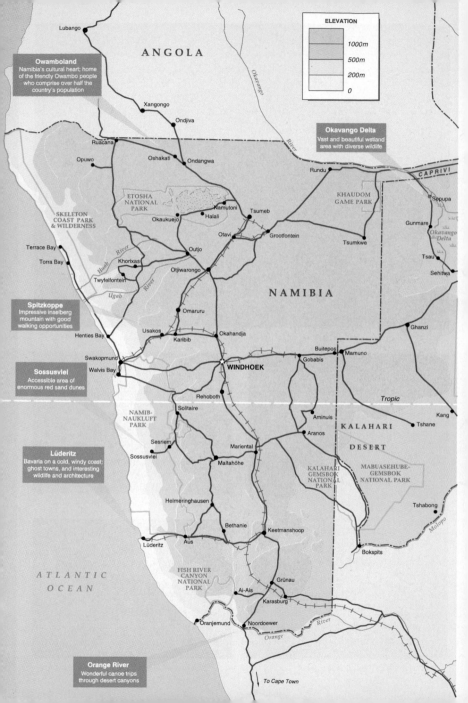

ELEVATION

1000m
500m
200m
0

**Owamboland**
Namibia's cultural heart; home of the friendly Owambo people who comprise over half the country's population

ANGOLA

Lubango

Xangongo

Ondjiva

Ruacana

Opuwo

Oshakati    Ondangwa

Rundu

**Okavango Delta**
Vast and beautiful wetland area with diverse wildlife

CAPRIVI

Sepupa

KHAUDOM
GAME PARK

Gunmare

Okavango
Delta

Tsau

Sehitwa

ETOSHA
NATIONAL
PARK

Namutoni

Halali    Tsumeb

Okaukuejo

Otavi    Grootfontein

Tsumkwe

SKELETON
COAST PARK
& WILDERNESS

Terrace Bay

Torra Bay

Huab    River

Khorixas

Twyfelfontein

Outjo

Otjiwarongo

Ugab    River

NAMIBIA

Ghanzi

**Spitzkoppe**
Impressive inselberg mountain with good walking opportunities

Henties Bay

Omaruru

Usakos    Okahandja
Karibib

Buitepos    Mamuno

Gobabis

Swakopmund

★ WINDHOEK

**Sossusvlei**
Accessible area of enormous red sand dunes

Walvis Bay

Rehoboth

Tropic

Kang

Solitaire

Aminuis

KALAHARI

Tshane

NAMIB-
NAUKLUFT
PARK

Sesriem

Mariental

Aranos

DESERT

**Lüderitz**
Bavaria on a cold, windy coast; ghost towns, and interesting wildlife and architecture

Sossusvlei

Maltahöhe

KALAHARI
GEMSBOK
NATIONAL
PARK

MABUASEHUBE-
GEMSBOK
NATIONAL PARK

Tshabong

Helmeringhausen

A T L A N T I C

O C E A N

Bethanie

Keetmanshoop

Bokspits

Lüderitz    Aus

FISH RIVER
CANYON
NATIONAL
PARK

Grünau

Molopo

Ai-Ais

Karasburg

**Orange River**
Wonderful canoe trips through desert canyons

Oranjemund    Noordoewer

Orange    River

To Cape Town

**ZAMBIA**

Zambezi

LUSAKA

**Mana Pools**
Game viewing on foot
in a remote and
natural setting

Lago de Cahora Bassa

Chirundu

**Victoria Falls**
Zimbabwe's number one
attraction; here the great
Zambezi River falls
more than 100m.
Great rafting trips and
other adrenaline sports.

Kariba

**MANA POOLS**
**NATIONAL**
**PARK**

Karoi

Centenary

Nyamapanda

Mvurwi
Mount Darwin
Kotwa

Katima
Mulilo

River

Kasane

**MATUSADONA**
**NATIONAL**
**PARK**

Sengwa
Siabuwa

Chinhoyi

Shamva

Mutoko

STRIP

Victoria
Falls

Hwange

Gokwe

Chegutu

**HARARE**

Chitungwiza

**NYANGA**
**NATIONAL**
**PARK**

Nyanga

**MOREMI**
**WILDLIFE**
**RESERVE**

**CHOBE**
**NATIONAL**
**PARK**

**CHIZARIRA**
**NATIONAL**
**PARK**

**Z I M B A B W E**

Juliasdale

Rusape

**HWANGE**
**NATIONAL**
**PARK**

Kwe Kwe

Chivhu

Mutare

**MAKGADIKGADI &**
**NXAI PANS**
**NATIONAL**
**PARK**

Gweta

Nata

**GWERU**

Shangani

Shurugwi

**CHIMANIMANI**
**NATIONAL**
**PARK**

Maun

Chimanimani

Toteng

**Ntwetwe**
**Pan**

**Bulawayo**

Khami

Zvishavane

Masvingo

**Sua**
**Pan**

Rakops

Plumtree

Gwanda

Chiredzi

Orapa

Lethlakane

Francistown

Shashe

**MATOBO**
**NATIONAL**
**PARK**

Triangle

**BOTSWANA**

Serule

Selebi-Phikwe

**GONAREZHOU**
**NATIONAL**
**PARK**

**Great Zimbabwe**
**National Monument**
Ruins of the largest ancient
city in sub-Saharan Africa

**CENTRAL KALAHARI**
**GAME RESERVE**

Serowe

Babonong

Beitbridge

Shoshong

Palapye

Zanzibar

River

**M O Z A M B I Q U E**

Mahalapye

Limpopo

of        Capricorn

**KHUTSE**
**GAME RESERVE**

Mochudi

**North-East Tuli**
**Game Reserve**
Large private wildlife reserves
with fabulous scenery

**Serowe**
Royal capital of the
Ngato clan and site of
Khama museum and
new rhino sanctuary

Khakhea

**GABORONE**

Thamaga

Kanye

Werda

Lobatse

River

Ramatlabama

**Mokolodi Nature Reserve**
Reserve emphasising
environmental education and
protection of endangered species

**MAPUTO**

**JOHANNESBURG**

**MBABANE**

**SWAZILAND**

**INDIAN**
**OCEAN**

Warrenton

**SOUTH AFRICA**

**MASERU**

**LESOTHO**

To Cape Town &
Port Elizabeth

# Zimbabwe,
# Botswana & Namibia

0    100    200 km

Kokerbooms, also known as quiver trees (Nam).

Glossy starling perched on flowering aloe (Zim).

In flower at Vumba Botanical Gardens (Zim).

The Great Zimbabwe ruins abound with aloes.

of these people are evidenced by their use of pigments. Although pigments had been used for bodily ornamentation for thousands of years, they now found their way into rock paintings. Whether the San or some other group were directly responsible for the paintings remains a matter of dispute. Although the artistic tradition in southern Africa chronologically and stylistically coincides with that of Europe, the spreading Sahara probably precluded any contact between the cultures and there's no substantial evidence supporting a theory of mutual influence.

## Early Bantu-Speaking Groups

The archaeological connection between the late Stone Age people and the first Khoisan arrivals isn't clear, but it is generally accepted that the earliest historically recognisable inhabitants of Zimbabwe, Botswana and Namibia were San, a nomadic people organised into extended family groups who were able to adapt to the severe terrain. The San seem to have come under pressure from the Khoi-Khoi with whom they share a language group. The Khoi-Khoi were tribally organised people who raised stock rather than hunted and who were probably responsible for the region's first pottery production. They seem to have migrated from the south and gradually displaced and absorbed the San in Namibia and dominated the country until around 1500 AD. Their descendants still live in Namibia and Botswana, but few maintain a traditional lifestyle.

During the early Iron Age, between 2300 and 2400 years ago, rudimentary farming techniques appeared on the plateaus of south-central Africa. Whether the earliest farmers were Khoisan who'd settled into a stationary existence or migrants fleeing the advancing deserts of northern Africa remains in question, but the latter is the favoured hypothesis. The arrival of these farmers in southern Africa marked the beginning of tribal society in the region. These people, commonly called Bantu, would more accurately be called Bantu-speaking, as the word actually refers to their language group. It has become a term of convenience to describe the black African peoples but the grouping is as ill-defined as American or Oriental. In fact, the Bantu-speaking ethnic group is made up of many sub-groups or tribes, each with its own language and cultural traditions.

These groups arrived in sporadic waves of southward movement over many hundreds of years. Groups moved slowly, perhaps only from one valley or fertile area to the next in an entire generation, but, as they pressed southward, dominant groups subsumed or displaced other groups.

The first agriculturalists and iron workers of definite Bantu-speaking origin in southern Africa belonged to the Gokomere culture. They settled the temperate savanna and cooler uplands of Zimbabwe and were the first occupants of the Great Zimbabwe site, which was an obvious and inviting natural fortification.

Between 500 and 1000 AD, the Gokomere and subsequent groups developed gold-mining techniques and produced progressively finer quality ceramics, jewellery, soapstone carvings and textiles. Cattle ranching became the mainstay of the community and earlier hunting and gathering San groups either retreated to the west or were enslaved and/or absorbed by the Bantu-speakers (this process continues to the present day).

As early as the 11th century, some foundations and stonework were already in place at Great Zimbabwe and the community, generally regarded as the nascent Shona society, came into contact with Swahili traders who'd been plying the coast of what is now Mozambique for over four centuries. They traded African gold and ivory for glass, porcelain and cloth from Asia. Great Zimbabwe thereby became the capital of the wealthiest and most powerful society in south-eastern Africa. The hilltop citadel came to serve not only as a fortress but as a shrine for the worship of Mwari, the pre-eminent Shona deity.

Around 1600, the Herero people, who

were Bantu-speaking pastoralists, arrived in Namibia from the Zambezi Valley and occupied the north and west of the country, where they came into conflict with the Khoi-Khoi over the best grazing lands and water sources. (It's thought that the present-day Nama are descended from early Khoi-Khoi, who resisted the Herero and, in fact, violent clashes between these groups continued right up to the 1870s and 80s.) Eventually, nearly all the indigenous Namibian groups submitted to the Herero, who displaced not only the San and Khoi-Khoi, but also the Damara, whose origins are unclear.

A later-arriving Bantu-speaking group, the Owambo, probably descended from people who had migrated from eastern Africa over 500 years earlier, had now settled in the north along the Okavango and Kunene rivers.

For the history of the colonial and post-colonial periods, see under History in the Facts about the Country chapters.

## FLORA & FAUNA

This section deals with flora, reptiles, insects, birds and fish native to Zimbabwe, Botswana and Namibia. Other animals and birds are pictured and discussed in the Safari Guide in this book.

### Flora

**Zimbabwe** Author TV Bulpin wrote of Zimbabwe 'there is not a more picturesque part than the wild garden of trees and aloes and flowering plants that lies between the Limpopo and Zambezi rivers ...'. Despite that lofty assessment, Zimbabwe's vegetation cover is undeniably rather uniform throughout. Most of the central and western plateau country is covered in bushveld – thorny acacia savanna and *miombo* (dry open woodland) while the drier lowlands of the south and south-east are characterised by lower thorny scrub and baobabs.

Generalisations, however, fail to convey the richly colourful array of species that enlivens this plain canvas: towering cactus-like euphorbias resembling pipe-organs, 30 diverse species of aloe (which flower in the cool, sunny days of midwinter), spreading poinsettia shrubs as big as cottages, flowering jacarandas, hibiscus, citrus trees, jasmine, banana trees, flame trees, bougainvilleas and a host of other succulents, tropical flowers, palms and perennials.

The Eastern Highlands and their unique climatic conditions provide another botanical environment altogether. The higher slopes around Nyanga are draped with very un-African pine forests – some admittedly planted by the paper industry – and down the eastern slopes of the Vumba, where Zimbabwe spills into Mozambique, you can find stands of tropical hardwood forest complete with ferns and lianas.

If you're after Africa's archetypal Tarzan jungles, however, you'll have to head for central Africa or keep within 100m of Victoria Falls, where the constant spray has created a lush stand of tropical rainforest.

**Botswana** Most of Botswana is covered by savanna – either acacia or low thorn scrub – which rolls on across the flat and almost unchanging landscape. In the heart of the Kalahari the vegetation reaches through the sands to access underlying aquifers.

The country's only deciduous *mopane* forests are in the north-east. Here, six Chobe District forest reserves harbour stands of commercial timber for paper and construction, as well as both *mongonga* and *marula* trees, whose edible nuts once served as staple foods for the San. The soft wood of the marula is used in local crafts and its fruit goes into a local beer.

The Okavango Delta enjoys a riparian environment dominated by marsh grasses, water lilies, reeds and papyrus, and dotted with well vegetated islands thick with palms, acacias, leadwood and sausage trees.

**Namibia** Namibia is mostly covered by tree-dotted, scrub savanna grasses of the genera *Stipagrostis*, *Eragrostis* and *Aristida*. In the south, the grass is interrupted by stands of quivertrees *(kokerbooms)* and eu-

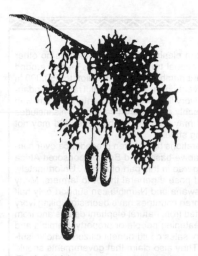

The fruits of the sausage tree (*Kigelia africana*) can grow up to a metre in length.

phorbias, with ephemeral watercourses lined with tamarisks, buffalo thorn and camelthorn.

In the sandy plains of south-eastern Namibia, raisin bushes *(Grewia)* and candlethorn grow among the scrubby trees, while hillsides are covered with the green-flowered *Aloe viridiflora* and camphor bush.

The eastern fringes of Namib-Naukluft Park are dominated by semidesert scrub savanna vegetation, including some rare aloe species *(Aloe karasbergensis* and *Aloe sladeniana)*. On the gravel plains east and north-east of Swakopmund grows the bizarre *Welwitschia mirabilis*, which is surely one of the world's most unusual plants (see the boxed text in the Central Namib chapter).

In higher rainfall areas, the characteristic grass savanna gives way to acacia woodlands, and Etosha National Park enjoys two distinct environments: the wooded savanna in the east and thorn-scrub savanna in the west. The higher rainfall of Caprivi and Kavango sustains extensive mopane woodland and the riverine areas support scattered

wetland vegetation, grasslands and stands of acacia. The area around Katima Mulilo is dominated by mixed sub-tropical woodland containing copalwood, Zambezi teak and leadwood, among other hardwood species.

## Fauna

**Reptiles** Africa's reptile extraordinaire is the Nile crocodile. Female crocodiles lay up to 80 eggs at a time, depositing them in sandy areas above the high-water line. After three months incubation in the hot sand, the young emerge. Newly hatched crocs are avocado green in colour and, like avocados, darken to nearly black as they age.

Other reptiles to watch for – but which

## Poachers

Each of the three countries covered in this book likes to blame the other two – as well as Zambia, Angola, Mozambique and South Africa – for their wildlife poaching problems. Wherever their place of origin, however, elephant and rhino poachers are ruthless businesspeople in pursuit of the high prices commanded for rapidly dwindling supplies of animal products such as ivory and, especially, rhino horn.

Rhino horn is highly sought after as a component for the sheaths of Yemeni dagger handles and is believed by some Asian cultures to have medicinal properties. Both markets shell out big money for the commodity and, as long as someone will pay (and the product isn't yet extinct), someone else is going to risk their neck to provide it.

Most African countries have a shoot to kill policy with respect to poachers, so the culprits are understandably jumpy about anyone seen travelling in the remote bush where they practice their heinous trade. Anything that stands between a poacher and their profits will be as endangered as the prey itself. Fortunately, few travellers wander far enough from the beaten routes to encounter poachers.

## CITES and the 1997 Directives

Among conservation issues, the fate of the African elephant raises passions as no other and, in October 1989, the cessation of an international trade in ivory was lauded around the world. After all, poaching has reduced elephant numbers from 1.3 million to 650,000 in less than 10 years. Until 1997, CITES (the Convention on International Trade in Endangered Species) declared the import and export of ivory illegal in every country on earth, with the listing of the elephant under Appendix I, the highly endangered category. This includes 'species threatened with extinction which are, or may be, affected by trade, and may not be traded without a valid permit from the receiving state'.

In southern Africa, however, economic considerations have taken precedence over conservation. According to John Hutton of the Zimbabwe-based and British-sponsored Africa Resources Trust, the elephant was 'never endangered in this part of Africa'. Unfortunately, elephant tend to destroy trees, ravage crops and pose a general threat to farmers. Many experts believe the wild lands of Zimbabwe, Botswana and Namibia can support only half the current elephant population. As a result, the three countries have been stockpiling ivory for nearly a decade, much of which has accumulated from natural elephant deaths and from elephant which have been culled or killed for threatening people or property. Namibia and Zimbabwe claim that part of the income from ivory sales could benefit citizens who've suffered property damage by elephantine mischief. They also claim that governments should be compensated for their efforts at elephant conservation.

In early 1997, the governments of Zimbabwe, Botswana, South Africa and other regional nations held an estimated US$8 billion in worthless ivory stocks: Zimbabwe had 32.3 tonnes, Botswana had 32.7 tonnes and Namibia had 45.6 tonnes, and all three nations had sustainable elephant populations. In January 1997, the three countries proposed annual sales of around 30 tonnes of culled ivory to Japan, where it's used for traditional personal carvings known as *hankos*. This might seem viable, but it would still deliver a message to poachers that there is indeed a legal outlet for illicit ivory sources. According to David Barrit, director of the International Fund for Animal Welfare, elephant poachers recently arrested in the Republic of Congo (Zaïre) defended themselves with claims that the ivory trade would soon be legal. (This was confirmed first-hand a week after the subsequent official downlisting of the elephant's endangered status, when we encountered signs of poachers in the

shouldn't inspire bush paranoia – are snakes. Southern Africa has a complement of both venomous and harmless snakes, 76 varieties in all, but most fear humans (they fear anything larger than they are) and travellers will be lucky even to see one.

The largest snake – and one that is normally harmless to humans – is the python, which grows to over 5m in length. It is found mainly in eastern Zimbabwe, from the lowveld north to Nyanga, and subsists mainly on small mammals.

There is a host of other harmless snakes – the bush snake, the green water snake, the mole snake, and so on – and quite a few

venomous species. The most sinister-looking – and for good reason – is the flat, fat and bloated gaboon viper. It has a massive triangular head and grows to over 1m in length. Although it's not common, watch for it on walking tracks in the Eastern Highlands of Zimbabwe; its bite means bye-bye unless antivenin is administered quickly.

The related puff adder also enjoys sunning itself on mountain tracks. It reaches about 1m in length and, although it isn't as hideous-looking as the gaboon viper, it's responsible for most snakebite poisoning in Zimbabwe. The puff adder isn't aggressive

wildest reaches of Zimbabwe's Chizarira National Park, who apparently hoped to participate in the newly liberalised market.)

Furthermore, Japan's internal controls for distinguishing between legal and illicit ivory are flawed, according to Marshall Jones, assistant director of the US Fish and Wildlife Service. 'Their registration system is flagrantly not followed.'

At the 10th CITES conference, held in Harare from 6 to 20 June 1997, over 1500 delegates representing 139 member nations attended. During the proceedings, southern African nations announced that they were unable to accept conservationists' concerns and argued that they were being punished for the sins of poachers in East, Central and West Africa and that southern Africa's elephant population and the international demand for ivory demanded changes in the regulations.

As a result, Zimbabwe, Botswana and Namibia, with the support of South Africa, Nigeria, Pakistan, Saudi Arabia, Russia, China, Egypt, Korea and Norway, proposed new rulings. (Norway expects reciprocal favours when it comes to the downlisting of the minke whale.) These would allow limited trade in ivory by downlisting the elephant from the highly endangered Appendix I category to Appendix II, which covers species which are threatened, or '... although not necessarily now threatened with extinction may become so unless trade in specimens of such species is subject to strict regulations in order to avoid utilisation incompatible with their survival.'

This gobbledygook allows export of hunting trophies for non-commercial purposes, export of live animals to appropriate and acceptable destinations, export of hides from Zimbabwe and export from Zimbabwe of leather goods and ivory carvings for non-commercial purposes. Otherwise, trade in Appendix II species requires only an export permit. From 18 March 1999, annual export quotas for raw ivory to Japan would not exceed 23.5 metric tonnes from Botswana, 13.8 metric tonnes from Namibia and 20 metric tonnes from Zimbabwe. To all other nations, trade in elephant ivory would be regulated by Appendix I regulations.

In the first round of voting, these measures, with South African amendments, netted 75 votes in favour and 41 opposed, with seven abstentions, which was three votes short of the two-thirds majority required to pass them. However, the measure was eventually passed in the final plenary session after several abstaining countries were won over.

---

but, because it's so lethargic, hikers should take care not to inadvertently kick one out of its sweet dreams.

Zimbabwe also boasts four species of cobra: the forest cobra, the rinkal, and the Egyptian cobra, all of which reach over 2m in length, and the 1m-long Mozambique spitting cobra, which can spit a stream of venom up to 3m. It aims for the eyes.

Other venomous snakes include the common vine snake; both the green and black mamba; and the *boomslang* (Afrikaans for tree snake), a slender 2m aquamarine affair that has black-tipped scales.

The dry lands of Botswana and Namibia boast more than 70 species of snake, including three species of spitting cobra. It is actually the African puff adder which causes the most problems for humans, since it inhabits dry, sandy, and otherwise harmless-looking riverbeds. Boomslangs and vine snakes are common in the Okavango and Caprivi areas but they generally don't bother humans. Horned adders and sandsnakes inhabit the gravel plains of the Namib, and the sidewinder adder lives in the Namib dune sea.

Lizards are ubiquitous in southern Africa, from Zimbabwe's eastern highlands to Namibia's Kaokoland, and from the bathroom ceiling to the kitchen sink. The largest of these is the *leguan* or water monitor, a docile creature that reaches over 2m in length, swims and spends a lot of time lying around water holes, perhaps dreaming of being a crocodile. A smaller version, the savanna leguan, inhabits *kopjes* (small hills) and drier areas. Also present in large numbers are geckos, chameleons, legless snake lizards, rock-plated lizards and a host of others.

The Namib Desert supports a range of lizards, including a large vegetarian species, *Angolosaurus skoogi*. The sand-diving lizard, *Aprosaura achietae*, is known for its 'thermal dance'. In order to get some relief from the heat of the sand, it lifts its legs in turn as if following a dance routine. The unusual bug-eyed palmato gecko inhabits the high dunes and there's also a species of chameleon.

**Insects & Spiders** Although southern Africa doesn't enjoy the profusion of bug life found in countries further north, a few interesting specimens buzz, creep, and crawl around the place. Over 500 species of colourful butterfly – including the African monarch, the commodore, and the citrus swallowtail – are resident, as well as many fly-by-night moths.

Some of the more interesting buggy types include the large and rarely noticed stick insects, the similarly large (and frighteningly hairy) baboon spider and the leggy chongalolo, a millipede that reaches a foot in length.

Common insects such as ants, stink bugs, grasshoppers, mopane worms and locusts sometimes find their way into frying pans and are served as snack and protein supplements.

Nuisance insects include malarial *Anopheles* mosquitoes, which are profuse in the Zambezi Valley, the Zimbabwean lowveld and north-eastern Namibia; and the tsetse fly, which carries sleeping sickness and is found in the lowveld and around Zimbabwe's Lake Kariba. There are also various stinging insects, such as the striped hornet, an evil-looking variety of house wasp. In the gravel plains of Namibia, you'll also encounter such nuisance insects as ticks, which favour the shade of thorn trees and areas where there are lots of grazing animals.

The Namib Desert in particular has several wonderful species of spider. The tarantula-like 'white lady of the dunes' is a white hairy affair which is attracted to light. It does a dance, of sorts, raising each of its eight hairy feet in turn. There is also a rare false spider known as a solifluge or sun spider. You can see its circulatory system through its light-coloured translucent outer skeleton. Much of the time, however, it remains buried in the sand.

The Namib dunes are also known for their extraordinary variety of tenebrionid beetles, which come in all shapes and sizes. They've adapted well to their desert environment and most of their moisture is derived from fog.

**Birds** Although southern Afric~ ~ffers an adequate sampling of LBJ's (little brown jobs), it is also home to an array of colourful and exotic birdlife.

Botswana's pan and the harbours and coastal wildfowl reserves of Namibia support an especially wide range of birdlife: white pelicans, grebes, herons, flamingoes, cormorants, ducks and hundreds of other wetland birds. In Namibia, the sheer number of birds, which survive on the fish stocks nurtured by the cold Benguela Current, has contributed to the country's lucrative guano industry. Near Walvis Bay, artificial offshore islands have been constructed to stimulate production. Further south, around Lüderitz, flamingoes and jackass penguins share the same desert shoreline.

The canyons and riverbeds slicing across the central Namib are home to nine species of raptor, as well as the hoopoe, the unusual red-eyed bulbul and a small bird known as the familiar chat. Around the western edge of the Central Plateau you may see the colourful sunbirds or emerald cuckoos. Central Namibia also has bird species found nowhere else, such as the Namaqua sandgrouse and Grey's lark.

The well watered areas of the Namibian far north and Botswana's Okavango Delta and Chobe Riverfront support an entirely different range of birdlife, including such colourful species as lilac-breasted rollers, psychedelic pygmy geese (actually a duck) and white-fronted, carmine and little bee-eaters. There are other fabulous wetland species: African jacanas, snakebirds, ibis, hoopoes, storks, egrets, parrots, shrikes, kingfishers, hornbills, great white herons and purple and green-backed herons. Birds of prey include Pel's fishing owl, the goshawk and both the bateleur and African fish eagles.

For more information on the region's birds, see the Safari Guide in this book.

**Fish** Zimbabwe, the wettest of the three countries covered in this book, has 117 fish species. Many of these were introduced by anglers during the colonial period, but every aquatic habitat in Zimbabwe has its own piscine community and angling remains a popular pastime and food source. Botswana's Okavango Delta and the Namib Coast also support fish species (and anglers). For more information, see Fishing under Activities in the Regional Facts for the Visitor chapter.

## SOCIETY & CONDUCT
Short of public nudity or openly vocal criticism of the government, there aren't really any unforgivable *faux pas* that must be avoided (for foreigners, anyway). However, in most places, any open displays of affection are frowned upon and show insensitivity to local sentiments.

A few straightforward courtesies, however, may greatly improve a foreigner's chances of acceptance by the local community, especially in rural areas. In all three countries, pleasantries are taken quite seriously, and it's essential to greet or say goodbye to someone entering or leaving a room. Learn the local words for hello and goodbye and use them unsparingly. In rural Zimbabwe, verbal greetings are often accompanied by a clap of the hands. For those out of earshot, it is customary to offer a smile and a pleasant wave, even if you're just passing in a vehicle.

Emphasis is also placed on handshakes. The African handshake consists of three parts: the normal western handshake, followed by the linking of bent fingers while touching the ends of upward-pointing thumbs, and then a repeat of the conventional handshake. In Botswana, offer your right hand for a conventional handshake while holding your right elbow with your left hand. Often, people continue to hold hands right through their conversation.

As in most traditional societies, the achievement of old age is an accomplishment worthy of respect and elders are treated with deference – their word should not be questioned and they should be accorded utmost courtesy. Teachers, doctors, and other professionals often receive similar treatment.

Likewise, people holding positions of authority – immigration officers, government officials, police, village chiefs, and so on – should be dealt with pragmatically. Officials in Zimbabwe, Botswana, and Namibia are not as sensitive as those in most neighbouring countries and are normally refreshingly open and friendly. However, if you do cross them or strike a nerve, all that may change. It is one thing to stand up for your rights but blowing a fuse, undermining an official's judgement or authority, or insulting an ego may only serve to waste time, tie you up in red tape and inspire closer scrutiny of future travellers.

At the other end of the spectrum, children rate very low on the social scale. They are expected to do as they're told without complaint and defer to adults in all situations. For example, it is considered rude for a child to occupy a seat in a bus if adults are standing. Foreigners are normally exempted. Similarly, southern Africa is largely still a man's country and a black man will not

## The Cultural Factor & Economics in Africa

Thanks to its European colonisers, southern Africa's infrastructure appears to work in much the same way as those of Europe, North America and Australasia. This superficial western veneer may tempt visitors to assume that locals share their own cultural values. However, when something unexpected happens, it quickly becomes clear that the African world view is quite different from that of most western societies.

While some ideals are shared – for example, respect for elders and the importance of family – there are prominent differences, including attitudes towards obligations and responsibilities. In fact, some standard African practices may well be questioned in the west. While most westerners emphasise looking out for their own interests, Africans place more importance on mutual help. People are members of families, communities and tribal groupings, in that order; after that, they're citizens of a nation. One's own interests, at least as far as westerners would probably define them – personal power, wealth and accumulation of possessions – would take a lower priority.

Nowhere is the cultural rift more pronounced than in the realms of economics. Throughout the developed world, Africa is often perceived as a languishing relation that doesn't seem to cope well with the modern western economic system. The UN is constantly debating what to do about 'the African problem' and many investors regard the continent as a hole into which capital and hope are irretrievably dumped or squandered. Although economic conditions are slowly improving across the continent – thanks largely to its vast resources, improving educational systems  and increasingly democratic leadership – the prevailing western economic system remains something of a stranger and, if a complete transition is possible, it will take many years.

First, western economics operates on the premise that 'time is money', yet in Africa – where money is regarded as fondly as it is anywhere – attitudes towards time and urgency differ greatly from those in the west. Time and punctuality take a back seat to less confining notions. If something doesn't get done today, it can wait until tomorrow or next week. If it never happens, it wasn't very important anyway. This concept is neatly illustrated by the supplanting of the word 'now' with such expressions as 'just now', which means anything from  'sometime soon' to 'in a few minutes' or 'tomorrow', and 'now-now', which conveys some degree of imminence, but is definitely not 'now' as most westerners would interpret it. The word 'tomorrow' is even more loosely interpreted and in many cases could be considered synonymous with 'never'.

Perhaps the greatest difference, however, is the prevailing – and perhaps fatalistic – African emphasis on the present rather than an unpredictable and potentially unpromising future. As an illustration, say that in a particularly good season, a family's harvest of mielies yields twice the amount required for the year. Instead of planting the following year as a hedge against drought or other misfortune – which may or may not occur – they're likely to take the year off and not plant again until supplies run low. In contrast, Europeans, who historically faced unforgiving but reasonably predictable winters, were forced to plan ahead or were quickly weeded out of the population. (In fact, this is thought to be a major factor in the evolution of the western economic system.)

The same concept carries over into business. When a businessperson has enough money to meet family responsibilities – but not necessarily such abstract concepts as financial obligations, client expectations or growth-promoting investments – the business may be neglected until the next shortfall. Because the western economic system simply doesn't accommodate this sort of thing, as yet only a few African-run businesses compete successfully on a large scale.

normally give up his seat to a woman, never mind that she is carrying a baby and luggage and minding two toddlers. It makes one wonder what they must think of the local whites and other westerners who habitually do.

When visiting rural settlements, it's a good idea to request to see the chief to announce your presence and ask permission before setting up camp or wandering through a village. You will rarely be refused permission. Women should dress and behave modestly, especially in the presence of chiefs or other highly esteemed persons.

Visitors should also ask permission before drawing water from community bore holes. If you do draw water at a community tap or bore hole, avoid letting it spill on the ground, especially in desert areas, where it's as precious as gold. If you wish to wash your body or your clothing, fill a container with water and carry it elsewhere.

Lone travellers may be looked upon with suspicion: women because they should be at home rearing families and men because, in many areas, foreigners are potentially spies for right-wing factions. It may help to carry photographs of your family or evidence of a non-espionage-related profession.

Most travellers will have the opportunity to share an African meal sometime during their stay and will normally be given royal treatment and a seat of honour. Although concessions are sometimes made for foreigners, table manners are probably different from what you're accustomed to. The African staple, maize or sorghum meal, is the centre of nearly every meal. It is normally taken with the right hand from a communal pot, rolled into balls, dipped in some sort of relish – meat gravy or vegetables – and eaten. As in most societies, it is considered impolite to scoff food, or to hoard it or be stingy with it. If you do, your host may feel that he or she hasn't provided enough. Similarly, if you can't finish your food, don't worry; the host will be pleased that you have been satisfied. Often, containers of water or home-brew beer may be passed around from person to person. However, it is not customary to share coffee, tea or bottled soft drinks.

Finally, if you do visit a remote community, please tread lightly and leave as little lasting evidence of your visit as possible. In some African societies, it isn't considered impolite to ask others for items you may desire. If you're besieged with requests, it's perfectly acceptable to refuse without causing offence. If you start feeling guilty about your relative wealth and hand out all your earthly belongings, you may be regarded as very silly indeed. As for gift-giving, reciprocation of kindness is one thing but superficial altruism is another. Indiscriminate distribution of gifts from outside, however well intentioned, tends to create a taste for items not locally available, erodes well established values, robs people of their pride and in extreme cases, creates villages of dependent beggars.

On the other hand, when you're offered a gift, don't feel guilty about accepting it; to refuse it would bring shame on the giver. To receive a gift politely, accept it with both hands and perhaps bow slightly. If you're receiving some minor thing you've asked for, such as a salt shaker or a pen, or getting back change at a shop, receive it with your right hand while touching your left hand to your right elbow; this is the equivalent of saying thanks. Spoken thanks aren't common and local people tend to think westerners say thank you too often and too casually, so don't be upset if you aren't verbally thanked for a gift.

# Regional Facts for the Visitor

## PLANNING

### When to Go

The biggest factors in timing your visit are probably climate, crowds and opportunities for wildlife viewing. While all three countries in this book lie within the tropics, they experience a range of climatic conditions, from the cool, moist climate of Zimbabwe's Eastern Highlands to the dusty heat of the Namib Desert and the tropical humidity of the Zambezi valley.

In much of the region, the year is divided into the dry winter season, which runs roughly from May to October, and the warmer, more humid summer wet season, from November to April. During the summer months, the bushland takes on a lush green hue, while through the winter, the prevailing colour is dry brown. From May to late July, the equivalent of autumn, the mopane scrub takes on colourful hues.

Although lots of winter-weary travellers from the northern hemisphere venture south between November and February, the rains may limit activities. Generally, winter is the most comfortable season, especially in the Zambezi and Okavango valleys, the Zimbabwean lowveld, and northern Namibia. Temperatures may drop below freezing at night, but days are typically warm, sunny and pleasant. However, along the Namibian coast, winter may bring cold, damp and windy conditions.

Wildlife viewing is generally most rewarding in the dry winter months, when animals gather around water holes in large numbers and are easy to observe. Only around Botswana's Nxai Pan, which is a destination for migrating herds of animals, are the concentrations greater during the summer.

To miss the crowds, avoid mid-April to mid-May or mid-July to mid-September, when residents of Zimbabwe, Botswana, Namibia and neighbouring South Africa have winter school holidays (dates vary from country to country and province to province). Book accommodation and National Parks facilities in advance or you may be out of luck.

June, which is normally the coolest and traditionally the quietest month, is an excellent time to travel, and is gaining popularity with overseas travellers. In early July, which is still chilly, visitor numbers pick up and build towards the high season, which begins later in the month. In August, southern Africa seethes with tourists, but by late September the crowds are gone, and although temperatures are climbing and there's always a chance of rain, the weather is generally good.

### What Kind of Trip?

Your style of travel depends mainly on your budget, available time and preparedness for unknowns. While southern Africa isn't a 'difficult' destination, it's impossible to construct a highly structured trip for a short period of time without spending lots of money. Low-budget travel requires sacrificing the security of structure and allowing time to accommodate uncertainties.

Of the three countries, Zimbabwe is the most negotiable on public transport. Services in Botswana and Namibia only connect population centres, while most sites of visitor interest are accessible only by private vehicle or organised tour or safari. This makes shoestring travel in both countries quite difficult.

Nicer hotels or lodges are typically quite expensive, although Zimbabwean hotels without multi-tier pricing (ie different rates for foreigners) can offer good deals. Of the three countries, Namibia offers the best value mid-range to top-end accommodation. Zimbabwe and Namibia have clean, good-value backpackers hostels, but for budget travel in Botswana or away from population centres, a tent is essential. Mid-range guest houses are quite popular in

Zimbabwe and Namibia, and a few places are now emerging in Botswana.

## Maps

The best regional map is Michelin's map 955 – *Central & Southern Africa, & Madagascar*, at a scale of 1:4,000,000. However, expect a few discrepancies between the map and reality. The Automobile Association (AA) in South Africa produces an excellent series of road maps, which are available at AA shops. For closer-up coverage, Lonely Planet publishes travel atlases for *Zimbabwe, Botswana & Namibia* and *South Africa, Lesotho & Swaziland*. Individual country maps are listed in the country chapters.

In the USA a good source of maps, including topographic sheets for all three countries, is Maplink (☎ (805) 965-4402), 25 E Mason St, Dept G, Santa Barbara, CA 93101. In the UK Stanfords (☎ (0171) 836 1321), 12-14 Long Acre, London WC2E 9LP has a similarly extensive selection of mapping. Alternatively, there's Latitude Map Mail Order (☎ (01707) 663090; fax 663029).

In Australia, try Map Land (☎/fax (03) 9670 4383), 372 Little Bourke St, Melbourne 3000 or Travel Bookshop (☎ (02) 9241 3554), 20 Bridge St, Sydney 2000.

## What to Bring

What items you'll need to bring from home will depend on your intended budget, itinerary, mode of travel, time of visit and length of stay. While travelling light always enhances trip enjoyment, some items are indispensable if you can't splash out on hotel accommodation.

There are three items no budget traveller in southern Africa should be without: a tent, a sleeping bag, and a torch (and batteries) or candle lantern. The tent and sleeping bag will keep accommodation costs to a minimum and the light source will let you remain awake past 6 pm in the winter/dry season. Also useful is a universal drain plug, which will allow you to use laundry sinks and bathtubs in a region of few showers and even fewer drain plugs.

Backpacks are usually recommended as the most practical and useful carry-all. Carry the sturdiest and best-made pack you can afford, paying attention to the strength of zippers, straps and tabs. In general, internal-frame packs are more sturdy and flexible than external-frame packs. A padlock will protect your pack from opportunistic riflers, but may also encourage thieves to take the whole bag! Generally, khaki or military-green bags aren't recommended, lest you even remotely resemble a soldier or mercenary.

For hiking, you need either track shoes or desert boots; sandals are unsuitable. For walking in the bush, gaiters are useful to protect your socks from thorns and little seeds that cling to every passing thing.

Bushwalkers will appreciate a lightweight stove, preferably one that will run on petrol or paraffin (kerosene), since white gas (Shellite/Coleman fuel) isn't readily available. Note that you may not carry stove fuel or butane cartridges on aeroplanes, and flights originating in the USA or New Zealand may restrict even empty fuel bottles. In the capital cities, there's little problem finding stove fuel or butane cartridges, but in Zimbabwe notched butane cartridges for Bleuet stoves are rare; try Fereday & Sons on Robert Mugabe Rd in Harare or Eezee Camping in Bulawayo.

In the dry season, you'll need a range of clothing, especially in the Kalahari, the Namib desert, Zimbabwe's Eastern Highlands or along the Namibian coast. You can expect T-shirt weather most days across the region, but overnight temperatures can dip below freezing and even in the tropical north, mornings and evenings can get chilly. You won't need thermal underwear, but a jacket, a woolly jumper, a hat, gloves and warm socks would be welcome.

Waterproofs are useful in the rainy season, or for winter visits to Zimbabwe's Eastern Highlands or the Namibian coast. A bathing costume will be welcome for swims in the Eastern Highlands or in hot springs and public pools (elsewhere, intentions to swim may be foiled by bilharzia – see

Health). For summer travel or visits to the deserts or the Zambezi, Chobe or Okavango valleys, bring cool lightweight cottons.

In rural areas and places with a high Afrikaner population, people tend to be conservative and swimwear or tight shorts aren't normally well received. In the cities, dress is generally more formal than in rural areas, so it's also useful to bring one change of 'glad rags' for nights on the town.

Other handy items include a travel alarm, Swiss Army-style knife, clothes line, basic first-aid kit, water bottle, water filter and/or purification tablets, towel, sewing kit, several passport-sized photos (for visa applications) and photographic equipment. Film is available in southern Africa, but you may not find your preferred brand and it's likely to be more expensive than at home. For Zimbabwe, take enough batteries to power all your gadgetry; Zimbabwean batteries have been known to expire in under 10 seconds!

## VISAS & DOCUMENTS
### Passport
All visitors to Zimbabwe, Botswana and Namibia must carry a current passport from their country of citizenship, which must be produced on entry to each country and when changing currency. For visa details, see the Facts for the Visitor chapters for the individual countries.

### Photocopies
With valuable documents such as passports, it's wise to prepare for the worst. Even if your passport is registered with your embassy, keep separate records of your passport number and issue date, and photocopies of the pages with the passport number, name, photograph, place issued and expiry date. It's also a good idea to carry copies of:

- visas
- travellers cheque receipt slips
- travel insurance policies and addresses
- personal contact addresses
- credit card numbers
- airline tickets

your birth certificate, if possible (to verify your citizenship should you lose your passport)

Keep these photocopies separate from your passport and money (hotels and backpackers hostels have a safe for valuables). Keep one copy with you, one copy inside your luggage and, if possible, deposit another with a travelling companion. Also slip US$100 or so into an unlikely place to use as an emergency stash.

### Travel Insurance
All travellers should consider a travel insurance policy, which can take some of the stress out of medical emergencies or the loss or theft of money or belongings. It may seem an expensive luxury, but if you can't afford a travel insurance policy, you probably can't afford a medical emergency abroad, either. Travel insurance policies can normally be extended to include baggage, flight departure insurance and other options. Buy your policy as early as possible, as last-minute purchase may exclude flight delays caused by industrial action.

Always check the small print. Some policies exclude 'dangerous activities', which may include white-water rafting, sandboarding or even trekking. A locally acquired motorcycle licence may not be valid under some policies.

You may prefer a policy that pays doctors or hospitals directly rather than one requiring you to pay on the spot and claim later. If you must claim after the fact, however, keep all your documentation. Some insurers ask you to phone (reverse charges) their centre in your home country where an immediate assessment of your problem is made.

Also, remember to check the policy's coverage of emergency transport or evacuation to your home country. If you have to stretch out across several airline seats, someone has to pay for it!

Finding the best deals will probably require lots of shopping around. Long-term or frequent travellers can generally find something for under US$200 per year, but these are normally issued by general business insurance companies rather than those specialising in travel. Policies offered by STA or other student travel organisations are usually good value. However, note that some inexpensive policies may exclude travel where health care costs are high, such as in the USA, and may offer very limited baggage protection. Always read the fine print!

To make a claim on your travel insurance, you must produce proof of the value of any items lost or stolen (purchase receipts are the best). In the case of medical claims, you'll need detailed medical reports and receipts for amounts paid. If you're claiming on a trip cancelled by circumstances beyond your control (illness, airline bankruptcy, industrial action etc), you must produce your flight tickets, tour agency receipts, itinerary and proof of whatever glitch caused the cancellation.

If you're taking an organised tour, the company will normally encourage you to purchase their own travel insurance policy, which may or may not be a good deal. Some unscrupulous companies – particularly in Europe – keep their tour prices low and appealing by requiring overpriced travel insurance with the package.

### Driving Licence

Most car rental agencies in Zimbabwe, Botswana and Namibia will accept your home driving licence but if you're buying a car or motorcycle locally, most insurers require non-residents to have an International Driving Licence from their home automobile association. For details, see Car & Motorcycle in the Getting Around chapters for the respective countries.

### International Health Card

Travellers entering southern Africa directly from an infected area need proof of vaccination against yellow fever.

### EMBASSIES

As a tourist, it's important to realise what your country's embassy can and can't do.

Generally speaking, it won't be much help in emergencies if the trouble you're in is remotely your own fault. Remember that you are bound by the laws of the country you are in. Your embassy will not be sympathetic if you end up in jail after committing a crime locally, even if such actions are legal in your own country. In genuine emergencies you might get some assistance, but only if other channels have been exhausted. For example, if you need to get home urgently, a free ticket home is exceedingly unlikely – the embassy would expect you to have insurance. If you have all your money and documents stolen, it might assist with getting a new passport, but a loan for onward travel is out of the question. Embassies used to keep letters for travellers or have a small reading room with home newspapers, but these days the mail holding service has been stopped and even newspapers tend to be out of date.

On the more positive side, if you are heading into very remote or politically volatile areas you might consider registering with your embassy, so they know where you are, but make sure you tell them when you come back as well. Some embassies post useful warning notices about local dangers or potential problems. The US embassies are particularly good for providing this information and it's worth scanning their noticeboards for 'travellers advisories' about security, local epidemics, dangers to lone travellers etc.

Detailed embassy listings are included in the Facts for the Visitor chapters for the individual countries.

### MONEY

The most readily recognised international currency is the US dollar, but British pounds, German marks and South African rand are also widely accepted. In banks and foreign exchange (forex) bureaus in the capital cities, you can normally also change Botswana pula, French francs, Italian lira, Dutch guilders, Swiss francs and Australian or Canadian dollars. Note that due to counterfeiting, old US$100 notes (those with the smaller picture of Benjamin Franklin) are not accepted in places without a device for checking validity.

## Costs

Generally, prices in southern Africa range from 50% to 75% of what you'd find in Europe, Australasia or North America. Obviously, there are exceptions: locally produced goods (including food and beer) may be cheaper while imports may cost twice what they would in the west.

For budget accommodation and transport, Zimbabwe offers the best value in the region while at the upper mid-range to luxury end (for foreigners), Namibia is the best value. Namibia also has the most equitable national parks fees (that is, foreigners and locals pay the same rates). For more specific information, see the Facts for the Visitor chapters for the individual countries.

### Carrying Money

To keep money, passports, air tickets, etc safe from pickpockets, the best place is out of sight under your clothes; it's easy to make a cloth pouch that hangs around your neck or waist, or is pinned under clothing. Other methods include belts with concealed zipper compartments, and bandages or pouches worn around the leg.

Try not to keep everything in one place; keep small change and a few banknotes in a shirt pocket, to pay for bus tickets and small expenses without having to extract wads of cash. It may help to distribute valuables about your person and baggage, especially if you must carry all your belongings at once (eg on the way to the bus terminal).

### Bargaining

In some areas, particularly at rural markets and craft stalls, bargaining for goods and services – produce, clothing, lifts and especially crafts and artwork – is a way of life. Such commodities are worth whatever their owners can get for them.

In markets that are frequented by foreigners, sellers will invariably make their asking price high. If you pay this price – whether out of ignorance or guilt feelings about your relative wealth – you may be considered foolish and create the impression that foreigners will pay any price named. You may also disrupt the local economy; by paying high prices, you may put some items out of reach of locals who generally have less disposable cash. And who can blame the sellers – why sell an item to a local when foreigners will pay twice as much?

At craft and curio stalls, where items are designed to be sold to tourists, bargaining should be conducted in a friendly and spirited manner. The vendor's aim is to identify the highest price you're willing to pay. Your aim is to find the price below which the vendor will not sell. There are all sorts of formulae for working out what this will be, but there are no hard and fast rules. Some craft vendors may initially ask a price four (or more) times higher than what they're prepared to accept, although it's usually lower than this. Decide what you want to pay or what others have told you they've paid; your first offer should be about half this. At this stage, the vendor may laugh or feign outrage, but the price will quickly drop from his or her original quote to a more realistic level. When it does, begin making better offers until you arrive at a mutually agreeable price. And that's the key – mutually agreeable; if you don't like a price, simply don't pay it.

If sellers won't come down to a price you feel is fair, it probably means that lots of high-rolling foreigners have passed through and if you don't pay what they're asking, someone else will. If you're fed up with an intransigent vendor or the effort seems a waste of time, politely take your leave. Sometimes vendors will change tack and call you back if they think their stubbornness may be losing a sale. If not, you can always look for another seller or try again the following day.

## INTERNET RESOURCES

Throughout this book, email and Web site

addresses are provided where applicable. For some of the most useful Web sites, see the Internet Resources sections in the individual country chapters. Other useful sites are listed in the Online Services boxed text.

## Travel Advice

The US State Department has a Web site with advice for travellers (www.stolaf.edu /network/travel-advisories.html). It does get a bit hysterical, but you may glean some useful information. Much better is its British counterpart, the Travel Advice Unit of the Foreign & Commonwealth Office (www.fco.gov.uk/).

## Laptop Adaptors

If you're carrying a laptop computer with you and need to access the Internet during your travels, you'll probably need an adaptor plug for your telephone linkup, as each country has its own configuration. A recommended source of information and plugs is the company TeleAdapt (www .teleadapt.com), which has offices at the following locations:

*TeleAdapt Ltd*, The Technology Park, Colindeep Lane, London NW9 6TA, UK (☎ (0181) 233 3000; fax 233 3132; <info@uk.teleadapt .com>)

---

## Online Services

If you have access to the Internet, you can get hold of all sorts of information about southern Africa. Some of the best Web sites are:

### Lonely Planet Online
(www.lonelyplanet.com)
The award-winning Lonely Planet Web site, containing destination updates, recent travellers' letters and a useful travellers' bulletin board.

### Wildnet Africa
(www.wildnetafrica.co.za/wildweb.html)
A companion site to Worldnet Africa, this is a wildlife site, offering links to the national parks and game reserves of southern Africa. It's extremely informative and comprehensive.

### Travelinfo Southern Africa
(www.rapidttp.com/travel)
This site wastes no time with graphics and is very ordinary-looking, but full of good info on where to stay and what to do, getting around, and health and safety. It covers Botswana, Lesotho, Madagascar, Malawi, Mozambique, Namibia, Swaziland, South Africa, Zambia and Zimbabwe.

### South Africa's Electronic Mail & Guardian
(www.mg.co.za/mg)
An interesting and entertaining off-the-beaten-track guide to holidays in southern Africa.

### Africanet
(www.africanet.com)
Although still under development, Africanet looks to be a fairly impressive and comprehensive site. There's country-specific information such as visa requirements and getting around, and the site has special interest information including beach resorts, photography in Africa, special events and exchange rates.

*TeleAdapt Inc*, 2151 O'Toole Ave, Suite H, San Jose, CA 95131, USA (☎ (408) 965-1400; fax 965-1414; <info@us.teleadapt.com>)
*TeleAdapt Pty Ltd*, Locked Bag 5340, Artarmon, Sydney 2064, Australia (☎ (02) 9433 8363; fax 9433 8369; <info@au.teleadapt.com>)

## BOOKS

If there's one place that sparks writers' imaginations and emotions, it's Africa. Bibliophiles with an interest in southern African works – particularly literature and historical and political treatises – may enjoy the bimonthly publication *Southern African Review of Books* (☎ (021) 462 2012; fax 461 5407), Sir Lowry Rd, PO Box 13094, Cape Town 7900, South Africa.

### Lonely Planet

Lonely Planet also publishes the *Zimbabwe, Botswana & Namibia travel atlas* to help you get around. If you're including South Africa in your itinerary you'll also find Lonely Planet's *South Africa, Lesotho & Swaziland* useful, as well as the accompanying *South Africa, Lesotho & Swaziland travel atlas*.

### Regional Titles

The following list outlines general regional titles dealing with historical, social and conservation issues, as well as general interest titles. Titles specific to individual countries are listed in the Facts for the Visitor chapter for each country.

Most books are published in different editions by different publishers in different countries. As a result, a book might be a hardcover rarity in one country while it's readily available in paperback in another. Fortunately, bookshops and libraries search by title or author, so your local bookshop or library is best placed to advise you on the availability of the following recommended books.

*At the Hand of Man* by Raymond Bonner holds that nature conservation will only work if Africans see real benefits themselves. He also rightly maintains that western-style conservation measures in-

volving laws, force, threats and insensitivity to local cultures and traditions only create animosity and suspicion. *Kakuli* by Norman Carr covers the same points, which the author (a leading southern African wildlife conservationist) first raised over 30 years ago. It's also a very readable account of life in the bush.

Elephant conservation has come to represent wider issues, as described in several books. *Dear Elephant, Sir* by Clive Walker, a well known southern African conservationist, attempts to explain to elephants why humans have treated them so abominably, and amazingly, it isn't as dizzy as it sounds.

*The Last Elephant* by Jeremy Gavron is a light and sympathetic introduction to debates about elephant poaching and culling, and the ivory trade issue. Particularly entertaining is the tale of the eponymous Last Elephant in Burundi, which managed to keep a step ahead of poachers and development.

*To Save an Elephant* by Allan Thornton & Dave Currey is a gripping tale outlining the undercover work by the Environmental Investigation Agency and its infiltration of the illicit ivory trade, from Kenya to Dubai to Hong Kong. In Zimbabwe, it discovered a sinister trail of 'accidental' death, which frequently befalls active opponents to the corruption that fuels the trade.

*Fantastic Invasion – Dispatches from Africa* by Patrick Marnham reveals the shambles created when western-style politics, government, boundaries, values and conservation efforts were superimposed upon established African cultures. *Banana Sunday – Datelines from Africa* by Chris Munion contains humorous accounts based on dispatches by a journalist covering various African wars.

Like Marnham and Munion, the author of *Fishing in Africa*, Andrew Buckoke, was a newspaper correspondent in Africa. This depressing exposé of chaos, corruption and violence from Sudan to Zimbabwe is lightened only by moments when the author wanders away from the breaking stories and power games to seek out secret fishing holes – and real people – off the beaten track.

*Blood on the Tracks* by Miles Bredin chronicles a hopeless attempt by the author and Harriet Logan to ride the rails between Angola and Mozambique – a tale of war, bureaucracy, corruption and inefficiency, neatly outlining the problems faced by modern Africa.

*The Scramble for Africa – White Man's Conquest of the Dark Continent from 1876 to 1942*, by Thomas Pakenham, details the colonial history of Africa in well written and entertaining prose. It was one of the first studies to tell both sides of the story and has become established as the standard work on the topic.

*The History of Southern Africa* by Kevin Shillington provides an overall historical discussion of Botswana, Namibia, South Africa, Lesotho and Swaziland in textbook form. It objectively and sensitively covers prehistory as well as black African and colonial history.

The idealistic *No Man's Land* by George Monbiot champions the rights of nomadic peoples living a traditional lifestyle to occupy game parks and other wilderness areas in Africa. It focuses on Kenya, but the issue is especially germane to the plight of the San of Botswana and Namibia.

A useful and entertaining choice is *Travellers' Literary Companion – Africa*, edited by Oona Stathern, which contains over 250 prose and poetry extracts from around Africa. There's also an introduction to each country's literature and a list of 'literary landmarks' – sites that appear in novels written about the country.

Motorcyclists will love the *Adventure Motorbiking Handbook* by Chris Scott, which reveals all there is to know about two-wheeling in remote places, particularly arid areas. A series of stimulating anecdotes by 'those who've done it' illustrates the thrills – and the glitches – that await you (see also the Web sites www.compass-star.co.uk/AMW.htm and www.uscrs.global net.co.uk/~ckscott/). *Africa by Road*, by Bob Swain & Paula Snyder, provides no-nonsense advice for African expeditions by private vehicle.

Finally, avid cooks may be interested in learning more about the local cuisines with *The African News Cookbook*, *A Zimbabwean Cookery Book* and *A Taste of Africa*.

**Field Guides**

In the UK, an excellent source for wildlife and nature titles is Subbuteo Natural History Books Ltd (☎ (01352) 756551; fax 756004; <sales@subbooks.demon.co.uk>), Pistyll Farm, Nercwys, near Mold, Flintshire CH7 4EW (international mail orders are welcome). In the USA, try the Adventurous Traveler Bookstore (☎ (1-800) 282-3963) or Nature Co (☎ (1-800) 227-1114). In Australia, check out Andrew Isles (☎ (03) 9510 5750), 115 Greville St, Prahran 3181, Victoria.

*Robert's Birds of Southern Africa* by Gordon Lindsay is a birdwatching requisite, but it's not a featherweight volume. The more luggable but less comprehensive *Bundu Guide to the Birds of Zimbabwe* is available at Kingston's outlets in Zimbabwe.

*Ian Sinclair's Field Guide to the Birds of Southern Africa* by Ian Sinclair is a comprehensive work with colour plates of all avian species in the region. An abridged version that concentrates on commonly observed species is the *Illustrated Guide to the Birds of Southern Africa*.

The comprehensive *Newman's Birds of Southern Africa* by Kenneth Newman is the standard work on the region's avifauna; all species are identified in colour or black-and-white illustrations. The same author's *Birds of Botswana* is the most complete guide to Botswana's species, and it includes full-colour plates.

*Birds of Southern Africa* by SASOL is a comprehensively illustrated book with a format that is readily accessible to amateur birdwatchers.

The *Field Guide to the Mammals of Southern Africa* by Chris & Tilde Stuart is a well illustrated field guide to just about every furry thing you're likely to encounter in this part of the world. The *Field Guide to*

*Mammals of Africa Including Madagascar* by Haltenorth & Diller is a good portable choice with lots of colour plates.

*Land Mammals of Southern Africa* by Reay Smithers, one of South Africa's best-known zoologists, is a rundown of the 200 most frequently observed species.

*Predators of Southern Africa* by Hans Grobler contains in-depth coverage and an identification guide for all predatory mammal species.

*Southern, Central & East African Mammals* by Chris & Tilde Stuart is a handy pocket guide containing photos and descriptions of the most commonly seen mammal species in the southern half of the African continent.

If you want to know what it is that's slithering underfoot – and whether or not it's dangerous – the *Field Guide to the Snakes and Other Reptiles of Southern Africa* by Bill Branch has the answer.

Frogophiles will love the comprehensive *South African Frogs*, by Neville Passmore and Vincent Carruthers. It concentrates on South Africa, but includes most species found 'north of the border'.

The *Field Guide to the Butterflies of Southern Africa* by Igor Migdoll isn't totally comprehensive, but you probably won't encounter a butterfly that isn't included in this guide.

The large-format *Flowers of Southern Africa* by Auriol Batten is less a field guide than a celebration of major flowering species, illustrated with colourful paintings.

*Trees of Southern Africa* by K Coates provides the most thorough coverage of the sub-continent's arboreal richness, illustrated with colour photos and paintings.

For background on regional medicinal plants, look for *Medicinal Plants of South Africa*, available from Briza Publications (☎ (012) 329 3896; fax 329 4525), PO Box 56569, Arcadia 0007, South Africa.

## NEWSPAPERS & MAGAZINES

Several southern African magazines are available internationally by subscription and can provide useful preparatory reading.

Publications specific to each country are described in individual Facts for the Visitor chapters.

*Getaway* is South Africa's largest and most popular travel magazine, and each issue contains at least one article on travel in Zimbabwe, Botswana or Namibia. Contact Getaway (☎ (021) 531 0404; fax 531 7303), PO Box 596, Howard Place 7450, South Africa. Foreign subscriptions cost the equivalent of R100 (around US$28) for 12 issues.

Outdoor adventure buffs will also enjoy *Out There*, a bimonthly publication that features activities in Africa and beyond. Contact Out There (☎ (011) 497 2711; fax 834 6246; <outthere@tml.co.za>), PO Box 1138, Johannesburg 2000, South Africa.

More specialised is the biannual *African Safari*, with articles on wildlife, safaris and game reserves. Contact the magazine (☎/fax (02) 9542 5054; <safarim@ozemail .com.au>) at PO Box 575, Engadine 2233, Australia; or 2 Sidney Rd, Old Costessey, Norwich NR4 5DR, UK.

The new quarterly magazine *Travel Africa* covers the entire continent, with an emphasis on travel-related articles. Subscriptions cost UK£15 in the British Isles, UK£22 elsewhere. Contact Travel Africa (☎ (01865) 434220), 2 Potland Cottages, Toot Baldon, Oxford OX44 9NH.

The semi-monthly *Africa Environment & Wildlife*, which is one of the finest productions you'll encounter anywhere, examines issues all over the continent, with an emphasis on events in southern Africa. Foreign subscriptions cost R105, US$32 or UK£21 annually; contact Subscriptions, Africa Environment & Wildlife (☎ (021) 686 9001; fax 686 4500), PO Box 44223, Claremont 7735, Cape Town, South Africa.

## PHOTOGRAPHY & VIDEO
### Film & Equipment

Photographers will probably want to bring their equipment from home, as it can be expensive in southern Africa. Although print film is now widely available, slide film is sold only in urban centres and you may not find your preferred brand. Video cartridges are widely available in Namibia, and in a few places in Botswana (Gaborone and Maun) and Zimbabwe (Harare, Bulawayo and Victoria Falls).

Useful accessories would include a small flash, a cable release, a polarising filter, a lens-cleaning kit (fluid, tissue and aerosol), and silica-gel packs to protect against humidity. Also, remember to take spare batteries for cameras and flash units and make sure your equipment is insured. If you're using a video camera, you'll normally find 12V plugs in taxis (cigarette lighters) and hotels where you can recharge batteries. Factors that can spoil your equipment include heat, humidity, fine sand and sunlight, so take appropriate precautions.

## Photography

Most people find 100 ASA adequate for most situations, but for morning or evening shots at longer focal lengths (ie 300 to 500mm), 400 ASA allows greater flexibility. For transparencies, you'll get the best results with Fujichrome Sensia 100, Provia 100 or Velvia 50, or Kodachrome 64.

On sunny days, the best times for photos are the first two hours after sunrise and the last two before sunset, when the shadows are the least harsh and colours are strongest (due to colour-enhancing rays cast by a low sun). At other times, colours may be washed out by harsh sunlight and glare, although you can counter this with a polarising (UV) filter. If you're shooting on sand or near water, always adjust for glare and keep your photographic equipment away from salt water and sand.

When photographing out of doors, take light readings on the subject and not the brilliant African background or your shots will be underexposed.

## Restrictions

Officials in Zimbabwe, Botswana and Namibia aren't as paranoid about photography as their counterparts in some other African countries, but photographing bridges, airports, military equipment, government buildings and anything that could be considered strategic or susceptible to sabotage is taboo.

## Photographing Animals

To score some excellent wildlife shots effortlessly, a good lightweight 35mm SLR camera, a UV filter, and a 70 to 300mm zoom or a minimum 300mm fixed-length telephoto lens should do the trick. If your subject is nothing but a speck in the distance, however, resist wasting film on it but keep the camera ready – anything can happen at any time. Unless you're an experienced photographer, you may want to carry a 'point and shoot' automatic camera rather than a manual camera; once you've adjusted the aperture, exposure and focus, your subject could be long gone.

## Photographing People

The quest for that perfect 'people shot' will prove a photographer's greatest challenge. While many Africans enjoy being photographed, others do not; they may be superstitious about your camera, suspicious of your motives, or simply interested in whatever economic advantage they can gain from your desire to photograph them. The main point is that you must respect the wishes of the locals, however photogenic or colourful, who may be camera-shy for whatever reason. If you can't get a candid shot, ask permission and don't insist or snap a picture anyway if permission is denied.

Often, people will allow you to photograph them provided you give them a photo for themselves, a real treasure in rural Africa. Understandably, people are sometimes disappointed not to see the photograph immediately materialise. If you don't carry a Polaroid camera, take their address and make it clear that you'll send the photo by post once it's processed. And never promise to send a copy and then fail to do so.

When photographing people, particularly dark-skinned people, remember to take the light reading from the subject's face and not the background.

## TIME

In the summer months (October to April), Zimbabwe, Botswana and Namibia are two hours ahead of GMT/UTC. Therefore, when it's noon Saturday in southern Africa, it's 10 am Saturday in London, 5 am Saturday in New York, 2 am Saturday in Los Angeles and 8 pm Saturday in Sydney. In the winter (April to October), Namibia turns its clocks back an hour, making it only one hour ahead of GMT/UTC and one hour behind Zimbabwe and Botswana.

## ELECTRICITY

All three countries generate electricity at 220V AC, 15 amps. Zimbabwe has both three-pin rectangular (UK type) and three-pin round plug sockets. In Botswana, most sockets take two-pin round plugs, and in Namibia they take either two or three-pin round plugs. Few continental European or North American plug adaptors will cope with the full range of sockets found in all three countries, and you may have to buy a plug locally and connect it yourself. Note that a voltage adaptor is needed for US appliances.

## WEIGHTS & MEASURES

All three countries covered in this book use the metric system. To convert between metric and imperial units, refer to the conversion chart on the inside back cover of the book.

## HEALTH

Travel health depends largely on predeparture preparations, day to day attention to health, and the handling of health problems that do arise. The following section may seem like a who's who of unpleasant diseases, but the chances of contracting something serious in southern Africa are slight. Travellers are exposed to different environmental factors, foods and sanitation standards, but following a doctor's advice and using common sense will minimise risks.

The following health information is not meant to replace professional diagnosis or

---

### Medical Kit Checklist

Consider taking a small medical kit, which should include:

☐ **Aspirin** or paracetamol (acetominophen in the USA) – for headaches, pain or fever.

☐ **Antihistamine** (such as Benadryl) – useful as a decongestant for colds and allergies, to ease itching from insect bites, or to prevent motion sickness. Antihistamines may cause sedation and interact with alcohol so care should be taken when using them.

☐ **Antibiotics** – useful if you're travelling off the beaten track. Most antibiotics are prescription medicines, so carry the prescription along with you. Be sure to carry details of any drug allergies you may have.

☐ **Loperamide** (eg Imodium) or diphenoxylate (eg Lomotil), or kaolin and pectin preparations (eg Kaopectate), for diarrhoea, to bung things up when long-distance travel is essential.

☐ **Rehydration** mixture – for treatment of the effects of severe diarrhoea; particularly important when travelling with children.

☐ **Antiseptic** liquid or cream and antibiotic powder for minor injuries.

☐ **Calamine lotion** or **aluminium sulphate spray** – to ease irritation from bites and stings.

☐ **Bandages** and Band-Aids (plasters).

☐ **Scissors, tweezers** and a **thermometer** – note that the carrying of mercury thermometers is prohibited by airlines.

☐ **Cold and flu tablets** and throat lozenges – pseudoephedrine hydrochloride (Sudafed) is useful if flying with a cold, to prevent ear damage.

☐ **Insect repellent, 15+ sunblock** (sunscreen), **suntan lotion, chap stick** and **water purification tablets** (or iodine).

☐ **Sterile syringes**, in case you need an injection in a country where sanitation may be a problem. Ask your doctor for a note indicating their purpose.

prescriptions, and travellers should discuss travel health matters with their doctor.

## Predeparture Planning

**Information** In the US, the Overseas Citizens Emergency Center provides health and safety bulletins on African countries. Write to the Bureau of Consular Affairs Office, State Department, Washington, DC 20520. There's also a phone line (☎ (202) 632-5525) for emergencies abroad.

In the UK, Medical Advisory Services for Travellers Abroad (MASTA), Keppel Street, London WC1E 7HT provides 'Health Briefs' (☎ (0891) 224100) and a range of medical supplies (☎ (0113) 239 1707). Another source of medical information and supplies is the British Airways Travel Clinic (☎ (0171) 831 5333). The Department of Health publishes leaflets SA40/41 on travellers' health requirements, and operates a Freephone service (☎ (0800) 555777). In Australia, contact the Travellers Medical and Vaccination Centre in Sydney (☎ (02) 9221 7133) for general health information.

On the Internet there are also several excellent travel health Web sites. Lonely Planet's Web site at www.lonelyplanet.com/weblinks/wlprep.htm#heal has links to the sites for the World Health Organization (WHO) and the US Centers for Disease Control & Prevention.

**Vaccinations** For entry into Zimbabwe and Namibia, a yellow-fever vaccination certificate is required if you are arriving from yellow fever endemic areas further north in Africa (including Zambia) or South America. The most commonly recommended vaccines for travel to southern Africa are typhoid, diphtheria & tetanus, polio and meningitis. Protection against hepatitis is also recommended.

In general, the further off the beaten track you go, the more necessary it is to take precautions. Children and pregnant women are often at a greater risk of disease.

Plan ahead for getting your vaccinations: some require an initial shot followed by a booster, while some should not be given together. It's recommended that you seek medical advice at least six weeks prior to travel. All vaccinations should be recorded on an International Health Certificate, which is available from your doctor or government health department.

Some vaccines to consider include:

- *Hepatitis A* This is the most common travel-acquired illness after diarrhoea, and can put you out of action for weeks. Havrix 1440 and Vaqta are vaccinations that provide long-term immunity (possibly more than 10 years) after an initial injection and a booster at six to 12 months.

  Gamma globulin is ready-made antibody collected from blood donations. It should be given close to departure because, depending on the dose, it only protects for two to six months.
- *Hepatitis B* This disease is spread by blood or by sexual activity. Travellers who should consider a hepatitis B vaccination include those visiting countries where there are known to be many carriers, where blood transfusions may not be adequately screened or where sexual contact is a possibility. It involves three injections, the quickest course being over three weeks with a booster at 12 months.
- *Typhoid* This vaccine is recommended for any country with hygiene problems. It's available either as an injection or oral capsules.
- *Diphtheria & Tetanus* Diphtheria is a throat infection and tetanus is transmitted through open wounds; both are potentially fatal. Vaccines are highly recommended for everyone; after an initial course of three injections, boosters are necessary at least every 10 years.
- *Meningococcal Meningitis* This disease, which is transmitted like a cold by healthy carriers, can be fatal within a few hours. Although the disease isn't a serious problem in the countries covered in this book, the vaccination is recommended for onward travel to Mozambique, Angola and central Africa. A single injection is good for up to three years.
- *Poliomyelitis* This serious, easily communicable disease is present in southern Africa. Although most westerners are immunised as children, it's necessary to keep the vaccination up to date with a booster every 10 years.
- *Rabies* Vaccination against this fatal disease should be considered by longer-term travellers to Africa, especially if they're cycling, handling animals, caving or travelling to remote

areas. It's also recommended for children, who may not report being bitten. Pretravel rabies vaccination involves three injections over 21 to 28 days. If someone who has been vaccinated is bitten or scratched by an animal, they will require two booster injections, while those not already vaccinated require more.

• *Cholera* The cholera vaccine is of limited efficacy, lasts only six months and is not recommended for pregnant women. There have been no recent reports of cholera vaccine requirements in Zimbabwe, Botswana or Namibia, but those travelling overland through Africa might want to have it to avoid possible delays at borders.

• *Tuberculosis* TB risk to travellers is usually very low, but for those who will be living closely with local people, there may be some risk. Vaccination is recommended for children living in the region for more than three months. Most healthy adults don't develop symptoms; a skin test before and after travel will determine whether exposure has occurred.

**Malaria Prophylaxis** There's currently no efficacious vaccination against malaria, but antimalarial drugs significantly reduce the risk of you becoming very ill or dying from malaria. These drugs do not prevent you from becoming infected but they can kill the malarial parasites during a certain stage in their development.

All endemic areas of southern Africa should be considered chloroquine-resistant (that is, the parasite does not respond to chloroquine-based antimalarial drugs). There are many factors to be considered, including the area to be visited, the risk of exposure to malaria-carrying mosquitoes, the side effects of medication, your medical history, your age and whether you are pregnant, so discuss the matter thoroughly with your doctor before deciding which course to take.

**Travel Health Guides** Several good books on travel health include:

*Bites, Bugs & Bowels*, by Jane Wilson Howarth (Cadogan). This witty guide is a useful companion for travellers in the developing world.
*Practice Guidelines for Wilderness Emergency Care*, by William W Forgey, MD (ICS Books, 1370 E 86th Place, Merrillville, IN 46410,

USA). This book includes the best available wilderness medical guidelines and advice on dealing with natural hazards.
*Staying Healthy in Asia, Africa & Latin America* (Moon Publications). This handy volume is probably the best all-round guide to carry.
*Travellers' Health*, by Dr Richard Dawood (Oxford University Press). This comprehensive and authoritative work is recommended reading.
*Where There is No Doctor*, by David Werner (Macmillan). This detailed guide is especially suitable for people living and working in remote areas.
*Travel with Children*, by Maureen Wheeler (Lonely Planet Publications). This one includes basic advice on travel health for children.

**Other Preparations** Make sure you're healthy before embarking on a long journey. Have your teeth checked and if you wear glasses or contacts, bring a spare pair and a copy of your prescription. Losing your glasses can be a real problem, but in southern Africa you can have a new pair made with little fuss. Also, a pair of good quality, UV-protective sunglasses is essential, as are a hat, sunscreen lotion and lip protection.

If you require a particular medication, contraceptive pills or vitamin tablets, take an adequate supply as they may not be available locally. Take a copy of any prescription with the generic rather than the brand name so it will be universally recognisable.

**Basic Rules**
**Food** Zimbabwe, Botswana and Namibia aren't particularly unhealthy countries, but in some places, sanitation and hygiene can be poor, so pay attention to what you eat. Stomach upsets, mostly minor, are the most common travel-health problem, but don't be paranoid about sampling local foods – it's all part of the travel experience and shouldn't be missed.

Salads and fruit should be washed with purified water or peeled where possible. Ice cream, even a reputable brand, may have been melted and refrozen, and is best

## Nutrition

If your food is poor or limited in availability, if you're travelling and therefore missing meals, or if you simply lose your appetite, you can soon start to lose weight and place your health at risk.

Make sure your diet is well balanced. Eggs, tofu, beans, lentils and nuts are all safe ways to get protein. Fruit that you can peel (bananas, oranges or mandarins for example) is always safe and a good source of vitamins. Try to eat plenty of grains (including rice) and bread. Remember that although food is generally safer if it is cooked well, overcooked food loses much of its nutritional value. If your diet isn't well balanced or if your food intake is insufficient, it's a good idea to take vitamin and iron tablets.

In hot climates, drink lots of liquids – don't rely on feeling thirsty to indicate when you should drink. Not needing to urinate or trickles of dark yellow urine are danger signs. Always carry a water bottle with you on long trips. Excessive sweating can lead to loss of salt and cause muscle cramping. Salt tablets are not a good idea as a preventative, but in places where salt is not used much, adding salt to food can help.

---

avoided. Take great care with shellfish or fish and avoid undercooked meat, particularly in the form of mince. Steaming does not make shellfish safe for eating.

In general, if a place looks clean and well run and the vendor also looks clean and healthy, the food is probably all right. Places that are packed with travellers or locals will be fine, while empty restaurants are questionable. Busy restaurants mean the food is being cooked and eaten quickly and is probably not being reheated.

**Water** Although some areas may have problems with contaminated water, tap water is generally safe to drink in Zimbabwe, Botswana and Namibia. Care should be taken when drinking from rural bores, however, since many are considered fit only for cattle. Except in the Okavango Delta and some areas of Zimbabwe's Eastern Highlands, surface water (ie from rivers, lakes and ponds) should not be drunk untreated.

Reputable brands of bottled water or soft drinks are normally fine although sometimes water bottles are refilled – use only containers with serrated seals, not caps or corks, and check the seals before buying. Take care with fruit juices since water may

have been added. Good quality pasteurised milk is available all over the region, but in rural areas milk is often unpasteurised and is best avoided due to the risk of TB.

**Water Purification** You may on occasion need to rely on surface water or rural bores, which may be contaminated. The simplest way to purify water is to boil it vigorously. At higher altitudes, water boils at a lower temperature and must therefore be boiled for longer to kill bacteria.

Alternatively, consider purchasing a water filter. There are two main types of filters and it's important to read and understand the specifications of the one you choose. Simple filters take out dirt and larger foreign bodies, allowing chemical solutions to work more effectively. They do not remove all dangerous organisms so you still need to boil the water or treat it with a chemical tablet.

Total filters, on the other hand, take out all organisms and chemical contaminants and make the water safe to drink. They are often expensive, but can be more cost-effective than buying bottled water.

Chlorine tablets (Puritabs, Steritabs and other brand names) kill many but not all pathogens. Iodine is very effective and is available in tablet form (such as Potable Aqua) but follow the directions carefully and remember that too much iodine is harmful.

## Medical Problems & Treatment
Self-diagnosis and treatment can be risky, so wherever possible seek qualified help. Although we do give treatment dosages in this section, they are for emergency use only. Correct diagnosis is vital.

An embassy, consulate or five-star hotel can usually recommend a local doctor. In some places standards of medical attention are so low that for some ailments the best advice is to get on a plane and go somewhere else. Fortunately, all three countries covered in this book have reasonably good standards of medical care and excellent care is also available in nearby South Africa (particularly in Johannesburg and Cape Town).

Just about any sort of remedy available at home can also be found in local pharmacies, but most drugs are available only on prescription. There are some exceptions, however, and some pharmacists will dispense treatment dosages of such things as praziquantel (Biltricide – for bilharzia) or malaria prophylaxis and treatment without a prescription.

Antibiotics should ideally be administered only under medical supervision. Take only the recommended dose at the prescribed intervals and use the whole course, even if the illness seems to be cured earlier. Stop immediately if there are any serious reactions and don't use the antibiotic at all if you are unsure that you have the correct one. Some people are allergic to commonly prescribed antibiotics such as penicillin or sulpha drugs; if you are, carry this information when travelling, for example on a bracelet.

When buying medications, especially outside major cities, be sure to check expiry dates. Also, bear in mind that some drugs available in Africa may be no longer recommended or even banned in other countries.

## Environmental Hazards
**Fungal Infections** Hot-weather fungal infections are most likely to occur on the scalp, between the fingers or toes (athlete's foot), in the groin (jock itch) and on the body (ringworm). You get ringworm (which is a fungus, not a worm) from infected animals or by walking on damp areas, such as shower floors.

To prevent fungal infections wear loose, comfortable clothes, avoid artificial fibres, wash frequently and dry carefully. If you do get an infection, wash the infected area daily with a disinfectant or medicated soap and water, and rinse and dry well. Apply an antifungal powder such as tolnaftate (Tinaderm) and expose the affected area to air or sunlight as much as possible. Wash towels and underwear, let them dry in the sun and change them often.

**Heat Exhaustion** Dehydration or salt deficiency can lead to heat exhaustion. Take time to acclimatise to high temperatures, drink sufficient liquids and don't do anything too physically demanding. Salt deficiency is characterised by fatigue, lethargy, headaches, giddiness and muscle cramps. Salt tablets will help, but it's better just to add salt to your food. Anhidrotic heat exhaustion, a rare form of the condition, is caused by an inability to sweat. It tends to affect people who have been in a hot climate for several months, rather than newcomers, and can progress to heatstroke. Treatment involves removal to a cooler climate.

**Heatstroke** This serious, sometimes fatal, condition can occur if the body's thermostat breaks down and the body temperature rises to dangerous levels. Excessive alcohol consumption, strenuous activity or long periods of exposure to high temperatures, especially if you've recently arrived in a hot climate, can leave you vulnerable to heatstroke.

Symptoms include minimal sweating, a flushed red skin, a high body temperature (39 to 41°C or 102 to 106°F) and generally feeling unwell. Severe throbbing head-aches, aggressive or confused behaviour and decreased co-ordination may also be signs of heatstroke. Eventually, the sufferer will become delirious or go into convulsions. Hospitalisation is essential, but in the interim, get the victim out of the sun, remove their clothing, cover them with a wet sheet or towel and then fan continually. If they're conscious, administer fluids.

**Hypothermia** Hypothermia occurs when the body loses heat faster than it can produce it and the core body temperature falls. It's surprisingly easy to progress from very cold to dangerously cold due to a combination of wind, wet clothing, fatigue and hunger, even if the air temperature is above freezing. Hikers, trekkers, hitchers, swimmers and anyone spending long periods in wet or windy conditions, or at temperatures below about 10°C, are particularly vulnerable. It's best to use the layering method when selecting clothing; silk, wool and new synthetics, such as polypropylene, are all good insulating materials. A hat is also essential, as lots of heat is lost through the scalp. A strong waterproof outer layer and a 'space blanket' (for emergencies) are essential. Carry sufficient fluids and snacks containing simple sugars (to generate heat quickly).

Symptoms of hypothermia are exhaustion, numbness (particularly toes and fingers), shivering, slurred speech, irrational or violent behaviour, lethargy, stumbling, dizzy spells, muscle cramps and violent bursts of energy. Irrationality may take the form of sufferers claiming that they are warm and then trying to remove their clothing.

To treat mild hypothermia, first get the person out of the wind and/or rain, remove their clothing if it's wet and replace it with warm, dry clothing (no clothing at all is better than wet garments) or get them into a sleeping bag. Give them hot liquids, high-carbohydrate food and a hot bath if possible. This should be sufficient to treat the early stages of hypothermia.

**Jet Lag** Many of the human body's functions (such as temperature, pulse rate, and emptying of the bowels and bladder) are regulated by internal 24-hour cycles. When we travel by air across three or more time zones, our bodies require time to adjust to the 'new time' at our destination. As a result, we may experience fatigue, insomnia, anxiety, disorientation, impaired concentration and loss of appetite. These effects normally disappear after a few days (the more time zones you cross, the more time required), but to minimise the impact of jet lag:

- Rest for a couple of days prior to departure.
- Try to select flight schedules that minimise sleep deprivation; arriving late in the day means that you go to bed soon after arrival. For very long flights, try to organise a stopover.
- Avoid excessive eating (which bloats the stomach) and alcohol consumption (which causes dehydration) during the flight. Instead, choose non-carbonated, non-alcoholic drinks such as fruit juice or water.
- Avoid smoking.
- Wear comfortable loose-fitting clothing and bring an eye mask and ear plugs to help you sleep.
- Try to sleep at the appropriate time for your destination.

**Motion Sickness** Eating lightly before and during a trip will reduce your chances of succumbing to motion sickness. If you know you're susceptible, try to find a place that minimises motion – near the wing on aircraft or near the centre on buses. Fresh air usually helps but reading and cigarette smoking don't.

Commercial motion sickness preparations, which can cause drowsiness, have to be taken before the trip commences; once you begin feeling ill, it's too late. Ginger (available in capsule form) or peppermint can be used as natural preventatives.

**Prickly Heat** Prickly heat is an itchy rash caused by excessive perspiration under the skin. It usually strikes those newly arrived in a hot climate whose pores have not opened enough to accommodate sweating.

Keeping cool, taking frequent baths and applying talcum powder may help.

**Sunburn** All three countries covered in this book lie mostly within the humid tropics where the sun's rays are more direct and concentrated than in temperate zones. Even in the cooler highland areas, everyone – particularly fair-skinned people – is susceptible to hazardous UV rays, even when it's cloudy. Use a sunblock with a UV protection factor of 15 or higher on exposed skin; wear a hat; protect your eyes with UV protective sunglasses; and perhaps use a barrier cream, such as zinc oxide, on your nose and lips.

## Infectious Diseases

**Diarrhoea** Simple things like a change of water, food or climate can cause a mild bout of diarrhoea, but a few rushed trips to the toilet with no other symptoms is not indicative of a serious problem.

Dehydration is the main danger with any diarrhoea, particularly in children or senior travellers, as it can occur quite quickly. The most essential treatment is fluid replacement – you need to drink at least the same volume of fluid that you are losing in bowel movements and vomiting. If urination produces only small amounts of concentrated urine, you need to drink more, and to drink more often. Soda water, flat soft drinks diluted with 50% water or weak black tea with a little sugar are all good.

With severe diarrhoea, a rehydrating solution is preferable to replace lost salts and minerals. Commercially available oral rehydration solutions (ORS) should be added to boiled or bottled water. In an emergency, you can make up a solution with six teaspoons of sugar, a half teaspoon of salt and a litre of boiled or bottled water. As you recover, stick to a bland diet.

Gut-paralysing drugs like Lomotil or Imodium can be used to bring relief to the symptoms, but they don't actually cure the problem. Only use them if you do not have access to a toilet – for instance, if you must make a long bus trip. Note that these drugs aren't recommended for children under 12 years of age, or when the diarrhoea is accompanied by severe dehydration or a high fever.

The drug bismuth subsalicylate may be useful in shortening the duration of travellers' diarrhoea, but it may not be available everywhere (eg it's unavailable in Australia). The dosage for adults is two tablets or 30mL and for children one tablet or 10mL. This dose can be repeated every 30 minutes to one hour, with no more than eight doses in a 24 hour period. Care should be taken, as side effects may occur, and medical advice is preferred.

In certain situations antibiotics may be required: diarrhoea with blood or mucus (dysentery), diarrhoea with fever, profuse watery diarrhoea, persistent diarrhoea not improving after 48 hours and severe diarrhoea. These indicate a more serious cause of diarrhoea. In these situations gut-paralysing drugs should be avoided.

A stool test is necessary to diagnose what is causing your diarrhoea, so you should seek medical help urgently in these situations. Where this is not possible the recommended drugs for treating bacterial diarrhoea (the most common cause of diarrhoea in travellers) are norfloxacin 400mg twice daily for three days or ciprofloxacin 500mg twice daily for five days, or one of their related drugs. These are not recommended for children or pregnant women. The drug of choice for children is a five day course of co-trimoxazole (Bactrim, Septrin, Resprim), with dosage dependent on weight. Ampicillin or amoxycillin may be given if the patient is pregnant, but medical care is necessary.

Two other causes of persistent diarrhoea are amoebic dysentery and giardiasis. **Amoebic dysentery** is characterised by a gradual onset of low-grade diarrhoea, often with blood or mucus. Cramping abdominal pain and vomiting are less likely with this than in other types of diarrhoea, and fever may not be present. It will persist until treated and can recur and cause other health problems.

The parasite causing **giardiasis** is found in contaminated water. Symptoms include stomach cramps, nausea, a bloated stomach, watery foul-smelling diarrhoea and frequent gas. Giardiasis can appear several weeks after you have been exposed to the parasite. The symptoms may disappear for a few days and then return; this can go on for several weeks.

You should seek medical advice if you think you may have amoebic dysentery or giardiasis, but where this is not possible, Tinidazole (Fasigyn) or metronidazole (Flagyl) are the recommended drugs. Treatment is a 2g single dose of Fasigyn or 250mg of Flagyl three times daily for five to 10 days.

**Hepatitis** Hepatitis is a general term for inflammation of the liver, and the disease occurs worldwide. Symptoms include fever, chills, headache, fatigue, weakness, and aches and pains, followed by loss of appetite, nausea, vomiting, abdominal pain, dark urine, light-coloured faeces and jaundice (yellow colouring) in the skin and eyes.

Hepatitis A is transmitted by contaminated food and drinking water, and may therefore be readily contracted by travellers. You should seek medical advice, but there's little you can do apart from resting, drinking lots of fluids, eating lightly and avoiding fatty foods. People who have had hepatitis should avoid alcohol for some time after the illness, to allow the liver time to recover.

Hepatitis B has nearly 300 million chronic carriers worldwide and is prevalent in southern Africa. It is spread through contact with infected blood, blood products or body fluids, for example through sexual contact, unsterilised needles, infected blood transfusions or contact with blood through minor wounds. Other risk situations are shaving, tattooing or body piercing with contaminated equipment. The symptoms of hepatitis B may be more severe than those of hepatitis A and may lead to long-term health problems.

The hepatitis C and D viruses are spread by contact with blood – usually via contaminated needles or transfusions – and can lead to chronic liver disease. The D strain, known as the 'delta particle', always occurs in concert with hepatitis B, never on its own. Hepatitis E is transmitted in the same way as hepatitis A and can be very serious in pregnant women. Expensive tests are available for these strains, but travellers shouldn't be too paranoid as they're fairly rare (so far) and following the same precautions as for A and B should be all that's necessary to avoid them.

**HIV & AIDS** Infection with the Human Immunodeficiency Virus (HIV), which may develop into Acquired Immune Deficiency Syndrome (AIDS), is a serious problem worldwide, but is prevalent in Africa and should be a major concern to all visitors. Known colloquially as 'Slim' because it causes victims to appear emaciated, AIDS is particularly rampant in East Africa – some areas of Uganda have already been depopulated by it – and it has spread southwards, particularly along trucking routes and in areas where men migrate to work far from their families. Therefore the most vulnerable segment of society is economically productive men, and often their wives.

Although it exists in all three countries covered in this book, Zimbabwe has the most serious problem and the statistics may seem frightening and difficult to accept. Zimbabwe's AIDS education programme has now taken off, but HIV was virtually ignored until the early 1990s. Currently 90% of all deaths in Zimbabwe are AIDS-related and in June 1997, papers reported that 50% of all children seen by doctors in Harare were HIV-positive. Botswana also has problems, and at the time of writing 30% of the country's sexually active population between 15 and 49 years of age were infected with the virus.

Any exposure to blood, blood products or body fluids may put the individual at risk. The disease is often transmitted through sexual contact or dirty needles – injections, acupuncture, tattooing and body piercing can be potentially as dangerous as intravenous drug use. If you do need an injection, ask to see the syringe unwrapped in front of you, or take your own needle and syringe pack. (However, fear of HIV infection should not preclude treatment for serious medical conditions.)

HIV/AIDS can also be spread through infected blood transfusions; Zimbabwe, Botswana and Namibia currently claim that all blood donations are screened for HIV. If you must have a transfusion, private clinics are preferable to public hospitals; if you're able, ascertain that the blood in question has been screened and is clear of the virus.

See also Sexually Transmitted Diseases below.

**Intestinal Worms** Worms are common throughout the humid tropics and different worms are transmitted in different ways, eg by eating unwashed vegetables or undercooked meat or by walking barefoot. Infestations may not show up for some time and although they aren't generally serious, they can cause severe health problems later if left untreated. Consider having a stool test when you return home to check for worms and determine the appropriate treatment.

**Meningococcal Meningitis** This very serious disease is spread by close contact with healthy carriers who spread it through coughs and sneezes. It attacks the brain and can be fatal. A fever, severe headache, sensitivity to light and neck stiffness that restricts bowing of the head are the first symptoms. There may also be blotchy purple patches on the skin. Death may occur in just a few hours, so urgent medical treatment is required. Treatment is large doses of penicillin given intravenously or injections of chloramphenicol.

**Schistosomiasis** Also known as bilharzia, this disease is prevalent in southern Africa and is caused by blood flukes, minute worms that infect certain species of fresh-

water snail found in rivers, lakes and dams. Once inside the snails, they multiply for several weeks before being released into the water.

The worms enter the body through the skin and attach themselves to the intestines or bladder. The first symptoms may be a general feeling of being unwell, and a tingling and sometimes a light rash around the area where it entered. Weeks later, a high fever may develop. Once the disease is established, from several months to a year after exposure, signs include abdominal pain and blood in the urine. At this stage, damage to internal organs is irreversible.

The best prevention is to avoid swimming or bathing in rivers, lakes and especially dams – the streams of Zimbabwe's Eastern Highlands and Botswana's Okavango Delta are significant exceptions. Since the intermediate hosts – snails – live only in fresh water, there's no risk of catching bilharzia in the sea. If you do get wet, dry off quickly and dry your clothes as well.

A blood test provides the most reliable diagnosis, but will not show up positive until a number of weeks after exposure. Bilharzia is normally treated with praziquantel (Biltricide), at a dose of 40mg per kg of body weight.

**Sexually Transmitted Diseases** The most common STDs are gonorrhoea and syphilis, which may appear as sores, blisters or rashes around the genitals and pain or discharge when urinating. In some STDs, such as wart virus or chlamydia, symptoms may be less marked, or not evident at all in women. The symptoms of syphilis eventually disappear but the disease continues and may cause severe problems later.

While abstinence from sexual contact is the only 100% effective prevention, using a condom is also effective. Antibiotics are used to treat both syphilis and gonorrhoea; there is currently no cure for herpes or AIDS (see HIV & AIDS above).

**Typhoid** Typhoid is a dangerous gut infection caused by contaminated food or water.

In its early stages, typhoid may resemble the flu or a bad cold, with a headache, body aches and a fever that slowly rises to around 40°C (104°F) or more while the pulse slowly drops (unlike other fevers, in which the pulse increases). These symptoms may be accompanied by nausea, diarrhoea or constipation.

In the second week, the fever and slow pulse continue and a few pink spots may appear on the body. Trembling, delirium, weakness, weight loss and dehydration may occur, as may complications such as pneumonia, meningitis or perforated bowel.

The fever should be treated by keeping the victim cool and administering fluids to prevent dehydration. The drug of choice is ciprofloxacin at a dose of 750mg daily for 10 days. The alternative, chloramphenicol, is also prescribed in many countries. The adult dosage is two 250mg capsules, four times daily. Children eight to 12 years old get half the adult dose and younger children one-third the adult dose.

### Insect-Borne Diseases

**Malaria** Malaria is caused by the blood parasite *Plasmodium*, which is transmitted by the nocturnal *Anopheles* mosquito. There are four types: *Plasmodium falciparum*, the deadliest; *Plasmodium malariae*, which is still universally sensitive to chloroquine; and *Plasmodium vivax* and *Plasmodium ovale*. The drug-resistant status of different malarial strains in different parts of the world is constantly in flux. Currently, the areas of greatest risk include the Zambezi and Chobe valleys, the Okavango Delta, the lowveld of south-eastern Zimbabwe and Namibia's Caprivi Strip.

Only female mosquitoes spread the disease. Malaria sporozoites enter the bloodstream and travel to the liver where they mature, infect the red blood cells and multiply. This process takes between one and five weeks (*P. falciparum* normally incubates in seven to 14 days). Only when the infected cells re-enter the bloodstream and burst do the dramatic symptoms begin. Therefore malaria can develop after the victim has left the malarial area, and may be improperly treated.

If you are travelling in endemic areas it is extremely important to avoid mosquito bites and to take tablets to prevent this disease. Symptoms range from fever, chills and sweating, headache, diarrhoea and abdominal pains to a vague feeling of ill-health. Seek medical help immediately if malaria is suspected, as most malaria deaths are due to delays in treatment.

If medical care is not available, malaria tablets can be used for treatment. You need to use a malaria tablet that is different from the one you were taking when you contracted malaria. The standard treatment dosage of mefloquine is three 250mg tablets and a further two six hours later. With Fansidar, take a single dose of three tablets. If you were previously taking mefloquine and can not obtain Fansidar, then other alternatives are Malarone (atovaquone-proguanil; four tablets once daily for three days), halofantrine (three doses of two 250mg tablets every six hours) or quinine sulphate (600mg every six hours). There is a greater risk of side effects with these dosages than in normal use if used with mefloquine, so medical advice is preferable. Be aware also that halofantrine is no longer recommended by the WHO as emergency standby treatment because of side effects. It is, however, the most widely used treatment in Zimbabwe and Namibia but should only be used if no other drugs are available.

Travellers are advised to prevent mosquito bites at all times. The main points are:

- wear light-coloured clothing
- wear long pants and long-sleeved shirts
- use mosquito repellents containing the compound DEET on exposed areas – (prolonged overuse of DEET may be harmful, especially to children, but its use is considered preferable to being bitten by disease-transmitting mosquitoes)
- avoid wearing perfume or aftershave
- use a mosquito net impregnated with mosquito repellent (permethrin) – it may be worth taking your own
- impregnating clothes with permethrin effectively deters mosquitoes and other insects

**Myiasis** This unpleasant disease is caused by the larvae of the tumbu or putse fly, which lays eggs on damp or sweaty clothing. The eggs hatch and the larvae burrow into the skin, producing an ugly boil. To kill the invader, place drops of hydrogen peroxide, alcohol or oil over the boil to cut off its air supply, then squeeze the boil to remove the bug. However revolting the process, at this stage the problem is solved.

### Cuts, Bites & Stings

**Cuts & Scratches** Thanks to the warm moist conditions in the tropical lowlands, even a small cut or scratch can become painfully infected and lead to more serious problems. Wash cuts well with soap and apply an antiseptic like povidone-iodine. Where possible, avoid bandages and Band-Aids (plasters), as these will keep wounds moist and encourage bacterial growth. If the wound becomes tender and inflamed, you may find that treatment with antibiotics is warranted.

**Bedbugs, Scabies & Lice** Bedbugs live in dirty mattresses and leave itchy bites in neat rows. They're evidenced by blood spots on bedding and walls. Calamine lotion or Stingose spray may help. Scabies mites are also harboured in bedding and burrow mainly into the abdomen, buttocks, wrists and ankles, creating itchy rash-like eruptions. To get rid of them, wash clothing, bedding and towels and shower several times in a lindane-based anti-scabies lotion, eg Kwell, or a malathion solution.

Lice make themselves at home in your hair (head lice), clothing (body lice) or pubic hair (crabs), causing itching and discomfort. They're caught through direct contact with affected people or their personal belongings. Powder or shampoo treatment will kill the lice. Affected clothing should be washed in very hot, soapy water.

**Bites & Stings** Ants, gnats, mosquitoes, bees and flies are as annoying in Africa as they are at home, but unless you're allergic, they're usually more painful than dangerous. Calamine lotion or Stingose spray will offer relief and ice packs will reduce pain and swelling. Tea tree oil works well on non-infected bites, to dry up the bite and minimise itching.

Several species of spider can also deliver a painful bite. The most venomous spider in southern Africa is the six-eyed crab spider, which is found in Botswana, Namibia and southern Zimbabwe, and for which no antivenin is available. It hunts by covering itself in sand and then leaping out at its prey. The rare button spider, which lives in the Zambezi Valley, is not aggressive and rarely life-threatening, although it bites instinctively when touched. Medical attention should be sought if bitten, as antivenin is available, although it is usually reserved for children or elderly people. Button spiders tend to reside in messy webs indoors or low down in short grass or other plants.

To avoid receiving spider bites, simple precautions should suffice, such as not walking barefoot outdoors and not sticking hands into places where spiders might be lurking.

Scorpion and centipede stings are notoriously painful but rarely fatal; always check your shoes and clothing before slipping them on.

**Leeches & Ticks** Leeches, which attach themselves to your skin to suck your blood, may be present in damp conditions and trekkers often get them on their legs or in their boots. Salt or a lighted cigarette end will persuade a leech to let go, but don't pull them off, as the bite is then more likely to become infected. Clean and apply pressure if the point of attachment is bleeding. An insect repellent may keep them away.

Always check your body after walking through tick-infested areas, as the insects can cause skin infections and more serious diseases, such as typhus. If a tick is found, press the skin around the tick's head with tweezers, grab the head and pull gently upwards. Don't pull the rear of the body, as this may squeeze parts of the tick into the skin, increasing the risk of infection. Serious hikers may want to have their boots and trousers impregnated with benzyl benzoate and dibutylphthalate, which will ward off ticks.

**Snakes** To minimise your chances of being bitten, always wear boots, socks and long trousers when walking through undergrowth. Don't put your hands into holes and crevices and be careful when collecting firewood.

Puff adders are the most common cause of snake bite in southern Africa. They especially like the loose sand in dry river beds so wear stout footwear rather than sandals when hiking. Other dangerous species include green mambas, black mambas, gaboon vipers and spitting cobras.

Snakebites do not cause instantaneous death and antivenenes are usually available, but it is vital to make a positive identification of the snake (a good field guide is essential for bushwalkers in Africa – see under Books earlier in this chapter). Immediately wrap the bitten limb as you would for a sprain and attach a splint to immobilise it. Keep the victim still and seek medical help immediately. Tourniquets and sucking out the poison are now comprehensively discredited.

### Less Common Diseases

The following problems are thankfully rare in travellers and therefore get only a light mention. You should seek medical attention if you think you have contracted any of these.

**Cholera** Cholera outbreaks are widely reported and travellers can usually avoid problem areas. The disease is characterised by acute diarrhoea with 'rice water' stools, vomiting, muscular cramps and extreme weakness. The risk of dehydration is severe as you may lose as much as 20L per day, so the most vital treatment is fluid replacement. If there is a delay in getting to the hospital, then begin taking tetracycline in 250mg doses four times daily (not recommended for children under nine or pregnant women). While the drug may help shorten the illness, adequate fluid replacement is the most essential factor in survival.

**Filariasis** Symptoms of this mosquito-transmitted parasitic infection include fever, pain and swelling in the lymph glands, inflammation of the lymph drainage areas, swelling of the limbs or scrotum, skin rashes and blindness. Treatment will eliminate the parasite from the body, but damage already caused may not be reversible.

**Leishmaniasis** This group of parasitic diseases is transmitted by sandfly bites, which are usually painless but itchy. Cutaneous leishmaniasis affects the skin tissue, causing ulceration and disfigurement, while visceral leishmaniasis affects the internal organs. Laboratory testing is required for diagnosis and treatment. The best prevention is to avoid sandfly bites by covering up and applying insect repellent. The usual treatment is a 21 day course of antimony.

**Rabies** Rabies is a fatal viral infection found throughout Africa, and transmitted in the saliva of dogs, rodents, bats, monkeys and cattle. Any bite, scratch or even lick from a mammal should be cleaned immediately and thoroughly. Scrub with soap and running water, then apply alcohol or iodine solution. This greatly reduces your risk of contracting rabies, but you must still seek medical help promptly. Treatment involves a series of injections to destroy the virus before it reaches the brain.

**Tetanus** Tetanus occurs when a wound or bite becomes infected by the bacterium *Clostridium tetani*, which can live in soil or animal faeces and enters the body through a break in the skin. Tetanus is also known as 'lockjaw' and the first symptom may be difficulty in swallowing and a stiffening of the jaw and neck followed by painful convulsions of the jaw and whole body.

The disease can be prevented by regular vaccination.

**Trypanosomiasis (Sleeping Sickness)**
This disease is carried by the tsetse fly, which is about twice the size of a housefly and recognisable by its scissor-shaped wings. Only a small percentage of the flies carry this potentially fatal disease, but no prevention is available except to avoid being bitten. The flies are attracted to large moving objects, such as vehicles, to colours such as dark blue, and to perfume and aftershave. The first sign of infection is swelling around the bite, followed after two or three weeks by irregular fevers, abscesses, inflammation of the glands and physical and mental lethargy. The illness is serious, but it responds well to treatment.

**Tuberculosis (TB)** TB is a bacterial infection normally transmitted through coughs. It may also be passed via unpasteurised milk from infected cattle, but milk that has been boiled or soured for yogurt or cheese is safe to drink. Travellers aren't at great risk, as close household contact is usually necessary to contract the disease.

**Typhus** Typhus is spread by ticks, mites and lice (see under Cuts, Bites & Stings earlier in this section), and begins as a cold followed by fever, chills, headache, muscle pains and, several days later, a rash. There is often a large painful sore at the site of the bite and nearby lymph glands become swollen and painful. Typhus is readily treated with medical supervision.

**Women's Health**
**Gynaecological Problems** Sexually transmitted diseases are a major cause of vaginal problems. Symptoms include a smelly discharge, painful intercourse and sometimes a burning sensation when urinating. Medical attention should be sought, and remember that HIV or hepatitis B may also be acquired during exposure. Metronidazole (Flagyl) is the most frequently prescribed drug. Male sexual partners must also be treated.

Fungal (yeast) infections, characterised by a rash, itch and/or discharge, can be treated with a vinegar or lemon-juice douche or with yoghurt. The usual treatments include nystatin, miconazole or clotrimazole vaginal cream or pessaries.

**Pregnancy** It's not advisable to travel to some places while pregnant, as some vaccinations used to prevent serious disease aren't advisable during pregnancy. In addition, some diseases, such as malaria, may increase the risk of stillbirth.

Most miscarriages occur during the first three months of pregnancy, and can occasionally lead to haemorrhaging. The last three months should also be spent within a comfortable distance of good medical care. A baby born as early as 24 weeks stands a chance of survival, but only in a good modern hospital. Pregnant women should avoid all unnecessary medication but vaccinations and malarial prophylactics should still be taken where possible (seek medical advice). Pay particular attention to diet and proper nutrition, avoid alcohol and nicotine, and take extra care to prevent illness.

## WOMEN TRAVELLERS
Generally, women travellers won't encounter specifically female problems, such as harassment from men, any more than they would elsewhere. For the most part sober men are polite and respectful, especially if you're clearly not interested in their advances, and in fact southern Africa is one place in the developing world where women can meet and communicate with local men – of any race – without their intentions necessarily being misconstrued. That doesn't mean that you can sally into a bar or disco unaccompanied and expect to be left alone. The 'loose foreigner' stigma that prevails in so many countries has arrived to some degree, but local white women have done a lot to refute the idea that women of European descent are willing to hop into bed with the first taker.

Particularly in rural areas and places with a large Afrikaner population, some degree of modesty is expected of women. Short sleeves are fine but hemlines shouldn't be much above knee-level. To avoid unwanted attention, prevent sunstroke and keep cool, it's best to cover up as much as possible.

The threat of sexual assault isn't greater in southern Africa than in Europe but women should still avoid walking alone in parks and backstreets, especially at night. See the relevant sections in the individual country Facts for the Visitor chapters for more information.

When it comes to evening entertainment, this region is very much a conservative, traditionally male-dominated society (for all races) and women travellers may run into barriers. Many bars are male only, either by order of the establishment or by tradition, and even where women are admitted, conventions often dictate that you don't go without a male companion. However distasteful this may seem, to force the issue may invite problems.

On the road, the best advice about areas to avoid will come from local women. However, local whites – men and women – are likely to be appalled at the notion of travelling alone (even in your own vehicle!) and may try to discourage you with horrendous stories (often of dubious authenticity).

Although Zimbabwe, Botswana and Namibia are safer than most in Africa, hitching alone cannot be recommended. Be prepared to refuse a lift if the driver is visibly intoxicated (a sadly common condition) or the car is chock-a-block with men (as is often the case with military vehicles). Never hitch at night and, if possible, find a companion for trips through sparsely populated areas. Use common sense and things should go well.

## GAY & LESBIAN TRAVELLERS

All three countries in this book are conservative in their attitudes towards gays and lesbians, and homosexuality is rarely seriously discussed in public. In the last couple of years, the presidents of Zimbabwe and Namibia, Robert Mugabe and Sam Nujoma, have spoken out publicly – and venomously – against homosexuality. However, some observers see these verbal attacks as just another way to deflect attention from dissatisfaction with the governments.

Although some homosexual activity does occur, especially between younger men, in most black African societies gay and lesbian relationships are a cultural taboo. In most places, any open displays of affection are frowned upon, whatever their orientation, and show insensitivity to local sentiments.

Male homosexual activity is illegal in all three countries and lesbian activities are illegal in Namibia and Zimbabwe. For information on HIV/AIDS, see Health earlier in this chapter.

## DISABLED TRAVELLERS

People with limited mobility will not have an easy time in southern Africa and although there are more disabled people per capita here than in the west, facilities are few. In the capital cities, some government buildings have ramps and lifts, but they're probably not places you'd be interested in visiting. On streets and footpaths, kerbs and uneven surfaces will often present problems for wheelchair users and only upmarket hotels and restaurants have installed ramps and railings.

In short, most wheelchair users will find travel easier with an able-bodied companion, but there is some good news: footpaths and public areas are often surfaced with tar or concrete; many buildings, including safari lodges, are single-storey; car hire is easy; and assistance is usually available on regional flights.

Similarly, the general local attitude towards disability is quite different from that in the west. On the one hand, you're unlikely to be treated in a patronising manner, but this can be carried to extremes. One blind traveller reported asking an official for help filling out her immigration forms and was told she had no business travelling if she couldn't see. On the other hand, many people will be more open and willing to strike up casual conversations than in the west, and disabled travellers who can discuss their jobs, educational background, opportunities and even problems may well inspire able-bodied Africans to re-evaluate their attitudes.

If you want to go the package route, the company Wilderness Wheels (☎ (011) 648 5737; fax 884 7883), PO Box 1133, Sunninghill 2157, South Africa, arranges regional bush safaris for disabled travellers.

## SENIOR TRAVELLERS

Southern Africa is generally good for senior travellers (on the assumption that they want to rough it less than the younger set), as high-quality hotels and restaurants are available in most places.

Many local seniors (mostly whites) tour their own countries – there's a thriving caravan scene – and visit neighbouring countries independently or on organised packages. If you're concerned about logistics, chances are you can pre-book and pre-pay for everything from your home country.

## TRAVEL WITH CHILDREN

Children love Africa and most Africans love children. Travellers with children will often find it easier to make local friends, and the children will easily make new friends, too. Note, however, that children rank very low on the black African social scale (see Society & Conduct in the Facts about the Region chapter).

Travellers who are considering taking the kids along will be happy to hear that there are fewer health risks in southern Africa than most other parts of the continent. That doesn't mean you should become blasé about health matters, but neither should you become hysterical.

When booking safaris and accommodation, ascertain whether children are welcome. Many safari companies, activity operators, lodges and game ranches don't allow anyone under either 12 or 16 years of age. Neither can children participate in most adrenaline activities. In some cases, this is because operators wish to foster an adult atmosphere, while in others, it's due to insurance restrictions or the presence of

dangerous wildlife. On the other hand, several agencies in Victoria Falls offer children's day-safaris to keep the kids occupied while the adults are off stimulating adrenaline production.

For further information and suggestions, see Lonely Planet's *Travel with Children*, which discusses these and other issues.

## USEFUL ORGANISATIONS

For information on cultural preservation and/or environmental conservation in the region, contact the following:

Australia
  *Greenpeace Australia Ltd*, 3/389 Lonsdale St, Melbourne 3000 (☎ (03) 9670 1633)
Botswana
  *Kalahari Conservation Society*, PO Box 859, Gaborone (☎ 314259; fax 374557)
Canada
  *Wildlife Preservation Trust Canada*, 17 Isabella St, Toronto, Ontario M4Y 1M7
Namibia
  *Africat*, Okonjima, PO Box 793, Otjiwarongo (☎ (0651) 304563; fax 304565; <africat@iwwn.com.na>)
  *Cheetah Conservation Fund*, PO Box 247, Windhoek (☎ (0651) 304216)
  *Namibian Association for the Protection of Abused Equines*, Helen Lohmann, PO Box 11662, Klein Windhoek (☎ (061) 238897)
  *Namibia Nature Foundation*, Pottie de Brain, PO Box 245, Windhoek (☎ (061) 248345; fax 248344; <nnf@iwwn.com.na>)
  *Save the Rhino*, PO Box 83, Khorixas (☎ (061) 222281)
  *Wildlife Society of Namibia*, Namib Centre, PO Box 483, Swakopmund (☎ (064) 405258)
South Africa
  *Endangered Wildlife Trust*, Private Bag X11, Parkview 2122 (☎ (011) 486 1102; fax 486 1506)
  *Worldwide Fund for Nature (WWF)*, PO Box 456, Stellenbosch 7599
  *Wilderness Trust of Southern Africa*, PO Box 577, Bedfordview 2008 (☎ (011) 453 7645)
Switzerland
  *Worldwide Fund for Nature (WWF)*, Département de l'Information et de l'Education, Avenue de Mont Blanc, 1196 Gland
UK
  *Minority Rights Group*, 29 Craven St, London WC2N 5NT (☎ (0171) 930 6659)

## The CAMPFIRE Programme

Nearly everyone agrees that tourism holds vast potential as a source of income for Zimbabwe. In past years, however, much tourism development has taken place at the expense of subsistence farmers on communal lands, and the maintenance of national parks and wildlife reserves has placed a strain on the people inhabiting the surrounding areas. Local people have seen these large tracts of usable land placed off limits, while being forced to suffer the ravages of wild animals on their crops and families.

Historically, a major part of the problem has been that the Zimbabwean government had formal authority over national parks, and attempted to manage wildlife areas from the central National Parks Department. All revenue from hunting and tourism in the parks was directed straight into the national treasury – or to the private owners of tour companies and safari lodge operators. Few locals saw any of the economic benefits that were being touted as justification for conservation and tourism development. The inevitable result was an increase in poaching, domestic encroachment onto protected land and a general resentment of the parks and wildlife by people living in the surrounding areas.

In response, in 1987 the government set up the Communal Area Management Programme for Indigenous Resources (CAMPFIRE). The idea was to encourage active popular participation in conservation by providing a means for local people to benefit from tourism on their lands. It hoped to vest in local people proprietary rights to wildlife resources and was intended to help them see wildlife and protected lands as assets rather than liabilities.

Three years after it was created, CAMPFIRE had already been extended to 12 districts surrounding wildlife-rich national parks and reserves. In 1994, the programme earned a total of US$1.2 million. Proceeds from big game hunting on the protected lands are divided equally between district councils and private safari operators. From their share, councils are permitted to take 15% of the proceeds for their general funds, while 35% goes to wildlife management (for example, to build electric fences to keep elephants out of the corn!). The remaining 50% is passed on to surrounding communities to spend as they wish.

Although CAMPFIRE's emphasis is on hunting revenues, some communities have carried the concept a step further and set up their own tourist facilities. Among these are the Mavuradonha Wilderness Camp and the Sunungukai Camp, both in north-eastern Zimbabwe. The former maintains basic accommodation in a magnificent wilderness hiking area, while the latter provides tourists with a glimpse of traditional village life in Zimbabwe. Revenue generated by Sunungukai has been channelled into the running of a community grist mill and the construction of a local primary school.

Inspired by the success of the CAMPFIRE programme, several other African countries – including Namibia – are currently setting up similar schemes. The Namibian programmes are still in the experimental stages, but have so far met with some success.

Bookings for camps and programmes may be made through CAMPFIRE (☎ (14) 747152), Mukuvisi Woodlands, Harare.

*Survival International*, 310 Edgware Rd, London W2 1DY (☎ (0171) 723 5535)
*Worldwide Fund for Nature (WWF)*, Panda House, Weyside Park, Godalming, Surrey GU7 1XR (☎ (01483) 426444)
*Zambezi Society UK*, Director of Conservation, Zoological Society of London, Regent's Park, London NW1 4RY

USA
*CAMPFIRE*, 1401 16th St, NW, Washington, DC 20036 (☎ (202) 939-9655)
*Conservation International*, 1015 18th St, NW, Suite 1000, Washington, DC 20036 (☎ (202) 429-5660)
*The Ecotourism Society*, 801 Devon Place, Alexandria, VA 22314

*Survival International USA*, 2121 Decatur Place, NW, Washington, DC 20006

*Wildlife Preservation Trust*, 3400 W Girard Ave, Philadelphia, PA 19104

*Worldwide Fund for Nature (WWF)*, 1250 24th St, NW, Washington, DC 20037

Zimbabwe

*CAMPFIRE*, 15 Phillips Ave, Belgravia, PO Box 4027, Harare (☎ (14) 790570)

*Natural Farming Network of Zimbabwe*, PO Box CY301, Causeway, Harare (☎ (14) 726538; fax 723056)

*Nature Experiences Eco-Tourism Implementation*, PO Box CH-69, Chisipite, Harare (☎ (14) 42858; fax 792342)

*Ornithological Association of Zimbabwe*, PO Box CY161, Causeway, Harare

*Wildlife Society*, Mukuvisi Woodland Environmental Centre, PO Box GD800, Greendale, Harare (☎ (14) 700451)

*Zambezi Society*, Mukuvisi Woodland Environmental Centre, PO Box HG774, Highlands, Harare (☎/fax (14) 747152; <zamsoc@zwe.toolnet.org>)

*Zimbabwe Council for Tourism*, 9th Floor, Travel Centre, Jason Moyo Ave, PO Box 7240, Harare (☎ (14) 733211; fax 794015)

*Zimbabwe National Environmental Trust*, 18 Mitchell Rd, Greendale, PO Box CY358, Causeway, Harare (☎/fax (14) 496105)

## ACTIVITIES

### Safaris & Wildlife Viewing

Most visitors to southern Africa want to meet the faces they've come to know over

---

## Close Encounters

The threat of attack by wild animals in Africa is largely exaggerated and problems are extremely rare, but compliance with a couple of guidelines will further diminish the chances of an unwelcome close encounter.

The five animals most potentially dangerous to humans have been grouped into a sort of game hunter's checklist known as the 'big five' – lion, leopard, buffalo, elephant and rhino. Since they're normally abroad only at night, you'd have to be extremely fortunate to see a leopard, let alone have problems with one. Because rhino are so rare these days, the threat of a rhino charge is negligible. If for some reason you are caught out, the advice normally given is to face the charge and step to one side at the last moment. The rhino can't really see you and will have too much forward momentum to turn quickly, anyway. If you are with other people, make sure that the entire group steps in the same direction or there could be complications.

Although buffalo are docile while in a herd, individuals who've somehow become estranged from buffalo society can be more irritable. Avoid such animals. If you do encounter one in the bush, however, back quietly away without making any sudden moves until you're out of sight. If there is a charge, head for the nearest tree or dive into the bushes posthaste.

Lion, though rarely interested in humans, have been known to attack on occasion. If you're camping out in the bush, be sure to zip your tent up completely and if you hear a large animal outside, lie still even if it brushes against the tent. This is easier said than done, of course, but lion don't really know what to make of tents and normally leave them alone. If you encounter a lion (or especially a lioness) while walking in the bush, try to avoid an adrenaline rush (also easier said than done) and back slowly away; whatever you do, don't turn and run. If you respond like a prey species, the lion could react accordingly.

Unless you're in a vehicle, elephant are best avoided; their size alone will probably put you off approaching them too closely anyway. Although elephant certainly aren't bloodthirsty creatures – they're vegetarian – it's been said that an elephant never forgets. An individual that's had trouble from humans previously may feel the need to take revenge. If an elephant is visibly holding its trunk erect and sniffing the air, it probably detects your presence and is worried; you should move away slowly. Cows with calves should also be avoided, and

the years through nature programmes. The term safari, which means 'we go' in Swahili, may conjure up the image of a single-file procession of adventurers stalking through the bush behind a large elephant gun, but modern usage is broader and may extend to river rafting, bushwalking, horse riding, canoeing or just warming a seat on a train or plane! Note that trips advertised as 'photographic safaris' don't normally have anything to do with photographic instruction. They're so-called because the participants carry cameras rather than guns.

Most safaris, however, do include wildlife-viewing. Most wildlife parks are off limits to pedestrians, cyclists and hitchers, so safaris allow travellers to appreciate the wildlife without having to pay for car rental. Don't let the prices of overseas-booked safaris put you off. Most of these are tailored for travellers who are willing to pay for all the comforts of home, and lots of more affordable options are available locally.

Shoestring travellers may sense that the rules and regulations are designed specifically to keep them out: there's no public transport into the parks; hitching on park roads is forbidden; the permit system is geared towards people with vehicles; and, with few exceptions, individual walking

---

do not approach any elephant with visible injuries, such as a damaged foot or trunk (an indication of having been caught in a snare). When camping, don't keep fresh fruit – especially oranges – in your tent, since it can attract elephant.

In addition to the big five, other large animals that can be dangerous to humans are the crocodile and the hippo. It's often repeated that hippo kill more humans in Africa than any other animal. Like elephant, they aren't vicious but they are large. When boating or canoeing, watch for signs of hippo and steer well away from them. Never pitch a tent in an open area along an otherwise vegetated riverbank or shoreline; this will probably serve as a hippo run. Hippo spend most of their time underwater munching tender plants growing on the river bottom, but when it's time to surface or to enter or leave the water, they don't much care what's in their way.

Nile crocodiles have provided hours of hair-raising campfire tales and they can be worthy adversaries. Although not as large as their Australian counterparts, the crocs, which spend most of their time lying motionless around water holes or on riverbanks minding their own business, grow up to 4m in length and have been known to cause problems for the careless.

Visitors should take care not to swim in rivers or water holes where crocs (or hippo) are present – if local advice is not available, assume there are crocs and don't swim (you may also be avoiding bilharzia) and use extreme caution when tramping along any river or shoreline. Crocodiles aren't readily recognisable as such; when they're snoozing in the sun, they look more like logs or branches.

Hyaena are also potentially dangerous, although they're normally just after your food. They aren't particularly fussy eaters, either; they'll eat boots, clothing and equipment left outside a tent and have been known to gnaw off headlamps and door handles from vehicles. One cheeky character at Zimbabwe's Mana Pools National Park spent several hours one night subduing – and flattening – one of our tyres! There are plenty of frightening tales of hyaena attacking people who are sleeping in the open or in an open tent – although this is rare, it's still wise to sleep inside and zip up your tent.

Smaller creatures such as hunting dogs and honey badgers can also be quite vicious but they are rarely seen.

tours and bush camping are prohibited. Persistence, however, normally pays off and anyone who really wants to see the parks generally does. Hitching may be prohibited, but hours spent waving your thumb outside the gates may result in a lift that takes you precisely where you want to go.

In East African parks, carnivores are the animals most seriously affected by tourism, and often find themselves being trailed by dozens of white minibuses while trying to hunt. In southern African parks, however, tourism is better regulated, so natural patterns are little altered by human onlookers. Just remember to keep as low a profile as possible; if an animal is obviously hunting, try to control your excitement and avoid the temptation to move in too close, lest you distract the predator or spook the intended prey.

### Canoeing & Rafting

The upper Zambezi River below Victoria Falls offers some world-class white water, and below Lake Kariba a more lethargic Zambezi accommodates those who prefer to take their thrills more slowly. Raft trips may be done on either the Zimbabwe or the Zambia side. For details, refer to the Victoria Falls section in the Western Zimbabwe chapter.

Middle Zambezi camping and canoe safaris run from three to nine days along the river between Kariba and Kanyemba near the Mozambique border, highlighted by overnight stops in Mana Pools National Park.

None of these trips is particularly cheap and nonresidents must pay in foreign currency or show bank receipts totalling at least the amount of the trip.

In Namibia, you won't find the same sort of thrills, but rafts and canoes will provide access to unimaginable wilderness landscapes. The most popular canoeing and rafting venue is the Orange River, which flows through lovely desert country along the boundary between Namibia and South Africa. The water is tame by anyone's standards, but the trips aren't expensive and the

scenery and sense of solitude provide all the motivation you'll need. For details, see the Southern Namibia chapter.

Alternatively, you can spend five days rafting the wild Kunene River, which forms the boundary between Namibia and Angola. There are a few decent white-water stretches and the presence of crocodiles adds a measure of excitement. Budget trips are now available, and as with the Orange River, they traverse territory that is otherwise practically inaccessible. See the North-Western Namibia chapter.

### Hiking

Some of the best bushwalking areas – Nyanga, Vumba and Chimanimani national parks – are in Zimbabwe's Eastern Highlands where you can spend an afternoon or a week walking, camping and enjoying the forests, streams and peaks. Other excellent hiking venues include Matobo National Park near Bulawayo, Matusadona National Park near Kariba (but only with an armed guide) and the Mavuradonha Wilderness in northern Zimbabwe.

In Botswana, most trips through the Okavango Delta include some hiking on the palm islands, and the Tsodilo Hills are particularly attractive for bushwalkers.

In Namibia, bushwalking is permitted in national parks without dangerous animals. The Waterberg Plateau and Skeleton Coast parks offer organised and accompanied hikes with rangers, which are good value but must be booked well in advance through the Ministry of Environment & Tourism (MET) in Windhoek.

Unfortunately for travellers without a fixed route, the popular MET-administered trails (Fish River Canyon, Waterberg unguided, Naukluft four/eight day and Daan Viljoen Sweet-thorn) must be booked and paid for in advance. Hikes may begin only on designated days and hikers must travel in groups of three to 10.

For some hikes, you must also present a doctor's certificate of fitness issued not more than 40 days prior to the hike. However absurd this may sound to experi-

## Minimum Impact Camping

- Select a well drained camp site and, especially if it's raining, use a plastic or other water-proof groundsheet to prevent having to dig trenches.
- Along popular routes, such as in Chimanimani National Park or Fish River Canyon, set up camp in established sites.
- Naturally burn or carry out all rubbish, including cigarette butts. Bio-degradable items may be buried but anything with food residue should be either burned or carried out, lest it be dug up and scattered by animals.
- Use established toilet facilities if they are available. Otherwise, select a site at least 50m from water sources, and bury waste at least 20cm deep. If possible, burn used toilet paper.
- Use only bio-degradable soap products (you'll probably have to carry them from home) and use natural temperature water where possible. When washing with hot water, avoid damage to vegetation either by letting the water cool before pouring it out, or by dumping it in a gravelly, non-vegetated place.
- Wash dishes, shave and brush your teeth away from watercourses.
- When building a fire, select an established site and keep fires as small as possible. Use only fallen, dead wood and when you're finished, make sure ashes are cool and buried before leaving.

---

enced hikers, the system is popularly defended in both Namibia and South Africa.

The good news is that many large private ranches have set up their own hiking routes and trails for guests. Notable ones include Zebra River Lodge and Namibgrens in the Namib region, and Fish River Lodge and Klein-Aus Vista in southern Namibia.

Although individual hiking in wildlife parks is forbidden (with the notable exception of Mana Pools) in all three countries, Zimbabwe allows organised hiking and backpacking safaris in certain areas. These rewarding trips are led by either national parks game scouts or licensed private guides who have gone through a stringent three year licensing programme. For suggestions, see the Organised Tours chapter later in this book.

### Rail Safaris

For serious rail buffs, Rail Safaris in Zimbabwe offers four day and nine day steam rail tours using 1st class and luxury carriages. These expensive but informative tours will take you by rail from Victoria

Falls to Mutare on the *Zambezi Special* and the *Eastern Highlander*.

Rail Safaris also organises connections with named trains in South Africa, and 'Runpast' and 'False Start' journeys for enthusiasts who specifically want to photograph the trains. In a runpast, the train stops at scenic spots, allowing photographers to get off and take photos of the train with the scenic backdrop; in a false start, the train chugs out of the station for photographs, then reverses to pick up the photographers. It's worth looking at their brochure *Rail Safaris Information*, which contains a good thumbnail history of rail in Zimbabwe.

For the tour from Victoria Falls to Mutare, prices range from US$1000 to US$1340, including sightseeing. For information, contact Rail Safaris, Mr & Mrs G Cooke, 2c Prospect Ave, Raylton, Bulawayo (☎ (19) 75575; fax 42217; <railsaf@acacia.samara.co.zw>).

If you have a really big pile of ready cash for a rail adventure, South Africa's luxurious *Blue Train* occasionally runs between

Johannesburg/Pretoria and Victoria Falls. Contact Blue Train Reservations (☎ (011) 773 7631; fax 773 7643), PO Box 2671, Joubert Park 2044, South Africa.

## Horse-Riding

If you're a fan of equine sports (or would like to be), Zimbabwe offers several good opportunities. Wild animals aren't normally frightened by horses and don't distinguish between the horse and the rider, so you can approach them without causing alarm. Several national parks and other game reserves run guided horse trails through wildlife reserves and other areas of interest. Trips normally last 1½ hours and cost around US$20. Participating parks include Lake Chivero, Mutirikwe, Matobo and Nyanga, as well as the Tshabalala Wildlife Sanctuary near Bulawayo.

In addition to the national parks, some private safari companies organise horseback safaris in such diverse places as Zambezi National Park, the Save Valley (near Gonarezhou National Park) and the Mavuradonha Wilderness in Zimbabwe, and in Botswana's Okavango Delta.

Zimbabwe's increasing number of private wildlife ranches and private conservancies also provide ideal conditions for equine exploration. Favourite inexpensive options include Clovelly Lodge near Masvingo and Mopani Park Farm near Kwe Kwe. The latter keeps thoroughbred horses, runs backpackers accommodation and conducts day rides and extended tours on horseback through the adjoining nature conservancy. It also provides riding lessons and teaches polo cross.

## Fishing

The swift streams of Zimbabwe's Eastern Highlands abound with rainbow (*Salmo gairdneri*), brown (*Salmo trutta*) and brook (*Salvelinus fontinalis*) trout, and the area's dams are stocked by the trout hatchery at Nyanga National Park.

In Lake Kariba and the Zambezi Valley, the most sought after are several species of tilapia or bream – mozambique (*Tilapia mossambica*), redbreasted bream (*Tilapia rendalli*) and greenhead (*Tilapia macrochir*). The lake is also popularly known for vundu (giant catfish – *Heterobranchus lonigilis*), barbel (*Clarias gariepinus*), chessa (*Distichodus schenga*), yellowbelly bream (*Serranochromis robustus*), bottlenose (*Mormyrus longirostris*), Hunyani salmon (*Labeo altivelis*), yellowfish (*Barbus mareuqensis* and *Barbus holubi*), nkupe (*Distichodus mossambicus*) and 'fighting' tiger fish (*Hydrocynus vittatus*). Other large dams hold bream, yellowfish, barbel, introduced black bass (*Micropterus salmoides*), bottlenose, Hunyani salmon and carp (*Cyprinus carpio*).

For more on licence fees and seasons for individual dams and streams, see the Zimbabwe National Anglers' Union in Harare or one of the country's 70 angling societies. Local tourist offices may also be of help.

In Namibia, the entire desert coast from Swakopmund to the mouth of the Ugab River is a sea angler's paradise. No licence is required but there are restrictions on the size and number of fish that may be taken. You need a licence for freshwater fishing in Namibia, which can be obtained from local tourist offices. The most popular species are black bass, carp, yellowfish, bream and barbel. The Lüderitz area is known for its crayfish.

## Golf

Zimbabwe is one of the world's least expensive and least crowded golfing venues, and if you don't mind warthogs digging on the fairways and crocodiles in the water hazards, you'll love it. There are over 70 courses around the country; 14 are within a 30km radius of Harare. The most renowned are the 18 hole Royal Harare golf club, 3km from the city, and the nine hole Leopard Rock course in the country's Eastern Highlands.

Note, however, that golf courses require lots of water to maintain, and in drier areas or times of drought, keeping the courses green for tourists cannot be justified.

## WORK

For information on paid work, see the Facts for the Visitor chapters for the individual countries. If you have skills that are in demand, an alternative to paid work is to apply for a volunteer position with a non-government organisation (NGO) or a government-sponsored volunteer organisation – however, there are no guarantees about where you'll end up. You will normally need to be a citizen of the country where the organisation is based. The organisations take care of the red tape and will normally help you settle in and find a place to live.

Agencies that have agreed to be mentioned are listed below. Note that only VOCA offers short-term placements; all the others require long-term commitment.

*Overseas Service Bureau (OSB)*, PO Box 350, Fitzroy 3065, Australia (☎ (03) 9279 1788; fax 9419 4280)

*Volunteer Service Abroad*, PO Box 12-246, Wellington 1, New Zealand (☎ (04) 472 5759; fax 472 5052)

*Voluntary Service Overseas (VSO)*, 317 Putney Bridge Rd, London SW15 2PN, UK (☎ (0181) 780 7200; fax 780 7300)

*VOCA*, 50 F St, NW, Suite 1075, Washington, DC 20001, USA (☎ (202) 383-4961)

# Getting There & Away

## AIR

Southern Africa isn't exactly a hub of international travel, nor is it an obvious transit point along the major international routes – and air fares to or from Europe, North America and Australia certainly reflect that. The greatest hope for inexpensive transport to the region is the current tourism boom in South Africa. There are some bargain fares to Johannesburg (and increasingly to Cape Town), from where you can easily travel overland or find decent short-haul flight deals to Harare, Gaborone or Windhoek.

### Buying Tickets

Your plane ticket will probably be the single most expensive item in your budget, and buying it can be an intimidating business. There is likely to be a multitude of airlines and travel agents hoping to separate you from your money, and it is always worth putting aside a few hours to research the current state of the market. Start early: some of the cheapest tickets must be purchased months in advance, and some popular flights sell out early. Talk to recent travellers. Look at the ads in newspapers and magazines (not forgetting the press of the African community in your country), consult reference books and watch for special offers. Then phone around travel agents for bargains. (Airlines can supply information on routes and timetables; however, except at times of inter-airline price wars, they don't supply the cheapest tickets.) Find out the fare, the route, the duration of the journey and any restrictions on the ticket. Then sit back and decide which is best.

You may discover that those incredibly good deals are 'fully booked, but we have another one that costs a bit more...' Or the flight is on an airline notorious for its poor safety standards and leaves you in the world's least favourite airport mid-journey for 14 hours. Or they may claim only to have the last two seats available for that country for the whole of July, which they will hold for a maximum of two hours. Don't panic – keep ringing around.

Use the fares quoted in this book as a guide only. They are approximate and based on the rates advertised by travel agents at the time of going to press. (Note that quoted air fares don't necessarily constitute a recommendation for the carrier.)

At certain times of the year and/or on certain sectors, many airlines fly with empty seats. This isn't profitable and it's more cost-effective for them to fly full even if that means selling drastically discounted tickets. This is done by off-loading them onto bucket shops, who sell them to the public at reduced prices. These tickets are often the cheapest you'll find, but you can't buy them directly from the airlines. Availability varies widely, of course, so you'll not only have to be flexible in your travel plans, you'll also have to be quick off the mark as soon as an advertisement hits the press.

As you can imagine, there's lots of scope in this business for shady dealings. Many bucket shops are reputable organisations but there will always be the odd fly-by-night operator who sets up shop, takes your money and then either disappears or issues an invalid or unusable ticket. If you're suspicious, don't hand over all the money at once – leave a deposit of 20% or so and pay the balance when you get the ticket. If they insist on cash in advance, go somewhere else. And once you have the ticket, ring the airline to confirm that your booking has actually been made.

Bucket shops advertise in newspapers and magazines and there's a lot of competition – especially in places like Bangkok and London, which are crawling with them – so it's wise to telephone and ascertain availability before rushing from shop to shop. Naturally, they'll advertise the cheapest available tickets, but by the time you get there those may be sold out and you may be looking at something which is slightly more expensive.

You may opt to sacrifice the bargains and play it safe with a better known travel agent. Firms such as STA, who have offices worldwide, Council Travel in the USA or Travel CUTS in Canada offer good prices to most destinations and they aren't going to disappear overnight, leaving you clutching a receipt for a nonexistent ticket.

Once you have your ticket, copy down the number, the flight number and other details, and keep this information safe and separate from the ticket. If the ticket is lost or stolen, this will help you get a replacement. It's sensible to buy travel insurance as early as possible; travel insurance purchased the week before you fly may not cover flight delays caused by industrial action.

**Low Season Travel** Fortunately, the low season partially coincides with the best times to visit the region. Low-season fares from Europe and North America are typically applicable from April to June while high season is between July and September. The rest of the year, with the exception of the several weeks around Christmas, which are also considered high season, falls into the shoulder-season category.

**Travellers with Special Needs**
If you have any special needs – you've broken a leg, you're vegetarian, you're travelling in a wheelchair, you're taking the baby or you're terrified of flying – let the airline know as soon as possible so that they can make appropriate arrangements. Then remind them when reconfirming your booking (at least 72 hours before departure) and again when checking in at the airport. It may also be worth ringing the airlines before making your booking to find out how they can handle your particular needs.

Airports and airlines can be surprisingly helpful, but they do need advance warning. Most international airports can provide

escorts from the check-in desk to the plane where needed, and most have ramps, lifts, accessible toilets and phones available. Aircraft toilets, on the other hand, are likely to present problems; discuss this with the airline at an early stage and, if necessary, with the airline's doctor.

Guide dogs for the blind must normally travel in a specially pressurised baggage compartment with other animals, away from their owner, though smaller guide dogs may be admitted to the cabin. All guide dogs are subject to the same quarantine laws (six months in isolation, etc) as any other animal when entering or returning to countries free of rabies such as the UK or Australia.

Deaf travellers can ask for airport and in-flight announcements to be written down for them.

Reputable international airlines usually provide nappies (diapers), tissues, talcum powder and all the other paraphernalia needed to keep babies clean, dry and half-happy. Airlines normally provide 'Skycots' for infants but these need to be requested in advance; they'll hold a child weighing up to about 10kg. Strollers (pushchairs) can often be taken as hand luggage.

**North America**
In the USA, the best way to find cheap flights is by checking the Sunday travel sections in the major newspapers such as the *Los Angeles Times* or the *San Francisco Examiner* or *Chronicle* on the west coast, and the *New York Times* on the east coast. The student travel bureaux – STA or Council Travel – are also worth a go but in the USA you must produce proof of student status and in some cases be under 26 years of age to qualify for their discounted fares.

North America is a relative newcomer to the bucket-shop traditions of Europe and Asia. You'll find tickets are cheaper but ticket availability and restrictions need to be weighed against what is offered on the standard Apex or full economy (coach class) tickets.

First do some homework. It may well be

## Air Travel Glossary

**Apex** An Apex (advance purchase excursion) ticket is a discounted ticket that must be paid for in advance. They usually cost 30 to 40% less than the full economy fare but there are restrictions. You must purchase the ticket at least 21 days in advance (sometimes more), travel for a minimum period (normally 14 days) and return within a maximum period (90 or 180 days). Stopovers aren't allowed and if you must change your dates of travel or destination, you'll incur extra charges. If you must cancel altogether, the refund is often considerably less than the price of the ticket. Take out travel insurance to cover loss or theft.

**Baggage Allowance** This will be written on your ticket: usually one 20kg item to go in the hold, plus one item of hand luggage.

**Bucket Shop** An unbonded travel agency specialising in discounted airline tickets.

**Cancellation Penalties** If you have to cancel or change an Apex ticket there are often heavy penalties involved; insurance can sometimes be taken out against these penalties. Some airlines impose penalties on regular tickets as well, particularly against 'no show' passengers.

**Check In** Airlines ask you to check in a certain time ahead of the flight departure (usually 1½ hours on international flights). If you fail to check in on time and the flight is overbooked the airline can cancel your booking and give your seat to somebody else.

**Children's Fares** Airlines will usually carry babies up to two years of age for 10% of the relevant adult fare, and some carry them free of charge. For children between two and 12 years of age, the fare on international flights is usually 50% of the regular fare or 67% of a discounted fare. These days, most fares are considered discounted.

**Confirmation** Having a ticket written out with the flight and date you want doesn't mean you have a seat until the agent has checked with the airline that your status is OK or confirmed. Meanwhile you could just be 'on request'.

**Discounted Tickets** There are two types of discounted fares – officially discounted and unofficially discounted. The lowest prices often impose drawbacks like flying with unpopular airlines, inconvenient schedules, or unpleasant routes and connections. A discounted ticket can save you things other than money – you may be able to pay Apex prices without the associated Apex advance booking and other requirements. Discounted tickets only exist where there is fierce competition.

**Economy-Class Tickets** Economy-class tickets are usually not the cheapest way to go, although they do give you maximum flexibility and the tickets are valid for 12 months. Most are fully refundable if you don't use them, as are unused sectors of a multiple ticket.

**Full Fares** Airlines traditionally offer first-class (coded F), business-class (coded J) and economy-class (coded Y) tickets. These days there are so many promotional and discounted fares available that few passengers pay full economy fare.

**Lost Tickets** If you lose your airline ticket an airline will usually treat it like a travellers cheque and, after inquiries, issue you with another one. Legally, however, an airline is entitled to treat it like cash and if you lose it then it's gone forever. Take good care of your tickets.

**MCO** MCO (Miscellaneous Charges Order) is a type of voucher (to the value of a given amount) that resembles a plane ticket and can be used to pay for a specific flight with any IATA (International Air Transport Association) airline. MCOs, which are more flexible than a regular ticket, may satisfy the irritating onward ticket requirement, but some countries are now reluctant to accept them. MCOs are fully refundable if unused.

**No Shows** No shows are passengers who fail to show up for their flight, sometimes due to unexpected delays or disasters, sometimes due to simply forgetting, sometimes because they made more than one booking and didn't bother to cancel the one they didn't want. Full-fare passengers who fail to turn up are sometimes entitled to travel on a later flight; the rest of us are penalised (see Cancellation Penalties).

**On Request** An unconfirmed booking for a flight.
**Open Jaws** A return ticket where you fly out to one place but return from another. If available this can save you backtracking to your arrival point.
**Overbooking** Airlines hate to fly with empty seats and since every flight has some passengers who fail to show up airlines often book more passengers than they have seats. Usually the excess passengers balance those who fail to show up but occasionally somebody gets bumped. If this happens guess who it is most likely to be? The passengers who check in late.

**Reconfirmation** At least 72 hours prior to departure time of an onward or return flight you must contact the airline and reconfirm that you intend to be on the flight. If you don't do this the airline can delete your name from the passenger list and you could lose your seat. You don't have to reconfirm the first flight on your itinerary or if your stopover is less than 72 hours. It doesn't hurt to reconfirm more than once.
**Restrictions** Discounted tickets often have various restrictions on them – Apex is the most usual one. Others are restrictions on the minimum and maximum period you must be away, such as a minimum of 14 days or a maximum of one year.
**Round-the-World (RTW) Tickets** Basically, there are two types: airline tickets and agent tickets. An airline RTW ticket is issued by two or more airlines that have joined together to market a ticket that takes you around the world on their combined routes. It permits you to fly pretty well anywhere you choose using these routes as long as you don't backtrack. Compared to the full-fare tickets, these tickets are much less flexible. They are, however, much cheaper. Other restrictions are that you (usually) must book the first sector in advance and cancellation penalties then apply. There may be restrictions on how many stops you are permitted. Usually, these tickets are valid for 90 days up to a year. The other type of RTW ticket, the agent ticket, is a combination of cheap fares strung together by an enterprising travel agent. These may be cheaper than an airline RTW ticket but the choice of routes will be limited. Many RTW tickets including Africa will be of this type. If you wish to include Africa on a RTW routing, you'll probably wind up flying into Nairobi from London or Delhi or into Harare or Johannesburg from London or Australia.

**Standby** A discounted ticket where you only fly if there is a seat free at the last moment. Standby fares are usually only available on domestic routes.
**Student Discounts** Some airlines offer student-card holders 15 to 25% discounts on their tickets. The same often applies to anyone under the age of 26. These discounts are generally only available on ordinary economy-class fares. You wouldn't get one, for instance, on an Apex or a RTW ticket, since these are already discounted.

**Tickets Out** An entry requirement for many countries is that you have an onward or return ticket – in other words, a ticket out of the country. If you're not sure what you intend to do next, the easiest solution is to buy the cheapest onward ticket to a neighbouring country or a ticket from a reliable airline that can later be refunded if you do not use it.

cheaper to fly first on an economy hop to London (you'll pay anywhere from US$225 one way), then buy a bucket shop or discount travel agency ticket from there to Africa. The magazines specialising in bucket-shop advertisements in London (see under Europe) will post copies so you can study current pricing before you decide on a course of action.

The recommended newsletter *Travel Unlimited* (PO Box 1058, Allston, MA 02134) publishes details of the cheapest air fares and courier possibilities for destinations all over the world.

Canadians may also find the best deals travelling via London. Travel CUTS has offices in all major Canadian cities and the Toronto *Globe & Mail* carries travel agents' advertisements.

**Discount Travel Agencies** North Americans won't get the great deals that are available in London, but a few discount agencies keep a lookout for the best air fare bargains. To comply with regulations, these are sometimes associated with travel clubs.

*Council Travel*, national toll-free line (☎ (800) 226-8624)
*Flight Centre*, 3030 Granville St, Vancouver, BC V6H 3J8 (☎ (604) 739-9539)
*High Adventure Travel*, 353 Sacramento St, Suite 600, San Francisco, CA (☎ (1-800) 428-8735/(415) 912-5600; fax 912-5606; <air treks@highadv.com>)
*Premier Travel*, 217 S 20th St, Philadelphia, PA 19103 (☎ (215) 893-9966). Specialises in Africa.
*STA Travel*, national toll-free line (☎ (800) 777-0112)
510 Grant Av, San Francisco, CA 94108 (☎ (415) 391-8407)
10 Downing St, New York, NY 10014 (☎ (212) 627-3111)
920 Westwood Blvd, Los Angeles, CA 90024 (☎ (310) 824-1574)
*Travel CUTS*, 187 College St, Toronto, Ontario M5T 1P7 (☎ (888) 838-2887/(416) 979-2406)
*Uni Travel*, PO Box 12485, St Louis, MO 63132 (☎ (314) 569-2501)

**Ticket Options** Excessive competition between carriers and governmental interfer-

ence mean that USA fare structures are subject to numerous restrictions and regulations. This is especially true of bargain tickets and, at best, anything cheaper than an economy fare must be purchased 14 to 30 days prior to departure.

You must also book departure and return dates in advance, and most tickets are subject to minimum and maximum stay requirements (usually seven days and six months respectively). It's often better to purchase a return ticket and trash the return portion than pay the one-way fare. You'll rarely find return tickets that allow an open return date within a 12-month period, and you're subject to penalties of up to 50% of the fare if you change flight dates.

From the USA, your main link to Africa is London, which is accessible via direct flights from most major US cities, including Los Angeles, Houston, Miami and Boston. Normally, economy fares must be purchased two weeks in advance, with a minimum stay of two weeks and maximum stay of three months.

Fares to London (low/high season) are around US$289 to US$731 (from New York JFK); US$469 to US$1058 (Los Angeles International); C$701 to C$1120 (Toronto); and C$789 to C$1165 (Vancouver).

Some sample fares (low/high season) from New York (JFK) are: to Harare, US$1399 to US$2780; to Gaborone, US$2279 to US$3181; and to Windhoek, US$1904 to US$2784. From Los Angeles International, fares are in the following ranges: to Harare, US$1819 to US$3521; to Gaborone, US$1986 to US$4135; and to Windhoek, US$3149 to US$5845. From Canada, flights from Toronto to Harare range from C$3579 to C$3988, and from Vancouver, from C$3905 to C$6754.

Budget-minded masochists can fly Balkan Bulgarian Airlines to Sofia from New York on a Friday evening. This flight ostensibly connects with the Saturday evening flight from Sofia to Johannesburg; unfortunately the airline no longer offers its connection from Sofia to Harare.

The best direct routing from North

America to southern Africa is South African Airways' direct flight from Miami to Cape Town and Johannesburg; it also flies from New York. In addition, American Airlines flies between New York and Johannesburg. From Johannesburg, you'll find easy air connections to Harare, Windhoek or Gaborone and overland connections to Harare and Gaborone. At the time of writing, going via Johannesburg was the cheapest route, usually connecting in London. Unfortunately, Johannesburg may not be the nicest introduction to Africa.

### Australia & New Zealand

When it comes to southern Africa, Australians and New Zealanders are at a disadvantage. On Monday and Thursday, Qantas and Air Zimbabwe fly a combined service to Harare direct from Sydney and Perth, Australia. They depart on the return trip to Sydney via Perth several hours after landing in Harare. These flights connect directly with a South African Airways flight to and from Johannesburg. There are no direct flights from New Zealand to southern Africa; kiwis must first get to Sydney.

Direct Sydney-Harare flights cost as little as A$1626 return in the low season, but one-way flights are normally available as part of a RTW package fare. The cheapest options normally include routings via Singapore, Mauritius and/or Nairobi.

An alternative to a RTW package is to fly from Sydney to Harare, and then travel on to London from Nairobi. Low-season combined fares for this route start at A$1689.

For the best deals look in the Saturday editions of the *Sydney Morning Herald* and the Melbourne *Age* or try STA Travel, which has branches at universities and in the state capitals.

### Discount Travel Agencies

In Australia and New Zealand, inexpensive travel is available mainly from STA:

855 George St, Ultimo, NSW (☎ (02) 9212 1255)
235 Rundle St, Adelaide, SA (☎ (08) 8223 2426)
111-117 Adelaide St, Brisbane, Qld (☎ (07) 3221 3722)
224 Faraday St, Carlton, Victoria (☎ (03) 9349 2411)
53 Market St, Fremantle, WA (☎ (08) 9430 5553)
10 High St, Auckland (☎ (09) 390458)

STA also has toll-free fast fares numbers in Australia (☎ 1300 360 960) and New Zealand (☎ 0800 100 677).

### Europe

**Bucket Shop Tickets** There are bucket shops by the dozen in London, Paris, Amsterdam, Brussels, Frankfurt and other places. In London, several magazines with lots of bucket shop ads can put you on to the current deals. The best ones include:

*The Star & SA Times* (☎ (01858) 435354; fax 432164; <satimes@atlas.co.uk>), Tower House, Sovereign Park, Market Harborough LE16 9EF, UK, is published mainly for South African visitors and expats in London, and naturally contains lots of good travel advertising. A year's subscription (50 issues) costs UK£55.

*Time Out* (☎ (0171) 813 3000), 251 Tottenham Court Rd, London W1P 0AB, is London's weekly entertainment guide and contains travel information and advertising. It's available at bookshops, newsagents and newsstands. Subscription inquiries should be addressed to Time Out Subs, Freepost (SWB569), Bristol BS32 0ZZ (☎ (01454) 620070).

*TNT Magazine* (☎ (0171) 373 3377), 14-15 Child's Place, London SW5 9RX, UK. This free magazine can be picked up at most London Underground stations and on street corners around Earls Court and Kensington. It caters to Aussies and Kiwis working in the UK and is therefore full of travel advertising. In this magazine, you'll find discounted fares to Cairo, Nairobi, Johannesburg and other parts of Africa.

*Trailfinder* This magazine is put out quarterly by Trailfinders (☎ (0171) 938 3444). It's free in London but if you want it mailed, it costs UK£8 for four issues in the UK or Ireland and UK£12/US$20 or the equivalent for four issues in Europe or elsewhere (airmail). Subscription inquiries should be addressed to Trailfinder, 23 Abingdon Rd, London W8 6AL (☎ (0171) 938 4615).

The latest deals are listed in the Saturday and Sunday travel sections of major London newspapers, but don't take agency advertised fares as gospel truth. To comply with UK advertising laws, companies must offer some tickets at their cheapest quoted price, but that may be only one or two per week. If you're not one of the lucky punters, you'll be looking at higher fares. To get a fair idea of what's available, seek out deals well before your intended departure.

On the continent, the newsletter *Farang* (La Rue 8 á 4261, Braives, Belgium) deals with exotic destinations.

**Discount Travel Agencies** Especially in London, there is a growing number of travel agencies offering very good deals on long-haul travel. The following are good places to initiate your price comparisons:

France
  *Council Travel*, Rue St Augustine, Paris (☎ (01) 42 66 20 87)
  *Council Travel*, 22 Rue des Pyramides, Paris (☎ (01) 44 55 55 44)
Germany
  *Alternativ Tours*, Wilmersdorferstrasse 94, Berlin (☎ (030) 881 2089)
  *SRID Reisen*, Bergerstrasse 1178, Frankfurt (☎ (069) 43 01 91)
  *SRS Studenten Reise Service*, Marienstrasse 23, Berlin (☎ (030) 281 5033)
Ireland
  *USIT Travel*, 19 Aston Quay, Dublin (☎ (01) 679 8833)
Italy
  *CTS*, Via Genova 16, off Via Nazionale, Rome (☎ (06) 46 791)
Netherlands
  *NBBS*, Rokin 38, Amsterdam (☎ (020) 624 0989)
  *Malibu Travel*, Damrak 30, Amsterdam (☎ (020) 623 6814)
Spain
  *TIVE*, Calle José Ortega y Gasset, Madrid (☎ (91) 401 1300)
Switzerland
  *SSR*, Leonhardstrasse 5-10, Zürich (☎ (01) 261 2956)
UK
  *Bridge the World*, 47 Chalk Farm Rd, London NW1 8AN (☎ (0171) 911 0900; fax 813 3350)
  *Quest Worldwide*, 4/10 Richmond Rd,

Kingston, Surrey KT2 5HL (☎ (0181) 547 3322)
  *STA Travel*, 86 Old Brompton Rd, London SW7 (☎ (0171) 581 4132)
  117 Euston Rd, London NW1 2SX (☎ (0171) 465 0484)
  *Trailfinders*, 42-50 Earls Court Rd, London W8 6FT (☎ (0171) 938 3366)
  194 Kensington High St, London W8 7RG (☎ (0171) 938 3939)
  *Travel Bug*, 125 Gloucester Rd, London SW7 4SF (☎ (0171) 835 2000)
  597 Cheetham Hill Rd, Manchester M8 5EJ (☎ (0161) 721 4000)
  *Travel Mood*, 214 Edgware Rd, London W2 1DH (☎ (0171) 258 0280)

**Ticket Options** About the cheapest consistently available fare directly to southern Africa from Europe is the long and laborious London to Johannesburg flight on Balkan Bulgarian Airlines, which runs on Saturday, stopping in Sofia for two hours. Although service is improving, given its bare-bones equipment, typically severe overbooking and reluctance to change reservations or tickets, it may be worth paying more for something more reliable. The return fare is £385 during the high season, but can be even lower at other times.

Air Zimbabwe flies from London to Harare four times a week: the low-season Apex return fare is £789; shoulder-season fares are over £200 more. The average flight time is 10 hours. British Airways, which flies four times a week between London and Harare, advertises high-season Apex fares starting at £602. A slightly cheaper option is British Airways' twice-weekly flight from London to Gaborone, with a two-hour stop at Johannesburg; however the flight time is 14 hours.

Kenya Airways flies twice weekly from London and Frankfurt to Harare via Nairobi, and this leg forms part of some round-the-world itineraries. Egypt Air flies from Cairo to Harare on Thursday and returns on Friday. Ethiopian Airlines does one weekly run from London via Addis Ababa (Ethiopia) and Mt Kilimanjaro (Tanzania). South African Airways has daily flights between London and Johannesburg with frequent connections to Harare, Gaborone and Windhoek.

Air Namibia operates flights direct to Windhoek International Airport from Frankfurt and London three times a week; the flight time is about 10 hours. Similarly, LTU International offers low/high-season return fares between Munich (with connections to London Stansted) and Windhoek for around £506/591; time restrictions apply. The flight stops at Mt Kilimanjaro in Tanzania en route to Windhoek and Durban.

If you're coming from the continent the most direct route is from Zürich to Harare with Swissair, which occasionally offers discounted deals. For what it's worth, Swissair is one of the world's most ecologically conscious airlines.

From other parts of Europe, it may be cheaper to find a scheduled flight to Johannesburg, Cape Town or Harare, then pick up a connecting flight to your destination.

### Elsewhere in Africa

Since Harare is the major hub between Nairobi and Johannesburg, many intra-Africa flights to Zimbabwe, Botswana and Namibia are routed through it. Unfortunately, there aren't really any bargain fares – you may get a reduction for advance purchase but that's about it – so it won't be worth doing too much shopping around.

Kenya Airways flies between Harare and Nairobi twice weekly for around US$235 each way. Air Zimbabwe flies the same route three times a week for US$375 each way. Air Mauritius has one direct weekly flight from Mauritius to Harare and three more with connections through Johannesburg. To fly between Harare and Antananarivo, Madagascar, you must make connections in Mauritius.

Both Air Zimbabwe and Air Tanzania fly between Harare and Dar es Salaam (Tanzania); Air Zimbabwe and Air Malawi fly to/from Lilongwe (Malawi) six times weekly (the Air Zimbabwe return fare is around US$245); Linhas Aéreas de Moçambique (LAM) flies to/from Maputo

and Beira in Mozambique; Zambia Airways and Air Zimbabwe each has three trips a week between Harare and Lusaka; and Egypt Air flies between Harare and Cairo once weekly.

South African Airways, Air Zimbabwe and Zimbabwe Express Airlines all have frequent flights between Harare and Johannesburg, where you'll find frequent connections to Cape Town and Durban. Between South African cities and Gaborone or Windhoek, you can take the South African commuter airline, Comair, which is owned by British Airways. Fares from Johannesburg to Gaborone/Windhoek are US$123/198. Between Harare and Gaborone, Air Botswana has two flights a week. Air Zimbabwe flies weekly between Harare and Windhoek, and Air Namibia has flights daily from Tuesday to Saturday between Harare and Windhoek, as well as numerous flights to South Africa. See also the Getting There & Away chapters for each country.

### Asia

The only reasonable way to travel between India or Pakistan and Africa is to fly. There are several bucket shops in New Delhi, Bombay and Calcutta. In New Delhi, Tripsout Travel, 72/7 Tolstoy Lane, behind the Government of India Tourist Office, Janpath, is recommended. It's very popular with travellers and has been in business for many years. Coming from Delhi, you can either fly Ethiopian Airlines to Harare via Addis Ababa for around US$650 one way or fly Air India to Nairobi and continue from there on another carrier or overland to southern Africa.

In addition, during the low season (November to March) the Russian airline Aeroflot runs a series of special flights between Moscow and Harare, via Bombay. They're cheap, but dates are very limited and they're likely to book up early.

For travel from South-East Asia, your best bet is Bangkok, where you'll find bucket shops galore. There, you should have little difficulty finding an inexpensive flight to Harare, which may be routed through Mauritius and/or Nairobi.

## LAND

With the exception of the Israel-Egypt connection, all overland travel to Africa must begin in Europe and even then will involve a ferry crossing at some point.

Whether you're hitching or travelling by bus or train across Europe, you should decide which of the two routes south through Africa you want to take – through the Sahara from Morocco and Mauritania to West Africa (the traditional route through Algeria is currently blocked by Islamic fundamentalists with a habit of shooting foreigners) or up the Nile from Egypt to Uganda and Kenya. It's very difficult to travel overland between the two routes in North Africa due to the roadblock imposed by Libya (which nevertheless may open up in the near future) so travellers between Morocco, Algeria or Tunisia, and Egypt will probably have to fly. Also bear in mind that even the fortunate travellers who somehow wangle a Sudanese visa may have problems south of Khartoum, so the Nile route would be greatly facilitated by a flight from Cairo – or ideally from Khartoum – to Kampala or Nairobi.

From Nairobi, there are several options for reaching Zimbabwe, Botswana and Namibia. A popular route is the TAZARA Railway between Dar es Salaam, Tanzania (accessible by bus or plane from Nairobi) and Kapiri Mposhi, Zambia, from where you can pick up an onward train to Lusaka and Livingstone. It's extremely inexpensive for the distance travelled – around US$60 1st class at the time of writing – but be prepared for a slow pace and frequently uncomfortable conditions.

Another option takes you across Tanzania to Kigoma on Lake Tanganyika, then by steamer to Mpulungu, Zambia, and over-

land to Chitipa, Malawi, or Lusaka, Zambia. It's also possible to enter Zambia at Nakonde or Malawi between Mbeya and Karonda. There's no public transport along the latter route so you'll have to hitch.

Other possibilities from Nairobi include travelling through Uganda, Congo (Zaïre), Rwanda and Burundi, catching the Lake Tanganyika steamer from Bujumbura, Burundi, and connecting up with the previously outlined route at Mpulungu, Zambia. However, this region remains politically highly volatile and the refugee crisis is ongoing. Due to shortages of food and supplies, travellers would be wise not to venture in and compound the problems.

In Zambia, it's straightforward reaching Lusaka or Livingstone and entering Zimbabwe at Chirundu, Kariba or Victoria Falls, or crossing into Botswana at Kazungula. See the Zimbabwe and Botswana Getting There & Away chapters (the former includes information on the route between Malawi and Zimbabwe via Mozambique).

### Car & Motorcycle

Explaining how to bring your own vehicle to southern Africa is beyond the scope of this book, but the good news for drivers is that you don't need a carnet de passage to travel through and around most of the southern African region.

Thanks to the Southern African Customs Union, you can drive through Botswana, Lesotho, Namibia, South Africa and Swaziland with a minimum of ado, and with the proper paperwork – a Blue Book sheet detailing the vehicle's particulars and proof of insurance and current registration – you can secure temporary import permits to visit Malawi, Mozambique, Zimbabwe and Zambia. To travel further north, however, will require a carnet de passage, which can amount to heavy expenditure, and more serious consideration.

# Organised Tours

Zimbabwe, Botswana and Namibia are safari countries, but independent travellers will quickly find that most places of tourist interest are well away from the public transport routes. For those without private vehicles or hire cars, this gap is often filled by local safari or tour operators, who can organise a practically unlimited range of adventures to places that would otherwise be difficult to reach.

There are basically two types of tour company: the overseas agents who do the booking and cobble together itineraries in conjunction with the locally based operators, and those locally based operators, who actually provide the tours. Within southern Africa, there is a large number of these tour companies, most of which run trips in small coaches, safari vehicles or minibuses. However, some overseas packagers merely provide self-guided itineraries, pre-booking flights, accommodation and vehicle hire.

This chapter includes lists of overseas packagers as well as a carefully selected list of local operators in each country who cater for independent travellers and/or offer particularly good value options. Although these operators may be mentioned elsewhere in the text, in many cases their contact details are found only here. Operators for some regions and/or activities – the Okavango Delta, middle-Zambezi canoe safaris, budget operators in Namibia and so on – have been described in detail in their respective chapter, and only a skeleton description appears here.

## OVERSEAS OPERATORS

Literally hundreds of tour and safari companies now organise package tours to Zimbabwe, Botswana and Namibia.

With packages, it always pays to shop around for deals. Especially in Europe, it's becoming increasingly popular to look for late bookings, which are available at a fraction of the normal price. First try the travel sections of weekend newspapers. In some cases, there are special late bookings counters at international airports. If you prefer a more independent approach, you can pre-book flights and hotels for the first few nights, then join tours locally.

While it would be impractical to include a comprehensive rundown of package operators, the following list will provide some idea of the range available, and includes some of the more creative and offbeat offerings. Any of these packages may be booked through your travel agent:

### Germany
*Namibia Travel Service*, Schottenstrasse 75, 78462 Konstanz (☎ (07531) 914491; fax 914492; <namibia.safaris@t-online-de>). Organises all facets of travel in Namibia.

### Japan
*Springbok Corporation*, Ishinkuru Bldg, 2F 214-3 Taishido, Setagayo-ku, Tokyo 154 (☎ (03) 5486 8185; fax 5486 5696). Guided tours including the northern and southern circuits through the major sites in Namibia.

### New Zealand
*Adrift*, PO Box 354, Ngongotaha (☎ (07) 347 2345; fax 346 3167). As the name suggests, this company specialises in liquid experiences, and in the case of Zimbabwe, that means rafting on the Zambezi below Victoria Falls.

### South Africa
*African Routes*, 164 Northway, Durban North 4051 (☎ (031) 833348; fax 837234; <aroutes@ iafrica.com>). This friendly company offers reasonably priced overland tours and hiking trips through Namibia and Zimbabwe, as well as other parts of Africa.

*Afro Ventures*, PO Box 2339, Randburg 2125 (☎ (011) 886 1524; fax 886 2349). Of primary interest are trips through the Central Kalahari Game Reserve and its camping, canoeing and bushwalking safaris in Zimbabwe and Namibia. They are not cheap, but low accommodation costs mean reasonably accessible prices.

*Clive Walker Trails*, PO Box 645, Bedfordview 2008 (☎ (011) 453 7645; fax 453 7649). Emphasis is on walking and ecology-oriented trips in the Okavango Delta and Tuli Block areas of Botswana. However, luxury isn't a component.

*Penduka Safaris*, PO Box 55413, Northlands 2116 (☎/fax (011) 883 4303). This recommended company operates mainly in Namibia, Botswana and South Africa. Its popular Kalahari tours include Kubu Island, Deception Pan, Nxai Pan, Mabuasehube, Tsodilo Hills and the Makgadikgadi Pans. The prices are mid-range.

*Wayfarer Adventures*, 4 Norwich Ave, Observatory, Cape Town 7925 (☎ (021) 470792; fax 474675). Wilderness adventure travel throughout southern Africa, including Land Rover tours around Namibia.

*Wilderness Safaris*, PO Box 651171, Benmore 2010 (☎ (011) 884 1458; fax 883 6255). This company offers a range of tours in Zimbabwe, Botswana, Namibia and other African countries. In addition to the standard lodge-based tours, it offers bushwalking, birdwatching, canoeing, photography and other activity-based trips. However, it is quite expensive and the tours seem a bit rushed.

*Wild Frontiers*, PO Box 844, Halfway House 1685 (☎ (011) 315 4838; fax 315 4850). Middle price range canoeing and walking trips in Zimbabwe.

## Spain

*Expediciones César Cañareras*, Roberto Franco, c/o Otumba 12 2°, 41001 Seville (☎ (95) 421 4737; fax 456 4009). This company specialises in tours through Etosha National Park and around northern Namibia.

## UK

*Abercrombie & Kent*, Sloane Square House, Holbein Place, London SW1W 8NS (☎ (0171) 730 9600). This well heeled company organises upmarket luxury safaris in southern Africa, with particular emphasis on the Okavango Delta.

*Adrift*, Collingbourne House, Spencer Ct, 140-142 Wandsworth High St, London SW18 4JJ (☎ (0181) 874 4969; fax 875 9236). This UK subsidiary of the New Zealand company of the same name specialises in rafting trips on the Zambezi River.

*Africa Exclusive Ltd*, Hamilton House, 66 Palmerston Rd, Northampton NN1 5EX (☎ (01604) 628979; fax 639879). Customised itineraries that will take you pleasantly off the beaten track. It concentrates on Zimbabwe, but also covers Namibia.

*Discover the World*, 29 Nork Way, Barnstead, Surrey SM7 1PB (☎ (01737) 218800; fax 362341). This company runs exclusive wildlife-oriented tours to various sites worldwide, including a two week excursion through Namibia.

*Explore Worldwide Ltd*, 1 Frederick St, Aldershot, Hampshire GU11 1LQ (☎ (01252) 319448; fax 343170). Organised group tours through Zimbabwe, Botswana and Namibia, focusing on adventure and hands-on activities.

*Himalayan Kingdoms*, 45 Mowbray St, Sheffield S3 8EN (☎ (0114) 276 3322; fax 276 3344; <expeditions@hkexpeds.demon.co.uk>). This well known company offers rock-climbing itineraries in Namibia.

*In the Saddle*, Laurel Cottage, Ramsdell, Tadley, Hampshire RG26 5SH (☎ (01256) 851 665; fax 851 667; <rides@inthesaddle.cix.co.uk>). This company appeals specifically to horse aficionados. In southern Africa, it offers riding safaris in the Okavango Delta, Namibia's Khomas Hochland, and Zimbabwe's Mzola and Mavuradonha wilderness areas.

*Naturetrek*, Chautara, Bighton, Alresford, Hampshire SO24 9RB (☎ (01962) 733051; fax 733368). This company's aim is to get you to where the animals are. It offers specialised wildlife-viewing itineraries in Zimbabwe, Botswana and Namibia, as well as other areas of southern Africa.

*Okavango Tours & Safaris*, Gadd House, Arcadia Ave, London N3 2TJ (☎ (0181) 343 3283; fax 343 3287). This company combines its forté, the Okavango Delta, with tours through Chobe National Park as well as Zimbabwe and Namibia.

*Peregrine Holidays*, 40/41 South Parade, Oxford OX2 7JP (☎ (01865) 511642; fax 512583). Upmarket wildlife and botanical safaris, including Botswana's Okavango Delta and Chobe National Park.

*Safari Drive Ltd*, Wessex House, 127 High St, Hungerford, Berkshire RG17 0DL (☎ (01488) 681611; fax 685055). With this company you can organise your own 4WD expedition through the wildest parts of southern Africa – with little risk. The 4WD vehicles come with all the equipment you'll need – including a radio and GPS to ensure you're never out of touch.

*Temple World*, 13 The Avenue, Kew, Richmond, Surrey TW9 2AL (☎ (0181) 940 4114; fax 332 2456). This very sophisticated and recommended company organises middle to upper-range tours to the best of Zimbabwe, Botswana and Namibia.

*Tusk Tours*, 143 High St, Newport, Isle of Wight PO30 1TY (☎ (01983) 530851; fax 530848). This friendly and down-to-earth company runs its own tours, which take in the major sights as well as some of Zimbabwe's smaller and more ignored destinations.

*Voyages Jules Verne*, 21 Dorset Square, London NW1 6QG (☎ (0171) 616 1000; fax 723 8629). This company specialises in luxury-tinted tours around the highlights of Zimbabwe and Botswana. It offers some particularly reasonable off-season prices. It also organises expensive 14-day rail safaris from Victoria Falls to Cape Town on the *Zambezi Express* and the *Pride of Africa*.

*Wild Africa Safaris*, 1st Floor, Castlebank House, Oak Road, Leatherhead, Surrey KT22 7PG (☎ (01372) 363100; fax 363500). This company runs two to three-week upmarket tours taking in Zimbabwe and Botswana highlights. It also uses local operators to organise speciality safaris, including tiger fishing, canoeing, walking safaris in the national parks (including tracking rhinos), rail safaris and even (very expensive) trips by Catalina flying boat.

*Wildwings*, International House, Bank Rd, Bristol BS15 2LX (☎ (0117) 984 8040; fax 961 0200). If you've always wanted to spend 22 days in search of birds in Namibia, here's your opportunity. Wildwings is interested in birds and if you see larger animals as well, they're frosting on the cake.

## USA

*Abercrombie & Kent*, 1420 Kensington Rd, Oak Brook, IL 60521 (☎ (708) 954-2944). This well-known tour operator runs short or long pricey organised tours around the Zimbabwe and Botswana highlights, with particular emphasis on luxury.

*Adventure Center*, 1311 63rd St, Emeryville, CA 91608 (☎ (510) 654-1879; <adventctr@aol.com>). This isn't actually a tour operator, but rather a travel agency specialising in adventure tours worldwide.

*Africa Adventure Company*, 1620 S Federal Hwy, Suite 900, Pompano Beach, FL 33062 (☎ (305) 781-3933; <noltingaac@aol.com>). This adventure travel company runs a range of safari options all over Africa, with a particular focus on Zimbabwe.

*Africa Travel Centre*, 23830 Route 99, Suite 112, Edmonds, WA 98026 (☎ (206) 672-3697; fax 672-9678). This is a travel and resource centre for prospective Africa travellers. There's a good chance that it will have information on the trip you're looking for.

*Desert & Delta Safaris*, 16179 E Whittier Blvd, Whittier, CA 90603 (☎ (213) 947-5100). Focuses on lodge-based tours in the Okavango, but also offers connecting packages around southern Africa.

*Global Adventures*, 8762 South Mourning Dove Lane, Highlands Ranch, CO 80126 (☎/fax (303) 791-9959; <escape@globaladventures .com>; Web site www.globaladventures.com /about.htm). Organises adventure tours in Zimbabwe, Botswana and Namibia.

*Journeys*, 1536 NW 23rd Ave, Portland, OR 97210 (☎ (503) 226-7200). Specialises in trekking and camping trips through the more remote areas of Zimbabwe and Botswana.

*Ker & Downey Inc*, 13201 NW Freeway, Suite 850, Houston, TX 77040 (☎ (713) 744-5260; fax 895-8753). This is far and away the most exclusive company operating in Botswana. It focuses on lodge-based tours in Chobe National Park and the Okavango Delta, including a frighteningly expensive elephant-back safari in the Delta.

*Legendary Adventure Co*, 13201 NW Freeway, Suite 800, Houston, TX (☎ (1-800) 324-9081; fax (713) 895-8753; <ssonier@aol.com>). Offers luxury camping, horse-riding and walking safaris in Botswana's Okavango Delta area.

*Mountain Travel/Sobek* (☎ (1-800) 227 2384; <info@mtsobek.com>). Adventure trips, including rafting and wildlife safaris, in Zimbabwe, Zambia and Botswana.

*Nature Expeditions International* (☎ (1-800) 869 0639; <naturexp@aol.com>). Upmarket wildlife and walking safaris in Zimbabwe and Botswana.

*Natural Habitat*, 2945 Center Green St, Suite H, Boulder, CO 80301 (☎ (303) 229-3711 or (1-800) 543-8917; fax (303) 449-3712). This company organises wild tours to Zimbabwe, Botswana, Namibia and South Africa, including special tours for women.

*Safariplan*, 673 E California Blvd, Pasadena, CA 91106 (☎ (818) 578-0510; fax 796-6365). Luxury, lodge-based tours for independent travellers, taking participants to the highlights of Zimbabwe.

*Spector Travel*, 31 St James Ave, Boston, MA 02116 (☎ (617) 338 0111). This company puts together budget tours all over Africa, and combines them with discounted airfares.

*United Touring Company*, 400 Market St, Suite 260, Philadelphia, PA 19106 (☎ (215) 923-8700; fax 985-1008). One of the largest tour operators in Africa, UTC does everything from day tours to longer itineraries.

*Voyagers*, PO Box 915, Ithaca, NY (☎ (1-800) 633-0299). Photographic and wildlife-viewing safaris.

*Wilderness Travel*, 801 Alston Way, Berkeley, CA 94710 (☎ (1-800) 358-8530; <info@wildernesstravel.com>). This company offers guided group tours with an emphasis on down-to-earth touring, including hikes, treks and other hands-on pursuits.

## Overland Companies

Although overlanding from Cairo to the Cape is quite difficult due to unrest in Sudan, some overland operators have taken up the trans-Sahara route through Morocco, Mauritania and west Africa, across the Central African Republic, Congo (Zaïre) and Uganda to Kenya and on to Zimbabwe, Botswana and South Africa.

While these trips are popular, they're designed mainly for inexperienced travellers who feel uncomfortable striking out on their own or for those who prefer guaranteed social interaction to the uncertainties of the road. If you have the slightest inclination towards independence or would feel confined travelling with the same group of 25 or so people for most of the trip (although quite a few normally drop out along the way), think twice before booking an overland trip.

Increasingly, many overland companies are opting for shorter hauls and some also provide transport – a sort of backpackers' bus and transfer service. Independent travellers may join overland trucks for around US$15 per day, plus food kitty contributions. Just visit an overland truck stop and ask the driver if there's space available. This is a particularly useful way to transfer quickly between Harare and Malawi or Nairobi, Victoria Falls and Maun, or even Harare and Windhoek.

For further information or a list of agents selling overland packages in your home country, contact one of the following operators dealing in African overland trips, all of which are based in the UK (many companies also have offices or representatives in Australia, New Zealand, the USA and Canada):

*Acacia Expeditions*, 23a Craven Terrace, London W2 3QH (☎ (0171) 706 4700; fax 706 4686)

*Dragoman*, Camp Green, Kenton Rd, Debenham, Stowmarket, Suffolk IP14 6LA (☎ (01728) 861133; fax 861127)

*Encounter Overland*, 267 Old Brompton Rd, London SW5 9JA (☎ (0171) 370 6845; fax 244 9737)

*Exodus Overland Expeditions*, 9 Weir Rd, London SW12 0LT (☎ (0181) 675 5550; fax (0171) 673 0779)

*Guerba Expeditions*, Wessex House, 40 Station Rd, Westbury, Wiltshire BA13 3JN (☎ (01373) 826611; fax 858351)

*Kumuka Expeditions*, 40 Earls Court Rd, London W8 6EJ (☎ (0171) 937 8855; fax 937 6664)

*Phoenix Expeditions*, College Farm, Far St, Wymeswold, Leicestershire LE12 6TZ (☎ (01509) 881818; fax 881822)

*Top Deck*, Top Deck House, 131/135 Earls Court Rd, London SW5 9RH (☎ (0171) 244 8641; fax 373 6201)

Alternatively, you could just begin your overland trip in South Africa, which has a growing number of operators:

*Karibu Safaris*, 53 Anthony Rd, Canford Park, Durban North 4051, PO Box 35196, Northway 4065 (☎ (031) 839774; fax 831957). South Africa's own overland company runs popular 'roughing it' safaris throughout southern Africa.

*Livingstone Zimbabwe Trails*, PO Box 11430, Ranhart 1457 (☎/fax (011) 867 2586). Inexpensive overland tours between South Africa and Zimbabwe, with emphasis on the highlights.

*Nomad Adventure Tours*, 28 Southern Cross Dr, Constantia 7800 (☎/fax (021) 794 1446). Overland camping safaris through Zimbabwe, Botswana and Namibia.

*Which Way*, 51B Lourens St, PO Box 2600, Somerset West 7130 (☎ (021) 852 2364; fax 852 1584). Lots of routes through Zimbabwe, Botswana and Namibia, and on to east Africa.

## ZIMBABWE

Tours of all sorts – bushwalking, rail, canoe and raft trips, sightseeing, wildlife viewing, birdwatching and even all-inclusive lounging around – are available from local operators.

In most cases, it's advisable to book these tours on the spot rather than through an overseas agent, which may cost you up to four times more for the same tour. The following list includes local operators who accept individual and on-the-spot bookings. Some specific tours are described in the relevant chapters, but addresses are listed only in this section.

*Africa Dawn Safaris*, PO Box 128, Bulawayo (☎/fax (19) 70488). This company focuses on Matabeleland, with day tours around Bulawayo and Matobo, as well as wildlife-viewing in Hwange National Park and tailor-made safaris countrywide.

*Africa Sun Safaris*, 389 Thurso Rd, Killarney, Bulawayo (☎ (19) 76523). Runs day tours to Matobo National Park for US$40, including meals and a game drive.

*African Explorations*, Safari House, 160 Samora Machel East, PO Box MP 222, Mount Pleasant, Harare (☎/fax (14) 721586). This Harare operator runs value tours to standard sites around Harare, including Domboshawa and the Bally Vaughn Game Sanctuary.

*African Wanderer*, PO Box 1976, Bulawayo (☎/fax (19) 72736). Owners Ken and Ian Harner run high quality day tours from Bulawayo to Matobo, Chipangali, Tshabalala and Khami.

*Backpackers Africa*, PO Box 44, Victoria Falls (☎/fax (113) 4510). This operation leads half-day to 12-day walking safaris in Chizarira, Kazuma Pan, Hwange and Zambezi national parks. You can choose between straight backpacking, hiking with porters or a combination of driving and hiking. Trainee guides may be hired for independent exploration.

*Birds of a Feather Tours*, PO Box BW 594, Borrowdale, Harare (☎ (14) 882478; fax 728744). This company runs ornithological tours in the Eastern Highlands, the middle Zambezi, Hwange and Victoria Falls, and a bird of prey (raptor) tour in Matobo.

*Black Rhino Safaris*, PO Box FM 89, Famona, Bulawayo (☎/fax (19) 41662). Black Rhino, one of Zimbabwe's best and most enthusiastic companies, specialises in day trips to Matobo, which it knows better than anyone else. It also runs superb trips to Mana Pools, Hwange and Chizarira for US$100 per day.

*Buffalo Safaris*, PO Box 113, Kariba (☎ (161) 2645; fax 2827; <buffalo@harare.iafrica.com>). This recommended company, which is well disposed toward backpackers, incorporates Zambezi Canoeing and Lake Wilderness Safaris and does middle Zambezi canoe trips

and walking safaris in Mana Pools and Matusadona. It also runs Lake Wilderness, Nyakasanga and Kushinga lodges, all around Kariba.

*Bukima Africa*, The Rocks, 18 Seke Rd, Hatfield, Harare (☎ (14) 796226; fax 753199). Bukima does overland transits between Harare and Victoria Falls from US$20, and circuits around Zimbabwe and Botswana for US$270, plus food and sightseeing.

*Bushbeat Trails*, VFR, 5th Floor Memorial Building, 35 Samora Machel Ave, PO Box H226, Hatfield, Harare (☎ (14) 780396; fax 708089; <vfrtours@harare.iafrica.com>). Bushbeat runs sightseeing tours around Harare (US$23 to US$55) and day trips to Tengenenge (US$55), Great Zimbabwe (US$140), the Eastern Highlands (US$140) and the Tangenhamo game reserve in Chivhu.

*Carew/Livingstone Safaris*, Private Bag 295A, 18th floor, Livingstone House, Samora Machel Ave, Harare (☎ (14) 735920; fax 795301). Carew runs unique and fabulous horse tours through the wild and beautiful Tingwa Valley in the Mavuradonha range. Special backpackers deals are available off-season or when there are last minute vacancies.

*Chikwenya Safaris*, PO Box 292, Kariba (☎ (161) 2525). This company operates Chikwenya Camp at Mana Pools National Park and Fothergill Island Lodge in Lake Kariba. It offers wildlife viewing by vehicle, boat, and on foot from these two lodges.

*Chipembere (Wild Frontiers) Safaris*, PO Box 9, Kariba (☎ (161) 2946). This South African company runs canoe trips on the middle Zambezi from Mana Pools to Kanyemba, and recommended walking and backpacking trips through the Chitake Springs area of Mana Pools. In South Africa, contact Wild Frontiers (☎ (011) 314 5838; fax 4850), PO Box 844, Halfway House 1685.

*Club Wununda Safaris*, PO Box 9084, Hillside, Bulawayo (☎/fax (19) 42379). This original company brings together golfing and photography. Tours range from a circuit of Zimbabwe's major golf venues to a countrywide photographic study.

*Dabula Safaris*, PO Box 210, Victoria Falls (☎/fax (113) 4453). Dabula organises game drives, walking safaris, booze cruises, fishing trips, bush dinners and transfers around Victoria Falls, Kasane (Botswana) and Livingstone (Zambia).

*Dendera Safaris*, Creek House, Cutty Sark Hotel, PO Box 328, Kariba (☎ (161) 2321 ext 326; fax 2575). Dendera runs three and four-day canoeing and camping trips to Matusadona and Mana Pools for US$395 to US$495.

*Eddie's Tours & Safaris*, 29 Campbell Ave, PO Box NE71, North End, Bulawayo (☎ (19) 65971; fax 65016). Eddie is pretty good for cultural tours in the communal lands around Bulawayo, but anything more complex would stretch this operation's organisational capacity.

*Far & Wide Zimbabwe*, PO Box 14, Juliasdale (☎ (129) 26329). This company's speciality is white-water rafting on the Pungwe River in the Eastern Highlands. It also runs a small safari camp near Mtarazi Falls.

*Footprint Safaris*, Trish Reynolds, PO Box BW 276, Borrowdale, Harare (☎ (14) 882883). This small, enthusiastic company offers personalised guided tours in Harare and around Zimbabwe.

*Foxtrot Tours*, 9 Adylinn Rd, Harare (☎ (14) 300294). Foxtrot runs transfers between Harare and Chimanimani for US$20.

*Frontiers*, Shop 1, Phumula Centre, Parkway, PO Box 35, Victoria Falls (☎ (113) 5800; fax 5801). Frontiers specialises in white-water rafting below Victoria Falls, and booze cruises and canoeing on the upper Zambezi. It also runs overnight and longer rafting trips right through Batoka Gorge.

*Goliath Safaris*, Suite 336, Brontë Hotel, PO Box CH294 Chisipite, Harare (☎ (14) 739836; fax 708843). This personable company is recommended for its canoe routes between Chirundu and Kanyemba and backpacking trips in Mana Pools.

*Gwaai Valley Safaris*, PO Box 17, Gwaai River (☎/fax (118) 575). Gwaai Valley specialises in game drives and custom safaris in Hwange National Park, and also runs the budget-oriented Nyati Lodge near Gwaai River outside the park.

*Ivory Safaris*, PO Box 9127, Hillside, Bulawayo (☎ (19) 61079). Ivory runs safaris through Hwange National Park based at its own camp, Ivory Lodge, which lies just outside the park boundaries.

*Kalambeza Safaris*, VFR Tours, 6th floor, 35 Samora Machel Ave, PO Box 4128, Harare (☎ (14) 793996; fax 791188) or PO Box 121, Victoria Falls (☎ (113) 4480; fax 4644). Kalambeza concentrates on day tours near Harare and Victoria Falls, and wildlife-viewing safaris through Hwange and Kazuma Pan national parks.

*Kamoto Tours* (☎/fax (14) 308991; <kamoto@ samara.iafrica.com>). This operator runs two and four-night visits to Madzimbawe, an African village an hour north of Harare, for

US$10 per day, including transfers and African-style meals.

*Kandahar Safaris*, Sopers Arcade Shop 9, Parkway, PO Box 233, Victoria Falls (☎ (113) 4502; fax 4556). Kandahar specialises in canoe day trips above Victoria Falls and camping trips along the Upper Zambezi between Kazungula and the Falls.

*Kasambabezi Safaris*, PO Box 279, Kariba (☎ (161) 2641). This company offers canoeing trips between Kariba and Chirundu. It's cheap for canoeing, especially if you're short on time.

*Khangela Safaris*, PO Box FM 296, Famona, Bulawayo (☎ (19) 49733; fax 68259; <secbird@ harare.iafrica.com>, mark 'Attn: Khangela Safaris'). This highly recommended operation is run by Mike and Anna Scott. Mike is a professional guide who leads walking, camping and wilderness backpacking trips through Chizarira, Hwange, Matobo and Gonarezhou national parks. You can choose between day walks from semi-permanent base camps or backpacking treks through the wilderness for US$140 per day. Either way, you'll have an unforgettable experience and a new bush perspective. Gonarezhou and Chizarira are especially recommended. All-inclusive eight-day walking/driving safaris in Chizarira and Hwange, or through Matobo, Gonarezhou and Great Zimbabwe, cost US$1120. With advance notice, they also run backpacking trips in Matusadona.

*Khatshana Tours & Travel*, 39 Fife St, PO Box 8253, Belmont, Bulawayo (☎/fax (19) 66538). Khatshana organises custom tours around Zimbabwe; the basic charge is US$0.60 per km, including transport and guide only.

*Landela Safaris*, 29 Mazowe St, PO Box 66293, Kopje, Harare (☎ (14) 734043; fax 708119; <landela@samara.co.zw>). Landela operates lodges all around the country, including Chokamella Camp near Hwange National Park, Gache Gache at Kariba, Landela Lodge near Harare, and Sekuti's Drift and Masuwe near Victoria Falls.

*Londa Mela Safaris*, PO Box 130, Queens Park, Bulawayo (☎ (19) 41286; fax 78319). This upmarket organiser specialises in tours around Bulawayo and further afield. Although it works mainly with overseas operators, you may be able to make late bookings for good rates.

*Matobo Tours*, PO Box 2405, Bulawayo (☎ (19) 72748; fax 72749). Matobo operates Bulawayo city tours and full and half-day tours to Matobo National Park, Khami Ruins and Great Zimbabwe. It also runs transfers to Masvingo and Hwange.

*Mia Falls*, 36 Athlone Ave, Northend, Bulawayo (☎ (19) 46448; fax 77300). This company, which is affiliated with Black Rhino safaris (see above) concentrates on day tours from Bulawayo to Matobo, including walking safaris.

*Miombo Safaris*, PO Box 90, Dete (☎ (118) 446). Miombo has a comfortable camp near Dete and organises economical transport and tours in Hwange National Park.

*Moomba Safaris*, Shop 2, Parkade Centre, Fife St & Ninth Ave, PO Box 369, Bulawayo (☎ (19) 79478; fax 69079). Moomba runs several sightseeing, camping and cultural tours in Matobo National Park and surrounding communal lands.

*Muvimi Safaris*, 89 Central Ave, PO Box 2233, Harare (☎ (14) 793107; fax 704960). This outfit does four-night tours to its luxury tented camp in Matusadona National Park (US$1000), as well as middle Zambezi canoeing safaris (US$460 to US$600) and four-night Mana Pools backpacking safaris with professional guides (US$470 to US$630). The minimum age is 16 years.

*Mzingeli Tours*, 133 Leopold Takawira Ave, PO Box 2827, Bulawayo (☎ (19) 540268; fax 540269). This company runs cultural tours around Bulawayo, including visits to communal lands, villages and rural self-help projects, as well as popular sites.

*Nemba Safaris*, PO Box 4, Gwaai River (☎ (135) 33). This company, owned by Chris and Val van Wyk, organises walking tours in the remote Mzola Wilderness area outside Hwange National Park.

*Ngamo Photo Safaris*, PO Box 467, Bulawayo (☎ (19) 61495; fax 74825). This company, which works in affiliation with the Zimbabwe Forestry Commission, generates revenue for Zimbabwean conservation programmes. Currently, it operates three lodges in forest areas of north-western Zimbabwe: Ganda Lodge at the edge of Hwange National Park; Sijarira Camp, between Lake Kariba and Chizariri National Park; and Jafuta Camp, in a forested area 13km from Victoria Falls.

*N'taba Trails*, 102 Pioneer House, Fife St, Bulawayo (☎ (19) 79563; fax 76658). N'taba offers budget day tours to the Matobo Hills, including a visit to an African village.

*Peter Ginn Birding Safaris*, PO Box 44, Marondera (☎/fax (179) 23411; <pgbs@mango .zw>). Peter Ginn does courses in bird identification and runs trips for clients who 'want to spend more time on birds than on big game'.

Specialities include the Save Valley Conservancy and the remote Haroni and Rusitu forest reserves.

*Purple Patch Tours*, PO Box BW1633, Borrowdale, Harare (☎/fax (14) 883217). Runs airport transfers and day tours around Harare, Nyanga and Great Zimbabwe, and longer tours to Kariba.

*Rail Safaris*, Mr & Mrs G Cooke, 2c Prospect Ave, Raylton, PO Box 2536, Bulawayo (☎ (19) 75575; fax 42217; <railsaf@acacia .samara.co.zw>). For rail buffs, this company runs expensive but informative tours from Victoria Falls to Mutare on the *Zambezi Special* and the *Eastern Highlander*. It also organises connections with named trains in South Africa. Low-season steam trips from Bulawayo to Victoria Falls cost US$315/350/450 in Heritage/Ivory/Emerald (posh/posher/poshest) class. Those who splash out on Emerald Class can even take a memorable bath on a moving train!

*Sabre Adventures & Expeditions*, Private Bag A6106, Avondale, Harare (☎ (14) 733711; fax 733718). If you want to go far beyond the end of the tourist track, here's your opportunity. How about joining the rhino-protection squads in the remote bush or learning navigation, tracking and bush survival on a foot expedition through the Zambezi Valley?

*Safari Par Excellence*, Third floor, Travel Centre, Jason Moyo Ave, Harare (☎ (14) 720527; fax 722872; <safpar@harare.iafrica.com>). This multi-faceted company is known for rafting trips below Victoria Falls and Zambia-side canoeing on the middle Zambezi. It also does walking and backpacking in Matusadona National Park. *Kayila Lodge* on the Zambian shore of the Zambezi near Mana Pools is characterised by pleasant rock-bound architecture, treehouses and even a toilet inside a baobab.

*Sandbank Safaris*, Shaka's Spear, Bulawayo (☎ (19) 69923). Owners Mike and Natalie Magee offer an enthusiastic perspective on the Matobo area, with emphasis on the rocks and paintings. From Bulawayo, 10 to 11-hour day tours cost US$40, including meals. They also organise horse trips in the Mazwi Game Sanctuary, a high protection zone for endangered wildlife near Bulawayo. A full day of riding, with meals, costs US$37.

*Senanga Safaris*, Victoria Falls (☎/fax (113) 4614). This company specialises in five-hour night-time game drives in and around Victoria Falls for US$40 per person. The price includes snacks around a campfire and, during cooler months, a loan of warm clothing.

*Shamwari Safaris*, PO Box 53, Dete (☎ (118) 248). This operator runs recommended safaris and game drives through Hwange National Park. The owner, Roberto 'Beat' Accorsi is one of the best photographic guides and naturalists around. You can choose between tailor-made itineraries or standard packages.

*Shearwater*, Edward Building, on the corner of First St and Nelson Mandela Ave, PO Box 3961, Harare (☎ (14) 757831; fax 757836; <shearwat@harare.iafrica.com>). This operator is Zimbabwe's largest organiser of rafting trips at Victoria Falls as well as middle Zambezi canoeing trips from Kariba all the way to Kanyemba. It also operates backpacking safaris in Mana Pools National Park and 'Breakaway Safaris' to Namibia and Botswana.

*Singing Bird Tours*, Dete (☎ (118) 255; fax 383). This small, recommended company has cottages for rent and runs inexpensive game drives in Hwange National Park.

*Stonegate Safaris*, PO Box 1375, Harare (☎/fax (14) 883002). This small operator specialises in tours to the sculpture gardens at Tengenenge Farm in northern Zimbabwe.

*Sunbird Safaris*, Great Zimbabwe Hotel, PO Box 644, Masvingo (☎ (139) 62718). Sunbird runs day tours from Masvingo, including Great Zimbabwe and the Mutirikwe Game Park, birdwatching, horseback riding trips, and cruises on Lake Mutirikwe.

*Supreme Raft*, Parkway, PO Box 295, Victoria Falls (☎ (113) 3300; fax 3299). This adrenaline-motivated company does a range of white-water rafting trips at Victoria Falls, and organises the original Gruesome 2-Some – a bungee-jumping/rafting combination – and the even more serious Awesome 4-Some, which adds microlighting and parachuting.

*Tchechenini Trails*, Mhangura (☎ (14) 727080). This small operator, based on a working tobacco farm, runs horse trips in Zambezi Escarpment wilderness areas. A small thatched lodge serves as a base for all trips.

*Time for Africa*, 14 Windsor Ave, PO Box HG940, Highlands, Harare (☎ (14) 703633; fax 703634; <safari@icon.co.zw>). This company is the booking agent for Inns of Zimbabwe and organises air safaris, and sailing and luxury 'paddlewheel' safaris on Lake Kariba.

*Touch the Wild*, Private Bag 6, Hillside, Bulawayo (☎ (19) 74589; fax 229088; <touchwld@harare.iafrica.com>). This up-market company runs tours and game drives around the country. It works mainly with over-

seas operators and is well out of range for budget-conscious travellers. It also runs the lovely Matobo Hills Lodge in Matobo National Park, but foreigners must pay top-tier rates.

*Tsika Tours*, 39 Hughes St, Masvingo (☎ (139) 65793). Tsika does day tours to Great Zimbabwe ruins and Mutirikwe.

*Tsoro River Safaris*, Stand 787 Sable Dr, Kariwa House, PO Box 161, Kariba (☎/fax (161) 2426). Operates middle Zambezi canoeing safaris between Chirundu and Mana Pools.

*United Touring Company (UTC)*, United House, 4 Park St, corner of Jason Moyo Ave, PO Box 2914, Harare (☎ (14) 793701; fax 792794). With tentacles all over Africa, UTC runs a range of day trips in Harare, Kariba, Bulawayo, Hwange National Park and Victoria Falls.

*Wamambo Cultural Tours & Safaris*, 9th Floor, Puzey Chambers, corner First St and Robert Mugabe Rd, PO Box 6928, Harare (☎ (14) 773883; fax 773884; <wamambo@teconet .co.zw>). This company specialises in budget, culturally-oriented tours around the country. In its own words, 'Experience a Zimbabwe that doesn't charge in US dollars'.

*Wilderness Safaris*, PO Box 288, Victoria Falls (☎ (113) 4527; fax 4224); <wildness@ zol.co.zw>). This company books Makalolo Plains Lodge in Hwange, Matusadona Water Lodge near Matusadona, Nduna Safari Lodge in Gonarezhou and walking safaris in Chizarira and Matusadona.

*Wild Horizons*, PO Box 159, Victoria Falls (☎ (113) 4219). Wild Horizons organises half-day and full-day game walks through Zambezi National Park. It also runs Imbabala Camp and Hwange's Jijima Safari camp.

*Wildlife Expeditions*, 72 King George Rd, Avondale, Harare (☎ (14) 335716; fax 335341; <wildlife_expd@compuserve.com>). Runs good value, longer camping safaris around Zimbabwe, as well as to South Africa, Mozambique, Malawi, Kenya, Tanzania, Botswana and Namibia.

*The Zambezi Safari & Travel Company*, The Heights Centre, PO Box 158, Kariba (☎ (161) 2632; fax 2291; <zambezi@harare.iafrica .com>; Web site <www.zambezi.com>). This travel agency/operator concentrates on safaris, tours and transfers in and around Kariba, Mana Pools and Matusadona.

*Zambezi Hippo Trails*, Dalmatia House, Speke Ave, PO Box 3158, Harare (☎/fax (14) 702148). This operator offers middle Zambezi canoeing from Mana Pools to Kanyemba.

*Zimbabwe Balloon Flights*, 316 Harare Drive,

Msasa, Harare (π/fax (14) 487035). These folks do balloon flights around the Harare area.

*Zindele Safaris*, Private Bag 232A, Harare (π (14) 721696; fax 702006; <zinsafari@zol :co.zw>). Zindele organises custom trips to main sites of interest, has a guest farm north of Harare and runs the Shumba Shaba Lodge in the Matobo hills near Bulawayo.

## BOTSWANA

The Botswana government heartily promotes organised tours and offers tour discounts on national park entry fees. Most interest focuses on the Okavango Delta area, but operators also offer options around Nata, Gweta, Shakawe and other places. In general, safaris may be more economically arranged through Botswana companies than through overseas agents.

The following list includes major operators. For more on specific tours, see the regional chapters (details on Maun and Okavango Delta operators are listed in boxed text in the Okavango Delta & North-Western Botswana chapter). Note that there are no area codes for telephone numbers in Botswana.

*African Encounters*, Private Bag BR102, Broadhurst, Gaborone (π 314252; fax 303201). African Encounters operates upmarket tours around Gaborone, Khutse, the Tuli Block, northern Botswana game reserves and northern South Africa.

*Bathusi Travel & Safaris*, Rileys Garage, Main Road, Private Bag 44, Maun (π/fax 660647)

*Bonaventures Botswana*, PO Box 201, Maun (π/fax 660502)

*Bush Camp Safaris*, Baagi House, PO Box 487, Maun (π/fax 660847)

*Chobe Flyfishing Safaris*, Andre Van Aardt, PO Box 206, Kasane (π 650414; fax 650223). This company specialises in fly-fishing expeditions on the Chobe River. The quarry includes pike, tigerfish and bream.

*Crocodile Camp Safaris*, PO Box 46, The Mall, Maun (π/fax 660265)

*Gametrackers*, PO Box 100, Maun (π 660351)

*Game Trails Safaris*, Private Bag 0062, Maun (π 660536; fax 660201)

*Go Wild Safaris*, PO Box 56, Kasane (π 650468; fax 650223). This popular company, based at Chobe Safari Lodge in Kasane, operates the morning and evening game drives in Chobe

National Park and cruises on the Chobe River, as well as safaris in Chobe, Moremi and the Okavango Delta.

*Gweta Rest Camp*, PO Box 124, Gweta (π/fax 612220). In addition to day and overnight tours, this reliable operation organises customised safaris throughout Botswana.

*Island Safaris*, PO Box 116, Maun (π/fax 660300)

*Kanana Safaris*, PO Box 2, Ghanzi (π/fax 596166). Kanana Safaris, owned by John Hardbattle, runs Kanana Safari Lodge near Ghanzi and organises cultural safaris in the area: visits to San villages (US$25), excursions with San guides (US$9 per hour) and horseriding in the Kalahari (US$15 per hour).

*Ker & Downey*, PO Box 27, Maun (π 660375; fax 661282; <kerdowny@abacus.global.bw>)

*Linyanti Explorations*, PO Box 22, Kasane (π 650505; fax 650342; <chobe@icon .co.za>). This upmarket operation runs remote luxury lodges in Chobe, Moremi and the Linyanti region. It also guides four-day walking and canoeing safaris in the Selinda Reserve, near Linyanti. All-inclusive packages for one/two people cost US$405/610 per day.

*Merlin Services*, Private Bag 0013, Maun (π 660635; fax 660036)

*Okavango Explorations (Hartley's Safaris)*, Private Bag 0048, Maun (π/fax 660528)

*Okavango Tours & Safaris*, PO Box 39, Maun (π 660220; fax 660589; <okavango@global .bw>)

*Okavango Wilderness Safaris*, Private Bag 014, Maun (π 660086; fax 660632)

*Phakawe Safaris*, PO Box 20538, Maun (π 660567; fax 660912; <phakawe@info.bw>; Web site www.phakawe.demon.co.uk). The best value in Botswana!

*Touch of Africa Safaris*, PO Box 127, Kasane (π 632058 or 632007; fax 632006). Runs two-day safaris in Chobe National Park and the Kazuma Pan area.

*Trans Okavango*, Private Bag 033, Maun (π 660023; fax 660040)

*Uncharted Africa Safaris*, PO Box 173, Francistown (π 312277; fax 213458). This company operates two remote safari camps – Jack's Camp and San Camp – deep in the Makgadikgadi Pans area, and the budget-oriented Planet Baobab and Kalahari Surf Club, near Gweta. Using the camps as a base, it runs game drives and excursions around the Pans. A new offering is a foray into the wildest Kalahari for a glimpse of the traditional San lifestyle; for a mere US$500 per day, you get luxury in the wilderness. (Don't miss their Jack's Camp brochure – it contains absolutely no information, but is a veritable work of art!)

*Wild Attractions/Traction Safaris*, PO Box 60, Serowe (☎ 430420; fax 430992). This small company puts together custom participation safaris through Moremi, Chobe and Nxai Pan, among other places, and runs transfers between Maun and Kasane, via the national parks.

*Wild Hog Tours & Safaris*, PO Box 213, Kasane (☎/fax 651140; <wildhog@info.bw>; Web site www.info.bw/~wildhog). This unique operator offers wild rides around southern Africa on Harley-Davidson motorbikes. Whether you're an aspiring Hell's Angel or you just appreciate a good solid machine, it's sure to be a thrill. Bikes – you can choose from a Dyna Wideglide, Superglide, Custom Softail, 1200 Sportster and 883 Hugger – cost US$300 per day, and you can add a passenger for US$90. Accommodation is anywhere from US$150 to US$350, depending on the standards required.

## NAMIBIA

Even if you're one who spurns organised trips, there's a good case for joining a basic camping tour to such out-of-the-way and difficult-to-reach places as the Skeleton Coast, Damaraland, the Kaokoveld, the Kunene Valley, the Owambo country, Bushmanland and the wild Namib Desert. If you can't muster a group for car hire, they also provide an alternative to hitching or battling with public transport to visit the more popular places. Many offer nothing but transport and camping options; participants do all the camp work and prepare their own meals.

The following list of reputable operators includes a range of possibilities. The most interesting tours and rates are outlined in the relevant chapters.

*Abenteuer Afrika*, PO Box 1490, Swakopmund (☎/fax (064) 404030; fax 464038). This German-oriented company runs half and full-day tours around Swakopmund and Walvis Bay. Three and four-day camping tours to the Namib and Damaraland range from US$360 to US$450.

*Africa Adventure Safaris*, 72 Tal Strasse, PO Box 20274, Windhoek (☎ (061) 234720; fax 230001; <afradven@iwwn.com.na>). Geared for those with limited time, it does Windhoek city tours and visits to Daan Viljoen, Etosha and Sossusvlei.

*Afri-Fishing & Safaris*, 6th St West 14, PO Box 2156, Walvis Bay (☎ (064) 209449; fax 209440). The name suggests waterborne tours, but in addition to fishing and dolphin-watching, this company also runs good-value day tours into the wilder reaches of the Namib Desert Park.

*Afro Ventures*, Hertzog Berlin Building, 14A Kaiser Wilhelm Strasse, PO Box 1772, Swakopmund (☎ (064) 463812; fax 400216). Afro Ventures does half and full-day tours around Swakopmund and Walvis Bay.

*!Ah N!hore Safaris*, PO Box 5703, Windhoek (☎/fax (061) 220124). This novel operation offers educational cultural tours with skilled Bushmanland hunters and trackers. Visitors learn about traditional San values, lifestyles and methods. The safaris generate funds for the Tsumkwe Trust.

*Anton's Day Tours*, PO Box 900, Swakopmund (☎ (064) 404060). Anton Thelen guides seven-hour day tours to sites around Swakopmund costing from US$32 to US$52.

*Baobab Tours*, PO Box 24818, Windhoek (☎ (061) 232314; fax 224017). Baobab's reasonably priced cultural and environmental camping tours emphasise national parks and benefits to local communities.

*Blue Marlin*, Swakopmund (☎ (064) 404134). If you've always wanted to haul in a big fish, US$54 will buy you a few hours on the open seas in quest of kob, steenbras, galjoen and shark. When snoek, yellowtail and larger game fish are the quarry, it costs US$66 per day. Whale-watching and photography cruises are US$34.

*Bona Safaris*, PO Box 804, Gobabis (☎/fax (061) 562988; <100554.3710@compuserve.com>). Bona specialises in Namibia's major tourist sites, as well as Bushmanland, the Caprivi and Khaudom.

*Byseewah Safaris*, PO Box 495, Outjo (☎ (06458) ask for 4222; fax (0651) 4294). Byseewah organises custom safaris in northern Namibia, particularly Etosha, for as little as US$83.50 per day, including accommodation (on its own 'cattle-free, fence-free' farm), food, walks, game drives and laundry.

*Chameleon Safaris*, PO Box 21903, Windhoek (☎/fax (061) 211490). Chameleon is geared for backpackers and runs seven-day all-inclusive loops through northern or southern Namibia, or transfers to Victoria Falls. For more, see the boxed text in the Windhoek chapter.

*Charly's Desert Tours*, 11 Kaiser Wilhelm

Strasse, PO Box 1400, Swakopmund (☎ (064) 404341; fax 404821). A variety of reasonably priced day tours around Swakopmund, including rock-hounding, the Spitzkoppe, Welwitschia Drive, Cape Cross and Sandwich Harbour.

*Crazy Kudu Safaris*, 15 Johann Albrecht Strasse, PO Box 86124, Windhoek (☎/fax (061) 222636; <crazykudu@hotmail.com>). The most economical safari company in Namibia, Crazy Kudu, run by Mike Godfrey, does 10-day all-inclusive adventures through northern and western Namibian highlights, a six-day northern highlights tour and a three-day Namib Desert circuit, as well as tailor-made safaris (including the unique 'Lonely Planet Tour'!). For details see the boxed aside in the Windhoek chapter.

*CTOA/Travel Magic*, PO Box 1754, Walvis Bay (☎ (064) 203400; fax 203401). This packager organises safaris to both well known sites and off-the-beaten-track destinations.

*Damaraland Trails & Tours*, 15 Cathy St, Ludwigsdorf, PO Box 3073, Windhoek (☎ (061) 234610; fax 239616). Rock art and desert tours in Damaraland and wildlife viewing in Etosha National Park.

*Desert Adventure Safaris*, Namib Centre, Roon Strasse, PO Box 1428, Swakopmund (☎/fax (064) 404459; fax 404072). This company runs inexpensive day tours around Swakopmund, the Spitzkoppe and Cape Cross, and longer tours to Damaraland and the Kaokoveld. It also runs Palmwag Lodge in Damaraland and the beautiful Serra Cafema Lodge on the Kunene.

*Eagle's Nest Tours*, Field Strasse 16, PO Box 2107, Swakopmund (☎ (064) 400932 or (081) 1244069). Guide Allin van Zyl leads sightseeing tours around Swakopmund and deep-sea fishing trips for as little as US$52 per day.

*Eco-Marine Kayak Tours*, Jeanne Meintjes, Walvis Bay (☎/fax (064) 203144). Jeanne guides kayaking trips around the beautiful Walvis Bay wetlands, as well as trips to Pelican Point and Bird Island.

*El Gekko Tours*, PO Box 505, Keetmanshoop (☎ (063) 224831 or (081) 1241207; fax (063) 222175). Inexpensive and informal tours around southern Namibia, including Lüderitz and Fish River Canyon.

*Ermo Safaris*, PO Box 80205, Windhoek (☎/fax (061) 51975) – or 1312, Kamanjab. This company, based at Ermo Safari Lodge near Etosha, runs multi-day camping safaris combining the Kaokoveld and Etosha National Park.

*Farm Hilton*, W & A Fritsche, PO Box 20706, Windhoek (☎ (0628) 1111). This Khomas Hochland farm runs horseback trips in the Hochland. Serious riding aficionados can join its popular 10-day riding/camping trip from the Hochland across the Namib Desert to Swakopmund. Book well in advance.

*Gondwana Tours*, Pension Gessert, 138 13th St, PO Box 690, Keetmanshoop (☎/fax (063) 223892). This company does day trips to the Kokerboomwoud, Lüderitz, Fish River Canyon and around southern Namibia.

*Honeyguide Safaris*, Hubertus Kreiner, PO Box 434, Windhoek (☎/fax (061) 239700). This one does hunting trips, so if you're opposed to that, look elsewhere. The company organises hunting and photographic safaris around Namibia.

*Inshore Safaris*, 12th Rd, PO Box 2444, Walvis Bay (☎ (064) 202609; fax 202198; <inshore@gem.co.za>). This is a good Walvis Bay operator for trips to Sandwich Harbour, the dunes, the nature reserves and Welwitschia Drive. It also does 10-day all-inclusive circuit tours of northern or southern Namibia for around US$1850.

*Kaokohimba Safaris*, PO Box 11580, Windhoek (☎/fax (061) 222378). Kaokohimba runs 12 to 15-day cultural tours through the Kaokoveld and Damaraland, wildlife-viewing trips in Etosha National Park and hiking around northern Namibia.

*Levo Tours*, PO Box 1860, Walvis Bay (☎ (064) 207555 or (081) 1247825; fax (064) 207555). Deep-sea day fishing trips and seal and dolphin-watching cruises.

*Lüderitzbucht Tours & Safaris*, PO Box 76, Lüderitz (☎ (063) 202719; fax 202863). In addition to Kolmanskop tours, this company also runs trips to other recently opened parts of the Sperrgebiet (Diamond Area 1) such as Elizabeth Bay, Atlas Bay and the Bogenfels. Tours are available in English, German or Afrikaans.

*Mola-Mola Safaris*, PO Box 980, Walvis Bay (☎ (064) 205511 or (081) 1242522; fax (064) 207593; <molamola@iwwn.com.na>). This water-oriented company runs half-day dolphin-watching cruises for US$34, seabird-watching trips for US$45 and day trips to Bird Island, Pelican Point and Sandwich Harbour, with a meal of Walvis Bay oysters, for US$68.

*Muramba Bushman Trails*, PO Box 689, Tsumeb (☎ (06738) ask for 6222; fax (067) 220916; <natron@lianam.lia.net>). This recommended company, owned by Reinhard Friedrich, provides a unique introduction to the Heikum San people. Participants learn bush skills and also experience the San traditions, lifestyles and natural pharmacopoeia.

*Namibia Pappot Safaris*, PO Box 130, Maltahöhe (☎ (063) 293042; fax 293150). This company, run by Piet and Kota van Zyl, does rugged circuits of southern Namibia with the 4WD enthusiast in mind.

*Namibia Photo Tours*, 8 Roon Strasse, PO Box 442, Swakopmund (☎/fax (064) 404561). This Swakopmund company does photographic and fishing tours. Day tours include Welwitschia Drive, Cape Cross, the Spitzkoppe, a sundowner on the dunes and shark-fishing.

*Namibian Tourist Friend*, Eros Airport, COMAV Flying School, PO Box 11099, Windhoek (☎ (061) 249408; fax 233485; <ntf@iwwn .com.na>). This company does 'tuk-tuk' city tours (US$30), canoe trips (US$79), sundowners (US$45) and flying tours over Namibia's main sights.

*Namib Sky Adventure Safaris*, PO Box 197, Maltahöhe (☎ (0663) 5703). For those who dream of looming over the dunes in a balloon, these people offer Namib desert balloon flights. The early morning flight departs before sunrise, when not a breath of wind is stirring. This operator is affiliated with the Namib Rand Guest Ranch.

*Nawa Safaris*, PO Box 22311, 3 Louis Botha Ave, Windhoek (☎/fax (061) 227893). Nawa runs well priced camping safaris, concentrating on northern Namibia. A 14-day all-inclusive trip through Windhoek, the Waterberg, Etosha National Park, the Kunene region and Damaraland starts at US$1450.

*Okakambe Trails*, PO Box 1591, Swakopmund (☎ (064) 402799). This company gives riding lessons and runs horseback tours around Swakopmund, including an overnight Swakop River tour to Goanikontes.

*Okashana Wilderness Tours*, PO Box 96, Okahandja (☎ (0621) 502802). On Okashana's multi-day cultural trips to the Kunene region and Owambo country, you'll come in contact with traditional lifestyles in north-western Namibia.

*Ondese Safaris*, PO Box 6196, Ausspannplatz, Windhoek (☎ (061) 220876; fax 239700; <ondese@iwwn.com.na>). Ondese does expensive, luxury-oriented tours in Namibia, as well as neighbouring countries.

*Oryx Tours*, 11 Van der Bijl St, Northern Industrial Area, PO Box 2058, Windhoek (☎ (061) 217454; fax 263417; <orxytours@iwwn.com .na>). Oryx does day tours and longer trips through the highlights, as well as Kavango, Caprivi, Victoria Falls and the Okavango

Delta. It concentrates on overseas bookings, but can also be booked locally.

*Otjimburu Trails*, PO Box 5144, Windhoek (☎ (061) 234359; fax 228461). Otjimburu runs Windhoek city tours and longer custom trips.

*Pasjona Safaris*, PO Box 24256, Windhoek (☎/fax (061) 223421). Pasjona operates northern and southern circuits through the major sites. It caters mainly for German travellers.

*Pleasure Flights*, PO Box 537, Swakopmund (☎ (064) 404500 or (081) 1294500; fax (064) 405325; <redbaron@iml-net.com.na>). Pleasure Flights runs 'flightseeing' tours from the Skeleton Coast right down to Fish River Canyon. For an economical price, you need a group of five people.

*Rhino Tours*, PO Box 4369, Vineta, Swakopmund (☎/fax (064) 405757). Rhino runs day tours around Swakopmund and longer safaris in the Namib, the Skeleton Coast, Damaraland and the Kaokoveld. Day tours cost from US$52 and longer tours average US$160 per day.

*Sandy Acre Safaris*, PO Box 9970, Windhoek (☎ (061) 248137; fax 238707). This company does luxury-level safaris around Namibia for US$315/225 per person per day, with groups of two/four.

*Shongololo Express Namibia* (☎ (061) 250378; fax 246428). This company operates unique luxury rail journeys in Namibia, with minibus tours to sites of interest along the way.

*Skeleton Coast Fly-In Safaris*, PO Box 2195, Windhoek (☎ (061) 224248; fax 225713; <sksafari@iwwn.com.na>; Web site www .iwwn.com.na/sksafari/brochure.html). This company offers all-inclusive four-day tours of the Skeleton Coast and Kunene River region for US$1860. Add Sossusvlei and it's US$2050. Five-day trips to the Skeleton Coast, the Kunene River, Etosha National Park and Sossusvlei are US$2280. Add the NamibRand Nature Reserve and Lüderitz and it's US$2710. Tours accommodate four to 10 people.

*Southern Cross Safaris*, 43 Independence Ave, PO Box 941, Windhoek (☎ (061) 221193; fax 225387). Southern Cross does wilderness camping safaris in wildest Kaokoland and Caprivi, and also into Zimbabwe and Botswana.

*Springbok Atlas Namibia*, PO Box 11165, Klein Windhoek (☎ (061) 215943; fax 215932). We've had lots of recommendations for this upmarket tour company, which offers a comfortable way to see the best of Namibia.

*Sunny South Tours*, PO Box 31039, Pionierspark, Windhoek (☎/fax (061) 246895). 4WD tours

on Farm Weenen in the rugged Gamsberg area
of the Khomas Hochland.

*SWA Safaris*, 43 Independence Ave, PO Box
20373, Windhoek (☎ (061) 237567; fax
225387; <swasaf@iwwn.com.na>). This company runs longer, mid-range tours around
Namibia, from Etosha to Fish River Canyon. It
caters mainly for the senior German market.

*Trans-Namibia Tours*, Shop 28, Gustav Voigts
Centre, 123 Independence Ave, PO Box
20028, Windhoek (☎ (061) 221549; fax
2982033; <tntours@iwwn.com.na>). Trans-
Namibia runs environmentally conscious day
tours, hiking tours and fly-in safaris, as well as
longer itineraries and self-drive tours. A highlight is the Fish Eagle Hiking Trail in southern
Namibia, which costs US$700 all inclusive.

*Weltvrede*, Private Bag X1009, Maltahöhe
(☎ (06632) ask for 3221). For photographing
the Namib Dunes, Weltvrede runs five-day
camping photography workshops based at its
rest camp near Solitaire. The price is US$363,
including camping, instruction and full board.

*Westcoast Angling Tours*, 9 Otavi Strasse, PO
Box 545, Swakopmund (☎ (064) 402377; fax
402532). This company specialises in fishing
tours, from deep-sea fishing to rock and surf
angling from the beach. Anglers can even try

for copper sharks, which may be caught from
the beach.

*Whitewater Eco Tours*, PO Box 30024, Windhoek
(☎ (081) 1220014; fax (061) 228259; <wet@is
.com.na>). This company is affiliated with
Kunene River Lodge and offers good value
white-water rafting on the Kunene River.

*Wild Dog Safaris*, PO Box 26188, Windhoek
(☎/fax (061) 257642; <awkirby@iafrica.com
.na>). This recommended budget operator
does swings through northern and southern
Namibia, as well as transfers between Windhoek and Victoria Falls. See the Budget Safaris
in Namibia boxed text under Windhoek.

*Wilderness Safaris Namibia*, The Namib Travel
Shop, PO Box 6850, Windhoek (☎ (061)
225178; fax 239455; <nts@iwwn.com.na>).
This company does camping safaris, rock-
hounding tours, Namib Desert tours and
Etosha game drives, as well as rafting trips on
the Kunene. The Swakopmund office (☎ (064)
405216; fax 405165) runs day tours around
Swakopmund and Walvis Bay.

*Wildlife Tours*, PO Box 24374, Windhoek
(☎ (061) 240817; fax 240818; <nts@iwwn
.com.na>). These folks offer 'ecologically oriented luxury', featuring walking, boating,
canoeing, ballooning and mountain biking.

# SAFARI GUIDE

# PRIMATES

**Bushbabies** *Otolemur crassicaudatus* (Greater or Thick-Tailed Bushbaby); *Galago moholi* (South African Lesser Bushbaby)

You could be forgiven for mistaking a bushbaby for a huge pair of eyes, big ears and a long bushy tail on four legs. While these features give bushbabies an exceptionally cute appearance, they have evolved this way for good reason. Bushbabies are strictly nocturnal, and because they live in trees and often feed on insects, they need excellent senses to survive. They also eat fruit, and the sap of some trees. Lesser bushbabies are smaller than thick-tailed bushbabies. Although common in some areas, they are difficult to see. However they sometimes give their presence away by bounding across the roofs of vehicles, chalets or rondavels at night.

**Size:** similar to a squirrel
**Distribution:** wooded or forested areas; greater bushbabies occur in eastern Zimbabwe, lesser bushbabies throughout the region
**Status:** common, but strictly nocturnal

PETER BROTHERTON

Lesser Bushbaby

## Chacma Baboon *Papio ursinus*

The dog-like snout of the baboon gives it a more aggressive appearance than most other primates, which have much more human-like facial features. However, when you watch baboons playing or merely sitting around, it's difficult not to make anthropomorphic comparisons. Baboons live in large troops of up to 150 animals, headed by a dominant male. Individuals spend much of their time searching for insects, spiders and birds' eggs. They also visit lodges, camp sites and picnic areas for easy pickings. Food should not be left, even in closed tents, when baboons are around – they have been known to destroy a tent while attempting to get at food inside it. Baboons may become such a nuisance that they have to be dealt with harshly by park officials, so resist the temptation to feed them.

**Size:** up to the size of a large dog
**Distribution:** throughout the region
**Status:** very common in many areas, and active during the day

MITCH REARDON

Baboons

Vervet Monkeys

### Vervet Monkey *Cercopithecus aethiops*

The playful vervet monkey is southern Africa's most common monkey. It is easily recognisable by its black face fringed with white hair. The hair is yellowish-grey elsewhere, except on the underparts, which are whitish. The male has an extraordinary bright blue scrotum. Vervet monkeys usually live in woodland and savanna, running in groups of up to 30. They're extremely cheeky and inquisitive, as you may find out when camping in the game reserves. Many have become used to humans and will stop at nothing to steal food or secure handouts, including making themselves welcome at dining tables or inside tents or cars.

**Size:** similar to a small dog
**Distribution:** Zimbabwe and the wetter parts of Botswana and Namibia
**Status:** often very common; bold and easy to see

### Samango Monkey (White-Throated Guenon) *Cercopithecus mitis*

Samango monkeys are pretty with a grey to black face, black shoulders, limbs and tail, and a reddish-brown back. Mature males make coughing sounds; females and young of both sexes make chirping and chattering sounds. They feed in the early morning and late afternoon in the higher treetops, descending into shady areas during the day. Samango monkeys normally live in social groups of between four and 12. Predators include leopard, pythons and eagles.

Samango Monkey

**Size:** similar to a medium-sized dog
**Distribution:** forests in eastern Zimbabwe
**Status:** locally common; active during the day, but often difficult to see among foliage

# SCALY ANTEATERS
### Ground Pangolin *Manis temminckii*

Pangolins, sometimes known as scaly anteaters, are covered with large rounded scales over the back and tail, with hair only around the eyes, ears, cheeks and belly. Their primary foods include ants and termites dug from termite mounds, rotting wood and dung heaps. They walk on the outer edges of their hands, with claws pointed inwards. They normally keep to dry scrubby country, especially areas with light sandy soil.

Ground Pangolin

**Size:** about the size of a dog
**Distribution:** throughout the region
**Status:** mainly nocturnal; difficult to see

# RODENTS

## Cape Porcupine *Hystrix africaeaustralis*

The prickly Cape porcupine, the largest rodent native to southern Africa, can weigh as much as 24kg and measure up to 1m in length. On cooler days, it may emerge during daylight hours. Porcupines are covered with a spread of long black-and-white banded quills from the shoulders to the tail. Along the ridge from the head to the shoulders runs a crest of long coarse hair, which stands on end when the animal is alarmed. For shelter, they either occupy caves or excavate their own burrows. Their diet consists mainly of bark, tubers, seeds and a variety of plants and ground-level foliage.

**Size:** up to the size of a large dog
**Distribution:** throughout the region
**Status:** common, but nocturnal and difficult to see

Cape Porcupine

## Springhare *Pedetes capensis*

In spite of its name and large ears, the springhare is not a hare, but a rodent. 'Springhare' is an anglicised form of the Afrikaans springhaas, which refers to the animal's bounding motion. As it hops along on its outsized hind feet, it is sometimes mistaken for a small kangaroo. Springhares dig extensive burrows, from which they emerge at night to feed on grass. Reflections of spotlights from their large, bright eyes often give them away on night safaris.

**Size:** similar to the European brown hare, but with a long tail
**Distribution:** throughout Namibia, Botswana and south-western Zimbabwe, but restricted to areas with sandy soils
**Status:** common, but strictly nocturnal

Springhare

## Cape Ground Squirrel *Xerus inauris*

Ground squirrels live in colonial burrows, often shared with meerkats. Males, which have very large testicles, wander between the female-dominated groups looking for mates. In tourist camps it is worth watching their playful antics during the heat of the day. Some individuals become quite tame, and will take food from humans very politely. They will also wander into open tents looking for food. They have an elegant fan-like tail, which they erect when alarmed while emitting a high-pitched whistle.

**Size:** similar to a grey squirrel
**Distribution:** drier parts of Botswana and Namibia
**Status:** common, and active throughout the day

Cape Ground Squirrel

# HYAENA

### Aardwolf *Proteles cristatus*

This small, curious relative of the hyaena is perhaps best known for its diet, which consists almost entirely of harvester termites. Aardwolves superficially resemble striped hyaena – which do not occur in the region – but are much smaller. They put up a spirited defence against danger, fluffing out their fur, erecting the hackles on their forequarters, and emitting surprisingly loud barks and roars.

Aardwolf

PHILLIP RICHARDSON/ABPL

**Size:** similar to a medium-sized dog
**Distribution:** throughout Namibia and Botswana, and everywhere in Zimbabwe except the far north-east
**Status:** uncommon; nocturnal, but occasionally seen at dawn and dusk

### Brown Hyaena *Hyaena brunnea*

Seen in poor light, with its long 'cape' of dark fur and purposeful stride, the brown hyaena is like some medieval messenger on a secret errand. They are not good hunters, and get most of their food by scavenging, often visiting the kills of other predators, and carrying off large parts to stash away. They forage alone, although groups co-operate to raise young and defend territories.

Brown Hyaena

ANDREW MacCOLL

**Size:** similar to a large dog
**Distribution:** throughout Botswana, the extreme south-west of Zimbabwe and all of Namibia except the south-east
**Status:** low numbers and declining; nocturnal, but often seen at dawn and dusk

### Spotted Hyaena *Crocuta crocuta*

The most remarkable physical feature of the spotted hyaena is the female's large erectile clitoris, which renders it almost indistinguishable from males. Spotted hyaena are massively built and appear distinctly canine, but they are not closely related to dogs. Carrion forms an important part of their diet, but spotted hyaena are also true predators. They can reach speeds of up to 60km/h and a pack of them will bring down wildebeest and zebra. The 'Ooooop' call of spotted hyaena at night is one of the most evocative, and loudest, natural sounds of Africa.

Spotted Hyaena

TONY WHEELER

**Size:** similar to a very large dog
**Distribution:** Zimbabwe, Botswana and northern Namibia
**Status:** common where there is suitable food; mainly nocturnal, but also seen during the day.

# CATS

### Cheetah *Acinonyx jubatus*

The cheetah is a magnificent cat: sleek, streamlined and graceful. Although it superficially resembles a leopard, the cheetah is longer and lighter, and has a slightly bowed back and a smaller and rounder face. Cheetahs hunt at dawn and dusk. They stalk their prey as closely as possible, and then launch into a sprint of up to 110km/h. This can only be sustained for a short distance because, with the explosive energy required for running, the animal begins to overheat. The prey, often a small antelope, may be brought down with a flick of the paw to trip it up. Other favourite meals include hares and young warthogs. Cubs reach maturity at around one year of age, but stay with the mother much longer to learn hunting and survival skills. Cheetah cubs are preyed on by lion, leopard and hyaena, which will also take the kills of adults.

**Size:** similar to a big dog
**Distribution:** throughout the region, except the driest and most forested areas
**Status:** usually occurs at low density, with individuals moving over large areas, but active by day, and frequently seen in Etosha and other national parks

JOHN HAY

Cheetah

### Leopard *Panthera pardus*

Leopards are heard more often than seen; their cry sounds very much like a hacksaw cutting through metal. This powerfully built animal often ambushes its prey, which consists mainly of birds, reptiles and mammals, including monkeys, baboons, large rodents, dassies, warthogs and small antelope. Leopards are agile and climb well, and often spend their days resting in trees up to 5m above the ground. They also protect their kills by dragging them up trees. They are solitary animals, except during the mating season, when the male and female stay in close association. A litter of up to three cubs is produced after a gestation period of three months.

**Size:** similar to a very large dog
**Distribution:** throughout the region, although they have been eradicated from much of central Zimbabwe
**Status:** common, but mainly nocturnal, they are the most difficult of the large cats to see

DAVID WALL

Leopard

## Lion *Panthera leo*

Although very popular, lions spend almost all their time doing nothing and can be boring to watch. They are most active in the late afternoon. They live in prides of up to about 30, which will defend a territory of between 20 and 400 sq km, depending on the terrain and the game available. Although they co-operate well, lions aren't the most efficient hunters and up to four out of five kill attempts are unsuccessful. Males leave the family group at the age of two or three, when they may form alliances with other young males and attempt to take over a pride of their own. Lions are dangerous, and do occasionally attack and kill people; remember that they could cover what might look like a big distance between you and them in seconds. Take the warnings seriously, and stay in your vehicle in national parks.

Lion

ANDREW MacCOLL

**Size:** similar to very large dog
**Distribution:** throughout Botswana, but confined to the extreme north and south of Zimbabwe and the north of Namibia
**Status:** common in many of the larger parks, and also outside them in Botswana; mainly nocturnal, but nonetheless obvious during the day

## Caracal *Felis caracal*

The caracal, despite its sometimes sleepy appearance, is the fastest cat of its size. They live in porcupine burrows, rocky crevices or dense vegetation. Their favourite prey are birds, rodents and other small mammals, including young deer. They stalk their prey until a quick dash or leap can capture it. Caracal are generally solitary animals, but might sometimes be seen in pairs with their young. They are believed to be territorial, marking the territory with urine sprays. Their calls are typical of cats – miaows, growls, hisses and coughing noises.

Caracal

DAVID WALL

**Size:** similar to a large dog
**Distribution:** throughout the region
**Status:** not common; strictly nocturnal, and difficult to see

## African Wild Cat *Felis lybica*

Closely resembling the household tabby, although with less distinct markings, the African wild cat is the species from which the cat was originally domesticated by the Egyptians. African wild cats differ most prominently from domestic cats in having reddish backs to their ears, longer legs and a generally leaner appearance. They cross freely with domestic cats anywhere close to human habitation where the two meet, and this is probably the biggest threat to the integrity of the wild species. Namibia and Botswana, where there are relatively few humans, harbour some of the purest wild cat populations in Africa. They subsist mainly on small rodents, but also prey on birds and insects, which they hunt alone.

**Size:** similar to the domestic cat
**Distribution:** throughout the region
**Status:** common; nocturnal, although sometimes spotted at dawn and dusk

ANDREW MacCOLL

African Wild Cat

## Serval *Felis serval*

The serval inhabits thick bush and tall grass around streams. It stands about 50cm high and measures 110cm in length, including the tail. The dirty yellow coat is dotted with large black spots, which form lines along the length of the body. Other prominent features include large upright ears, a long neck and a relatively short tail. It's an adept hunter, favouring birds, hares and rodents, and can catch birds in mid-flight by leaping into the air.

**Size:** similar to a medium-sized dog
**Distribution:** throughout Zimbabwe, but confined to wetter areas in northern Namibia and Botswana
**Status:** common, but mainly nocturnal; sometimes seen in the early morning and late afternoon

DAVID WALL

Serval

# FOXES & DOGS (CANIDS)

## Bat-Eared Fox *Otocyon megalotis*

The huge ears of this long-legged fox look, and function, like radar dishes. While foraging they listen for the faint sound of insects below ground. By lowering their head towards the soil, ears pointed, they can use a sort of triangulation to get an exact fix on potential food. This is followed by a burst of frantic digging to capture the prey. The bat-eared fox eats mainly insects, especially termites, but also takes small animals and wild fruit. Its tail is very bushy and seems to be used to distract enemies when being chased. They are monogamous, and are almost always seen in pairs or family groups. They are very slow to get off roads away from traffic, and whole families are often wiped out. Their natural enemies include large birds of prey, hyaena and lion.

Bat-Eared Fox

**Size:** similar to a small to medium-sized dog
**Distribution:** Namibia, Botswana and the south-west of Zimbabwe
**Status:** locally common, especially in parks; mainly nocturnal, but often seen in the late afternoon and early morning

## Cape Fox *Vulpes chama*

A dainty fox, with a beautiful plume of a tail, it trots without its feet seeming to touch the ground. Solitary outside the breeding season, it feeds on insects, small mammals and reptiles. In some parks, individuals visit tourist barbecues to scrounge food; they sit, wrapped in their tail, on the edge of the firelight, waiting to be thrown scraps. In farming areas they are blamed for losses of lambs and goat kids, and are heavily persecuted as a result.

Cape Foxes

**Size:** similar to a red fox, or to a small to medium-sized dog
**Distribution:** drier parts of Botswana and Namibia (Etosha National Park and Namib-Naukluft Park)
**Status:** widespread; most often seen at night or in the early morning, especially in the summer months, when often seen close to breeding burrows

## Wild Dog *Lycaon pictus*

The wild dog's Latin name means painted wolf, and the blotched black, yellow and white coat, together with its big, round ears, makes it unmistakable. Wild dogs are highly sociable, living in packs of up to 40, although today packs bigger than a dozen animals are rare. They are very efficient hunters and rarely scavenge. Once the prey has been selected it is chased relentlessly until exhausted, before being pulled down by the pack. Favoured prey include mid-sized antelope, but they can kill animals as large as buffalo.

**Size:** similar to a large dog
**Distribution:** mainly Botswana, but also Zimbabwe
**Status:** declining severely from a naturally low density, it is a real privilege to see these animals

MITCH REARDON

Wild Dog

## Side-Striped Jackal *Canis adustus*

This jackal superficially resembles the black-backed jackal, from which it is most easily distinguished by its having a white-tipped tail. They eat less meat than other jackals, relying extensively on wild fruit, although they do also eat small mammals and insects. They hunt alone or in pairs, in a territory that they defend. They have a varied vocal repertoire, including explosive yaps and owl-like hoots.

**Size:** similar to a medium-sized dog; very similar in size to the black-backed jackal
**Distribution:** woodland in Zimbabwe, northern Botswana and northern Namibia; found in Hwange, Mana Pools and Chobe national parks
**Status:** widespread but not abundant; active at night and in the early morning

CLEM HAAGNER/ABPL

Side-Striped Jackal

## Black-Backed Jackal *Canis mesomelas*

Black-backed jackals are real opportunists and quickly make the best of any situation. They commonly hang around kills awaiting morsels but they will also hunt insects, birds, rodents and even the occasional small antelope. They will frequent human settlements, and take domestic stock. As a result they are persecuted by farmers and tend to be restricted to parks and reserves. Black-backed jackals form long-term pair bonds, and each looks after a home territory of around 250 hectares.

**Size:** similar to a medium-sized dog
**Distribution:** throughout the region, except the north and east of Zimbabwe
**Status:** common and easily seen; active both night and day

ANDREW MacCOLL

Black-Backed Jackal

# MUSTELIDS

### Cape Clawless Otter *Aonyx capensis*

The Cape clawless otter has a light greyish brown back; the snout, face and throat are white or cream-coloured and each cheek has a large rectangular spot. Unlike most otters, only the hind feet of Cape clawless otters are webbed, and although some are truly clawless, others have short pointed claws on the third and fourth toes. The otters are normally active by day, and with a bit of luck may be seen playing, swimming and diving throughout the afternoon. In areas where they're hunted by humans, however, the otters have adopted a nocturnal schedule. Their main foods include fish, crabs, frogs, and both bird and crocodile eggs. Their only known natural enemy is the crocodile.

**Size:** similar to an otter
**Distribution:** by water in Zimbabwe and northern Botswana
**Status:** locally common; active both day and night but usually seen in the early morning and late afternoon

Cape Clawless Otter

ROGER DE LA HARPE/ABPL

### Honey Badger or Ratel *Mellivora capensis*

The honey badger is of a similar size and shape to the European badger and is every bit as ferocious. They've even been known to attack creatures as large as the Cape buffalo! They are normally active between dusk and dawn. Honey badgers subsist on fish, frogs, scorpions, spiders and reptiles, including poisonous snakes; at times they'll even take young antelope. They also eat a variety of roots, honey, berries and eggs, and are adept at raiding rubbish bins.

**Size:** similar to a badger or medium-sized dog
**Distribution:** Zimbabwe, Namibia and north-eastern Botswana
**Status:** common; mainly nocturnal, but seen during the day

Honey Badger

LORNA STANTON/ABPL

# VIVERRIDS

**Genet** *Genetta genetta* (Small-Spotted Genet); *Genetta tigrina* (Large-Spotted Genet)

Genets vaguely resemble domestic cats, although the body is considerably longer, the long, coarse coat has a prominent crest along the spine and the tail is longer and bushier. The tail is banded with nine or 10 dark rings. Genets live singly or in pairs in riverine forests and dry scrub, savanna and open country, and are agile climbers. By day they sleep in abandoned burrows, rock crevices or hollow trees, or on high branches, apparently returning to the same spot each day. Genets may also climb trees to seek out nesting birds and their eggs, but normally hunt on the ground. Their diet consists of small rodents, birds, reptiles, insects and fruits. Like domestic cats, they stalk prey by crouching flat on the ground, and spit and growl when angered.

**Size:** similar to a long, thin cat
**Distribution:** small-spotted genets are distributed throughout the region, except the north and east of Zimbabwe; large-spotted genets are confined to Zimbabwe, and the north of Botswana and Namibia
**Status:** common, but strictly nocturnal

Large-Spotted Genet

## African Civet *Civettictis civetta*

Civets have a set of anal musk glands that produce a foul-smelling oily substance used to mark their territory. This musk was once collected from captive animals for use in perfume manufacture, but it has now been replaced by synthetic compounds. Civets are solitary animals; by day they nestle in thickets, tall grass or abandoned burrows. They have a varied diet consisting of amphibians, birds, rodents, eggs, reptiles, snails, insects (especially ants and termites), berries, young shoots and fruit.

**Size:** similar to a medium-sized dog
**Distribution:** Zimbabwe, northern Namibia and Botswana
**Status:** common, but mainly nocturnal and difficult to see

African Civet

## Meerkat or Suricate *Suricata suricatta*

Meerkats are the stars of wildlife films that have gained them a fame far beyond their small distribution. They are not cats, but mongooses. Highly sociable and intelligent, they live in groups that viciously defend their territories. Meerkats sleep in burrows, from which they emerge to warm themselves in the first rays of the sun. Most of the day is

Meerkat

spent foraging for reptiles, insects and scorpions. They are constantly at risk from martial eagles and jackals, against which they mount continuous guard. Meerkats with their heads down digging are constantly reassured by the sentry's peeping calls, and individuals are never far from a bolt hole when the alarm is sounded. A dominant male and female monopolise breeding, but the young are cared for by other group members.

**Size:** similar to a small cat
**Distribution:** drier parts of Botswana and Namibia (Namib-Naukluft Park)
**Status:** common, and easily seen in open habitat, especially when sunning themselves at sunrise

## Mongooses

In Africa, many of the small mammals that dash across roads in front of cars are mongooses. Most species are solitary, and are often seen only fleetingly. Others are more or less sociable and are always worth stopping to watch. Yellow mongooses live in colonies of up to 20, but scatter to forage. Banded and dwarf mongooses are intensely sociable, and do almost everything in groups. Bandeds are easily identified by the dark bands across their backs. Dwarf mongooses are much smaller, and live in larger groups. Dwarf and banded mongooses keep contact while foraging by incessant twittering, and are quick to give alarm calls at the approach of danger.

Dwarf Mongooses

**Size:** from stoat to cat-sized; varies depending on species, but all are small
**Distribution:** widely distributed and common
**Status:** many species are common where they occur; sociable species are active during the day, solitary species tend to be nocturnal

## Aardvark (Antbear) *Orycteropus afer*

The pig-like aardvark has thick and wrinkled pink-grey skin with very sparse and stiff greyish hair. It has an elongated tubular snout and a round, sticky, pink tongue, which is used to lap up ants and termites dug from nests and rotting wood with the long claws of its front feet. Aardvarks are astonishingly good at digging burrows, which are used by many other species. They normally emerge only at night, but in the morning after a cold night they may bask in the sun a while before retiring underground.

Aardvark

**Size:** similar to a pig
**Distribution:** throughout the region
**Status:** nocturnal, and very difficult to see; this is the one safari connoisseurs are looking for

# ELEPHANT

## African Elephant *Loxodonta africana*

Elephants are gregarious animals, and usually live in herds of between 10 and 20. Elephant society is matriarchal, and herds are dominated by old females. Elephants communicate using a range of sounds, including a very deep rumble that is almost felt, rather than heard, by humans. They also produce a high-pitched trumpeting when they're frightened or want to appear threatening. An adult's average daily food intake is about 250kg. In drought years, they're capable of destroying dense woodland by felling trees. This may lead to them being perceived as a threat to fragile environments, but elephant damage may be necessary in the natural cycle of the bushveld. An elephant's life span is about 60 to 70 years, though some individuals may reach 100 or more. A fully grown bull can weigh more than 6500kg and his tusks as much as 50kg each.

**Size:** very large
**Distribution:** northern Namibia and Botswana, and the northern and western borders of Zimbabwe
**Status:** still very common in some parts of southern Africa, and easy to see

Elephants

# ROCK DASSIE

## Rock Dassie or Rock Hyrax *Procavia capensis*

Rock dassies occur practically everywhere there are mountains or rocky outcrops. They are sociable animals and live in colonies of up to 60 individuals. They feed on vegetation but spend much of the day sunning themselves on rocks or chasing each other in play. Where they're used to humans they're often quite tame, but otherwise they dash into rock crevices when alarmed, uttering shrill screams. Despite its small size, the dassie is thought to be more closely related to the elephant than any other living creature, but the exact relationship is unclear.

**Size:** similar to a hare
**Distribution:** widely distributed, but absent from eastern Namibia and much of Botswana
**Status:** common, and easy to see, especially where used to humans

Rock Dassie

# ODD-TOED HOOFED ANIMALS

**Rhinoceros** *Ceratotherium simum* (White Rhinoceros); *Diceros bicornis* (Black or Hook-Lipped Rhinoceros)

The white rhino's name does not refer to its colour, but is a corruption of wide (lipped) rhino. Poaching has made the rhino Africa's most endangered large animal: in many countries it has been completely exterminated. Black rhino are browsers, living in scrubby country, while white rhino are grazers and prefer open plains. While white rhino are generally docile, black rhino are prone to charging when alarmed. Their eyesight is extremely poor and they've even been known to charge trains or elephant carcasses! Adult black rhino weigh up to 1100kg while the much larger white rhino may be 500kg heavier. Both species are solitary, only socialising during the mating season.

**Size:** very large
**Distribution:** black rhino are now found only in small areas in northern Namibia, northern Botswana, and the Zambezi valley in Zimbabwe; white rhino are found only in a few reserves
**Status:** remarkably difficult to see for such enormous animals, but a good chance in specialist reserves (Matobo, Hwange and Etosha national parks, and Waterberg Plateau Park)

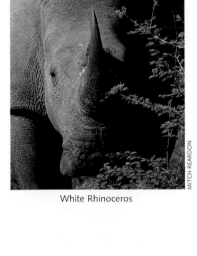
MITCH REARDON

White Rhinoceros

**Zebra** *Equus burchellii* (Common or Burchell's Zebra); *Equus zebra hartmannae* (Hartmann's Mountain Zebra)

Burchell's zebras have shadow lines between the black stripes; mountain zebras don't have shadows but do have a gridiron pattern of black stripes just above the tail. Zebras are grazers but occasionally browse on leaves and scrub. They need water daily and rarely wander far from a water hole. They often mingle with other animals, such as wildebeest, elephant and impala. During the breeding season, stallions engage in fierce battles for control of a herd of mares. Lions are the zebra's worst enemy, but they're also taken by hyaena and wild dogs.

**Size:** similar to a horse
**Distribution:** Burchell's zebras are found in northern Namibia and Botswana, and much of Zimbabwe; mountain zebras are found in the mountains of central Namibia
**Status:** common and easy to see

JULIET COOMBE

Burchell's Zebras

# EVEN-TOED HOOFED ANIMALS

### Bushpig *Potamochoerus porcus*

The hairy bushpig is similar in many ways to the wild boar of Europe. They are sociable, and live in 'sounders' (groups) of up to a dozen animals, which are lead by a dominant boar and sow. Boars defend their sounder against the unwanted attentions of interlopers. They eat fallen fruit, and root up rhizomes, bulbs and tubers. As a result they are a pest where crops are grown, and are often controlled outside protected areas. Bushpigs are dangerous to humans when cornered or wounded.

**Size:** similar to a pig
**Distribution:** forested and thickly vegetated areas in Zimbabwe and northern Botswana
**Status:** common, but difficult to see in dense vegetation; seen from hides at water holes

ANTHONY BANNISTER/ABPL

Bushpig

### Warthog *Phacochoerus aethiopicus*

Warthogs live in family groups, also known as 'sounders', which include a boar, a sow and three or four young. Their most endearing habit is the way they trot away with their thin tufted tail stuck straight up in the air like antennae. They grow two sets of tusks: the upper ones curve outwards and upwards and grow as long as 60cm; the lower ones are usually less than 15cm long. Warthogs feed mainly on grass, but also eat fruit and bark. In hard times they'll burrow with their snout for roots and bulbs. They also rest and give birth in abandoned burrows, or sometimes excavate cavities in abandoned termite mounds.

**Size:** similar to a pig
**Distribution:** Botswana and Zimbabwe, and all but the driest areas of Namibia
**Status:** common and easy to see

ANDREW MacCOLL

Warthog

### Hippopotamus *Hippopotamus amphibius*

Hippo are always found close to, or in, freshwater. They spend most of the day in the water, feeding on bottom vegetation and socialising. Only at night do they emerge to graze, and they can consume about 40kg of vegetable matter each night. They disperse their faeces with a propeller-like action of the tail. They're very gregarious animals and live in large herds. Adult bulls defend territories against each other very aggressively. Virtually every male hippo bears the scars of such conflicts. For humans, hippos

DAVID CIMINO

Hippopotamus

are Africa's most dangerous animal. Most accidents occur when hippo surface beneath boats or when someone blocks a hippo's retreat route to the water. Hippos live for about 30 years, and when fully grown weigh in between 950 and 2000kg. The hippo's only natural predators are lion and crocodiles, which prey on the young.

**Size:** very large
**Distribution:** Zimbabwe and northern Botswana
**Status:** common and easy to see

### Giraffe *Giraffa camelopardalis*

The name giraffe is derived from the Arabic zarafah (the one who walks quickly). Males are around 5m tall, while females average 4.5m. Both sexes have 'horns', which are short projections of skin-covered bone and may be a remnant of what might once have been antlers. Despite the giraffe's incredibly long neck, it still has only seven cervical vertebrae – the same number as all mammals, including humans. Giraffe browse on trees, especially acacia. They must go through all sorts of contortions to drink. They're at their most vulnerable at water holes and always appear hesitant and visibly nervous when drinking. If they feel the slightest uncertainty about the safety of the situation, they'll often forgo their drink altogether.

**Size:** large and very tall
**Distribution:** from northern Namibia through northern and central Botswana to southern Zimbabwe
**Status:** common and easy to see

Giraffes

MITCH REARDON

### African Buffalo *Syncerus caffer*

Both sexes of the African (or Cape) buffalo have the distinctive curving horns that broaden and almost meet over the forehead, but those of the female are usually smaller. Buffalo have a penetrating gaze, and one safari operator has noted that 'buffalo always look at you as if you owe them a lot of money'. Although they're generally docile and stay out of humans' way, these 800kg creatures can be very dangerous and should be treated with caution. Solitary rogue bulls and females protecting their young are the most aggressive. African buffalo are territorial, but when food and water are plentiful the herds, which normally consist of 100 or more individuals, may disperse over an area 100km in diameter.

**Size:** similar to a bull
**Distribution:** northern Namibia, Botswana and Zimbabwe
**Status:** common and easy to see

African Buffalo

JEAN-BERNARD CARILLET

# ANTELOPE

## Blue Wildebeest or Brindled Gnu
*Connochaetes taurinus*

Blue wildebeest are very gregarious and sometimes move about in herds up to tens of thousands strong, often in association with zebras and other herbivores, and accompanied by a cacophony of amusing snorts and low grunts. In southern Africa, numbers are now much smaller. The wildebeest's ungainly appearance makes it unmistakable. It has been described as having the forequarters of an ox, the hind parts of an antelope and the tail of a horse. Males are territorial, and attempt to herd groups of females. Wildebeest are grazers, and move constantly in search of good pasture and water. Because they prefer to drink daily and can survive only five days without water, wildebeest will migrate large distances to find it. During the rainy season they graze haphazardly, but in the dry season they coalesce around waterholes. Major predators include lion, hyaena and wild dogs.

**Size:** similar to a horse
**Distribution:** Botswana, western and northern Namibia, and southern Zimbabwe
**Status:** very common

Blue Wildebeest

## Hartebeest *Alcelaphus buselaphus* (Red Hartebeest); *Sigmoceros lichtensteinii* (Lichtenstein's Hartebeest)

The hartebeest is a medium-sized antelope easily recognised by its long, narrow face and short horns, which are distinctively angular and heavily ridged. In both sexes, the horns form a heart shape, hence their name (heart beast in Afrikaans). Hartebeest feed exclusively on grass and prefer grassy plains for grazing but are also found in sparsely forested savanna or hills. They're social animals and often mingle with other grazers such as zebra and wildebeest. Predators are mainly hyaena, the large cats and hunting dogs.

**Size:** similar to a pony
**Distribution:** red hartebeest are found throughout Botswana, and in the north and east of Namibia; Lichtenstein's hartebeest are found only in small areas of southern Zimbabwe (Gonarezhou National Park)
**Status:** red hartebeest are common where they occur, and easy to see; Lichtenstein's hartebeest are fairly easy to see where they occur

Red Hartebeest

Tsessebe (Topi)

### Tsessebe (Topi) *Damaliscus lunatus*

The tsessebe is like the hartebeest in appearance but darker – in some cases appearing almost violet – with black patches on the rear thighs, front legs and face. The horns, carried by both sexes, curve gently up, out and back. A highly gregarious antelope, it lives in herds and often mingles with other grazers. Although tsessebe can live on dry grasses spurned by other antelope, they prefer flood plains and moist areas that support lush pasture. They are capable of surviving long periods without water as long as sufficient grass is available.

**Size:** similar to a pony
**Distribution:** northern Botswana and central Zimbabwe
**Status:** common and easy to see

Common Duiker

### Common or Grey Duiker *Sylvicapra grimmia*

Duikers are usually solitary, but are sometimes seen in pairs, and prefer areas with good scrub cover. The common duiker is greyish light-brown in colour, with a white belly and a dark brown vertical stripe on the face. Only the males have horns, which are straight and pointed, and grow to only 20cm in length. Common duikers are almost exclusively browsers, though they appear to supplement their diet with insects and even bird chicks. They're capable of going without water for long periods but will drink whenever water is available.

**Size:** similar to a small goat
**Distribution:** throughout the region
**Status:** common; active throughout the day, except where disturbance is common

Springbok

### Springbok *Antidorcas marsupialis*

Springbok are the only gazelles in southern Africa. Both males and females have ribbed, lyre-shaped horns of medium length. They are one of several species of antelope known for their pronking (leaping vertically in the air). Male springbok are territorial during the rutting season, when they collect harems of females and defend them against other potential suitors. At other times, herds consist of mixed groups of males and females, although groups of bachelors are often observed. Occasionally, in conditions of severe drought, huge herds migrate in search of water; in the great migration of 1896, herds 220km long and 25km wide were recorded.

**Size:** similar to a small pony
**Distribution:** drier areas of Botswana and Namibia
**Status:** very common

### Klipspringer *Oreotragus oreotragus*

The delicate little klipspringer, which stands at about 50cm at the shoulder, is shy and easily disturbed. It's easily recognised by its curious tip-toe stance – the hooves are adapted for balance and grip on rocky surfaces. The widely spaced 10cm-long horns are present only on the male. Klipspringers normally inhabit rocky outcrops; they also venture into adjacent grasslands, but when alarmed they retreat into the rocks for safety. These amazingly agile and sure-footed creatures are capable of bounding up impossibly rough rock faces.

**Size:** similar to a medium-sized dog
**Distribution:** on rocky outcrops in Zimbabwe, central Namibia and south-eastern Botswana
**Status:** common

Klipspringer

### Damara Dik-Dik *Madoqua kirkii*

Dik-diks are best identified by their small size, but other tell-tale features include the negligible tail and the tuft of dark hair on the forehead. Only the males have short horns. Dik-diks are monogamous, and the males territorial. They are usually seen singly, in pairs or in family parties of three, in woodland, or bush where there is good cover.

**Size:** similar to a small dog
**Distribution:** northern Namibia
**Status:** common, but shy and easy to miss; active in the morning and afternoon

Damara Dik-Dik

### Oribi *Ourebia ourebi*

Oribi are a uniform golden brown with white on the belly and the insides of the legs. The males have short straight horns about 10cm long. The oribi's most distinguishing mark is a circular patch of naked black skin below the ear, which is actually a scent gland. Another identifying characteristic is the tuft of black hair on the tip of the short tail. Oribi have many predators, including the larger cats. They usually graze on high grass savanna plains, where they're well sheltered from predators. When alarmed, they bolt, making erratic bounces with all four legs held rigid. After 100m or so, they stop to assess the danger. Oribi are territorial and usually live in pairs or small groups.

**Size:** similar to a large dog
**Distribution:** northern Botswana and central Zimbabwe
**Status:** common, but patchily distributed and difficult to see

Oribi

### Steenbok *Raphicerus campestris*

The steenbok bears a resemblance to both the duiker and the grysbok, with a short tail and proportionally long and slender legs. The back and hindquarters range from light reddish brown to dark brown, and on the upper edge of the nose is a black, wedge-shaped spot. Males have small, straight and widely separated horns. Steenbok live mainly on open plains, but can be found almost anywhere in this region. They're solitary animals, and only have contact with others during the mating season. Steenbok are active in the morning and evening, and may also continue activity when there's a bright moon. At other times, they seek out high grass for protection from enemies, which include leopard, hyaena and jackals.

**Size:** similar to a medium-sized dog
**Distribution:** throughout the region, apart from northern Zimbabwe
**Status:** common

Steenbok

DEANNA SWANEY

### Sharpe's Grysbok *Raphicerus sharpei*

Sharpe's grysbok is a small, stocky antelope, reddish-brown with a pale red underside. The back and sides are speckled with individual white hairs, from the nape of the neck to the rump, hence the Afrikaans name grysbok, or grey buck. Only the males have horns, which are small, sharp and straight. Grysbok are found in both bushy and woodland savanna country and on rocky kopjes, feeding primarily on shoots and leaves.

**Size:** similar to a medium-sized dog
**Distribution:** throughout Zimbabwe
**Status:** common, but predominantly nocturnal

Grysbok

NIGEL DENNIS/ABPL

### Suni *Neotragus moschatus*

This tiny antelope is best looked for from observation hides at water holes. It is often given away by the constant flicking of its tail. Suni are probably monogamous, and use secretions from the large scent gland in front of the eye to mark their territories. They nibble selectively on leaves and fallen fruit. When surprised they will freeze, sometimes for prolonged periods, before bounding away accompanied by a high-pitched call.

**Size:** similar to a big cat or a lamb
**Distribution:** wooded areas of eastern Zimbabwe (Mana Pools National Park)
**Status:** common, but difficult to see because it is small, shy and lives in thickets; active in the early morning and late afternoon

Suni

ANTHONY BANNISTER/ABPL

## Impala *Aepyceros melampus*

Impala are very graceful antelope. Males have long, lyre-shaped horns averaging 75cm in length. They are gregarious, and during the rut males defend harems. Single males form bachelor groups. Impala are known for their speed and ability to leap; they can spring as much as 10m forward in a single bound, or 3m into the air – and frequently do – even when there's nothing to jump over! And it's lucky they can; impala are the rabbits of Africa, and make a tasty meal for all large predators, including lion, leopard, cheetah, wild dogs and even hyaena.

**Size:** similar to a fallow deer
**Distribution:** throughout Zimbabwe and in north-eastern Botswana; there is an isolated population in northern Namibia distinguished by their black faces
**Status:** common and easy to see

ANDREW MacCOLL

Impala

## Roan Antelope *Hippotragus equinus*

The roan is one of southern Africa's rarest antelope. As a grazer, it prefers tall grasses and sites with ample shade and freshwater. It is the third largest antelope, after the eland and kudu, reaching up to 150cm at the shoulder. The coat varies from reddish-fawn to dark reddish-brown, with white underparts and a conspicuous mane of stiff, black-tipped hairs stretching from the nape to the shoulders. The ears are long, narrow and pointed, with a brown tassel at the tip. The face has a distinctive black and white pattern. Both sexes have curving, back-swept horns up to 70cm long. For most of the year roans are arranged in small herds of normally less than 20 individuals, led by a master bull.

**Size:** similar to a cow
**Distribution:** northern Botswana, and northern and eastern Zimbabwe
**Status:** one of the less common antelope, roan populations are declining, but not difficult to see where they occur

JEAN-BERNARD CARILLET

Roan Antelope

### Sable Antelope *Hippotragus niger*

Sable are slightly smaller than roan, but are more solidly built. The colouring is dark brown to black, with a white belly and face markings. Both sexes have long sweeping horns, but those of the male are longer and more curved. These and their black colouring give them a slightly satanic appearance. Sable feed mainly on grass, but foliage accounts for around 10% of their diet. Female and young sable live in herds. Males are territorial, or form bachelor groups. Like the roan, the sable is a fierce fighter and has been known to kill lion when attacked. Other predators include leopard, hyaena and hunting dogs.

**Size:** similar to a donkey
**Distribution:** Zimbabwe and north-eastern Botswana
**Status:** common and easy to see

Sable Antelope

### Gemsbok (South African Oryx) *Oryx gazella*

The gemsbok is a large beige antelope, standing around 120cm at the shoulder. It is a solid but stately animal, with impressively long, straight horns, an attractive grey-fawn body with black on the flanks and white on the underside, and a black and white pattern on the face. The tail is hairy like a horse's. Gemsbok are principally grazers, but will also browse on thorny shrubs. They can survive for long periods without water. Herds vary from five to 40 individuals, but the bulls normally prefer a solitary existence.

**Size:** similar to a pony
**Distribution:** Botswana and Namibia
**Status:** common where it occurs, and easy to see

Gemsbok

### Kudu *Tragelaphus strepsiceros*

The beautiful greater kudu is one of the largest antelope. Their bodies are light grey in colour with between six and 10 white stripes down the sides and a white chevron between the eyes. The horns, carried only by males, form large spirals; an old buck can have up to three complete twists. Kudu live in small herds of females and their young. The normally solitary males occasionally band into small herds. Kudu are mainly browsers and can eat a variety of leaves. When on the move kudu can easily clear obstacles of over 2m and are known for their unhealthy habit of leaping in front of oncoming vehicles. They prefer savanna with fairly dense bush cover.

**Size:** similar to a donkey
**Distribution:** throughout the region, except in the driest areas
**Status:** common, but sometimes difficult to see in the dense vegetation it prefers

Kudu

## Nyala *Tragelaphus angasii*

The nyala is one of Africa's rarest and most beautiful antelope. Males are grey with a mane and long hair under the throat and hind legs. They also have vertical stripes down the back and long, lyre-shaped horns with white tips. Females are a ruddy colour with vertical white stripes, but have no horns. They browse on trees and bushes. During the dry season they're active only in the morning and evening, while during the rains, they more often feed at night. Female nyala and their young live in small groups. Nyala defend themselves bravely against humans and predators – mainly leopard and lion. The young may even be taken by baboons and birds of prey.

**Size:** similar to a pony
**Distribution:** very restricted, in woodland in the extreme north and south of Zimbabwe
**Status:** common where it occurs, but well camouflaged

PETER LILLIE/ABPL

Nyala

## Bushbuck *Tragelaphus scriptus*

Shy and solitary animals, bushbuck inhabit thick bush close to permanent water. They are chestnut to dark brown in colour and have a variable number of white vertical stripes on the body between the neck and rump, as well as a number of white spots on the upper thigh and a white splash on the neck. Normally only the males grow horns, but females have been known to grow them. The horns are straight with gentle spirals and average about 30cm in length. When startled bushbucks bolt and crash loudly through the undergrowth. They're nocturnal browsers and rarely move far from their home turf. Though shy and elusive they can be aggressive and dangerous when cornered. Their main predators are leopard, lion and hyaena, and their lambs are often taken by pythons.

**Size:** similar to a roe deer
**Distribution:** Zimbabwe, northern Botswana and Namibia
**Status:** common, but difficult to see in the dense vegetation of their habitat

ANDREW MacCOLL

Bushbuck

### Eland *Taurotragus oryx*

The eland is the largest antelope; a mature bull can weigh up to 1 tonne. Both sexes have horns about 65cm long, which spiral at the base and sweep straight back. The male has a much hairier head than the female, and its horns are stouter and shorter. Eland prefer savanna scrub, and feed on grass and tree foliage in the early morning and late afternoon. They normally drink daily, but can go for a month or more without water. Eland usually live in groups of around six to 12, but herds can contain as many as 50 individuals. A small herd normally consists of several females and one male, but in larger herds there may be several males.

**Size:** similar to a cow
**Distribution:** Botswana, eastern Namibia, and the west and east of Zimbabwe
**Status:** common and easy to see

### Common Reedbuck *Redunca arundinum*

The dusky brown reedbuck is found on wetlands or river areas. It never strays more than a few kilometres from a permanent water source. Males have distinctive forward-curving horns. The underbelly, inside of the thighs, throat and underside of the bushy tail are white. Reedbuck are not gregarious, and are usually seen in pairs or small family parties. Their diet consists almost exclusively of grass and some foliage. At mating time, competing males fight with spirit. Predators include hyaena, big cats and hunting dogs.

**Size:** similar to a pony
**Distribution:** Zimbabwe, northern Namibia and Botswana
**Status:** common, and easy to see

Eland

DAVID WALL

Common Reedbuck

PAUL WEEKS

### Waterbuck *Kobus ellipsiprymnus*

The waterbuck has a bull's-eye ring around its rump, and white markings on the face and throat. It's a solid animal with a thick, shaggy, dark brown coat. Only the males have horns, which curve gradually outwards before shooting straight up to a length of about 75cm. The bulk of the waterbuck's diet consists of grass. They never stray far from water and are good swimmers, readily entering the water to escape predators. Herds are small and consist of cows, calves and one mature bull, while younger bulls live in small groups apart from the herd. Predators go for the young calves and females, but mature waterbucks are not favoured prey because of their tough flesh and the distinct odour of the meat.

**Size:** similar to a pony
**Distribution:** wet areas in Zimbabwe and northern Botswana
**Status:** common and easy to see

Waterbuck

### Red Lechwe *Kobus leche*

Lechwe are majestic antelope of the wet grasslands and flood plains. They take freely to water, and swim well. Males carry large lyre-shaped horns, but females are hornless. Lechwe occur in small herds of 15 to 20, and occasionally in huge aggregations of thousands. They graze on swamp and flood-plain grasses. To see a herd of lechwe bounding and leaping through water is a wonderful sight.

**Size:** similar to a pony
**Distribution:** wet areas in northern Botswana and Namibia (Okavango Delta)
**Status:** common and easy to see

Red Lechwe

### Puku *Kobus vardonii*

Puku are similar to lechwe in appearance, and in the type of habitat they prefer. However they are smaller and more lightly built than lechwe. They also use less extensive wet areas than lechwe, along rivers and in woodland, grazing on a range of grasses. They occur in small herds of about half a dozen animals, and males defend territories on which they will try to herd passing females.

**Size:** similar to a pony
**Distribution:** riverine areas in northern Botswana (Chobe National Park)
**Status:** rare and very restricted in distribution; active at dawn and dusk

Puku

# BIRDS

Birds rate highly among the many attractions of southern Africa. For sheer abundance and variety few parts of the world offer as much for the bird-watcher, whether expert or beginner. Southern Africa is host to nearly 10% of the world's bird species – around 920 species have been recorded in the region.

With the exception of nocturnal, cryptic (camouflaged) or rare species, birds can be easily seen – not just in national parks and game reserves, but at popular tourist destinations and even in the middle of large cities.

Bird-watching is a popular pastime for residents and visitors alike; birds and birdlore are not only intrinsic to ancient African customs, they have been assimilated into the lives of white settlers, and there is an English and an Afrikaans name for nearly every species. Visitors will find ample books and other publications on the region's birds.

The astonishing variety of the region's birdlife can be attributed to the number of habitats. The climate ranges from cool temperate with winter rainfall in the south-west to a hot tropical zone with summer rains in the north-east. The main habitats can be separated into seven categories: forest; savanna/woodland; fynbos; grassland/semi-desert; Karoo; freshwater areas (rivers, marshes, lakes, pans, and their adjoining shores); and seashore areas (including areas of brackish water where freshwater meets salt in lagoons and estuaries).

Many species of bird are wide-ranging, but the vast majority have feeding, breeding or other biological requirements that restrict them to a habitat or group of habitats. Therefore, to see a wide variety of birds a visitor should try to take in as many different habitats as possible.

All the national parks and game reserves feature a great range of birdlife. (For a complete rundown, refer to the National Parks and Wildlife Reserves sections in the Facts about Zimbabwe, Botswana and Namibia chapters.) In Namibia, Etosha National Park and the Caprivi Strip are both good for all sorts of birds. Many seabirds – including pelicans and flamingoes – can be seen along the coast at Walvis Bay, and boat trips are available from Lüderitz to visit an offshore penguin colony. Northern Botswana, including the Okavango Delta and Chobe National Park, is excellent for bird-watching. The eastern highlands of Zimbabwe, including Nyanga and Chimanimani national parks, are especially good for forest birds,

Flamingoes

MITCH REARDON

including the spectacular jewel-like sunbirds. The Zambezi valley in the north is also rich with birds.

## Bird Groups

The following is a group-by-group description of some of the birds you'll see in southern Africa. This is not a comprehensive list; the focus is on common, unusual and spectacular species. Using the colour photos in this section, you should be able to identify most bird families and a few common species. For more detailed descriptions refer to one of the readily available field guides.

**Ostrich** The largest and heaviest of all birds, the ostrich is a wide-ranging inhabitant of grassland and savanna.

**Waterfowl** This large group includes the familiar ducks and geese. As their collective name suggests, they are found almost exclusively around waterways. Some species are found at inland swamps, while others have a broader habitat preference and can be seen on coastal lagoons or even in city parks and gardens. Only the South African shelduck and Cape shoveler are endemic to the region; other members of this highly mobile group roam across the continent looking for suitable places to feed and breed.

**Seabirds** Into this broad category can be lumped a number of bird families that hunt over the open sea. They include Africa's one resident penguin, the jackass penguin; the various petrels, shearwaters and albatrosses, which usually live far out to sea and only return to land to breed; the beautiful gannets and their tropical relatives the boobies, which feed by plunging from a great height after fish; frigatebirds, which because of their marauding habits have also been known as man o'war birds; and the fish-eating cormorants (shags), which also make use of brackish and freshwater habitats.

**Birds of Prey** Southern Africa's hawks, eagles, vultures, falcons and the unique secretary bird fall under this broad heading and together number nearly 70 species. Their presence is almost ubiquitous and you'll soon notice a few different species, from soaring flocks of scavenging vultures to the stately bateleur perched atop a kopje, from where it surveys the surrounding plain for prey. Many have specialised prey or habitat requirements: the osprey and the striking fish eagle of large waterways feed almost exclusively on fish; and the pygmy falcon is so small it nests in the colonies of sociable weavers.

DAVID WALL

Ostrich

RICHARD DU TOIT/APL

Jackass Penguins

MITCH REARDON

Fish Eagle

Wattled Cranes

Saddlebilled Stork

Blacksmith Plover

**Cranes** These graceful, long-legged birds superficially resemble storks and herons, but are typically grassland-dwelling birds. The crowned crane is eccentrically adorned with a colourful crest. Look out for the wattled crane, an endangered species.

**Long-Legged Wading Birds** Virtually any waterway will have its complement of herons, egrets, spoonbills, ibis and/or storks. All species have long legs and necks, and bills adapted to specific feeding strategies: herons and egrets have dagger-like bills for spearing fish and frogs; spoonbills have peculiar, flattened bills, which they swish from side to side to gather small water creatures; ibis have long, down-curved bills to probe in soft earth or seize insects; and storks have large powerful beaks to snap up small animals and fish. Members of this group range in size from the tiny, secretive bitterns to the enormous Goliath heron (standing 1.4m tall) and the hideous marabou storks, which often gather around a kill and feed on carrion. Some storks are migratory and may be absent from a region until they arrive in autumn, often in vast numbers; Abdim's stork is particularly noteworthy because large flocks arrive suddenly when on migration. An unusual member of this group is the hamerkop, a small heron-like bird that makes an enormous nest of twigs and grass.

**Waders** Every year millions of shorebirds arrive in southern Africa for the southern summer after completing a journey of many thousands of kilometres from their breeding grounds in the northern hemisphere. Generally nondescript in their non-breeding plumage, these migratory waders present an identification challenge to the keen bird-watcher. The migrants include sandpipers, curlews and small plovers. A number of other wading species are resident; these include the boldly marked blacksmith plover, the very noisy crowned plover, the painted snipe, jacanas, avocets and the odd dikkops – a lanky, cryptic, nocturnal species with weird wailing cries. With few exceptions these birds are found near fresh and saline waterways, feeding on small creatures or probing the intertidal mud for worms.

**Pigeons & Doves** Familiar to city and country dwellers alike, members of this worldwide family make up for their lack of colour by their ubiquity. The various species of the region have adapted to virtually every habitat: the rock pigeon to crags and peaks; the cinnamon dove to forest floors; and the African green pigeon to a nomadic life following the fruiting of trees.

**Louries** In southern Africa, three beautifully coloured species of these medium-sized birds inhabit forests – Ross's lourie, the purplecrested lourie and the Knysna lourie. They can be difficult to see because they hide in the canopy; often you will only catch a tantalising view as one flies across a clearing, showing its broad, rich-crimson wing patches. A fourth species, the grey lourie, is often seen in noisy parties in thornveld; its raucous call has earned it the alternative name of the go-away bird.

**Barbets & Woodpeckers** There are a few species of woodpecker in the region, but perhaps more conspicuous are their colourful, tropical cousins the barbets. Rather than drilling into bark after grubs like woodpeckers, barbets have strong, broad bills adapted to eating fruit and a variety of insect prey.

ELIOT LYONS/ABPL

Crested Barbet

**Mousebirds** This uniquely African group comprises a small group of common but rather plain birds. They are so named because they forage by crawling up tree trunks and along branches, dragging their long tails behind them and looking, as their name suggests, like tree-dwelling rodents.

**Honeyguides** Honeyguides display one of the most remarkable behaviour patterns of any bird: they seek out mammals such as the honey badger, or even humans, then guide them to a bees' nest. Once it has attracted the attention of a 'helper', the honeyguide flies a short way ahead then waits to see if it is being followed. In this way it leads its 'helper' to the hive. While the obliging creature, which could also be a genet, mongoose or baboon, breaks open and robs the hive, the honeyguide feeds on the wax and bee larvae and eggs.

NIGEL DENNIS/ABPL

Greater Honeyguide

**Kingfishers** Colourful and active, the 10 species found in southern Africa can be divided into two groups: those that typically dive into water after fish and tadpoles (and as a consequence are found along waterways); and those that usually live away from water for much of their lives, preying on lizards and large insects. Of the former, the giant kingfisher reaches 46cm in height and the jewel-like malachite and pygmy kingfishers a mere 14cm. The less brightly coloured 'forest' kingfishers are inhabitants of woodland and forest.

LANZ VON HORSTEN/ABPL

Malachite Kingfisher

**Bee-Eaters, Rollers & Hoopoe** The various species of bee-eater and roller are colourful relatives of the kingfishers; they are commonly seen perched on fences and branches, sometimes in mixed flocks, from where they pursue flying insects – particularly,

TIM LIVERSEDGE/ABPL

Little Bee-Eaters

Lilacbreasted Roller

Cape Eagle Owl

Pearlbreasted Swallow

Masked Weaver

as their name suggests, bees and wasps. The most stunning of all is the carmine bee-eater. Mention should also be made of the bizarre hoopoe, a salmon-pink migrant from Europe and Asia that sports a dashing black and white crest.

**Owls** Many African tribes have deep superstitions about these nocturnal birds of prey. Owls have soft feathers (which make their flight inaudible to prey), exceptional hearing and can turn their heads in a 180 degree arc to locate their prey. The prey varies according to the species: from insects, mice and lizards among the smaller species to the roosting birds and small mammals favoured by others. One of the region's most splendid examples is the Cape eagle owl.

**Nightjars** Another nocturnal group, these small birds are not related to owls, although their plumage is soft and their flight silent. Nightjars roost on the ground by day, their subtle coloration making a perfect camouflage among the leaves and twigs. At dusk, they take to the wing and catch insect prey. Although these birds are fairly common, you may be oblivious to their presence until one flies up near your feet. The identification of several species is difficult and often relies on call, but when flushed during the day, nightjars typically fly to a nearby horizontal branch and perch there, allowing you a closer look.

**Swifts & Swallows** Although unrelated, these two groups are superficially similar and can be seen chasing flying insects just about anywhere. Both groups have long wings and streamlined bodies adapted to lives in the air, both fly with grace and agility after insect prey, and both are usually dark in coloration. However, the two differ in one major aspect: swallows can perch on twigs, fences or even the ground while swifts have weak legs and rarely land except at the nest. In fact, swifts are so adapted to life in the air that some are even known to roost (sleep) on the wing!

**Finches, Weavers & Widows** This large group includes many small but colourful species, readily seen in flocks at camping grounds, along roads and wherever there is long grass. All are seed eaters and while some, such as the various sparrows, are not spectacular, others develop showy courtship plumage and tail plumes of extraordinary size. The sociable weaver makes an enormous communal nest of grass and straw that can literally cover the crown of a tree and resembles a thatched cottage (other species will perch on the 'thatch' and even build a nest on top). The sparrows come typically in shades of brown and grey; widows are similar while not breeding, but males moult into black plumage with red or yellow highlights when courting. Whydahs are predominantly black with a lighter breast coloration and develop striking tail plumes during courtship. The bishops moult from drab coloration to brilliant reds and yellows – during courtship, a field can have a black and red dot every few metres as males perch on top of stems trying to attract a mate.

**Larks & Pipits** Larks and pipits may not be the most spectacular group of birds, but in southern Africa they are diverse and, biologically, are significant to the grasslands they inhabit. Many are endemic to the region and for the keen bird-watcher their identification can pose some real challenges.

**Sunbirds & Sugarbirds** Sunbirds are small, delicate nectar feeders with sharp down-curved bills. The males of most species are brilliantly iridescent while the females are more drab. Sunbirds are commonly seen feeding on the flowers of proteas etc. Of the two species of sugarbird, only Gurney's sugarbird is found outside the Cape: in Zimbabwe. While sugarbirds are less colourful than their relatives the sunbirds, the males sport long, showy tail feathers.

**Starlings** At any of the game parks sooner or later you'll see fast-flying flocks of iridescent starlings. Starlings in Africa have evolved into intelligent, opportunistic and adaptable birds. Colourful, noisy and gregarious, there are many species, including the glossy starling, the bizarre wattled starling, and the red-billed oxpecker (often seen clinging to game, from which they prise parasitic ticks and insects).

LANZ VON HORSTEN/ABPL

Lesser Double Collared Sunbird

NIGEL DENNIS/ABPL

Cape Sugarbird

# Zimbabwe

# Facts about Zimbabwe

## HISTORY

By the 11th century, the site of Great Zimbabwe had been settled and foundations and stonework constructed. For history prior to this era, see the History section in the Facts about the Region chapter at the beginning of this book.

### The Shona Kingdoms & the Portuguese

It's generally believed that in the 11th century, the nascent Shona society at Great Zimbabwe encountered the Swahili traders who'd been plying the Mozambique coast for over four centuries. They traded gold and ivory for glass, porcelain and cloth from Asia and Great Zimbabwe became the capital of southern Africa's wealthiest and most powerful society.

By the 15th century, Great Zimbabwe's influence had begun to decline. Although the cause of its downfall in the 16th century remains a mystery to historians, possibilities include overpopulation, overgrazing by cattle, popular tribal uprisings and political fragmentation.

During Great Zimbabwe's twilight period, Shona dynasties scattered into autonomous states. The most prominent was the Mutapa dynasty, which after a series of raids on Zambezi Valley tribes, took in most of northern and eastern Zimbabwe and much of Mozambique. Their powerful *mambo* or king, Mutota, came to be known as Mwene Mutapa or 'the great raider', and his Mutapa Empire grew wealthy by policing and taxing the trade routes between Zimbabwe and the coast.

Upon Mutota's death in 1450, his son and successor, Motope, moved the seat of empire to Fura Mountain, 50km or so north of the present-day Zimbabwean capital. Motope's successor, a weaker character called Nyahuma, lost the southern two-thirds of Mutapa territory (and his life) to Motope's son, Changa, who later founded

### ZIMBABWE AT A GLANCE

**Area:** 390,580 sq km
**Population:** 11,423,000
**Population Growth Rate:** 1.26%
**Capital:** Harare
**Head of State:** Robert Gabriel Mugabe
**Official Language:** English
**Currency:** Zimbabwe dollar
**Exchange Rate:** Z$18.65 = US$1
**Per Capita GNP:** US$500
**Time:** GMT/UTC +2

the Changamire dynasty which would spawn the Rozwi dynasty in the late 17th century.

Another Shona kingdom, the Torwa, emerged in 1480 in south-western Zimbabwe, with its capital at Khami. This kingdom is generally considered the successor to the Great Zimbabwe state and its ruling class amassed considerable wealth from cattle and the ongoing gold trade.

In 1502, the Portuguese voyager Vasco da Gama landed at Sofala on the Mozambique coast and heard tales from Swahili traders of marvellous wealth and golden cities on the plateau. They also told of the vast empire of Mwene Mutapa (Monomatapa to the Europeans) whom the Portuguese assumed to be the custodian of King

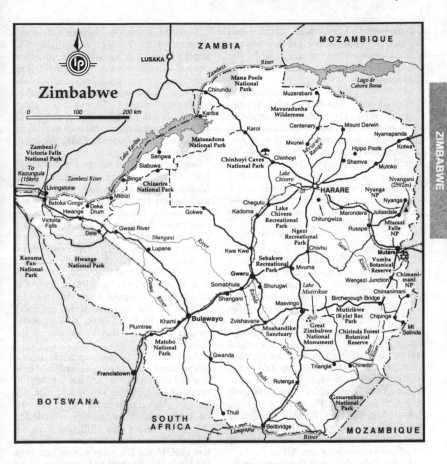

Solomon's mines and the mysterious land of Ophir. In 1512, the Portuguese government sent the exiled Antonio Fernandez on a fact-finding mission.

Over the next century, both Portuguese and Swahili traders exploited internal African squabbles to collect as much gold as they could cart off. In 1565 when the mambo of Manyika (a state in the Eastern Highlands) challenged the incumbent Mwene Mutapa, Portuguese forces under the command of Francisco Barreto, governor of loosely defined Portuguese East

Africa, attempted to help the Mwene Mutapa seize control of Manyika. The mission failed, however, and the Portuguese resorted to bribery and manipulation of African ruling classes to gain influence over the interior.

In 1629, Mwene Mutapa Kapararidze tried and failed to drive the Portuguese out for good, and was summarily replaced by Mwene Mutapa Mavura, a Catholicised Portuguese vassal. Portuguese interests were thereby given free reign until the southern state of Guruhuswa and the

Changamire dynasty attacked Mutapa and deposed his puppet leader. The new Mwene Mutapa formed an alliance with the Changamire and forced a Portuguese retreat to Mozambique.

Meanwhile, in 1684 the Torwa dynasty in the south-west was conquered by the Changamire (the clan which first conquered southern Mutapa in the late 15th century). The resulting Rozwi state took in over half of present-day Zimbabwe and had its capital at Danangombe (Dhlo-Dhlo). Its power and influence continued until 1834 when Nguni forces from the south, under Soshangane and Zwangendaba, stormed the Shona fortifications and assassinated the Rozwi leader.

## The Ndebele

After Portuguese influence withered, most of Zimbabwe was controlled by various Shona groups. South of the Limpopo River, however, several loosely associated Sotho-speaking tribes, the Nguni, competed for territory and power. In 1780 Dingiswayo, chief of the Mtetwe (a clan of the Nguni), forcibly confederated these dispersed groups into a larger and more respectable force. In 1818, however, an ambitious youngster called Shaka, from a minor clan, engineered the commander's death and took control of the Mtetwe. He renamed the tribe Zulu, after his own humble clan, and launched into a campaign of military despotism and expansionism that would reverberate across southern Africa.

As the Zulu plundered their way across Natal, some conquered Nguni tribes fled northward on a *difaqane* or *mfecane* (forced migration), an African version of the Exodus. These tribes ploughed their way through existing political entities and by the 1820s, the Soshangane had reached southern Mozambique and eastern Manyika. They established the Gaza state, installed a ruthless and oppressive military government and enslaved the local population. (In the late 19th century Gaza was reined in by the Portuguese, whose rule of Mozambique was then internationally recognised.)

In the 1830s, the Rozwi government was dismantled by Zwangendaba, who was aiming for greener pastures further north in central Africa. However, Rozwi's final knockout punch was delivered by the Ndebele (those who carry long shields) under the command of Xumalo clan chief, Mzilikazi, whose father had alienated the clan (and brought about his own execution) by failing to hand over to Shaka the spoils of a cattle raid.

As Mzilikazi fled northward, he peacefully encountered the missionary Robert Moffat, and also took several beatings from northbound Boer trekking parties. Upon reaching the Matobo (Matopos) Hills, he established a settlement and attempted to confederate all Nguni tribes within his sphere of influence. After a foray northward to assess the country beyond the Zambezi River, he discovered that his *indunas* (captains or councillors) had elected his son to take his place. Legend has it that those involved in the treason were promptly executed on the hill, Thabas Indunas, north-east of Bulawayo, thereby cementing the Ndebele state.

Mzilikazi set up his capital at Inyati, 60km north of Bulawayo, and in 1859, allowed Robert Moffat and his son John to establish a London Missionary Society mission. Although Mzilikazi never converted to Christianity, he initially extended to the missionaries the full measure of Ndebele hospitality. He took exception, however, to the Christian notion that even the lowliest individual had access to God's personal attention and relations began to break down. As a result, the Ndebele reception to Christianity was only lukewarm and in 1864 Moffat left Inyati.

During the 1850s, missionary and geographer David Livingstone and his wife, Mary Moffat (the daughter of Robert Moffat), briefly made their home there. Whether it was religious fervour or simply wanderlust that drew Livingstone north towards the Congo Basin and the Nile source remains a matter of dispute, but he eventually left his family in the care of the

London Missionary Society and set off towards his 'presumptuous' meeting with Stanley in Ujiji, Tanzania.

When Mzilikazi died in 1868, he was mourned with the words *Uku dilika kwe ntaba* (a mountain has fallen). His son Lobengula ascended to the throne and shifted the Ndebele capital to Bulawayo. Meanwhile, European gold seekers and ivory hunters from the Cape were moving into Shona and Ndebele territory. Frederick Courteney Selous' reports of abandoned gold workings, artist Thomas Baines' gold find in Mashonaland and Adam Renders' 1868 'discovery' of Great Zimbabwe launched a wholesale European grab for the region's presumed wealth.

## Enter the British

The best known of the opportunists was Cecil John Rhodes, whose fortune was made in the Kimberley diamond fields. Keen to take Queen Victoria's interests – and his own enterprise – into the exploitable country north of the Limpopo, he envisioned a great corridor of British-style civilisation and a railway stretching from the Cape to Cairo.

In 1888, Rhodes tricked Ndebele leader Lobengula into agreement with the Rudd Concession by presenting a deliberately mistranslated version. This agreement permitted British mining and colonisation of lands between the Limpopo and the Zambezi rivers while prohibiting Boer activity in Matabeleland. In exchange, the king would receive £100 monthly, 10,000 rifles, 100,000 rounds of ammunition and a river gunboat. Lobengula had apparently hoped the agreement would eliminate European competition for minerals and limit the number of prospectors and other itinerants entering his territory. In fact, it had just the opposite effect.

In 1889, Rhodes formed the British South Africa Company (BSAC) and received a royal charter allocating the power to 'make treaties, promulgate laws, maintain a police force ... make land grants and carry on any lawful trade', installing on his board such heavyweights as the dukes of Abercorn and Fife, and Earl Grey.

The next year, Rhodes mustered an army of 500, the 'Pioneer Column', and a contingency of settlers who marched northward into Mashonaland. On 27 June, they hoisted the Union Jack over Fort Victoria (Masvingo) and on 12 September established Fort Salisbury. Their next target was Manyika, still occupied by the Portuguese, but they were able to coerce Africans to join their efforts and, after a skirmish resulting in a border shift, the BSAC established Umtali (Mutare) as an eastern headquarters on the new frontier.

Finding little gold, the colonists appropriated farmlands on the Mashonaland plateau. In 1893, Lobengula, who still hadn't realised he'd been duped by the British, sent Ndebele raiders to Masvingo to put down a band of Shona attempting to drive a wedge between the Ndebele and the British by sabotaging colonial telegraph lines. Leander Starr Jameson, commander of Fort Victoria (Masvingo), mistook this action as an offence against the British and prepared to invade Matabeleland.

For the Ndebele, it was an unequal contest against superior arms, and anticipating a humiliating defeat, Lobengula burned his capital at Bulawayo and fled. He died of smallpox shortly after the Ndebele thrashed enemy forces at the Battle of Shangani River 150km north-west of Bulawayo. Although the Ndebele continued to resist the BSAC forces, their leader's death caused a drop in morale and their resistance foundered. By 1895, the spoils had been divided among white settlers, and Africans had been relegated to marginal scrubby and tsetse fly-infested lands. Not surprisingly, this provided incentive to remain on white lands as indentured workers. Those who failed to work for the landowner at least four months per year were required to pay a substantial 'hut tax' to be allowed to remain.

By 1895, the new country was known as Rhodesia after its heavy-handed founder. Shortly thereafter, Mark Twain wrote in

*More Tramps Abroad*: 'Rhodesia is the right name for that land of piracy and pillage, and puts the right stain upon it'.

## The First Chimurenga

The new European government of Rhodesia was set up 'for, by, and of' the whites. Although the Ndebele had been conquered, the Shona continued trading with the Europeans until it became apparent that the latter intended to control the entire country.

After the BSAC failed in a March 1896 raid against Kruger's Boers in the Transvaal, the Ndebele recognised a weakness and gathered forces to drive the enemy from their land. This warlike spirit proved contagious and by June they were joined by their traditional enemies, the Shona.

This crusade, called *Chimurenga*, or 'war for liberation', was led by two African *mhondoro* (spiritualists), Nehanda Charwe Nyakasikana (believed to be a female incarnation of the oracle spirit Nehanda) and Sekuru Kaguvi, who preached solidarity and co-operation among the Shona and Ndebele. Although the revolt gained some momentum, it was effectively stalled in 1897 when the leaders were captured and hanged. Nehanda's parting words, 'my bones will rise again', prophesied the Second Chimurenga which culminated in Zimbabwean independence.

The Ndebele indunas came to a tenuous peace agreement with the BSAC, but the fragmented Shona groups were only quelled after violent BSAC persuasion.

In 1899, a white Legislative Council was installed and European immigration then began in earnest. By 1904 there were some 12,000 European settlers in the country and double that number by 1911. Conflicts between black and white came into sharp focus after the 1922 referendum in which the whites chose to become self-governing rather than become part of the Union of South Africa (the Cape and Natal combined with the conquered Boer Republics of Transvaal and Orange Free State). The following year Rhodesian profits were not meeting expectations, and so the BSAC

happily handed Southern Rhodesia over to the British crown.

Although Rhodesia's constitution was in theory non-racial, suffrage was based on British citizenship and annual income and only a few blacks qualified. White supremacy was legislated in 1930 in the form of the Land Apportionment Act, which excluded Africans from ownership of the best farmland and, in 1934, by a labour law which excluded them from skilled trades and professions or settling in white areas (including all towns and cities). The effect was to force Africans to work on white farms and in mines and factories.

## Rumbles of Nationalism

The first black resistance to their unequal status surfaced in the 1920s and 30s with the formation of the Rhodesia Bantu Voters' Association, the Southern Rhodesia Native Association and the Southern Rhodesia African National Congress. These represented only middle-class Africans (the only group able to vote), and sought to reform the system rather than dismantle it. They were effectual only in that they raised black consciousness of the realities of inequality.

Abysmally poor wages and conditions led to the gradual radicalisation of the African labour force. During the 1940s, active resistance surfaced in the form of the African Voice Association, headed by Benjamin Burombo. Nationalistic fervour was fanned with the passage of the Native Land Husbandry Act of 1951 in which common pasture land on Native reserves was divided into tiny plots and allocated to individual families, some of whom were recent evictees from white lands. Herd sizes had to be reduced to reflect the amount of grazing land available.

By 1953, when Southern Rhodesia, Northern Rhodesia and Nyasaland were politically joined into the Federation of Rhodesia and Nyasaland, mining and industrial concerns favoured a more racially mixed middle class as a counterweight to the increasingly dissatisfied labour force. Pressure from the British government eliminated several of the economic segregation policies and allowed blacks to enter skilled professions and work in city centres, but no concessions were made to the sort of democracy envisioned by the nationalist movements.

At the same time, white farmers, business people and skilled workers perceived that growing nationalistic sentiments posed a threat to their privileged status. When Garfield Todd, the Federation's prime minister, attempted to satisfy some moderate African demands, he was thrown out. In 1962, the same thing happened to his successor, Sir Edward Whitehead, who had approved a new constitution which envisaged African-European parity sometime in the distant future.

In Salisbury in 1955, adamant nationalist leaders formed the City Youth League, which merged two years later with the Southern Rhodesian African National Congress to form a new ANC under labour activist Joshua Nkomo. Although the organisation was banned in 1959, it continued briefly under the guise of the National Democratic Party (NDP). In response to the State of Emergency declared on 26 February 1959, resistance took the form of *zhii* (vengeful annihilation of the enemy) and turned violent. In response to the protests, labour strikes and sabotage, the government banned the party and violently repressed one Bulawayo rally. Unfazed, the NDP re-emerged on 17 December 1961 as the Zimbabwe African People's Union (ZAPU) with Joshua Nkomo at the helm.

ZAPU was banned after just a few months, and in 1962 the newly elected right-wing government of Winston Field's Rhodesian Front Party also banned all black assemblies and political debates and instituted a mandatory death sentence for arson.

Nkomo bandied about the possibility of setting up a government in exile, but internal disputes caused a rift in ZAPU and the dissident members were ousted. The disaffected included Ndabaningi Sithole, Robert Mugabe, and Leopold Takawira, who shortly thereafter formed the Zimbabwe African National Union (ZANU). After squabbles between the two groups in the aftermath of the Federation's 1963 breakup – which later resulted in the independence of Northern Rhodesia (Zambia) and Nyasaland (Malawi) – both ZAPU and ZANU were banned and most of the leadership imprisoned.

## Ian Smith & UDI

In April 1964, Ian Smith took over both the Rhodesian Front and the presidency and began actively pressing for Rhodesian independence. British prime minister Harold Wilson countered by outlining a series of conditions which had to be met before Britain would even consider cutting the tether. These conditions included guarantees of internal racial equality, evidence of a charted course towards majority rule, and majority sanction of the prospect of independence. In 1965, realising he had a snowball's chance in hell of securing such concessions from the white constituency, Smith pressed for a Unilateral Declaration of Independence from Britain (UDI). In the election of May 1965, Smith's party picked up all 50 seats in government and declared UDI in December.

Britain reacted by declaring Smith's action illegal and imposing economic sanctions in an attempt to bring him to heel. The UN eventually (1968) voted to make these sanctions mandatory but with South Africa openly assisting Smith, and Mozambique still under colonial rule, the loopholes were enormous. The sanctions were ignored by most western countries and even by some British companies (including British Petroleum), and action that was intended to force Smith to the negotiating table failed miserably. The Rhodesian economy actually prospered; sanctions provided the incentive to increase and diversify domestic production. In fact, laws were passed to restrict export of profits and to impose import controls. Smith refused to even countenance any concessions; he considered the revocation of the UDI and especially acceptance of majority rule entirely out of the question.

'Never in a thousand years,' Smith declared, would black Africans rule Rhodesia. Given such intransigence, both ZANU and ZAPU decided that only by armed conflict could power be wrested from Smith and his Rhodesian Front.

On 28 April 1966 (now known as Chimurenga Day), the Second Chimurenga began when ZANU guerrillas launched an attack on Rhodesian forces at Chinhoyi, north-west of the capital. This, and subsequent guerrilla actions, failed due to lack of cohesion and the vulnerability of training facilities within the country. However, after anti-colonial Frelimo guerrillas liberated substantial areas of neighbouring Mozambique from the Portuguese, ZANU nationalists were able to establish bases there and escalate the conflict.

Following suit, ZAPU (combined with South Africa's ANC) set up its own Zimbabwe Peoples' Revolutionary Army (ZIPRA) bases in Zambia and training camps were organised in Tanzania.

The increasingly organised nationalist movements didn't faze Smith nearly as much as Britain's refusal to budge on the issue of independence. His response was to submit a new constitution guaranteeing blacks eight out of 66 seats in parliament. However, Britain was intent upon hearing the will of the people and organised the Pearce Commission to solicit black African opinion before it would consider taking any action.

Despite the Rhodesian Front's massive and costly campaign to secure black acceptance of the new constitution, the Smith government – which had apparently been on holiday from reality for some time – was surprised to find its scheme summarily and forcefully thrown back in its face.

As the liberation movement gained momentum, Josiah Tongogara, commander of ZANLA (Zimbabwe African National Liberation Army), ZANU's military force, went to China for Maoist tactical training. As a result, the civilian public was drafted into co-operation; young men operated as scouts and messengers, and women assisted and cooked for guerrilla troops. When the government got wind of all this, it set up 'protected villages' and, to shield them from 'intimidation', forcibly relocated those suspected of helping or harbouring guerrillas and terrorists.

The nationalist forces struck with ever-increasing ferocity throughout the country: ZANLA from Samora Machel's Mozambique and ZIPRA from Kaunda's Zambia. Whites, most of whom had been born in Africa and knew no country but Rhodesia, gradually realised the gravity of their situation. Many abandoned their homes and farms, particularly in the Eastern Highlands, and emigrated to South Africa or the Commonwealth countries. It finally dawned on Smith that all was not well in Rhodesia.

The Lisbon Coup and subsequent overthrow of the fascist regime in Portugal in April 1974, which brought independence, pseudo-Marxism and eventual chaos to both Angola and Mozambique, completely altered the balance of power in the region. It forced such powers as the USA and South Africa to reappraise their political positions in southern Africa. Surprisingly, both countries advised Smith to accommodate the nationalists.

On 8 December 1974, at Lusaka, Zambia, the various nationalist groups were united under Abel Muzorewa's African National Congress. On 11 December on the Zambezi Bridge at Victoria Falls, the unlikely duo of South Africa's John Vorster and Zambia's Kenneth Kaunda persuaded Smith to call a ceasefire and release from detention the highest ranking members of the nationalist movement – Nkomo, Sithole, and Mugabe among them – to allow peace negotiations to begin.

The talks, however, were hardly peaceful and broke down in an atmosphere of recrimination between Smith and the nationalists on one hand and between nationalist leaders on the other. ZANU split, Joshua Nkomo had differences with ANC leader Muzorewa and was expelled from the organisation, and Robert Mugabe, a highly respected former teacher and 10-year detainee under Smith, made his way to Mozambique where he replaced Sithole as the leader of ZANU. The following year, ZANU chairman Herbert Chitepo was assassinated in Lusaka by Rhodesian intelligence.

Nationalist groups continued to fragment and reform in an alphabet soup of 'Z' acronyms. In January 1976, in Geneva, ZANU and ZAPU were induced to form an alliance known as the Patriotic Front, with Sithole and Muzorewa leading separate delegations. Although the desired spirit of co-operation between the two was never realised, the Patriotic Front survived in name. Similarly, ZIPRA and ZANLA combined to form ZIPU (Zimbabwe People's Army) under Rex Nhongo.

Robert Mugabe has led Zimbabwe since independence in 1980.

At this stage, Ian Smith, faced with wholesale white emigration and a collapsing economy, was forced to change his strategy to one of internal settlement. Both Sithole and Muzorewa were persuaded to join a so-called transitional government in which the whites were to be guaranteed 28 out of 100 parliamentary seats as well as a veto over all legislation for the next 10 years. In addition, white property would be guaranteed and white control of the armed forces, police, judiciary and civil service would continue. In exchange, Patriotic Front guerrillas would be granted amnesty.

The effort failed dismally, as might have been expected, and indeed this conditional agreement only resulted in escalation of violence. To save the settlement, Smith entered into secret talks with Nkomo, offering to ditch both Sithole and Muzorewa, but Nkomo wouldn't be swayed.

Finally, with support for Smith waning among the white population and the country's largest fuel depot sabotaged by Patriotic Front guerrillas, Smith opted to call a general election by both blacks and whites. On 1 May 1979, he handed the office of prime minister over to Muzorewa, who was effectively a puppet, and opened up 50% of European-designated lands to people of any race. Government structure was, however, much the same as that pro-

posed under the 'internal settlement'. The changes weren't taken very seriously; no-one was cheering and international diplomatic recognition of Zimbabwe-Rhodesia, as it was now called, wasn't forthcoming. At best, a few countries regarded Zimbabwe-Rhodesia as simply a passable transitional government.

## Independence

In Britain, the Conservatives won the 1979 election and Margaret Thatcher immediately began pressing for a solution to the Rhodesian problem. It was finally decided that any new constitution would have to be satisfactory to Britain and be ratified in free and well-monitored elections.

On 10 September 1979, the delegations met at Lancaster House in London to draw up a constitution satisfactory to both the Patriotic Front represented by Nkomo and Mugabe and the Zimbabwe-Rhodesia government, represented by Muzorewa and Smith. Also attending were Kenneth Kaunda and Julius Nyerere, to encourage the Patriotic Front towards a settlement, and Margaret Thatcher, who would pressure Smith to compromise. For several months, the talks accomplished nothing; Mugabe, who wanted ultimate power in the new government, refused to make any concessions whatsoever.

After 14 weeks of talks and some heavy-handed coercion by the British, the racially imbalanced Lancaster House Agreement, which guaranteed whites (3% of the population) 20 of the 100 seats in the new parliament, was reached. The agreement also stipulated that private land-holdings could not be nationalised or appropriated without adequate compensation, a more logical 'concession' to whites than the race-dictated imbalance in parliamentary representation. Despite the agreement's failings, the way for independence was paved and the various factions got down to the business of jostling for a position in the queue for power.

In the carefully monitored election of 4 March 1980, Mugabe and ZANU won 57 of the 80 seats available to blacks, Nkomo's ZAPU party won 20, and Muzorewa's UANC won only three. Zimbabwe joined the ranks of Africa's independent nations from this date, under an internationally recognised majority government headed by Robert Mugabe. In Salisbury (Harare) on 16 April 1980, the Reverend Canaan Banana was officially sworn in as the first president of independent Zimbabwe and Robert Mugabe took the helm as prime minister.

Despite the long and bitter struggle, Mugabe displayed restraint and kept vengeful tendencies at bay in the new society. (Interestingly, Ian Smith himself stayed on and still lives quietly in Harare, beside the Cuban embassy.) The remaining whites were a nuisance but Mugabe wasn't keen to throw out the baby with the bathwater and lose their wealth, technical expertise and access to foreign investment – all necessary to the fulfilment of the dream he, as a committed Marxist, had of creating a one-party socialist state. He appointed white ministers of Agriculture and Commerce & Industry, made assurances that 'there is a place for everyone in this country ... the winners and the losers', and that he aimed not to bring about a new Mozambique or a new Kenya,

but a new Zimbabwe. The economy soared, wages increased and basic social programmes – notably education and health care – were reconstituted or established.

It was a promising start, but the euphoria and the optimistic sense of national unity brought on by independence quickly faded. There was a resurgence of the rivalry between ZANU and ZAPU, which escalated into armed conflicts between supporters of the two parties. Mugabe ordered five prominent Nkomo supporters to be arrested in 1980 and ousted Nkomo from his cabinet position in 1981. Tensions were further inflamed by the arrest of the Minister of Manpower Planning, Edgar Tekere, for the alleged murder of a white farmer. Although Tekere was found not guilty, the arrest effectively marked the end of his political career.

Nkomo was accused of plotting to overthrow the government and there was a resurgence of guerrilla activity in Matabeleland, the area from which ZAPU drew the bulk of its support. In early 1983, Mugabe sent in the North Korean-trained Fifth Brigade to quell the disturbances, but they launched into an assault in which several thousand civilians fell victim. Villagers were gunned down and prominent members of ZAPU were systematically eliminated in order to rout out dissidents. Bodies are still being uncovered in rural Matabeleland. Essentially, the conflict was a tribal one between the majority Shona (largely ZANU supporters) and the minority Ndebele (largely ZAPU supporters).

Nkomo meanwhile fled to England and was to remain there until Mugabe, realising Zimbabwe's enemies were watching with interest as internal strife threatened to escalate into civil war, publicly relented and guaranteed his safe return.

At this point, Mugabe and Nkomo began the talks that would result in the combining of ZANU and ZAPU. An amnesty was offered to the dissidents and the entire affair, but not the underlying discontent, was thereby masterfully swept under the carpet.

## Reform, Scandal & Discontent

Despite the tragic examples of Kaunda's Zambia, Nyerere's Tanzania, and the violent and oppressive revolutionary government in Mozambique, Mugabe still harboured dreams of transforming Zimbabwe into a one-party state. The long overdue abolition in mid-1988 of the law guaranteeing 20 parliamentary seats to whites, the imposition of strict and strangling controls on currency, foreign exchange and trade and later, in April 1990, a review of land-ownership guarantees for whites (after the British-brokered constitution expired on the 10th anniversary of independence) all seemed to indicate steps in this direction.

However, the main features of the late 1980s were scandal and government corruption. Some MPs and cabinet ministers were loudly professing socialism, some sincerely, but many of the same group were privately greasing their own palms. In 1988, the government was linked with shady practices at the Willowvale car assembly plant near Harare. The corruption was exposed by the press, and students at the University of Zimbabwe launched a protest against Mugabe for having allowed crooked government to exist in Zimbabwe when he'd pledged it would never happen. Mugabe felt threatened by the uprising, and cut off some areas of university funding, refusing to restore them until the students admitted their mistake.

Late 1990 saw further student unrest when riot police resorted to using tear gas to break up a demonstration against a proposed increase in government control over University of Zimbabwe policy.

Some dirty business surrounding the March 1990 elections revealed similar facets of the president. The newly formed ZUM (Zimbabwe Unity Movement) party under the leadership of Edgar Tekere, which promoted a free-enterprise economy and a multiparty democratic state, played mouse to the elephant and challenged ZANU in several electorates. Like the elephant, Mugabe overreacted and engineered some last minute gerrymandering to waylay any possible ZUM victories. Shortly following the election (a ZANU landslide all around) the ZUM candidate who'd shown promise in the Gweru North electoral district, Patrick Kombayi, was wounded in an apparent assassination attempt and anyone having ties with ZUM quickly sought a low profile.

Finally, at a government (essentially ZANU) central committee meeting in August 1990, 22 of 26 members voted against any one-party notions. They argued that introducing a one-party state at a time when the worldwide trend was in the opposite direction could be interpreted as a step backward and affect Zimbabwe's credibility in the eyes of potential investors.

## Increasing Taxes & Tensions

In February 1995, with Mugabe's popularity waning and elections due the following month, he revealed vote-catching plans for a US$160 million 'anti-poverty programme' aimed at training workers, developing rural areas and providing a safety net for the poor. He also paid lip service to nationalisation of white lands and promised to reduce unemployment, which would inevitably mean an increase in the public service sector.

The election, however, was characterised by general apathy and was boycotted by the growing opposition groups, who voiced concerns that both the cards and the constitution were stacked against everyone but the ruling party. The voters, feeling powerless to change the situation, stayed away en masse.

On a positive note, Zimbabwe slowly recovered from the initial shocks brought on by the ESAP (see boxed text on the following page) and by the catastrophic drought of the early 1990s. However, in August 1997, the social event of the season, with 20,000 guests, was President Robert Mugabe's marriage to his 32-year-old former secretary, Grace Marufu, with whom he has two children. Many disgruntled public workers, who had received a rather paltry 6% pay rise (in the face of 22% annual inflation)

ZIMBABWE

## The Land Issue & ESAP

At independence in 1980, 270,000 whites lived in Zimbabwe. There are now only 90,000 to 100,000, making up less than 1% of the population, but they still own one-third of the country's arable land and produce 42% of the nation's annual export income. When Robert Mugabe came to power in 1980, he promised to resettle 162,000 black families on white-owned lands. However, under the British-brokered peace agreement of 1980, the government could not force farmers to sell their land. This issue has been the bugbear of the Mugabe government.

During the first decade after independence, only four million acres had been purchased and 55,000 families resettled, far short of the original goal. The government sought another six million hectares for the resettlement of 110,000 more families, leaving six million hectares for commercial farming ventures.

Under the 'willing buyer, willing seller' scheme, which operated through the 1980s, the government had the power to set land prices – although the government itself was the buyer. Farmers could each sell only one farm; absentee landlords would automatically lose their claims; land could not be sold to foreigners; and farmers would be compensated in Zimbabwe dollars, effectively preventing their leaving the country after selling out. The proposed methods of land takeover, however, were protested against by the Commercial Farmers Union (which not surprisingly is comprised mostly of white farmers).

Over subsequent years, whenever public support waned, Mugabe paid lip service to this resettlement scheme (and continues to do so). However, he has also tried to remain pragmatic. One official, recognising commercial farmers' gripes, admitted the government didn't want to 'kill the goose that lays the golden eggs' or frighten away foreign investors. Eventually, the land reformers had no choice but to return to the drawing board.

In 1990, the 'willing buyer, willing seller' clause expired. The National Farmers Association and the Zimbabwe National Farmers Union (both mainly non-white organisations) wisely suggested that resettlement continue to be handled on a mutually willing buyer and seller basis, but that the government offer easy-terms loans to allow small or peasant farmers to purchase their own land.

The government, however, ignored this advice, and in late 1990 and early 1991, proclaimed that it would redistribute 50% of the land held by white commercial farmers to black subsistence farmers. This meant risking nearly half of Zimbabwe's foreign exchange earnings, turning the country into a food importer, inviting international criticism and thwarting foreign investment.

In late 1991, however, in an about-turn aimed at courting foreign investment and aid, the Zimbabwe government revealed the Economic Structural Adjustment Programme (ESAP),

while government ministers saw a pay rise of 130%, viewed the lavish affair as an affront and walked off the job in protest. The government refused to negotiate with the unions and sacked all striking employees. Many saw this as an attempt at paring down the bloated public sector work force and creating better conditions for the remaining skilled professionals. However, most of Zimbabwe's population lies within the unskilled sector and the affair further eroded support for the government.

The years from 1996 to 1998 saw growing economic and political tension, and increasing dissatisfaction with the government, which reacted by promising to take more land from white farmers and redistribute it among communal peasant farmers. It claimed, however, that it lacked the means to pay compensation except for

which had been recommended by the International Monetary Fund and the World Bank. The goal was economic liberalisation, which required a realistic official exchange rate, lifting of price controls, and allowing competition from imports, in order to bring about long-term economic vitality and usher Zimbabwe into the international community.

Naturally, these drastic measures inspired immediate price increases, which were accompanied by hardship among the poorer classes (some suggested the acronym ESAP really stood for Ever-Struggling African Peoples). These hardships were compounded by the drought of the early 1990s which had caused widespread crop failure. The result was a rash of migration to urban areas, along with increased unemployment and crime.

With all these problems, popular disenchantment with the Mugabe government reached an all-time high, and naturally the land issue again showed its face. In March 1992, the Land Acquisition Act was unanimously approved in Parliament. The new goal was to seize five million hectares of mostly white-owned commercial farmland for the resettlement of one million black subsistence farmers. The former landowners would be compensated in near worthless government bonds.

The underlying intent of all this was to court the goodwill of the common people. However in international aid and investment circles, it set off alarm bells and the new law was criticised as being irreconcilably at odds with ESAP. In hopes of rekindling some international goodwill, Mugabe inserted palatability clauses in the legislation providing for fair cash compensation for farmers and landowners' right to judicial appeal. There was, however, little he could do about the major international concern, which was the creditworthiness of a country which had disenfranchised the source of half its export income.

Thus far, most white farms taken over have been abandoned property or second farms which have been reallocated to government officials, in blatant defiance of the spirit of the plan. One well-publicised farm takeover was that of 260-hectare Churu Farm, which was owned by Ndabaningi Sithole, the hot-headed Black leader of the small opposition party, ZANU-Ndonga. Mr Sithole described the move as 'politically motivated theft' (and given the circumstances, one could hardly disagree with him). Immediately thereafter, 4000 families illegally settled on the farm and remained, despite government intentions to evict them on health grounds. Unfortunately for Mr Sithole, a last minute court order allowed them to stay.

As yet, there are no solutions to the land quandary. Perhaps the most interesting proposal put forth comes from Diana Mitchell, writing in the Zimbabwean tourist paper, *Travellers' News* in mid-1994. In a nutshell, she suggested that the government approximate traditional African custom and convert all private and communal lands to leasehold land, granting leases to those who use it.

improvements (houses, barns and other structures) on the lands of dispossessed farmers. After written assurances that the takeover would be handled in a 'rational' way, the World Bank and EU promised to finance any shortfalls. The racial overtones applied to this land policy fostered increased bitterness and racial tensions.

War veterans, aroused by the discovery in late 1996 that top government officials and ministers had illegally obtained huge sums from the War Victims' Compensation Fund, began demonstrating and demanding their rightful compensation. The demonstrations grew progressively more violent and culminated in an uncomfortable confrontation with President Mugabe at the August 1997 Heroes' Day rally. The president hastily promised money for the ex-guerrillas. In November 1997 the Ministry of Finance increased personal income taxes by 5%, raised the GST from 15 to 17.5% and increased fuel taxes. Payments to veterans would include 'gratuities' of Z$50,000 (at the time, US$4100) each, plus life pensions of Z$2000 (US$170) per month.

The normally passive Zimbabweans, already heavily burdened by excessive taxes, found the new levies unsustainable if they were to feed and clothe their families and make ends meet. As a result, they rebelled and eagerly took up a trade union call to boycott work on 9 December 1997. Throughout the country, blacks, whites, Asians and coloureds united in a peaceful demonstration of disapproval, but in Harare, police attempted to prevent people from attending the demonstration by firing tear gas into the crowds.

Parliament, however, saw reason and decided to reject the proposed 5% income tax increase, and also mandated that the fuel price be dropped on 31 December 1997. The president and his ministers were incensed.

Meanwhile, on 14 November 1997, the Zimbabwe dollar lost over 50% of its value against the US dollar and British pound. The increased cost of imports caused immediate price hikes for most goods, including basic foodstuffs. In Harare, protesters again took to the streets and rioting ensued, causing millions of dollars worth of property damage and looting. The police and army were called in to quell the disturbances and a number of people were killed. Even so, the government refused to reduce the sales taxes or to even discuss alternative measures.

In the face of this intransigence, the Zimbabwe Congress of Trade Unions called on the government to address and right the problems by 27 February 1998 or face a two-day work stoppage. The government still declined to discuss the matter and threatened 'stern action' if the boycott went ahead. Undaunted by the intimidation, workers stayed home on 3 and 4 March 1998. Trade worth an estimated Z$7 million (at the time, nearly US$300,000) was lost.

Riot police came out in force and waited for a demonstration which never happened. Shops and factories were closed, but otherwise, people went about their business peacefully.

Still the government ignored the popular dissatisfaction and demands for reduced taxation, and instead of taking remedial action, accused white industrialists of paying members to strike in an attempt to destabilise and overthrow the ZANU government. (As a side note, on 5 March, the Zimbabwe Congress of Trade Unions building in Bulawayo burned down, and the police suspected arson.) Currently, discontent among all races and classes of Zimbabweans is running high and, unless the government hears their grievances and attempts to rectify the mess it has made with the economy, violence is a very real possibility.

## GEOGRAPHY

Zimbabwe, a landlocked country in south-central Africa, lies entirely within the tropics – between 15 and 22°S latitude. Most of the country consists of highveld and middleveld plateau lying between 900 and 1700m above sea level and enjoys a remarkably temperate climate. It is bound on the north-west by Zambia, on the east and north-east by Mozambique, on the south-west by Botswana, and on the south by the Republic of South Africa. Four countries – Zambia, Zimbabwe, Botswana and Namibia – meet at a single point at the country's westernmost extreme.

Zimbabwe's maximum width is 725km, while north to south it stretches 835km. The total area is 390,580 sq km, roughly half the size of Australia's New South Wales or the same size as the British Isles with an extra Scotland thrown in.

A low ridge across the country from the Mvurwi Range in the north-east to the Matobo Hills in the south-west marks the divide between two of Africa's great river systems, the Zambezi in the north-west and the Limpopo-Save in the south-east. The former consists mostly of plateau, sloping gently away from the ridge before dropping dramatically to the broad Zambezi plain in the north-east and into the tangled hills and valleys around Lake Kariba in the north-west. This landscape is characterised by bushveld dotted with small rocky outcrops, known locally as *kopjes,* and bald knob-like domes of slickrock called *dwalas.*

The hot, dry lowveld of southern Zimbabwe is comprised mostly of the relatively flat savanna lands of the Save Basin, sloping almost imperceptibly towards the Limpopo River.

The only significant mountainous region in Zimbabwe is the Eastern Highlands, which straddles the Zimbabwe-Mozambique border from the Nyanga region in the north to the Chimanimani Mountains in the south. Zimbabwe's highest peak, Nyangani, rises 2592m near the northern end of this range.

## CLIMATE

What surprises people about Zimbabwe's climate is that it's not as hot as the latitude would suggest. Although it lies entirely within the tropics, the country stretches over a high plateau averaging 900m above sea level and, during the dry season, it enjoys a pleasantly temperate climate.

Winters (May to October) are like luscious Mediterranean springs, with warm, sunny days and cool, clear nights. It never snows, not even in the Eastern Highlands, but overnight frosts and freezing temperatures aren't uncommon on the plateau. Winter is also the best time for wildlife viewing since animals tend to gather around pans and never stray far from water sources.

The lowveld and Zambezi valley reguins experience hotter and more humid temperatures but in the winter months, there's still a minimum amount of rainfall. Although

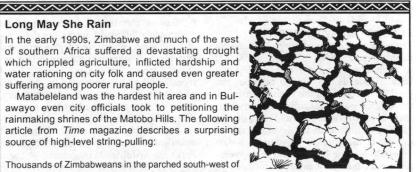

### Long May She Rain

In the early 1990s, Zimbabwe and much of the rest of southern Africa suffered a devastating drought which crippled agriculture, inflicted hardship and water rationing on city folk and caused even greater suffering among poorer rural people.

Matabeleland was the hardest hit area and in Bulawayo even city officials took to petitioning the rainmaking shrines of the Matobo Hills. The following article from *Time* magazine describes a surprising source of high-level string-pulling:

Thousands of Zimbabweans in the parched south-west of the country pleaded with Britain's Queen Elizabeth II to stay longer after rain coincided with her visit to Bulawayo. People cheered the queen when a torrential downpour suddenly started at the onset of her visit. The first rain of the season on the parched Matabeleland plains interrupted her speech in the country's second largest city, which had only enough water in its reservoirs to last a few more weeks. As the queen proclaimed 'I pray that the drought may end soon, and that you have ample rain in the coming year', the showers began.

Queen Elizabeth again demonstrated her rainmaking skills on her March 1995 visit to South Africa, where her arrival in drought-stricken Natal and Transvaal coincided with copious rainfall which revived desiccated vegetation and crops. She thereby earned the African name *Motlalepula,* 'she who brings rain'.

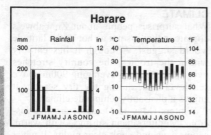

**Harare**

spring and autumn aren't really obvious as seasons, the highveld mopane trees change colours throughout the winter and provide touches of orange, yellow and red reminiscent of a European or North American autumn.

Most of Zimbabwe's rain falls in brief afternoon deluges and electrical storms in the summer (November to April) and brings only fleeting relief from the stifling humidity. Although temperatures rarely exceed 30°C, the air can feel oppressive.

## ECOLOGY & ENVIRONMENT
Since the turn of the century, Zimbabwe's human population has grown from 500,000 to 12 million. As pressures to develop and farm wild lands increase, so too does the need for retreat from the chaos. Currently, the official policy regarding the environment is one of 'sustained yield use'; that is, hunting is limited to the level of natural growth in the wildlife population. Safari areas allow game hunting and the government cites their annual net of millions of dollars in foreign exchange as justification for their existence and therefore, for wildlife conservation.

### The CAMPFIRE Programme
In 1989, increasing disquiet over the government's 'shoot to kill' policy to combat poaching gave rise to the CAMPFIRE programme, which channelled revenue from hunting on communal lands, where wildlife can become a nuisance to subsistence farmers, back into affected communities in the form of schools, hospitals and other infrastructure. In some areas, households receive as much as US$225 a year – a fortune in rural Zimbabwe. Since its inception, CAMPFIRE participation has grown from 9000 to 103,000 households and land in Zimbabwe dedicated to conservation has more than doubled. Poaching has slowed and populations of endangered species – including rhino – are rising.

About 90% of CAMPFIRE's revenue is derived from leases on sport hunting and tourism concessions to commercial safari operators, with large contributions from foreign sources, including USAID (US Agency for International Development).

For further information, see the boxed text in the Regional Facts for the Visitor chapter.

### National Parks
Tourism accounts for 6.6% of Zimbabwe's GDP and the main draw is the wildlife-rich national parks and safari areas, which make up about 13% of the country. Unfortunately, they're chronically underfunded and maintenance of roads, water supplies, accommodation, campgrounds, reservations systems and other infrastructure has declined greatly in recent years. Until recently, all money generated by the parks went into the government's central treasury, where it was swallowed in bureaucracy. While entrance fees have risen dramatically – ostensibly to cover the deficit and directly fund the Department of National Parks & Wildlife Management – there hasn't yet been any visible improvement in the facilities and it remains to be seen what will become of the languishing parks system.

### Private Efforts
In 1975, control of wildlife on private ranches was ceded to the ranchers, but currently the Ministry of Environment & Tourism hopes to place the control of privately-owned wildlife under the care of the district councils and CAMPFIRE. However, alleged government mismanagement of elephant and rhino translocation

projects, the policy of 'indigenisation' (granting new licences only to black Zimbabweans) of the safari industry, and government attempts to take over white-owned lands have cast a veil of uncertainty over the future of private conservation.

On a happier note, in an effort to foster an appreciation for wildlife and wilderness in school children, several amateur conservation groups have purchased small, protected reserves in urban areas, mainly for the education of city children. These include Mukuvisi Woodlands near Harare, Cecil Kop near Mutare and Tshabalala near Bulawayo.

### The Elephant 'Problem'

According to many biologists and zoologists, Zimbabwe's wildlife reserves face ecological disaster due to the destructive habits of the country's 65,000 elephant. The Zambezi Valley's estimated 17,000 elephant have already proven a menace by invading and destroying thousands of hectares of cropland. In Hwange National Park, covering 14,600 sq km, 20% of the woodland has already been lost and 25% of the baobabs in Mana Pools National Park have been severely damaged and are expected to die within a few years.

It has been suggested that the optimal elephant population would be 35,000, and that numbers could be reduced by culling and trophy hunting. Currently, hunters pay up to US$20,000 to shoot a bull elephant, providing badly needed revenue. On the other hand, many conservation groups contend that Zimbabwe and other southern African countries can support their elephant populations, and that while elephant destruction of the environment may be unsightly to tourists, it's all part of a grand natural cycle.

For further information, see the Elephant Control boxed text in the Western Zimbabwe chapter.

### FLORA & FAUNA

Zimbabwe's enormous popularity with visitors is largely due to its wild element, and offers a wonderful and relatively accessible range of fauna and flora. The country's national parks are rife with the creatures that visitors come to see: elephant, buffalo, lion, cheetah, hyena, jackals, monkeys and a wide range of antelope and smaller animals. For sheer numbers, Hwange is the best park to visit, but Mana Pools, Chizarira, Matusadona, Gonarezhou and Zambezi national parks also offer rewarding wildlife viewing.

Species which are unique to Zimbabwe, or are found in only limited ranges elsewhere, include the rare nyala, which is found only in Gonarezhou and Mana Pools national parks; the king cheetah, which is endemic to Gonarezhou; and the samango monkey, which inhabits the Eastern Highlands.

Zimbabwe is also one of the last rhinoceros ranges, and both white and black rhino are present, albeit in small numbers. The best and most accessible viewing is in Matobo national park, but you also have a chance of seeing rhino in Hwange and Matusadona national parks.

Zimbabwe also enjoys an interesting floral realm. Much of the natural vegetation is comprised of *msasa* and *mopane* bushveld, but the country also hosts a variety of bizarre aloes, as well as euphorbias, cycads, palms and other dryland vegetation.

For an overview of flora and fauna, refer to the Flora & Fauna section of the Facts about the Region chapter.

### National Parks & Wildlife Reserves

If your ideal African adventure includes rambling through forest and savanna bushlands and photographing Africa's wild menagerie, Zimbabwe is for you. Without the commercial assembly-line feeling of Kenya, the expense of Botswana or Tanzania, the cushy development of South Africa or the political uncertainties of most other countries, Zimbabwe's wilderness and its wildlife reserves offer pristine natural habitats, large animal populations and as much variety of species as any country on the African continent.

**ZIMBABWE** *(side tab)*

## ZIMBABWE'S NATIONAL PARKS & WILDLIFE RESERVES

| Region | Features |
|---|---|
| **Northern Zimbabwe** | |
| Chinhoyi Caves | This tiny 'roadside' national park protects a series of limestone sinkholes and underground pools. |
| Mana Pools | Contains lovely Zambezi landscapes and is popular for canoe trips and walking safaris. It's the only wildlife park where visitors may walk without a guide. |
| Matusadona | High and wild mountain country contrasts with the Lake Kariba shoreline. It's known for large numbers of elephant, buffalo and lion. |
| **Eastern Highlands** | |
| Chimanimani | This roadless park includes Zimbabwe's most dramatic mountains and best bushwalking country. |
| Mtarazi Falls | This small appendage to Nyanga National Park focuses on Mtarazi Falls, which plunges 762m over the Honde Escarpment. |
| Nyanga | Long established as a weekend getaway for Harare people, this former estate of Cecil Rhodes contains lovely highlands, picturesque waterfalls, great fishing and Mt Nyangani, Zimbabwe's highest mountain. |
| Vumba | High and misty forests and botanical gardens. A popular retreat for city dwellers and homesick British. |
| **Midlands & South-Eastern Zimbabwe** | |
| Gonarezhou | Formerly home to some of Africa's largest elephants, Gonarezhou (the abode of elephants) is still worth a visit for the grand scenery and increasing wildlife numbers. |
| Great Zimbabwe | The ruins complex of sub-Saharan Africa's greatest ancient city, set amid a lovely, haunting landscape. |
| **Bulawayo** | |
| Matobo | The hills and balancing rock kopjes form Zimbabwe's most bizarre landscape, and the attached Whovi Game Park has healthy populations of white and black rhino. |
| **Western Zimbabwe** | |
| Chizarira | Zimbabwe's wildest national park blends stunning scenery and relatively undisturbed wildlife habitat. |
| Hwange | The country's largest and most wildlife-packed national park. Its relative accessibility makes it a favourite with visitors. |

| | |
|---|---|
| Kazuma Pan | The centrepiece of this wild and little-visited park is a large grassy pan surrounded by teak and mopane forest. It contains Zimbabwe's only gemsbok and is also home to the rare oribi antelope. |
| Zambezi/Victoria Falls | This beautiful park encompasses 40km of Zambezi River frontage backed by wildlife-rich mopane forest and savanna. The Victoria Falls National Park extension contains the falls themselves, as well as the Zambezi gorges and a small rainforest reserve. |

**ZIMBABWE**

In fact, 13% of Zimbabwe is protected or semi-protected wildlife habitat, either in national parks or unfenced national safari areas. This doesn't include privately protected areas such as game ranches and nature conservation areas, which add considerably to the total amount of protected land. In addition, there are several dam-oriented recreational parks, which include Lake Chivero, Lake Mutirikwe, Sebakwe Dam, Ngezi Dam, Lake Manyame, Lake Manjirenji and Lake Cunningham. See the boxed text for an outline of the main parks and reserves.

**Visiting the Parks** Fees for national parks admission and accommodation are standardised, and foreigners or clients of tour operators pay several times the resident rates (rates quoted here are for foreigners). Entry costs US$5/10 per day/week plus US$1 per car or US$2 per truck/4WD vehicle (with the exception of Victoria Falls, which is open to pedestrians only and costs US$10 per entry).

Unfortunately, much of the park revenue (of which 30.6% is derived from hunting) goes into the central treasury and little returns to the parks, resulting in chronic budget problems: artificially pumped water holes go dry, facilities become shabby and the reservations system remains a shambles.

Organised activities are limited, but in some parks you can go horse riding or hire a game scout for a walk in the bush. Horse-riding tours cost US$20 for two hours, and must be booked in advance. All-day horse tours are available at Nyanga for US$40. Walks led by game scouts cost US$15 per hour for up to six people (except at Hwange Main Camp, where a two hour walk is US$5 per person). Longer wilderness treks with a game scout, for up to six people, cost US$80 for the first day and US$35 for each subsequent day. For more on parks accommodation and the tedious booking system, see Accommodation in the Zimbabwe Facts for the Visitor chapter.

Note that hitching is technically forbidden in parks, so the only legitimate economical way of visiting them is to muster a group, hire a vehicle and organise everything yourself. Note that in the wildlife-oriented parks, such as Hwange and Mana Pools, you must be back in camp prior to dusk, or face a fine of US$5.

In Zimbabwean national parks, as well as most private campgrounds and caravan parks and some general stores, pre-cut firewood is sold in bundles for reasonable prices. Wilderness campers, however, are advised to carry a fuel stove for cooking and, if possible, to avoid building fires.

## GOVERNMENT & POLITICS

The Republic of Zimbabwe's legislative body consists of the executive president and a 150-member parliament. The president, who serves a six year term, is in theory elected by national popular vote every six years, and is the official head of state and commander-in-chief of the armed forces.

In the legislative branch, the unicameral House of Assembly, 120 of the 150 seats are filled by general vote for five-year terms. Each of Zimbabwe's eight provinces has its own local government, headed by a state-appointed governor, who is also a member of parliament. Of the remaining parliamentary seats, 10 are filled by chiefs, who are nominated and elected by an electoral college of other chiefs (although only the president can authorise the title of 'chief'), and the remaining 12 members of parliament are directly appointed by the executive president.

The judicial branch consists of both General and Appellate Divisions, with power in both civil and criminal matters. The chief justice is appointed by the president in council with the prime minister. Appellate justices are appointed by the president in concordance with the Judicial Commission.

## Politics

Officially, the Republic of Zimbabwe is a parliamentary democracy, while unofficially, it would be more accurately described as a one-party state. In the April 1995 election, the ruling Zimbabwe African National Union-Patriotic Front (ZANU-PF), which is the voice of Zimbabwe's Shona majority, won 82.3% of the vote and 118 seats. The ZANU-Ndonga which, in spite of its name, is a conservative opposition party, won 6.5% and two seats. Although the centrist Forum Party of Zimbabwe received 6.3% of the vote, it captured no parliamentary seats. Another opposition party, the Liberty Party of Zimbabwe, was founded in South Africa in February 1998 as a voice for the Ndebele minority, many of whom were living and working in South Africa.

The current executive president, 74-year-old Robert Mugabe, has served as chief of state, head of government and commander

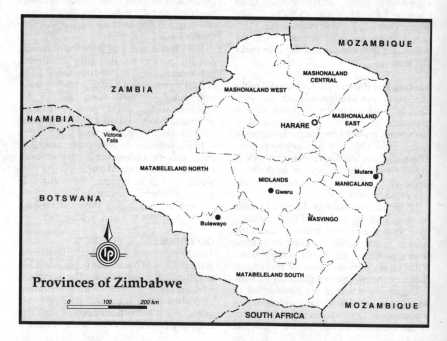

**Provinces of Zimbabwe**

of the armed forces since Zimbabwean independence in 1980. In the popularly boycotted March 1996 presidential elections, he was re-elected with 92.7% of the vote. However, ongoing economic strife, accusations of corruption and rifts in the ZANU-PF party have resulted in calls for Mugabe's resignation which, given his current attitude, seems highly unlikely. Former freedom fighter Simon Muzenda and Ndebele leader Joshua Nkomo serve as vice presidents.

Ndabaningi Sithole, a co-founder and first president of ZANU-PF, became disaffected with the ruling party and went on to lead the opposition ZANU-Ndonga party and represent Manicaland in parliament. ZANU-PF doesn't take kindly to opposition and in February 1998, Sithole was accused and convicted of masterminding a 1995 plot to assassinate Mugabe. Despite his strong denial of the accusation and an ongoing appeal, he was suspended from parliament. Sadly, many other would-be opposition leaders may well take this case as a warning about the consequences of vocal dissent.

## ECONOMY

Zimbabwe's economic potential is considerable; its temperate climate, ample natural resources and increasingly skilled workforce are all factors. Despite the slowdown and economic stagnation experienced during the Second Chimurenga (or bush war as the whites referred to it), the effects of Rhodesia's necessary industrial diversification during UDI-related international sanctions are still being felt, and the country does have a reasonably sound industrial base. However, during the first decade of independence, the economy suffered serious setbacks under strict isolationist policies – an artificially valued Zimbabwe dollar, strict currency controls and crippling import duties.

In late 1991, however, the government conspired with the World Bank and the International Monetary Fund to implement the Economic Structural Adjustment Programme (ESAP), which was intended to liberalise the Zimbabwean economy. It brought the official exchange rate more or less into parity with the parallel rate, and lifted price controls and stifling import restrictions with the aim of stimulating competitive trade and turning the country into an international player.

ESAP also brought about changes in the restrictive currency laws for residents. Zimbabwe citizens and residents were suddenly permitted to hold foreign bank accounts and were also given a 'holiday allowance', which permitted them to export up to US$2000 annually. Few could afford foreign travel, however, and the price increases brought about by ESAP (see earlier boxed text) were initially devastating, particularly for the country's poorest people.

The structural changes notwithstanding, a major obstacle to international trade and economic prosperity is transport. Landlocked Zimbabwe is dependent upon its neighbours for access to port facilities. The Zambezi River route is blocked by Mozambique's moribund Cahora Bassa hydro project, and the crippling war in that country left the Mutare-Beira rail link in dubious condition. Currently, the country relies mainly on South Africa for access to the sea.

Although about 80% of Zimbabwe's population is dependent upon agriculture, it accounts for only 20% of the GNP because the majority of farmers and pastoralists operate on the subsistence level while many larger, commercially viable farms are being purchased by the government for resettlement. Currently, less than 15% of arable land is under cultivation.

The staple food crop is maize, while cotton, coffee, tea, burley and Virginia tobacco (tobacco is the largest export earner in the economy), wine grapes (Zimbabwe's white wines are palatable but the reds still have a way to go) and sugar cane are the primary cash crops. The country also supplies small quantities of fresh flowers, citrus fruits and vegetables for the European market.

The sugar cane, which is grown in the lowveld, is turned into table sugar, molasses and 40 million litres of ethanol annually. When it's available, sugar-cane ethanol is blended with petrol and used as fuel to supplement the imported petrol entering the country via the carefully guarded but vulnerable pipeline through the Beira corridor.

Livestock, the major indication of wealth in precolonial Zimbabwe, remains a major commodity. The country is nearly self-sufficient in milk, beef, poultry, pork and mutton. In addition, more than a million goats roam the communal lands (grazing them into wastelands) and provide subsistence-level protein. Game ranching is also increasing, particularly of antelope.

Mining interests account for around 40% of exports; gold is the major earner. Coal, chromite, nickel, asbestos, copper, iron ore and tin are also exported in significant quantities. Recently, oil exploration by Mobil in the Zambezi Valley east of Mana Pools revealed nothing. Thanks to pressure from the Zambezi Society, a private conservation group, environmental impact was considered.

Forestry is an up-and-coming venture, especially in the Eastern Highlands, where vast tracts of softwood forests have been planted and are being harvested for pulp, and in the south-west where mahogany and teak provide raw materials for railway construction and a growing furniture industry.

Manufacturing comprises only a small sector of the economy and is dominated by textiles, including spinning, weaving and dyeing enterprises. Other manufacturing concerns include hardwood furniture, leather goods, food processing and tobacco products. Perhaps Zimbabwe's most controversial foreign exchange earner is the export arms industry. It revolves around two Harare factories which employ 300 people making ammunition and filling grenades, shells and mortar bombs with high explosives. Currently, the major markets are trouble spots in Africa.

Tourism in Zimbabwe is on the increase, and the setbacks faced by the tourist industry during the war are now behind it. Hordes of package tours descend on Hwange and Victoria Falls, and the country is figuring in more and more African itineraries. There are concerns about security problems, but they're out of proportion to the real dangers – Zimbabwe is still more secure than Kenya, for example.

Currently, South Africa sends the greatest number of tourists, but most of Zimbabwe's tourism revenue comes from British and US visitors. Interestingly, hunting brings in more money than any other sector of the tourist industry.

For information on investment in Zimbabwe, contact the Zimbabwe Investment Centre (☎ (14) 790991), PO Box 5950, Harare or the national export promotion organisation, ZimTrade (☎ (14) 731020; fax (14) 707531), PO Box 2738, Harare.

## POPULATION & PEOPLE

By the latest estimates Zimbabwe has a population of 11,515,000, expected to increase by one million by the year 2000. Of these, 73% live in rural areas and 45.5% are under 15 years of age. The average life expectancy is approximately 60 years.

Most Zimbabweans are of Bantu origin; 76% belong to various Shona groups (Ndau, Rozwi, Korekore, Karanga, Manyika and Zezuru) occupying the eastern two-thirds of the country, 18% are of Ndebele background (including the Kalanga) living primarily in south-western Zimbabwe, and the remainder are divided between Batonka (2%) of the upper Kariba area, Shangaan or Hlengwe (1%) of the lowveld, Venda (1%) of the far south and European, Asian and Coloured (2%), scattered around the country.

After independence, the European population declined steadily, and in the early 1980s, white emigration averaged 17,000 people annually. The European population has now stabilised at around 100,000. In addition, there are about 25,000 coloureds (people of mixed European and African descent) and 10,000 Asians, mainly of Indian origin.

### The Shona

The Shona people, who make up Zimbabwe's ruling class and over 75% of its population, originated in the Shaba region of Congo (Zaïre) and migrated southward in the 10th and 11th centuries AD. The original range of Shona settlement extended from the Indian Ocean westward to the Kalahari sands and from the Zambezi in the north to the Limpopo in the south. Over the course of the 11th century, the Karanga confederated several previously unaffiliated chiefdoms – probably asa consequence of its wealth in cattle and reputation as a religious force. As this clan accumulated regional and economic power, it began collecting tribute from subordinate groups, which were eventually absorbed. This entity developed into the Rozwi, which built the Great Zimbabwe complex and eventually developed into the modern Shona culture.

### The Ndebele

The Ndebele people, who make up less than 25% of Zimbabwe's population, occupy the area around Bulawayo and Victoria Falls. They're made up mostly of Nguni groups who moved northward on the *mfecane* (the 'crushing' or forced migration) when Shaka, who ruled the relatively minor Zulu tribe, set about creating a Zulu confederacy in the Natal and Transvaal. In fact, the modern-day Ndebele are descended from this group, as well as the many people encountered and absorbed along the route to the north (see History, earlier in this chapter). Initially, these warrior-like peoples exercised control over – and indeed exacted tribute from – the incumbent Shona, who were forced eastward.

Recently, however, Zimbabwe's Ndebele minority has suffered at the hands of the Shona rulers in Harare, including a brutal massacre in Bulawayo during the early days

ZIMBABWE

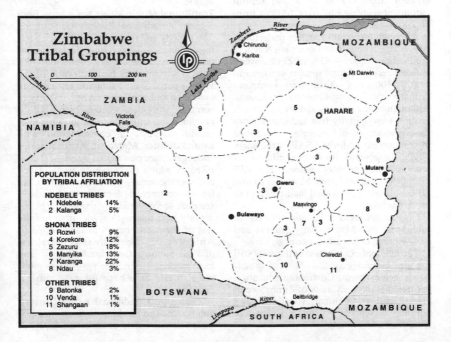

Zimbabwe Tribal Groupings

0    100    200 km

**POPULATION DISTRIBUTION BY TRIBAL AFFILIATION**

NDEBELE TRIBES
1 Ndebele        14%
2 Kalanga        5%

SHONA TRIBES
3 Rozwi          9%
4 Korekore       12%
5 Zezuru         18%
6 Manyika        13%
7 Karanga        22%
8 Ndau           3%

OTHER TRIBES
9 Batonka        2%
10 Venda         1%
11 Shangaan      1%

of independence and subsequent governmental discrimination. Although the amalgamation of the ZANU and ZAPU military forces improved tribal relations, animosities remain between predominantly Shona Harare and mostly Ndebele Bulawayo.

## EDUCATION

Prior to independence in 1980, education was only free and compulsory for students of European background. Schools were segregated, and black African children were required to pay tuition fees. Despite the staggering odds against them, over 40% managed to attend at least one term of schooling. It's not surprising then that the overall literacy rate stayed at around 50% until the new majority government established a universal, integrated and compulsory educational system. Between 1979 and 1992, the number of schools increased from 177 to 1517 and school enrolment increased by over 1000%, from 66,200 to 687,742.

Although education remains underfunded – texts, materials and qualified teachers are in short supply – 93% of Zimbabwean children receive at least some education and nearly 100% of those who complete primary school go on to secondary school. Although both a primary and secondary education were initially free and compulsory for everyone, school fees were reintroduced in conjunction with the ESAP in the early 1990s. In general, however, children attending rural primary schools are still exempt from school fees. Most whites and affluent blacks pay to send their children to private schools.

Classes are held from mid-January to mid-April, mid-May to early August and mid-September to early December.

The national examination authorities still use the Cambridge System of assessing academic achievement. Continuing education is offered at the University of Zimbabwe in Harare and at technical, vocational and agricultural schools in Harare, Bulawayo, Kwe Kwe and Mutare.

## ARTS

Visitors to Zimbabwe are normally surprised by the scope and degree of artistic talent that Zimbabweans seem to take for granted. From even the humblest practical ceramic pot or basket created in a remote village emerges evidence of artistic sensitivity and attention to detail.

Artists are held in high esteem in Zimbabwean society and a greater percentage of artists make a viable living at their trade than in most other countries. In Harare and Bulawayo arts centres seek out those with the greatest talents for special training. One problem for the artists is the abundance of talent and therefore, of competition. This means that pieces that would fetch huge sums elsewhere are scarcely noticed. As a result, however, quality pieces are affordable for most visitors and the work thereby gains international exposure.

## Music

**Traditional Music** Music has always been a given in traditional Zimbabwean culture. The melody and rhythm of repetitive chanting becomes a mesmerising declaration of unity between the singers, while individuality is sustained by harmonisation of the various parts. Shared song has served as an evocation and confirmation of solidarity in common struggles, whether battle with a neighbouring tribe, co-operation on a successful harvest, or confrontation with natural disaster. Moreover, African stories and legends are punctuated by musical choruses in which the audience participates, and social events – weddings, funerals, religious ceremonies, harvests, and births – are each accompanied by unique songs.

Only over the past decade or so has the rest of the world begun to take notice of African music – especially since the release of Paul Simon's *Graceland* album – and most modern Zimbabwean artists use traditional music as a base for new musical direction.

Zimbabwe's traditional musical instruments, though fashioned from natural materials on hand, produce an array of effects. The best known is the marimba, a wooden xylophone that creates tones similar to those in western music and is often used for pieces with strong European influences. The keys of the best marimbas are made from the hard wood of the *mwenje* tree of northern Mozambique, which produces optimum resonance. Sound boxes are normally made of dried gourds.

Another instrument which enjoys popularity among souvenir hunters as well as musicians is the *mbira*, known in English as a thumb piano. It was originally used to accompany historical epics set to music. Although there are several variations, most mbira consist of 22 to 24 narrow iron keys mounted in rows on a wooden sound board. The player plucks the ends of the keys with the thumbs or specially grown thumbnails. An accomplished mbira player is known as a *gwenyambira*.

Percussion instruments include an array of rattles and drums. Rattles can be made of seeds, gourds and even bottle caps. *Hosho* rattles (maracas) are held in the hands, while *magagada*, *majaka*, *madare* (bells) and Ndebele *mahlwayi* rattles are attached to the legs and ankles of dancers. The *ngoma*, a tapered cylindrical drum made from the *mutiti* or lucky bean tree, comes in all sizes. Although the standard skin covering these days is cowhide, the optimum skins are considered to be zebra and *leguaan* (a waterloving lizard). For maximum resonance, drums are treated with beeswax and dried over a flame before a performance.

Probably the oddest percussion instrument ever used in Zimbabwe was the *mujejeje*, the stone bells. Many stones in granite kopjes around the country have exfoliated in such a way that when struck, they'll resound with a lovely bell-like tone (Zimbabwe's first rock music?). Historically, special occasions were held around these stones in order to take advantage of this novel musical opportunity. The most famous of these can be seen today at the Khami Ruins near Bulawayo.

The woodwind group is represented by

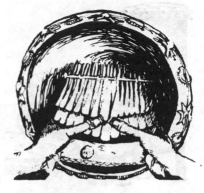

Zimbabwe's traditional music is based on the rhythms and melodies of the *mbira*.

several types of flute, including pan pipes and the *nyanga* or horn, which is, logically, fashioned from animal horn. Although traditional string instruments (mostly bow-shaped like the Shangaan *makweyana*) have been used historically in Zimbabwe, they are rarely played these days.

Kwanongoma College in Bulawayo was established to promote the revival of these traditional instruments, particularly the marimba and mbira. It focuses on training musicians and makers of musical instruments, and fosters popular appreciation for age-old Zimbabwean tones and rhythms.

**Popular Music** In Shona culture, as in so many African cultures, music is incorporated into almost every aspect of life. Through traditional songs, stories are told, games are played and important lessons passed from generation to generation. These songs use the traditional rhythmic structures of Zimbabwean music and are often accompanied by various percussion instruments (such as dried gourd rattles and skin drums), the mbira, marimbas and the nyanga.

In the period between WWII and the start of Zimbabwe's war of independence in the early 1970s, little attention or even interest was afforded by the music industry to these

ZIMBABWE

The *mutandarikwa* drum (left) is commonly found among the Karanga of Masvingo province.

traditional musical forms. Musically, Zimbabwe was inundated with foreign material – from swing in the 1940s through to South African pennywhistle in the 1950s to Otis Redding and other US soul music in the 1960s. Many local groups, including some of today's famous names such as Thomas Mapfumo and Oliver Mtukudzi, began their careers doing Beatles and Elvis covers.

To the great benefit of Zimbabwean music lovers, the war of independence inspired musicians to write, perform and record original protest songs, which were based on traditional Shona sounds, transposed onto western instruments. These songs, known as Chimurenga, form the musical basis for much of Zimbabwean popular music today. Particularly in Harare, there is no shortage of excellent groups performing their own variations on this essentially Zimbabwean style, mostly with lyrics sung in Shona. Some of the best musicians have been snapped up by overseas audiences, but the majority are still in Harare, which is very fortunate indeed for the traveller. The recordings of Thomas Mapfumo, Zimbabwe's best known musician, are sold around the world. The Bhundu Boys with their fast *jit* dance music

went international in 1987. Sadly, the group has been plagued by AIDS and since the band's inception it has lost some of its members to this disease.

Zimbabwe has also over the past decade become a kind of asylum for South African exiles – there are quite a number of musicians hanging around there until the time is right to return to their homeland. This, and the fact that so many foreign bands include Zimbabwe on their tours, combine to make Harare one of Africa's great musical centres. One way to tap into what's current and popular is to take your own radio and tune in to one of the Shona stations which play great local and not-so-local music.

As well as popular Shona and Shangaan styles, there is a strong market for Zaïrois *kwasa kwasa* music, which tends to be based on the rhumba beat. In fact, so admired is the rhumba that Zimbabwean record shops have four categories for African music: local, South African, reggae and rhumba. The general rule is: if it's not obviously local, South African or reggae, you'll find it under rhumba! There's also some great West African music around (under rhumba, of course).

For any sort of African music, try the Pop Shop on the corner of First St and Baker Ave in Harare – the staff are as helpful and enthusiastic as they can be and if you ask them to play something local, they may even dance to it as you listen! Good sources of African music by mail order are Africa Sounds, PO Box UA 553, Harare or Dandemutande (see Further Information later in this section).

**Groups & Musicians** Some of Zimbabwe's better-known music names include the following: Thomas Mapfumo and the Blacks Unlimited, Oliver Mtukudzi, The Four Brothers, New Black Montana (in the Mapfumo genre), Robson Banda and the Black Eagles, Joseph Mutero, Steve Dyer, The Real Sounds of Africa, the Khiami Boys, the Ngwenya Brothers, Leonard Dembo, Black Umfolosi, John Chibudura and the Tembo Brothers.

Bands, however, are constantly breaking up, changing members and changing names, so don't be discouraged if you can't find a group you know of – those helpful and enthusiastic people in the record shop can be a useful source of information. Or just keep your eye out for the posters to get an idea of who's around.

**National Anthem** Until recently, Zimbabwe – like much of Africa – used as its national anthem the hymn of African nationalism *Nkosi Sikilele iAfrica* (God Bless Africa). In 1987, however, a competition was launched to find a unique anthem for the country. It attracted over 1600 entries and it took nine years to select a winner.

## African A Cappella: Black Umfolosi

Zimbabwe's most internationally famous singing group is probably Black Umfolosi, an a cappella ensemble from Bulawayo. The name is derived from the Umfolosi River in South Africa, and the group added 'Black' to emphasise their identity. The eight male members of the group, who hail from Matabeleland, have been singing together since 1982.

Black Umfolosi sing their a cappella pieces in both Ndebele and English, in a style known as *imbube*. Their songs address general human concerns – love, family, God – as well as contemporary problems – wars, apartheid, the environment and AIDS. Their music is fresh and surprising not only for the interesting texts and lyrics, but also for the typically intricate rhythms, unusual harmonies and interspersed clicking, clapping and shouting, which combine to produce a natural, funky and rugged aura.

MARTIN POPE

Black Umfolosi consider their music not just as entertainment or a route to renown, but as a means of reviving Zimbabwean – particularly Ndebele – culture and introducing it abroad. They achieve this not just by singing their songs, but also by performing traditional dances on stage – including such modern additions as the miners' gumboot dance, which usually closes their performances (see photo). For several years now, Black Umfolosi have been collecting funds to build a cultural centre in Bulawayo, to be called the Enkundleni Cultural Centre. This centre serves not only as a performance venue, but also as a training centre for new groups, a children's educational centre, a community events facility and a site for the documentation of African music and dance.

Currently, Black Umfolosi have two CDs on the World Circuit label: *Unity* and *Festival-Umdalo*. A portion of the proceeds from record sales go to the Enkundleni Cultural Centre. Black Umfolosi also offer their services to tourist groups through the Black Umfolosi Performing Arts Project. Their office (☎ (19) 77409; fax 65016) is on the corner of George Silundika St and 3rd Ave in Bulawayo. For further information, write to the Chairperson, Black Umfolosi Project, ZIMFEP, PO Box 673, Bulawayo or fax (19) 65016.

**Norbert Schürer, USA**

That turned out to be *Ngaikomborerwe Nyika Yezimbabwe* (Blessed be the Land of Zimbabwe), which was introduced at the April 1994 Independence Day celebrations.

**Further Information** Fans of Zimbabwean music should contact Paul Novitski at *Dandemutande – a resource for Zimbabwean music and culture* (☎ (1-206) 323 6592; fax 329 9355), 1122 East Pike St, #1163, Seattle, WA 98122-3934, USA. Check out the Web site www.dandemutande.com for lots of good information, pictures and their catalogue. The name means spiderweb, network or complex arrangement, with reference to the intricate weaving of melodic lines in Shona music and 'a nod in passing to the spider-egg casings used as buzzers in Zimbabwean music'. It's self-described as 'a web connecting lovers of Zimbabwean marimba and mbira music and related arts – throughout the world'. There's a calendar of events worldwide and a quarterly magazine with articles on trends, personalities and hints on making and playing traditional Zimbabwean instruments. Annual subscriptions cost US$15/25 inside/outside the USA for the calendar and magazine.

The Zimbabwe Entertainment Directory Web site features all the latest on Harare's music scene. It can be reached through the Web site of The Tube night club at http://thetube.cybergate.co.zw.

Other useful contacts for music fans include:

*International Library of African Music*, Andrew Tracy, Rhodes University, Grahamstown 6140, South Africa (☎ (0461) 318557; fax 24411). This is the world's largest and most comprehensive collection of African ethnomusicological recordings and academic writings, including music from numerous Zimbabwean cultural groups.

*Kunzwana Trust*, Keith Goddard, 3 Maxwell Rd, Groombridge, Harare, Zimbabwe (☎/fax (14) 301519). The aim of this organisation is to help Zimbabwean musicians and instrument makers become commercially self-sufficient. It also sponsors the fabulous annual Houses of Stone music festival in Harare. Write for advance information and specific dates.

*The Kutsinhira Center*, Joel Lindstrom, PO Box 26111, Eugene, OR 97402, USA (☎ (1-503) 461 3442). This is a school for Zimbabwean musical arts, focusing on mbira and marimba.

*Mother Earth*, Stella Chiwashe, PO Box 66513, Kopje, Harare, Zimbabwe (☎/fax (14) 301519). An organisation of female performing artists which sponsors performances and educational workshops, such as the Pasirisangana International Women's Voices Workshop, held in May 1995.

*Ozema Studio*, Joseph Oze Matare, Breisacherstr 60, Basel, CH-4057, Switzerland (☎/fax (61) 692 5705). This school of Zimbabwean musical arts focuses on song and percussion.

*The Rufaro School of Marimba*, Michael and Osha Breez, 161 Dougherty Lane, Friday Harbor, WA 98250, USA (☎ (1-360) 378 6649). A school for Zimbabwean musical arts, also focusing on mbira and marimba.

## Traditional Crafts

Traditional African crafts, though utilitarian, display a degree of art that reflects and reveals ancient traditional values and the spiritual attitude of the culture. Tools and implements are consciously designed to be both functional and aesthetically pleasing. Women in particular have perpetuated characteristically African themes and shapes by integrating them into everyday items, such as pottery, basketry, textiles, and jewellery, while men have focused on woodcarving, iron sculpture and architecture in the context of tool-making and home construction.

**Textiles & Basketry** Even before Arab traders brought cloth from India, Zimbabweans were spinning and weaving garments from wild cotton that grew on the plateau, and making blankets, mats and clothing from strands of the soft and pliable tree bark known as *gudza*. This art is still practised.

The quality of woven baskets in Zimbabwe is phenomenal and the patterns well thought out and beautifully symmetrical. As in many cultures, baskets are used for a variety of purposes, from trapping fish underwater to storing food and belongings. They are common almost everywhere.

A number of materials, such as *imizi* grass, reeds, *ilala* palm, and sisal, are used, and the characteristic earth-tone dyes are derived from a variety of tree barks. The largest baskets, which typically contain well over a cubic metre, are a favourite with tourists who take them home to use as laundry baskets.

More recently, Zimbabwean women have proven highly skilful at crocheting, batik, tie-dyeing and clothing design. Although these aren't traditional Zimbabwean arts, these inexpensive creations are typically of optimum quality.

**Pottery** Ceramics, another traditionally female activity in Zimbabwe, has played an essential role in the development of its cultures. Pots were used for storage, cooking, serving, carrying, preparing curdled milk and even the brewing of yeast beer. While their various shapes have always been undoubtedly practical, their understated colours and intricate but unpretentious designs make Zimbabwean pottery an enduring art form.

**Carving** Although souvenir hunters will be tempted by row upon row of identical soapstone elephants and hippos and rough-hewn wooden giraffes and lions in kitsch gift shops and public squares, there's much more to Zimbabwe's carving heritage than such assembly-line productions would suggest. Traditionally, such tools as hoes, axe handles, ladles, bowls, and *umncwado* (penis sheaths) were all carved from wood in simplistic and practical designs. Spear, knobkerrie and dagger handles were decoratively rendered and shields were mounted on a carved wooden frame. Even small canoes were typically hewn out of a single bit of wood.

Carved *mutsago* or *umqamelo* (Shona and Ndebele words for headrest) were considered emblematic of family responsibility, and headrests of distant ancestors were passed down male lines and called upon to evoke ceremonially the spirits of earlier owners. Various theories have arisen about the extent of their early use – whether for afternoon rests, protection of elaborate coiffures, or as concessions to the comfort of the elderly. Now, their worth lies primarily in their antique or heirloom value.

Wooden stools, whose expertly intricate decorations reach their highest level in the Batonka culture of western Lake Kariba, are carved from a single piece of wood. Historically, only men were allowed to sit on them and male heads of household used them as a 'throne' from which to oversee family affairs.

Divining devices or *hakata* are carved from bone, wood or ivory and are used in traditional rural areas to forecast future events, determine guilt and communicate with ancestors. There are four tablets in a set: *chirume*, which has a male value; *kwami*, with a female value; *nhokwara*, with 35 triangular cuts representing good luck; and *chitokwadzima*, which represents bad luck and bears the image of a crocodile. Interpretations are made by a reader based on the configuration of the tablets after being thrown.

### Literature

Prior to the 1960s, most of Zimbabwe's written literature was produced by the white sector of the population. Popular novelists like Cynthia Stockley and Gertrude Page wrote simplistic but well-received novels during the early part of the century. The first work to express scepticism of Rhodesia's social structure was *The Bay Tree Country* penned by Arthur Cripps, a British-born poet and missionary, published in 1913. In the same vein, in 1950, Doris Lessing produced the very successful *The Grass is Singing*.

Although both Shona and Ndebele oral traditions had perpetuated a large body of stories, legends, songs and poetry, the first written works by black authors didn't appear in print until the publication (in Shona) of *Feso* by S Mutswairo in 1956. The first published Ndebele novel was *Umthawakazi* by PS Mahlangu, which appeared in 1957.

Subsequent works by both groups fall mainly into two categories: those dealing with pre-colonial traditions, myths and folk tales and those focusing on the social and political experiences of black Africans under a white regime. Although numerous protest pieces were written during the following 10 years, the first serious treatise on the topic was Stanlake Samkange's *On Trial for my Country* published in 1966.

However, Zimbabwean independence in 1980 ended oppression-inspired literature. Although some axe-grinding continues, most independence-era literature has focused on the liberation effort and the struggles to build a new society. In 1992, the Commonwealth Prize for Literature went to Zimbabwean writer Shimmer Chinodya for *Harvest of Thorns*, his epic novel of the Second Chimurenga. Another internationally renowned Zimbabwean writer is Chenjerai Hove, who authored the war-inspired *Bones*, the tragic *Shadows*, and the rather humorous *Shebeen Tales*.

Thanks to increasing literacy rates, better education and higher wages over the past decade, Zimbabwean literature is enjoying a boom. New novels, nonfiction and poetry titles in English, Shona and Ndebele are appearing frequently and are being studied as serious literature, as evidenced by the University of Zimbabwe offering a university degree in Shona literature.

For information on other titles and players, see Books in the Zimbabwe Facts for the Visitor chapter.

## Shona Sculpture

Although it's a relatively recent addition to Zimbabwe's cultural arts – it has no functional or ceremonial value and therefore wasn't significant in traditional society – Shona sculpture has garnered most of the laurels as far as international recognition is concerned. It isn't simply considered great African art but great art in the broadest sense.

Although the movement is known as Shona sculpture, the Shona tribe has no exclusive rights to the genre and smaller tribal groups are participating as well. Today's sculpture has been evolving over the past 30

years or so, a product of welding African themes and ideas with European artistic training.

African folklore provides themes for a majority of the work and pieces are populated by stylised animals, gods, spirits, ancestors and totems as well as deeply emotional humans heavily involved in life. One recurring theme is the metamorphosis of man into beast, the prescribed punishment for violation of certain social interdictions – such as making a meal of one's totem animal. Most of the work is superb.

Four of the major practitioners are considered to be among the world's greatest sculptors. The late John Takawira, highly acclaimed in Europe, was best known for his facility with a number of forms, sizes and themes.

Minimalist Nicholas Mukomberanwa, on the other hand, tends to utilise consistently bulky masses while striving to simplify the designs into only their essential components. The third, Henry Munyaradzi, learned his art at the Tengenenge colony in northern Zimbabwe. Although his pleasant and instantly recognisable works seem reminiscent of the cubist tradition and he's been highly successful, his work risks becoming repetitious.

Bernard Matemera, Tengenenge's best known artist, experiments with deliberately surreal dimensions and forms, and tests responses. In 1986, Matemara won a major international award in India. Other acclaimed sculptors include Joram Mariga, Sylvester Mubayi and Joseph Ndandarika.

In addition to these, Zimbabwe has hundreds of exceptionally talented sculptors, many at schools, art centres, and sculpture communities around the country.

## Architecture

Zimbabwe's architectural greatness lies largely in its past. The ancient Zimbabweans who designed and constructed the great stone cities of Khami, Great Zimbabwe and other Rozwi sites lacked the western inclination to subdue nature, but instead integrated it into their work in a very practical (and pleasantly labour-saving) manner. Although many smaller dwellings occupied foundations of earth and stone, the larger 'great stone houses' rambled over the natural relief and integrated large boulders and other features into their walls and interior spaces. While earlier structures seem to have been primarily utilitarian, time and practice honed the skills of early builders and their later efforts include some very fine work. This progress can be most readily traced in the overlapping walls of the Great Enclosure at Great Zimbabwe, which clearly reveal the increasing proficiency of the builders as they worked their way around the gracefully curved walls.

In modern Zimbabwe, little emphasis has been placed on architecture and, apart from the work of a few inspired colonials and some innovative safari lodges, structures are mostly functional and travellers may be reminded of Kansas or parts of Queensland. Interesting exceptions include the relatively ornate Douslin House in Bulawayo, several government buildings in Harare and the historic districts of Shurugwi and Kwe Kwe. In rural areas, the main construction components are mud and thatch, and several safari lodges have expanded on that theme.

The most successful is probably The Lodge at Victoria Falls, which surely ranks among the loveliest buildings in Africa. Here, local materials and rustic open-plan construction have provided natural air conditioning and a mirror of the expansive spaces beyond the eaves. Other superb lodges include the Matobo Hills Lodge, which enhances a spectacular rocky landscape in the Matobo, near Bulawayo.

## Film

To date, the most successful film to come out of Zimbabwe is *Flame*, by British director Ingrid Sinclair. This mainly donor-funded, politically sensitive film surprised everyone by winning numerous international awards, including Best Film at the Nestor Almendros International Human Rights Film Festival and the Best Actress, Best Director and OAU Special Award for Best Film at the Southern African Film Festival in Harare. The story follows the tale of Florence and Nyasha, alias Flame and Liberty, who travel to Mozambique to join the Zimbabwean liberation struggle under the charismatic Comrade Danger. In addition to the daily horrors of war, the women are subjected to discrimination, rape and other disillusioning experiences that have been written out of the official history of the Second Chimurenga. The Zimbabwean government has not reacted favourably, but their threats to ban it made it all the more popular. To quote Ms Sinclair, 'What they wanted was a glorious epic, not the story I wanted to tell'.

*Jit*, directed by Michael Raeburn, is a romantic comedy about a young man's travels in search of fame, fortune and the woman of his dreams. The young man, called UK by his friends because they're sure he'll go far, falls in love with a woman named Sofi whose current boyfriend is a gangster and whose father wants an especially high bride price for his prize of a daughter. The story unfolds to the beat of some of Zimbabwe's finest musicians.

*Everyone's Child*, directed by Tsitsi Dangarembga (author of the fabulous autobiographical book *Nervous Conditions* and Zimbabwe's first female director), is the story of two children who are catapulted into the world of adult responsibility when their family is struck by AIDS.

Another widely lauded film with a social message is *Neria*, the story of a successful Zimbabwean family who worked their way into the good life in Harare. When the man of the family is tragically killed, his wife Neria and her children must endure a nightmare struggle against greedy relations back in her home village. Its aim is to educate Zimbabwean women regarding their legal rights in a society currently in transition between older traditional life and progressive modern ways. The last three of these films (and other titles dealing with social issues) are available from DSR Inc, 9111 Guilford Rd, Columbia, MD 21046 USA

(☎ (1-301) 490 3500; fax 490 4146; <dsr@us.net>).

## Theatre

Western and African theatre troupes in both Harare and Bulawayo now present a range of productions for theatre-goers. Among the finest is the African-oriented Amakhosi Theatre in Bulawayo, which performs both national and international productions at the Township Square Cultural Centre (☎/fax (19) 76673) in Bulawayo. In Harare, the best venue is Gallery Delta (☎ (14) 792135), which stages both European and African productions.

## RELIGION
## Christianity

Between 40 and 50% of Zimbabweans belong to Christian churches, but their belief system is characterised more by a hybrid of Christian and traditional beliefs than by dogmatic Christianity.

In 1859, Reverend Robert Moffat of the London Missionary Society established Zimbabwe's first Christian mission at Inyati near Bulawayo. He was followed by black African representatives of the Dutch Reformed Church from South Africa and the Jesuits who set up their headquarters at Lobengula's Kraal in Matabeleland in 1880. Anglicans and Methodists came later. All the Protestant groups set up schools, agricultural assistance and medical facilities.

Many Zimbabwean Christians identify with some Protestant sect (the result of numerous early missions zealously competing for converts) but the Roman Catholic church, with 800,000 members in Zimbabwe, claims more adherents than any of the Protestant denominations, which include Methodist, Salvation Army, Seventh-Day Adventist, Dutch Reformed, Presbyterian, Congregational, Episcopalian, North American fundamentalist groups and a number of African splinter organisations.

Although the Portuguese first brought Catholicism to Zimbabwe in 1561, it wasn't a recognised presence until 1890 and only became significant in the 1950s. In 1972, the church established the Catholic Commission for Justice & Peace to monitor human rights violations in the country and promote peace and justice. Although it was most active during the Second Chimurenga, it has continued its work to the present day. Another organisation, the Catholic Development Commission, is working to upgrade socioeconomic conditions in rural areas. The church also operates a number of private schools in Namibia.

## Mwari Worship

The majority of Zimbabweans profess traditional religious beliefs as well as those introduced by Europeans. The Mwari Cult, a monotheistic animist belief system which entails ancestor worship and spiritual proxy and intercession, has predominated at least since the height of Great Zimbabwe. Because of its rather clandestine nature, however, little is actually known about the scope of the cult's current influence.

Of the numerous Mwari cave shrines evident in Zimbabwe, only the Matonjeni grouping near Bulawayo – Njelele and Wirarani in the Matobo and Dula near Esigodini – are thought to be still active. These shrines remain officially off limits to outsiders.

The original concept of Mwari, the supreme deity, was probably brought by southward migrating Bantu groups who arrived in Zimbabwe during the 14th century. The new religion spread quickly across southern Africa and took a firm hold. In fact, it was one of the few elements of the Rozwi Empire that survived the Nguni invasions of the early 19th century, and the conquering Ndebele were themselves absorbed into the Rozwi religion. Even Christianity could not displace it and converts to European sects took it that Mwari and the Christian God were one and the same. In Shona, the Christian God is still known as Mwari.

Mwari theology is quite simple. Occasionally referred to as Musiki (Creator), Musikavanhu (Origin of Man), or Nyadenga (Father of the Skies), Mwari is the unknowable supreme being. He speaks to his human subjects (or victims) through The Voice of Mwari, a cave-dwelling oracle who is most often female. The oracle not only serves as a vehicle for divine will, but also as intercessor between the spirits, the god and the people, especially in cases of natural disaster or outside aggression, both considered deserved punishments for religious infractions. It was the oracle, in fact, who received the go-ahead to begin the First Chimurenga in 1896.

## Midzimu, Mhondoro & Mambo

Although Mwari is the pre-eminent god, followers also believe that spirits of their ancestors or *midzimu*, all the way back to the *tateguru* (the common ancestors who lived at some hazy point in the distant past and ultimately deliver messages to Mwari), continue to inhabit the human world. These spirits, whose afterlife status is determined by the length of time since their deaths, retain a great deal of influence over the physical world. A person with happy midzimu will be kept out of harm's way while those whose forbears are dissatisfied may meet with all sorts of misfortune.

When that happens, a medium is contacted and the disgruntled ancestor is identified. Normally, a *bira* or family gathering is held in which the unhappy mudzimu (singular form of midzimu) is invited to enter the victim's body, state the complaint and make suggestions for remedying the problem. If all goes well, the victim becomes the family *svikiro* or medium for the now appeased mudzimu.

The *mhondoro* ('lions' in Shona) operate under much the same principle as the midzimu but rather than confining attentions to their descendants, the mhondoro are often territorial spirits and can affect entire communities of people. When a problem such as a plague or drought strikes, these are the spirits who must be consulted.

Svikiros of individual mhondoro spirits may appear erratically through many generations (one such incarnation is the Mutota of the Mavuradonha mountains, who currently inhabits a Mozambican who received his calling in a dream). Due to their ferocity and fearlessness, they are normally associated with a lion character, hence their name, and the svikiro of a mhondoro takes on the aspect of a lion. Prior to the fall of Rozwi, the Rozwi *mambo* or king most often served as the svikiro. His growled directives were incoherent to the lay populace but readily interpreted by the Mwari priesthood.

In the early 19th century, one mambo fell afoul of Mwari himself, which was a serious infraction for someone in his position. Before long, the offended god made known to the priests that Rozwi was doomed and would soon fall at the hands of outsiders. Soon thereafter, the Nguni invasions began.

## LANGUAGE

The official language of Zimbabwe – used in government, legal and business proceedings – is English, but it is a first language for only about 2% of the population. The rest of the people are native speakers of a Bantu language, the two most prominent of which are Shona, spoken by 76% of the population, and Ndebele, the language of the Ndebele people, spoken by 18%.

Shona, which is actually an amalgamation of several Bantu languages, is spoken in the central and eastern parts of the country. The 'high' dialect and the one used in broadcasts and other media is Zezuru which is indigenous to the Harare area.

Ndebele is spoken primarily in Matabeleland in the western and south-western parts of Zimbabwe. It is derived from the Zulu group of languages and is not mutually intelligible with Shona.

Another dialect, Chilapalapa, is actually a pidgin version of Ndebele, English, Shona, and Afrikaans, among other things, and is used primarily as a lingua franca for communication between employers and employees. It isn't overly laden with niceties and it's a safe bet that Zimbabweans would prefer to hear straight English than this aberration.

## Pronunciation

Since both Shona and Ndebele were first written down by phonetic English transliteration, most letters are pronounced as they would be in English. The major exceptions are the Ndebele 'clicks': drawing of the tongue away from the front teeth (dental), slapping it on the roof of the mouth (palatal) or drawing it quickly sideways from the right upper gum (lateral). Each of these comes in four different varieties: voiced, aspirated, nasal, and aspirated nasal. For interest only – non-native speakers rarely get the hang of this – the following table outlines standard transliterations of each of these sounds:

|         | voiced | aspirated | nasal | aspirated nasal |
|---------|--------|-----------|-------|-----------------|
| **dental**  | gc | ch | nc | ngc |
| **palatal** | gq | hn | qn | ngq |
| **lateral** | gx | xh | nx | ngx |

Other Ndebele differences of note include:

**b**   pronounced implosively

**m**   pronounced as a little hum when placed before a word-initial consonant

**n**   pronounced as a hum with an 'n' sound when placed before a word-initial consonant

**o**   as the 'aw' in 'law'

**th**   aspirated like the 't' in 'tarmac'

Shona differences of note are:

**dya**   try pronouncing 'jga' in as near to one syllable as possible

**m, n**   same as in Ndebele when placed before a word-initial consonant

**sv**   similar to the Chinese (Pinyin) 'x'. If that's not familiar, say 's' with your whole tongue touching the roof of your mouth.

**tya**   say 'chka' quickly

**zv**   similar to 'sv' but say 'z' instead of 's'

Although most urban Zimbabweans have at least a little knowledge of English, many rural dwellers' English vocabulary is very limited, so it may help to know a few pleasantries in the local lingo. Even those Zimbabweans who speak English well will normally be pleasantly surprised to hear a foreigner make an attempt to speak a few words of Shona or Ndebele.

If two translations are given for the same word or expression, the first is used when speaking with one person, the second with more than one.

## Zimbabwean English

In addition to the indigenous languages, Zimbabweans have some unique ways of expressing themselves in English. Some words have been adopted from Afrikaans, Shona or Ndebele, some are common words adapted to local usage, and others are entirely new. The following is a rundown of several you can expect to encounter:

*ablutions block* – a building which contains toilets, baths, showers and washing up areas. It's also known as an 'amenities block'.

*baas* – boss, subservient address reserved mainly for white males

*babalass* – a hangover; those who indulge in *chibuku* are particularly vulnerable

*bakkie* (pronounced bucky) – utility or pick-up truck

*bashas* or *bashers* – thatched A-frame chalets

*bazaar* – inexpensive department store

*bhundu* – the bush, tules, sticks, boonies, ie wilderness

*biltong* – dried and salted jerked meat that can be made from just about anything from eland or ostrich to mutton or beef

*bioscope* – a cinema

*blair toilet* – high-tech outdoor toilet which was developed in Zimbabwe and used in rural areas. It has an odd spiral long-drop with a black-painted interior to drive flies up air vents toward daylight where they are trapped in a mesh just short of freedom.

continued on page 149

| | **Shona** | **Ndebele** |
|---|---|---|
| **Greetings & Civilities** | | |
| Hello. (initial) | Mhoro/Mhoroi. | Sawubona/Salibonani. |
| Hello. (reply) | Ahoi. | Yebo. |
| How are you? | Makadii/Makadi-ni? | Linjani/Kunjani? |
| I'm well. | Ndiripo. | Sikona. |
| Thank you. | Ndatenda/Masvita. | Siyabonga kakulu. |
| Welcome. | Titambire. | Siyalemukela. |
| Good morning. | Mangwanani. | Livukenjani. |
| Good afternoon. | Masikati. | Litshonile. |
| Good evening. | Manheru. | Litshone njani. |
| Goodbye. (person staying) | Chisarai zvakanaka. | Lisalekuhle. |
| Goodbye. (person leaving) | Fambai zvakanaka. | Uhambe kuhle. |
| Please. | Ndapota. | Uxolo. |
| Excuse me. | Pamsoro/ipindeo. | Ngicela ukwedlula. |
| Sorry/pardon. | Pamsoro. | Ngiyaxolisa. |
| Do you speak English? | Unodziva kutawura chirungu? | Uyakwazi ukukuluma isilungu? |

| | | |
|---|---|---|
| **Useful Words & Phrases** | | |
| Yes/No. | Ehe/Aiw. | Yebo/Hayi. |
| What is your name? | Unonzi ani zita rako? | Ibizo lakho ngubani? |
| My name is ... | Ndini ... | Elami igama ngingu ... |
| I'm from ... | Ndinobva ku ... | Ngivela e ... |
| sir/madam | changamire/mudzimai | umnimzana/inkosikazi |
| men/women | varume/vakadz | amadoda/abafazi |
| boy/girl | mukomana/musikana | umfana/inkazana |
| friend | shamwari | mngane |
| Where is the station? | Chiteshi chiri kupi? | Singapi isiteshi? |
| When does the ... leave? | ... richaynda rihni? | Izawuhamba nini ...? |
| bus | ehazi | bhasi |
| train | chitima | isitimela |
| car | motokari | imoto |
| Where is the ...? | Arikupi ...? | Ungaphi ...? |
| Go straight | Ufambe dzwa. | Uhambe uqonde nta. |
| Turn left. | Bvoshikwe. | Ukone kwesobuxele. |
| Turn right. | Bvushikwe. | Ukone kwesokudla. |
| far | kure | katshana |
| near | paduze | duze |
| What time is it? | Dzavanguvai? | Yisikhati bani? |
| today | nhas | lamhla |
| tomorrow | mangwana | kusasa |
| yesterday | nezuro | izolo |
| market/shop | musika/chitoro | imakethe/isitolo |
| I'd like ... | Ndinoda ... | Ngicela ... |
| How much? | I marii? | Yimalini? |

ZIMBABWE

|  | Shona | Ndebele |
|---|---|---|
| **Useful Words & Phrases,** *continued* | | |
| small/large | diki/guru | okuncane/ncinyane |
| tampon | kubvara ropa reshikadzi | umuciko wesifazana |

**Food & Drink**

|  | Shona | Ndebele |
|---|---|---|
| beef | mombe | nkomo |
| beer | doro/whawha | utshwala |
| bread | chingwa | isinkwa |
| butter | bhat | ibatha |
| chicken | huku | nkukhu |
| coffee | kofi | ikofi |
| eggs | mazai | amaqanda |
| fish | hove | ininhlanzi |
| fruit | michero | izithelo |
| ground nuts | nzungu | amazambane |
| maize | chibage | umbila |
| maize porridge (grits) | sadza | sadza |
| meat | nyama | inyama |
| milk | mukaka | ucago |
| potatoes | mbatatisi | amagwili |
| salt | muny | isaudo |
| sugar | shuga | ushukela |
| tea | ti | itiye |
| vegetables | muriwo | imbhida |
| water | mvura | amanzi |

**Animals**

|  | Shona | Ndebele |
|---|---|---|
| baboon | gudo | ndwangu |
| buffalo | nyati | nyathi |
| dog | imbwa | nja |
| elephant | nzou | ndhlovu |
| giraffe | twiza | ntundla |
| goat | mbudzi | mbuzi |
| hippopotamus | mvuu | mvubu |
| horse | bhiza | ibhiza |
| hyaena | bere | mpisi |
| impala | mhara | mpala |
| leopard | mbada | ngwe |
| lion | shumbai | silwane |
| monkey | bveni | nkawu |
| rabbit | tsuro | mvundla |
| rhinoceros | chipembere | ubhejane |
| warthog | njiri | ungulube yeganga |
| zebra | mbiz | ndube |

ZIMBABWE

|  | Shona | Ndebele |
|---|---|---|
| **Days of the Week** | | |
| Sunday | *svondo* | *ngesonto* |
| Monday | *muvhuro* | *umbulo* |
| Tuesday | *chipiri* | *olwesibili* |
| Wednesday | *chitatu* | *ngolwesithathu* |
| Thursday | *china* | *ngolwesine* |
| Friday | *chishanu* | *ngolwesihlanu* |
| Saturday | *mugovera* | *ngesabatha* |
| **Numbers** | | |
| 1 | *potsi* | *okukodwa* |
| 2 | *piri* | *okubili* |
| 3 | *tatu* | *okutathu* |
| 4 | *ina* | *okune* |
| 5 | *shanu* | *okuyisihlanu* |
| 6 | *tanhatu* | *okuyisithupha* |
| 7 | *nomwe* | *okuyisikhombisa* |
| 8 | *tsere* | *okuyisitshiyangalo mbila* |
| 9 | *pfumbamwe* | *okuyisitshiyangalo lunye* |
| 10 | *gumi* | *okuli tshuml* |
| 50 | *makumi mashanu emadhora* | *amathumi-mahlanu* |
| 100 | *makumi mashanu epondho* | *amathumi-ahkulu* |
| 1000 | *churu chemadhora* | *amakulu-amabili* |
| 1 million | *one million* | *one million* |
| **Emergencies** | | |
| Help! | *Ruphatshiro!* | *Akeli ncede!* |
| Call a doctor. | *Taidza patshirai na doctor.* | *Biza udokotela.* |
| Call the police. | *Taidza mapurisa patshirai.* | *Biza amapolisa.* |
| Leave me alone. | *Ndiregerei ndonga.* | *Akelingixolele.* |
| I'm lost. | *Ndara tsika.* | *Sengilahlekile/Ngiduhile.* |

*continued from page 146*

*boerewors* – a spicy Afrikaner sausage which ranges from the consistency of mince meat to solid and bricklike. No braai could happen without it.

*braai* – a barbecue which normally includes several varieties of meat grilled on a braai stand or pit. It's a southern African institution, particularly among whites.

*buppies* – black yuppies

*chibuku* – the 'beer of good cheer'. Both inexpensive and revolting, this grain and yeast concoction is stored in vats and served up in buckets, or available in takeaway cartons (when it's known locally as shake-shake) or plastic bottles called *scuds*.

*Club Special shandy* – a nonalcoholic drink made from lemonade, ginger beer and Mazowe orange

*Comrade* (or *Cde*) – a Marxist title used mainly by the media when referring to black Zimbabwean citizens, especially government officials

*dam* – what some English speakers call a reservoir

*dam wall* – what some English speakers call a dam

*daga hut* – a traditional African round house consisting of a wooden frame covered with mud and manure walls reinforced with straw, also known as 'pole and daga hut'

*dagga* (pronounced dakha) – 'grass', marijuana

*donkey boiler* – it may sound cruel but it has nothing to do with donkeys. It's an elevated watertank positioned over a wood fire and used to heat water. (Also known as a Rhodesian boiler, which may also seem a bit cruel.)

*drift* – a river ford; most are normally dry

*Dutchman* – term of abuse for a white of Afrikaner descent. Offence is always taken.

*flotty* – a hat for canoe safaris, with a chinstrap and a bit of cork in a zippered pocket so that it floats in case of a capsize

*gap it* – to 'split' in the sense of making a quick exit; alternatively, 'take the gap' – what Rhodeys did who 'escaped' to South Africa after Zimbabwean independence

*guti* – dank and drizzly weather that afflicts the Eastern Highlands in the winter

*Izzit?* – rhetorical question which most closely translates as 'Really?' and is used without regard to gender, person, or number of the subject. Therefore, it could mean 'Is it?', 'Are you?', 'Is he?', 'Are they?', 'Is she?', 'Are we?' etc.

*jesse* – dense thorn scrub normally impenetrable to humans

*just now* – reference to some time in the future but intended to imply some degree of imminence. It could be half an hour from now or two days from now, that is at the appropriate time.

*kaffir* – highly derogatory reference to a black person

*kapenta* – *Limnothrissa mioda*, a salty small fry caught in Lake Kariba

*kloof* – a ravine or small valley

*koeksesters* – small doughnuts dripping in honey, very gooey and figure-enhancing

*kopje* (pronounced coppie) – this translates from Afrikaans as 'little hill'. In Zimbabwe, any old heap of rocks qualifies.

*kraal* – Afrikaans version of the Portuguese *curral*. It can refer to an enclosure for livestock or fortified village of daga huts.

*lekker* (pronounced lakker) – very good, tasty

*location* – another word for township, but used more in Namibia and South Africa than Zimbabwe

*make a plan* – to 'sort things out'; can refer to anything from working out a complicated procedure to circumventing bureaucracy

*Malawi shandy* – nonalcoholic drink made from ginger beer, Angostura bitters, orange or lemon slices, soda and ice

*Mazowe orange* – sweet orange cordial made from citrus grown in the Mazowe area. It's a Zimbabwe staple.

*mielie pap* – maize porridge; a black African staple

*mopane worms* – the caterpillar of the moth *Gonimbrasiabelina*; these lovely larval delicacies are available in mopane trees and some Zimbabwe markets

*murunge* – this is actually a Shona word referring to a white European

*não faz mal* – Portuguese expression meaning, literally, 'it doesn't make bad', used in Zimbabwe as 'no problem'

*now now* – definitely not now but sometime sooner than 'just now'

*peg* – milepost

*peri-peri* – ultra-hot pepper-based sauce that usurps the flavour of your *sadza ne nyama* (mielie pap with meat relish)

*PK* – the WC, the toilet

*pronking* – gleeful leaping by several species of antelope, apparently for fun

*Rhodey* – a normally derogatory term for a white Zimbabwean. It's roughly the equivalent of 'ocker' or 'redneck' in Australia and the US.

*robot* – no, not R2-D2, just a traffic light.

*rock shandy* – a wonderful nonalcoholic concoction made of lemonade, soda water and angostura bitters. In a variation known as a 'sneaky puff adder', vodka replaces the soda water.

*rondavel* – a round, African-style hut

*rooibos* – 'red bush' in Afrikaans; a herbal tea reputed to have therapeutic qualities

*rusks* – solid bits of biscuit-like bread which are made edible by immersion in coffee or tea

*scuds* – two-litre plastic bottles of chibuku

*Shake-shake* – Chibuku sold in waxed cardboard cartons

*Shame!* – half-hearted expression of commiseration

*shebeen* – an illegal drinking establishment cum brothel; nonregulars are unwelcome without an invitation

*sjambok* – whip

*Snice!* – equivalent of Wow!

*spruit* – a little streambed, which rarely contains any water

*squaredavel* – see under rondavel, and work out the rest

*Sus!* – the opposite of *snice*, roughly the equivalent of 'yuck'

*tackies* – trainers, tennis shoes, gym shoes

*TAB* – 'That's Africa, baby.' Standard utterance when things are AFU, that is, not going according to plan.

*TIZ* – 'This is Zimbabwe', same connotation as TAB

*Tonkies* – derogatory word for members of the Tonga tribe, or for anyone/thing basic, simple, or 'gone bush'

*township* – high-density black residential area outside a central city or town

*toxic sludge* – a disgusting mixed drink comprised of tequila or vodka combined with brandy or schnapps and hot cherry jelly (that's jello for Americans)

*tsotsis* – hoodlums, thieves

*TWOGs* – acronym for Third World groupies, used by white Zimbabweans in reference to foreigners who travel to underdeveloped countries and consciously sink to the lowest level of local society

*van der Merwe* – archetypal Boer country bumpkin who is the butt of jokes throughout southern Africa

*veld* – open grassland, normally in plateau regions. One variation, 'bushveld', has the grassland replaced with thorn scrub.

*veldskoens* or *vellies* – comfortable bush shoes of soft leather, like moccasins

*vlei* – any low open landscape, sometimes marshy

*Ziko ndaba* – Zimbabwean version of the Swahili *Hakuna matata*, has the same meaning as *não faz mal* (see earlier)

# Facts for the Visitor

## PLANNING

### When to Go

Generally, the dry winter months (May to October) are the most comfortable for travelling, but you'll miss the lovely green landscapes that characterise the hotter, wetter summer season (November to April). In the winter, daytime temperatures are optimum, but at night they can drop below freezing. Summer daytime temperatures can climb to the mid-30s Celsius, but may be tempered by afternoon thunderstorms.

Winter is also the best season for wildlife viewing because the animals tend to congregate close to water holes and are easily observed. In the summer, the presence of water allows them to spread over a wider area, making viewing less predictable.

National parks and tourist sites are most crowded during South African school holidays, so if you want to avoid the throngs and find accommodation, don't travel between mid-April and mid-May or from mid-July to mid-September. There's a smaller rush during Namibian school holidays in December and early January. For these months, national parks accommodation must be booked well in advance. A good month for avoiding the worst crowds is June, which is normally the coolest and quietest month.

### Maps

Plans of larger towns are available at Publicity Associations (municipal tourist offices), but maps of other towns are more difficult to come by. Some Publicity Associations sell photocopied national parks maps (most of which were produced by Shell Oil in the 1960s). If you're spending time in Harare, you may want to look for the detailed *Greater Harare Street Guide*, an atlas of large-scale maps of all the suburbs. It was once sold by the Harare Publicity Association, but now appears to be out of print. You may be able to find a copy somewhere. A similar Bulawayo atlas remains in print and is sold by the Bulawayo Publicity Association.

The best map is *Zimbabwe Carte Générale*, 1:1,000,000, published by the French Institut Géographique Nationale. A close second is International Travel Maps *Zimbabwe* at 1:1,250,000. Another decent map is *Zimbabwe Relief*, 1:1,000,000, published by the Surveyor General ($\pi$ (14) 794545) in Electra House on Samora Machel Ave, Harare, and sold for US$5. All three of these depict relief using colour and cover railroads, mines, rural missions, hydrography and roads, right down to minor country tracks.

The Surveyor General also sells 1:50,000 ordnance survey topographic maps, covering the entire country, for US$2.50 per sheet, and a range of thematic maps. These include some national parks maps ranging from US$2 to US$4 and a large-scale Harare street plan at 1:15,000 for US$2.50. The salesperson may ask to check your ID when purchasing maps but usually they only want your name and home address on the chit. For a catalogue, write to PO Box 8099, Causeway, Harare, Zimbabwe.

Occasionally, you'll find the updated version (ie with town-name changes) of the old Shell Oil maps. On one side is a fairly good road map of the country; the reverse side includes larger scale insets of areas of tourist interest. An even better map (which nevertheless does contain a few printing oddities) is the Automobile Association's *AA Tourist Map of Zimbabwe* at a scale of 1:1,800,000. The reverse side has insets of the most popular national parks. It's available at tourist shops or directly through the AA (see under Useful Organisations in this chapter) for less than US$2.

Finally, there's the *Mini-map of Zimbabwe* published in South Africa by Map Studio. This compact little map depicts the country at a scale of 1:2,000,000, and includes inset maps of national parks and street plans of Harare and Bulawayo. It costs around US$4, but is unfortunately hard to find in Zimbabwe itself. To order, contact the publisher directly: Map Studio, PO Box 624, Wynberg 2012, South Africa (☎ (011) 444 9473).

A decent road map covering the entire region is Michelin's map 955 – *Central & Southern Africa, & Madagascar*. It's available internationally.

## HIGHLIGHTS
Zimbabwe has a lot to offer and to enjoy it thoroughly requires more time than most travellers allow. If you're rushed, you may want to include some of the sites and experiences described in the highlights table on the following page, which provides a sampling of Zimbabwe's many attractions.

## SUGGESTED ITINERARIES
### Low-Budget Tour
This option includes low-cost options which can be reached on public transport or inexpensive tours, with budget accommodation available. Some of these are accessible by overnight train, allowing you to avoid additional days travelling between attractions.

1. Harare (two days)
2. Hippo Pools (three days)
3. Drifters, near Mutare (two days)
4. Vumba Botanical Reserve (two days)
5. Great Zimbabwe (one day)
6. Mopane Park Farm in Kwe Kwe (two days)
7. Bulawayo, with day tour to Matobo National Park (two days)
8. Hwange National Park, with two game drives (two days)
9. Victoria Falls (three days)

### Hikers Tour
This option is for those who love walking. Most of these places are accessible by public transport, but may require adding extra days in case of uncertainties. Alternatively, contact one of the companies listed under Tours in the Zimbabwe Getting Around chapter and book a walking expedition

through one or several of the country's wildlife reserves.

1. Harare, with a day trip to Domboshawa and Ngomakurira (two days)
2. Mavuradonha Wilderness – access is by private vehicle only (three days)
3. Mana Pools – access is by private vehicle only (three days)
4. Nyanga National Park – climb Mt Nyangani (one day) or walk from Mt Nyangani to Honde Valley (four days)
5. Vumba Botanical Reserve (one day)
6. Chimanimani National Park (three days)
7. Matobo National Park (two days)
8. Victoria Falls (two days)

### Activities Tour
This option includes some of the increasingly popular outdoor activities available, particularly around Victoria Falls.

1. Harare (two days)
2. Hippo Pools – wildlife walks and excursions (two days)
3. Canoe trip on the middle Zambezi (trips run from two to 10 days)
4. Horse-riding on Mopane Park Farm near Kwe Kwe (two days)
5. Matobo National Park – day tour from Bulawayo (one or two days)
6. Camping safari in Hwange National Park (three days)
7. Victoria Falls – rafting, kayaking, microlighting, wildlife-viewing, bungee jumping, fishing, etc (five days)

### Historical & Cultural Tour
This option takes in both cultural and historical highlights, in addition to Zimbabwe's most popular attractions. Although most of these historical and cultural sites of interest can be reached by public transport, you will need a car to make the most of this option.

1. Harare – Chapungu Kraal, National Gallery, Mbare, Domboshawa and Ngomakurira (three days)
2. Tengenenge Farm or Nyanga National Park (two days)
3. Masvingo – Great Zimbabwe National Monument, Serima Mission (three days)

## ZIMBABWE HIGHLIGHTS

| Region | Feature |
|---|---|
| **Harare** | |
| Domboshawa & Ngomakurira | These highly recommended Harare day-trips offer spectacular scenery, fine hiking and some of the country's most inspiring rock paintings. |
| Harare & Bulawayo | Zimbabwe's urban scenes provide opportunities for shopping, people-watching and nightlife. |
| **Northern Zimbabwe** | |
| Lake Kariba | For many Zimbabweans, the fishing, boating, wildlife-viewing and camping around Lake Kariba represent paradise on earth. |
| Mana Pools National Park | Remote Mana Pools is one wildlife park where visitors may strike out on foot. Many travellers arrive by canoe safari along the Zambezi River. |
| **Eastern Highlands** | |
| Chimanimani National Park | A lack of roads turns Chimanimani's rugged mountain wilderness into Zimbabwe's finest bushwalking country. |
| Nyanga National Park | Nyanga's 'civilised' mountain country, and that of adjoining Mtarazi Falls National Park, make this area the highland escape for affluent Harare dwellers. |
| Vumba | Vumba's forests and botanical gardens offer far-ranging vistas over lush green mountains. |
| **The Midlands & South-Eastern Zimbabwe** | |
| Gonarezhou National Park | This incredibly beautiful park is packed with wildlife and remains well off the trodden track. It's not to be missed by anyone who wants a taste of the real wild Africa. |
| Great Zimbabwe Ruins | Great Zimbabwe, sub-Saharan Africa's greatest archaeological site, is a serene setting for relaxation and exploration. |
| **Bulawayo** | |
| Matobo National Park | The kopje-studded terrain and weird balancing rocks of the Matobo Hills near Bulawayo shelter hundreds of caves and rock paintings. It's also one of the best places in Africa to see white and black rhino. |
| **Western Zimbabwe** | |
| Hwange National Park | Hwange is the most accessible of Zimbabwe's wildlife parks and offers its greatest variety and concentration of wildlife. |
| Victoria Falls | The popularity of Victoria Falls has turned the town into a tourist circus, but the falls themselves remain relatively unspoilt. |

4. Bulawayo – Natural History Museum, Mzilikazi Arts and Crafts Centre, Khami Ruins, Cyrene Mission, Nalatale and Danangombe Ruins (three days)
5. Matobo National Park (two days)
6. Hwange National Park (two days)
7. Victoria Falls (two days)

## Wildlife Tour

If you're in Africa for the wildlife, the field is wide open. Most of the following places either require a private vehicle (4WD in some cases) or a booking with a safari operator. See the Organised Tours chapter for more information.

1. Harare, visit Mukuvisi Woodlands and/or Lake Chivero (one day)
2. Mana Pools National Park (three days)
3. Matusadona National Park (three days)
4. Bulawayo – Natural History Museum, Tshabalala Wildlife Reserve and Chipangali Wildlife Orphanage (two days)
5. Matobo National Park (one day)
6. Hwange National Park by camping safari (four days)
7. Victoria Falls, with a visit to Zambezi National Park (three days)

## TOURIST OFFICES
## Local Tourist Offices

Local publicity associations distribute maps and information about their respective areas, but some are considerably more helpful and better organised than others. Mutare, Chimanimani and Bulawayo are generally excellent; Victoria Falls, Nyanga and Masvingo are competent; and Harare and Kariba are not particularly useful except for the most basic of information.

*Bulawayo*
Bulawayo Publicity Association, City Hall Car Park, PO Box 861 (☎ (19) 72969 or 60867)
*Chimanimani*
Chimanimani Tourist Association, PO Box 75 (☎ (126) 2294 or 2840)
*Gweru*
Gweru Promotional Council, City Hall, Livingstone Ave, PO Box 730 (☎ (154) 2226)
*Harare*
Harare Publicity Association, African Unity Square, 95 Jason Moyo Ave, PO Box 1483 (☎ (14) 705085)

Zimbabwe Council for Tourism, PO Box 7240 (☎ (14) 794016; fax 794015)
*Kariba*
Kariba Publicity Association, PO Box 86, (☎ (161) 2328)
*Masvingo*
Masvingo Publicity Association, Robert Mugabe St, PO Box 340 (☎ (139) 62643)
*Mutare*
Manicaland Publicity Association, Market Square, Milner Ave, PO Box 69 (☎ (120) 64711)
*Nyanga*
Nyanga Tourist Association, PO Box 110, (☎ (129) 8435)
*Victoria Falls*
Victoria Falls Publicity Association, Stand 412, Parkway, PO Box 97 (☎ (13) 4202)

## Tourist Offices Abroad

*Australia*
Zimbabwe Travel Bureau, Level 7, 75 Miller St, North Sydney, NSW (☎ (02) 959 4922)
*Germany*
Zimbabwe Fremdenverkehrsamt, An der Hauptwache, 60313 Frankfurt am Main, Germany (☎ (069) 920 7730; fax 920 77315)
*South Africa*
Zimbabwe Tourist Board, Tower Mall, Upper Shopping Level, Carlton Centre, Commissioner St, PO Box 9398, Johannesburg 2001 (☎ (011) 331 6970)
Zimbabwe Tourist Board, 2 President Place, Jan Smuts Ave, Rosebank, Johannesburg 2196 (☎ (011) 788 1748)
*UK*
Zimbabwe Tourist Board, Zimbabwe House, 429 The Strand, London WC2R OSA (☎ (0171) 836 7755; fax 379 1167)
*USA*
Zimbabwe Tourism Office, Rockefeller Center, Suite 1905, 1270 Avenue of the Americas, New York, NY 10020 (☎ (1-212) 332 1090; fax 332 1093)

## VISAS & DOCUMENTS
## Visas

Everyone needs a valid passport, but visas are not required by nationals of Commonwealth countries, the European Union, Japan, Norway, Switzerland or the USA. South African citizens can pick up entry cards at the port of entry. Direct inquiries to the Zimbabwe embassy or high commission

ZIMBABWE

in your country or the Chief Immigration Officer, Private Bag 7717, Causeway, Harare, Zimbabwe.

Unless you're arriving by car, Immigration officials at land borders may want to see an onward ticket – although a ticket out of a neighbouring country or even Kenya will usually suffice – and they rarely ask to see cash or credit cards unless you can't produce a ticket. If you're entering by bus or rail, a return ticket via the same route may work but don't count on it; they normally want a ticket back to your home country. Miscellaneous Charge Orders are not acceptable.

If you arrive without an onward ticket or at least a major credit card, you may be refused entry or be carefully scrutinised for 'sufficient funds'. Officers may even require a refundable deposit of up to US$1000 in cash or travellers cheques.

Immigration forms will ask for your address in Zimbabwe. To minimise hassles, don't write 'camping' or 'don't know'. Rather, select the name of a mid-range hotel in Harare or the next city you'll be visiting. Travellers visiting friends in Zimbabwe are expected to provide names, addresses, telephone numbers and any other details the officer may want.

In the box marked 'occupation', if you write in anything related to publishing, the media or any sort of military or government position, you'll be issued with a 'Notice to Visitor' (NTV) document, and the letters 'NTV' will be inscribed on your entry stamp. This is intended to alert officials that you're involved in what they consider a sensitive profession. This doesn't really mean much, but it may invite closer scrutiny when dealing with officials. Note also that journalists may be issued a 24-hour visa and asked to secure a temporary employment permit and a Zimbabwe Press Card (normally valid for only 14 days) from the Ministry of Home Affairs, 7th floor, Liquenda House, Nelson Mandela Ave, Harare.

**Visa Extensions** The maximum length of

stay granted is normally 90 days, which can readily be extended by any Immigration office for one month at a time, up to a maximum of six months. The procedure is normally hassle-free; you'll only have to fill in a form and demonstrate that you have enough money for the longer length of stay.

## Visas for Other Countries

Harare is one of the best places in southern Africa to pick up visas for other African countries. Requirements are constantly changing but nearly all require a fee – some must be paid in US dollars – and multiple passport-sized photos. If you plan to do a lot of border hopping, carry a stack of these photos. The contact details for the relevant embassies can be found in the Embassies & Consulates in Zimbabwe section below.

*Congo (Zaïre)*
The Congo Embassy accepts visa applications in the morning (from 8 am) and visas are issued at 4 pm the same day. Three-month visas cost (sit down please) US$195 single entry and US$255 multiple entry (they're cheaper in Nairobi and elsewhere).

*Ethiopia*
Visas are issued in 24 hours with one photo. A one-month visa costs US$28 and a three-month one is US$42. US citizens can also get a two-year multiple entry visa for US$70.

*Kenya*
The Kenya High Commission issues three-month single-entry visas for US$30. They require two photos and are issued in 24 hours. Multiple-entry visas are slower to obtain, so you're better off getting a single-entry visa and changing it in Nairobi.

*Mozambique*
The Mozambique Embassy is open Monday to Friday from 8 am to noon. A one-way/return transit visa for the Tête corridor through Mozambique to Malawi costs US$9/14 (this is certain to increase in the near future), requires three passport photos and is issued in 24 hours with little fuss. Visas must be used within seven days of issue. One-month single-entry tourist visas are US$20 (also sure to increase) and take 24 hours to issue (same-day service costs an additional US$5). Multiple entry visas good for three or six months are also available. Before leaving the office, check your visa for any irregularities.

*Namibia*
Few travellers need visas for Namibia, but for those who do, they're free, require two photos and are issued in 24 hours.

*Tanzania*
The Tanzanian High Commission issues visas in under 48 hours and requires two passport photos, plus fees which are dependent on nationality. British subjects pay US$42; USA citizens, US$32; Germans, Danish and Israelis, US$9; Dutch, US$18/24 for one/three months; Swiss, US$12; and South Africans, US$25. Note that there's no Tanzania consulate or High Commission in Malawi, so be sure to pick up your visa here or in Lusaka.

*West Africa*
The French Embassy in Harare issues visas for the Cote d'Ivoire, Senegal, Burkina Faso, the Central African Republic and Gabon, and provides information on visas for other former French West African countries. Note that the Nigerian High Commission won't issue visas if you could have obtained them in your home country prior to your journey.

*Zambia*
Visas are required by all except nationals of the Irish Republic, Romania, Sweden and the former Yugoslavia. Citizens of Commonwealth countries (except the UK) only need a visa if they've been resident in East Africa and are of Bangladeshi, Indian, Pakistani or Chinese descent. Prices vary according to nationality. A one-day visa for US citizens costs US$10; multi-day visas are US$25. For British subjects, the fee is £35 for one day and £45 for multiple days, but visa requirements are waived if the individual is 'introduced' to the country by a 'Zambian tour company'. This includes everything from rafting and microlighting companies to hotels and lodges, so it pays to pre-book at least one activity.

## Other Documents

If you're entering Zimbabwe from Zambia or further north in Africa, you may be asked for a yellow fever vaccination certificate.

A driving licence from your home country is sufficient to drive in Zimbabwe provided it's written in English. Otherwise, you'll need an authenticated translation plus a photograph. Driving licences from Zambia, Malawi, Namibia, South Africa, Botswana and Swaziland are valid until their expiry dates and other foreign licences are valid for 90 days.

## EMBASSIES & CONSULATES
### Zimbabwe Embassies & Consulates

Zimbabwe is diplomatically represented at the following missions (telephone numbers include area codes in brackets):

*Australia*
High Commission of Zimbabwe, 11 Culgoa Circuit, O'Malley, Canberra, ACT 2606 (☎ (02) 6286 2270; fax 290 1680)

*Botswana*
High Commission of Zimbabwe, 1st floor, IGI Building, PO Box 1232, Gaborone (☎ 314495; fax 305863)

*Canada*
High Commission of Zimbabwe, 332 Somerset St West, Ottawa, Ontario K2P OJ9 (☎ (613) 237-4388; fax 563-8269)

*France*
Ambassador of Zimbabwe, 5 Rue de Tilsitt, 75008, Paris (☎ 01 53 81 90 10; fax 01 53 81 90 190)

*Germany*
Ambassador of Zimbabwe, Villichgasse 7, Bonn (☎ (0228) 356071; fax 356309)

*Kenya*
High Commission of Zimbabwe, 6th floor, Minet ICDC Building, Mamlaka Rd, PO Box 30806, Nairobi (☎ (02) 721071)

*Malawi*
High Commission of Zimbabwe, 7th floor, Gemini House, PO Box 30187, Lilongwe (☎ 784988)

*Mozambique*
High Commission of Zimbabwe, Ave Kenneth Kaunda 816/820, Caixa Postal 743, Maputo (☎ (1) 499404; fax 492239)
Consulate of Zimbabwe, 617 Rua Francisco Dechage Almelda, Ponde Gea, PO Box 649, Beira (☎ (3) 327950; fax 328942)

*Namibia*
High Commission of Zimbabwe, Gamsberg Building, PO Box 23056, Windhoek (☎ (061) 227738; fax 226859)

*South Africa*
High Commission of Zimbabwe, 798 Mertons, Arcadia, Pretoria (☎ (012) 342 5125)
Consulate of Zimbabwe, 20 Anderson St, Johannesburg 2000 (☎ (011) 838 2156; fax 838 5620)
Consulate of Zimbabwe, 55 Kuyper St, Cape Town (☎ (021) 461 4710)

*Tanzania*
High Commission of Zimbabwe, 6th floor, New Life House, Sokaine Drive/Ohio St, PO Box 20762, Dar-es-Salaam (☎ 514 6259)

ZIMBABWE

*UK*
High Commission of Zimbabwe, Zimbabwe House, 429 The Strand, London WC2R 0SA (☎ (0171) 836 7755; fax 379 1167)
*USA*
Ambassador of Zimbabwe, 1608 New Hampshire Ave NW, Washington, DC 20009 (☎ (202) 332-7100; fax 438-9326)
*Zambia*
High Commission of Zimbabwe, 4th floor, Ulendo House, Cairo Rd, PO Box 33491, Lusaka (☎ (01) 229382; fax 227474)

## Embassies & Consulates in Zimbabwe

It is often a good idea to register with your embassy or consulate if you are spending a lot of time in a remote area or an unstable region. All of the following are in Harare.

*Angola*
Doncaster House, Speke Ave and Angwa St (☎ (14) 790675)
*Australia*
Karigamombe Centre, 53 Samora Machel Ave (☎ (14) 757774)
*Botswana*
22 Phillips Ave, Belgravia (☎ (14) 729551)
*Canada*
45 Baines Ave, corner of Moffat St, PO Box 1430 (☎ (14) 733881)
*Congo (Zaïre)*
24 van Praagh Ave, Milton Park, PO Box 2446 (☎ (14) 724494)
*Ethiopia*
14 Lanark Rd, Belgravia (☎ (14) 725822)
*France*
Renelagh Rd near Orange Grove Drive, PO Box 1378, Highlands (☎ (14) 498096)
*Germany*
14 Samora Machel Ave, PO Box 2168 (☎ (14) 731955)
*Kenya*
95 Park Lane, PO Box 4069 (☎ (14) 790847)
*Malawi*
Malawi House, 42/44 Harare St, PO Box 321 (☎ (14) 752137)
*Mozambique*
152 Herbert Chitepo Ave (☎ (14) 790837)
*Namibia*
31A Lincoln Rd, Avondale (☎ (14) 497930)
*Netherlands*
2 Arden Rd, Highlands (☎ (14) 776701)
*New Zealand*
Eastgate Centre, 8th floor, corner Second St and Robert Mugabe Rd (☎ (14) 759221)

*South Africa*
Temple Bar House, corner of Nelson Mandela Ave and Angwa St (☎ (14) 753147 – the visa section (☎ (14) 776712) is at 1 Princess Drive, Newlands Shopping Centre, Highlands, Harare)
*Tanzania*
23 Baines Ave, PO Box 4841 (☎ (14) 721870)
*UK*
7th floor, Corner House, corner of Leopold Takawira and Samora Machel (☎ (14) 772990)
*USA*
Arax House, 172 Herbert Chitepo Ave, PO Box 3340 (☎ (14) 794521)
*Zambia*
6th floor, Zambia House, Union Ave, PO Box 4698 (☎ (14) 773777)

For general information on what your embassy can and can't do for you when you are travelling in a foreign country, see Embassies in the regional Facts for the Visitor chapter.

## CUSTOMS

Visitors may import a maximum of Z$1000 in non-trade items, excluding personal effects. Travellers over 18 years of age can also import up to five litres of alcohol, including two litres of spirits. Firearms must be declared at the border.

Motor vehicles may be imported temporarily if they bear current number plates and are licensed, registered and titled in the home country. See under Car & Motorcycle in the Zimbabwe Getting Around chapter.

Travellers bringing a pet or a guide dog (unless they reside inside the Southern African customs union) need a permit from the Director of Veterinary Services, PO Box CY52, Causeway, Harare, Zimbabwe. The procedure takes at least three months, so apply well in advance of your visit. There are no animal quarantine laws, but all animals require vaccination certificates and a clean bill of health from a government veterinary office in their home country. Animals belonging to residents of Botswana, Lesotho, Namibia, South Africa or Swaziland need only a clean bill of health from a government veterinary office at home.

## MONEY
### Costs
Although hotels, national parks and tour operators employ a two-tier (or three-tier) pricing system, in which foreigners pay considerably more for goods and services than Zimbabwe residents, Zimbabwe is still not an expensive country for foreigners, unless they're using the international-class hotels, safari lodges, fine dining establishments and package safaris that support the bulk of the country's tourist industry.

Fortunately for budget travellers, inexpensive accommodation alternatives, such as backpackers hostels, are springing up around the country and, although prices for foreigners have risen phenomenally in recent years, national parks are still generally good value. In addition, you'll find comfortable and inexpensive campgrounds and caravan parks in and around most cities, towns and places of interest.

Food is mostly inexpensive and eating at small local establishments or self-catering will allow you to eat heartily on a tight budget. A meal of the Zimbabwean staple, *sadza ne nyama* (mielies with meat relish) in a local eatery costs around US$0.75. Hotels offer good value buffet meals for US$5 to US$20.

Any item that must be imported (and therefore purchased with foreign exchange) is expensive. This is less of a headache with the new economic restructuring, but Zimbabweans must still save for years to buy imported items such as televisions or computers. Even cheap digital watches are expensive and would make well-appreciated gifts for local friends. Consumer goods produced in Zimbabwe, on the other hand, may be of varying quality but are normally quite affordable.

Consumer taxes, which are normally factored into marked prices, are 16% on retail items (excluding food) and 19% on 'luxury' items (electronic equipment, airline tickets, furniture and automobiles). There's also a 15% tax on hotel rooms, safaris and other tourist services. Travellers can avoid this expense by pre-paying their accommodation in their home country, but agency commissions and mark-ups may eat up any potential savings.

Inflation has been rampant in Zimbabwe over the past few years, making it difficult to give an accurate price for goods and services in local currency. Therefore, all prices are given in US dollars, as this value will tend to remain more accurate due to the fluctuating exchange rate cancelling out the effects of inflation. However, this does not mean that you should pay for everything in US dollars – it is merely intended to help you calculate your potential expenditure in Zimbabwe. Local currency should be used except when paying for hotels and organised activities such as rafting or canoeing.

### Currency
The unit of currency is the Zimbabwe dollar (Z$1=100 cents). Notes come in denominations of two, five, 10, 20, 50 and 100 dollars. Coins are valued at one, five, 10, 20 and 50 cents, and Z$1 and Z$2.

Although it's no longer necessary to declare currency and travellers cheques on arrival, immigration forms still ask for this information to ascertain whether you have enough for your intended length of stay. Even though the currency black market is defunct, customs officers occasionally ask to see bank receipts as you leave the country, as proof you've exchanged your foreign currency at the official rate, so don't throw them away.

Bear in mind that import of Zimbabwean banknotes is limited to Z$500 per person per visit and export is limited to the equivalent of US$200. However, now that local residents may hold overseas bank accounts, Zimbabweans have a US$2000 annual holiday allowance and exporters can retain up to 50% of their foreign earnings. This regulation is likely to be further relaxed in the future.

### Currency Exchange
At the time of writing, the Zimbabwe dollar had the following values against other currencies:

ZIMBABWE

| Australia | A$1 | = | Z$10.95 |
|-----------|-----|---|---------|
| Botswana | P1 | = | Z$4.49 |
| Canada | C$1 | = | Z$12.25 |
| France | 1FF | = | Z$2.99 |
| Germany | DM1 | = | Z$10.06 |
| Japan | ¥10 | = | Z$1.27 |
| Malawi | MK10 | = | Z$6.95 |
| Mozambique | Mt1000 | = | Z$1.53 |
| Namibia | N$1 | = | Z$3.44 |
| New Zealand | NZ$1 | = | Z$8.92 |
| South Africa | R1 | = | Z$3.45 |
| UK | UK£1 | = | Z$29.33 |
| USA | US$1 | = | Z$17.95 |

## Changing Money

Banks are open Monday, Tuesday, Thursday and Friday between 8.30 am and 3 pm. On Wednesday, they close at 1 pm and on Saturday they're open from 8 to 11.30 am. The exchange desk at Harare airport is open whenever there's an incoming flight, but often limits transactions to US$100. Hotel reception desks will sometimes exchange currency but the service is normally reserved for hotel guests and includes a substantial commission.

All brands of travellers cheques in US dollars or UK pounds may be exchanged for Zimbabwe dollars at any bank, but you must fill out an 'Application for Permission to Sell Foreign Exchange to an Authorised Dealer'. Major international currencies are also welcomed, but due to rampant counterfeiting, no-one currently accepts US$100 notes.

For exchanging travellers cheques, Zimbank charges 2% commission, with a minimum of Z$10, while Barclays and Standard Chartered Banks charge only a 1% commission with a Z$20 minimum. However, Barclays Bank gives especially good rates on Visa travellers cheques. To exchange Thomas Cook travellers cheques, some banks may ask to see your purchase receipts.

You may purchase foreign currency travellers cheques but never at a good rate since the transaction is converted from foreign currency into Zimbabwe dollars and then back to foreign currency, and each step yields a commission for the bank. Funds transferred from outside the country can only be received in Zimbabwe dollars or foreign-currency travellers cheques – at the same loss ratio as when buying travellers cheques outright.

**Credit Cards** Credit cards – American Express, Diner's Club, MasterCard and Visa, as well as Eurocheques – are accepted by establishments catering to tourists and business people. Petrol credit cards – even those issued by oil companies represented in Zimbabwe – aren't accepted at all.

When purchasing currency with a credit card, you're limited to a very small amount of foreign currency per transaction, although you can buy as many Zimbabwe dollars as you like. With a Visa card, you can draw instant cash at Barclays Bank automatic teller machines. Otherwise, prepare to wait a while for authorisation, especially in smaller towns.

### Black Market

The Economic Structural Adjustment Programme (ESAP) and the relaxation of import regulations have put an end to the black market in currency. However, informal currency exchange remains illegal in Zimbabwe.

If you do encounter street money changers offering higher than official rates, you can be guaranteed it's an attempt at scamming. If you bite, they'll either turn you over to the police or attempt to separate you and your money; many people wind up with a wad of clipped newspaper sandwiched between two Z$20 notes (this is rife in Victoria Falls). Don't let greed sell you short!

### Tipping

Tips of approximately 10% are expected by taxi drivers and in tourist-class hotels and restaurants. Some establishments automatically add a 10% service charge to the bill, however, which replaces the gratuity.

## POST & COMMUNICATIONS
### Postal Rates

At the time of writing, international postal

services were relatively cheap. Approximate rates were as follows: a 10g airmail letter to Europe, North America or Australia cost around US$0.25; domestic letters went for US$0.05. Sending air- or surface-mail parcels weighing under 2kg is relatively cheap if you send them as letters. They go for about US$2 each and in fact, it works out cheaper to send five 2kg parcels than one 10kg parcel. Figure that one out!

### Sending Mail

The Zimbabwean postal system is generally reliable, especially in urban areas, but it's wise to register anything of value (US$0.15 for anything valued under Z$50). When joining a typically long and apparently stagnant post office queue, check the notices over the windows, which list services available at that window and the time the attendant is scheduled for a lunch break. Make sure your postcards, letters and parcels are clearly addressed and stickered (green stickers for surface mail; yellow for SAL or surface airlifted; and blue for airmail). Overseas parcels require a green customs declaration.

For air-freighting handicrafts and artwork, an inexpensive option is Affretair at Harare International Airport. You must box it up yourself, but they charge just US$3.20 per kilogramme to Europe, North America or Australasia. Another company, which does the boxing for you, is AirLink (☎ (14) 736783), on the corner of Boshoff Drive and Conald Rd in Graniteside, Harare. For large items or bulk freight, try the freight consolidators, TNT Express Worldwide (☎ (14) 722129; fax 796689), Caprivi Carriers Ltd, 100 Central Ave, Harare. Federal Express courier services are also available in Harare (☎ (14) 737693), Bulawayo (☎ (19) 61519) and Mutare (☎ (120) 66030).

### Receiving Mail

Poste restante services are available in all major cities and towns but Harare is probably the best and most efficient. Have mail sent to you c/o Poste Restante, GPO, Inez Terrace, Harare, Zimbabwe. The address for American Express Customer Mail is PO Box 3141, Harare.

### Telephone

The Zimbabwean telephone system may be the butt of jokes but it is improving – or so they say. Local calls are the most notorious. Although there are lots of public telephone boxes, habitual foul-ups in local services combined with staggeringly crowded party lines result in long queues for the phones, especially in Bulawayo and Harare. Signs on public phones ask you to deposit a minimum of Z$0.20, but unless you insert Z$0.50 or more, the line will cut off when your party answers.

Overseas services are considerably better but there are no telephone offices where you can book and pay for calls without plugging coins into the box. To make overseas calls, your best bet is to use telephone cards, which are sold at post offices for Z$30, Z$50, Z$100 and Z$200. Otherwise, find a private telephone (hotels charge double or triple the official rates) or carry a huge stack of coins. Oddly, international calls are cheaper from rural areas than from urban centres. Reverse-charge calling is available to a few countries but only from private lines.

The international access code is 110. Calls to Australia, most of Western Europe and North America cost around US$9 for the first three minutes and US$2 for each subsequent minute. To other places, you'll pay around US$11 for the first three minutes and US$2.50 for each extra minute.

Zimbabwe's country code is 263; if you're calling from outside the country, drop the leading 1 from the internal trunk code. For domestic directory inquiries, dial 962; for international, dial 966. If you're phoning the USA from Zimbabwe, you can get an AT&T USA Direct operator on ☎ 110-899.

### Fax & Email

Public fax services are available at post offices in larger towns. Within southern

Africa, you can send a fax for US$2.50 per A4 sheet. To other countries, you'll pay US$6 for each A4 sheet.

In Harare, the public fax number is (263-4) 731901 and the office is open from 8.30 am to 5 pm Monday to Friday and from 8 to 11.30 am on Saturday. If you wish to receive faxes at this number, advise correspondents to mark your name, contact address and telephone number clearly at the top of the fax. Other public fax numbers include Bulawayo (19) 78053; Gweru (154) 51638; Kadoma (168) 2893; Kwe Kwe (155) 2169; Masvingo (139) 63897; and Mutare (120) 64238.

Email and Internet access is available at the Internet Cafe (☎ (14) 758194; <baboon@icafe.co.zw>), Fourth floor, Eastgate shopping centre, at the corner of Robert Mugabe Ave and Second St in Harare. Long-stay visitors may set up accounts. There's also an Internet facility at The Tube night club (<thetube@baobab.cszim.co.zw>), at 125 Mbuya Nehanda St, Harare.

## INTERNET RESOURCES

Various pages of the Lonely Planet Web site at www.lonelyplanet.com have information, advice and travellers' reports regarding Zimbabwe. The Zimbabwe Information Services Web site (www.mother.com/~zimweb/Tourism.html) has lots of useful information on topics such as tourist offices, airlines and transport.

Addresses of other useful Web sites are given in the book in places where they're most relevant. (For a couple of good choices, see the Newspapers & Magazines section in this chapter.)

## BOOKS

Many foreign writers have heard the call of Africa and committed their sentiments to paper. Now, as Africans realise their own unique perspective, there is an increasing body of local literature. The country's largest popular book chain is government-owned Kingston's, which has outlets in most cities and towns. For the largest selection of Zimbabwean titles, try the Book Cafe in Harare, which carries lots of African literature and numerous works on history, economy, politics, music, languages and natural history. Foreign publications are expensive in Zimbabwe, but you'll find plenty of pulpy reading material at the commercial book exchanges in Harare and Bulawayo.

Anyone interested in the African publishing scene can check out the Zimbabwe International Book Fair, which is held in Harare in late July or early August. In Europe, contact the Zimbabwe International Book Fair (☎ (0181) 348 8463; fax 348 4403; <margaret.ling@geo2.poptel.org.uk>; Web site www.mediazw.com/zibf/), 25 Endymion Rd, London N4 1EE, UK. In Zimbabwe, the address is Zimbabwe International Book Fair Trust (☎ (14) 702104; fax 702129; <zibf@samara.co.zw>), Harare Gardens, New Book House, PO Box CY1179, Causeway, Harare.

### Non-Fiction

Lonely Planet's *Songs to an African Sunset – A Zimbabwean Story*, by Sekai Nzenza-Shand, is the intriguing tale of a Zimbabwean expat who returns to her native village with her Australian husband.

*Mukiwa – A White Boy in Africa*, by Peter Godwin, is a sensitive and delightfully non-political account of Rhodesian life in the 1960s.

The word 'introduction' in the title of *An Introduction to the History of Central Africa – Zambia, Malawi, and Zimbabwe* by AJ Wills is misleading. Although it's a bit disorganised, this 500-page work, generally considered the best on the history of the region, will probably tell you more than you wanted to know on the subject.

*The Great Betrayal* by Ian Smith, the autobiography of colonial Rhodesia's most controversial leader, chronicles a tumultuous, emotion-charged period in modern Zimbabwean history.

*Great Zimbabwe Described & Explained* by Peter Garlake attempts to sort out the history, purpose and architecture of the ancient ruins at Great Zimbabwe.

*Mapondera 1840-1904* by DN Beach is a biography of Kadungure Mapondera, a descendent of the Changamire and Mutapa dynasties, who resisted settler encroachment into north-eastern Zimbabwe.

*Mugabe* by Colin Simpson & David Smith, the biography of Robert Mugabe, traces his rise to the office of executive president of Zimbabwe.

*The Struggle for Zimbabwe: the Chimurenga War* by David Martin & Phyllis Johnson is a popular history of the Second Chimurenga which describes in detail the Zimbabwean perspective of the tragic war that led to the country's independence. It is also available in Zimbabwe in an edition published by Zimbabwe Publishing House.

If you're interested in colonial history, look for the biographies and diaries of Robert Moffat, David Livingstone, Cecil John Rhodes, Frederick Courteney Selous, Leander Starr Jameson, and so on, which are available in libraries.

Other titles of historical interest include *Mapondera: Soldier of Zimbabwe* by Solomon Mutswairo and *Robert Mugabe of Zimbabwe* by Richard Worth.

## Fiction

There are several established and emerging names in Zimbabwean literature whose works are available in the Heinemann African Writers Series, Longman African Classics and a couple of locally published series. Tsitsi Dangarembga's *Nervous Conditions* is highly acclaimed and shouldn't be missed. Set in eastern Zimbabwe, it's the tale of a young woman attending a mission school in 1960s Rhodesia.

Also worthwhile are the works of Charles Mungoshi, one of Zimbabwe's first internationally recognised black writers, who masterfully captures the despair of black Africans in pre-independence Rhodesia. His most highly acclaimed work is *Coming of the Dry Season*. If you like it, look for his other works which are published in the Heinemann African Writers Series. They are available at most Zimbabwe bookshops.

Other writers to watch for include Dambudzo Marechera, John Munoye, Ngugi and John Nagenda. The late Stanlake Samkange, whose 1967 book *On Trial for my Country* raised the ghosts of both Lobengula and Cecil John Rhodes, is a favourite. *Bones* by Chenjerai Hove is a highly acclaimed account of a soldier in the liberation war and his more recent *Shebeen Tales* humorously exposes everyday life in Harare.

Doris Lessing, the most widely known serious writer to examine the Rhodesian experience and expose its inequalities, sensitively portrays Zimbabwe and its people in *The Grass is Singing*, published in the Heinemann African Writers Series in 1973. She's also compiled two anthologies of African stories, *Sun Between Their Feet* and *This was the Old Chief's Country*. During the 1980s and early 1990s, she returned to the country (after being banned for opposition to the Rhodesian government) four times; these trips resulted in *African Laughter*, a treatise on the changes observed since independence. She also has a number of other works.

Most Zimbabwe travellers have also read something by Wilbur Smith, who has written over a score of adventure novels set in southern Africa, past and present. They may not exactly qualify as great literature, but they are 'page-turners'. Those which take place in Zimbabwe include *A Falcon Flies*, *Men of Men*, *The Angels Weep*, *Power of the Sword*, *Elephant Song*, *The Leopard Hunts in Darkness* and *A Time to Die*. The last two are currently banned in Zimbabwe, mainly because they side with Ndebele factions, expose gruesome realities of the war in Mozambique and speculate in some detail about corruption in the Zimbabwean government.

## Travel Guides

The *Guide to Southern African Safari Lodges*, by Peter Joyce, provides a rundown of National Parks camps and private safari lodges in Zimbabwe and around southern Africa.

*Backpacker's Africa – East and South-ern*, edited by Hilary Bradt, outlines hiking possibilities in Zimbabwe (and every country from the Sudan to South Africa). Most information is dated, but an update should be forthcoming.

For general background and enticing colour photos, see the *Spectrum Guide to Zimbabwe*, by Camerapix. It's especially useful for trip-planning, but the prose does get excruciating.

If you read German, DuMont's worth-while *Zimbabwe* volume, by Astrid & Marcus Cornaro, is full of background on history, arts, culture, sights, wildlife and landscapes.

### Language

Several English-Shona and English-Ndebele dictionaries are sold locally. If you want to pick up some Shona, the pamphlet-sized book *Fambai Zvakanaka mu Zimbabwe – Have a Nice Trip in Zimbabwe* offers some basic grammar and vocabulary.

### Art & Music

*Images of Power – Understanding Bushman Rock Art* by David Lewis-Williams is a comprehensive examination of rock art sites in southern Africa and educated speculation about their history and meaning.

*The Painted Caves – An Introduction to the Prehistoric Art of Zimbabwe* by Peter Garlake contains explanations and locations of major prehistoric rock art sites in Zimbabwe. This is an essential companion for anyone searching out Zimbabwe's prehistoric art works.

*Life in Stone* by Oliver Sultan outlines the 15 top-rated Zimbabwean sculptors, with a short biography of each, and brilliant black and white photos.

Although the photographs in *Shona Sculpture* by F Mor are superb, the text seems utterly inaccessible, and particularly heavy on artsy hyperbole. Maybe I'm just out of touch.

*Serima* by Albert B Plangger is a history and outline of the beautiful Serima Mission

near Masvingo and its modern sculpture and woodcarving traditions.

*The Material Culture of Zimbabwe* by H Ellert is the most complete coverage of all aspects of Zimbabwe's material crafts cultures, both ancient and modern, including weapons, musical instruments, tools, pottery, jewellery, basketry and so on.

*Roots Rocking in Zimbabwe* by Fred Zindi covers Zimbabwe's pop-music scene including background information on the music itself and data on all the major players.

*Making Music – Musical Instruments in Zimbabwe Past & Present* by Claire Jones outlines teaching, playing and construction of Zimbabwean musical instruments.

*The Soul of Mbira – Music & Traditions of the Shona People of Zimbabwe* by Paul F Berliner is a scholarly treatise on the mbira and marimba musicians of Zimbabwe and includes an appendix with instructions on how to build and play an mbira (thumb piano). These last two books are available through *Dandemutande* (see under Music in the Facts about Zimbabwe chapter).

### NEWSPAPERS & MAGAZINES

Zimbabwe's two daily papers – the Harare *Herald* and the Bulawayo *Chronicle* – are long on local, national and sports news, while international events get short shrift. Similar is the *Standard*, which appears weekly on Sunday.

Of much greater interest – and a better source of world news – is the politically vocal and controversial *Zimbabwe Independent* (<newsdesk@zimind.samara.co.zw>; Web site www.samara.co.zw/zimind/), which is run by Zimbabweans, both black and white, with a decidedly anti-government editorial stance. It comes out on Friday. The Friday *Financial Gazette* also offers some outside news but the best coverage of world events is in *Time* and *Newsweek*, both of which are available from hotels, bookshops and street vendors.

The Catholic monthly magazine *Moto*, first published in 1959, became a weekly newspaper in 1971 and now covers national, cultural and political issues. It was banned by the Smith government in 1974 but resurfaced to become one of the greatest pre-independence influences on the black population. A similarly liberal and politically outspoken black publication is *Horizon*. Both are available at newsstands.

The excellent monthly tourist paper *The Travellers' Times* is distributed free via hotels, lodges and tour agents and operators. (The 12-issue subscription rate of US$20 to Europe and US$24 elsewhere covers postage only.) Contact Travellers Times (☎/fax (14) 301348; <shamba@ mail.pci.co.zw>; Web site www.mediazw .com/travel/), 148 Nelson Mandela Ave, PO Box EH75, Emerald Hill, Harare.

Another useful publication is *Zimbabwe Travel News* (☎ (14) 752125; fax 751802), 6th floor, Memorial Building, Samora Machel Ave, PO Box 4128, Harare. The alternative address is Tourism in Print, 4th floor, Grosvenor Crescent, London SW1X 7EE, UK. It keeps up with the latest tourism developments, but it makes a rather corporate meal of things and is expensive outside Zimbabwe (US$57 per year).

## RADIO & TV

Zimbabwe's two television and four radio stations are overseen by ZBC, the Zimbabwe Broadcasting Corporation. TV 2 and Radio 4 are funded by the government; both are commercial-free and education-oriented. Radio 1 broadcasts interviews in English and emphasises classical music. Radio 2 focuses on African music and broadcasts mostly in Shona but has a few programmes in Ndebele. Radio 3 broadcasts in English and plays popular top 40-style music.

BBC World Service broadcasts four times daily; for times and frequencies, contact the BBC African Service bureau (☎ (14) 793961), 4th floor Frankel House, Second St, Harare. The Voice of America is heard twice daily. When atmospheric conditions are ideal, you can also pick up Radio Australia's South East & North Asian service.

## ELECTRICITY

Electricity is generated at 220V AC, so for use of US appliances you'll need an adaptor. Both round and rectangular three-prong plugs and sockets are in use.

## LAUNDRY

All mid-range hotels in Zimbabwe offer laundry services to their guests for very reasonable prices while upmarket hotels tend to charge significantly more. If you're camping or staying in hostels, coin-operated commercial laundries/dry-cleaners are available in Harare, Bulawayo and Victoria Falls. Nearly all National Parks and private campgrounds are equipped with laundry sinks, but you'll need your own universal drain plug.

## HEALTH

This section includes information on health services specific to Zimbabwe. For a rundown on keeping healthy in southern Africa, see Health in the Regional Facts for the Visitor chapter.

Medical services in Zimbabwe are generally quite good, and both Harare and Bulawayo have excellent general hospitals. However, for potentially serious problems or complications, it's probably best to arrange to go home, or at least get to Johannesburg, which offers a full range of medical services.

In hospitals and private clinics, medical equipment is well sterilised and blood products are carefully screened, so despite the proliferation of HIV/AIDS in Zimbabwe, there's little chance of infections from needles or transfusions. However, bush clinics operate on much stricter budgets and proper equipment may not always be available, especially in emergency situations. To ease any concerns, you may want to carry a couple of sterile syringes; see Predeparture Preparations in the Health section at the beginning of the book.

The nationwide emergency telephone number is (☎ 99). If a medical emergency arises while you're on safari, you're likely to be treated or evacuated by the very

**ZIMBABWE**

efficient Medical Air Rescue Service (☎ (14) 793642; fax 734517), on Elcombe Ave in Belgravia, Harare. Ascertain whether your safari operator subscribes to this service, and if you have a specific medical condition – diabetes, epilepsy, a heart condition, bee-sting allergy etc – advise the operator at the time of booking.

## Traditional Medicine

In Zimbabwe, traditional healers and folk practitioners (n'anga and chiremba) are shamans, whose powers are thought to be derived from two types of spirit. The first type, midzimu, are ancestral protective spirits and are bestowed by a direct ancestor of the healer. The second type, shave, are the spirits of deceased strangers who lived nearby and were not properly buried. This powerful entity honours the recipients by selecting them to be shamen. In rural Zimbabwe, about one person in 1000 practices the profession.

Although some shamans are called as children, callings are most often accompanied by a chronic mental or physical sickness which occurs during young adulthood, together with dreams of herbal remedies and 'medical' practices. The cause of this distress is usually diagnosed by someone who's already a shaman and, if the elected person agrees to accept the calling, he or she is initiated in a special ceremony.

As with most physicians, n'anga have three main aims: prevention of illness, finding the cause of illness and working out a cure. For some ailments, a n'anga may simply prescribe herbs but, if the patient suggests that the ailment is derived from a spell or magic, some form of divining may be necessary to isolate the cause of the problem and make a prognosis for survival. This is often done by consulting with the spirits or reading the hakata (wooden divining bones, used in central Mashonaland), shoro (animal bones, used mainly in eastern Zimbabwe) or mungomo (seeds, used in Matabeleland).

Often, the problem is determined to be an intervening spirit, such as a muroyi (witch), ngozi (avenger) or a shave, which is affecting the protection normally afforded by his or her mudzimu (singular of 'midzimu'). It may also be determined that the patient brought on the illness by failing to perform a required ritual, such as ignoring a special holiday, or by breaking a taboo, such as eating one's totem animal. The n'anga then decides on an appropriate muti (treatment). This may involve powders, ointments, teas or scarification. The disease may be determined to have been caused by an uroyi (evil spirit) or muroyi (witchcraft), willed upon the patient. Historically, a perpetrator – most often a woman – would have been identified and punished, but these practices are now illegal in Zimbabwe and are rare.

If the person has been possessed, the n'anga exorcises the spirit and casts it into an animal, which carries it away. If the victim has been jinxed by a witch, treatment normally involves the ingesting of herbs. Alternatively, the bad luck may be lured into a specially prepared bottle and left in the bush; the spell is then cast upon the person who finds it.

Currently, traditional healers are gaining increased credibility and patronage among the masses. This is largely due to rising health costs, which place much western medicine out of reach of most Zimbabweans. Such organisations as the Zimbabwe National Traditional Healers Association (ZINATHA) have established clinics and are now manufacturing and packaging traditional remedies for the mass market. In fact, the president of ZINATHA, Dr Gordon Chavunduka, has announced that a potential AIDS cure has been identified by traditional healers and is now undergoing tests.

Despite its bid to be taken seriously by western practitioners, ZINATHA has rejected suggestions that the two treatment systems be integrated. Traditional healers have opted instead for co-operation, as many feel that western medicine has little to teach them and there are fears of being regarded as subordinates.

Independent travellers can purchase insurance against evacuation costs directly from the Medical Air Rescue Service for a nominal fee. However, if something does go wrong, you'll have to get to a phone or radio to alert them.

Pharmacies and chemists are found in major towns, but they only dispense medicines and drugs with a doctor's prescription. Zimbabwe is also blessed with an outstanding natural pharmacopoeia, and a fine homeopathic/naturopathic shop, The Herbalist, has opened in First Street Mall in Harare, near Jason Moyo Ave. It carries everything from sausage tree (*Kigelia africana*) cream, which is used as a remedy for some forms of skin cancer, to natural sunblocks made from sausage tree extracts, Zimbabwean aloes (*Aloe excelsa*) and lavender trees (*Heteropyxis dehniae*). These products are also sold at regional pharmacies.

### GAY & LESBIAN TRAVELLERS

Although homosexual activities are certainly present in Zimbabwe, they're officially scorned – and technically illegal – and discretion is strongly advised. The Reverend Canaan Banana, Zimbabwe's first president, is currently under investigation for alleged homosexual offences and Robert Mugabe, the current president, is conducting a very high-profile anti-homosexuality campaign and is on record as saying that: '... gays can never, ever stand as something we approve in Zimbabwe'. The only bar known to encourage gay patronage is The Tube Nite Club in Harare.

### USEFUL ORGANISATIONS

The Automobile Association of Zimbabwe (☎ (14) 707021), which dates back to 1923, offers a wide range of member services, including technical and legal advice, maps and touring assistance, emergency breakdown services and access to services of similar organisations worldwide. Members receive discounts on auto-related services. Contact them at Fanum House, 7th floor, Samora Machel Ave, PO Box 585, Harare.

UK residents with a particular interest in Zimbabwe may want to contact the British Zimbabwe Society, Marieke Clark, 5a Cricke Rd, Oxford OX2 6QJ, UK (☎ (01865) 57807). It publishes a newsletter and organises Zimbabwe-related events.

### DANGERS & ANNOYANCES
#### Con Artists & Scams

Mainly in Harare, Bulawayo and Victoria Falls, adept con artists take tourists for staggering amounts of money and the victims may not even realise they've been conned. There are countless fabricated sob stories, all tailored to separate you from your cash.

Many scams are fairly innocuous. If someone approaches you claiming to be hungry (they know this one is difficult to ignore), don't give money, but perhaps buy an inexpensive snack or direct them to a church mission which dispenses free meals.

There are also characters running around with notes, ostensibly from the Ministry of Health, stating that the bearer is mentally indigent (or some such thing) and therefore dependent upon public generosity for support. This is all rubbish, of course and few locals ever fall for it.

Even more rife are 'sponsorship scams', and some Zimbabweans are expert and inventive. Someone will approach you requesting donations for one good cause or another – anything from their school building fund to a kidney transplant for their grandmother.

Other people approach foreigners and ask them to loan their watch, camera etc, and arrange a date and time to meet for the return of the loaned goods. It's practically inconceivable that anyone falls for this!

Another scam involves betting. Foreigners are invited for an informal game of cards, billiards or whatever. One instigator suggests a 'friendly bet' and teams up with the foreigner, who is entrusted to hold winnings and temporarily make good the losses for their team so the game can progress. There seem to be a lot of losses for the befuddled foreigner's team – but that's chalked up to being unfamiliar with the rules. At some point, the foreigner's team-mate counts up wins and losses, ostensibly to settle the team's share of the debt. Once the cash is in hand, all the instigators split, leaving the foreigner deservedly feeling very stupid indeed.

In short, it's fine to be friendly and polite when interacting with strangers, but don't be naïve. Don't fall for ridiculous stories, don't add your name to the bottom of a list of Z$100 donations, never reach for your money when people are crowding around (some thieves want to see where your cash is kept so they can grab it), and never let greed affect your good judgement.

More sinister scams are thankfully not so common. Sometimes, someone may claim to have seen you smoking dope or changing money illegally or whatever and threaten to report the incident to the police. Don't panic. Sometimes, this ploy is merely used to distract you from your belongings momentarily. At other times, especially if you are guilty of whatever infractions they're alleging, it's simply attempted extortion.

## Theft

In addition to scams, which give alert victims a fighting chance, theft and mugging are also concerns. As a result of the recent drought in Zimbabwe, many subsistence farmers migrated to the cities in search of employment. However, many lacked marketable skills and few were successful. Some took to hawking fruit and other goods in the city centres, but others were recruited into criminal gangs, which descended to take advantage of an opportunity. The resulting crime wave left Harare less secure than it had been. When the country's reputation began to slide in tourism circles, extra police were hired to patrol the city centre, but at night it's still risky.

The warning should be obvious: don't walk around at night in the cities. Even by day, avoid youths loitering outside hotels; they're invariably pickpockets. Have a supply of loose change handy for purchases, but never pull out a stash of cash. Leave

your passport in a safe place and carry only a photocopy.

Places which warrant special caution, particularly at night, are bus terminals, crowded discos and the big parks in Harare and Bulawayo. Many camp sites and caravan parks have guards to watch over campers' belongings (Coronation Park in Harare is a notorious exception) but occasionally things go missing, so don't leave valuables in your tent. If you have a car, don't leave tempting items anywhere in sight if you're going to be away from it for any length of time. Also, be especially wary when driving foreign-registered vehicles in Harare. Occasionally, when you're stopped at a traffic light, someone might puncture your tyre and, when you stop to repair it, they offer to help but wind up helping themselves.

Another problem in Harare involves taxi drivers who drop clients far enough from their door to allow accomplices to attack with knives. The drivers then receive a share of the booty. Before climbing into a taxi, note the number plate and, especially at night, insist on being dropped right at your door.

## Racism & Tribalism

Although Zimbabwe has been independent for some time, visitors will notice that racism based on skin colour or tribal origin still exists, and the fact that the country is governed by the Shona majority has had little effect on old habits. It's tempting to sweep the issue under the rug and present Zimbabwe in the image its tourist industry would most appreciate – that it's a free country where all races and tribes are treated equally – but that's simply not the case.

The situation is not, as many foreigners are conditioned to believe by the western media, merely an issue of black and white. Although the economic disparity between those of European and African origin is more obvious and exploitation of inexpensive labour is a serious problem, the long-standing animosity between the majority Shona and the minority Ndebele is also serious and has caused untold grief.

### Police & Military

Compared to most African countries, Zimbabwe's police and military are friendly and courteous, and problems are rare. However, drivers are sometimes asked for food or money at routine roadblocks, but there's no obligation to comply with these requests. Those who offer something get a smile and thanks; those who don't are normally told to have a nice day and waved on.

The Zimbabwe military wear green soldierly uniforms and are easily recognisable – they'll often be carrying an automatic weapon. The police normally wear khaki – long trousers in the winter and shorts in the summer – with peaked caps. Traffic police wear all-grey uniforms. Other units wear grey shirts and blue trousers or all-blue uniforms with white caps.

Should you encounter an officer behaving unprofessionally, note their name and ID number. Report any serious offences to the Public Relations Officer at the Central Police Station in Harare.

### Land Mines

Travellers in the eastern highlands, particularly around Mutare and Chimanimani National Park, should be aware of dangers involving land mines and unexploded ordnance. The mines were planted both by Renamo rebels from Mozambique and by the Zimbabwe military in hopes of discouraging cross-border guerrilla activities. Some ordnance may even date from the Second Chimurenga.

Despite efforts by the Zimbabwean authorities to remove the mines, many remain and are regularly detonated by wild animals. The well-publicised 1989 land mine fatality near Skeleton Pass in Chimanimani National Park should provide sufficient warning to hikers tempted to wander off marked tracks. If you do find yourself away from well-trodden areas, don't touch anything vaguely resembling weaponry.

### BUSINESS HOURS

Most shops are open between 8 am and 5 pm Monday to Friday, with occasional early closing on Wednesday and lunch closing from 1 to 2 pm. Saturday hours are from 8 am to noon. Petrol stations open up at 6 am and most close at 6 pm, although several in Harare and Bulawayo, and others along well travelled routes, keep later hours. Banks are open from 8.30 am to 2 pm Monday to Friday (although some close at noon on Wednesday), and from 8.30 to 11 am on Saturday. Post offices are open 8.30 am to 4 pm Monday to Friday and 8.30 to 11.30 am on Saturday.

### PUBLIC HOLIDAYS & SPECIAL EVENTS

#### Public Holidays

Zimbabwe observes the following public holidays:

1 January
  *New Year's Day*
March or April
  *Good Friday, Easter Sunday, Easter Monday*
18 April
  *Independence Day*
1 May
  *Workers' Day*
25 & 26 May
  *Africa Days*
11 & 12 August
  *Heroes' Days & Defence Forces Day*
25 December
  *Christmas Day*
26 December
  *Boxing Day*

#### Special Events

Zimbabwe's finest cultural events are probably those which are run across incidentally: a rural agricultural fair, a school theatre production, a traditional wedding or a town anniversary (Bulawayo's 1994 Centenary celebrations carried on for months).

Most Zimbabweans are pleased and proud when strangers take an interest in their special events, and travellers are almost invariably welcome to share in the festivities. However, to get the most from such opportunities, your itinerary must allow flexibility.

There are also several fixed events. On 18 April, Independence Day festivities are celebrated around the country and in late May, Africa Day commemorates all African independence struggles. On 11 and 12 August, the Zimbabwean military forces are fêted and national heroes – particularly those from the independence movement – are remembered and honoured.

Those with an interest in African literature and publishing won't want to miss the annual Zimbabwe International Book Fair, which is held in Harare in late July or early August. For details, see Books earlier in this chapter.

Music lovers will appreciate the annual Houses of Stone Music Festival in Harare, which celebrates traditional Zimbabwean music. The date varies from year to year, but Kunzwana Trust (see Music under Arts in the Facts about Zimbabwe chapter) can provide specific information.

The Zimbabwe Agricultural Society Show, held at the showgrounds in Harare around the end of August, attracts farmers and agriculture students from around the world. In Bulawayo, the big event is the Zimbabwe International Trade Fair, held in late April or early May. It draws over 1000 exhibitors and 200,000 visitors from around the country and worldwide.

## ACTIVITIES

In Zimbabwe, the scope for activity tourism grows daily, and in the Victoria Falls/Livingstone area alone, you can choose from white-water rafting, canoeing, kayaking, riverboarding, microlighting, parachuting, wildlife viewing, horseback riding, cycling and even the world's highest bungee jumping (off the Zambezi bridge between Zimbabwe and Zambia).

Other parts of the country also present possibilities. The Mavuradonha Wilderness and the national parks of the Eastern Highlands offer superb hiking. In addition, you can go white-water rafting on the Pungwe River near Nyanga National Park; the

Kariba area offers sailing, houseboating and other water activities; the middle Zambezi is ideal for long-distance canoeing; several private ranches in the Midlands offer horseback riding; and a growing number of operators conduct foot safaris through wildlife-oriented national parks.

For further choices, see the Organised Tours chapter.

## WORK

Although it isn't impossible to secure permission to work in Zimbabwe, neither is it easy and officials definitely prefer that intending workers organise permits in their home country. If you've simply run out of money, however, and have a skill that's in demand, you may be able to convince them that your case warrants hardship considerations (however, advising them of such a situation may also qualify you for deportation). In this situation, it's best to seek out an employer, secure a solid job offer, and then set about arranging a permit with the prospective employer's help.

Upper or A level teachers, especially science teachers, engineers, computer experts and medical personnel, will have the most luck. Those in professions for which there are sufficient qualified Zimbabwean citizens, such as nursing or primary school teaching, have less success.

In government schools, teachers may currently teach up to the level they have completed. Therefore, a university degree and/or education certificate is not necessary to teach A level courses, but those with a higher degree can command a higher starting salary than those who've completed only A levels. Private colleges pay better than government schools (usually about twice the salary), but require a university degree in education. Harare's two best colleges are Speciss College on Herbert Chitepo Ave and ILSA Independent College on Fife Ave.

If you're really committed to teaching and are prepared for a challenge, you can improve your chances of success by requesting a rural posting. Government teaching contracts are normally negotiated for an extendable two years, and paid leave at both government and private schools amounts to about four months annually.

Wages in Zimbabwe are very low by European, North American or Australasian standards, and salaries are paid only in Zimbabwe dollars. With special permission, some people may export a portion of their salaries, but otherwise, you're subject to the same currency controls as Zimbabwean citizens (see Money earlier in this chapter). Also, be aware that government employees, including teachers, may sometimes wait months for a pay cheque.

Applications for permanent residence or work permits must include a doctor's certificate stating the applicant has had a recent chest x-ray and shows no evidence of tuberculosis or other serious illness.

## ACCOMMODATION

Most visitors are pleasantly surprised at the juxtaposition of pleasant standards and reasonable prices. However, unless you can pay for five stars, a holiday will be most enjoyable if you take a *laissez-faire* attitude towards accommodation and service.

Happily, accommodation for budget travellers to Zimbabwe is becoming more plentiful. In addition to the National Parks facilities and municipal caravan parks, there is a growing number of backpackers hostels and B&Bs, so those without tents are no longer relegated to quirky youth hostels or brothel hotels.

Accommodation rates, save for camping fees, are subject to a 15% government bed tax. Except at backpackers hostels and B&Bs, foreigners must pay in foreign exchange, but note that hotel exchange rates are generally lower than banks offer. Always double check hotel arithmetic and query any discrepancies!

### Camping

All larger cities and towns have well-maintained caravan parks for both caravans and tent camping. Most are clean, and all offer toilet, bath and shower facilities. The most popular ones are attended 24 hours a day, so your belongings are reasonably secure when left inside your tent.

Camping in rural areas or communal lands is generally discouraged and often prohibited. If you're caught without accommodation, seek permission from property owners or villagers before setting up camp.

For information on National Parks campsites, see National Parks Accommodation later in this section.

### Hostels & Backpackers Lodges

Zimbabwe has only one youth hostel (in Bulawayo), but fortunately, a boom in backpackers lodges is providing a popular alternative. Most places offer dormitory beds, double rooms and camping space as well as a range of services: bars, swimming pools, tourist information, transfers to and from transport terminals and budget tour bookings.

All backpackers options at the time of writing have been covered in this book, but things change frequently. A source of heavily politicised information on southern African lodges is the *Backpackers Up-to-Date Guide (BUG)*, by Kirk Hall, Port St Johns Backpackers, c/o Post Office, Port St Johns, Eastern Cape Province, South Africa.

### B&Bs

Zimbabwe has recently started an association of home and farm-stay B&Bs. For the latest listings and information, phone or visit Bed & Breakfast (☎ (14) 724331), 161 Second St Extension, Harare.

### Hotels

For a quiet night, avoid the cheapest hotels, which normally cater to the sex and swill crowds rather than travellers. You also risk misunderstandings with the personal services squads.

Mid-range accommodation is comfortable, adequate and fairly reasonably priced. Middle- to upper-range hotels are rated on a zero to five-star scale based on an

## The Three-Tier Pricing System

In the days when the government controlled hotel rates, hoteliers' applications for price increases were often rejected and hotel owners were faced with increasing overheads but limited income. The solution, which was approved by the government, was to charge overseas guests in hard foreign currency. Somehow, this evolved into a three-tier pricing system in which overseas guests pay European-level rates.

Although price controls are no longer in place, most safari lodges and some four- and five-star hotels (Zimbabwe Sun Hotels, Rainbow Hotels, Meikles, Sheraton and Holiday Inn, among others) cling to this system. Foreign rates can be up to two or three times those paid by Zimbabwe residents. 'Regional' guests (including South Africans) get marginal discounts off the foreign rates. However, the Cresta/Best Western Hotels group (Web site www.cresta hospitality.com) has abandoned this practice; for this standard of accommodation, they offer foreigners the best value for money.

Over the years, this issue has become a matter of heated contention and debate. Although some travellers feel guilty about their relatively high incomes and happily pay the higher rates, it's worth considering several things:

- Many companies charging multi-tier rates are owned by foreign corporations, so often, the profits are soaked out of the country.
- You can be certain that the Zimbabwean resident rates are not below the cost value of the accommodation; that is, no one is taking a loss on the local rates.
- No tax dollars are contributed towards the support of these businesses, which might entitle local taxpayers to a discount (in theory, that's the rationale behind the two-tier National Parks' fees, although it's not quite that simple since the fees don't actually go towards National Parks' maintenance).
- Foreigners don't inherently consume more goods or services than locals do, necessitating a higher tariff (although in the case of some safari lodges, the higher rates do include activities not available on the local rate, such as game drives).
- Lastly – and perhaps most importantly – overhead costs in Zimbabwe are commensurate with the local economy, and the staff are paid the same typically low wages (by European standards, anyway), whether they're serving foreigners or locals. Unless staff salaries are brought into line with those of their European counterparts, there's little justification for charging European-level rates.

---

elaborate points system for service, cleanliness and amenities. One- or two-star hotels average US$15 to US$30 for a double room and three-star hotels range from US$25 to US$50. In most four- and five-star hotels, foreigners pay up to 200% more than Zimbabwe residents (see the boxed text on the Three-Tier Pricing System).

### Game Ranches

Many white commercial farms and cattle ranches have now been allowed to revert to bushland and are being stocked with wildlife. These game ranches now repre-sent a rapidly growing accommodation sector in Zimbabwe, and many also breed various animals for sale to other game ranches.

On most ranches, the emphasis is on wildlife viewing and photography, and the main attractions are the quality of accommodation and catering. On hunting-oriented ranches, the accommodation tends to be incidental to the hunting trip. While pro-hunting crowds maintain that their activities demonstrate to local people that there's a pay-off in wildlife conservation, anyone who has problems with hunting should check the orientation of the ranch before booking.

Game ranches aren't budget options, but several have recognised the budget market and set up camping areas or basic cottages. For information, contact Zimbabwe Safari Farms (☎ (14) 733573), PO Box 592, Harare.

### National Parks Accommodation

Zimbabwe's national parks offer over 250 chalets, cottages and lodges as well as well-appointed campsites. Chalets, the least expensive option, provide furniture, fridges, bedding and towels. Cooking is done outside the main unit and amenities are communal. The more upmarket cottages add kitchens and private baths, and the lodges are fully self-contained and serviced by National Parks staff. All three types offer one- or two-bedroom units with two beds per room. Hwange, Matusadona, Mana Pools and other parks also offer exclusive camps which are occupied by a single party.

National Parks campsites offer braai pits and ablutions blocks (hot showers are made possible with donkey boilers), but larger camps cater more to caravans than tents. Most sites consist of a patch of cement-like terra firma that resists wimpy aluminium or fibreglass tent pegs, so use equipment that's up to the challenge.

Foreigners and clients of tour operators pay two to five times the Zimbabwe resident rates (rates quoted here are for foreigners). National Parks campsites with toilets and baths cost US$3 per site. Large exclusive camp sites, accommodating parties of up to 12 people, exist in all wildlife-oriented parks and cost US$5. The same fee applies to 12-person fishing camps in Gonarezhou and Zambezi national parks, and picnic site camps in and around Hwange National Park. Most camps have braai pits and long-drop toilets, but a few have running water, flush toilets and showers.

One- or two-bedroom chalets cost US$2.50 per bed; cottages are US$5 per bed and fully-equipped one/two bedroom lodges are US$7.50 per bed (except at Udu Dam, Nyanga, where you'll pay US$40 for eight beds and at Mana Pools and Mutirikwe, where lodges cost US$60 for eight beds). The overpriced mountain hut at Chimanimani costs US$10 per person.

**Bookings** Bookings are essential for National Parks accommodation and campsites, but the current reservations system isn't exactly a well-oiled machine (see boxed text). National Parks accommodation bookings are most reliably made through the Central Booking Office (☎ (14) 792782), near the National Botanical Gardens, on the corner of Borrowdale Rd and Sandringham Drive, PO Box CY826, Harare. Less reliable is the Bulawayo Booking Agency (☎ (19) 63646), at the corner of Herbert Chitepo St and Tenth Ave, PO Box 2283, Bulawayo. Both offices are open Monday to Friday 8.30 am to 3 pm.

Bookings are available up to six months in advance, but for January, April, May, August, September and December, reservations are handled on a draw basis. At other times, they're on a first-come, first-served basis (except for Matusadona exclusive camps, which are always on a draw basis). Note that if you can't check into your accommodation before 5.30 pm, inform the attendant or you'll forfeit the booking and the money.

### FOOD

Zimbabwean cuisine, the legacy of bland British fare melded with normally stodgy African dishes, makes for some pretty ordinary eating. The dietary staple is *sadza* – the white maize meal porridge upon which nearly all local meals are built.

### Meat & Fish

The second main meal component is meat (or *nyama* – sadza with meat gravy is known as *sadza ne nyama*). Zimbabwe is one of the world's great producers of beef, which is available nearly everywhere. Chicken is also a staple and on occasion, game meat, including crocodile, kudu and

~~~~~~~~~~~~~~~~~~~~~~~~~~~~~~~~~~~~~~~~~~~~~~~~~~~~~~~~~~~~~~~~~~~~~~~~~~~~

### The National Parks Reservation System

When dealing with National Parks accommodation bookings, the best advice is to book early and hang onto your receipt. If they tell you everything is full, don't despair – there are typically lots of no-shows. The catch is that you must wait until 5.30 pm on the day you wish to stay, so you'll need an alternative plan in case you're turned away. The following letter describes a typical experience:

The National Parks central reservations system is a disaster. You can only book centrally in Harare (or Bulawayo). I tried to book Hwange Main Camp, Sinamatella and Zambezi National Park but everything was fully reserved months in advance. Both Hwange and Zambezi national parks were practically deserted in May/early June, yet people were being told they were full, both in Harare and on site.

The problem is that people can book and not pay, or they can book and pay and not turn up. The camps themselves don't know until 5.30 pm whether a unit will be taken or available, so no booking means you have to hang around until then. If you want to stay more than one night, you must check out every day and wait. Unless you ring Harare, of course. An Australian couple we met spent 2½ hours at Hwange Main Camp reception trying to phone Harare – and failed.

On three occasions at Zambezi, we were told all accommodation was full – that all 19 lodges were paid for and everyone had turned up, but when I checked the registration book there were only two or three signatures. But after 10 to 15 minutes of persistence we were given a lodge.

**Catherine Webster, UK**

~~~~~~~~~~~~~~~~~~~~~~~~~~~~~~~~~~~~~~~~~~~~~~~~~~~~~~~~~~~~~~~~~~~~~~~~~~~~

impala, is available. In rural communal lands, people eat lots of goat and mutton.

*Biltong*, a normally anonymous dried meat, can be anything from beef to kudu or ostrich. It's usually delicious and makes a great snack, but it can be deceptively salty so it's a good idea to have lots of water handy.

The most popular domestic fish include bream from Lake Kariba, which is available only occasionally, and the anchovy-like dried *kapenta (Limnothrissa mioda)*, also from Kariba. Trout is a speciality in the eastern highlands and is superb. Until just a couple of years ago, heavy import restrictions meant that it was practically impossible to find any other sort of fish or seafood in Zimbabwe, apart from some very expensive – and smuggled – Mozambican prawns. Now, the market has opened up and you'll find seafood from all over the region.

### Fruit & Vegetables

The supply of fruit and vegetables is limited but what's available is quite good. Gems squash, a type of marrow, is popular and delicious. Tomatoes, cucumbers, maize, pumpkins, courgettes (zucchini, marrows), and tropical fruits such as papayas, mangoes and bananas are also cheap and plentiful.

### Buffets

For hearty appetites and medium budgets, nothing can beat the hotel buffets. For breakfast, you can get unlimited fresh and tinned fruit, cereals, breads, porridge, bacon, sausages, eggs, cheese, yoghurt, coffee, etc for an average of US$5.

Lunch buffets normally include salads, several meat dishes, casseroles and desserts for a similar price, and in some places, vegetarians can opt out of the meat for a price reduction. At the Holiday Inn in Harare, for example, a vegetarian lunch costs only US$3 compared to nearly twice that for the full board.

All-you-can-eat dinners aren't as popular, although several places in Victoria

Falls offer major pig-outs, with table after table of European and African dishes, meats, salads, casseroles, breads and myriad sweets. The three or four hours you'll spend gorging and socialising are worth every bit of the price, which averages around US$15.

### Fast Food

Bus terminals brim with cheap and greasy snack stalls where you can pick up groundnuts, corn on the cob, eggs, sweets, and even deep-fried beetles. Basic cooked meals are available in market dining areas, but aren't recommended for anyone with a weak stomach or keen olfactory receptors.

One step up are the Mum & Pop style takeaways which serve chips, sausages, meat pies, sandwiches, burgers, etc, and normally offer good value. Next up the scale (although not necessarily better) are the fast-food chains – Wimpy, Chicken Inn, Kentucky Fried Chicken, Nando's, etc – which are found around the country.

### Restaurants

In major cities, especially around transportation terminals, you will find lots of small food halls serving up plain but filling fare – usually some variation on sadza ne nyama – for just a dollar or two. These places are normally happy to try their hand at vegetarian fare as well, but the best they'll probably manage is sadza overlain with tinned baked beans, boiled cabbage and onions, or a boiled green known as *rape* (the best of the lot).

Around central business districts and suburban shopping centres you'll find a variety of pleasant coffee houses and international restaurants serving up Continental, Italian, Chinese, Greek, Indian and so on. Restaurants in the big tourist hotels concentrate on international fare, and several elegant places in Harare and Bulawayo admirably attempt gourmet cuisine.

There are normally dress restrictions in bars and restaurants after about 4 pm but the definition of the standard 'smart casual dress' will vary from place to place. At the very least, it excludes anyone wearing shorts, jeans, T-shirts or thongs (flip-flops).

### Self-Catering

Zimbabwean supermarkets are improving all the time and, in the cities, the variety of goods available is now nearly as wide as that found in Botswana or Namibia. With this increase in convenience, however, has come a corresponding increase in prices, and self-catering is no longer the fabulous deal it once was. Township markets and bus terminals offer especially good value on fresh produce, but your choices are often limited.

### Vegetarian

Vegetarians find it particularly difficult to travel in Africa since most of the inexpensive fare is based upon meat. Eggs and groundnuts, both good sources of protein, are readily available in southern Africa and fresh breads and vegetables can be found nearly everywhere, but to form an interesting meal from them, you'll probably have to resort to self-catering. Although some places now offer a vegetarian opton, in those that don't, vegetable dishes politely concocted for vegetarian foreigners may turn out bland or stodgy.

### DRINKS
### Nonalcoholic Drinks

Southern Africa's refreshing contribution to liquid enjoyment is the shandy, which comes in three varieties. The Malawi shandy is comprised of ginger beer, angostura bitters and soda water with ice and lemon. The delicious rock shandy is a smoother alternative, made with lemonade, soda water and angostura bitters. The club special shandy is a mixture of lemonade, ginger beer and Mazowe orange, a ubiquitous orange cordial which fills the noncarbonated drink niche. Some travellers love it; others find it too sickly sweet.

If you just want a glass of water, which is safe to drink straight from the tap in Zimbabwe, order a Zambezi cocktail ('...but hold the crocs').

**Hot Drinks** Coffee addicts who want to kick the habit should think about a holiday in Zimbabwe. Both tea and coffee are grown on plantations in the Eastern Highlands, but the best of it is reserved for export. Although more restaurants are picking up on the demand for good local or imported coffee, what you'll normally get, even in big hotels, is a revolting blend of instant coffee and chicory known as Daybreak, Riccoffy, or half a dozen other brands.

It isn't of optimum quality, but locally-grown Nyanga tea is available throughout the country.

## Alcohol
**Beer** *Chibuku*, the alcoholic tipple of the Zimbabwean masses, may be advertised as 'the beer of good cheer', but it's not at all tasty. Brewed from indigenous ingredients (yeast, millet, sorghum and mielies) and served up in buckets, it has the appearance of hot cocoa, the consistency of thin gruel and a deceptively mellow build up to the knockout punch. The idea is to mess oneself up as cheaply as possible. For the mass market, chibuku is sold either in paper cartons, (and called shake-shake) or large

plastic bottles which, after the Gulf War, came to be known as *scuds*.

You wouldn't go into a pub and order chibuku. It's drunk mainly by men in high-density township beer halls or in shebeens, those not-quite-legal drinking dens where admission is reserved for invited guests. It's also used for ceremonial purposes.

A step down from chibuku is *skokiaan*, a dangerous and illegal grain-based swill spiked with anonymous (and questionable) ingredients. It was common 50 years ago but is fortunately no longer popular.

The beer you're probably more used to is available in the form of lager, which is served as cold as they can get it. The most popular brand is Castle, followed by Bohlinger's, Lion and the misnamed Black Label. You can also try the excellent Zambezi Lager, which until recently was only for export.

**Wine** Although Zimbabwe's climate isn't ideal for grapes, it does sustain a limited wine industry in the region east and southeast of Harare. Although Zimbabwean wine doesn't have the best international reputation, the opening up of South Africa has brought experts north to Zimbabwe and the

---

### Glass vs Aluminium
The first thing to remember about soft drink consumption in Zimbabwe is that the bottle is worth more than the drink inside. Bottles represent money and aren't taken lightly. A Coke drunk on the spot costs a mere 30 cents, but to take it away in the bottle, you'll pay at least a 50 cent deposit – that is if the establishment will let the bottle out of sight.

Normally, to take a bottle one must exchange an empty. Everyone must obey the laws of bottle conservation; unless they pay for new bottles, merchants can only sell as many bottles of soft drink as they can supply empties to the distributor. The major pluses are the employment created by manufacturing and cleaning bottles and the limited amount of unsightly litter.

In 1994, both glass-bottle manufacturers and environmentalists were up in arms when the government debated allowing the import of beverages in aluminium cans. If you want to see what can happen when aluminium cans are introduced to replace glass, just visit Botswana, where mountains of empty cans roll and scatter about the streets and fields. Clearly, the benefits of returnable glass more than compensate for the inconvenience of returning the bottles.

country now produces some decent white and very palatable red wines.

The best-known winery is Mukuyu (☎ (14) 620410), near Marondera, which produces white wines (Chardonnay, Chenin blanc, Pinot blanc, Sauvignon blanc, Colombard, Muscat), reds (Cabernet Sauvignon, Merlot, Pinot Noir and Shiraz blends), rosés, Port (red and tawny) and sparkling wines. Stapleford (☎ (14) 308341; fax 303083), with wineries in Gweru and north of Harare, does Cordon Rouge, Colombard, Cabernet/Merlot, Emerald Steen, Muscat and Blanc Fumé.

**Spirits** Spirits are generally inexpensive, but quality varies. The local produce is, of course, cheaper, and it can be bearable, although Zimbabwean ouzo, whisky and brandy all taste a bit odd.

## ENTERTAINMENT

As in most countries, Zimbabwe enjoys a range of pubs, discos, nightclubs, cinemas and sporting events, but of most interest to visitors will be the unique style of music that has become a national trademark (see Arts in the Facts about Zimbabwe chapter). Many travellers make a point of attending a live African music performance sometime during their visit.

**Music Venues** The easiest way to find out what's on is to watch the newspaper entertainment sections. Lesser-known bands (which are often excellent!) usually advertise on posters around town fringes or near railway lines. Most hotels have house bands and ask US$1.50 to US$2 cover charges.

**Pungwes** The exact origin of the word *pungwe* is unknown, but it's believed to derive from *ngwe*, which means 'from darkness to light'. It was first used in the 1960s to refer to all-night urban discos. In the Second Chimurenga (1972-80), however, all-night celebrations of nationalistic unity between villagers and guerrillas, accompanied by morale-inspiring song and dance, were also called pungwes. Nowadays, any

sort of disco or musical performance may be advertised as a pungwe, meaning it begins in the evening and carries on through the night.

**Night Life Guidelines** Upmarket pubs and hotel bars require 'smart casual' dress, which normally means sporty dress for men, skirts or suits for women, and no trainers (joggers, sandshoes), thongs (flip-flops), denims or T-shirts. Although this is interpreted less rigidly than in the past, it's wise to err on the side of conservatism.

Foreigners are welcomed in African bars, discos and nightclubs, but prepare for attention. Some interest will be the product of friendly curiosity, but an equal share may be mercenary. To many Zimbabweans, foreigners represent wealth and their presence may inspire requests for money and drinks. Also, if you're dancing at a crowded performance or disco, leave your cash with a member of your group back at your table. Even better, leave money and valuables at the hotel and carry only enough to cover the evening's expenses, including a taxi home.

Unaccompanied women are especially prone to uncomfortable situations at discos, drinking establishments and live music venues. Unless you can face them head on, either attend with a male companion or try to gravitate towards local women.

## SPECTATOR SPORTS

Sporting events are popular in Zimbabwe, and football matches in Harare and Bulawayo attract large crowds.

International cricket is growing phenomenally in popularity. The earliest match in was held in 1890. In 1981, Zimbabwe was elected as an associate member of the International Cricket Council and scored a famous victory over Australia early in the 1983 World Cup. In 1992, the Zimbabwe Cricket Union staged its first home-based Test series, but was defeated by India. Although Zimbabwe is the lowest-ranked Test-cricketing nation, the team is improving and, in 1997, it drew with England in a home-staged Test series. The best-known international players are Graeme Hick (who played for England) and Grant and Andy Flower. The main venues are the Harare Sports Club and the Queens Club Ground on the north side of First Ave at Fife St, in Bulawayo. Zimbabwe's domestic competition is known as the Logan Cup.

Zimbabwe's Nick Price is one of the world's leading golfers and has won two of the four major international tournaments – the PGA in the USA and the British Open – and was world number one in 1995. The annual Zimbabwe Open Golf Tournament is held at the Royal Harare Golf Club in November.

The tennis-playing brothers Byron and Wayne Black beat Australia in the Davis Cup in early 1998. At the same time, their sister, Cora, was the number one junior women's tennis player.

No discussion of sport in Zimbabwe is complete without a mention of the country's most renowned sports export, Bruce Grobbelaar, who had a distinguished, if somewhat unorthodox, career in English league football. In 1981, after fighting on the side of the colonists in the Zimbabwean bush war, he migrated to the UK and joined Liverpool FC where he played until 1992, when he was transferred to Southampton.

In 1996 and 1997, Grobbelaar made international headlines when he was accused of belonging to an Asian betting syndicate which rigged English football league games. He allegedly accepted bribes to fix matches from 1991 to 1994. After two trials he was acquitted in 1997.

You can watch – and bet on – horseracing at Borrowdale and Ascot in Harare and Bulawayo, respectively.

## THINGS TO BUY

Curio shops in Zimbabwe dispense a remarkable amount of tourist kitsch. Notwithstanding the soapstone and wooden carvings which line roadsides and city footpaths, serious sculpture is a new and well-received form of expression in Zimbabwe. The big-name sculptors will naturally command high prices, but there are sculpture gardens, arts centres and gallery shops in Harare and Bulawayo where you can pick up some competent work by budding artists for very competitive prices. When looking for Shona sculpture, beware of scamsters attempting to pass off second-rate tourist carvings for work by the big names. Before parting with your hard-earned cash, get a feel for quality work by visiting a reputable art gallery, the National Gallery, Chapungu Kraal or Gallery 2000 in Harare.

Precious and semiprecious stones such as malachite, verdite, serpentine and low-grade emeralds are carved or set into jewellery and make pleasant mementoes. If you're intrigued by unusually beautiful natural patterns and 'meditation' pieces, some of the most interesting stone specimens are polished into egg-shaped chunks and sold for around US$4.50.

Another recent artistic manifestation is crochet, and magnificently intricate lace table coverings and bedspreads are hawked for very low prices – as little as US$10. Competition and therefore the lowest prices seem to be concentrated in the Kariba area but it's hard to avoid guilt pangs paying so little for the considerable time and expertise involved in their creation.

Baskets also display a rare level of skill and facility with design and are excellent value. They are sold along roadsides and in shops nationwide.

Around Binga and the upper Zambezi Valley you'll find Batonka stool seats with their roughly carved wooden bases. These are a speciality item and not easy to come by but if you're looking for something unusual to take home, they're a great choice. They're more readily available in Victoria Falls than in the area of origin.

Along the roadsides and in craft markets and curio shops around the country, you'll see row upon row of appealing – and often lovely and well-executed – African faces, hippos, rhinos and gracefully elegant giraffes carved from stone or wood. These can be very good value when purchased directly from the producer, and bargaining is expected. You should aim to pay around 40% of the initial asking price.

When purchasing wooden carvings, be aware that carvings and creations made of low-grade wood are often stained in hot tar and passed off as mahogany, mukwa, ebony or other prestigious and expensive woods. Some are quite skilfully done, but sometimes, just a whiff will reveal the deception.

If you prefer something more unusual, you may want to take home a toilet seat made of *mukwa* wood, a Zimbabwean speciality. They're available in Harare at hardware shops, such as PG Timbers. In Bulawayo, try J&F on the corner of Herbert Chitepo St and Fourth Ave or UBM on Fife St between Fifth and Sixth Aves.

On the issue of ivory, carvings sold in tourist shops around Zimbabwe will come with a certificate stating it's 100% culled ivory, which may or may not be legitimate. It is illegal to import non-certified ivory products into countries which are signatories to the CITES agreement – which includes virtually all western countries. Don't buy anything without such certification or it won't be allowed into your home country. Potential buyers should also consider the environmental impact of their purchase. Tourists who buy ivory and other wildlife products – even certified items – bolster the market for these products and indirectly support the illicit trade in endangered wildlife.

# Getting There & Away

This chapter covers access into Zimbabwe only from neighbouring countries. Information about reaching southern Africa from elsewhere in Africa or from other continents is outlined in the regional Getting There & Away chapter.

## AIR

Harare is the obvious hub for travel between Zimbabwe and neighbouring countries.

### Botswana

Air Botswana flies between Harare and Gaborone (US$220) and covers the safari market with three weekly flights between Maun and Victoria Falls (US$85).

### Namibia

Air Zimbabwe flies on Friday between Harare and Windhoek (US$285) and Air Namibia flies the same route on Tuesday and Friday (US$243). Air Namibia's Monday and Wednesday service between Windhoek and Victoria Falls (US$195) is a real milk run, stopping en route in Tsumeb, Rundu and Katima Mulilo (Mpacha). The Friday service runs via Maun and Katima Mulilo.

### South Africa

Both Air Zimbabwe (US$185) and Zimbabwe Express Airlines (US$191) have frequent services between Harare and Johannesburg.

There are also international services to and from Bulawayo and Victoria Falls. South African Airways, for example, has three nonstop flights weekly between Bulawayo and Johannesburg (US$115). SAA also flies on Tuesday and Saturday between Johannesburg and Victoria Falls (US$163), and offers occasional package discounts. Zimbabwe Express Airlines flies between Victoria Falls and Johannesburg five times weekly (US$191).

## LAND

For temporary entry to Zimbabwe with a hired vehicle, you need a 'Blue Book sheet', detailing the vehicle's particulars, as well as proof of insurance in the vehicle's country of registration. At the border, you must procure a temporary import permit, which must be presented when you depart.

Before accepting lifts from neighbouring countries, especially on trucks, ascertain what's in the back. Travellers have reported that drivers may try to force passengers to pay fines on illicit goods they're smuggling across borders.

### Overland Trucks

An increasingly popular option for A-to-B travel is on overland trucks. Although they were once known for exhausting long-haul routes across Africa, most companies also run shorter itineraries and, when there's space, you can ride along for around US$15 per day plus a food kitty contribution. Just speak with the drivers at overland stops (such as The Rocks in Harare or the Town Council Caravan Park in Victoria Falls). Currently, the most popular routes are from Harare to Nairobi (via Zambia, Malawi and Tanzania) or between Harare and Windhoek, Namibia. Most routes run via Victoria Falls, as well as Chobe and the Okavango Delta in Botswana and the Caprivi Strip and Etosha National Park in Namibia.

### Botswana

**Border Crossings** The Kazungula-Kasane crossing is open from 6 am to 6 pm daily. The Plumtree-Ramokgwebana land crossing is open from 6 am to 8 pm daily and the rail border crossing opens whenever a train passes. There's also a minor crossing at Pandamatenga, west of Hwange National Park, open 6 am to 4 pm.

The Kazungula ferry crossing between Zambia and Botswana is just 2km from the Zimbabwe-Botswana border post at Kazun-

180

gula; 55km further to the west is the Botswana/Namibia border post at Ngoma Bridge.

**Bus** By bus, the Plumtree-Francistown route is served by a twice-weekly Chitanda & Sons (☎ (14) 621657) express bus from Harare to Gaborone via Bulawayo and Francistown, departing from the Holiday Inn in Harare and the President Hotel in Gaborone.

On Thursday and Sunday at 6 am, the less reliable Express Motorways (Harare: ☎ (14) 796934; Bulawayo: ☎ (19) 61402) runs from the corner of Rezende St and Nelson Mandela Ave in Harare, via Bulawayo, to Gaborone (US$50). From Gaborone (☎ (267) 304470), they depart from the African Mall and the Gaborone Sun Hotel on Tuesday and Saturday at 6 am.

There's also a daily (except Sunday) no-frills coach service between Bulawayo and Francistown (US$3), departing early from the Lobengula St terminal in Bulawayo. Book through the Zimbabwe Omnibus Company (☎ (19) 67291) on Lobengula St, Bulawayo.

The only public transport between Victoria Falls and Kasane is the UTC bus which costs US$35 each way. UTC is at the post office complex in Victoria Falls.

**Train** The daily train between Bulawayo and Gaborone departs Bulawayo at 2.30 pm and arrives the following morning at 6.30 am. From Gaborone, it leaves at 9 pm and arrives in Bulawayo at 12.25 pm the next day. The fares between Bulawayo and Gaborone are US$33/27/9.10 in 1st/2nd/ economy class. This service no longer runs through to South Africa.

There is meant to be a buffet car on most services, but it's still wise to bring snacks and drinks. Note that Zimbabwe dollars aren't accepted on international trains, so have some Botswana pula or other hard currency. Sexes are separated in 1st and 2nd class sleepers unless you book a whole compartment or a two person coupé.

Botswana customs and immigration are handled on the train at the Plumtree border, and it's a relatively relaxed procedure. Arrivals to Zimbabwe go through immigration at the Plumtree border, but they must then clear customs at the station in Bulawayo. Foreign travellers with nothing to declare are rarely subjected to much scrutiny.

Rail travellers from Zimbabwe to either Botswana or South Africa must show their passport when booking the ticket.

**Hitching** For general comments on hitching in Zimbabwe, see the Hitching section in the Zimbabwe Getting Around chapter.

Hitching between Francistown and Bulawayo via Plumtree is fairly easy. Mornings are best for hitching into Botswana, while most afternoon traffic is headed towards Bulawayo. For lifts between Victoria Falls and Kazungula-Kasane, wait at the Kazungula Rd turn-off about 1km south-east of Victoria Falls town.

### Mozambique & Malawi
Everyone needs a visa for Mozambique, even if they're only transiting to Malawi. The most direct route between Harare and Blantyre in Malawi is across Mozambique's formerly infamous Tête Corridor via the Zimbabwe/Mozambique border at Nyamapanda and the Mozambique/Malawi border at Zóbué/Mwanza.

Travellers between Zimbabwe and Mozambique may only import or export US$200 in Zimbabwe dollars.

For the latest Mozambique road information and details on import and immigration fees phone the Beira Corridor Group (☎ (14) 739302; fax 721956), 207 Josiah Tongogara Ave, Harare.

**Border Crossings** The land border crossings at Mutare and Nyamapanda are open from 6 am to 6 pm daily. At the crossings, officials impose an informal 'border tax' of US$5, payable only in hard currency.

**Bus** Stagecoach Malawi has coaches between Harare and Blantyre (US$50, nine

ZIMBABWE

## The Beira Corridor

The Beira corridor is a 32km-wide swathe along the Mutare-Beira railway line to the Indian Ocean. The corridor has been opened and closed from time to time over the last 25 years, reflecting the political situation inside Mozambique and relations with its neighbours.

In 1974, the Portuguese colonial government in Mozambique was overthrown and replaced by the rebel government of FRELIMO (Frente pela Liberacão de Moçambique or Mozambique Liberation Front). Skilled labour and technical expertise fled for Portugal, leaving in its wake a trail of sabotaged buildings and equipment. The new government, professing a Marxist ideology, took up where the fleeing Portuguese had left off and proceeded to dismantle what remained of the country's economy, infrastructure and educational system. The railway line to Beira was closed and the enemy, Rhodesia, was left cloistered.

The reaction of the Smith government was clandestinely to establish an insidious counter-revolutionary destabilisation force called RENAMO (Resistência Nacional de Moçambique or MNR). Its engagement of FRELIMO's defence forces launched Mozambique into a devastating civil war.

When Zimbabwe gained independence in 1980, the new government aligned itself with the FRELIMO regime in Mozambique against RENAMO. The railway line was reopened to freight traffic between the two friendly neighbours. However, it was repeatedly being shut down by South African-backed RENAMO saboteurs, as the civil war continued until 1990.

In that year, FRELIMO ditched its Marxist ideology and announced that the country would switch to a market economy, thereby pulling the carpet out from under RENAMO. Following two rounds of peace talks in Rome in 1990, a cease-fire was arranged.

Miraculously, the situation in Mozambique now appears to have calmed. The widespread droughts of the early 1990s didn't help matters any but, in 1994, democratic elections were held, investors are cautiously returning and the economy is slowly rebounding from what once seemed to be a hopeless collapse. As a result, the Beira corridor is now open again for trade and a growing flow of tourists is reaching the Beira coast.

to 14 hours) three times weekly in either direction. They can be found at the bus terminal in both Blantyre and Lilongwe. A smaller company, Munorurama (☎ (14) 776651 or 751210), runs daily Harare-Blantyre transfers, via Mozambique, for US$20 (plus an additional US$10 to Cape Maclear or Monkey Bay). They depart from Monkey Bay at 6.30 am, Blantyre at 8.30 am and Harare at 7.30 am. Services fill up quickly, and pre-booking is strongly advised; they do pickups at most Harare backpackers lodges or you can meet them along Enterprise Rd.

Hitching isn't difficult, but minibuses also run daily between Nyamapanda, Tête and Zóbué and express buses connect the Mwanza/Zóbué border with Blantyre. If you're Beira bound, buses from Harare via

Mutare and Chimoio cost US$15; in Harare phone (☎ (14) 727231 or (14) 721658).

**Via Zambia** The easiest Zambia route between Zimbabwe and Malawi is via Lusaka (see Zambia later in this section), where frequent buses run to Lilongwe (US$15) from the Dedan Kimathi Rd terminal. Book tickets a day in advance. It's also easy to find buses from Lilongwe to the Zambian border, where minibuses leave for Chipata in Zambia, and then on to Lusaka.

Three daily Lusaka-Harare buses (US$8) depart at 6 am and arrive in Harare at around 4 pm, but there's no advance booking, so be at the Inter-City bus station at around 5.30 am. (Don't worry about finding a bus – the touts will rope you in!) The more comfortable Giraffe service

(US$8) runs twice weekly and can be booked on Cairo Rd opposite Mr Rooster in Lusaka or opposite the Holiday Inn in Harare.

Alternatively, catch a bus from Lusaka to Livingstone and enter Zimbabwe at Victoria Falls; from Livingstone, taxis to the border cost US$3 and a twice daily rail service is US$1.50.

### Namibia

Although Zimbabwe and Namibia share one common point in the middle of the Zambezi, there's no direct border crossing. The most straightforward route between them is from Victoria Falls to the Caprivi Strip via Botswana, which entails driving or hitching to Kazungula (over the Botswana border from Victoria Falls) and thence across the free transit route through Chobe National Park (which is exempt from park fees) to the Namibian border crossing at Ngoma Bridge. From there, it's a short hitch to Katima Mulilo in the Caprivi. See also Botswana, earlier in this section.

### South Africa

**Border Crossings** The only direct crossing between Zimbabwe and South Africa is at Beitbridge either on the road or the Trans-Limpopo rail link. The crossing is open from 5.30 am to 10.30 pm daily.

Fortunately, Zimbabwean economic reforms and the South African government have inspired liberalisation of customs procedures. Zimbabwean officials still watch for locals smuggling in South African goods without paying duty, but don't seem concerned about foreigners. If you're crossing into Zimbabwe and intend to return to South Africa, it's still wise to declare photo equipment, radios etc on the form provided, including serial numbers.

**Bus** The comfortable Mini-Zim Luxury Mini-Coaches (☎ (19) 72495), Budget Tours, at 1 Beverley Place, corner of Fife St and Tenth Ave, Bulawayo leave from the Bulawayo Holiday Inn for Johannesburg's Rotunda terminal on Wednesday and

Sunday at 6.30 am and arrive at 5.15 pm the same day. The fare is US$55.

The more personal Zimi-Bus services (Harare: ☎ (14) 481797; Johannesburg: ☎ (011) 678 2308) operate between the Harare Holiday Inn and Johannesburg's Rotunda terminal on Monday, Wednesday and Friday (US$60). Advance bookings are essential. Jacaranda Coach Lines (☎ (14) 754460) runs minibuses from Century House East on Nelson Mandela Ave in Harare at 6 am Monday and Friday and from Rotunda in Johannesburg at 7 am on Wednesday and Sunday. The one-way fare of US$63, includes light refreshments.

Silverbird Coach Lines (☎ (14) 729771, ext 109) departs from the Harare Sheraton on Monday and Friday at 1 pm and arrives in Johannesburg at 6.30 am the next day. From Rotunda it leaves at 1 pm Wednesday and 6.30 am Sunday and arrives in Harare at 7 am Thursday and 9.50 pm Sunday, respectively. The fare between Harare and Johannesburg is US$76. Zimbabwe Travel (☎ (19) 76644; <zimtravl@iafrica.com>) has Wednesday and Sunday services between Bulawayo and Johannesburg (US$50).

More comfortable are the Blue Arrow and Trans-Lux coaches, which have TVs, videos, reclining seats, air-con, toilets and first-aid trained attendants who serve drinks. Blue Arrow (Johannesburg: ☎ (011) 830 1411; Harare: ☎ (14) 729514; fax 729572; Bulawayo: ☎ (19) 65548; fax 65549) runs four times weekly between Johannesburg and Bulawayo (US$69) and daily except Saturday between Johannesburg and Harare (US$55). Twice weekly, the Bulawayo services connect with buses to and from Victoria Falls (US$21).

Trans-Lux (☎ (011) 774 3333), in Johannesburg, has services daily, except Monday and Wednesday, from Johannesburg at 9 pm, arriving in Beitbridge (US$28) at 7 am the next day and in Bulawayo (US$50) at 11.20 am. The Tuesday and Friday services continue to Victoria Falls (and return on Thursday and Sunday to connect with Johannesburg runs). From Bulawayo, they

ZIMBABWE

depart daily except Wednesday and Friday, arriving in Jo'burg the next afternoon. In Harare book at Trans-Lux (☎ (14) 725132; fax 725247), Third Floor, Hungwe House, 69 Jason Moyo Ave; in Victoria Falls, through UTC (☎ (113) 4771); and in Bulawayo, at Trans-Lux (☎ (19) 66528; fax 78347), LAPF House, Eighth St, between Fife and Jason Moyo Sts, or through Manica Travel (☎ (19) 540531). Their Harare terminal is at the Holiday Inn and in Bulawayo, it's the Bulawayo Rainbow Hotel.

Express Motorways (Harare: ☎ (14) 796934; Bulawayo: ☎ (19) 61402) runs daily between their St Barbara House terminal at the corner of Leopold Takawira St and Nelson Mandela Ave, Harare, and the Park Lane Hotel in Johannesburg, via City Hall car park in Bulawayo (US$50/37 from Harare/Bulawayo).

Commuter minibuses to Johannesburg, which operate on no fixed schedule (you could wait 30 minutes or six hours), depart when full from the Crowne Plaza Hotel in Harare (US$30) and the City Hall Car Park in Bulawayo (US$27).

If you're travelling to or from Cape Town, the new Route 49 Minibus Line (☎ (27-21) 799 7904 or mobile (27-83) 454 3791; fax (27-21) 788 2925; <zimcaper@dockside.co.za>), PO Box 151, St James 7946, South Africa, has weekly departures in a 10-seater VW bus for US$110/200 one-way/return. They leave on Saturday northbound and Tuesday southbound. The trip runs via Botswana and takes 24 hours, with only petrol stops en route. In Zimbabwe, the booking agents are UTC and Frontiers (☎ (19) 61402).

**Train** Rail connections between Zimbabwe and South Africa pass through Beitbridge; there are no rail services via Botswana. The *Trans-Limpopo Express* to Johannesburg leaves Harare at 7 am Sunday and arrives in Johannesburg at 9 am Monday. Northbound, it leaves Johannesburg at 8.30 am on Friday and arrives in Harare at 9.55 am Saturday. The Bulawayo Express leaves

Johannesburg on Tuesday at 3.25 pm and arrives in Bulawayo at 4.20 pm Wednesday; from Bulawayo, it leaves at 9 am Thursday and pulls into Johannesburg at 9.01 am Friday.

The 1st/2nd class fares from Johannesburg are US$80/55 to Harare and US$60/43 to Bulawayo. Between Harare and Johannesburg, double compartments cost US$247/240. There's also a daily run from Beitbridge to Johannesburg, departing at 1 pm and arriving at 5.30 am the next day. The 1st/2nd class fares are US$41/28.

Bookings are essential on all routes; in South Africa, contact Main Line Trains (☎ (011) 773 2944), PO Box 2671, Joubert Park 2044, Johannesburg. In Harare, the contact number is (☎ (14) 700011).

**Hitching** For general comments on hitching in Zimbabwe, see the Hitching section in the Zimbabwe Getting Around chapter.

Hitching into South Africa via Beitbridge is relatively easy, but expect waits. Unfortunately, South African immigration officials seem to regard hitchhikers as a lower form of humanity. If there's a best time to cross the border, it's around 12.30 pm when the shift is changing or just before the border closes, when everyone is ready to go home without delay.

In South Africa, the Dial-a-Lift system helps bring lifts and riders together. There's a small fee, but riders may only have to help with petrol. In Johannesburg, they're at Bizarre Cut, Shop 9, on the corner of Rockey and Raymond Sts, Yeoville 2198 (☎ (011) 648 8136 or 648 8602).

### Zambia
**Border Crossings** The land border crossings at Chirundu and Kariba are open from 6 am to 6 pm daily; the Victoria Falls crossing is open from 6 am to 8 pm daily.

The Kazungula ferry crossing between Zambia and Botswana is just 2km from the Zimbabwe-Botswana border post at Kazungula; 55km further to the west is the Botswana/Namibia border post at Ngoma Bridge.

**Bus** From Harare's Mbare bus terminal, ZUPCO and Giraffe run several daily buses to Lusaka (US$8), via Chirundu. The first departure is at 6 am; the buses get crowded so arrive early. The trip takes nine hours.

The more comfortable Power Coach Express (☎ (14) 668716), 10 Williams Ave, Ardbennie, Harare, has daily services between Mbare and Lusaka for US$12. The thrice weekly Big 5 Travel bus (Harare: ☎ (14) 700332; Lusaka: ☎ (260-1) 288971; fax 289362) runs between Harare and Lusaka via Kariba and costs US$22. Express Motorways runs between Lusaka's Pomodzi Hotel and Johannesburg, via its Harare terminal. Services run southbound on Tuesday, Thursday and Saturday and northbound on Monday, Wednesday and Friday. The more comfortable Trans-Lux has a similar southbound service on Sunday and northbound on Friday. For Express Motorways and Trans-Lux contact details, see earlier in this chapter.

**At Victoria Falls** It's a 1km walk (or US$1 taxi ride) between the Zambian and Zimbabwean border posts at Victoria Falls, and you're rewarded with great views of the falls from the Zambezi bridge. The Zimbabwean border post lies 1km from Victoria Falls town and the Zambian post is 7km south of Livingstone. Taxis between the border and Livingstone cost around US$3 and the twice daily rail service is US$1.50. For details on day trips/activity trips between Victoria Falls and the Livingstone area, see the Western Zimbabwe chapter.

### LEAVING ZIMBABWE
For non-residents over 12 years of age, the airport departure tax is US$20 (residents pay Z$20). At the airport, it must be paid in US currency and only US$10 and US$20 notes are accepted. You can also pre-pay the departure tax in Zimbabwe dollars at any commercial bank at the official exchange rate.

# Getting Around

At independence, Zimbabwe inherited good rail links between all major centres and a superb network of tarred roads and, although things have deteriorated, they're still among the best in Africa.

What Zimbabwe lacks, however, is sufficient foreign exchange to purchase and maintain public transport commensurate with the quality of its infrastructure. The Economic Structural Adjustment Plan and Export Retention Schemes have improved things considerably, but it's still often difficult to find spare parts and, while Zimbabweans are adept at jerry-rigging repairs, equipment remains in short supply.

One corollary of the transport shortage is that buses run only where and when demand justifies it. Unfortunately for tourists, the masses are more interested in population centres than national parks and tourist sites, and people who do visit those sites are likely to have their own vehicles.

## AIR
### Domestic Air Services
Air Zimbabwe, the national carrier, flies domestic routes between Harare, Bulawayo, Kariba, Victoria Falls, Hwange National Park and Gweru. Services to Masvingo and Buffalo Range (Triangle/Chiredzi) have now been handed over to United Air Charters. The well organised Zimbabwe Express Airlines also serves domestic routes between Harare and Bulawayo, Hwange and Victoria Falls, and also flies to and from Johannesburg. Foreigners may purchase

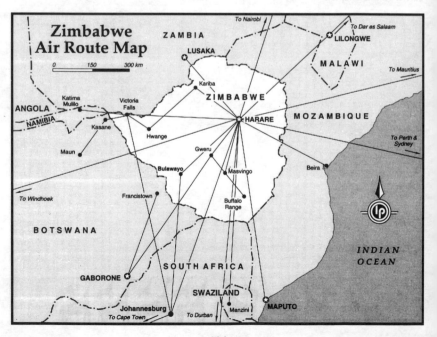

Zimbabwe Air Route Map

Zimbabwe domestic (but not international) flight tickets with Zimbabwe dollars.

## Airline Offices

You'll find Air Zimbabwe offices/agents at the following addresses:

*Bulawayo*: Treger House, Jason Moyo St, PO Box 1000 (☎ (19) 72051)

*Chiredzi*: Lowveld Travel, Mutual House, 77 Knobthorne Rd (☎ (131) 2295)

*Gweru*: Manica Travel Services, corner of Robert Mugabe St and Fifth Ave, PO Box 1347 (☎ (154) 3316)

*Harare*: City Air Terminal, corner of Third St and Speke Ave, PO Box 1319 (☎ (14) 794481)

*Hwange National Park*: United Touring Company, Hwange Safari Lodge, PO Box DT 5792, Dete (☎ (118) 393)

*Kariba*: Kariba Airport, PO Box 13 (☎ (161) 2913)

*Masvingo*: Travel World, Allan Wilson St (☎ (139) 62131)

*Victoria Falls*: Air Zimbabwe Terminal, Livingstone Way, PO Box 60 (☎ (113) 4316)

Zimbabwe Express is at 1st Floor, Kurima House Annexe, 89 Nelson Mandela Ave, PO Box 5130, Harare (☎ (14) 729681; fax 737117; <zimexair@hre.iafrica.com>).

## Charter Airlines

United Air Charters, a subsidiary of the United Touring Company (UTC), runs charter flights to Lake Kariba camps as well as between domestic airports. It's now the exclusive operator for the airfields at Masvingo and Buffalo Range (Triangle/Chiredzi). It also operates the Flight of the Angels at Victoria Falls. It's headquartered at Harare International Airport (☎ (14) 731713), with branch offices in Kariba (☎ (161) 2305) and Victoria Falls (☎ (113) 4220).

## BUS

Zimbabwe has two types of bus – express and local (most commonly known as African buses). A third option is overland trucks, which often serve as a travellers' no-frills bus service (see the Zimbabwe Getting There & Away chapter).

## Express Bus

Express buses are relatively efficient, operating according to published timetables and making scheduled snack and toilet stops along the way. The best scheduled services between major cities and towns are operated by Blue Arrow/United Transport Group (☎ (14) 729514; fax 729572; <spring@harare.iafrica.com>). If you're doing a lot of travelling in a short time, Blue Arrow offers a good-value travel pass. Avoid travel agency commissions by booking through Blue Arrow's offices in Harare or Bulawayo (see the Getting There & Away sections in the Harare and Bulawayo chapters for details).

## Local (African) Bus

Local buses, on the other hand, go just about anywhere people are living. They're good value and services are frequent between main centres. Some of the best companies are Tenda, Phumulani, Tauya, Shu-Shine, Zimbabwe Omnibus, ZUPCO, Hwange Special Express and the ominously named Tombs Motorways. Levels of service and reliability vary, but they're sometimes just as quick as express buses.

These buses are also fairly crowded (although not by Asian or Latin American standards) but are ultra cheap – for instance only US$4 between Harare and Bulawayo. The novelty of having a foreigner aboard will scarcely be containable for most people and you're more likely to meet Zimbabweans than on the express buses, which cater mainly to foreign travellers.

We caught the local bus to Mutare, which was great fun. I thought we had a lot of luggage until I saw people putting double beds on top of the bus! Well, what do you do if you want a new bed and don't have a car? You go to town, buy a bed and take it home on the bus, don't you? One man tried to get on the bus with a goat in a carrier bag, but the conductor asked him to tie its legs together and put it on top. Fortunately, it didn't seem any worse for wear when he lifted it down at the end of his journey.

**Julie Sheard, UK**

African buses normally depart from the *musika* (*renkini* in Ndebele), township markets which lie outside the town centre. Larger cities and towns also have an 'in-town bus terminal', where you can be picked up or dropped in the city centre. The problem will be finding a seat – or even standing spaces – once the bus has left the musika.

Although you'll hear vague murmurings about average numbers of buses per day, they follow no real timetables. Don't get flustered if no-one seems to have specific information. Between major population centres, buses depart when full throughout the day, usually until mid-afternoon, but if you're unsure about departures, turn up as early as possible. Sometimes, the only bus of the day leaves at 6 am!

As enjoyable and interesting as the local buses can be, finding the right bus can be frustrating. Especially at Harare's Mbare musika, travellers and locals alike are assailed by touts who cluster around and create confusion. Try not to get rattled. If you need help finding a particular bus, try asking a woman or an older man.

Try to avoid travelling on weekends after pay day – normally the end of the month – or at the beginning and end of school holidays, when pandemonium reigns at bus terminals. People spend up to two nights queuing for transport and tourists aren't accorded any special treatment.

## TRAIN

Zimbabwe has a good railway network which connects Harare, Bulawayo, Victoria Falls and Mutare. Trains are very cheap, especially in 3rd or economy class.

Zimbabwean rolling stock includes 1920s passenger cars, complete with beautiful brass- and wood-trimmed interiors, even in 2nd class. Although the romantic scheduled steam service between Bulawayo and Victoria Falls was discontinued in 1993, there are still expensive steam 'rail safaris' on this route, and steam locomotives are still used for shunting duties in the Bulawayo rail yard. Travellers report the

occasional use of steam on some runs (perhaps when the diesel engines are being serviced).

Most trains run at night and, because of the relatively short distances, move very slowly in order to arrive at stations at a convenient hour of the morning. Sleeping compartments and bedding are inexpensive and well worth the investment if you require a comfortable night's sleep.

Sexes are separated at night unless you book a family compartment or a coupé (two-person compartment) in advance for an additional charge. Second class compartments hold six adults but children are not counted and, as most Zimbabwean women bring their children, single women may prefer a coupé.

Few domestic trains pull buffet cars, so bring food and drink. On international trains, you must pay for food and drink in the currency of the country you're travelling through. Unless you have a private coupé (which can be locked by the conductor) don't leave your gear unattended.

For domestic trains, bookings open 30 days ahead and for international services to Johannesburg, you can book 90 days ahead. Book as early as possible and advise them whether you're bringing your own bedding.

Direct questions to the inquiries desks in Harare (☎ (14) 733901), Bulawayo (☎ (19) 363111, after hours ☎ (19) 322284) and Victoria Falls (☎ (113) 4391).

### Timetables

For information on international rail connections between Zimbabwe and Botswana and South Africa, see the Zimbabwe Getting There & Away chapter.

**Harare to Mutare**  The 1st/2nd/economy class fares between Harare and Mutare are US$7/6/2. Trains run daily:

| Station | Departs | Station | Departs |
| --- | --- | --- | --- |
| Harare | 9.30 pm | Mutare | 9.00 pm |
| Marondera | 11.41 pm | Nyazura | 11.05 pm |
| Rusape | 2.54 am | Rusape | 12.04 am |
| Nyazura | 3.30 am | Marondera | 3.28 am |
| Mutare | 5.25 am | Harare | 5.20 am |

**Bulawayo to Harare** There is a nightly run in both directions, with all classes available. Between Bulawayo and Harare, the 1st/2nd/economy class fares are US$11/9/4.

| Station | Departs | Station | Departs |
|---|---|---|---|
| Bulawayo | 9.00 pm | Harare | 9.00 pm |
| Gweru | 1.15 am | Kadoma | 12.01 am |
| Kwe Kwe | 2.30 am | Kwe Kwe | 1.24 am |
| Kadoma | 4.00 am | Gweru | 3.00 am |
| Harare | 6.50 am | Bulawayo | 6.40 am |

**Bulawayo to Victoria Falls** Between Bulawayo and Victoria Falls, the 1st/2nd/economy class fares are US$21/16.50/8. There is no longer a scheduled steam locomotive service on this route.

| Station | Departs | Station | Departs |
|---|---|---|---|
| Bulawayo | 7.00 pm | Victoria Falls | 6.30 pm |
| Dete* | 1.29 am | Hwange | 10.22 pm |
| Hwange | 3.04 am | Dete* | 12.50 am |
| Victoria Falls | 7.00 am | Bulawayo | 7.00 am |

*Dete is the station for Hwange Park

## CAR & MOTORCYCLE

The easiest way to travel is in a private vehicle; you can stop where you like, visit national parks at leisure and reach places not served by public transport. Motorbikes also perform well on open highways but aren't permitted in national parks.

Foreign-registered vehicles can be imported temporarily (free of charge) but unless you already have third-party insurance which is valid in Zimbabwe, you must purchase an inexpensive policy at the border when entering the country. Travellers in foreign-registered rental cars may have to buy commercial insurance.

A driving licence from your home country is valid for visits of up to 90 days, provided it's written in English. Otherwise, you need an authenticated translation plus a photograph.

At the time of writing, petrol or 'blend' (which may be mixed with varying amounts of sugar cane ethanol) cost around US$0.50 per litre.

### Rules of the Road

As in the rest of southern Africa, traffic keeps to the left. Use of seat belts is technically compulsory in the front seat and motorists must use headlights between 5.30 pm and 5.30 am. The speed limit on the open highway is 120 km/h, while villages and towns are posted lower – normally from 60 to 90 km/h. Note that police now use radar in rounding up speeders, particularly around Beitbridge, where many South Africans quickly learn that 210 km/h (not uncommon in South Africa) isn't acceptable here.

Drivers must pull over if they see the presidential motorcade (identifiable by the accompanying police motorbikes with sirens and blue flashing lights) and wait for it to pass before proceeding.

Take special care to watch for wildlife. Antelope (especially kudu) may leap onto the road from nowhere and elephant saunter into your path without warning. A collision would write off the car. On communal lands, highways become footpaths for people and their domestic animals; drivers who run down a suicidal goat or sheep are expected to compensate the owner financially.

### Rental

Hiring a vehicle in Zimbabwe can be expensive so, if you're on a tight budget, it's most feasible with a group. Rental vehicles are in short supply, however, so book well in advance. If your rental vehicle is registered in a neighbouring country, carry adequate proof of insurance or you may have to buy a Commercial Vehicle Guarantee at the border, an insurance policy which can cost as much as the insurer thinks you're able to pay.

**Insurance & Restrictions** Hire cars from Botswana, Namibia or South Africa may be brought into Zimbabwe with permission from the car hire company, but at the border you must secure a temporary export permit from the vehicle's home country and a temporary import permit for Zimbabwe. Ask the hire company to provide relevant paperwork.

Most larger car hire companies insist on a completed credit card payment slip as a deposit (do not leave the card itself), but smaller companies often accept a cash deposit of Z$1000 to Z$5000. The minimum rental age varies, but it's usually between 23 and 25 years. With some agencies the maximum age is 65 years.

With all rental agencies, CDW (collision damage waiver) insurance, normally with an excess of between US$175 and US$300, is charged on top of the hire rate. (Opting out of it means that the driver is responsible for any damage.) If you're making a cash deposit, you'll probably have to increase it by the amount of the excess (deductible). Note that CDW does not cover 2WD vehicles in Mana Pools or on many gravel roads; for these, you must hire a 4WD.

**Rental Agencies** The major rental companies – Avis, Hertz, and Europcar/Inter-Rent – accept their own credit cards as well as major credit cards (Visa, MasterCard, American Express and Diners Club). There are also numerous cheaper agencies, but vehicle maintenance may not be a high priority and, in the case of a breakdown, few provide rescue service or replacement vehicles. Some may even hold renters responsible for routine maintenance and repairs, so read the fine print carefully!

Currently, the big companies charge around US$30 per day plus US$0.35 per kilometre for the cheapest Group A car (a Mazda 323 or similar). For longer periods – normally more than five days – you'll pay US$60 per day with up to 250 or 300km free per day. Smaller firms start at around US$25 per day plus US$0.32 per kilometre, or US$60 per day with unlimited kilometres. For a 4WD, rates start at US$55 per day plus US$0.60 per kilometre, or US$140 per day with unlimited kilometres.

*Amaswazi Car Hire*
 93B George Silundika and Ninth Ave, Bulawayo (☎ (19) 79778)
 Singing Bird Curios, Dete (☎ (118) 255)

*Avis*
 5 Samora Machel Ave, Harare (☎ (14) 720351; fax 750526)
 Harare International Airport, Harare (☎ (14) 575144)
 99 Robert Mugabe Way, Bulawayo (☎ (19) 68571; fax 68572)
 Livingstone Ave & Mallet Drive, Victoria Falls (☎/fax (113) 4532)
*Bulawayo Car Hire*
 Vundla Safari Tours, Zimnat House, Jason Moyo St, Bulawayo (☎ (19) 65133; fax 61324)
*Compact Car Hire*
 1 Avon House, Queensway shopping centre, Hatfield, PO Box UA473, Harare (☎ (14) 577747)
*Compass Car Hire*
 28 George Ave, Msasa, PO Box AY912, Amby, Harare (☎ (14) 720026)
 Shop 2, Parkade Centre, Ninth Ave and Fife St, PO Box AC181, Ascot, Bulawayo (☎ (19) 78576; fax 61430)
*ERB Car Hire*
 198 Herbert Chitepo Ave, PO Box 6390, Harare (☎/fax (14) 721023)
*Hertz*
 Beverley Court & Nelson Mandela Ave, Harare (☎ (14) 706254; fax 792793)
 George Silundika St and Fourteenth Ave, Bulawayo (☎ (19) 74701; fax 63383)
 Hwange Safari Lodge, Dete (☎ (118) 393; fax 367)
 Lake View Hotel, Kariba (☎ (161) 2411; fax 2662)
 43 Hughes St, Masvingo (☎ (139) 62131; fax 64205)
 Holiday Inn, Mutare (☎/fax (120) 64784)
 Bata Building, Parkway Drive, Victoria Falls (☎ (113) 4267; fax 2097)
*Ike's Bikes Motorbike Hire*
 Harare (☎ (14) 792202)
 Kariba (☎ (161) 2839)
*Impexo Car Hire*
 24 East Rd, Belgravia, PO Box 1360, Harare (☎/fax (14) 705780)
*Interrent/Europcar*
 19 Samora Machel Ave, PO Box 3430, Harare (☎ (14) 752559; <europcar@mail.pci.co.zw>)
*Rent-a-Jeep*
 12 Market St, Eastlea, Harare (☎ (14) 703730; fax 793384)
*Thrifty Car Rental*
 10 Samora Machel Ave, corner Harare St, HP Box HG92, Highlands, Harare (☎ (14) 736587; <bellbar@harare.iafrica.com>)

88A Robert Mugabe Way, Bulawayo (☎/fax (19) 64550)

*Transit Car & Truck Hire*
80 George Silundika Ave, Harare (☎ (14) 706919; fax 734121)
86 Robert Mugabe Way, Bulawayo (☎ (19) 76495; fax 76394)
18 Sopers Centre, Victoria Falls (☎ (113) 2109)

*Victoria Falls Car Hire*
Suite 7/8, Phumula Centre, PO Box 236, Victoria Falls (☎/fax (113) 4357)

## Purchase

Unless you're staying for an extended period, it's not worth buying a vehicle in Zimbabwe. Not only are vehicles generally expensive and in less-than-optimum condition, they're also in short supply. You'd find it considerably easier and less expensive to buy a car in South Africa, especially in Johannesburg, but be sure to secure the paperwork necessary to take it to Zimbabwe temporarily. Note that you won't be permitted to sell a vehicle in Zimbabwe without officially importing it and paying a substantial duty.

## BICYCLE

Most major routes in Zimbabwe are surfaced and in excellent repair. Road shoulders are often sealed and separated from the mainstream of vehicular traffic by painted yellow lines, so they may be used as bicycle lanes. Although there are certainly rough, hilly sections, the relatively level landscape over much of the country (particularly along major roads) further facilitates long-distance cycling. However, bicycles are not permitted in game parks.

The predictable climate helps cyclists considerably. Winter weather is especially ideal, with cool, clear days, and the generally easterly winds are rarely strong enough to hinder cycling. Although distances between towns and points of interest are long by European standards, there are plenty of small stores between towns where you can stop for a drink and a chat.

If you're riding a lightweight bicycle, bear in mind that next to nothing is available in terms of spares, not even in Harare. Local cycles take 26- or 28-inch tyres, so you can sometimes find these, but 27-inchers or 700C tyres are almost impossible to obtain. Bring with you all the tools and spares you think may be necessary. The best cycle shops in Harare are Zacks, on Kenneth Kaunda Ave opposite the railway station, and nearby Manica Cycles on Second Ave. Bicycles may be hired in Harare, Bulawayo and Victoria Falls.

## HITCHING

Hitching is never entirely safe in any country in the world, and we don't recommend it. Travellers who do decide to hitch a ride should understand that they are taking a small but potentially serious risk. However, many people do choose to hitch, and the advice that follows should help to make their journeys as fast and safe as possible.

Hitching is easy in Zimbabwe and is many locals' standard means of transport. It offers a good opportunity to meet Zimbabweans, and many travellers consider hitching easier and more reliable than taking the local buses. Many drivers accept passengers in order to help pay for their journey, so ask about charges before you climb in; the rate will never exceed the local bus fare.

It's probably not wise to hitch in the afternoon or evening on weekends or public holidays, when a large proportion of drivers are under the influence of alcohol.

Although it's better to hitch in pairs, it is possible for women to hitch alone if there are women and/or children in the car. Obviously it is not worth the risk of accepting a lift from a car full of men. It is also best to determine the driver's degree of sobriety before climbing in to the car; drunken driving is a serious problem in Zimbabwe. Hitching at night is not advisable, nor is it permitted in national parks.

It's important to note that away from the main road system vehicles are few and far between so, if you're headed for the hinterlands, plan on walking and waiting. Even on some major highways – the approaches to Beitbridge from Masvingo or Bulawayo, or the long haul from Bulawayo to Victoria Falls – there isn't an abundance of traffic. Vehicles that do pass, however, are more than likely to offer a lift.

In cities or towns, the best place to solicit lifts is at petrol pumps, especially at the last station before the open road where nearly everyone heading in your direction will stop to top up the tank. Don't feel uncomfortable about asking; locals do it too, and it's a straightforward way to select the right lift and determine prices.

At its best, hitching does provide opportunities to meet interesting people. Readers have sent the following stories about hitching in Zimbabwe:

Remember that a car is never full, even if you think it is. Two of us and our backpacks had a ride in an ancient Peugeot 404 together with 12 other people.

**Marc van Doornewaard, Netherlands**

I could not believe how easy hitching was, despite foolishly deciding to hitch around the eastern part of the country in a group of four. We always managed to get a lift within 20 minutes of setting up camp beside the road. One such lift managed to cram all of us plus our packs into his car, drove 77km out of his way to drop us off, and then three days later came to collect us and take us to his farm to stay for as long as we wished. It is occurrences like this which made travelling worthwhile.

**Stephen Millward, UK**

I was lucky enough to be offered transport to Mlibizi in response to a message I left on the camp site notice board in Victoria Falls. It was with a lovely South African couple who, despite my offers to pay my way, said all they wanted was company and conversation. Although they wanted to leave at 4 am to catch the ferry the next day, we cracked open some student plonk red wine that night to celebrate our meeting. I staggered back to my cabin at midnight thinking how lucky I was. The 300km drive the next morning went smoothly and for me, the bonus was meeting a couple of socially conscious and environmentally committed South Africans.

**A traveller, New Zealand**

I hitched everywhere – a lone white female – and I never felt uncomfortable with the people who picked me up. In fact, I met some of the most fascinating types – a fellow who'd just discovered gold in his yard, an entrepreneur refurbishing an historic hotel, etc. I hitched in rural areas as well, with the same experiences. I always asked if they charged, but almost never had to pay. I really felt hitching was a part of seeing Zimbabwe!

**Susan Loucks, USA**

## WALKING

For the majority of Zimbabweans, recreational walking is unheard of, but since walking is the cheapest method of transport, people often resign themselves to foot travel, particularly in rural areas where hitching is difficult. It's not uncommon to meet someone without luggage who's strolling off to a market or to visit friends or relatives in a village 30km away.

Away from the main bus routes, where visitors – particularly hitchhikers – may find themselves in a similar situation, time allowances should be made for this sort of thing.

## BOAT

Since Zimbabwe is a landlocked country, the only boats of any consequence are two ferry systems that operate on Lake Kariba between Kariba town and Binga or Mlibizi near the western end of the lake. They're handy especially if you want to do a circular tour of Zimbabwe without retracing your steps between Victoria Falls and Bulawayo.

The more popular and comfortable option is with Kariba Ferries, whose two car ferries, the *Seahorse* and *Sea Lion*, each sail twice weekly between Kariba and Mlibizi. The more basic DDF ferry connects National Parks Harbour in Kariba with Binga and Gache Gache. The Binga ferry departs fortnightly, with overnights in Chalala and Sengwa. There are also weekly runs to Tashinga and Gache Gache. For further details about both ferries, see Kariba in the Northern Zimbabwe chapter.

Transport to Binga and Mlibizi can be difficult; without a vehicle, you'll have to rely on lifts from fellow passengers. There are local buses from Bulawayo to Binga via Dete Crossroads, but they only pass within 15km of Mlibizi.

## LOCAL TRANSPORT
### To/From Harare International Airport
For the 15km trip from Harare's international airport to the centre, taxis cost around US$7. There's also an express bus which costs US$2 and stops at most hotels and guesthouses in the centre; in the other direction, it departs from Meikles Hotel (☎ (14) 720392 for schedules). The Meikles Hotel, the Sheraton and the Crowne Plaza offer free airport shuttles for guests. There are no hotel-booking facilities at the airport but currency exchange is available whenever international flights arrive.

### Bus
Both Harare and Bulawayo have city bus and minibus services connecting the centre with suburban areas. In both cities, try to board the bus at the terminal if at all possible, otherwise it will be packed to overflowing. Once people are hanging out the windows and doors, the driver won't bother to stop to pick up more. Local bus fares currently range from US$0.10 to US$0.25. Pay in Zimbabwe dollars.

### Emergency Taxi
Emergency taxis are easily recognised – look for clunky stripped-down Peugeot station wagons with 'emergency taxi' painted across one door. The name has nothing to imply about the urgency of their condition; most just keep plugging along against all odds. They're licensed to operate only within city limits along set routes and charge a standard nationwide rate to anywhere they're going. This works out at roughly US$0.25 – pay in Zimbabwe

dollars. Their routes aren't advertised, so you'll have to ask for help from the driver or one of the numerous locals certain to be milling around in the terminal.

### Taxi
By western standards, city and suburban taxis are inexpensive in Zimbabwe – generally less than US$2 anywhere in the city centres and US$4 to US$5 into the Harare or Bulawayo suburban areas.

Most legal taxis are metered, but if you're boarding at a railway station or bus terminal, especially if you're headed for a hotel, drivers will often try to forego the meter. This may well be an attempt at overcharging you or ripping off the taxi company. If you think you're being taken for a ride, insist on using the meter.

Unlicensed taxis aren't actually any cheaper than licensed taxis (they're constantly having to pay fines and bribes) and there are plenty of horror tales about high-speed chases involving unlicensed taxis and pursuing police vehicles.

A problem in Harare has been caused by unscrupulous taxi drivers who collaborate with thieves. They drop clients far enough from their door to allow accomplices to mug disembarking passengers. The drivers then get a share of the booty. Before you climb into a taxi, always note the number plate and, especially at night, insist on being dropped right at your door. In Harare, Rixi Taxi and Cream Line are recommended as the most reliable companies. Unlicensed taxis often take similar sounding names, such as Pixi or Dream Line, so be aware.

## ORGANISED TOURS
For a list of organised tours, see the Zimbabwe section in the Organised Tours chapter earlier in this book.

# Harare

Harare, with a metropolitan population of over 1.6 million, is not only Zimbabwe's capital, but also the heart of the nation in nearly every respect. In short, whatever Harare lacks, Zimbabwe probably doesn't offer.

The city inherited a distinctly European flavour from its colonisers, and it continues as Zimbabwe's showpiece city and centre of commerce and government, replete with high-rise buildings, traffic and their attendant urban action.

Most visitors have their first taste of Zimbabwe here, but if it's not the Africa you expected – and chances are it isn't – what you're looking for isn't far away. The bustle of the African marketplace hums at Mbare *musika*, only a few kilometres from the city centre, and giraffe and zebra roam at Lake Chivero, half an hour away by car.

## History

The first Shona inhabitants of the marshy flats near the kopje where Harare stands today called themselves Ne-Harawa after the regional chief, whose name meant The One Who Does Not Sleep. The Mbare, under rule of the lower Chief Mbare, controlled the kopje itself. Later, another small clan led by Chief Gutsa settled in what is now Hillside, south-east of the city centre. When the two groups inevitably clashed, latecomer Gutsa emerged victorious. He not only killed his rival, Mbare, but also sent the Mbare people packing into the rugged plateaus above the Zambezi Valley.

On 11 September 1890, however, a new intruder arrived. The Pioneer Column of the British South Africa Company, led by Major Frank Johnson, saw Chief Gutsa's kopje and decided it would make an ideal site for agriculture and was therefore ripe for colonial expropriation. He even suggested to Leander Starr Jameson that the kopje was destined to be the capital of the new country they were founding.

## HIGHLIGHTS

- Stroll around Zimbabwe's largest market at Mbare
- Appreciate African material arts at the National Gallery
- Eat, drink, shop, dance and enjoy the nightlife in Zimbabwe's vibrant capital city
- Hike to the ancient rock paintings at Domboshawa and Ngomakurira

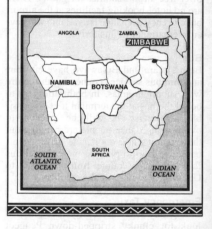

On 13 September 1890, the Union Jack was raised at what is now African Unity Square and the settlement named Fort Salisbury, after British prime minister Robert Cecil, the Marquis of Salisbury. The next winter brought the first influx of white settlers from the south, arriving to collect on promises of fertile farm lands and lucrative gold claims along the Zambezi.

Over the following seasons, more white settlers and merchants arrived to develop the low-lying lands immediately east of the kopje. By now the government had decided the higher ground to the north-east was eminently more suitable and set about

ZIMBABWE

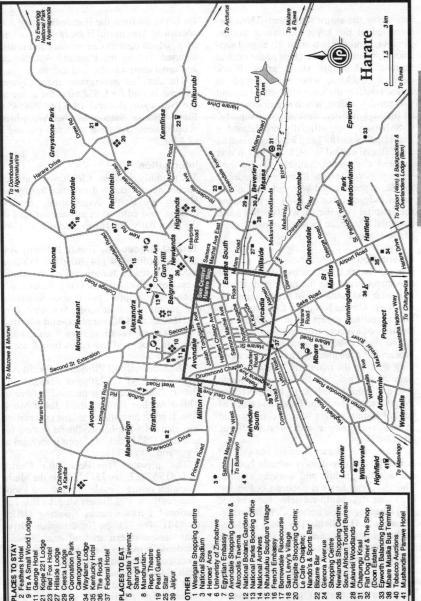

**Harare**

0    1.5    3 km

To Arcturus

To Ewanrigg
National Park
& Nyamapanda

To Mutare
& Ruwa

To Ruwa

To Domboshawa
& Ngomakurira

To Mazowe & Mvurwi

To Chinhoyi
& Kariba

To Bulawayo

To Masvingo

To Chitungwiza

To Airport (4km) & Backpackers &
Overlanders Lodge (8km)

Cleveland
Dam

See Central
Harare Map

**PLACES TO STAY**
2   Feathers Hotel
9   It's A Small World Lodge
11  George Hotel
21  Kopje 221 Lodge
23  Red Fox Hotel
27  Hillside Lodge
29  Cresta Lodge
30  Coronation Park
    Camground
34  Wayfarer Lodge
35  Kentucky Hotel
36  The Rocks
37  Federal Hotel

**PLACES TO EAT**
5   Aphrodite Taverna;
    Shangri La
8   Manchurian;
    Reps Theatre
19  Pearl Garden
25  Sitar
39  Jaipur

**OTHER**
1   Westgate Shopping Centre
3   National Stadium
4   Heroes' Acre
6   University of Zimbabwe
7   Egyptian Embassy
10  Avondale Shopping Centre &
    Akrooolis Taverna
12  National Botanic Gardens
13  National Parks Booking Office
14  National Archives
15  Nhukutuku Sculpture Village
16  French Embassy
17  Borrowdale Racecourse
18  Sam Levy's Village
20  Chisiplse Shopping Centre;
    Le Cafe Chisiplse;
    Nando's & Scots Bar
22  Bizarre Bar
24  Glenora Avenue
    Shopping Centre
26  Newlands Shopping Centre;
    South African Tourist Bureau
28  Mukuvisi Woodlands
31  Chapungu Kraal
32  Flat Dog Diner & The Shop
    (Coon Estate)
33  Epworth Balancing Rocks
38  Mbare Musika Bus Terminal
40  Tobacco Auctions
41  Mushandira Pamwe Hotel

relocating the entire settlement. Those entrenched at the kopje refused to budge, however, and the two areas developed separately, resulting in the clash of the central Harare and Kopje street grids. Black African workers, who were forced to remain outside the main city, settled around present-day Mbare, which remains the heart of the high-density, working-class suburbs.

Salisbury was officially proclaimed a municipality in 1897 and was recognised as the colonial capital in 1923. In 1935, it was granted city status. Salisbury languished through WWII and the following decades of unrest, sanctions and war, but at Zimbabwean independence in 1980, it was made the capital of the new Republic and renamed Harare, an incorrect transliteration of Ne-Harawa.

## Orientation

Central Harare is formed by the collision of two street grids. On the main grid, streets run north and south whilst avenues run east and west. On the Kopje grid, streets run in both directions except those which are extensions of avenues from the main grid.

The city centre is compact, making it a breeze for pedestrians. The central shopping area, on the main grid, stretches from Samora Machel Ave to Kenneth Kaunda Ave and from Fourth St to Julius Nyerere Way. Cheaper shops and hotels and much of central Harare's night life are concentrated in the lively Kopje area west of Julius Nyerere Way.

The rest of Harare sprawls outward in both high and low-density suburbs housing the wealthy, middle and working classes. The industrial heart is concentrated in the high-density, south-western suburbs of Workington, Southerton, Willowvale, Mbare and Highfield. The most densely-packed dormitory community is sprawling Chitungwiza, which could actually be considered a separate city.

**Maps** The useful *Greater Harare Street Guide*, a gazetteer of large-scale maps, takes in the entire metropolitan area. It sells

for US$2.50 from the Harare Publicity Association. Also useful is the *Harare Visitors Map*, which contains advertising and is distributed free by the Publicity Association and most tourist hotels and lodges.

The detailed government map, *Central Harare*, is sold for US$2.50 at the office of the Surveyor General (☎ (14) 794545), Electra House, Samora Machel Ave, which is open weekdays from 8 am to 1 pm and 2 to 4 pm.

## Information

The monthly *Sunshine City Harare* outlines upcoming events; it's distributed free by the Harare Publicity Association. Sports, cinema, and cultural events are outlined in the local daily, the *Harare Herald*.

**Tourist Offices** The Harare Publicity Association office (☎ (14) 705085), PO Box 1483, Causeway, Harare, sits on the southwest corner of African Unity Square. It's not overly helpful, but it does distribute the monthly publication, *Sunshine City Harare*, as well as pamphlets and advertising. It's open weekdays from 8 am to noon and 1 to 4 pm and Saturdays from 8 am to noon.

The more helpful Zimbabwe Tourist Authority (☎ (14) 758730; fax 758828), PO Box CY286, Harare, is on the 7th floor of Three Anchor House, at 54 Jason Moyo Ave. It provides national tourist information and also sells Zimbabwe-theme posters for less than US$1 each. It's open from 8 am to 1 pm and 2 to 4.30 pm.

The private Travellers Info Centre (☎ (14) 757727; fax 757728) is in the Metro shopping centre, beside the Eastgate shopping centre at 109 Robert Mugabe Rd. The National Parks Central Booking Office (☎ (14) 706077), on Sandringham Drive near the northern end of the Botanic Gardens, provides park information and takes parks bookings. It's open weekdays from 9 am to 3 pm.

If you're heading south, the South African Tourist Bureau is in Newlands shopping centre on Enterprise Rd.

**Foreign Consulates** For embassy and consulate details, see the Zimbabwe Facts for the Visitor chapter.

**Money** All banks change US dollars and UK pounds sterling, both in cash and travellers cheques. The exchange desk at Harare airport opens for international arrivals, but it's often short of cash and often limits transactions to around US$100. Larger hotels normally exchange currency, but at poor rates. Harare also has a growing number of ATMs which accept VISA and ATM cards (the Cirrus and Plus systems seem to be the most widespread).

**Post & Communications** The main post office, on Inez Terrace, has stamp sales and poste restante upstairs in the arcade, and a parcel office in a separate corridor near street level. The philatelic bureau, which sells colourful and historical stamps, is on the 2nd floor. The poste restante (only available at the main post office) and stamp sales counters are open from 8.30 am to 4 pm weekdays and until 11.30 am on Saturday.

There are other branches on the corner of Third St and Julius Nyerere Way and near the corner of Second St and Union Ave. Each suburb also has its own post office.

The central telecommunications office, upstairs in the main post office, is basically a chronically busy block of public telephone boxes, and overseas calls still require a sackful of coins (a better place to queue is along First St Mall, which has several clean, mostly functional telephone boxes). Long distance calls are much easier on private phones or with telephone cards. You'll find card phones in front of the Courteney Hotel, at the main post office, in the international airport lounge and on First St Mall. Directory assistance is available on ☎ 92. For fax details, see Post & Communications in the Zimbabwe Facts for the Visitor chapter.

Email and Internet access is available at the Internet Cafe (☎ (14) 758194; <baboon@icafe.co.zw>), 4th floor, Eastgate shopping centre, at the corner of Robert Mugabe Ave and Second St. Long-stay visitors may set up accounts. ZimSurf Internet Cafe (☎ (14) 750297; fax 751046; <cybercafe@email.zimsurf.co.zw>) provides similar services at the corner of Jason Moyo Ave and First St. There's also an Internet facility at The Tube night club (<thetube@baobab.cszim.co.zw>), at 125 Mbuya Nehanda St.

**Immigration** The relatively amenable Department of Immigration Control (☎ (14) 791913) organises visa and length-of-stay extensions on the 1st floor of Liquenda House, on Nelson Mandela Ave between First and Second Sts.

**Travel Agencies** Thomas Cook (☎ (14) 728961) is in the Pearl Assurance building on Jason Moyo Ave between Third and Fourth Sts. American Express is represented by Manica Travel (☎ (14) 704012) on the 2nd floor of the Eastgate shopping centre. They change travellers cheques and also make bookings for major coach lines.

On the 5th floor of the same building is Safaris Incorporated (☎ (14) 728256; fax 728255), which books a range of safaris. If you're after a Lake Kariba houseboat booking, the specialist to call is Rhino Rendezvous (☎ (14) 735912; fax 795344; <rhinoren@mail.pci.co.zw>), 56 Samora Machel Ave, PO Box GD334, Greendale, Harare.

For overland trips, international flights, adventure safari bookings, adrenaline activities and information on tours and transfers, see Worldwide Adventure Travel (☎ (14) 773364; fax 734724; <wwathre@primenet .zw.com>), PO Box 7071, Ottawa House, Suite 5, 14 Angwa St.

**Film & Photography** The novel Strachan's Photo Chemist & Tea Terrace at 66 Nelson Mandela Ave near Second St does one-hour photo processing and, while you wait, you can enjoy muffins, light meals and Zimbabwean coffee. Just as good for print film processing is Goldprint at 7 George Silundika Ave, between First and Angwa

Sts. Both slides and print film are sold at Photo Inn on the corner of First St and Nelson Mandela Ave.

**Bookshops** The largest source of popular books, magazines, foreign paperbacks, African literature, textbooks and coffee-table books is the government-owned chain, Kingston's, which has major outlets in the Parkade shopping centre on First St between Samora Machel and Union Ave, and on the corner of Second St and Jason Moyo Ave.

Upstairs in the Fife Ave shopping mall is the Book Cafe (☎ (14) 792551), formerly the recommended Grass Roots bookshop. It has a wide range of books and sometimes presents poetry-reading and storytelling sessions in the evenings. The adjoining rooftop cafe serves up light meals and drinks. On occasions they also stage live entertainment.

The book exchanges, Booklover's Paradise at 48 Angwa St and the Treasure Trove at 26C Second St, on the corner of George Silundika Ave, will provide pulp reading material. The latter is a real Ali Baba's cave, with stacks of second-hand books as well as used clothing, knives, and sports and camping equipment.

**Left Luggage** For left luggage, the Air Zimbabwe office on Speke Ave charges Z$10 per piece per day, and the railway station charges Z$3. The latter is open Monday to Friday 6 am to 1 pm and 2 to 9.30 pm; on Saturday, it's open 6 am to 10 pm and on Sunday, from 5.30 to 9.30 pm.

All backpackers lodges offer safe luggage storage, but avoid leaving valuables at cheaper hotels.

**Parking** Street parking isn't advisable for vehicles bearing foreign number plates. Multi-storey parking garages (parkades) are found on Julius Nyerere Way near the main post office and on First St. The entrances to the First St parkade are on Samora Machel Ave and Union Ave. The parkades are open from 6 am to 11 pm.

**Laundry** Harare's only coin-operated laundry is the Fife Avenue Laundrette, in the Fife Ave shopping centre near the corner of Fife Ave and Fifth St. It's open from 7 am to 7 pm every day, and costs US$2 to wash and US$1.20 to dry.

Mid-range hotels also provide laundry services, and charge around US$1 for a T-shirt and US$1.20 to US$2 for trousers. Top-end hotels charge considerably more. Many budget places also have laundry sinks, but normally you must provide your own drain plug.

**Camping Equipment** Limited camping equipment, including butane Camping Gaz canisters for Bleuet stoves, is available at Fereday & Sons on Robert Mugabe Rd between First and Angwa Sts. You can hire camping equipment at Rooney's Hire Service (☎ (14) 792724) at 144 Seke Rd, south of the centre. They hire tents, sleeping bags, propane lamps and cookers, hurricane lamps, cooking gear, cool boxes, and camp tables and chairs but it's mostly heavier stuff that's better suited to mobile safaris than backpacking.

**Medical Services** A recommended doctor in Harare is Dr JR Hulme (☎/fax (14) 723051 office; ☎ (14) 223626 home), whose office is at 25 Medical Centre, 52 Baines Ave.

**Emergency** For police, fire and ambulance services dial 99. For non-emergency police calls, phone ☎ (14) 733033. Alternatively, call the private MARS ambulance (☎ (14) 734513).

**Dangers & Annoyances** During the drought of the early 1990s, many desperate rural farmers migrated into Harare and, lacking marketable skills, wound up unemployed and living in marginal conditions. Unscrupulous factions saw an opportunity and began organising criminal gangs. As a result, the city saw an alarming increase in violent crime, with tourists as prime targets.

When word spread that the city was

unsafe, tourist numbers dropped dramatically and the city countered by increasing its police force and posting officers all over the centre. By day, you're at little risk if you use common sense and watch for pickpockets but there are still security problems, especially in the areas around the Avenues. Also, anyone passing along Selous Ave past the Earlside Hotel and Palm Rock Villa must beware of muggers. After dark everything changes; never walk around the city at night and only use official taxis!

Chancellor Ave, an extension of Seventh St which eventually turns into Borrowdale Rd, is the site of both the Executive President's residence and the State House. It's off limits between 6 pm and 6 am and guards are under orders to fire without question at any person or vehicle caught beyond the barricades between those hours (even if the booms haven't been lowered).

### National Archives

Founded in 1935, the National Archives (☎ (14) 792471), Private Bag 7729, Causeway, Harare, harbours historical records of both colonial Rhodesia and modern Zimbabwe. It's on Ruth Taylor Rd, Gun Hill, near Borrowdale Rd, 3km north of the centre.

The upstairs foyer contains striking artwork by Zimbabwean youngsters, and the Beit Trust Gallery displays colonial historical artefacts and photos as well as original accounts by European explorers and colonists. The downstairs foyer contains alternating exhibits and biographies of Zimbabwean war heroes. In separate rondavels are old photos and newspaper clippings from the Second Chimurenga; one is dedicated to war statistics and the other salutes ZANU. As one reader put it, 'you get to know the people whose names you read on street signs all over the country'. Even non-history buffs will enjoy the aloe gardens.

Historical researchers should head for the ground floor reading room, which harbours an exhaustive collection of Zimbabwean records and literature. You can also buy prints of old African maps and Thomas Baines paintings for US$3 each.

The archives are open from 8.30 am to 4 pm Monday to Friday and 8 am to noon on Saturday; admission is free. Take the Borrowdale or Domboshawa bus from the market square terminal. The archives are signposted on Borrowdale Rd.

### Queen Victoria Museum

The best things at this small and easily digestible rundown on the history of life and rocks in Zimbabwe are the appealing concrete creatures standing guard at the front – a chameleon, a praying mantis, a pangolin and a snail. The museum can't compare to its Bulawayo counterpart, but the fossils and the dioramas are good, and the other exhibits will occupy an hour or so.

The museum is in the Civic Centre complex between Pennefather Ave and Rotten Row. It's open from 9 am to 5 pm daily, including weekends. Foreigners pay US$2 admission.

### National Gallery of Zimbabwe

Zimbabwe's National Gallery (☎ (14) 704666) is the final word on African art and material culture from around the continent. It was founded in 1957 around a core of works by European artists and was later enhanced by the fruits of an African sculptors workshop established by the late Frank McEwen, who was the museum's first director. Although most early Zimbabwean works catered to commercially profitable European tastes, African expression eventually blossomed and Shona sculpture has now become an internationally recognised art form. The gallery's crowded outdoor sculpture garden and small indoor display exemplify some of the genre's best work.

On the ground floor are drawings and paintings from the original collection and others from the colonial and post-colonial eras. There's nothing gripping, but you will find a few gems.

The captivating 1st floor display of vibrant and earthy African art and material culture presents an insight into a private

ZIMBABWE

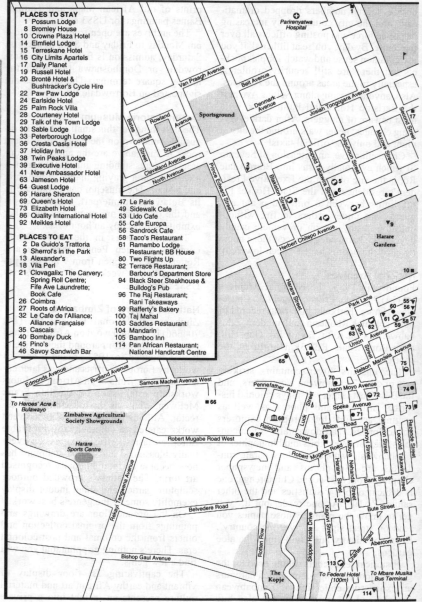

**PLACES TO STAY**
1 Possum Lodge
8 Bromley House
10 Crowne Plaza Hotel
14 Elmfield Lodge
15 Terreskane Hotel
16 City Limits Apartels
17 Daily Planet
19 Russell Hotel
20 Brontë Hotel &
   Bushtracker's Cycle Hire
22 Paw Paw Lodge
24 Earlside Hotel
25 Palm Rock Villa
28 Courteney Hotel
29 Talk of the Town Lodge
30 Sable Lodge
33 Peterborough Lodge
37 Holiday Inn
38 Twin Peaks Lodge
39 Executive Hotel
41 New Ambassador Hotel
63 Jameson Hotel
64 Guest Lodge
66 Harare Sheraton
69 Queen's Hotel
73 Elizabeth Hotel
86 Quality International Hotel
92 Meikles Hotel

**PLACES TO EAT**
2 Da Guido's Trattoria
9 Sherrol's in the Park
13 Alexander's
18 Vila Peri
21 Clovagalix; The Carvery;
   Spring Roll Centre;
   Fife Ave Laundrette;
   Book Cafe
26 Coimbra
27 Roots of Africa
32 Le Cafe de l'Alliance;
   Alliance Française
35 Cascais
40 Bombay Duck
45 Pino's
46 Savoy Sandwich Bar

47 Le Paris
49 Sidewalk Cafe
53 Lido Cafe
55 Cafe Europa
56 Sandrock Cafe
58 Taco's Restaurant
61 Ramambo Lodge
   Restaurant; BB House
80 Two Flights Up
82 Terrace Restaurant;
   Barbour's Department Store
94 Black Steer Steakhouse &
   Bulldog's Pub
96 The Raj Restaurant;
   Rani Takeaways
99 Rafferty's Bakery
100 Taj Mahal
103 Saddles Restaurant
104 Mandarin
105 Bamboo Inn
114 Pan African Restaurant;
   National Handicraft Centre

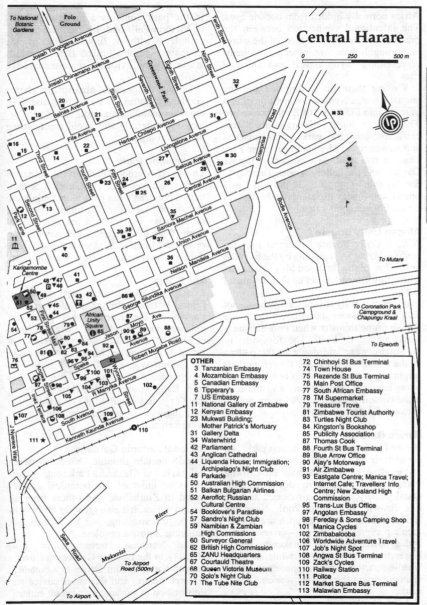

# Central Harare

0    250    500 m

ZIMBABWE

**OTHER**

3 Tanzanian Embassy
4 Mozambican Embassy
5 Canadian Embassy
6 Tipperary's
7 US Embassy
11 National Gallery of Zimbabwe
12 Kenyan Embassy
23 Mukwati Building;
   Mother Patrick's Mortuary
31 Gallery Delta
34 Waterwhirld
42 Parliament
43 Anglican Cathedral
44 Liquenda House; Immigration;
   Archipelago's Night Club
48 Parkade
50 Australian High Commission
51 Balkan Bulgarian Airlines
52 Aeroflot; Russian
   Cultural Centre
54 Booklover's Paradise
57 Sandro's Night Club
59 Namibian & Zambian
   High Commissions
60 Surveyor General
62 British High Commission
65 ZANU Headquarters
67 Courtauld Theatre
68 Queen Victoria Museum
70 Solo's Night Club
71 The Tube Nite Club

72 Chinhoyi St Bus Terminal
74 Town House
75 Rezende St Bus Terminal
76 Main Post Office
77 South African Embassy
78 TM Supermarket
79 Treasure Trove
81 Zimbabwe Tourist Authority
83 Turtles Night Club
84 Kingston's Bookshop
85 Publicity Association
87 Thomas Cook
88 Fourth St Bus Terminal
89 Blue Arrow Office
90 Ajay's Motorways
91 Air Zimbabwe
93 Eastgate Centre; Manica Travel;
   Internet Cafe; Travellers'
   Info Centre; New Zealand High
   Commission
95 Trans-Lux Bus Office
97 Angolan Embassy
98 Fereday & Sons Camping Shop
101 Manica Cycles
102 Zimbabalooba
106 Worldwide Adventure Travel
107 Job's Night Spot
108 Angwa St Bus Terminal
109 Zack's Cycles
110 Railway Station
111 Police
112 Market Square Bus Terminal
113 Malawian Embassy

Africa normally hidden from outside eyes. The intentional connection between the practical and aesthetic natures of the works is thoroughly haunting, especially in items representing mythological and spiritual rites.

Visiting thematic exhibitions and the annual Baringa/Nedlaw competition offer a glimpse into the future of Zimbabwean art. The museum shop sells art publications, crafts and sculptural works by both masters and newcomers. The entrance is on Park Lane at the south-east corner of Harare Gardens and the gallery is open Tuesday to Sunday from 9 am to 12.30 pm and 2 to 5 pm. From Monday to Saturday admission is US$1; on Sunday it's free.

### African Unity Square

African Unity Square is a great spot for reading, lazing and lunching by the fountain or strolling along the Jason Moyo Ave side, where flower vendors set up their colourful stalls.

It was originally named Cecil Square, not after Cecil Rhodes, but Robert Cecil, the British prime minister when Fort Salisbury was founded in 1890. The footpaths in the square were laid down in the pattern of the Union Jack and the flower gardens originally memorialised colonial settlers. Now, however, the gardens and the new name commemorate the 1988 unity accord between ZANU and ZAPU.

### Harare Gardens

Harare Gardens, the city's largest park, is a popular picnic spot, with expansive lawns and gardens. Clustered around the Crowne Plaza Hotel at its southern edge are the National Gallery, an open-air theatre and the Les Brown Swimming Pool. Near the Herbert Chitepo Ave entrance are a children's playground, an open-air restaurant, and a bowls club. On weekends, music blares from the bandstand while strolling wedding parties pose for photographs and visitors browse through the weekend crafts market.

A small island-like stand of rainforest in the park contains a miniature model of Victoria Falls and the Zambezi Gorges, complete with a tiny replica of the Zimbabwe-Zambia bridge. Below the falls is a small pond, evidently representing Lake Kariba.

Despite the peaceful atmosphere, Harare Gardens is notorious for robbery and rape, the latter mainly after dark. Watch your belongings carefully and avoid short-cutting through at night.

### Greenwood Park

This neighbourhood park on the corner of Herbert Chitepo Ave and Seventh St contains a children's fun park with a miniature railway and cable car. The fun park operates on Saturday from 2 to 5 pm and Sunday from 10 am to 1 pm and 2 to 5 pm. It's also open on Monday, Wednesday and Friday during school holidays from 9 am to noon.

### The Kopje

Rising above the south-west corner of central Harare is the granite 60m-high hill known as the Kopje. This prominent outcrop once served as Chief Mbare's capital and, at its foot, white colonists first set up their shops and businesses. Access to the summit, where the Eternal Flame of Independence was lit on 18 April 1980, is from Bank St and Rotten Row. However, the Kopje has acquired a nasty reputation for muggings, so avoid going alone or carrying valuables.

### National Botanic Gardens

The 58 hectare Botanic Gardens between Belgravia and Alexandra Park contain specimens of most of the botanical species found in Zimbabwe and others from all around Africa. It's also great for birdwatching or just strolling, but be warned that mugging is now a problem.

The National Herbarium (☎ (14) 303211), in the Botanic Gardens at Downie Rd and Sandringham Drive, is a botanical research centre, and dispenses advice and information to gardeners and plant enthusiasts by appointment. There's a map of the gardens at the parking area off Sandring-ham Drive, south of the herbarium.

The gardens are open daily between sunrise and sunset and admission is free. To get there, walk for 25 minutes north of Herbert Chitepo Ave along Fifth St or the Second St Extension. Alternatively, take a northbound bus along Second St Extension and get off at Downie Ave, where there's a signpost for the gardens. It's then two blocks east to the herbarium.

### Historic Buildings

Harare's remaining colonial architecture, which is concentrated along Robert Mugabe Rd, is outlined in *Historical Buildings of Harare* by Peter Jackson. If it's not in the shops, contact Quest Publishing (☎ (14) 704076) at Makomva House, 107 Leopold Takawira St, Harare.

**Market Hall** The recently renovated market hall, built in 1893, still functions as a market and forms a backdrop for the market square bus terminal near the corner of Bank and Mbuya Nehanda Sts.

**Mother Patrick's Mortuary** This tiny place, in front of the Mukwati building on Livingstone Ave between Fourth and Fifth Sts, is one of Harare's oldest buildings. Built in 1895, it was used to store the deceased until their relatives could be contacted and brought in from the countryside. Mother Patrick, born Mary Patrick Cosgrave, was an Irish missionary who organised hospitals around Zimbabwe in the late 19th century. Today, there's a small display about Mother Patrick and her work.

**Parliament Buildings** The parliament buildings, at the corner of Nelson Mandela Ave and Third St, were originally conceived as a hotel in 1895 by South African politicians Daniel Mitchell and Robert Snodgrass. The following year, however, the partially completed building was commandeered by the Rhodesian army for use as a barracks. In 1898, when Mitchell and Snodgrass failed to repay their building loan, the

building, which was being referred to as the Cecil Building, was repossessed by the government, with the intention of turning it into a post office.

However, the new Legislative Assembly took a liking to it and on 15 May 1899 it was taken over as the parliament building. It has since undergone several renovations (in 1969 it grew to six storeys) but is still used by the Senate and Legislative Assembly for official proceedings. The current plan is to construct new parliament buildings on the Kopje but, by present indicators, that project is still a few years off.

To attend a free weekly guided tour and an explanation of government operations, or sit in the gallery seats during sessions, apply to the Chief Information Officer (☎ (14) 700181), Parliament of Zimbabwe, PO Box 8055, Causeway, Harare.

**Anglican Cathedral** Harare's first church, which was constructed of African-style mud and pales by Canon Balfour in 1890, stood at the corner of Second St and Nelson Mandela Ave. That site is now occupied by the Anglican Cathedral of St Mary & All Saints, an uninspiring granite-block structure designed by South African architect Sir Herbert Baker. (The only remaining artefact from the original church is an altar cross fashioned from cigar boxes, which is housed in St George's chapel of the main cathedral.)

Although construction began in 1913, the cloisters weren't completed until the late 1940s and the remainder of the project was not finished until 1964. Part of the delay was attributed to a dispute over the shape of the bell tower (which was finally completed in 1961). The architect originally envisioned a Great Zimbabwe-like conical tower, but that was rejected in favour of a square, prison-like structure. The ten bells in the tower were cast in London by Whitechapel Foundry and chime daily at 6 pm.

If you'd like to attend an African church service, a good choice is the Baptist church on the corner of Second St and Fife Ave.

ZIMBABWE

**Town House** The Town House, on Julius Nyerere Way, dates back to 1933 and serves as Harare's town hall. This primarily Italian Renaissance-style structure houses the mayoral, city council and town clerk's offices. The centrepiece of the gardens is a colourful floral clock. Appointments to view the interior are necessary (☎ (14) 706536).

**ZANU Headquarters** Don't miss catching a glimpse of the modern ZANU headquarters, near the Sheraton Hotel, which is topped by the Mugabe government's cockerel crest. The building, is shaped like a *chibuku* beer carton, and is known as the shake-shake building, taking the nickname of the cartons.

### Mukuvisi Woodlands

The nearest thing to a zoo in Harare is the Mukuvisi Woodlands Environmental Centre (☎ (14) 747152), PO Box GD 851, Greendale, Harare, which lies 7km east of the city. Over half of the 265 hectare reserve is natural *msasa* parkland used for picnics, walking and birdwatching, while the rest has been set aside as a wildlife park. The resident zebra, giraffe, warthogs and antelope and the hand-reared elephants, Shungu and Tendai (which are fed at 3.30 pm daily) can be observed from a viewing platform. There's also a large aviary and the Wildlife Society's Woodland Shop, which sells curios, maps and a range of nature-oriented books, stationery and field guides.

The reserve is open from 8.30 am to 5 pm daily and admission is US$1.50. Two-hour guided foot safaris are conducted daily at 2.30 pm and cost US$3. One hour horse tours are available Monday to Friday for US$5; they must be booked in advance.

Mukuvisi lies just off Glenara Ave South on the Hillside Rd extension, which is a 20 minute walk from Coronation Park. Take the Msasa bus from Market Square or from the corner of Fourth St and Robert Mugabe Rd, or the Greendale bus from the Rezende St terminal, and ask to be dropped as near to Mukuvisi as possible.

### Chapungu Kraal

Chapungu Kraal and Shona Village (☎ (14) 786648) is an attempt to create a cultural theme park for tourists. Gallery Delta may strive to be the 'artistic heartbeat of Harare', but this place touts itself as the lifeblood for the entire continent – 'the pulse of Africa'. You can't get much more vital than that!

*Chapungu* is the Shona word for the bateleur eagle, the spirit messenger of the Shona people. A half hour guided tour of the worthwhile Shona sculpture garden explains the granite, jasper and verdite works of Zimbabwe's most renowned artists, providing an overview of the genre. Many works, you'll notice, deal with the hazards of social failure – excessive drinking, for example, or (horror of horrors) eating your totem animal, which as you will see can yield very unpleasant results.

Chapungu lies 8km from the city centre on the Doon Estate, 1 Harrow Rd, Beverley East, Msasa. Take the Greendale bus from the Rezende St terminal and walk from Coronation Park or hitch east on Mutare Rd past the Beverley shopping centre. Turn right into the industrial site and after a sharp right turn, pass the security gate at the Sorbaire sign.

The garden, museum, craft shop, bar and tearoom are open Monday to Friday from 8 am to 6 pm and on weekends from 9 am to 5.30 pm. Admission costs US$0.50 and guided tours are US$2.50. African dance performances are held on weekends at 3 pm. The resident *nyanga* (shaman) is available daily except Monday.

### Heroes' Acre

On a hill overlooking Harare, the dominating obelisk of Heroes' Acre serves as a monument to the ZIPRA and ZANLA dead during the struggle for liberation from the Rhodesian oppressor. It holds the tombs of the war heroes (as well as several who died in car accidents) and a war museum is to be built there.

This North Korean-designed canonisation of the dead heroes – as well as the Leninisation of Robert Mugabe – is quite an impressive production. However, the liberators' just cause is mocked by a preoccupation with military violence, 'raised fist' posturing and lip service to socialism. The most recent inductee into Heroes' Acre is the late wife of Robert Mugabe, Ghanaian Sarah 'Sally' Mugabe, who died of kidney failure in 1994 at the age of 60.

If you aren't put off by the propaganda, Heroes' Acre is worth a visit. You must first pick up a visitor's permit from the Ministry of Information, (Room 514 of Liquenda House on Nelson Mandela Ave) which is normally issued immediately to foreigners (Zimbabweans have more difficulty getting permits).

To reach Heroes' Acre, which is 5km from the city centre on the Bulawayo Rd, catch the Warren Park bus from the terminal just west of Chinhoyi St along Samora Machel Ave. Admission and guided tours of the site are free.

### Tobacco Auctions

Zimbabwe is one of the world's largest tobacco producers, and the evil weed currently draws in more foreign exchange than any other commodity. Between April and October (dates vary depending on the harvest), auctions are held daily from 8 am to noon at the world's largest tobacco auction floor, on Gleneagles Rd in Willowvale. In a single day an average of 16,000 bales change hands – that's one every six seconds.

Visitors are welcome to watch the trading and guided tours of the floor are available, as well as commentary on the complex tobacco industry. Take the Highfields bus from the corner of Fourth St and Robert Mugabe Rd. To confirm dates and times of trading activity, contact the Tobacco Sales Floor (☎ (14) 668921) or the Tobacco Marketing Board (☎ (14) 666311).

### Mbare

Mbare, 5km from the centre, is probably the only Harare suburb worth visiting in its own right. Before independence, when Harare was called Salisbury, Mbare was known as Harare Township. The current name honours the Shona chief Mbare, who was headquartered on the Kopje in what is now central Harare.

All Mbare's activity is centred on the musika, Zimbabwe's largest, busiest and most hectic market and bus terminal. Between 6 am and 6 pm it hums constantly, crowded with shoppers, travellers, and business people. Shoppers will find everything from second-hand clothing, appliances and recycled bits of junk to herbal remedies, African crafts and jewellery. Fresh fruit and vegetables are sold in produce stalls at a fraction of supermarket prices. A good time to visit is Sunday afternoon; while the rest of Harare shuts down, Mbare keeps buzzing.

At the Canon Paterson Art Centre on Chaminuka Rd, founded by the Bulawayo reverend Canon Paterson in the 1940s, you can watch artists carving soapstone, verdite, wood and serpentine into souvenirs which are sold around the country. You can also buy curios for slightly less than you'd pay elsewhere.

Buses, commuter buses and emergency taxis run to Mbare every few minutes from the corner of Cameron St and Charter Rd. A taxi for up to five passengers costs around US$2; unlicensed taxis can be cheaper but riskier and aren't really a good idea.

For information on the Mbare musika inter-city bus terminal, see Getting There & Away later in this chapter.

### Zimbabwe Agricultural Society Show

The Zimbabwe Agricultural Society Show is held at the showgrounds, near the Sheraton Hotel, around the end of August. It's a national showcase for agricultural, commercial and manufacturing industries – much like a state fair in the midwestern USA. It was first held in 1897 as a cattle and produce show, and has grown into an annual event attracting over 150,000 spectators and 150 commercial exhibits, along with traditional dance performances, live music and military demonstrations. Check with the Publicity Association for dates and scheduled events.

## Activities

The Olympic-sized Les Brown Swimming Pool in Harare Gardens behind the Crowne Plaza Hotel is open daily from 10 am to 6.30 pm from late August to early May. The rest of the year, hours are 11 am to 4 pm. Admission costs about US$0.10. Alternatively, visit Waterwhirld, 2km east of the centre on Samora Machel Ave, which offers water slides and an artificial beach.

The popularity of golf in Harare is illustrated by seven courses, including the internationally acclaimed Royal Harare Golf Club, 20 minutes walk north of the centre on Josiah Tongogara Ave. Green fees are some of the world's lowest: a round of 18 holes costs under US$3 on weekdays and US$5 on weekends. Club hire costs US$2 per day and caddies charge around US$2 per game. Mini-golf is available at Waterwhirld.

The Mountain Club of Zimbabwe runs monthly climbing, birdwatching and bushwalking outings, and visitors are welcome. Contact numbers are listed in *Sunshine City Harare*.

For information on tennis and squash, contact the Harare Sports Club (☎ (14) 791151). Alternatively, phone for squash (☎ (14) 722234) or tennis (☎ (14) 724424) court bookings. The Hash House Harriers (☎ (14) 664618) meet weekly on Monday.

If you've always wanted to learn skydiving, courses are available for just US$90. Contact Bruce on (☎ (14) 787404).

## Organised Tours

Several companies operate Harare-area day tours to museums and historical buildings, Ewanrigg National Park, Chapungu Kraal, Mukuvisi, Epworth Balancing Rocks, Domboshawa, the Kopje, the tobacco auction floors (weekdays, April to September only), Mbare, Larvon Bird Gardens, the Lion & Cheetah Park and Lake Chivero, as well as longer trips further afield. Departures are normally guaranteed with two or more participants. Main companies include African Explorations, Bushbeat Trails and UTC; contact details are listed in the Organised Tours chapter.

## Places to Stay – Budget

**Camping** At *Coronation Park* camp site (☎ (14) 486398), 7km east of the centre on the Mutare road, the incredibly cheap camp sites (US$1.20 for up to four people) are offset by poor security. Basic chalets cost US$26 for up to four people. The Menara and Greendale buses from Rezende St terminal pass the entrance and the Msasa bus from Market Square terminal stops a few minutes walk away, but hitching isn't difficult.

*The Rocks* (mobile ☎ (111) 403029; fax (14) 734724), at 18 Seke Rd, Sunningdale, is a great place to connect with overland trucks to Nairobi or elsewhere, and managers Wayne and Sparky set the laid-back mood in an immense outdoor bar surrounded by 2.6 hectares of boulder-studded bushland. Camping costs US$1.50 (tents may be hired), dorm beds are US$3 and doubles US$7. A laundry service is available, mainly for arrivals caked in overland dust. Take a Hatfield emergency taxi from the Mobil station on the corner of Robson Manyika and Julius Nyerere; or the Zengeza or St Mary's bus from the Angwa St terminal. It's a five minute walk from Seke Rd.

The similar *Duck Farm* (☎ (173) 2494), also called Spey Bay, lies out of town on Chiremba Rd in Ruwa, 1km south of the Mutare road. It's extremely popular with overlanders and its vehicle repair facilities have fulfilled many a mechanic's dream. Camping costs US$1.50 per person and basic chalets are US$10.

Most backpackers lodges also allow camping.

**Hostels & Backpackers Lodges** The friendly *Kopje 221 Lodge* (☎ (14) 499097), at 221 Enterprise Rd, Chisipite, has camping for US$2.10, dorms from US$3 to US$4 and doubles for US$10. Amenities include a bar, kitchen, laundry, fabulous pizzas, braais on Sunday, town transfers and twice daily pickups (9.30 am and 4 pm) from the Sandrock Cafe. You can also join weekly wine tours (US$8) and day trips to Ngomakurira (US$5), and travellers love the safe, laid-back atmosphere. Take a Chishawasha bus from the main post office and get off at the Shell station beyond Chisipite shopping centre. (Don't confuse this place with the much less appealing Kopje View Lodge, opposite the power plant on Rotten Row.)

*Possum Lodge* (☎ (14) 726851; fax 722803; <possum@zol.co.zw>), on Deary Ave, charges US$3 for camping, US$5 for dorms, and US$13 to US$15 for private doubles or 'garden sheds'. There's a pool, volleyball court, sauna, TV lounge and bar, but the big plus is its location, a 20 minute walk from the centre. What's more, it backs onto chronically hectic Second St, which will ensure that your Harare days begin bright and early!

More secluded is the quirky *Hillside Lodge* (☎ (14) 747961), an old colonial home at 71 Hillside Rd. The extraordinary decor may leave you feeling dizzy, but you won't see anything else like it in Zimbabwe. Doubles are US$10, dorm beds are US$3.50, mattresses are US$3, and camping beneath the jacaranda trees is US$2.10. They also rent one-speed bicycles (US$6.50 per day), provide a book exchange, run free pick-ups from town and do town/airport transfers (US$1/3.50 per trip). Alternatively, take the Msasa, Tafara or Mabvuku bus from the corner of Speke Ave and Julius Nyerere Way, get off at the Children's Home, and walk up Robert Mugabe Rd to Helm Road, which will take you to Hillside Rd.

*It's a Small World Lodge* (☎/fax (14) 335341), run by Shaun and Claire Chapman at 72 King George Rd, Avondale (handy for Avondale shopping centre), has received mixed reviews – many people feel it's too much like a youth hostel – but it's inexpensive at US$5 for dorm beds (with linen), from US$12 to US$14 for doubles and

US$3 for camping. Initial pickup is free, but they charge for subsequent transfers. There's a pool, volleyball court, laundry services, a bar (which closes at 10 pm) and a communications centre, with phone, fax, email and postal services.

*Peterborough Lodge* (☎ (14) 796735 or (14) 738459), 11 Peterborough St, is favoured by aid volunteers and travellers seeking a home away from home, so don't expect a raucous backpackers scene. Dorms cost from US$2.50 to US$3.50 and double rooms are US$8.

The recently renovated *Sable Lodge* (☎ (14) 726017) at 95 Selous Ave is now quite a smart place. Dorm beds cost US$4, mattresses are US$3 and doubles are US$10, all with use of the kitchen and pool.

The *Daily Planet* (☎ (14) 750353), at 94 Josiah Chinamano Ave, and *Talk of the Town* (☎ (14) 730344), at 92 Central Ave, cater mainly to import/export people and local business travellers. The latter, run by Shepherd, Rhoda and Luke, gets excellent marks for friendliness and cleanliness. At either place, dorm beds cost US$7 and singles/doubles US$9/13.

A friendly but crowded place to meet travelling businesspeople is the centrally-located *Guest Lodge* (☎ (14) 735450; fax 707900), at 164 Harare St. Dorm beds cost US$6.50 and twin or double rooms (which are named after African rivers) are US$20. A big plate of *sadza ne nyama* (mielies with meat gravy) costs just US$0.80.

The cosy *Palm Rock Villa* (☎ (14) 700691), 39 Selous Ave, has dorm beds at US$6; single/double rooms are US$13/15, including the use of kitchen facilities. The self-contained family room costs US$18. Use caution walking to and from the centre.

Scruffy *Paw Paw Lodge* (☎ (14) 724337), at 262 Herbert Chitepo Ave, charges US$5/4 for dorm beds/mattresses (you need a sleeping bag). Guests may use the lounge and kitchen facilities, but they're often filled with friends of the owner. The similarly spartan *Twin Peaks Lodge* (☎ (14) 730537), at 130 Samora Machel Ave, has dorms for US$4 and doubles for US$10.

The cramped but pleasant *Wayfarer Lodge* (☎ (14) 572125), at 47 Jesmond Rd, Hatfield, is out of town, but offers free initial pickup from the centre. Camping costs US$2.50, dorm beds are US$5, set tents are US$3 and single/double thatched chalets US$12/14. They offer cooking facilities, TV/video, a pool, tent hire (US$2 per night) and town/airport transfers (US$1/2.20), and also organise Zimbabwe tours for around US$40 per day, including meals, transport, camping and guide.

Women may like *Bromley House* (☎ (14) 724072) at 182 Herbert Chitepo Ave, opposite Harare Gardens, which is a spotless hostel for female students and office workers. Rooms are available only between school terms, but it's a bargain at US$5, with tea and dinner, and is excellent for meeting local women.

**Hotels** Many bottom-end hotels in Harare are noisy and double as brothels; if you don't want to risk being misconstrued, you may want to try other options.

A central option is the *Elizabeth Hotel* (☎ (14) 721101) on the corner of Julius Nyerere Way and Robert Mugabe Rd. Singles/doubles with shared facilities cost US$11/15 with breakfast. The nicer rooms over the street may be noisy but they're preferable to the dark, prison-like cells at the back. Entertainment – either live or disco music – is featured nightly.

Similar is the *Queens Hotel* (☎ (14) 738977) on Kaguvi St near the corner of Robert Mugabe Rd, which has a restaurant, live bands or disco on Friday, Saturday and Sunday nights and an occasional *pungwe* performance in the garden. Singles/doubles cost US$13/22 with breakfast.

The *Federal Hotel* (☎ (14) 752406) near the southern end of Kopje at 9 Harare St, is the most distinctly African of the inexpensive places. You'll pay US$13/22 for single/double rooms with breakfast. *Elmfield Lodge* (☎ (14) 728041) at 111 Fife Ave is good value at US$5 to US$9 per person, but the area is risky – especially at night – and security is negligible.

At 102 Fife Ave, the one-star *Terreskane Hotel* (☎ (14) 707031) has singles/doubles with shared bath for US$8 per person and en suite doubles for US$19. The weekend disco rages until 4 am so, if you relish quiet, ask for a room at the back.

The *Earlside Hotel* (☎ (14) 721101), at Fifth St and Selous Ave, looks seedier than it is, but security is definitely a big problem – as are the unsavouries who loiter around the entrance. Single/double rooms cost US$12/14.

The respectable *Russell Hotel* (☎ (14) 790565) at 116 Baines Ave charges US$23/33 for a single/double with breakfast and its annexe, the *City Limits Apartels* (☎ (14) 791895), at Second St and Baines Ave, costs US$15/26. Reception is at the Russell.

The recommended *Executive Hotel* (☎ (14) 792803), on Samora Machel Ave near Fourth St, has a dining room, private baths, telephones, TV and a sundeck. Singles/doubles cost US$25/28.

On the corner of Greendale Ave and Stewart Rd, 5km from the centre, is the two-star *Red Fox Hotel* (☎ (14) 495466), done up as a black and white English cottage. Singles/doubles with bath cost US$20/27. There are two attached pubs and the restaurant, The Huntsman, specialises in fish and beef.

The suburban *Feathers Hotel* (☎ (14) 228472), at Sherwood Drive and Notley Rd in Mabelreign, has single/double rooms for US$18/23. It features a swimming pool, grill, three bars, a conference centre, and even an adjoining 18 hole golf course.

### Places to Stay – Mid-Range
Mid-range hotels offer comfortable choices but, in some, foreigners pay higher rates than Zimbabweans and must also settle up in foreign currency (quoted rates are those for foreigners).

The *Quality International Hotel* (☎ (14) 729439), on the corner of Nelson Mandela Ave and Fourth St, is centrally located but lacks a pool or television. Singles/doubles with breakfast cost US$50/65.

The Courteney Hotel (☎ (14) 704400), on the corner of Selous Ave and Eighth St, has a secluded pool area, the Old Crow bar, a coffee shop and the excellent L'Escargot dining room. For singles/doubles with bath, you'll pay US$28/37.

Now affiliated with the Rainbow Group, the quiet *New Ambassador* (☎ (14) 708121; fax 708126), at 88 Union Ave, charges US$50/58 for single/double rooms with breakfast, telephones, TV and private baths.

The recommended *Cresta Lodge* (☎ (14) 487154; fax 487009; <cresta@samara .co.zw>), 7km east of the centre at the corner of Samora Machel Ave and Mutare Rd, has singles/doubles with bath, TV and breakfast for US$39/48. It's excellent value and considerably nicer than the rates would suggest.

Straddling the middle and top ranges, the three-star *Cresta Oasis* (☎ (14) 704217; fax 790865; <jamgm@samara.co.zw>), 124 Nelson Mandela Ave, offers high standards and a quiet location. Rates are US$47/61 for singles/doubles with breakfast.

The clean, quiet and delightfully olde worlde *Brontë Hotel* (☎ (14) 796631; fax 721429), set in quiet gardens at 132 Baines Ave, makes a great splash-out. Unfortunately, it's chronically full, so book at least a month in advance. In the main building, single/double rooms cost US$45/55, with breakfast. In the annexe across the street they're US$36/49.

The less central *George Hotel* (☎ (14) 336677; fax 723230), on King George Rd near Avondale shopping centre, represents good value at US$29/37 for singles/doubles with bath.

The *Kentucky Hotel* (☎ (14) 570109), on St Patrick's Rd, Hatfield, is convenient for early arrivals or late departures from the airport. Singles/doubles cost US$45/70. Airport transfers are available.

### Places to Stay – Top End

Harare hotel prices and quality aren't always proportional, so if you're looking for high standards, don't be put off by low rates. Hotels which employ a multi-tier pricing scheme are more pricey for foreigners than those with equivalent standards in which everyone pays the same rate.

The four-star *Jameson Hotel* (☎ (14) 774106; fax 774119; <jamsales@msasa .samara.co.zw>), on Samora Machel Ave at Park St, is excellent value right in the heart of high-rise Harare. Single/double rooms cost from US$67/83 to US$100/125, with breakfast.

The *Holiday Inn* (☎ (14) 795611; fax 735695), on Samora Machel Ave between Fifth and Sixth Sts, is pretty much like Holiday Inns everywhere. Foreigners pay US$111/175 for standard singles/doubles and deluxe rooms are US$132/178.

The five-star *Meikles Hotel* (☎ (14) 795655; fax 707754), on Jason Moyo Ave, served as the foreign correspondents' watering hole during Zimbabwe's liberation war and still boasts a range of restaurants and bars. Hotel snobs will love it, but the atmosphere may prove too stuffy for some tastes. For standard single/double rooms, foreigners pay US$175/195.

It may not draw a passing glance elsewhere, but in Harare, the Yugoslav-designed *Harare Sheraton* (☎ (14) 729771; fax 796678), between Samora Machel Ave West and the end of Pennefather Ave, stands out as a monument to modernity. It boasts all the regular amenities: shops, hairdressers, a conference centre, snack bars, gourmet restaurants and pubs. For standard singles/doubles including breakfast foreigners pay US$185/200.

Size-wise, the daddy-of-'em-all is the immense, wave-like *Crowne Plaza* (☎ (14) 704511; fax 791920) – formerly the Monomatapa – on Park Lane, overlooking Harare Gardens. For standard rooms with breakfast, foreigners pay US$116/156.

### Places to Stay – Out of Town

South of the Ruwa crossing on Kilwinning Rd is the *Backpackers & Overlanders Lodge* (☎ (14) 5074115), which charges US$4.50 for dorms, US$2.50 for camping, US$10 for A-frame doubles, and US$13 for large doubles with en suite facilities. It could be described as a backpackers resort, with a bar, swimming pool, billiards, kitchen, lots of travel information and 72 hectares of gardens and bushland for rambling. It's a long way from town, but they do free airport pickups during business hours and daily runs to (9 am) and from (1 and 5 pm) the Lido Cafe in the centre. Meat-oriented meals are available nightly.

The recommended *Setanga Lodge* (☎/fax (173) 2381) in Ruwa charges US$31/50 for single/double rooms with half board. They also offer horse-riding, tennis, squash, a swimming pool and access to the 18 hole Ruwa Country Club golf course. Follow the Mutare road to the 25.5km peg, turn right on a gravel drive and continue to the end.

The lively and good-value *Mwena Lodge* (☎ (162) 8270) provides comfortable, laid-back accommodation for around US$50 per person, including gimmicky game drives in a Model-T Ford. Equestrian activities are also available. The lodge is one hour's drive south of Harare and they provide transfers from the centre.

The *Mbizi Game Park* (☎ (173) 572886; fax 700812), PO Box US358, Harare, off Delport Rd 7km south-east of the airport, features fishing, birdwatching, some wildlife viewing and an 11km Manyame River canoe route. The unique architecture – particularly the swimming pool – is integrated into a garden landscape of balanced rocks. Lodges or rondavels cost from US$60 to US$70 per person, including meals, and self-catering bush cottages range from US$40 to US$80. Day entry is US$3, game walks or drives cost US$3 per hour and transfers from the city are US$8 (with a minimum of two people). They also hire out mountain bikes, horses, canoes and fishing gear.

*Wild Geese Lodge* (☎ (14) 860466; fax 860276), PO Box BW 198, Borrowdale, just beyond the northern suburbs, sits amid the savanna grasslands of the upper Mazowe valley with views towards the Great Dyke. Standard singles/doubles cost US$125/170 with breakfast and the luxury lodge is US$150/220.

At the *Pamuzinda Safari Lodge* (☎ (14) 333581; fax 333584), PO Box CY 633, Harare, standard lodges start at US$150 and luxury or 'royal' lodges are US$200, including meals, walks and game drives. This well-known wildlife retreat sits on a game farm near Selous, 80km south-west of Harare on the Bulawayo road. Horse-riding, canoeing and game drives are available, but they don't allow children under 12.

*Mwanga Lodge* (☎ (174) 432; fax 430), lies 44km north-east of Harare at the 20.5km peg on the Shamva road. For foreigners, A-frame thatched cottages amid the low granite hills of Bally Vaughn Bird and Game Sanctuary cost US$160 per person (locals pay US$63), including meals, canoe trips and sometimes elephant rides. Book through Sunlink (☎ (14) 786521; fax 746212). The sanctuary is open for day visits from Tuesday to Sunday; contact African Explorations (☎/fax (14) 721586). They charge US$44 for a full day, with lunch.

At 3 Albert Glen Close in Glen Lorne, 20km from the centre, is *Imba Matombo* (☎ (14) 499013; fax 499071; <imba@harare.iafrica.com>). It occupies a posh, thatched colonial home that features a pool, lawns, gardens, a gourmet dining room, colonial furnishings and a collection of crafts and sculpture. Standard singles/doubles including family-style meals are US$160/220, while veranda rooms are US$180/ 260.

*Landela Lodge* (☎/fax (173) 24330; <landela@samara.co.zw>), PO Box 66293, Kopje, Harare, in Ruwa, 40 minutes east of Harare on the Mutare road, has a small wildlife park and a colonial farmhouse which is reminiscent of the *Out of Africa* film set. Rates start at US$210/280 for single/double units; bookings are essential. Airport transfers may be arranged.

## Places to Eat

For updates on Harare's dining options, look for the free quarterly publication *Harare on a Plate*, which is distributed by the Publicity Association and some hotels.

**Breakfast** The highly recommended *Lido Cafe* (☎ (14) 726316), at 51 Union Ave, serves excellent full breakfasts. *Cafe Europa* is recommended for its coffee. *Le Cafe Chisipite*, in the Chisipite shopping centre 10km north-east of the city centre, serves excellent 'health breakfasts' of fresh fruit, yoghurt and oatmeal, as well as more decadent pastries and full English breakfasts. Their coffee is undoubtedly Harare's best.

In the centre, you'll find real filtered coffee at *Brazita's* in the First St Parkade. Nearby *Le Paris* on the Samora Machel Ave side of the Parkade also has good coffee and is better for a chat. It also does sandwiches, snacks and light meals.

Zimbabwe's extravagant buffet breakfasts and lunches at the four and five-star hotels will fill you up for most of the day. See Buffets later in this section.

**Snacks & Lunches** The *Lido Cafe* is recommended for burgers, which start at US$1.20. More creative concoctions – such as delicious sandwiches, curry, grills and goulash – average from US$2.50 to US$4 and there's a range of sweets: shakes, apple pie and lemon pancakes. On weekdays, it's open for dinner.

The *Sidewalk Cafe* on First St does inexpensive burgers, chicken, salads, sweets and vegetarian dishes, as well as a mean apple pie, accompanied by a pleasant atmosphere and good music. The trendy and popular *Sandrock Cafe*, on Julius Nyerere Way, serves up excellent pizzas, sandwiches, rolls, burgers and other light meals. It has a pleasant integrated atmosphere and is popular with the local Rastafarian crowd.

For great sandwiches and pies, try the *Savoy Sandwich Bar* on Second St near Samora Machel Ave. *Rafferty's Bakery*, on Robert Mugabe Rd near First St, does basic, healthy lunches which have been repeatedly recommended by readers. However, there's nowhere to sit inside. Also recommended is the *Spring Roll Centre* in the Fife Avenue shopping centre, which is open seven days a week.

For a sunny place to sit, drink coffee and write post cards, go to the laid-back *Terrace Restaurant* on the third level of Barbour's Department Store. Nearby, also on First St Mall, is *Two Flights Up*, which serves coffee and light lunches, and boasts a popular salad bar. Try *Dagwood's* in the First St Parkade for sandwiches and sadza ne nyama.

The patio at *Sherrol's in the Park* (☎ (14) 725535), in Harare Gardens, serves acclaimed light lunches: salads, toasted sandwiches, quiche and steak and kidney pie. It's open seven days a week. The attached Palm Dining Room, which emphasises Mediterranean cuisine, serves lunch Tuesday to Friday from noon to 3 pm, and dinner on Tuesday to Saturday from 6.45 pm.

The food stalls in the *Farm and City Centre* on Wynne St, near Kenneth Kaunda Ave, have great value filled rolls, curried fish, samosas, etc. Around the centre, takeaways do chips, burgers, samosas, soft drinks and other quick nosh. For cheap and filling fast food or African fare, the takeaways in the Kopje grid are good value.

For more institutionalised fast food, try *Chicken Inn*, with several outlets in central Harare. The affiliated *Bakers Inn* sells sticky pastries and doughnuts and *Creamy Inn* scoops up ice cream. For Portuguese-style peri-peri chicken, you can't beat *Nando's*, on Mbuya Nehanda St near Robert Mugabe Rd, and in the Avondale, Sam Levy's Village, Chisipite and Westgate shopping centres.

Westgate and Chisipite both have fast food dining halls, and upstairs at Eastgate shopping centre, you'll find a bewildering selection, from pasta, quiche and vegetarian lunches at the *Healthy Choice*, to Indian takeaways at the *Eastern Deli* and beefy concoctions at the *Black Steer Takeaway*.

If you're out at Chapungu Kraal, you may want to check out the unusual *Flat Dog Diner*, which has a recommended restaurant and a bar with live music. The outdoor seating is great for Sunday lunch, and there are specials on Wednesday evenings.

ZIMBABWE

**Buffets** The big hotels – the *Sheraton*, *Crowne Plaza*, *Meikles* and the *Holiday Inn* – put on extravagant buffet meals. In the morning you can try the English or continental breakfasts or wait until midday for the lunch version. Either could satisfy an appetite for most of the day.

The best breakfast deals are at the Crowne Plaza and Holiday Inn, where a pig-out costs around US$3.50 (less for a continental breakfast). The Sheraton and Meikles both charge US$5. Lunch buffets include salads, meat dishes, vegetables, casseroles and desserts for around US$6. Vegetarians can opt for the cheaper salad bars at US$3. If you prefer to pig out at just the dessert table, you'll only pay around US$2.50. For dinners, you'll pay around US$9. However, don't turn up at any of these hotels looking like you've just crawled out of a sleeping bag or you may be asked to leave.

**Dinners** Gourmets may not relish Harare, but when locals want to impress visitors they might suggest *Alexander's* (☎ (14) 700340), at 7 Livingstone Ave, which is often lauded as the city's most prestigious venue. It specialises in continental cuisine, including vegetarian options.

All the big hotels and most smaller ones offer both fine dining and mid-range restaurants. In the Sheraton are *La Chandelle*, for gourmet fare, and *Harvest Garden*, serving more down-to-earth meals. On Thursday nights, the Harvest Garden puts on an African buffet, complete with traditional dancing. *L'Escargot* (☎ (14) 706411) at the Courteney Hotel is also touted as one of Harare's finest and most highly acclaimed restaurants. Meikles Hotel has a quartet of fine restaurants: the table d'hôte *Mirabelle*, the Mediterranean buffet *Pavilion*, the French-oriented *Bagatelle* and the à la carte *La Fontaine*.

The following is a selection of the city's laudable but good-value restaurants.

**Beef & Seafood** In the *Quality International Hotel*, you can opt for a three-course meal featuring an obscenely large steak for US$8. Another option for large chunks of beef is the mid-range *Carvery* in the Fife Ave shopping centre. *Wombles* (☎ (14) 882747) in the Ballantyne Park shopping centre also does consistently good steaks and other beef options. There's a branch of the South African chain *Black Steer Steakhouse & Bulldog Pub* in the Westgate centre and another opposite the Eastgate centre, on Jason Moyo Ave. *Saddles*, a branch of another South African steakhouse chain, can be found on Robert Mugabe Rd at Second St.

For fish and seafood, a good choice is *Pino's* (☎ (14) 792303) at 73 Union Ave. The fresh kingclip from South Africa and the paella Valencia are recommended, and they often serve crab, crayfish, vegetarian dishes and other treats. Plan on spending around US$10 per person, without drinks.

**Italian** Travellers normally love *Da Guido Trattoria* (☎ (14) 723349) in the Montagu shopping centre, on the corner of Harare St and Josiah Chinamano Ave. Nightly pasta specials cost around US$3.50, meat dishes are US$5, and you'll also find pizza, salads and other Italian standbys (including espresso and cappuccino). It's open for lunch from noon to 2 pm; dinner starts at 6.30 pm.

Another Italian choice is *Clovagalix & Luigi's Pasta Bar* (☎ (14) 721850), in the Fife Avenue shopping centre, which is open daily for lunch and dinner. The seafood dishes and homemade pasta are especially recommended.

**Indian** For Indian lunches and dinners, try the exceptional *Taj Mahal* (☎ (14) 700207) at 88 Robert Mugabe Rd in the centre, or the *Bombay Duck* (☎ (14) 723657) at 7 Central Ave. The adjoining takeaway serves curry and rice for US$1.50. The *Rani* (☎ (14) 729242) and the *Raj* (☎ (14) 708101), both at 56 Speke Ave, offer Indian meals and takeaways, respectively. Another Indian choice is the *Sitar* (☎ (14) 746215) at Newlands shopping centre on Enterprise

Rd. The *Jaipur* (☎ (14) 740849), at the Sunrise Sports Club on Hurtsview Rd in Ridgeview serves up Indian cuisine, including vegetarian, for lunch and dinner from Tuesday to Sunday.

**Oriental** The best Chinese options are the *Bamboo Inn* (☎ (14) 759092) and the *Mandarin*, both on Robert Mugabe Rd near First St, and the *Pearl Garden* (☎ (14) 495199) on Enterprise Rd, south of the Chisipite shopping centre. At the *Shangri-La* (☎ (14) 302730), on Suffolk Rd in Strathaven, you can choose from Chinese, Japanese, Thai, Vietnamese or North Indian cuisine, including several vegetarian choices.

Hard-core carnivores may prefer the Mongolian barbecue at the *Manchurian* (☎ (14) 36166), on Second St Extension in Avondale. An all-you-can-eat buffet costs US$8.50. *Meridian's* (☎ (14) 700332), at the corner of Nelson Mandela Ave and Fourth St, is open for breakfast, lunch and dinner, seven days a week, for European and Oriental cuisine.

**African** Quality African cuisine is on offer at *Roots of Africa* (☎ (14) 721494), at the corner of Seventh St and Livingstone Ave. It's open for lunch and dinner seven days a week. Also recommended is the *Tawanda* (☎ (14) 730003) at Fifth St and Selous Ave, but note that the location is a bit dodgy. The *Pan African* restaurant and tea garden (☎ (14) 721816) at the National Handicraft Centre, on Chinhoyi St and Grant St, serves Zimbabwean dishes and other traditional African fare.

Perhaps in emulation of Nairobi's renowned Carnivore restaurant, *Ramambo Lodge* (☎ (14) 775335) serves a spread of wild game dishes, from impala and warthog to ostrich steak, eland stroganoff and crocodile in cheese sauce. If that's not your bag, they also do traditional cuisine, beef, vegetarian meals and seafood. As you'd expect, the decor reflects a 'safari lodge' theme, and you can almost forget that Harare's widest street bustles just below. Lunches are backed up by a marimba band and in the

evening, they stage a 'traditional dance cabaret'. You'll find it upstairs in BB House, on the corner of Samora Machel Ave and Leopold Takawira St. It's closed on Sunday.

**Other Ethnic Cuisine** The *Coimbra*, at 61 Selous Ave, does Portuguese-style seafood and legendary peri-peri chicken. Portuguese alternatives include the *Vila Peri* (☎ (14) 790565), on Third St between Baines and Josiah Chinamano Aves, and the *Cascais* (☎ (14) 724869), at 139 Samora Machel Ave.

*Taco's Restaurant* (☎ (14) 750298), in Lintas House at 46 Union Ave, serves approximations of Mexican food. It's open for lunch and dinner seven days a week.

Harare's Cypriot/Greek choices include the recommended *Akropolis Taverna* (☎ (14) 339181), behind Avondale shopping centre, which serves Greek dishes for under US$7, and the *Aphrodite Taverna* (☎ (14) 35500) at Strathaven shopping centre, Strathaven.

The best French/continental bistro is *Le Cafe de l'Alliance* (☎ (14) 720777) at Alliance Française, near the eastern end of Herbert Chitepo Ave. The affiliated *Le Cafe Chisipite* (☎ (14) 494034), in the Chisipite shopping centre, specialises in breakfasts and European-style breads. For more up-market French cuisine, try *Le Français* (☎ (14) 704501), in the Crowne Plaza Hotel.

**Deliveries** If you're too tired to go out, between noon and 9 pm you can use Dial-a-Delivery (☎ (14) 336336) to order from restaurants all over Harare. Delivery charges range from US$1 to US$2; phone and ask where you can pick up a comprehensive menu.

**Self-Catering** There's a TM supermarket on Nelson Mandela Ave between First and Angwa Sts and a Woolworth's on the First St pedestrian mall. The supermarket at the Fife Ave shopping centre, on the corner of Fife Ave and Fifth St, is open Monday to

Saturday until 6.30 pm and on Sunday from 8 to 11.30 am.

## Entertainment

Harare is a great place to hear African music – both live and disco. A good place to find information on upcoming events is the monthly tourist office booklet *What's on in Harare*, which lists cultural, sports and musical events which they deem of interest to tourists. More obscure venues and cinema schedules are normally listed in the daily *Herald*.

Most pubs, hotel bars and nightclubs are conservative and smart casual dress rules apply. And remember, don't walk from late-night spots after dark; take a taxi to your front door!

**Cinema** In the afternoon and evening, cinemas run three or four screenings of popular foreign films. Popular cinemas include the *Rainbow* on Park Lane near Herbert Chitepo Ave, *Cinemas 1, 2, 3* and *4* on Nelson Mandela Ave near Leopold Takawira St, several complexes near the corner of Julius Nyerere Way and Union Ave, the *Liberty Theatre* on Cameron St and the four screens at *Westgate shopping centre*. Admission averages US$1.50. Check the daily *Herald* for listings.

**Theatre** Harare doesn't have much in the way of theatre; for information on the current month's activities, either phone or check *Sunshine City Harare*.

*Gallery Delta* (☎ (14) 792135) bills itself as the artistic heartbeat of Harare, and hosts quality art exhibitions, theatre and jazz performances. It's housed in Harare's oldest home, that of landscape artist Robert Pauls, at 110 Livingstone Ave, which dates from 1894. It's open Monday to Friday, 8.30 am to 5.30 pm, on Saturday from 8.30 am to 1 pm, and after hours by appointment.

*Harare Reps* (☎ (14) 336706), which stages solid middle-of-the-road productions, has its auditorium in the Belgravia shopping centre at the corner of Thurston Lane and Second St Extension, Avondale.

Spotlight (☎ (14) 308159), in the theatre foyer, handles ticket sales Monday to Friday from 8.30 am to noon and 1 to 4 pm and on Saturday from 9 to 11 am. Visiting theatre groups normally appear at the *Seven Arts Theatre*, a large auditorium also in Avondale.

On weekdays at lunchtime, the Zimbabwe Association of Community Theatre puts on 20-minute mini-performances in *Harare Gardens* for US$2.70, including a sandwich. Purchase advance tickets at the Kine 4 box office on Union Ave near Julius Nyerere Way.

**Live Music** Many night-owl visitors to Harare want to attend a pungwe – an all-night drinking and dancing musical performance by one of Zimbabwe's top musicians. The Publicity Association rarely keeps up with such things, so your best bet is to cruise the streets of Kopje, where upcoming gigs are advertised on walls, lampposts and shop windows. Live performances always carry a cover charge (and some places also charge for disco music). For some practical night spot guidelines, see Entertainment in the Zimbabwe Facts for the Visitor chapter.

The *Federal*, *Queen's* and *Elizabeth* hotels stage live performances on Friday and Saturday nights. There's not much quality control and there are some duds, but occasionally, well-known jit jive names, such as the Bhundu Boys, do drop by. On other nights, African and western pop and disco music blares from antiquated sound systems until 11.30 pm.

The garden bar at the *Nyagonzera Skyline Motel* (☎ (14) 67588), at the 19km peg of the Beatrice-Masvingo road, also attracts superb talent. However, it's an expensive taxi ride from town, so phone and ascertain whether the trip is worth the effort.

Another possible weekend venue for big names like Thomas Mapfumo or Ilanga is *Job's Night Spot*, owned by Job Kadengu, in the Wonder shopping centre on Julius Nyerere Way. For the more intrepid, three closely-grouped Highfields nightclubs – the

*Machipisa*, *Club Saratoga* and *Mushandira Pamwe* – feature live bands on weekends and often attract the likes of mbira player and spirit-singer Stella Chiweshe, soul man Oliver M'tukudzi, and even Thomas Mapfumo and the Blacks Unlimited.

Other possible venues for well-known names include the outdoor *Hideout 99*, on Cedrella Ave in Lochinvar; the New Yorkish *Playboy Club* at 40 Union Ave; and *Turtles*, at 66 Jason Moyo Ave. *Le Cafe de l'Alliance*, on Herbert Chitepo Ave near Enterprise Rd, stages live bands on Friday nights.

*Taco's*, on Union Ave near Julius Nyerere Way, attracts a mixed clientele and has an emphasis on reggae music. On weekends, *Aguila's* in Sam Levy's Village, Borrowdale, puts on live European pop music performances.

Marimba bands, including the renowned Jairos Jiri Marimba Band, give free performances in the bandstand at Harare Gardens. On weekend afternoons, local bands play at the Mbare drinking halls, and there is plenty of cultural interest, but lone women should attend with a male companion or give them a miss.

Major musical events – national celebrations or concerts by international stars – are held in the National Stadium. For such concerts, half of Zimbabwe seems to descend on Harare so book tickets well in advance.

**Pubs, Discos & Night Clubs** Anyone who's propelled by beer won't want to miss the new *Harare Beer Engine*, on Park St beside the Jameson Hotel. Named for the hand-operated draughts, this boutique brewery produces three excellent brews – Coxswain ale, Navigator bitter and Lighthouse lager. Zimbabwe's landlocked nature renders the nautical names somewhat inexplicable, but it's a great place to eat, drink and socialise.

Currently, the most popular night spot for white Zimbabweans is *The Tube Nite Club & Platform Pub* (☎ (14) 704919), with a London tube station theme, at 125 Mbuya Nehanda St. Check out their Web site

(thetube.cybergate.co.zw) for information about forthcoming attractions. It also has links to various other sites, including the Zimbabwe Entertainment Directory, which gives details of events all over Harare. Also popular is *Archipelago* (☎ (14) 792094), in Liquenda House on Nelson Mandela Ave. Both are open nightly. On weekends, they rock until 4 am. Many Harare backpackers hostels provide discount entry coupons.

The glitzy *Solo's* (☎ (14) 794088), housed in an old synagogue on the corner of Jason Moyo Ave and Harare St, is open daily for African-style lunches and nightly for disco or live performances. It's known for its lively but relaxed and low-risk atmosphere.

The *Time and Place*, at 32 Nelson Mandela Ave, is open nightly for disco, with live bands on weekends. *Turtles* (☎ (14) 794957), in a basement at 66 Jason Moyo Ave, between First and Second Sts, has a disco on Friday and Saturday nights, and live music on Sunday (it's a favourite haunt of Thomas Mapfumo and the Blacks Unlimited).

*Sandro's* (aka The Sandrose), at Julius Nyerere Way and Union Ave, attracts an older and more pretentious professional crowd. There's a US$5 cover charge. More pedestrian tastes will be satisfied with the nonstop large-screen sports broadcasts (on 70 screens!) at the formidably popular *Sports Cafe/Bar* (☎ (14) 498581) in the Chisipite shopping centre. They serve up lots of beef and beer, and on Wednesday, Friday and Saturday, there's disco dancing.

Lively *Sarah's Rave Club*, at Jason Moyo Ave and Park St, caters to a young and trendy mixed crowd, and *Smuggler's*, in the Glenara Ave shopping centre, between Samora Machel Ave and Enterprise Rd, is mainly a middle-class African hang-out. The latter imposes a US$6 cover charge.

For pub atmosphere, Zimbabwe-style, try the *Londoner* in the Strathaven shopping centre or the *Keg and Sable* in Sam Levy's Village, Borrowdale. The liveliest Irish-theme pub is *Tipperary's*, near Fife Ave and Leopold Takawira St.

Hotel bars present a range of choices. The popular patio watering hole at the *Terreskane Hotel* and the *Bird and Bottle* at the New Ambassador Hotel are favourite spots with a loyal and lively clientele and are often packed.

The *Elizabeth* and *Queen's* hotels bask in African pop and disco music – and alcoholic effluvium – until 11.30 pm nightly. The *Quality International Hotel*, at Fourth St and Nelson Mandela Ave is, according to one reader, 'a low-life drinking hole that's good fun'.

If you reluctantly missed the golden days of Empire, The *Explorers Club* at the Meikles Hotel may fulfil fantasies. *Harpers* at the Cresta Oasis puts on excellent live jazz performances weekly. For sedate low-light drinking, opt for the *Old Crow* at the Courteney Hotel.

## Spectator Sports

Spectator sport events are announced in the *Herald* and held regularly at the Chinese-constructed National Stadium, west of the city centre on the Bulawayo road (take Samora Machel Ave). The cricket ground, which hosts big international matches, is on Josiah Tongogara Ave.

A football match is one of the few things you can do on a Sunday and it's great fun. We saw the Dynamos, one of the Harare teams, known as the Glamour Boys. You couldn't get away with a name like that in England surely! Imagine what the rugby boys would do to you! And be sure to swot up on your English footy gossip before you go; as with every country, if you can talk English footy, it's easy to make friends.

**Becky, UK**

On weekends, you can watch and bet on horse racing in the 'mink and manure' suburb of Borrowdale. Harare boasts 600 active thoroughbred horses and there's a good chance of catching this popular sport at one of Mashonaland Turf Club's 41 annual meets at the Borrowdale Park track. Alternatively, trotting races are held on Sundays at the National Trotting Club's Waterfalls Stadium on Seke Rd.

## Things to Buy

All souvenir shops and hotel gift shops dispense crafts and curios, but they aren't the cheapest options and similar or superior items may often be found at informal markets and lower-overhead outlets. For real works of art, particularly Shona sculpture, the National Gallery and several commercial galleries offer a range of names and prices.

With the downlisting of the elephant at the 1997 CITES (Convention on International Trade in Endangered Species) conference (which was held in Harare), ivory products are now legally available. Most shops provide certification that their ivory has been taken in accordance with CITES regulations. However, the system has flaws which widen as tourist demand increases, and visitors are still advised to avoid ivory products.

Mall rats will appreciate Sam Levy's Village in Borrowdale, which is patrolled by a force of English-style bobbies, or the Westgate shopping centre on the Kariba road, which is Zimbabwe's largest shopping mall.

**Sculpture Galleries & Art Dealers** For original Shona sculpture, check the major commercial galleries, which deal mainly in works by known sculptors. Stone Dynamics at 56 Samora Machel Ave specialises in serpentine and verdite works by older, well-known and established artists. Vhuku-tiwa Gallery, north of town on the corner of Harvey Brown Ave and Blakiston St, is in a pleasant old suburban home. Besides sculpture by well-knowns and newcomers, it deals in handicrafts, including Batonka material arts.

At 110 Leopold Takawira St is Matombo Gallery which also emphasises big names and promotes emerging talents. Pangolin Place, on Masotsha Ndlovu between Airport and Seke roads, specialises in the works of renowned sculptor, Adam Madebe. Another renowned and tasteful gallery is Gallery Delta (see Theatre under Entertainment earlier in this chapter).

The gallery at Ramambo Lodge restaurant sells a selection of Shona sculpture. Gallery 42, at 42a Enterprise Rd in Newlands, concentrates on metal sculpture and original paintings. Other places for sculpture include the Nyati Gallery, on Spitzkop Rd, 18km out of town towards Bulawayo; Pierre Gallery, at 9 Normandy Rd in Alexandra Park; Springstone, at 5 Idlehurst Way in Avondale; and Similitudes, at 1 Bodle Ave in Eastlea, off Robert Mugabe Rd beyond Enterprise Rd. For antiques or traditional, esoteric or ritual items – and if money is no object – see Dendera Gallery at 65 Speke Ave, between First and Second Sts.

The Gallery of Shona Sculpture at Chapungu Kraal is at Doon Estate, 1 Harrow Rd, Msasa, Beverley East. The sculptures are spread across a grassy lakeside – and the sales people are easy-going. The admission charge buys you a guided tour and a spoon-fed appreciation for the inspiration behind some of the works. It's open daily from 8 am to 4.30 pm. A similar place is the Nhukutuku Sculpture Village at 18135 Griffin Road, Gun Hill; it's just north of the city on Borrowdale Rd.

**Crafts & Material Arts** Plenty of reasonably priced crafts outlets exist around Harare. The best and cheapest are found at the large outdoor craft market on Enterprise Rd and at Mbare musika, where stall upon stall of carvings and practical items – as well as kitsch souvenirs – may be purchased at negotiable prices. You'll also find craft peddlers set up in Harare Gardens and along Jason Moyo Ave in the centre.

For something more inspired – and more expensive – visit the National Handicraft Centre, on the corner of Grant and Chinhoyi Sts in Kopje. You'll find musical instruments, mats, carvings, handmade toys, baskets, pottery, leatherwork, weavings, crocheted and knitted items, and handprinted textiles. It's open daily from 9.30 am to 5 pm. The attached Pan African Restaurant and tea garden serve up local and traditional delicacies.

The Shop, on Doon Estate, Harrow Rd, Msasa, features Kudhinda Fabrics, which sells beautiful and unusual wall-hangings, bags, clothing, cushions, tablecloths, etc, which have been block-printed by hand in local designs. In the same complex is Ros Byrne Pottery, selling hand-decorated ceramics and Malawi wickerwork, and The Works, which produces African design screen prints, recycled paper products and scented items, such as aromatherapy oils, soap, tea, candles and potpourri. They're open from 8 am to 5 pm Monday to Friday and 8 am to 1 pm on Saturday.

Zimbabalooba, which creates popular, vibrantly patterned cotton clothing has its main outlet (☎ (14) 487708) at 80 Kenneth Kaunda Ave and a factory shop at 7 van Praagh Ave in Milton Park. The latter sells seconds at good rates. Another place for hand-painted textiles and batiks is Zenga (☎ (14) 776308) at 61 Speke Ave.

The Danhiko Project School on Mutare Rd sells locally made clothing and carpentry items at below shop prices. The colourful fabrics are produced with Scandinavian aid by disabled and low-income Zimbabweans. Also, check out the shops selling inexpensive African-print clothing between South and Kenneth Kaunda Aves, near the railway station.

The Jairos Jiri Shop, which benefits disabled Zimbabweans, is in the Park Lane building on Julius Nyerere Way opposite the National Gallery. In the centre, the cheapest T-shirts are found at Zimcraft Co-operative Shop in the First St Parkade, at 30% less than at the trendy Rado Arts on the First St Mall.

See also under Mbare, earlier in this section, and Cold Comfort Farm Society in the Around Harare section.

**Getting There & Away**
**Air** Harare international airport, 15km south-east of the city, handles all international and Air Zimbabwe domestic traffic. Charter flights and light aircraft operate out of Charles Prince airport, 18km north-west of Harare.

Air Zimbabwe and/or Zimbabwe Express have frequent domestic services between Harare and Bulawayo, Buffalo Range, Kariba, Masvingo, Hwange National Park and Victoria Falls (see the Zimbabwe Getting Around chapter). Information on international services to Harare is found in the Getting There & Away chapters.

Main airline offices include:

*Aeroflot* Karigamombe shopping centre, Samora Machel Ave (☎ (14) 731971)
*Air Botswana* Suite 501, Jameson Hotel, on the corner of Samora Machel near Park St (☎ (14) 733836)
*Air Mauritius* 13th floor, Old Mutual shopping centre, on the corner of Third St and Jason Moyo Ave (☎ (14) 735738)
*Air Namibia* 29 Mazowe St (☎ (14) 739878; fax 739879)
*Air Zimbabwe* City Air Terminal, on Speke Ave near Third St (☎ (14) 575111; fax 575068)
*American* Leopard Rock Hotel Group, 95 Jason Moyo Ave (☎ (14) 733073; fax 791484)
*Balkan Bulgarian* Trustee House, 55 Samora Machel Ave (☎ (14) 759271; fax 757684)
*British Airways* Batanai Gardens, on the corner of First St and Jason Moyo Ave (☎ (14) 759173; fax 756670)
*Kenya Airways* Stanley House, Jason Moyo Ave (☎ (14) 792181)
*KLM* 1st floor, Finsure House, corner of Union Ave and Second St (☎ (14) 731042; fax 736021)
*Lufthansa* 99 Jason Moyo Ave, (☎ (14) 793861; fax 708696)
*Qantas* 5th floor, Karigamombe shopping centre, 54 Union Ave (☎ (14) 794676)
*South African Airways* 2nd floor, Takura House, 69-71 Union Ave (☎ (14) 738922)
*Zambia Airways* Pearl Assurance Building, First St (☎ (14) 793235)
*Zimbabwe Express Airways* corner of Silundika Ave and Fourth St (☎ (14) 708867)

**Bus** Express Motorways (☎ (14) 796934) departs daily for Mutare (US$6.40) and Bulawayo (US$13). It also serves Masvingo/Great Zimbabwe (US$8.50) on Friday at 5 pm, Kariba (US$11) on Friday at 1 pm and Gaborone (US$35) on Thursday and Sunday. For Victoria Falls (US$26), you must change in Bulawayo, entailing an overnight stop. The booking office and terminal are at the corner of Nelson Mandela Ave and Leopold Takawira St. There have been reports of difficulties with Express Motorways services lately.

Blue Arrow services (Harare: ☎ (14) 729514; fax 729572; Bulawayo: ☎ (19) 65548) are more comfortable. Their offices are at Chester House, Speke Ave, between Third and Fourth Sts, Harare and Unifreight House, 73a Fife Ave, Bulawayo. Services run between the two towns several times daily, via Chivhu (US$19, six hours), Kwe Kwe (US$19, 5½ hours) or Masvingo (US$28, nine hours). On Friday and Sunday, they run to and from the Holiday Inn in Mutare (US$13, 4¼ hours).

Trans-Lux (☎ (14) 725132) uses the terminal at the Holiday Inn, Harare. The booking office is in Hungwe House on Jason Moyo Ave. For details of routes see the Zimbabwe Getting There & Away chapter.

For Juliasdale (US$11, three hours), Nyanga (US$13, 3½ hours) and Troutbeck (US$13.50, four hours), DSB Coachlines (☎/fax 734837) leaves from the Sheraton on Wednesday at 7 am and Friday at 2 pm. To Masvingo (US$13, four hours) and Great Zimbabwe (US$15.20, 4½ hours), it leaves on Sunday and Thursday at 1 pm.

Jacaranda Luxury Coach Lines (☎ (14) 754460), 7th floor, Century House East, on the corner of Nelson Mandela Ave and Angwa St, runs return services to Great Zimbabwe on most days for US$120.

Long-distance African buses depart from the Mbare musika terminal, 5km from the centre in Mbare. Signs indicate destinations and buses are grouped according to which road they take out of the city (Mutare, Beatrice, Bulawayo, Chinhoyi etc). Crowding is only a problem on weekends and holidays, when buses are packed to overflowing.

To smaller villages, there may only be one bus daily, and it's likely to depart at, or shortly after, 6 am. In particular, if you want a seat on a bus to Masvingo, Kariba or Mutare, don't arrive much after 6 am. For Mutare (US$2.50), buses depart half-hourly from Mbare or from Msasa on the Mutare road. Bulawayo buses (US$4) depart when full from early morning to mid-afternoon; you shouldn't wait more than a few minutes. From Mbare to Kariba (US$3.50), take the Mucheche or ZUPCO buses. To Masvingo (US$3), the recommended company is Mhunga, departing from Mbare in the early morning. Musanbi has buses to Beitbridge four times weekly at 8 am.

For international bus routes, see the Zimbabwe Getting There & Away chapter.

**Train** The railway station is on the corner of Kenneth Kaunda Ave and Second St. Trains run to Bulawayo nightly at 9 pm and to Mutare at 9.30 pm. The *Trans-Limpopo Express* pulls out of Harare at 7 am Sunday and arrives in Johannesburg (US$80/55 in 1st/2nd class) at 9 am Monday.

The reservations office (☎ (14) 733901, ext 3416) is open from 8 am to 1 pm and 2 to 4 pm Monday to Friday and from 8 to 11.30 am Saturday. The ticket office opens Monday to Friday from 8 am to 1 pm, 2 to 4 pm, and 7 to 9.30 pm. On Saturday, it's open from 8 to 11.30 am and 7 to 9.30 pm. On Sunday, it's only open from 7 to 9.30 pm.

### Getting Around
**The Airport** Express Motorways (☎ (14) 796934) runs an hourly airport bus to and from the centre (US$3), to connect with arriving or departing flights. The in-town terminal is at Speke Ave and Second St, near Meikles Hotel, but it also picks up booked passengers from anywhere in the central area. Coming from the airport, it drops passengers at central hotels and guesthouses.

Taxis to the airport cost around US$7. Larger hotels – Meikles, Sheraton, Crowne Plaza etc – send mini-vans to pick up booked guests for around US$5 per person.

**Bus** Harare's old smoke-spewing ZUPCO buses are gradually being replaced by more comfortable and convenient 15-seater mini-vans, known as commuter buses. However,

they exist mainly to connect the city centre with suburban areas and do get very crowded, especially at peak hours. Fares range from US$0.10 to US$0.20.

Buses and commuter buses are best caught at one of the five central city bus termini: Market Square, between Harare and Mbuya Nehanda Sts; the Fourth St terminal, on Robert Mugabe Rd between Fourth and Fifth Sts; the Angwa St terminal, on the corner of Angwa St and Robson Manyika Ave; the Rezende St terminal, on Rezende St between Jason Moyo and Nelson Mandela Aves; and the Chinhoyi St terminal, on Speke Ave between Cameron and Chinhoyi Sts. Buses to the Mbare musika intercity bus terminal depart from the Angwa St terminal. There's also a string of bus stops along Jason Moyo Ave, near the corner of Fourth St.

**Taxi** Taxi ranks are found in front of all hotels; on the corner of First St and Nelson Mandela Ave; on Samora Machel Ave near First St; and on Union Ave between Angwa St and Julius Nyerere Way. Official services include Rixi Taxi (☎ (14) 753080) and the economically priced A1/Cream Line Taxis (☎ (14) 725254). It's risky to use the uncontrolled maverick taxis, of which there are hundreds.

Taxi meters all run at different speeds, and controls are nonexistent. Rixi, based on the corner of Samora Machel Ave and Harare St, appears to be the most reliable. Fares around the city centre range from US$0.60 to US$1. Trips to the suburbs costs between US$2 and US$2.25, and to the airport costs about US$7.

Look for emergency taxis around the corner of George Silundika Ave and Fourth St, or on Rezende St between Jason Moyo and Nelson Mandela Aves. Emergency taxis cost US$0.20 to anywhere along their fixed routes, but working out which goes where requires some research.

**Car & Motorcycle** Ike's Bikes (☎ (14) 792202), Flat 24, Shawdon Flats, 186 Herbert Chitepo, hires motorbikes for

ZIMBABWE

US$12.50 per day plus US$0.10 per kilometre. For a more information on hiring vehicles and a list of car hire firms, see the Car and Motorcycle section in the Zimbabwe Getting Around chapter.

**Bicycle** Harare lends itself well to bicycle exploration, even for those unused to cycling, but remember to lock up your bike. Between 9 am and 2 pm, you can hire bikes for US$15 per day from Bushtrackers (☎ (14) 303025), in the Brontë Hotel, 132 Baines Ave. Alternatively, Pedal Power Cycle Hire & Bike Shop (☎ (14) 752848; fax 752854), at 28 Park St, hires mountain bikes for similar rates.

# Around Harare

## CHITUNGWIZA

With the unchecked urban drift after Zimbabwean independence, it appeared that Harare would burst at the seams, and city planners realised something had to give. The result was the creation of the massive satellite of Chitungwiza south of the airport. It is effectively a city in its own right and is now home to nearly one million people. When counted as separate from Harare (which it certainly is – at least physically), Chitungwiza is Zimbabwe's third largest city, after Harare and Bulawayo. When Chitungwiza is included in statistics for metropolitan Harare, the capital's population practically doubles.

Chitungwiza is divided into several units. Unit B is the wealthiest, while units C and D are considerably poorer. A visit to this sprawling high-density community may prove to be an interesting social experience, but it's much like a bigger version of Mbare.

### Getting There & Away

Catch a bus from in front of the London Bakery on Rezende St in Harare. Alternatively, wait anywhere along Hatfield Road.

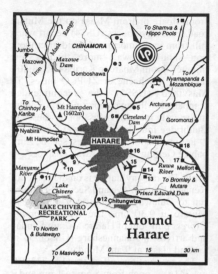

**PLACES TO STAY**
1  Mwanga Lodge
6  Imba Matombo
7  Wild Geese Lodge
13  Mbizi Game Park & Lodge
14  Backpackers & Overlanders Lodge
17  Setanga Lodge
18  Landela Lodge

**OTHER**
2  Ngomakurira Rock Paintings
3  Domboshawa Rock Paintings
4  Ewanrigg National Park
5  Chishawasha Mission
8  Charles Prince Airport
9  Cold Comfort Farm Society
10  Larvon Bird Gardens
11  Lion & Cheetah Park
12  Nyagonzera Skyline Motel
15  Harare International Airport
16  Epworth Balancing Rocks

## EPWORTH BALANCING ROCKS

Although there are better examples of balancing rocks all over Zimbabwe, the ones at Epworth, a mission and former squatter camp 13km south-east of Harare, are probably the most famous. The big attraction is the group known as the Bank Notes, catapulted to rock stardom when they were featured on Zimbabwe paper currency. Admission to the site is US$1, and children offer guide services for around US$0.50.

Visitors should note that Epworth itself isn't Harare's most appealing suburb and, although the government has attempted to deal with its sanitation and social problems, this remains one of Zimbabwe's least hopeful communities.

By car, follow Robert Mugabe Rd east and turn right on Chiremba Rd, which will take you directly to Epworth. Alternatively, take the Epworth bus from the Fourth St and Jason Moyo Ave terminal and get off at either Munyuki shopping centre or the Epworth Primary School turn-off. From the latter, it's 500m along the road to the park entrance. You'll be surrounded by the balancing boulders – and Epworth kids – for the entire walk.

## EWANRIGG NATIONAL PARK

This small, loosely defined national park 40km north-east of Harare consists of an elaborate 40 hectare botanical garden and 200 hectares of woodland. The garden is characterised by an array of prehistoric-looking aloes, cacti and palm-like cycads. During the winter, the slopes glow with the brilliant red and yellow blooms of the succulents and the variegated hues of tropical flowers. Along with the flowering plants, there's a stand of bamboo, a herb garden, a water garden and an arboretum.

Originally, Ewanrigg was the farm and personal hobby garden of botanist Harold Basil Christian, who set up housekeeping on the site in 1891. It was named *Ewanrigg* (Manx for Ewan's Ridge) after the family holdings on the Isle of Man. Upon Christian's death on 12 May 1950, his holdings were bequeathed to the state.

For most of the week, Ewanrigg stays serene, but sunny weekends draw droves of Harare residents for braais, cricket, football and strolling. Facilities include picnic tables, braai pits, water taps, toilet blocks and firewood. However, there are no camp sites. Foreigners pay US$5.

### Organised Tours

Kalambeza Safaris runs daily Ewanrigg tours for US$15.

### Getting There & Away

As early in the morning as possible, take the Shamva bus from Mbare and get off at the Ewanrigg turn-off, which is a 3km walk from the gardens. Alternatively, hitch from along Enterprise Rd/Mutoko Highway to the Shamva turn-off (the A15). It's then 20km to the Ewanrigg turn-off.

## HARARE TO LAKE CHIVERO
### Larvon Bird Gardens

Larvon Bird Gardens, with over 400 bird species, is a great place to familiarise yourself with southern African avifauna. At the bird orphanage and conservation reserve, larger birds roam free and waterfowl enjoy a pleasant natural lake. It's open weekdays except Thursday from 10 am to 5 pm and on weekends from 9 am to 5 pm. Admission is US$1.50. On weekends, light snacks and drinks are served at the tea garden beside the lake.

Larvon lies 18km south-west of Harare, off the Bulawayo road. Take any Bulawayo bus from Harare and get off at Oatlands Rd. From the intersection, it's just 1km to the entrance. Larvon Bird Gardens is also included in a UTC tour, described under Lion & Cheetah Park later in this section.

### Cold Comfort Farm Society

The well-established Cold Comfort Farm Society (☎ (14) 703372) is an artists cooperative on Cowie Rd, 13km from Harare and 2km off the Bulawayo road. It sells farm produce and makes African tapestries from local wool and natural dyes. The proceeds are used to support co-operative agricultural, carpentry and metalworking ventures.

The Amon Shonge Gallery, which is housed in a former barn, sells original but pricey material arts by rural Zimbabwean women. It's open to visitors Monday to Friday from 10 am to 5 pm and on weekends from 10 am to 4 pm.

### Lion & Cheetah Park

The Lion & Cheetah Park (☎ (162) 27564), 24km from Harare off the Bulawayo road, is the only place in the area to see big cats. It's on a large private estate which also boasts a population of baboons and crocodiles.

The collection of serpents at the attached Snake Park displays some harmless varieties as well as such renowned baddies as spitting cobras, gaboon vipers, puff adders, boomslangs and mambas. The parks are open daily from 8 am to 5 pm and admission to both costs US$13 per vehicle and US$3 per adult.

From Harare, UTC, Kalambeza and Bushbeat Trails run tours (including Lake Chivero) for around US$50. Otherwise, you need a private vehicle, as walking and hitching are forbidden.

### LAKE CHIVERO RECREATIONAL PARK

The 5500 hectare national recreational park, 32km south-west of Harare, focuses on 57 sq km Lake Chivero, a reservoir created by the 1952 damming of the Manyame (also known as the Hunyani) River. The lake was originally named after Sir Robert McIlwaine, first chairman of the board of National Resources. The water level has been quite low for several years now and the shore is becoming choked with rapidly spreading water hyacinth.

Few travellers are set alight by Lake Chivero, but it's all the rage with middle-class Harare day-trippers, who love to spend their weekends fishing, boating, partying and organising lakeshore braais.

### The North Shore

The commercialised California-esque north shore of Lake Chivero is lined with private boat harbours and special-interest group camps, all with big iron gates and fences. Fishing, boating, water-skiing (away from the croc-infested shoreline), lazing, dazing and boozing are the big attractions. Peace and quiet don't figure in the equation.

The Admiral's Cabin (☎ (162) 27144),

with picnic sites and a snack bar, charges US$1.30 admission to the shoreline. You can hire a motorboat for US$8 per hour, pontoon boats for US$13 and paddle canoes for US$1.50 to US$2.50.

From the Hunyani Hills Hotel, a view of the zealously guarded dam wall is a 25 minute lakeshore stroll, via the Mazowe Sailing Club.

### The South Shore

Most of the south shore of the lake lies within the 1600 hectare Chivero Game Park, where you can see antelope, zebra, giraffe, a couple of well-protected white rhino and lots of smaller beasts, such as birds and frogs. Foreigners pay US$10 for day use (US$5 with a tour operator). Guided horse safaris (US$20, 1½ hours) may be booked in advance.

**Rock Paintings** Bushman's Point at the end of the south shore drive has a designated picnic site and walking area within the game park. A set of rock paintings just beyond the traffic turnaround features human figures: hunters, dancing women and a row of 13 kneeling figures of undetermined sex. One painting depicts the felling of a tree, but perhaps the most prophetic painting is of several large fish, which was done long before the lake just beneath them was even a gleam in some ancient angler's eye.

Other rock paintings at the west end of the game park – Crocodile Rock, Pax Park and Ovoid Rock – are accessible only with a park service guide; inquire at the game park gate. The panel at Crocodile Rock (nothing to do with Elton John) depicts two detailed and stylised crocodiles and a procession of 10 individualistic hunters. The Pax Park paintings incorporate hunters, food gatherers and animals, and Ovoid Rock features some unexplained ovoid shapes.

### Places to Stay & Eat

**North Shore** At The Admiral's Cabin (☎ (162) 27144) basic double rooms cost

ZIMBABWE

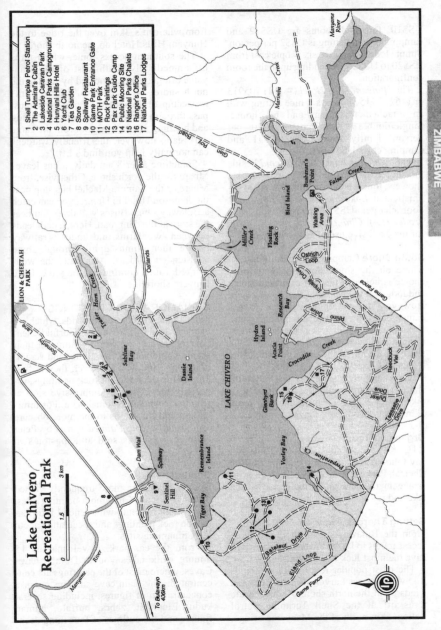

Lake Chivero Recreational Park

0   1.5   3 km

To Bulawayo 406km

Manyame River

Somerset Lane

LION & CHEETAH PARK

Trigger Horn Creek

Oatlands

Glen Roy Road

Manyame River

Marimba Creek

False Creek

Bushman's Point

Walking Area

Bird Island

Floating Rock

Miller's Creek

Research Bay

Hydro Island

Acacia Point

Crocodile Creek

Ostrich Loop

Kudu Drive

Rhino Drive

Reedbuck Vlei

Duiker Drive

Tsessebe Drive

Game Fence

LAKE CHIVERO

Sublime Bay

Dassie Island

Granhyrd Bank

Varley Bay

Preparation Ck

Bateleur Drive

Eland Loop

Game Fence

Dam Wall

Spillway

Remembrance Island

Sentinel Hill

Tiger Bay

1   Shell Turnpike Petrol Station
2   The Admiral's Cabin
3   Lakeside Caravan Park
4   National Parks Campground
5   Hunyani Hills Hotel
6   Yacht Club
7   Tea Garden
8   Store
9   Spillway Restaurant
10  Game Park Entrance Gate
11  MOTH Park
12  Rock Paintings
13  Pax Park Guide Camp
14  Public Mooring Site
15  National Parks Chalets
16  Ranger's Office
17  National Parks Lodges

US$10, four-bed rooms are US$12 and camping or caravaning is US$2 per person. Simple lodges for up to six people cost from US$20 to US$25, depending upon the room configuration.

The *Hunyani Hills Hotel* (☎ (14) 705913 or (162) 27152) enjoys a nice setting with an attached restaurant and tea house. Single/double rooms cost US$20 per person, family rooms are US$51 and camping costs US$3 per person.

The *National Parks campground* beside the hotel has camp sites with baths, showers, toilets and braai pits. The more sophisticated *Lakeside Caravan Park* next door charges US$3.50 per person. The *Trader Horn Club camp site* further east is for the exclusive use of club members.

**South Shore** Camping isn't permitted anywhere on the south shore, so your only choice is between the self-catering chalets and lodges at the *National Parks rest camp*. However, non-emergency access to the camp is forbidden between 6 pm and 6 am. Crocodiles and bilharzia make lake swimming a bad idea, but guests may use the swimming pools at the camp, as well as the tennis and volleyball courts.

There are no restaurants on the south shore. The nearest shop is at the Shell Turnpike petrol station on the Bulawayo road, 5km north-east of the Manyame bridge.

### Organised Tours
UTC, Kalambeza and Bushbeat Trails run day tours to Lake Chivero and the Lion & Cheetah Park for around US$50. With prior arrangement, you can normally stay at the lake and rejoin the tour on another day.

### Getting There & Away
From the Bulawayo road, there are three access routes to Lake Chivero. Hitchers will have the most luck at weekends.

The most popular route is via Oatlands Rd, which passes Larvon Bird Gardens and winds up at the north shore. Another route turns off at the Shell Turnpike petrol station, 5km north of the Manyame bridge,

from where it's 3km over the ridge to the Hunyani Hills Hotel on the north shore.

The southern access route, which turns off immediately south-west of the Manyame bridge, isn't connected by road to the north shore. To reach the National Parks rest camp or Bushman's Point, you must pass through the game park where walking and hitching are prohibited. From the game park gate, however, the friendly wardens can normally help you find a lift.

Sometime after 8 am daily, a bus leaves Mbare for the north shore. Otherwise, from Mbare or the Samora Machel bus stop near the Jameson Hotel in Harare, you can catch a Bulawayo bus. Buses will drop you near the store at the dam road. Here, a path leads between two farms and under a railway bridge, then climbs uphill through some well-tended gardens. At a gate, the well-marked route continues along the Lake Chivero shoreline.

### CHINAMORA ROCK PAINTINGS
The Chinamora communal lands, which are characterised by stark and colourful lichen-covered domes, are worth visiting for their scenic value and their walking and scrambling opportunities. However, they're best known for their ancient rock paintings, especially the extremely impressive sites at Domboshawa and Ngomakurira. For information and directions to the more obscure sites, refer to *The Painted Caves* by Peter Garlake, which is sold at Kingston's in Harare.

### Domboshawa
Domboshawa, the more frequently visited of the two main Chinamora painting sites, has a small museum with general information on rock paintings and speculation about the Chinamora sites.

From the car park, a well-marked 15 minute walk takes you to Domboshawa Caves, where most of the paintings are concentrated. The main cave contains a dense concentration of figures, including several kudu. Elephant, zebra, buffalo, human figures and the outlines of four rhino decorate the interior walls. In a fracture to the left of the main cave, seven stick figures attack an irritable elephant. A faded panel about 30m to the right of the cave depicts a troupe of dancing, long-waisted beings colloquially known as the rainmakers.

The site is open until 5 pm. Foreigners pay US$2 admission.

### Ngomakurira

It's generally agreed that Zimbabwe's finest, readily accessible rock paintings are found at Ngomakurira, (mountain of drums). The name is derived from an acoustic effect which is believed to represent the beating drums of festive spirits. (This effect is most in evidence in several sacred caves which are off limits to visitors.) Foreigners pay US$2 admission.

From the base, take the obvious earthen track to a pronounced ridge, then follow the brown painted arrows across a valley and over bare rock for about 2km. The best paintings, which include two yellow elephants, several antelope and spear-wielding hunters, occupy a dark cave in the precipitous western slope of the rock. Well-treaded footwear is essential.

Alternatively, from the valley, turn upstream and follow the green arrows to the foot of a lichen-stained cliff which bears a procession of four very large elephant flanked by human figures: women, couples, sleeping children and hunters. On the head of the third elephant, a violent confrontation is depicted between a man with a club and his terrified unarmed victim. Other human figures dance across the rock or perform daily tasks while anonymous animals meet their doom at the hands of hunters. This site is best seen in the afternoon.

### Getting There & Away

For Domboshawa, take the Bindura via Chinamora bus from Mbare or the Domboshawa bus from in front of Kingston's bookshop, near African Unity Square (these buses may also be caught anywhere along Seventh St, Chancellor Ave or Borrowdale Rd). With the former bus, get off 4km north of Domboshawa village (30km north of Harare) and follow the side road 1km east to the base of the rock. The latter bus stops at Domboshawa village, requiring a 5km walk to the hill.

The Bindura via Chinamora bus continues to Ngomakurira village, 15km north of Domboshawa. To visit the Ngomakurira paintings, get off at Sasa Road and walk 2km east to the base of the mountain.

### CHISHAWASHA

The Chishawasha Catholic Mission, 21km north-east of Harare, lies on a little-travelled road midway between the Shamva turn-off on the Mutoko road and the Arcturus road. It was founded on 31 July 1892 by the German priest, Francis Richartz. After the First Chimurenga, it became a farming, printing and teaching centre. The interior murals and nearby cemetery have both historical and aesthetic value.

# Northern Zimbabwe

With the exception of eastern Kariba and Mana Pools national park, the country north of Harare draws a geographical blank from many Zimbabweans and visitors alike. This beautiful rolling landscape supports numerous small villages and such little-visited gems as the Mavuradonha Wilderness, the Umfurudzi Safari Area, the middle Zambezi wilderness and the sculptors community at Tengenenge Farm.

## History

If the high incidence of prehistoric rock paintings around Mutoko is any indication, north-eastern Zimbabwe has been inhabited for millennia. In the mid-16th century, Fura, the small mountain now called Mt Darwin, was taken by the Portuguese to be a corruption of Ophir. For several centuries, Europeans wildly speculated that the Empire of Monomatapa guarded the biblical land of Ophir and the elusive King Solomon's mines. The British, who arrived in the late 19th century, settled around Harare because they believed the area to the north was as rich in minerals and precious metals as South Africa's Kimberley and Witwatersrand regions.

Later, the wild northern region attracted the exiled and dispossessed of other areas, including the people of the defeated chief Mbare who had ruled from the Kopje at present-day Harare, and the charismatic 19th century Shona outlaw, Mapondera, who died in prison on a hunger strike after admitting defeat in his attempts to resist encroaching colonial rule.

# The North-East

## NYAMAPANDA

The only reason to visit Nyamapanda is to connect with the run across Mozambique's

Tête Corridor to Malawi. For details, see Mozambique & Malawi in the Zimbabwe Getting There & Away chapter.

## MAZOWE

Mazowe, Zimbabwe's citrus capital, lies in a fertile agricultural area 40km north of Harare. The idea of planting orange, lemon and lime groves at Mazowe stemmed from the early discovery of wild Indian lemon trees, which had apparently been imported by 15th century Swahili and Portuguese traders. The plantation's first commercial citrus crop was harvested in 1913 on

Mazowe Citrus Estates, a subsidiary of the British South Africa Company (BSAC). The 700 hectare plantation area now boasts 200,000 citrus trees.

The blue Mazowe Dam nearby draws weekend visitors from Harare for boating and braais.

### Places to Stay

The colonial-style *Mazowe Hotel* (☎ (75) 2243), which dates from 1895, has a bar and licensed restaurant. *Zindele Guest Farm* (☎ (14) 721696; fax 702006), 30km north of Mazowe, is a working tobacco farm and game ranch. Day trips cost US$70 and overnight stays US$125 per person.

### TENGENENGE FARM

The remote Tengenenge Farm sculptors community, at the foot of the Great Dyke near Guruve, offers a worthwhile detour from the trampled route and an enjoyable introduction to – and appreciation of – Shona sculpture (see boxed text).

The farm is supported by sales as well as outside sponsorships and is always looking out for new talent. However, don't envision a bohemian utopia in the wilderness, as

ZIMBABWE

---

## Tengenenge – One Man's Dream

The sculptors community at Tengenenge Farm is the realised vision of tobacco farmer Tom Blomefield who discovered Great Dyke chrome on his land during the UDI (Unilateral Declaration of Independence) days and from it earned enough money to abandon farming and concentrate on his consuming interest in art. In 1966, local soapstone sculptor Crispen Chakenyoka revealed deposits of magnificent black serpentine in the hills surrounding the property; fate had seemingly dictated that Blomefield's focus would be on sculpture. In Blomefield's words:

The world is like a cattle kraal; you can only see what is in it, the earth and the cattle, the stockade and the sky and the passing birds. Sometimes you may find a small hole in the back ... and you can escape from this world into the mists of the invisible universal field. You may discover new realities there, and dare to dream and desire great things and – visualising them – put out your hands into the swirling mist, grasp them and bring them back to become creatures of the real world.

Malawian sculptor Lemon Moses was the first to join the community and, before long, artists were arriving from around southern Africa, carrying with them the artistic traditions of their respective cultures. Zimbabwean Shona artists were consumed with defining in stone the mystical aspects of their own folklore. Angolans sculpted mask-like faces and the Chewa of Malawi created hulking, monolithic pieces, while their compatriots, the Yao, infused their beliefs in a more abstract iconography.

Although Tengenenge lay in an area of guerrilla conflict during the Second Chimurenga, Blomefield respected the local cause as well as their spiritual motivation and was left to peacefully carry on his work.

The National Gallery provided the community's only Harare sales outlet until 1969 and its director, Frank McEwen, encouraged Blomefield to concentrate on a few outstanding artists and regulate the flow of new talent at Tengenenge. Blomefield's principles wouldn't permit this and more and more artists were welcomed and provided with food, tools, stone and exhibition space. By the time the formal school closed in 1979, over 500 sculptors had lived and worked there, among them such greats as Sylvester Mubayi, Bernard Matemera and Henry Munyaradzi.

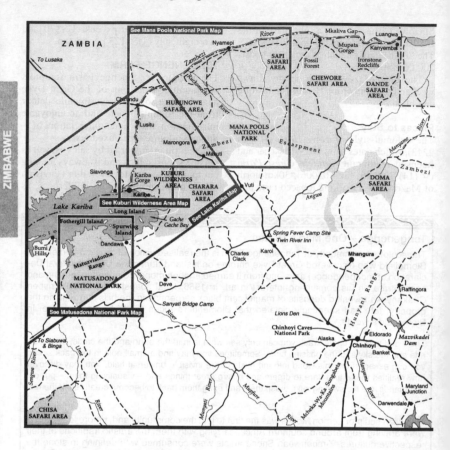

Tengenenge is now a solidly commercial operation. Although the patrons try to avoid a mass-production mentality, some artists have surrendered to market forces. Some of the original artists now maintain farms at the community while others have established more accessible studios on well used routes to Harare.

Visitors can stroll through the extensive sculpture gardens, which contain 17,000 original pieces. Room and board costs US$25 and the basic camp site is US$3 per person. Visiting foreign sculptors are welcome, but must still pay tourist rates.

For information, contact Tengenenge Farm (☎ (158) 1223), PO Box 169, Mvurwi.

### Organised Tours
Stonegate Safaris and Bushbeat Trails, both in Harare, offer day tours to Tengenenge for US$55. For contact details, see the Organised Tours chapter.

### Getting There & Away
From Harare, follow the Mazowe road to Mazowe Dam and turn left. After 56km (at a big dome rock), turn left again, towards Mvurwi. Once through Mvurwi, turn right

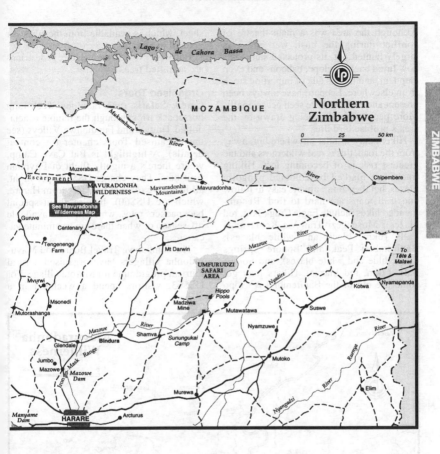

towards Guruve. After 34.5km (12km south of Guruve), take the right turning onto Gurungwe Rd, which is signposted Gurungwe Arts Centre. After 11km, you'll run out of tar. Continue for 2km on the gravel and turn left; it's then 5km to Tengenenge.

The best option on public transport is the bus which leaves Mvurwi for Tengenenge in the afternoon and returns in the morning. If you don't catch this bus, other buses from Mvurwi or the Guruve bus from Harare's Mbare terminal stop at Gurungwe Rd (the Tengenenge turn-off) 12km south of Guruve. Unless you're lucky with a lift, you

will have to walk the remaining 19km through grasslands and upland msasa country. To improve your chances of getting within striking distance in a single day, get a very early start from Mbare.

## MAVURADONHA WILDERNESS

In 1988, the Zimbabwe government set aside a 500 sq km chunk of the Mavuradonha Range above the Zambezi Escarpment as a wilderness area and game reserve. Characterised by rugged, mountainous uplands, the wild landscape is simultaneously beautiful and daunting.

Although the area was a main theatre of conflict during the bush war and was largely hunted out, its protected status has now lured back antelope, baboons and even elephant, and there's talk of importing stock from elsewhere. Leopard have always been present and even lion are seen occasionally. More people are also being drawn by the area's profuse bird life.

Hikers may wander anywhere but, away from the road, this is real wilderness and the greatest risk is of becoming lost. Hiking tracks are marked by coloured pangolin blazes, but they aren't always easy to follow and trail maps are hard to find. Recommended hikes include Eagle Crag (3km, red blazes); Musengezi Trail via Kemavanga Falls (6km, black and white blazes); Banirembizi Peak and Bohore Springs (7km, blue and white blazes); and Sohwe Falls (7km, red blazes). Hikers may get some use out of the Banirembizi A3 topo sheet, which is available from the surveyor general in Harare.

Entry is US$1.50 per vehicle, pedestrians are admitted free.

## Organised Tours

Carew Safaris runs fabulous week-long horseback trips through the remote acacia-dotted Tingwa and Fundumwe Valleys (see the Organised Tours chapter for contact details). A highlight is Bat Cave Camp, where there's a nightly flight of Egyptian fruit bats. They charge US$180 per night, all inclusive (except transfers from Harare, which are US$60). Inquire about special backpackers rates, which may be available off-season or when there are last minute vacancies.

The Zimbabwe Travel Board and Mavuradonha villagers have organised a rural tourism programme for Murota village. For US$63, visitors spend a weekend in a

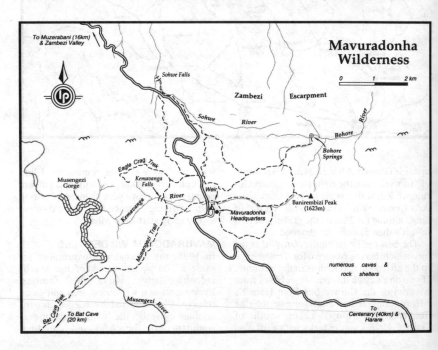

village, including transfers from Harare, simple accommodation, meals, drinks and information on village life. They leave Harare at 7 am Saturday and return on Sunday afternoon. Contact the Zimbabwe Travel Bureau (☎ (14) 702941), PO Box UA 534, Harare. Book by the Thursday prior to the weekend you want to go.

### Places to Stay & Eat
The *Mavuradonha CAMPFIRE Camp Site* is maintained by the local community, which benefits from the income generated. Tent camping is US$2 per person and camping in thatched two-person A-frames costs US$4.50. There's no bedding and you sleep on a mattress of straw, so bring a sleeping bag. Basic toilets and showers are available, and the staff sell bundles of firewood for US$1.20. Lodges are under construction at the main camp and at Sohwe Falls. Book through CAMPFIRE (☎ (14) 747152), Mukuvisi Woodlands, Harare, or the Wildlife Society of Zimbabwe (☎ (14) 700451), PO Box 3497, Harare.

For supplies and a glimpse of another world, try the country supermarket in Muzerabani, 12km from the Zambezi Escarpment.

### Getting There & Away
The Mavuradonha headquarters lies two hours by car from Harare at the 50.5km peg on the Muzerabani road north of Centenary. Petrol is available at Muzerabani from Monday to Saturday; on Sunday you have to go to Mvurwi, 115km away.

From Mbare (Harare), you can reach Mavuradonha on a Centenary/Muzerabani bus; the park office lies 200m off the road.

## UMFURUDZI SAFARI AREA
This relatively little-known wilderness (which, despite its name, does not permit hunting) comprises 76,000 hectares of dry, lonely hills north of the Mazowe River. This magnificent walking country is rich in wildlife – hippo, large cats and antelope, including the rarely observed roan. For longer trips, you'll need a guide and must be self-

sufficient. Foreigners pay US$10 admission.

### Hippo Pools
*Hippo Pools* (☎ (14) 738341 or 739836; fax 731273), PO Box 90, Shamva, a budget resort set idyllically on the wildlife-rich banks of the Mazowe River, makes a pleasant Umfurudzi base and is ideal for canoeing, fishing, relaxing and hiking on 250km of maintained trails (maps are available).

There's a wildlife-viewing hide 300m from camp and owners Sue and Iain Jarvis organise guided game walks, drives and excursions around the Umfurudzi Safari Area. Worthwhile sites include ancient rock paintings, a basic gold-mining operation, old Shona and Portuguese forts and the communal lands across the river (the source of all that drumming at night). A wonderful all-day game drive takes you to Fantasy Pools, where you can picnic and swim. At high water (January to April), they run two-night canoeing trips on the Mazowe River. Alternatively, you can strike out on the 50km of walking tracks.

Camping costs US$7 per person, accommodation in cabins (or in the hide 7m off the ground) is US$15. In chalets, it's US$20, including use of the self-catering facilities. Meals cost US$10. Special four-day budget safaris, with transfers, accommodation and half-board, cost US$77.

**Getting There & Away** Transfers from Harare (US$9) run on Monday and Friday at 2.30 pm from Kopje 221 Lodge and the Brontë Hotel. Book through Goliath Safaris, Brontë Hotel, Harare, or contact Hippo Pools directly.

Hippo Pools is accessible without 4WD except in the wet summer months. From Harare, take Enterprise Rd and turn north on the Shamva road. Continue past Shamva for 33km and take the second right into Madziwa village. Immediately beyond the village shop (which sells basic supplies), turn right down a hill, follow the road to the

T-junction and turn left. It's 6km of tarred road to the Amms Mine turning; don't turn here, but continue on to the National Parks entrance. After 6km, you'll reach the National Parks office turn-off. Continue straight on for 12km, mostly downhill, to Hippo Pools.

### Sunungukai Camp

The CAMPFIRE camp Sunungukai ('welcome and be free'), on the banks of the Mazowe River, sits at the edge of the Umfurudzi Safari Area near the village of Nyagande. It's quite basic, but is an honest effort by local villagers to bring tourism to this lovely and quiet corner of Zimbabwe and, in 1994, it won the British Airways Tourism for Tomorrow award.

The area is good for fishing, birdwatching and hiking, and a nearby mountain has ancient rock paintings. Revenue from the project is ploughed into such community development projects as a local school, clinic and grist mill.

Simple four-bed rondavels cost US$8.50 per person, camping (no caravans) is US$5 and meals cost US$1.50. For bookings, contact CAMPFIRE (☎ (14) 747152) at Mukuvisi Woodlands, Harare.

**Getting There & Away** From Harare, there are two daily Kukura Kurerwa buses. The first, marked Nyava via Shamva and Mazowe Bridge, leaves Mbare musika at around noon and the second, to Nhakiwa via Bindura and Glendale, departs around 4 pm. Alternatively, buses marked Katiyo-Mutawatawa via Shamva depart at 6 am and 12.30 pm.

By car from Harare, take the Mutoko road to Murewa and turn left onto the tarred road leading into the Uzumba Maramba Pfungwe communal lands. After 55km, turn left at the Sunungukai signpost and continue for 3km to the Nyagande General Dealer shop, where you should turn right. After 1.5km, you'll see the camp on your right. You can also take the scenic route via Shamva, but the road along the Mazowe River may not be passable after rain.

# Harare to Chirundu

The tarred road between Harare and Chirundu is well travelled and hitchers should have few problems (especially at weekends).

If you want to fish for bream (tilapia) or tiger fish at Kariba, pick up fishing worms around Chinhoyi town, where salespeople hang sacks of worms from small roadside tripods.

### CHINHOYI

Chinhoyi town, 120km north-west of Harare, serves as the administrative centre for a rich tobacco, maize and cattle-farming region. Alaska Mine, 20km north-west of town, began producing export quantities of copper in 1959.

Chinhoyi's place in history was secured on 28 April 1966, when ZANLA forces, led by Bernard Mutuma, and well-armed Rhodesian Security Forces met in the 12 hour clash now known as the Battle of Chinhoyi. The skirmish resulted in the loss of seven ZANLA guerrillas and launched the Second Chimurenga which eventually led to Zimbabwean independence. In Zimbabwe, 28 April is now commemorated as Chimurenga Day.

### Places to Stay

The clean and comfortable *Orange Grove Motel* (☎ (167) 2785; fax 3095) is the only place to stay in the town itself. Standard single/double rooms cost US$23/33; with TV, they're US$28/37. Ask about special backpackers rates. Campers pay US$1.60 per tent or US$2 per caravan, and may use the swimming pool.

Another option is the small *Mazvikadei Dam Lodge* (☎ (14) 573766), beside the dam of the same name north-east of Chinhoyi. It's reasonably priced at US$13 per person, with bed, breakfast and transport from Harare or Chinhoyi. Meals are available and there are opportunities for walking and birdwatching around the dam. Book by

## The Great Dyke

The Great Dyke is a spine of low rocky hills 530km in length, stretching north to south down Zimbabwe, from the Zambezi Escarpment near Guruve all the way to Mberengwa and Shurugwi in the Midlands. Its northern anchor is the jumbled Mvurwi Range, which rises to nearly 1700m at the western end of the Mavuradonha Mountains. At its southern end, it rears up beneath the Chironde Range, near Shurugwi.

The ridge is of volcanic origin, an exposed extrusion of erosion-resistant igneous material which is 70% serpentine and extremely rich in platinum, chrome, asbestos and magnesium. The easiest places to view it from the road are at Great Dyke Pass, which offers long-ranging views across the surrounding maize and tobacco farmlands, and on Wolfshall Pass in the Chironde Range east of Shurugwi.

phone or through Shane Maurel, 11 Manondo Rd, Hatfield, Harare.

See also under Chinhoyi Caves National Park.

## CHINHOYI CAVES NATIONAL PARK

This small but worthwhile 'roadside' national park, 1½ hours from Harare, is riddled with limestone and dolomite caves and sinkholes which have been used for storage and refuge for nearly 1500 years. The largest caves were once well-decorated with stalactites and stalagmites, but most of those in accessible passages have long since been broken off.

The main pool is called Sleeping Pool or Chirorodzira (Pool of the Fallen), and maintains a constant temperature of 22°C). The name may suggest commemoration of an accident or a battle but, in fact, the 'fallen' were local people intentionally cast into the formidable hole by the invading Nguni

tribes in the early 19th century. In 1887, colonial hunter Frederick Courteney Selous found the area occupied by the subjects of Chief Chinhoyi and took the pocked landscape (which resembled that around the modern copper mines a few kilometres away) to be evidence of ancient mine workings.

From the park entrance, a footpath descends 46m to water level, affording views into the cave's dark recesses, as well as its 91m-deep aquamarine pool and its plants and fish.

From Dark Cave (the rear entrance to Chirorodzira), the view through the shadows to the sunlit waters below reveals a magical effect. The clear water so perfectly admits light that the water line disappears and the pool takes on the appearance of a smoky blue underworld. Divers have discovered an underwater passage leading from the Bat Cave, a

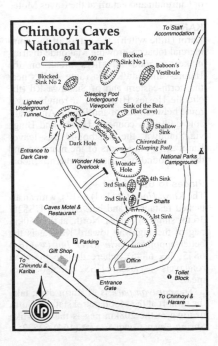

Chinhoyi Caves National Park

sub-chamber of Dark Cave, to another cavity known as Blind Cave.

The park is open during daylight hours all year round and admission is US$5. The hotel sells petrol.

### Places to Stay & Eat

The *Caves Motel* (☎ (167) 2340) at the park entrance charges US$21/27 for singles/doubles, with breakfast. There's also a restaurant with a surprisingly varied menu: paella, schnitzel, lasagne, trout, venison and German dishes. The *National Parks Campground* charges US$2.50 per person for tent or caravan camping. Use of picnic facilities costs US$2 and firewood sells for US$3.50 per bundle.

### Getting There & Away

You'll find the entrance on the Harare-Chirundu road, 8km north-west of Chinhoyi. From Harare, take any bus to Kariba or Chirundu and get off at the Caves Motel.

## KAROI

Karoi (little witch), the centre of the commercial tobacco-growing Makonde district, makes a good travellers break on the Harare-Chirundu/Kariba route. It lies near the north-eastern end of Siabuwa Rd (the Nicolle Hostes Highway), a rough gravel route between Karoi and Binga. An unreliable daily bus connects Harare and Binga via Siabuwa; the westbound bus leaves Karoi at varying hours of the morning and the eastbound one passes in the afternoon.

### Places to Stay & Eat

The *Karoi Hotel* (☎ (164) 6317), with an attached restaurant and bar, charges US$25/36 for singles/doubles. North, at the 250km peg of the highway toward Kariba, is the better-appointed *Twin River Inn* (☎ (164) 6845; fax 6846), where double thatched rondavels cost around US$21. It also serves meals.

The *caravan park* is at Karoi dam; take the turnoff at the Mobil petrol station. North of town at the 208km peg is the park-like *Spring Fever Camp Site* (☎ (164) 625325),

with electricity and braai stands. There's a tea room and it also serves breakfasts and light lunches, and sells petrol and self-catering supplies. Braais are organised on Sundays.

Simple meals are available at the *As You Like It* takeaway on the main road through town.

## MAKUTI

Makuti sits on the edge of the Zambezi Escarpment, where the land spills down from jumbled forested hills towards Kariba, 66km away. The tiny settlement is little more than a road junction, motel and the last petrol station before Kariba or Mana Pools. All Kariba buses pass through Makuti.

### Places to Stay & Eat

Makuti's action focuses on the *Cloud's End Hotel* (☎/fax (163) 526). Surrounded by pleasant but unkempt gardens and backed by a far-ranging view, it's a favourite of Kariba-bound travellers. There's a dilapidated swimming pool and a dining room which serves up a mean buffet breakfast. Singles/doubles cost US$26/34 and family rooms are US$63, all with breakfast. Adjoining the petrol station is a pub, bottle store and small food shop.

## MARONGORA

In the beautiful hills near the lip of the Zambezi Escarpment sits Marongora, the administrative offices for Mana Pools National Park (☎ (163) 512). Prospective Mana Pools visitors (including those who've pre-booked accommodation) must secure a park entry permit at Marongora *before 3.30 pm* on the day of entry into the park. You need both accommodation reservations and transport before permits will be issued.

For visitors without private vehicles, who cannot pre-book Mana Pools accommodation, Marongora offers a chance to find transport and park accommodation. If you have a guaranteed lift and lodges or camp sites are available, the rangers will help you with arrangements. Otherwise, pick up a day entry permit and hope that accommodation comes available. (For details, see Permits under Mana Pools National Park, later in this chapter.)

## Places to Stay

If you must wait for accommodation in the park, you can stay in Makuti, 10km south of Marongora, or camp behind the park office, where there's a *camp site* with braai pits, cold showers and toilets. The nearest shop and restaurant are at Makuti.

## CHIRUNDU

This uninspiring border town on the Zambezi is one of several put-in points for middle Zambezi canoe safaris. Here, Zambia and Zimbabwe are joined by the impressive Otto Beit Bridge (no photos allowed). Its name honours the younger brother of Alfred Beit, the philanthropist who established the Beit Trust and financed the bridge construction.

Chirundu is known for its wildlife and

visitors should watch out for elephant, buffalo, hippo and crocodiles. A sign at the motel swimming pool reads 'Swim at your own risk – elephants drink here'. Although the thirsty pachyderms have been staying away recently, elephant, buffalo and other animals still drink at the camp site water hole.

## Activities

Willy Reed of Tiger Safaris (☎/fax (163) 7633), PO Box 1, Chirundu, runs speedboat fishing trips on the Zambezi (no tackle provided) for US$59/50 per full/half day for up to three people, including a driver. Fuel and National Parks permits are extra. The Tiger Safaris camp lies 1km downstream from the bridge. Book Zambezi canoe safaris in either Harare or Kariba.

## Places to Stay & Eat

The riverside *Zambezi Angling Club Camp Site*, downstream from the bridge, offers basic sites for US$2. Wildlife is profuse; campers should zip their tents, watch for

## The Zambezi Valley

In ancient geological history, the Zambezi flowed from what is now southern Angola to join the Limpopo on its trip to the Indian Ocean. Subsequent igneous upheavals, however, diverted the northern headwaters into the Kalahari, where it disappeared into the sands and formed the vast swamplands of the Okavango Delta and the Linyanti Marshes. Another branch of the river spilled into the Luangwa Valley, a tributary fault of Africa's remarkable Great Rift Valley.

The pools for which Mana Pools National Park is named are leftovers from the gradual northward migration of the main Zambezi River channel. Elsewhere, they'd be called billabongs, bayous or oxbows – puddles occupying the low-lying patches of the former riverbed. On the northern bank of the Zambezi, the rugged green mountains of Zambia abut the flood-plain but, as the river pushes further northward, they're doomed to the same erosion that flattened out the broad series of river terraces to the south.

The abrupt and dramatic escarpment delineating the southern edge of the Zambezi Valley extends from the Mozambique border in the east, through Mana Pools National Park to Kariba in the west. Above it are the cooler, undulating highlands of the Mavuradonha Range and below, an expansive mopane-covered plain stretching away to the river itself. The best views are to be had on the Chirundu Rd between Marongora and the Mana Pools National Park entrance, and from near Centenary, where the view extends all the way to Mozambique's Cahora Bassa Dam.

hippo and avoid venturing outside after dark. Pay only the angling club, not 'the caretaker.

The *Chirundu Valley Motel* (☎ (163) 7618) is decent value at US$17/28 for single/double units with bath, including a full breakfast, but camping costs a whopping US$5.50. Staples are sold in a small shop beside the hotel.

At *Tiger Safaris Lodge* (☎/fax (163) 7633), 1km downstream of the bridge, self-catering chalets with two double bedrooms, bath, kitchen, veranda and car port cost US$75 for up to four people and US$19 for each extra person. There's a pool and recreation area, and self-catering supplies are sold on request.

### Getting There & Away

Thanks to commercial traffic on the main Harare-Lusaka (Zambia) route, hitching isn't difficult. Daily bus services connect Harare and Chirundu from Mbare musika, or you can take the more frequent Kariba buses to Makuti and hitch from there.

All buses between Harare and Lusaka also stop at Chirundu. The first of several daily services leaves Mbare at 6 am but arrive early to get a seat. For more comfort, Power Coach Express (☎ (14) 668716) has a service from Mbare at 8 am daily. The fare to Chirundu is US$4.

# The Middle Zambezi

Locally, the stretch of the Zambezi below Kariba and above Kanyemba is often known as the Lower Zambezi, apparently relative to Kariba (the centre of some Zimbabweans' universe!). However, it's more accurately called the Middle Zambezi, as an awful lot of the river lies in Mozambique territory further downstream.

Beyond Chirundu and Mana Pools National Park, this bit of river is inaccessible from the highway system without 4WD. In fact, for many locals, the river *is* the

highway system. To take advantage of this lovely wilderness route, canoe safari companies run two- to nine-day river trips between Kariba and Kanyemba on the Mozambique border.

## MANA POOLS NATIONAL PARK

Mana Pools is magnificent, but allow it more than a quick glance, or it may disappoint. Mana's magic stems from a pervading sense of the wild and remote (unlike Hwange with its artificial dams and petrol-generated waterholes) but away from the riverbanks, the landscapes are less than overwhelming and the wildlife density pales in comparison to Hwange's.

In 1982, this magnificent wilderness was saved from flooding when successful lobbying by the Zambezi Society convinced the government to abandon plans for a dam at Mutapa Gorge. In recognition of their ecological significance, UNESCO has designated Mana Pools and neighbouring Chewore Safari Area as a World Heritage Site.

Mana Pools is open to motor vehicles only during the dry season, from 1 May to 31 October. The National Parks lodges remain open year-round, but from 1 November to 30 April, they may be accessed only by boat or on foot.

### Information

**Bookings & Permits** Visitors must book accommodation through the National Parks Central Booking Office in Harare (or the alternative method outlined in the Marongora section, earlier in this chapter). Visitors must demonstrate that they have transport; if you're asked how you intend to travel to the park, don't say you're hitching, because it isn't permitted. Nor should you say you're hiring a vehicle, unless it's a 4WD, as car hire agencies don't allow their 2WD cars into Mana Pools on the grounds that the road is too rough.

Your best option is to convince them you've borrowed a vehicle from a local friend. Alternatively, hitch to Marongora and hope there's a camp site and a lift avail-

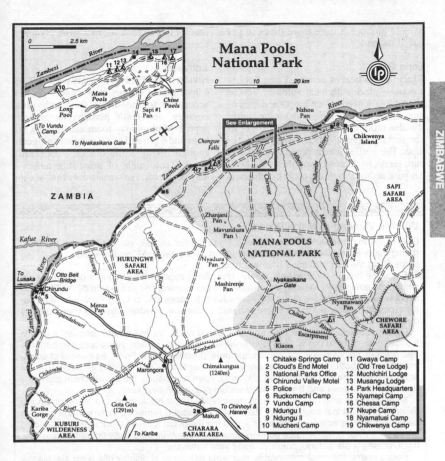

Mana Pools
National Park

ZAMBIA

See Enlargement

MANA POOLS
NATIONAL PARK

SAPI
SAFARI
AREA

Nyakasikana
Gate

CHEWORE
SAFARI
AREA

HURUNGWE
SAFARI
AREA

Kafue River

To
Lusaka

Otto Beit
Bridge

Chirundu

KUBURI
WILDERNESS
AREA

Kariba
Gorge

Gota Gota
(1291m)

To Kariba

Chimakungua
(1240m)

To Chinhoyi &
Harare

CHARARA
SAFARI AREA

Makuti

ZIMBABWE

| | |
|---|---|
| 1 Chitake Springs Camp | 11 Gwaya Camp |
| 2 Cloud's End Motel | (Old Tree Lodge) |
| 3 National Parks Office | 12 Muchichiri Lodge |
| 4 Chirundu Valley Motel | 13 Musangu Lodge |
| 5 Police | 14 Park Headquarters |
| 6 Ruckomechi Camp | 15 Nyamepi Camp |
| 7 Vundu Camp | 16 Chessa Camp |
| 8 Ndungu I | 17 Nkupe Camp |
| 9 Ndungu II | 18 Nyamatusi Camp |
| 10 Mucheni Camp | 19 Chikwenya Camp |

able when you arrive. Hitchers can't be added to their driver's permit, so it's wise to buy a permit which is valid beyond your intended stay, thus allowing time to find a lift out of the park.

After booking accommodation, you must secure an entry permit, which for foreigners costs US$5/10 per day/week. This must be picked up from the Marongora office before 3.30 pm on the day you enter the park. Once the permit is issued, you must reach the Nyamepi park headquarters (☎ (163) 7533) that day. If the Marongora office says the

park camps are fully booked, you can get a US$5 day entry permit. However, it's difficult to extend a day permit into a multi-day permit at Nyamepi because no-shows aren't confirmed until 5.30 pm and should nothing become available, you wouldn't have time to exit the park before the gate closes.

Before you reach the Zambezi, your permit will be scrutinised four times – at Marongora, at the park turn-off, at the park boundary and at Nyamepi – so don't even consider trying to sneak in without one. Once you've arrived, don't lose it; you'll have to produce it three more times to get out of the park.

## Long Pool

Except in the heat of midday, Long Pool is a popular place with local wildlife. You're almost guaranteed to see hippo and crocodiles in the water and basking on the shore. It's also more than likely that you'll get to see zebra, elephant and a variety of antelope. The entire human population of the park seems to descend upon the Long Pool car park at dusk, so this is probably the best time of day to look for lifts from Nyamepi Camp.

## Activities

**Hiking** Mana Pools is the only park in Zimbabwe where visitors may wander on foot according to the dictates of individual courage, and that's perhaps its greatest appeal. Visitors may roam at will between 6 am and 6 pm and some people can't get in enough hiking while others – especially after a tense night of unsettling noises – may be put off. For some safety tips, see the

---

### Wildlife Viewing at Mana Pools

Only in the rainy season do any of Mana Pools' larger animals venture far from the river; during the drier months, wildlife is concentrated on the several-kilometres-wide alluvial terraces along the park's riverine northern boundary.

Since the heat of the Zambezi Valley days sends most of the creatures under cover of shade, the best wildlife viewing is done early in the morning and just before dusk. The most popular viewing areas are along the Mana River terraces and at Long Pool, where crocodiles and hundreds of hippos share the water hole with anyone else who may come to quench a thirst.

Common antelope include the kudu, eland and nyala, as well as the ubiquitous impala that seem to mill and pronk around everywhere. Baboon, buffalo, zebra and elephant are also present, sometimes in staggering numbers. Birdlife at Mana Pools, as in most of southern Africa, is both diverse and abundant, augmented by the meeting of several avian habitats – mopane and jesse scrub, savanna, open woodlands, the environment along the newest river terraces and the fish-filled waters of the Zambezi itself.

Mana Pools is also one of the final strongholds of the black rhino, but its numbers are dwindling fast. At last count, fewer than 1000 individuals remained in Africa and, despite dehorning and transplanting schemes – and the wardens' ruthless treatment of suspected poachers – rhino continue to be gunned down at a staggering and sadly uncontrollable rate. If you do see a black rhino, count yourself very fortunate.

For campers, the most memorable moments will come at night, while lying sleeplessly (and breathlessly?) listening to the surrounding evidence of timeless nocturnal activity. Elephant splash and trumpet beside the river while hippo grunt nearby. The almost incessant roaring of lions reverberates through camp (remember, hungry lions don't roar lest they send prey species scattering to all quarters; roaring lions are normally fat and satisfied lions!) and hyaena yelp with their odd characteristic crescendos. Anonymously stealthy footfalls approach and retreat outside the tent and unidentified raucous cacophonies erupt and subside in the bush. For many – at least for the first night – sleep is fitful if it comes at all!

**Safety on Foot** While the risks are very real and the (often sensationalised) stories reiterated in travellers haunts Africa-wide can get pretty gory, the reality is that humans have safely coexisted with African wildlife for aeons and generations of bush wisdom are at the disposal of modern visitors. Although caution is warranted, paranoia is not, and following

boxed text Wildlife Viewing at Mana Pools below.

If you prefer more structured exploration, several companies offer four- to six-day walking safaris.

**Fishing & Canoeing** Without a licence, visitors may take up to six fish per day from the Zambezi. Three-person canoes can be hired from the Nyamepi headquarters for US$14 per day. However, you still need a vehicle to transport the canoes from the office to the river. For information on or-

ganised canoe safaris, see later in this section.

**Places to Stay**

Advance booking is strongly advised, especially during Zimbabwean and South African school holidays, but cancellations and low periods occasionally permit last-minute bookings from Marongora.

Most visitors stay at *Nyamepi Camp*, near park headquarters, which has showers, toilets and sinks. Firewood is sold at the office, but National Parks prefers that

time-honoured (and some relatively new) guidelines will practically ensure only pleasant encounters:

- Oranges and other fresh fruits, particularly citrus, may attract elephant. Park rangers confiscate oranges brought into the park, but all fruit should be locked up in a vehicle.
- If you want to observe wildlife, don't dazzle it with shocking pink, fluorescent yellow or even (unlikely once you've arrived at Mana!) freshly scrubbed white. It's best to wear natural earthy colours the animals are accustomed to seeing.
- Avoid heavy bush or high grass where you can't observe what's lurking ahead. If you must pass through thick brush, climb a tree every so often and have a look around before proceeding. Listen carefully and watch for ripples in the grass.
- Keep a lookout for larger animals and scan tree lines for felines; also keep an eye on what's happening behind you. If you do encounter elephant, lion, buffalo or rhino, try to pass quietly downwind of them, especially if they're with young ones, and don't block their escape route to the water or bush. If they're moving in your direction, move quietly away but never run, especially in the case of large cats. Your retreat may trigger their reflex to give chase.
- While avoiding the big guys, don't forget to watch where you're putting your feet. Black mambas also thrive along the middle Zambezi as do such other nasties as centipedes and scorpions. Carefully check your shoes in the morning and your sleeping bag at night!
- When walking along river banks, beware of logs that could turn out to be crocodiles and steer away from hippo runs. Before drawing water from any source, make a slow and careful assessment of what's occupying the water in question.
- Don't even think about swimming in the Zambezi. The bilharzia risk may be minimal, but crocodiles, hippos and the strong, fast current are all deadly hazards.
- Keep a good distance from all animals and don't be seduced into carelessness by what may appear to be the ultimate photo opportunity. On foot, you're lucky to approach within even telephoto range.
- Although the Milky Way or full moon may tempt you to sleep in the open on a clear Zambezi night, it's best to zip up your tent and stay quietly inside, as lion, elephant and hyaena often prowl around camp sites at night. The obvious corollaries are to drink liquids in moderation before bedtime and use the toilet before crawling into the sack.

campers use their own stoves. Individual collection of firewood is prohibited.

There are also several smaller campgrounds. *Mucheni Camp*, 8km west of Nyamepi, has four sites. *Chessa Camp*, immediately east of Nyamepi, *Nkupe Camp*, east of Mana Mouth, and *Gwaya Camp* (Old Tree Lodge), near the national park lodges, each accommodates groups of up to 12 people. *Ndungu Camp*, 11km west of Nyamepi, has two organised group camp sites which also hold 12 people each.

*Vundu Camp*, 13km upstream from Nyamepi, has sleeping huts, a cooking area, a living area and an ablutions block with hot water and showers. It accommodates up to 12 people and is hired out in six-day blocks.

West of the Nyamepi office are the popular *Musangu* and *Muchichiri* National Parks lodges, with eight beds each. They cost US$50 and are normally allocated by lottery.

In addition, there's the recently established *Chitake Springs Camp*, 30km inland near the Zambezi Escarpment. It's accessible only by 4WD.

There are no shops or restaurants in the park; visitors must be self-sufficient.

**Luxury Camps** Two lodges which occupy private concessions within the park provide more comfort than the National Parks accommodation. Both stay open from early April to mid-November and employ professional hiking guides for their guests.

*Ruckomechi Camp*, near the park's western boundary, offers well-appointed single/double chalets and full-board for US$340/480 in high season and US$260/360 in low season. It's accessible by road, plane, boat or canoe, and Shearwater uses it as a scheduled stop on its canoe safaris. Return transfers from Kariba cost US$100; from Chirundu, they're US$50. Children under 16 years aren't permitted. Book through Shearwater in Harare.

The comfortable *Chikwenya Camp* sits in a grove of Natal mahogany at the confluence of the Sapi and Zambezi rivers. All-inclusive single/double packages cost

US$445/690 and air transfers are US$343 return. Book through Acacia Hotels (☎ (14) 707438), which has headquarters at the George Hotel in Harare, or through Chikwenya Safaris (☎ (161) 2525) in Kariba.

### Getting There & Away

From Marongora, the Chirundu road continues northward to the lip of the Zambezi Escarpment then steeply descends 900m into the broad Zambezi Valley. The Mana Pools turn-off lies just below the escarpment. Once past the turn-off gate, it's a long, corrugated route through dense and thorny *jesse* scrub to the Nyakasikana park entrance on the Ruckomechi River. Once over the bridge, sign in at the boom gate and then turn left. Everyone must check in at the Nyamepi office before proceeding to their lodge or camp site.

If you have a vehicle and would like to share petrol and expenses to Mana Pools, post notices at Harare backpackers hostels. You'll be enthusiastically received by those who might have given up hope of ever getting there!

See under Chirundu for information on public transport to Marongora, where you must pick up a park permit. Alternatively, you can enter Mana Pools on a canoe safari; see the following section for details.

### MIDDLE ZAMBEZI CANOE SAFARIS

A number of operators offer a little soft adventure in the form of multi-day Middle Zambezi canoe safaris. The entire route extends from Kariba Gorge to Kanyemba, on the Mozambique border. Trips are normally done in stages: Kariba to Chirundu, Chirundu to Mana Pools and Mana Pools to Kanyemba, but any west to east combination is possible.

In addition to wildlife viewing, the big attraction of these low-impact safaris is the wilderness silence. To relax and fully appreciate the river's rhythm and moods, a single three day stage may not be enough. If you can do only one stage, Chirundu-Mana Pools offers the broadest wildlife diversity and best scenery. This may easily

## Canoe Safari Operators

*Buffalo Safaris*, PO Box 113, Kariba (☎ (161) 2645; fax 2827; <buffalo@harare.iafrica.com>). Year round, this friendly, professional and highly recommended company operates three- to 10-day trips on all stages from Kariba to Kanyemba.

*Chipembere Safaris*, PO Box 9, Kariba (☎ (161) 2946). Chipembere (black rhino) has five-day runs from Chirundu to Mana Pools on Sunday and Wednesday; four-day walking safaris from Chitake Springs or the Mana Pools riverfront (US$340); and Mana Pools backpacking trips (US$265 – participants carry their own food and camping equipment).

*Goliath Safaris*, Suite 336, Brontë Hotel, PO Box CH 294, Chisipite, Harare (☎/fax (14) 708843). This small and personable company is also recommended and is gaining popularity with travellers. Goliath covers the routes between Chirundu and Kanyemba and tends to be the least 'routine' of the operators.

*Kasambabezi Safaris*, PO Box CY420, Causeway, Harare (☎/fax (14) 787012) or Stand 787 Sable Drive, Andora Harbour, Kariba (☎/fax (161) 2641). This company does the 60km run from Kariba to Chirundu and on to Mana Pools. Since access to both the start and finish are relatively easy, it's an inexpensive option.

*Muzo's Canoe Safaris*, PO Box 255, Kariba (☎/fax (161) 2777 or ☎ (14) 700002; fax 700001). This company runs inexpensive two- to four-day canoeing safaris between Kariba and Mana Pools.

*River Horse Safaris*, Andora Harbour, PO Box 224, Kariba (☎ (161) 2447; fax 2422; <riverhse@icon.co.zw>). River Horse offers two- to five-night canoe safaris from Kariba to Chirundu and Chirundu to Mana Pools, as well as day activities. The novel offerings include a one day canoe trip (US$120) as well as Two-in-One (boating and game driving, US$30), Three-in-One (the same, plus canoeing, US$55) and Four-in-One (all the above plus a hike, US$120) day trips from Kariba. It has also launched two budget canoe safaris, for a minimum of four people. Kariba to Chirundu (two nights, three days) costs US$150; Chirundu to Mana (three nights, four days) is US$230. Participants provide their own food, drink, tents and sleeping gear, River Horse covers the rest, including transfers to and from the safari area, canoe permits and camp fees.

*Safari Par Excellence*, 3rd floor, Travel Centre, Jason Moyo Ave, PO Box 5920, Harare (☎ (14) 700911; fax 722872). Safari Par Excellence runs three- to five-day luxury canoe safaris from the Zambian shore, between the mouths of the Kafue and Chikwenga Rivers. Overnights are at fully-equipped tented camps. Alternatively, there's a more basic – and less expensive – four day camping safari which runs between Chirundu and Chongwe Falls. It also offers a five day combination walking and canoeing package through Mana Pools National Park, which costs US$250 per day.

*Shearwater/Royal Zambezi Canoeing*, Edward Building, First St and Nelson Mandela Ave, PO Box 3961, Harare (☎ (14) 757831; fax 757836; <shearwat@harare.iafrica.com>). Shearwater offers numerous itineraries and accommodation options (from river island camping to plush Ruckomechi Camp in Mana Pools) along the 10 day route from Kariba to Kanyemba. It also runs a soft option four day Mana Pools trip. The affiliated Royal Zambezi Canoeing (☎ (260-1) 224334; fax 223504), 6th floor, Findeco House, Cairo Rd, PO Box 31455, Lusaka, Zambia, does three- to five-day camp-based itineraries from the Zambian shore, between the Kafue River mouth and Jekki Camp in the Lower Zambezi National Park. In Kariba, book through the Kariba Breezes Hotel.

*Sobek*, PO Box 30263, Lusaka, Zambia (☎ (260-1) 224248; fax 224265). For a different twist, this company begins its tours in Siavonga, on the Zambian side of Kariba Dam, for three-day trips to Chirundu or beyond into Lower Zambezi National Park and the Mozambique border. Along the way, armed guides lead walking tours through this little-visited area.

*Tsoro River Safaris*, PO Box 161, Kariba (☎/fax (161) 2426). This company runs four-day canoe safaris between Chirundu and Mana Pools for under US$450 per person.

*Zambezi Hippo Trails/Muvimi Safaris*, 89 Central Ave, PO Box 2233, Harare (☎ (14) 793107; fax 704960; <afadvent@id.co.zw>). This company does the five day section from Mana Pools to Kanyemba, starting on Wednesday and Sunday.

be extended to include the wild section from Mana Pools to Kanyemba. The very motivated can go for the whole 10 day extravaganza from Kariba to Kanyemba and experience the slow metamorphosis of the Zambezi from its newly-liberated frolic below Kariba Dam to its self-assured amble into Mozambique.

Most companies camp on the riverbanks, but safaris may not stray more than 50m from the river unless they're accompanied by a licensed foot safari guide. July to October are peak months for wildlife viewing. On the river, hippo and crocs are almost constant companions, but guides know how to steer clear.

## Information

The various canoe operators use different camps and a range of approaches, so shop around. Buffalo Safaris and Goliath Safaris are especially recommended for independent travellers while upmarket patrons may prefer the Shearwater approach, which includes overnights at plush camps rather than bush camping.

Zimbabwean canoe guides are licensed and well-experienced in the bush. All operators use 5.7m Canadian-design fibreglass canoes. In Zimbabwe, operator numbers are limited and each one is restricted to specific days of the week; as a result, some companies have set up on the Zambian banks. Zambian authorities are less stringent about environmental impact, so please encourage your operator to avoid wood fires and to carry out all rubbish.

Most companies include transport from Harare or Kariba, but you'll get a discount by arranging your own transport. They may also offer discounts for groups of four or more people. Foreigners must normally pay in foreign currency.

Single travellers can often find places on the spot, but with several people, one to three months advance booking is advised, especially during peak months or school holidays. Most companies operate from April-May to October-November, but some offer trips year-round. Some operators, such

as Buffalo Safaris, offer reduced rates for low-season travel (June, November, the first half of December, the last half of January and from February to April).

Use the following table as a basic rate guide for camping safaris (those using safari camps and lodges charge more):

| Stage | Days/ Nights | Low Season Price | High Season Price |
|---|---|---|---|
| Kariba-Chirundu | 3/2 | US$263 | US$315 |
| Chirundu-Mana Pools | 4/3 | US$378 | US$525 |
| Mana Pools-Kanyemba | 5/4 | US$441 | US$630 |
| Kariba-Mana Pools | 6/5 | US$504 | US$620 |
| Chirundu-Kanyemba | 8/7 | US$630 | US$804 |
| Kariba-Kanyemba | 10/9 | US$714 | US$977 |

Zambian shore trips range from US$765 to US$1095, plus transfer fees.

## Kariba to Chirundu

As both Kariba and Chirundu are accessible by public transport, this stage makes a convenient introduction to the Zambezi. The dark recesses of dramatic Kariba Gorge are quickly left behind and you're issued abruptly onto the open savanna plains, where you'll pass the African villages that dot the Zambian shore. From the mouth of the gorge to Chirundu, you're likely to see elephant and perhaps even lion.

## Chirundu to Mana Pools

The most popular and interesting stage is the three day paddle from Chirundu through Mana Pools National Park. Downstream of Chirundu, you'll notice the transition as village life, especially on the Zambian shore, gives way to wildlife-rich reserves on both banks. Here the broad, flat Zambezi allows canoeists to paddle safely within close range of wildlife. Overnight stops may include Vundu, Nyamepi and Nyamatusi camps.

## Mana Pools to Kanyemba

Mana Pools to Kanyemba is the wildest and most thrilling stage on the Middle Zambezi. Upon leaving Mana Pools, the river slides between Zimbabwe's Chewore Safari Area and Zambia's Lower Zambezi National Park. It then enters a region of low and nondescript hills before picking up velocity and slotting between the high walls of 30km-long Mupata Gorge, a dramatic slice in the Chewore Mountains. With no villages and little wildlife, it's a profoundly silent place.

Beyond Mupata, fishing canoes appear and there's evidence of traditional life along the riverbanks. This is the home of the Va Dema (Two-Toed) people, which is Zimbabwe's only nonagricultural society. (The moniker is derived from a genetic mutation affecting a small percentage of families.) Although many have resettled in communal lands, some independent Va Dema, who have been successful at eluding even tenacious western anthropologists, still enjoy a hunting and gathering lifestyle.

Most safaris include transfers out of Kanyemba, or you can use the bus which connects Kanyemba and Harare.

# Eastern Lake Kariba

## KARIBA

The name of this strung-out town of 13,000 is derived from *kariwa*, the Shona word for trap. It was originally applied to Kariba Gorge, into which the Zambezi waters were sucked as if into a drainpipe. Now that they're trapped by the dam wall, the metaphor continues to apply and may be extrapolated even further, as Kariba has also become a trap for tourists!

It's only natural that ocean-starved upper-class Zimbabweans love Kariba. While foreigners flock to Victoria Falls, Zimbabweans who can afford the luxury of a holiday – mostly whites and professional blacks – spend their leisure time and Zimbabwe dollars fishing, relaxing and puttering around the lake. Most sites of interest are scattered around the lake, where transport and accommodation are extremely expensive, and foreign travellers who can't afford to join the beautiful people at play may not fully appreciate Kariba's appeal.

### Orientation

Kariba town is an unconsolidated two-level jumble without a definable character and as a result, no-one knows exactly where Kariba is. The developed area stretches for over 10km along the lakeshore between the airport and the Zambian border, but there's no central focus and hotels intentionally keep their distance from competitors. The MOTH camp site and Andora boat harbour are separated from the main highway by Mahombekombe township, which has a post office, shops and bus terminal. Kariba Heights, a cooler and more prestigious neighbourhood in the clouds, 600m above the shore, has a bank, shopping centre, country club, bakery, supermarket and post office.

### Information

The Publicity Association (☎ (161) 2814) at Kariba Dam Observation Point may be friendly, but it's not particularly useful. You'll get better information from The Zambezi Safari & Travel Company (☎ (161) 2532; fax 2291; <zambezi@ harare.iafrica.com>; Web site www .zambezi.com) in Kariba Heights. They can also book accommodation and organise safaris and lake activities.

**Money** You can change foreign currency and travellers cheques at the bureau de change beside the supermarket in Kariba Heights.

There's a Barclay's ATM at the petrol station next to Polly's Takeaways.

**Dangers & Annoyances** Kariba is hot. In the summer, anticipate average temperatures of 40 to 42°C accompanied by stifling humidity and frequent rain. In winter – June to August – expect daytime temperatures of around 25°C.

Lake Kariba is home to 25,000 crocodiles, which kill several people every year, so swimming around the lakeshore isn't an

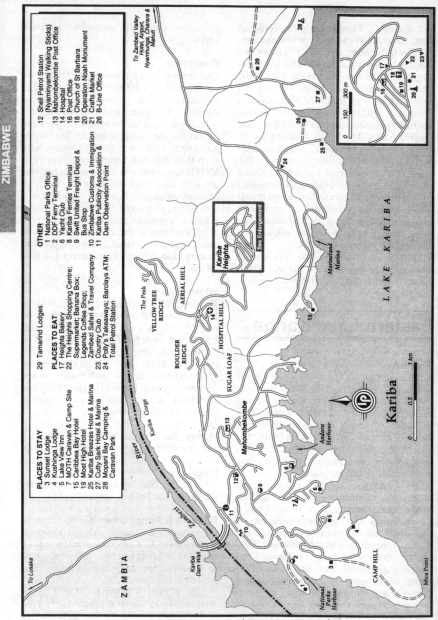

PLACES TO STAY
3 Sunset Lodge
4 Kushinga Lodge
5 Lake View Inn
7 MOTH Caravan & Camp Site
15 Caribbea Bay Hotel
19 Most High Hotel
25 Kariba Breezes Hotel & Marina
27 Cutty Sark Hotel & Marina
28 Mopani Bay Camping & Caravan Park
29 Tamarind Lodges

PLACES TO EAT
17 Heights Bakery
22 The Heights Shopping Centre; Supermarket; Banana Box; Legends Coffee Shop; Zambezi Safari & Travel Company
23 Country Club
24 Polly's Takeaways; Barclays ATM; Total Petrol Station

OTHER
1 National Parks Office
2 DDF Ferry Terminal
6 Yacht Club
8 Kariba Ferries Terminal
9 Swift United Freight Depot & Bus Stop
10 Zimbabwe Customs & Immigration
11 Kariba Publicity Association & Dam Observation Point
12 Shell Petrol Station (Nyaminyami Walking Sticks)
13 Mahombekombe Post Office
14 Hospital
16 Post Office
18 Church of St Barbara
20 Operation Noah Monument
21 Crafts Market
26 B-Line Office

option! Other dangers include elephant, which march into town, especially during dry periods. They drink from swimming pools, trample flower gardens and uproot trees. Both of the Kariba campgrounds are favourite habitats for elephant, which are best avoided. Although most elephant pose little threat when left alone, several people in Kariba have been killed by less tolerant individuals. Buffalo and hippos also pose dangers in urban areas.

### Kariba Dam Wall

On 17 May 1960, with the Queen Mother officiating, the switch was flipped on the first Kariba generator. Until Egypt's Aswan High Dam was completed in 1971, Kariba was Africa's largest hydroelectric project. With the rising lake, which eventually covered 5200 sq km and had a capacity of 186 billion cubic metres of water, Kariba also rose, becoming the holiday and service centre it is today.

The hulking 579m-wide dam wall towers 128m above the Zambezi River between Zimbabwe and Zambia and comprises nearly one million cubic metres of concrete which, at its base, is 24m thick. At maximum capacity, it can handle 9000 cubic metres of water per second. At the foot of the spillway, the drainage has eroded a 60m-deep hole in the riverbed. To visit the dam wall, leave your passport at Zimbabwe immigration and walk down onto the dam, which unsettlingly vibrates to the rhythm of the 700-megawatt generators that power most of Zimbabwe and Zambia.

The best dam view is from the observation point, uphill from the Shell petrol station. The vulnerability of the dam wall is of grave concern to both Zimbabwe and Zambia and border guards of both these countries take the boundary very seriously. Boaters are not permitted past the nets and floating markers at the gorge entrance.

### Church of Santa Barbara

This circular church in Kariba Heights is dedicated to Santa Barbara, the patron saint of engineers, as well as the Virgin Mary and St Joseph, the patron saint of carpenters. Workers from Impresit (the Italian company which built Kariba dam) built it in memory of their 86 colleagues who died during construction from accidents, heat stroke, malaria and so on. A stone plaque lists their names.

The open circular shape of the building represents a coffer dam; the open walls are a concession to the climate. Inside are five Carrara-marble sculptures: St Catherine, St Joseph, the Virgin Mary, St Barbara and St George (the last is a copy of the renowned original by Donatello).

### Operation Noah Monument

The rising lake waters caused problems not only for the Batonka people but also for animals trapped on mid-stream islands threatened with inundation by the rising Kariba waters.

Word of the crisis got around and the resulting public outcry prompted the Rhodesian government to assign Rupert Fothergill and a team of 57 wildlife personnel to effect a rescue project. They worked throughout the dry season – from March to December, 1959 – tracking, trapping and relocating over 5000 creatures of at least 35 species, including reptiles (even black mambas!) and small mammals, as well as lion and rhino. It was all orchestrated to the tune of much pomp and ceremony in the world media. The project, dubbed Operation Noah after a similar operation quite a few years earlier, resulted in artificially dense concentrations of game on the southern shore, particularly in Matusadona National Park.

A monument commemorating the efforts behind Operation Noah has been erected at the lake viewpoint in Kariba Heights.

### Crocodile Farm

Kariba's crocodile park lies 20km from town, on the lakeshore beyond the airport, so it isn't convenient for anyone without a vehicle. It's open from 8 am to noon and 2 to 5 pm daily except Monday and admission is US$1.20.

---

## The Trials of Kariba Dam

The history of Kariba is the history of Kariba Dam. The town of Kariba, with a current population of approximately 13,000, sprang up in 1955 as a work camp to house engineers and labourers from Impresit, the Italian firm which worked on the dam during its trouble-fraught construction.

The Batonka people of the upper Zambezi Valley, threatened with inundation or displacement by the proposed lake, called in desperation upon the fish-headed and serpent-tailed Zambezi River god, Nyaminyami. They asked him to intervene in order to preserve his own environment, and also to do something about the predicament of his faithful neighbours, the Batonka.

Edward Abbey's *Monkey Wrench Gang* would have been proud of Nyaminyami, who either complied with his charges' request or simply went into a raging fit over the whole matter. On Christmas Eve 1955, the river rose dramatically, swept away the workers' pontoon bridge and swamped the foundations of the unfinished coffer dam. The next setback came in the form of scorching temperatures which stifled work on the project and slowed progress to a crawl. In July (the dry season) 1957, a torrential storm on the upper Zambezi sent floodwaters roaring through the work site, damaging the main coffer dam.

The following March, yet another climatic anomaly – a once-in-1000-years flood – unleashed 16,000 cubic metres of water per second, again destroying the coffer dam and also collapsing the highway suspension bridge across the Zambezi. In all, 86 project workers were killed during construction, including 18 who were buried in wet concrete. Several of the bodies were never recovered and are dubiously honoured with what must be the world's largest tombstone.

After weathering the unprecedented climatic setbacks and fatal tragedies, the 10,000-strong Impresit crew completed the main dam wall in December 1958 and the waters began to rise and fill in the valleys and branches of the middle Zambezi. In 1959, stranded animals were rescued in the public-inspired Operation Noah (see under Operation Noah Monument in this chapter), and the 50,000 displaced – and justifiably disgruntled – Batonka people were resettled on higher ground. The river god, apparently having spoken his piece, cooled

---

### Organised Tours

Town tours (US$11) with UTC (☎ (161) 2453), PO Box 93, Kariba, depart at 10.30 am from the Cutty Sark Hotel, with pickups at Caribbea Bay Hotel and Lake View Inn. Morning or evening game drives in the Charara Safari Area cost US$21. You can also take a flight over the lake; these 'flight-seeing' trips cost US$60 for 15 minutes, US$86 for 30 minutes and US$172 for a full hour.

Cruise Kariba (☎ (161) 2697), PO Box 1, Kariba, runs two daily booze cruises (US$13 each): the Siesta Cruise which departs from the Cutty Sark jetty at 2 pm (returning in time for the airport transfer) and the Sunset Cruise, at 4.30 pm.

Rick Taylor at the Kariba Breezes Hotel marina runs inexpensive lake cruises. Backpackers rates start at US$85 per day for up to six people, including fuel, plus US$5 per person for lunch. Overnight trips cost US$99 per 24 hours, plus US$9 per person for lunch and dinner. Book at the MOTH campground.

Due to popular request by budget travellers, Buffalo Safaris (☎ (161) 2645; fax 2827) now offers all day canoe paddles on Lake Kariba for US$21, including transport, a picnic lunch and a qualified canoe guide.

For US$70, River Horse Safaris (☎ (161) 2447; fax 2944) offers day paddles through the Zambezi Gorge. Lunch is provided and

his wrath – at least for the time being.

No sooner had the lake begun to fill, however, than a pesky and destructive weed, the appropriately named *Salvinia molesta* or Kariba weed, began creeping across its surface. By 1962, it covered 20% of the lake and was spreading rapidly, transported by the wind. It became so thick that it created an underwater shadow which prevented sunlight from nourishing the plankton and aquatic plants which sustain fish and other lake dwellers. To combat it, the deadly chemical paraquat was sprayed across the lake. Several biological solutions were also considered, and in 1970, amphibious South American grasshoppers were imported to devour the green scourge.

The little nibblers succeeded, but a new problem surfaced. Salvinia mats cut loose by grasshoppers were dying and washing up around the lake shoreline, and ecologists were concerned about possible negative effects on wildlife. In the end, however, it decomposed nicely into a mulch that stimulated the prolific growth of *Panicum repens* or torpedo grass, which in turn provided shoreline grazing for large mammals whenever fodder was scarce further inland. Although the creation of such a large artificial lake severely altered the Zambezi ecosystem, it seems that a new ecology has arisen and has apparently stabilised satisfactorily.

In the early 1990s, however, tragedy again threatened. This time it came in the form of a drought which caused water levels to drop to crisis lows. There wasn't enough water passing through the dam's turbines to generate sufficient power for both Zimbabwe and Zambia. As a result, Zimbabwe suffered frequent power cuts and was forced to purchase electricity from South Africa to make up the slack.

Meanwhile, the still-agitated Batonka people maintain that Nyaminyami isn't yet through with the nuisance dam – and that he won't be satisfied until Kariba's monumental obstruction has been flushed away. Although the rains thankfully returned to southern Africa in 1993, the lake level remains low. Furthermore, there are now tenuous plans for a second large dam in Batoka Gorge (or alternatively, Devil's Gorge) farther upstream, to supply the country's growing electricity needs (see the Western Zimbabwe chapter). Given Nyaminyami's penchant for havoc, however, officials may be playing with fire.

---

you can extend the trip and camp on the riverbank.

For Crocodile Farm tours (US$17) or early morning and afternoon game drives in Kuburi Wilderness (US$20), contact Pesha Safaris (☎/fax (161) 2247). Trips depart from the Cutty Sark Hotel. Kasambabezi (☎ (161) 2224) runs two-hour game drives in Kuburi Wilderness and Charara Safari Area for US$18 and one-day paddles on the lake for US$51.

### Activities
**Water Sports** Crocodiles and bilharzia present such a threat to water activities that there is now a ban on swimming at Caribbea Bay beach. UTC (☎ (161) 2662)

hires powerboats for US$39/52 for a half/full day, excluding petrol, fishing tackle and bait. Parasailing and waterskiing (away from the shore) cost US$20/10 respectively. Phone Tobin Langbrenner (☎ (161) 2475 or 2771).

**Fishing** The Kariba Bream Farm, 2km off the main road on the Chawara turnoff in the Kuburi Wilderness Area, charges US$1 admission and US$1.50 per kilogram of fish you keep. Braai stands, fishing equipment and snacks are available on the site. It's open daily 9.30 am to 6 pm.

**Boat Hire & Charter** The best agents for organising Kariba yacht and houseboat hire

is The Zambezi Safari & Travel Company
(☎ (161) 2532; fax 2291; <zambezi@
harare.iafrica.com>), PO Box 158, Kariba,
or Rhino Rendezvous (☎ (14) 735912; fax
795344), 56 Samora Machel Ave, PO Box
A131, Avondale, Harare.

**Yachts** Yachts for up to four adults may be
hired from *Kariba Yachts* (☎ (161) 2983;
fax 2575) at the Cutty Sark Marina, PO Box
80, Kariba. Four- or six-day hire costs
US$250 per person. It also runs 14-day sails
to Binga and 21-day trips to Devil's Gorge
for US$250 and US$300 per person, respectively. The main office is at 6 Fairfield
Rd, Hatfield, Harare.

*Sail Safaris* (☎ (14) 339123; fax
339045), 4 Cheshire Rd, Mt Pleasant,
Harare, hires sailboats for four- or seven-
day lake cruises. In low season (March to
May), seven-day hire for four/six people,
including meals, drinks, fuel, bedding,
crew, sailing instruction (if necessary) and
insurance starts at US$1189/1504.

**Houseboats** Simpson's Cruises (☎ (161)
2308), owned by Rowena and Barry
Simpson, runs lake cruises aboard the
*Queen II* for US$145 per night for up to
eight people, including pilot, fuel and
wildlife viewing. Meals are US$15 per
person per day or you can self-cater.

The pontoon houseboat *What a Pleasure*
costs US$385 per day for up to 10 people,
including meals and pilot. Contact Pleasure
Cruises (☎ (167) 22785; fax 23095) at the
Orange Grove Motel in Chinhoyi, or write
to PO Box 16, Kariba.

*MV Manica* Touring Services (☎ (14)
736091), PO Box 429, Harare, runs cruises
in a floating hotel. In high/low season, they
charge US$775/625 per day, with pilot,
meals, booze and all fishing gear. It takes up
to 10 people and cruises as far as Masana,
near Devil's Gorge.

Kariba Houseboats (☎/fax (161) 2922;
<houseboa@samara.co.zw>) hires out the
22m 16-passenger pontoon houseboats
*Peregrine* and *Shikra* for US$800 per day,
plus US$40 per person for meals. It also has

larger boats. The *Zambezi Rebel*, which is
booked through The Zambezi Safari &
Travel Company (see earlier in this
section), accommodates 12 passengers and
hires for US$285 per day, without meals.
The 22m pontoon houseboat *Navistar* accommodates 12 people and costs US$350
per day plus US$20 per person per day for
meals. Book with the Anchorage Marina
(☎ (161) 2245; fax 2246).

**Motor Cruisers** The 15m motor cruisers
*Charisma* and *Viking* accommodate four
and six people, respectively, but the latter is
air conditioned and has a lounge. The
former costs US$292 per day, plus meals,
and the latter option is US$512 per day plus
meals. Contact Kariba Boating & Safaris
(☎/fax (161) 2227). The same company
rents out the 30m, 14-passenger luxury
cruiser *Concorde,* which offers five-star accommodation – including air conditioning,
a bar, lounge, jacuzzi and five crew
members – for just US$2600 per day.

### Places to Stay – Budget

The cheapest accommodation at Kariba is
mainly camping. The popular *MOTH
Caravan & Camp Site* (☎ (161) 2809), PO
Box 67, Kariba, lies 20 minutes walk from
Mahombekombe township. It charges
US$1.75 per person for camping and US$3
in pre-erected tents. Furnished six-person
self-catering chalets cost US$25 and double
rooms are US$8.50. Bookings are essential
on weekends and school holidays.

On site you can buy braai packs and firewood, and there's laundry service and a
small library. Thanks to guards and other
measures, security is now fairly good.
Advise them if you're arriving after 6.30
pm and watch out for wildlife:

At night, elephants came through the fence to eat
the trees, we heard a lion roaring just 50m away
and hippos bellowed through the night from the
lakeshore. There are elephant everywhere, and
buffalo, so don't walk around in the evening –
and watch your step.

**Andy Bollen, Australia**

Also thrilling but less secure is *Mopani Bay Camping & Caravan Park* (☎ (161) 2555), on the shore 2km from the Cutty Sark Hotel. Camp sites cost US$0.75, plus the following per person: power and braais, US$3; without power, US$2.50; undeveloped, US$2. Tents are available for US$2 to US$3. Note that nocturnal visits by elephant are common and grounds maintenance is handled by hippos, who keep the grass closely chopped.

Whatever your budget, a superb choice in Kariba is the friendly, secluded and beautifully-situated *Kushinga Lodge* (☎ (161) 2645; fax 2827), on Camp Hill, which overlooks a pristine shoreline. Green four-person tent/caravan sites cost US$4/7; charming thatched double A-frames for backpackers cost US$12; double self-catering rondavels on the lakeshore are US$27; family chalets are US$37; and self-catering lodges for six/12 people are US$53/100.

## Places to Stay – Mid-Range

The two-star *Kariba Breezes* (☎ (161) 2433; fax 2459) is one of Kariba's nicest mid-range hotels at US$46/86 for singles/doubles with breakfast. Everyone pays the same rate, so standards are better than the price would imply.

The quiet *Cutty Sark Hotel* (☎ (161) 2221; fax 2575) affords a good view of the lake and distant hills – and a breath of fresh air, as foreigners and Zimbabweans pay the same rates. Standard singles/doubles cost US$53/82, deluxe rooms are US$67/107 and budget rooms are US$33, all with breakfast.

Near the Cutty Sark is *Tamarind Lodges* (☎ (161) 2697), a self-catering complex with open-air stone and thatch construction. At US$35/50, the single/double lodges represent good value for groups. Anglers may use the fish freezer at reception and guests can use the Cutty Sark swimming pool and tennis court.

In a quiet location high above the lakeshore is spacious *Sunset Lodge* (☎ (161) 2645; fax 2827), a beautiful self-catering unit with four bedrooms. Meals or a private chef are available on request. For foreigners, the entire building costs US$126 for up to 10 people, plus US$12 for each extra person. Breakfast/lunch/dinner is US$11/16/21. The affiliated *Kushinga Lodge* (see Places to Stay – Budget) also offers lovely self-catering units for US$27 to US$100.

The *Most High Hotel* (☎/fax (161) 2965), run by Lester and Peggy Seiler, does sit at the highest altitude in town (and also has the best view), but the name of this Christian hotel at Kariba Heights actually has more religious connotations. Note that alcohol is forbidden, smoking is permitted only in the garden and unmarried couples of the opposite sex may not share the same room. Singles/doubles with breakfast cost US$32/60 (breakfast for non-guests is US$3.50). On the terrace they serve homemade cakes and ice cream, and huge table d'hôte dinners cost just US$7.

The *Zambezi Valley Hotel* (☎/fax (161) 2926), in Nyamhunga township near the airport, is the place to go for high-volume African-style entertainment and boozing. Happily, its reputation is improving, and it's now a viable choice. Singles/doubles cost US$25/35.

In Charara, 25km out of town toward Makuti, is the self-catering *Mauya Lodge* (☎ (14) 725213; fax 725224; <afadvent@ id.co.zw>), run by African Adventures. This four-bedroom thatched lodge costs US$79.

## Places to Stay – Top End

The upmarket *Caribbea Bay* (☎ (161) 2453; fax 2765) can get nearly as noisy as the Zambezi Valley Hotel but here the boozing is Rhodey-style. This sparkling monument to pseudo-Mexican stucco architecture could have inspired the Eagles' *Hotel California*. With its beach, palm trees, tennis courts and casino, it aims to fulfil holiday fantasies by transporting patrons away from Africa to an imaginary tropical paradise Somewhere Else. For standard single/ double rooms with breakfast, foreigners pay US$115/144.

Caribbea Bay's main attraction is the casino. Monte Carlo or Las Vegas it's not, but you can still immerse yourself in roulette and blackjack or relax while feeding hungry one-armed bandits. Smart casual dress is strictly enforced.

The *Lake View Inn* (☎ (161) 2411; fax 2413) offers average accommodation and, as its name would imply, a glorious view of the lake. Single/double rates for foreigners are US$80/100 with breakfast. Zimbabwe residents pay US$44/55.

### Places to Stay – Zambian Shore

If you've had enough of the Zimbabwean Riviera and want to get back to Africa – or if you're transiting to Zambia – you can also stay on the Zambian lakeshore. Unfortunately, the border post and visa requirements make short visits awkward and expensive.

*Eagle's Rest* (☎ (260-1) 511168), 4km off the main road in Siavonga East, is recommended. It has double chalets for US$20 per person, but bring your own food and cooking gear (if you're travelling light, the owner may loan you a saucepan or two). Camping costs US$6.50. On the same stretch of coast, the smart *Manchinchi Bay Hotel* (☎ (260-1) 511599) offers well appointed self-contained singles/doubles for US$53/88.

*Leisure Bay Lodge* (☎ (260-1) 511136), on the shore in town, has basic self-contained chalets for US$28/38. The *Lake View Council Resthouse* (☎ (260-1) 511279) has clean, basic rooms for US$22 (up to four people) and meals for US$4. The Kariba North Bank bus to Lusaka (US$2.50, four hours) departs from here daily at 5 am.

West of town, the *Zambezi Lodge* (☎ (260-1) 511148) has simple bungalows with superb views for US$40/60 and *Lake Kariba Inn* (☎ (260-1) 511358) charges US$57/90 for large rooms with full board, plus use of the sauna and gym.

### Places to Eat

A great place for cheap eats is the *Country Club* in the Heights where a hearty spread

costs about US$3. People have been ignoring the 'members only' sign for years, but non-members may be asked to pay a 10% surcharge. It's closed Mondays.

*Polly's Takeaways*, at the Kariba Breezes turn-off emphasises takeaways – burgers, pasties, chips, chicken and ice cream – but you're welcome to eat on the shady lakeview terrace out the side. It's closed on Mondays.

In the lower town, the cheapest snacks, groceries and basic meals are available in Mahombekombe, where there's a Spar Market and an inexpensive bakery and butchery. The beer hall sometimes features live music, and you don't have to be close to hear it. In the Heights is the *Supermarket*, as well as the *Banana Box* greengrocer, and the excellent *Heights Bakery*.

Hotel dining room prices are pretty much proportional to their room rates. The *Cutty Sark* does a good buffet breakfast for US$3.50. The *Lake View Inn*, a quick uphill jaunt from the MOTH camp site, has great views. The *Caribbea Bay Hotel* dining room offers a very nice dinner buffet for US$10; bookings are essential. If you need a big home-cooked meal, try the *Most High Hotel* in Kariba Heights. Big buffet breakfasts cost US$3.50 and its set menu dinners (US$7) are typically enormous US-country-style.

### Things to Buy

At the Shell petrol station near the dam wall, you'll find the famous (and fabulous) Nyaminyami walking sticks carved by master carver, Rainos Tawanameso. In fact, both the Queen Mother and Pope John Paul II own examples of these original creations. Beautiful locally crocheted tablecloths and bedcovers are sold for very good prices in the Heights and at the dam observation point.

### Getting There & Away

**Air** Air Zimbabwe (☎ (161) 2913) has daily 45-minute flights between Kariba, Harare (US$35) and Victoria Falls (US$45). Note that Air Zimbabwe seems to have rules of its own in Kariba, and flights have been known to leave early.

**Bus** Several daily buses link Kariba's Mahombekombe terminal with Mbare (Harare). The most convenient is MB Luxury Coaches, with 12 buses daily. Once or twice weekly, African buses run from Mahombekombe to Binga via the Siabuwa road, with an occasional branch service south to Gokwe.

The Express Motorways (☎ (161) 2662) Kariba service (US$11, 5½ hours) leaves Harare at 1 pm Friday and calls in at the Cutty Sark, Caribbea Bay and Lake View hotels in Kariba. It leaves the same hotels for Harare around 2 pm Sunday.

**Hitching** The Harare-Kariba road is fairly well travelled. Coming from Harare, weekend visitors make hitching easiest late on Friday or early on Saturday. It follows, then, that the optimum time to return is Sunday afternoon or evening.

**Ferry** Two ferry services link Lake Kariba's eastern and western ends; Kariba Ferries connects Kariba with Mlibizi and DDF runs between Kariba and Binga. Although Kariba Ferries doesn't stop at Bumi or Binga, you can arrange for transfers between the ferry and shore with B-Line Lake Passenger Services (☎ (161) 2473).

When sailing on the lake, watch for boats fishing for *kapenta* (*Limnothrissa miodom*), a salty small fry which was introduced to Kariba in 1967 by the Zambian government and is now a local staple. Kapenta are caught in purse-seine nets, dip nets and lift nets suspended beneath a light, which attracts the fish. They're also used by sport anglers to attract tiger fish and other larger fish.

**Kariba Ferries** The popular Kariba Ferries boats lack cabins but they have comfortable seats which recline into beds and fares include meals. The *Sea Lion*, which carries 16 cars, sails at 9 am Monday and Thursday from Kariba and at 9 am on Tuesday and

Friday from Mlibizi. The *Seahorse* carries eight cars and sails at 9 am on Tuesday and Friday from Kariba and at 9 am on Wednesday and Saturday from Mlibizi. At busy times, there may be additional, unscheduled sailings.

Foot passengers are advised to pre-book, but with a vehicle, you need to reserve between two and 12 months in advance. The disparity between fares for foreigners and Zimbabweans is probably the most shocking in southern Africa: with an ordinary car/4WD vehicle, locals pay US$36/59 and non-residents, US$165/270. Fares for Zimbabwean/foreign foot passengers are US$50/245. If you can handle this sort of gouging, book through Kariba Ferries Ltd (☎ (161) 4162; fax 4161; <ferries@mail .pci.co.zw>), PO Box 578, Harare.

Without a vehicle, reaching the Mlibizi ferry terminal entails catching a Binga bus from Dete Crossroads on the Victoria Falls road; one or two buses run daily (see Dete in the Western Zimbabwe chapter). Get off at the Binga turn-off and make the hot, dry 15km slog to Mlibizi (bring plenty of water!). If your visit is synchronous with the ferry departure, you may get a lift, but hitching is normally more successful in the opposite direction.

**DDF Ferries** The basic DDF ferry (☎ (161) 2694) connects Kariba's National Parks Harbour with Binga and Gache Gache. The ferry *Chaminuka* departs Kariba fortnightly on Thursday at 11 am and arrives in Binga at 5 pm on Saturday. From Binga, it sails at 10 am Monday and chugs into Kariba at 2 pm Wednesday. There are stops in Chalala, Sabilobilo, Mackenzie, Sengwe, Chibuyu, Sinamwenda and Chete (which has a small game park).

No food is available on board, though there is a cooker to boil water for sadza. Passengers either sleep on deck and cope with swarms of mosquitoes or stay on shore. Overnights are in Chalala (where you can stay at *Brooke-Mee Chalets*, in a lakeside oasis, for US$20 with breakfast) and Sinamwenda, a navigation-control post and crocodile-breeding centre with camping and private local accommodation. The basic *hunting and fishing lodge* at Sengwe may be booked through Sunshine Tours (☎ (19) 67791; fax 74832) in Bulawayo. (For information on the budding resort town of Binga, see the Western Zimbabwe chapter.)

On Monday, the *Nyaminyami* runs to Chalala via Kings Camp, Tashinga (Matusadona National Park), Musamba, Musango and Bumi Hills, arriving in Chalala at 5 pm the same day. On Wednesday at 10 am, the ferry *Mbuya Nehanda* leaves Kariba for Gache Gache, returning the same afternoon.

DDF has recently installed a two-tier pricing system to match that of Kariba Ferries. From Kariba, fares for Zimbabweans/foreigners are as follows: Binga (US$7/16), Mlibizi (US$7.50/17), Kings Camp (US$1.50/4), Spurwing (US$1/4), Tiger Bay (US$1.50/7), Sengwe (US$4/8), Tashinga (US$2/5) and Chalala (US$3/7).

### Getting Around

**The Airport** UTC (☎ (161) 2305) does transfers between the airport and the Lake View, Caribbea Bay and Cutty Sark hotels for US$3.

**Bus & Taxi** Less convenient is the bus which connects the Swift United Freight Depot with Nyamhunga suburb, near the airport, via a circuitous route through Mahombekombe and Kariba Heights. It appears every 30 to 60 minutes.

Taxi services (☎ (161) 2454) operate from the Caribbea Bay Hotel.

**Bicycle** Mountain bikes may be hired for US$1 per hour from the Mopani Bay and MOTH campgrounds, or at any of the hotels except Zambezi Valley. You must leave your passport as a deposit.

**Hitching** Walking around sprawling, up-and-down Kariba is a hot, tiring and time-consuming pursuit, and hitching is the standard means of getting around. You'll rarely wait more than a few minutes for a lift from one part of town to another.

## KUBURI WILDERNESS AREA

Carved from part of the Charara and Hurungwe safari areas, the Kuburi Wilderness Area is leased from the Ministry of Natural Resources & Tourism by the Zimbabwe Wildlife Society. Bounded on the south by Lake Kariba, the west by Kariba Gorge and the north by a series of minor gorges, this rugged landscape of peaks and watersheds takes in 37,700 hectares and harbours a variety of wildlife, including 67 bird species.

As a condition of the lease, the reserve is divided into usage areas, which are variously intended for educational tours, game drives, wild camping, game hides, hiking, game walks, picnics, administration and organised camping.

### Information

The new Kuburi Information Centre (☎ (161) 2705) on the Makuti road dispenses tourist information and sells books and local crafts. Kuburi entry permits cost US$1 per person plus US$1 per vehicle. It's open every day from 7 am to 1 pm and 2 to 5 pm.

### Places to Stay

Sites at the Kuburi headquarters *campground* cost US$1.50 per person. You can also stay in the *Kuburi Platform* game hide, which costs US$5 for groups of up to 12 people. A small, thatched six-person *rondavel and camp site* at the Muto River picnic site, in the east of the area, costs US$5.50 for up to 12 people.

The National Parks *Nyanyana Camp* (☎ (161) 2337), 25km from Kariba and 5km off the Makuti road at the mouth of the Nyanyana river, has camp sites with braai pits and ablutions. Foreigners pay US$5 and locals US$2.50. Pre-booking is recommended for weekends and holidays.

The *Mushuma Bush Camp* (☎ (161) 2705) has twin-bedded safari tents under thatch with en suite facilities and a communal kitchen. In high season (16 June to 15 January) self-catering rates are US$63 per tent.

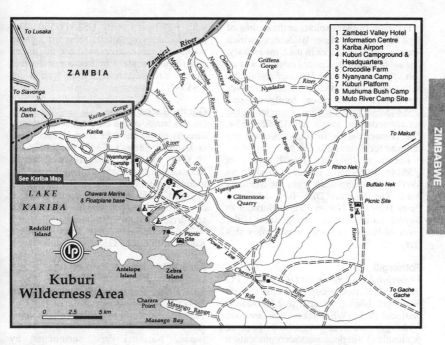

| | |
|---|---|
| 1 | Zambezi Valley Hotel |
| 2 | Information Centre |
| 3 | Kariba Airport |
| 4 | Kuburi Campground & Headquarters |
| 5 | Crocodile Farm |
| 6 | Nyanyana Camp |
| 7 | Kuburi Platform |
| 8 | Mushuma Bush Camp |
| 9 | Muto River Camp Site |

## Getting There & Away

Kuburi lies on the main Kariba-Makuti road. All camps are accessible in private vehicles.

## LAKE KARIBA RESORTS

The shores of Lake Kariba, especially around Matusadona National Park, support a growing number of resorts. The larger ones cater only to those with bigger budgets, and try to maintain a sense of isolated luxury where guests can experience solitude without sacrificing comfort. The only concession to budget travellers is Nyakasanga Lodge, a beautifully situated houseboat moored in the waters of Matusadona National Park.

Kariba Breezes Marina (☎ (161) 2475) runs water transfers to lake lodges; rates average US$50 per person for up to eight people, plus fuel. Flights to lodges can be organised through Float Plane Services

(☎ (14) 724705; fax 724659), 3rd Floor, Goldbridge, Southside, Eastgate, Harare or (☎ (161) 2432) in Kariba.

## Bumi Hills, Water Wilderness & Katete Lodges

*Bumi Hills Safari Lodge* (☎ (161) 2453; fax 2354), PO Box 41, Kariba, of the Zimbabwe Sun hotels group, is a beautiful three-star wilderness resort west of Matusadona National Park. It caters mainly to an upmarket crowd looking for low-key adventure: organised fishing, wildlife viewing, water sports, bushwalking and other activities.

Bumi Hills charges US$384/614 per night for single/double accommodation, with meals and wildlife viewing. Book through Zimbabwe Sun central reservations (☎ (14) 736644; fax 736646), Travel Centre, Jason Moyo Ave, PO Box 8221, Harare.

For even further exploits in the realms of high finance, visit *Water Wilderness*, which features floating lodges in the Ume estuary. The more luxurious *Katete Lodge* evokes an *Out of Africa* or *White Mischief* ambience, with huge rooms, candlelit meals and silver service. At either place, foreigners pay US$445/690 for all-inclusive single/double accommodation; locals pay US$234/354. The contact details for these two are the same as for Bumi Hills Lodge.

Return air transfers from Kariba cost US$146. Bumi Hills is also accessible by 4WD via a rough track from the Siabuwa road. The Monday DDF ferry connects Bumi Hills with National Parks Harbour in Kariba but anyone who wants Bumi Hills' level of luxury probably won't enjoy this ferry.

### Fothergill

*Fothergill Island Resort* (☎ (161) 2253), PO Box 2081, Kariba, occupies a bushy area on Fothergill Island, adjacent to Matusadona National Park. (When lake levels are low, Fothergill and Spurwing islands become peninsulas.) Single/double accommodation

with full board costs US$317/530. The price includes organised fishing trips, game walks and game drives, and use of canoes and fishing tackle. Children are welcome. Return air/boat transfers from Kariba are US$141/121.

### Gache Gache Lodge

On the banks of the Gache Gache estuary, directly across the lake from Kariba town, is Landela Safari's *Gache Gache Lodge* (☎ (161) 2905; fax 2902). It's well east of Matusadona National Park, but there's still a fair bit of wildlife. The single/double rate of US$425/550 includes accommodation in open-fronted chalets, meals, game walks and drives, and use of canoes.

The Wednesday DDF ferry connects Kariba with Gache Gache.

### Lake Wilderness & Nyakasanga Lodges

*Lake Wilderness Lodge* (☎ (161) 2645; fax 2827), Lake Wilderness Safaris, PO Box 113, Kariba, comprises a large houseboat and two floating lodges moored in Matusadona National Park, surrounded by

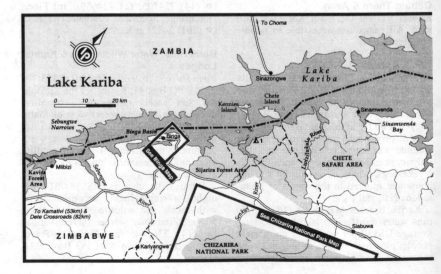

Kariba's archetypal drowned tree landscape. It's run by game guide Hans van der Heiden and his wife, Valerie. For the single/double rates of US$205/336 (high season) or US$164/274 (low season), you get three hefty meals plus two excursions daily: canoe trips, pontoon trips or guided game walks in Matusadona National Park.

The affiliated *Nyakasanga Lodge*, a houseboat moored alongside Lake Wilderness Lodge, is a wonderful concession to budget travellers. If you're feeling Kariba was made only for the wealthy, here's your chance to enjoy the scenic serenity without the expense. For US$45 per person you get accommodation, full board and use of canoes, but you can self-cater for a discounted rate; it's especially nice to sleep under the stars on the roof. If you can muster at least six people, you can weigh anchor and cruise around the lake aboard Nyakasanga. Fishing tackle is available, but bring your own hooks and bait. Transfers from Kariba, game walks and pontoon trips cost extra. Bookings are essential.

For either lodge, transfers from Kariba cost US$79 per person.

## Kipling's of Kariba

*Kipling's of Kariba*, on an island at the mouth of the Ume River, offers brick and thatch chalets with views of the lake and mountains. (From a distance, it resembles a Burmese temple on the road to Mandalay.) For bookings, contact Shearwater (☎ (161) 2433; fax 2459; <shearwat@harare.iafrica .com>).

Activities include canoeing, fishing, boat and pontoon trips, game walks and drives, and scenic flights. For foreigners, all inclusive single/double packages cost US$340/480 in the high season and US$260/360 in the low season. Transfers from Kariba cost US$100.

## Matusadona Water Lodge

*Matusadona Water Lodge*, run by Brian and Lindi Worsley, is a series of floating chalets anchored offshore just east of the Tashinga Peninsula. For singles/doubles, including meals, they charge US$360/520. Return air transfers from Kariba cost US$110 per person. Book through Wilderness Safaris (☎ (161) 4527; fax 4224; <wildness@ zol.co.zw>), PO Box 288, Victoria Falls.

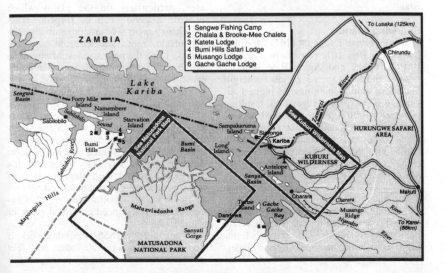

## Musango

*Musango Lodge* (☎ (14) 735929; fax 795301; <livsa@mail.pci.co.zw>), PO Box UA 306, Harare or (☎ (161) 2899) in Kariba sits on an island/peninsula between the Ume River mouth and Bumi Hills. The single/double rate of US$310/500 in high season and US$270/440 in low season includes accommodation in the Maronga or Musango tented camps, meals, game walks with professional guides, and canoe safaris. Because Musango lies outside Matusadona National Park, they're permitted to run night game drives. Return transfers by plane/boat cost US$100/50.

## Sanyati

*Sanyati Lodge* (☎/fax (14) 703000), PO Box 4047, Harare or PO Box 2008, Kariba, which accommodates 16 guests, is an exclusive venue. The area isn't known for wildlife, but Sanyati is acclaimed for its fabulous food, and enjoys a superb hillside setting at the mouth of Sanyati Gorge. All-inclusive accommodation in thatch and stone chalets costs US$270 per person; transfers are extra. A notable treat is the 'moonlight' supper, served on a small lake island.

## Spurwing Island

*Spurwing Island Lodge* (☎ (161) 2466; fax 2301), PO Box 101, Kariba, overlooking Buffalo Creek and Agate Bay, is a bit smaller and less expensive than Fothergill but offers similar amenities. Its biggest advantage is its sparser vegetation, resulting in better wildlife viewing. Tented accommodation, with meals and activities, costs US$170 per person. Boat transfers from Kariba are US$70. The resort also organises three-day backpacking trips into the Matuzviadonha Range.

## Tiger Bay

The name of *Tiger Bay Safari Resort* (☎ (161) 2569), PO Box 102, Kariba, refers not to stray Asian cats but to Kariba's fighting tiger fish. Its thatched A-frame chalets sit beside the Ume River just outside Matu-sadona National Park and offer a pleasantly inexpensive choice. As the name suggests, the emphasis is on tiger fishing and equipment is available to guests. All-inclusive single/double rates start at US$122/230; at the affiliated *Chura River Safari Camp*, they're US$94 per person. Return air transfers for either camp are US$77. Book through Tiger Bay (☎/fax (14) 791034), PO Box W41, Waterfalls, Harare.

## MATUSADONA NATIONAL PARK

If you're intrigued by those photos of fish eagles sitting in dead trees before a mountain backdrop, Matusadona National Park is where you'll find the real thing. The trees, of course, are drowning victims, having been inundated by rising Kariba waters in the late 1950s. The mountain backdrop is the Zambezi Escarpment, which cleverly masquerades here as the Matuzviadonha Range.

The 1407 sq km park lies between the Sanyati River, which runs through a gash-like gorge, and the broad, islet-studded Ume River. Much of the wildlife displaced by Lake Kariba eventually settled in this area, particularly on the plains which provide a good crop of torpedo grass (*Panicum repens*) for grazing animals such as buffalo, zebra and assorted antelope. Thanks to all the prey species, Matusadona also boasts Zimbabwe's densest lion population – at least 300 at last count.

For Zimbabweans, the most popular recreational activity is fishing, and in October the Kariba International Tiger Fishing Tournament is held in the lake's eastern basin. The predatory tiger fish (*Hydrocynus vittatus*), which can weigh up to 15kg, is a worthy adversary for anglers. It's also quite beautiful, with silvery black sides and a yellow, orange and black tail.

The walking opportunities are also excellent, but you'll need an armed guide or game scout.

Foreigners pay US$5/10 per day/week. If you're staying in a private lodge, park fees are normally included in the package.

Can you resist the urge to buy souvenirs? (Zim)

Decorative baskets (Zim)

Mural fresco with motifs (Zim)

Fine wickerwork brooms (Zim)

Carved wooden mask (Zim)

Shona carving, Nyanga (Zim)

Printing traditional designs with potato cuts, Mutare (Zim)

MITCH REARDON

Taking time out in the sun, Lake Kariba (Zim).

DAVID WALL

Malindidzimu – the dwelling place of benevolent spirits, Matobo NP (Zim).

## Organised Tours

From Tashinga, guided walks with armed game scouts cost US$67 per day for up to six people. Book through the National Parks office in Harare (☎ (14) 706077). Most safari lodges (see Lake Kariba Resorts earlier in this chapter) also organise walking trips and game drives in the park. For longer trips, Graeme Lemon Safaris (☎ (161) 2538) runs four-day wilderness backpacking and camping trips. They aren't cheap at US$160 per day, all inclusive, but they're one of the best ways to see Matusadona.

## Places to Stay

National Parks runs two campgrounds near the shore: *Sanyati West Camp*, near the Sanyati River mouth, and *Tashinga Camp*, at park headquarters. The latter has the airstrip and the larger campground, as well as pre-erected sleeping shelters. Both hire

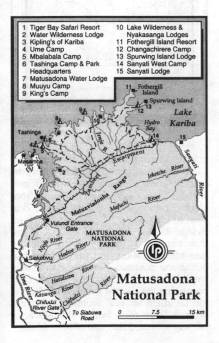

| | |
|---|---|
| 1 Tiger Bay Safari Resort | 10 Lake Wilderness & |
| 2 Water Wilderness Lodge | Nyakasanga Lodges |
| 3 Kipling's of Kariba | 11 Fothergill Island Resort |
| 4 Ume Camp | 12 Changachirere Camp |
| 5 Mbalabala Camp | 13 Spurwing Island Lodge |
| 6 Tashinga Camp & Park | 14 Sanyati West Camp |
| Headquarters | 15 Sanyati Lodge |
| 7 Matusadona Water Lodge | |
| 8 Muuyu Camp | |
| 9 King's Camp | |

Matusadona
National Park

camping equipment and have showers, baths, toilets and laundry sinks. The smaller *Changachirere Camp*, on the shore near Spurwing Island, accommodates groups of up to 10 people.

Three exclusive chalet camps accommodate up to 12 people. *Ume* and *Mbalabala* are both on the estuary of the Ume River, and *Muuyu* lies near Elephant Point, not far from Tashinga. Each consists of two two-bedroom chalets with three beds in each room, a bathroom, toilet, kitchen, dining room, and storeroom. Cooking implements and linen are provided. However, they're available only for six-day periods.

On Siabuwa Rd, overlooking the confluence of the Chiroti and Sanyati rivers, is the basic *Sanyati Bridge Camp*. As part of the CAMPFIRE programme, it's great for experiencing traditional Zimbabwean life. Camping costs US$2 and the three self-catering double rondavels are US$8. Shona-style meals are available on request. Book through the Wildlife Society of Mashonaland (☎ (14) 747500), Mukuvisi Woodlands, Harare.

See also Lake Kariba Resorts earlier in this chapter.

## Getting There & Away

However you look at it, access to Matusadona is tricky. For most of the year, you need 4WD for the road into Tashinga, as well as for wildlife viewing on park roads. The Matusadona access road turns off the Siabuwa road 150km west of Karoi, from where it's 10km to the Chifudze River gate into the park. For foreigners, park entry per day/week costs US$10/20.

The daily early morning Bumi Hills/Peter Store buses between Mbare (Harare) and Binga (via Karoi) only skirt the southern park boundary, 82km south of Tashinga, but they do pass within 1km of Sanyati Bridge Camp.

The crowded DDF ferry *Nyaminyami* stops at Chalala via Tashinga every Monday but, as you may not hike in the park without a guide, there isn't much to do until the ferry returns or you can catch a lift out.

# Eastern Highlands

Few first-time travellers to Zimbabwe expect anything like Manicaland – better known as the Eastern Highlands – and it's true that this narrow strip of mountain country isn't the Africa that normally crops up in armchair fantasies. Homesick colonists have been reminded of Ireland, Scotland and the English Lake District but, whatever your vision, these uplands make a pleasantly cool retreat from the summer heat of the lowlands and, in the brisk, dry winters, they provide Zimbabwe's finest hiking opportunities.

Public transport in Manicaland exists mainly to connect the region with Harare and provide access to communal lands in the western part of the province. Areas of tourist interest aren't well-served, so it's much more convenient to have a private vehicle.

## MARONDERA

Although it's not actually in Manicaland, Marondera (population 22,000) gives travellers their first whiff of high-country pine amid the eucalyptus. Just 72km east of Harare, it's the highest town in Zimbabwe and its temperate climate is ideal for sheep, maize, garden vegetables and orchards.

### Wineries

Marondera's climate may not be optimum for viticulture, but it's the nearest Zimbabwe has and several wineries are now turning out palatable products. The Mukuyu division of Monis wineries produces the most renowned vintages, and has an outlet in town where you can taste its offerings. The main winery (☎ (179) 24501) lies a half-hour drive along the Ruzawe road and offers tours and tastings, but it's difficult to reach without a vehicle. Tours, including tasting, cost less than US$1 per person.

### Markwe Cave Paintings

The Markwe paintings portray a host of

## HIGHLIGHTS

- Hike and camp in Chimanimani National Park
- Climb Mt Nyangani in Nyanga National Park
- Stroll through the Vumba Botanical Gardens
- Soak in the hot springs at Nyanyadzi
- See the patchwork patterned Honde Valley from lovely Mtarazi Falls

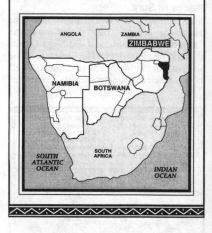

human figures involved in various unidentified tasks interspersed with a menagerie of animal forms. However, access is difficult without your own vehicle. Coming from Harare, turn right on Watershed Rd, 2km west of Marondera. After 3km, turn left on Bridge Rd and follow it for about 35km, then turn left at the sign-posted Markwe turn-off. After 4km, turn right at the farmhouse and continue 1km to the base of a small hill, above which you'll find the cave containing the painted panel. If Markwe is too far afield for you, another panel decorates a large rock behind the Macheke railway station, 35km east of Marondera.

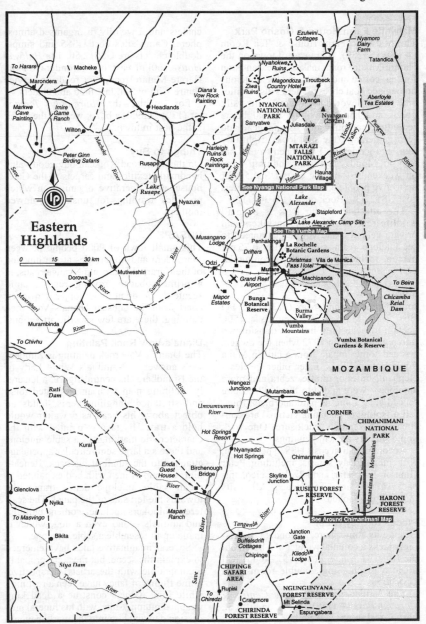

## Malwatte Farm House & Gosho Park

The Malwatte Farm House & Tea Room (☎ (179) 23239), 10km east of town on the Harare-Mutare road, makes a pleasant stop for tea, coffee and meals; try the delicious homemade goat cheese. There's also a tailor and shops devoted to sweets, gifts, silk goods and hand-weavings, herbal home remedies, camping and fishing gear and 'eco-gardening' (the sign looks frightfully like 'ego-gardening'). It's open from 8 am to 5 pm Monday to Friday, and until 9 pm on weekends. Camping costs US$4.50 for up to five people and single/double chalets cost US$22/30. Book on ☎ (14) 344112.

The attached Gosho Park is a small wildlife reserve accessible to hikers and private vehicles, and you're guaranteed to see antelope. Admission is just US$0.75 per person, including overnight accommodation in small huts.

## Imire

Imire Game Ranch (☎/fax (122) 354), PO Box 3750, Marondera, began as a 4500 hectare tobacco farm but was transformed into a game park in 1972 when the owners rescued some impala from a cull in Mana Pools National Park. Later, other species – elephant, buffalo, giraffe, zebra and more antelope – were added to the 2000 hectare fenced area. Lion, leopard and black rhino (all offspring of poaching victims) are confined to a separate enclosure. One rock kopje shelters ancient paintings.

Accommodation costs US$85 per person, with meals. Day safaris, including Peter Ginn birding safaris and 2½ hour elephant-back safaris, are US$67 each. All visits must be pre-booked.

## Places to Stay & Eat

Despite its atmosphere, Marondera surprisingly lacks a colonial wonder of a hotel, but the *Hotel Marondera* (☎ (179) 24005) will do at a pinch. Single/double rooms cost US$30/50.

The Indian-run *20/19 Play Centre & Caravan Park* (☎ (179) 23564), on Fifth St, has a restaurant, takeaway, tea garden, chalets and a weirdly disorganised atmosphere. Camp sites cost US$5 and simple double chalets are US$12.50. The *Halfway House*, 60km east of Marondera on the Harare-Mutare road, is a roadside service centre with petrol, fast food and chalets.

For meals, the *Burgundy Terrace* (☎ (179) 24895), a block west of the hotel, is the best in town.

## Things to Buy

On the main road, you can buy good-value handmade textiles and carpets at the Gate-house, a co-operative organisation which provides training for unskilled, unwed mothers.

## RUSAPE

This small town of 9000 people between Marondera and Mutare lies at the junction of the Harare, Mutare and Nyanga roads, in a prime tobacco-growing region, amid scenic *dwala* domes and kopjes. However, apart from the unusual Diana's Vow rock painting, there are few specific attractions.

## Diana's Vow Rock Painting

The Diana's Vow rock painting is Zimbabwe's answer to Namibia's White Lady of the Brandberg. Its central figure, a leisurely reclining man with an elongated torso and stretched dangling penis, holds an object above his head as a waiter would hold a tray. His face is painted with the characteristic markings of a sable antelope and there's a large semi-circular appendage attached to the small of his back. Beneath him, a group of men with bodies painted to recall sable antelope dance trance-like towards the left side of the panel. The scattered onlookers include women, children and animals – and even a dog, which is made up to resemble a sable antelope.

Several imaginative tales have emerged to explain the scene, but most are probably incompatible with the artists' perspective. Some flights of fancy have seen a reclining white king. Others construe a dead king wrapped mummy-like, with his funeral procession dancing him into the world beyond.

The most widely accepted interpretation suggests that the players are honouring the sable antelope and have entered a trance-like state to generate potency in the central figure, which is represented by the object on his back.

The best way to reach Diana's Vow is in a private vehicle. The paintings are sheltered beneath a rock overhang about 200m from the gate of Diana's Vow Farm. From Rusape, turn east off the Harare road onto route A14. After 29km, turn left on Constance Rd and continue 13km to Silver Bow Rd, where you should turn left. After 200m, turn left again through a gate; this track leads about 1km to a small clearing where you can leave your vehicle. The painting is 100m away on foot.

From Harare, ERB Tours (☎/fax (14) 721023) runs day trips to Diana's Vow for US$65 (see the Zimbabwe Getting Around chapter).

### Places to Stay

The lively colonial-style *Hotel Balfour* (☎ (125) 2945) serves as the rest stop for Harare-Mutare express buses. Singles/ doubles cost US$33/50. The more modern one-star *Crocodile Motel* (☎ (125) 2404), west of town, charges US$34/41. At *Rusape Dam Caravan Park*, 10km south of town, camp sites cost US$5.

### Places to Eat

Your best meal option is *Joe's Place* (☎ (125) 3583), on the main road, which does snacks, light meals and meat-oriented main courses. On a sunny day, the garden is especially inviting.

### ODZI

Odzi is mainly a tobacco-growing, wine-producing and tungsten-mining village 35km west of Mutare.

### Places to Stay

At *Mapor Estates* (☎ (130) 03013), a working tobacco farm 16km south of the village, you can observe the harvesting, drying or curing processes in the appropri-

ate season. Guests can try bouldering and rock climbing, or explore the hills, caves and rock paintings on foot or horseback. There's a basic shop, swimming pool, petrol pump and kitchen (but no cooked meals). Day visits cost US$1 and overnight camping is US$2.50. Farmhouse accommodation must be pre-booked.

Coming from Harare, turn south at the bridge immediately before the Odzi River, 32km west of Mutare. Follow this road for 6km to Odzi post office and turn left at the sign marked Maranke-Mapembe. After 10.5km, turn left at the Mapor Estate signpost. Continue 2.5km along this road to another signposted left turn and then follow the signs to the farmhouse.

Alternatively, phone and arrange to be picked up (for a minimal charge) from the Odzi River bridge (on the Harare-Mutare bus route) or get off at the bridge, walk 6km to Odzi post office and phone from there.

## MUTARE

Mutare, Zimbabwe's fourth-largest city, is beautifully situated in a bowl-like valley surrounded by mountains. It has an odd cold-country feel and, indeed, some of the surrounding hills are cloaked in pine woods and the main route into town is called Christmas Pass. However, Mutare's palm-lined main street should quickly sort out any high-latitude delusions.

### History

The first Umtali, as Mutare was known until Zimbabwean independence in 1980, was a white gold-mining settlement near present-day Penhalonga. When Fort Umtali was built further down Penhalonga Valley in 1891 (thanks to an 1890 border dispute between the British and Portuguese), the name was commandeered and the new Umtali grew around the fort. In 1896, the town was shifted again, this time over the mountain to its present location 16km south of the old fort, to accommodate the railway line to Beira.

Early local authorities were known as the sanitary boards, as their primary function

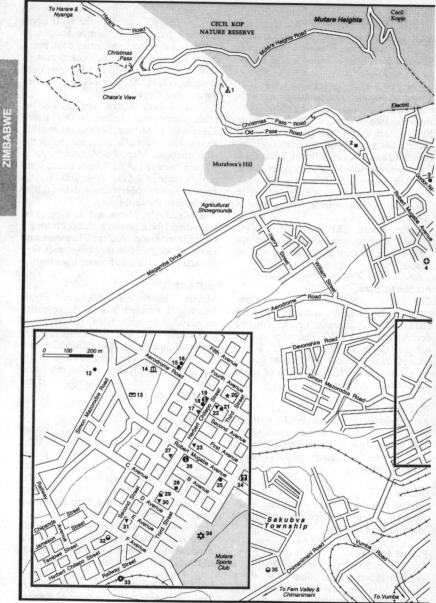

ZIMBABWE

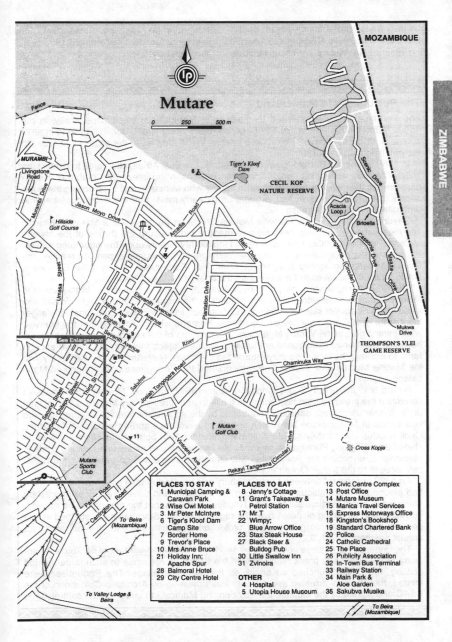

**Mutare**

0    250    500 m

MOZAMBIQUE

MURAMBI

Fence

Livingstone Road

Murambi Drive

Jason Moyo Drive

Hillside Golf Course

Umasa Street

Tiger's Kloof Dam

CECIL KOP NATURE RESERVE

Acacia Loop

Broella

Scenic Drive

Rekayi Tangwena (Circular) Drive

Cassonia Drive

Maasa Drive

Mukwa Drive

THOMPSON'S VLEI GAME RESERVE

Arcadia Road

Bain Drive

Plantation Drive

Eleventh Avenue

Ninth Ave
Tenth Avenue
Eighth Ave
Seventh Avenue

See Enlargement

River

Sakubva

Josiah Tongogara Road

Chaminuka Way

Mutare Golf Club

Cross Kopje

Second Street
Harben Street
Chitepo Street
Third St

Mutare Sports Club

Vincent Ave

Rekayi Tangwena (Circular) Drive

Park — Road

Carrington Road

To Beira (Mozambique)

To Valley Lodge & Beira

To Beira (Mozambique)

**PLACES TO STAY**
1  Municipal Camping & Caravan Park
2  Wise Owl Motel
3  Mr Peter McIntyre
6  Tiger's Kloof Dam Camp Site
7  Border Home
9  Trevor's Place
10  Mrs Anne Bruce
21  Holiday Inn; Apache Spur
28  Balmoral Hotel
29  City Centre Hotel

**PLACES TO EAT**
8  Jenny's Cottage
11  Grant's Takeaway & Petrol Station
17  Mr T
22  Wimpy; Blue Arrow Office
23  Stax Steak House
27  Black Steer & Bulldog Pub
30  Little Swallow Inn
31  Zvinoira

**OTHER**
4  Hospital
5  Utopia House Museum

12  Civic Centre Complex
13  Post Office
14  Mutare Museum
15  Manica Travel Services
16  Express Motorways Office
18  Kingston's Bookshop
19  Standard Chartered Bank
20  Police
24  Catholic Cathedral
25  The Place
26  Publicity Association
32  In-Town Bus Terminal
33  Railway Station
34  Main Park & Aloe Garden
35  Sakubva Musika

was the provision of a honey wagon to cart off the town's sewage. The sanitary board's first meeting in Mutare's present location was held on 29 September, 1897, thus justifying the town's prolonged 1997 centenary celebrations.

## The Portuguese in Manicaland

The Portuguese first established themselves in Manicaland, albeit superficially, in the 1560s. Although King Sebastiano entertained grand designs of a dominion taking in all of southern Africa, the primary Portuguese interest in the area lay in the access it afforded to the goldfields further north.

In 1569, Francisco Barreto, governor of Portuguese East Africa, attempted to contact the Mwene Mutapa to negotiate gold-mining concessions in the interior. An outbreak of sickness among the men was blamed on Arab traders who were accused of poisoning the water supply (the problem was, in fact, brought on by early rains) and the two groups became embroiled in a bloody skirmish.

Several years earlier, the Manyika Mutasa Chikanga (*mutasa* was a Manyika dynastic title established in the 16th century) had made a bid to usurp the throne of the Mwene Mutapa, but the incumbent naturally hadn't looked favourably upon the attempted mutiny. By the time the decimated and somewhat bedraggled Portuguese expedition reached the Mwene Mutapa, he agreed to open the territory to Portuguese mining if the Europeans would assist in the revenge he was scheming against Mutasa Chikanga.

The showdown, which took place near Nyanga, ended in stalemate. In the end, the Mwene Mutapa's goldfields proved less productive than rumoured and Barreto himself was killed in a subsequent skirmish north of the Zambezi. However, the Europeans' indefatigable lust for gold lured a successor, Fernandes Homem, who discovered that the Manyika were mining gold in the Vumba Mountains. Observation of the arduous mining techniques, however, dampened Portuguese enthusiasm for the project; they weren't a great enough force to enslave the locals, so they returned to the coast. Nevertheless, a 1629 treaty with the Mwene Mutapa and Mutasa Chikanga granted the Portuguese a feeble grip on Manicaland.

By the time the British South Africa Company (BSAC) arrived, Mutasa Chifambausiku controlled the province from his capital on a hilltop near present-day Mutare. The highland areas further south were effectively controlled by the aggressive bandit Gungunyana, who was based in Mozambique but whose sphere of havoc had spread considerably further. Cecil Rhodes immediately sought diplomatic relations with both chiefs. His objectives included annulling any Portuguese claims to the region, as well as securing mining rights in Manicaland, encircling the Boer states with British influence and guaranteeing the BSAC safe access to the Indian Ocean at Beira.

An 1890 agreement between Lord Salisbury and the Portuguese government, however, had placed the Mozambique border along the Masheke and Save rivers, leaving eastern Manicaland within Portuguese territory. Rhodes' demands that the agreement be rescinded resulted in mounting disputes over the region. Leander Starr Jameson stepped in and coerced the Mutasa into guaranteeing protection of British interests in Manicaland for annual payments of £100.

The unhappy Portuguese countered by sending a slave-trader, Manoel de Souza, to encourage the Mutasa to break relations with the British. In response to such underhanded dealing, the British launched an attack on the Mutasa's village. The Portuguese were ousted, their leaders arrested and a treaty was drawn up by Archibald Colquhoun of the BSAC and signed by the Mutasa, thereby bringing Manicaland under British control.

**Orientation & Information**

Mutare lies at or near the intersection of several roads, so travellers to the Eastern Highlands will probably pass through at least once.

**Tourist Office** Zimbabwe's most helpful tourist office, the Manicaland Publicity Association (☎ (120) 64711), sits on Market Square, near the corner of Herbert Chitepo St and Robert Mugabe Ave. In addition to dispensing information, it produces the entertaining monthly, *Mountain Digest* which, they like to point out, has a readership as far away as Tunisia (and now Alaska, I might add!). It's open Monday to Friday from 8.30 am to 12.45 pm and 2 to 4 pm.

**Money** The Bhadella Bureau de Change at 18/20 Chipanda St changes cash and travellers cheques.

**Travel Agencies** Manica Travel Services (☎ (120) 64112), on the corner of First St and Aerodrome Rd, is the local American Express representative. ChiVuNya (☎/fax (120) 65165; <chivunya@harare.iafrica .com>), in Bhadella Arcade on Herbert Chitepo St near First Ave, books Eastern Highlands and south-eastern Zimbabwe safaris and accommodation.

**Internet Resources** You can pick up and send email messages from Walter's House, 63-67 Fourth St.

**Bookshops** You'll find pulpy reading material at the Time Bookshop on Herbert Chitepo between Second and Robert Mugabe Aves. Kingston's is just a block away, between Second Ave and Aerodrome Road, and there's a book exchange just up the stairs at MB Home Videos, near Kingston's.

**Mutare Museum**

The Mutare Museum has a well-mounted agglomeration of exhibits covering geology, history, anthropology, technology, zoology and the arts. The Manicaland wildlife habitat dioramas are populated by pitiable creatures who made the ultimate sacrifice to bring you this production, but the assembly of lethargic snakes has been granted amnesty for the time being.

The collection of 16th to 19th century armaments includes stone-, iron- and agricultural-age exhibits and the transportation museum features what must be the world's most unusual flightless aeroplane. Out the back is an active beehive, with a cross section cut for easy viewing, and a walk-in aviary.

The museum is on Aerodrome Rd within walking distance of the centre, and is open daily from 9 am to 5 pm. Foreigners pay US$2 admission.

**Main Park & Aloe Garden**

Mutare's main park and aloe garden, at the south end of D and E Aves, are great for sunny afternoons reading or picnicking on the lawns. In the aloe garden, which blooms in midwinter, you'll find approximately 250 species native to southern Africa and Madagascar, including prehistoric cycad palms.

**Cathedral**

Mutare's Catholic cathedral, built in 1971, is worth a look for its lovely stained glass and inspired architecture.

**Utopia House Museum**

Utopia House, just off Jason Moyo Drive, was the home of Rhys and Rosalie Fairbridge and their son, Kingsley (1885-1924), a colonial poet and founder of Fairbridge Farm Schools for homeless and neglected children.

The home was built in 1897 but, to enhance the colonial homestead ambience, it has been restored and refurnished in the style of the 1920s. The statue of Kingsley Fairbridge, which once overlooked Christmas Pass, has been moved to the garden at Utopia House. It's open from 2.30 to 4 pm on Friday and Saturday and 2.30 to 4.30 pm on Sunday. Foreigners pay US$2 admission.

## Cross Kopje

A short track leads from Circular Drive, at the eastern end of Mutare, to the top of the small hill, Cross Kopje, which overlooks the Mozambique border. The cross on the summit is a memorial to black Zimbabweans and Mozambicans who died in the WWI campaigns in East Africa. Follow Robert Mugabe Ave east past the park to Park Rd, then take a left and carry on one block to Vintcent Ave where you should turn right. This turns into Circular Drive, which passes near the foot of Cross Kopje.

## Mutare Heights

Mutare Heights offers a view of the entire bowl. The quickest route up follows the steep footpath from the suburb of Murambi. For a longer, more level hike with decent views, hitch to Christmas Pass and walk the 6km along the ridge on Mutare Heights Road to the top.

## Murahwa's Hill

There are great walks in the maze of tracks in the national trust nature reserve on Murahwa's Hill rock kopje. You can see rock paintings and the well-crumbled ruins of an iron-age village, but the real attractions are the views and access to nature so near Mutare. Look also for the *mujejeje*, a slice of exfoliated granite rock which produces a chime-like sound when struck with a wooden mallet. Monkeys and leopards both make their home here, but the latter tend to be quite retiring.

Access is from Magamba Drive near the Agricultural Showgrounds. The route from Old Pass Rd above the Wise Owl Motel is overgrown and difficult.

## Cecil Kop Nature Reserve

The 1700 hectare Cecil Kop Nature Reserve wraps around the northern end of Mutare and abuts the Mozambique border. In 1977, the Wildlife Society of Zimbabwe leased the land from the city council and, since then, improvements and management have been supported by public donations and volunteer interest. Foreigners pay US$2 admission to all three sectors of the reserve. Avoid the fence along the eastern perimeter – this is the Mozambique border and land mines still riddle the area.

**Tiger's Kloof Dam** Without a vehicle, you're limited to Tiger's Kloof Dam, 3.5km from the centre, which is fed by springs high in the forested hills which are home to 200 of Zimbabwe's 500 butterfly species. Tiger's Kloof also has other wildlife, but it's a bit like a zoo, especially from 4 to 4.30 pm when the giraffe, elephant, zebra, buffalo and antelope congregate to be fed. Admission is US$2.

Take Herbert Chitepo St north from the centre. The car park lies 1km after it turns into Arcadia Rd. Snacks and soft drinks are sold at the kiosk and tea garden daily from 9.30 am to dusk.

**Thompson's Vlei** With a vehicle, you can explore the Thompson's Vlei sector and observe zebra, monkeys, nyala, wildebeest, buffalo, warthog and the usual antelope range – impala, kudu, waterbuck, duiker and so on. Near the entrance gate is a pan with a wildlife-viewing platform where you can watch the world pass by. For a great view over the city, the Vumba Mountains and Mozambique, drive up the winding road to the peak at the reserve's north-eastern corner. Foreigners pay US$2 per person admission plus US$0.75 per vehicle.

**Wilderness Sector** The wilderness sector, which takes in the western half of the reserve, is characterised by steep mountainous terrain. Some hiking trails have been constructed but they're not very well maintained and may be difficult to follow.

## Organised Tours

The cheapest day tours to Vumba, Burma and Essex Valleys, Penhalonga, La Rochelle, Nyanga or Honde Valley are with Pickup Tours (☎ (120) 63061), run by Cornelius with his open bed pickup (ute). The transport isn't all that comfortable, but it's cheap and lots of fun. A day tour of the

Vumba, including Burma and Essex valleys, costs US$16/11/8 per person with two/four/eight people. Nyanga day tours, including a peek into Honde Valley, are US$31/21/15. Book directly or through Mutare backpackers lodges.

Similarly novel transport – emergency taxis – is used by loosely organised Vimbiso Tours (☎ (120) 64711; fax 64298), 2nd floor, Suite 31, Compensation Building, PO Box 521, Mutare. It offers visits to the Vumba, Penhalonga, Nyanga and Honde Valley, with emphasis on traditional Manicaland culture. You'll learn how people lead their daily lives: farming, herding, preparing meals, brewing local beer, building homes, etc.

If pickup trucks and ETs aren't your style, UTC (☎ (120) 64784) runs Vumba day tours (US$26); a run around Burma and Essex Valleys (US$24); half-day trips to Odzi, including the winery and Mapor Estates (US$19); day trips to Nyanga (US$59); and a circuit to Nyanyadzi Hot Springs and Birchenough Bridge (US$46). All tours (except Odzi) include a light lunch.

Three times weekly, Mherepere Tours runs unintrusive and culturally sensitive half-day visits to Eastern Highlands communal lands for US$21. Book through ChiVuNya (☎/fax (120) 65165) in the Bhadella Arcade.

## Places to Stay

This section includes places in and around Mutare. Vumba accommodation is described under Vumba, later in this chapter.

## Places to Stay – Budget

The *Municipal Camping & Caravan Park* is near Christmas Pass 6km from town (US$2.50 by taxi), but lies just metres from the noisy Harare highway. Coming from Harare by bus, get off at the Christmas Pass summit – drivers won't stop on the downhill slope – and walk 2km downhill to the campground. Sites cost US$1.60 per person. The more convenient *Tiger's Kloof Dam camp site*, 3.5km from the centre,

charges US$2.50. For extra seclusion and solitude, try the *camp site* at Lake Alexander, over the mountains toward Nyanga, where camping is US$1 per person.

Mutare also has a clutch of backpackers hostels. A recommended choice is *Mrs Anne Bruce* (☎ (120) 63569) at 99 Fourth St. Beds cost US$4, doubles are US$8 and meals, including vegetarian, are available for reasonable rates. However, it's not for anyone who's allergic to cats (the feline population is reportedly down to two, but that's still too many for some people).

*Mr Peter McIntyre* (☎ (120) 63968) runs a highly recommended place at 5 Livingstone Rd in Murambi. He charges US$3.50 per person for rooms, US$2 for dorm beds and US$7 for a caravan that sleeps four people. Every morning, he offers free lifts to the centre; at other times, transfers to the centre or Sakubva cost US$0.80. To the Mozambique border post costs US$2.

The centrally located *Trevor's Place* (☎ (120) 67762) at 119 Fourth St, corner of Eighth Ave, has cooking, laundry, braai facilities and bicycle hire. Dorm beds cost US$4, singles/doubles are US$5/10 and camping is US$2.50. Reviews are mixed, but it's an option if other places are full.

The clean *Border Home* (☎ (120) 63346), 3A Jason Moyo Drive, charges US$3.20 for a dorm bed and US$4.50 per person in family rooms. Private doubles and cottages range from US$6.50 to US$16.50 and camping is US$2 per person. Meals, laundry service and bicycle hire are available. Booked guests can be picked up from anywhere in Mutare.

The cheapest hotel is the *Balmoral* (☎ (120) 61435), on C Ave, which charges US$9 per person, with breakfast. The *City Centre* (☎ (120) 62441), on Herbert Chitepo St and C Ave, charges US$16/18 for singles/doubles. It's decidedly downmarket but you'll meet the local drinking crowd.

If you don't have to stay in town, head for the friendly *Drifters* (☎ (120) 62964) backpackers lodge, 21km west of town on the Harare road. Dorm beds cost US$5; single/double rondavels are US$11; two- or four-bed rooms cost from US$5 to US$7 per person; and camping is US$2/4 per person in tents/caravans. Transfers are free to and from town or the Nyanga turn-off. There's a pool for guests and a large bar and restaurant upstairs serves drinks and meals (US$2). On Friday they hold a pizza bake in the outdoor oven, and on Sunday there is a Mongolian barbecue. Braai packs cost US$2.

There's plenty to do at Drifters, including game walks on the surrounding reserve, and game drives on a larger ranch nearby. You can also climb to the ruins, rock paintings and ancient gold smelting works on Chikanga mountain, over the road; guides are available for this four hour walk.

In Fern Valley, 13km south of Mutare, the *Hillside Enigma Backpackers Lodge* (☎ (120) 218910) has dorm beds for US$3, mattresses for US$2 and camping for US$1.75 per site plus US$0.50 per person. Turn east on Fern Valley Rd, 8km south of Mutare and continue for 4.5km, then turn left on Orpen Rd. The guest house is on the left. You can also get there on the Fern Valley commuter minibus from Sakubva *musika* (US$0.50).

## Places to Stay – Mid-Range

In a quiet setting on the far side of Christmas Pass, 10km from town, is the colonial-style *Christmas Pass Hotel* (☎ (120) 63818; fax 63875), which has a garden and a swimming pool in a quiet setting. Singles/doubles cost US$41/57 with half board.

The *Wise Owl Motel* (☎ (120) 64643; fax 64690) is about 3km from the centre on Christmas Pass Rd. Singles/doubles with breakfast cost US$47/65. It's clean and acceptable, and there's no multi-tier pricing, but check your bill and insist on a fair exchange rate.

On the Beira road, 6km from Mutare, is the pleasantly situated *Valley Lodge* (☎ (120) 62868). Accommodation is in individual lodges, all with lounges and private facilities. Single/double lodges cost US$46/61 with breakfast; suites are

US$55/73. They don't accept children under 12.

## Places to Stay – Top End

The only top-end accommodation in town is the three-star *Holiday Inn* (☎ (120) 64431; fax 64466), one of those cast-in-a-mould expense-account hotels, on Aerodrome Rd near Third St. Foreigners pay US$99/118 for singles/doubles and residents pay US$64/86.

West of Drifters, 26km from Mutare on the Harare road, German-run *Musangano Lodge* (☎ (120) 42267; fax 42263; <musangano@odzi.icon.co.zw>; Web site www .icon.co.zw/musangano) offers basic double chalets for US$40 per person, including breakfast, and five/seven-bed self-catering lodges for US$70/80 for two people, plus US$15 for each additional person. You can either cook for yourself or opt for table d'hôte meals. There is a pool and local activities include hiking, fishing, mountain biking, horse-riding and visiting ancient rock paintings.

## Places to Eat

For US$3.50 at the *Holiday Inn* you'll get a continental breakfast buffet of fruit, breads, pastries, cereals and cheeses. For US$4.50, they do a full English breakfast, with all of the above, plus sausage, bacon, kidneys, eggs and fried potatoes. They also serve lunch and dinner. The attached *Apache Spur Steak Ranch* (☎ (120) 64431) is another of the ubiquitous South African chain, which serves family-oriented meals and recommended salads.

*Jenny's Cottage* (☎ (120) 60747), a craft shop at 130 Herbert Chitepo St, does light lunches, salads and afternoon teas. The *Portuguese Club* serves pub meals in the evening and lunches on weekends; it now has tablecloths and glasses. Vegetarians will love *Grant's Takeaway* at Grant's Petrol Station, which does vegetarian stir-fries, veggie burgers, spinach and feta pies and vegetarian pizza.

*Mr T*, on Herbert Chitepo St at Second Ave, is fine for takeaways, ice cream, greasy burgers, chicken and chips and other snacks, but it's only open until 8 pm. There's also the ubiquitous *Wimpy* on Herbert Chitepo St.

The nicest mid-range place is the friendly *Stax Steak House* in the Norwich Union Centre arcade. Try the potato-based veggie burgers, salads, eggs and toast, cappuccino and Belgian waffles piled with cream and berries. Another steak place is *The Carvery* (☎ (120) 63615), in the Courtauld Theatre (near the civic centre complex), which is open daily until late. A new steak house, the *Black Steer* in Meikles Department Store does a range of beef dishes, plus three vegetarian options.

At the *Wise Owl Motel*, continental meals start at US$4 and the Sunday braai costs US$5. The *Fantails Restaurant* (☎ (120) 62868) at Valley Lodge, 6km out on the Beira road, offers rather elegant dining, including superb vegetarian options, for around US$10. Advance bookings are required.

For sadza ne nyama and other African fare, try the *Little Swallow Inn*. Alternatively, there's *Zvinoira* on E Ave near Herbert Chitepo St. The Sakubva musika market sells a range of produce.

### Entertainment

It's evening, you're not tired and everything seems to be closed – not a rare situation in Mutare. In such circumstances, why not check out *The Place*, a sane boozing joint and a mildly entertaining night spot, with live music at weekends. Two other popular places are the *Portuguese Club* (off Simon Mazorozde Road) and the *Motoring Club* (at the Mutare Sports Club). The former has served as the watering hole of choice for the European players in all recent conflicts in Zimbabwe and Mozambique. For something more local and lively, the *City Centre Hotel* sees riotous drinking nightly, with live music in the beer garden on weekend afternoons.

Mutare's cinemas show mostly rubbishy North American films and the Courtauld Theatre puts on amateur theatre produc-

tions. All are near the civic centre complex on Robert Mugabe Ave.

The Olympic-sized pool, also near the Civic Centre, is open daily except Monday from late August to mid-May.

### Getting There & Away

**Air** There is no scheduled air service to or from Mutare. Charter and commuter flights use the military airport over the hill at Grand Reef.

**Bus** The in-town bus terminal is between Herbert Chitepo and Tembwe Sts, near F Ave. Get off here unless you're heading for Sakubva musika, several kilometres from town. There are plenty of local buses and taxis (US$1.50) from Sakubva to the centre. Most buses leave Sakubva between 6 and 7 am, so it's wise to prearrange a morning taxi. Note that buses heading south from Sakubva (eg to Chimanimani) are often swamped and most of them don't stop at the in-town terminal.

For the seven hour trip to Harare, buses leave hourly from the in-town terminal. On Friday and Sunday, Blue Arrow has express services to and from Harare (US$10; 4¼ hours); the terminal is at the Holiday Inn. Express Motorways (☎ (120) 62501) runs once or twice daily between Harare and the Holiday Inn (US$8).

From Sakubva musika and the in-town terminal, ZUPCO, Zvinoira and Masara buses leave nine times daily for Juliasdale and Nyanga (US$1; two hours) between 6 am and 1 pm.

There is also at least one daily bus from Sakubva to Birchenough Bridge, Honde Valley, Cashel Valley, Chipinge and Masvingo and periodic services to Chiredzi, Triangle and Beitbridge. Tenda runs a daily video bus to Bulawayo (US$8), via Masvingo, but you need to be at Sakubva by 5 am to get a seat.

Fortunately, services to Chimanimani are more reliable than in the past. Daily ZUPCO and Msabaeka buses run from Sakubva (they don't call at the in-town terminal) to Chimanimani at around 7 am and

**ZIMBABWE**

10.30 am; return services leave Chimanimani three times daily. A scenic alternative is to take the Chipinge bus, get off at the intersection 7km north of Chipinge, and hitch to Skyline Junction and Chimanimani Village. Alternatively, take any bus to Birchenough Bridge, get off at Wengezi Junction, 67km south of Mutare, and hitch to Skyline Junction and Chimanimani. Allow a long day for either option.

**Train** The easiest way to travel between Harare and Mutare is by overnight train. The service departs from Harare nightly at 9.30, arriving in Mutare at 6 am. From Mutare, it leaves at 9 pm and arrives at 6 am in Harare. The 1st class fare is US$5, 2nd class is US$3.50 and economy is US$2.30. The reservations and ticket offices at the station are open from 8 am to 12.30 pm and 2 to 4 pm weekdays.

### Getting Around

There are taxi stands at Sakubva musika, the in-town bus terminal, the Holiday Inn and the Manicaland Publicity Association. Phone for a taxi on (☎ (120) 63344 or 63166). Urban buses run between Sakubva musika and the centre.

You can hire vehicles from Hertz Rent-a-Car (☎ (120) 64784) at the Holiday Inn.

### AROUND MUTARE
### La Rochelle Botanic Gardens

Over the mountain in Imbeza Valley north of Mutare is La Rochelle, the former estate of Sir Stephen and Lady Virginia Courtauld. It was bequeathed to the nation upon Lady Courtauld's death in 1972. After several years of deterioration in the late 1980s, La Rochelle became less a botanical garden than a trampled and weed-ridden back-to-nature experience. Since then it has been cleaned up considerably and the gardens now contain plants and trees imported from around the world. The guided Braille trail at La Rochelle is a unique attraction and a far sight better than its only other African counterpart, which is found at Kirstenbosch in Cape Town.

The gardens are open daily from 8 am to 5 pm, and snacks, light lunches (US$2.50) and teas are served in the tearoom from 9.30 am to 4.30 pm. You can also hire bicycles. Admission for foreigners is US$1. For accommodation information see Places to Stay under Penhalonga.

**Getting There & Away** From the petrol station over Christmas Pass, turn north on the Penhalonga road. After 6km, turn right and continue 3km to the entrance. Otherwise, take any Penhalonga bus from the in-town bus terminal, get off at the intersection 6km up the Penhalonga road and walk the last 3km.

### Penhalonga

The mines at the secluded village of Penhalonga (from the Portuguese for long rocky cliff) were first worked by the Manyika people in the 16th century. In the late 19th century, AR Colquhoun arrived with a contingent from the Pioneer Column, built a fort – ostensibly against Portuguese aggression from the east – and founded the first Umtali.

The mines were reactivated by gold-crazed colonial prospectors and settlers in the 1920s. By the 1960s, the ore had begun to play out but, in 1968, the discovery of a new lode revitalised the operations.

Apart from mining, forestry also contributes to the economy. The first pines were planted by John Meikle in 1905 and by the 1930s local tree plantations were booming.

Little remains of Penhalonga's colourful history but it's set in a picturesque bowl of hills and, as with so many mining towns, it's full of character. It's worth seeing the 1906 Anglican Church of St Michael and All Angels, constructed of corrugated iron. Lake Alexander/Odzani Dam, 20km north of Penhalonga, provides a watery playground for Mutare residents.

**Places to Stay** *La Rochelle Botanic Gardens* (☎/fax (120) 22250), in Imbeza Valley, has seven en suite rooms in the main house for US$25 per person, singles/doubles with half board for US$38/59 and garden cottages for US$11 per person. Camping costs US$4.50 for up to six people. Penhalonga village also has a pleasant little *caravan park*, and there's an *Eastern Angling Society camp site* (☎ (120) 60775) at Smallbridge Dam, just off the Odzani-Smallbridge Rd. The latter offers fine fishing and costs US$1 per person plus US$1 per vehicle.

**Getting There & Away** Buses to Penhalonga depart several times daily from Mutare's in-town bus terminal.

## VUMBA MOUNTAINS

The Vumba Mountains, 28km south-east of Mutare, are characterised by cool, forested highlands alternating with deep, almost jungled valleys. In Manyika, Vumba (or Bvumba as it's often spelt) means mist, and it's a valid name. English travellers who are prone to homesickness should probably stay away – when the mist settles over the forests, meadows, apple orchards and country gardens, it'll be too late!

### Altar Site Ruins

A few kilometres south-east of Mutare just north of the Vumba road is a small archaeological site amid a thick stand of msasa trees. In 1905, archaeologist EM Andrews uncovered 134 human and animal effigies in soapstone near the hilltop platform now presumed to have been an altar, hence the ruin's name.

The information plaque at the site indicates that the structure probably served a ritual purpose similar to the Shona *chikuva*, small platforms placed behind huts for offerings to ancestral spirits. Another theory suggests that the altar was actually a high throne.

Indications are that this was a large settlement and the remains of many hut platforms have been uncovered in the surrounding district. An 80m length of paving runs through the site from two monoliths on the south-east corner and smaller strips of pavement connect other prominent structures. Although you can't determine much from what's left at the site, excavators speculate that it may have served as a provincial capital of the Great Zimbabwe state sometime around 1450. A map at the site details the presumed layout.

### Vumba & Bunga National Botanical Reserves

The Vumba and Bunga botanical reserves are two small protected enclaves just over 30km from Mutare in the Vumba Mountains. The tiny Bunga Botanical Reserve, which has no facilities, encompasses 39 hectares straddling the Vumba road.

Until the 1950s, the Vumba section was the very English private estate of former Mutare mayor Fred Taylor, and was known as Manchester Gardens. It consists of 200 hectares of sloping ground, 30 beautifully manicured hectares of which make up the Botanical Gardens. Unspoilt indigenous bushland characterises the remaining 170 hectares, comprising the Vumba Botanical Reserve.

In the gardens, you'll find an international sampling of botanical wonders as well as wide lawns and the obligatory teahouse. The fine views stretch past several ranges of hills to the tropical lowlands of Mozambique, 1000m below. The wilder section of the park is criss-crossed with footpaths through natural bush. These can all be hiked in a couple of hours, but a more leisurely pace is recommended if you want to fully appreciate the unique semi-tropical vegetation.

Forest wildlife includes samango monkeys, unique to the Eastern Highlands, as well as eland, duiker, bushbuck, sable and flashy tropical birds. Watch the forest floor for the odd little elephant shrew, a tiny but ferocious beast that hops like a kangaroo and has long ears and an elongated, trunk-like nose.

The gardens are open to day visitors from 9 am to 5 pm daily and the teahouse from 10 am to 4 pm daily except Monday. Foreigners pay US$2.60 admission.

ZIMBABWE

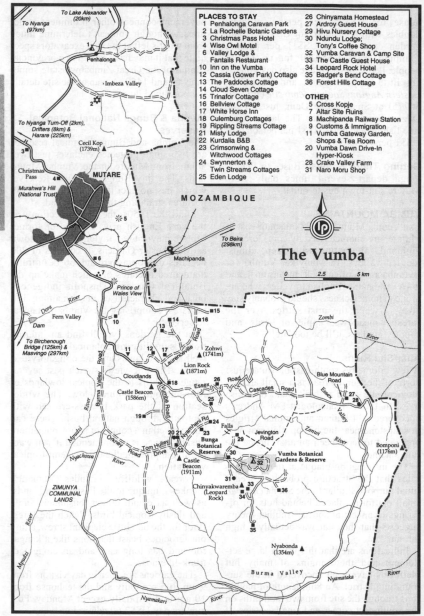

**PLACES TO STAY**
1  Penhalonga Caravan Park
2  La Rochelle Botanic Gardens
3  Christmas Pass Hotel
4  Wise Owl Motel
6  Valley Lodge &
   Fantails Restaurant
10 Inn on the Vumba
12 Cassia (Gower Park) Cottage
13 The Paddocks Cottage
14 Cloud Seven Cottage
15 Trinafor Cottage
16 Bellview Cottage
17 White Horse Inn
18 Culemburg Cottages
19 Rippling Streams Cottage
21 Misty Lodge
22 Kurdalia B&B
23 Crimsonwing &
   Witchwood Cottages
24 Swynnerton &
   Twin Streams Cottages
25 Eden Lodge

26 Chinyamata Homestead
27 Ardroy Guest House
29 Hivu Nursery Cottage
30 Ndundu Lodge;
   Tony's Coffee Shop
32 Vumba Caravan & Camp Site
33 The Castle Guest House
34 Leopard Rock Hotel
35 Badger's Bend Cottage
36 Forest Hills Cottage

**OTHER**
5  Cross Kopje
7  Altar Site Ruins
8  Machipanda Railway Station
9  Customs & Immigration
11 Vumba Gateway Garden,
   Shops & Tea Room
20 Vumba Dawn Drive-In
   Hyper-Kiosk
28 Crake Valley Farm
31 Naro Moru Shop

**The Vumba**

0     2.5     5 km

MOZAMBIQUE

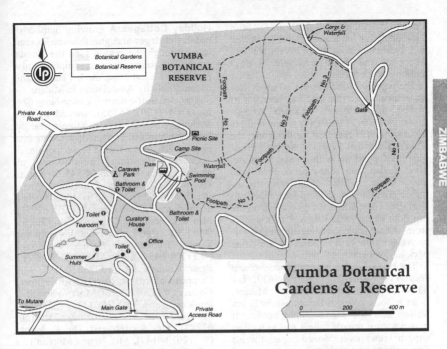

**Vumba Botanical Gardens & Reserve**

ZIMBABWE

### Chinyakwaremba (Leopard Rock)

The Chinyakwaremba (sitting down hill) monolith, also known as Leopard Rock, may be easily climbed via a signposted track from Vumba Rd about 2km east of the Botanical Reserve turn-off. The views from the top are naturally excellent. For information on the imposing hotel, see Places to Stay below.

### Burma & Essex Valleys

These two lush and densely populated lowland valleys, nearly 900m lower than Vumba, are accessed by a 70km scenic loop road. The Burma Valley Rd turns off 12km from Mutare and you can reach Essex Valley by continuing past the Vumba turn-off at Cloudlands, 18km from Mutare. Along the partially tarred route you pass through coffee, banana, tobacco and cotton plantations and over beautiful heavily forested mountains with frequent views into

Mozambique. Essex Valley in particular is a taste of Africa as it is further north, reminiscent in places of Uganda and the Kenyan highlands.

The Crake Valley Farm, 20km out on the Essex Valley road, produces the soft, ripe Vumba cheese, for which the region is famous; Pepperoni Cheese, made with green peppercorns from Chipinge; solid and mild Dutch cheese; Zonwe cheddar cheese; and soft Alpine cheese. What is the secret of their success? Well, the cheesemakers 'credit ... the cows that set the ball rolling'. (That's credit where credit is due!) Samples are free, but you should probably buy something afterward. It's open Monday to Saturday from 10 am to 3 pm.

### Places to Stay

**Camping & Hostels** The idyllic *campground* and *caravan park* in the Botanical Gardens has all the standard National Parks amenities: braai pits and ablutions facilities – including hot baths and showers – as well as a swimming pool. It's a lovely place to disappear and spend a couple of days ambling in the forests.

The popular Cloud Castle Cottage is now under new ownership and has been refurbished, upgraded and renamed *Ndundu Lodge* (☎ (120) 217620). It's set amid misty mountains 10 minutes walk from the Vumba Botanical Reserve and the atmosphere is topped off with a cosy fireplace, quiet garden, bar, sunny patio, braai area and kitchen facilities. Don't miss the attached Tony's Coffee Shop (see Places to Eat)! Beds cost US$4.50; try for one on the top floor of the main house. Free transfers from Mutare leave the Manicaland Publicity Association daily around 11 am; trips back to town leave at 7 am.

The beautiful and historic *Ardroy Guest House* (☎ (120) 217121 or 65622; fax 63743), PO Box 3150, Paulington, Mutare, is an historic colonial farmhouse in Essex Valley near the Mozambique border. It makes a great remote retreat and as well as superb views over Mozambique, there's fine walking and birdwatching. Tennis and squash courts are available at the neighbouring sports club where you can take out temporary membership. Single beds cost US$10 and private doubles with use of kitchen facilities are US$25. Breakfast and dinner, including vegetarian choices, are available for US$5.

If driving or hitching on the winding Essex Rd from Mutare, make sure you don't get lost in the wattle plantation. You can take the Mapofu bus, which leaves between 6 and 7 am from Mutare's in-town bus terminal, and get off at the Mapofu stop. Continue along the road for 1km to Blue Mountain road and turn left. The guesthouse lies 1km to the north. Alternatively, you can catch the 11 am Mutare-Burma Valley bus, which travels anticlockwise around the Burma-Essex Valley loop. Get off at the corner of Essex Rd and Blue Mountain Rd, turn right and walk 1km north to Ardroy.

**Holiday Cottages** A growing number of holiday cottages and guesthouses lie scattered through the region (see the Vumba map). The following is a sampling only; pick up the latest complete list from Manicaland Publicity Association in Mutare.

The two self-catering *Culemburg Cottages* (☎ (120) 66755), owned by Mrs Vermuelen, lie 18km from Mutare near the Essex Rd turn-off. They accommodate four people each and cost US$13 per person.

Other self-catering possibilities, all charging from US$25 to US$45 for four to six people, include *Trinafor Cottage* (☎ (120) 64522) owned by Mrs Hayden-Tebb; *Forest Hills Cottage* (☎ (120) 62911), Mrs J Coleridge; *Cloud Seven Cottage* (☎ (120) 219617; fax 64238), Jenny and Sandy Robertson; *Bellview Cottage* (☎ (120) 64522), Mr Mattison; *Badger's Bend Cottage* (☎ (120) 210310), Mrs Campbell-Morrison; *Cassia (Gower Park) Cottage* (☎ (120) 62612), Mrs P Wilde; *Willowbrae Farm* (☎ (120) 219122), Mrs Paterson; *Hivu Nursery Cottage* (☎ (120) 63885), Mrs Simlet; and *The Paddocks* (☎ (120) 60149), Mrs Nancy Morgan (for animal lovers only – there are cats).

*Seldomseen Farm* (☎ (120) 215125), on a rough track off Nyamheni Rd, has several self-catering cottages. *Swynnerton* and *Twin Streams* cost US$10 each, and *Crimsonwing* and *Witchwood* lodges cost US$13 and US$17, respectively. Guests pay US$2.50 for guided birdwatching walks with bird expert Peter Mwadziwana at the Seldomseen Ornithological Study Centre (others pay US$5).

The pleasant *Chinyamata Homestead* (☎ (120) 63321), owned by Mrs Jill Dix, has a six-bed cottage with a swimming pool for US$63/42 in high/low season. Mrs Colleen Taylor's recommended *Misty Lodge* (☎ (120) 60115) accommodates four people for US$40 or up to 10 people for US$75. Amenities include a wood stove, kitchen facilities, a braai and a balcony overlooking Misty Lake. Canoes are available to guests for fishing on the lake.

The *Kurdalia B&B*, owned by Mrs

Hayter, has one double and one single room and costs US$5 per person. To book, go through Manicaland Publicity Association in Mutare (☎ (120) 64711).

*Genaina Lodge* (☎ (120) 217620), an exquisite stone and thatch cottage deep in the forest, has a fabulous view and space for nine people. You'll pay US$34 per person with meals and US$21 with breakfast. The two-bedroom basement flat is suitable for couples. It sits at the 24km peg of the Vumba Rd.

**Hotels & Lodges** Hotels in the Vumba area seem to be struggling to outdo each other in the charm competition, yet each fills a different niche. Nearest Mutare is the *Inn on the Vumba* (☎/fax (120) 60722). Families are welcomed and there's a swimming pool and playground for the kids. Standard rooms, all with a mountain view, cost US$46/73 for singles/doubles with half board. Deluxe self-catering cottages for up to four people cost US$84 for double accommodation, plus US$17 for each extra adult. The pub is a local favourite and transfers from Mutare are available.

A more exclusive place is the *White Horse Inn* (☎/fax (120) 60325), beautifully situated on Laurenceville Rd, in a deep valley amid trees and gardens. It's known for its elegant dining room and French menu; in the evening, guests must dress for dinner – no jeans or T-shirts. Each room is pleasantly (if a bit ostentatiously) trimmed in a different floral theme, reminiscent of an English country B&B. Singles/doubles cost US$40.25/56.50, with breakfast. Carrying the Anglo theme even further, there's also a garden cottage, which affords more privacy, for US$54 plus US$13 per adult.

*Eden Lodge* (☎ (120) 62000; fax 62001), on Freshwater Rd, is more like a transplanted safari lodge than an Old Country estate. Its immense lounge and dining room have high ceilings and hardwood floors and overlook what may be the best view in the Vumba. For a lovely single/double cottage in the trees, you'll pay US$37/56, including vouchers entitling you to use the facilities at the Leopard Rock Hotel. Try for one of the two wooden cottages which overhang the precipice. Unless the proprietors are going to town, transfers from Mutare cost US$10 per party.

At *The Castle Guest House* (☎ (120) 210320), a secluded, medieval-looking mountain-top hideaway near Leopard Rock, the management spares nothing to provide a cosy and luxurious stay. The three singles/doubles cost US$63.50/109, including meals (minimum charge US$136). They accept groups of up to six and bathroom facilities are shared. If you're conjuring up visions of Transylvania, note the warning on their brochure: 'During the rainy season (November to March), it is recommended that groups should not exceed four in number, to avoid use of the tower bedroom, access to which can be daunting on a stormy night'. For weekends, book up to a year in advance.

Below the flanks of Chinyakwaremba (Leopard Rock) is the palatial *Leopard Rock Hotel* (☎ (120) 60115; fax 61165), with vast lawns and lavish gardens. It was built entirely of stone by Italian prisoners of war during WWII and its mark in history was made when the British Queen Mother, Elizabeth, made a royal visit in 1953. It was devastated in 1978, during the Second Chimurenga, but has been renovated and is now one of Zimbabwe's poshest hotels. Due to three-tier pricing, foreigners who pre-book overseas pay excruciating prices, which range from US$161/220 (local rate US$82/114) for a single/double room near the casino to US$346 (local rate US$179) for a honeymoon suite. Rack rates are about 30% lower.

For 18 holes of golf, hotel guests pay US$8 and outsiders, US$11. Clubs, carts and caddies are available for hire. Other facilities include a croquet pitch, bowling green, billiards, tennis courts and a swimming pool, sauna and gym. Horse-riding on the Campbell-Morisson farm nearby costs US$5 per hour and 2½ hour birdwatching tours in the mountain forests of Seldomseen Ornithological Study Centre cost US$5.

ZIMBABWE

## Places to Eat

For meals, there's little apart from the hotels and lodges. About 10 minutes walk from the Botanic Gardens is *Tony's Coffee Shop*, where you may regret the calories but not the quality; the coffee and sweets are the best I've had anywhere in the world, but don't just take my word for it. Try the chocolate truffle cake, which has been dubbed 'Rebirth by Chocolate'.

Self-caterers can pick up staples at the *Naro Moru* shop (maybe someone was reminded of Mt Kenya?), 500m from Ndundu Lodge. From the Vumba Botanical Gardens turn-off, head west and take a left at the first opportunity. It's closed on Monday.

The elaborate-looking *Vumba Gateway*, on the road from Mutare, has a crafts shop, bar and tea room serving weak coffee, tea and sweet cakes. They also serve light meals and fast food.

## Things to Buy

If you're craving such Vumba specialities as pickles, honey, Vumba cheese, biltong, coffee from the Zimbabwean highlands, locally grown protea flowers and even greeting cards made from elephant and rhino dung (no joke), visit the Vumba Dawn Drive-In Hyper-Kiosk (the name reflects its creator's sense of humour) at the 21km peg of the Vumba road.

Majig Animals (☎ (120) 219124; fax 60949), 4km beyond the White Horse Inn, produces unique wooden African animal puzzles. Hi-Vu Nursery, near the Vumba Botanical Gardens, sells local plants and basketry. For other options, see Crake Valley Farm under Burma & Essex Valleys, earlier in this section.

## Getting There & Away

Without a vehicle, access to the Vumba area is quite limited. From the in-town bus terminal in Mutare, there's a bus to Leopard Rock at 8 am and 3 pm on Friday, Saturday and Sunday, returning to Mutare just over an hour later. There's also a bus departing from Mutare at 6 am for Essex Valley and a Burma Valley bus leaves at 11 am.

# Nyanga Area

Nyanga National Park, the scenic wonderland around which the Nyanga region revolves, is more a popular and developed resort area than a real wilderness. However, there's scope for some remote bushwalking around the perimeter, especially in the park's southern extremes. Mtarazi Falls National Park, an appendage of Nyanga, is almost completely undeveloped – little more than a camp site – and the only vehicle access is a steep, rutted track leading to the park's namesake attraction. Just east of the park lie the tropical agricultural lowlands and tea estates of the Honde Valley.

## JULIASDALE

Piny Juliasdale, it seems, is simply a holiday cottage settlement and a repository for scattered hotels and private holiday cottages in need of a town name in their address. It boasts a petrol station, a post office, and a couple of small shops. From the centre, inasmuch as Juliasdale has one, you'll have good westward views across the farm lands, intermittent forests and granite domes.

## Organised Tours

Far and Wide Zimbabwe (☎ (129) 3011 or 2440; fax 3012; <farnwide@pci.co.zw>), PO Box 14, Juliasdale, offers white-water rafting and kayaking trips which give participants close-up views of the wild Pungwe River. The trips run between November and May, water levels permitting, and range from half-day to seven-day expeditions. The five hour white-water paddle, which costs US$65, departs from 6km out on Brackenridge Rd. Far And Wide also run abseiling, rock climbing, mountain biking, fishing and hiking programmes, which last from one to five days. As well as this, they have several wilderness cabins, lodges and camp sites. Book at their office beside the BP petrol station.

## Nyanga Vegetation & Wildlife

The Nyanga landscape ranges from subtle to spectacular. Much of the upland regions, typically 2000 to 2300m above sea level, are comprised of gentle granite mountains and heath-covered moors. The Nyanga highlands are also a stronghold of Zimbabwe's national flower, the flame lily, whose colour ranges from red to orange. Many of Nyanga's stone ruins have been overcome by red aloes and protea trees, whose pink blooms come straight out of a Dr Seuss fantasy. Lower areas, like the steep-walled gash of Pungwe Gorge and the precipitous Nyanga escarpment, offer some indigenous semi-tropical vegetation and views down into entirely separate, rather jungly ecosystems, where ferns, orchids and tropical hardwoods replace the heath and grasslands of the higher regions.

Although you won't find vast herds of African beasts at Nyanga, the park isn't completely empty of wildlife. The Eastern Highlands are the sole Zimbabwean home of the samango monkey, which is blue-grey in colour with yellow highlights, black legs and a brown face. Another inhabitant native only to this region is the blue duiker, Zimbabwe's smallest antelope. These rarely observed forest-dwellers are grey-brown in colour except for a white throat and a dark line from the nose to between the short ringed horns. Other animals to watch for include baboon, hyaena, klipspringer, kudu and reedbuck. There are also leopard around but they're as elusive as leopard everywhere. Occasionally, someone even finds evidence of lion or buffalo, but such animals are rarely seen.

### Places to Stay & Eat

*Juliasdale Camp & Cabin* (☎ (129) 2202), which fills the budget niche, is a great for chilling out in the mellow mountain air. Garden camp sites cost US$3 per person and simple cabins cost US$5 per person. Horse tours near Rusape cost US$2 per hour.

The recommended *Pine Tree Inn* (☎/fax (129) 388), deep in a dark piny forest, is known for its excellent meals. Standard single/double rooms cost US$46/73, with breakfast. Luxury suites in the Garden Wing cost US$55/82. Rates include half board.

The four-star *Montclair Casino Hotel* (☎ (129) 441; fax 447), which boasts a full casino, attracts an elegant crowd with its tennis courts, swimming pool, croquet, horse-riding, golf and so on. Foreigners pay single/double rates of US$91/114, including breakfast.

The three-star *Brondesbury Park Hotel* (☎ (129) 2341), 30km west of Juliasdale on the Rusape road, has singles/doubles for US$46/63, with half board and use of the swimming pool, tennis courts and bowling green. A golf course adjoins the hotel grounds and camping is also available. The area is known for its butterflies, which are especially profuse in the rainy season.

Self-catering cottages with a pool are available at *Silver Rocks Holiday Farm* (☎ (129) 2394), 10km off the Rusape road. The recommended *Punch Rock Chalets* (☎ (129) 224422), beneath a lovely kopje and an incredible spread of *Acacia abyssinica* trees, has comfortable English-style self-catering cottage chalets for US$10 per person. The popular Swiss-style *York Cottages* (☎ (129) 2360) sleep six people for US$30, but it's very hard to get a booking.

The *takeaway* beside the petrol station bakes excellent chicken pies, and between Juliasdale and Nyanga is the Claremont Orchard Shop ('exciting biting'), which sells Nyanga trout and local apples.

### Getting There & Away

The only express service between Harare, Rusape, Juliasdale and Nyanga is DSB Coachlines (☎ (129) 202), which leaves from the Harare Sheraton on Wednesday at 7 am and Friday at 2 pm. The trip to Juliasdale takes three hours, to the Village Inn in Nyanga, 3½ hours and Troutbeck Inn in Troutbeck, four hours. In the opposite direction, the bus runs from Troutbeck on Sunday at 7 am and Wednesday at 1 pm, passing Nyanga (Nyamhuka Township) half an hour later and Juliasdale an hour later. Fares between Harare and Juliasdale, Nyanga or Troutbeck are US$11/13.

The Sabi Star transfer service, operated by Sun Hotels (☎ (14) 736644; fax 736646), runs transfers between Harare and the Montclair Casino Hotel (or Troutbeck) or between Juliasdale/Troutbeck and Great Zimbabwe, for US$18.

The Masara bus line runs a service from Mbare to Juliasdale and Nyanga (Nyamhuka township) daily except Saturday at 7 am. In Harare, catch the bus marked Nyanga/Nyamaropa from the corner of Glenara Rd and Robert Mugabe Rd, or flag it down from opposite the Chicken Inn in Msasa, on the Mutare road. The fare is around US$4. Alternatively, take a bus to Rusape and connect there with the hourly services to Juliasdale and Nyanga.

From the in-town bus terminal in Mutare, ZUPCO, Zvinoira and Masara buses depart for Juliasdale and Nyanga hourly until midday and cost US$1.50.

## NYANGA NATIONAL PARK
Although it can hardly be described as pristine – nearly all the naturally occurring vegetation in easily accessible areas was cleared for farming long ago – 33,000 hectare Nyanga National Park is a scenically distinct enclave in the Eastern Highlands. Cecil Rhodes fell in love with it and, as only he could have done, bought it for his own residence. Not surprisingly, the park, like the entire country, acquired his name and it's still sometimes referred to as Rhodes Inyanga. The African name, Nyanga, means 'the shaman's horn'.

### Information
Information is found at the park headquarters near Nyanga Dam.

### Around Nyanga Dam
The Nyanga National Park service centre focuses on Nyanga Dam, which was the site of the Rhodes homestead. Indeed, Rhodes'

## Forestry in Zimbabwe
Many areas of the Eastern Highlands – around Nyanga National Park, the Vumba and Chimanimani – are characterised by the rolling, forested hillsides, striped with logging roads and occasional clearcuts, which provide most of Zimbabwe's characteristically pulpy paper.

These slopes originally bore hardwood forests, but these were cleared by early inhabitants for agriculture. The vast stands of conifers, eucalyptus and wattle that replaced them are little more than tree farms. Zimbabwe's first modern tree-planting scheme was started in 1905 by John Meikle in the Penhalonga area and, 25 years later, when the government became involved, the plantations began spreading northward. This spreading area of forests now covers over 1000 sq km and lends the Eastern Highlands landscape a rather North American feel.

To many tourists, the large-scale logging activities may seem an affront to the aesthetics of an otherwise superb countryside. However, the logging of non-indigenous forests conserves foreign exchange capital. The pine forests, which account for 700 sq km, are used for lumber and paper production. Over 300 sq km are covered in eucalyptus, which is used for firewood and lumber. The newest and (it seems) fastest-growing forestry scheme is producing the fernlike black wattle for tanbark.

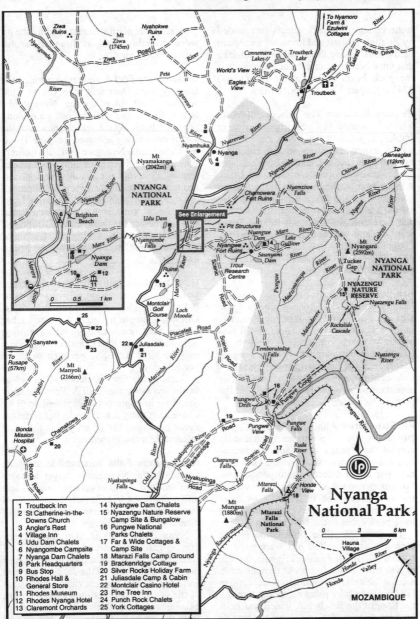

ZIMBABWE

**Nyanga National Park**

1 Troutbeck Inn
2 St Catherine-in-the-Downs Church
3 Angler's Rest
4 Village Inn
5 Udu Dam Chalets
6 Nyangombe Campsite
7 Nyanga Dam Chalets
8 Park Headquarters
9 Bus Stop
10 Rhodes Hall & General Store
11 Rhodes Museum
12 Rhodes Nyanga Hotel
13 Claremont Orchards
14 Nyangwe Dam Chalets
15 Nyazengu Nature Reserve Camp Site & Bungalow
16 Pungwe National Parks Chalets
17 Far & Wide Cottages & Camp Site
18 Mtarazi Falls Camp Ground
19 Brackenridge Cottage
20 Silver Rocks Holiday Farm
21 Juliasdale Camp & Cabin
22 Montclair Casino Hotel
23 Pine Tree Inn
24 Punch Rock Chalets
25 York Cottages

stone cottage residence stands surrounded by English gardens and imported European hardwoods beside the small artificial lake that once bore his name. Near the chalets is the park headquarters office (☎ (1298) 274384), open 7 am to 6 pm daily.

**Rhodes Museum** The Rhodes Museum, which is housed in Cecil Rhodes' former stables, is worth a good look round. One would expect devotion to the coloniser himself, but the museum also dedicates space to several positive facets of black African history: the struggles of the Second Chimurenga and its spirit-inspired elements; and the good works of Zimbabwean war hero and philanthropist Rekayi Tangwena. Then of course there are the obligatory Rhodes relics! The museum is open daily except Monday from 9 am to 1 pm and 2.30 to 5.30 pm.

**Brighton Beach** Between the Nyanga Dam complex and the Nyangombe camping area is a natural wide spot below a cascade in the Nyangombe River. There you'll find a sandy beach, unofficially known as Brighton Beach, a green lawn, changing rooms and bilharzia-free swimming – although the temperature of the chilly mountain water is likely to deter all but the hardiest swimmers.

**Pit Structures** Although there are unrestored pit structures strewn haphazardly around the Nyanga landscape, the reconstructed pit structure near Nyanga Dam may help put the architecture into perspective. For comparison, take a look at the similar but unrestored one in a grove of trees behind the main pit. These particular sites have been dated to the 16th century.

The most plausible explanation is that these dry-stone-walled pits were used as corrals for small livestock: goats, sheep, pigs or small cattle. Entry was through dark, narrow tunnels; the animals were kept in (and protected) by pales extending through the floor of the family hut, which was built on a level stone platform above the tunnel.

Smaller stone platforms surrounding the pit were probably used as foundations for grain-storage huts.

**Chawomera Fort** A pleasant morning hike from Nyanga Dam will take you to Chawomera Fort, 6km up the Nyangombe River; follow the well-defined path along the north bank. With a vehicle, however, the fort is more easily accessed from the Troutbeck road. Like Nyangwe Fort, Chawomera Fort is one of a series of similar structures stretching across the Nyanga region. Although they resemble defence structures, it's more likely they served as simple lookouts. Local sources have suggested that sentries posted in these hilltop structures, which are mutually visible on clear days, communicated by blowing on the spiral kudu horn.

**Udu Dam** Udu Dam, 2km west of Nyanga Dam, lies at the bottom of a grassy parabolic valley sloping up towards the hills. Guests staying in the quiet A-frame basher lodges may use a convenient swimming hole in the Udu River, and rowing boats may be hired for US$2 per hour or US$6 per half-day.

Because the low vegetation allows good visibility, both the Udu Valley and surrounding hills are easily explored on foot. There aren't any actual tracks but National Parks personnel can direct you to the most interesting unexcavated ruins.

**Nyangombe Falls** Just outside the park boundary, the Nyangombe River tumbles over terraced stacks of cuboid boulders and into a shallow gorge. In fact, it may remind you more of an abstractly sculpted fountain than a work of nature.

Nyangombe Falls is 5km from Nyangombe campground and 3km from Udu Dam. Wear shoes with a good tread because the short descent from the car park is steep and slippery. For the best views, follow one of the several well-worn tracks to the right as you approach the river. Downstream from the upper falls, which are depicted on brochures and postcards, a narrower and more dramatic drop feeds a deep river pool. Stay off the flanking rocks, as the moss fostered by the flowing water can be hazardously slick.

**Nyangwe (Mare) Dam Trout Research Centre** At the Trout Research Centre near Nyangwe Dam, pisciphiles can learn from the experts about breeding and hatching rainbow *(Salmo gairdneri)* and brown trout *(Salmo trutta)* to stock Zimbabwe rivers. The staff conduct free 15-minute tours of the site whenever there's interest. It's open daily except Saturday from 2 to 3 pm and 4.30 to 5 pm.

**Nyangwe Fort** Nyangwe Fort and other hilltop enclosures have traditionally been ascribed to defence but, as with Chawomera Fort, they were more likely used as lookouts. Although the hilltop sites might have been favourable for defence, the placement of the structures away from water sources would have prevented resistance under longer periods of siege. Despite rock loopholes, which resemble gun sights, their small size and odd positioning would have commanded no field of fire. Furthermore, the enclosures are so broad that the occupants would have been subjected to fire by assailants.

Whatever its purpose, Nyangwe is the best preserved of the Nyanga fort structures. The main enclosure, full of storage-hut platforms and partially overgrown with aloes and msasa trees, is surrounded by five smaller fort-like enclosures. Nyangwe is just a 2km walk from Nyangwe Dam along a driveable road.

**Mt Nyangani**
Rising to 2592m, flat-topped and myth-shrouded Mt Nyangani is Zimbabwe's highest mountain. Viewed from the park, it's not dramatic by any description, and its loftiness only becomes apparent from the context of Honde Valley, over 1000m lower than the high moors west of the mountain. Nearly every visitor with a bit of stamina

makes the obligatory climb to the summit. From the car park 14km east of Nyanga Dam, this can take anywhere from 1½ to three hours.

While there are plenty of reasons to climb Nyangani, there are also plenty of reasons not to. The weather can change abruptly; wind-driven rain can render the trip very unpleasant and when the *guti* mists drop around the marshy peak, the view becomes irrelevant. Local inhabitants, however, believe there are more implicit reasons for avoiding Nyangani, and few black Africans are interested in climbing it (although on my last climb I encountered several groups); this hallowed mountain has earned a reputation for devouring hikers.

Park regulations ask prospective walkers to register at park headquarters before setting off, and to check back in once the trip is completed. At the base, you're met with an intimidating warning sign which outlines the climatic uncertainties and forbids hiking with children. If you remain undaunted, set out as early as possible to make the best use of decent weather. Hitch-hiking is best from the Nyanga Dam area. Otherwise, it's a 15km walk each way.

**Mt Nyangani to Honde Valley Walk**
For a fairly easy – but not entirely straightforward – three or four day walk, consider the increasingly popular route from Mt Nyangani into the Honde Valley.

From the car park at the base of Mt Nyangani, a southbound track skirts the base of the mountain. Once you've reached the summit of Mt Nyangani, either return to the car park the way you came, then follow the track southward; or descend along the south-western slope of the mountain, where you'll strike the track 4km south of the car park (this option is for experienced hikers only).

From Mt Nyangani, a rough but driveable track winds for 12km over grass-covered hills and passes through the lovely Nyazengu Nature Reserve (entry costs US$4.50 per vehicle plus US$2.50 per person), which takes in stunning forested and gorge-studded landscapes between Mt Nyangani and the Honde Lowlands. The reserve has two camp sites – including an undeveloped site beside dramatic Nyazengu Falls. A lovely bungalow, *Stonechat Cottage*, with two double and two single rooms costs US$46. Book through Nyangani Farms (☎ (14) 303518; fax 339679; <vet@samara.co.zw>), 128 East Rd, Avondale, Harare.

South of Nyazengu, you have 10km of excellent views along the lip of the escarpment before descending into the upper reaches of Pungwe Gorge at Pungwe Drift. Here you'll find several National Parks chalets, which were destroyed in the Second Chimurenga but have now been rebuilt. From here, a one hour return side trip leads to the top of 240m Pungwe Falls. The chilly eddies above the falls make for refreshing, teeth-chattering swimming. Further downstream are several possible camp sites with plenty of fresh water available from the hell-bound Pungwe River. The most favoured site is the prominent sand bar near Pungwe Drift.

From Pungwe Drift, follow the little-travelled road back onto the escarpment and on to the car park at Mtarazi Falls. Along the way, don't miss Pungwe View, where a magnificent vista of the gorge, the falls and the now-distant Mt Nyangani opens up along a short detour from the main road. About 4km beyond the Mtarazi Falls turn-off from Scenic Rd is Honde View, which reveals an enticing panorama of Honde Valley, nearly 1000m below, and the Mozambique frontier.

After a further 3km downhill, you'll arrive at the Mtarazi Falls National Parks campground. There, a footpath leads 700m to a view of 762m Mtarazi Falls (Africa's second or third highest waterfall, depending upon your source) as it plunges over the escarpment.

The steep 9km farm workers' track (actually a tangle of tracks) over the escarpment and into Honde Valley begins several hundred metres from the Mtarazi Falls campground. It's a bit tricky to find –

it starts about 500m back up the road from the campground – but the isolated car park attendant would probably welcome the opportunity to offer direction. The track branches on the way down; take the right fork and you'll emerge on the Honde Valley road about 1km above Hauna, from where you can connect with a Mutare bus. Incidentally, the Honde Valley is well known as a favourite haunt of black mambas, so be especially cautious where you step.

### Nyamziwa Falls

Nyamziwa Falls lies 1km north of the northern loop road between Nyanga Dam and Mt Nyangani. The upper part of the falls resembles an immense slippery slide (but don't be tempted into trying it!) giving way to a 30m drop into the gorge below. It's ideal for a couple of hours relaxation on a sunny day, especially after a morning climb of Mt Nyangani, which is an easily walkable 5km away.

### Troutbeck

The lovely *Troutbeck Inn* (☎ (1298) 305; fax 474), founded by Irishman Major Robert McIlwaine, sits at an altitude of 2000m. It serves 100% typically English food – cream teas, Yorkshire puddings and game pies – and has the weather and the country estate atmosphere to match. Among the amenities to be found on the estate are tennis and squash courts, a swimming pool, a shooting range, a golf course, a private trout lake, lawn bowls and stables. Tradition has it that the log fire roaring in the main hall has been burning since the hotel was founded in 1950! Unfortunately, three-tier pricing has reared its ugly head and foreigners now pay US$115/144 for standard single/double rooms that include breakfast and a lake view while locals pay US$63/79.

The pretty and immaculately maintained Church of St Catherine-in-the-Downs in Troutbeck village merits a look. In the tiny churchyard is the grave of Major Robert McIlwaine, who died in 1943. Services are held on Sunday at 8.30 am.

## Connemara Lakes

These stunning lakes, surrounded by lovely pine forests, were created and named by the same homesick Irishman who founded Troutbeck Inn. Unfortunately, they're sadly inaccessible to the public. In fact, it's scarcely possible to even catch a glimpse of them with all the fences, gates, dogs, security systems and Keep Out signs!

## World's View

World's View, atop the Troutbeck Massif, sits perched on a precipice, 11km up the winding mountain road from Troutbeck. As its name implies, this National Trust site affords a broad view across northern Zimbabwe. Visitors pay a fee of US$0.25 for the upkeep of the landscaped lawns and picnic facilities.

Buses run infrequently from Troutbeck, but since World's View is on most Nyanga itineraries, finding a lift isn't too difficult. It's also a pleasant and straightforward walk up from Troutbeck or along the steep 4km footpath which leads up the scarp from 6km north of Nyanga village.

## Pungwe View & Pungwe Gorge

The dramatic Pungwe View overlook, on the back roads between Nyanga and Mtarazi Falls, affords a dramatic view down the Pungwe Gorge. In the distance rise the slopes of the truncated Mt Nyangani and nearer is 240m-high Pungwe Falls, where the wild Pungwe river is swallowed up in the lush vegetation of the gorge.

The turn-off to Pungwe Drift lies 4km along Scenic Rd north of Pungwe View. From there, it's a pleasant half-hour walk downstream to a series of swimming holes immediately above the falls. Alternatively, follow the walking track down to the Drift from Pungwe View. The hiking route from Mt Nyangani to Honde Valley crosses the Pungwe River at Pungwe Drift.

North-east of Pungwe Drift, the track climbs back onto the heath. After 10km, it deteriorates and passes through the Nyazengu Private Nature Reserve; 12km later, it emerges at the Mt Nyangani car park.

For information on white-water rafting and kayaking trips, see Organised Tours under Juliasdale.

## Activities

Nyanga streams and lakes are stocked with rainbow, brook and brown trout. Fishing licences cost US$3.50 per day at all sites except the Gairezi River (US$7 per day) and at Gulliver and Saunyami (Purdon) dams (US$5 per day). Fishing is permitted between 5 am and 6.30 pm. Seasons are as follows: Mare Dam, December to August; Nyanga Dam, August to April; Udu Dam,

---

## The Pungwe in Peril

The wild Pungwe may not stay that way for much longer. The Zimbabwean cabinet has approved the controversial Pungwe Water Supply Project, which is intended to provide Mutare with a reliable water supply. Essentially, this involves blasting a 4km tunnel through the rocks and building a pipeline to carry the water to the Odzani water works.

No environmental impact assessment has been done, but it's believed the effects will be far-reaching. The Pungwe River's decreased flow will diminish Pungwe Falls and cut water availability in the agricultural Honde Valley. Furthermore, less water will also mean saline intrusion into the Pungwe Flats wetlands in Mozambique, and will probably affect Beira's water supply. A less damaging proposal – a water pipeline from the Odzi River – would cost about US$30 million less, but has been rejected. The World Bank has said that financing will be approved upon completion of feasibility studies and environmental impact assessments.

April to December; Gulliver and Saunyami dams, October to July; and all rivers, October to May.

Guided 1½ hour/six-hour pony trails around the archaeological sites of the Nyanga Dam area cost US$20/40. Book through the National Parks office (☎ (1298) 274384) near Nyanga Dam.

### Places to Stay

**Camping** The National Parks *Nyangombe* camp site lies between the Nyangombe River and the highway. It's full of big piny woods – reminiscent of Yogi Bear cartoons – and has hot showers, braai pits and toilets.

Camping elsewhere in the park is officially prohibited but unofficially tolerated. The park administration can't fathom why anyone would undertake an overnight hiking trip, but they don't organise sting operations to reel in violators. Just use discretion. Mt Nyangani presents a special case; hikers are technically expected to register at headquarters before climbing and to sign out the same day, which can be a problem if you're en route to Pungwe Gorge. Again, use your own discretion.

**Lodges & Cottages** The cosy *National Parks chalets* at Udu Dam, Nyanga Dam and Nyangwe Dam all lie within a few kilometres of the main park service area. Pungwe Drift at the south end of the park also has two remote National Parks lodges.

Self-catering options include the rudimentary *Brackenridge Cottage* (☎ (179) 26321 or (14) 475002), which enjoys an ideal location on a fruit farm 3km from Pungwe Falls. It costs US$22/26 for four/six people. *Follie's Mountain Haven* (☎/fax (14) 721696), PO Box 101, Kopje, Harare, is at Connemara Lakes.

The quiet *Ezulwini Cottages* (☎ (1298) 61121), 1700m up the slopes of Mt Rukotso (north of Troutbeck), border the Nyangui Forest Reserve and overlook an idyllic stream broken by pools and waterfalls. They cost US$8 per person (minimum US$16.50, or US$32 during school holidays). *Tara Hill B&B* (☎ (1298) 415) is

14km past St Catherine's church, near the junction of Church Road and Gairezi Scenic Drive. This English-style cottage rents for US$15 per person, with breakfast.

The remote *Kafukuto Chalets*, in the Cherenje Mountains 95km north of Troutbeck, offer hiking, climbing, fishing and a glimpse of traditional rural life. Camping (US$2), solar-powered chalets (US$10) and local cuisine are available. Book with Kafukuto (☎/fax (14) 301214), c/o Stand 702 Brig Atif Rd, Mt Pleasant, Harare.

The Manicaland Publicity Association in Mutare can provide updated lists of country cottage options. Note that there are no shops or services within walking distance of any of these places.

**Hotels** The friendly *Rhodes Nyanga Hotel* (☎ (1298) 377; fax 477) at Nyanga Dam boasts a tropical veranda and well-kept gardens, recalling the days of its namesake who once lived on the site. Singles/doubles with breakfast cost US$58/74. See also under Troutbeck, earlier in this section.

### Places to Eat

*Nyamoro Farm* (☎ (1298) 30212), run by John and Jen Stables, has a tea room and sells fresh dairy products and local organic produce. It's open daily except Saturday from 8.30 am to noon and 3 to 5.30 pm. Take the road north of Troutbeck and turn left at the top of the hill past the Jersey cow sign, then turn left again at the signposted gate.

### Getting There & Away

Between 7 and 8 am, buses leave Nyamhuka (Nyanga village) for Harare, Mutare, Masvingo and Bulawayo (see Getting There & Away under Juliasdale). In the national park, the bus stops at Nyangombe campground.

### NYANGA VILLAGE

Separated from the Nyamhuka township by 1km of highway, Nyanga village may unsettle visitors with its beautifully manicured gardens and well-tended hedges. The village common, tiny library (which houses the tourist office) and little stone church, all beneath the towering Troutbeck Massif, apparently intentionally call to mind the English Lake District.

## Information

**Tourist Office** The friendly folks at the Nyanga Tourist Association (☎ (1298) 435), PO Box 110, Nyanga, in the library, provide information about the entire Nyanga region. It's open weekdays from 9 am to 1 pm and 2 to 4.30 pm and on Saturday from 9 to 11.30 am.

**Money** The Zimbank does currency exchange on Monday, Tuesday, Thursday and Friday from 8 am to 1 pm; on Wednesday from 8 am to noon; and on Saturday from 8 am to 4 pm. The Rochdale grocery also changes cash and travellers cheques.

## Nyamhuka Township

Relaxed Nyamhuka township is a world apart from the neatly manicured village, so when you've had enough Anglo nostalgia and are again longing for Africa, head this way. It has a couple of shops and stalls selling inexpensive snacks and a craft village, opposite the bus terminal, which sells mats, basketry, ceramics, batik, tie dye, woven rugs and Shona sculpture.

## Places to Stay

The friendly *Village Inn* (☎ (1298) 336339) makes a great alternative to camping. You can curl up beside the log fire in the lounge, plonk away on the piano or enjoy a relaxing set meal featuring home-grown vegetables. Single/double rooms with half board are US$39/77. Budget singles with shared facilities and no meals cost US$25 and cottages are US$30 per person.

The clean and basic *Mangondoza Country Hotel* (☎ (1298) 588), north of the village, offers half board in simple single/double rooms for US$14/26.

The recently resurrected *Angler's Rest* (☎ (1298) 436; fax 9713) – known locally as Rest Angels – 4km from the village, orig-

inally dates from the 1930s, but during the bush war it was abandoned and invaded by squatters. It was brought back to life by a local trio who whimsically call themselves BADGERS (Betty & Diana's Get Excessively Rich Scheme). In fact, no-one is likely to get rich, but it now offers camping for US$2 per person, caravan sites for US$4, backpackers dorms for US$4.50 and en suite doubles for US$30. The views are great, there are cooking facilities and the staff can arrange guided hikes to World's View for negotiable rates. Turn west on Angler's Rest Rd, 2km north of the Nyamhuka turnoff, and continue 1.5km to Angler's Rest; you can phone for a lift from Nyanga or Nyamhuka.

## Places to Eat

The Rochdale *grocery shop* stocks a wide enough range for basic self catering. Fresh vegetables are available from the *gardener* living behind the Village Inn, and you'll find staples, produce and snacks at the *market* in Nyamhuka township. There's also the *Eastern Highlands Takeaway*, with simple snacks. For prepared meals, you're limited to the *Village Inn* dining room.

## Things to Buy

The excellent Zuwa Weaving Co-operative (the name means either 'day' or 'sun'), behind the post office, sells sturdy and well-executed wool and cotton blankets and rugs, and mohair scarves. It's open Monday to Friday from 8 am to 4 pm and Saturday from 8 am to 2 pm. Dilly's Craft Shop sells handmade knives with ebony handles, among other craft products, and the Bloo Zoo, which serves tea and snacks, sells locally made craftwork.

## Getting There & Away

Nyamhuka is the terminal for buses to and from Mutare, Rusape and Harare (see Juliasdale, earlier in this chapter).

## Getting Around

Bicycle hire is available at Angler's Rest (see Places to Stay) for US$5 per day.

## NORTH OF NYANGA

The highlands north of Nyanga were formerly used as a Frelimo guerrilla-training zone, but visitors no longer require military permission to enter. This region holds the greatest concentration of pre-colonial ruins in Zimbabwe, but for the most part, they're accessible only by private vehicle. However, some of the best sites lie just 22km from Nyanga village, so walking is possible.

### Ziwa & Nyahokwe Ruins

As you drive north from Nyanga village, you'll constantly come across examples of the ancient terraces that characterise the region. The most extensive expanse of ruins in the Nyanga area is the Ziwa complex, which sprawls over 80 sq km. These were formerly known as Van Niekerk's Ruins, after the Boer who brought them to the attention of archaeologist Donald Randall McIver in 1905, but have now been renamed Ziwa after the 1745m-high mountain which rises in their midst. (The mountain itself was named Sa Ziwa after a 19th-century Karanga chief.)

The parallel walls, housing platforms, agricultural terraces, circular enclosures, pit corrals and disjointed rubble that litters the intermediate ground are thought to be evidence of a Karanga agricultural community – everyday farmers closely associated for defence purposes. Stone seats and built-in grinding niches are also in evidence. With the exception of some excavation for artefacts, these post-Great Zimbabwe ruins have remained much as they were when their inhabitants left them. A small interpretive display outlines what little is known about the complex.

Although it's thought to be the work of earlier stonemasons, Nyahokwe, named for the Karanga chief Hokwe from the same era as Sa Ziwa, is more of a consolidated village than the extensive Ziwa. Although it was inhabited as recently as the 19th century, this hilltop site is attributed to the migrating tribes who are also credited with constructing Great Zimbabwe. The inhabitants were probably involved in iron smelting and the ruin is believed to be the remains of a rudimentary ore-crushing operation. For novelty value, don't miss the lonely juniper tree (*Juniperus procura*) which, as far as anyone knows, is the only one in Zimbabwe.

### Getting There & Away

The shortest route to Ziwa Ruins turns west from the main road about 1km south of Nyanga village; after 11km, turn right and continue another 10km to the site. A better alternative is via Nyahokwe; the road turns west 14km north of Nyanga village. After 5km, you'll come to the turn-off for Nyahokwe Ruins, which are 1km away. If, instead of turning, you continue straight on for 8km, you'll arrive at Ziwa. Without a private vehicle, your only option is to walk, which is pleasant, or attempt hitching, which is nigh hopeless. You can camp anywhere in the area.

## MTARAZI FALLS NATIONAL PARK

Mtarazi Falls National Park, a southern appendage to Nyanga National Park, protects Mtarazi Falls, a spindly trickle of water that plummets 762m down the escarpment and disappears into a series of cascades through the forest below.

According to Mark and Hazel Igoe in *The Manicaland Guide*, the pool at the bottom is inhabited by water spirits who drag the unwary down into its depths. Perhaps it's fortunate that access to this pool is quite difficult.

### Honde View

Drivers on the Mtarazi Falls road aren't normally aware of the sharp escarpment dropping off next to them. Then they pull off at Honde View and receive a dramatic awakening when they behold the patchwork of agricultural patterns in the broad valley below.

### Places to Stay

A National Parks *campground* operates beside the falls parking area.

**Getting There & Away**
From the main Mutare-Nyanga road, take the Honde Valley turn-off and after 2km, bear left onto Scenic Rd. After an occasionally rough 16km, take the right turning and follow that road 7km to the car park. From there, it's a 750m walk to the most spectacular falls vantage points.

Hitching isn't impossible, but expect long waits and remember that most drivers visit Mtarazi Falls as a whistle-stop on a longer Nyanga tour. See also the description of the Mt Nyangani to Honde Valley walk in the Nyanga National Park section.

## HONDE VALLEY

A former haunt of Mozambican MNR raiders, the picturesque Honde Valley sits vulnerably cut off from the rest of Zimbabwe by the Nyanga Mountains, and offers awesome views of the brooding Nyanga Escarpment. This low-lying and well-watered basin holds some of Zimbabwe's richest communal lands and is ideal for growing coffee, tea and tropical fruit.

At the Aberfoyle Tea Estates, which were established in the 1940s, most of Zimbabwe's export tea is grown and in the summer, the idyllic rolling landscape turns as green as Ireland. Have a look around the tea estates, tour the factory and stroll to a series of idyllic cascades about 5km away.

From near Hauna village, a footpath leads to a haunting forest pool beneath Mtarazi Falls. The trail to the top of the falls, which is used mainly by Hauna people working in the highlands, turns off the main road about 1km south of the village.

### Places to Stay & Eat

The *Aberfoyle Country Club* (☎ (128) 385), on the tea estates 30km north-east of Hauna, has comfortable rooms enhanced by gardens, a golf course, squash and tennis courts, a swimming pool, great hiking and fishing and a superb setting. Singles/doubles cost US$20/37 with half board. Camping is normally permitted, but you may have to get out of sight. A small workers' shop sells food staples, but don't miss the memorable three-course meals at the Country Club restaurant.

The *Katiyo* (☎ (129) 392) and *Eastern Highlands* (☎ (129) 251) tea estates nearby also offer accommodation. The latter, known as *Honde Red Dragon Lodge*, charges US$42 per person for accommodation in log cabins and US$38 for camping (tent hire is US$4.50). Rates include transfers, hiking, meals and use of the tennis courts, swimming pool, satellite TV, kitchen and braais.

### Getting There & Away

From Sakubva musika in Mutare, early morning buses depart daily for Hauna, but they don't reach the tea estates. Get off at the end of the line and look for a local bus continuing to Aberfoyle. Hitching is possible, but unpredictable.

Coming from Nyanga, a good road turns off 27km south of Juliasdale and passes through pine forests before it descends and twists steeply down the escarpment and into the valley. There's also a steep and tedious 4WD route which descends from Troutbeck into the northern end of Honde Valley.

# Chimanimani Area

Chimanimani likes to call itself 'the best kept secret in Zimbabwe', but the secret is now out. Enclosed by green hills on three sides and open on the fourth side to the dramatic wall of the beguiling Chimanimani Range, its appeal is undeniable.

The first European visitor to Chimanimani was George Benjamin Dunbar Moodie of Melsetter on the Orkney island of Hoy. He duly attached the name of his home town to the mountain district and spread word of its beauty to Martinus Martin, who subsequently led a contingency of settlers from South Africa in November 1894.

The post-independence name, Chimanimani, is derived from the Manyika name for

ZIMBABWE

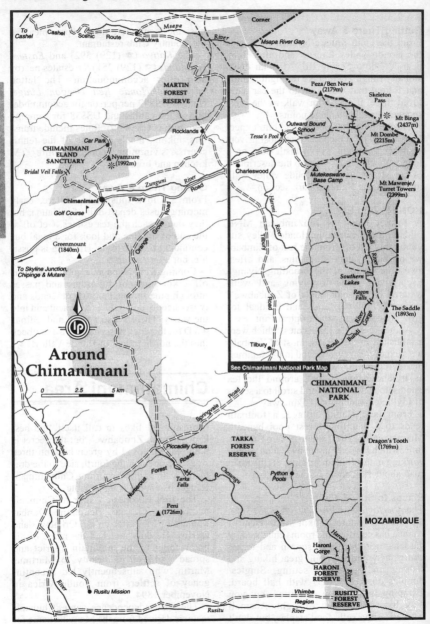

# Around Chimanimani

0    2.5    5 km

To Cashel
Cashel Scenic Route
Chikukwa
Msapa River
Corner
Msapa River Gap

MARTIN FOREST RESERVE

Rocklands

Peza/Ben Nevis (2179m)
Skeleton Pass
Mt Binga (2437m)

CHIMANIMANI ELAND SANCTUARY
Car Park
Nyamzure (1992m)
Bridal Veil Falls

Outward Bound School
Tessa's Pool
Mt Dombe (2215m)

Charleswood
Mutekeswane Base Camp
Mt Mawenje/Turret Towers (2399m)

Chimanimani
Golf Course
Tilbury
Zunguni River
Zunguni Road

Haroni River
Tilbury Road

Greenmount (1840m)

To Skyline Junction, Chipinge & Mutare

Southern Lakes
Ragon Falls
Bundi River
Bundi River Gorge

Orange Grove Road

Tilbury

The Saddle (1893m)

See Chimanimani National Park Map

Tilbury Road

CHIMANIMANI NATIONAL PARK

Springvale Road

Piccadilly Circus

TARKA FOREST RESERVE

Numerous Forest Roads
Tarka Falls

Chesungu River

Python Pools

Dragon's Tooth (1769m)

Peni (1726m)

MOZAMBIQUE

Nyahodi River

Haroni River
Haroni Gorge

HARONI FOREST RESERVE

RUSITU FOREST RESERVE

Rusitu Mission

Vhimba Region

Rusitu River
Rusitu River

DAVID WALL

Great Zimbabwe, the ancient Shona capital.

DAVID WALL

Hike through the cool Eastern Highlands (Zim).

JULIET COOMBE

The remote Diana's Vow is the site of an intriguing rock painting (Zim).

Homework done, lunch packed, ready for school, Bulawayo (Zim).

An African interpretation of biblical stories at Cyrene Mission, near Bulawayo (Zim).

a place that must be passed single file, presumably referring to the narrow gap where the Msapa River flows through the range from Zimbabwe to Mozambique, followed closely by a narrow footpath. The name has been enlarged to include the entire mountain range, as well as the village.

## CASHEL VALLEY

The fertile Cashel Valley was named after Colonel R Cashel of the British South Africa Police, who retired there after WWI. In the 1970s, it was the site of a successful agricultural scheme but, after independence, this unravelled and agriculture has largely been abandoned. The valley lies amid some lovely mountain scenery and, if you have a car, it's worth a quick side trip from the Wengezi-Chimanimani road.

## CHIMANIMANI

Chimanimani village is the main service centre for the district, and a good base for visits to the surrounding mountain country.

### Information
**Tourist Office** The helpful Publicity Association (☎ (126) 2294), PO Box 75, offers tourist information and sells the *Milkmaps Guides* (US$0.75), which detail local hill walks, as well as sketch maps of park hiking routes and Chimanimani area topo sheets. It's open daily from 10 am to noon and 2 to 4.30 pm.

Note that the Chimanimani Eland Sanctuary and Bridal Veil Falls have recently been combined into a sort of Chimanimani National Park annexe, requiring payment of National Parks fees. For foreigners that's US$5 per day.

**Money** The Commercial Bank of Zimbabwe does currency exchange on Monday, Tuesday, Thursday and Friday from 8 am to 2.30 pm; Wednesday from 8 am to 1 pm; and Saturday from 8 to 11 am.

**Emergency Services** For Mountain Rescue services, dial (☎ (126) 2411) and ask for the officer in charge.

**Bookshop** Zvokupona Bookshop & Stationery sells limited reading material and offers photocopy services on weekdays

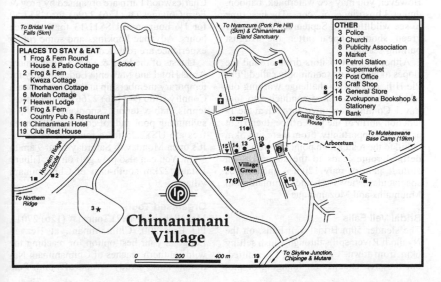

**PLACES TO STAY & EAT**
1 Frog & Fern Round House & Patio Cottage
2 Frog & Fern Kweza Cottage
5 Thorhaven Cottage
6 Moriah Cottage
7 Heaven Lodge
15 Frog & Fern Country Pub & Restaurant
18 Chimanimani Hotel
19 Club Rest House

**OTHER**
3 Police
4 Church
8 Publicity Association
9 Market
10 Petrol Station
11 Supermarket
12 Post Office
13 Craft Shop
14 General Store
16 Zvokupona Bookshop & Stationery
17 Bank

To Bridal Veil Falls (5km)
To Nyamzure (Pork Pie Hill) (5km) & Chimanimani Eland Sanctuary
School
Cashel Scenic Route
To Mutekeswane Base Camp (19km)
Arboretum
Northern Ridge Route
To Northern Ridge
Village Green
Chimanimani Village
To Skyline Junction, Chipinge & Mutare
0    200    400 m

from 8 am to 5 pm. Film is sold at the Chimanimani Arms Hotel gift shop.

## Arboretum

The small forested area in front of the Publicity Association was first fenced in 1960 and is now home to a range of bird and tree species. It's maintained by local volunteers and funds raised by Publicity Association map sales, and makes a nice spot for a stroll or a picnic.

## Chimanimani Eland Sanctuary & Nyamzure

The 18 sq km Chimanimani Eland Sanctuary was established to protect eland and other antelope which found it difficult to resist young shoots of maize and coffee and pine saplings in the surrounding agricultural and timber lands.

Eland are Africa's largest antelope, reaching nearly 2m in height and weighing up to 1000kg. The odd thing about the Eland Sanctuary is the conspicuous absence of eland. Apparently, the sanctuary concept was flawed and they were all poached, ostensibly by Mozambican insurgents. However, you may see waterbuck, baboon, duiker, klipspringer or zebra. The best time to see wildlife is in September, when new green shoots appear after the August burning season.

Although most visitors drive around the slopes of Nyamzure (commonly called Pork Pie Hill, and it's no challenge working out why), the track is more conducive to foot travel. Coming from town, turn left at the T-junction north of the post office, then right at the first opportunity. From there, it's 5km uphill to the road's high point, where a well-defined route leads to the summit – an altitude gain of only 120m – and affords spectacular views of the Chimanimani Mountains and Mozambique.

## Bridal Veil Falls

The slender 50m Bridal Veil Falls, on the Nyahodi River, spills through a lush setting 6km from town. Camping isn't permitted, but the area is super for lounging or picnicking in the tree-filtered sunlight. The waterfall pool may invite swimming, but the icy water in this shaded niche will put off all but determined swimmers (or anyone carelessly climbing on the slippery, slimy rocks around the pool).

From town, it's an easy and pleasant 6km walk along the road, which twists, climbs and descends around wooded slopes to the falls car park. Note that robbery is a problem on this route; avoid going alone or carrying valuables.

For a longer walk, keep following the road to a cattle grid 2km beyond the falls. Here, turn left up the fence line until you gain the ridge, then turn left along the southern boundary of the Chimanimani Eland Sanctuary and follow it for 4km. At this point, descend the ridge to the road and turn left. You'll meet up with the Bridal Veil Falls road less than 1km from Chimanimani. Allow four hours for the entire loop.

## Activities

For novices, horse-riding trips around the village are available for US$5 per hour; contact Tempe (☎ (126) 2496). Rides on Charleswood Farm are organised by Frog & Fern Cottages (☎ (126) 2294) for US$7.50 for 1½ hours and US$11/13 for two/three hours. Advance bookings and some riding experience are required.

Guests of the Frog & Fern, Chimanimani Arms Hotel and Mawenje Lodge qualify for temporary membership at the Chimanimani Country Club (☎ (126) 2266), which offers tennis, table tennis, snooker, squash, a swimming pool and, of course, golf. Green fees are US$2.25 for a round of 18 holes. It's open Monday to Saturday from 9 am to 5 pm. You can also play golf on the Tilbury Estate, 22km south-east of Chimanimani village.

## Organised Tours

Mahobahoba (MH2) Tours (☎ (126) 2701), PO Box 200, Chimanimani, at Heaven Lodge is your best option for reaching the wild southern reaches of Chimanimani National Park. Andy Woodruff and Pete

Baxter lead hikes to and through the Haroni River Gorge; around the Mozambican plateaux; and into the Vhimba communal lands near the Haroni and Rusitu Forest Reserves. They also run mountain biking trips and even organise abseiling into a 350m limestone sinkhole. Five-day hiking and camping trips average around US$100 per person (with a minimum of three people), including food but not park fees.

MH2 also runs transfers, sells butane cartridges and hires sleeping bags and camp stoves.

## Places to Stay

The most popular budget accommodation is quirky *Heaven Lodge* (☎/fax (126) 2701; <heaven@harare.iafrica.com>), 300m out on the national park road. This unpretentious crash pad oscillates between sedate and wild, but the music can be good and it enjoys one of the best views in town. Dorm beds/mattresses cost US$4.50/3.50, doubles are US$13, draughty A-frame huts are US$21 and camping is US$2.50 per person. Cooked meals include vegetarian choices and an hour of mountain steam in the sauna is US$2. There have been reports of thefts from the safe here but new, more vigilant management has recently taken over. It might still be wise to make a careful note of how much cash you leave in the safe.

The alternative budget choice is the quieter *Club Rest House* (☎ (126) 2266), 500m from the village. Claustrophobic huts cost US$10/13 for one/two people, a dorm mattress is US$2 and camping costs US$2.50 per tent plus US$0.50 per person.

The *Frog & Fern* (☎ (126) 2840 or 2294), in the heights, consists of three lovely cottages. The architecturally interesting stone and thatch Round House is divided into four rooms, accommodating a total of six people. The smaller Patio Cottage is adjacent to the Round House, and Kweza Cottage, also of stone and thatch, has one double and three twin rooms. Self-catering costs US$25 per person; B&B is US$32. Guests may use the common lounge, kitchen and dining room.

*Moriah Cottage* (☎ (126) 2595; fax 2884), which sits on the slopes of Pork Pie Hill, sleeps six people and offers stunning views of the Chimanimani range. Bed and breakfast costs US$23 per person and self catering is US$20. The self-catering *Thorhaven Cottage* costs US$8.50 per person for up to three people, or US$25 for four. To book, see Lauren at the petrol station.

The Sheraton set is out of luck in Chimanimani, but next best are the beautifully-located stone and thatch chalets at Wally And Leslie Johnson's *Mawenje Mountain Lodge* (☎ (126) 25441; fax 2886), run by Wally and Leslie Johnson. Mawenje lies on Charleswood Estate en route into Chimanimani National Park. Accommodation costs US$100 per person.

The three-star *Chimanimani Arms Hotel* (☎ (126) 2511; fax 2515) is a grand but faded colonial wonder (completed in 1953), surrounded by gardens and overlooking some of Zimbabwe's finest mountain views. Single/double rooms with fireplaces, balconies and big antique bathtubs cost US$36/56 – ask for a mountain view. Family rooms for up to four people are US$62.50. If you want to immerse yourself in luxury (or a deep hot bath) after a tramp around the mountains, this is the place. The laundry service is also useful.

You can camp in the hotel gardens and use the hotel baths for US$3.50 per person. There's a guard at night, but theft is still a problem (the perpetrators are as frequently simian as human) so lock up your valuables and baboon-tempting goodies in the hotel storeroom. While visiting the national park, hotel guests may leave their luggage for no charge.

## Places to Eat

The *Chimanimani Arms Hotel* dining room offers an international menu at suitably low prices. The partially buffet-style English breakfast is good value but other meals are less predictable.

At the once-popular *Beta Restaurant & Bar* the emphasis is now on the bar, but the walls still bear the doodles of travellers past and it may someday revert to its former glory. It's open 6 am to 11 pm. Fortunately, a new restaurant is being opened and promises to be extremely good.

Several village shops sell essential groceries and the market has a selection of produce. *Heaven Lodge* sells delicious Chimanimani cheese, which goes well on mountain hikes.

### Things to Buy
Near the village market you'll find a small co-operative shop selling local handicrafts, particularly *gudza* (chewed bark) dolls and bags. Another local speciality is the delicious garlic and peppercorn Chimanimani cheese, which is produced on a farm 20km out of town on the Cashel scenic route and is distributed through Heaven Lodge, the Frog & Fern Cottages, the Chimanimani Bottle Store and the Nyanyadzi Hot Springs resort. Don't miss it!

### Getting There & Away
Two or three daily buses leave Sakubva in Mutare between 7 and 10.30 am. From Chimanimani, they leave around 5 am, 11 am and noon (US$2.50).

Hitching isn't bad, but may result in a series of short lifts rather than a single lift to or from Mutare. The route from Chipinge is normally easier than from Wengezi Junction (between Mutare and Birchenough Bridge). Don't consider hitching the scenic route through Cashel Valley unless you can handle a good long walk.

### Getting Around
Mahobahoba (MH2) Tours (☎ (126) 2701), PO Box 200, Chimanimani, runs transfers to Mutekeswane Base Camp (US$5 return) from Heaven Lodge at 8 am daily (at busy times, there's also an early run at 7 am) and from Mutekeswane at 5 pm. Transfers to Corner cost around US$10 per person and transfers to Haroni and Rusitu forest reserves can be arranged when they're heading down to pick up hiking groups. MH2 also hires out mountain bikes for

US$3.50/6 for two/four hours or US$12 for the whole day.

## CHIMANIMANI NATIONAL PARK
The formidable mountain wall opposite Chimanimani village is the heart of Chimanimani National Park, a wilderness wonderland of steep sandstone peaks and towers, clear rivers, savanna valleys and forests of stone columns. The water is good to drink and the pools safe for swimming; orchids and hibiscus grow on the tangled slopes; and lobelia, heather, aloes and many species of meadowland wildflowers carpet the intermittent savanna plains.

Chimanimani isn't a game park, but it does have baboons, which screech through the night, and several species of retiring antelope, including blue duiker, klipspringer and waterbuck. Rangers report that leopard are common (though rarely observed) and that lion and buffalo are occasional visitors to the park's remote southern extremes.

### Tessa's Pool
On a marked track off the Outward Bound approach road lies Tessa's Pool, where you'll find a classic swimming hole and a rope swing, along with a barbecue shelter with braai pits. It's actually one of series of three pools on government land outside the national park. Most visitors stop on their way to the mountains, but it's even more welcome after a long hike, especially the Hadange River descent.

The nearby Outward Bound school (☎ (126) 25440), which leases this land, uses the pool for some of its courses, so phone in advance to find out when it's available. They restrict visits to the pool to between 9 am and 4 pm and prohibit picnicking or climbing. Visitor numbers are limited to groups of 10. (Note that Outward Bound has also asked us to discourage tourists from inquiring about their courses.)

### Mutekeswane Base Camp
For most hikers, Mutekeswane Base Camp, 19km from Chimanimani village, is the entry point to Chimanimani National Park.

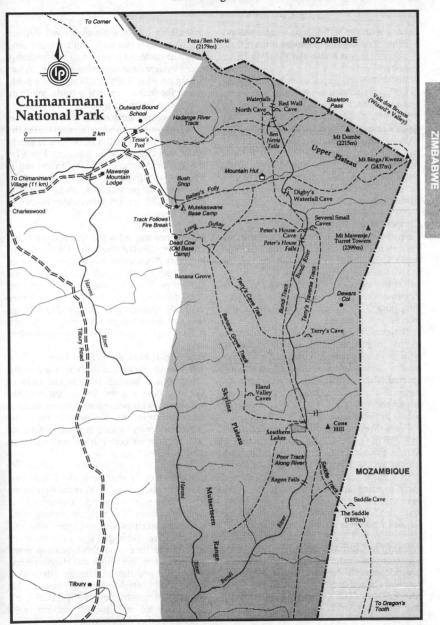

ZIMBABWE

There's a ranger station and a campground with hot showers and elaborate braai pits. If you're driving, it's also the place to leave your car.

In the summer, the office is open Monday to Friday from 6 am to noon and 2 to 5 pm, and on Saturday from 6 am to 12.30 pm. In the winter, it's open 7 am to noon and 2 to 4 pm weekdays, and 8 am to 12.30 pm Saturday. Here visitors must report, sign in and pay fees (foreigners pay US$4.20 for the first day or US$8.50 for two to seven days, plus US$5 per night) before proceeding into the park. You can also pick up Bundi River fishing permits.

## Corner

This appendage to Chimanimani National Park is a salient which juts into Mozambique, separated from the rest of the park by the Martin Forest Reserve and the communal lands along the Mozambique border. The two sections are connected by a 10km-long and 300m-wide swathe along the international boundary.

National Parks has discussed constructing lodges in Corner but, as yet, it remains wild and undeveloped. The highlight is the narrow 'chimanimani' through the constricted Msapa River Gap, which gave its name to the entire region. You can camp anywhere in Corner, but firewood collection is prohibited.

From Chimanimani, Corner is accessible by vehicle on the Cashel scenic route via Martin Forest Reserve and the village of Chikukwa. A daily bus to Chikukwa Business Centre leaves Chimanimani in the early evening and returns early the next morning, but from there, it's a good 10km walk into Corner. Park fees are collected by rangers who greet arriving visitors.

## Walking in Chimanimani

Chimanimani National Park, which is accessible only to foot traffic, is a hikers' paradise. Whether you're day-hiking from Mutekeswane Base Camp or making a five-day wilderness trek, this place will get a grip on you.

Walking tracks are mostly well defined but if you lose the way, don't wander onto a trail of flattened grass – this was probably made by someone else who was lost. When hiking on wide trails or through thick bush, watch for snakes; on major trails, you may even see a lounging python.

Moving surface water in Chimanimani is potable (quick-flowing streams are the cleanest), but it's still a good idea to purify water (see Health in the Regional Facts for the Visitor chapter). Walking in the sun is hot, dry work; you should carry at least 1L of water per person and, away from the Bundi River, top up your water bottles at every opportunity.

**Maps** Photocopied walking maps are available sporadically from the Chimanimani Publicity Association and at Heaven Lodge, but the map in this book should suffice for most trips. The Ordnance Survey mapping dates from the early 1930s (the Melsetter 1:50,000 quadrangle, sheets C1, C3 and D4) and doesn't depict walking tracks, but it's essential for cross-country exploration.

**Warning** Hikers around the higher peaks and back country must remain aware of the Mozambique border. It's marked only at Skeleton Pass and the Saddle but possible encounters with unexploded mines make it especially relevant. Keeping to the Zimbabwe side won't guarantee your safety but your chances are better. It's safest to stick to well-travelled tracks.

The only track to the park's southern extremes leaves Zimbabwe at the Saddle and passes through 8km of Mozambique territory before re-entering Zimbabwe at Dragon's Tooth. To reach the remote south without entering Mozambique, you can either drive through Rusitu Forest or attempt the long slog through deep grass and bush along the Bundi and Haroni rivers. While the popular Mt Binga climb also loops briefly into Mozambique (in fact, Mt Binga is Mozambique's highest peak), it's well travelled and doesn't present more risks than other park hiking routes.

**Bailey's Folly** Bailey's Folly is the shortest and most popular route between Mutekeswane and the mountain hut. It's a straightforward track which leads up through groves of msasa trees, then levels off a couple of times before passing through a magnificent forest of standing rocks. After crossing a meadow, it winds down to the mountain hut above Bundi Valley. The walk takes two to three hours, depending on how may times you are distracted by the scenery.

**Hadange River Track** This alternative route to the mountain hut begins near the Outward Bound school and follows the Hadange River up a shadowy ravine to connect with the Bundi River track just below North Cave. If it has recently rained or the track is wet, the passage may be muddy, slippery and generally difficult, so you may prefer to opt for the easier Bailey's Folly route.

However, lots of hikers descend by this route, thanks to the incentive provided by Tessa's Pool at the bottom. The track tends to be quite muddy and slippery, so take it easy.

**Skeleton Pass** Skeleton Pass, once notorious as a guerrilla route between Zimbabwe and Mozambique, is now a major trade route between the two countries. At the top is a sign denoting the frontier, an easy 40 minute walk from the mountain hut, and beyond this the path winds into the Vale dos Bruxos (Wizard's Valley).

Many people rush up to Skeleton Pass in the morning, yawn and retreat from the singularly unspectacular sight of a bright glaring sun and hazy hills fading into a nondescript horizon. In the late afternoon, however – provided the sun is shining – you'll be treated to an unsurpassed view into the Vale dos Bruxos. You'll be thrilled by the sight of range after range of green Mozambican mountains divided by plunging valleys laid out before you. On a clear day, the distant blue line of the Indian Ocean meets the horizon.

**Mt Binga** The highest point in the Chimanimani Range, 2437m Mt Binga on the Mozambique border (again, it's also the highest point in Mozambique), is a stiff two to three hour climb from the mountain hut. If you have fine weather, don't miss it. The view from the top encompasses a vast amount of territory and you can sometimes see right across Mozambique to the Indian Ocean.

Carry at least 1L of water per person. The last stream is less than halfway between the hut and the summit, so drink deeply and fill your water bottle for the steep, hot climb to the peak. There's a reasonably level camp site 150 to 200m below the peak, but no water is available.

**Southern Lakes** Little more than wide spots in a U-turn bend of the Bundi River, the murky pools known as Southern Lakes provide a nice lunch spot or, if you have a tent, a passable camp site.

From Southern Lakes, another track heads south-east towards the Saddle. Ragon Falls are 4km south along the river on a less clear track. They're not terribly exciting, but make a pleasant day trip from Southern Lakes.

**The Saddle** The Saddle, at 1893m, is another pass into Mozambique. To get there, cross the Bundi River between the first and second Southern Lakes and walk south along the river until you reach a steep track heading up the slope. From there, it's about an hour to the top.

**Banana Grove & Long Gulley** These two routes up to the first level of peaks begin south of Mutekeswane. The Banana Grove Track, named for the grove of strelitzia trees growing alongside it, is a gentler ascent than the more popular Bailey's Folly. It is also a considerably longer route to the caves and mountain hut, but provides access to Southern Lakes. The lush, rocky ravine known as Long Gulley is a bit steeper, but provides ready access to Digby's Waterfall Cave.

Both routes begin at Mutekeswane. Descend steeply from the south side of the road, about 250m west of the ranger's office. At the bottom, slop your way through the small and disagreeable swamp, then follow the up-and-down fire break to the old base camp, enigmatically known as Dead Cow. Here, the track turns sharply to the east and winds upward. At the very faint fork about 500m above Dead Cow (look for a patch of bare red earth to your left), you must choose your route. The left fork ascends Long Gulley and the right one climbs to Banana Grove. At the ridgetop, hikers for Southern Lakes should follow the downward-trending track, which hits the Bundi River at the northernmost Southern Lake. Allow four to five hours for this hike.

The Banana Grove route is most often used by hikers making a circuit of the park to Mutekeswane via Southern Lakes. Coming from the mountain hut, head south along the Bundi River, watching carefully on your right as you approach the first Southern Lake. There you'll see the red-earth track, which climbs steeply about 30m above the main river route before levelling off. Allow seven to nine hours to walk from the mountain hut to Mutekeswane via Southern Lakes and Banana Grove.

### Places to Stay
If you walk from Chimanimani village to the park, you may spend the first night at *Mutekeswane Base Camp*, where steep slopes mean that camp sites occupy stone-walled terraces. From there you'll have broad vistas of nearby forested hills and the red-earth coffee plantations beyond. Amazingly, hot baths and showers are available, but there's no electricity in the ablutions block so bring a torch!

Overlooking the Bundi Valley, across the first range of peaks, two to three hours from Mutekeswane, is a classic stone mountain hut, complete with wooden bed bases, propane cooking rings (but no cutlery or cooking implements) and cold showers. It comfortably sleeps from 20 to 30 people but foreigners must pay US$10 per person

– which is absurdly high by Zimbabwe standards – and it remains empty most of the time. Non-guests may use the burners to cook for US$1 per meal, but there's often no propane.

Your best bet is to camp. The Bundi Valley is riddled with small caves and rock overhangs which make ideal sites, so you don't necessarily need a tent. The nicest and most accessible caves lie near the valley's northern end. North Cave, a 30 minute walk from the mountain hut, overlooks a waterfall and opens onto views of the highest peaks. Above the waterfall is a pool, good for a cold swim, and Red Wall Cave lies 10 minutes further along. These are the first caves to be occupied, so get an early start from base camp.

Down the valley from the hut is Digby's Waterfall Cave, where the river provides a swimming hole, and beyond that is Peter's House Cave. Still further along, 2.5km north of Southern Lakes and two hours from the hut, is Terry's Cave, which is divided into two rooms by an artificial stone wall. It's above the eastern bank of the river and not easily found, but there's a faint track leading from the river.

However, don't leave anything edible in the caves while you're out and about – baboons will plunder anything and ravenous rodents and birds will happily gnaw through your pack to get at whatever's inside.

### Getting There & Away
Since the park road is now tarred as far as Charleswood, traffic is increasing and hitching is easier than it once was. Inquire at Heaven Lodge or the Chimanimani Arms Hotel to find someone heading in your direction.

Three people in Chimanimani village now provide transfers to Mutekeswane. Thanks to the road conditions beyond Charleswood, they charge US$16.50 per trip, but this is reasonable if you have a full complement of six people. For information, contact the Publicity Association, Frog & Fern B&B or Heaven Lodge.

Otherwise, you can walk the 19km road to Mutekeswane. It's not an unpleasant prospect but takes four hours in either direction. From Chimanimani village, set out along the Tilbury road for 9km to Charleswood. Turn left at the coffee plantation and immediately take the right fork. After 5km, you'll reach the Outward Bound/Tessa's Pool turn-off. From there, it's a further 5km to Mutekeswane Base Camp.

An occasional bus goes as far as Charleswood, but it leaves in the evening and is therefore of limited use for travellers heading for the national park.

## HARONI & RUSITU FOREST RESERVES

These two remote reserves take in parts of the Haroni and Rusitu valleys, bordering the southernmost extreme of Chimanimani National Park. Known locally as Chizire and Nyakwaa, they're considered sacred to people in the adjacent Vhimba Communal Lands. Along with the neighbouring Makurupini area in Chimanimani National Park, they represent Zimbabwe's only lowland rainforests, and harbour wild orchids, ferns and such rare trees as wild coffee (*Coffea salvatrix*) and large-fruited rinorea (*Rinorea arborea*). They're best known, however, for their unique birdlife: the chestnut-fronted helmet shrike, the eastern honey-guide, the slender bulbul, Pel's fishing owl, black-headed apalis, blue-spotted dove, green coucal, Angola pitta and the Vanga flycatcher, among others. Other rare wildlife includes the Argus tree frog, the tree civet and Grant's lesser bushbaby.

The Wildlife Society of Zimbabwe plans to mark and fence the reserve boundaries, then establish a hardwood nursery and interpretive centre at nearby Vhimba School. Children would learn to tend seedlings and thereby provide financial support for the school. For information, contact the Secretary, Wildlife Society of Zimbabwe, Chipinge Branch, PO Box 382, Chipinge.

Currently, there are also plans to develop a CAMPFIRE programme, with a camp site, chalets, a fishing dam, and an introduction to traditional lifestyles. For a progress report, contact Ms Helen Steward (☎ (126) 2272 or 2616), The Campfire Unit, Chimanimani Rural District Council, PO Box 65, Chimanimani.

### Organised Tours

Mahobahoba (MH2) Tours in Chimanimani runs adventure hiking tours in the Haroni and Rusitu forest reserves, the Vhimba communal lands and the southern part of Chimanimani National Park. For more information, see Organised Tours under Chimanimani.

Peter Ginn, on the Southdown Tea Estate near Marondera (☎ (179) 23411; <pgbs@mango.zw>) PO Box 44, Marondera, runs birdwatching tours through both reserves. He charges US$300 per day for up to 10 participants.

### Getting There & Away

These remote reserves lie on the Mozambique border, 35km down a rugged 4WD track from the junction of the roads between Chimanimani, Chipinge and Birchenough Bridge. There's no public transport and precious little chance of finding a lift to this remote corner of the country.

## CHIPINGE

Chipinge, named after a local chief, lies in the heart of a rich agricultural district. This sleepy little town, with its corrugated iron roofs, jacaranda-lined streets and bougainvillea gardens, may remind you of a town somewhere in rural Australia. Most commercial farmers in Chipinge are descended from the Boers who arrived with the Moodie Trek and created a rather unique cultural enclave.

Much of the local wealth derives from the coffee and tea plantations spread across the rolling landscape towards the Mozambique border. There's a coffee research institute just off Mt Selinda road, and logging and wattle extraction operations on surrounding hillsides. Chipinge is also a dairying centre.

ZIMBABWE

## Places to Stay & Eat

The *Chiping Hotel* (☎ (127) 2226) has certainly seen better times but, unless you're set up for camping, it's your only option. Singles/doubles cost US$20/32 with attached bath or US$18/30 without a bath. The hotel restaurant is only average but otherwise there isn't much choice apart from the market snacks, the supermarkets or the *Busi-Grill* snack bar and takeaway.

The secluded riverside *campground* and *caravan park* lies 500m west of the confusion of the centre. Sites cost US$1.30 per tent, plus US$0.75 per person. For caravans, they charge US$3/4 without/with electric hook-ups.

*Kiledo Lodge* (☎/fax (127) 2944) is a self-catering getaway on a tea and coffee estate 18km east of Chipinge on the Eastern Border road. In this unique area, with stocked dams for fishing and an attached botanical reserve, there's a chance of seeing samango monkeys. It's also a good base for exploring the Haroni and Rusitu forest reserves. Thatched self-catering cottages cost US$46/72, with half board – and the meals are reputedly excellent. Book through Time for Africa (☎ (14) 703633; fax 703634; <safari@icon.co.zw>) in Harare.

Beside the Tanganda River on the Birchenough Bridge road is *Buffelsdrift Cottages* (☎ (127) 226220). These two self-catering cottages cost US$12 for two people and US$3 for each additional person, up to 12 people. The farm produces tobacco, coffee, wheat and tropical fruits, and enjoys a wealth of birdlife.

## Getting There & Away

Chipinge is the gateway to Mt Selinda, but otherwise, it's nothing to go out of your way for. Hitchers to or from Chimanimani are often stuck there. The bus terminal at the market square (three blocks east of the main street) serves adjoining communal lands, Birchenough Bridge, the lowveld and occasionally Chimanimani. There are also three or four buses daily to both Mutare and Masvingo and frequent services to nearby Mt Selinda.

## MT SELINDA

The village of Mt Selinda sits in a hilltop hollow above the Chipinge district coffee plantations. It revolves around a health mission founded by the American Board of Commissioners in 1893 and developed over the years into a vocational and agricultural training centre. In fact, the Mt Selinda mission was responsible for the first irrigation scheme in the dry scrubland around Nyanyadzi Hot Springs. The village abuts the Mozambique border and served as a refugee camp during that country's recent civil war.

Monument buffs may want to hunt up Swynnerton's Memorial, just north of the road into the village. This long-untended slab commemorates the work of the 19th century British naturalist and entomologist who settled in Chimanimani to catalogue local bugs and flora. His accomplishments include extensive studies on tsetse flies and, after WWI, service as the first game warden in Britain's newly acquired territory of Tanganyika (now Tanzania).

### Chirinda Forest Reserve

The Chirinda Forest Reserve, a 949 hectare slice of hardwood forest, is in fact the southernmost tropical rainforest in Africa. The red mahogany is relatively common on the eastern slopes of Zimbabwe's Eastern Highlands, and normally reaches heights of 20 to 30m. Its small, white and fragrant flowers bloom in early spring and the red wood polishes brilliantly. Africans use its bark to make an infusion against pneumonia, abdominal pains, gonorrhoea, and as an aphrodisiac, and the seeds of its brownish fruit to make aromatic oils.

Several other species of mahogany are also present; the most common is the *Trichilia dregeana* (forest mahogany) which has pinkish fine-grained wood. Stands of both types, as well as ironwood and other large trees, grow throughout Chirinda, particularly in the region known as Valley of the Giants. Birdwatchers may want to watch for Swynnerton's robin, which has one of its only habitats here.

Chirinda's dark and dank depths are criss-crossed with paths, but lovers of superlatives will gravitate towards the Big Tree route. This obvious track turns off the Mt Selinda road, just up the 'tree tunnel' from the mission hospital. And it leads to – you guessed it – Zimbabwe's biggest tree (or so it's claimed). This 1000-year-old, 66m-high and 15m round behemoth belongs to the species *Khaya nasica* (red mahogany).

An excellent book, *Chirinda Forest – a Visitors' Guide*, by Jonathan Timberlake and Phil Shaw, is available at the Chirinda Forest camp site or from the Zimbabwe Forestry Commission (☎ (14) 496878; fax 497066), PO Box HG595, Orange Grove Drive, Highlands, Harare.

### Places to Stay

There's now a tiny, organised 12-site *campground* (☎ (127) 224116) amid the trees of Chirinda Forest Reserve. In a bizarre twist of logic, however, someone determined that campers couldn't see the forest for the trees and decided to clear-cut a broad swathe to afford a view over the hill. Camping costs US$2.50 per tent and simple two-bed chalets with braai facilities are US$4.50. Note the unconventional toilet facilities. Bookings are available by phone or through the Ngungunyana Research Patrol, PO Box 6, Mt Selinda.

### Getting There & Away

Frequent but unscheduled buses do the 30km run between Chipinge and Mt Selinda, but hitching is a better option. The road may be sparsely travelled, but since Mt Selinda sits at the end of the line (the road continues into Mozambique but the border is closed), everyone will know where you're going.

## BIRCHENOUGH BRIDGE

Above the braided Save River, Birchenough Bridge rises like a mirage from the ruddy thorn and baobab scrub. If it appears that someone has simply lifted the Sydney Harbour Bridge and plopped it down in a most unlikely place, that's not far off the mark. Not surprisingly, this 378m-long span was designed by Ralph Freeman, who was also responsible for Sydney's 'Coat Hanger'.

Birchenough Bridge was named after Sir Henry Birchenough, chairman of the Beit Trust which financed its construction in 1935. His ashes now rest in one tower of the bridge. This strategic bridge, which appears on Zimbabwe's 20 cent coin, is guarded day and night against terrorist attacks and photography is prohibited from the span itself.

In addition to the stark beauty of the Save Communal Lands, Birchenough Bridge village boasts a vibrant rural market out of all proportion to the size of the population.

### Places to Stay

The friendly but seedy *Birchenough Bridge Hotel* (☎ (127) 225819) has single/double rooms for US$20/27; the dining room is just acceptable, but don't venture beyond the sadza. Campers may set up tents on the lawn, where they have a front-row view of the bridge itself. An alternative is the small *Enda Guest House* (☎ (124) 8221) west of town – go 2.5km towards Masvingo then right at the sign.

*Mapari Ranch* (☎ (120) 62671 or (124) 259), 12km west of town, sprawls over 23,000 hectares of the Save Valley. The *Stop-In*, on the main road, has four-bed chalets with en suite facilities for US$17 per chalet plus US$5 per person. Attached is a restaurant and caravan/camp site (US$3 per vehicle plus US$1 per person). Self-catering chalets at the Sabi River Camp, 16km off the road, cost US$11 per person. The wild camp site at Sabi River Bush Camp, 22km off the road on a 4WD track, has braai and ablutions facilities and costs US$2 per person. The Devuli River Bush Camp, 4km off the road, costs US$5 per person and is accessible by 2WD.

### Getting There & Away

At the bus terminal, you can make connections to Harare, Mutare, Chimanimani, Chipinge, Masvingo and even Chiredzi and

**ZIMBABWE**

Beitbridge. On Friday, most buses to Masvingo leave after 6 pm.

## NYANYADZI HOT SPRINGS

The *Nyanyadzi Hot Springs Resort* (☎ (126) 2367; fax 2328), which lies 32km north of Birchenough Bridge, was reduced to a heap of rubble during the war, but it has now been rebuilt by Lollie and Theo Nel. The large pool is filled by a piping hot natural spring, which reputedly has magical powers and curative properties. The relaxing spell is enhanced by its peaceful setting on communal lands between the dry highlands and the Odzi River.

Comfortable single/double lodges cost US$46/67, including three good meals. In the backpackers section, camping costs US$4 per person (including use of facilities), but there's a limit of five tents at a time. Day use costs US$2 per person.

There's a shop, open-air video lounge and a dam-view dining area for imaginative buffet lunches and dinners. There's always a vegetarian option – this is a health resort after all – and a range of breads and cheeses, including the famous Chimanimani cheese. Breakfast costs US$4.50, lunch is US$6.50 and dinner is US$8. Health treatments are available, including nutritional assessments, heat treatments, facials, aromatherapy, acupressure and reflexology massage.

### Getting There & Away

Transfers from Mutare with the resort staff cost US$2.50 per person. Alternatively, take any bus between Mutare and Birchenough Bridge. The resort lies 100m off the highway. North of Nyanyadzi along the Mutare road, watch for the river with the curious name of Umvumvumvu – a reference to the sound made by the water splashing over rocks.

# The Midlands & South-Eastern Zimbabwe

Travellers who seek out areas regarded by the tourist industry as uninteresting will find plenty of joy in the Midlands and south-eastern Zimbabwe. In fact, the region holds a great deal of interest, and only at Great Zimbabwe, the stone houses that gave their name to the entire country, will you encounter a lot of other tourists.

The Midlands are known as the highveld, while warmer, lower-lying south-eastern Zimbabwe is referred to as the lowveld. At the transition between the uplands and the south-east lies the town of Masvingo.

The highveld, sliced neatly through by the metal and mineral-rich Great Dyke, is the historical heart of Zimbabwean mining. Several thousand mines were already working when the European colonists arrived and the veins still produce enough gold, nickel, chromium, chrome and asbestos to keep the Midlands humming.

In the late 19th century, the route between Chegutu and Bulawayo came to be known as the Hunters Road, after the ivory hunters who travelled through this district when it was rich in elephant. Today, the region's only elephant roam the empty hill country around the remote town of Gokwe.

The scrubby lowveld, on the other hand, is dedicated mainly to ranching and agriculture. The eradication of the tsetse fly allowed ranchers to establish large cattle holdings and manage a meagre living on dry and previously uninhabited land. More recently, rivers such as the Save, Chiredzi and Limpopo have been tapped to transform parts of the lowveld into green and productive agricultural areas. Former thorn scrub now produces wheat, sugar cane and cotton, and fuels Zimbabwe's textile and refining industries.

The lowveld's finest attraction is the magnificent and little-visited Gonarezhou National Park. During Mozambique's civil war, this scenic park was used as a bush

## HIGHLIGHTS

- Visit the lovely Chilojo Cliffs and look for enormous elephant in Gonarezhou National Park
- Play polo-crosse at Mopani Park Farm
- Visit the historic mining town of Shurugwi
- Explore Great Zimbabwe, the largest ruins complex in sub-Saharan Africa
- Climb to the small but beautiful ruins at Nalatale

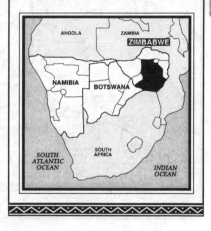

larder by cross-border insurgents and it remained closed to foreigners until 1994.

# The Midlands

Perhaps inspired by their own thrilling Midlands, early British colonists passed the moniker on to the open and nearly flat country from Harare south-west to Bulawayo and south to Masvingo.

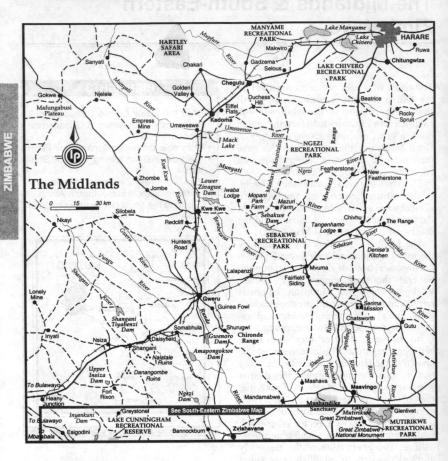

**The Midlands**

0    15    30 km

See South-Eastern Zimbabwe Map

## MANYAME RECREATIONAL PARK

The dam wall which created the 9 sq km Manyame Recreational Park (formerly Darwendale-Lake Robertson), 40km west of Harare, was constructed in 1976 to supply water to the capital. The lake brims with tiger fish, Hunyani salmon and five types of bream.

The National Parks picnic and camp sites have braai pits and ablutions; fishing permits are available from National Parks in Harare. Foreigners pay US$10 per day admission. From Harare, public buses go only as far as Darwendale and Norton; weekends are best for hitching.

## CHEGUTU

This soporific town of 22,000, formerly called Hartley, began as an 18th century Portuguese trading post. Sitting at the heart of Zimbabwe's cotton and maize farming, cattle ranching and gold and nickel mining districts, it likes to consider itself an administrative and commercial centre. In fact, anything that might liven things up typically whizzes through without looking back, making Chegutu a contender for Zimbabwe's least happening town.

## Places to Stay & Eat
The *Chegutu Hotel* provides rollicking poor-value accommodation for US$38. For light, trendy treats, see the *Dodhill Restaurant and Garden Centre*, north along the Harare road. Near the centre is the *Flying Pot Restaurant and Takeaway*, marked by two stranded and decrepit Dakota aircraft. Other choices include the *Sol y Mar Portuguese Takeaway*, specialising in peri-peri chicken, and the *Dairy Den*, which offers fast food and a quick exit.

## KADOMA
Although its name means 'silent', Kadoma (population 50,000) is louder than neighbouring Chegutu. It was founded by an enterprising trader in 1906 as a service centre for surrounding gold mines and its rich deposits of gold ore – as well as magnesite, nickel and copper – earned it the nickname Africa's Klondike.

Mining continues at nearby Eiffel Flats and along the tangled roads of Golden Valley, but Kadoma's current emphasis is on cotton, and the town now boasts weaving, spinning and dyeing mills, as well as a cotton research institute and a textile-industry training facility.

For visitors, the town's colonial architecture is of interest, as are the steam engines, steam roller and Mozambican coach lined up on the Kadoma Ranch Hotel grounds.

## Places to Stay & Eat
Kadoma is proud of its three-star *Kadoma Ranch Hotel* (☎ (168) 2321; fax 2325), complete with green lawns and even strutting peacocks. Single/double chalets cost US$46/68, lodges are US$54/78 and deluxe 'villas' are US$58/85. Rates include breakfast.

On Union St in the centre is the cheaper *Speck's Hotel* (☎ (168) 3302). The *Grand Hotel* (☎ (168) 4035), at Cameron Square, has a nice retro facade from the 'Klondike' days, but it's otherwise less than grand –

unless you're in the market for boozing followed by a brief romantic liaison.

## Getting There & Away
The express bus terminal is at the Kadoma Ranch Hotel.

## SEBAKWE & NGEZI NATIONAL RECREATION PARKS
These twin dams, lost in the bush between the Masvingo and Bulawayo roads, mainly attract the fishing crowd (swimming is out due to bilharzia). However, they're often deserted, so if you like quiet relaxation, consider visiting these forgotten parks.

### Sebakwe Dam
The height of the dam wall at the 27 sq km Sebakwe park was increased by 7m in the late 1980s. When full, the resulting dam, which is pinched in the middle by two fingers of the Great Dyke, is Zimbabwe's fourth largest lake.

### Ngezi Dam
The 63 sq km Ngezi park is quite a long way from anywhere. It has camp sites and lodges, which should be booked through National Parks. For information, contact the senior ranger (☎ (1557) 2405), Ngezi Recreational Park, PO Box 8046, Kwe Kwe.

### Getting There & Away
Sebakwe lies 10km from the Kwe Kwe-Mvuma road (the turn-off is 18km east of Kwe Kwe) and, by road, Ngezi lies about 90km north-west of Chivhu and 93km north-east of Kwe Kwe. There's no public transport to either park and hitching is probably a waste of time.

## KWE KWE
The unusual name of this midlands town of 60,000 people is derived from the sound made by croaking frogs along the river banks, but the frogs have now been drowned out by the hum of progress. In the town's promotional tourist hand-out, which features enticing photos of 'rolled barbed

ZIMBABWE

wire awaiting transport', an 'automatic mixer and bagging of castable material', and 'a view of the water pumping station at Dutchman's Pool', you'll learn that Kwe Kwe is, in fact, 'Where Industry Leads the Nation'. It then goes on to boast that 'Kwe Kwe could fill 1500 swimming pools with water every day'. The frogs may be happy to hear that, but one wonders why we're not all rushing off to visit Kwe Kwe!

If you do pass through, however, stroll around the town centre, which is crowded with lovely colonial architecture. The town also has one of the country's finest museums.

## History
Despite its faded present, Kwe Kwe has enjoyed a rich past and has the tailings dumps to prove it. This gold-producing region has been known for at least a thousand years and the district brims with ancient workings. In the late 19th century, rumours of an African El Dorado attracted hordes of English fortune-seekers from South Africa. Although the pickings never reached the levels they did in the fabulously rich goldfields further south, Kwe Kwe produced enough booty to justify its existence.

Kwe Kwe's first modern gold-mining operation, one of Zimbabwe's oldest, was the Globe and Phoenix. In later years, iron smelting and steel production arrived in Kwe Kwe and similar operations were set up by ZISCO (Zimbabwe Iron and Steel Company) at nearby Redcliff. The gold veins are almost exhausted but the area produces chromium, silica and copper, and mining remains the town's major earner.

## Mosque
Visitors to Kwe Kwe may be surprised to find a dominating and colourfully painted mosque in the centre. The town is the unlikely headquarters of Zimbabwe's Islamic Mission.

## National Museum of Gold Mining
This friendly, worthwhile stop provides a fascinating introduction to commercial gold mining in Zimbabwe, past and present. You're greeted by a working scale model of the Globe and Phoenix mine which bears a startling resemblance to the real thing which grinds away just off the museum grounds.

The Paper House, Zimbabwe's first prefabricated building, really is made of paper. The outer walls are constructed of wire mesh-reinforced papier-mâché mounted on a wooden frame, while the inner panels are of cardboard. It was imported from Great Britain in 1894 as the residence of the Globe and Phoenix mine's general manager but, in fact, became the mine office.

The mechanical detritus scattered about the lawns – pumps and crushers, graders and compressors – represent 100 years of gold mining in southern Africa and the museum attendant can explain the function of every piece. There are also tentative plans to construct an artificial mine shaft on the grounds, allowing visitors to go underground. It's open from 9 am to 5 pm daily; foreigners pay US$2 for admission and a guided tour.

## Lower Zivagwe Dam (Dutchman's Pool)
Lower Zivagwe dam, constructed in 1954 to provide water for Kwe Kwe, is set amid peaceful woodland 6km north of town. Birdlife includes ducks, herons, hornbills, African jacanas, cormorants, francolins and even fish eagles.

Use of the Angling Society picnic site and campground costs US$1 per person, and fishing is permitted. Head 2km north of town on the Harare road and take the signposted turning east; it's then 4km to the dam.

## Sable Park Game Park & Snake Farm
Just 300m from Lower Zivagwe dam is a small but scenic game park with sable, tsessebe, kudu, impala, steenbok, eland, duiker, wildebeest, dassies, zebra and warthog. It's open on weekends and public holidays, but you must have a vehicle. The

adjacent snake enclosure displays various serpentine specimens – pythons, gaboon vipers etc – as well as a few crocodiles. Admission to both the game park and the snake enclosure is US$1.

## Places to Stay

Kwe Kwe's *caravan park*, behind the cemetery on Ely Drive, south of town, is dirty, ill-kept and occupied mainly by full-time tenants working in local industry. There's no guard so don't leave anything of value.

Of the several forgettable accommodation choices, the best is the three-star *Golden Mile Motel* (☎ (155) 3711; fax 3120). Standard singles/doubles cost US$42/50, and there's a nice pool-side bar. Breakfast is an additional US$2.50.

The decent one-star *Shamwari Hotel* (☎ (155) 2387; fax 2388), on the main street, costs US$31/42. Next down the scale is the no-star *Sebakwe Machipisa Hotel* (☎ (155) 2981), a cheap but clean digs where the main attraction is boozing. Singles/doubles with shared bath cost US$17/21. The *Phoenix Hotel* (☎ (155) 3748) on Second St is the local bottom end in nearly every way and the dilapidated *Sumba Hotel*, on Nelson Mandela Way near Second St, is actually just a local bar.

## Places to Stay – Out of Town

Kwe Kwe is now emerging as a travellers destination thanks to several remote farms which have opened their doors to budget travellers.

The popular *Mopani Park Farm* (☎ (155) 247822; fax 4039), 49km from Kwe Kwe, caters especially to overland trucks and offers a friendly party atmosphere in the bush. Owners Kathie and Rudy have combined their property with seven other farms to form a 3800 hectare private nature reserve and rhino conservation area, which has become extremely popular with equestrians. They have 55 horses and welcome experienced riders and beginners.

Accommodation in rooms or tree houses with/without breakfast and game-based dinners costs US$13/7, camping is US$9/2

per person (plus US$1 to use the pool, bar and video). Horse rides cost US$9 for a sunrise jaunt and US$30 for a six hour picnic ride. Riding lessons for novices are US$9 per hour and anyone can attempt polo-crosse, which is extremely popular, for US$7 per hour. Advanced equestrians can try cross-country riding and jumping for US$7 per hour. Two/three-day horseback safaris in the rhino conservation area or to Sebakwe dam cost US$200/300, with full board and camping. Transfers from town are US$2.

The more upmarket 5600 hectare *Mazuri Farm* (☎ (155) 247523; fax 3027), run by Eleanor, Rob and Debbie Lowe, charges US$33 per person for lodges and full board. They also cater to backpackers, with A-frames overlooking a lake for US$5 and camping for US$3. Amenities include a swimming pool and tennis courts. Horse-trekking, elephant rides, game drives and game walks are also available. Transfers from Kwe Kwe cost marginally extra; guests are met at the Odds and Ends shop on Third St in Kwe Kwe between 12.30 and 1.30 pm, but it's wise to phone and confirm.

The *Iwaba Lodge* (☎ (155) 20144; ☎/fax 24245; <tae31@dial.pipex.com>) is a 100 sq km private reserve in the Munyati Valley. Run by Justin and Ruth Seymour-Smith, it was a pioneer in rhino conservation and currently has over 10 black and 20 white rhino. Daily rates start at US$150 per person; for accommodation, meals and activities, you'll pay US$220. Road and air transfers are available on request.

## Places to Eat

For meals, the *Que Que Grill* at the Shamwari Hotel is Kwe Kwe's best eating spot. There's also a *Wimpy* just opposite the mosque. For inexpensive African fare, try either the *Africa Centre Restaurant* or the *Siyapambili Restaurant*.

## Getting There & Away

The Express Motorways terminal is at the Golden Mile Motel, 2km south of town on the Bulawayo road. Local bus services operate from the market. Trains between Harare and Bulawayo call in at Kwe Kwe in the small hours of the morning.

## GWERU

Gweru (population 105,000), Zimbabwe's third-largest city, may not be a tourist destination, but most overland travellers pass through at some stage and comment on its friendly small-town feel – a lot like 1950s Hill Valley in the film *Back to the Future*.

### History

Gweru's backdrop, Senga Hill, has been worked by agriculturalists almost continuously since the stone age, but modern Gweru wasn't founded until 1894, when Leander Starr Jameson thought the site would make an ideal service centre for the Midlands goldfields. The original name, Gwelo, meant 'steep' in the local vernacular, and probably referred to the sloping

banks of the Gweru River. Growth began in earnest in 1902 with the arrival of the Harare-Bulawayo railway line. On 18 June 1914, Gweru gained municipal status and officially became a city in October 1971.

### Information

The Publicity Association (☎ (154) 226), in City Hall on the corner of Eighth St and Robert Mugabe Way, is open from 8 am to 4.30 pm Monday to Friday. The American Express representative is Manica Travel Service (☎ (154) 23316) at Meikles on the corner of Robert Mugabe Way and Fifth St.

### Midlands Museum

Gweru is the home of Zimbabwe's military academy and its largest air base, and the Midlands Museum fittingly traces the country's military and police history and technology, from the earliest tribal wars through the Rhodesian years to modern

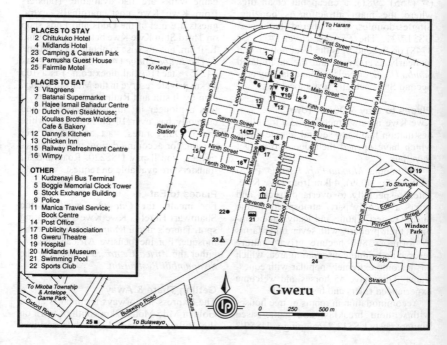

**PLACES TO STAY**
2  Chitukuko Hotel
4  Midlands Hotel
23  Camping & Caravan Park
24  Pamusha Guest House
25  Fairmile Motel

**PLACES TO EAT**
3  Vitagreens
7  Batanai Supermarket
8  Hajee Ismail Bahadur Centre
10  Dutch Oven Steakhouse;
     Koullas Brothers Waldorf
     Cafe & Bakery
12  Danny's Kitchen
13  Chicken Inn
15  Railway Refreshment Centre
16  Wimpy

**OTHER**
1  Kudzenayi Bus Terminal
5  Boggie Memorial Clock Tower
6  Stock Exchange Building
9  Police
11  Manica Travel Service;
     Book Centre
14  Post Office
17  Publicity Association
18  Gweru Theatre
19  Hospital
20  Midlands Museum
21  Swimming Pool
22  Sports Club

Gweru

times. Of particular interest are the historical military and police uniforms, and the descriptions of pre-colonial weapons and warfare. Most worthwhile is the attached aviation exhibit, which features more than 50 vintage and military aircraft.

The Midlands Museum is open daily (apart from Christmas and Good Friday) from 9 am to 5 pm. Foreigners pay US$2 admission.

### Historic Buildings
In the municipal gardens near the city hall, the 315-seat theatre is a 'civic pride and joy'; note the carved wooden mural depicting theatre through the ages. The colonial stock exchange, constructed in 1898, is Gweru's oldest building.

### Boggie Memorial Clock Tower
You can't miss the clock tower, which blocks Gweru's two main streets. This non-attraction was erected by Mrs Jeannie Boggie in 1937, as a memorial to her husband, Major WJ Boggie (who had died nine years earlier), and to 'all colonial pioneers and their beasts of burden'. Mr Boggie's remains were interred in the tower but, one post-independence morning in 1981, they were removed and the clock ceased functioning. Until they were repaired 10 years later, the hands on all four faces remained frozen at 10.50 am.

### Antelope Game Park
The zoo-like Antelope Game Park, 9km from Gweru, has most of Zimbabwe's antelope species, as well as giraffe, zebra and other wildlife. Large cats inhabit a separate enclosure.

Follow Bulawayo Rd (Robert Mugabe Way), turn right at Tratford Rd, then take a left on Oxford Rd and follow it out of town through Mkoba township to the park. It's open from 10 am to 5 pm daily, with feeding at 3 pm. Admission is US$1.

### Places to Stay
Gweru's green *Camping and Caravan Park* (☎ (154) 2929) abuts the sports club about 500m from the centre on the Bulawayo road. Campers pay US$5 for a car or caravan, US$1 per person, and US$3.50 to US$5 for a tent. Check in at the bar in the sports club.

The rather forgettable three-star *Midlands Hotel* (☎ (154) 2581; fax 3784), which is frequented by business travellers, charges US$47/62 for singles/doubles.

The *Fairmile Motel* (☎ (154) 4144; fax 3189), on Bulawayo Rd, enjoys a three-star rating, but avoids pretences to luxury. Basic singles/doubles cost US$41/50, with breakfast; rooms in the new wing are US$50/67.

Another good choice is the bright and airy *Pamusha Guest House* (☎ (154) 3535), at 75 Kopje Rd. Singles/doubles cost US$36/40 with shared bath and US$41/55 with en suite facilities.

The local drinkers' venue is the *Chitukuko Hotel* (☎ (154) 2681), alias Gunsmoke, on the corner of Third St and Moffat Ave. From the outside it looks more like a hospital clinic than a hotel. Singles/doubles cost US$23/41 or US$46 for a twin. The resident band provides decent African entertainment nightly.

### Places to Eat
*The Dutch Oven Steakhouse* on Fifth St is a diner catering for passing travellers. It proudly announces that it serves 'Food American Style'. As the name implies, the speciality is steak – not surprising here in cattle country. You can neutralise the saturated fats on the next block at the *Vitagreens* greengrocer.

In the Hajee Ismail Bahadur Centre, off Fifth St, you'll find *Nommy's Chinese Kitchen*, *Holly's Pizza*, *Sno-Flake Ice Cream* and the *Quick-Bake Bakery*. *Danny's Kitchen*, a Muslim-run takeaway on Fifth St, is great for quick snacks, but don't look for pork sausage rolls. *Koullas Brothers Waldorf Café* serves greasy African fare, but the attached bakery is fine.

The *Chicken Inn*, at Sixth St and Robert Mugabe Way, is like all Chicken Inns with billiards, deep-fried chicken and chips. For

Chinese takeaway, go to the *Railway Refreshment Centre* approximately opposite the railway station. It's open late.

### Entertainment

Apart from the cinema and Gweru's flashy theatre, which stages visiting performances, there's the Midlands Hotel's *Dandaro bar and disco* which occasionally features live bands at weekends.

The *Chitukuko Hotel* stages live African-style music and boozing and the *Msopero Midnight Club* at 62 Seventh St serves meals by day and cranks up its Jungle Mix Disco from 9 pm to 5 am.

Alternatively, head for the swimming pool near the Midlands Museum. It's open throughout the summer from 10 am to 2 pm and 3 to 6 pm on Tuesday to Friday and from 10 am to 12.30 pm and 2.30 to 6 pm on weekends.

### Getting There & Away

All Harare-Bulawayo buses stop in Gweru. African buses use the Kudzenayi terminal near the market on Robert Mugabe Way between Second and Third Sts and Express Motorways stops at the Fairmile Motel. Book express services through Manica Travel (☎ (154) 23316) at Meikles on the corner of Robert Mugabe Way and Fifth St. Trains between Bulawayo and Harare stop at Gweru in the wee morning hours.

### AROUND GWERU

Lost in the back roads between Shangani and Nsiza, south-west of Gweru, are some fascinating and little-visited Torwa ruins. Prior to its conquest by the Rozwi, the Torwa state is thought to have risen from the declining Great Zimbabwe culture further east, improving upon its architecture and material culture. Nalatale, Danangombe, Bila and Zinjanja are clustered within a 40km radius. (The other Torwa centre, Khami, is discussed in the Bulawayo chapter.)

In this sparsely-populated region, access is limited to private vehicles, and hitchers face long waits. Even in the relatively busy

months of August and September, only three or four vehicles may pass in a day and in June, a week may pass without activity.

### Nalatale Ruins

Though smaller and less elaborate than Great Zimbabwe, Nalatale rates among the finest of Zimbabwe's 150 walled ruins. This simple structure on a remote granite hilltop enjoys a commanding view across the hills, plains and kopjes of Somabhula Flats. (On one hill, Wadai, which is visible across the flats, is the most northerly nesting colony of protected Cape vultures.)

Nalatale's main wall exhibits all the decorative patterns found in Zimbabwe: chevron, chequer, cord, herringbone and ironstone. The wall was originally topped by nine plinths, but only seven haphazardly reconstructed ones remain. The plaster on the top of the wall was added in 1937 to prevent deterioration.

Archaeologist Donald Randall McIver dug at the site in 1905 and 1906, but found only two iron spearheads, a pair of elephant tusks, copper tools and a couple of soapstone pipes. From the scant evidence that has been unearthed, Nalatale has been attributed to the Torwa dynasty and, in the early 17th century, it probably served as the Torwa capital. It's thought to have fallen to the Rozwi state sometime in the 1680s.

In the centre of the roughly elliptical complex are the remains of the principal hut, which probably belonged to the Torwa king. Its walls radiate from the main complex like spokes of a wheel. All other huts are at least 2m lower.

**Places to Stay** There are no facilities or services at Nalatale. Visitors can rough camp outside the enclosure, but must bring all their food and water.

**Getting There & Away** Nalatale (also spelt Nalatela or Nalatele) is well signposted. Coming from the north, turn south off the Gweru-Bulawayo road at Daisyfield. From the south, turn east from Shangani, follow the gravel road for 27km and take the sign-

ZIMBABWE

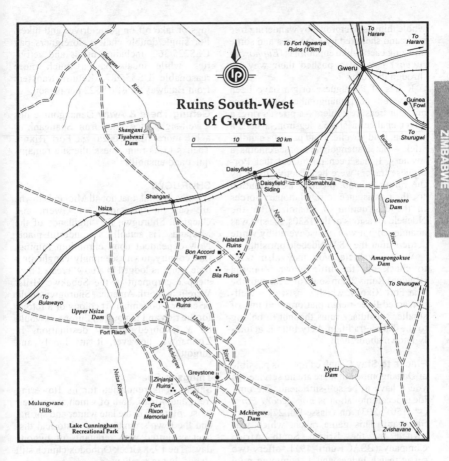

**Ruins South-West of Gweru**

0    10    20 km

---

posted left turn to Nalatale. From the parking area, it's 1km uphill to the site. On weekdays, the ruins guide, who lives in the cottage near the car park, may be able to organise lifts with local farm trucks to Shangani.

### Bila Ruins

On the back road which connects Nalatale and Danangombe are the small, signposted Bila Ruins. They consist mainly of a small stone enclosure, and were probably just a kraal for animals.

### Danangombe & Zinjanja Ruins

Commonly known as Dhlo Dhlo (the approximate pronunciation is hshlo hshlo), Danangombe isn't as lovely or well preserved as Nalatale but it covers a larger area and has a most interesting history.

It was originally designated a royal retreat under the Torwa dynasty but, after the Torwa people were defeated by the Changamires, it probably became the Rozwi administrative centre. The most interesting feature is a crumbling enclosure formed partially by natural boulders. The whole thing is overgrown by wandering tree roots and sheltered by large trees and some amazing cactus-like euphorbias (*Euphorbia ingens*) have also pushed their way up through the ruins.

Relics of Portuguese origin have been uncovered at Danangombe by ruthless amateur treasure hunters – a priest's ring, a silver chalice, a slave's leg-iron, a bell, a cannon, gold jewellery and part of a candlestick – but Danangombe's past remains a mystery. It has been postulated that Portuguese traders were held captive there by the ruling *mambo*, possibly as retribution for their assistance to revolutionary forces in the destruction of Khami. After the Ndebele invasions of the 1830s, the site was abandoned but was re-discovered by white settlers after the 1893 Ndebele uprising.

With a vehicle, you may also want to check out the little-known Zinjanja (Regina) Ruins 29km south of Danangombe (via Fort Rixon), which consist of a well-preserved three-tiered platform and lots of smaller subsidiary ruins thought to belong to the Torwa tradition. Very little is actually known about them.

**Places to Stay** Rough camping is possible at Danangombe but there are no services so you'll have to be self-sufficient. The only local accommodation is *Bon Accord Farm* (☎ (150) 3303), on Glasse Rd, 27km from Shangani. This game ranch, which was owned by the British South Africa Company (BSAC) until 1911, offers two rustic thatch lodges and a swimming pool overlooking a water hole. Activities include game walks and drives, swimming in a natural swimming hole and fishing in nearby dams. It's not bad value, but isn't a budget option.

A new option is *Embukisweni Safari Lodge* (☎ (150) 2708 or (19) 79726; fax (19) 65959), run by Tom and Salie Goddard on Endura Ranch near Shangani. They have all the standard amenities – en suite rooms, bar, restaurant, pool and braai facilities, as well as a 10,000 hectare cattle/game ranch where you can watch the day-to-day work-

ings or take off on game drives and hikes. For single/double chalets, foreigners pay US$225/360, including meals and activities, while locals pay a much more reasonable US$55/87. Return transfers from Bulawayo cost US$22 per person.

**Getting There & Away** Danangombe lies a well-signposted 32km from Shangani, or a bit more from Nsiza via Fort Rixon. Thanks to its remoteness, the site remains quiet and unspoilt.

## SHURUGWI

It's nice to think that not all Midlands towns are cast in the mould of Gweru and Chegutu. Shurugwi, the 'highlands of the Midlands', is actually a wonderful place. Now dependent upon chromium mining, this country town, seemingly caught in a time warp, is lodged in a bowl created by a steep escarpment in the Sebakwe Hills. Were it in North America, Shurugwi would be either a bohemian art colony or a retreat for the rich and famous; in Europe, it would be a favoured holiday destination. In Zimbabwe, however, it sits lonely and forgotten.

### Things to See

Shurugwi is renowned for its flowering trees and *msasa*, both of which are at their most colourful in the late winter and spring, and the town's tumbledown historical district is dotted with remnants of bygone days. The 1938 Greek Orthodox church still stands, but is rarely used.

From Monday to Saturday, a Disneyland-like narrow-gauge train moves mine workers between the town and the mine, high on the mountain; it also shifts chrome ore from the mine to the crushing yard. The Shurugwi Peak scenic drive crosses the railway and climbs for 8km to the town's eponymous peak for a great view. If you prefer your own steam, follow the Hospital Hill scenic walk just east of town, which also renders a view.

Historically, oxen teams pulled heavy wagon-loads of asbestos up to the plateau from the Zvishavane mines via the scenic Wolfshall Pass approach. From a lay-by on the pass, 3km outside Shurugwi, a walking track leads to perennial Dunraven's Falls, deep in a forested valley.

### Places to Stay & Eat

The *Ferny Creek Caravan Park* (☎ (152) 220) lies 2.5km from town, past the sun-baked golf course and down a red dirt road into a wooded valley. It has apparently seen better days, evidenced by descriptions of it in long outdated tourist literature. You can choose between camping or staying in extremely basic chalets.

The unkempt *Garden Motel* (☎ (152) 6548), which really does occupy a garden, lies 1.5km off the main road west of town. It's good value at US$17 per person, or US$25 for a basic double. On Friday and Saturday nights, the place rocks to Shurugwi's only disco.

For meals, your best choice is the Garden Motel dining room, which serves staples. There's also a basic fish-and-chip shop and the *Balmain Supa Market and Supa Snax* (the spelling says it all).

### CHIVHU

Chivhu, originally called Enkeldoorn or lone thorn (the Dutch maintain it's 'ankle thorn'), was established in the late 1890s by Afrikaners from the Orange Free State. Today, it's mainly a cattle ranching area and makes a pleasant lunch or overnight stop between Harare and Masvingo.

### Places to Stay & Eat

The Cape Dutch-style *Vic's Tavern* (☎ (156) 2797), a small and friendly country hotel in the centre, has en suite singles/doubles for US$29/39, with an enormous breakfast. Backpackers accommodation with communal facilities costs US$19/27.

The *Tangenhamo Lodge* (☎ (156) 25308; <denise@baobab.cfzim.co.zw>), on Tangenhamo Game Ranch, lies 16km south of town on the Masvingo road. This secluded stone and thatch lodge is cleverly integrated into a lovely landscape of trees and boulders. Accommodation costs US$70 per person; activities – game walks and drives; birdwatching; bass, bream and barbel fishing; horse-riding; and yes, even elephant rides (US$20) – cost extra. Bushbeat Trails (see the Organised Tours chapter) offers day tours from Harare.

Chivhu's best in-town eatery is the veranda restaurant at *Vic's Tavern*. Quicker meals are found at *Palate Takeaways*, on the square. For a treat, check out the famous *Denise's Kitchen* (☎ (156) 25309), opposite Tangenhamo Lodge. Here, owner Denise Tennant serves up steaks, chicken dishes, salads, baked potato specialities, vegetarian meals and snacks, and the wildlife may even stop by for handouts (a bit off-putting if you're eating the impala burgers!). Check out the Tarzan and Jane toilets.

### MVUMA

The name of Mvuma, a gold-mining and railway community, was taken from the Mvuma River which means 'place of magic singing' after a river pool where mysterious singing, drumming and the lowing of cattle were once heard. This small community is the site of the historic Falcon Mine, abandoned in 1925, which pioneered Zimbabwe's oil flotation smelting process. Today, only the Athens Mine is still worked.

The town's landmark is the crumbling Falcon Mine stack, a 40m-high remnant dating from 1913. Town residents are waiting for it to collapse which, given its current condition, appears imminent.

### SERIMA MISSION

Serima Mission is a treasure house of African art based on the traditions of west and central Africa where the genre reached its peak. Although the church exterior is now a bit worn, the spacious interior and all its artistic enhancements remain intact and are certainly worth the effort of visiting. For further information, look for *Serima* by Albert Plangger, which details its history, art and architecture in words and photos. It's sold at the National Gallery in Harare.

## History

Serima was founded in 1948 by Swiss Catholic priest and art instructor Father John Gröber who had earned a degree in architecture before his 1939 calling to teach on the rural missions of southern Africa. At Serima, he was impressed by the level of artistic talent in young Shona people. Beginning with sketch drawings of masks, he helped students progress to clay models and finally to carvings and sculpture, encouraging them to express themselves without pandering to European sensitivities.

The students' first projects were to decorate the school building with carved pillars and patterns. Father Gröber then invoked his ultimate missionary objective, but chose to emphasise the spiritual rather than dogmatic elements of Christian tradition. With his encouragement, students infused their African expressionism with Christian influences, which resulted in the potpourri of carvings which grace the church today.

## Church

The Serima Mission church, which was designed by Father Gröber, encloses an open, airy and brilliantly lit space. The room and its simple furnishings emphasise the dense and diverse frescoes, sculptures and carved pillars and reliefs, yet seem to relate well to the altar, which is the focus of the room. In his book *A Tourist in Africa*, Evelyn Waugh predicted that Africans would one day see it with the same reverence as Europeans behold the medieval cathedrals of Europe.

The bell tower comprises a circle of African angels gripping musical instruments and, on shelves above the church entrance, shepherds and wise men labour towards a nativity scene. Biblical events are depicted in a series of frescoes above the arcaded interior walls, including a masterful Last Supper scene above the main altar. Except for the reed-matted ceiling beams, not a single piece of wood in the building remains uncarved.

## Places to Stay

Serima lacks formal accommodation, but the Catholic sisters normally allow travellers to camp in the grounds.

## Getting There & Away

A Bream Express bus runs to Serima several times weekly in the early morning from Mucheke musika in Masvingo, passes Great Zimbabwe, then continues to Serima, where it stays overnight before returning to Masvingo early the next morning. The Felixburg bus from Masvingo can drop you at the turn-off 10km from Serima. Alternatively, take a bus from Masvingo towards Harare, and get off at Fairfield Siding, where the railway crosses the road south of Mvuma. From there, three buses run to Serima daily.

With a vehicle, turn east from the Harare-Masvingo road onto the Felixburg road 60km north of Masvingo. After 6km, you'll cross the railway; continue for 4km and turn right again. From there, it's about 10km to the mission, which is on the right side of the road past a small dam.

## MASVINGO

Masvingo, with a population of 40,000, is neatly divided by the Mucheke River. The name Masvingo, which was adopted after Zimbabwean independence, is derived from *rusvingo*, the Shona word for walled-in enclosures, in reference to the nearby Great Zimbabwe ruins. While the centre emits a clean, small-town laziness, Mucheke township, 2km away, is vibrant Africa and has one of Zimbabwe's liveliest markets.

## History

Historically, Masvingo prided itself on being the first colonial settlement in Zimbabwe (a distinction which few people cared about one way or another). The pioneer column of the BSAC, led by Frederick Courteney Selous, moved through Lobengula's stronghold in Matabeleland and across the dry lowveld to the cooler plateaux. In August 1890, they paused at a spot now known as Clipsham Farm, south of present-day Masvingo, to establish Fort Victoria and construct a rude fortification

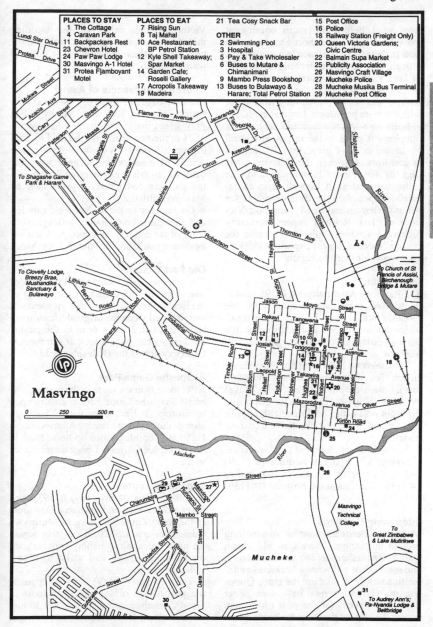

PLACES TO STAY
1 The Cottage
4 Caravan Park
11 Backpackers Rest
23 Chevron Hotel
24 Paw Paw Lodge
30 Masvingo A-1 Hotel
31 Protea Flamboyant Motel

PLACES TO EAT
7 Rising Sun
8 Taj Mahal
10 Ace Restaurant; BP Petrol Station
12 Kyle Shell Takeaway; Spar Market
14 Garden Cafe; Roselli Gallery
17 Acropolis Takeaway
19 Madeira
21 Tea Cosy Snack Bar

OTHER
2 Swimming Pool
3 Hospital
5 Pay & Take Wholesaler
6 Buses to Mutare & Chimanimani
9 Mambo Press Bookshop
13 Buses to Bulawayo & Harare; Total Petrol Station
15 Post Office
16 Police
18 Railway Station (Freight Only)
20 Queen Victoria Gardens; Civic Centre
22 Balmain Supa Market
25 Publicity Association
26 Masvingo Craft Village
27 Mucheke Police
28 Mucheke Musika Bus Terminal
29 Mucheke Post Office

ZIMBABWE

Masvingo

0    250    500 m

from mud before the main contingent moved north to found Fort Salisbury, the next in their line of defence installations. A drought two years later forced the removal of Fort Victoria to a more amenable location between the Shagashe and Mucheke Rivers, the site of present-day Masvingo, where a more permanent fort was built.

In its early years, Masvingo served as a jumping-off point to the mines of central Mashonaland and grew into Rhodesia's largest town. However, the Ndebele uprisings of the First Chimurenga and the subsequent defeat of Lobengula in Matabeleland opened up the Bulawayo area for white settlement and lured many Fort Victoria settlers towards more promising pickings elsewhere. Bulawayo became the country's second-largest city while Masvingo has now dropped to eighth.

## Information

The Publicity Association (☎ (139) 62643) distributes maps, advertising and the monthly publication *This is Masvingo!*, which outlines events and local news. It's open weekdays from 8 am to 1 pm and 2 to 4.30 pm.

The Belmont Press Cottage Shoppe, on Josiah Tongogara Ave, sells curios and tourist-oriented publications, and Travel World (☎ (139) 62131; fax 64205), opposite the main post office on Hughes St, is your best option for transport, hotel and tour bookings.

You'll find card phones at the post office. Masvingo's public fax number is (139) 64238. Emergency services include police (☎ (139) 62222) and the hospital (☎ (139) 62112).

## Interesting Buildings

Masvingo merits an hour or so strolling around the centre. There's an old steam engine languishing in the railway station and the modern civic centre beckons to conventioneers. Next door are the green Queen Victoria Gardens, which have seen better days. The tower near the post office was one of the lookout turrets in the second Fort

Victoria. Other relics of the building include a small section of the wall and the bell tower, which was used as a colonial warning alarm.

## Church of St Francis of Assisi

The Church of St Francis of Assisi was constructed between 1942 and 1946 by Italian POWs, and inside are interred the remains of 71 of their compatriots who died in Zimbabwe between 1942 and 1947. The simulated mosaics in the apse were the work of an Italian engineer while the wall murals were completed 10 years later by Masvingo artists.

Go 3km east on the Mutare road, turn left and then turn immediately left again. In front of the military barracks, turn left yet again and you'll see the church 100m away.

## Old Fort Victoria

The original Fort Victoria, 10km south of Masvingo, lies on Clipsham Farm, east of the Beitbridge road. Masvingo's present site was selected when the original location ran short of water. It's not open to the public, but visitors can have a look at the Pioneer Cemetery across the Beitbridge road.

## Shagashe Game Park

After more than six years in the making, the small Shagashe Game Park is finally open to visitors. It lies 10km from Masvingo along the Harare road. Admission is US$0.50. For information on horse tours in Shagashe, see Clovelly Lodge under Places to Stay.

## Organised Tours

Sunbird Safaris (☎/fax (139) 65793) runs tours of Masvingo and environs. Day tours to the Great Zimbabwe ruins or Mutirikwe Game Park cost US$20. It can also organise horse rides, birdwatching trips, cruises on Lake Mutirikwe and visits to Shona villages.

Tsika Tours (☎ (139) 65793), opposite the post office, runs US$42 day tours to Great Zimbabwe commencing at 9.30 am. After visiting Great Zimbabwe, you get lunch and take a boat transfer across the lake for a game drive in Mutirikwe Game Park. Morning tours of the ruins cost US$18 and morning/afternoon game drives in Mutirikwe Game Park are US$24/27.

For something different, how about a home stay in the lovely Zaka Communal Lands with the Sekiwe Madanhire family (☎ (134) 2754), Gunguvu Schook, PA Jichidza, Masvingo? You'll enjoy fabulous rural hospitality and catch a glimpse of the real Zimbabwe. It's 65km south-east of Masvingo. Note, however, that sensitivity is requisite if this opportunity is to remain intact for future travellers. Please leave any western notions behind and let the experience affect you rather than the other way around! Access is by bus from Mucheke musika.

### Places to Stay – Budget

Masvingo's *Caravan Park* (☎ (139) 62431), with green lawns and a riverside setting, charges US$2 per person. Non-guests may use the picnic sites and showers for a nominal fee.

A great spot is the friendly *Clovelly Lodge* (☎ (139) 64751), run by Bruce and Iris Brinson, which nestles among the gum trees 6km west of the centre. It's on the small side, so advance booking is advised. Comfortable dorms cost US$9 and doubles are US$11, including breakfast, family-oriented dinners (including vegetarian choices) and transfers to and from town and Mucheke. You can also cool off in a small swimming pool. Horse-riding costs US$4 per hour, riding lessons are US$4.50 and three-hour trail rides in Shagashe Game Reserve cost US$12, including a picnic lunch. For transport from town, phone from the post office.

Barry Binder's *Backpackers Rest* (☎ (139) 65503), centrally located in the Dauth Building, has dorm beds for US$6 and, with half-board, singles/doubles cost US$8/15. The food isn't that memorable – it comes from the affiliated takeaway – but the price is right. Self-caterers may use the cooking facilities, pickups from Mucheke

are free and anyone (even non-residents) can hire one-speed/mountain bikes for US$3.25/6.50 per day.

*Paw Paw Lodge* (☎ (139) 65231), 18 Kirton Rd, has very basic dorms with cooking and laundry facilities for US$7 and double rooms for US$15. Rates include breakfast.

The friendly and quirky *Breezy Brae B&B* (☎ (139) 64650) lies perched beside an immense *dwala* dome, 5km west of town on the Bulawayo road. The six upstairs rooms have baths and the downstairs four have showers. Those arriving on public transport can phone for a pickup from town. Singles/doubles cost US$17/24 including breakfast; with dinner, they're US$20/29. Special backpackers rates are US$8.50 per person.

Another B&B option is *The Cottage* (☎ (139) 63340), at 6 Citrus Ave, run by Mrs Martha Percival. The attitude is rather colonial, but it's clean and provides an in-town alternative to the hotels. B&B accommodation costs US$13 and self-catering is US$10 per person. Meals are also available.

*Audrey Ann's Accommodation* (☎ (139) 51315; fax 52178), lies 1km from Riley's Truck-Inn, 4km out on the Beitbridge road. This homely little place has six-bed chalets for US$8.50 for one person, plus US$5 for each additional person. B&B costs US$13 per person or US$11 for a bed only.

### Places to Stay – Mid-Range

The central *Chevron Hotel* (☎ (139) 62054; fax 65961) has been upgraded and now charges US$45/58 for singles/doubles, with breakfast. The nicer *Protea Flamboyant Motel* (☎ (139) 52835; fax 52899), marked by a leaning Norfolk Island pine, has singles/doubles with bath for US$46/61, with breakfast. Family suites for up to six people cost US$88.

The *Masvingo A-1 Hotel* (☎ (139) 62917), on a hilltop in Mucheke township, has slightly cheaper rooms at US$33/42 for singles/doubles with breakfast, but you may not appreciate the alcohol-induced noise, which is incessant. Unaccompanied women may not feel comfortable.

On the game farm of Graham and Cally Richards, 11km out on the Beitbridge road, is *Pa-Nyanda Lodge* (☎ (139) 53084 or 63412; fax (130) 62000). For a basic, but unique, open-air chalet, locals/foreigners pay US$41/62 per person with half-board. The self-catering lodges accommodate up to five people and costs US$64/85 per lodge plus US$17 per person.

Other options are described in the sections on Great Zimbabwe, Lake Mutirikwe and Mushandike Sanctuary.

### Places to Eat

The best eatery is the *Garden Cafe*, behind Roselli Gallery, which serves up daily lunch specials, including vegetarian dishes. It's open weekdays from 8.30 am to 4.30 pm and Saturdays from 8.30 am to 2 pm.

Petrol stations cater to hungry travellers in a rush. The takeaways at *Kyle Shell* and the *Ace Restaurant* at the BP station are best for snacks. Kyle Shell has an attached *Spar Market*, which is open every day from 7 am to 8 pm, and the Balmain Shell has the handy *Supa Market*. The *Breadbasket Bakery* on Josiah Tongogara St is good for pies and bread.

You won't have a memorable meal at the *Acropolis Takeaway* on Herbert Chitepo St, but it's a viable choice in the evening. Several other restaurants and takeaway places (some ethnically named: the *Taj Mahal*, *Rising Sun*, *Madeira*, etc) stick close to the usual chicken, burgers, chips and deep-fried snacks themes. The *Tea Cosy Snack Bar* at Meikles on Robert Mugabe St serves up tea, cakes, pastries and light snacks. The ubiquitous *Wimpy* does its usual breakfast and burger thing on the Beitbridge road.

The terrace at the *Chevron Hotel* does great snacks and drinks, and the dining room has vastly improved in recent years. Even better is the *Protea Flamboyant Hotel*, which does breakfast buffets, à la carte lunches and snacks and, on weekend evenings, a buffet braai.

The *Pay & Take* wholesaler offers good deals on groceries, but you must buy in bulk. Lots of produce, snacks and junk food are sold around Mucheke musika (ever had the urge to try deep-fried stink bugs?).

### Things to Buy

The Masvingo Craft Village lies just uphill from the Publicity Association, near the Mucheke turn-off. It has a range of carvings, baskets, sculpture and other items, some pleasantly original.

The Roselli Gallery, at 39 Hughes St, sells paintings, sculpture and ceramics by local artists. It's open weekdays from 9.30 am to 4 pm and on Saturday from 9 am to 12.30 pm.

Along the Beitbridge road south of Masvingo is at least a score of impromptu craft markets, some of which sell good work. The fierce competition also means competitive prices.

### Getting There & Away

United Air Charters flies to and from Harare every Monday, Wednesday and Friday.

Express Motorways buses leave Harare for Masvingo and Great Zimbabwe (US$12) on Fridays at 5 pm. DSB Coachlines runs between Harare, Masvingo and Great Zimbabwe (US$13) on Sunday and Thursday. Blue Arrow has services from Harare to Masvingo and from Masvingo to Bulawayo on Monday, Wednesday and Friday. Services from Bulawayo and to Harare run on Tuesday, Thursday and Saturday. Express buses between Harare and Johannesburg also call in at the Trans-Lux terminal on the Beitbridge road; see South Africa in the Zimbabwe Getting There & Away chapter.

Most African buses stop in the town centre en route to Mucheke musika, 2km away. Harare buses arrive at and depart from Mucheke frequently and there are also several daily services to Bulawayo and Mutare. At least one bus leaves for Beitbridge daily between 6 and 11 am. The recommended long-haul company is

Masara Transport Ltd. Access to Mucheke from Masvingo is by bus or emergency taxi.

The population density of the Masvingo province communal lands also put smaller destinations in relatively easy reach via local bus services. There's no passenger rail service to Masvingo.

### Getting Around

For a taxi, phone Masvingo Taxis (☎ (139) 65866; 52825 after hours).

## GREAT ZIMBABWE NATIONAL MONUMENT

Great Zimbabwe, the greatest medieval city in sub-Saharan Africa, provides evidence that ancient Africans reached a level of civilisation not suspected by earlier scholars. As a religious and secular capital, this city of between 10,000 and 20,000 people dominated a realm which stretched across what is now eastern Zimbabwe and into present-day Botswana, Mozambique and South Africa. Archaeologists have attributed over 150 tributary zimbabwes to the Great Zimbabwe society, which was actually an amalgamation of smaller groups gathered under a central political system.

The name *Zimbabwe* is believed to derive from one of two possible Shona origins; either *dzimba dza mabwe* (great stone houses) or *dzimba woye* (esteemed houses). The grand setting and history-filled walls certainly qualify as highlights of southern Africa. The site is open from 6 am to 6 pm daily; foreigners pay US$5 admission, which includes entry to the attached reconstructed Karanga village, open from 8 am to 5 pm. Three-hour guided tours are available six times daily for US$1.50 per person.

### History

Several volumes have been written about Great Zimbabwe and speculations over its purposes and origins have been hashed over for centuries now. If you're keen to learn more, the most comprehensive and scholarly work on the subject is *Great Zimbabwe Described and Explained* by Peter Garlake. It's available at Kingston's bookshops, or failing that contact the publisher: Zimbabwe Publishing House (☎ (14) 790416), 144 Union Ave, PO Box 350, Harare.

Despite nearly 100 years of effort by colonial governments to ascribe the origins of Great Zimbabwe to someone else – anyone else – conclusive proof of its Bantu origins was already in place in 1932, after British archaeologist Gertrude Caton-Thompson spent three years examining the ruins and their artefacts.

One can almost forgive the scepticism of early colonists – the African peoples they encountered seemed to have no tradition of building in stone and none of the stone cities were inhabited at the time of colonisation. However, even up to the time of Zimbabwe's independence, the Rhodesian government ignored the evidence and supported far-fetched fantasies of foreign influence and habitation. Despite results based on radiocarbon dating of materials found at the site, many Rhodesian officials perpetuated the nonsense that Great Zimbabwe dated from the pre-Christian era. Not a scrap of proof for Phoenician, Jewish, Greek, Egyptian, Arabic or any other origins has ever surfaced.

Other outside influences did, however, play a role in the development of Great Zimbabwe. Swahili traders were present along the Mozambique coast from the 10th century through the height of Rozwi influence in the 14th and 15th centuries. Trade goods – porcelain from China, crockery from Persia and beads and other trinkets from India – have been unearthed on the site, and the Africans undoubtedly adopted and adapted some of the outsiders' ways.

The first society to occupy the Great Zimbabwe site arrived in the 11th century. It probably comprised several scattered groups which recognised safety in numbers. Construction of their first project, the royal enclosures on the Hill Complex, commenced sometime during the 13th century, while the remainder of the city was completed over the next 100 years or so.

Apparently, Great Zimbabwe was primarily a blue-collar project. Despite the

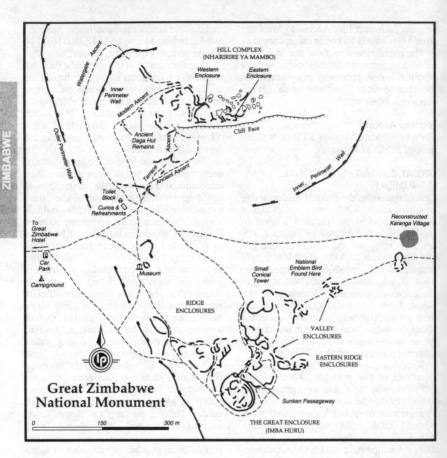

**Great Zimbabwe National Monument**

0        150        300 m

Labels on map:
HILL COMPLEX (NHARIRIRE YA MAMBO)
Watergate Ascent
Inner Perimeter Wall
Western Enclosure
Eastern Enclosure
Modern Ascent
Outer Perimeter Wall
Ancient Daga Hut Remains
Terrace
Ancient Ascent
Cliff Face
Inner Perimeter Wall
Toilet Block
Curios & Refreshments
To Great Zimbabwe Hotel
Reconstructed Karanga Village
Car Park
Campground
Museum
Small Conical Tower
National Emblem Bird Found Here
RIDGE ENCLOSURES
VALLEY ENCLOSURES
EASTERN RIDGE ENCLOSURES
Sunken Passageway
THE GREAT ENCLOSURE (IMBA HURU)

ZIMBABWE

beauty of the ruins, the remains do not provide evidence of superior architectural skills and it seems that only a sketchy overall plan was devised before work began. Construction was a labour-intensive venture, requiring thousands of hands to hew out millions of granite blocks for the extensive walls. Since the main walls and platforms weren't intended to support roofs, precise measurements and straight lines were unnecessary. The structure's wonderfully haphazard curving and twisting lines either circumvented or incorporated natural features into the buildings, resulting in an impressive harmony with the landscape.

Fuelled by the Swahili gold trade, the city grew into a powerful and prestigious religious and political capital; in every way it was the heart of the Rozwi culture. Royal herds increased and coffers overflowed with gold and precious trade goods.

In the end, however, Great Zimbabwe probably became a victim of its own success. By the 15th century, the growing human and bovine populations and their environmental pressures had depleted local resources, necessitating emigration to more productive lands. One contingent, under the Mwene Mutapa, relocated its capital to Fura Mountain in northern Zimbabwe. Another group migrated westwards to Khami, the new capital, and later to Danangombe and Nalatale. Great Zimbabwe declined rapidly and, when the Portuguese arrived in the 16th century, the city was nearly deserted.

At this point, the site was taken over by the Nemanwa dynasty, which endured until the late 18th century, when it was over-thrown by the Mugabe dynasty. The Mugabe were in turn toppled in 1834 by a contingent of Nguni under Zwangendaba, throwing the conquered leaders from the cliffs and ruthlessly seizing power. By the time German-US hunter Adam Renders stumbled upon Great Zimbabwe in 1868, only ruins remained.

## Hill Complex

Once known as the Acropolis, the Hill Complex was probably the first of the Great

### Visiting Great Zimbabwe

Great Zimbabwe merits at least a full day of exploration. If you're staying overnight at the ruins, either camping or at the hotel, you should try to witness morning light on the ruined walls. The gates open at 8 am and the effects of a low sun and its long red rays add a be-guiling dimension.

The following is just a suggested itinerary which moves chronologically through the site. Other possible routes are outlined in the pamphlet *A Trail Guide to the Great Zimbabwe National Monument*, available from the museum for US$1, and in *Trails of Discovery*, a pho-tocopied brochure which may be purchased at the hotel for the same price.

To see the site in the order it was constructed, begin with the Hill Complex, which prob-ably first served as the earliest royal enclave and later became a religious centre. From the curio shop, climb the Ancient Ascent, the oldest of the four summit routes. The rambling walls and intermittent boulders covering the hilltop are good for a couple of hours explor-ing. West of the Hill Complex, three other routes (the Modern, Terrace and Watergate Routes) connect the level ground with the summit and also merit exploration.

Next, continue along to the remains of the inner perimeter wall and return to the curio shop, where you'll connect with a track leading to the easternmost ruins and the recon-structed Karanga village. This slightly tacky compound (note the plaster of paris inhabitants) will provide some idea of how common folk lived at Great Zimbabwe. While nobility occu-pied the stone buildings, it's thought that more than 10,000 other people occupied huts scattered around the city perimeter.

From the village, continue to the Valley Enclosures, perhaps the most intriguing struc-tures on the site, where heaps of overgrown rubble and crumbling walls suggest that wealthier commoners made their homes. One can almost imagine an inhabited version of the reconstructed Karanga village spread over the raised platforms. For the tour de force, climb the aloe-decked Sunken Passageway to the crowning achievement of the Rozwi Culture, the fabulous Great Enclosure and its instantly recognisable conical tower.

En route to the museum, notice the Ridge Enclosures, which were rough additions to the original structure by post-Great Zimbabwe occupants, possibly Karanga. In the museum, you can peruse some of the material residue discovered around the site. The highlight is the lineup of the world-famous Zimbabwe birds, probably totems of the ruling dynasty, which now serve as the national emblem. Once armed with the new perspective offered by the museum, it may be tempting to repeat the entire circuit and have a look at each site from a new angle.

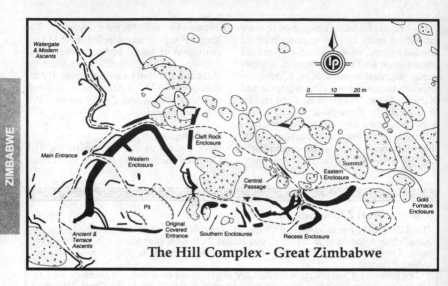

The Hill Complex - Great Zimbabwe

Zimbabwe structures to be built. This clearly wasn't a fortress, but rather a series of royal and ritual enclosures. Instead of ripping out the boulders to install the chambers, builders followed the path of least resistance, integrating the boulders into the structures as best they could. Evidence indicates that the Hill Complex was occupied for at least 300 years.

The most salient feature of the Hill Complex is the Western Enclosure, where the Ancient and Terrace ascent routes converge. On the 8m-high western wall, note the small upright towers for which no purpose has yet been determined. The pit in the centre is a recent excavation, clearly revealing the layered floors of the consecutive huts that have stood on the site. When the site was inhabited, collapsing huts were razed and their floors smoothed over with wall material to provide floors for subsequent structures.

Leading through the eastern wall of the Western Enclosure is the Covered Entrance, which leads into a passageway through to the Southern Enclosures. Beyond them lies the small three-sided Recess Enclosure,

from which a series of steps leads into the wall. This is the entrance to the Eastern or Ritual Enclosure, where artificial and natural elements combine to form a well-protected site, possibly used for ritual purposes. Stone Zimbabwe birds once stood on six of the pillars around its periphery. On a lower level east of the Eastern Enclosure, traces of gold-smelting operations have been found, hence the name, Gold Furnace Enclosure.

Both the Watergate and Modern ascents skirt the northern wall of the Western Enclosure and pass through a collapsed entrance into the Cleft Rock Enclosure, a large area bounded by boulders, where it's believed the female spirit mediums once performed their rites. A passage through from its eastern end leads to the Eastern Enclosure.

### Valley Enclosures

This series of 13th century enclosures, *daga* hut platforms and even a small conical tower, stretches from the Sunken Passageway, below the Great Enclosure, towards the Karanga village reconstruction. They

have yielded some of the site's finest archaeological finds, including metal tools
and the strange Zimbabwe birds, with their
mammalian feet, that became the national
symbol.

### Great Enclosure

The elliptical Great Enclosure is the structure normally conjured up by the words
Great Zimbabwe. It's the most often photographed and perhaps the most photogenic
of all the ruins. Nearly 100m across and
255m in circumference, it is the largest
ancient structure in sub-Saharan Africa.
The mortarless walls reach heights of 11m
and are 5m thick in places.

The outer wall appears to have been built
in an anticlockwise progression. Builders
began with the roughly constructed north-
west entrance, honing their techniques as
they moved around to the north-eastern
side, where the walls are highest and most

skilfully completed. This is another indication that no pre-determined plan had been
formulated.

It is commonly accepted that the Great
Enclosure was used as a royal compound
and a sort of cloister for the king's mother
and senior wives. The object of greatest
speculation is, of course, the 10m-high,
convex Conical Tower, tucked away
beneath overhanging trees at the south-
eastern end. This solid and apparently
ceremonial structure is probably of phallic
significance, but no conclusive evidence
has yet been uncovered. Treasure hunters of
yore believed the tower sheltered the royal
treasury (it now contains only rocks and
dirt) while current speculation is that it
served as the king's granary. The tower was
originally capped with three rows of
chevron designs.

In the reconstructed version, the Great
Enclosure has three entrances, all of which

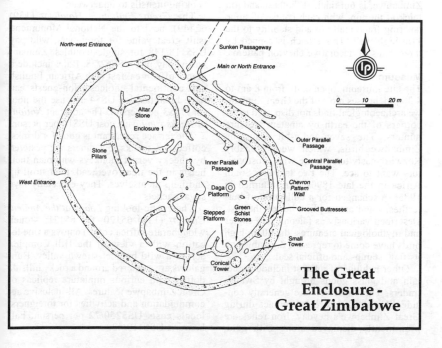

The Great
Enclosure -
Great Zimbabwe

were probably lintelled and covered in the original, opening through rounded buttresses. The North Entrance, probably the main gate, is met outside by the Sunken Passageway connecting it to the Valley Enclosures.

Leading away north-east from the Conical Tower is the narrow 70m-long Central Parallel Passage. This may have been a means of moving from the North Entrance to the Conical Tower without being detected by those in the living area of the Enclosure. It's also possible that the Parallel Passage's inner wall was intended to be an outer wall but, by the time the builders had completed that far around, their construction methods had improved so dramatically that they decided to continue building around the former perimeter, leaving the superior work visible from the outside. The outside wall of the Central Parallel Passage, perhaps the most architecturally advanced structure in Great Zimbabwe, is 6m thick at the base and 4m thick at the top, with each course of stone tapering fractionally to add stability to the 11m-high wall. This stretch is capped by three rings of decorative chevron patterns.

## Museum

The site museum, open daily from 8 am to 4.30 pm, houses most of the Great Zimbabwe archaeological finds not dispersed to far corners of the earth by amateur treasure hunters. The seven-and-a-bit soapstone Zimbabwe birds, which were probably Rozwi dynasty totems, are what most visitors want to see. The two taken to South Africa in the late 1890s were returned in 1985 – exchanged for a collection of butterflies – and are in place beside the rest. Described variously as falcons, fish eagles and mythological creatures, the 40cm-high birds have come to represent Zimbabwe on its flag, stamps and official seal.

Other exhibits of interest include porcelain and glass goods brought by Swahili traders. These artefacts are generally considered proof of foreign contact during Great Zimbabwe's heyday. Iron relics are prominently displayed along with gold, bronze and copper items, soapstone dishes and clay pottery. Some of the iron pieces were ritual objects and owned by the king, while others were practical items treasured by common folk.

## Organised Tours

Tours are available from Sunbird; see Organised Tours under Masvingo.

## Places to Stay & Eat

Campers have the best deal here. The *National Museums & Monuments Camp Site* (☎ (139) 7052) occupies a lovely field within sight of the Hill Complex, just over a rise from the other ruins. Camping costs US$2 per person. Cold showers are available and security guards are posted to watch your belongings while you're off exploring. Don't leave anything outside your tent – baboons and vervet monkeys aren't picky and will abscond with anything from cooking utensils to underwear.

The *Great Zimbabwe Hotel* (☎ (139) 62449), next to the National Monument, isn't great value for foreigners, who pay US$118/148 for singles/doubles. Zimbabweans pay just US$62/78. Rates include a great buffet breakfast with African, English and continental choices. Non-guests can have breakfast for US$4 and use the pool for US$3 per person. The adjacent *National Parks rondavels* cost US$10 per person.

The terrace restaurant is good for drinks, coffee and snacks, but diners are pestered by cheeky vervet monkeys who plan their heists in the trees overhead, then stroll up and help themselves. They especially love sugar sachets.

The exotic-looking *Lodge at the Ancient City* (☎ (139) 65120; fax 65121; <touch wld@harare.iafrica.com>) enjoys a fine location with a view of the Hill Complex across a wild boulder-strewn valley. Bungalows are scattered around a rocky hillside dotted with curious miniature replicas of Great Zimbabwe features. All-inclusive accommodation and activities for foreigners/locals costs US$250/72 per person; half board is US$119/42.

## Getting There & Away
**Bus** ZUPCO runs three buses daily from Mucheke in Masvingo at 8 am, noon and 3.30 pm. The crowded minibuses to Morgenster Mission run from Mucheke more or less hourly, but you'll have to hustle for a seat. Get off at the Great Zimbabwe Hotel turn-off (drivers know where tourists are going) and walk the 1km to the hotel. You can also continue to Morgenster Mission to see the rock pillars known as Finger Rocks, which guard the mission gate, and the impressive vista from World's View.

Jacaranda Luxury Coach Lines (☎ (14) 754460) has a US$63 return service from Harare to Great Zimbabwe on Wednesday and Sunday at 6 am; it allows four hours at Great Zimbabwe before returning to Harare. On Tuesday, Thursday and Saturday, departures require at least five booked passengers.

Sabi Star transfers, run by Zimbabwe Sun hotels, cost US$18 to or from Masvingo and US$36 from Harare; these services also connect Great Zimbabwe with the Chilo, Mahenye and Senuko Lodges near Gonarezhou for US$18.

In addition, several bus services have through services from Harare, via Masvingo. See Getting There & Away for Masvingo.

**Taxi** Taxis to Great Zimbabwe charge around US$10 for up to five passengers. See under Masvingo for contact numbers.

## MUTIRIKWE (KYLE) RECREATIONAL PARK
A decade of drought has caused the waters of Lake Mutirikwe (still commonly called Lake Kyle) to fall to record low levels and the lake has shrunk to one-hundredth of its capacity. Although the rains have picked up substantially since 1993, the irrigation-intensive farming in the lowveld still hasn't fully recovered. Therefore, the lake itself is currently of limited recreational value, but the surrounding scenic area is worthwhile and combines nicely with a visit to Great Zimbabwe.

## Pokoteke Gap
The signposted access road to Pokoteke Gap leads to the steep-walled water gap where the Pokoteke River flows through the Beza Range on its way to Lake Mutirikwe. It lies 2.5km south of the Masvingo-Mutare road, 20km east of Masvingo. This scenic stop is ideal for picnicking but camping is prohibited.

## Mutirikwe Dam Wall
The 305m-wide Mutirikwe dam wall forms Lake Mutirikwe by blocking the impressive Mutirikwe Gorge. It was completed in 1961 as part of a scheme to irrigate the parched lowveld and allow cultivation of such thirsty crops as cotton and sugar cane.

## Rock Paintings
Two relatively accessible rock painting sites can be seen near the lakeshore. The easier to reach is a small unnamed one about 2km south-west of the dam wall and 100m off the road. It's well signposted.

The better known Chamavara paintings at Chamavara Cave lie 18km north-west of the dam wall on Murray McDougall Drive, then 5km south-east on the signposted turn-off. You'll probably have to walk much of the way due to boulders blocking the road.

Most of the painted human and animal figures are confusingly dense on the cave wall and are at times hard to discern. Because many figures have white faces, speculation has connected the paintings with unlikely Arab and European influences. The cave's main figure, known as the Giant Man of Chamavara, who is surrounded by several elegantly painted kudu, is unique in Zimbabwe.

## Mutirikwe (Kyle) Game Park
It may seem a bit artificial, but the Mutirikwe Game Park offers the possibility of seeing white rhino and many more species of antelope than any other national park in Zimbabwe. On the 64km of dirt roads you'll readily see warthog, impala, kudu, tsessebe, wildebeest, waterbuck, giraffe, zebra, buffalo and baboons. Oribi and eland

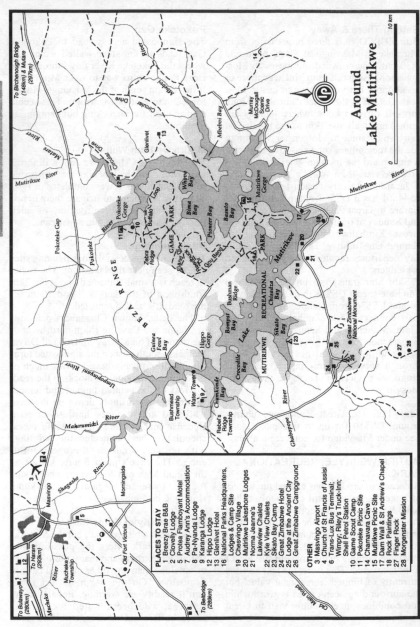

**Around Lake Mutirikwe**

**PLACES TO STAY**
1 Breezy Brae B&B
2 Clovelly Lodge
5 Protea Flamboyant Motel
7 Audrey Ann's Accommodation
8 Pa-Nyanda Lodge
9 Karanga Lodge
12 Hippo Lodge
13 Glenlivet Hotel
16 National Parks Headquarters,
   Lodges & Camp Site
19 Chesvingo Village
20 Mutirikwe Lakeshore Lodges
21 Norma Jeanne's
22 Lakeview Chalets
23 Kyle View Chalets
24 Skato Bay Camp
25 Great Zimbabwe Hotel
26 Lodge at the Ancient City
26 Great Zimbabwe Campground

**OTHER**
3 Masvingo Airport
4 Church of St Francis of Assisi
6 Trans-Lux Bus Terminal;
   Wimpy; Riley's Truck-Inn;
   Shell Petrol Station
10 Game Scout Camp
11 Pokoteke Picnic Site
14 Chamavara Cave
15 Mutirikwe Picnic Site
17 Dam Wall & St Andrew's Chapel
18 Rock Paintings
27 Finger Rock
28 Morgenster Mission

are seen occasionally, but there are no elephant or big cats. The gates close at 6 pm.

Walking is permitted only around Mushagashe Arm near the National Parks lodges and camp site. It's actually outside the game fence, so you won't observe much wildlife, but hippos and crocodiles are often seen in and around the water. The area north of the dwala, around the National Parks lodges, is an arboretum, with over 150 species of indigenous trees. However, be warned that the way hasn't been cleared for some time.

### Activities
National Parks guided horseback trips through the game park allow wildlife viewing from closer range than a vehicle would permit. They depart at 7.45 am from park headquarters and return at 10.30 am. Advance bookings are essential.

### Places to Stay
**South Shore** Most Mutirikwe accommodation is along the lake's southern shore. Camping is available at the beautiful National Parks *Sikato Bay Camp* (☎ (139) 67150), 6km north of Great Zimbabwe National Monument for US$3 per person.

To the east of this, the laid-back *Kyle View Chalets* (☎ (139) 67202) has standard/executive one-, two- and three- bedroom self-catering chalets with en suite facilities for US$14/17 per person; camping costs US$2. Amenities include a swimming pool, tennis courts and a relaxed restaurant and pub.

Further east are the *Mutirikwe Lakeshore Lodges* (☎ (139) 67151). These two-storey self-catering rondavels with en suite facilities accommodate up to six people. Economy/executive lodges are good value at US$11/17. Camping is US$2 per person. There's a swimming pool, shop and pub.

*Norma Jeanne's Lakeview Chalets* (☎ (139) 65083; fax 64879), on Dunollie Estate at the 42km peg of Mutirikwe Rd, is recommended for its friendly, homely atmosphere. Self-catering chalets cost US$17 per person. Go 200m east of Kyle View

Chalets and look towards the hillside on the right. Meals are available on request.

At *Chesvingo Village* (☎ (139) 67157), PO Box 773, Masvingo, near the southern shore of the lake, Shona villagers share their traditions and lifestyles with visitors. Camping costs US$2 per person. Guided four-hour walks to painted caves cost US$5 and excursions to other villages are US$7. From Mucheke in Masvingo, buses run daily at 6 am and 2 pm.

The pleasant and informal *Karanga Lodge* (☎/fax (139) 65793), overlooking Lake Mutirikwe, lies 8km down the Bushmead turn-off from the Masvingo-Great Zimbabwe road. Too bad it discriminates so heavily against foreigners, who pay US$175 per person for half-board accommodation, while locals pay US$34.

**North Shore** The *National Parks camp* (☎ (139) 62913), on the northern shore, has self-contained two- and three-bedroom lodges. The camp site has the standard features – showers, baths and braai pits – and costs US$3 per person. Book through National Parks in Harare.

The secluded *Glenlivet Hotel* (☎ (139) 67611; fax 62846), in the hills east of the lake, dates from the 1940s. For relaxation, guests can use the sauna, tennis courts and swimming pool. The surrounding hills provide several excellent hikes, including a steep climb to a mountain-top shelter and a pleasant stroll to the spring which supplies the hotel's water. Single/double rooms cost US$35/49, including bed and breakfast and a table d'hôte dinner. Family rooms cost US$18.50 per person.

The affiliated *Hippo Lodge* (☎/fax (139) 66041; <glenlivt@mvo.samara.co.zw>) has friendly and excellent value accommodation in a remote area of the north shore. The three stone and thatch self-catering chalets, with linen, blankets and hot showers, cost US$40 for up to four people. Backpackers double rooms with half-board (or use of self-catering facilities) and daily pickups from the Masvingo Publicity Association cost US$10 per person.

**Places to Eat**

Apart from the nearby *Great Zimbabwe Hotel* dining room, *Kyle View Chalets* has the only restaurant. Both Mutirikwe Lakeshore Lodges and Kyle View Chalets sell staples and beer (considered by some to be a staple).

The game park has two picnic sites; Mutirikwe, on the point at the end of Ostrich Loop, and Pokoteke Gorge, where the river flows into Lake Mutirikwe.

**Getting There & Away**

Once you're at Great Zimbabwe, it's an easy 6km walk or hitch to the south shore of Mutirikwe, but the main sites of interest are further along. The only public transport is the infrequent Glenlivet bus and hitching is poor along the sparsely travelled Murray McDougall scenic drive and Circular Drive between Great Zimbabwe and the Masvingo-Mutare road.

To reach the game park, it's probably easier to go the other way round, from Great Zimbabwe via Masvingo. The northern shore is best accessed from the turning off the Mutare road, 13km east of Masvingo.

When the lake is full, it may be possible to hitch a boat ride from Mutirikwe Lakeshore Lodges to the game park with one of the rangers. Phone the warden or senior ranger (☎ (139) 62913) during office hours (7 am to 6 pm daily).

See also under Masvingo in the Organised Tours chapter.

**MUSHANDIKE SANCTUARY**

A well-kept secret, the 13,360 hectare Mushandike Sanctuary lies 11km south of the Masvingo-Bulawayo road; the turn-off is 25km west of Masvingo. Its focus is Mushandike Dam, a blue jewel filling valleys between serene wooded hills. Look for sable, kudu, tsessebe, klipspringer,

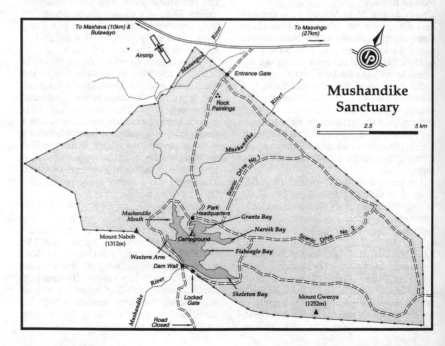

steenbok, grysbok, duiker, waterbuck, impala and wildebeest, as well as zebra, leopard and warthog.

The Mushandike campground may well be the most beautiful in the Zimbabwe National Parks system. For much of the year, you're likely to have it to yourself, but there's still an attendant on hand to look after the boiler and chop firewood. Especially in the winter, you'll find superb solitude, the air is cold and clear and the *mopane* forest puts on brilliant golds, reds and oranges.

The nearest shops are at Mashava and Masvingo. The information office or the National Parks officer training school, near the dam, can help with inquiries. You may also visit the eland research institute. Foreigners pay US$10 admission.

### Getting There & Away

To reach the Mushandike entrance, either hitch or take any Masvingo-Bulawayo bus. From there, access to park headquarters will probably entail an 11km walk as lifts are very rare. Note that the scenic drives in the eastern part of the sanctuary are rough. The gates on the boundary are locked and there's no access to the Beitbridge road.

### Getting Around

Mushandike is one of few parks where hiking and mountain biking are permitted.

# South-Eastern Zimbabwe

Much of south-eastern Zimbabwe is comprised of hot lowveld, characterised mainly by low scrub. Add water, however, and the desert blossoms, as it has around the well-irrigated sugar cane-growing area of Triangle. For tourists, the main draw to this region is the recently re-opened – and, as yet, little-visited – Gonarezhou National Park.

### MANJIRENJI DAM

In the beautiful transition zone between the highveld and lowveld, Manjirenji Dam Recreational Park lies lost in communal lands, 12km off MacDougall Rd (the untarred back route between Chiredzi and Masvingo). You'll find pleasant hiking tracks, ample picnic sites, and free camping in the basic shelters, but it's not a wilderness area and is heavily used by local people. There's no public transport into this area.

### RUNDE RIVER

The village of Runde River, on the Beitbridge-Masvingo road, enjoys a lovely setting beside the slow and shallow Runde River. It may remind you of an ancient Chinese painting, with rounded monolithic hills, dwala domes and lush vegetation. There's a craft centre in the village and lots of rock-climbing potential, but no amenities. If 'the road less taken' appeals to you, be sure to bring a tent.

### TRIANGLE

It's pretty easy to deduce that Triangle is a company town. Neat and square cornered (despite its name), it appears to have been prefabricated elsewhere and transplanted wholesale to the lowveld sea of waving sugar cane. Here, the company and its workers melt into one beehive of bland cooperation, and everyone and everything is stamped with the Triangle logo.

The success of Triangle – and it is successful – may be attributed to the persistence of an unconventional Scot by the name of Thomas Murray McDougall, who single-handedly introduced lowveld irrigation and converted the area into a productive agricultural region (see boxed text on page 329).

### McDougall Museum

Housed in McDougall's home, the McDougall museum sits on a hill about 1.5km off the highway. Here, you get the lowdown on events leading to the birth of Triangle Sugar Estates and its takeover by the Sugar

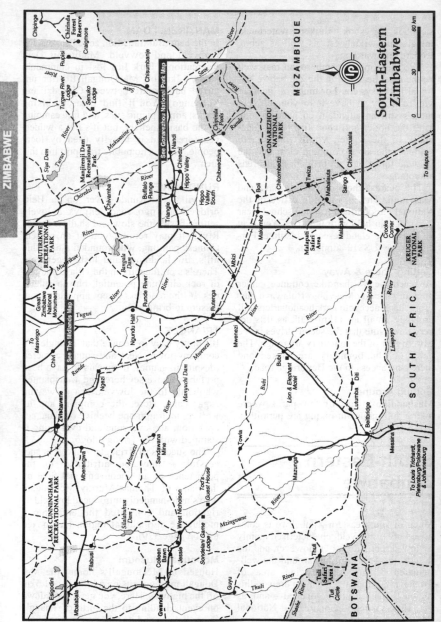

ZIMBABWE

South-Eastern Zimbabwe

Industry Board. There is also information about McDougall and the sugar industry in general. The building is now designated a national monument. It's open daily except Monday from 8.30 to 9.30 am and 3.30 to 4.30 pm. There's a nominal admission charge.

### Places to Stay & Eat

The only accommodation is at the *Country Club* (☎ (133) 6492), which charges US$10 per person. It also serves cheap basic meals.

### Getting There & Away

The airport for Triangle is at Buffalo Range. United Air Charters flies to and from Harare via Masvingo on Monday, Wednesday and Friday.

Daily buses between Harare, Masvingo and Chiredzi pass through Triangle.

### CHIREDZI

Hot and malaria-infested Chiredzi sprang up with the lowveld irrigation schemes of the mid-1960s. It's mainly a sugar town these days, but isn't as anomalous or interesting as nearby Triangle.

### Places to Stay & Eat

The one-star *Planter's Inn* (☎ (131) 2281), which sits on a hill in the centre, has a pub and a reasonable dining room. Singles/doubles cost US$27/39, including breakfast. Chalets for four people cost US$54, without breakfast.

The two-star *Tambuti Lodge* (☎ (131) 2575; fax 3187) is 12km from town on the Birchenough Bridge road. It has recently improved its image and the Chiredzi riverside setting is pleasant. Singles/doubles with bath cost US$20/30 with breakfast.

The *Country Club* at Hippo Valley, 10km from Chiredzi, is surrounded by endless expanses of sugar cane. Meals are available most of the day and they're now building chalets to provide accommodation.

The friendly *Continental Restaurant*, with odd, mirrored decor, whips up a surprising range of dishes. The raucous *La Bamba Night Club* next door offers a bar and nightly entertainment. A lesser option is the *dining room* at the Planter's Inn. The adjoining township, 2km from the centre, has a plethora of inexpensive snack stalls and takeaways.

---

### Thomas Murray McDougall

As a young man, Thomas Murray McDougall ran away from Scotland to the British Guiana (now known as Guyana) sugar plantations at the age of 14 but, by 1908, he found himself in lowveld Rhodesia. The purchase of a herd of cattle – all bearing a triangle brand – from a bankrupt rancher led to his first attempt at enterprise in the lowveld but, at that stage, the vast, flat and dry territory was far from productive.

When his ranch failed, McDougall hatched a new scheme; he saw the exotic waters of the Mutirikwe and other lowveld rivers as the key to agriculture in the otherwise desert country. The following seven years saw him digging and blasting two 425m irrigation tunnels through solid granite to divert the river waters onto his property.

By 1931, McDougall was growing cotton, vegetables, tobacco and cereal grains and tending orchards, but before long, his efforts were decimated by swarms of locusts. As a last resort, he used his early experience in South America and turned to sugar cane. Although the government was less than enthusiastic, it allowed him to import three stalks of cane from Natal in South Africa. The rest he had to smuggle in, merely a formality for this determined character. The events that led to the foundation of Triangle Sugar Estates and its takeover by the Sugar Industry Board are detailed in the museum on the site, which has now been designated a national monument.

The nearest camping is at Gonarezhou National Park; see later in this chapter.

### Getting There & Away

Chiredzi's airport, which serves mainly agricultural business traffic, is at Buffalo Range, 15km west of town. United Air Charters flies to and from Harare via Masvingo on Monday, Wednesday and Friday.

Bus services connect Chiredzi's township bus terminal with Harare, Masvingo, Mutare, Bulawayo and Beitbridge, as well as nearby Triangle, Hippo Valley and Buffalo Range.

### GONAREZHOU NATIONAL PARK

When large scale agriculture began encroaching on south-eastern Zimbabwe's wildlife habitat in the late 1960s, tsetse fly control measures (both large-scale bush burning and wildlife culling) claimed the lives of 55,000 large animals. In response, Nuanetsi District Commissioner Alan Wright suggested a wildlife refuge and poaching control corridor along the border. The result was the scenic 5000 sq km Gonarezhou Game Reserve, which is virtually an extension of South Africa's Kruger National Park. In 1975, it became a fully fledged national park. For more information, seek out copies of *Valley of the Ironwoods* and *Grey Ghosts of Buffalo Bend*, written by Alan Wright about his 10 years in the area.

The park's impressive parched scrublands are laced by the broad Mwenezi, Save and Runde rivers, which form ribbon-like oases for wildlife. In wetter times, when Great Zimbabwe was flourishing, traders probably navigated up the Save River as far as Chivilila Falls. The falls still impede saltwater species – Zambezi sharks, sawfish and tarpon – and have fostered the evolution of such rare species as freshwater goby (*Chonophorus aeneofusucus*), black bream (*Oreochromis placida*) and the bright turquoise killifish (*Nothobranchius furzeri*), which inhabits only tiny desert pools in the Mwenezi area.

Gonarezhou is also one of only two Zimbabwean habitats of the nyala (the other is Mana Pools) and the tiny suni antelope reach their highest concentrations here. The rare king cheetah, a marbled or striped model of the world's fastest animal, inhabits the park's furthest reaches.

### History

In Shona, *gona-re-zhou* means 'abode of elephants', but poaching has taken its toll. In the 1920s, one of Africa's most notorious poachers, Stephanus Barnard, shot his way through some of the continent's largest tuskers. His kills included the famous Dhulamithi, thought to have been the largest elephant ever taken in southern Africa – his tusks reportedly weighed in at over 110kg.

More recently, during the Mozambican civil war, guerrillas regularly crossed the border to escape pursuers and used the park as a bush larder. At the height of the conflict in the late 1980s and early 1990s, the park remained closed to non-Africans. The drought of the early 1990s also took its toll, and 750 Gonarezhou elephants were translocated. Most went only as far as the private Save Valley Conservancy, while around 150 wound up in South Africa. Gonarezhou has now reopened, but park elephants remember too many close calls with elephant guns and AK47s, and many bear grudges against humans, so keep a respectable distance.

### Information

Gonarezhou is divided into two administrative regions: the Save-Runde subregion in the north and Mwenezi subregion in the south. Some roads are passable to cars, but most require 4WD. The park is open to day visitors from 6 am to 6 pm from May to October. From November to April, access is restricted to Chipinda Pools, Mabalauta and Swimuwini.

Fishing is permitted only at camp sites unless you pick up a permit from the Department of National Parks and Wildlife Management at Chipinda Pools or Harare. Below Chivilila Falls on the Save and

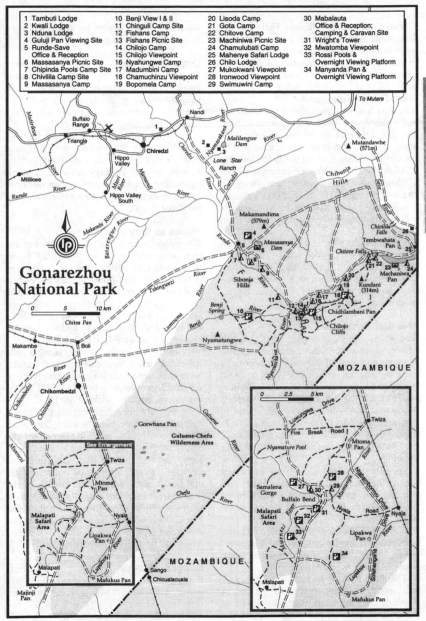

| | |
|---|---|
| 1 Tambuti Lodge | 10 Benji View I & II |
| 2 Kwali Lodge | 11 Chinguli Camp Site |
| 3 Nduna Lodge | 12 Fishans Camp |
| 4 Guluji Pan Viewing Site | 13 Fishans Picnic Site |
| 5 Runde-Save | 14 Chilojo Camp |
| Office & Reception | 15 Chilojo Viewpoint |
| 6 Massasanya Picnic Site | 16 Nyahungwe Camp |
| 7 Chipinda Pools Camp Site | 17 Madumbini Camp |
| 8 Chivilila Camp Site | 18 Chamuchinzu Viewpoint |
| 9 Massasanya Camp | 19 Bopomela Camp |
| 20 Lisoda Camp | 30 Mabalauta |
| 21 Gota Camp | Office & Reception; |
| 22 Chitove Camp | Camping & Caravan Site |
| 23 Machiniwa Picnic Site | 31 Wright's Tower |
| 24 Chamulubati Camp | 32 Mwatomba Viewpoint |
| 25 Mahenye Safari Lodge | 33 Rossi Pools & |
| 26 Chilo Lodge | Overnight Viewing Platform |
| 27 Mukokwani Viewpoint | 34 Manyanda Pan & |
| 28 Ironwood Viewpoint | Overnight Viewing Platform |
| 29 Swimuwini Camp | |

ZIMBABWE

Chitove (or Selawondoma) Falls on the Runde, bream, tiger fish and even some saltwater species have been caught.

Admission for foreigners is US$10 for one day and US$20 for up to a week.

## Save-Runde Subregion

The park's most photogenic attraction, the red sandstone Chilojo (or Tjolotjo) cliffs, rise like a Rajasthani fortress near the confluence of the Runde and Save Rivers. The area offers the park's best wildlife viewing.

With 4WD, you can drive right to the Chilojo and Chamuchinzu viewpoints, at the top of the cliffs. In a 2WD vehicle, you'll only get as close as Fishans Camp, which affords good views of the cliffs from below.

On the short side trip to the two Benji View viewpoints, you won't see much wildlife, but you'll love the stark, silent landscape. There are picnic sites at Massasanya and Fishans Camps, both accessible by ordinary cars in the dry season.

## Mwenezi Subregion

The scenic pools and pans that dot the Mwenezi subregion offer excellent wildlife viewing and Rossi Pools has an overnight viewing shelter. Other pools of interest include Mwatomba, deep in a rock shelter; Mukokwani, with a small picnic shelter; Manyanda Pan, with an overnight viewing platform; and Makonde. Makonde is overlooked by Wright's Tower, which was built by Alan Wright to facilitate wildlife viewing.

On clear days, the view from Ironwood viewpoint extends to Mozambique and sometimes even into South Africa's Kruger National Park. It's framed by large ironwood trees on a sharp ridge near Swimuwini. The shallow Samalena Gorge (the place of execution), on the Mwenezi River, is filled with semi-permanent rock pools and may be explored on foot.

The large ox-bow lake, Majinji Pan, lies just outside the park west of the Mwenezi River. It once attracted enormous flocks of water-loving birds, but siphoning of the

Runde and Save rivers for lowveld irrigation is causing it to dry up.

## Organised Tours

From May to October at the full moon, groups of up to six people can join four-day, ranger-guided game walks through the Mwenezi subregion. Overnight camps are made at permanent water holes.

For the best of Gonarezhou on foot, go with Khangela Safaris (see the Organised Tours chapter), which runs backpacking safaris as well as day-walks from semi-permanent camps. Scheduled trips last from six to 10 days, and custom safaris are also available.

## Places to Stay

**Camping** In the Save-Runde subregion, the most accessible camp site is idyllic *Chipinda Pools*, which lies down a corrugated gravel road from Chiredzi. Sites have shelters and braai areas, and overlook the lush pools, which teem with hippo. Further upstream is *Chinguli Camp*. Both camps have showers and flush toilets and, in the dry season, are accessible without 4WD.

Primitive *camp sites*, strung along Runde River between Chipinda Pools and Runde-Save confluence, are limited to one party of up to 12 people at a time. Only *Fishans Camp* is accessible without 4WD.

In the Mwenezi subregion, the nicest camp is *Swimuwini* (place of baobabs), which overlooks Buffalo Bend in the Mwenezi River. It's accessible in an ordinary car and offers both camping and chalets. It's also a haunt of both elephant and lion, and the small pond attracts nyala. The more basic *Mabalauta Camping and Caravan Site* has five sites and an ablutions block. Two wildlife-viewing hides, *Rossi Pools* and *Manyanda Pan*, may be occupied overnight by individual parties.

**Lodges** Outside Gonarezhou National Park, on the 40,000 hectare Lone Star game ranch, lie two Malilangwe Conservation Trust safari lodges (☎ (113) 4527; fax 4224; <wildness@zol.co.zw>), which cycle profits back into the reserve. At *Nduna Lodge*, which caters for adults, foreigners pay US$225 per person for sandstone and thatch bungalows with en suite facilities, game walks, fishing and wildlife-viewing hides. Gonarezhou day trips are available at extra cost. The family- and art-oriented *Kwali Lodge* accommodates 18 people in thatched wooden bungalows with communal ablutions for US$75 per person, including meals.

*Mahenye Safari Lodge*, magically set on an island at the Runde-Save confluence, features rustic single/double chalets inspired by the local Shangaan architecture. Its sibling, *Chilo Lodge*, lies on the Save River a short distance upstream. Both charge US$256/454, including meals and activities (locals pay a more reasonable US$69/95). Both can be booked through Sun Hotels (☎ (14) 736644; fax 736646). For air taxi transfers from Chiredzi, foreigners pay US$87 and locals US$47.

The nearest supplies are at Rutenga and Chiredzi.

### Getting There & Away
The only public transport into the region is with Zimbabwe Sun's Sabi Star transfer service, which goes to the Chilo, Mahenye and Senuko lodges, and costs US$36 from Harare and US$18 from Masvingo.

### SAVE & CHIREDZI RIVER CONSERVATION AREAS
These adjoining conservation areas comprise 340,000 hectares of wildlife-rich lowveld scrubland. They were formed in the early 1990s by merging several private landholdings and effectively extend an already vast protected area which takes in Gonarezhou National Park, South Africa's Kruger National Park and Mozambique's Banhine and Zinave national parks. Projects include elephant translocation, black rhino breeding and conservation of predators, particularly wild dog.

### Places to Stay
The stone and thatch *Makwekwete Lodge*

(☎ (131) 2865; fax 3026), run by Mungwezi Safaris, PO Box 297, Chiredzi, lies amid the granite kopjes of the Chiredzi River Conservation Area and offers hiking, riding and lowveld wildlife viewing. It accommodates only one group at a time and costs under US$80 per person.

The *Turgwe River Lodge* (☎/fax (14) 307921; <bushveld@mail.pci.co.zw>), lies on Humani Ranch in the Save River Conservation Area and occupies a classic lowveld landscape of granite kopjes, savannas, and mopane, baobab and ilala scrub. Bungalow accommodation costs US$145 per person.

The *Senuko Safari Lodge* (☎ (131) 7241; fax 7244; <senuko@svc.icon.co.zw), run by conservationist Clive Stockil, is a new Zimbabwe Sun hotel, built of local materials on a granite kopje. For single/double bungalows with meals and activities, foreigners pay US$381/478 and locals pay US$118/147. Transfers from Buffalo Range airport cost US$14; Zimbabwe Sun's Sabi Star bus service charges US$36 from Harare and US$18 from Great Zimbabwe.

### BEITBRIDGE
Beitbridge was named after the Limpopo River bridge, which was in turn named after Alfred Beit of the Beit Trust, which financed it. Exciting in name only is the 'great grey-green greasy Limpopo', an unimpressive green channel sliding through a scrubby flood-plain. However, you won't catch even a glimpse of the river unless you're crossing the border.

This is Zimbabwe's only border crossing with South Africa, and hot, tedious waits are possible. Most travellers stop in Beitbridge only long enough to fill up with petrol (Beitbridge must have more petrol stations per capita than anywhere else in Zimbabwe) and, for many, even that's too much time there.

### Places to Stay
If you're caught out after the border crossing closes, try *Peter's Hotel* (☎ (186) 2309), where singles/doubles cost US$15/26.

The more upmarket *Beitbridge Inn* (☎ (186) 2214; fax 2413), has single/double cottages for US$20/33. Rooms in the main building are US$17/31.

Travellers on the Masvingo road can stop at the pleasant *Lion & Elephant Motel* (☎ (186) 336; fax 358) at Bubi River, 78km from Beitbridge. The beautiful riverside camp site costs US$2 per person, including use of facilities. Singles/doubles with bed and breakfast are US$26/32. A similar place on the Bulawayo road, 120km from Beitbridge, is *Tod's Guest House* (☎ (116) 5403), Private Bag N5244, Bulawayo, which charges US$17 per person, with breakfast; camping is US$2 per car plus US$1 per person.

Near West Nicholson, 125km from Beitbridge on the Bulawayo road, is the lovely *Sondelani Game Lodge* (☎ (19) 68739; fax 64997). At this private game ranch, foreigners pay US$150 to US$220 per person for accommodation, meals, game drives and walks, elephant rides and transfers from Beitbridge or Bulawayo. Locals pay US$38.

### Places to Eat

The *Bird Cage Restaurant and Snack Bar* at the Beitbridge Inn is only an option if you really can't control your hunger. If you'd wisely prefer to pick up supplies and press on, *Sunrise Takeaways* serves snacks and there's also a small supermarket. The South African side offers more variety but at higher prices.

### Getting There & Away

The Mangena minibus runs to Bulawayo on Monday, Wednesday and Friday at noon and on Tuesday and Thursday at 8 am, and numerous African buses connect Beitbridge with Masvingo, Harare and Bulawayo.

Note that motorists leaving Zimbabwe are charged a 'toll' of US$6 to cross South Africa's Limpopo Bridge. For information on cross-border buses, see South Africa in the Zimbabwe Getting There & Away chapter.

## GWANDA

Gwanda, a railway cattle-loading station on the Bulawayo-Beitbridge road, began as a service centre for the gold fields. The former gold mine at Colleen Bawn, 25km south-east of Gwanda, was first claimed in 1895 by Irish prospector Sam Daly, who named it after his girlfriend back in Dublin. Daly himself was perpetually short of luck but, in 1905, a marginal vein was discovered. Although gold-mining is no longer profitable, the mountain behind Colleen Bawn is now being removed and converted into cement.

### Places to Stay

Gwanda has little to attract visitors but, if you're caught out, there's a *caravan park* east of town and on the main street is rundown *Hardy's Inn* (☎ (184) 476).

## TULI CIRCLE

The geographically anomalous Tuli Circle, an odd semi-circular Zimbabwean bridgehead on the western bank of the Shashe River, is the result of the 1891 definition of magisterial jurisdiction over a 16km radius of Thuli village. The name is derived from the Shona word *uthuli*, meaning dust.

This 416 sq km area now comprises the Tuli Safari Area, created in 1963, which takes in some stunning riverine scenery. Although mainly a hunting area, it also contains three small botanical reserves which protect mopane woodland and riverine forest. Admission for foreigners costs US$5.

### History

Fort Tuli, which was built in 1890 by the Rhodesian Pioneer Column, is best-known as the site of Zimbabwe's first rugby match (1890), which pitted the Pioneers against the Fort Tuli soldiers in the Shashe riverbed. The following year, a contingent of Lobengula's army visited (most likely to assess the feasibility of an attack) and were treated to an impressive demonstration of British firepower. No confrontation ever materialised.

During the Boer Wars, Fort Tuli served as a supply and training depot and attracted a Catholic nursing mission led by Mother Patrick, of Harare fame. In 1897, however, the new railway between South Africa and Bulawayo bypassed the Tuli Circle and, by the turn of the century, most colonists had left. All that remains is a monument, a cemetery and a flag marking the fort site.

### Getting There & Away

Access is tough – you can approach on the rough track along the Limpopo from north of Beitbridge, or the equally rough route south from the Beitbridge-Bulawayo road, midway between Gwanda and Beitbridge. A daily Bulawayo-Beitbridge bus runs via Thuli (the village north of the Shashe River), but it's a slow trip.

# Bulawayo

ZIMBABWE

Originally called Gu-Bulawayo – the killing place – Bulawayo (population 900,000) is Zimbabwe's bright and historically intriguing second city. The name presumably resulted from the executions that accompanied the development of the Ndebele state under Mzilikazi. These took place on Thabas Indunas (Hill of Chiefs), which occupied a site near present-day Bulawayo. However, because Harare became the seat of government in the colonial era, Bulawayo has been largely free from political tension, and now emits a peaceful, relaxed ambience.

## History

In early 19th century Transvaal (now in South Africa), newly unified Zululand suffered a series of political disturbances. After the overthrow of Zulu leader Dingiswayo by an ambitious young captain, Shaka, the realm was brought to its knees when the ruthless new king launched a reign of terror. Several subordinate groups, now called the Nguni, fled his wrath on what was called the *mfecane* (forced migration). One refugee, Mzilikazi, who'd had irreconcilable differences with Shaka, arrived in south-western Zimbabwe with his Kumalo clan in the 1830s and took the name Ndebele, 'those who carry long shields'.

On Mzilikazi's death in 1870, his son Lobengula assumed the throne and moved his capital to Bulawayo. He soon found himself face to face with the British South Africa Company (BSAC), and in 1888 Lobengula had his first meeting with Cecil Rhodes. At this meeting, the king was duped into signing the Rudd Concession, which granted the foreigners mineral rights in exchange for 10,000 rifles, 100,000 rounds of ammunition, a gunboat and £100 monthly.

A series of misunderstandings followed, with disastrous consequences. Lobengula

## HIGHLIGHTS

- Explore the rocky hills and painted caves, and spot rhino in Matobo National Park
- Look for the past at Bulawayo's famous Museum of Natural History
- Visit the Khami ruins, Zimbabwe's second-largest complex
- Discover Zimbabwe's artistic roots at the Mzilikazi Arts and Crafts Centre

sent a contingent of Ndebele raiders to Fort Victoria (Masvingo) to prevent Shona interference in relations between the British and the Ndebele. The British mistook this as aggression against them and launched an attack on Matabeleland, the Ndebele territory (which incidentally was rumoured to hold vast mineral deposits). As a result, Lobengula's kraals were destroyed, Bulawayo was burned and the king fled the pursuing BSAC troops.

Lobengula sent the BSAC a peace offering of gold, but it was commandeered by company employees and never reached Rhodes. The vengeful British dispatched

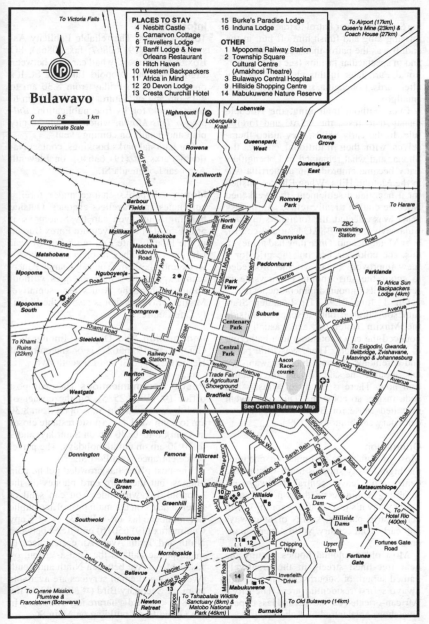

## Bulawayo

0    0.5    1 km
Approximate Scale

**PLACES TO STAY**
4 Nesbitt Castle
5 Carnarvon Cottage
6 Travellers Lodge
7 Banff Lodge & New
  Orleans Restaurant
8 Hitch Haven
10 Western Backpackers
11 Africa in Mind
12 20 Devon Lodge
13 Cresta Churchill Hotel

15 Burke's Paradise Lodge
16 Induna Lodge

**OTHER**
1 Mpopoma Railway Station
2 Township Square
  Cultural Centre
  (Amakhosi Theatre)
3 Bulawayo Central Hospital
9 Hillside Shopping Centre
14 Mabukuwene Nature Reserve

ZIMBABWE

the Shangani River Patrol to track down the missing king and finish him off but, in the end, it was the patrol that was finished off, and in spectacular fashion (see Matobo National Park later in this chapter). Shortly afterwards, Lobengula, still in exile, died of smallpox.

Even without their king, the Ndebele managed to resist the BSAC and foreign rule. In the early 1890s, they allied themselves with their traditional enemy, the Shona, and what remained of Lobengula's army became embroiled in a guerrilla war in the Matobo Hills. When Rhodes pushed for a negotiated settlement, the weakened Ndebele couldn't really refuse. An uneasy peace was effected, the foreigners invaded Bulawayo and the BSAC assumed control over Matabeleland. Once they had achieved this, the colonists laid out the grid for a 'new improved' Bulawayo and proceeded to scour the surrounding countryside in search of its rumoured mineral deposits.

On 1 June 1894, Dr Leander Starr Jameson climbed onto a soapbox outside the Maxim Hotel bar and casually announced the city's founding to a gathering of boozy revellers. There was little pomp and ceremony: 'I don't think we want any talk about it', he said. 'I make the declaration now. There is plenty of whisky and soda inside, so come in.' This little event provided cause for Bulawayo's extensive centenary celebrations in 1994.

### Orientation

Most of Bulawayo's population occupies the high-density suburbs north-west of the centre. This leaves central Bulawayo resembling a middle-sized town in Kansas (and by day it's just about as exciting), with centre-strip parking, scores of takeaways and early 20th century North American architecture.

Most older colonial homes occupy the neat tree-lined streets in the creatively named suburb of Suburbs, which was Bulawayo's first residential area. The city's African-oriented businesses and less expensive shops are centred on Lobengula St.

### Information

**Tourist Office** The reliable Publicity Association (☎ (19) 60867; fax 60868), PO Box 861, is at the city hall car park between Eighth Ave and Leopold Takawira St. It's open Monday to Friday from 8.30 am to 4.45 pm and on Saturday from 8.30 am to noon. Look for its free publication, *Bulawayo This Month*, which includes a city plan and details on coming events.

For national parks bookings, contact National Parks (☎ (19) 63646), on Eleventh Ave near Lobengula St.

**Money** All banks change major foreign currencies and travellers cheques. Outside banking hours, you can try Solomons at 56B Fife St or the Adventure Forex Bureau in the Fidelity Life Centre on Fife St near Eleventh Ave. They're open seven days a week until 4.30 pm. You can change American Express travellers cheques without commission at the AmEx representative, Manica Travel, which is also in the Fidelity Life Centre.

**Immigration** The Dept of Immigration Control (☎ (19) 65621) is on the corner of Herbert Chitepo St and Eleventh Ave.

**Post & Communications** The main post office (☎ (19) 62535), on the corner of Eighth Ave and Main St, is open from 8.30 am to 5 pm weekdays (poste restante closes at 4 pm); 8 to 11.30 am on Saturday; and 9 to 10.30 am on public holidays. The parcel office entrance is on Fort St.

The post office has crowded public coin phones, but there are card phones on the Leopold Takawira side. You can send or receive faxes on the main post office public fax number (fax (19) 78053) or at Copy Centre (fax (19) 65016) on Fife St between Ninth and Tenth Aves. An easier place to make phone calls is the Dial-a-Vision, on Jason Moyo Ave between Ninth and Tenth Aves. Fax and email services are available from the Secretary Bird (☎ (19) 68230; fax 78081; <secbird@harare.iafrica.com>) in the Grand Hotel building on Main St.

**Travel Agencies** The American Express Representative is Manica Travel (☎ (19) 540531) on Tenth Ave between Main and Fort Sts.

For tour information and bookings, try Sunshine Tours (☎ (19) 67791; fax 74832; <sunshine@msasa.samara.co.zw>) at 5 Basnic House near Twelfth Ave and Fife St, or Adventure Travel (☎ (19) 66525; fax 74832), on Ninth Ave between George Silundika St and Robert Mugabe St.

**Bookshops** Kingston's outlet is on Jason Moyo St between Eighth and Ninth Aves and is well stocked. Book Centre, on Eighth Ave between Main and Jason Moyo Sts, has a more sophisticated selection, including a range of Africa-theme books and pulp novels. The best book exchange is Book Mart at 103 George Silundika St. For maps, see the Surveyor General in the Tredgold Building on the corner of Fort St and Leopold Takawira Ave.

**Camping Equipment** Eezee Kamping, on George Silundika St between Ninth and Tenth Aves, is probably the best outdoors shop in Zimbabwe, which isn't really saying a lot. To hire tents, stoves, cooking implements and warm clothing, try Iverson's (☎ (19) 61644) on the Khami road west of town. However, its equipment is designed for motor safaris and isn't suitable for hiking.

**Left Luggage** You can leave luggage at the railway station indefinitely for US$0.15 per piece per day.

**Laundry** The Bulawayo Laundrette, 109A Josiah Tongogara Ave, is open daily and charges US$3 per load for washing and drying. The Fife Street Laundrette, in the Fidelity Life Centre on Fife St near Eleventh Ave, has coin-operated machines and 75-minute laundry services. It's closed Wednesday and Sunday afternoons.

**Emergency Services** The emergency services number is ☎ 99. For non-emergency

police calls, dial ☎ (19) 72515. The best equipped hospital is Bulawayo Central (☎ (19) 72111) on St Lukes Ave, Kumalo, near Ascot Race Course. The recommended Galen House Emergency Medical Clinic (☎ (19) 540051), on Josiah Tongogara St near Ninth Ave, is open 24 hours and charges just US$8 for a consultation.

**Dangers & Annoyances** Although personal security in laid-back Bulawayo is much better than in Harare, lone women should avoid remote parts of Centenary and Central parks. Also, avoid walking between the city centre and the Municipal Caravan Park and Camp Site, especially after dark.

### Centenary & Central Parks
The vast Central and Centenary parks separate the commercial centre from the upmarket suburbs and provide a lunchtime green fix for harried office workers, a nap spot for idle hours and playing fields for children. Centenary Park further attracts the younger set with a playground, a miniature railway and a model-boat pond. It also boasts an aviary, well-tended botanical gardens, the Museum of Natural History and the Bulawayo Theatre. Central Park offers swathes of true bushland as well as shady lawns, benches and small gardens. The Municipal Caravan Park & Camp Site occupies a fenced enclosure in Central Park.

### City Hall Square
Along the Fife St footpath at City Hall Square, souvenir hawkers, needle-workers, artists and flower vendors display their wares. The city hall building houses the city council chambers and the Bulawayo archives. Also, note the renovated town well, which once supplied all the city's water; it was rediscovered in 1951.

### Museum of Natural History
Bulawayo's famous Museum of Natural History in Centenary Park probably merits a half day visit. Well-realised displays and dioramas include 75,000 examples of all

ZIMBABWE

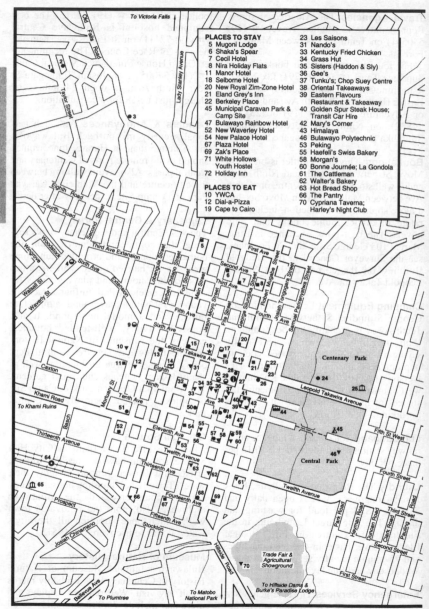

**PLACES TO STAY**
5 Mugoni Lodge
6 Shaka's Spear
7 Cecil Hotel
8 Nira Holiday Flats
11 Manor Hotel
18 Selborne Hotel
20 New Royal Zim-Zone Hotel
21 Eland Grey's Inn
22 Berkeley Place
45 Municipal Caravan Park &
Camp Site
47 Bulawayo Rainbow Hotel
52 New Waverley Hotel
54 New Palace Hotel
67 Plaza Hotel
69 Zak's Place
71 White Hollows
Youth Hostel
72 Holiday Inn

**PLACES TO EAT**
10 YWCA
12 Dial-a-Pizza
19 Cape to Cairo

23 Les Saisons
31 Nando's
33 Kentucky Fried Chicken
34 Grass Hut
35 Sisters (Haddon & Sly)
36 Gee's
37 Tunku's; Chop Suey Centre
38 Oriental Takeaways
39 Eastern Flavours
Restaurant & Takeaway
40 Golden Spur Steak House;
Transit Car Hire
42 Mary's Corner
43 Himalaya
46 Bulawayo Polytechnic
53 Peking
55 Haefeli's Swiss Bakery
58 Morgan's
60 Bonne Journée; La Gondola
61 The Cattleman
62 Walter's Bakery
63 Hot Bread Shop
66 The Pantry
70 Cypriana Taverna;
Harley's Night Club

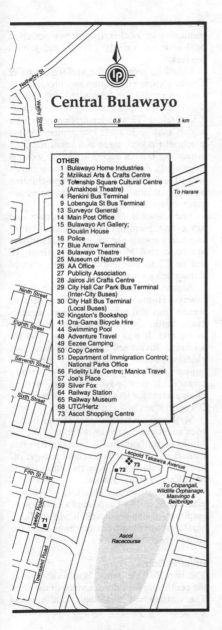

**OTHER**
1  Bulawayo Home Industries
2  Mzilikazi Arts & Crafts Centre
3  Township Square Cultural Centre
   (Amakhosi Theatre)
4  Renkini Bus Terminal
9  Lobengula St Bus Terminal
13 Surveyor General
14 Main Post Office
15 Bulawayo Art Gallery;
   Douslin House
16 Police
17 Blue Arrow Terminal
24 Bulawayo Theatre
25 Museum of Natural History
26 AA Office
27 Publicity Association
28 Jairos Jiri Crafts Centre
29 City Hall Car Park Bus Terminal
   (Inter-City Buses)
30 City Hall Bus Terminal
   (Local Buses)
32 Kingston's Bookshop
41 Dra-Gama Bicycle Hire
44 Swimming Pool
48 Adventure Travel
49 Eezee Camping
50 Copy Centre
51 Department of Immigration Control;
   National Parks Office
56 Fidelity Life Centre; Manica Travel
57 Joe's Place
59 Silver Fox
64 Bulawayo Station
65 Railway Museum
68 UTC/Hertz
73 Ascot Shopping Centre

**Central Bulawayo**

sorts of wildlife indigenous to Zimbabwe: birds, antelope, predators, fish and reptiles (a few are still alive). It even claims the world's second-largest stuffed elephant, and one room is dedicated entirely to bugs.

Historical displays present African and European cultures, arts and artefacts in sections dedicated to humanity and weaponry, both ancient and modern. In one corner, an artificial mine emphasises Zimbabwe's mineral wealth and explains extraction methods through the ages. There's also an extensive rock and mineral collection, with explanations of Zimbabwe's prominent topographical features.

The museum is open from 9 am to 5 pm daily except Christmas and Good Friday. Foreigners pay US$2 admission.

### Railway Museum

The Railway Museum tells the story of rail in Zimbabwe. It boasts a collection of historic steam locomotives, railway offices and buildings, passenger carriages and a model of an historic railway station with period furnishings. Check out Cecil Rhodes' opulent private carriage, which dates from the 1890s; the Service Coach No 0831; and the beautiful 9B Class Locomotive No 115, built at the North British Loco Co in 1912 and sold for £8124.

Bulawayo's Railway Museum pays tribute to Zimbabwe's rail heritage.

It's open from 9.30 am to noon and 2 to 4 pm Tuesday to Friday, and weekends from 3 to 5 pm. So far, it has resisted multi-tier pricing; admission is still just US$0.15.

Rail buffs can also join the engineers in the steam locomotives in their shunting duties. For arrangements or photography permits, see the National Railways publicity officer, on the 6th floor of the National Railways of Zimbabwe building on Fife St, near Haefeli's Swiss Bakery.

The museum is lost amid the rail lines and unpaved streets of the Raylton suburb, and the quickest foot access is a roundabout circuit through the station and over the tracks.

### Douslin House & the Bulawayo Art Gallery

The imposing Douslin House, on the corner of Main St and Leopold Takawira Ave, is one of Bulawayo's finest buildings. Originally known as the Willoughby Building, this beautiful colonial structure was completed in 1900 and first occupied the following year by the Willoughby Consolidated Co, a mining and ranching firm. Due to cement costs at the time of construction, the foundations extend only 15cm below the surface.

In 1956, the building was taken over by African Associated Mines and ominously renamed Asbestos House. After the Bulawayo Art Gallery purchased it in 1980, the name was changed to Douslin House in honour of its original architect, William Douslin. The building now houses the Bulawayo Art Gallery's permanent collection, including modern African art and paintings by Bulawayo artists.

It's open from 10 am to 5 pm Tuesday to Friday and Sunday, and on Saturday from 10 am to noon. Admission is a mere US$0.15 and, believe it or not, students get a discount.

### Mzilikazi Arts & Crafts Centre

Mthwakazi Crafts Bulawayo, headquartered in Princess Margaret Park at the corner of Leopold Takawira Ave and Samuel Parirenyatwa St, is an umbrella organisation of local crafts groups made up of 800 artisans, mainly women and school leavers.

Of all its projects, the Mzilikazi Arts & Crafts Centre is a Bulawayo highlight. It was originally established by the city in 1963 to provide art training for otherwise latent talent. This concentration of artistic ability may seem more like a museum than a school (indeed, there is a small museum where the best of recent students' work is displayed). Full-time enrolment now stands at 150 and nearly 500 school-age children attend part-time. Proceeds from sales are returned to the school.

The school is divided into ceramics and stoneware, painting, iron and stone sculpting and carving classrooms. Guided tours are conducted Monday to Friday from 10 am to 12.30 pm and 2 to 5 pm, except during school holidays.

Across the lawn beside the library is Bulawayo Home Industries, where artisans weave rugs and produce sweaters, needlecraft, batik, crochet, tapestries and other home arts. It was first set up in 1964 for widows, divorcees and abandoned and elderly women with no other means of support, and was subsidised by the city council. It now pays for itself, selling choice items for less than curio shop prices. It's open 9 am to 4 pm weekdays.

Mzilikazi and Bulawayo Home Industries are 3km from the town centre. Take the Mpilo or Barbour Fields (marked BF) bus from the Lobengula St terminal and get off at either Bulawayo Home Industries or the Mzilikazi Primary School.

Another affiliate, Buhlaluse, which was established in 1989, produces a selection of inspired African beadwork. It's in the Tshabalala suburb 6km from the centre, near the Khami road.

### Hillside Dams

The two Hillside dams, 5km south-east of the centre, are now dry for much of the year. The surrounding rock kopjes and gardens are great for picnics, braais, and strolling amid the aloes. Unfortunately, crime has increased here, so stay vigilant. Take the Hillside Rd or Burnside bus from the city hall terminal, get off at Moffat St and walk the remaining 1km to the dams. The site is open from dawn to dusk.

### Mabukuwene Nature Reserve
This 12 hectare park in Burnside provides a bit of bushland within city limits. In addition to a range of indigenous trees, plants and bird life, there's a wild aloe garden and a gazebo with a view across the entire city. It lies 1km west of Burnside Rd, via Chipping Way.

### Old Bulawayo
A project is now in progress to develop an historical theme park and restore the ruins of Old Bulawayo and its Jesuit mission to their former state. You can still see the 1881 remains of the wagon garage of Ndebele king Lobengula, several hut floors and the walls of the old Jesuit mission. It's scheduled for completion by 2000, but is already open to casual visitors. Take Hillside/Burnside Rd for 18km from the centre, turn right on Criterion Mine Rd and follow it for 6km to Old Bulawayo.

### Lobengula's Kraal
The original Bulawayo was established by Lobengula in 1881 at the site of the present-day State House, in the Highmount suburb north of town. In 1886, however, it was burned as the chief fled the approaching BSAC forces. All that remains of his kraal is the indaba (meeting) tree, which oddly escaped the fire, where he met with his tribal council to conduct official business. There's now a small museum in a rondavel originally constructed for Cecil Rhodes on one of his official visits. However, the museum is rarely open to the public so check first with the Publicity Association.

### Activities
Golf is available at the Bulawayo Country Club, the Bulawayo Golf Club and the Harry Allen Golf Club, all within a few kilometres of the city centre. The gym on the corner of Ninth Ave and Fort St has a weights room, aerobics classes, a sauna and squash courts, and charges reasonable daily, weekly and monthly rates.

The municipal swimming pool in Central Park on Samuel Parirenyatwa St is open from late August to late May, 10 am to 2 pm and 3 to 6 pm. Admission costs US$0.25.

### Organised Tours
UTC (☎ (19) 61402), at Fourteenth Ave and George Silundika St, does half-day city tours (US$17) taking in the Museum of Natural History, Centenary Park, Mzilikazi Arts and Crafts Centre and Bulawayo Home Industries, or just the Museum of Natural History and the Railway Museum (US$10). Other excursions include Khami Ruins (US$13) and Chipangali (US$11).

The recommended Black Rhino Safaris (☎/fax (19) 41662) does tours to Khami (US$25), Chipangali (US$25) and half-day or full-day Matobo tours (US$35/45), with a picnic lunch. Sandbank Safaris (☎ (19) 69923 or 43865 after hours) organises Matobo tours or wildlife-viewing trips on horseback in the Mazwi Reserve for US$55, including transport, guide and three picnic meals.

Ms Alice Nkomo's Mzingeli Tours (☎ (19) 540268; fax 540269), 133 Leopold Takawira Ave, specialises in cultural tours, including Old Bulawayo, the high density suburbs, the Mzilikazi Arts and Crafts Centre and Amakhosi Theatre at the Township Square Cultural Centre. She also visits Tshabalala; the Matobo, Kezi, Chipangali and Cyrene communal lands; and several cultural self-help programmes. Prices range from US$15 to US$45.

Unique tours of the townships are run by the grass roots Umzabalazo Theatre Resource Consultancy Team (☎ (19) 72939; fax 78053), at the Bulawayo Art Gallery. Tours take in Mzilikazi Arts and Crafts Centre; Barbourfields Stadium; Amakhosi's Township Square Cultural Centre; Church St, with the townships' earliest educational and recreational facilities; and

ZIMBABWE

MaKhumalo's Big Beer, which may be Zimbabwe's largest beer hall.

African Wanderer (☎/fax (19) 72736), run by Ken and Ian Harmer, does half-day tours to Tshabalala, Chipangali, Khami or Cyrene Mission, as well as city tours and cultural heritage tours; each costs US$25.

A unique option called Mbowe Inspan attempts to recreate pioneer days with five-hour ox-wagon rides on a private farm in Marula. You can choose between a champagne breakfast and snacks or a lunch and snacks. Locals/foreigners pay US$25/65. Book through Sunshine Tours in Bulawayo.

For more information on Matobo Tours, see Organised Tours under Matobo National Park, later in this chapter.

### Events

Bulawayo's big annual event is the Zimbabwe International Trade Fair, held during the last week in April or the first week in May at the Trade Fair & Agricultural Society Show Ground south of the centre. The displays and booths on technology and commercial ventures draw at least 200,000 visitors and 1000 exhibitors from around Zimbabwe and the world. Peripheral events provide further entertainment.

### Places to Stay – Budget

The *Municipal Caravan Park & Camp Site* (☎ (19) 63851), on Caravan Way, Central Park, occupies a garden setting just 10 minutes walk from the centre. It's clean and well guarded, with hot showers or baths. Sites cost US$1/3 per tent/caravan plus US$1 per person. Basic chalets are US$6 per person. Taxis from the centre cost around US$1.50; don't even consider walking there after dark.

The greatly-improved *White Hollows Youth Hostel* (☎ (19) 76488), 20 minutes walk from the centre, is in an old house in a predominantly wealthy neighbourhood. There's a TV lounge, cooking facilities and hot showers. It costs US$2/3 per person for Hostelling International members/non-members. It's no longer locked up during the day.

At the *Country Rest Camp* (☎ (19) 229551), 19km out on the Victoria Falls road, camping costs US$2/2.50 per person in tents/caravans plus US$2 per vehicle, and dormitory beds are US$5. Self-catering chalets are US$16 for up to three people.

The success and popularity of the rollicking *Shaka's Spear* (☎ (19) 69923 or 61385), 4 Baron Flats, at the corner of Second Ave and Jason Moyo, is thanks mainly to its enthusiastic proprietors, Mike and Natalie Magee. Dorm beds cost US$4.50, with use of cooking and laundry facilities. This is the only backpackers lodge in Bulawayo's central area.

The basic *Western Backpackers* (☎ (19) 44100), at 5 Nottingham Rd, Hillcrest, lies 600m off Hillside Rd and offers a bar, pool table, swimming pool and braais. It's run by Rachel and Charity, who create a friendly and lively atmosphere. Dorm beds cost US$4 and doubles are US$9. Guests are picked up at the city hall car park at 5 pm, and booked guests are also met at the railway station and bus terminals.

*Africa Sun Lodge* (☎ (19) 31528 or 46824), 398 Thurso Rd, Killarney, run by Anthony, Lilly and Sebastian Kruger, occupies a large old house 7km from the centre. They offer free pickups from the bus or train and there's a regular shuttle service to the centre. Facilities include a kitchen, swimming pool, bar, braai area, a video lounge and optional meals. It's good value at US$4 per person for dorms and US$9 for doubles. From Ascot shopping centre, take Coghlan Ave, which turns into Tayport Rd. Turn right on Flisk and then right again on Thurso; it's the first house on the right.

At 11 Inverleith Drive in the Burnside suburb (5km from the town centre) you'll find the friendly, secure and quiet *Burke's Paradise Lodge* (☎ (19) 46481; fax 64576; <paradise@harare.iafrica.com>), run by Allan Burke. Camping costs US$4 per person and dorm beds or doubles (even 'honeymoon suites' with private facilities) are US$6 per person, including linen and use of the pool, sun deck, barbecue, videos and laundry and cooking facilities. Pickups and transfers to and from town are free, or you can catch a commuter minibus from Twelfth Ave and Josiah Tongogara St for US$0.25. It's on a large and leafy estate and the entrance is only 200m from Mabukuwene Nature Reserve.

Another cosy backpackers place is *20 Devon Lodge* (☎ (19) 41501), in Hillside, run by Carol and Cliff Correia. They offer free pickups from town and amenities include a bar, outdoor dining area, TV lounge, volleyball, cooking facilities and a family atmosphere. Take the Hillside Rd bus from Stand II at City Hall bus terminal and get off at the corner of Weir and Hillside Rd. It's two blocks from there. Dorm beds in the cottage cost US$5 and doubles are US$13 for one or two people. Camping costs US$3 per person. Home-cooked meals are served on request.

*Hitch Haven* (☎ (19) 46274; <online@ coldfire.dnet.co.zw>) at 7 Hillside Rd has dorm beds for US$3, doubles for US$8 and camping for US$2. Meals and cooking facilities are available. Take the Hillside Rd bus from City Hall bus terminal.

*Mugoni Lodge* (☎ (19) 540679), at the corner of First Ave and Fort St, has simple, centrally located self-catering singles/ doubles for US$10/13.

A good bet, with only favourable reports, is the friendly, secure and recently upgraded *Berkeley Place* (☎ (19) 67701). Doubles (most with shower) cost US$15, including breakfast. No alcohol is served and it's hassle-free for women travelling alone. There is a laundry service and also a UTC representative.

Other budget hotels aren't recommended for lone women. The cheapest is the *New Waverley* (☎ (19) 60033), on Twelfth Ave near Lobengula St, which charges US$8/10 for singles/doubles. The bar is one of Bulawayo's liveliest African night spots. The *New Palace Hotel* (☎ (19) 64294), on Jason Moyo St near Tenth Ave, starts at US$15/18 for a single or double without/with bath. A touch plusher is the *Plaza Hotel* (☎ (19) 64280), at Fourteenth Ave and Jason Moyo St. Singles/doubles without bath cost

US$17/20; with bath they're US$25/28. The spartan *Manor Hotel* (☎ (19) 61001) on Lobengula St has single/double rooms with bath for US$14/15 and without bath for US$12/13; all with breakfast.

You may enjoy the out of town 'bush camp' at *Chipangali Wildlife Orphanage* (☎ (19) 70764; fax 72187; <chipanga@ harare.iafrica.com>). Basic bungalows with cooking facilities cost US$6 per person. For access, see Around Bulawayo.

## Places to Stay – Mid-Range

The clean and comfortable *Cecil Hotel* (☎ (19) 60295), on the corner of Fife St and Third Ave, straddles the middle and lower ranges at US$19/22 for singles/doubles with breakfast. There's a restaurant and disco, but security may be a problem.

The oddly named two star *New Royal Zim-Zone Hotel* (☎ (19) 65764), at George Silundika St and Sixth Ave, charges US$37/42 for singles/doubles and US$50 for a four-bed room.

The popular but deteriorating *Eland Grey's Inn* (☎ (19) 540318), on Robert Mugabe St near Leopold Takawira Ave, charges US$39/47 for singles/doubles with bath.

Another dilapidating favourite, the *Selborne Hotel* (☎ (19) 65471), on the corner of Leopold Takawira Ave and George Silundika St, has singles/doubles for US$39/47, with breakfast. Note that the smaller rooms in the back are within earshot of the clunky kitchen fans.

Although it's better known for the New Orleans restaurant, the quiet *Banff Lodge* (☎ (19) 43176; fax 44402) is also a pleasant guest house. Singles/doubles cost US$39/43, with breakfast. The friendly Dutch-run *Travellers Lodge* (☎/fax (19) 46059), next door, is in a class by itself – a cross between a B&B, guest house and backpackers place. Doubles with private bath and use of the braai, pizza oven, TV lounge and pool (and the chance to meet Steve the hyper-dog) cost US$30 with breakfast. With bath and shower they're US$40. Phone for a pickup from town.

The trendy and centrally located *Zak's Place* (☎ (19) 540129; fax 540190), 129 Robert Mugabe St, offers 'executive' single/double B&B accommodation for US$38/50.

*Africa in Mind* (☎/fax (19) 46225), 17 Limerick Rd, Hillside, offers rondavel accommodation in a private suburban garden. Singles/doubles cost US$21/38, plus US$10/5 for each additional adult/child. *Carnarvon Cottage* (☎/fax (19) 41209; <jp scales@coldfire.dnet.co.zw>), at 5 Carnarvon Rd, Hillside, charges US$80 for up to five people self-catering or US$40 per person with breakfast.

*Nira Holiday Flats* (☎ (19) 79961; fax 79963), 41 George Silundika St, has inexpensive self-catering flats for US$17 per person or US$51 for four people.

Bill and Elizabeth MacKinney's *Coach House* (☎ (19) 229551) occupies a peaceful setting 27km out on the Turk Mine road. Take the name literally; it's a repository for coaches and horse-drawn vehicles, some of which have been used in Zimbabwean films. Camp sites with braai pits and cooking facilities cost US$6, and you can hire tents or caravans for an additional US$7. Lodge rooms cost US$17 per person and the double chalet – a replica of an 1894 trading store – costs US$13 per person with breakfast. Horse-riding is also available.

When it was built in 1933, the location of the two-star *Hotel Rio* (☎ (19) 41384; fax 49407) on the Old Esigodini road was determined by early Bulawayo liquor laws, which permitted only out-of-town 'travellers' inns to serve alcohol on Sunday. Singles/doubles are US$45/55, with breakfast.

A new rural choice is *Sunbird Cottage* (☎ (184) 3509), 53km out the Victoria Falls road, then 5km west to Edwaleni Farm. This secluded self-catering cottage accommodates six people and makes a quiet retreat. It costs US$35 for two people, plus US$17 for each extra person.

### Places to Stay – Top End

The imposing and centrally located *Bul-awayo Rainbow Hotel* (☎ (19) 540273; fax 61739) serves as Bulawayo's business and package-tour hotel. However, it's particularly expensive for foreigners, who pay US$94/126 for singles/doubles.

The mock-Tudor *Cresta Churchill Hotel* (☎ (19) 41016; fax 44247), 5km out of town on Matopos Rd at Moffat St, has singles/doubles for US$100/121.

The third upmarket hotel, near Ascot shopping centre a half-hour walk from the city centre, is the *Holiday Inn* (☎ (19) 72464; fax 76227). For singles/doubles foreigners pay US$103/134 while Zimbabwe residents pay US$58/72.

For a foray into decadence, consider the luxurious *Nesbitt Castle* (☎ (19) 42726; fax 41864), a cross between a medieval castle and an English country estate, at 6 Percy Ave, Hillside. It was constructed at the turn of the century by a former Bulawayo mayor. Amenities include a sauna, gymnasium, library, gardens, swimming pool and billiard table. For suite-like singles/doubles, you'll pay US$116/163, with dinner and a champagne breakfast. Advance bookings are essential.

*Induna Lodge* (☎ (19) 45684; fax 45627), south-east of the centre at 16 Fortunes Gate Rd, Matsheumhlope, has singles/doubles for US$100/200 with half board and US$70/130 with breakfast only. Airport transfers are US$35 per person. At the small *McAllister's Lodge* (☎/fax (19) 44462), a large thatched home at 57 Southway Drive, Burnside, locals pay US$38 per person with full board and foreigners, who apparently eat a lot more, have to pay US$100 per person.

The name of *Chief's Lodge* (☎ (19) 79583; fax 76658), formerly N'tabazinduna (hill of chiefs) Lodge, honours the fallen indunas which gave Bulawayo its grisly name (the killing place). Before opening the lodge, the owners consulted a *n'anga* (shaman) to learn about the implications of building on a sacred site. Apparently, the chiefs were pleased to be commemorated in that way. Don't be put off by the directions in the lodge's brochure, simply head 16km out on the Harare road and continue west for 5km on N'tabazinduna Rd. Solar-powered lodges cost US$70 on a half-board plan. Transfers from Bulawayo are US$15.

## Places to Eat

**Breakfast** At the friendly *Grass Hut* on Fife St, between Eighth and Ninth Aves, odd decor is an asset and the breakfast menu includes eggs, omelettes, bacon, sausage and toast. The really hungry will appreciate *Homestead*'s (☎ (19) 60101) ample breakfast buffet in the Bulawayo Rainbow Hotel between 7 and 10 am. All you can eat costs US$5 and a continental breakfast is US$3. Note that it includes real, unadulterated coffee.

**Lunch & Snacks** Bulawayo has a range of takeaway places but naturally some are better than others. *Oriental Takeaways* (☎ (19) 72567), near the corner of George Silundika St and Eighth Ave, is one of the best. Vegetarians can fill up on veggie burgers, samosas, curries and other vegetarian dishes.

Near the corner of Twelfth Ave and Fife St, the *Hot Bread Shop* serves ordinary takeaway meals as well as more creative concoctions. *Dagwood's* (☎ (19) 63934), at the corner of Tenth Ave and Josiah Tongogara St, specialises in sandwiches, salads and filled baked potatoes.

Chinese standards are the speciality at *Tunku's* and the *Chop Suey Centre*, neighbouring takeaways on Eighth Ave between Robert Mugabe St and George Silundika St. For traditional Zimbabwean fare, try *The Pantry*, open from 5 am to 3 pm, on Fifteenth Ave between Main and Fort Sts.

The *YWCA* on Lobengula St is open for lunch from 12.30 to 3 pm. For US$1.50, you get a filling plate of *sadza* ladled over with the relish of the day, normally some sort of beef stew.

For a pizza, fish and chips, peri-peri chicken or a range of filled jacket potatoes, check out the recommended *Dial-a-Pizza* (☎ (19) 66847) on Lobengula St. It's open daily from 10 am to 9 pm and delivers any-

where in Bulawayo. Fast food is also available at the rather plush *Kentucky Fried Chicken*, on Jason Moyo between Eighth and Ninth Aves. Just down the street between Eighth Ave and Leopold Takawira St is *Nando's* (☎ (19) 72198), which offers spicy Portuguese chicken.

If you don't mind playing guinea pig for cooking students, try the *Bulawayo Polytechnic* around the corner from the caravan park, which serves potentially great three-course lunches for US$2. It's closed for school holidays in May and August.

The Portuguese-owned *Bonne Journée* (☎ (19) 64839), on Robert Mugabe St between Tenth and Eleventh Aves, specialises in espresso, cappuccino and ice cream as well as steaks, burgers, omelettes, peri-peri chicken, and snacks such as chips and hot dogs.

Another place for sweet treats is *Mandy's Coffee Shop* (☎ (19) 75224), at 112 Josiah Tongogara St. It's great for goodies – chocolate cake, quiche, biscuits, muffins and coffee – and also does pub lunches and salads. The popular *Mary's Corner* (☎ (19) 76721), 88 Josiah Tongogara Ave, serves pizzas, Greek specialities and chicken and beef dishes, as well as sweet snacks and coffee. It's wise to book for lunch.

For English-style teas and excellent light lunches, including small but well-conceived buffets for under US$2, you can't beat *Sisters* (☎ (19) 65511), on the 2nd floor of Haddon and Sly department store. You'll also find light meals at the *Old Vic Pub*, in the Bulawayo Rainbow Hotel. *Esther's Tea Room* (☎ (19) 70721) at the Bulawayo Art Gallery is popular for its pastas, salads, cream teas and especially its waffles.

**Dinner** A fine mid-range Italian choice is *La Gondola* (☎ (19) 62986), at 105 Robert Mugabe St, which serves up home-made pasta, steaks, pizza, fish, seafood and vegetarian dishes, as well as such African specialities as ostrich and crocodile. An alternative is *Cypriana Taverna* (☎ (19) 62081), at the Trade Fair Show Ground, specialising in Cypriot and Greek cuisine.

More exotic meals may be ordered 24 hours in advance. For Spanish food, there's *Granada* (☎ (19) 70716) on the 1st floor of the Parkade Centre, on Fife St between Ninth and Tenth Aves. It's open Tuesday to Friday for lunch and dinner, Monday for lunch only and Saturday for dinner only.

Gone are the days when seafood was like gold in Zimbabwe. Bulawayo's finest seafood choice, *It's Fishy* (☎ (19) 75360), below the Granada, serves up fish dishes from smoked salmon to mussels, prawns and calamari.

An increasingly popular restaurant and night spot is the *Cape to Cairo* (☎ (19) 72387). This tasteful restaurant/bar with a colonial theme specialises in game dishes but also does super steaks and laudable seafood and peri-peri chicken. It's open for lunch and dinner from Monday to Friday and on Saturday evenings.

A good Chinese choice is the *Peking* (☎ (19) 60646) on Jason Moyo St, with tasty Sichuan and Cantonese fare. Plan on US$4 for a meat and rice dish or a hearty set lunch. It's open weekdays for lunch and dinner and on Saturday for dinner only.

*Morgan's* (☎ (19) 79404), in the Ramji Centre on Eleventh Ave, offers pub meals in the bar as well as beef, chicken, seafood, pork and vegetarian choices. It's open Monday to Saturday for lunch and dinner.

The popular *Himalaya* (☎ (19) 67068), on the corner of Ninth Ave and Josiah Tongogara St, dishes up excellent vegetarian thali as well as other Indian-oriented fare. *Eastern Flavours* (☎ (19) 74617), on the same block, offers an equally fine Indian menu and takeaways.

The *Homestead* (☎ (19) 60101), in the Bulawayo Rainbow Hotel, is open from 12.30 to 2.30 pm for lunch and 6 to 10 pm for dinner. For steak and other meals heavy on Zimbabwean beef, there's the *Golden Spur Steak House* (☎ (19) 70318) on Robert Mugabe St between Eighth and Ninth Aves. Even better is *The Cattleman* (☎ (19) 76086) on the corner of Josiah Tongogara and Twelfth Ave. Many restaurants have kudu heads on the wall, but here a re-

proachful bovine watches diners as they eat some of the tenderest steaks this side of Texas. It also does a bounteous lunch buffet for just US$5.

The *Arizona Spur*, at the Holiday Inn, is a popular family restaurant featuring steaks and one of Zimbabwe's best salad bars. It's part of the ubiquitous South African chain which prides itself on consistent quality. Another beefy chain is the *Black Steer* (☎ (19) 75521), in Meikles at the corner of Jason Moyo and Leopold Takawira. In addition to the steaks, barbecue ribs and burgers, it features fish and vegetarian dishes.

The *Highwayman* (☎ (19) 60121), at the Eland Grey's Inn, serves good, simple cuisine; the speciality is chicken Kiev with salad and chips, but the beef choices aren't bad. *Buffalo Bill's* (☎ (19) 65741), a pizzeria and steak house in the Selborne Hotel, serves steaks for US$4, pizza for US$2.50 and has a salad or dessert bar for US$1.50 each. It's open every day and is popular with travellers.

Haute cuisine in Bulawayo comes in three forms – à la *Les Saisons* (☎ (19) 77292) at 71 Josiah Tongogara St, *Maison Nic* (☎ (19) 61884) on Main St near Fourth Ave, or *New Orleans* (☎ (19) 43176) on Banff Rd in Hillside. The best is Les Saisons, run by the former owner of Maison Nic (which, under his tutelage, took Zimbabwe's best restaurant award after year). Despite the exclusive atmosphere, prices aren't prohibitive. Try the antelope venison or the nicely prepared vegetarian options and fish dishes, including Malawi *chambo*, Kariba bream and whitebait. The new Maison Nic remains very good, and is a bit cheaper. The New Orleans serves continental and Cajun cuisine. Advance bookings are recommended for all three places.

**Self-Catering** For cheap fruit and vegetables the best place is Makokoba market on the road beyond Renkini bus terminal. A good greengrocer is *Gee's*, on Eighth Ave between George Silundika and Fife Sts.

*Haddon and Sly*, at Eighth Ave and Fife St, has a supermarket on the ground floor. For refined tastes, the supermarket at the Ascot shopping centre is probably the best stocked in town.

You'll find wholemeal bread, doughnuts, European-style cakes, pies and pastries at *Haefeli's Swiss Bakery* on Fife St between Tenth and Eleventh Aves. Also recommended is *Walter's Bakery* (☎ (19) 61071) at 124 Robert Mugabe St.

If you're just after a bit of a tipple, you may want to reward the honest folks who named the *Boozer's Paradise Bottle Store*, at the corner of Fourteenth Ave and Robert Mugabe St.

## Entertainment

**Nightspots** Compared to those in Harare, most Bulawayo pubs and clubs are strict about 'smart casual' dress requirements. That means no open-top shoes, no trainers, no denim and nothing that could remotely be construed as grubby after 4.30 pm.

The *Alabama*, in the Bulawayo Rainbow Hotel, is a pleasant, crowded bar with live jazz music almost every evening. Fortunately, the smart-casual dress code is very loosely enforced. The more upmarket *Top of the Sun*, at the same hotel, offers live music nightly.

The rather sleazy *Silver Fox*, at 101 Robert Mugabe St, has disco music until 2.30 am Monday to Saturday, and until midnight on Sunday. The lively *New Waverley Hotel* has live performances, but women – even accompanied – experience a measure of hassle.

For Saturday night disco dancing, a respectable option is *Talk of the Town* in the Monte Carlo Building on the corner of Fife St and Twelfth Ave; no jeans or trainers are allowed. *Morgan's*, which serves both food and drinks, attracts over-25 white crowds. For a glimpse of the Rhodey teen scene, check out Harley's (☎ (19) 62081) at the Trade Fair Show Ground, but avoid walking around here after dark.

For Anglo-Zimbabwean atmosphere, try the *Old Vic Pub* in the Bulawayo Rainbow or the *Knight's Arms* in the Holiday Inn. *Joe's Place* (☎ (19) 77460), at Eleventh Ave and George Silundika St, is a sports bar with TV action. The atmospheric *Picasso's*, in the Granada restaurant, 1st floor, Parkade Centre, on the corner of Fife St and Ninth Ave, isn't a bad hangout, but it can get rough at weekends.

On Fridays, the public bar at the *Cresta Churchill Hotel* has live music and occasionally features well-known names. On Friday and Saturday nights, the *Hilltop Motel* (☎ (19) 72493), east of town, offers disco music.

**Cinemas** Bulawayo has a good choice of quality cinemas. The best are the *Kine 600* and *Elite 400* on Robert Mugabe St between Tenth and Eleventh Aves, the *Rainbow Vistarama* on Fife St between Eleventh and Twelfth Aves and the *Seven-Arts* on Jason Moyo St between Tenth and Eleventh Aves. The *Bulawayo Art Gallery* occasionally sponsors lunchtime films – inquire at the gallery or the Publicity Association.

*Alliance Française* (☎ (19) 30814, after 5 pm) at 60 Josiah Tongogara St screens French films with English subtitles several times a month.

**Theatre & Dance** The *Bulawayo Theatre* (☎ (19) 65393) in Centenary Park stages dramatic productions and occasionally hosts visiting troupes. The fabulous African-oriented *Amakhosi Theatre* stages productions of local interest and organises the annual Inxusa Festival, which involves national and international theatre, plus music and film productions and workshops. It's housed in the Township Square Cultural Centre (☎/fax (19) 76673), off the Old Falls road. You can also sample African cuisine.

For the pounding rhythms and articulate movements of African dance, don't miss a practice session of the dance troupe *Sunduza*, which rehearses Monday to Friday from 10 am to noon at the Pumula Hall in the Pumula Suburb. Access is by minibus from the TM supermarket in town.

Admission to the two hour session costs US$6.50.

Consult the *Daily Chronicle* or *Bulawayo This Month* for information on current productions.

### Spectator Sport

Most sports have Bulawayo clubs to accommodate them. *Bulawayo This Month* lists all the clubs; for information on their activities, contact numbers and meeting times, check with the Publicity Association.

The cricket ground is on the corner of Robert Mugabe St and First Ave. Catch horse racing at Ascot on alternating Sunday afternoons.

### Things to Buy

The Jairos Jiri Craft Centre (☎ (19) 69147), at the eastern end of city hall car park, sells the work of disabled Zimbabwean artisans and offers good value on Ndebele pottery and basketry, and Batonka stools from western Kariba. Along the Fife St footpath at City Hall Square, street souvenir hawkers, needle-workers, artists and flower vendors display their wares. You could also try the Mzilikazi Arts & Crafts Centre and Bulawayo Home Industries (see details earlier in this chapter).

The African Heritage shop in the Tshaka Centre, on Fife St between Tenth and Eleventh Aves, specialises in jewellery and African-look clothing – ethnic prints, tie-dye and batik.

The recording *Blue Skies Bulawayo* is a compilation of Bulawayo archives, revivals and contemporary music from 1948 to 1994. It's sold for US$4 at the National Gallery or from Phaphama Promotions (☎ (19) 78159; fax 78053), PO Box 2792, Bulawayo.

### Getting There & Away

**Air** Air Zimbabwe (☎ (19) 72051; fax 69737) offers several flights daily to and from Harare and connections to Kariba, Hwange National Park and Johannesburg. Zimbabwe Express (☎ (19) 229797) has twice-daily services to and from Harare.

United Air Charters has non-stop flights between Bulawayo and Kariba on Monday and Friday; book through Air Zimbabwe.

**Bus** There are two long-distance African bus terminals. Renkini musika on the Sixth Ave Extension, opposite the Mzilikazi police station, serves Harare, Masvingo, Beitbridge and the Eastern Highlands, while Entumbane, near Luveve Rd in the north-western suburbs, has buses to Victoria Falls and Turk Mine. Harare, Masvingo, Beitbridge and Victoria Falls services depart daily when full, starting around 6 or 7 am. Each morning, Hwange Special Express buses leave Entumbane for Gwaai River, Safari Crossroads (US$6) and Victoria Falls (US$8). To Beitbridge, the Mangena minibus (☎ (19) 41475) leaves from Renkini on Monday, Wednesday and Friday at 6 am and on Tuesday and Thursday at noon. To Masvingo, ZUPCO and Shu-Shine leave Renkini daily except Sunday.

Trans-Lux (☎ (19) 66528; fax 78347) has services to Harare daily except Wednesday and Saturday at 11.55 pm. Buses leave from the Bulawayo Rainbow hotel. Book at Trans-Lux, LAPF House, Room 705, near Fife St and Eighth Ave. Blue Arrow (☎ (19) 60176) runs at least two coaches daily to Harare via either Chivhu or Kwe Kwe. The terminal is at the Unifreight House at 73a Fife St.

Mini-Zim Mini-Coaches (☎ (19) 72495; fax 78319) departs for Johannesburg from the Holiday Inn on Wednesday and Sunday at 6.30 am and arrives at 5.15 pm the same day. From Johannesburg, it leaves on Monday and Friday at 6.30 am. The fare is US$55; seniors pay US$45. Book through Budget Tours on the corner of Fife St and Tenth Ave.

Minibuses leave for Johannesburg from the city hall car park bus terminal when full; the fare is US$23.

Chitanda & Sons runs twice weekly to Francistown and Gaborone (Botswana); book through Manica Travel Services (☎ (19) 540531).

**Train** The reservations and ticket offices (☎ (19) 322411) at the station are open variable hours for different service classes, so phone before going out there. When booking or purchasing international tickets, you must present your passport (see the Zimbabwe Getting There & Away chapter).

The daily trains between Bulawayo and Harare depart at 9 pm in both directions, arriving before 7 am the following day. To Hwange and Victoria Falls, the service departs at 7 pm, arriving at Dete (Hwange National Park) at 1.30 am and Victoria Falls at 7 am. The train from Victoria Falls also departs at 7 pm, passes Dete at 12.45 am and arrives in Bulawayo at 7.05 am. The 1st/2nd class one-way fares to Harare or Victoria Falls are US$9/6.

The daily train to Gaborone (Botswana) leaves at 2.30 pm and arrives in Gaborone at 6.30 am the following day. From Gaborone, it leaves at 9 pm and arrives in Bulawayo at noon the next day. Fares are US$33/27/10 in 1st/2nd/economy class.

The rail connection between Bulawayo and Johannesburg now passes through Beitbridge rather than Botswana. The service leaves Bulawayo at 9 am Thursday and arrives in Johannesburg at 9.01 am Friday. The 1st/2nd class fare is US$49/35. Tickets must be pre-booked and purchased at least a week before travel.

### Getting Around

**To/From the Airport** The Air Zimbabwe bus runs between the Bulawayo Rainbow Hotel and the airport for US$3 per person. Taxis cost at least US$5 each way.

**Bus** Bulawayo has two suburban bus terminals. The city hall terminal (☎ (19) 67172) on Eighth Ave, between Robert Mugabe St and George Silundika Sts, serves the more affluent northern, eastern and southern suburbs. Note that the published timetable is often inaccurate.

The Lobengula St terminal (☎ (19) 74059), on the corner of Lobengula St and Sixth Ave, serves the high-density suburbs west and south-west of the centre.

**Taxi** Most Bulawayo taxis are metered, but on popular runs you can normally bargain for a lower price. Both Rixi Taxi (☎ (19) 60666 or 61933) and York's Taxi (☎ (19) 72454) are reliable.

**Bicycle** As Bulawayo is situated in an area of relatively level countryside, the town is particularly suitable for exploration by bicycle. You can hire mountain bikes for US$6.50 per day from Miles Ahead Cycle Hire (☎ (19) 46503); ask for Geoff or Sandy. Alternatively, look for Barry from Miles Ahead at the Municipal Caravan Park & Camp Site. Dra-Gama's (☎ (19) 72739), near the corner of Eighth Ave and Josiah Tongogara St, has bicycle hire for US$5 per day. It's open daily from 8 am to 5 pm.

# Around Bulawayo

Bulawayo's surroundings feature scenic and unusual landscapes of balancing rocks, ancient ruins and rock paintings. The highlight, of course, is Matobo National Park and its rhino-rich game park. This impressive region once served as the spiritual capital of the Mwari-worshipping Rozwi empire. Later, it so impressed Cecil Rhodes that he requested to be buried there, at the summit of the hill he called View of the World.

## CHIPANGALI WILDLIFE ORPHANAGE

Chipangali was founded in 1973 by Viv Wilson and his son Kevin. It was conceived as a centre for rearing the offspring of poached animals and caring for injured, illegally captured or sick birds and animals, for eventual release into the wild, but unfortunately it now feels more like a zoo than intended. The highlight is the large walk-through aviaries, which house both raptors and smaller birds.

It's open daily, except Monday, from 10 am to 5 pm; the animals are fed at 3.30 pm. Admission costs US$1.80.

ZIMBABWE

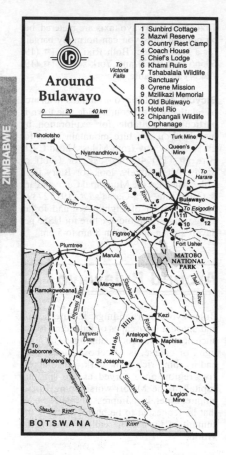

**Around Bulawayo**

0    20    40 km

1 Sunbird Cottage
2 Mazwi Reserve
3 Country Rest Camp
4 Coach House
5 Chief's Lodge
6 Khami Ruins
7 Tshabalala Wildlife Sanctuary
8 Cyrene Mission
9 Mzilikazi Memorial
10 Old Bulawayo
11 Hotel Rio
12 Chipangali Wildlife Orphanage

the internal and external walls of the thatched chapel are painted with frescoes depicting African interpretations of biblical accounts and scenes from African history. The mission was named after the African, Simon of Cyrene, who was forced to carry the cross at Jesus' crucifixion (Luke 23:26).

The mission was established in 1939 by Canon Edward Paterson, an artist himself, who served as mission principal until his retirement in 1953. In addition to basic education and practical vocational training, Canon Paterson required his students to participate in art classes. His emphasis was on individual creativity in several media – drawing, sculpture, wood carving and painting – and no European examples were provided.

The paintings and carvings that cover the chapel today are almost entirely the work of students (Paterson himself is responsible for a couple of the works). All of them depict African characters, animals, homes and backdrops. Some are brilliant, others merely competent, but the variety of styles employed is worth examining.

### Getting There & Away

From the Renkini bus terminal in Bulawayo, take the Figtree or Plumtree bus (or the Francistown bus from the Lobengula St terminal) and get off at Cyrene Rd, 8km short of Figtree. From there, it's a 2.5km walk to the mission. Alternatively, hitch out on the Plumtree road to Cyrene Rd and walk the remaining distance.

Coming from Matobo National Park, Cyrene lies 10km along the infrequently travelled Cyrene Rd from Cecil Rhodes' old rail terminal, just outside the park near the arboretum gate. Hitching will be tough so plan on walking the entire distance; it's a hot, dry area so carry lots of water.

### ESIGODINI

This tiny settlement, formerly called Essexvale, lies 42km out on the Beitbridge road from Bulawayo. The main interest is the *Eland Country Inn* (☎ (188) 226), which offers a pleasant restaurant and quiet out-of-

### Getting There & Away

Chipangali lies 200m from the Beitbridge road, 24km east of Bulawayo. For lifts, wait anywhere past Ascot shopping centre. Alternatively, take an Esigodini bus from the Renkini terminal. Several tour companies run day tours to Chipangali; see Organised Tours under Bulawayo.

### CYRENE MISSION

The artistically rich Cyrene Mission, 32km from Bulawayo on the Plumtree road, may not be as overwhelming as Serima, but both

town accommodation. For locals/foreigners double chalets, including breakfast, cost US$33/115. Excellent lunches or dinners are US$7.

## KHAMI RUINS

The peaceful and deserted ruins of Khami (also spelt Kame or Khame) aren't as expansive as those of Great Zimbabwe, but visitors can wander through the crumbled 40 hectare city and see more or less what remained after its former inhabitants fled the fire that destroyed it. UNESCO has now proclaimed Khami a World Heritage Site.

A small museum on the site attempts to piece together an explanation of Khami's history. Before exploring the ruins, pick up the pamphlet *A Trail Guide to the Khami National Monument*, is sold at the museum. The site is open from 8 am to 5 pm daily; for foreigners, admission is US$3.

### History

The Khami area was inhabited by Stone Age people for perhaps 100 millennia before the construction of the now-ruined city. By 1000 AD, southern Africa was well into the Iron Age and subsistence cultures had settled down to agriculture and trade. Among them were the Leopard's Kopje culture, which had settled in a *daga* hut village north of the Khami River. Here they raised cattle and carried on trade with the Swahilis from the Indian Ocean coast.

By the late 15th century, Leopard's Kopje had been absorbed, along with other scattered groups, into a political entity called the Torwa state, which established its capital at Khami. (Torwa was probably initiated, or at least influenced, by refugees from the collapsing Great Zimbabwe state, 250km away.)

In the late 17th century, Torwa's ruling Changamire dynasty was conquered by Rozwi people from the north. Khami was burned and levelled and Torwa was absorbed by Rozwi, which had its capital at Danangombe, 100km to the north-east.

In the early 1830s, Rozwi was in turn overcome by Ndebele raiders. Europeans

first saw Khami around 1893. Until Lobengula's death in the same year, the Ndebele guarded it from the colonists, perhaps as a royal retreat or a sacred site.

### The Hill Complex

At the northern end of Khami is the hill complex, which served as the royal enclosure and home to the Torwa *mambo*. There are several hut platforms and Khami's greatest concentration of stone walling. At the foot of the three-step stairway leading to a semi-circular hut platform (which was probably a ritual site) was a small royal treasury, which revealed ivory divining pieces, copper items, iron and bronze weapons and ritual drinking pots (these are now displayed at Bulawayo's Museum of Natural History). The main supports to this hut are still standing.

At the northern end of the hill complex is an odd platform with a stone Dominican cross, reputedly placed there by an early Portuguese Catholic missionary. Evidence suggests that commoners occupied the peripheral areas, particularly the eastern slopes of the main hill.

### Southern Ruins

Khami's southern reaches contain several scattered sites. The Vlei Platforms near the museum were probably cattle kraals, and nearby is the *mujejeje*, a resonant stone near the dam wall, which rings like a bell when struck. Carved into the rock near the car park and along the track to the dam wall are *tsoro* game boards. This complicated game is now played on carved wooden boards with four rows of holes. For playing pieces, the Khami dwellers probably used small rounded stones.

The beautifully decorated 6m by 68m retaining wall of the Precipice Platform, just east of the dam, bears a chequerboard design along its entire length. However, the dam prevents close-range viewing.

### Places to Stay

Self-catering chalets at the *Khami Ruins Lodge* (☎ (19) 43954) cost US$60 for up to

ZIMBABWE

ZIMBABWE

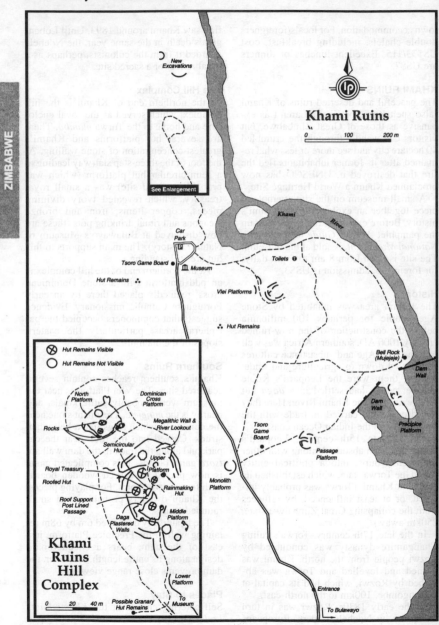

five people and US$11 for each additional person up to 10 people. A camp site is planned.

### Getting There & Away

There are no buses along the little-travelled Khami road, and most travellers hire bicycles for the flat 22km ride from Bulawayo to the ruins. Take Eleventh Ave beyond Lobengula St and follow the signs to Khami. Several tour companies include Khami in their itineraries; see Organised Tours under Bulawayo.

### MAZWI RESERVE

This city council-sponsored game reserve has harmless wildlife: zebra, giraffe and various antelope. Take the Khami road for 15km, turn west onto Khami Prison Rd and follow it for 6km to the signposted reserve turn-off; the gate is 6km from there. Sandbank Safaris runs horse-riding in Mazwi (see Organised Tours under Bulawayo).

### MATOBO NATIONAL PARK

You need not be in tune with any alternative wavelength to sense that the Matobo Hills are one of the world's power places. These otherworldly formations appear as though some very young deity has been playing with thousand-tonne building blocks, stacking them precariously into fanciful castles and towering imaginary cities, then populating them with stone-faced human figures – women in billowing dresses, men working and socialising and children following or looking on. It's no wonder that the Rozwi regarded Matobo as their spiritual capital; its latent and pervasive power cannot be denied.

Dotted around the modern park are numerous signs of former habitation. In addition to the wealth of ancient San paintings, which decorate the rocks, and bits of pottery scattered around the hills, there are examples of old grain bins, where Lobengula's warriors once stored their provisions. Some hidden niches still shelter clay ovens which were used as iron smelters in making the infamous *assegais*, or spears, to be used

against the growing colonial hordes. Some peaks, such as Shumba Shaba, Shumba Sham, Imadzi (the bald one), Efifi and Silozwane, are now considered sacred, and locals believe that even to point at them will bring misfortune. Hidden in a rock cleft is the Ndebele's sacred rain shrine, Mjelele, where people still pray to Mwali and petition for rain. During the droughts of the early 1990s, even government officials came to pull some strings here.

With the history comes a superb array of wildlife. You may have the chance to see the African hawk eagle (*Hieraaetus spilogaster*) or the rare Cape eagle owl (*Bubo capensis mackinderi*). Matobo is also home to the world's greatest concentration of black eagle (*Aquila verreauxi*) nesting sites and you may well observe these birds soaring above their kopje-bound nests. (Interestingly, the park is even shaped like an eagle.) The bad news is that the eagles are coming under pressure from poachers, who lift chicks and eggs from nests to supply illicit overseas pet markets.

The Whovi Game Park portion of Matobo offers a variety of wildlife, but is best known for its zealously guarded population of white and black rhino.

An encouraging story is told of two Zambians who arrived at the Bulawayo railway station carrying long – and ominously rifle-shaped – canvas bags and asking directions to Matobo National Park (they might as well have worn flashing neon signs reading 'We are rhino poachers'). One local woman immediately became suspicious and took the story to the police. A massive sting operation was organised and the would-be poachers were thwarted.

### History

As many as 100,000 years ago, the first hunting and gathering societies appeared around the Matobo Hills. Evidence of their inhabitation and apparent fascinations are preserved in hundreds of rock paintings which decorate caves, shelters and overhangs throughout the region, both inside and outside the park. From these ancient

ZIMBABWE

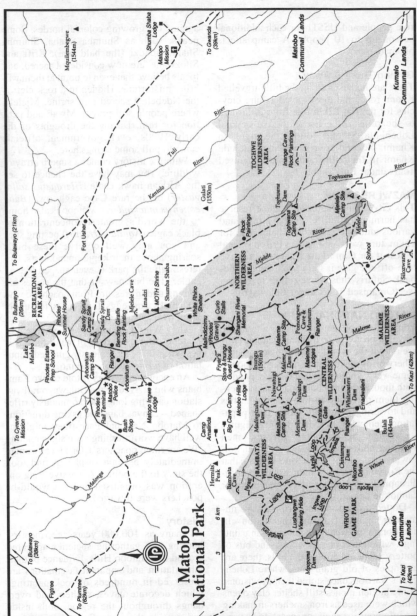

Matobo National Park

0   3   6 km

works of art, we've learned that the Matobo area was indeed a natural haunt of the white rhino, justifying its recent reintroduction there, as well as the quagga, the giant zebralike wild horse, for which it's now too late for reintroduction.

It would be difficult to imagine such a place escaping religious attention. In the late 17th century, the Torwa state, whose capital was at nearby Khami, was conquered by the Rozwi, who invaded from the north and absorbed rather than wiped out the incumbent dynasty.

After Khami was burned and razed by the invaders, a new political centre was established at Danangombe, while the enigmatic Matobo Hills became a ritual capital and religious retreat. Here, the cult of Mwari took hold and it dominated Rozwi thinking until the Ndebele swept in from the south and finished them off. Interestingly, the Ndebele were so taken by the Mwari religion – or they were afraid not to be – that they adopted it for their own purposes. King Mzilikazi himself bestowed the name *Amatobo*, meaning bald heads.

Even the next wave of conquerors, the white Matabeleland farmers, hedged their climatic bets by petitioning Mwari for rain during the prolonged post-WWII drought. It is believed that Mwari and his mediums, priests and other subsidiaries still thrive at several shrines in the communal lands around Matobo today. (For details on the Mwari belief system, see Religion in the Facts about Zimbabwe chapter.)

Once heavily farmed, the Matobo area was subject to considerable controversy in the mid-1900s between whites and blacks over the fate of the land. While whites struggled to protect the area as a natural preserve and national shrine to Cecil Rhodes, blacks argued that the farmland was needed by subsistence farmers to feed their families. Whites countered that unnatural erosion caused by domestic animals and outdated farming techniques would render the land useless anyway. Blacks reminded them that the Matobo country held religious significance as the headquarters of Mwari, a figure at least as important as the whites' revered Rhodes.

In 1962, the white government won out, moving Matobo resident farmers to communal lands outside the proposed park boundaries, which now contain an area of 43,200 hectares. Resistance was stiff but the land, rather than the government, suffered

---

### The Matobo Hills – a Geological Perspective

Geological analyses tell us that the Matobo Hills are the final remnants of a granite batholith, a vast igneous intrusion which worked its way up from the earth's molten mantle and thrust up the crustal material around Matobo into a high dome of peaks. As erosion took its toll and slowly dragged off the softer overlying material, the mountains diminished in size. The resistant rock that remained – now exposed to the weather – heated, cooled, cracked and crumbled along weaker fissures and left dwala domes as well as piles and crenellated pinnacles of the strongest rock. The domes exfoliated or peeled off in sheets that sloughed away into the valleys. Steeper features eroded more slowly along cracks. (Interestingly, the builders of Great Zimbabwe used fire and water to artificially simulate the exfoliation process in the rock they used for construction.)

In short, the balancing boulders of Matobo weren't stacked that way, as one would be inclined to believe (and wonder who hefted them up there), but rather, were eroded *in situ* and separated from each other by the forces of natural weathering. By all indications, they will continue to do so and eventually crumble into an entirely new – if perhaps not quite so interesting – landscape.

as the new park was vandalised. After Zimbabwean independence in 1980, people began to move back into the park, mistakenly assuming that the Mugabe government would reverse the white decision that created the preserve. In 1983, Matobo was the scene of bloodshed as the powers in Harare sent armed forces to eliminate the dissidents. After the 1988 Unity Accord, which combined the ZAPU and ZANU armies into one national force, calm returned to the area.

Since the surrounding communal grasslands have now all been cut or chewed to the roots by goats, Matobo National Park has recently been opened to local residents for thatch-cutting. Rhodes still sleeps peacefully at View of the World, the white and black rhino tenuously hang on and the park has been earmarked for inclusion in the register of UNESCO World Heritage Sites. Perhaps in the end – at least as regards Matobo – everyone will win.

### Central Wilderness Area

It may seem oxymoronic calling a wilderness area 'central', but this one lies at the heart of the park. It's not a wilderness in the traditional sense – it's threaded by roads and contains several developed enclaves – but there are plenty of opportunities for escape into the hills, which can provide the appropriate illusion.

**Maleme Dam** The dam, which serves as park headquarters, is the busiest part of Matobo, with lodges and chalets, a general shop, the main campground, horse stables, ranger offices and picnic sites. Because most overnight visitors wind up here, it tends to fill up, especially on weekends and holidays. These are the best times to hitch in but not always the most pleasant to *be* there. In the winter and during the week, however, you'll share Maleme with only a few travellers and the baboons, dassies and klipspringer which inhabit the surrounding bouldery hills. The area immediately west and north-west of the dam also supports antelope and zebra.

**Nswatugi Cave** An easy and scenic 7km walk north-west of Maleme dam and 200m up a steep track will bring you to Nswatugi cave and its well-preserved array of rock paintings. Note especially the accuracy in the motion of the galloping giraffe and running zebra. Also note the excellent perspective paintings of giraffes. Other well-represented figures include numerous kudu bulls and cows, a hunting party and eight apparently sleeping human figures.

Excavations at Nswatugi have revealed human bones over 40,000 years old, which are believed to be the oldest human remains uncovered in Zimbabwe. Overlying layers of ash and artefacts date from around 10,000 years ago. Foreigners pay US$2 admission, which also includes entry to Pomongwe cave and Rhodes' grave.

**Pomongwe Cave & Museum** Pity the well-meaning soul who made his mark in history at Pomongwe cave in the 1920s. He is destined to be forever maligned by generations of tourists for an undeniably stupid mistake: in an attempt to preserve the gallery of ancient artwork from the elements, he applied shellac over all the cave figures – before ascertaining the effects of shellac on ancient paintings. Where giraffe and ancient hunters once featured, there remain only splotchy brown stains and one kudu that somehow escaped the brush-off.

An information board at the site explains what was once depicted and a new museum houses the great piles of tools and pottery uncovered in several levels of archaeological deposits. The most recent layers have been dated to about 6500 BC while the deepest excavations have yielded artefacts over 35,000 years old. Admission is US$2, but you must buy the ticket at either Nswatugi cave or Rhodes' grave (both of which are included in the price).

Pomongwe is accessed from Maleme either by road or by scrambling over the steep kopje.

**Inungu** Although it's outside the park, the granite dome of Inungu is a landmark, topped by a large cross which was erected in June 1982, on the occasion of the 70th birthday of Father Odilo, a local Catholic priest. It's a half-day return walk and climb from the Maleme camp site.

### Northern Wilderness Area
Near the park's north-eastern entrance, you'll have a nice view down the Mjelele Valley. Surprisingly, it's not unusual to see rhino *outside* the game park, grazing on the dry grasses of the valley floor.

### Mjelele Cave
Just outside national park boundaries, the Mjelele cave paintings are on the northern faces of two very large boulders 8km north of White Rhino Shelter a few hundred metres east of the road. They depict a human-crocodile figure and there are also some detailed ancient paintings blotted out by the amateurish work of later imitators.

### Arboretum & Rhodes' Rail Terminal
Not much remains of Cecil Rhodes' rail terminal 2km outside the park's north-west entrance. The line was originally built so that turn-of-the-century Bulawayo socialites could have easy Sunday afternoon access to the rocky wonders of Matobo Park.

The arboretum is just inside the park boundary from the rail terminal. If you're after greenery, the camp site will prove pleasant.

### White Rhino Shelter
The White Rhino Shelter lies several hundred metres along a clearly marked path from the signposted car park about 5km north of the turn-off to Malindidzimu. Here you'll find paintings with a difference: outline drawings rather than the polychrome paintings more commonly found in Matobo and, indeed, all over Zimbabwe. Most prominent are the finely executed outlines of five white rhino and the head of a black rhino, with human figures visible behind them, and five well observed and exquisitely drawn wildebeest. Peripheral figures include a procession of human hunters and a prominent polychrome lion, which are believed to post-date the other paintings by many millennia. Sadly, they must be enclosed in a cage to prevent vandalism.

### MOTH Shrine
This pleasant little garden shrine, dedicated to the Memorable Order of Tin Hats (MOTH), contains one tree in memory of each MOTH killed in WWII. Even today, whenever a MOTH dies, they are cremated and brought here to be scattered in the garden.

### Malindidzimu
The lichen-streaked boulders around Cecil Rhodes' grave, atop the hill which Rhodes called View of the World, seem to have been placed there deliberately to mark the spot. The old boy wasn't quite so influential, but he did unknowingly choose the mountain which the Ndebele knew as Malindidzimu, 'the dwelling place of benevolent spirits' (see the boxed text).

While some of the more traditional Rhodeys still make an annual pilgrimage to the site on the anniversary of his death (26 March) most visitors just appreciate the solitude and the view that so strongly gripped Rhodes nearly a century ago.

Just down from Rhodes' grave is that of Dr Leander Starr Jameson, a good friend of Rhodes, who commanded Fort Victoria (Masvingo) after its 1890 founding. He died in England on 26 November 1917 but, because of WWI, was not brought to View of the World until 1920. Also interred at View of the World is Charles Patrick John Coghlan, the first premier of Southern Rhodesia, buried there on 14 August 1930.

The Shangani River (Allan Wilson) memorial, an imposing structure downhill from Rhodes' grave, was erected in 1904 to the memory of Allan Wilson and the 33 soldiers of his Shangani River Patrol. The entire troop was wiped out by the forces of General Mtjaan and his 30,000 Ndebele warriors, of whom more than 400 were slain by the patrol's superior firepower. Mistakenly believing that Lobengula's impis (spear-carrying soldiers) had committed acts of war against the British at Fort Victoria, the patrol had been sent in pursuit of the fleeing king. Lobengula himself conceded that their battle was bravely fought – a moving human reaction from a singularly intriguing individual.

The bodies were brought at Rhodes' request from Great Zimbabwe, where they had previously been interred. The inscription reads simply: 'Erected in the enduring memory of Allan Wilson and his men who fell in a fight against the Matabele on the Shangani River, December 4th, 1898. There was no survivor.'

Another Malindidzimu attraction is its population of lizards (the females are grey-green and the males rainbow-coloured) which skitter over the equally rainbow-coloured lichen-encrusted rocks. Several times daily, a long-time park attendant proffers lumps of mielies and forces them to jump for a share of the meal – the original leaping lizards.

Although the easiest access to the summit is via a road leading up the from the eastern side of the hill, an alternative and more scenic walking route ascends from the picnic area directly south of it. A display at the bottom of the hill outlines highlights of Rhodes' life and career.

Foreigners pay US$2 admission, which also includes admission to Pomongwe and Nswatugi caves.

### Whovi Game Park

The well-guarded white rhino population at Whovi (pronounced HOO-vee) is relatively healthy (at last count, there were around 35) and lucky visitors may even spot the more elusive black rhino, of which there were nine, at last count. What's more, the

---

### Cecil Rhodes & Malindidzimu

The Ndebele name of the hill Malindidzimu means 'dwelling place of the benevolent spirits'. This is where they believe the more saintly of their ancestors dwell in peace. Ironically, they now share their lovely mountain top haunt with a sort of colonial Heroes' Acre.

Cecil John Rhodes, the source of everything Rhodesian, didn't spend much time at his estate near Rhodes dam just outside Matobo National Park, but was taken with the surrounding country and its spell. After one foray into the hills with Lord Grey, he returned home to exclaim: 'We have found a hill from the top of which a marvellous view is to be seen ...'. The same day he returned to the site with friends and declared: 'I shall be buried here, looking towards the north, and the remains of Allan Wilson and his party must be brought from Fort Victoria and placed inside the memorial I shall put up to their memory ... I call this one View of the World'.

When Rhodes died of heart failure in South Africa on 26 March 1902, at the age of 49, his body was carried to the spot and buried in the way he'd requested. The funeral party included a band of Ndebele who requested that no saluting volley be fired lest the benevolent spirits of the place be disturbed. Instead, they offered the respectful salute *Hayate*, the only time such an honour has been accorded to a European.

scenery, with Matobo's most precarious and imaginative pinnacles and boulder stacks, is as good as the wildlife.

The relatively dense wildlife population includes klipspringer, kudu, reedbuck, sable, impala, wildebeest, dassies, warthog, giraffe, zebra, ostrich and even tiny elephant shrews. Leopard are also at home in the rambling rock ramparts – Matobo is reputed to have Africa's densest leopard concentration – but you'd be lucky to catch a glimpse of one.

Gates open at 8 am and close at dusk.

### Emadwaleni

Emadwaleni village, on the communal lands outside Matobo National Park, offers a village atmosphere, including opportunities to sample local foods, traditional dancing and Ndebele cultural demonstrations. Admission is US$1 and guided walks around the surrounding communal lands to visit ancient granaries and cave paintings cost US$5. Phone for information (☎ (19) 48889).

### Bambata Cave

The well painted Bambata cave, in the tiny Bambata wilderness area, west of the main body of Matobo Park, is best known for its rendition of a cheetah, a clearly individual cat which appears to have striped legs. Elephant and eland figure prominently in other sections of the work. Extensive excavations in the cave have uncovered tools and pottery from the first few centuries BC and have given the name Bambata to similar finds from the same period elsewhere in Zimbabwe. The cave is a 40 minute walk off the Whovi-Bulawayo road. (Note that this road isn't really suitable for low-clearance vehicles.)

### Toghwe Wilderness Area

The remote eastern third of Matobo lies in the Toghwe wilderness area, the wildest of all the park's wilderness areas. It contains parts of the scenic Mjelele and Toghwana valleys, as well as Inange cave and its fine collection of rock paintings. Roads are rough with some very steep bits and vehicles are infrequent; low-slung cars may encounter problems. After rains, low-lying stretches of the rough roads may become impassable without 4WD.

**Mjelele Dam** This long, narrow and nearly empty dam at the park's southern edge is becoming choked with vegetation. It doesn't attract many visitors at the moment but the road has been improved and the camp site upgraded. It's a long walk from anywhere so, without a car, access is nearly impossible. The road between Mjelele dam and Toghwana dam is horrid, requiring a lion-hearted and preferably high-clearance 4WD vehicle.

**Togwhana Dam** This remote and lovely spot, set amid tightly packed peaks, has a wonderful camp site. A good three day, 45km return walk will take you from Maleme dam to the Inange cave paintings, which are 7km on foot from Toghwana. If you return via Mjelele dam, it's a 60km return walk. Alternatively, walk one-way via the 27km route through communal lands to or from Sandy Spruit at Matobo's north entrance.

The access roads have some very steep sections and although 4WD isn't essential, you'll need a strong vehicle.

**Inange Cave** This cave (sometimes spelt Inanke), which sits atop a high whaleback *dwala*, is a four to six hour return walk from the Toghwana dam camp site. In this remote site, you'll encounter one of the most complex and well executed of Zimbabwe's cave paintings. Herds of well-observed African animals march in confused profusion across the walls, interspersed with hunters, and geometric and stylised designs. The greatest of these is a puzzle, a series of 16 rectangles overlying layers of egg-like ovals. Across and around the whole thing strut parades of giraffe. Large and bizarre human figures also make appearances around the panel.

Inange is a rough – and often steep – 7km

walk from Toghwana dam. It's a good idea to get there early, which will be facilitated if you stay at Toghwana dam. Most of the route is marked by green-painted arrows and small rock cairns and, although the way may become confusing as it passes over a series of nearly identical ridges and valleys, you shouldn't have problems.

**Silozwane Cave** Silozwane, a little-visited cave in the communal lands south of the park, is more easily reached than Inange. The panel is a dense mishmash of delicately executed figures, a wall full of doodles bearing little apparent relationship to each other. Particularly interesting are the rows of intricate human figures involved in various domestic tasks.

From Maleme, go 6km north-east to the Mjelele and Toghwana dam turn-off. Turn right and follow that road for 12km, then take the signposted right fork onto a very rough road and follow it for nearly 2km to the car park. This section of the road is in very poor condition, so you may have to walk it (but don't leave anything of value in your vehicle). From there, it's a short, steep walk over the dome to the cave hollow, with beautiful views along the way. Hitching prospects are poor.

### Organised Tours
Numerous Bulawayo operators offer Matobo day tours. Russell and Colleen Pumfrey, of the widely recommended Black Rhino Safaris (☎ (19) 41662; fax 77300), operate Matobo tours as a labour of love, and their infectious enthusiasm for Matobo shines through on every tour. (Beware of impersonators who have recently been ambushing backpackers at Bulawayo railway station and bus terminals.) They're happy to drop you at Maleme dam after the tour and pick you up on another day. Five/nine-hour tours cost US$35/45, including lunch and a Whovi game drive (and sometimes a rhino walk) but no two tours are identical. Advance booking is advised.

Sandbank Safaris (☎ (19) 69923 or 43865 after hours), at Shaka's Spear in Bu-lawayo, also offers an enthusiastic perspective. Day tours lasting 10 to 11 hours cost US$55, including three light meals.

Mzingeli Tours (☎ (19) 540268; fax 540269) visits cultural sites in both the park and surrounding communal lands. Out of respect for local tradition that outsiders not be admitted to sacred Matobo sites, you may want to avoid tours which visit Mzilikazi's Grave at Nthumbane or the Mjelele shrine, where people still come to petition the god Mwari.

Another recommended company is Chris and Cate Ferreira's Adventure Travel (☎ (19) 46982). Guide Tom Everett is one of only a few who can show you the game park on foot and one reader has described it as 'live comedy with wildlife thrown in as a bonus'. African Wanderer (☎ (19) 72736), charges US$45/40 for full/half-day tours and picnic lunch. It also does simple transfers to Maleme for US$20 from Bulawayo and for US$5 as a drop-off after its day tour.

### Activities
Guided 1½ hour horseback trips are available from the National Parks rangers at Whitewaters dam (near the Whovi Game Park entrance). If you lack a vehicle and aren't lucky with hitching, this is an option for access to the game park. Advance booking is essential.

A bit more expensive is hot-air ballooning over Matobo with Wildfire Balloons (☎/fax (19) 85383), 57 Josiah Tongogara St, PO Box 157, Bulawayo. A morning spin over the wondrous Matobo landscape will set you back US$194; locals pay US$146.

### Places to Stay
**National Parks Accommodation** It costs US$3 per person to camp in the park. The main camp site is at Maleme dam. The site at Sandy Spruit dam, near the northern park entrance, may be too close to the highway, but it's convenient if you're arriving late. The Toghwana dam site in the Toghwana wilderness area and Mjelele dam, 8km south of Toghwana, are both remote but extremely appealing. Near the Arboretum

entrance is a very civilised site and there's also a small and beautiful camp site at Mezilume dam near Nswatugi cave.

At Maleme are two luxury lodges, the *Black Eagle* and *Fish Eagle*, which afford a boulder-studded hilltop vista of Maleme Dam and surroundings. For one/two bedrooms, you'll pay US$13/26; they're well worth it, but bookings are essential. Chalets with one/two bedrooms are US$5/10.

Be warned that all park waters are infected with bilharzia and drinking water at all camp sites should be boiled or purified.

**Hotels & Lodges** *Inungu Guest House*, adjacent to Fryer's Store, 10km north of Maleme, accommodates one party of up to six people. The rates – US$44 for up to four adults plus US$6 per additional person – and the magical setting make it a great Matobo getaway. Book through Sunshine Tours (☎ (19) 67791) in Bulawayo.

The friendly *Matopo Ingwe Lodge* (☎ (183) 8233; fax 8217), on Gladstone Farm outside the Matobo boundary, has accommodation in comfortable single/double rondavels for US$32/44, with breakfast.

If I could cast a vote for Zimbabwe's loveliest lodge, it would go to *Matobo Hills Lodge* (☎ (19) 74589; fax 229088; <touch wld@harare.iafrica.com>), lost amid magnificent natural rock gardens west of the northern wilderness area. The simple stone and thatch architecture blends assiduously with its setting, the pool is hewn from natural rock and the spacious and airy bar overlooks a sublime landscape of standing rocks. All that detracts from it is the three-tier pricing, which places it out of reach for most foreigners. The international rate is US$250 per person; locals pay US$72. These rates include family-oriented meals and two game drives daily. If you opt out of the game drives, the rate is US$150/60 for foreigners/residents.

At *Camp Amalinda* (☎ (19) 46443 or (183) 8268; fax (19) 46436; <landa@msasa .samara.co.zw>) north of the Bambata wilderness area, you'll find such original features as a dining table made from sleep-

ers from Cecil Rhodes' Matopos rail line and a cave bar inside the Matobo rock, as are some of the rooms. A London *Daily Mail* reviewer called it 'a little corner of the cartoon town of Bedrock'. There's also a tiny swimming pool and a cosy fire circle for cold evenings. From 1 May to 1 November, accommodation for foreigners/ Zimbabweans costs US$220/49, The price includes meals, most drinks, and two game walks, drives or horseback rides. For US$30, the camp, run by Londa Mela Safaris, also organises rides on Tusker, Duma and Ishe, three orphaned elephants from Gonarezhou.

*Big Cave Camp* (☎ (19) 77176; fax 77300; <bigcave@harare.iafrica.com>) sits on a dwala 5km off the Whovi-Bulawayo road. The surrounding wilderness supports antelope, leopard and over 110 bird species. Foreigners pay US$75 for B&B or US$160 for thatched A-frame chalets, with meals, game drives and most drinks. Transfers from Bulawayo are US$45.

East of the park, off the Gwanda road, is Zindele Safaris' *Shumba Shaba Lodge* (☎ (188) 662; fax (19) 64128). The name means 'red lion', after the dwala on which it's perched. For accommodation and full board, everyone pays US$50.

Further afield, on the Stone Hills Game Sanctuary south of the Plumtree road, is Run Wild's (☎ (14) 795841) beautiful and acclaimed *Malalangwe Lodge* (☎ (19) 74693; fax 76917). The name means 'place where the leopard sleeps' and the decor features furnishings made out of *mukwa* (African mahogany). The area boasts at least 70 examples of the rare Transvaal red balloon tree (*Erythrophysa trasvaalensis*, also called wild jacaranda) and offers rewarding hiking and birdwatching. For single/double bungalows foreigners pay US$220 per person, with meals, drinks, game drives, walks and day tours. Locals pay US$110. Discounts are available in June and from December to March. The turn-off from the Plumtree road, 70km west of Bulawayo, is marked by a green sign reading 'Richard Peek'.

Also west of Figtree, *Izintaba Safari Lodge* (☎/fax (183) 256) occupies a photogenic 6000 hectare game ranch in the Matobo Hills. Contact Intaba Safaris (☎ (19) 60137; fax 63120), 4 Elgar Building, corner of Twelfth Ave and Robert Mugabe St, Bulawayo.

### Places to Eat
Apart from the hotels and lodges, there are no restaurants in the Matobo Hills. Maleme has a basic shop, but Fryer's Store, outside the park boundary 6km upstream from Maleme dam (10km by road), offers a bit more variety.

### Getting There & Away
Without a vehicle, budget access to Matobo can be difficult. Taxis aren't permitted in the park and hitching is slow, so nearly everyone takes a tour. The undaunted can hire bicycles in Bulawayo and cycle to the park, but note that cyclists aren't permitted in the game park.

Alternatively, the Kezi bus from Renkini in Bulawayo passes three Matobo turn-offs. From the first turn-off, you can cycle, walk or hitch the 6km to Sandy Spruit camp site. From the second turn-off at Rhodes' rail terminal, it's 5km to the arboretum camp site. To reach Maleme, get off at the Whovi access road and take the 6km shortcut or the 12km circuit past Mezilume, Nswatugi and Madingizulu dams, and Nswatugi cave.

### PLUMTREE
This tiny cow town on the Botswana border is the customs and immigration post for the highway and rail line between Bulawayo and Francistown. If you're entering Zimbabwe, try not to get stuck behind a bus or you may be delayed. You can stay at the basic *Plumtree Hotel* (☎ (180) 226).

### TSHABALALA WILDLIFE SANCTUARY
This small sanctuary, 10km from Bulawayo, was established on the former landholding of Fairburn Usher, a British sailor

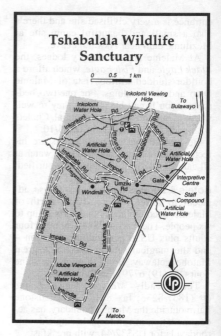

who arrived in 1883, and his Ndebele wife, who was a daughter of King Lobengula. It's perfect for a relaxing day and there are no predators – only antelope, zebra, giraffe, warthog and the like. Walking, horse-riding and picnicking are encouraged.

Tshabalala is open from 6 am to 6 pm in the summer and 8 am to 5 pm in winter. Foreigners pay US$10 admission and horse hire costs US$10 per hour. You may cycle, walk or drive on the sanctuary roads, but no motorbikes are allowed.

### Getting There & Away
The chances of hitching a lift aren't bad once you get out of Bulawayo. The Kezi bus from the Renkini terminal passes Tshabalala, and the Matobo Rd bus from the city hall terminal will drop you at Retreat, 3km from Tshabalala.

# Western Zimbabwe

With Zimbabwe's major attractions – Victoria Falls and Hwange National Park – and a few less well known ones, Western Zimbabwe looms big on most travellers' southern African itineraries. Naturally Hwange and The Falls, as they're known with local familiarity, are the main draws, but there are also other wonderful places. Western Lake Kariba, a wild alternative to its eastern counterpart, offers leisurely stays at the casual Mlibizi Resort; Binga, with its unique Batonka culture; and rugged and remote Chizarira, Zimbabwe's wildest – and arguably most beautiful – national park.

## GWAAI RIVER
Gwaai River, also called Dahlia Siding, is an almost obligatory stop for highway travellers between Bulawayo and Victoria Falls. Most travellers just drop in for petrol and a snack or drink at the Gwaai River Hotel, but the area also offers pleasant day walks and fishing streams. The local co-operative, Gwaai Valley Pottery, still uses traditional techniques and visitors are welcome to try out their own pottery-making skills.

### Places to Stay & Eat
Virtually all travellers between Bulawayo and Victoria Falls stop for tea and snacks in the sunny garden of the charming *Gwaai River Hotel* (☎ (118) 355; fax 375). The hotel pub is the hub of Gwaai River nightlife (and daylife, for that matter). Standard single/double units cost US$34 per person with half board. Plusher half board options include Syringa Suites (US$47/75), Jacaranda Square (US$40/67) and Acacia Lodge (US$53/80). Camping isn't advertised, but budget travellers may be permitted to pitch a tent in the grounds.

Another choice is *Halfway House Hotel* (☎ (189) 281), at the 221km peg of the Bulawayo-Victoria Falls road. Singles/doubles with hot showers cost US$22/35, self-catering is US$50 and meals are US$5 to

### HIGHLIGHTS

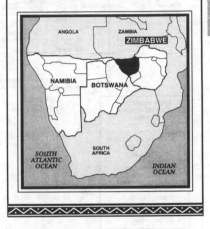

- Stroll around the rainforest park at world-famous Victoria Falls
- Raft the mighty Zambezi gorges
- Go on safari in wildlife-rich Hwange National Park
- Take a walking or backpacking safari in Chizarira National Park
- Learn about the Tonga culture at Binga on the shores of Lake Kariba

US$7. Plus points include a 24-hour petrol station, a bar, a pool and friendly staff.

See also Hotels, Camps & Lodges under Hwange National Park.

## MZOLA FOREST RESERVE
Nemba Safaris (☎/fax (189) 271 or fax (19) 78081; <secbird@harare.iafrica.com>) runs Mzola Wilderness Safaris – remote walking trips near the Mzola Forest Reserve. The trips aren't strenuous, as luggage is carried by oxcart and the distance between camps – Carmine, Mzola and Figtree – is only 7km. Hiking trips for one/two people cost US$210/360 and horseback tours are

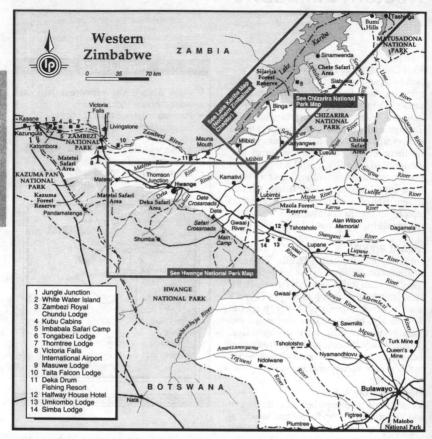

# Western Zimbabwe

ZAMBIA

0    35    70 km

**Key (numbered)**

1 Jungle Junction
2 White Water Island
3 Zambezi Royal Chundu Lodge
4 Kubu Cabins
5 Imbabala Safari Camp
6 Tongabezi Lodge
7 Thorntree Lodge
8 Victoria Falls International Airport
9 Masuwe Lodge
10 Taita Falcon Lodge
11 Deka Drum Fishing Resort
12 Halfway House Hotel
13 Umkombo Lodge
14 Simba Lodge

---

US$230/400, including accommodation at the three bush camps. Two nights at their lodge, The Ridge, including half board, drinks, transfers and wildlife-viewing, cost US$380 per person. Contact Chris and Val van Wyk, Nemba Safaris, PO Box 4, Gwaai River.

## DETE

The village of Dete has the rail terminal for Hwange National Park. Unfortunately, trains between Bulawayo and Victoria Falls in both directions arrive at a red-eye hour of the morning and you're still faced with a 12km walk or hitch to the park entrance and another 7km to Hwange National Park Main Camp.

### Places to Stay

The basic *Wildside Hostel* (☎ (118) 446) backpackers lodge, run by Paul and Val DeMontille, charges US$7.50 per person (US$5 if you arrive on the Blue Arrow bus), including transfers from the bus or train and use of cooking facilities.

The affiliated *Miombo Safari Lodge*

(☎ (118) 446) lies 3km east of Dete along the Hwange Main Camp road. This simple but lovely operation offers camping, comfortable chalets and family-oriented buffet meals in a nice bush setting, and the adjacent rail line means that train-spotters will find as much joy as bird and wildlife enthusiasts. Chalet accommodation costs US$60/75 on a B&B/full-board basis. Camping costs US$40 per person, including a four hour game drive, park entry fees, firewood, use of the swimming pool and transfers from Dete. The Blue Arrow bus will drop you at the Miombo entrance.

The *SSET Budget Hostel* (☎ (118) 483), run by Singing Bird Safaris, has camping in a stark compound for US$3 per vehicle and US$2 per person, and dorm beds in the old brick railway hostel for US$5. Self-catering cottages for up to six people cost US$40. The office is beside the Dete post office.

The *Game Reserve Hotel* (☎ (118) 256; fax 269), currently under renovation, may seem overdone for its setting, but it offers a decent mid-range option at US$30/50 for Zimbabweans and US$58/80 for foreigners.

If all else fails, you can crash on the concrete floor of the '1st class' lounge at the railway station, but it gets cold so bring a thermal pad and sleeping bag.

### Getting There & Away

All trains between Bulawayo and Victoria Falls stop in Dete. By bus, the best option is with Blue Arrow (☎ (19) 60176 in Bulawayo), which stops in Dete on its daily services between Bulawayo and Victoria Falls. The trip costs US$13 from Bulawayo and US$9 from Victoria Falls.

### HWANGE

Hwange town, like the national park, was named for an early Ndebele chief. For years, it was spelt Wankie and this mispronunciation has endured to the present day (much to the amusement of international visitors), although some Zimbabweans pronounce it 'HWAN-gay'.

Nestled amid mountains of mine tailings, Hwange owes its existence to coal. The proposed copper belt railway line was originally intended to cross the Zambezi River into Zambia at Chirundu, but construction was held up by the Boer Wars and the route was diverted westward to provide coalfields access. The main tourist interest revolves around seven German Henschel steam locomotives which serve the colliery.

### Places to Stay

The two-star *Baobab Hotel* (☎ (181) 323) on the hill offers agreeable singles/doubles for Z$50/70, with breakfast.

### Getting There & Away

All buses and trains between Bulawayo and Victoria Falls pass through Hwange.

### HWANGE NATIONAL PARK

Hwange National Park may be Zimbabwe's most accessible and wildlife-packed park, but by East African standards it's scarcely visited, and most organised safaris concentrate on the short and rewarding loop drives within 10km of Main Camp.

During the dry season (September and October), wildlife is readily observed as it congregates around water sources (most Hwange water holes are pumped with petrol-powered compressors). When the rains come, however, animals spread out across the park's 14,650 sq km for a bit of trunk and antler room, and viewing is less predictable.

### History

Hwange National Park sits at the ragged edge of the Kalahari sands and although the area was once home to nomadic families of San people, it was considered by other groups to be too hot, dry and sandy for permanent habitation. Originally, it wasn't thickly populated with wildlife, either; although animals spread across the region during the rainy season, they retreated to the perennial waters of the Zambezi Valley during the dry. However, as human pressure cut off favourable lands to the east, north and west, wildlife was driven into areas of poor soil and scarce surface water, such as

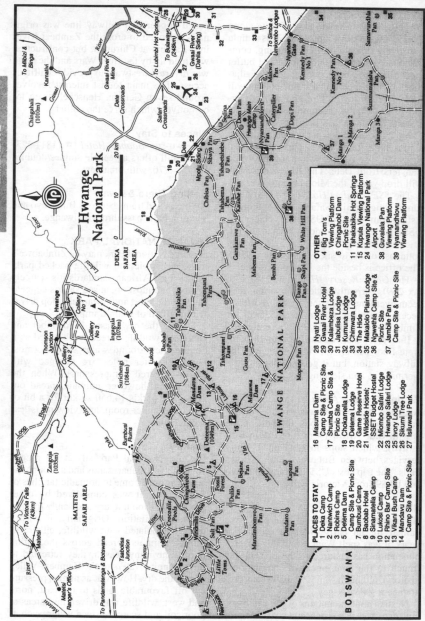

**Hwange National Park**

DEKA SAFARI AREA

HWANGE NATIONAL PARK

MATETSI SAFARI AREA

BOTSWANA

To Mlibizi & Binga
To Lubimbi Hot Springs
To Bulawayo (248km)
To Simba & Umkombo Lodges
To Victoria Falls (43km)
To Pandamatenga & Botswana

PLACES TO STAY
1 Deka Camp
2 Nantwich Camp
3 Robins Camp
5 Detema Dam
7 Camp Site & Picnic Site
8 Baobab Hotel
9 Bumbusi Camp
10 Lukosi Camp
12 Sinamatella Camp
13 Rhino Bar Camp Site
14 Vikani Bush Camp
Mandavu Dam
Camp Site & Picnic Site

16 Masuma Dam
Camp Site & Picnic Site
17 Shumba Camp Site &
Picnic Site
18 Chokamella Lodge
19 Detema Lodge
20 Game Reserve Hotel
21 Wildside Hostel;
SSET Budget Hostel
22 Miombo Safari Lodge
23 Hwange Safari Lodge
25 Ivory Lodge
26 Sikumi Tree Lodge
27 Isiluwani Park

28 Nyati Lodge
29 Gwaai River Hotel
30 Kalambeza Lodge
31 Jabulisa Lodge
32 Kumuna Lodge
33 Chimwara Lodge
34 The Hide
35 Makalolo Plains Lodge
36 Ngwethla Camp Site &
Picnic Site
37 Jambile Pan
Camp Site & Picnic Site

OTHER
4 Big Tom's
Viewing Platform
6 Chingahobi
Picnic Site
11 Tshakabika Hot Springs
15 Kupula Viewing Platform
24 Hwange National Park
Airport
38 Guvalala Pan
Viewing Platform
39 Nyamandlovu
Viewing Platform

Hwange, which were considered unsuitable for human habitation.

In the 19th century, Hwange served as a hunting reserve for both the Ndebele kings and European settlers, and was subsequently overhunted, but in 1928 it gained national park status and became a wildlife-viewing stop-off for tourists en route to Victoria Falls. Settlers created 60 artificial water holes fed by underground water, and by the 1970s the region had one of Africa's densest wildlife concentrations.

Since Zimbabwe's independence, wildlife management has taken a low budgetary priority. Financial shortfalls permitted an increase in poaching – particularly of rhino – and during the drought of the early 1990s many artificially-pumped waterholes dried up. Much of the credit for recent conservation efforts goes to Mike Edwards and the Hwange Conservation Society, which has established an anti-poaching unit and oversees the drilling, pumping and maintenance of bore holes. As a result, Hwange still provides some of Africa's finest wildlife-viewing.

### Orientation

Travellers on the Hwange Special Express bus arrive at Safari Crossroads; Air Zimbabwe arrives at Hwange National Park Airport; and railway passengers disembark at Dete railway station. From Safari Crossroads, it's 7km to the airport turn-off and 11.5km to Hwange Safari Lodge. From there, it's another 5km to the railway line and park entrance (Dete lies 12km northwest of this point), and 7km further to Main Camp.

The Main Camp area is characterised by savanna and thorny acacia scrub while the area around Ngwethla camp site, to the south-east, boasts broad grassy *vleis*, acacia-dotted plains and wildlife concentrations reminiscent of the great parks of Kenya. Here you'll find some of the largest herds of antelope, zebra, buffalo and elephant in Zimbabwe, as well as throngs of baboons.

West of Main Camp, around Shumba

---

### Buffalo Thorn

Conventional wisdom has it that buffalo thorn trees (*Ziziphus mucronata*) also known as 'wait-a-bit' (*blinkblaar wag 'n bietjie* in Afrikaans) grow only over sub-surface streams and therefore make an excellent indicator of underground water supplies. The small edible fruit is also quite tasty, but this tree isn't to be taken lightly. The sinister backward-pointing thorns can rip flesh and clothing at the slightest brush and legend has it that this tree was used to make the crown of thorns when Jesus was crucified.

---

camp site, the savanna gives way to rolling thorn and *mopane*-covered hills. Although this area doesn't support the staggering numbers of animals found elsewhere, there's a good chance of observing such predators as lion, leopard, cheetah, hyaena, jackal and wild dog.

### Information

Park information and sketchy photocopied maps are available at the ranger offices at Main, Sinamatella and Robins camps.

### Organised Tours

**Game Drives & Mobile Safaris** Geared especially for backpackers, the friendly Shamwari Safaris (☎/fax (118) 248) offers inexpensive game drives and camping safaris with owner and guide, Roberto 'Beat' Accorsi. He runs transfers between Hwange National Park airport, Dete railway station, Hwange Safari Lodge, Main Camp, Gwaai River Hotel, the Mlibizi ferry and Safari Crossroads; two-, six- and 12-hour game drives (including return trips between Main Camp and Sinamatella Camp), and all-inclusive group camping (or National Parks accommodation) safaris for up to six people, including transfers, meals and camping equipment. Budget safaris are available, without the transfers, meals or camping gear, from US$50 per day. Booking is strongly advised.

Paul and Val de Montille of Miombo Safaris (☎ (118) 446), the owners of Wildside Hostel and Miombo Lodge, run two-hour game drives starting at US$30 or ranger-guided hikes around Ngwethla for US$65, including lunch and park fees.

O'Brien Masawi's Singing Bird Safaris (☎ (118) 255; fax 383) runs three-hour/half-day/full-day Hwange game drives for US$25/40/70; the full day trips include lunch. Short game walks and night drives cost US$30. Intundla Safaris (☎ (118) 325), in Dete, has two-hour game drives for US$25 and half-day/full-day drives cost US$38/67. Village tours cost US$21.

Gwaai Valley Safaris (☎/fax (118) 515),

PO Box 17, Gwaai River, does half-day/full-day game drives for US$25/50 (full-day includes lunch). It also runs longer, tailor-made safaris and clients can be picked up from Gwaai River, Hwange Main Camp or Dete. Backpacker Special Safaris are also available.

United Touring Company offers two-hour game cruises around the 10 Mile Drive from Hwange Safari Lodge or Hwange Main Camp for US$25. Full-day drives with lunch are US$50. UTC is based at Main Camp but also maintains an office at Hwange Safari Lodge. Touch the Wild offers more informative two-hour/full-day game drives for US$48/154 but it caters mainly for pre-booked package tours.

Many other companies park outside the

---

## Elephant Control

The Zimbabwe National Parks Department's culling of elephant remains highly controversial. Although an average of 16 to 20 elephant is poached every week, the country now has over 65,000 elephant, and that, officials claim, is 30,000 more than Zimbabwe's capacity. Culling proponents say that for evidence of the destruction that results from elephant overpopulation, one need only look at Botswana's Chobe National Park, which has four times the ideal elephant population. It's true – in places, the bush appears to have experienced nuclear holocaust. Although the culling is done relatively humanely – entire herds are destroyed, rather than individuals, in order to prevent emotional stress on the survivors – many argue that nature should simply be allowed to take its course. Others favour translocation as an alternative to culling.

The flaw in this argument, according to officials, is that humans have interfered so drastically with lands outside game reserves – setting up farms and veterinary control fences; grazing domestic stock; and clearing the tasty bushland trees that elephant bulldoze, uproot and devour in staggering quantities – that the herds can't spread out as they'd be inclined to if there had been no human interference.

When elephant do decide to spread out, they create problems for local farmers, who get no benefit from the huge parcels of land set aside as national parks. Historically, culling has provided a sort of compensation for local people in the form of meat. The drought of the early 1990s compounded the problem. Instead of controlling the elephant population, it forced record numbers into urban areas, especially Kariba, where they've taken to drinking from swimming pools, and destroying trees and gardens. This has produced a dangerous situation for local people, their property, their crops and their animals.

Even the large number of elephant in wild and wonderful Hwange National Park is a feat of human engineering. Because the park's dams and artificially pumped water holes are unnatural creations, many ecologists agree that Hwange's wildlife must be carefully managed. Otherwise, they say, the park will face an irreconcilable conflict between conservation and tourism. Tourists come to see wildlife, so new water holes are created to

main camp offices in the afternoon and compete for game drive clients, but their quality is inconsistent. Note also that many are unlicensed and using them is unfair to operators who follow the rules.

**Walking** For walking, camping and backpacking trips, you can't beat Khangela Safaris in Bulawayo (☎ (19) 49733; fax 68259), run by professional guide Mike Scott. He leads two- to eight-day trips through the park's back country, either backpacking from camp to camp or doing day walks from a base camp. There's a good chance of seeing lion and leopard, or tracking black rhino through thick bush. These wonderful trips are great value at US$137 per day, including meals.

Backpackers Africa in Victoria Falls (☎/fax (113) 4510) does three to eight-day walking safaris, including occasional trips in the remote Shakwankie Wilderness, where buffalo and elephant gather to drink from natural springs rising from the Kalahari sands. It also offers 12-day walking trips through western Zimbabwe's four national parks (Hwange, Zambezi, Kazuma Pan and Chizarira). These fully catered trips aren't cheap but are still quite popular.

### Hwange Main Camp

Impressive landscapes and the possibility of spectacular wildlife encounters lure visitors into Hwange's outer reaches, but for sheer density and variety of animals you need not wander far beyond Main Camp.

attract more animals to visitor areas. Thanks to the presence of water, wildlife populations increase in these areas. Because of this wildlife density, tourist numbers increase and so does pressure on the environment, exerted by both the animals and increased demand for tourist facilities. The environment begins to degrade and, at this stage, it becomes clear that something has to give. In the past, park managers have opted for culling.

The opposite camp argues very convincingly that elephant play a vital role in complicated bush ecosystems and that culling interferes with these natural processes. The mopane tree (*Colophospermum mopane*), for example, covers much of the elephant's habitat in southern Africa and is a favoured food of the pachyderms. The fact that they strip leaves and turn tall mopane trees into stunted hedge shrubbery means that the trees begin to grow tender new leaves before their taller counterparts, providing food for impala, kudu, eland and other browsers to see them through the end of the dry season. The young leaves also contain more energy, protein and nitrogen – and less indigestible tannin – than mature leaves.

Elephant also strip the bark from the mopane trees. While this may look unsightly, it opens the tree up to colonisation by termites, which hollow out the centre of the tree and make way for helpful cocktail ants. When an animal begins to browse on the tree, it's attacked by these ants, who rush to the tree's defence. Thus, elephant are actually part of a larger and less obvious cycle than simple observation would indicate.

What's more, the culling of elephant clearly isn't popular with sentimental western tourists. They not only lament the killing, they also want to imagine they've stumbled upon a bit of wild Africa and rankle at the thought of complex management plans. On the other hand, few tourists relish the sight of decimated bush and starving elephant. As an alternative, the wildlife managers have experimented with translocating elephant out of overcrowded areas, but such operations are very expensive and park budgets don't stretch that far. To help fund these efforts, parks are now being allocated a larger share of the revenues they earn, but visible progress will take several years.

**The 10 Mile Drive** All that many visitors experience of Hwange is the convenient 10 Mile Drive loop around the most wildlife-packed part of the park, which can be easily completed in a two hour game drive. The route takes in several popular water holes, including Dom Pan (an apocryphal story explains that its name comes from the sound made by its water pump – dom-dom-dom ...). The highlight, Nyamandhlovu Pan, features a high-rise viewing platform and a good view over a favoured waterhole.

**Activities** From the office at Main Camp, two-hour ranger-guided walks to the wildlife-viewing hide at Sedina Pan depart at 6.30 and 10 am and 4 pm and cost US$10 each. Don't miss this safe and easy opportunity to strike out on foot among the herds of antelope, zebra and giraffe. Occasionally, even elephant, buffalo, lion or cheetah are spotted. Doing the whole regimen will familiarise you with the animals' daily routines.

Each month for three nights around the full moon, weather permitting, Main Camp rangers lead a convoy of vehicles into the park for two hours to see what's brewing at night. Hitchhikers are normally welcome; just ask the ranger or anyone with space in their vehicle.

**Places to Stay & Eat** *Main Camp* contains most park services: ranger headquarters, pub, restaurant, shop, petrol station, a campground, cottages and lodges. The shop is open from 8 to 10 am, noon to 2 pm and 4 to 7 pm. Behind it, a small museum displays aspects of Hwange's natural history.

To pitch a tent or park a caravan on the concrete-hard camp site costs US$3 per site. As Zimbabwe's most popular camp, Main Camp gets more crowded every year and during South African school holidays, it may resemble a small city. Advance booking may not offer any guarantees, but it's still wise.

**Ngwethla Loop**
On the open savannas around Ngwethla picnic site you'll see great concentrations of animals, and the nearby Kennedy Pans are magnificent, especially at dusk, when herds of elephant pack into the water to bathe, frolic and churn the pans into thick mud holes. Via Kennedy Pans, Ngwethla is accessible to any car, but the entire Ngwethla loop drive requires a sturdy vehicle. The Ngwethla and Jambile picnic sites are also available for overnight camping (see under Other National Parks Camps later in this section).

**Sinamatella Camp**
Sinamatella Camp, the nicest of Hwange's three large camps, sits atop a 50m mesa and enjoys a commanding 50km view in all directions. Services include a ranger office, museum, curio shop, small kiosk selling food and general items, petrol pumps, and a restaurant and pub.

Although wildlife is profuse around Sinamatella, it lacks the diversity of grazers or browsers found near Main Camp. By day, buffalo and antelope often amble into the grassy patch below camp and at night, Sinamatella comes alive. Vicious little honey badgers skitter around the restaurant awaiting hand-outs and you're almost certain to hear the contented roaring of lions and disconcerting yowls of hyaena at the foot of the hill – as well as a host of unidentified screeches, thumps, bumps and howls.

Accommodation comprises camping, chalets, cottages and lodges. Ranger-escorted walks are available for US$67 per day for groups of up to six people; a popular walk is a return cross-country walk to Mandavu Dam. Three-day treks with an armed game scout, also limited to six people, cost US$125 and must be pre-arranged through the National Parks Harare booking office.

**Robins & Nantwich Camps**
Robins and Nantwich camps, near the park's north-west corner, lie in prime lion, cheetah and hyaena country. The campground at Robins has been described as rough and is subject to nocturnal invasion

by lion and hyaena. You're advised not to venture out at night and once you've heard the hyaena whooping and yelping beneath your windows, you won't want to anyway.

Chalets include outdoor cooking facilities. Robins Camp also has a sparsely stocked grocery, the Hyaena Shop. The Hyaena Restaurant (open at mealtimes) and Hyaena Bar (open 10.30 am to 10.30 pm) occupy the ground floor of the fire tower. You can also arrange guided day walks and overnight trips with armed game scouts (see under Sinamatella for details).

Nantwich Camp, which lacks a campground facilities, has three two-bedroom lodges, each accommodating up to six people, but there are no other facilities.

## Other National Parks Camps

**Exclusive Camps/Picnic Sites** Exclusive park service camps cater for groups of up to 12, and include cooking facilities and the services of a resident walking guide. *Bumbusi Camp* near Sinamatella is the nicest of the lot, but for holiday periods it's booked up six months in advance.

*Deka Camp*, 25km west of Robins Camp, and *Lukosi Camp*, 5km south-east of Sinamatella Camp, offer fine amenities but little wildlife. Deka is accessible by 4WD vehicle and Lukosi is open only during the non-hunting season between November and April. You're permitted to walk within an 8km radius of Lukosi even without a guide.

Other exclusive camps include those such as *Vikani Bush Camp* and *Rhino Bar*, which are booked mainly by organised safari groups (see the Organised Tours chapter).

The fenced public picnic sites at *Shumba*, *Mandavu Dam*, *Masuma Dam*, *Ngwethla*, *Jambile*, *Kennedy Pan I* and *Detema Dam* are available to groups of up to eight people as exclusive camps. Lion are frequently seen around Shumba, but the site isn't especially appealing. Mandavu has a nice big expanse of water, Kennedy Pan I has lots of elephant and the Ngwethla site is a favourite with wildlife. At Masuma Dam, you can hole up in the hide overlooking the

water and listen to the belching hippo and trumpeting elephant and watch the endless parades of thirsty antelope, zebra, giraffe and predators.

## Private Hotels, Camps & Lodges

Around Hwange, luxury camps and lodges have sprouted like mushrooms and only Nyati Lodge and Isiluwani Park are accessible to budget or mid-range visitors. The following is a list of the latest offerings:

*Chimwara Lodge* (☎ (14) 795841; fax 795845; <runwild@mail.pci.co.zw>). This Run Wild tented camp sits near the border of Hwange National Park, 15km from Gwaai River. The mostly savanna region invites walking safaris from the camp. High season single/double rates are US$295/440.

*Chokamella Lodge* (☎ (14) 734046; fax 708119; <landela@samara.co.zw>). Set atop the bluffs overlooking the Chokamella River, this Landela Safaris camp occupies a private game reserve adjacent to the Nchonlomela railway siding and has one of the nicest settings of any safari lodge in the region. All-inclusive accommodation in single/double thatched chalets costs US$425/550.

*Detema Lodge* (☎ (14) 700661; fax 735080). This pleasant lodge is on a private farm in Dete near the national park border. For accommodation in thatched one- or two-bedroom chalets, foreigners pay US$169 per person.

*The Hide*, 11 Rossal Rd, PO Box GD305, Greendale, Harare (☎ (14) 498548; fax 498265). Lies amid mopane, teak and acacia woodland inside Hwange National Park and evokes romantic Hollywood images of Africa. This basic tented camp organises twice-daily game walks and drives to water-hole viewing hides with licensed guides. For less than plush singles/doubles foreigners pay US$425/590, including meals, activities and a concept. Locals pay only US$73 per person.

*Hwange Safari Lodge* (☎ (118) 332). The most accessible of Hwange's luxury accommodation and set on the road from Safari Crossroads to Hwange Main Camp. Amenities include a swimming pool and tennis and volleyball courts, and restaurant diners are treated to a front-row view of wildlife lumbering up for a drink from the hotel's own watering hole. Some bedrooms have a glass wall facing the watering hole, so guests can watch the wildlife in comfort, day or night. For single/double rooms, foreigners pay US$176/220 and Zimbabwe residents, US$76/94. Buffet lunches are US$7, but non-guests pay an additional US$2 'membership fee'.

*Isiluwani Park*, Lions Den Enterprises, PO Box 19, Gwaai River (☎/fax (118) 295). Offers secluded tent or caravan camping 7km east of Gwaai River and within easy reach of Hwange National Park. Sites are US$2 plus US$5 per person, with use of laundry facilities and electrical hookups. Accommodation in simple chalets is US$9 per person.

*Ivory Lodge* (☎ (118) 224). Set in the dense bush of a private game ranch near Safari Crossroads. It's opposite Zingweni Vlei, where animals congregate to •scratch for water. Accommodation in elevated teak and thatch bungalows costs US$240 per person for foreigners.

*Jabulisa Lodge*, PO Box 23, Gwaai River Jabulisa Lodge (☎ (118) 2306; fax 295). The Ndebele name means 'place of delight'. Built around a converted colonial farmhouse dating from 1922, a low ridge affords a commanding view over Sikumi Vlei. For foreigners, accommodation in thatched chalets costs US$222 per person, with meals, Hwange game drives, night drives, horse-riding and tours of nearby communal lands. For accommodation and meals only, it's US$121.

*Kalambeza Lodge* (☎ (113) 4480; fax 4644). This luxury camp on the banks of the Gwaai River lies on a 30,000 hectare private game ranch, where they conduct game walks and night drives. They also run excursions into the national park. Singles/doubles in A-frame chalets cost US$225/360, with meals. It's just off the main Bulawayo-Victoria Falls road and is accessible by ordinary vehicles. Bus travellers may be picked up from Gwaai River Hotel.

*Kumuna Lodge*, PO Box 19, Gwaai River (☎ (118) 2308; fax 295). The Batonka name means 'place of peace'. Set beside a mineral spring 20km outside the national park, it occupies a large private estate with plenty of wildlife, and the owners, Mr and Mrs De Vries, have 50 years-worth of riveting bush stories. Foreign/local rates for their thatched rondavels are US$192/96 per person with activities and full board. Camping costs US$2 per site plus US$1.50 per person.

*Makalolo Plains Lodge* (☎ (113) 4527; fax 4224; <wildness@zol.co.zw>). This Wilderness Safaris tented camp lies beside Somavundhla Pan in the remote southern savannas of Hwange National Park. Activities include

game drive and foot safaris. High-season single/double rates are US$395/590.

*Nyati Lodge* (☎/fax (118) 515). A rare budget choice in the area, with comfortable lodges on the Hankano Ranch private game reserve. Singles/doubles including full board cost US$66/110. With breakfast only the cost is US$47/78 and self-catering is US$39/64. Participants on Gwaai Valley's Backpacker Special Safaris can use the no-frills camp site. Hwange National Park game drives cost US$32/70 for a half/full day and transfers are free from Gwaai River and US$15 from Hwange National Park.

*Sikumi Tree Lodge* (☎ (118) 273; <touchwld@ harare.i.frica.com>). In these thatched bungalows you won't be sleeping in the treetops, but they do sit on stilts 2m off the ground. In addition to game drives in the national park and night drives on the private estate, guests can opt for game walks and visits to nearby African villages. Rates start at US$275 per person, all inclusive, and children are welcome.

*Simba Lodge*, 167 Enterprise Rd, Chisipite, Harare (☎/fax (14) 495057). Lies 20km off the Victoria Falls road and 45 minutes from Hwange's Nyantwe Gate. The lodge occupies a 600 hectare concession in the Gwaai Forest Reserve; the sandstone and thatch lodges sit at the edge of forest lands, overlooking an open grassy plain. Foreigners/locals pay US$180/105 per person.

*Umkombo Lodge* (☎ (14) 700002; fax 700001). These solar-powered thatch and timber chalets east of Simba Lodge offer simple but spacious accommodation amid giant acacias for US$50 per person. They're accessible by private vehicle.

## Getting There & Away

**Air** Air Zimbabwe has daily services to and from the following: Harare (via Kariba); Bulawayo (via Kariba and Harare; no Bulawayo to Hwange service on Monday, Wednesday or Saturday); Kariba; Victoria Falls; and Johannesburg (via Harare and/or Kariba or Victoria Falls; no Johannesburg to Hwange service on Monday, Wednesday or Friday).

UTC meets incoming flights and provides transfers to Hwange Safari Lodge or Main Camp for US$10 per person (minimum US$60).

**Bus** The Hwange Special Express bus from Bulawayo or Victoria Falls stops at Safari Crossroads, which lies an 11.5km hitch to Hwange Safari Lodge, 5km from the Dete turn-off. Hitching isn't permitted beyond the railway line so you must wait at the entrance for a lift into the park.

Alternatively, you can get off the bus east of Hwange town and hitch along the rough 40km road into Sinamatella Camp. Expect long waits.

**Train** In either direction, the train between Bulawayo and Victoria Falls passes Dete in the small hours of the morning. See under Dete earlier in this chapter.

### Getting Around
**Car** The park speed limit is 40km/h, so don't try to see the whole park in a single day. Unless you're racing to reach your camp before closing time, there's no reason to rush, anyway. However, if you're booked into a camp, don't turn up after the gates close, or the rangers will mount a search for you and you may have to foot the bill for their efforts.

Petrol is sold at Hwange Safari Lodge, Main Camp and Sinamatella Camp.

**Hitching** The rule that hitchhikers aren't permitted inside the park is intended to prevent hitchers being caught out among the lion and elephant and to shield those with vehicles from annoying petitions for lifts. Having said that, officials sometimes tolerate discreet hitching outside the park entrances or around Main Camp.

# Victoria Falls

The world-famous Victoria Falls is Zimbabwe's supreme contribution to the list of the world's great attractions and miles of film and videotape are gobbled through cameras here every year. Over this incredible 1.7km-wide precipice, an average of 550,000 cubic metres of water plummets 90 to 107m into the Zambezi gorges every minute but, during the March to May flood stage, the volume increases to about five million cubic metres per minute.

### VICTORIA FALLS
Victoria Falls town was built on tourism but, unfortunately, the falls' ample natural beauty has now been compromised by an archetypal tourist circus, complete with kitsch curio shops, pseudo-traditional dance

---

### Name Games
Humans have been living around Victoria Falls for hundreds of thousands of years. The first known name of the falls was Shongwe, given to it by the Tokaleya people who inhabited the area prior to the Nguni invasions. Later, the Ndebele changed the name to Amanza Thunquayo, or Water Rising as Smoke. The late-arriving Makalolo, a tribe of refugees from the Nguni invasions, changed it yet again, this time to Mosi-oa-Tunya or Smoke that Thunders. On 16 November 1855, Scottish missionary David Livingstone was brought to the falls by the Makalolo in a dugout canoe and, following the established procedure, promptly renamed it in honour of the queen.

During the Zimbabwean name games going on shortly after independence, Victoria Falls was not renamed Mosi-oa-Tunya as it was pointed out that the country couldn't afford to sacrifice the familiarity of Livingstone's choice of names. They feared that, by any other name, the tourism potential and income generated by Zimbabwe's monumental drip just wouldn't smell as sweet.

ZIMBABWE

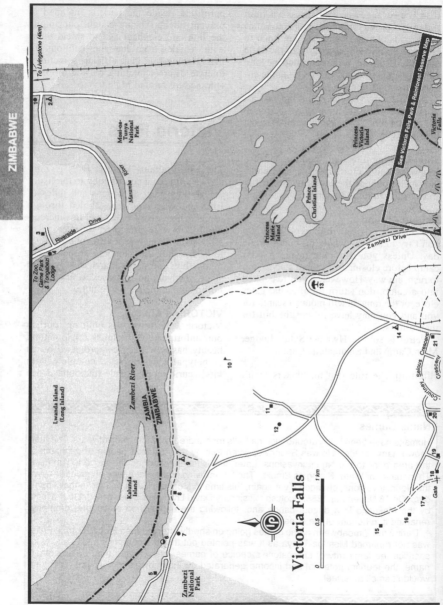

To Livingstone (4km)

1
2

Moni-oa-Tunya
National Park

Marambe River

See Victoria Falls Park & Rainforest Reserve Map

Victoria
Falls

Princess
Victoria
Island

3
Riverside Drive

To Zoo,
Game Park
& Tongabezi
Lodge

Prince
Christian Island

Princess
Marie
Island

Zambezi Drive

13

10

14

Zambezi River

ZAMBIA
ZIMBABWE

Lwanda Island
(Long Island)

11

12

21

Courtenay Selous Crescent
Crescent

20

Kalunda Island

9

19

8

18
Gate

17

Victoria Falls

15

16

7

6

5

0        0.5        1 km

Zambezi National
Park

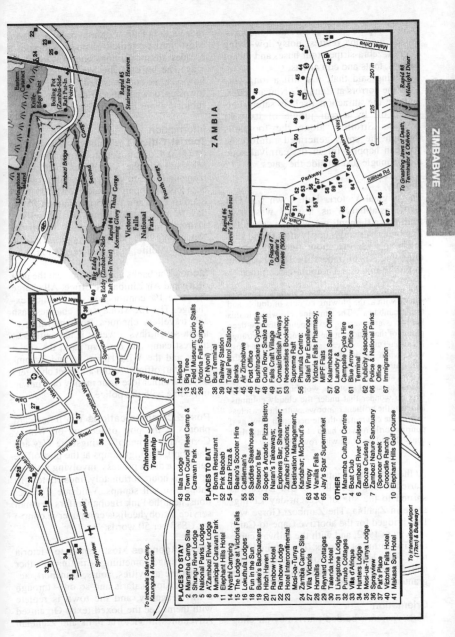

ZIMBABWE

**PLACES TO STAY**
2 Maramba Camp Site
3 Shungu River Lodge
5 National Parks Lodges
8 A'Zambezi River Lodge
11 Municipal Caravan Park
11 Elephant Hills Hotel
14 Nyathi Camping
15 The Lodge at Victoria Falls
16 Lokuthula Lodges
18 Fun in the Sun
19 Burke's Backpackers
20 Hitch-Haven
21 Rainbow Hotel
22 Rainbow Lodge
23 Hotel Intercontinental
   Mosi-oa-Tunya
24 Zambia Camp Site
27 Villa Victoria
28 Hornbills
29 Reynard Cottages
30 Taterda Hotel
31 Livingstone Lodge
32 Pumulo Cottages
33 Villa d'Afrique
34 Hunters Lodge
35 Mosi-ua-Tunya Lodge
36 Sprayview
37 Pat's Place
40 Victoria Falls Hotel
41 Makasa Sun Hotel

43 Ilala Lodge
50 Town Council Rest Camp &
   Caravan Park

**PLACES TO EAT**
17 Boma Restaurant
52 Pink Baobab
54 Eatza Pizza &
   Beano's Scooter Hire
55 Cattleman's
58 Saddles Steakhouse &
   Stetson's Bar
59 Soper's Arcade; Pizza Bistro;
   Explorers Bar; Shearwater;
   Zambezi Productions;
   Destination Management;
   Kandahar; McDonut's
63 Wimpy
64 Vanilla Falls
65 Jay's Spar Supermarket

**OTHER**
1 Maramba Cultural Centre
4 Boat Club
6 Zambezi River Cruises
   (Booze Cruises)
7 Zambezi Nature Sanctuary
   (Spencer Creek
   Crocodile Ranch)
10 Elephant Hills Golf Course

12 Helipad
13 Big Tree
25 Field Museum; Curio Stalls
26 Victoria Falls Surgery
   (Dr Nyoni)
38 Bus Terminal
39 Railway Station
42 Total Petrol Station
44 Banks
45 Air Zimbabwe
46 Post Office
47 Bushtrackers Cycle Hire
48 Curio Row; Snake Park
49 Falls Craft Village
53 Necessities Bookshop;
   Comair/British Airways
51 Supreme Raft
56 Phumula Centre;
   Safari Par Excellence;
   Victoria Falls Pharmacy;
   MIPF Flats
57 Kalambeza Safari Office
60 Laundry &
   Campsite Cycle Hire
61 Blue Arrow Office &
   Terminal
62 Publicity Association
66 Police & National Parks
   Office
67 Immigration

shows, reptile parks, adrenaline sports, muzak marimba revues, noisy low-flying aircraft, zebra-striped tour buses and lots of hassles, touts and con artists.

Having said that, it's still a long way from the horrors at Canada's Niagara Falls, and the big attraction itself is safely cordoned off by a real jungle of its own creation. Strolling along the footpaths through the spray-generated rainforests, you can happily forget the carnivalesque tourist jungle just outside the gates.

### History

The original Victoria Falls town was Old Drift, established as a wild west-style trading settlement on what is now the Zambian riverbank, shortly after David Livingstone's reports about the Falls began attracting Anglo traders. In 1865 he wrote in purple-tinted and comma-laden prose:

The morning sun gilds these columns of watery smoke with ... the glowing colours of double and treble rainbows ... The sunshine, elsewhere in this land so overpowering, never penetrates the deep gloom of that shade. In the presence of the strange Mosi-oa-Tunya, we can sympathise with those who, when the world was young, peopled the earth, air and river with beings not of mortal form ... The ancient Batoka chieftains used mid-river islands as sacred spots for worshipping the deity. It is no wonder that under the cloudy columns, and near the brilliant rainbows, with the ceaseless roar of the cataract, with the perpetual flow, as if pouring forth from the hand of the Almighty, their souls should be filled with reverential awe.

At the turn of the century, however, malaria started taking its toll and Old Drift was shifted to the site of present-day Livingstone in Zambia. The Zambezi Gorge was first bridged for the abortive Cape-to-Cairo railway in 1902, and with the railway came the first influx of tourists. The original Victoria Falls Hotel was constructed in 1906 and, 66 years later, the growing village was granted town status.

### Orientation

Most visitors who don't arrive by air chug into Victoria Falls' colonial railway station. Most tourist-oriented businesses nestle in arcades around Livingstone Way or Parkway. The bulk of the town's population, however, is concentrated in Chinotimba township, down Pioneer Rd, with its colourful local shops and rollicking beer hall.

### Information

**Tourist Office** The Publicity Association (☎ (113) 4202), under chief tourism officer Mkhululi Bhebhe, distributes local advertising and sells town maps and information booklets. It's open Monday to Friday from 8 am to 1 pm and 2 to 5 pm, and on Saturday from 8 am to 1 pm. It also sells *A Visitor's Guide to Victoria Falls* by Mrs M Newman (1987), with information on local history, wildlife, birds and vegetation.

**Money** The banks are lined up near the post office and Air Zimbabwe office. All charge the same 1% commission on currency exchange. The FX Moneycorp changes cash and travellers cheques from morning to night, seven days a week; it has outlets at the rest camp and caravan park, the snake park, and the Wild Horizons and Kalambeza safari offices. Avoid all street changers or you'll either lose your money or wind up in trouble with the police.

**Post & Communications** You'll find card phones at the post office and on Wimpy Corner (the corner of Livingstone Way and Parkway). Buying stamps at the post office can be a tedious process, involving waits of up to an hour; fortunately, most hotel gift shops also sell stamps. Wildside Connections, near the Pink Baobab, offers an email service (<tobyheelis@compuserve.com>) for US$3 per 50 words.

**Travel Agencies** Most visitors to Victoria Falls arrange something – rafting or other adrenaline activities, tours, transport, accommodation, safaris and so on – through a travel agency, and the town is replete with them. See the boxed texts, Organised Adventures in Victoria Falls and Zambian

## Organised Adventures in Victoria Falls

The following travel agencies can organise a range of tours; safaris; booze cruises; transfers; scenic flights; horse or elephant-riding; transport; and adrenaline activities, including rafting, riverboarding, bungee jumping, microlighting, canoeing, kayaking, and so on.

*African Bush Safaris* (☎ (113) 5990). Does inexpensive morning and evening game drives (starting at US$30) through Zambezi National Park, including snacks and beverages.

*Backpackers Africa*, PO Box 44, Victoria Falls (☎/fax (113) 4510). Runs game walks and backpacking trips through Zambezi, Kazuma Pan, Hwange and Chizarira national parks.

*Dabula Safaris*, 309 Parkway Drive, PO Box 210, Victoria Falls (☎ (113) 4453; fax 4609). Dabula books all the usual activities – tours, transfers, game drives, canoeing and booze cruising, and it's also the booking agent for Zambia's Raft Quest rafting trips.

*Destination Management Zimbabwe*, Shop 18, Soper's Arcade, Victoria Falls (☎ (113) 4729; fax 2109 or 5959). This friendly agency books everything from adrenaline activities to transfers, transport, hotels and day trips around Zimbabwe, Zambia and Botswana.

*Frontiers Adventures*, PO Box 117, Victoria Falls (☎ (113) 5800; fax 5801). Organises upper Zambezi booze cruises, white-water rafting, game drives, Kariba sailing, and all other area activities. It also books the Safari Express steam train tours. Its popular canoe safaris are provided in conjunction with Siansimba Safaris & Canoeing, 425 Pioneer Rd, PO Box 241, Victoria Falls (☎ (113) 4236; fax 2149).

*Kalai Safaris*, 414 Clark/Livingstone Way, Victoria Falls (☎ (113) 5842; fax 5855). Kalai specialises in day tours around Victoria Falls, Zambia, Hwange and Chobe.

*Kalambeza Safaris*, 306 Parkway Drive, PO Box 217, Victoria Falls (☎ (113) 4480; fax 4644). Books booze cruises, scenic flights, rafting, bungee jumping, guided tours and accommodation at its own lodge in Hwange National Park.

*Kandahar Safaris*, Shop 9, Soper's Arcade, Parkway Drive, Victoria Falls (☎ (113) 4502; fax 2014). Specialises in canoeing safaris on the upper Zambezi.

*Safari Par Excellence*, Phumula Centre, PO Box 44, Victoria Falls (☎ (113) 4424; <zaibmgll@ibmmail.com>). As one of Zimbabwe's largest agencies, Safari Par Excellence books anything and everything you might like to do in the region. Specialities include rafting and canoeing trips in Zimbabwe and Zambia. It also books Bush Birds Microlighting safaris, Zambezi Horse Trails in Zambezi National Park, day tours to Botswana's Chobe National Park, and Ulinda Safaris trips through Hwange National Park.

*Safari Travel Agency*, PO Box 185, Victoria Falls (☎ (113) 4571; fax 4426). Books all area transport and activities, but specialises in river/booze cruises and game drives.

*Shearwater*, Soper's Arcade, PO Box 125, Victoria Falls (☎ (113) 4531; fax 4341; <shearadv@zol.co.zw>). Shearwater operates Upper Zambezi canoeing safaris and both Zimbabwe- and Zambia-side rafting, and is the Zimbabwe booking agent for Batoka Sky microlighting.

*Tatenda*, Town Council Rest Camp & Caravan Park (☎ (113) 4210). This grass roots operation does three-hour game drives in Zambezi National Park for US$35 and Hwange day tours for US$150.

*Vundla Safari Tours*, Suites 6 & 7, Phumula Centre, PO Box 236, Victoria Falls (☎/fax (113) 4357). Organises transfers, car hire, ferry tickets, package tours and adrenaline activities.

*Wild Horizons*, PO Box 159, Victoria Falls (☎ (113) 4219; fax 4349). This company runs morning and afternoon elephant-back safaris through the Woodlands Estate, half an hour from Victoria Falls, for US$112. Half/full-day walks in Zambezi National Park are US$30/65 and overnights are US$120.

ZIMBABWE

Side Tour Operators, for a rundown of the main players and their offerings.

**Film** Film – including slide film – is available at the Zambezi Productions photo shop (which produces those rafting photos and videos) in Soper's Arcade or at the Photo Fast on Parkway. You'll pay around US$9 for a roll of Fujichrome 100-36.

**Dangers & Annoyances** Beware when leaving your valuables in rafting companies' safe box while you're off shooting the rapids. Some travellers have reported large notes going missing, so be vigilant and count your cash before and after your trip.

**Medical Services** Dr Nyoni (☎ (113) 3356), whose surgery is on West Drive, is recommended.

**Bookshops** For pulp reading material, try the Upmarket Book Exchange, upstairs in the Phumula Centre, which also sells ethnic jewellery and clothing. You can find a range of souvenir books and maps at Necessities bookshop on Parkway.

**Laundry** Cheap laundry services are available at the town council rest camp and caravan park. A coin laundrette is in preparation and should be open in town by the time you read this.

### Victoria Falls Park & Rainforest Reserve

Before setting off for the falls, think about water and the effects it will have on what you're carrying. Protect your camera equipment and wrap cash and valuables vulnerable to water in plastic. It's also wise to wear either waterproofs or clothing that won't create a public scandal when soaked. You can hire waterproofs from Raincoat & Camping Equipment Hire (☎ (113) 4528), Stand 307, Parkway.

**Visiting the Park** You can approach the park entrance from Livingstone Way east of town or down the track from the Victoria Falls Hotel. For foreigners, a single-entry ticket for the park is now US$10.

Along the rim, a network of surfaced tracks – laid down to limit damage to the fragile rainforest ecosystem – leads to a

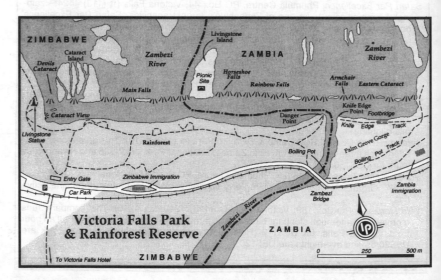

## A Matter of Air, Mist & Light

The time of year and time of day when you visit will affect your experience of the Victoria Falls. The flow of water is greatest between April and June so these are the times for the misty views. When the wind is blowing, rainbows form over the gorge. During low water from September to November, you'll get the clearest views and photos with the most rock showing between segments of the falls. During midsummer, the humidity will be at its most stifling and the rains will be hard and frequent, making viewing a generally hit-or-miss proposition.

Sunrises and sunsets are the best from late October to December when the sun is in the south, humidity is rising, clouds are most dramatic and the river is still low enough not to obscure the view with spray. During the dry season, the best sunset view is normally from the viewpoints opposite the main falls while sunrise is best from Cataract View. However, Cataract View is low in the gorge, so the morning sun won't be seen here until a good hour after it's already shining brightly elsewhere.

During the dry season, you may want to return to Cataract View in the mid-afternoon when the sun shines directly into the gorge and the refraction rainbow is strategically placed for an ideal photograph. For something really special, however, time your visit to coincide with the rising of the full moon. The park stays open later to allow you to witness the magical lunar rainbow over the falls.

Having said all that, it's important to point out that these are all just guidelines. Air, mist and light conditions could combine to offer magnificent surprises from any vantage point at any time of the year!

series of viewpoints. One of the most dramatic is Cataract View, the westernmost point of the park, at the bottom of a steep stairway.

At the aptly named Danger Point, you'll have a stunning view into the First Zambezi Gorge, but terraces of soaking and slippery moss-covered rocks and a sheer, unfenced 100m drop-off conspire to rattle your nerves. You can then follow a side track for a view over the gracefully precarious Zambezi Bridge which connects Zimbabwe with Zambia. This is now a favourite vantage point for locals, who gather to watch insane foreigners diving off the Zambezi Bridge on giant rubber bands.

While walking through the rainforests, note the profusion of unusual species – ebony, ferns, fig trees and a variety of lianas and flowering plants – growing in this unique little enclave. Also, watch for the bushbuck which browse right up to the lip of the gorge.

### Along the Zambezi

The free walk along the Zambezi above the falls is an excellent and potentially thrilling experience, but don't take it too lightly. This thin strip of Victoria Falls National Park is packed with wildlife: warthog, crocodiles, hippo, antelope and even elephant, buffalo and lion.

Avoid walking near the shore – the crocs are thick along the riverbank and can appear without warning. Some silly travellers do swim in this stretch of the river, but it's extremely unwise. If you aren't fazed by crocs and hippos, consider the bilharzia.

**Livingstone Statue** Most Zambezi walks begin at the Livingstone statue, which overlooks Cataract View at the upper end of the Victoria Falls Park track. Here you can gaze across the Zambezi as it steepens and gains momentum before disappearing over the edge. A gate topped with barbed wire prevents access to the rainforest reserve.

**The Big Tree** As an attraction, the Big Tree is, well, a big tree, but it makes a fine excuse for a walk. This is a giant baobab referred to as an 'upside-down tree', so called because a distant ancestor reportedly offended a deity and in punishment, was uprooted, turned over and stuck back into the ground upside down. The Big Tree served as a camp and a gathering site for early white settlers and traders awaiting passage across the Zambezi to Old Drift on the opposite shore. Although this specimen stands only about 25m high, its 20m circumference makes it seem much larger.

### Falls Craft Village

In this fortified mock-up of historical Zimbabwean life, you'll see a collection of prefabricated ethnic huts from around the country. You can also watch craftspeople at work and consult with a *n'anga*, (shaman) who will reveal your future – if you really want to know it. However, they may not mention that your destiny includes an exit through an immense curio shop. The village is open from 8.30 am to 4.30 pm Monday to Saturday, and on Sunday from 9 am to 1 pm. Guided tours are conducted at 9.30 am, and a live traditional dance production is staged from 7 to 8 pm nightly.

### Curio Row & Snake Park

The area's first white settler, Percy Clark, opened the first in a long line of Victoria Falls curio shops in 1903, but the real boom arrived with the railway. One of the original places, *Soper's Curios*, has been in business since 1911. Outside its rustic shop is a pool where the original owner, Jack Soper, kept his commercial gimmick – a live croc. Not surprisingly, there's still a crocodile whiling away its days in the very same pool. Near the end of the street is the Victoria Falls Aquarium, which has a range of Zimbabwean freshwater fish and crocodiles; the idea is to draw you into the curio shop which specialises in fish-inspired carvings, jewellery and clothing. Predators are fed daily at 2 pm.

If you've always wanted to buy a copper cut-out in the shape of Zimbabwe, drilled through and installed with clock workings, etched with a giraffe-and-acacia design and mounted on a bit of anonymous wood, here's your chance. The kitsch value of the stuff sold in this cluster of curio shops staggers the imagination. When you've finished browsing, you can check out the Zambezi Taxidermy Snake Park and pay US$1.50 to watch snakes being milked.

For value and quality, however, visit the craft halls at the end of the street, where local women display their creations and you can bargain over already competitive prices. Skilful bargainers can pick up great deals while contributing directly to the local economy.

### Zambezi Nature Sanctuary (Spencer Creek Crocodile Ranch)

If you're impressed by those photos of tourists cuddling up to crocodile hatchlings, here's the place for the hands-on experience. With 5000 crocodiles of all sizes, the Zambezi Nature Sanctuary (formerly Spencer Creek Crocodile Ranch) offers lots of crocs for your US$2 admission fee. It also screens informative crocodile videos and there's a crocodile museum, a tearoom, a cat enclosure, an aviary, a collection of insects, domestic animals and a curio shop.

It's open from 8 am to 4.30 pm daily except Christmas.

### Activities

Victoria Falls is quickly becoming the greatest adrenaline-capital-cum-tourist-playground west of New Zealand and the town is full of agencies and operators (for details, see the boxed texts, Organised Adventures in Victoria Falls and Zambian Side Tour Operators). Given the competition, it sometimes pays to shop around for deals. On the Zimbabwe side, all river activities are subject to a National Parks river use fee of US$2 per person.

Parents, note that children's day safaris are available from most Victoria Falls agents. While you're off adrenaline-tripping, your kids can visit the reptile parks, take a forest walk and game drive, and have a bush picnic for US$40 per child.

**Flight of the Angels** The name of this 10 to 15 minute buzz over the falls is derived from an overworked quote by an awe-struck David Livingstone, who wrote in his journal that: 'on sights as beautiful as this, angels in their flight must have gazed'.

Most of today's angels are produced in Pennsylvania by Piper Aircraft, and the privilege of briefly joining them in their flight costs an appropriately sky-high US$47 per person. Flights, which are operated by United Air (☎ (113) 4530), depart the Sprayview Airfield roughly every 15 minutes. A longer 30 minute version includes a buzz over the falls and a game flight over Zambezi National Park's Chundu Loop, and costs US$65 per person. Alternatively, go by seaplane with Seaplane Safaris Africa for US$60/90 for 20/30 minutes. Book directly or through local tour agencies.

Other scenic flights are organised by Southern Cross Aviation (☎ (113) 4618), which runs 15-minute helicopter flights over the falls (US$48 per person), 30-minute flights up the Zambezi (US$82), 25-minute flights over the falls by Cessna (US$32) and a 40 minute Cessna flight along the Zambezi Gorges (US$48). It also flies by helicopter to a mid-river island for a two hour champagne breakfast, which costs US$390 for up to four people.

**Microlighting** Batoka Sky (☎ (260-3) 323672; fax 324289) organises microlight flights over the falls from the airport at Livingstone in Zambia. They cost US$65 for 15 minutes and US$130 for 30 minutes, including a spin over Mosi-oa-Tunya National Park. The catch is that photography is not permitted; you must buy the photos provided by the company. It also runs instruction courses in microlight piloting. Book directly or through Sobek in Livingstone or Shearwater in Victoria Falls.

Alternatively, contact Bush Birds Flying Safaris through Safari Par Excellence or Supreme Raft. Flights over the falls and gorges cost US$85/125 for 35/60 minutes.

**White-Water Rafting** Although it's splashing out in more ways than one, white-water enthusiasts travel from all over the world to be flung headlong down the angry Zambezi below the falls. The rapids of the Gorges are among the world's wildest but they are also among the safest, largely because of the deep water, steep canyon walls and lack of rocks mid-stream. During low water the roughest rapids are considered class IV and V (on the I to VI ratings scale). Rafters can leave the work to an experienced oarsperson or they can paddle themselves, which is considerably more challenging as it's impossible to hold on. Whatever your method, you're bound to get wet (those who manage to hold onto the rafts are known as short swimmers; those who don't, and shoot the rapids without a raft are called long swimmers), but the operators use the best safety gear available and injuries are very rare. Bear in mind, however, that the river god Nyaminyami normally demands some sort of offering from river travellers; don't take anything you're not prepared to lose. If you need rafting shoes, buy them from the Bata shop near Vanilla Falls (the rafting companies charge considerably more).

One challenging element is the steep and slippery slog back up to the rim while your body is still jittery with adrenaline from the ride down. If you were so busy holding on that you missed the experience, operators feature the day's runs on video nightly, and you can also purchase videos and photo stills of your own run.

High-water runs through rapids 11 to 18 (or 23), which are relatively mundane, can be done either from the Zimbabwean or Zambian side between 1 July and 15 August, though in low rainfall years they may begin as early as mid-May. Wilder, low-water runs, taking in the winding 22km from rapids four to 18 (or 23) in Zimbabwe or rapids one to 18 (or 23) in Zambia, operate from roughly 15 August to late December. The put-in points for these are Big

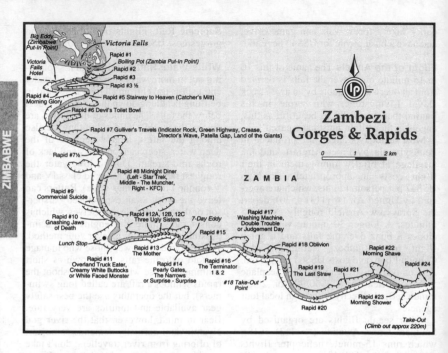

Eddy on the Zimbabwean side and the Boiling Pot on the Zambian shore. If you definitely want to continue to rapid 23, make it clear when booking the trip; otherwise, they'll pull out at rapid 18 (known as Oblivion). All operators walk around rapid nine, which is affectionately nicknamed Commercial Suicide.

For a half/full day's rafting, you'll pay US$80/100 on the Zimbabwe side and US$75/95 on the Zambia side. Most companies provide long-sleeved wetsuits, which temper the icy blast of winter spray. Several companies also offer a full day of rafting followed by a beach dinner and overnight camp for around US$145. Some companies, such as Safari Par Excellence, also offer three- to eight-day downstream trips to such enigmatic locales as Cimamba Rapids, Moemba Falls, Batoka Gorge and the Matetsi River mouth for US$100 to US$125 per day.

**Canoeing & Kayaking** You may see photos of kayakers being tossed around in the Boiling Pot below the falls, but most Victoria Falls canoeing and kayaking tours are run above the falls (and fortunately stay there). It's lots of fun to paddle this wide river, exploring its mid-stream islands and shooting its mini-rapids. It's ideal for a relaxing time punctuated with stretches of rolling water, walks around uninhabited river islands and lots of wildlife.

Zambezi Canoe & Safari (Shearwater), which uses inflatable canoes, offers several options, from a half-day dawdle around Kandahar Island to a three-day/two-night camping tour, beginning above Katombora Rapids. Accommodation is at its tented river camp in Zambezi National Park.

Kandahar Safaris runs half-day to four-day trips. It runs the course at a more leisurely pace than the Zambezi Canoe Company and finishes at the Big Tree.

The awesome spectacle of Victoria Falls from the air (Zim).

For a fish eagle's view of Victoria Falls take a microlight flight (Zim).

Navigating the Zambezi sedately ...

... or energetically (Zim).

Traditional dances enliven many festivals (Zim).

Frontiers offers the same full-, half- and multi-day options in either inflatable or Canadian canoes. Zambezi Odyssey (Safari Par Excellence) uses Klepper kayaks, but it offers only half-day and two-day options.

All companies charge roughly the same rates. Morning trips (with breakfast) or afternoon trips (with tea) cost US$55; three-hour afternoon canoe booze cruises are US$45; all-day trips cost US$90; and multi-day trips (1 April to 15 October) cost US$240/390/540 for one/two/three nights.

**Guiding Courses** The Zambezi International White Water School (☎/fax (113) 3300), PO Box 295, Victoria Falls, offers guiding and first aid courses, from introductory half-day kayaking courses for US$35 to an intensive 21-day rafting guide's course for US$1650.

**Riverboarding** If you want all the thrills of rafting without the raft (which many rafters

manage to jettison anyway), this new adrenaline activity is for you. Imagine surfing the Zambezi with nothing between your body and the swirling maelstrom except a piece of foam. Zambezi Riverboarding offers half-day Zambia-side expeditions from rapids one to five for US$85, including a T-shirt and lots of liquid refreshment. Book through Safari Par Excellence.

**River/Booze Cruises** There is a variety of river and booze cruises on the Zambezi above the falls, some of which include a stop on Kandahar Island in midstream. Oddly, the African-sounding name of this island isn't African at all; it was named after Lord Roberts of Kandahar, whose title was, in turn, derived from his victory at Kandahar in Afghanistan in 1880, the decisive battle of the second Afghan war.

Some excursions, such as the sundowner cruise, include drinks in the price and are good value; others have a very expensive

---

### The Zambezi Gorges

The geology behind the curiously formed gorges at Victoria Falls is fascinating. Since the Zambezi flows through alternating soft and resistant rock formations, the character of the river changes accordingly. Along the easy stretches, it follows a broad channel and the river becomes dotted with sandy islets carried and deposited by silty and slow-moving water.

Where the water encounters rough stretches, erosion rather than deposition is the primary force. In Zimbabwe's case, these resistant regions of basalt were laid down, layer upon layer, by volcanic eruptions during the Jurassic period. Subsequent uneven cooling of the layers caused them to crack and, in one place, opened up a gaping rift over 1700m wide. Over the following aeons, erosion continued and the entire area apparently did a brief stint underwater, as evidenced by the remains of aquatic creatures which have been discovered in the area.

However, climatic changes (some undoubtedly caused by continental drift) subsequently caused the surface water to dry up, leaving two rivers flowing on either side of the basaltic plateau – the Matetsi to the north and the Zambezi to the south. Subsequent tectonic uplifting south of the Zambezi shifted that river's course further and further north. At the point where it encountered the previously mentioned 250m-deep, 1700m-wide fissure, it plunged in and was forced to cut itself a new course through the difficult material – and eventually join up with the Matetsi. This original Victoria Falls was 8km downstream from the present falls. Weaknesses in the basalt perpendicular to the river's flow – and two million years of erosion – have allowed the river to cut through seven subsequent gorges, each further upstream from the previous one. The waterfall we see today is actually Victoria VIII!

cash bar. You can choose between a champagne breakfast (6 to 8 am), a morning tea cruise (10 am to noon), a lunch cruise (12.30 to 2.30 pm) or an afternoon tea cruise (2 to 4 pm) for US$27. There's also a no-frills morning backpackers cruise for US$18; an afternoon champagne cruise (4 to 6 pm) for US$27; a sunset cruise (4 to 6.30 pm) for US$21; and the most popular, a sundowner booze cruise (5 to 6.30 pm) for US$25. The boats don't stop anywhere and neither does the alcohol so things can get rowdy, but it's fun and the sunset may never seem more brilliant. A lighter variation on the sundowner cruise opts for small boats and combines booze and birdwatching. A sundowner cruise combined with an evening braai in the bush costs US$37.

Boats leave from the jetties near A'Zambezi River Lodge. Book at Dabula Safaris or Safari Par Excellence. Transport from hotels is included in the price, and leaves 30 minutes prior to cruise departures.

**Bungee-Jumping** Bungee-jumping from the Zambezi Bridge costs US$90 per jump and, contrary to popular belief, the rescues are no longer made in white-water rafts (unless you're doing the Gruesome 2-Some – see Combinations later in this section) as they were when the concession first opened. Instead, dangling jumpers are actually retrieved and dragged back up to the bridge by a guy who must feel a bit like a yo-yo at the end of the day. As a result, bungee-jumping can go on year round.

**Parachuting** If bungee-jumping seems too tame, you can visit the Zambezi Vultures Skydivers Club, which offers one-day sky-diving courses for US$105, including a static line jump from 1000m. Tandem dives from 2500m cost US$150. Book through Safari Par Excellence (☎ (113) 2051) in the Phumula Centre.

**Mountain Biking** From September to April, Bushtrackers (☎ (113) 2024) has organised four-hour mountain bike trails around Victoria Falls for US$40.

**Fishing** For keen anglers, Dabula Safaris runs Zambezi fishing trips; the main prey is yellow bream, tiger fish, squeakers and barbel (catfish). For two-hour, half-day or full-day trips, including drinks and all fishing tackle, you'll pay US$11 per boat per hour, plus US$2.50 per person per hour.

**Steam Trains** The Victoria Falls Safari Express (☎ (113) 4682; <fallsexp@mail.pci.co.zw>) allows rail buffs to enjoy a Zambezi-side breakfast, lunch, tea or moonlight dinner aboard a 1st class coach from 1900 pulled by a 1922 Class 10 steam locomotive. Book directly or through Frontiers Adventures.

**Combinations** The novel Supreme Raft company caters to adrenaline junkies with its US$185 Gruesome 2-Some. It begins with a bungee jump off the bridge, from which you're lowered into a waiting raft for a run through rapids 1 to 23 on the Zambian shore. More serious punters can pay double the cost and check out the Awesome 4-Some, which involves bungee-jumping, rafting, microlighting and parachuting.

### Places to Stay – Budget
However spacious, the *Town Council Rest Camp and Caravan Park* (☎ (113) 4210; fax 4308) still gets crowded with tents and overland trucks. Camping costs US$5 per person, but don't leave your tent unzipped; the camp is fairly secure against human intruders but, like teenage thugs, gangs of thieving monkeys and baboons make daily rounds dumping rubbish bins and looting camps. Three-bed chalets cost US$8 per person (with a minimum charge of US$12/16 for single/double occupancy) including use of bedding, a fridge, and pots and pans. Six-bed self-contained cottages cost US$10 per person, with a minimum of US$27. Dorm beds cost US$7, but security is slack and we've had reports of packs sometimes disappearing. The small informal safari company in the camp office runs good, inexpensive tours to Chobe and elsewhere; ask for Learnmore.

The smaller better-maintained *Nyathi Camping* has recently opened next door to the Rainbow Hotel. Facilities are clean, it's quiet, and shady, grassy tent sites cost US$5. Chalets cost US$9 per person and cottages US$12 per person.

For more solitude, try the larger, out-of-town *municipal caravan park* near the A'Zambezi Lodge. Elephant wander through at night, and by day you may see warthogs, baboons and antelope. Camping prices are the same as in town, but there are no dorms or chalets.

The recommended *Burke's Backpackers* (☎ (113) 2179), 357 Gibson Rd, run by Moyra and Vic Enslin, is a wonderful leafy retreat with cooking facilities, 20 minutes walk from town. Dorm beds or thatched A-frame tents cost US$13 and double rooms are US$30. Mountain bikes cost US$5/10 per half/full day. It fills up quickly, so phone before you traipse out there.

*Pat's Place* (☎ (113) 4375), owned by Pat and Ian Finaghty at 209 West Drive, has received mixed reviews. Four- and eight-bed dormitories cost US$9 per person, the three double rooms are US$21 each and triples are US$25. All rates include use of the pool, jacuzzi, braai and kitchen.

Another new place is *Hitch Haven* (☎ (19) 46274; <online@acacia.samara .co.zw>), at 332 Wood Rd, which is affiliated with the Bulawayo hostel of the same name. It hasn't yet decided what sort of atmosphere it will foster, but the rates are good. Dorm beds cost US$9 and camping is US$5. Meals and laundry services are also available.

At the time of writing, a large, budget complex, *Victoria Falls Wanderers*, was under construction 1.5km east of town on the Kazungula road. Camping will cost (US$8), dorms (US$12/15), and chalets (US$60/80). There will be a pool, spa, bar and braai area in spacious lawns and free transfers to town. Check the Web site (www .vicfallswanderers.co.zw) for progress reports and further details.

See also under Livingstone and Zambezi National Park in this chapter.

**Places to Stay – Mid-Range**
At the *Sprayview* (☎ (113) 4344) on Livingstone Way, everyone pays US$43/58 for comfortable singles/doubles, but it's difficult to get a booking. The bar and disco are popular haunts and the pool terrace is great for a cold beer.

*Villa Victoria* (☎ (113) 4386), 165 Courteney Selous Crescent, run by Sue Peacock and Tony Moore, has quiet, comfortable rooms for US$15 per person. Guests may use the pool, braai and self-catering facilities. It fills quickly, so ring first.

Lilian Machena's pleasant two-storey *Livingstone Lodge* (☎ (113) 5903), Stand 449, PO Box 13, Victoria Falls, has dorm beds for US$13 and singles/doubles with veranda for US$32/49. *Hornbills* (☎ (113) 4495 or 4468), 376 Squire Cummings Rd, has doubles for US$20. Guests have access to the kitchen and swimming pool.

*Fun in the Sun* (☎ (113) 4556), owned and run by Naas and Mabeleen Terblanche, is a single-room cottage with four beds and self-catering facilities; rates start at US$13 per person.

The very friendly *Villa d'Afrique* (☎ (113) 5945) has self-catering facilities for four people for US$79. *Gabriel Cottages* (☎ (113) 2160) charges US$20 per person, with a minimum charge of US$42. *Hunters Lodge* (☎ (113) 4614 or 5977) charges US$40/60 for singles/doubles and *Pumulo Cottages* (☎ (113) 4334), on Reynard Rd, has motel-style cottages starting at US$50, with a full English breakfast and use of the pool, braai and kitchen facilities.

The recommended *Mosi-ua-Tunya Lodge* (☎ (113) 4403) has singles/doubles in a two-storey thatched building for US$40/50, including breakfast and use of the kitchen.

The *Tatenda Hotel* (☎ (113) 3349 or 5988), whose name means 'thanks', is set in lovely gardens and offers friendly accommodation as well as a pool, braais, TV, a security guard and reliable mosquito nets. Singles/doubles cost US$30/35.

The homely *Reynard Cottages* (☎ (113) 4418) charges US$30/42 for simple single/

ZIMBABWE

double B&B accommodation with laundry and braai facilities. The *Mining Industrial Pension Fund (MIPF) Flats* (☎ (113) 4397), in the Phumula Centre, charge from US$34 to US$50 for double self-catering flats.

### Places to Stay – Top End

All top-end hotels in Victoria Falls charge three-tier rates. Architecturally, one of the best is *Ilala Lodge* (☎ (113) 4737; fax 4417), near the post office. The pleasant natural decor, sunny terrace bar and restaurant, green lawns and nearby bushland provide a bush-like atmosphere right in the heart of town. For singles/doubles foreigners pay US$167/246 and residents pay US$84/123.

When you step off the train and pass through the Edwardian railway station, the three-star *Victoria Falls Hotel* (☎ (113) 4203, fax 4586) provides a fitting climax to the grand colonial illusion. This stately structure, which dates back to 1905, simply oozes atmosphere and its setting above the second Zambezi gorge is nothing short of spectacular. Unfortunately, it's shamefully overpriced for foreigners, who must pay US$288/360 for singles/doubles; locals, meanwhile pay US$123/154.

The glitterati, sheikhs and gangsters haven't yet arrived in Victoria Falls, but the casino has – at the *Makasa Sun Hotel* (☎ (113) 4275). From the outside, this three-star hotel that was somehow awarded four stars may remind you of a subsidised housing project, but it's quite nice inside. The rate for foreigners is US$170/212 for singles/doubles while locals pay US$71/95. The one-armed bandits wake up at 10.30 am and the rest of the casino opens at 8 pm nightly. The bars remain open until 11 pm and non-guests may use the pool for a nominal fee.

A short walk from the centre is the three-star *Rainbow Hotel* (☎ (113) 4585; fax 4654). It's set amid green lawns and gardens, but its Moorish-Swahili architecture may seem incongruous. Foreigners pay

---

## Victoria Falls Hotel

The elegant Edwardian-style Victoria Falls Hotel, which many travellers know for its lavish buffet breakfast (now only available to residents) and evening braai, was Victoria Falls' first. The earliest tourists had to arrive overland, either on foot or in wagons, travelling for days along the Pandamatenga Trail from Botswana.

Once the railway arrived in 1904, tourism took a great leap forward. For the first year, visitors were required to bed down in railway carriages. As railway bridge workers and increasing numbers of tourists arrived, the need for a real hotel became evident. In 1905, work was begun on the first Victoria Falls Hotel, a wood and corrugated-iron structure perched between the railway station and the second Zambezi Gorge. Reports were that it wasn't very comfortable and, in 1914, the rudimentary structure was replaced with a more permanent brick building. Meanwhile, a trolley track was laid to transport tourists to the falls in carts pushed by servants. Once a hard-won destination only for the intrepid, Victoria Falls had availed itself to wimpy tourism.

The current hotel is actually the product of several additions to the second early building but it still hangs together well. The equally appealing grounds are planted with green lawns, bougainvillea, frangipani, royal poinciana, palms and other tropical finery.

For many years, hotel guests were greeted by the popular head concierge, Odwell Makamure, who never lost an item of luggage and sported a top hat, red jacket and waistcoat festooned with badges given to him by visitors and friends from around the world. Sadly, this legendary character died in 1997 and the hotel will have a hard time filling his shoes.

US$115/170 for singles/doubles and residents pay US$58/85.

The *A'Zambezi River Lodge* (☎ (113) 4651; fax 4536) offers quiet – and over-awarded – three-star accommodation but it's quite a distance from town. For foreigners, singles/doubles cost US$120/180; locals pay US$47/61. Between the hotel and the Zambezi is a spacious lawn with a pool and terrace area where they serve up evening buffet braais.

Capping a nearby hill, the *Elephant Hills Hotel* (☎ (113) 4793; fax 4655) dominates all it surveys. All rooms enjoy a thatched balcony and a view, and the standards of comfort are among the highest in Victoria Falls. However, the hotel is frequently nominated for the title of Zimbabwe's ugliest building. From a distance, you'd be forgiven for mistaking this immense grey concrete structure for a prison fortress (complete with bars on some windows) or, at best, a mound of stacked egg cartons. For singles/doubles foreigners pay US$214/268 and locals pay US$87/108. Every half hour from 8 am to 5 pm, a shuttle service runs to and from the Makasa Sun Hotel in town.

New on the Victoria Falls hotel scene is *The Lodge at Victoria Falls* (☎ (113) 3201; fax 3205; <saflodge@vfsl.gaia.co.zw>). This immense and beautifully designed place, which resembles a vast, open-plan tree house, has sunset views for everyone and merits its five-star rating. The ecological theme is backed up with recycled toilet paper and stationery, natural history reference books in every room, a garden full of indigenous species and educational lectures on environmental issues. For foreigners, single/double low-season rack rates start at US$210/308; locals pay US$114/167.

At the adjacent *Lokuthula Lodges* (☎ (113) 4725; fax 4792), foreigners pay US$215/290 for two/three-bedroom self-catering units. The more reasonable local rates range from US$65 to US$99 for a two-bedroom lodge to US$87 to US$133 for three bedrooms. Each lodge has airy open-plan architecture and accommodates up to six people.

## Places to Stay – Safari Lodges

The luxury *Imbabala Safari Camp* (☎ (113) 4219; fax 4349), run by Wild Horizons, lies nestled in dense forest near Kazungula, with a view over the Zambezi riverbanks. Rates start at US$175 per person, including accommodation in thatched A-frame chalets, meals, guides, game drives, boat trips and fishing gear.

Landela Safaris' *Masuwe Lodge* (☎/fax (113) 4699) is 7km from town beside the Masuwe River west of the Bulawayo road. The name of this tented camp means 'place of soft stone' after a type of oxidised rock traditionally used for cosmetics. It occupies a 300 hectare private game ranch which abuts Zambezi National Park, so there's plenty of wildlife around. The light tents are set on raised wooden platforms and the dining area sits perched over the valley for the maximum views. Prices start at US$425/550 for singles/doubles with full board and activities.

Landela's other lodge, *Sekuti's Drift* (☎ (113) 426524; fax 4699), lies just 15 minutes from Victoria Falls on a private estate bordering Zambezi National Park. Accommodation in colonial-style lodges with long wilderness views costs US$425/550 for single/double lodges including meals and activities.

## Places to Eat

After several days of hotel breakfasts you'll appreciate *Naran's Takeaways*, in Soper's Arcade, which has a 'campers breakfast' of steak, bacon, egg, toast, chips and Mazoe orange for US$2. For lunch and snacks, you can't beat their curries, samosas and vegetarian specialities (try the vegetarian curry *sadza*). Closing time is between 4.30 and 6 pm, depending on afternoon business.

The *Wimpy* fries up greasy breakfasts and, for the rest of the day, serves its standard menu of burgers, chicken, chips and so on; you'll eat for around US$2. Sweet snacks are the speciality at *McDonut's*, upstairs in Soper's Arcade.

The *Pink Baobab* (☎ (113) 4436), which claims that Hemingway would have eaten there had it been open in his day, serves up real Zimbabwe-grown coffee and tea, fruit juice, soft drinks and a range of snacks: waffles with cream, fresh fruit pancakes, crepes, pies, salads, sandwiches, quiche, kebabs and other treats. Their recommended breakfasts start at US$3.50 and healthy lunch specials are US$5. Afterward, check out *Vanilla Falls*, which dishes up ice cream whips and a rainbow of flavours in scoops, shakes and frozen yoghurt. McDonut's, The Pink Baobab and Vanilla Falls are open until about 4 pm.

*Pizza Bistro* in Soper's Arcade may well be the town's most popular eatery. From 9 to 11 am, they serve breakfasts, including omelettes, crepes, pancakes and a breakfast pizza with bacon, mushrooms, fried egg, tomato and mozzarella. From lunchtime until late you can get a variety of meals, including pasta, burgers, filled baked potatoes, salads and of course, a variety of pizzas. They don't take bookings, but if you're caught short, the popular *Explorer's Bar* next door also has a restaurant.

The *Eatza Pizza* takeaway is open from 10 am to midnight daily and will deliver pizzas to the caravan park. At the *Cattleman's* (☎ (113) 4767) and *Saddles Steak House*, both in the Phumula Centre area, the speciality is beef.

The *Summit Seafood Restaurant* in the Makasa Sun Hotel specialises in a maritime menu and the *Palm Restaurant* at Ilala Lodge offers Asian cuisine and a sampler of African dishes. The *A'Zambezi River Lodge* serves full meals and bar snacks all day on its pool terrace. The *Boma Restaurant* (☎ (113) 4725) at Lokuthula Lodges has received awards for its food. For US$16 you get a four course African buffet, including game dishes and traditional local cuisine – sadza, rice, salad, potatoes, bread and sauces – complete with an Ndebele choir performing in the background. A vegetarian version is US$10. It's out of town, but free pick up is available from the big hotels.

**Buffets** The various hotels/lodges also offer buffet breakfasts, lunches and dinners,

and some are veritable banquets. Unfortunately, the buffet breakfast at Victoria Falls Hotel has now been placed off limits to backpackers and other outsiders.

The *Sprayview* offers the best deal at US$3 for breakfast and US$6 for dinner. The recommended evening braai at the *Victoria Falls Hotel* costs US$14 and will satisfy even the most excessive appetites. Vegetarians can fill up on table-loads of salads, breads, casseroles and sweets while non-vegetarians can choose between a range of hors d'oeuvres, four braaied meats and sadza with various relishes. You won't want to move afterwards.

The buffets at *Elephant Hills Hotel* are also excellent (US$4.50 breakfast, US$9 lunch and US$10 dinner), as are the highly recommended US$3.50 buffet breakfast and the US$2 pub lunch at the *Ilala Lodge*. Decent buffet breakfasts/lunches/dinners at the *Rainbow Hotel* cost US$5.50/7/8.50.

For a decidedly unusual dining experience, Dabula Safaris (☎ (113) 4453) organises an outdoor *Bush Dinner* in a private wildlife reserve adjoining Zambezi National Park. The menu begins with a crocodile tail starter and runs through soup, sadza with venison relish and a dessert. All the while, you can envision reproachful eyes staring at you from the bush. The price is US$30 per person, including transport and drinks.

**Self-Catering** For self-catering, the best all around shop is the relatively well-stocked *Jay's Spar Supermarket*. There's also the *Fruit & Veg Centre* greengrocer in Soper's Arcade and a decent *butcher* near the bus terminal in Chinotimba township.

### Entertainment
**Video Nights** In the evenings, the various adrenaline companies run video shows of the day's adventures (at various locations) and non-participants are welcome to attend for a bit of inspiration and courage-building. Stills and videos are sold to those who participated, but they're quite expensive. You can save a bit of money if you get

them to copy their footage onto your own video cassette.

**Bars & Discos** Until early evening, the *beer hall* near the bus terminal in Chinotimba township is good for local action. The bars in the larger *hotels* offer toned-down live music, often pseudo-African 'banana boat' revues and insipid marimba muzak that resembles the drivel you hear while waiting on hold. Beyond these and the *Makasa Sun casino*, choices are limited.

Most travellers enjoy the *Sprayview* disco which offers a good helping of reggae music as well as a lot of mundane local stuff nightly from 7.30 to 11 pm. A favourite bar is *Explorers* in Soper's Arcade, which is popular with raft jockeys and overland truck drivers – as well as anyone who'd otherwise be stuck in a dark tent in the caravan park. *Stetson's Bar*, attached to the Saddles Steak House, is open from midday until late evening and the bartenders dress up like Texans and serve up 500mL draught Castles for US$1 each. They also do bar snacks; a burger with chips or onion rings costs US$4.

The *Downtime Night Club* (US$2.50 cover charge) at Ilala Lodge is frequented mainly by expats, tour operators, raft jockeys, truck drivers and backpackers – the whole circus, in fact. It's open nightly from 8 pm until late. The rooftop bar at the *Makasa Sun Hotel* is enhanced by good views and free bar snacks at 6 pm nightly.

**Falls Craft Village** At night, the Falls Craft Village (☎ (113) 4309) stages traditional dancing performances at dusk (around 7 pm) for US$3.50. The dancing is punctuated with such intriguing attractions as ominous, myth-perpetuating drumming and even a circumcision ritual. Even if you don't attend, you're welcome to listen from almost anywhere in town.

**Africa Spectacular** *The* grand tourist show at the falls is Africa Spectacular, staged nightly at the Victoria Falls Hotel. Although the performers must be getting weary of it all after thousands of performances, they manage to convey a sense of enthusiasm. If not entirely authentic, it does appeal as an entertaining introduction to traditional African dancing. It begins nightly at 7 pm in the pavilion behind the hotel and costs US$4.

### Getting There & Away
All tourist trails converge at Victoria Falls, which sits near the intersection of four countries, and nearly every visitor to Zimbabwe, Zambia, Namibia and Botswana passes through here. As a result, getting there and away is easy.

**Air** Air Zimbabwe and Zimbabwe Express both fly at least twice daily between Victoria Falls and Harare; some flights run via Kariba and/or Hwange National Park.

There are also direct flights between Victoria Falls and Johannesburg, as well as Katima Mulilo in Namibia, and Maun in Botswana. The flight to Katima Mulilo with Air Namibia costs US$45, takes 25 minutes and provides a wonderful bird's-eye view over the falls – a sort of incidental Flight of the Angels. In fact, some pilots kindly spend 10 minutes of the flight providing passengers with superb photo opportunities.

**Bus** The terminal for African buses to Hwange town, Dete Crossroads (for connections to Binga), Safari Crossroads (for Hwange National Park) and Bulawayo is near the market, on Pioneer Rd in Chinotimba Township. There are at least three to five buses daily, departing when full.

The only public access to Kazungula and Kasane is with the UTC transfer buses, which leave every morning and cost US$35. The border crossing is straightforward. Book through UTC in the post office complex or through another travel agent. Otherwise, stand on the Livingstone Way, the road to Bulawayo, opposite Wimpy, and flag down the vehicle – it passes between 7.20 and 7.30 am.

Twice weekly the Blue Arrow service (Harare: ☎ (14) 729514; fax 729572;

Bulawayo: ☎ (19) 65548; fax 65549) between Johannesburg and Bulawayo connects with buses to and from Victoria Falls.

For information on connections to Namibia, see To/From Zimbabwe in the Namibia Getting There & Away chapter.

**Train** Until the early 1990s, the romantic highlight of a Zimbabwe trip was riding the steam train to Victoria Falls; now everything is diesel. The trains leave Bulawayo at 7 pm daily, passing Dete at 1.30 am. From Victoria Falls, they also leave at 7 pm, passing Dete at 12.45 am. The 1st/2nd class fare is US$9/6. Economy class costs US$4. The former two have a sleeper service while the latter offers seats only.

There's also a twice-daily passenger service to Livingstone on the goods train over the Zambezi Bridge. Trains leave from Victoria Falls at 8 am and 6 pm and from Livingstone at 6.15 am and 3.30 pm. The trip takes 30 minutes and costs US$1. Zambian visas are available from the immigration officer on the train.

The station booking office is open from 7 am to noon and 2 to 4 pm on weekdays and on mornings at weekends.

**Hitching** Traffic between Bulawayo and Victoria Falls isn't heavy, but you'd be unlucky not to find a lift. For Botswana, wait at the Kasane turn-off early in the morning and you'll most probably get a lift.

### Getting Around

The tracks that carried earlier visitors around Victoria Falls on hand-pushed trolleys were long ago ripped up, but there are other options until one reaches Victoria Falls Park; there, everyone has to walk.

**To/From the Airport** The Victoria Falls airport is 20km out of town along the Bulawayo road and thanks to recent (and occasionally violent) taxi wars, transport to town is less than straightforward. Foreigners may initially be quoted US$45 or more, but you should refuse to pay over US$20. Otherwise, opt for the Air Zimbabwe or South African Airways US$3 shuttle bus, which connects with arriving and departing flights.

**Taxi** Midnight Taxis (☎ (113) 4290), which isn't as dodgy as the name would imply, is the company serving the vicinity. The taxi stand is opposite the Total petrol station. Host Taxis (☎ (113) 3245) are available 24 hours a day.

**Motorcycle** Anyone over 18 with a driving licence can hire a 50cc motor scooter from Beano's Scooter Hire (☎ (113) 3398), in the alley behind Dubula Safaris. You'll pay US$5 per hour or US$15/20/30 per 6/12/24 hours, with insurance and unlimited kilometres. Bring your home driving licence.

**Bicycle** Bushtrackers (☎ (113) 2024), near the banks, Baobab (☎ (113) 4436), beside Necessities bookshop, and Camp Site Cycle Hire, beside the Publicity Association, all hire mountain bikes for US$1.50 per hour or US$7/13 for a half/full day.

# Victoria Falls – the Zambian Side

The Zambian side of Victoria Falls provides an alternative experience to its Zimbabwean counterpart. First, the views are different: you can sidle right up to the falling water, walk a steep track down to the base of the falls and follow spindly walkways perched over the abyss. The views may not be as picture-postcard-perfect as those in Zimbabwe, but they allow close-up observation of the mesmerising water, and Zambia's less manicured surroundings foster a more pristine atmosphere.

Citizens of some countries – including Britain, France, Germany and the USA – require Zambian visas, which are issued at the border. US citizens pay US$10 for day trips and US$25 for multi-day visits. British citizens pay £35 for a one day visa and £45 for multiple days, but the fees are waived if they're 'introduced' to the country by a Zambian tour operator (loosely-defined as any Zambian lodge or tour company). This means that it pays to pre-book activities, tours and accommodation from Zimbabwe or elsewhere. A similar scheme may soon be available to USA travellers. Zimbabwean tour companies organise visas for their participants, but visa charges typically aren't included in activity prices.

To call the numbers in this section from outside Zambia, preface the number with the country code (260) and the area code, minus the leading zero. To phone from Victoria Falls, Zimbabwe, dial 8 in place of the country and area codes.

## MOSI-OA-TUNYA NATIONAL PARK

Mosi-oa-Tunya, Zambia's smallest national park, is comprised of two sections, the Victoria Falls area in the east and the game park, further west along the riverbank. Admission to the park is US$3. If you need a few kwacha to use in the falls area, you can change cash or travellers cheques at the Hotel InterContinental Mosi-oa-Tunya. However, it's better to change money at a bank in Livingstone.

### Victoria Falls Area

From the park entry gate at the falls, a network of paths leads through thick vegetation to several stunning viewpoints. A fabulous view of the Zambezi Bridge and main river gorges is reached via a path alongside the border fence. For close-up shots, nothing beats the Eastern Cataract or Knife Edge Point, where you cross a hair-raising (but safe) footbridge through swirling clouds of spray to a cliff-girt chunk of rock looming above the Zambezi River. The view is often obliterated by drenching spray, but at low water, you'll have a unique view of the falls and the yawning abyss below the bridge. Once you're good and wet, descend the steep track to the Boiling Pot to see the tortured river as it passes through hell.

Near the falls, several stalls offer inexpensive curios, and the salespeople are keen to barter; foreign T-shirts with slogans are always in demand. At the small field museum, archaeological finds from an adjacent excavation provide evidence that humans have inhabited this region for 2½ million years. The 'donation' for foreigners is US$2 – and it's not worth it.

**Livingstone Island Picnic Site** Thanks to Tongabezi Lodge, you can enjoy a three-course champagne lunch at the 'world's most exclusive picnic spot' on Livingstone Island. On this chunk of rock, which splits Victoria Falls in half, David Livingstone spent several days in 1855 taking biological samples. The US$75 price includes car and boat transfers from Zimbabwe or Zambia, a three course meal, drinks and park fees. You can also opt for overnight camping trips which normally take place during the full moon to view lunar rainbows over the falls. Tours run from 1 June to 15 January; book with Safari Par Excellence (☎ (03) 323349; fax 323542) at the Hotel Intercontinental Mosi-oa-Tunya.

If you don't mind a dose of adrenaline with your meal, you can organise your own Livingstone Island picnic. At times of very low water, as in late winter, you can pick your way to Livingstone Island along stepping stones from the Zambia side. (There's no charge for doing this, so ignore demands for payment.) This creates quite a spectacle for viewers on the Zimbabwe side, but it's not for the dizzy or faint-hearted.

### Mosi-oa-Tunya Game Park

The little Mosi-oa-Tunya Game Park, near the boat club north of the Maramba River, once had a few indigenous rhino but they were all poached. In 1994, they were replaced by six white rhino from South Africa. One has since died from dehorning complications but, to the credit of the park guards, those that remain have survived for at least two years now. If you go on your own, you'll pay about US$0.50 for a short walking safari.

## Zambian Side Tour Operators

Zambian tour operators can arrange free visas for British clients who book from the Zimbabwean side, but other travellers must normally purchase their own visas.

*Batoka Sky*, PO Box 60305, Livingstone (☎ (03) 323672; fax 324289; <batoka@ zamnet.zm>). Batoka Sky offers microlighting trips over Victoria Falls, as well as microlighting instruction.

*African Horizons/Botswana Bus*, Richard Sheppard, PO Box 61170, Fawlty Towers, 216 Mosi-oa-Tunya Rd, Livingstone (☎/fax (03) 323432). Runs inexpensive tours from Livingstone to Chobe National Park and the Okavango Delta. The nine-day safaris visit the Chobe riverfront, Savuti, Makwena Camp, Mahango Game Reserve, Ngepi Camp and the Caprivi for US$595, including transport, camping, meals and guide. It also runs two-week Namibia trips for US$595, and shuttles between Livingstone, Victoria Falls and Maun for around US$295, including a short Eastern Delta trip.

*Bundu Adventures*, Plot 699, Industrial Rd, PO Box 60773, Livingstone (☎ (03) 324407; fax 324406; <zambezi@zamnet.zm>). This enthusiastic company does half/full-day raft trips for US$85/95, half/full-day upper Zambezi canoeing for US$55/75 and six-hour tours through Mosi-oa-Tunya National Park.

*Bwaato Adventures*, New Fairmount Hotel, PO Box 60672, Livingstone (☎/fax (03) 324227; <vfrtours@harare.iafrica.com.zw>). Bwaato offers breakfast or lunchtime booze cruises for US$25 and sundowner cruises for US$20. Game drives in the Mosi-oa-Tunya National Park cost US$28, including drinks, plus US$3 park fees.

*Jolly Boys Backpackers* (☎ (03) 324229). Runs trips to Maun via Nata for US$295; you spend nine days in Zimbabwe and Botswana, including transport, visas, camping and park fees. It also has two-day trips to the Chobe Riverfront for US$180 and transfers to Malawi, via Kafue and Luanga National Parks, for US$350.

*Makora Quest*, PO Box 60420, Livingstone (☎ (03) 321679; fax 320732). With this company you can do upper Zambezi canoe safaris and day tours through Livingstone's scenic and historical attractions – Old Drift, Mosi-oa-Tunya National Park, the museums, a local market and Victoria Falls.

*Raft Quest* (☎ (03) 322086; fax 320732). Operates half/full-day Zambia-side rafting for US$85/95.

*Shungumufu Tours* (☎ (03) 324092). Runs day tours to Mosi-oa-Tunya National Park and books Zambia-side rafting, microlighting and booze cruises.

*Sobek*, PO Box 60305, Livingstone (☎ (03) 323672; fax 324289; <sobek@zamnet.zm>). Sobek was the first rafting operator in the Victoria Falls area and is still running.

### Organised Tours

All hotels and lodges in south-western Zambia, including backpackers options, can organise a whole range of adrenaline activities such as white-water rafting, bungee jumping and microlighting, as well as booze cruises and other amusements. For agency contact details, see the boxed text Zambian Side Tour Operators.

### Places to Stay

The *Hotel Intercontinental Mosi-oa-Tunya* (☎ (03) 321121; fax 321128), beside the falls, has singles/doubles for US$145/180, with breakfast. Rates are negotiable in low season. The government-owned *Rainbow Lodge* (☎ (03) 322473) is less organised, with double rondavels for US$75.

The barren *Zambia Camp Site*, looked

after by the Rainbow Lodge, charges US$5 per person, including use of hotel facilities. Although it's conveniently located, your belongings aren't safe and should be locked in the hotel baggage room when you're away. Watch for hippo grazing on the hotel lawns.

Your other option is the *Taita Falcon Lodge* (☎/fax (03) 321850), downstream from the Zambezi Bridge. It's perched right over the gorge, with splendid views of the river (and rafters) far below. Single/double accommodation in rustic bungalows costs from US$100/160 with full board and transfers from Livingstone.

### Places to Eat
The *Hotel Intercontinental Mosi-oa-Tunya* offers fine, expensive dining. Special theme evenings range from Chinese to Italian and weekend buffets for US$16 are good value.

### Getting There & Away
The Zimbabwe-Zambia border is open from 6 am to 8 pm, but get an early start because queues can be long, particularly in the late morning and early afternoon. Taxis between the Zimbabwean and Zambian border posts cost around US$0.50, but many people walk across to enjoy great views from the Zambezi Bridge. Alternatively, you can hire a bike in Victoria Falls, but keep your rental receipt to show the border guards. Note that many travellers on foot or bicycle have reported muggings on the road to Livingstone (7km further), so these methods of travel are not advised.

If you're driving, be sure to buy Zambian third party insurance at the border (around US$30), or you'll be fined and turned back at the Maramba police roadblock, 3km from the border. Fuel in Zambia currently costs US$0.90 per litre.

Taxis between the Zimbabwe border and Victoria Falls cost US$1, and the fare from the border to Livingstone is US$5. Minibuses leave the Livingstone bus terminal when full and run to the Zambian border for around US$0.80 per person.

Note that you may export only Z$400 in Zimbabwean currency.

## LIVINGSTONE
After malaria prompted the shift of the original Old Drift settlement 7km north, to the site of present-day Livingstone, the new town began to develop and eventually became the tourism hub and service centre for the entire region. However, in the 1970s (when Zambia started down the road to economic and political chaos), the town was eclipsed by the noisy upstart on the Zimbabwean side. Nowadays, things are changing again, and Livingstone is becoming a centre of commerce and an increasingly welcoming escape from the tourist jungle across the falls.

### Information
**Tourist Office** The tourist office (☎ (03) 321404) can arrange hotel bookings, but it provides only limited information, and actually tries to charge for advertising leaflets and brochures.

**Money** To exchange currency or travellers cheques, try the Barclays Bank, Continental Bureau de Change or Finance Bank on Mosi-oa-Tunya Rd, or the New Fairmount Hotel.

**Immigration** For trips to Victoria Falls, single-entry visas can be upgraded to multientry for US$4 per visit at the immigration office on Mosi-oa-Tunya Rd.

### Railway Museum
The Railway Museum (☎ (03) 321820), which bears the somewhat grandiose official title of the Zambezi Sawmills Locomotive Sheds National Monument, lies west of Mosi-oa-Tunya Rd as you enter town from the south.

The yards fell into disuse in 1973 and now contain a charmingly mixed collection of old engines and rolling stock, as well as rail-related antiques and exhibits on railway history. The museum is open daily from 8.30 am to 4.30 pm. However, foreigners pay US$5 admission and unless you're an ardent railway buff, it isn't worth it. If you really don't feel like paying that much,

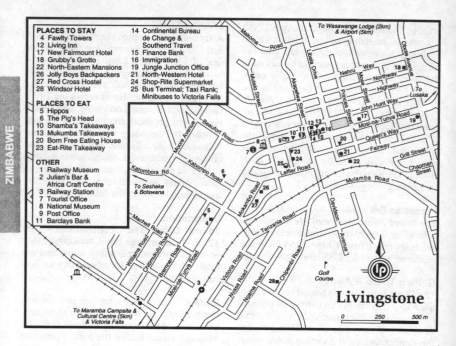

**PLACES TO STAY**
4 Fawlty Towers
12 Living Inn
17 New Fairmount Hotel
18 Grubby's Grotto
22 North-Eastern Mansions
26 Jolly Boys Backpackers
27 Red Cross Hostel
28 Windsor Hotel

**PLACES TO EAT**
5 Hippos
6 The Pig's Head
10 Shamba's Takeaways
13 Mukumba Takeaways
20 Born Free Eating House
23 Eat-Rite Takeaway

**OTHER**
1 Railway Museum
2 Julian's Bar &
   Africa Craft Centre
3 Railway Station
7 Tourist Office
8 National Museum
9 Post Office
11 Barclays Bank

14 Continental Bureau
   de Change &
   Southend Travel
15 Finance Bank
16 Immigration
19 Jungle Junction Office
21 North-Western Hotel
24 Shop-Rite Supermarket
25 Bus Terminal; Taxi Rank;
   Minibuses to Victoria Falls

however, it's often possible to work out some sort of discount.

## National Museum

The National Museum (☎ (03) 321204), adjacent to the tourist office, houses an interesting collection of archaeological and anthropological relics, including a copy of a Neanderthal skull estimated at over 100,000 years old. The original Broken Hill Man (formerly known as Rhodesian Man and now Kabwe Man) was uncovered near Kabwe (north of Lusaka), during the colonial era and is now displayed in the UK.

There are also examples of ritual artefacts and Tonga material crafts, an African village mock-up, a collection of David Livingstone paraphernalia and a display of Africa maps dating back to 1690. Ask Mr Sitale to show you the back room where they keep an amazing – and rather horrifying – collection of bizarre witchcraft

paraphernalia. Admission for foreigners is a whopping (but eminently negotiable) US$5.

## Maramba Cultural Centre

The Maramba Cultural Centre is 5km south of Livingstone, towards Victoria Falls. On Saturday from 3 to 5 pm it stages traditional dance performances, which are more authentic than the Africa Spectacular on the Zimbabwean side.

## Places to Stay

A great place to camp is the friendly *Maramba Camp Site* (☎/fax (03) 324189; <maramba@zamnet.zm>), with a bar, hot showers and a secure and beautiful location beside the Maramba River. Camping costs US$5, the tree house is US$8 per person and comfortable two/three/four-bed chalets are US$25/35/45.

*Livingstone Overnight* (☎ (03) 320371; fax 323095), run by Allan and Anita

Goodyear, offers camping for US$5 per person and wheelchair-accessible three-bed chalets for US$30 per person, including a full breakfast. Table d'hôte dinners cost US$4. It's west of the Victoria Falls road, about 4km from town.

The friendly new *Shungu River Lodge* (☎ (03) 321248), owned by Joan, Guy and Rian Butler, has camping in sheltered sites for US$5 per person and simple four-bed chalets for US$34 with shared ablutions facilities (labelled 'He-po' and 'She-po'). Amenities include an open-plan kitchen, braai stands, laundry facilities and bicycle hire. It's 7km south-west of town – take Riverside Drive by the cultural centre.

Livingstone's hopes of attracting backpackers are greatly aided by *Jolly Boys Backpackers* (☎ (03) 324229; <jboys@zamnet.zm>), 559 Mokambo Road, run by friendly Paul Quinn. Dorm beds cost US$6, camping is US$2, and guests may use the pool, sauna and cooking facilities. Breakfast is US$3 and dinner US$4 – including pizzas and vegetarian options. Fax and email services are available. They also organise good-value tours to national parks and other sites of interest around Zambia.

Another friendly choice is *Fawlty Towers* (☎/fax (03) 323432), at 216 Mosi-oa-Tunya Rd. Dorms cost US$5, twin rooms are US$12 and camping costs US$2. Facilities include all the standards plus safari options and luggage storage.

Also promoting the Livingstone backpackers scene is *Gecko's Guesthouse* (☎ (03) 322267), at 84 Limilunga Rd, near the railway station. Dorm beds cost US$6, doubles are US$10 per person and camping costs US$5 per tent. Guests have access to the kitchen, braais, bar, luggage storage, laundry service and free border transfers.

*Grubby's Grotto* (☎/fax (03) 322370; fax 324157), in the large colonial railway staff house, is surrounded by broad green lawns. It offers camping (US$2.50 per person) for overland trucks exclusively.

The basic *Red Cross Hostel* (☎ (03) 322473), Mokambo Rd, has clean doubles with washbasin and communal facilities for US$6. Its reputation is as safe accommodation for local businesspeople. The decrepit *North-Eastern Mansions* has doubles for US$12, but its reputation is dodgy at best.

The most upmarket place, the *New Fairmount Hotel* (☎ (03) 320723; fax 321490), has self-contained rooms with television for US$34/39, but discounts are available in low season. It also has a low-key casino, which operates in the evenings. The *Living Inn* (☎ (03) 324203; fax 324380), 95 John Hunt Way, has acceptable rooms for US$15/23. The attached Dreamland Takeaway offers simple snacks. The basic and locally popular *Windsor Hotel* (☎ (03) 320100), at 78 Chipembi Rd, offers camping for US$1 and simple self-contained singles/doubles for US$8/10.

The comfortable *Wasawange Lodge* (☎ (03) 324066; fax 324067), 2km out, on the airport road, makes a quiet alternative to in-town accommodation. Single/double lodges cost US$70/100.

## Places to Eat

The *Pig's Head* pub, in the old Masonic Hall, does appetising bar meals – omelettes, sandwiches, chips, salads, burgers, chicken and steaks – in a friendly atmosphere. Your only formal restaurant option is the *Tamarind* in the New Fairmount Hotel.

The *Born Free Eating House* on Queen's Way offers good local fare and atmosphere. *Eat-Rite Takeaway* is OK for greasy lunches, but a better choice is the *Mukumba Restaurant*, a block back from the main street. Attention focuses on the TV and music videos, but the food is quite acceptable. Otherwise, grab a takeaway from *Shamba's* or another of the places on Mosi-oa-Tunya Rd.

For alcohol, try the *Pig's Head* or the *New Fairmount Hotel* bar. The latter sometimes stages live music performances.

## Getting There & Away

**Bus** Buses and minibuses to Lusaka start running daily from the main bus terminal at around 8 am and cost US$10 and US$9 respectively. The clean, punctual post bus runs daily at 7 am from the post office to Lusaka. Buses to Sesheke, on the Namibian border, leave from the terminal at 6 am daily. Southend Travel is the agent for Trans-Lux and Blue Arrow routes in Zimbabwe.

Minibuses leave for Victoria Falls from the main bus terminal; alternatively, take a taxi (around US$3) or hitch. Because of frequent muggings, walking and biking aren't advised.

**Train** Trains to Lusaka (US$10/9 in 1st/2nd class, 13 hours) leave daily at 9 am. The TAZARA train to Dar es Salaam (Tanzania) leaves on Tuesday and Friday at 2.15 pm. Fares are US$50/33 in 1st/2nd class. For details on crossing to Zimbabwe by train, see Getting There & Away under Victoria Falls.

**Hitching** For lifts to Lusaka, Katima Mulilo or Kasane, the best place to wait is the truck park near the railway station.

### Getting Around

Jolly Boys Backpackers (☎ (03) 324229) hires bicycles for US$6/10 per half/full day.

### THE ZAMBEZI RIVERFRONT

Upstream from Victoria Falls, the Zimbabwean shore of the Zambezi is protected by Zambezi National Park, but the Zambian side is open to development and promises to become one of Zambia's greatest tourist draws. Whether this is a good thing is open to debate, but in a country desperate for tourist recognition and foreign exchange, it's bound to have an impact.

### Places to Stay

The lovely and luxurious *Tongabezi Lodge* (☎ (03) 323235; fax 323224; <tonga@ zamnet.zm>) emphasises originality and has become a favourite getaway for regional travellers. Imaginatively designed tented accommodation costs US$376/536 for singles/doubles and secluded suites are US$474/676. One amazing open-air honeymoon suite, set on a bluff, has a private garden, sunken bathtub and romantic four-poster bed. Rates include meals and transfers from Livingstone. Other themed suites include the Bird House, Tree House, Dog House and the delightfully Andy Warholesque Coca-Cola House.

The lodge also runs *Sindabezi Camp*, on a mid-river island just downstream, which costs US$376/536 for singles/doubles. For the same price, you can view lunar rainbows on a full-moon Livingstone Island camping safari, just above the falls.

*Thorntree Lodge* (☎ (03) 320823; fax 320732) is a family-owned tented camp on private land inside Mosi-oa-Tunya National Park 7km east of Tongabezi. Each unit sits on the riverbank and affords a front-row view of elephants using this stretch of the Zambezi as a crossing-point. In high season, foreigners pay US$295/390 for single/double tented lodges including meals and drinks. Locals pay US$156/216.

*Chundukwa Camp* (☎/fax (03) 324452), just upstream from Tongabezi, has three thatched chalets built on stilts over the river and fronted by an open veranda. This comfortable well-run place has a small pool and an open lounge area. Accommodation and meals cost US$135 per person. It also runs canoeing, hiking and backpacking safaris.

The collection of thatched riverside cottages at Roelf Bosman's *Kubu Cabins* (☎/fax (03) 324091; <kubu@zamnet.zm>; Web site www.zamnet.zm/zamnet/zntb /kubu.html), PO Box 60748, Livingstone, 25km from Tongabezi, is a good base for birdwatching, walking and relaxing. Single/double rates are US$121/176, with meals, drinks and transfers. The honeymoon suite features a river-view bathtub and a living canopy bed and costs US$245. Riverside tent sites cost US$9 per person plus US$20 for transfers from Livingstone. The restaurant offers both African and European cuisine (campers must pre-book meals). River cruises and day tours start at US$30 per person.

The *Zambezi Royal Chundu Lodge* (☎/fax (03) 321772; <chundu@icon.co .za>; Web site www.icon.co.za/~creative2)

has comfortable riverside accommodation on a broad stretch of the Zambezi below the Katombora Rapids. For comfortable single/double chalet accommodation and meals, foreigners pay US$190/300. Add guided tours, fishing, birdwatching and other activities, and it's US$280/480. Locals pay 30% less.

At *Jungle Junction* (☎ (03) 324127; <jungle@zamnet.zm>), on a lush island at Katombora Rapids, care is taken to ensure that local people benefit directly from tourism. Rough shelters – fishermen's huts – cost US$20 per person, camping is US$11 per person, and everyone pays a one-off transfer/canoe-hire fee of US$50; pre-booking is essential. They pick up guests at the Zimbabwe border post at noon daily; otherwise, book in at the office at 21 Obote Ave, Livingstone. You're bound to hear more about this place on your travels through the region.

Not far downstream is another wild camp site, *White Water Island* (☎ (03) 321772), Room 104, New Wing, Mosi-ua-Tunya House, PO Box 60889, Livingstone. Camp sites cost US$12 per person, including *mokoro* transfers.

The small village of Mwande lies on the Zambezi about 145km west of Livingstone. *Soka Fishing Camp* has self-catering ron-davels for US$10 per person and camping for US$5. Book in advance through Gwembe Safaris.

# Around Victoria Falls

## ZAMBEZI NATIONAL PARK

The 56,000 hectare Zambezi National Park, which is vaguely associated with Victoria Falls National Park, consists of 40km of Zambezi River frontage and a spread of wildlife-rich inland mopane forest and savanna. The park is best known for its herds of sable, but is also home to other antelope species, elephant, zebra, giraffe, lion and buffalo.

The park headquarters office is open from 6 am to 6.30 pm. The cordoned off area west of the park office was mined during the Second Chimurenga and remains riddled with dangerous unexploded mines. Heed the signs and keep out!

### Activities

**Horse-Riding** Horseback safaris accommodate up to eight riders at a time, but children under 12 must prove they've had a year's riding experience or completed a riding course. Experienced riders pay US$50 for three-hour rides and novices US$35 for two hours. All-day tours cost US$113 and longer trips are also available. Book through Shearwater, Safari Par Excellence or other Victoria Falls agencies.

**Game Drives** Game drives in Zambezi National Park are available for around US$35 (plus US$3 for park entry). They start between 6 and 8 am and finish between 9 and 11 am and also run from 3 to 6 pm. Full-day drives cost around US$95, with lunch. Providers include Safari Par Excellence, African Bush Safaris and Dabula Safaris.

**Game Walks** Half/full-day game walks are run by Wild Horizons and Dabula Safaris for US$45/85 per person. They also run occasional overnight walks for US$140, all inclusive. Backpackers Africa does half/full day game walks for US$52/85; overnight trips are US$120 and 2½ day walking safaris cost US$280. Locals pay only half-price.

The only place you can walk on your own is between picnic sites one and 25, near the eastern park boundary.

### Places to Stay

National Parks operates a variety of accommodation in the park. The riverside lodges at the park entrance have two two-bed rooms, a living area and a veranda, but they book up well in advance. Make reservations at the central booking office in Harare.

At the three fishing camps, *Mpala-Jena*,

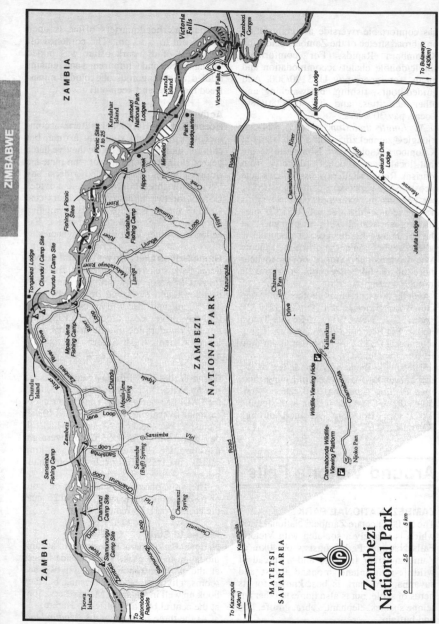

Zambezi
National Park

*Kandahar* and *Sansimba*, all beautifully located along the river, you can fish for yellow bream and tiger fish. Each camp has rudimentary shelters and toilets and no licences are necessary to fish in these international waters. The road is closed from November to April, but the camps remain open and accessible by canoe. At this time of year, advance bookings may be made in Victoria Falls.

There are also five exclusive camps. Visitors may camp overnight at the remote *Chamabonda Wildlife-Viewing Platform*, in the far south-west of the park, which has piped water, a flush toilet and a cold shower. *Chundu 1* and *Chundu 2*, between Mpala-Jena and Sansimba, occupy a magical stretch of riverbank. *Chamunzi* lies on the riverbank 40km west of the reception area and *Siamunungu* is 7km west of Chamunzi. Each camp may be used by parties of up to 12 people.

### Getting Around
Independent visitors to Zambezi National Park need a car; bicycles and motorbikes aren't allowed, except on the transit route to Kazungula. Although it's discouraged, you can walk from Victoria Falls town to the park entrance gate and look for a lift.

## KAZUMA PAN NATIONAL PARK
In Zimbabwe's extreme north-west corner, the 31,300 hectare Kazuma Pan National Park is an unusual enclave of savanna in otherwise teak and mopane-wooded country. The heart of the park is a large grassy pan, more typical of Botswana than Zimbabwe. It's home to Zimbabwe's only gemsbok, as well as such rare species as eland, roan, wild dog and oribi (which are found nowhere else in Zimbabwe). Lion and cheetah are fairly common, and many antelope species, as well as buffalo and elephant, inhabit the pan area.

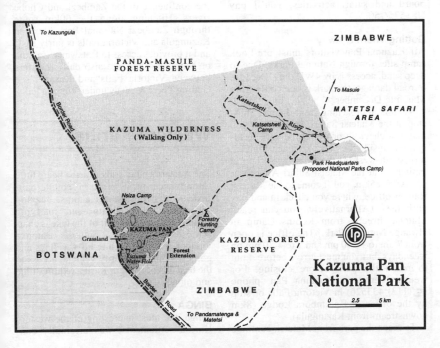

Kazuma Pan National Park

## Organised Tours

Backpackers Africa runs two- to four-day backpacking trips in Kazuma Pan between April and December.

## Places to Stay

Facilities are limited to two primitive camp sites with braai pits and long-drop toilets, and only two visitor parties are accommodated at a time. Further improvements are planned, but currently, the nearest services are at Victoria Falls.

Graced by a prominent baobab and a grove of teak trees, *Nsiza Camp* is just a shady spot at the pan's edge. It's more accessible than remote *Katsetsheti Camp*, which lies beside the marshes flanking the Katsetsheti river.

The nearest safari lodge is the posh *Matetsi Lodge* (π (14) 431520), which is one of Zimbabwe's most exclusive options. For single/double accommodation, full-board and safari activities, you'll pay US$575/750.

## Getting There & Away

All Kazuma Pan visitors must pre-book camp sites through National Parks. Due to deep sand, access is by 4WD only. Because of road damage, the park is open only from March to December.

Visitors approaching from the east must stop at the Matetsi Safari Area office; you may not check in or out at the park headquarters inside the park. To reach Matetsi, turn south-west off the Bulawayo-Victoria Falls road at the Matetsi Safari Area turn-off. After 25km, you'll come to the Matetsi Ranger office, where you check in and pay park fees. (Alternatively, you can reach Matetsi directly from Robins Camp in Hwange National Park.) The office is open from 7 am to 12.30 pm and 2 to 4.30 pm on weekdays, but you must arrive before 4 pm to reach the park before closing. For weekend entry to Kazuma Pan, phone (π (113) 433526) in Victoria Falls or stop by the office at Katombora Lodge (8km downstream from Kazungula).

To reach the park from Matetsi, continue for 12km to Tsabolisa Junction and turn right, then continue 27km to Pandamatenga, where there's a Botswana border crossing. Here you must register at the police station to use the border road; it's open from 8 am to 5 pm. At Pandamatenga, the road turns north-west and straddles the international boundary for 25km before entering the park. There is no direct park access via the border road from Victoria Falls, Kazungula or Botswana; you must check in at Matetsi.

If that isn't enough red tape, you'll also have to check out of the park. Heading east, stop at Matetsi. If you're exiting along the Pandamatenga road to Kazungula and Victoria Falls, check out at Katombora Lodge, 8km downstream from Kazungula.

## KAZUNGULA

Four countries – Zimbabwe, Zambia, Namibia and Botswana – meet at the Kasane/Kazungula border crossing, near the confluence of the Zambezi and Chobe rivers. Hitching along the 60km route through Zambezi National Park between Kazungula and Victoria Falls is fairly easy, and it provides access to Botswana, Zambia or Namibia. There are also daily transfers between Victoria Falls and Kasane; see Getting There & Away under Victoria Falls.

# Western Kariba

The western end of Lake Kariba bears little resemblance to its eastern counterpart. Instead of hotels, safari camps, buzzing speedboats, houseboats and partying holiday-makers, this half of the lake is characterised by wilderness outposts, Batonka villages and wild, rolling hills, valleys and gorges. Without a sturdy vehicle, access to the best bits of western Kariba requires time and money.

## BINGA

Binga, the most interesting of the western Kariba settlements, was originally constructed as a government administrative centre. It was also intended as a resettlement site for the Batonka people, who were displaced by the rising Lake Kariba waters from their riverside homes to this higher and less productive ground.

Binga isn't exactly an action spot, but the lake offers good fishing and relaxation. The area is also known for much sought-after Batonka crafts – such as baskets, decorative stools, headrests and drums.

Without a vehicle, you're in for some hot, dry walks just getting around. Binga may be a planned community, but it straggles from the shore to the hills and you may spend awhile looking for it before realising you're already there. Petrol is available at the DDF ferry terminal and Kulizwe Lodge.

### Crocodile Farm
The Crocodile Farm, beyond the elite dacha complex, is good for a brief look around but it doesn't really cater to visitors. It's attended daily except Sunday.

### Chibwatatata Hot Springs
The Chibwatatata Hot Springs, uphill from

the rest camp, have long been considered a 'power place' by the Batonka, and formerly served as a rainmaking site. The larger and hotter 'spring' would more accurately be described as a fumarole (a hole in the ground from which steam is emitted). The less violent hot spring nearby provides naturally heated water for the rest camp swimming pool. It's also used as a laundry and bath, and has become rather polluted.

### Chilangililo Co-operative
The Chilangililo Co-operative project, a novel and successful tourism concept, is the brainchild of anthropologist Dr Peta Jones. Her interests include promoting donkeys as transport and encouraging talented local artisans. The attached Binga Craft Centre sells unique material arts, particularly wood carvings and basketry.

Village Visits, run by the co-operative, offers a glimpse into Tonga culture. It takes visitors by boat to traditional Tonga kraals, where they'll meet local people and sample traditional foods. This region can't accommodate mass tourism, so you'll need to muster a group and book well in advance. Visitors are encouraged to relax, avoid the appearance of wealth and resist the temptation to dole out gifts (donations to local projects are gratefully accepted). The price of an all-inclusive trip is US$125 (one to five people) or US$209 (six to 10 people) plus US$100 for the boat.

Contact Chilangililo through the Kasambabezi Kiosk (☎ (115) 2407). Coming from Dete Crossroads/Kamativi, get off at the bus stop immediately after the Chilila gate, turn north (right) on the next track and follow the yellow backpacker signs.

### Places to Stay & Eat
*Chilangililo Co-operative's* lakeshore stilt huts are Binga's most interesting accommodation. With two basic sleeping huts and a separate cooking hut, they're ideal for backpacking travellers. Accommodation costs US$3 per person, but you must bring your own food and sleeping bag.

At *Binga Rest Camp* (☎ (115) 2244),

Lake Kariba

Chilila Gate

To Comednze
Tonga Crafts
Kamativi, Chizarira &
Dete Crossroads

To Airstrip

**Binga**

0    2    4 km

| | |
|---|---|
| 1 Intale Houseboat Marina | 10 Chilila Lodges |
| 2 Kulizwe Lodge | 11 Masumu Lodge |
| 3 Petrol Station | 12 Bus Stop |
| 4 Binga Crocodile Farm | 13 DDF |
| 5 Binga Rest Camp | Ferry Terminal |
| 6 Chibwatatata Hot Springs | 14 Police |
| 7 Kasambabezi Store/Kiosk | 15 Post Office |
| 8 Chilangililo Co-operative | 16 Shops |
| 9 Chilangililo Stilt Huts | 17 Hospital |

## The Tonga

Until the tribe was permanently displaced by the rising Kariba waters in the late 1950s, few outsiders had ever heard of the Tonga people of the Zambezi Valley. Nowadays, they command almost a cult following. Even colonial remnants refer to someone who has, to them, become inordinately liberal or countercultural in their thinking, as having 'run off to join the Tonkies'.

The Tonga are believed to have migrated to the Zambezi Valley from the area of Lake Malawi during the 15th or 16th century and settled in the Gwembe Valley area of present-day Zimbabwe and Zambia. The Tonga language is a more archaic dialect than Shona or Ndebele, both of which have undergone great changes through interaction with other groups. Although the Tonga came in contact with Portuguese traders and suffered occasional Ndebele mischief, they were naturally sheltered by the Zambezi Escarpment and were mostly left to go their own way.

During the colonial era and after Zimbabwean independence, however, their domain was split by superimposed international boundaries. Lake Kariba simply drove the wedge deeper. Today, the government has tarred the road into their capital at Binga and is trying to absorb the Tonga into mainstream Zimbabwe by providing schools and medical services.

For the Tonga, as for Rastafarians, smoking *mbanje*, or cannabis, has long been a way of life, and only in this tiny enclave of Zimbabwe is the dreaded weed tolerated by the authorities. In reality, however, it's not so popular and any images travellers may have of a utopian Kaţhmandu-by-the-Lake are largely unjustified.

Although there are still a few red half-mast eyes around, the traditional Tonga culture appears to be sadly and permanently disappearing into history. The stereotypical image of the Tonga will invariably include an elderly woman smoking mbanje in a long gourd pipe. Thanks to some unusual and long moribund aesthetic values, her nose will have been pierced by a length of bone and her front teeth knocked out when she was a young girl. Today, however, it's unlikely you'll encounter such a person in Binga.

---

housed in the former district commissioner's home, you can camp and use the pool facilities for US$3 per person. Singles/doubles cost US$15/18 and chalets are available for families. The attached restaurant serves very good fare, but it receives less patronage than the bar, which is *the* local gathering place. You can also pitch a tent at a spot near the Somabhula Houseboat, away from the main populated area.

At *Kulizwe Lodge* (☎ (115) 286), which is more an agglomeration of holiday homes, you'll pay from around US$50 per person. Out of town are the *Chilila Lodges* (☎ (19) 72568; fax 76854), five traditional self-catering lodges in a forested setting beside a lovely harbour.

The *Masumu River Lodge* (☎ (115) 2207), on the lakeshore east of Binga, offers a luxury alternative in a quiet setting. Bed, breakfast and dinner in a shared room costs US$130.

### Things to Buy

In addition to the excellent value Binga Craft Centre, you can check out Comednze Tonga crafts, near the corner of the Binga and Siabuwa roads, and other roadside stalls, which sell a similar variety of Tonga material arts.

### Getting There & Away

The new high-speed tarred road to Binga is smooth as silk but hitching from Dete Crossroads remains difficult due to sparse traffic. Heading for Binga, you'll have the most joy on Saturday mornings; leaving is easiest on Sunday afternoons.

The bus stop is at the supermarket, 5km from Binga Rest Camp. A Country Boy bus leaves for Victoria Falls at 5 am daily, and heads back toward Binga at 11 am. There's also a daily bus in either direction between Bulawayo and Siabuwa via Binga. To continue to Karoi or Harare, you'll have to stay overnight in Siabuwa (camping only), and catch a bus (or a series of buses) to Karoi and Harare the following morning.

For information on the DDF ferries between Kariba and Binga, see Kariba in the Northern Zimbabwe chapter. Informal fishing trips or boats to Mlibizi may be arranged privately from the Intale houseboat marina, down the road opposite Binga Rest Camp.

## MLIBIZI

Unless they're fishing, most Kariba ferry travellers spend only one night at laid-back Mlibizi.

### Places to Stay

At the ferry terminal is the *Mlibizi Zambezi Resort* (☎ (115) 272), where you can stay in Mediterranean-style chalets for US$125 a double, or camp for US$2 per person. Note that all drinking water must be boiled.

Further along is the more affordable *Mlibizi Safari Lodge* (☎/fax (115) 271), which is set on a hill and bills itself as 'the place you never want to leave – the best place to do nothing'. For a single/double stone and thatch bungalow, you'll pay US$35/45; a simpler bungalow without a veranda costs US$30/40. Garden villas with six-bed dormitories cost US$20 per person. To while away the time until the ferry arrives, there's a restaurant, bar, children's playground, tennis courts and swimming pool. They also arrange sunset cruises, crocodile cruises and boat trips through spectacular Devils Gorge. If you're walking from Mlibizi Zambezi Resort for an evening meal, carry a torch and arrange to have the gate left open for your return.

Alternatively, you can hire a six-bed self-catering bungalow for US$10 per person. Contact Janet (☎ (19) 70466 or 77538).

### Getting There & Away

The Binga bus from Dete Crossroads passes within 15km of Mlibizi, but it's a hot dry walk from the junction so carry lots of water. Transfer services from Victoria Falls and Hwange National Park average around US$80 for one to six people. With a large group, you can hire a UTC minibus from Victoria Falls for US$93. Taxis cost around US$25 from Victoria Falls, but beware of drivers (mostly unlicensed) who quote good prices but demand much more at the time of departure, knowing it would be difficult to find another option to get you to Mlibizi before the ferry leaves.

To get lifts from Bulawayo or Victoria Falls, leave notices at hotels and camp sites, stating whether you'll share petrol and expenses. Otherwise, you can hitch from Dete Crossroads (where the petrol station owner sometimes offers lifts to Mlibizi starting at around US$20). Hitching out of Mlibizi is more difficult because vehicles arriving on the ferry are normally full.

Ferries depart for Kariba several times weekly at 9 am; for details, see Kariba in the Northern Zimbabwe chapter. In Victoria Falls, you can book ferries upstairs in the Zimbank Building.

### DEKA DRUM

The *Deka Drum Fishing Resort* (☎ (181) 50524) idles beside the confluence of the Deka and Zambezi rivers, near the entrance to Devils Gorge. At this beautiful spot you can sit and fish in the river to your heart's content. Camping costs US$2 per person and basic self-catering chalets are US$12 per person. Petrol is available and a small on-site restaurant prepares meals and snacks. Access is by road from Victoria Falls or Hwange town, but there's no public transport.

### CHIZARIRA NATIONAL PARK

The name of this remote and magnificent 192,000 hectare park is derived from the Batonka word *chijalila*, meaning 'closed off' or 'barrier', which aptly describes its position. Topographically, Chizarira is actually three parks – the Zambezi Escarpment, the Uplands and the Busi Valley – and it seems worlds away from the dusty, goat-ravaged scrub of the Gwembe communal lands at the foot of the Zambezi escarpment.

ZIMBABWE

---

## The Power Struggle

At the time of Zimbabwean independence in 1980, the country's optimistic new leaders set about laying down plans to meet Zimbabwe's future power needs. Among other ideas were plans to construct a new hydroelectric project on the Zambezi River by the year 2002, to supplement the output of Kariba Dam.

The initial proposal was for a new dam in the Mupata Gorge, between Mana Pools and the Mozambican border. However, the inevitable result would have been the flooding and destruction of the magnificent Mana Pools flood plain. Fortunately, environmental pressure groups (particularly the Zambezi Society) were able to bring the matter to worldwide attention. Mana Pools was subsequently placed on the World Heritage List and, in the end, the idea was scuppered.

Once the notion of a dam on the middle Zambezi had been abandoned, attention turned to the upper Zambezi, and specifically, Batoka Gorge, 54km downstream from Victoria Falls. Conservationists weren't exactly happy with the prospect, but conceded that it was considerably more acceptable than the Mupata Gorge proposal, and plans were drawn up.

Construction was set to begin in 1996, to be completed in 2002. However, a series of snags arose. Zambia, which was expected to pay half the cost, balked at the projected US$3 billion price tag and pulled out in early 1995. In any case, after heated disputes over Kariba, Zambians continue to mistrust Zimbabwean promises to fairly allocate energy resources and profits. Furthermore, Zambian villagers living along the riverbanks are determined not to leave their homes and fields, and have refused to accept the fate that befell the Batonka people when Kariba Dam was built. Another drawback – albeit relatively minor in the overall scheme of things – would be the flooding of the Zambezi gorges and the cessation of white-water rafting potential below Victoria Falls.

As opinions heated up, UNESCO called for an environmental-impact assessment of the project and conservation groups suggested a series of smaller and less imposing dams. In the end, the Batoka Gorge idea was set aside and alternatives were sought. One prospect was the development of recently discovered coal reserves at Sengwa, near Lake Kariba. Unfortunately, the Sengwa fields are estimated to hold only 35 years-worth of reserves, and a thermal power plant there would produce an unacceptable level of carbon dioxide emissions. Furthermore, the scale of mining required would severely alter an environmentally sensitive area for an admittedly meagre return.

Another possibility would be to tap into the power about to be generated by Mozambique's Cahora Bassa dam, which lay dormant through that country's years of civil war. However, Mozambique has already agreed to sell the power to South Africa, so any small surplus available to Zimbabwe would quickly diminish as South Africa's power needs increase.

Other more feasible possibilities would include power rationing, the development of Zimbabwe's immense solar potential, or plugging into the enormous new Inga Barrage, currently being constructed on the Zaïre River. It's projected that Inga will have the capacity to power the entire African continent.

Whatever happens, the Zimbabwean government has determined that if no viable alternative is found, it will eventually go ahead with the Batoka Gorge project but, given the recent setbacks, it seems unlikely to happen anytime in the near future.

ZIMBABWE

Until recently, Chizarira was the last great stronghold of the black rhino but, unfortunately, they have now completely disappeared from the area. The few which avoided death at the hands of the poachers have been translocated to Matusadona where, in theory, they can be more readily monitored and guarded.

## The Zambezi Escarpment

In the north, cutting through the edges of the dramatic Zambezi Escarpment, are the deep green gorges of the Mucheni and Lwizilukulu (also spelt Ruziruhuru) rivers. Both drainages are readily accessible by road from the Manzituba headquarters. In the north-east, the Zambezi Escarpment is capped by 1500m Tandezi (which many western visitors liken to a squashed hat). According to a Batonka folk tale, a large and volatile snake lies coiled on its bald summit.

## The Uplands

South of the escarpment, the landscape changes to msasa-dotted upland plateau, which is prime wildlife country. The solitary summits of Chingolo and Gongoriba provide impressive vantage points. The highlight, however, is the emerald-coloured pools of the Chimbovo River Gorge.

## The Busi Valley

South of the Sinamagoga Ridge, the land slopes gently into the Busi Valley whose wild and remote beauty makes it a favourite destination in Chizarira. The wildlife-rich banks of the Busi, which strongly resemble the Mana Pools river frontage, boast everything from porcupine and warthog to elephant, lion and leopard, and the lovely riverine vegetation includes the stately winterthorne acacia *(Acacia albida)*. Also magical are the dramatic Mvurwi Gorge and the frog-filled soda spring at Mujima.

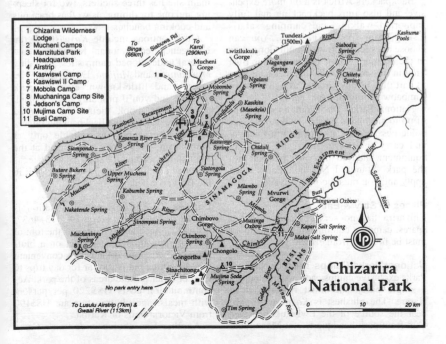

1 Chizarira Wilderness Lodge
2 Mucheni Camps
3 Manzituba Park Headquarters
4 Airstrip
5 Kaswiswi Camp
6 Kaswiswi II Camp
7 Mobola Camp
8 Muchaninga Camp Site
9 Jedson's Camp
10 Mujima Camp Site
11 Busi Camp

Chizarira National Park

## Organised Tours

Chizarira is often considered Zimbabwe's most scenic national park, but most of its few visitors are confined to their vehicles and a crumbling system of 4WD bush tracks. The only way to reach the park's greatest wonders is on foot with National Parks game scouts or licensed walking guides. If you splash out on only one extravagance in Zimbabwe, make it a Chizarira walking safari.

Your best bet is Khangela Safaris (☎ (19) 49733; fax 68259; <secbird@harare.iafrica.zw>), PO Box FM296, Famona, Bulawayo. Leader Mike Scott knows and loves Chizarira, and ensures that every trip is unique. You can choose between backpacking safaris, where you carry everything on your back, or walking safaris, where daily forays are made from semi-permanent base camps. The daily rate is US$140, including meals and transport.

Backpackers Africa is a bit more expensive and also runs backpacking and fully supported walking and camping safaris lasting from five to 12 days. You can choose between the Lwizilukulu Gorge area in the northern sector or the popular Busi Trail in the south. It also includes Chizarira as part of a 12 day circuit through Western Zimbabwe's four national parks.

National Parks game scouts escort groups of up to six hikers on day walks or longer wilderness treks. Participants must supply and carry their own food and camping equipment, and find their own transport into the park. Standard National Parks rates apply and you must book in advance.

## Places to Stay & Eat

Chizarira has no services and all food, spares, camping equipment, fuel and so on must be brought from elsewhere.

**National Parks Camps** The four National Parks exclusive camps each accommodates a single party and must be booked in Harare. The plushest is *Kaswiswi Camp*, near the source of the Lwizilukulu River 6km from park headquarters at Manzituba.

This wilderness compound has two raised sleeping huts, a cooking and dining area, hot showers and flush toilets. It's scenically unspectacular, buried in dense scrub, but is well placed for viewing the small herds of elephant and buffalo.

On a ridge overlooking Mucheni Gorge are the two dramatically situated *Mucheni* camp sites, which share long-drop toilets, a picnic shelter and a spectacular view.

The other northern camp, *Mobola Camp*, lies beside the Mucheni River 6km from Manzituba. The site sits beneath trees which are favoured by bats and often suffers guano bombardment. It lacks shelters but does have a concrete cooking bench, a table and pumped-in river water, as well as flush toilets.

*Busi Camp*, which is actually two exclusive camp sites, lies 35km down a rough 4WD track from Manzituba on the acacia-dotted floodplain of the Busi River. The main site has three shelters, two for sleeping and one for dining, as well as braai pits and cooking benches.

Other options include *Kaswiswi II* (an emergency camp near Kaswiswi) and several undeveloped camp sites, including *Muchaninga* and *Mujima*. However, they're remote and little-known, even by park rangers, and you'll probably draw a blank trying to pre-book them. They're used mainly by walking and backpacking safaris.

The water supply is reliable only at Mabolo and Kaswiswi camps, and at the Manzituba headquarters. At Busi, water is obtained elephant-style by digging for it in the Busi riverbed.

**Lodges** The nearest accommodation is *Chizarira Wilderness Lodge* (☎ (113) 4637; fax 4417), outside the park near the foot of the escarpment. Scenically set on a bluff above the communal lands, it's convenient for Manzituba but is too far for day trips to Busi or other remote areas of the park. Accommodation costs US$220 per person, with meals, and air transfers are US$190 from Victoria Falls or Kariba.

Another fine choice is *Jedson's Camp*

(☎ (19) 60490; fax 67609), PO Box NE88, North End, Bulawayo. Perched on a 100m ridge above the wild Mujima Springs region, it has one of the finest settings of any lodge in Zimbabwe. All-inclusive accommodation is US$300 per person.

## The Tsetse Fly

The tsetse fly, one of Africa's several big scourges, resembles a common housefly except for its distinctive scissor-fold wings and its habit of sucking blood. It's best known for carrying the fatal cattle disease *trypanosomiasis* or *nagana*, which is occasionally passed along to humans as 'sleeping sickness'. Historically, the threat of this disease rendered large swathes of Africa – including the Zambezi Valley and the Okavango area – uninhabitable to pastoralists and their cattle.

Naturally, some conservationists count this as a blessing and, indeed, many of Africa's remaining wilderness areas owe their existence to this fly. Developers and cattle ranchers, however, are naturally at odds with this assessment and have been working with local governments to eradicate the fly.

In Zimbabwe, the earliest national eradication attempts, which were developed in the 1960s, focused on the Zambezi Valley and were rather basic. The first plan involved very simple components: a tiny round enclosure, which was just large enough to hold one cow and one man on a stool. The concept was simple enough – whenever a tsetse fly landed on the cow, the man would swat it. Naturally, this optimistic programme, which hoped to keep zillions of potentially threatening flies at bay, met with limited success. You'll still see these enclosures dotted around Chizarira National Park and other areas near the Zambezi.

The next proposed plan of attack was to build a fence along the base of the Zambezi Escarpment and shoot everything north of the fence. For some reason, this suggestion wasn't enthusiastically received and it was dropped before it got off the ground.

Because the fly inhabits forested areas, deforestation was another mooted plan of attack, and the banks of Zimbabwe's Shangani River were zealously stripped of trees. However, the flies quickly adapted and scarcely noticed the change, thus sparing the remainder of Zimbabwe's trees.

Inevitably, it was decided that the answer was aerial spraying of insecticides, and the environment was liberally misted with a cocktail of DDT, deltamethrin and endosulphan. In fact, this method is still used in Botswana's Okavango Delta and, although it's clearly a threat to the delta's aquatic ecosystems, it conveys the unambiguous message that cattle come first in Botswana. (In fact, the Botswana government has gone so far as cutting trees, to deprive the fly of shelter, and killing buffalo and kudu to wipe out its food supply.)

On a brighter note, the latest method of tsetse control – which began in the early 1970s and thankfully doesn't require drastic environmental sacrifice – appears to be the most effective. Strips of material impregnated with the hormone component in bovine breath are placed in known tsetse habitats. The flies don't realise – until it's too late – that these strips also contain a poison brewed up specifically for them. You'll often see these strips attached to metal frames throughout affected areas around northern Zimbabwe and north-western Botswana, including the Okavango Delta.

There's no independent access; you arrive via either the Lusulu airstrip, 25km away, or an exclusive back road from Hwange; transfers are US$150 each way.

### Getting There & Away
Without a 4WD, you'll have to join a tour; Chizarira just doesn't see enough traffic to make hitching even marginally feasible. On public transport, you can reach the park turn-off west of Siabuwa on the Karoi-Binga track; from there, it's 24km uphill to the Manzituba park headquarters. However, walking is not permitted past the park entrance at the mouth of Mucheni Gorge.

Petrol is sometimes sold at Siabuwa; otherwise you must reach Binga, 90km away.

### Getting Around
Both 4WD and high clearance are required for travel south of Manzituba and, although the park is open all year round, many areas are inaccessible in the summer wet season (November to April).

# Botswana

**BOTSWANA AT A GLANCE**

Area: 600,370 sq km
Population: 1,861,000
Population Growth Rate: 1.4%
Capital: Gaborone
Head of State: Festus Mogae
Official Language: English
Currency: Pula
Exchange Rate: US$1 = P5.31
Per Capita GNP: US$3,300
Time: GMT/UTC +2

# Facts about Botswana

## HISTORY
### Early San & Bantu Groups

The original inhabitants of Botswana were San (Bushmen), who continue to live throughout the Kalahari regions of eastern Namibia and western Botswana. Their origins are unknown but they are believed to have occupied the area for at least 30,000 years. They were followed by the Khoi-Khoi (Hottentots), who probably originated from a San group cut off from the mainstream. Sheep remains and pottery in late Stone Age diggings provide evidence that they eventually adopted a pastoral lifestyle.

Next arrived the agricultural and pastoral Bantu groups, who migrated from the north-western and eastern regions of the African continent – there is evidence that they originated in the area of present-day Cameroon – sometime during the 1st or 2nd century. It is likely, however, that this 'Bantu migration' bypassed or just skirted the edges of present-day Botswana, avoiding the harsh Kalahari sands and continuing into the more amenable areas of the Transvaal and the Cape, where the newcomers inevitably encountered the San and Khoi-Khoi. Relations between the three societies appear to have been amicable and they apparently mixed freely, traded and intermarried.

The Bantu of southern Africa have been divided into groups by anthropologists, based on similarities in their languages and social structures. The earliest such group probably arrived in Botswana during the first centuries AD and settled along the Chobe River. The Sotho-Tswana, a later Bantu arrival, consisted of three distinct tribal entities: the Northern Basotho, or Pedi, who settled in the Transvaal; the Southern Basotho of present-day Lesotho; and the Western Basotho, or Tswana, who migrated northwards into present-day Botswana. The Kgalagadi, the first Tswana-speaking tribe to colonise Botswana,

## BOTSWANA AT A GLANCE

**Area:** 600,370 sq km
**Population:** 1,500,765
**Population Growth Rate:** 1.48%
**Capital:** Gaborone
**Head of State:** Festus Mogae
**Official Language:** English
**Currency:** Pula
**Exchange Rate:** P3.96 = US$1
**Per Capita GNP:** US$2800
**Time:** GMT/UTC +2

arrived from the Transvaal around the 14th century and settled in the relatively arable and well watered south-eastern strip of the country between present-day Francistown and Gaborone.

At that time, north-eastern Botswana lay within Shona territory and was affiliated with the Torwa and later the Rozwi dynasties (see History in the Facts about Zimbabwe chapter). Indications, however, point to its earlier occupation, probably by the Leopard's Kopje, who were based in the Khami area of south-western Zimbabwe. These Shona speakers, now known as the Babirwa, were later completely absorbed into the Tswana culture, adopting the Tswana language and customs.

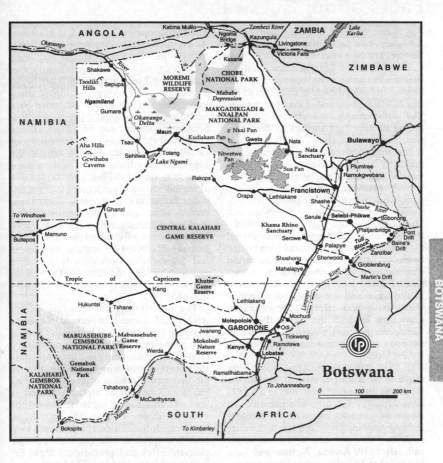

Between the 15th and 18th centuries the majority of the Bantu in Botswana lived east of the Kalahari sands, but during the early 18th century peaceful fragmentation of tribal groups became the standard. Familial and power disputes were solved amicably, with the dissatisfied party gathering followers and tramping off to establish another domain elsewhere.

Fragmentation was an ideal solution to disputes as long as there remained an 'elsewhere' to set oneself up; in the case of the people living in south-eastern Botswana, it was the vast expanses of country to the west, areas previously inhabited only by the San and Khoi-Khoi. In the north-west, where the Lozi Empire dominated, it was the Okavango Delta region and around the shores of Lake Ngami.

Perhaps the most significant split in Botswana history was that of Kwena, Ngwaketse and Ngwato, the sons of a chief called Malope (or Masilo) whose domain took in the Boteti River area of central Botswana. When the three brothers quarrelled, Kwena went to Ditshegwane,

Ngwaketse set himself up at Kanye in the far south-east and Ngwato settled at Serowe. The Ngwato clan split further with a quarrel between Chief Khama I and his brother Tawana, who subsequently left Serowe and established his chiefdom in the area of Maun at the end of the 18th century. The three major modern-day Tswana groups all trace their ancestry to this three-way split.

Late in the 19th century, the nomadic and primarily pastoral Herero, faced with German aggression in Namibia, began migrating eastwards and settling in the north-western extremes of Botswana.

## The Zulu

By 1800, all suitable grazing lands around the fringes of the Kalahari had been settled by pastoralists and peaceful fragmentation was no longer a feasible solution to disputes. Furthermore, Europeans had arrived in the Cape and were expanding northwards, creating an effective barrier against movement towards the south. By 1817, Kuruman, the first Christian mission in Tswana territory, had been founded by Robert Moffat.

In 1818 came an event that would alter the face of southern Africa. Shaka, the fierce and determined new chief of the Zulu confederation, forcibly amalgamated all area tribes and set out with his ruthless fighting machine on a rampage to conquer or destroy all tribes and settlements in his path. By 1830, Kwena, Ngwato and Lozi had fallen and Mzilikazi (see History in the Facts about Zimbabwe chapter) had broken away and fled northwards on a similar crusade with the Kumalo clan, later known as the Ndebele.

Mzilikazi stormed his way across the Transvaal and Botswana, sending raiding parties into the Tswana villages and scattering them north and westwards. Some were dispersed as far as Ghanzi and the Tshane cluster of villages in the dead heart of the Kalahari. Ngwaketse was rousted out in the process and sent fleeing into the desert, finally settling near Lethlakeng.

## The Missionaries

As a result of all the displacement and scattering, the Tswana realised that their divided nation would be particularly vulnerable to subsequent attacks. They began to regroup and developed a highly structured society. Each nation was ruled by a hereditary monarch and aristocracy whose economic power was based on tribute labour and the ownership of large herds of cattle. In each of the Tswana nations, the king's subjects lived either in the central town or in satellite villages. Each clan was allocated its own settlement, which fell under the control of village leaders. These leaders were responsible for distributing land and recruiting tribute labour for work in the monarch's fields and pastures. By the second half of the 19th century, some towns had grown to a considerable size. For example, by 1860 the capital of the Ngwato clan at Shoshong had an estimated population of 30,000.

The orderliness and structure of the town-based society impressed the early Christian missionaries at Kuruman Mission. The prime mover behind the missionary effort was the dogmatic and uncompromising Robert Moffat, who was responsible for the first transliteration of the Tswana language into the Roman alphabet as well as the first translation of the Bible into written Tswana. Even after years in Africa, however, Moffat couldn't be distracted long enough to appreciate the continent's unique characteristics and problems, instead remaining uninterested in – and intolerant of – traditional cultures and beliefs.

In 1841 came the inquisitive and charismatic Dr David Livingstone who based himself at Kuruman and married Robert Moffat's daughter, Mary. With a scientific background, Livingstone found it difficult to settle down to sedentary family and missionary life. Instead, he left the mission and staged a series of forays north to Lake Ngami and into the domain of the Lozi Empire. In the end, Livingstone's itchy feet got the better of him; he sent his family to England and struck out for parts unknown –

to Victoria Falls and beyond. It is significant that before Livingstone left he was unjustly accused by the Boers of selling firearms to the Tswana and rallying local people against them. In a Boer attack on the Tswana, Livingstone's Kuruman home was destroyed and his weapons stolen.

None of the missionaries converted great numbers of Tswana, but they did manage to advise the locals, sometimes wrongly, in their dealings with the Europeans that followed – explorers, naturalists, traders, miners and general rabble. The traders provided firearms and, in the name of commerce, sent the Tswana to gun down and practically exterminate the country's elephant, rhino and hippopotamus populations, especially around Lake Ngami. So great were the numbers killed that the European market for animal products was flooded, and prices could scarcely have justified the slaughter. At the same time, the Tswana, having been paid for the skins and ivory they bagged, were dragged into the European cash economy.

## The Boers
While Mzilikazi was wreaking havoc on the Tswana and the missionaries were busy trying to Christianise them in the northwest, the Boers, feeling pressure from the British in the Cape, embarked on their Great Trek across the Vaal River. Confident that they had Heaven-sanctioned rights to any land they might choose to occupy in southern Africa, 20,000 Boers crossed the Vaal into Tswana and Zulu territory and established themselves as though the lands were unclaimed and uninhabited (indeed some were, having been cleaned out earlier by Mzilikazi).

Each male farmer staked his claim by riding out an area of 3000 *morgen* (about 2400 hectares) and set up his farm. The remaining local people were either forced to move or were pressured into working as servants and farm hands.

When Mzilikazi came up against the Boers in 1837, the superior Boer firepower under the command of Hendrik Potgieter

stalled his campaign and sent him fleeing north-eastwards to settle in the Bulawayo area. Between 1844 and 1852, the Boers, bent upon establishing trade links with the Dutch and Portuguese, set up a series of fragmented republics that were independent of the British connection in the Cape.

At the Sand River Convention of 1852, Great Britain recognised the Transvaal's independence and the Boers immediately informed the Batswana (as the people of Botswana are often known) that they were now subjects of the new South African Republic. Boer leader MW Pretorius notified the British that the Tswana were acquiring weapons from white traders and missionaries and preparing for war. Maintaining that this rendered his country unsafe for travellers, he closed off the road through the Transvaal. Pretorius' allegation was technically true: the Tswana were obtaining muzzle-loading rifles to bring down the big game they were busy decimating.

Meanwhile, the prominent Tswana leader of the Kwena clan, Sechele I, and Mosielele of the Kgatla clan decided to rebel against white rule, but the Boers came back with a vengeance, launching a destructive rampage in the Tswana communities. Incurring heavy human and territorial losses, the Tswana sent their leaders to petition the British for protection from the Boers. Britain, however, already had its hands full in southern Africa and was in no hurry to take on and support a country of dubious profitability. Instead, Britain offered only to act as arbitrator in the dispute. By 1877, however, animosity had escalated to such a dangerous level that the British finally conceded and annexed the Transvaal, launching the first Boer War. War continued until the Pretoria Convention of 1881, when the British withdrew from the Transvaal in exchange for Boer allegiance to the British Crown.

## The Protectorate
With the British out of their way, the Boers looked northwards into Tswana territory, pushing westwards into the Molopo Basin

of what had become known as Bechuana-land. They managed to subdue the towns of Taung and Mafeking (now Mafikeng) in 1882 and proclaimed them the republics of Stellaland and Goshen. The British viewed this encroachment as threatening to their 'road to the north' – the route into Rhodesia and its presumed mineral wealth.

Meanwhile, the Tswana lobbied for continued British protection from the Boers, as well as from a possible renewal of the Ndebele threat in the north-east. John Mackenzie, a close friend of the Christian Ngwato chief, Khama III of Shoshong, travelled to London and actively campaigned for British intervention to stop the erosion of Tswana territory by the expansionist Boers. Mackenzie was appointed Deputy Commissioner of the region, a post that was quickly and underhandedly taken over by Cecil Rhodes. Rhodes saw Mackenzie's opposition to Bechuanaland's incorporation into the Cape Colony as a threat to Rhodes' 'Cape to Cairo' scheme (Rhodes dreamt of British domination of Africa from the Cape to Cairo, and planned to link the two with a railway line through the heart of the continent). Rhodes also complained that Boer control was cutting off the labour supply from the north to his British South Africa Company (BSAC).

In 1885, Britain finally resigned itself to the inevitable. The area south of the Molopo River became the British Crown Colony of Bechuanaland, which was attached to the Cape Colony. At the same time, British jurisdiction and protection were extended to cover the newly created British Protectorate of Bechuanaland, which took in all lands north of the Cape Colony, south of 22°S latitude and east of 20°E longitude. This inadvertently divided Khama III's Ngwato territory in half, but Khama, grateful for the protection, chose to ignore the issue.

The rationale behind the protectorate was to prevent Boer expansion to the north and west and stall encroachment by other European powers, particularly the Germans in German South West Africa (Namibia). Only

secondarily was it to provide protection for the existing Tswana power structures. Unfortunately, the new 'protectors' remained blasé about Bechuanaland and tried to transfer control to the Cape Colony, which refused on the grounds that the expense would be too great.

## Rhodes Loses Ground

A new threat to the Tswana chiefs' power base came in the form of Rhodes, who remained keen to take control of the country. By 1894, the British had more or less agreed to allow him to do so.

Realising the implications of Rhodes' aspirations, three high-ranking Tswana chiefs, Bathoen, Khama III and Sebele, accompanied by a sympathetic missionary, WC Willoughby, sailed to England to appeal directly for continued British government control over Bechuanaland. Instead of taking action, Colonial Minister Joseph Chamberlain advised them to contact Rhodes directly and work things out among themselves. Chamberlain then conveniently forgot the matter and left on holiday.

Naturally, Rhodes was immovable, so they turned to the London Missionary Society (LMS), who in turn took the matter to the British public. Fearing that the BSAC would allow alcohol in Bechuanaland, the LMS and other Christian groups backed the devoutly Christian Khama and his entourage. The public in general felt that the Crown had more business administering the empire than did Cecil Rhodes, with his business of questionable integrity. When Chamberlain returned from holiday, public pressure had mounted to such a level that the government was forced to concede to the chiefs. Chamberlain agreed to continue British administration of Bechuanaland, ceding only a small strip of the south-east to the BSAC to allow construction of a railway line to Rhodesia.

In 1890, the strip between 22°S latitude and the Chobe and Zambezi rivers came under British control by agreement with the Germans. Rhodes was still scheming to gain control in the protectorate. Posing as

MITCH REARDON

Giraffes browsing on acacia trees – their favourite food, Savuti, Chobe NP (Bot).

DAVID CIMINO

Driving across the white and empty expanse of a salt pan (Bot).

DAVID WALL

The stately Baines' Baobabs grace the skyline of the Kalahari Desert (Bot).

DEANNA SWANEY

The rugged Female Hill, Tsodilo Hills (Bot).

DEANNA SWANEY

The 700-million-year-old Aha Hills (Bot).

an agent of Queen Victoria, he tricked the Tawana king, Sekgoma, into signing a treaty of 'friendship' with Britain, which incidentally granted the BSAC mineral extraction rights. (This treaty, known as the Bosman Concession, was later disallowed by the British government.) In 1896, the government persuaded Sekgoma to open the Ghanzi area to white settlement in exchange for the guarantee of Tawana sovereignty over the remainder of Ngamiland. Rhodes lost ground, but wasn't yet defeated.

Much to the embarrassment of the British government, in 1895, Rhodes' associate Leander Starr Jameson launched an abortive private military foray into the Transvaal, aiming to rein it into some sort of southern African confederation. The Boers were not impressed and as a result Jameson was imprisoned and Rhodes was forced to give up his position as prime minister of the Cape Colony. This time, Rhodes was forced to admit defeat.

## Colonial Years

Now that British rule had settled in, the chiefs more or less accepted that their tribal rites, traditions and lifestyles would be forever altered by the influences of Christianity and western technology. The cash economy had been solidly emplaced and the Tswana had begun to participate actively. As a result, taxes were levied in the Bechuanaland Protectorate, and a capital was established at Mafeking (which was actually in South Africa, outside the protectorate).

Each chief in the protectorate was granted a tribal 'reserve' in which he was given authority over all black residents. The British assigned the chiefs, who still had some degree of autonomy in governing their tribes, to collect taxes, offering them a 10% commission on all moneys collected.

In 1899, Britain decided it was time for a consolidation of the southern African states and declared war on the Transvaal. The Boers were finally overcome in 1902, and in 1910 the Union of South Africa was created, comprising the Cape Colony,

Natal, the Transvaal and the Orange Free State – with provisions for the future incorporation of Bechuanaland and Rhodesia.

By selling cattle, draught oxen and grain to the Europeans streaming north in search of farming land and minerals, Bechuanaland enjoyed some degree of economic independence. However, any sense of security this may have offered didn't last long. The construction of the railway through Bechuanaland to Rhodesia (built at the rate of a mile a day!) and a serious outbreak of foot-and-mouth disease in the 1890s destroyed the transit trade.

By 1920, commercial maize farmers in South Africa and Rhodesia were producing grain in such quantities that Bechuanaland no longer had a market. Furthermore, in 1924 South Africa began pressing the Tswana chiefs to vote for Bechuanaland's amalgamation into the Union of South Africa. When they refused, economic sanctions were brought against the recalcitrant protectorate and its beef market dried up completely.

Economic vulnerability, combined with a series of drought years and the need to raise cash to pay British taxes, sent protectorate subjects migrating to South Africa for work on farms and in the mines. As much as 25% of Botswana's male population was abroad at any one time. This accelerated the breakdown of traditional land-use patterns and eroded the chiefs' powers, leaving the traditional leaders no longer in charge of the economy. Agriculture and domestic work were left in the hands of women, who remained at home. Some aristocrats and cattle barons turned the situation to their advantage by increasing their areas of cultivation and the size of their herds.

In 1923, Ngwato chief Khama III died at the age of 89 and was succeeded by his son Sekgoma, who died himself after serving only two years. The heir to the throne, four-year-old Seretse Khama, wasn't ready to rule over the largest of the Tswana chiefdoms, so his 21-year-old uncle, Tshekedi Khama, left his studies in South Africa to become regent over the Ngwato. This intelligent and competent leader was criticised by colonial authorities for his handling of local disputes according to tribal law. Punishments he ordered included flogging Phineas McIntosh, a white resident of Serowe, for the rape of a local woman. Tshekedi Khama was deposed by Resident Commissioner (well, not quite resident since he was based in Mafeking) Sir Charles Rey, but public opposition to the decision forced the chief's reinstatement.

Rey, who was keen to develop the territory in his charge, realised that no progress would be forthcoming as long as the people were governed by Tswana chiefs. He issued a proclamation turning the chiefs into local government officials answerable to colonial magistrates. So great was popular opposition to this decision – people feared it would lead to their incorporation into South Africa – that Rey was ousted from his job and his proclamation voided.

During WWII, 10,000 Tswana volunteered for the African Pioneer Corps to defend the British Empire. At the end of the war the heir to the Ngwato throne, Seretse Khama, went to study in England, where he met and married Ruth Williams, an Englishwoman. (For more about this story, see the boxed text under Serowe in the Eastern Botswana chapter.) Tshekedi Khama was furious at this breach of tribal custom (although he was accused of exploiting the incident as a means to gain real power in his nephew's place) and the authorities in South Africa, still hoping to absorb Bechuanaland into the Union, were none too happy either. Seretse's chieftaincy was blocked by the British government and he was exiled from the protectorate to England. Bitterness continued until 1956, when Seretse Khama renounced his right to power in Ngwato, became reconciled with his uncle, and returned with his wife to Bechuanaland to serve as vice-chairman of the Ngwato Council.

### Independence
The first signs of Tswana nationalist thinking occurred as early as the late 1940s, but during the 1950s and early 1960s, political changes were spreading across Africa and many colonies were gaining their independence. As early as 1955 it was apparent that Britain was preparing to release its grip on Bechuanaland. University graduates returned from South Africa with political ideals, and although the country had no real economic base, the first Batswana political parties surfaced and started thinking about independence.

Following the Sharpeville Massacre in 1960, South African refugees Motsamai Mpho of the African National Congress (ANC) and Philip Matante, a Johannesburg preacher affiliated with the Pan-Africanist Congress, joined with KT Motsete, a teacher from Malawi, to form the Bechuanaland People's Party. Its immediate goal was independence for the protectorate.

In 1962, Seretse Khama and Kanye farmer Ketumile 'Quett' Masire formed the more moderate Bechuanaland Democratic Party (BDP). They were soon joined by Chief Bathoen II of the Ngwaketse. The BDP formulated a schedule for independence, drawing on support from local chiefs and traditional Batswana. Their first acts were to promote successfully the transfer of the capital into the country, from Mafeking to Gaborone, draft a new nonracial constitution and set up a countdown to independence. The British gratefully accepted their peaceful plan for a transfer of power, and when general elections were held in 1965, Seretse Khama was elected president. On 30 September 1966 the country, now called the Republic of Botswana, was peacefully granted its independence.

Sir Seretse Khama (he was knighted shortly after independence) was certainly no revolutionary. He guaranteed continued freehold over land held by white ranchers and adopted a strictly neutral stance (at least until near the end of his presidency) towards South Africa and Rhodesia. The reason, of course, was Botswana's economic dependence upon the giant to the south. He stood at the helm of one of the world's poorest nations and the wages of Batswana mine workers in South Africa formed an important part of the country's income. Furthermore, Botswana was heavily reliant upon South African food imports.

Nevertheless, Khama refused to exchange ambassadors with South Africa and officially disapproved of apartheid in international circles. He also courageously committed Botswana to supporting the so-called 'Front Line' states of Zambia, Tanzania and Mozambique in opposing the Smith regime in Rhodesia and South African control in Namibia, but pragmatically refused to set up training camps for Zimbabwean liberation fighters. When Rhodesian armed forces carried out 'hot pursuit' raids into Botswana and bombed the Kazungula ferry to Zambia, Botswana's only frontier with a majority-ruled country, Botswana reacted by forming an army, the Botswana Defence Force.

## Modern Developments

Economically, Botswana was catapulted into new realms with the discovery of diamonds near Orapa in 1967. The mining concession, which was given to De Beers, allowed Botswana 75% of the mining profits. Although most Batswana remain in the low income bracket, this mineral wealth has provided enormous foreign currency reserves – almost US$5 billion at the time of writing – so that Botswana now actually lends hard currency to the International Monetary Fund. Between 1975 and 1990, Botswana was the world's fastest-growing economy, and the pula remains Africa's strongest currency. In the early 1990s, the market for pula in neighbouring countries eclipsed that for even the South African rand, which declined steadily.

Sir Seretse Khama died in 1980, shortly after Zimbabwean independence, but his Botswana Democratic Party (BDP), formerly the Bechuanaland Democratic Party, continued to command a substantial majority in the Botswana parliament. Sir Ketumile 'Quett' Masire, who succeeded him as president, continued to follow the

path laid down by his predecessor, while the government generally followed cautiously pro-western policies.

During the 1980s, South Africa accused Botswana of harbouring ANC members and other political refugees from the South African regime. It carried out two helicopter raids on Gaborone in 1986 in which several innocent civilians were killed (none of whom were affiliated with the ANC).

Although economic dependence on South Africa is declining slightly, the two countries remain active trading partners and most of Botswana's food imports originate in South Africa. Currently, Botswana's biggest problems are unemployment, urban drift and a rocketing birth rate – the third highest in the world – but economic growth has thus far managed to keep apace.

Botswana remains a peaceful country, the overall character of which is a positive force on the continent. In fact, it is one of just a handful of African countries – others include Namibia, Senegal, South Africa and Zambia – that enjoys scheduled popular elections and a democratic, multiparty, nonracial government.

There is, however, growing urban support for the BDP's rival party, the Botswana National Front (BNF), which supports redistribution of wealth and an isolated, artificial economy, which – if there are lessons to be learned from similar experiments in Tanzania, Zambia, Mozambique and Zimbabwe – would severely affect Botswana's relatively stable affluence. Most of its support is from Batswana youth and from unskilled migrants to urban areas, who are swelling the numbers of Gaborone's unemployed.

The October 1994 electoral results indicated that most Batswana were content with the status quo; the BDP won a landslide victory for the sixth time, retaining the presidency and all but 13 of the 40 parliamentary seats. However, support for Kenneth Koma's BNF continues to grow, thanks largely to its opposition to the slaughter of Ngamiland cattle to prevent the spread of cattle lung disease; its opposition to the government's awarding of development contracts to foreign firms; and to the 1997 reduction of the voting age from 21 to 18 years. As a result the BNF captured the remaining 13 seats. The centrist BPP (Botswana People's Party) won 4.6% of the vote, but failed to capture any parliamentary seats.

In late March 1998, Sir Ketumile 'Quett' Masire took voluntary retirement, which fortifies claims that Botswana is Africa's most peaceful democracy. He was replaced by Vice President Festus Mogae, who is a former minister of finance and development planning and governor of the Bank of Botswana, and an extremely competent financial manager. He also holds an honours degree in economics from Oxford University, as well as a degree in development economics from the University of Sussex. However, he's obviously not a typical 'people's politician' and there's no indication whether his popular support will match that of his predecessor. A key issue in the 1999 elections will be Mogae's selection of a vice president. Presidential affairs and public administration minister Ponatsehgo Kedikilwe is currently considered the favourite for the position, but retired army commander Ian Khama is also a possible contender.

Only time will tell whether President Festus Mogae will be as popular as his predecessor.

The most contentious recent political issue has been the forced relocation in March 1998 of the San from the Central Kalahari Game Reserve, which had been set aside as a traditional hunting and gathering ground for them in 1961. In spite of vocal protests from the San, who realised that removal from their traditional lands would be likely to result in what would effectively amount to indentured servitude on private ranches, they were shifted from the village of Xade to a settlement called New Xade – which has neither water nor permanent buildings – outside the reserve. They were advised that failure to move would result in decreased government expenditure for health and educational facilities.

Officially, motivations for this action included wildlife preservation, tourism development and the need to 'rescue the Bushmen from their way of life and integrate them into mainstream society'. Cynics might also suggest that vast expanses of potential cattle grazing land and suspected diamond deposits within the reserve might also have played a part. For more information on the San, you might like to contact Survival International (see Useful Organisations in the Regional Facts for the Visitor chapter).

## GEOGRAPHY
With an area of 582,000 sq km, landlocked Botswana extends over 1100km from north to south and 960km from east to west. It's about the size of Kenya or France and somewhat smaller than Texas. It's bounded on the south and south-east by South Africa, across the Limpopo and Molopo Rivers. In the north-east is Zimbabwe while Namibia wraps around the western and northern frontiers. At Kazungula, four countries – Botswana, Zimbabwe, Zambia and Namibia – meet at a single point midstream in the Zambezi River. Therefore, Botswana has a border crossing with Zambia, although the two countries don't actually share a common border.

Most of Botswana lies at an average elevation of 1000m. Much of the country consists of a vast and nearly level sand-filled basin characterised by scrub-covered savanna. In the north-west, the Okavango River flows in from Namibia and soaks into the sands, forming the 15,000 sq km of convoluted channels and islands that comprise the Okavango Delta. In the lower elevations of the north-east are the great salty clay deserts of the Makgadikgadi Pans. Covering nearly 85% of Botswana, including the entire central and south-western regions, is the Kalahari (Kgalagadi), a semi-arid expanse of wind-blown sand deposits and long sandy valleys (which sporadically serve as stream channels) and ridges stabilised by scrubby trees and bushes. The shifting dunes that comprise a traditional 'desert' are found only around Bokspits in the far south-west.

Although Botswana has no mountain ranges to speak of, the almost uniformly flat landscape is punctuated occasionally by low desert hills, especially along the south-eastern boundary and in the far north-west. Botswana's highest point is 1491m Otse Mountain near Lobatse, but the three major peaks of the Tsodilo Hills, in the country's north-western corner, are more dramatic.

## CLIMATE

Although it straddles the Tropic of Capricorn, Botswana experiences a variable climate. In the winter (late May to August), the days are normally clear, warm and sunny, and nights are cool to bitterly cold. In the Kalahari, subfreezing night-time temperatures are normal, especially in June and July, and in more humid areas, frosts are common.

Fortunately, this mostly desert country also has a pronounced summer rainy season (November to March) when afternoon showers and thunderstorms bring *pula* (rain), which is so precious that Botswana's currency was named after it.

The in-between periods – April/early May and September/October – still tend to be dry, but the days are cooler than in summer and the nights are warmer than in winter.

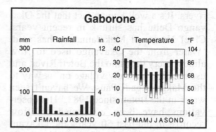

## ECOLOGY & ENVIRONMENT

As a relatively large country with a very low population density, Botswana is one of Africa's wildest regions. However this doesn't mean human activities have not greatly impacted on the fragile ecology of its magnificent deserts, wetlands and savannas. Some of the current major ecological and conservation issues are discussed below.

For further information on ecological issues in Botswana, see Useful Organisations in the Regional Facts for the Visitor chapter.

### The Okavango River

The Okavango River is a precious source of water not only for Botswana but also for Angola and Namibia. According to international law, Namibia has the rights to any river flowing through its territory and in November 1997, after prolonged drought in the central and southern parts of the country, the Namibian government proposed the construction of a 1250km pipeline from the Okavango River to its growing capital, Windhoek. Originally, the project was given 'emergency' status and was earmarked for completion by 1998, but thanks to increased rainfall in 1997, it slipped in priority and is now scheduled for completion by 2000.

Because a decrease in the flow of the Okavango River would affect the hydrology of the Okavango·Delta, Botswana has encouraged the Namibian government to examine other possibilities, such as desalination or use of the Kunene or Zambezi

BOTSWANA

rivers. It's a well known fact that the Okavango Delta has shrunk in recent years. Chief Nxaku of Makalamabedi has said: 'Water from the Okavango used to flow almost every year into the Boteti River, and used to flow past my village on its way to the Makgadikgadi Pans. We haven't seen water in the Boteti since 1983.' His observations have been confirmed by flow records: in the past 50 years, the Okavango's annual volume has decreased by nearly 20%. In the light of Namibia's pipeline proposal, a central issue in the debate is how much water is necessary to maintain the ecosystem.

Pipeline proponents maintain that the natural flow of water through the Okavango Delta may vary by as much as 10 billion cubic metres each year. On the other hand opponents point out that a pipeline would rob the ecosystem of water just when it's most needed – during prolonged periods of drought. They also fear that in years to come Namibia's water demands will increase to unsustainable levels with the growth of the country's population and industrial base.

## The Buffalo Fence

If you've been stopped at a veterinary checkpoint in Botswana or visited the eastern Okavango Delta, you'll be familiar with the country's 3000km of 1.5m-high 'buffalo fence', officially called the Veterinary Cordon Fence. It's not a single fence, but a series of high-tensile steel wire barriers that run cross-country through some of Botswana's wildest terrain. The fences were first erected in 1954 to segregate wild buffalo herds from domestic free-range cattle and thwart the spread of foot-and-mouth disease. However, no-one has yet proved that the disease is passed from species to species.

The issue, however, isn't whether the fences work or not. The problem is that they not only prevent contact between wild and domestic bovine species, but also prevent other wild animals from migrating to water sources along age-old seasonal routes.

While Botswana has set aside large areas for wildlife protection, these areas don't constitute independent ecosystems.

As a result, Botswana's wildebeest population has declined by 99% over the past decade and all remaining buffalo and zebra are stranded north of the fences. Mark and Delia Owens, authors of the book *Cry of the Kalahari*, spent several years in the central Kalahari, and reported seeing tens of thousands of migrating wildebeest – as well as herds of zebra, giraffe and other animals – stopped short by the Kuke Fence that stretches along the northern boundary of the Central Kalahari Game Reserve. Some became entangled in it, while others died of exhaustion searching for a way around it. The remainder were cut off from their seasonal grazing and watering places in the north and succumbed to thirst and starvation. The last great wildlife tragedy occurred during the drought of 1983, in which wildebeest heading for the Okavango waters were barred by the Kuke Fence. They turned east along the fence towards Lake Xau, only to find the lake already dried up. Thousands died as a result.

Cattle ranching is a source of significant wealth and a major export industry, but all exported beef must be disease-free, so naturally ranchers have reacted positively to the fences. According to Sedia Modise, Botswana's wildlife director, the fences do impede wildlife migrations, but in years of drought they have been unjustly blamed for deaths that he believes would have occurred anyway. In addition, the fences have to some extent kept cattle out of the Okavango Delta, which is essential if the Delta's wildlife is to survive. However, the new 80km-long Northern Buffalo Fence north of the Delta has opened a vast expanse of wildlife-rich – but as yet unprotected – territory to cattle ranching. Safari operators wanted the fence set as far north as possible to protect the seasonally flooded Selinda Spillway; prospective cattle ranchers wanted it set as far south as possible, maximising new grazing lands; and local people didn't want it at all, for they were concerned it would act as a barrier to them as well as to wildlife. The government sided with the ranchers; the fence opens 20% of the Okavango Delta to commercial ranching.

Although there have been creditable proposals to create migration corridors between the fences, nothing has yet come of them. International groups, including Conservation International, are attempting to persuade Botswana to rethink its position. Tourism plays an ever increasing role in the country's economy and anything that harms wildlife will also inevitably affect its attraction to tourists. Currently, officials in Botswana and Namibia are discussing removing non-vital fences during migration periods. Namibia has also agreed to keep cattle away from border areas. Another possible solution is to create 'trans-national' parks, which would allow the unrestricted movement of wildlife across international borders.

However, because much of Botswana's cattle ranching industry is subsidised by the EU and the World Bank, and international guidelines require strict separation of domestic cattle and wild buffalo, it's unlikely that the fences – or the issues they raise – will go away any time soon.

### Cattle Lung Disease – Emergency Measures

The interests of cattle and people versus those of wildlife continues to be a salient political issue in Botswana, and never has it been more hotly debated than during the recent outbreak of contagious bovine pleuropneumonia, commonly known as cattle lung disease. This serious problem is caused by a bacterium called *Mycoplasma mycoides* and kills up to 50% of the animals it infects, causing heavy production losses to farmers and ranchers.

In 1939, the Bechuanaland administration eradicated the disease, but it resurfaced in 1995, when it was re-introduced across international borders – probably from Namibia – and quickly spread across the cattle-rich Ngamiland district. The government attempted to contain its spread by

constructing four veterinary fences around the north-western corner of the country, but the disease was not contained and authorities wound up slaughtering 320,000 head of cattle to eliminate the epidemic.

To guard against recurrence, the government constructed a system of impenetrable, parallel, electrified steel fences along the Namibian border and around Ngamiland. However, an environmental impact study was only completed after the fact and although opponents don't expect a massive ecological catastrophe, the fences do restrict the migrations of elephant, buffalo, giraffe and antelope and no-one yet knows what long-term impact they'll have on wildlife.

### FLORA & FAUNA

If you're looking for the Africa of your dreams – vast open savannas with free-roaming wildlife – Botswana is the best place to find it. Much of the country is protected in wild, undeveloped national parks and reserves, and areas outside the reserves are only lightly populated by humans.

While the wildlife density in Chobe National Park and Moremi Wildlife Reserve may boggle the mind, the open spaces of the Central Kalahari and Khutse game reserves and the Makgadikgadi & Nxai Pan and Mabuasehube-Gemsbok national parks present Africa largely as it has been since time immemorial.

Thanks to the Okavango and Chobe rivers, most southern African species, including such rarities as the puku, red lechwe, sitatunga and wild dog, are present in Moremi Wildlife Reserve and parts of Chobe National Park and the Linyanti Marshes. In addition, the Makgadikgadi & Nxai Pan National Park has the migration of herds of wildebeest, zebra and other ungulates between their winter range on the Makgadikgadi Plains and the summer lushness of Nxai Pan.

Realistically, rhino may be seen only in the Gaborone Game Reserve and Mokolodi Nature Reserve, both near Gaborone, and in Serowe's Khama Rhino Sanctuary. It's

BOTSWANA

likely that the rest of Botswana's rhino have succumbed to poachers, although unconfirmed sightings have been reported in Chobe and Moremi.

Most of Botswana is covered with scrub and savanna grassland, although small areas of deciduous forest – mainly mopane, msasa and Zambezi teak – exist along the Zimbabwean border. The Okavango and Linyanti wetlands of the north-west are characterised by riparian and swamp vegetation – reeds, papyrus and water lilies – as well as larger trees, such as acacia, jackalberry, leadwood and sausage trees.

## Rhino & Conservation

No large southern African animals are more endangered than the white and black rhinoceroses and, as with the elephant, their rapidly dwindling numbers have raised cries of alarm and outrage both locally and around the world. And with good reason: over the past 25 years, nearly 70,000 black rhino and uncounted white rhino have been slaughtered by poachers, thanks mainly to the mistaken Asian belief that rhino horn has medicinal and aphrodisiac properties, and the Yemeni notion that all real men need a dagger made of rhino horn.

In traditional Chinese medicine, rhino horn has been used mainly as a fever-reducing agent, and although it works to some extent, its efficacy is considerably less than that of aspirin or paracetamol. Attempts at promoting substitution of other products, such as water buffalo horn, have met with resistance from Chinese pharmacists, who claim that the 'delicate constitutions' of the relatively sedentary modern Chinese wouldn't be able to absorb such 'rough' medicines.

The dramatic decline in rhino populations has caused prices for African rhino horn to rise to around US$5700 per kg on the Asian market (Asian horn is valued at a whopping US$52,000 per kg!) and the cycle grows more vicious. As a result, in several African and Asian countries, rhino have been completely exterminated.

One can hardly blame the poachers – the risks may be great but they can net as much from a single rhino horn (from US$100 to US$350) as from a lifetime of farming. The potential rewards are so great that although around 200 poachers have been shot and killed in Zimbabwe alone, many more have got away with the goods, and poaching continues unabated. Determined conservation efforts around southern Africa have been unable to keep pace with the losses from poaching and most programmes are faring poorly. Many translocated animals die of stress. Radio collaring only reveals the location of dead animals and park patrols are daunted – and endangered – by the poachers' utter ruthlessness. There's also a lack of funding.

Dehorning programmes were once thought to be the answer, as it was thought that they'd render the animals commercially worthless. However, they've enjoyed only limited success (mainly in Namibia and South Africa, where poaching activity isn't as rampant as in other countries).

First of all, poachers will kill a rhino for the smallest stump of horn that may remain. Secondly, after a poacher has spent four or five days tracking a hornless rhino, it's shot so it won't have to be tracked again. Thirdly, Asian dealers realise the rhino's extinction will render priceless the estimated 5 to 10 tonnes of horn they currently have stockpiled in Taiwan alone (worth US$35 to US$70 million). Mainland China is estimated to have around 9 tonnes, most of which is offcuts from Yemen. To that end, dealers have ordered poachers to shoot every rhino they encounter, whether it has a horn or not. In September 1993, 90 rhino were poached in Hwange National Park in Zimbabwe; of these, 84 had been

For a more complete treatment of vegetation zones, birds and wildlife, see Flora & Fauna in the Facts about the Region chapter.

## National Parks & Wildlife Reserves

Botswana's national parks are undoubtedly among Africa's wildest, and are characterised by open spaces where nature still reigns. Even the popular parks – Chobe National Park and Moremi Wildlife Reserve – are dominated by wilderness, and although they do support private safari concessions, there's little infrastructure and

---

dehorned. To further complicate the matter, the horn grows back at a rate of around 6cm annually.

As a result, the prognosis for the black rhino is not good; their numbers in Africa have declined from 60,000 in 1970 to perhaps 3300 today, and they're being poached much faster than they can reproduce. This scarcity of black rhino has already been reflected in increased poaching of white rhino in Zimbabwe, South Africa and Swaziland.

The most effective local answer, it seems, is to educate people living in rhino country about the value of wildlife and to demonstrate that for their communities, rhino are worth more alive than dead. Many people have advocated permitting limited high-priced hunting of rhino in order to provide funding for both conservation and local communities. However, seeing some people killing the rhino that others are committed to saving from extinction may send mixed signals to local subsistence farmers, who have little experience with outside economic practices.

On a global scale, everyone can help simply by attacking the rhino horn market. The worst offender, Taiwan, is a modern industrial nation, the economy of which depends heavily on exports. The USA has already stopped the import of all wildlife products from Taiwan, but few conservationists think that goes far enough and they advocate a full-blown boycott of all goods manufactured by (or in affiliation with) Taiwanese interests. It's hoped that this may inspire the Taiwanese government to get serious about enforcing its own laws against trade in endangered species.

Other proposed solutions include commercial dehorning; after all, if the rhino aren't slaughtered, the horn becomes a renewable resource. To flood the market with legal horn would cause the collapse of the illicit trade because the market would no longer promise huge amounts of cash. The counter argument runs that dehorning currently costs around US$1000 per animal, which would make it commercially unfeasible at a price low enough to cut out the illicit trade.

Happily, some recent news has been good. First, the National Association of Chinese Medicine Practitioners & Research in the USA has advocated support for the crusade against rhino poaching and is currently seeking herbal replacements for animal products. At the same time, researchers in both China and the west have concluded that rhino horn remedies have little effect. This, along with the fact that rhino have become increasingly scarce and therefore difficult to track, has apparently stalled many poachers, and wildlife experts and conservation campaigners agree that poaching declined between 1995 and 1998 and that rhino populations in Zimbabwe, Namibia and South Africa have grown by as much as 20% (increases in Botswana are due to translocation from South Africa). In Zimbabwe, no black rhino were poached during that same period and the population increased from a low of 270 to around 330 animals. However, poaching is a growing problem in South Africa (71 white rhino and seven black rhino were poached between 1990 and 1995), which long thought itself immune.

BOTSWANA

## BOTSWANA'S NATIONAL PARKS & WILDLIFE RESERVES

| Region | Features |
|--------|----------|

### Eastern Botswana

**North-East Tuli**

This odd park is cobbled from large chunks of private land, which are operated as exclusive private game reserves. The largest is Mashatu Game Reserve, followed by Tuli Game Reserve. Remaining pieces of protected private land fall into the area collectively referred to as the North-East Tuli Game Reserve.

### North-Eastern Botswana

**Chobe**

This diverse and popular park takes in a range of habitats, from the lush elephant-rich Chobe riverfront to the mopane forests of Ngwezumba and wildlife-packed savannas around the ephemeral Savuti Marsh.

**Makgadikgadi/Nxai Pan**

When the Nata-Maun road was tarred, these two complementary reserves, which are the scene of one of Africa's last great wildlife migrations, were combined. In the dry season, the herds graze in the Makgadikgadi Pans section, but with the rains, they migrate north to the water-filled Nxai Pan.

### Okavango Delta & North-Western Botswana

**Moremi**

At the north-eastern end of the Okavango Delta, Moremi is surely Botswana's most beautiful and popular reserve, and is home to dense and diverse concentrations of large mammals.

### The Kalahari

**Central Kalahari**

This 52,000 sq km reserve is among the world's largest national parks. It was set aside exclusively for research and groups of nomadic San and Bakgalakgadi. In Deception Valley, in the north, Mark and Delia Owens conducted the brown hyaena study that resulted in *Cry of the Kalahari*. Access is extremely difficult and most tourism is confined to the northern sectors.

**Khutse**

This wild and remote reserve, the nearest to Gaborone, supports a variety of antelope and predators as well as smaller creatures like the porcupine, caracal, bush squirrel and bat-eared fox.

**Mabuasehube-Gemsbok**

This two-part park takes in most of south-western Botswana and is one of Africa's last great wilderness areas. The immense and roadless Gemsbok National Park section is accessible only from South Africa's Kalahari Gemsbok National Park. The Mabuasehube section is a beautiful wilderness of red dunes with six main waterholes that attract gemsbok and other desert wildlife.

few amenities. Only a few national park camp sites even have a long-drop loo.

For a rundown of Botswana's national parks and wildlife reserves, see the boxed text.

**Visiting the Parks**

In 1989, national park entrance fees for foreigners were hiked by a whopping 600%, and they now constitute budget travellers' biggest thorn in the side. For all parks and reserves (except the western section of Mabuasehube-Gemsbok National Park), foreigners pay US$14 (P50) per day, plus US$6 (P20) per person for camping. Children from eight to 15 years of age get a bit of a break at US$7 (P25) for entry and US$3 (P10) for camping. Botswana-registered vehicles (including aircraft) pay US$0.60 (P2) and foreign-registered vehicles pay US$3 (P10). For booking details, see Accommodation in the Botswana Facts for the Visitor chapter.

Because the government discourages independent travel, organised tour participants pay only US$9 (P30) per day for admission and US$3 (P10) to camp. Botswana residents pay US$3 (P10) per day for entry and US$1.50 (P5) to camp and Botswana citizens pay US$0.75 (P2) entry and US$1.50 (P5) to camp. For booking information, see National Parks Camps under Accommodation in the Botswana Facts for the Visitor chapter.

The multiple-level pricing is not, as some may believe, due to economic disparities between Botswana and some foreign countries – all foreigners pay higher rates, regardless of their country's economic situation. Another myth is that park fees go to maintain the parks and pay staff. In fact, park revenues are channelled into the central treasury, and the parks themselves operate on a shoestring budget.

Having said that, the rationale behind the fees seems at least partially sound. The government hopes to maximise tourism revenue while minimising expenditure on infrastructure and limiting the negative effects of mass tourism (just look at Kenya, it says). However, since few Botswana citizens have the time, inclination and means to visit the parks, the national parks and reserves are essentially private playgrounds for wealthy foreigners, tour companies, expatriate workers and overseas volunteers.

## GOVERNMENT

Botswana is one of Africa's success stories, with a stable and functioning multiparty, democratic government, which oversees the affairs of a peaceful and neutral state. Freedom of speech, the press and religion are constitutionally guaranteed.

The constitution, which was drafted prior to independence in 1966, provides for three governmental divisions. The executive branch consists of the president, who is the head of state and the head of government, as well as 11 cabinet ministers and three assistant ministers. The ministers are selected by the bicameral parliament while the president is elected by the non-compulsory vote of all citizens over 18 years of age.

The legislative branch is made up of the aforementioned parliament, which is in turn composed of the 44 seat National Assembly and the executive president. Of the Assembly members, 40 are elected by voters every five years unless the body is dissolved by an interim popular election. The remaining four members are appointed by the ruling party. Before acting on issues of land tenure, local government or traditional law, parliament must first consult the House of Chiefs. This 15-member advisory body (which has recently been fighting for expanded powers) is made up of the chiefs of the eight principal tribes, four elected sub-chiefs and three additional members jointly selected by the other 12.

Judicial responsibilities are divided between the national and local governments, with the *dikgotla* or town councils handling local civic and domestic disputes. Rural issues and services are overseen by district councils.

After each general election, the National Assembly elects the president from its ranks, and the presidential term coincides with that of the National Assembly.

## ECONOMY

Botswana's economy is one of the world's fastest growing. Aided by a stable political climate and vast natural resources, the pula is Africa's strongest currency, making Botswana's economic outlook fairly good. In 1996, the GDP was estimated to be over US$6 billion, with a per capita GDP of US$3700. By western standards, it may not sound like much, but when you consider that most people exist at subsistence level and generate little income at all, it becomes apparent that urban dwellers working at professional and vocational levels aren't doing badly.

Since independence, Botswana has experienced one of the world's highest rates of economic growth – between 7 and 13% annually. Until 1992 even the per capita growth rate was 8.5% annually, and despite an official unemployment rate of 21% (and unofficial figures of up to 40%), the predicted annual economic growth rate for 1998-2002 is 8%. In addition, Botswana's external debts are not excessive and the government actually operates within its budget, despite such excesses as its lavish military spending – for example, on the vast Mapharangwane air base west of Gaborone.

The country is also poised to become a regional free-trade financial centre. There has been a considerable relaxation of restrictions on foreign currency holdings and repatriation of profits by foreign investors. These factors, along with low personal and corporate taxes, continue to encourage foreign investment in both manufacturing and tourism.

### Mineral Resources

To some extent, Botswana's booming economy is a product of government stability, but it's also derived from a natural geological wealth, created by terrestrial heat, pressure and time working on carbon deposits laid down some 300 million years ago. The diamond-bearing geological formation in Botswana is known as the Karoo, a layer of sediments that underlies the entire Kalahari region. Within these deposits are natural intrusions known as kimberlite pipes, igneous dykes that have pushed through the Karoo rock and provided sufficient heat and pressure to form diamonds.

Botswana's diamond industry represents 40% of the country's GNP, 50% of its government revenue and 70% of its foreign exchange. It's overseen by the De Beers Botswana Mining Company Ltd (Debswana), which mines, sorts and markets the diamonds. The country's largest known deposits lie around Jwaneng (the world's most lucrative diamond mine), Orapa and Lethlakane. Between them, they produce a combined annual yield of over 13.2 million carats, and profits of over US$750 million. Debswana expects to increase diamond output to 24 million carats a year by 2000.

Other mineral resources, although not as economically important as the shiny rocks, provide further foreign exchange income. Copper and nickel are mined in large quantities at two major deposits near Selebi-Phikwe (oddly enough, the town is named after the mines, which are called Selebi and Phikwe!).

Some gold is still mined around Francistown and limited amounts of coal are taken from eastern Botswana. The most recent large-scale project is the soda ash (sodium carbonate) and salt extraction plant recently brought into operation on Sua Pan. This has been set up as a joint Botswana-South African venture to diversify Botswana's currently diamond-dependent economy. It will involve pumping over 16 million cubic metres of brine per year from 40 wells into 25 sq km of solar evaporation ponds. The expected annual yield is 300,000 tonnes of soda ash and 700,000 tonnes of sodium chloride.

### Agriculture

Because of Botswana's large extent of desert, beyond cattle ranching commercial agriculture doesn't play a major role in its economy. However 80% of the country's population depends upon agriculture to some extent.

Currently, Botswana's grasslands support over twice as many cattle as people, and since the 1950s the national herd has grown from around 400,000 to three million. Nowadays, most of these cattle are controlled by just 5000 large-scale ranchers, who are supported by World Bank loans. This is largely due to the ill-conceived Tribal Grazing Lands Policy adopted in 1975, whereby most communal lands were parcelled out to individual ranchers. About US$100 million worth of this beef is exported to the European Union annually under favourable trade agreements in which Botswana receives well above the market rates.

This encouragement to increase the cattle population has led to destructive overgrazing of large-scale ranching areas. What's more, many of the remaining traditional pastoralists in this dry land cluster around sparsely scattered bore holes. However, many of these water sources are unreliable, and in dry years, widely dispersed people herd their cattle, sheep and goats to those bore holes that remain productive. The resulting congestion puts a severe strain on the environment, and the overgrazed land suffers irreversible desertification. In the end, everyone loses.

In addition to herding, people cultivate maize, sorghum, beans, peanuts, cottonseed and other dry land crops on a subsistence scale. Larger cotton and citrus projects are evolving in the irrigated Tuli Block along the Limpopo River and dry land farming of sorghum and other crops is being tested at Pandamatenga near the Zimbabwe border.

## POPULATION & PEOPLE

Botswana has an estimated population of 1.46 million, about 60% of whom claim Tswana heritage. It currently has one of the world's highest birth rates – about 3.5% – and the average Batswana woman will bear five children. The Batswana are overwhelmingly youthful, with half the population under the age of 20. Since independence, the national average life expectancy has climbed from 49 to 69 years.

Botswana is also one of the world's most predominantly urban societies. The adoption of Christianity and a European-style central government has resulted in most traditional practices being phased out and rural villages shrinking as people migrate into urban areas in search of cash-yielding vocational and professional jobs. This demographic shift has created population centres along the south-eastern corridor between Lobatse and Francistown. Botswana's small percentage of Europeans and Asians lives mainly in larger cities, and other groups – Herero, Mbukushu, Yei, San, Kalanga and Kgalagadi – are distributed through the remote west and north-west.

In the predominant language, Tswana, tribal groups are denoted by the prefix 'Ba'. Therefore, the Herero are known as Baherero and the Kgalagadi as Bakgalagadi. The San are occasionally known as Basarwa, a Tswana word meaning 'people of the bush' or, more colloquially, Bushmen. The Tswana themselves are called Batswana, but all Botswana citizens, regardless of colour, ancestry or tribal affiliation, are also known as Batswana.

### Tswana

The Tswana are divided into a number of lineages, the three most prominent having descended from the three sons of 14th century Tswana chief Malope: Ngwato, Kwena and Ngwaketse. The Ngwato are centred on the Serowe area, the Kwena west of Molepolole, and the Ngwaketse in the south-east. An early split in the Ngwato resulted in a fourth group, the Tawana, who are concentrated around Maun in the northwest. Another group, the Kgalagadi, are probably an offshoot of the Tswana who broke away sometime around the 15th century. Since then they've mixed with the San and other peoples to form a new group, generally considered separate from the Tswana.

A typical Tswana village is a large, sprawling and densely populated affair comprised mainly of pole and *daga* huts. The individual homes are normally arranged around some commercial venture such as a food and bottle store, and a *kgotla*, a traditionally constructed community affairs hall.

Historically, the village chief lived at the village centre with the hierarchy of *wards* or family groupings arranged in concentric circles around him. Although he had councillors and advisers, the chief was considered the ultimate authority in all matters and the nearer one lived to him, the higher the family's community status.

Family units typically have three homes: one in the village, one at their fields and one at their cattle post, where village boys or San men look after the herds. As in many African societies, family wealth was once – and in some cases still is – measured by the number of cattle owned. Land, however, was not owned but rather held in a village trust and used by individual families, allocated at the discretion of the chief.

## San

Much has been written about and attributed to the San (Bushmen) of the Kalahari. The San have probably inhabited southern Africa for at least 30,000 years, but unfortunately their tenure hasn't yielded many benefits. Although they're being catapulted into the modern world, most San are still regarded as second-class citizens in both Botswana and neighbouring Namibia. One of the most fascinating peoples on Earth, they are now sadly resigned to the changes that have ended forever their traditional way of life, in which they enjoyed complete integration and harmony with their harsh desert domain.

Historically the San had no collective name for themselves, but there's evidence that some referred to themselves as 'the harmless people' or in similarly self-deprecating terms. The early Europeans in southern Africa knew them as Bushmen and that name stuck for several centuries. The Tswana generally refer to them by the rather derogatory name Basarwa, which

essentially means 'people from the sticks'. The word 'San' originally referred to the language of one group of indigenous people in southern Africa (the entire language group was known as Khoisan, and included Khoi-Khoi dialects), but when the term Bushmen fell from grace as both racist and sexist, San was adopted by Europeans to refer to several groups of non-Negroid peoples of southern Africa.

Although their characteristics and languages are distinct, all Khoisan languages share the dental and palatal clicks that have been adopted even by some Bantu groups, such as the Ndebele (see the Language section in the Facts about Zimbabwe chapter). The San clicks are of three types: '!' is the palatal click made by pulling the tongue away from the roof of the mouth. 'X' or '/' is the lateral click, formed by pulling the tongue away from the upper right teeth. 'C' or '//' is a dental click, made when the tongue is pulled from the upper front teeth.

The traditional San were nomadic hunters and gatherers who travelled in small family bands. They had no chiefs or system of leadership and individualism was respected. Personal decisions were made individually and group decisions by the group. In fact, there was no pressure to conform to any predetermined ideals, and anyone with itchy feet could leave the group without placing stress on the whole. During times of plenty, groups could swell to as many as 120 people, while during hard times, when people had to spread out to survive, they diminished to family units of 10 or fewer people.

A thoroughly mobile society, the San followed the water, the game and the edible plants. They had no animals, no crops and no possessions. Everything needed for daily existence was carried with them. Women spent much of their time caring for children and gathering edible or water-yielding plants, while the men either hunted or helped with the food gathering.

One myth has it that the San are unable to distinguish colour because most San languages contain few colour-related words. In fact, the languages are more concerned with tangibles than abstracts. It's simply considered unnecessary to separate linguistically an object from its attributes. Similarly, there's no word for work, which is a fundamental facet of life.

Another myth is that the San possess extremely keen senses of hearing, eyesight and direction. Although their awareness of their surroundings certainly seems phenomenal to the technology-dependent world, anthropological studies have determined that it's been learned as a result of necessity rather than a physiological adaptation. It's generally agreed that anyone, given the right circumstances and healthy faculties, can develop a similar awareness.

Early San encounters with other groups were probably happy ones. It's generally believed that they peacefully coexisted, and perhaps even traded, with early community-minded Bantu groups who moved in from the north. Eventually, however, the pressure of the Bantu numbers forced the San to take action. Some made themselves quite unpopular by purloining the Bantu herders' cattle. Others opted to attempt integration with the black communities, but they almost invariably wound up as slaves. Still others abandoned their traditional hunting grounds and sought out unpopulated areas to continue their nomadic ways.

However, the choice of unpopulated areas was quickly diminishing. The Europeans who arrived at the Cape in the mid-17th century saw the San and Khoi-Khoi as little more than wild animals and potential cattle raiders. The early Boers hatched an extermination campaign that lasted 200 years and killed as many as 200,000 people.

Of the remaining 55,000 or so individuals, approximately 60% live in Botswana, 35% in Namibia and the remainder are scattered through South Africa, Angola, Zimbabwe and Zambia. Of these, perhaps 2000 still live by hunting and gathering. The remainder work on farms and cattle posts or languish in squalid, handout-dependent and alcohol-plagued settlements centred on bore holes in western Botswana and north-eastern Namibia. Among many other Batswana and Namibians, their reputation as cattle rustlers and undesirables places them at the bottom of the human heap.

It would be pleasant to end on a more hopeful note, but the outlook for the San isn't good. The pattern, already in place among Australian Aborigines and Native Americans, is summed up in the San concept of life as a burden. Sadly, the Botswana government, which once permitted the San to use the Central Kalahari Game Reserve for traditional lifestyles, has begun allowing mineral exploration and started looking at the cattle ranching and tourism development potential of the vast reserve. Most San express the desire to join the Batswana mainstream, with access to land, education and health care, and the same rights and privileges as other citizens, but as yet, racism, prejudice and their own growing sense of worthlessness have thwarted any progress in that direction.

## Kalanga

Most of the Kalanga, who are related to the Shona, now live in western Zimbabwe, but they still comprise the second-largest group in sparsely populated Botswana. They are generally considered to be descendants of the people of the Rozwi Empire, who were responsible for building Great Zimbabwe and what is now the series of ruins centred on Bulawayo. The Rozwi were overcome and scattered by the Ndebele in the 1830s, spreading as far west as the Thamalakane River in northern Botswana and south to the Boteti River, where some were partially absorbed by the Ngwato branch of the Tswana.

## Mbukushu & Yei

The Mbukushu, who now inhabit the Okavango Delta area of Ngamiland, were originally refugees from the Caprivi in north-eastern Namibia. They were forced to flee southwards in the late 18th century after being dislodged by the forces of Chief Ngombela's Lozi Empire. The fleeing Mbukushu, in turn, displaced the Yei, who occupied the Chobe and Linyanti valleys of north-western Botswana.

The Mbukushu carried on to south-eastern Angola, just north of present-day Andara, Namibia. There, they encountered Portuguese and African traders who began purchasing Mbukushu commoners from the tribal leadership to be used and resold as slaves. The local rain-making deity also had a taste for Mbukushu infants and many people decided it was in their best interest to move on. Essentially a riverine tribe, some of the Mbukushu headed down the Okavango to farm maize and sorghum in the Panhandle area of the Delta. Their running days were finally over and, having mixed with later-arriving Tawana, many remain in and around the villages of Shakawe and Sepupa.

Meanwhile, the Yei scattered down the Panhandle, roaming as far south as Lake Ngami. Essentially a matrilineal society, they never settled in large groups and eventually melted into the islands and channels of the Okavango Delta where they travelled around the shallow waters by *mokoro*, or pole boat.

Like the Mbukushu, many Yei have now mixed with the Tawana, who arrived in the mid-19th century, although the connection wasn't entirely voluntary. The Yei were conquered by the more powerful Tawana and forced into clientship, a sophisticated form of enslavement in which the client's lot was similar to that of a serf in a fiefdom. Interestingly, the Yei (who were second-class citizens in Tawana society) themselves took clients from among the San, who wound up at the bottom of the heap. Many Yei still inhabit the Delta, depending mainly upon fishing and hunting.

### Herero

The colourfully dressed Herero women, attired in their full-length Victorian-style finery on even the most stifling days, will be noticed by most visitors to Maun and western Botswana. The unusual dress, which is now a tribal trademark, was forced upon them by prudish German missionaries in the late 19th century. The men, when traditionally dressed, wear a variation on the Scottish tartan kilt.

The Herero probably originated in eastern or central Africa and migrated across the Okavango River into north-eastern Namibia around the early 16th century. There, the group apparently split: the Owambo settled down to farming along the Kunene and Okavango rivers and the Herero moved south to the Central Plateau. Disputes with the Nama sent one contingent into the Kaokoveld of north-western Namibia (where they developed into the Himba). Subsequent disputes created another sub-group, the Mbanderu, which moved eastwards and adopted a pastoral lifestyle in the western Kalahari.

The nomadic Herero never practised farming and were dependent upon their cattle, which took on a religious significance as the source of Herero life. The Herero dietary staple was *omaeru* (sour milk).

In 1884 the Germans took possession of South West Africa (Namibia) and summarily took over the Herero grazing lands in that country. While the Germans were engaged in a war with the Nama, the Herero, hardened by their own years of war with the Nama, seized the chance to take revenge for injustices meted out by the colonials and attacked a German settlement, killing about 150 people. Predictably, the Germans came back with a vengeance and the remaining Herero were forced to abandon their herds and flee into Botswana.

The refugees settled among the Tawana and were initially subjugated to clientship, but eventually regained their herds and independence. Today they are among the wealthiest herders in Botswana and, now that Namibia is independent, many speak of returning to the 'old country' with which they still seem to feel strong kinship. The Botswana government, however, has stipulated that returnees to Namibia must do so permanently and without their animals or other personal assets that were acquired while in Botswana. So far, only a handful have made the move.

## EDUCATION

Sadly, the colonial government almost entirely neglected matters of health and education of the Batswana, and five years after independence, literacy was still at less than 15%. Over the next 10 years, however, diamond funds became available and the government used them to step up its primary education programmes. By 1981, an amazing 84% of primary school-aged children (years one to seven) were attending classes and secondary and tertiary education was offered as well.

Approximately 97% of Botswana's primary school-aged children – both boys and girls – are now attending school. Currently, however, only 33% of the population has access to a full secondary education. In rural areas, only seven to nine years of schooling are available locally.

### The Brigades

The Brigades movement was founded in 1965 by Patrick van Rensburg, headmaster of the Swaneng Hill Secondary School in Serowe. It was designed as a means of providing vocational training in carpentry, horticulture, forestry, welding, construction and other subjects for early school-leavers. Brigades schools operate on an apprentice system whereby classroom and practical training are given concurrently.

### The University of Botswana

On 1 January 1964, the University of Basutoland, Bechuanaland and Swaziland opened in Lesotho in answer to black Africans' need for an alternative to a South African university education. After Lesotho nationalised the university campus in 1975, Batswana and Swazi students removed themselves to a new campus in Swaziland – the University of Botswana and Swaziland. In 1980, the two divided into fully independent schools, and on 23 October 1982,

the University of Botswana was founded at Gaborone. It now has a total enrolment of over 3000 full-time undergraduate students and 400 part-time students. Staff from all over the world are employed to assist with the institution's rapid growth and graduate programmes have been developed.

## ARTS

### Material Arts

The original Batswana artists were everyday people who managed to inject individuality, aesthetics and aspects of Batswana life into their utilitarian implements. Baskets, pottery, fabrics and tools were decorated with traditional designs. Europeans introduced a new sort of art, some of which was integrated and adapted to local interpretation, particularly in weavings and tapestries. The result is some of the finest and most meticulously executed work in southern Africa.

Hoping to provide a cash income for rural Batswana, the Botswanacraft Marketing Company was set up by the government-run Botswana Development Corporation to identify the best of cottage creativity and purchase it for resale or export. The company has now been privatised and sells baskets and artwork from all over Africa, but still ensures that the bulk of the profit goes to the producer. In addition, it holds an annual basketry competition and awards bonuses for the highest-quality work. For more information or a catalogue, contact Botswanacraft (☎ 312471, fax 313189), PO Box 486, Gaborone.

Visitors to rural areas have the opportunity to purchase crafts directly from the producers. Alternatively, you can visit one of the several weaving and craft cooperatives around the country. Whether you're buying or just appreciating the artisans' skill, you can't fail to be impressed by the quality of what's on offer.

**Botswana Baskets** Botswana baskets are the most lauded of the country's material arts. Interestingly, some of the most beautiful designs aren't indigenous, but were brought to north-western Botswana by Angolan Mbukushu refugees in the last century.

Although the baskets are still used practically – for storage of seeds, grains and *bojalwa* mash for sorghum beer – the art has been finely tuned and some of the work is incredibly exquisite, employing swirls and designs with such evocative names as Flight of the Swallow, Tears of the Giraffe, Urine Trail of the Bull, Knees of the Tortoise, Roof of the Rondavel, Forehead of the Zebra, Back of the Python and The Running Ostrich.

The baskets are made from fibrous shoots from the heart of the mokolane palm (*Hyphaene petersiana*), which are cut and boiled in natural earth-tone dyes. Dark brown comes from motsentsila roots and tree bark, and pink and red are derived from a fungus that grows in sorghum husks; blood, ochre, clay and cow dung are also used as dyes. The mokolane strips are wound around a base of coils made from vines or grass. From start to finish, a medium-sized basket may require two to three weeks to make.

Generally, the finest and most expensive work comes from Ngamiland; more loosely woven but still beautiful Shashe baskets are produced mainly around Francistown.

**Weavings** Contemporary weavings – tapestries, rugs, bed covers and the like made from *karakul* wool – combine African themes with formats adopted from European art to produce work that appeals to both cultures. Most of the country's output is produced at two weaving co-operatives in south-eastern Botswana: the Lentswe-la-Odi weavers in Odi village and the newer Tiro ya Diatla in Lobatse, where artists are given free reign to choose their own themes, colours and presentation. Some of the results are truly inspired.

**Woodcarving** Woodcarving has been used traditionally in the production of such practical items as tools, spoons, bowls and containers from the densely grained wood of the mopane tree. Artists are now using mopane wood to produce jewellery, as well as both realistic and fantastic figurines of animals and renditions of more modern innovations such as tractors and aeroplanes.

**Pottery** The original pottery used in Botswana was constructed from smoothed coils and fired slowly, leaving it porous. Therefore, evaporation through the pot was possible and provided a sort of refrigeration system, keeping the liquid inside cool and drinkable on even the hottest days. Although today's productions are more modern in appearance, traditional patterns and designs are still used at pottery workshops around the country. The most accessible are Thamaga Pottery in Thamaga and Pelegano Pottery in Gabane, both in small villages west of Gaborone.

**Other Material Arts** The San of western Botswana are adept at creating seed-and-bead bracelets and necklaces, and beaded leather bags and aprons. The beads were traditionally handmade from ostrich eggshells, but nowadays plastic beads are the norm. It's just as well: not only are the ostriches happier, but some countries don't allow the import of ostrich egg products.

Herero women are skilled at making dolls dressed in Herero costume from fabric and other natural materials. The dolls are much in demand and may be found around Maun and Ghanzi.

**Literature**

Since the indigenous languages have only been written since the coming of the Christian missionaries, Botswana doesn't have much of a literary tradition. What survives of the ancient myths and praise poetry of the San, Tswana, Herero and other groups has been handed down orally and only recently written down.

Botswana's most famous modern literary figure was South African-born Bessie Head, who settled in Sir Seretse Khama's village of Serowe. Her writings, many of which are set in Serowe, reflect the harshness and the beauty of African village life and indeed of the physical attributes of Botswana itself. Her most widely read works include *Serowe – Village of the Rain Wind*, *When Rain Clouds Gather*, *Maru*, *A Question of Power*, *The Cardinals*, *A Bewitched Crossroad* and *The Collector of Treasures*; the last is an anthology of short stories. Bessie Head died in 1988.

## Architecture

A typical Tswana village is comprised mainly of pole and daga rondavels, known as *ntlo*. Some of these traditional homes are constructed from bricks (*dipolwane*), which are made from soil taken from termite mounds. The final product is then plastered with a mixture of termite mound soil and cow dung (*boloko*). In places short of termite mounds, homes are built from woven sticks plastered with ordinary mud and cow dung.

The roof poles (*maotwana*) to support the thatching are taken from strong solid trees and lashed together with flexible branches. The thatching grass itself, called *motshikiri*, is then sewn onto these flexible branches. When it's finished; the thatch is coated with oil and ash to discourage infestation by termites. Barring weather-related problems, a good thatching job can last five to 15 years and a rondavel can last 30 years or more.

Often, the outside of the hut is then decorated with a paint made from a mixture of cow dung and different coloured soils. Most of these are lovely and can be quite fanciful.

## RELIGION

Botswana's early tribal religions were primarily cults in which ancestors directed family matters from their underworld domain and were contactable only through the heads of family groups. Religious rites included the *bogwera* and *bojale* – or male and female initiation ceremonies – and the *gofethla pula* or rain-making rites. The supreme being and creator, who was incidental in the scheme of things, was known as Modimo.

Polygamy was practised. The head wife wasn't necessarily the first wife, but rather the one with whom an inheritance agreement had been made prior to marriage. A man's estate was inherited by the children of his head wife, while his cattle were typically transferred to that woman's family.

San folklore is rich with the sort off supernatural explanations for natural events that pervade many cultures. Their traditional religious beliefs are quite simple and not burdened with dogma or ritual. Their two supernatural beings represent good and evil, order and entropy. N!odima, the good, is the omnipotent creator who seems to have little time to meddle in the affairs of mortals. His opponent, Gcawama, is a mischievous trickster who spends his time trying to create disorder from the perfect natural organisation laid down by N!odima. Gcawama, unfortunately, seems to take a bothersome amount of interest in the lives of humans.

Like that of most Africans, the religion of the Herero was based upon ancestor worship. In their estimation the first ancestor, Mukuru, surpassed even Ndjambi, their supreme deity. So revered were the ancestors that Herero men set aside up to 200 head of cattle for their purposes. When a man died, his reserved beasts were sacrificed to keep the ancestors in a pleasant mood lest his family suffer.

When the first Christian missionaries arrived in the early 19th century, they brought with them an entirely new set of ideas that dislodged nearly all the Tswana traditions and practices, as well as those of many other tribes. The Christians naturally forbade ancestor veneration and the rites associated with it, as well as polygamy, inheritance practices and the consumption of alcohol.

Christianity is currently the prevailing belief system in Botswana, with the largest number of Christians belonging to the United Congregational Church of Southern Africa. The Lutheran, Roman Catholic, Anglican and Methodist churches also have significant followings in the country.

## LANGUAGE

English is the official language of Botswana and the medium of instruction from the fifth year of primary school on. The most common language, however, is Tswana (also known as Setswana), a Bantu language in the Sotho-Tswana group, which is understood by over 90% of the population. It is the language of the dominant population group, the Tswana, and is used as a medium of instruction in early primary school. The second Bantu language is Kalanga (or Sekalanga), a Shona derivative spoken by those

### Greetings & Civilities

| | |
|---|---|
| Hello. (to woman/man) | *Dumêla mma/rra.* |
| Hello. (to group) | *Dumêlang.* |
| Hello! (hailing someone from your door) | *Ko ko!* |
| Goodbye. (to person leaving) | *Tsamayo sentle.* |
| Goodbye. (to person staying) | *Sala sentle.* |
| Please. | *Tsweetswee.* |
| Thank you. | *Kea itumela.* |
| Yes/No. | *Ee/Nnyaa.* |
| Excuse me/Sorry. | *Intshwarele.* |
| Pardon me. | *Ke kopa tsela.* (lit: I want road.) |
| OK/No problem. | *Go siame.* |
| How's it going? | *O kae?* |
| I'm fine. (informal) | *Ke teng.* |
| I'm fine. (polite) | *Ke tlhotse sentle.* |
| How are you? | *A o tsogile?* (lit: how did you wake up?) |
| Did you wake well? | *A o sa tsogile sentle?* |
| Yes, I woke up well. | *Ee, ke tsogile sentle.* |
| How are you? (pm) | *O tlhotse jang?* |
| Come on in! | *Tsena!* |

### Useful Phrases

| | |
|---|---|
| Do you speak ...? | *A o bua Se?* |
| Do you speak English? | *A o bua Sekgoa/ Seenglish?* |
| Where are you from? (birthplace) | *O tswa kae?* |
| I'm from Australia. | *Ke tswa kwa Australia.* |
| Where do you live? | *O nna kae?* |

| | |
|---|---|
| I live in (Maun). | *Ke nna kwa (Maun).* |
| Where are you going? | *O ya kae?* |
| What's your name? | *Leina la gago ke mang?* |
| My name is ... | *Leina la me ke ...* |
| Which way is ...? | *Tsela ...e kae?* |
| Where is the station/hotel? | *Seteseine/hotele se kai?* |
| Is it far? | *A go kgala?* |

### Food & Drink

| | |
|---|---|
| What would you like? | *O batla eng?* |
| I'd like ... | *Ke batla ...* |
| Cheers. | *Pula.* |
| bread | *borotho* |
| food | *dijo* |
| meals | *bogobe* |
| meat | *nama* |
| milk | *mashi* |
| water | *metsi* |

### Women's Health

| | |
|---|---|
| I need tampons/ pads. | *Ke mose tswalong/ Ke kopa go itshireletsa.* |
| I'm suffering from thrush. | *Ke na le bogwata mo bosading.* |

### Emergencies

| | |
|---|---|
| Help! | *Nthusa!* |
| Call a doctor. | *Bitsa ngaka.* |
| Call the police. | *Bitsa mapodisi.* |
| Leave me alone! | *Ntlhogela!* |
| I'm lost. | *Ke la tlhegile.* |

Kalanga who live in the area around Francistown.

Most of Botswana's population is of Tswana heritage, and the Tswana are known as Batswana (although the word has also come to apply to any citizen of Botswana), just as the Yei are known as Bayei. By the same token, a Tswana individual (or individual citizen of Botswana) is called Motswana. The English designations for most Bantu languages take the name of the people who speak them – for example, the Tswana speak Tswana, the Kalanga speak Kalanga, and so on. Bantu speakers refer to the English language as 'Seenglish'. The land of the Tswana is, of course, Botswana.

## Tswana

Tswana is pronounced more or less as it's written. Exceptions are: 'g', which is pronounced as 'h' or, more accurately, as a strongly aspirated 'g'; and 'th', which is pronounced as a slightly aspirated 't'.

The greetings *dumêla rra* when speaking to men and *dumêla mma* when speaking to women are considered compliments and Batswana appreciate their liberal usage. When addressing a group, say *dumêlang*. Another useful phrase (normally placed at the end of a sentence or conversation) is *go siame*, meaning the equivalent of 'all right, no problem'.

To show gratitude when accepting a gift, receive it with both hands or take hold of it with your right hand and hold your right arm with your left.

The book *First Steps in Spoken Setswana* is useful; it's available from the Botswana Book Centre in Gaborone and Francistown. The list of words and phrases in the boxed text should get you started.

# Facts for the Visitor

## PLANNING

### When to Go

If you want to hit the back roads, enjoy wildlife viewing or explore the Okavango, summer isn't the best time. Wildlife is harder to spot and prolonged rains may render sandy roads impassable and rivers uncrossable, and may even close off Chobe National Park and Moremi Wildlife Reserve. In addition, animals disperse when water is abundant, as it is then unnecessary to stick close to perennial water sources. Summer (October to April) is also the time of the highest humidity and the most stifling heat; daytime temperatures of over 40°C aren't uncommon.

In the winter – late May to August – days are normally clear, warm and sunny, and nights are cool to cold. Wildlife never wanders far from water sources so viewing is more predictable than in the summer. Bear in mind, however, that this is also the time of European, North American and South African school holidays, although June, early July and mid-to-late September are reasonably uncrowded times to visit.

### Maps

The Department of Surveys & Mapping in Gaborone publishes topographic sheets, city and town plans, aerial photographs, geological maps and Landsat images. Various regional and national maps are available to the public for US$2 to US$4 per sheet from its office in Gaborone. For a catalogue, write to the Department of Surveys & Mapping, Private Bag 0037, Gaborone. For Geological Mapping, contact The Director, Department of Geological Survey, Private Bag 14, Lobatse.

The most accurate country map by far is the *Shell Road Map*, which shows major roads and includes insets of tourist areas and central Gaborone. It's available from bookshops in southern Africa. Almost as good is the South African Automobile

Association's 1:2,500,000 *Motoring in Botswana*. The 1:1,750,000 *Republic of Botswana* map, published by Macmillan UK, contains insets of Gaborone and the tourist areas.

If you're sticking to the main routes, you can use the *Botswana Mini-Map*, published by the Map House in South Africa and distributed by B&T Directories (☎ 371444; fax 373462), PO Box 1549, Gaborone. There are several editions of this map, which variously include insets of the national parks and city plans of Gaborone. B&T publishes the *Botswana Map Pack*, which contains town plans of Francistown, Selebi-Phikwe and Lobatse on one sheet. A second sheet is devoted to Gaborone and its suburbs.

## SUGGESTED ITINERARIES

### Budget Tour

Although there's no such thing as a low-budget tour in Botswana, the following suggestions will take you to places accessible by public transport where camping options are available.

1. Kasane – camp at Chobe Safari Lodge and take river trips and game drives into Chobe National Park (two days)
2. Nata – camp at Nata Lodge and visit Nata Sanctuary (two days)
3. Gweta – camp at Gweta Rest Camp and take camping and wildlife-viewing tours
4. Maun and the Okavango Delta – camp at Audi Camp and take budget *mokoro* camping trip in the Eastern Delta (three to seven days)
5. Shakawe – camp at one of the riverside camps (two days)

### Cultural & Historical Tour

As with most trips through Botswana, this tour will require access to a 4WD vehicle and good desert wilderness driving skills. Other sites of interest not included in this itinerary are the Kgalagadi Village Cluster in the central Kalahari and Kubu Island on Sua Pan in north-eastern Botswana.

1. Gaborone – National Museum, Mochudi, Mokolodi Nature Reserve and a couple of the arts and crafts centres in Gaborone's hinterlands (two to three days)
2. Serowe (one day)
3. Nata – Nata Sanctuary (one day)
4. Kasane and Kazungula (one day)
5. Chobe National Park (two days)
6. Moremi Wildlife Reserve (two days)
7. Maun and the Okavango Delta (three days)
8. Gcwihaba Caverns and the Aha Hills (three days)
9. Shakawe and the Tsodilo Hills (three days)

## Wildlife Tour

Botswana offers some of the world's finest wilderness wildlife viewing, with rich ecosystems and wide open spaces that will present the Africa you've always dreamed about. However, unless you're booked onto a comprehensive safari package, most of the following suggestions will require a 4WD vehicle.

1. Chobe National Park – both the riverfront and the Savuti area (three days)
2. Moremi Wildlife Reserve (three days)
3. Maun and the Okavango Delta – fly-in trip to the Inner Delta, with visits to Chiefs Island (five days)
4. Makgadikgadi and Nxai Pan National Park – with game drives through the Makgadikgadi Pans region and visits to Baines' Baobabs and Nxai Pan (three days)
5. Nata Sanctuary (one day)
6. Serowe and Khama Rhino Sanctuary (one day)
7. Gaborone and Mokolodi Nature Reserve (one day)
8. Khutse Game Reserve (two days)

## HIGHLIGHTS

Outside the cities, there's little that's artificial or pretentious about Botswana. What it lacks in diversity, it happily makes up for in inspiration. Although it's missing the diverse attractions found in neighbouring countries, its appeal lies in the pristine wildness of its empty spaces, the friendly, unhurried pace of its rural villages and the stability and security inherent in its peaceful nature. See the Botswana Highlights boxed text on the following page for details of the top attractions.

## TOURIST OFFICES
### Local Tourist Offices

The national tourism office in Gaborone (☎ 353024; fax 371539) is conveniently located on The Mall, the heart of all activity in the capital. It has maps, pamphlets and brochures and the staff are quite helpful with queries. Less useful are the offices in Kasane (☎ 250327) and Maun (☎ 260492), opposite the airport.

## VISAS & DOCUMENTS
### Visas

All foreign travellers need a valid passport. For tourist visits, no visas are required by citizens of the following: Commonwealth countries (except Ghana, India, Mauritius, Nigeria and Sri Lanka), EU countries (except Spain and Portugal), Iceland, Israel, Liechtenstein, Namibia, Norway, Pakistan, San Marino, South Africa, Switzerland, the USA, Uruguay and Samoa. Others may apply for visas through Botswana diplomatic missions or, where there is no Botswana representation, a British High Commission. Alternatively, apply by post to the Immigration and Passport Control Officer (☎ 374545), off Khama Crescent, PO Box 942, Gaborone.

Text on the following pages includes lists of embassies and diplomatic missions.

**Visa Extensions** Visitors are initially granted 30 days, which may be extended for up to a total of three months. You may be asked to show an onward airline ticket or sufficient funds for your intended stay.

For tourist visits lasting over three months, apply to the Immigration Office (☎ 374545), PO Box 942, Gaborone before your trip. Otherwise, you may remain for a maximum of 90 days in any 12-month period. Renewable three-year residence permits are generally available to those with skills that are in demand. See under Work later in this chapter.

### Other Documents

Visitors may use their home driving licence for up to six months (licences not in English

## BOTSWANA HIGHLIGHTS

| Region | Feature |
|---|---|
| **Eastern Botswana** | |
| Tuli Block | Lying along the Limpopo River, the private wildlife reserves and Old West scenery of the Tuli Block make it appealing for wealthy, well heeled travellers. |
| Serowe | Sprawling Serowe, home of Sir Seretse Khama and his forebears, is said to be the largest village in sub-Saharan Africa. The museum devoted to the history of the Khama clan merits a visit. The new Khama Rhino Sanctuary outside Serowe protects Botswana's last rhinos. |
| **North-Eastern Botswana** | |
| Chobe National Park | Actually several parks in one, the wildlife-rich and elephant-ravaged Chobe riverfront and the inland marshes and savannas make Botswana's most accessible game park the country's second most visited area. |
| Sua Pan | The vast, featureless expanses of Sua Pan have been immortalised in the popular 1985 film *The Gods Must Be Crazy* and in the more recent spectacular film *March of the Flame Birds*. Sua Spit, which juts into Sua Pan, is the site of Botswana's lucrative soda ash mining. |
| Makgadikgadi & Nxai Pan National Park | The beautiful grasslands of Makgadikgadi provide habitat for most species of Botswana wildlife. The grassy expanses of the ancient Nxai Pan lake bed are a unique rainy season gathering place for migrating wildlife. Nearby are Baines' Baobabs, an incongruous stand of misanthropic trees. |
| **Okavango Delta & North-Western Botswana** | |
| Okavango Delta | Botswana's supreme tourist destination is an African highlight – a maze of channels and wildlife-rich islands. Pristine Moremi Wildlife Reserve supports a full complement of archetypal African landscapes and wildlife. |
| Tsodilo Hills | Brought to world attention by Laurens van der Post in *Lost World of the Kalahari*, the remote and mystical Tsodilo Hills are an incredible gallery of ancient San paintings. They're not only the country's most impressive peaks, but also one of its best hiking areas. |
| Gcwihaba Caverns | Remote and forgotten, the Gcwihaba Caverns (Drotsky's Cave) in the heart of the Kalahari offer an undeveloped underground experience for adventurous travellers. |
| **The Kalahari** | |
| The Kalahari | Although several of the other Top 10 attractions lie in the Kalahari, the land itself offers the opportunity to experience a spectacular solitude all its own. If possible, don't miss a starry night camping in its wild expanses. Botswana's aboriginal inhabitants, the San, maintain that at night in the Kalahari 'you can hear the stars in song'. |

must be accompanied by a certified English translation), after which they must apply for a Botswana licence. There's no driving test involved; just present your old licence and pick up the local one.

Those entering by vehicle need current vehicle registration papers from the vehicle's home country and evidence of third-party insurance from somewhere in the Southern African Customs Union (South Africa, Botswana, Namibia, Lesotho, Swaziland). Otherwise, drivers must purchase insurance at the border. All foreign vehicles are subject to a road safety levy of US$1.50 (P5) upon entry.

## EMBASSIES & CONSULATES
### Botswana Diplomatic Missions

In countries where Botswana has no diplomatic representation, information and visas are available through British embassies or high commissions.

*EU (European Union)*
   Botswana Embassy & Mission to the EU, 169 Ave de Tervueren, 1150 Brussels, Belgium (☎ (027) 356110; fax 356318)
*South Africa*
   Botswana High Commission, 24 Amos St, Colbyn (☎ (012) 342 4760; fax 342 1845)
*UK*
   Botswana High Commission, 6 Stratford Place, London W1N 9AE (☎ (0171) 499 0031; fax 495 8595)
*USA*
   Botswana Embassy, 1531 New Hampshire Ave NW, Washington, DC 20008 (☎ (202) 244-4990; fax 244-4164)
*Zambia*
   High Commission of the Republic of Botswana, 5201 Pandit Nehru Rd, PO Box 31910, Lusaka (☎ (01) 250019; fax 253895)
*Zimbabwe*
   High Commission of the Republic of Botswana, 22 Phillips Ave, Belgravia, Harare (☎ (14) 729551; fax 721360)

### Foreign Embassies & Consulates in Botswana

The addresses of all the diplomatic missions below are in Gaborone. As yet, South Africa has no representation in Botswana.

*Angola*
   Angolan Embassy, 5131 Nelson Mandela Rd, Private Bag 111, Broadhurst (☎ 300204; fax 375089)
*EU*
   Delegation of the EU to Botswana, 68 North Ring Rd, PO Box 1253 (☎ 314455; fax 313626)
*France*
   French Embassy, 761 Robinson Rd, PO Box 1424 (☎ 353683; fax 356114)
*Germany*
   German Embassy, 3rd Floor, Professional House, Broadhurst, PO Box 315 (☎ 353143; fax 353038)
*Namibia*
   Namibian Embassy, BCC Building, 1278 Lobatse Rd, PO Box 1586 (☎ 372685)
*Netherlands*
   Netherlands Consulate, 2534 Nyerere Dr, PO Box 10055 (☎ 302194; fax 351200)
*UK*
   British High Commission, Queens Road, The Mall, Private Bag 0023 (☎ 352841; fax 356105)
*USA*
   US Embassy, Government Enclave, Embassy Dr, PO Box 90 (☎ 353982; fax 356947)
*Zambia*
   Zambia High Commission, Zambia House, The Mall, PO Box 362 (☎ 351951; fax 353952)
*Zimbabwe*
   Zimbabwe High Commission, Orapa Close, The Mall, PO Box 1232 (☎ 314495; fax 305863)

For general information on what your embassy can and can't do for you when you are travelling in a foreign country, see Embassies in the Regional Facts for the Visitor chapter.

## CUSTOMS

Botswana is a member of the Southern African Customs Union, the members of which allow unrestricted duty-free carriage of items between them. Goods brought into Botswana from any other country are subject to normal Botswana duties unless they're to be re-exported.

Visitors may import up to 400 cigarettes, 50 cigars and 250g of tobacco duty-free. South African alcohol is subject to duty, but

BOTSWANA

otherwise you can import up to 2L of wine and 1L of beer or spirits duty-free. Cameras, film and firearms must be declared upon entry but aren't subject to duty. All edible animal products, including untinned meat, milk and eggs, are confiscated at the border.

Special regulations apply to importing items such as unworked metals and precious stones, live plants, game trophies, pets and firearms. Information and application forms for bringing in animals or birds are available from the Director of Veterinary Services, Private Bag 0032, Gaborone, Botswana.

## MONEY

Travellers must declare their currency upon entry, and when departing must estimate the amount of money spent in Botswana; this is to determine how much tourists are spending and to ensure no-one takes more money out than they brought in (which would be a bad idea without a work permit).

Officially, foreigners may export up to US$185 (P500) in cash or up to US$370 (P1000) in foreign bank notes. Any more than that should be in travellers cheques. You may hear of meticulous scrutiny at the border, but people are rarely asked to show either their currency or their travellers cheques.

### Costs

If you want to enjoy your Botswana visit, the first thing to remember about money is to bring a lot of it. Botswana's tourism policy makes things difficult for budget travellers, and travelling cheaply, while not impossible as long as hitchhiking is permitted, will prove frustrating. If you can't afford a flight into the Okavango, a day or two at Moremi Wildlife Reserve or Chobe National Park, or a 4WD-trip through the Kalahari, think twice before visiting Botswana.

Supermarket, fast-food and restaurant prices are comparable to those in Europe, North America and Australasia. Small local food halls are normally a cheap option but

don't expect much variety beyond *bogobe* (sorghum porridge) and relish. Buses and trains aren't too expensive but they won't take you to the most interesting parts of the country. The cheapest vehicle hire is expensive by anyone's standards and to hire a 4WD formidably so.

### Currency

Botswana's unit of currency is the pula, which is divided into 100 thebe. *Pula* is also the national motto of Botswana and appears on the national coat of arms, but that doesn't mean that the Batswana are inordinately preoccupied with money. Rather, pula means rain, which is as precious as money in this largely desert country. Predictably, *thebe* means raindrop. Bank notes come in denominations of P1, 2, 5, 10, 20 and 50, and coins in denominations of 1t, 2t, 5t, 10t, 25t, 50t and P1.

Note that in some rural areas, someone may occasionally refer to the *pondo* (pound) as a unit of currency. It hails from the colonial days of pounds, shillings and pence, and is normally valued at P2.

The pula is currently stronger than even the South African rand. Generally, South African imports are priced the same in pula as they are in rand across the border, making shopping approximately 35% dearer in Botswana.

### Currency Exchange

Full banking services are available in Gaborone, Francistown, Mahalapye, Palapye, Selebi-Phikwe, Serowe, Jwaneng, Kanye, Maun, Mochudi, Ghanzi, Molepolole and Kasane. In major towns, banking hours are from 9 am to 2.30 pm on Monday, Tuesday, Thursday and Friday, from 8.15 am to noon on Wednesday, and from 8.15 to 10.45 am on Saturday. On Saturday, Barclays Bank at the Gaborone Sun Hotel is open from 8.30 am to 2 pm. The Sir Seretse Khama International Airport branch is open for foreign exchange from 9.30 am to 5 pm weekdays. Barclays Bank and Standard Chartered Bank charge US$1.50 commission on travellers cheques.

In remote towns and villages where there are no established banks, mobile banks are available at regular intervals, normally for an hour or two at the end of the month, after pay day. In Lethlakane, the bank arrives on the Debswana (De Beers of Botswana) payday, because all the town's income is generated by Debswana. In Shakawe and Gumare it comes on the government payday. Some villages have banking services once or twice weekly. For specific days and hours, which change periodically, inquire at branches in larger towns. These rural banking services may change foreign travellers cheques but not cash.

Avoid exchanging money at the end of the month or you'll face several hours in a sinuous queue of recently paid workers.

### Exchange Rates
At the time of writing the pula had the following values against other currencies:

| Australia | A$1 | = | P2.37 |
| Canada | C$1 | = | P2.72 |
| France | 1FF | = | P6.65 |
| Germany | DM1 | = | P2.23 |
| Japan | ¥100 | = | P2.82 |
| Namibia | N$10 | = | P7.69 |
| New Zealand | NZ$1 | = | P2.01 |
| South Africa | R10 | = | P7.67 |
| UK | UK£1 | = | P6.50 |
| USA | US$1 | = | P3.96 |
| Zimbabwe | Z$10 | = | P2.19 |

### Credit Cards
Most major credit cards – especially Barclays Visa – are accepted at tourist hotels and restaurants in larger cities and towns, although you can't use them to buy petrol. You can use Barclays Visa to purchase Barclays US$ or UK£ travellers cheques with little or no commission. Credit card cash advances are available in Gaborone, Lobatse, Maun and Francistown through Barclays Bank or Standard Chartered Bank. In smaller towns, you can apply at the banks for credit card cash advances but authorisation can take hours or even days.

Cash transfers from foreign banks are most convenient at Barclays where the money will be received by the Barclay House Branch on Khama Crescent, Gaborone. If the money isn't sent through a Barclays branch overseas, allow seven to 10 working days for the process to sort itself out. All money is converted to pula on receipt (with a commission plus a transfer fee deducted). To convert it into US$ or UK£ to purchase travellers cheques, yet another commission is taken.

### Tipping
While tipping isn't exactly required, the official policy of promoting only upmarket tourism has raised expectations in many tourist hotels and restaurants. In most places a service charge is added as a matter of course, but if your service has been excellent, leave about 10%. Taxi drivers generally aren't tipped.

## POST & COMMUNICATIONS
### Post
Although generally reliable, the post can be painfully slow; allow at least two weeks for delivery to or from an overseas address. In major towns, post offices are open between 8.15 am and 4 pm, closing for lunch from 12.45 to 2 pm. Expect long, slow-moving queues while the lackadaisical postal employees chat on the phone or among themselves between customers.

**Postal Rates** Currently, for letters or postcards weighing up to 10g, postal rates are 60t within Botswana, Namibia, Zimbabwe or South Africa; P1 to the rest of Africa; P1.75 to Europe; and P2 to anywhere else. Items weighing from 10 to 20g cost P2 to Europe and P2.50 elsewhere.

**Sending Mail** To post or receive parcels, go to the parcel office at the main post office, fill out the customs forms and/or pay duties. Parcels may be plastered with all the sticky tape you like, but they must also be tied up with string and sealing wax; bring matches to seal knots with the red wax provided. To pick up parcels, you must present a passport or other photo ID.

BOTSWANA

Aerogrammes (sold at post offices) and postcards are the least expensive to send, followed by 2nd class airmail letters, which are designated by clipping the corners off the envelope.

**Receiving Mail** The best poste restante address is the main post office on The Mall in Gaborone. If you are staying for a while, get on the waiting list for a post box as soon as possible. It can take years to get a box and meanwhile, you'll have to rely on poste restante or receive mail via your employer's private bag.

**Telephone**
Botswana's country code is 267; there are no regional area codes, so when phoning Botswana from outside the country, you should dial 267 followed by the telephone number. When dialling an outside number from Botswana, the international access code is 00; this should be followed by the desired country code, area code and telephone number.

Reliable call boxes may be found around post offices in all major towns. Direct dialling is available to most locations within Botswana, but for international calls you'll have to use the operator and have pockets full of coins to slot into the box.

Gaborone and Francistown have good but slow telephone offices for international calling. The offices are only open during normal business hours, so if you're phoning Australia or North America you'll probably be dragging someone out of bed.

Few if any countries have reciprocal reverse charges agreements with Botswana, but time and charges information is available for private telephones immediately after you hang up; request it when booking the call.

**Fax**
Fax services are now commonly used by businesses in Botswana. A good place to send or receive faxes is the Copy Centre in Gaborone. See Post & Communications in the Gaborone chapter.

## INTERNET RESOURCES
The Lonely Planet Web site (www.lonely planet.com) has several pages with information relevant to visitors to Botswana. The *Botswana Focus* magazine has an online version (www.africantravel.com /stbrob.html). Other useful addresses are given in relevant places throughout the Botswana chapters.

## BOOKS
The Botswana Book Centre on The Mall in Gaborone is one of the region's best-stocked bookshops, with international literature, novels, reference books, school texts and souvenir publications. For book exchange, see J&B Books upstairs at Broadhurst North Mall. There's also an excellent bookshop on The Mall in Selebi-Phikwe. Smaller and more limited selections are available at several bookshops in Francistown and Maun.

### Literature & Fiction
Perhaps because Botswana hasn't had the sort of tumultuous history that inspires creative outpouring of social statement, Botswana's indigenous literature is limited to the writings of Bessie Head (see Arts in the Facts about Botswana chapter) and the turn-of-the-century works by Sol Plaatje.

Neither has the country inspired much foreign fiction. For light reading, try Wilbur Smith's *The Sunbird*, two fanciful, well told tales about the mythical 'Lost City of the Kalahari', or *A Story Like the Wind* and its sequel *A Far Off Place*, Sir Laurens van der Post's fictional treatments of a meeting between European and San cultures.

### History
The best historical treatment of Botswana is the *History of Botswana* by T Tlou & Alec Campbell. The colourfully insightful *Monarch of All I Survey: Bechuanaland Diaries 1929-1937*, by Sir Charles Rey, chronicles the author's eight years as Resident Commissioner of Bechuanaland and the ho-hum attitude of the British towards the protectorate.

*A Marriage of Inconvenience: The Persecution of Seretse and Ruth Khama* by Michael Dutfield details negative responses to the marriage of Ngwato heir Seretse Khama and Englishwoman Ruth Williams in the 1950s.

*Serowe – Village of the Rain Wind* by Bessie Head straddles the division between history and literature, revealing the village of Serowe through interviews with its residents. It's marvellous reading for its insight into modern village life in Botswana.

### Personal Accounts

*Cry of the Kalahari* by Mark & Delia Owen is an entertaining and readable account of an American couple's seven years studying brown hyaenas in Deception Valley in the Central Kalahari. This book is to Botswana what *The Snow Leopard* is to Nepal and *Gorillas in the Mist* is to Rwanda.

The memoir *Starlings Laughing*, by June Vendall-Clark, chronicles 43 years at the end of Africa's colonial era. The author spent many years in the Maun area.

Elizabeth Marshall Thomas' hard-to-find work *The Harmless People* is a collection of informal and sensitive observations of the Kalahari San by an American woman living among them.

The well written anthropological classic *Lost World of the Kalahari*, by Laurens van der Post, is essential reading for anyone interested in the lifestyles of traditional San people. The author's quest for an understanding of their religion and folklore is continued in his subsequent works, *Heart of the Hunter* and *The Voice of Thunder*.

### Natural History

*Kalahari – Life's Variety in Dune and Delta* by Michael Main studies Kalahari vegetation, wildlife, geology and cultural history. Colour photos and lots of personality keep it moving along smoothly. *Okavango – Jewel of the Kalahari* by Karen Ross is a typical BBC production, filled with stunning photos outlining the Okavango's natural and cultural wonders.

The *Shell Field Guide to the Common Trees of the Okavango Delta & Moremi Reserve* by Veronica Roodt includes scientific data on Okavango vegetation, as well as legends about its trees. The informative descriptions are accompanied by useful paintings and drawings.

### Language

There are a couple of English-Tswana dictionaries as well as the useful *First Steps in Spoken Setswana*, available at the Botswana Book Centre in Gaborone. The 19th-century *Setswana-English Phrasebook*, by Molepolole missionary A J Wookey, provides some of the most amusing available insights into colonial thinking.

## NEWSPAPERS & MAGAZINES

The government-owned *Daily News*, published by the Ministry of Information and Broadcasting, is distributed free in Gaborone and features Botswana government issues as well as national and international news. There are also four weekly independent papers: the *Gazette* (Thursday), the *Botswana Guardian* (Friday) and the *Midweek Sun* (Wednesday) take a middle-of-the-road political stance and present general national news; for something more politically vocal, check out the left-leaning *Mmegi* (Reporter), published on Wednesday. Its relentless criticism of Botswana's government is a tribute to tolerance for dissent.

South African dailies provide an array of voices, and some hotels and bookshops sell the *International Herald Tribune* (sometimes a week late), *Time* and *Newsweek*. The widely distributed *New African* is an Africa-oriented news magazine.

For news on local events, pick up the free *Botswana Advertiser* in Gaborone or the *Northern Advertiser* in Francistown. They're published every Friday.

Air Botswana's in-flight magazine, *Marung*, includes travel-related articles and features on Batswana arts and culture. It's available by subscription from Marung (☎ (011) 463 3350), PO Box 98034, Sloane Park 2152, South Africa.

BOTSWANA

The free *Hello Botswana*, based in Gaborone, has articles describing local events, travel and business. For subscription information, contact Hello Botswana, Desk Top Publishing & Office Services (☎ 374134; fax 357433), Private Bag 0053, Gaborone.

## RADIO & TV

Nationwide programming is provided by Radio Botswana, which broadcasts in English and Tswana. With a short-wave set, you can pick up the BBC World Service, Radio Australia, the Voice of America and the quirky American Armed Forces Radio.

Botswana's single television station, the Gaborone Broadcasting Corporation (GBC), transmits nightly beginning at 7 pm and provides a blend of British and American programming, alongside local productions. It's picked up only in Gaborone. In Maun, satellite television beams in from various sources.

Four South African stations are also available. The clearest reception is on BOP-TV, which originates in Mafikeng. The other three come from Johannesburg and broadcast South African game shows, news programmes and sitcoms in English or Afrikaans.

## LAUNDRY

Gaborone has a self-service laundrette and there's a commercial dry-cleaning and laundry service at No Mathatha shopping centre in Gaborone. Large hotels offer laundry services, but at a premium, while in smaller villages, local women fill the laundry gap for a few pula.

## HEALTH

Botswana enjoys comparatively high health care standards, and in Gaborone and Francistown hospitals provide facilities comparable to those in Europe. Dental services are available in Gaborone and Francistown, and all main towns have well stocked pharmacies.

Although the malaria risk in Botswana isn't great, prophylaxis is recommended for

travel in the Tuli Block, the north-east and the Okavango Delta. For more information, see under Health in the Regional Facts for the Visitor chapter.

## DANGERS & ANNOYANCES

Botswana's greatest dangers are posed by the natural elements combined with a lack of preparedness. For guidelines on travel in remote areas, see the Getting Around chapter.

### Police & Military

Although police and veterinary roadblocks, bureaucracy and bored officials may become tiresome, they're mostly just a harmless inconvenience. Careful scrutiny is rare, but drivers may have to unpack their luggage – or their entire vehicle – for close inspection. Officials are usually just looking for meat products.

The Botswana Defence Force (BDF), on the other hand, takes its duties seriously and is best not crossed. The most sensitive base, which is operated jointly with the US government, lies in a remote area off the Lobatse road, south-west of Gaborone. Don't stumble upon it accidentally! Also avoid the State House in Gaborone, especially after dark.

### Theft

Although theft occurs, Botswana enjoys a low crime rate compared to other African (and most western) countries. However, you should allow lots of time if you have to report a robbery to the police for insurance purposes.

## BUSINESS HOURS

Normal business hours are from around 8 am to 5 pm, often with a one or two hour lunchtime closure, normally from 1 to 2 or 3 pm. On Saturday shops open early and close at noon or 1 pm, while on Sunday there's scarcely a whisper of activity anywhere.

For banking hours, see under Money earlier in this chapter. In major towns, post offices are open from 8.15 am to 4 pm, closing for lunch from 12.45 to 2 pm. On Saturday they're open between 8 and 11 am. Government offices are open from 7.30 am to 12.30 pm and from 1.45 to 4.30 pm, Monday to Friday.

Bottle shops generally open mid-morning and close at precisely 7 pm. If you want to purchase alcohol after that hour, you will need to resort to hotel and restaurant bars.

## PUBLIC HOLIDAYS

Botswana observes the following public holidays:

1 January
*New Year's Day*
2 January
*Day after New Year's Day*
March or April
*Good Friday and Easter Saturday, Sunday & Monday*
April or May
*Ascension Day*
July
*President's Day*
*Day After President's Day*
30 September
*Botswana Day*
1 October
*Day After Botswana Day*
25 December
*Christmas Day*
26 December
*Boxing Day*
27 December
*Day After Boxing Day*

## ACTIVITIES

Because Botswana is a high-budget, low-volume tourist destination, activity tourism focuses mainly on softer or more expensive options: wildlife-viewing, 4WD safaris, mokoro trips and the like. If you're really flush with cash, however, the sky is the limit, and you can choose between elephant-back safaris in the Okavango, learning to fly in Maun or hiring a 4WD and heading off into the Kalahari. Hiking opportunities are limited to the Tsodilo Hills in the north-west and several small ranges in the south-eastern part of the country.

## WORK

Botswana is developing rapidly and the educational system can't keep up with the growing demand for skilled professionals in several fields, so if you have a skill that is in demand, the country will probably welcome you with open arms.

Those with training and experience in a variety of professions – medical doctors, secondary school teachers, professors, engineers, computer professionals and so on – will have the best chances. At the present time there is no shortage of primary school teachers or nurses, but the situation may change, so it wouldn't hurt to look for something anyway.

Most people want to remain around Gaborone or Francistown but if you are willing to work in the back of beyond your chances of finding work will probably improve considerably.

Foreign workers are normally granted a three-year renewable residency permit. Application forms and information are available from the Immigration and Passport Control Officer (☎ 374545), off Khama Crescent, PO Box 942, Gaborone, Botswana. Applications must be submitted from outside the country.

Prospective Gaborone residents should realise that the city is the world's fastest-growing capital and experiences sporadic housing shortages. Construction can't keep up with demand and many expatriate professionals live in temporary housing.

International volunteer organisations – including Danish, German, Swedish and Norwegian volunteers and the US Peace Corps – are active in Botswana.

## ACCOMMODATION

All accommodation in Botswana, with the exception of camping, is now subject to a 10% government bed tax.

### Camping

Several hotels and lodges provide camping areas with varying amenities for campers. Most have showers as well as a cooking and washing area. Campers may use hotel bars and restaurants but shopping areas are rarely accessible without a vehicle. These camps average US$6 per person per night.

Outside national parks and away from government freehold lands, wild camping is permitted. There is no legal prohibition, and if you can get out of sight – as you can throughout most of Botswana – and are self-sufficient in food, water, transport, petrol and so on, you can set up camp just about anywhere, cook over an open fire and soak up the unbelievable Kalahari night skies, sounds and smells. This could well be Botswana's greatest appeal. However, if you're near a village, enquire after the local chief or visit the police station to request permission to camp and directions to a suitable site. Remember to carry out all rubbish with you, and keep cooking fires to a minimum size.

**National Parks Camps** The national parks camps are normally rudimentary. There are several reasonably comfortable camp sites with *braai* pits and flush toilets in Moremi Wildlife Reserve and Chobe National Park, but the rest are simply cleared spots in the dust. For your money, expect lots of wildlife activity in the night.

Foreigners, who pay US$14 (P50) per day just to *be* in the park, must shell out another US$6 (P20) to set up a tent. Bookings for park entry and camp sites (maximum six people per site) are required for all parks in north-eastern and north-western Botswana – Chobe, Moremi and Makgadikgadi/Nxai Pan (at the time of writing, advance bookings aren't needed for Mabuasehube-Gemsbok, Khutse or Central Kalahari). No bookings are available at the park gates, and without a booking, you'll be denied entry to these parks.

Bookings are available up to 12 months in advance and are most readily made through the Parks & Reserves Reservations Office (☎ 661265; fax 661264), PO Box 20364, Boseja, Maun, Botswana. You can book either by fax or in person. For Chobe bookings, you can also contact the Kasane Wildlife Office (☎ 650235) at the

Kasane Chobe National Park Gate. In Gaborone, book through the National Parks offices (☎ 371405) in Tsholetsa House, opposite Debswana House on The Mall. By post or fax, be sure to include the name of the park, the camp site requested, the dates of arrival and departure, the total number of campers and whether they are citizens, residents or non-residents of Botswana. Payments (in Botswana pula) must be received within one month or you forfeit the booking. Alternatively, you can book the parks through Botswana embassies and consulates and overseas tour operators.

### Camps & Lodges

Most of Botswana's safari camps and lodges are found in Chobe National Park, the Tuli Block and the Moremi/Okavango Delta areas. They're difficult to generalise; some lie along the highways and others occupy remote wilderness areas. They range from tent sites to established tented camps, brick or reed-built chalets and luxury lodges – or any combination of these. Prices range from US$10 to camp at Gunn's Camp in the Okavango to over 100 times that at Abu's Camp, also in the Okavango, which features circus elephant rides.

Most upmarket camps are pre-booked overseas in conjunction with an organised tour or through a local travel agency or company representative. The main exceptions are some downmarket camps around Maun and Kasane, where travellers can turn up at any time.

Many lodges and camps, especially in the Okavango Delta, lie in remote areas. Access is normally arranged by the booking agency or tour organiser and is included in the package price. Other camps are readily accessible by road and are open to anyone with a suitable vehicle.

### Hotels

Hotels in Botswana are much like hotels anywhere. Every town has at least one and the larger centres offer several price ranges. However, you won't find anything as cheap as the budget end in other African countries and the most inexpensive hotels are likely to double as brothels.

Although Gaborone's housing shortage is tapering off, some hotels still provide interim housing for expatriate residents. Therefore, room availability is erratic. For upmarket accommodation, it's always wise to pre-book.

## FOOD

While eating in Botswana isn't particularly exciting – there's no delectably refined national cuisine to knock your socks off – self-caterers will find the pickings among the best in Africa. The restaurants, however expensive, normally serve decent, if unimaginative, fare.

### Snacks & Meals

Both takeaway and fast-food outlets figure prominently in Botswana's cities and towns; cheap eating in Gaborone and Francistown revolves around quick chicken and burger fixes.

As for beef, just because it's one of Botswana's main export commodities doesn't mean you'll find a cheap, high-quality supply. The best beef is exported, while a few choice cuts are reserved for upmarket hotels and restaurants. The inexpensive meat served in local establishments is evidence that cattle are considered more as a sign of wealth than a food source – they aren't slaughtered until they're ready to drop dead anyway.

To our knowledge, there's only one health-food-cum-vegetarian restaurant in Botswana – The Kgotla in Gaborone. The normally pretentious hotel dining rooms and finer restaurants concentrate heavily on beef, although fish, lamb and chicken dishes are also served.

International cuisine is available only in Gaborone, where Chinese, Indian, French, Italian, Portuguese and other cuisines are represented. In smaller towns, however, expect little menu variation. Chicken, chips, beef and greasy fried snacks are the standards, as well as *mabele* or *bogobe* (millet or sorghum porridge, respectively), or

*phaletshe* (mielies), served with some sort of meat relish. Beyond the staples, you may want to try *vetkoek* (an Afrikaans word, which is pronounced as and means 'fat cake'). This variation on the doughnut is available nearly everywhere.

### Traditional Foods

Historically, men were responsible for tending the herds and subsisted primarily on meat and milk, while women were left to gather and eat wild fruits and vegetables. The Tswana staple was beef, but each of the several Tswana groups had its own food taboos. No-one ate fish or crocodile – the latter being the totem of the tribe as a whole – and other groups were forbidden to eat their own totems. Some tribes relied upon different food staples: the Yei of the Okavango were dependent upon fish, the Kalanga ate mainly sorghum, millet and maize, while the Herero subsisted mostly on thickened, soured milk. Nowadays, *mabele* or *bogobe* form the centre of most Batswana meals, but these are rapidly being replaced by imported maize mielies, sometimes known by the Afrikaans name, *mielie pap*, or just *pap*.

Before South African imports reached the furthermost corners of the Kalahari, the desert was dishing up a diverse array of wild edibles to augment the staples. Although most of modern Botswana derives its food from agriculture or the supermarket, remote communities still supplement their diets with these items.

One of the most useful desert plants is the *morama*, an immense underground tuber, the pulp of which contains large quantities of water and serves mainly as a source of liquid for desert dwellers. Above ground, the morama grows leguminous pods that contain edible beans. Other desert delectables include *marula* fruit, wild plums, berries, tubers and roots, *tsama* melons, wild cucumbers and honey.

There's also a type of edible fungus related to the European truffle but now known to marketing people as the Kalahari truffle. This San delicacy has now been discovered by outsiders, who think it may be well received in western markets. The truffle's spores grow on the root of the woody *Grewia flava* bush, which has a small shrivelled berry locally used to make *kadi* wine. In Kalahari mythology, the truffles are thought to be the eggs of the lightning bird because the truffles' presence is revealed by rings of cracked soil around the bush after electrical storms.

The nutritious and protein-rich *mongongo* nut, similar to the cashew, is eaten raw or roasted, and has historically been a staple for some San groups.

People also gather wild animal products when available: for example, birds and their eggs, small mammals and reptiles, and even ant eggs!

Mopane worms, caterpillar-like inhabitants of the mopane tree, may remind Australians of their own beloved witchetty grub. They're normally gutted and cooked in hot ash for about 15 minutes. Alternatively, they're boiled in salt water or dried in the sun for several days to be deep-fried in fat, roasted, or ground up and eaten raw.

Because of the scanty water supply, traditional crops are limited to *monoko* (ground nuts or peanuts), *digwana* (gourds), *magapu* (melons), *dinawa* (beans) and *mabelebele* (millet).

### Self-Catering

To visitors entering Botswana from Zimbabwe and other places to the north, the quantity and variety of food available in some Botswana supermarkets may well seem amazing. You can buy anything from Marmite to taco shells, corn chips to freshly ground coffee, fresh prawns to grapefruit. If you've been haunted by food fantasies while travelling across Africa, Botswana is where they can be fulfilled.

The reason for the abundance is Botswana's long-standing trade links with South Africa. The only food items originating in Botswana are beef, mielies, bitter melons and groundnuts. In the right season, you'll also find citrus fruits, mainly oranges, being cultivated in the Tuli Block.

Prices in Botswana supermarkets and bush shops are comparable to or slightly lower than those in North America, Australasia and Europe. Open-air markets aren't as prevalent as in Zimbabwe and other countries, but there are a few. In Gaborone, the market sprawls beside the railway station and there's also a small impromptu produce market between Broadhurst North Mall and the BBS building. In Francistown, there's a small market building on Baines St just off Blue Jacket St, and lots of impromptu stalls clustered around the railway station.

### DRINKS

A range of natural fruit juices from South Africa are sold in casks in supermarkets in the major cities and towns. You'll also find a variety of teas, coffees and sugary soft drinks.

Botswana's alcohol production is limited to beer; the three domestic options are Castle, Lion and Black Label. Otherwise, bottle shops are well stocked with imported beer, wine and spirits at prices comparable to those in Europe or North America. You may want to sample some of the superb red and white wines produced in the Cape, which are available for very reasonable prices. Note that alcohol may not be sold before 10 am and that bottle stores close at 7 pm nightly and all day on Sundays.

Traditional drinks are plentiful. Several of the more popular ones are less than legal, including *mokolane* (palm) wine, a potent swill made from distilled palm sap. Another is *kgadi*, made from distilled brown sugar and berries or fungus; the flavour is enhanced with any of a variety of additives.

Legal home brews include the common *bojalwa*, an inexpensive, sprouted-sorghum beer, which is brewed commercially as Chibuku. Another serious drink is made from fermented marula fruit. Light and non-intoxicating *mageu* is made from mielies or sorghum mash. Another is *madila*, a thickened sour milk that is used as a relish or drunk ('eaten' would be a more appropriate term) plain.

## THINGS TO BUY

The standard of Botswana handicrafts is generally very high, particularly the beautifully decorative Botswana baskets, that were originally produced in Ngamiland, the district that takes in all of north-western Botswana. If you think they're too inspired to use as bins, laundry hampers or magazine holders, they make lovely wall decorations.

In Gaborone, they're sold at Botswanacraft on The Mall and at several other cooperatives, including an excellent one in the Naledi Industrial Site on Old Lobatse Rd, run by a school for disabled Batswana. A range of basketry is available in Maun curio shops, but in such villages as Gumare, the Etshas, Shorobe and Shakawe, where you can buy directly from the artists and craftspeople, you'll pay less and contribute directly to the local economy.

In the remote western regions, beaded San jewellery and leatherwork are normally of excellent quality and you'll be deluged with offers. You'll find the famous leather aprons, ostrich eggshell beads (which may not be imported into some countries) and strands of seeds, nuts, beads and bits of carved wood. The genuine articles, however, will probably grow scarcer as tourism pushes further into the desert areas and demand increases for mass-produced items. They already make some concessions to tourists, making and selling the tiny bows and arrows that foreigners often associate with the San.

Beautiful weavings and textiles are also available. Although the most inspired pieces can be quite pricey, they'll probably cost a lot less than you'd pay at home and the handmade quality and individuality easily justify the expense. The best and least expensive work is normally found right at its source at weavings co-operatives around Gaborone and Francistown.

The Herero people in the north-west sell dolls representing Herero women in the four stages of life: pre-puberty, puberty, adulthood and old age. All but the last are normally dressed in the distinctive Herero women's dress. The old-age dolls are arrayed in traditional leather costumes, which were used prior to European contact. The Herero also produce milk jugs, which are carved from a single chunk of hardwood, and containers for storing cooking fat, which have been made from wet bits of leather that have been moulded into shape.

The philatelic desk at the Gaborone main post office sells Botswana's colourful and interesting stamps, most of which are wildlife-oriented. For information, write to the Philatelic Bureau, Botswana Postal Services, PO Box 100, Gaborone.

For more on Botswana's material crafts, see Arts in the Facts about Botswana chapter.

### Export Permits

In theory, an export permit is required for any item made from animal products, including ostrich eggshells, game skins and feathers. If you purchase the item from a handicraft outlet it will have been registered upon acquisition, but anything bought directly from locals must technically be registered with the Veterinary Office.

# Getting There & Away

## AIR

Air Botswana and Air Zimbabwe fly nonstop between Harare and Gaborone twice weekly. Air Botswana flies nonstop between Lusaka and Gaborone on Monday and Friday. However, air fares to and from Gaborone and elsewhere in Botswana are generally more expensive than to Harare, Windhoek or Johannesburg.

Air Namibia serves both Windhoek airports – Eros in the city and Windhoek International 42km east of town. A straightforward way to travel between Botswana and Namibia is on Air Botswana's US$175 flights between Windhoek Eros and Maun, connecting with Air Botswana flights to and from Gaborone. There is also a weekly return flight between Maun and Katima Mulilo, Namibia.

Air Botswana and South African Airways have convenient links between Gaborone and Johannesburg twice daily with connections to and from Durban and Cape Town.

In Harare, the Air Botswana office (☎ (14) 733836) is on the 5th floor of Southampton House, at the corner of 1st St and Union Ave. In Gaborone, the office is in the IGI Building on The Mall, and also serves as the agent for Air India, Air Mauritius, Air Zimbabwe, Lufthansa, Royal Swazi Airlines, South African Airways, SAS, Swissair, Air Tanzania, Air Malawi and KLM. The Zambia Airways office (☎ 312027) is at Zambia House on The Mall in Gaborone.

## LAND

### Border Crossings

Overland entry into Botswana is normally straightforward and respectful treatment of the officers will help you avoid undue hassles. Overland travellers must wipe their shoes (sometimes even those packed away in luggage) in a disinfectant dip to thwart foot and mouth disease. Vehicles must also pass through a pit filled with the same disinfectant.

Drivers of vehicles registered outside Botswana pay US$1.50 (P5) for a road-safety levy disc. You're allowed multiple entries without paying again, so hang onto your disc.

**Border Opening Hours** Border opening hours change frequently so use these opening times as guidelines only and check locally before turning up at remote posts, especially on weekends. Some posts close for lunch between 12.30 and 1.45 pm. The international airport immigration offices at Gaborone, Francistown, Kasane and Maun open whenever scheduled flights arrive or depart. (During the winter months, Namibia is one hour behind Botswana.)

Namibia
   Mamuno/Buitepos, 6.30/7.30 am to 4/5 pm
   Ngoma Bridge, 8 am to 4 pm
   Mohembo/Shakawe, 6 am to 6 pm
   Kasane/Mpalila Island, 7.30 am to 12.30 pm and 1.45 to 4.30 pm
South Africa
   (Note: Molopo River crossings close at times of high water)
   Bokspits/Gemsbok (Molopo River), 8 am to 4 pm
   Bray (Molopo River), 8 am to 4 pm
   Martin's Drift/Groblersbrug (Limpopo River), 8 am to 6 pm
   McCarthysrus (Molopo River), 8 am to 4 pm
   Middelpits, 8 am to 4 pm
   Parr's Halt/Stockpoort (Limpopo River), 8 am to 4 pm
   Pioneer Gate (Lobatse)/Skilpadsnek (Zeerust), 7 am to 8 pm
   Pitsane (Molopo River), 8 am to 4.30 pm
   Platjanbridge (Limpopo River), 8 am to 4 pm
   Pont Drift (Limpopo River), 8 am to 4 pm
   Ramatlhabama/Mmabatho (road & rail), 7 am to 8 pm
   Ramotswa, 8 am to 4 pm
   Saambou (Limpopo River), 8 am to 4 pm
   Sikwane/Derdepoort (Mochudi), 8 am to 4 pm

Tlokweng (Gaborone), 7 am to 10 pm
Werda (Molopo River), 8 am to 4 pm
Zanzibar (Limpopo River), 8 am to 4 pm
Zambia
  Kazungula Ferry (Zambezi River), 6 am to 6 pm
Zimbabwe
  Kazungula Rd (Kasane/Victoria Falls), weekdays 6 am to 6 pm
  Mpandamatenga/Pandamatenga, weekdays 6 am to 4 pm
  Ramokgwebana/Plumtree (road & rail), 6 am to 6 pm

## Namibia

There are four land crossings between Botswana and Namibia: Ngoma Bridge between the Caprivi and Chobe National Park; Mohembo/Shakawe in the upper Okavango Panhandle; Mamuno/Buitepos, west of Ghanzi in the Kalahari; and Kasane/Mpalila Island in the far north. The first three are open to all vehicles, while Kasane/Mpalila is by boat only and mainly serves lodges on the island.

Public transport links include minibus services between Harare, Victoria Falls and Windhoek, which cross into Namibia at Ngoma Bridge. See Zimbabwe in the Namibia Getting There & Away chapter.

The Star Line bus between Ghanzi and Gobabis, Namibia (US$11), leaves Ghanzi at 8 am Saturday, crosses the border at Mamuno/Buitepos at noon and arrives in Gobabis at 4 pm. Intercape Mainliner has a bus between Windhoek and Gaborone, which leaves Windhoek at 5 am on Sunday, Tuesday and Friday and arrives the same day at 10 pm. It costs US$67.

On the Botswana side, petrol is available at Kasane, Ghanzi, Gumare, Etsha 6 and Maun. In Shakawe, it's sold by the Brigades from steel drums and costs double the price in Maun; you'll find them 5km upstream from the village.

**Hitching** Ngoma Bridge is the easiest access for hitchhikers, as the 54km transit route through Chobe National Park is relatively well travelled, and if you avoid the riverfront tourist drives you won't pay park fees. The roads through Namibia's Caprivi Strip are relatively well maintained and because most drivers stop to refuel in Kasane, it's probably best to wait for a lift at the petrol station near Chobe Safari Lodge rather than the Chobe transit route turn-off near Kazungula.

In Ghanzi, enquire about lifts into Namibia at the Kalahari Arms Hotel petrol station; most drivers leave early in the morning. Shared taxis are available as far as the border, from where you can continue along the smooth gravel road to Gobabis.

On the Namibian side of the border, inexpensive accommodation is available at the East Gate Service Station & Rest Camp. On the Botswana side, there's a shop and restaurant at Charles Hill, 5km east of the border.

## South Africa

Thanks to the Southern African Customs Union and the good nature of most Botswana immigration officials, travellers entering from South Africa encounter a minimum of fuss. Most traffic between Botswana and South Africa passes through the crossings at Ramatlhabama/Mmabatho; the Tlokweng Gate, less than 20km from Gaborone; or Lobatse/Zeerust further south. Other border posts serve back roads across the Limpopo in the Tuli Block or across the Molopo River in southern Botswana; these are open only from 8 am to 4 pm.

**Bus** An easy way to reach Johannesburg is by minibus; they leave when full from the main bus terminal in Gaborone and cost US$15. To be assured of a departure, arrive at the terminal as early as possible. Similarly, minibus services leave Mafikeng for Lobatse at around 10 am and cost US$4.

Indaba Services (☎ 660351; fax 660978) in Maun has comfortable weekly minibus trips from Maun airport to the Sandton Holiday Inn in Johannesburg for US$113.

**Train** There is currently no passenger rail service between Botswana and South Africa.

**Hitching** Hitching between South Africa and Gaborone is easy and straightforward if you stick to the Ramatlhabama, Tlokweng and Lobatse borders. Tlokweng is reportedly the most relaxed border crossing into South Africa, with few searches and well disposed officials.

### Zambia

Apart from the air route, your only straight-through option between Zambia and Botswana is the ferry across the Zambezi at Kazungula.

**Road & Ferry** However you look at it, the ramshackle ferry across the Zambezi is an experience, although perhaps not as interesting as it used to be. Once upon a time, a heavy truck had to speed on board the ferry and slam on the brakes in order to provide the ferry with enough momentum to break away from the shore. If the truck stopped a little long or a little short, the ferry was known to flip and the system would have to close down while everything was righted and cleaned up.

Fortunately, it has now been renovated and is able to cast off under its own steam. Under normal circumstances, the ferry operates from 6 am to 6 pm daily. The crossing is free for vehicles registered in Botswana, but those with foreign registration pay US$10 for cars and US$20 for pickups.

Without a vehicle, it's a quick, straightforward crossing. In Kasane or on the Zambian shore, you can pick up trucks going through to Livingstone, Lusaka and points beyond. Once in Livingstone, you can also choose between buses and trains to Lusaka.

If the delays are too long, or if the ferry isn't operating, you can cross into Zimbabwe at Kazungula, hitchhike to Victoria Falls, and enter Zambia at Livingstone, but Zimbabwe immigration may require an onward ticket.

There's also a Tuesday and Thursday bus service between Gaborone and Lusaka, which runs via Francistown, Nata, Kasane, the Kazungula ferry and Livingstone. Check at bus terminals for the best details you're likely to find. The fare between Gaborone and Lusaka is a reasonable US$60 each way.

### Zimbabwe

There are two well used border crossings between Zimbabwe and Botswana: the road and rail link at Ramokgwebana/Plumtree and the Kasane/Kazungula border west of Victoria Falls. There's also a lesser-used back-road crossing at Mpandamatenga/Pandamatenga near Kazuma Pan National Park in Zimbabwe and Kazuma Forest Reserve in north-eastern Botswana. If you're driving, fuel is considerably cheaper on the Zimbabwe side.

**Bus** Buses are operated by Express Motorways (☎ 304470) from the African Mall and the Gaborone Sun Hotel (both in Gaborone) to Francistown, Bulawayo and Harare on Tuesday and Saturday at 6 am. Although things are improving, plan on lengthy delays at the border. Between Kasane and Victoria Falls, the United Touring Company operates a transfer service for US$35.

The no-frills, Bulawayo-based Zimbabwe Omnibus Company operates a direct service daily (except Sunday) between Francistown and Bulawayo. The trip takes from three to six hours, depending on the delay at the border. Mach Coach Lines, also in Bulawayo, offers a slightly posher service six days a week at 4 pm.

The bus and minibus lines between Livingstone (Zambia), Victoria Falls (Zimbabwe) and Windhoek (Namibia) pass through Kasane en route. For details, see Zimbabwe and Zambia in the Namibia Getting There & Away chapter.

**Train** Trains run daily from Gaborone to Bulawayo, departing at 9 pm and arriving in Bulawayo at noon the following day. You can choose between 1st and 2nd class sleepers or economy class seats. Security is dodgy in any case, but in economy class, people are packed in like cattle and belongings are at risk. These trains normally have a buffet car, but never leave your luggage unattended. Fares are US$33/27/9.10 in 1st/2nd/economy class.

Sexes are separated in 1st and 2nd class sleepers unless you book a whole compartment or pay a surcharge for a two-person coupé. When there is a buffet car, you must pay for everything in pula or South African rand; Zimbabwe dollars aren't accepted on the train in Botswana.

Customs and immigration formalities are handled on the train. For further information on this route, see the Botswana section in the Zimbabwe Getting There & Away chapter.

**Hitching** Hitching between Francistown and Bulawayo via the Plumtree border crossing is fairly easy. Mornings are best for hitching into Botswana, while most afternoon traffic is headed towards Bulawayo.

Hitching is easy past the Haskins and Guy Sts roundabout in Francistown. You can also catch a minivan to the Zimbabwean border from the Francistown bus terminal for about P5 (about US$1.50). Cash-strapped minivan drivers will be waiting on the other side of the customs border to shoehorn you into one of their vans to Bulawayo for about the same price. For the reverse trip, catch a Kombi in town on Fort St between 10th and 11th Aves to Bellevue. Minivans – and the larger, slower buses – leave from the Shell station parking lot for the Botswana border. Those with any significant packs/luggage will want to try the larger bus!

**Joseph Copeland, UK**

Wait at the Kazungula road turn-off about 1km south-east of town for lifts from Victoria Falls to Kazungula/Kasane. From Kasane, the direct route to Maun across Chobe National Park should essentially be considered unhitchable. It's very rough 4WD terrain most of the way and although some people have been lucky, this is certainly the exception to the rule. Although it's laboriously roundabout, the route from Kasane to Maun via Nata will prove far quicker.

# Getting Around

Botswana's public transport network can be summed up in a couple of words: pretty limited. Although air services are relatively good, domestic Air Botswana and charter flights are pricey and the country's small population means that only a few locations are regularly served. Botswana's single railway line offers slow but reliable service, while bus services are restricted by the highway system – only a handful of main routes are viable for bus traffic.

## AIR
### Domestic Air Services
The national carrier, Air Botswana, operates scheduled domestic flights between larger communities around the country. It also runs occasional packages between Maun and Gaborone, including hotels and sightseeing. The frequently changing prices are generally quite high, but student fares are often available and you may get some relief with 14-day advance purchase.

Air Botswana has four flights weekly between Gaborone and Francistown (US$123), and daily flights between Gaborone and Maun (US$173). On Mondays, Wednesdays and Fridays you can fly between Francistown and Maun via Gaborone (US$120). Kasane is served from Francistown (US$110) on Mondays and from Gaborone (US$193) and Maun (US$143) on Mondays, Thursdays and Saturdays. Air Botswana runs special weekend fares, including a popular US$75 return ticket between Gaborone and Francistown.

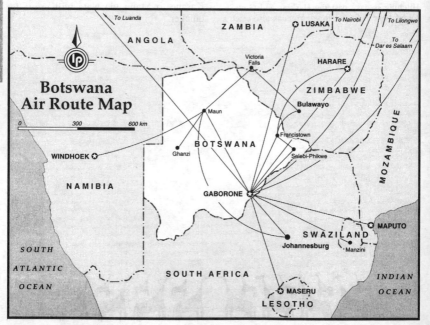

Air Botswana has offices at Blue Jacket Mall, PO Box 222, Francistown (☎ 212393; fax 213834); IGI Building, The Mall, PO Box 92, Gaborone (☎ 351921; fax 374802); and at Airport Rd, PO Box 191, Maun (☎ 660391; fax 660598). There are also offices in Kasane (☎ 650161) and Orapa (☎ 270250).

### Air Charters

Air charters provide the best access to remote tourist lodges and isolated villages. They're expensive when booked individually, but are generally better value when arranged through travel agencies or safari operators. If seats are available, you may be able to turn up just prior to departure. Otherwise, you'll pay by the kilometre for a *return* trip to your destination (they must return to their home base after dropping you off).

Agency-arranged charters from Maun to the Inner Delta average around US$100 return. Individually organised charters in a five-passenger plane cost around US$225 per hour or US$1.20 per kilometre. Naturally, more passengers mean lower prices per person; for example, flights between Kasane and Victoria Falls cost around US$73 per person with two people and US$45 per person with five. Between Maun and Kasane flights cost US$600 for the whole plane or US$119 per person, with a minimum of five people.

The major charter companies are:

*Aer Kavango* PO Box 169, Maun Airport, Maun (☎/fax 660393)
*Delta Air* PO Box 39, Maun (☎ 660044; fax 660589)
*Elgon Air* PO Box 448, Maun (☎ 660654; fax 660037)
*Executive Air* Private Bag SK-6, Sir Seretse Khama international airport, Gaborone (☎ 375257; fax 375258)
*Kalahari Air Services* PO Box 41278, Broadhurst, Gaborone (☎ 351804; fax 312015)
*Ngami Air* PO Box 119, Maun (☎ 660530; fax 660593)
*Northern Air* PO Box 40, Maun (☎ 660385; fax 660379)

*Okavango Air Services* PO Box 54, Selebi-Phikwe (☎ 313308; fax 356949)
*Quicksilver Enterprises (Chobe Air)* PO Box 280, Kasane (☎ 650532; fax 650223)
*Swamp Air* Private Bag 13, Maun (☎ 660569; fax 660571)

### BUS

Most bus and minibus services operate in the populated areas of eastern Botswana. Potential passengers should turn up early in the morning as schedules are erratic and buses normally run according to demand, departing only when full. Many travellers find all this too time-consuming and, especially along the Lobatse-Francistown route, it's sometimes better to hitch or take the slow but scheduled train.

The most frequently served bus routes follow the highway corridor between Ramatlhabama and Francistown, though often only part of the way. Buses may connect Gaborone and Mahalapye six times a day, for example, but perhaps only three of these continue to Palapye and only two go through to Francistown.

Other services operate between Francistown and Bulawayo (Zimbabwe); Serule and Selebi-Phikwe; Palapye, Serowe and Orapa; and Francistown, Nata and Kasane. Mahube Express also has services between Nata and Maun, and Maun and Shakawe.

There's no bus service through Chobe National Park between Kasane and Maun but safari companies offer reasonable three-day trips via Moremi (see the Okavango Delta & North-Western Botswana chapter). A daily minibus connects Kasane and Maun, via Nata. Between Kasane and Victoria Falls, UTC operates a pricey transfer service; book through any Kasane lodge.

Among the major bus companies are Sesennye (☎ 212112) and Mahube Express (☎ 352660), both in Gaborone. They serve Gaborone and Francistown and the latter also runs to Maun and Shakawe. KB Transport (☎ 410202) in Mahalapye runs between Gaborone and Mahalapye. Between Palapye and Selebi-Phikwe, the main operator is Loedza (☎ 810025) in Selebi-Phikwe.

## TRAIN

Although it's slow, rail travel provides a relaxing and effortless way through vast stretches of dusty and virtually featureless Botswana scrub. The railway line runs through the country between Ramokgwebana on the Zimbabwean border and Ramatlhabama on the South African border, although services currently only extend as far south as Lobatse. The main stops are Gaborone, Mahalapye, Palapye, Serule and Francistown. Second class commuter services also run between Gaborone, Pilane and Lobatse.

For further information see the Zimbabwe and Botswana Getting There & Away chapters.

### Classes & Fares

In 1991, comfortable new carriages were purchased from South Africa. Between Gaborone and Francistown, the crowded economy class carriages cost only US$8. In 2nd class, six-passenger sleeper compartments, the trip costs US$25.50. In 1st class carriages with four-passenger compartments, it's US$31.50. Bedding is an additional US$2 per night in either 1st or 2nd class. Other 1st/2nd/economy class fares from Gaborone include Mahalapye (US$19/14/4), Palapye (US$23/19/6) and Ramokgwebana/Plumtree (US$41/30/10). The fare to Lobatse (economy class only) is US$2.

### Reservations

Information, reservations and tickets are available at the Gaborone station on weekdays from 7 am to 1 pm and 1.45 to 4.30 pm. In Francistown, the office is open on weekdays from 8 am to noon and 1 to 4 pm. For 1st and 2nd class sleepers, advance bookings are essential.

### CAR & MOTORCYCLE

To see the best of Botswana, you need a vehicle (or plenty of time to wait for buses or to hitch lifts). Road journeys in Botswana fall into three categories: a high-speed rush along the excellent tarred road system; an uncertain rumble over typically poor secondary roads; or an expedition through the wildest terrain in a sturdy, high-clearance 4WD passenger vehicle or truck.

Conventional motorbikes perform well on the tarred roads and high-powered dirt bikes can be great fun on desert tracks, but in-between are roads where clouds of dust and sand kicked up by other vehicles will make for a miserable experience on a motorbike. It's important to note that motorbikes aren't permitted in national parks or reserves.

### Roads

At the time of independence in 1966, Botswana's only tarred road extended for 5km from Lobatse station to the High Court in Lobatse; it was completed in 1947 in preparation for the visit by King George VI.

Most of Botswana's population centres are now connected by beeline highways, and road-tarring projects are moving ahead at a record pace. Ghanzi-Sehitwa is the only major segment yet to be tarred, although there are also dim and distant plans to complete a highway between Rakops and the Nata-Maun road.

However, apart from the Trans-Kalahari Highway between Lobatse and Mamuno, via Kanye and Kang (with tarred spurs to Ghanzi and the Kgalagadi village cluster), the central and south-western parts of Botswana are accessible only with 4WD. Off main routes, the roads range from good, high-speed gravel to deep, rutted sand. Few roads are passable without 4WD, and some are challenging even with it. If you do venture onto remote routes, leave your planned itinerary and estimated time of return with someone who can sound the alarm if you're not in touch at a pre-specified time.

### Road Rules

As in most other southern African countries, traffic keeps to the left side of the road. The national speed limit on tarred roads is 120km/h, while through towns and villages you should assume a speed limit of 60km/h, even in the absence of a sign. Note that the highway police now use radar, as one reader learned:

We were stopped by an arm-waving uniformed police officer on the outskirts of Nata. Their tripod radar had clocked me doing 82km/h in a 60km/h zone. According to his Speed Trap sheet (that was the title!), my fine came to P142. It's a graduated scale, depending on one's speed.

Seat belt use is compulsory, as is proof of no-fault insurance. If you have an accident causing injury, it must be reported to the authorities within 48 hours. If vehicles have sustained only minor damage and there are no injuries – and all parties agree – you can exchange names and addresses and sort it out later through your insurance companies. Note that vehicles registered outside Botswana are subject to a road-safety levy of US$1.50 (P5) upon entry.

In theory, livestock owners are responsible for keeping their animals off the road, but in practice animals wander wherever they want, making it especially risky to drive at night. If you do hit a domestic animal, your distress (and possible vehicle damage) will be compounded by the effort involved in finding the owner and the red tape encountered when filing a claim. In the end, it will probably come to nought, and may backfire if the owner can prove driver negligence.

### Rental

Hiring a vehicle, especially a 4WD, will allow you the freedom to explore some of Africa's most pristine wilderness areas. However it requires a large cash outlay and the vast distances quickly rack up the kilometre charges, so it's not for low-budget travellers. To hire a vehicle in Botswana, you must be at least 25 years of age. Your home driving licence is valid for six months in Botswana, but if it isn't in English you must provide a certified translation.

Be aware of add-on charges (especially insurance-related charges), check the paperwork carefully, and thoroughly examine the vehicle before accepting it; make sure

the 4WD engages properly and that you understand how it works. Also check the vehicle fluids, brakes, battery and so on. The Kalahari is a harsh place to find out that the agency has overlooked something important.

Holiday Car Hire tends to offer the best value. For a Hyundai Accent, they charge US$28 per day plus US$0.28 per kilometre, US$55 per day with unlimited kilometres (minimum seven-day rental period), or US$730 per month with 100 free kilometres per day. A single-cab Toyota Hilux 4WD, with a 150L reserve fuel tank, costs US$50 per day plus US$0.50 per kilometre, US$98 per day for unlimited kilometres (minimum seven-day rental period), or US$1285 per month with 100 free kilometres per day. For an additional charge, they can provide camping gear and safari outfitting.

For a Toyota Corolla, Avis charges US$25 per day plus US$0.25 per kilometre, or US$40 per day with 200 free kilometres (minimum six-day rental period). For a double-cab Toyota Hilux 4WD, you'll pay US$75 per day plus US$0.75 per kilometre, or US$115 per day with 200 free daily kilometres (minimum six-day rental period).

For a Toyota Corolla, Imperial charges US$24 per day plus US$0.24 per kilometre, or US$37 per day with 200km included (minimum six-day rental). A Toyota Hilux 4WD costs US$60 per day plus US$0.55 per kilometre, or US$146 per day with 200km (minimum six days).

The following is a list of the rental offices in Botswana:

*Avis*
Sir Seretse Khama international airport, Gaborone (☎ 375469; fax 312205)
Francistown (☎ 216646)
Maun (☎ 660039; fax 660258)
Mowana Lodge, Kasane (☎ 650144; fax 650145)
*Economic Car Hire*
PO Box 1999, Gaborone (☎ 375491)
*Holiday Car Hire*
Nakedi Rd, Broadhurst Industrial Area, Gaborone (☎ 312280; fax 357996)

## Wild Driving in Botswana

Adventurous drivers in Botswana will find some of the continent's most challenging and rewarding routes. Hopefully, the following guidelines will help you successfully negotiate the bush track to insanity. For tested tips, techniques and descriptions of remote routes, see the *Visitors' Guide to Botswana* by Mike Main and John & Sandra Fowkes, which is sold in Botswana bookshops as well as in overseas travel book and map shops.

**Bush Driving** Little of Botswana's maze of criss-crossing ruts and bush tracks appears on maps, and the Department of Surveys & Mapping has given up trying to keep track of them. Most of these spontaneously created routes are maintained only by use, and they can utterly confound drivers. They'll usher you into sandy villages where tracks radiate in all directions, without a clue as to which leads where. Some provide access to remote cattle posts and then disappear, often to re-emerge somewhere on the other side of the post. Some tracks take you to larger roads or water sources. Once a route becomes too rutted, flooded or muddy to pass, a new route is created. Indicative of changing surface conditions, multiple parallel tracks split and join, cross, wander off and back, and even disappear altogether on occasion, leaving you stranded, with no way to turn but back the way you came.

**Four-Wheeling in the Kalahari** The following tips should help drivers negotiate the wildest regions of central, western and south-western Botswana:

- Take the best set of maps you can find. The Department of Surveys & Mapping in Gaborone has reasonably accurate and up-to-date maps of remote areas. Tracks change frequently, however, so ask directions locally whenever possible.
- Carry a Global Positioning System (GPS), or at least a good compass, and take readings periodically. Note that vehicular mechanisms create their own magnetic fields; to get an accurate compass reading, stand at least 3m from the vehicle.
- A reserve fuel tank of at least 150L is essential for off-road travel in central or western Botswana. In western Botswana, fuel is available consistently only in Maun, Ghanzi, Kang, Etsha 6 and over the border in South Africa and Namibia.
- Carry at least 5L of water per person per day (allowing for delays and breakdowns when calculating the trip length). Water travels best in an indestructible metal container, as plastic may not stand up to constant bumping.
- Even for relatively well travelled routes, confirm that your 4WD and other vehicular mechanisms are functioning before you set off. Spares are rarely available locally and although you'll be astounded by the ingenuity of some villagers in jerry-rigging repairs, you can spend lots of time and money waiting for a part's delivery from a larger centre.
- Travellers in remote regions must be entirely self-sufficient. This means that you'll need vehicle spares, tools and the expertise to repair problems that may arise. The minimum you should carry is a tow rope, torch, shovel, extra fan belt, vehicle fluids, spark plugs, baling wire, jump leads, fuses, hoses, a good jack (and a wooden plank to act as a base in sand or salt), several spare tyres (or a tyre lever and a puncture repair kit) and a pump. A winch and a short-wave radio would also be great safety assets and provide greater peace of mind.
- Wrap tools and solid or heavy objects in blankets or other soft packing materials and place them in the bottom of the boot or truck bed. Food should be wrapped and packed tightly in solid unbreakable containers – cardboard boxes will disintegrate on back roads. Aluminium packing boxes are available in Gaborone for under US$15. Once packed, strap everything down tightly. Keep plastic drink bottles, fragile snacks and poorly packaged items in the vehicle cab.

- A camping kit should include a tent and a warm sleeping bag as an absolute minimum. Camp beds are normally unnecessary – the soft Kalahari sand works adequately. For fire cooking, follow the locals' example and use a three-legged cast-iron *potjie* (pronounced POY-kee). A plastic basin and soap for washing up are essential to conserve precious water, and don't forget pots and pans, eating implements, a tin opener and waterproof matches.
- Sand tracks are most easily negotiated and least likely to bog vehicles in the cool mornings and evenings, when air spaces between sand grains are smaller. To further prevent bogging or stalling, move as quickly as possible and keep the revs up, but avoid sudden acceleration. Shift down in advance of deep sandy patches or the vehicle may stall and bog. When negotiating a straight course through rutted sand, allow the vehicle to wander along the path of least resistance. Anticipate corners and turn the wheel slightly earlier than you would on a solid surface – this will allow the vehicle to ski smoothly round – then accelerate gently out of the turn.
- Much Kalahari driving is through high grass and the seeds it scatters quickly foul radiators and cause vehicle overheating. If the temperature gauge begins to climb, stop and remove as much of the plant material from the grille as possible.
- Unbogging or driving on loose sand may be facilitated by lowering the air pressure in the tyres, thereby increasing their gripping area.
- When driving on the salt pans, keep to the tracks of vehicles that have gone before, or stick to within a couple of hundred metres of the pan's edge. The tempting flat, grey expanses easily become graveyards for vehicles that stick, sink and even break through into hidden subsurface cavities.
- For details of animal hazards, see Close Encounters under Activities in the Regional Facts for the Visitor chapter.

**Driving on the Pans** Prospective drivers on the salt pans should remember other standard rules. The pans have a mesmerising effect and create a sense of unfettered freedom. Once you drive out onto the salt, direction, connection, reason and common sense appear to dissolve, and you may be tempted to speed off with wild abandon into the white and empty distances – but restrain yourself.

First, follow the tracks of other drivers (unless you see bits of vehicles poking above the surface, of course), which are good indications that the way is dry. When in doubt, keep to the edges of the salt. Also, stay aware of where you are at all times by using a map and compass or (preferably) a GPS. In confusing areas around the edges of the pans, make a note of any islands or landmarks.

If you're unsure about whether the pan is dry, stick to the edges. If it has recently rained, however, don't venture onto the pans at all unless you're absolutely sure that both the salty surface and the clay beneath it are dry. Foul-smelling salt means a wet and potentially dangerous pan, very similar in appearance and character to wet concrete. When underlying clay becomes saturated, vehicles can break through the crust and become irretrievably bogged.

If you do get bogged and have a winch, anchor the spare wheel or the jack – anything to which the winch may be attached – by digging a hole and planting it firmly in the concrete-like pan surface. Hopefully, you'll be able to anchor it better than the pan has anchored the vehicle!

Merlin Travel, Maun (☎ 660635; fax 660036)
Kasane (☎ 650336; fax 650437)
*Imperial Car Rental*
  Sir Seretse Khama international airport, Air
  Botswana Headquarters, Gaborone
  (☎ 308609; fax 304460; <info@imperial
  .ih.co.za>)

## Purchase

Unless you're in Botswana for several years, it's probably not worth purchasing a vehicle. Even used vehicles are expensive and a 4WD will be out of the question for most people. A second-hand Botswana-standard Toyota Hilux, for example, starts at around US$20,000. Land Rovers cost less, but they're hard to find.

If you do buy a vehicle with hard currency and resell it in Botswana, you can remit the same amount of hard currency to your home country without hassles. Just keep the papers and inform the bank in advance.

An alternative would be to buy a used vehicle in South Africa. It's fairly easy to find a Land Rover in Johannesburg, for example, where prices are lower, then return to South Africa and sell it when you're finished. You can't sell a South African vehicle in Botswana without paying heavy import duties.

## BICYCLE

Botswana is largely flat, but that's the only concession it makes to cyclists. Some travellers still take a bike in the hope of avoiding the uncertainties of hitching and public transport, but unless you are an experienced cyclist and are equipped for the extreme conditions, abandon any ideas you may have about a Botswana bicycle adventure.

Distances are great, horizons are vast; the climate and landscape are hot and dry; and, even along major routes, water is scarce and villages are widely spaced. What's more, the sun is intense through the clear and semi-tropical desert air and prolonged exposure to the dry heat and burning ultraviolet rays is potentially hazardous.

On the tarred roads, which are mostly flat

and straight, the national speed limit of 120km/h doesn't prevent traffic cranking up the speed. When a semitrailer passes at 150km/h, cyclists may unwittingly be blown off the road. To access areas off the beaten track, bicycles are also unsuitable; and even experienced cyclists have pronounced most of the country's roads and tracks uncyclable. Along untarred roads, vehicles howl past in billowing clouds of sand and dust, and on lesser-used routes, you're likely to encounter deep drifted sand. Unless you're prepared to carry your bike and luggage over long, uninhabited distances, don't venture off the main routes. Also bear in mind that neither bicycles nor motorbikes are permitted in Botswana's wildlife reserves.

However, if you are not discouraged by the above and have a go anyway, please write in and let Lonely Planet know how you get on!

## HITCHING

Because public transport is somewhat erratic, many locals and travellers rely on hitchhiking as their primary means of getting around. On main routes, there should be no major problems.

The equivalent of a bus fare will frequently be requested in exchange for a lift. However, to prevent uncomfortable situations at the end of the ride, determine a price before climbing in. The standard charge is one or two thebe per person per kilometre, and drivers who do charge normally bring this up before prospective passengers climb aboard.

Hitching the back roads is another issue. If you're travelling between Lobatse and Ghanzi, through the Tuli Block or from Maun to Chobe, Moremi, Ghanzi or Namibia, carry camping equipment and enough food and water for several days of waiting. For trips even further afield, such as to the Makgadikgadi Pans or Gcwihaba Caverns, lifts must be arranged in advance. Your best chances of finding lifts to remote destinations are the lodges at Maun, as well as at Nata, Gweta, Shakawe and Ghanzi.

For the Lobatse-Ghanzi trip, try the Botswana Meat Corporation in Lobatse.

From Kasane, the direct route to Maun across Chobe National Park is a very difficult and expensive hitch (park fees!). Although it's laboriously roundabout, the Kasane-Nata-Maun route is easier and far more practical. (Please see the hitching warning in the Zimbabwe Getting Around chapter.)

## WALKING

Distances between towns are great in Botswana and the intervening spaces are typically empty and waterless. Outside the cities and towns, not even the local people will attempt to walk from place to place, and walking is not a practical way for you to get around in Botswana.

As for hiking and bushwalking, the best venues are the Tsodilo Hills in northwestern Botswana and the low hills around Gaborone and Lobatse. In the Okavango Delta and Moremi Wildlife Reserve, guided walks are available through private lodges and safari companies.

## LOCAL TRANSPORT

Gaborone and Francistown have public transport systems, but Gaborone's isn't really adequate for the city's growing population. Solidly packed little white minibuses, recognisable by their blue number plates, circulate according to set routes. The standard city route passes all the major shopping centres. Minibuses to outlying villages depart from the main bus terminal. Francistown's bus network is also minimal.

### To/From the Airport

The only reliable transport between Gaborone, Francistown and Selebi-Phikwe and their respective airports are the minibuses operated by big hotels for their guests. If you're not a guest and there's space available, you can sometimes talk the driver into a lift, but a tip of at least several pula is expected. Taxis turn up at the airport only occasionally; if you need one, you'll normally have to phone.

### Taxi

Although the public transport minibuses in Gaborone are known as taxis, conventional taxis are generally thin on the ground – even in Gaborone – so it's hardly worth searching for one on the street. Your best hope is to phone the taxi company and have them send one out. If you do find one, you'll have to negotiate a price with the driver. Licensed taxis are recognisable by their blue number plates.

### ORGANISED TOURS

For details of operators organising tours in Botswana, see the Organised Tours chapter earlier in the book.

BOTSWANA

# Gaborone

Botswana's capital, Gaborone, is little more than a sprawling village suffering from the growing pains, drabness and lack of definition that accompany an abrupt transition from rural settlement to modern city. Although it has a few sights – and urban planners may be drawn by curiosity about the extent of the disaster – few visitors want to linger.

What went wrong – or rather, what is going wrong – is Gaborone's lack of integration and its uncontainable sprawl. It's a bit like a nascent, microcosmic Los Angeles. Distances are long and uninteresting, and heavy traffic and lack of footpaths place pedestrians at risk. Beyond The Mall, which was an early attempt to provide the city with a heart, Gaborone lacks a central business district. New buildings and suburbs sprout like mushrooms wherever there's a block of land to fit them, resulting in a mix of low-cost housing, blocks of flats, shopping centres and industrial complexes.

## History

Archaeological evidence indicates that the site of Gaborone has been inhabited since the middle Stone Age. Excavations below Gaborone Dam in 1966 uncovered ancient tools and artefacts and nearly every new building site yields similar finds.

The first modern settlement was built on the banks of the Notwane River in 1884 by Kgosi (Chief) Gaborone of the Tlokwa clan. Whites in the area came to know it as Gaborone's village, which was inevitably abbreviated to Gaborones. The railway came through in 1897, passing just 4km west of the original village. Before long, a tiny settlement with a hotel and a few shops – known as Gaborones Station – appeared around the station.

Unlike Harare, Gaborone wasn't intended to be a capital, but in 1962 Botswana was confidently treading the road to indepen-

## HIGHLIGHTS

- Spend a day or two at the lovely Mokolodi Nature Reserve
- Appreciate Botswana's artistic diversity at the National Museum
- Climb Mt Kgale for a view over Botswana's sprawling capital
- Visit Mochudi to see the Phuthadikobo Museum and experience a typical Batswana village

dence and, thanks to its proximity to water and the railway line, this unlikely spot was selected to replace the former absentee capital, Mafikeng in South Africa.

In 1964, the task of designing the new city fell to the Department of Public Works. In their vision, it was never intended to accommodate more than 20,000 people. By 1990, however, the population was six times that and it is now among the world's fastest growing cities, with nearly 250,000 people.

In 1968, the 's' was dropped from Gaborones, in honour of the original chief's real name. Now, most of the rest of the word has also been dropped, and the city is affectionately known as just Gabs.

## Orientation

Because Gaborone lacks a defined centre, the urban action focuses on its dispersed shopping malls. The largest, imaginatively called The Mall, is a concrete slab between the town hall and the government complex of ministries and offices that is cradled in the sweep of Khama Crescent.

Five blocks south is the more down-to-earth African Mall, with several good restaurants and inexpensive shops. In Broadhurst, the area north of Julius Nyerere Drive, are the upmarket Broadhurst North Mall, and the Middle Star (Julius Nyerere) and Maru-a-Pula (No Mathatha) shopping centres. East of town is the smaller Village Mall; the Metro Mall is in the Broadhurst Industrial Estate west of the Francistown road; the expanding Gaborone West suburb has its own Gaborone West Mall; and the Kgale Mall has sprung up at the junction of the Western Bypass and the Lobatse road.

**Maps** B&T Directories (☎ 371444; fax 373462), PO Box 1549, Gaborone, publishes a town plan showing inner suburbs and shopping centre insets. It comes in the US$6 *Botswana Map Pack*, which includes a map of the country and street plans of main towns.

The *Botswana Mini-Map* contains a Gaborone inset map and the 1:1,750,000 map *Republic of Botswana* (Macmillan UK) includes a layout of The Mall. The useful *Gaborone City Centre Street Map*, published by Tru-Ads and Promotions, costs US$5.

The Department of Surveys and Mapping (☎ 372390), at the corner of Station and Old Lobatse Rds, publishes a large-scale city plan in several sheets, costing US$4 each. However, unless you're a surveyor, the detail is greater than you'll need.

## Information

The friendly Mall tourist office (☎ 353024; fax 308675) dispenses brochures, advertis-

ing and helpful advice. It's open Monday to Friday from 7.30 am to 12.30 pm and 1.45 to 4.30 pm. National tourist information is available at the National Museum Information Centre.

The free weekly *Botswana Advertiser* contains advertising, TV and cinema listings, and a calendar of events.

For reliable information on wilderness conservation, visit the Kalahari Conservation Society (☎ 314259), PO Box 859, on Independence Ave, diagonally opposite the National Museum. For national parks information, contact the Department of Wildlife and National Parks (☎ 371405).

**Money** Several banks on The Mall do currency exchange, but the most efficient option is Barclays Bank in the Gaborone Sun Hotel. It's open Monday to Friday from 8.30 am to 2.30 pm and on Saturday from 8.15 to 10.45 am. Cash transfers should be directed to the Barclay House branch of Barclays Bank.

**Post & Communications** The main post office, on The Mall, is open from 8.15 am to 1 pm and 2 to 4 pm Monday to Friday, and from 8.30 to 11.30 am on Saturday. Expect queues and generally lethargic service at any time of day.

At Botswana Telecom on Khama Crescent international calls cost an average of US$3.70 per minute. It's open Monday to Friday from 9.15 am to 1 pm and 2.15 to 4.30 pm and on Saturday from 8.15 to 11.30 am. No reverse charge calls are accepted. There are payphones and cardphones outside the post office and the National Museum. Phonecards are sold at the post office, Botswana Telecom and the chemist on The Mall.

For fax services, see the Copy Shop (fax 359922), north of Queen's Rd. Have correspondents mark faxes clearly with your name, and the name and telephone number of your hotel.

**Immigration** The Department of Immigration (☎ 374545), near the corner of State

Drive and Khama Crescent, handles visa extensions and enquiries.

**Travel Agencies** There are several travel agencies on The Mall, all about equally useful.

The American Express representative is Manica Travel Services (☎ 352021; fax 305552) in Botsalano (Debswana) House. A good choice for safari and transport bookings is Kudu Travel (☎ 372224), on Queensway.

**Bookshops** The Botswana Book Centre on The Mall sells maps, souvenir books, reference books and a wide selection of novels and literature. For new, used or exchange books, see J&B Books beside the Kgotla Restaurant, upstairs at Broadhurst North Mall. Also at Broadhurst is a branch of the Zimbabwean chain, Kingston's. On Saturday mornings, the Lions Club runs a book exchange on The Mall, opposite the Cresta President Hotel.

For descriptions of rock paintings, caves, abandoned mines, ruined villages and other sites of interest around Gaborone, look for the now scarce National Museum booklet *Sites of Historic and Natural Interest in and Around Gaborone*.

**Libraries** The Botswana Room at the University of Botswana library contains books and periodicals dealing with national topics. The Botswana National Library, east of The Mall on Independence Ave, also has a Botswana reference room. It's open Monday to Friday from 9 am to 6 pm and on Saturday from 9 am to noon. Researchers should also try the National Museum library.

The British Council on The Mall has a comfortable reading room with British periodicals. At the American Library, in the government enclave, you can read *Time*, *Newsweek* and other US publications. The Alliance Française (☎ 351650), on Mobutu Drive, screens French films, runs language courses and has a library of French-language books and periodicals.

**Left Luggage** The left-luggage service at the railway station is open at rather inconvenient hours: from 8 am to 1 pm and 2 to 4 pm, on weekdays only. If you might need to pick up your things at any other times, think twice before depositing them.

**Laundry** Kofifi Laundrette on Allison Crescent has coin-operated washing machines. Dry-cleaning services are available beside Maru-a-Pula (No Mathatha) shopping centre in southern Broadhurst. All the hotels also offer laundry services.

**Film** Both print and slide film are available, but they're expensive. There are several one-hour photo-processing services on The Mall and at Broadhurst North Mall.

**Camping Equipment** The best place for camping equipment, including butane cartridges, is Safari Centre (☎ 301999), in the Broadhurst Industrial Estate. More convenient is the appropriately named Explosions guns and ammunition shop in the African Mall. Gaborone Hardware on The Mall also sells outdoor supplies.

**Emergency Services** The Princess Marina Hospital (☎ 353221), on the North Ring Rd at Hospital Way, two blocks east of The Mall, is equipped to handle standard medical treatments and emergencies. For anything more serious, however, you'll probably have to go to the considerably more expensive Gaborone Private Hospital, opposite Broadhurst North Mall on Segoditshane Way. Consultations, by appointment, cost US$18.

The police (☎ 351161) are based on Botswana Rd opposite the Cresta President Hotel. The general emergency number is 999; other emergency numbers cover police (☎ 499), ambulance (☎ 997) and fire (☎ 998). Bush rescue services are available from Medrescue (☎ 301601).

**National Museum & Art Gallery**
The museum complex, on Independence Ave north-east of The Mall, features stuffed

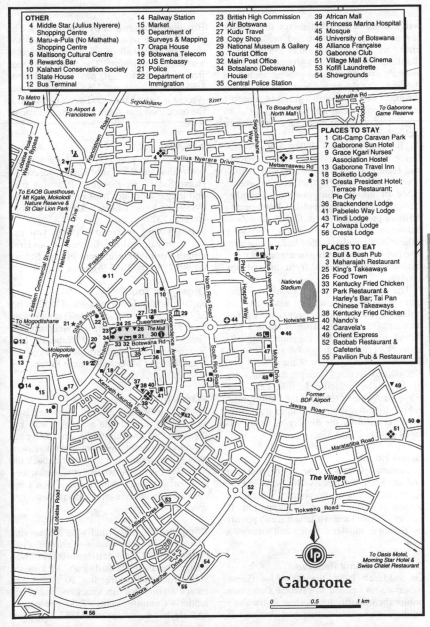

**OTHER**
4 Middle Star (Julius Nyerere) Shopping Centre
5 Maru-a-Pula (No Mathatha) Shopping Centre
6 Maitisong Cultural Centre
8 Rewards Bar
10 Kalahari Conservation Society
11 State House
12 Bus Terminal
14 Railway Station
15 Market
16 Department of Surveys & Mapping
17 Orapa House
19 Botswana Telecom
20 US Embassy
21 Police
22 Department of Immigration
23 British High Commission
24 Air Botswana
27 Kudu Travel
28 Copy Shop
29 National Museum & Gallery
30 Tourist Office
32 Main Post Office
34 Botsalano (Debswana) House
35 Central Police Station
39 African Mall
44 Princess Marina Hospital
45 Mosque
46 University of Botswana
48 Alliance Française
50 Gaborone Club
51 Village Mall & Cinema
53 Kofifi Laundrette
54 Showgrounds

**PLACES TO STAY**
1 Citi-Camp Caravan Park
7 Gaborone Sun Hotel
9 Grace Kgari Nurses' Association Hostel
13 Gaborone Travel Inn
18 Boiketlo Lodge
31 Cresta President Hotel; Terrace Restaurant; Pie City
36 Brackendene Lodge
41 Pabelelo Way Lodge
43 Tindi Lodge
47 Lolwapa Lodge
56 Cresta Lodge

**PLACES TO EAT**
2 Bull & Bush Pub
3 Maharajah Restaurant
25 King's Takeaways
26 Food Town
33 Kentucky Fried Chicken
37 Park Restaurant & Harley's Bar; Tai Pan Chinese Takeaways
38 Kentucky Fried Chicken
40 Nando's
42 Caravela's
49 Orient Express
52 Baobab Restaurant & Cafeteria
55 Pavilion Pub & Restaurant

BOTSWANA

Gaborone

0      0.5      1 km

wildlife and cultural displays that neatly reveal Botswana's past and present. The craft, art, hunting and other ethnographic displays provide background on Botswana's diverse cultural groups, including the San. The desultory junkyard spreading through the museum grounds doesn't reflect poor clean-up policies – it's an exhibit of colonial Bechuanaland's early technology.

The small National Gallery is a repository for both traditional and modern African and European art. The San artwork, which revolves around the ostrich egg, is given a place of honour, but most of the other African art originates outside Botswana (a brilliant piece is *Cops & Robbers* by Zimbabwean artist Obert Sithole). Visiting exhibitions are also staged and the museum also holds the annual Botswana basket competition, with entries from around the country.

The complex is open Tuesday to Friday from 9 am to 6 pm, and on weekends and holidays (except Easter weekend, Christmas and Boxing Day) from 9 am to 5 pm. Admission is free. The museum shop sells artwork, crafts and books and is open Tuesday to Friday from 9 am to 4.30 pm. Occasional lectures and presentations are given at the museum lecture hall. The *Pitse-ya-Naga* (zebra), the prominent zebra-striped museum vehicle, transports museum exhibits for display in small villages around Botswana.

### Orapa House

Debswana's Orapa House, at the southern end of Khama Cres, is Botswana's Fort Knox, from where the country's diamond wealth is sorted, stored and exported. If you're in town for a while and aren't put off by red tape, muster a group and arrange a tour.

### Gaborone Game Reserve

On 1 March 1988, the Gaborone Game Reserve was opened to give the Gaborone public the opportunity to view Botswana's wildlife in a natural setting, just 1km east of

Broadhurst. Access is by vehicle only. The park is home to a variety of antelope, and there are two well guarded white rhinos in a separate enclosure. The reserve is open from 6.30 am to 6.30 pm daily and costs US$2 per vehicle and US$3.70 per person. Access is from Limpopo Drive; turn east on the back road just south of the Segoditshane River.

### Activities

If you want to play cowboy in the scrubby bush 40km north-west of Gaborone, Arne's Horse Safaris in Kopong offers day trips and longer camping trips on horseback for US$9 per hour. Contact Arne or Salmona (☎ 312173).

For a very reasonable price, you can get a private pilot's licence in under a month from the Kalahari Flying School (☎ 309775; fax 309776) at the airport.

### Organised Tours

Kalahari Holiday Tours (☎ 313528; fax 357594), in the African Mall, runs organised half/full-day tours to Mochudi, the Gaborone Game Reserve, Molepolole, Livingstone's Cave and mission station, Mt Kgale and the Mokolodi Nature Reserve for US$15/33.

### Places to Stay – Budget

Finding accommodation in Gaborone isn't as much of a headache as it once was, but there are still few budget options. There are no reliable hostels and not even a reasonably priced dump of a hotel to fall back on. The YWCA does not accept guests, and foreign volunteer organisations don't accommodate anyone apart from their own workers.

**Camping** Gaborone finally has a camp site. The friendly *Citi-Camp Caravan Park* (☎/fax 377972; <citicamp@info.bw>) beside the Bull & Bush Pub, 15 minutes walk from the centre, has 50 places and caters mainly for backpackers and overlanders. Camping costs US$7 per person and electric hook-ups are US$2. At night, the river frogs provide riveting performances and the adjoining rail line keeps lesser noises at bay.

The *St Clair Lion Park* (☎ 304230), 17km south of town, has camping for US$5 per person, plus US$1.75 entry. At night, you can hear caged lions roaring just outside your tent.

Wild camping isn't permitted immediately around Gaborone, but you may set up a tent outside government freehold land west of Mogoditshane, north of Mmamashia (Odi junction) or south of the Ramotswa junction. Just hitch or take the bus to and from the city.

**Hostels** If there's space, the *Grace Kgari Nurses' Association Hostel*, at 2684 Phiri Crescent near the Gaborone Sun Hotel, will take travellers for US$26 per night single/double, but it's usually filled with live-ins from outside the city.

**Lodges** The spartan *Pabelelo Way Lodge* (☎ 351682), Plot 838, Pabelelo Way, near the African Mall, charges US$9/16 for basic singles/doubles.

The chalets at the *Mokolodi Nature Reserve* (☎ 353959; fax 313973), 12km south of town, are the region's most appealing accommodation. Set beside a dam in the game reserve, they're a super wild retreat from the city bustle. Dormitory accommodation at the Environmental Education Centre costs US$13 per person with breakfast, while three/six-bed self-catering chalets cost US$43/67 on weekdays and US$56/87 at weekends. The acclaimed outdoor restaurant offers a wonderful bush atmosphere. For more information, see under Mokolodi Nature Reserve, later in this chapter.

**Hotels** The inexpensive *Mogotel Hotel* (☎ 372228; fax 301154), off the Molepolole road in Mogoditshane, is erratically accessible by minibus. Rooms cost US$17/24 for a single/double with breakfast, and are just about the cheapest around. 'Resting rooms' (use your imagination) cost US$15 for a

couple of hours. The new management has improved the ambience, but women travelling alone still may not feel comfortable.

## Places to Stay – Mid-Range

**Lodges** A pleasant recent development is the emergence of a clutch of privately run B&Bs. *Lolwapa Lodge* (☎ 301200), Ext 10, Lot 2873, Mobutu Drive, near the Notwane Rd roundabout, has singles/doubles with en suite facilities and cooking facilities starting at US$24/39, including breakfast. There is 10% discount on stays of over a week.

The cosy *Brackendene Lodge* (☎ 312886; fax 306246), PO Box 621, Gaborone, three minutes walk from The Mall, has singles/doubles with shared bath starting at US$25/31, with breakfast. Rooms with bath are US$28/33 and family rooms accommodating two children cost US$70. Meals are available on request.

The central *Boiketlo Lodge* (☎ 352347 or 300845) offers single/double B&B accommodation with shared facilities for US$21/31. Lunch and dinner are served. *Tindi Lodge* (☎ 302599), at Plot 487 on the South Ring Rd, charges US$20/34 for singles/doubles with shared bath and US$23/37 with en suite facilities.

At the *EAOB Guest House* (☎ 373138; fax 373173), on Makhubu Hill Rd, Block 5, Gaborone West, you'll find simple single/double B&B accommodation in a residential home for US$17/34. Book through Tswana House (☎ 811883; fax 311001), Suite 11, on The Mall.

Near Kopong, north-west of Gaborone, the Swedish-run *Arne's Horse Safaris* (☎ 312173 or pager 150-10018) has double accommodation for US$28 and camping for US$3 per person. If you have a vehicle, drive 16km north-west of Gaborone on the Molepolole Rd to Metsemotlhaba and turn north-east on Lentsweletau Rd. The guest house is on this road 10km north of Kopong village. Otherwise, phone for a lift or take a minibus to Kopong or Metsemotlhaba, and look for onward transport there.

**Hotels** On Tlokweng Rd, 7km from town,

is the *Morning Star Hotel* (☎ 328301; fax 356844). Indicative of its disposition, the reception area is shielded by a wire cage. Singles/doubles cost from US$14/20 to US$20/23. There's no public transport from the centre, but plenty of traffic makes hitching relatively easy.

Considerably better but sliding downhill is the *Oasis Motel* (☎ 356396; fax 312968), also in Tlokweng. Singles/doubles cost US$28/38. There's no public transport from town.

The much nicer *Gaborone Travel Inn* (☎ 322777; fax 322727), north of the railway station, has a pleasant restaurant, a takeaway and a great bar (it prides itself on being the longest in Botswana), with live music at weekends. Singles/doubles with bath and TV cost US$47/56. It's understandably popular so it's wise to pre-book.

### Places to Stay – Top End

The *Cresta Lodge* (☎ 375375; fax 300635; <crestabs@iafrica.com>), on the south side of Samora Machel Drive near Old Lobatse Road, has singles/doubles for US$68/86. English/continental breakfasts cost US$6/4.50. Walking tracks lead from the hotel to scenic Gaborone Dam.

Once known for its highbrow atmosphere, the *Gaborone Sun Hotel & Casino* (☎ 351111; fax 302555) on Julius Nyerere Drive has now been humbled by competition. Singles/doubles cost US$84/106; an English/continental breakfast is an additional US$10/7 and both the Savuti Grill and Giovanni's restaurant specialise in upmarket dining. An annual membership fee of US$30 allows access to the swimming pool and squash and tennis courts.

The *Cresta President Hotel* (☎ 353631; fax 351840; <crestabs@iafrica.com>), on The Mall, offers friendly, central accommodation. Standard singles/doubles cost US$83/91 and a buffet English/continental breakfast is US$8/6. The attached Terrace Restaurant overlooking The Mall serves up healthy European cuisine, including vegetable-rich lunches, coffee and pastries.

The immense *Grand Palm Hotel*

(☎ 312999; fax 312989) – formerly the Sheraton – between Gaborone West and Mogoditshane offers five-star international standards at surprisingly reasonable rates: for standard singles/doubles, they charge US$78/98.

### Places to Eat

**Snacks & Lunches** For a cheap food fix, try the *Food Town* dining hall on The Mall, which is very popular with lunchtime crowds. A filling dose of stew or mielies and relish costs US$2. Alternatively, market stalls near the railway station dish up such offbeat lunch specialities as pickled spinach, goat, mopane worms or bojalwa (sorghum beer). For cheap burgers, chips and other snacks, try the office workers' favourite, *King's Takeaways*, on The Mall.

You'll also find the familiar *Kentucky Fried Chicken* on The Mall and in the African Mall; lunch specials start at around US$3. Competing with the Colonel are the *Nando's* outlets in the African Mall and Broadhurst North Mall, which do Portuguese-style peri-peri chicken. Downstairs from the Cresta President Hotel, on The Mall, *Pie City* bakes up tasty savoury pies. Other pie shops include *Mr Pie Man* on The Mall and *Pie City* in the Kagiso centre, Broadhurst North Mall.

The recommended *cafe* at the entrance to the Gaborone Private Hospital, immediately south of Broadhurst North Mall, will give you a whole new perspective on hospital food.

The *Terrace Restaurant,* appropriately located on the Cresta President Hotel terrace, serves crepes, quiche, fish dishes, vegetable soups and curries. Alternatively, linger over a frothy cappuccino and chocolate éclairs while surveying the passing mall scene below. In the evenings, they feature good-value steak specials.

For an exhaustive menu of sweets and vegetarian options, try the *Kgotla Restaurant* (☎ 356091) in Broadhurst North Mall. It's open from 9 am to 9 pm daily. The salads, desserts, cappuccino and iced coffee are all appealing.

A good choice for breakfast, lunch or dinner is the *Baobab Restaurant & Cafeteria* (☎ 584184), in the BNPC industrial complex near Tlokweng Rd and Mobutu Drive. The cafeteria, open from noon to 9 pm daily, does buffet meals, particularly traditional Batswana dishes, while the restaurant serves good value salads, grills, pasta and game dishes. During happy hour, from 5 to 6.30 pm, you'll get beer for US$0.75 and free bar snacks.

*Hot & Crusty* in Broadhurst North Mall does great one-person pizzas as well as breads and sweets.

**Dinners** The upmarket *Reflections* (☎ 356396), in the Oasis Motel, features a choice of seafood. Your meal will be rounded off with a free glass of sherry and chocolates. Book in advance for this popular dinner spot. You'll find continental and traditional cuisine at the *Pavilion Pub & Restaurant*, off Samora Machel Drive.

*Mike's Kitchen*, in the Kgale shopping centre on the new Lobatse road, belongs to a family-oriented South African chain and dishes up standard chicken, beef and seafood dishes. Another popular South African chain is represented by the *Diamond Creek Spur* steak house in the Kagiso centre, Broadhurst North Mall.

The African Mall has several good options. Most popular is the folksy *Park Restaurant* (☎ 351456), which serves pub meals and full dinners, including fabulous pizzas, steak, chicken, crepes, ribs, salads and other delights. It's open seven days a week from 11.30 am to 2.30 pm and 6 to 10.30 pm.

Next door is *Tai Pan Chinese Takeaways* and also the *Taj* (☎ 313569), which dishes up Indian, Mauritian and continental cuisine and excellent salads. Their US$8 buffet lunch is served seven days a week.

*Da Alfredo* (☎ 313604) at Broadhurst North Mall specialises in seafood and Italian cuisine. It's open every day for lunch and dinner, and also does takeaways. Another southern European choice is *Caravela's* (☎ 314284), in a quiet neighbourhood, which specialises in Portuguese fare (ever tried caldo verde?). Europe's higher side is represented at the *Swiss Chalet* (☎ 312247), on Tlokweng Rd, which serves both Swiss and Italian dishes.

The *Moghul* (☎ 375246), in the Middle Star shopping centre, serves Indian and Pakistani fare; their popular Indian buffet lunch costs US$8. The well acclaimed *Orient Express* (☎ 356287) in The Village is a pleasant and exclusive Chinese restaurant. In the Maru-a-Pula (No Mathatha) shopping centre is the popular *China Restaurant* (☎ 357254), open for lunch from noon to 2 pm and dinner from 6.30 to 11 pm.

If you prefer a British twist or a nice patio meal, see the *Bull & Bush Pub* (☎ 375070) off Nelson Mandela Drive; look for the west-pointing sign reading Police Housing Bull & Bush. The extensive menu offers everything from beef, pizza and pasta to elaborate vegetarian starters and main dishes; plan on US$7 to US$10 for a memorable meal. The new *Maharajah Restaurant* next door specialises in Indian cuisine and has also received favourable reviews.

Most hotel dining rooms feature menus heavy on beef dishes. *Chatters* (☎ 313234) at the Cresta Lodge is recommended. The more expensive *Giovanni's* (☎ 351111) at the Gaborone Sun Hotel dishes up live entertainment along with their Italian and international fare. On Thursday evenings, the same hotel's *Savuti Grill* offers an all-you-can-eat oyster bar.

The atmospheric outdoor restaurant and bar at the *Mokolodi Nature Reserve* (☎ 328692; fax 328568) serves up creative meals, including game meat. Diners who take a game drive don't pay admission to the reserve. They also organise sundowner bush braais at a lofty vantage point from 5.30 to 10 pm for US$37 per person, with a minimum of six people.

**Self-Catering** Gaborone doesn't have a traditional open market, but near the railway station and the Broadhurst North

BOTSWANA

Mall you'll find spreading expanses of impromptu stalls. Well stocked supermarkets include the Food Marts at the Middle Star shopping centre and Broadhurst North Mall, the Score in the Station House shopping centre, and the Corner Market on The Mall.

At *Tony's* in the African Mall you can stock up on fruit and fresh vegetables for bargain prices; in season, 50 oranges cost only US$2.50. The good-value *Gaborone Meat Centre* in the African Mall also sells seasonal Oriental groceries. The Broadhurst North and Metro malls both have recommended *Mr & Ms Veg* fresh produce shops.

## Entertainment

### Theatres & Cinemas

The 450-seat theatre in the Maitisong Cultural Centre (☎/fax 371809; <maitison@global.co.za>) at Maru-a-Pula (Rain Cloud) Secondary School was opened in 1987 as a venue for cultural events. Productions are well attended and advance booking is essential. A roster of coming events is posted on a bulletin board outside the centre, and listed each Friday in the *Botswana Advertiser*. The more serious local theatre groups, including some excellent new African troupes, perform exclusively at Maitisong, and in March it holds the fabulous nine-day Maitisong Performing Arts Festival.

The local amateur troupe Capital Players (☎ 372120) is also good fun. Performances are held at the Memorable Order of Tin Hats (MOTH) Hall just off the Molepolole road, near the bus terminal; they also participate in the Maitisong Performing Arts Festival. For upcoming events, check the *Botswana Advertiser* or write to Capital Players, PO Box 65, Gaborone.

The Stardust and The Village cinemas provide mostly escapist Hollywood entertainment. The Gaborone Film Society and the Alliance Française (☎ 351650) screen classic films. Refer to the *Botswana Advertiser* for information.

### Casinos

The Gaborone Sun and Grand Palm hotels both boast casinos with slot machines, blackjack and roulette. You must be at least 18 years of age to gamble in Botswana.

### Discos & Nightclubs

The *Diamond Club* at the Oasis Motel in Tlokweng emphasises live soul music. A long-standing hit with the affluent youth of Gaborone is the *Night Shift* in the Broadhurst North Mall. The bar is upstairs and the rather trendy disco rocks below.

For African disco music and dancing, try the well attended *Platform* in the Gaborone Sun Hotel. The popular local dance spot, the *Blue Note*, at the Entertainment Centre beyond the Spark market in Mogoditshane, specialises in kwasa-kwasa music from Congo (Zaïre). Another kwasa-kwasa venue is *Club La Bistro* in Gaborone West. Also in Mogoditshane is the *Club W*, with a disco on Saturday nights. Standards are preserved with a US$4 cover charge.

A strong favourite is *Sinatra's* (formerly called Visions and Club 585) in the Maru-a-Pula shopping centre. They charge US$6 admission and smart dress is required. The disco operates every night from Thursday to Sunday. On Sunday, the theme is jazz. You'll also hear jazz at the trendy *Duke's*, in the African Mall.

The popular *Bull & Bush Pub*, in the sticks off Nelson Mandela Drive, produces a respectable Anglo-African pub atmosphere. *Rewards*, on Julius Nyerere Drive, is popular with sports fans.

For good ol' boys and girls, *Harley's* at the Park Restaurant successfully emulates a southern USA rebel watering hole with its Budweiser and Harley-Davidson decor. The rebel theme is developed by a large Confederate flag, motorbike posters and a neon legend over the bar proclaiming 'Harley's – a Botswana Tradition'. There's live music on Friday and Saturday nights and the billiard table will keep you busy on other evenings. Cover charges apply only when live bands are booked.

The *Gaborone Club*, Okwa Rd, The Village, stages folk music performances at 7.30 pm on the first Saturday of each month. The *Sports Club* bar, opposite the Gaborone Sun Hotel, offers non-stop sports telecasts.

**Sports** The sports club scene includes groups devoted to tennis, cycling, running, golf, squash, cricket, riding and yachting. The *Gaborone Club* (☎ 356333) and the *Village Health & Recreation Club* (☎ 300990), both in The Village, offer swimming, tennis, squash, rugby and bowls. Paying members may invite visitors free of charge.

You can use the pool and the squash and tennis courts at the Gaborone Sun Hotel for an annual US$75 membership fee. At the *Notwane Club* (☎ 352399) and the *Gaborone Squash Racquets Centre* (☎ 314620), both of which are near the National Stadium, annual memberships cost US$100. Information on other participatory sports clubs is published in the *Botswana Advertiser* and *Consumer Info Gaborone*.

**Things to Buy**
The Botswanacraft Marketing Company (☎ 312471; fax 313189) on The Mall sells material arts and crafts – San pouches, hunting bows and jewellery, as well as Ngamiland and Shashe baskets, wooden animal carvings from Francistown, Odi weavings, silk-screen prints from Mochudi and pottery from the Gaborone hinterlands. They provide quality control, but many items may be cheaper at the point of origin.

Mokolodi Crafts (☎/fax 359416), 12km south of Gaborone on the Lobatse road, then 3km east, started by producing passport-toting teddy bears for the international market, but wool shortages dictated a change. It now specialises in original potato-printed fabrics, wall hangings, quilts and other textiles, hand-fired ceramic beads, carved bone jewellery and toys. It's open Monday to Saturday, 8 am to 4 pm.

The National Museum is also good for inexpensive Botswana baskets. See also under Gabane, Mochudi, Odi and Thamaga in the Around Gaborone section, later in this chapter.

**Getting There & Away**
**Air** The Sir Seretse Khama international airport is 14km from the centre. Air Botswana, British Airways, Air France, Air Zimbabwe, Air Namibia and South African Airways serve Gaborone, and Air Botswana operates scheduled domestic flights to and from Kasane (US$285), Maun (US$173) and Francistown (US$111). For general flight information, phone ☎ 314518.

**Bus** Intercity buses, as well as minibuses to outlying villages, use the main bus terminal near the Molepolole flyover. Local buses – to Gabane, Molepolole, Kanye etc – normally leave when full, starting in the early morning.

Larger domestic buses operate according to tentative timetables. Services are available (although not always direct or when you'd like to go) to Lobatse, Ramatlhabama, Mahalapye, Palapye, Serowe, Selebi-Phikwe, Francistown, Nata, Kasane and Maun, with connections to Shakawe. All bus trips to the north require an overnight stop in Francistown. From Gaborone to Francistown costs US$10 each way. Mochudi is served more regularly and the trip costs just US$1.50. For transport to Ghanzi, see under Lobatse, later in this chapter.

Minibuses to Johannesburg (US$15) leave when full from the northernmost lane at the terminal. Seabelo's Express has services to Francistown, Bulawayo, Gweru and Harare at 6 and 10 am daily. Chitanda & Sons goes to Bulawayo from the African Mall and Gaborone Sun Hotel. For more international information, see the Botswana Getting There & Away chapter.

**Train** Gaborone has daily rail connections to and from Bulawayo, Francistown and Lobatse. The northbound train departs at 9 pm and arrives in Bulawayo at noon the following day. You can choose between 1st, 2nd or economy classes; 1st and 2nd class both have sleepers. The fare to Bulawayo is US$37/30 in 1st/2nd class and US$9 in economy; to Francistown it's US$25/21 in

1st/2nd class and US$7 in economy. The day trains to Francistown carry economy and club class carriages (US$6 and US$9, respectively). Lobatse trains run on weekdays only and are limited to economy class (US$2). Phone Botswana Railways (☎ 351401) for the latest information.

Top-end hotels send minibuses to the station to pick up pre-booked guests.

**Hitching** Hitchers headed for Francistown should take the Broadhurst 4 minibus and get off at the standard hitching spot north of town (the drivers all know where it is). There's no need to wave down vehicles; anyone with space will stop for passengers. Expect to pay around US$6 per person.

### Getting Around

Gaborone's local public transport system is scarcely adequate for the city's growing population and people have a real battle making their way between home and work.

**The Airport** The only reliable transport between the airport and town is the courtesy minibuses operated by the top-end hotels for their guests. Non-guests can sometimes talk the driver into a lift for a small tip. The Kalahari Holiday Tours SSK Airport Shuttle (☎ 313528) provides airport transfers 24 hours a day, but you must pre-book.

Bizarrely, taxis rarely turn up at the airport. If you do connect with a taxi, you'll pay US$3 to US$12 per person for the 14km trip to the centre. Alternatively, walk down the road a few hundred metres and try hitching a lift.

**Minibus** The crowded white minibuses, or kombis, recognisable by their blue number plates, circulate on set routes and cost P1 per ride. The standard city circuit passes all the major shopping centres. Minibuses to surrounding villages depart from the main bus terminal, but follow no real schedule; the best sources of information are the drivers or other prospective passengers.

**Car** Holiday Car Hire (☎ 312280; fax

357996) is on Nakedi Rd, in the Broadhurst Industrial Area. The Avis (☎ 375469; fax 312205) headquarters is at Sir Seretse Khama international airport.

The addition of the Western Bypass and other road upgrades has made driving in Gaborone considerably less hectic than it was in the early 1990s.

**Taxi** Although the public minibuses in Gaborone are known as 'taxis', Gaborone has few conventional taxis, known locally as 'special taxis'. For a radio taxi, call the Cab Co (☎ 357308 or 309927). If you're intent on searching for a roving cab, look for vehicles with blue number plates. Fares are left to the whims of the drivers.

# Around Gaborone

Once you've exhausted your interest in Gaborone sightseeing, head for the desert hinterlands, where there are several natural, historical and cultural attractions to keep you occupied.

### MOCHUDI

The most interesting village in southeastern Botswana, Mochudi was first settled by the Kwena in the mid-16th century, as evidenced by a few remaining stone walls in the surrounding hills. In 1871 it was settled by the Kgatla people, who had been forced from their lands by Boers trekking northwards.

#### Phuthadikobo Museum

This Cape Dutch-style museum, established in 1976, focuses on the history of Mochudi in particular and the Kgatla people in general. It sits atop sacred Phuthadikobo Hill, which was a ceremonial site and the domain of Kwanyape, the rain-making gaboon viper.

The museum is housed in the first secondary school in Botswana, the Mochudi National School, which was founded in

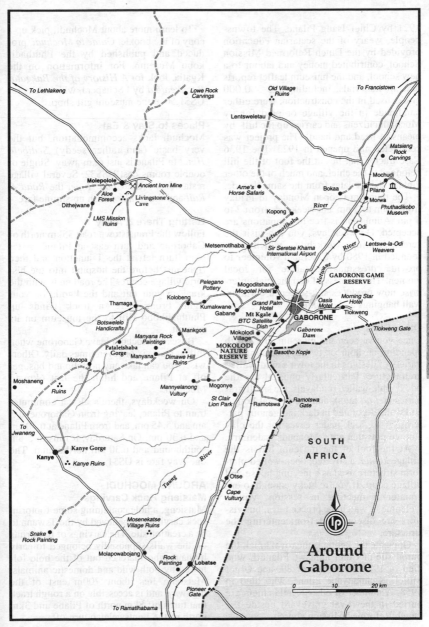

To Lethlakeng

Lowe Rock Carvings

Old Village Ruins

To Francistown

Lentsweletau

Matsieng Rock Carvings

Mochudi

Molepolole

Ancient Iron Mine

Aloe Forest

Livingstone's Cave

Arne's Horse Safaris

Bokaa

Pilane

Morwa

Phuthadikobo Museum

Dithejwane

LMS Mission Ruins

Kopong

River

Odi

Lentswe-la-Odi Weavers

Metsemotlhaba

River

Thamaga

Metsemotlhaba

Sir Seretse Khama International Airport

Notwane

GABORONE GAME RESERVE

Pelegano Pottery

Mogoditshane
Mogotel Hotel

Morning Star Hotel

Kolobeng

Grand Palm Hotel

Oasis Motel

Kumakwane

Gabane

BTC Satellite Dish

Mt Kgale

GABORONE

Tlokweng

Botswelelo Handicrafts

Mankgodi

Mokolodi Village

Gaborone Dam

Tlokweng Gate

Manyana Rock Paintings

MOKOLODI NATURE RESERVE

Pataletshaba Gorge

Manyana

Dimawe Hill Ruins

Basotho Kopje

Mosopa

Moshaneng

Ruins

Mannyelanong Vultury

Mogonye

St Clair Lion Park

Ramotswa

Ramotswa Gate

To Jwaneng

SOUTH AFRICA

Kanye Gorge

Kanye

Kanye Ruins

River

Taung

Otse

Cape Vulture

Snake Rock Painting

Mosenekatse Village Ruins

Molapowabojang

Rock Paintings

Lobatse

Pioneer Gate

To Ramatlhabama

## Around Gaborone

0      10      20 km

**BOTSWANA**

1921 by Chief Isang Pilane. The towns-people, weary of the sectarian education provided by the Dutch Reformed Mission School, contributed money and labour to a new school, and the museum leaflet reports that all materials, including the 300,000 bricks used in the construction, were either handmade in the village or paid for by Mochudi citizens and carried up the hill 'by means of head and hand'. The project was completed and opened in 1923. The 1936 Case tractor that lies at the foot of the hill belonged to the chief, and much of the other vintage debris dates from the same decade.

The museum is open Monday to Friday from 8 am to 5 pm and weekends from 2 to 5 pm. Admission is free but donations are accepted. On weekdays, you can visit the screen-printing workshop, which was founded in 1980 by a German volunteer to provide dressmaking fabric for local women. This successful commercial enter-prise now produces silk-screened curtains, wall hangings and clothing.

## Other Sites

Once you've seen the museum, it's worth spending an hour or two appreciating the variety of designs in the town's mud-walled architecture. Particularly unusual are the odd double-walled rondavels, the small gra-naries (*sefala* huts), and the several homes and walls decorated in dark indigenous pat-terns. Also, look under eaves for the clay storage pots that are a Mochudi trademark.

At the foot of the museum hill is the village *kgotla*, a covered, open-walled plat-form structure used as a meeting house and village court. If you're lucky enough to en-counter a meeting in session, you're welcome to watch the proceedings, but vis-itors are discouraged from entering the structure.

Opposite the kgotla is the royal kraal, the burial site of Chief Lentswe Pilane I, who died in 1924 at the age of 89, and Chief Molefi Kgamanyane Pilane, who died in 1958. A number of other Kgatla chiefs are buried in the royal graveyard beside the Dutch Reformed Mission church.

To learn more about Mochudi, pick up a copy of the booklet *Guide to Mochudi*, pro-duced and published by the Phuthadi-kobo Museum. For information on the Kgatla, look for *A History of the Bakgata-Bagakgafêla* by I Schapera, which sells for US$1.50 at the museum gift shop.

## Places to Stay & Eat

Mochudi lacks accommodation, but the very basic (and rather seedy) *Sedibelo Hotel* in Pilane is just 6km away. Single or double rooms cost US$32. Several village restaurants – the *Good Hope*, the *Road & Rail* and the *Ranko* – dish up simple fare.

## Getting There & Away

Follow the Francistown road 35km north of Gaborone and turn east at Pilane. After 6km, turn left at the T-junction and then right just before the hospital into the his-toric village centre. The road ends with the kraal on your left and the kgotla on your right. From there, a track winds up Phuthadikobo Hill to the museum on its summit.

Buses to Mochudi leave Gaborone when full, at least six or seven times daily. Other-wise, you can take any northbound bus, get off at Pilane and hitch the last 6km to Mochudi.

On weekdays, there's also a commuter train to Pilane, leaving from Gaborone at 5 am and 5.45 pm, and from Pilane at 6.30 am and 6.30 pm. On Saturday, it runs at 5 am southbound and 6.30 am northbound. The one-way fare is US$1.

## AROUND MOCHUDI
### Matsieng Rock Carvings

Matsieng, a hole containing some footprint rock carvings, is believed by the Tswana to be a creation site. The carvings of footprints on the walls supposedly belonged to early humans who marched out of the hole fol-lowed by both wild and domestic animals. Matsieng lies about 700m east of the highway, and is accessible on a rough track that turns off 8km north of Pilane and 3km north of the Lentsweletau turn-off.

## ODI

The small village of Odi is best known for the internationally acclaimed Lentswe-la-Odi (Rocky Hills of Odi) weavers (☎ 392268). The co-operative was established in 1973 by Swedes Ulla and Peder Gowenius, who hoped to provide an economic base for the villages of Odi, Matebeleng and Modipane.

Wool, hand-spun and dyed over an open fire, is woven into spontaneous patterns invented by the individual artists. Most of these depict African wildlife and aspects of rural life in Botswana. The richly coloured products include handbags, table mats, bed covers, hats, jackets, tapestries and table-cloths, all of which are available at the workshop. They'll even weave customised pieces based on individual pictures, drawings or stories. The tapestries, unusually, are sold by the square yard, with apparently no judgments made about their relative aesthetic value. Unfortunately, quality has apparently slipped in recent years, but that could change so it's still worth a visit.

The workshop is open 8 am to 4.30 pm on weekdays and 10.30 am to 4 pm on weekends. Coffee, tea, biscuits and *vetkoek* are served at the shop.

### Getting There & Away

Follow the Francistown road 18km north from Gaborone and turn east at the Odi signpost. From there it's 5km to the railway line and the bridge over the Notwane River. The road takes a sharp left turn at the 'two hills of Odi', from where it's about 1.5km through the village to the weaving co-operative.

By public transport, take any northbound bus or minibus from Gaborone and get off at the Odi turn-off. From there, either walk or hitch the remaining distance into the village.

## WEST OF GABORONE

### Gabane

Gabane village lies 12km south-west of Mogoditshane, 23km from Gaborone. Some of the ancient hilltop settlements around Gabane date from between 800 and 1200 AD. The early Bangologa people who once inhabited this area were skilled iron smelters and artisans, but most of the present-day residents migrated from Ramotswa in 1885.

Gabane's claim to fame is the renowned Pelegano Pottery, where you can buy a variety of lovely and original hand-painted ceramics. Popular items include masks, finely decorated bowls and charming animal figurines. It's open Monday to Friday from 8 am to 4.30 pm.

### Manyana

With a vehicle, you can visit Manyana village, south-west of Gaborone, which has some Zimbabwean-style rock paintings, a rarity in south-eastern Botswana. About 500m north of the village, on the road west of the river, is an 8m-high rock face. Opposite an overhang at its southern extreme are paintings of three giraffes, an elephant and several antelope.

### Molepolole

The tongue-twisting name of this hillside village (pronounced MO-lay-po-LO-lay), 52km north-west of Gaborone, means let him cancel it. It's thought to be derived from the utterance of the chief in response to a spell placed upon the land where the village now stands. It was first inhabited by the Kgwatleng tribe in the 16th century, but they were displaced by the Kwena who stayed for nearly 100 years before abandoning it. A Kwena group returned to Molepolole in the mid-19th century and has occupied the site ever since.

When you're there, have a look at the Scottish Livingstone Hospital, where students of two local schools have taken to covering the walls with painted murals.

**Places to Stay & Eat** John and June Byrne's *Mafenya-Tlala* (☎ 350522; fax 320663) has singles/doubles for US$31/37. There's also a camp site with electricity. The hotel name means hunger defeated, and accordingly the restaurant cooks up

BOTSWANA

anything from mielies to seafood dishes. There's also a bottle store and a disco operates on weekends.

**Getting There & Away** From Gaborone, minibuses leave for Molepolole when full. In your own vehicle, take the Molepolole flyover and follow the tarred highway to the village.

### Around Molepolole

If you have a sturdy vehicle, the Molepolole area is good for a day of exploration. In the village itself, note the stone-walled enclosures constructed by the Kwena to divide the settlement into family groups.

One kilometre west of the Scottish-run Livingstone Hospital is a large and eerie forest of Marloth aloes (*Aloe marlothii*). Legend has it that in 1850, the Boers trekked into Molepolole to punish Chief Sechele of the Kwena for befriending David Livingstone. Approaching stealthily on a dark night, they encountered the extraneous aloes and fled in fear, having mistaken them for ranks of Kwena warriors!

Six kilometres along the Lethlakeng road from Molepolole, in the gullies immediately north-west of the airstrip, are large deposits of silica asbestos, which resemble petrified wood. Collecting stones is forbidden at this protected site.

Between 2 and 6km south of Molepolole, west of the road towards Thamaga, is a trio of interesting sites. The first is an ancient trench excavation where the Kwena once mined iron. Two km beyond it is a hillside cave, visited by David Livingstone despite a Kwena shaman's warning that to do so would bring about a speedy death. His survival supposedly prompted Chief Sechele's conversion to Christianity.

One km south of the cave is the ruin of the LMS mission that operated from 1866 to 1884 under Reverend Roger Price and his wife, Elizabeth, who was a daughter of Robert Moffat. West of the stream, below the ruin, is a high rock face from which the Kwena flung unauthorised witches and wizards.

### Lowe Rock Carvings

You'll need a 4WD vehicle to visit the Lowe rock carvings, which depict some animal and human tracks as well as crude bovine figures. To get there, follow the Botlhapatlou track about 30km north of Molepolole, turn right onto a side track and proceed 5km to Kopong. From there, you must walk the remaining couple of kilometres to Lowe.

### Thamaga

Thamaga is best known for the Thamaga Pottery Workshop, which produces and sells original – if slightly kitsch – ceramic work, including dishes, ashtrays and other practical items. At Botswelelo Handicrafts, you can buy folding kgotla chairs; they're ornately carved from wood and the seats are woven from leather thongs. They're not too heavy and are relatively portable.

Fifteen kilometres from Thamaga, off the Gaborone road, is the ruin of Kolobeng, once the home and mission of David Livingstone in the 1840s. It was actually Botswana's first European-style settlement, and the site of the country's first Christian church. The only remnants are the decaying floor of Livingstone's home and several graves, including that of Livingstone's daughter. A museum is planned for the site.

### THE LOBATSE ROAD
### Mt Kgale

The 'sleeping giant' peak overlooking Gaborone is easily climbed and affords the capital's best view. Take any Lobatse bus to the Kgale siding or hitch 8km along the new Lobatse road to the satellite dish. Nearly opposite the dish is a concrete stile over a fence. Cross it, turn left, and follow the fence until it enters a shallow gully, where you'll see a set of whitewashed stones leading up the hillside to the summit. Beyond a small quarry, you'll have to scramble under a cattle fence.

### Basotho Kopje

Immediately east of the railway line, 9km south of Gaborone, lies Basotho Kopje, which was the site of a Boer War campaign in February 1900. The railway bridge was destroyed in the skirmish, but was repaired shortly thereafter and a rude fortress was established by Rhodesian forces to protect it from further sabotage. Some graves and part of a stone wall are still visible. North of the hill is the river ford used by the Voortrekkers' oxen-drawn wagons in the 1830s.

## Gaborone Dam

Gaborone Dam, on the Notwane River, provides the capital's water and serves as a marginal recreational site. From the satellite dish, 8km out on the new Lobatse road, it's 3km down the old Lobatse road to the lake. Follow the tarred road until you reach a barricade and walk from there to where the road disappears beneath the water. There's good bird-watching amid the drowned trees and bushes but watch for crocodiles. Swimming is not permitted.

To visit the dam wall, you need permission from the Water Utilities Corporation on Luthuli Rd, just south of the Khama Cres roundabout near the Gaborone railway station. To reach the dam wall, head down Mobutu Drive/Samora Michel Drive and turn left at the Sanitas Nursery sign north of the Cresta Lodge; it's 5km along that road.

## Mokolodi Nature Reserve

The Mokolodi Nature Reserve (☎ 353959; fax 313973), 12km south of Gaborone, covers 3000 hectares and aims to promote wildlife and conservation education and to establish new reserves in south-eastern Botswana. It also operates as a research facility, a breeding centre for rare and endangered species and a sanctuary for orphaned, injured or confiscated birds and animals.

This scenic reserve is Botswana's only protected habitat for mountain reedbuck, and white rhino have been reintroduced from South Africa. You'll also see zebra, baboons, warthogs and hippo as well as the more retiring leopard, honey badger, jackal, hyaena, genet and civet, and a range of an-

telope species including gemsbok, kudu, impala, waterbuck, klipspringer, steenbok, duiker and red hartebeest.

Also of interest are the well preserved stumps of 1500-year-old leadwood trees, which were cut 100 years ago to make sleepers for the colonial railway – they're too dense to rot or suffer termite damage – and the well worn stones that have been used by rhino for millennia as scratching blocks.

All the reserve's elephant are stabled, but during the day they roam free to feed (visitors can watch them bathing at 12.30 and 3.30 pm daily for US$1 per person). On Saturday and Sunday, you can ramble with them for five or six hours for US$42 per person (two to eight people). Also on weekends, you can spend six hours tracking the white rhino on foot for US$42 per person. Either walk must be booked in advance.

Admission costs US$3 per vehicle plus US$3 per person, and guided two-hour day/evening game drives cost US$12/14. Game walks are US$9. There are also comfortable chalets and a superb restaurant (see Places to Stay and Places to Eat under Gaborone). It's wise to pre-book accommodation and game drives.

Take a Lobatse minibus 12km south of Gaborone and get off at the turning 2km south of the signposted road to Mokolodi village. Then walk the final 1.5km west to the reserve entrance. Pick-up services from town cost US$17 for up to three people plus US$6 per extra person.

## St Clair Lion Park

If you don't mind seeing lions in enclosures, the St Clair Lion Park may be of interest. There's also a small children's zoo, and horse rides around the attached wildlife area cost US$10 per hour. Other activities include bird-watching, vulture-feeding and guided walks to a nearby Stone-Age site. However, the real emphasis is on quarterly off-road vehicle competitions and they aim to attract devotees from around the world.

St Clair is also a camp and caravan site. See Places to Stay under Gaborone.

BOTSWANA

## Otse

Otse (pronounced OOT-see), a former manganese-mining and forestry village, 45km south of Gaborone, is known for Mannyelanong Hill, one of Botswana's two Cape vulture nesting sites (the other site is also called Mannyelanong – the place where vultures shit – near Mogonye village). Above the southern end of Otse's backdrop hill, once a nesting site for thousands of mating pairs, the ungainly birds wheel around their lofty nests. In the late 1960s, the population dropped to 60 pairs, but numbers have since increased. Coming from Gaborone, turn left into Otse at the Shell petrol station, bear right and follow the rutted road to the obvious track leading to the cliffs where the vultures nest.

Nearby, north along the western side of Mannyelanong Hill, is Refuge Cave, a large fault 50m up the cliff. Pottery has been found here, and the cave was probably used as a hiding place during the Boer invasions of the 1870s.

## LOBATSE

Despite its scenic setting, Lobatse has a reputation for dullness and is best known as the site of the national mental hospital and the country's largest abattoir. Established by the Ngwaketse in the late 18th century, it served as the site of the High Court of Bechuanaland Protectorate when Mafikeng was the seat of government. In the early 1960s, it narrowly missed out being selected as the national capital, thanks mainly to water shortages.

### Information

Most Lobatse visitors live in Gaborone, so there's little need for a tourist office. The Choppy's Cash & Carry complex has a decent bookshop.

### Arts Co-operatives

Tiro Afrique Knitwear creates designer woollens from New Zealand Accorda wool for export and sells quality knitwear for reasonable prices. The workers also serve

---

### Vultures

Along with hawks and eagles, vultures belong to the Accipitridae family. Many different species are represented in southern Africa, but the most common are the Egyptian (*Neophron percnopterus*), hooded (*Neophron monarchus*), white-backed (*Pseudogyps africanus*) and white-headed (*Trigonoceps occipitalis*) varieties. All vultures prefer savanna country with high animal concentrations, and are found in large numbers in Hwange, Chobe, Moremi, Mana Pools, Chizarira and Etosha, but are present in all the smaller parks, as well.

The largest birds have 3m wing spans and can weigh up to 5kg. Vultures are fairly inefficient fliers and must rely on rising hot-air thermals to ascend and glide. For this reason you won't see them in the air until well into the morning when the updraughts have started.

They feed almost exclusively by scavenging and, fortunately for them, have no sense of smell. This means, however, that they must depend totally on their superb eyesight to locate food. Once a kill has been spotted, a vulture will descend rapidly and await its turn at the carcass. Of course, other vultures will follow the first downwards, and before long vultures will be winging in from as far as 50km away.

They are very efficient feeders and a large flock of vultures – they often congregate in mobs of up to 100 – can strip an antelope to the bone in half an hour. However, they're no good at ripping into a completely intact carcass. Due to their poor flying ability, they're unable to get off the ground with a full belly, so after a good gorging, they retreat from the carcass until the meal is digested.

refreshments to visitors and conduct informal tours around the work area.

The Tiro ya Diatla Weavers, opposite the Botswana Meat Corporation (BMC), started out producing durable karakul rugs and have now expanded into karakul tapestries and clothing, which are sold at factory prices. Tours are available.

### Anglican Church

Lobatse's most beautiful structure is St Mark's Anglican Church, a thatch-roofed stone building that would be more at home in a rural English village. Visitors are welcome whenever the door is unlocked.

### Botswana Meat Corporation

Imperial Cold Storage opened in 1934 and Lobatse has been known as a meat town ever since. At independence in 1966, after ICS had closed, re-opened and changed hands several times, it was taken over by the government and the BMC was formed. They've been in charge ever since.

The Lobatse BMC abattoir is the country's largest and conducts tours, which enjoy considerable popularity. However if you're looking for lots of gore, don't bother: the company proudly asserts that its work is 'humanely' executed.

### Places to Stay & Eat

At a pinch, the hills behind Lobatse would be suitable for unofficial camping, but there's no water. Otherwise, you're limited to the *Cresta Cumberland* (☎ 330281; fax 332106), on the Gaborone road. Singles/doubles with en suite baths cost US$42/49, including breakfast, and executive suites are US$55 for a single or double. The dining room does buffet English/continental breakfasts for US$5.50/3.50, while grill dinners range from US$8 to US$12.

The *El Shaddai* in the Madiba shopping centre (which resembles a Rubik's Cube) serves takeaways and pizzas, pasta, steak and seafood. On the main street are the simple *Danna Restaurant* and *Machado's Chicken Village & Pie Bake*. The *Chicken Licken* and *Cookie's Takeaway* lie along the

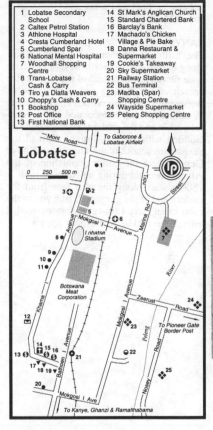

| | | |
|---|---|---|
| 1 | Lobatse Secondary School | 14 St Mark's Anglican Church |
| 2 | Caltex Petrol Station | 15 Standard Chartered Bank |
| 3 | Athlone Hospital | 16 Barclay's Bank |
| 4 | Cresta Cumberland Hotel | 17 Machado's Chicken Village & Pie Bake |
| 5 | Cumberland Spar | 18 Danna Restaurant & Supermarket |
| 6 | National Mental Hospital | 19 Cookie's Takeaway |
| 7 | Woodhall Shopping Centre | 20 Sky Supermarket |
| 8 | Trans-Lobatse Cash & Carry | 21 Railway Station |
| 9 | Tiro ya Diatla Weavers | 22 Bus Terminal |
| 10 | Choppy's Cash & Carry | 23 Madiba (Spar) Shopping Centre |
| 11 | Bookshop | 24 Wayside Supermarket |
| 12 | Post Office | 25 Peleng Shopping Centre |
| 13 | First National Bank | |

**Lobatse**

street parallel to the railway line. For self-catering, there are *Choppy's Cash & Carry*, *Trans-Lobatse Cash & Carry* and two *Spar* supermarkets.

### Getting There & Away

Frequent buses connect Gaborone and Lobatse, and commuter trains leave Gaborone daily at 6.05 and 10 am and 3.10 and 5.45 pm. From Lobatse, they run at 6.05 and 11.10 am and at 2 pm. The fare is US$2. The weekly bus between Lobatse and Ghanzi (12 hours, US$15) departs from

Lobatse at 9 am on Friday and Ghanzi at 9 am on Monday.

## KANYE
The hilltop settlement of Kanye, 50km along the tarred road north-west of Lobatse, once served as the capital of the Ngwaketse branch of the Tswana and is now one of Botswana's loveliest villages. The Ravos Vocational School is decorated with colourful murals and the students produce and sell clothing with original designs. East of the Seepapisto school is the impressive Kanye Gorge where the entire population of the village once hid during an Ndebele raid. A 1500m walk along the cliff face from the eastern end of the gorge will take you to the ruins of an early 18th-century stone-walled village, nestled between rocky kopjes.

## Places to Stay & Eat
Despite its name, Kanye's cosy hotel, *The Center* (☎/fax 340885), is actually east of the town. Standard singles/doubles cost US$28/35 and suites are US$45/65. When they have space, you can stay at the German-run *Ramatea Hostel*, in a lovely valley setting, for US$14.

The renowned *Mmakgodumo Restaurant* (☎ 340392; fax 340642), near the police station, is run by the Rural Industries Commission and serves excellent meals; it's closed Monday. The *Ko Gae Cafe* (☎ 341323) serves up traditional and vegetarian food; on Fridays, they stage jazz performances. The basic *Marapalalo Hotel* (☎ 340308) also has a restaurant, or you can choose between the *Halley's Comet* or *Lempu* snack bars.

# Eastern Botswana

In the winter it may bear a strong resemblance to a desert, but the scrubland strip along much of the South African and Zimbabwean borders is the part of Botswana most amenable to agriculture and human habitation. It's not exactly lush, but in the summer months the land does turn pleasantly green.

## FRANCISTOWN

Francistown, Botswana's second city, is without pretences. This randomly organised mining and industrial centre may have had a rich history, but for most visitors its *raison d'être* is retail and wholesale shopping.

Apart from the small museum, there's hardly anything of tourist interest – not even historical monuments or interesting churches. However, someone apparently took to heart the observation in previous editions of this book that Francistown lacked even a statue for the pigeons or a bit of kitsch architecture to liven up the scene; there's now a miniature replica of the Statue of Liberty in the grounds of the Cresta Thapama Lodge!

### History

Ancient stone tools and rock paintings reveal that this area has been inhabited for at least 80,000 years, probably by the San or their predecessors. Agriculture was introduced by Bantu groups around 200 AD, and evidence from ancient gold workings suggests that during the Great Zimbabwe era (the 12th to 15th centuries) the region lay along Swahili and Portuguese trade routes. It was later incorporated into the Torwa and Rozwi Shona states, which controlled much of present-day Zimbabwe until the early 19th century. As a result, the predominant language is the Shona dialect, Kalanga, rather than Tswana, and ruins in the district more resemble those around Bulawayo than early Tswana settlements.

In the 1820s, the Ndebele stormed

## HIGHLIGHTS

- Learn about Botswana's heritage at Serowe, the home of Sir Seretse Khama
- Look for Botswana's largest concentration of rhino at the Khama Rhino Sanctuary
- Enjoy the wild rocky scenery and diverse wildlife in Mashatu Game Reserve
- Camp beside the Tati River at Francistown's Marang Hotel

BOTSWANA

through before coming to rest near Bulawayo, bringing their influences and taxation to the Kalanga territory of northeastern Botswana. The first European to visit Nyangabgwe (the nearest village to present-day Francistown) was missionary Robert Moffat. He was followed by geologist Karl Mauch, who discovered gold along the Tati River in 1867 and sparked off southern Africa's first gold rush. It drew prospectors from as far as California and Australia. Without deference to the local Kalanga people, an impromptu settlement

483

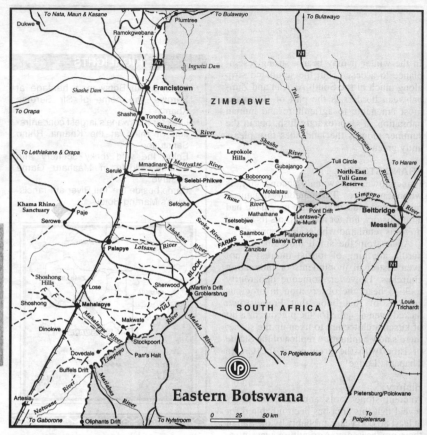

Eastern Botswana

0    25    50 km

sprang up on the Tati River to accommodate the incoming white population.

In 1869 came a group of Australian miners, along with Englishman Daniel Francis, who sunk a productive 20m mine shaft and thereby established a mining operation, Tati Concessions. Although he pulled up stakes in 1870 and headed for the newly discovered Kimberley diamond fields, he returned 10 years later to negotiate local mining rights with the Ndebele king, Lobengula, and laid out the town that now bears his name.

The foundations for Francistown's current industrial boom were established just prior to Zimbabwean independence, when Rhodesian firms threatened by economic sanctions migrated south and turned the town into the economic hub of eastern Botswana. Currently under construction is the Letsibogo Dam on the Motloutse River, south of town, which will provide water for Gaborone.

### Orientation

Francistown's central area is concentrated

between the railway line on the west, Khama St on the east, Selous Ave on the north and the Cresta Thapama Lodge on the south. The main shopping malls – The Mall, Blue Jacket Mall, the Smart Centre (or Barclays Plaza) and Blue Jacket Plaza – are lined up on Blue Jacket St. (The odd street name is taken from that of the Blue Jacket Gold Mine, which was in turn derived from the nickname for the Danish miner Sam Andersen, who always wore a blue denim jacket.)

Wholesale outlets are concentrated in the industrial area west of the centre. Further afield lies a dusty, desultory periphery characterised by Botswana's most squalid shanty towns – pockets of real poverty in this otherwise prosperous country.

## Information

There's no tourist office – and no need for one – but you can direct queries to the Supa-Ngwao Museum. For coming events, see the free weekly paper, the *Francistown News & Reviews* (☎/fax 212040); it's issued on Fridays.

**Money** Most banks lie along Blue Jacket St. Only at the end of the month are there long queues.

**Post & Communications** The main post office is on Blue Jacket St. The Botswana Telecom telephone office on Lobengula Ave is open weekdays, 7.45 am to 12.30 pm and 1.45 to 4 pm, and on Saturday, from 8 to 11 am.

**Bookshops** Blue Jacket Mall has a large branch of the Botswana Book Centre. The Francistown Stationers Bookshop on Haskins St, opposite the railway, has a few light novels and magazines. Glossy souvenir books on African topics are sold at BGI Tanning, over the railway from the centre.

**Laundry** Automatic laundry service is available at the Polina Laundrette at the northern end of Blue Jacket St.

**Camping Equipment** The best bet for camping equipment is Ebrahim Store on Tainton Ave.

**Left Luggage** The left luggage office at the railway station is open Monday to Friday from 4.45 am to 12.30 pm and from 2 to 9 pm and on Saturday from 4.45 to 10.30 am and 5 to 9 pm.

**Emergency Services** Nyangabgwe Hospital lies a few hundred metres east of the Cresta Thapama roundabout. For emergency medical services dial ☎ 997. The Hana Pharmacy in Blue Jacket Plaza and Pharma North Pharmacy, diagonally opposite it, are the best stocked. The police station (emergency ☎ 999) is on Haskins St, north of the central area.

## Supa-Ngwao Museum

Francistown isn't the most exciting place, but the Supa-Ngwao regional museum, in the old Francistown Court House, has displays on the region's culture and history, and hosts visiting exhibitions and events. In the small shop you can purchase regional maps, books and scholarly publications. It's open Tuesday to Saturday from 9 am to 1 pm and from 2 to 5 pm.

## Places to Stay

Francistown's upmarket choice is the *Cresta Thapama Lodge* (☎ 213872; fax 213766), which now has a casino and caters mainly for business travellers. Singles/doubles with breakfast cost US$78/99.

The good-value *Marang Hotel* (☎/fax 213991) is 5km from the centre on the old Gaborone road; follow the Matsiloje road from the Thapama roundabout. You can camp on the grassy lawn beside the banks of the Tati River for US$5 per person, including use of the hotel's showers, swimming pool and laundry. Comfortable single or double rooms or rondavels on stilts cost US$69, and single caravans with bath and toilet are US$28. Transfers are free from the centre and US$4 from the airport.

The *YWCA* (☎ 213046) has dormitory

**PLACES TO STAY**
6 Grand Lodge
32 Thapama Lodge

**PLACES TO EAT**
5 Chicken Run
7 Tasty Eats
8 Kismet Takeaways
18 Francistown Cafe
19 Ho Cafe
20 Tina's Coffee Shop
25 House of Pizza
26 Bus Stop Cafe & Takeaway
27 Silver Spur Steak House
35 Francistown Sports Club & Barbara's Bistro

**OTHER**
1 Supa-Ngwao Museum
2 Police
3 Nite Moves
4 Polina Laundrette
9 Standard Chartered Bank; Francistown Stationers Bookshop
10 Barclays Bank
11 Fruit & Vegetable Market
12 Post Office
13 Sam Edward City Park
14 Botswana Telecom Office
15 Blue Jacket Mall: Botswana Book Centre; Air Botswana; Pie City; Chicken City
16 Railway Station
17 BGI Tanning
21 First National Bank
22 The Mall: Hot & Crusty Bakery; Spar Supermarket; Snack Box; Nando's
23 Smart Centre (Barclays Plaza)
24 Ebrahim Store
28 Ritzma Sounds Bar
29 Bus Terminal
30 Blue Jacket Plaza: Hana Pharmacy; Kentucky Fried Chicken; Pie City; Milano Pizza & Chicken
31 Pharma North Pharmacy
33 Bank of Botswana
34 Nyangabgwe Hospital

**Francistown**

0     200     400 m

To Bulawayo

To Nata & Maun

To Nata & Maun

To YWCA, Satellite Guest House (2km) & Marang Hotel (4.5km)

To Gaborone

accommodation for US$12. Follow the Matsiloje road from the Thapama roundabout, turn right onto Teemana Drive at the Botsalano Bar, past the Nyangabgwe Hospital, and the YWCA is 200m further on the left.

If you prefer the town centre, the newly refurbished *Grand Lodge* (☎ 212300; fax 212309) has singles/doubles with toilet and shower for US$34/40.

The *Satellite Guest House* (☎ 214665; fax 202115), in the Satellite township, is in a walled compound and welcomes guests

with some unease. Air-conditioned singles/doubles cost US$33/44 and lunch and dinner are available during set hours. From the Thapama roundabout, follow the Matsiloje road for 3km, turn left opposite the school for the deaf and continue about 250m.

On the banks of the Shashe River, 30km south of town, is the three-star *Oasis Lodge* (☎ 284880), where prices start at US$34/40 for singles/doubles.

**Places to Eat**

For English/continental breakfasts, the

*Marang Hotel* offers excellent value at US$7/5, and in the evening there's a salad bar and fixed menu for around US$10 per person. The buffet breakfast at *Cresta Thapama Lodge* costs US$8; for dinner try their Ivory Grill, which serves carvery and curry dishes. Light snacks are available at the pool terrace in the afternoon and the cocktail bar serves light meals and snacks.

*Barbara's Bistro* at the Francistown Sports Club serves up tasty and inexpensive takeaways, lunches and dinners daily except Monday; visitors must pay US$2 for temporary club membership. Members also have access to the miniature golf course from noon to 2 pm and 7 to 11 pm from Monday to Saturday. Across the car park from the Blue Jacket Plaza is the *Silver Spur Steak House*, which predictably sizzles up slabs of local beef.

The Botswana chicken theme is perpetuated by the *Kentucky Fried Chicken* in Blue Jacket Plaza, *Chicken City* near Blue Jacket Mall, *Nando's* in The Mall (the best!) and *Chicken Run*, at the northern end of Blue Jacket St. Opposite the last-named is *Tasty Eats*, with curries, rotis, grills and savoury snacks. A fast food alternative is *Pie City*, with outlets in Blue Jacket Plaza and Blue Jacket Mall. For rice and stew, chicken, *sadza*, muffins, pies, cakes and coffee in a cosy atmosphere, try *Tina's Coffee Shop* on Blue Jacket St.

The popular *House of Pizza* cooks its pizzas in a wood stove and also does chicken, kebabs and pasta dishes. You'll also find tasty pizzas at *Milano Pizza & Chicken*, off the Blue Jacket Plaza car park. The *Bus Stop Café & Takeaway*, on Haskins St, fills the halal Chinese niche, and also serves chicken, burgers and steaks.

Cheap 'boozing and billiards' takeaways lie on or near Haskins St, including *Ma Kim's Café*, the *HO Café*, the *Snack Box*, *Kismet Takeaways* and the *Francistown Café*.

In addition to four well stocked supermarkets, Francistown has a small outdoor market and bus-terminal food stalls selling fruit, vegetables and light hot snacks. The

*Hot & Crusty Bakery* in The Mall bakes fresh bread and sweet treats. *Downing's Bakery* in the Industrial Sites specialises in British-style hot cross buns and other fresh bread confections.

### Entertainment
*Ma Kim's Café* has a lively and well patronised bar. A popular dance spot is the *Ritzma Sounds Bar* on Doc Morgan Ave beyond the Tati bridge. It's open for alcohol and fast food from 6 am to midnight, with jazz and dancing in the evenings. The young set also frequents the rather animated *Nite Moves*, on Blue Jacket St.

The *Marang Hotel* bar is always crowded. The pub at the *Cresta Thapama Lodge* attracts business travellers, but on one Friday per month it features a well attended happy hour, with live bands and a disco.

### Things to Buy
BGI Tanning, across the pedestrian bridge over the railway line, produces leather goods and stuffed African wildlife (imagine buying a stuffed kudu – 'the ideal decorative piece as a reminder of your visit to Africa'). It's also a source of Shashe baskets, which are more loosely woven than their Ngamiland counterparts.

Marothodi (☎ 213646) produces brilliant colour-fast fabrics and clothing handprinted with original wildlife motifs and traditional basketry patterns. Five km out on the Gaborone road, turn right into the BMC road; after 200m, look for the Marothodi sign on your left.

### Getting There & Away
**Air** The Air Botswana office (☎ 212393) is in the Blue Jacket Mall. Between Gaborone and Francistown (US$111), Air Botswana has morning and afternoon flights on Tuesday and Friday.

**Bus** Because it's at the intersection of the Gaborone, Nata/Kasanc, Bulawayo and Orapa roads, Francistown is a transportation hub. There are bus services to

Gaborone (US$10) from 10 am to noon daily and three daily services to Nata (US$3) and Maun (US$11). The bus terminal is wedged between the rail line and the frontage road connecting Haskins St and Doc Morgan Ave. The Mahube Express bus departs for Maun daily at 9.30 and 10.30 am.

For international connections, see the Botswana and Zimbabwe Getting There & Away chapters.

**Train** The daily trains between Bulawayo and Gaborone pass through Francistown at 9.20 pm southbound and 6.45 am northbound. The 1st/2nd class fares to Gaborone are US$25/21. The ticket office at the station is open weekdays from 7.30 am to 12.30 pm and 2 to 4.30 pm, and on Saturday from 7.30 to 10.30 am. For further timetable information, see the Zimbabwe Getting There & Away chapter.

**Hitching** To hitch to Maun, go to the tree near the airport turn-off where locals wait for lifts; just ask anyone and they'll show you where it is. Heading south, wait either at the Thapama roundabout or further out along the Gaborone road.

### Getting Around
As well as the ubiquitous minibuses, Francistown has taxis (☎ 212260) that resemble the minibuses and operate much like Zimbabwe's emergency taxis. They're most easily found at the railway station. Minibuses and share taxis are US$0.50 anywhere in the central area; look for their blue number plates.

When driving in the town centre, be mindful of the one-way streets between Haskins and Blue Jacket Sts.

### SELEBI-PHIKWE
This pleasant and scenic company town lies surrounded by small rock kopjes, savanna scrub and low, rugged hills. Prior to 1967, the site of Selebi-Phikwe was little more than a cattle post, but thanks to the Bamangwato Concessions Ltd (BCL) dis-

covery of the twin copper, nickel and cobalt deposits of Selebi and Phikwe, 14km apart, it's now Botswana's third largest community. Mining commenced in 1973 and the mines now produce a combined annual output of 2.5 million tonnes.

### Information
On The Mall, the heart of town, are the police, Botswana Telecom and post offices and a few eating places, as well as one of Botswana's finest bookshops. For a rundown of what's on at the many sports clubs, pick up a copy of the *Phikwe Bugle*, which is published on Friday.

### Things to See & Do
Admirable zoning policies and community efforts have resulted in a business district adorned with flowering trees and plants, but once you've strolled around The Mall, there's little to do. This could change, however, if they ever start up mine tours and allow visitors to gaze into the impressive Phikwe mine shaft.

### Places to Stay & Eat
The pleasant *Cresta Bosele Hotel* (☎ 810675; fax 811083) on Tshekedi Rd near The Mall owes its existence to mining business. Singles/doubles cost US$75/90. It has a standard dining room that puts on braais and buffets for bargain prices. Booked guests can be picked up at the airport or bus stop. The attached Menateng Casino provides a new attraction for Selebi-Phikwe.

Away from the centre is *Syringa Lodge* (☎ 810444; fax 810450), on the corner of Independence Ave and Airport Rd, and the attached *Red Lobster Restaurant* is the best in town. Singles/doubles with en suite facilities are US$75/90.

On The Mall, you can choose between *Pioneer Restaurant & Takeaways*, *Southern Fried Chicken Takeaways* and *Copper & Nickel Takeaways* (the name honours the mine and has nothing to do with the food). Further east on Independence Ave is the *Old Spice Catering Restaurant &*

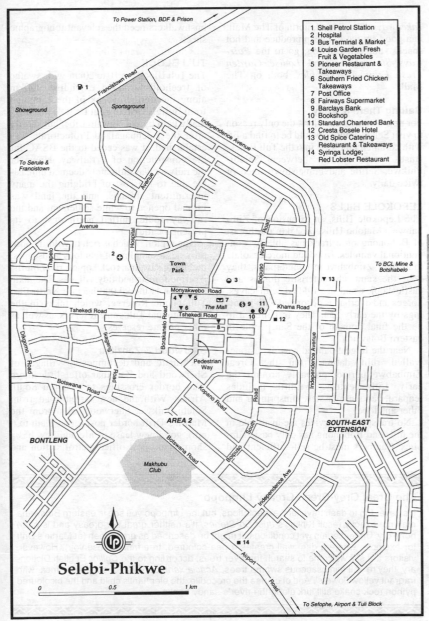

1 Shell Petrol Station
2 Hospital
3 Bus Terminal & Market
4 Louise Garden Fresh
  Fruit & Vegetables
5 Pioneer Restaurant &
  Takeaways
6 Southern Fried Chicken
  Takeaways
7 Post Office
8 Fairways Supermarket
9 Barclays Bank
10 Bookshop
11 Standard Chartered Bank
12 Cresta Bosele Hotel
13 Old Spice Catering
   Restaurant & Takeaways
14 Syringa Lodge;
   Red Lobster Restaurant

BOTSWANA

Selebi-Phikwe

0       0.5       1 km

*Takeaways.* The market, north of The Mall, is a good source of cheap produce and hot snacks. For self-catering, go to the *Fairways Supermarket* and *Louise Garden Fresh Fruit & Vegetables*, both on The Mall.

### Getting There & Away
For non-business travellers, the only reason to visit Selebi-Phikwe would be to find a lift with commercial traffic into the Tuli Block. Buses normally run between Selebi-Phikwe, Serule and Francistown once or twice daily.

## LEPOKOLE HILLS
The Lepokole Hills, an extension of Zimbabwe's Matobo Hills, lie 25km north-east of Bobonong on a track passable by conventional vehicles. Drier and more desolate than their Zimbabwean counterparts, they bear the same characteristic domes and castle kopjes and are riddled with caves, gorges and overhangs decorated with paintings by the early San. They're believed to be the final domain of the San people in eastern Botswana.

Near the largest painted cave is a stone-walled ruin dating from the Great Zimbabwe period, probably around the early 15th century. Wildlife includes leopard, baboons, dassies, klipspringer and other antelope.

No transport or services are available in the hills and Bobonong has only basic supplies. Campers must be self-sufficient and bushwalkers need the relevant topographic sheets.

## TULI BLOCK
The Tuli Block is a 10 to 20km-wide swathe of freehold farmland extending 350km along the northern bank of the Limpopo from Buffels Drift to Pont Drift. It was originally held by the Ngwato tribe, but shortly after the Bechuanaland Protectorate was established, it was ceded to the BSAC for the construction of a railway. However the railway was ultimately deemed unfeasible due to the cost of bridging the many intermittent streams, and the land was instead opened to white settlement and the railway route shifted north-west to its present location.

The region, which is rich in wildlife, also provides a sampling of fabulous landscapes, including savanna, rock kopjes, river bluffs, riverine forests and tidy villages. The main attraction is the 90,000 hectare North-East Tuli Game Reserve, which takes in the Mashatu and Tuli game reserves, as well as other private reserves.

### Sherwood & Zanzibar
The rustic and decomposing villages of Sherwood and Zanzibar offer little more than border crossings to or from South Africa. With the new tarred road from Selebi-Phikwe, Sherwood, 8km from the Martin's Drift border post (open 8 am to 6 pm), got a new lease of life and now has a shop, bank, post office, petrol station and

---

### The Great Grey-Green Greasy Limpopo
It's never fun to dash travellers' expectations, but the Limpopo you see in eastern Botswana may not exactly recall Kipling's *Just So Stories*. It's neither great nor greasy and is often bone dry. Under certain wet conditions, it might be described as grey-green (at Martin's Drift for example, where a dam wall creates a pea-coloured, tree-fringed reservoir). However, visitors are still welcome to search for fever trees; according to the *Collins* English Dictionary, they're 'tall mimosaceous swamp trees, *Acacia xanthophloea*, of southern Africa, with fragrant yellow flowers'. And of course the crocodile, the elephant's child and the bicoloured python rock snake still lurk along the river's sandy banks ...

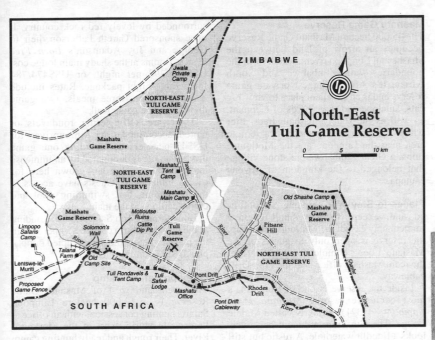

North-East
Tuli Game Reserve

ZIMBABWE

0    5    10 km

SOUTH AFRICA

bottle store. Zanzibar has only a small shop and bottle store.

The 105km rough gravel road between Sherwood and Zanzibar is a horrid series of dips through dry river crossings. Between Zanzibar and Pont Drift are two insignificant border crossings, Saambou and Platjanbridge, which close at 4 pm. From near Baine's Drift, which has a police checkpoint, you'll have a long-range view of South Africa's dramatic Blaberg Range.

### Pont Drift

Pont Drift, Botswana's easternmost village, is also a border crossing to or from South Africa. There's no bridge, so when the Limpopo is too deep to be forded, vehicles may not cross. Passengers are carried across the river on the rustic Pont Drift cableway, which costs US$4 per person. Immediately beyond the immigration post is the Mashatu Game Reserve office.

### Motloutse Crossing

The intermittent Motloutse (large elephant) River enters the Limpopo 27km west of Pont Drift. At the crossing, where deep sand necessitates 4WD, the 30m-high dolerite (a coarse-grained granite-like basalt) dyke known as Solomon's Wall cuts through the landscape on either side of the riverbed. On the western bank, this bizarre formation can be explored on foot (the eastern bank lies in the Mashatu Game Reserve). Look for agates and quartzite crystals in the riverbed.

Immediately east of the crossing, the road enters a small detached chunk of the Mashatu Game Reserve where you'll see some lovely landscapes and lots of wildlife. Travellers were once allowed to camp in the riverside mashatu trees west of the crossing (which belong to Talana Farm) but, due to the level of local prejudice against budget travellers, this practice has now been officially prohibited.

## Mashatu Game Reserve

The 45,000 hectare Mashatu Game Reserve occupies an arrow of land between the Shashe and Limpopo rivers, which form the boundaries with Zimbabwe and South Africa. It's Africa's largest private game reserve and is an excellent place to view big cats, antelope and large herds of elephant, as well as the stately mashatu trees after which the reserve is named. In a remote area near the Limpopo are the Motloutse ruins, a Great Zimbabwe-era stone village that belonged to the kingdom of Mwene Mutapa.

**Places to Stay** Wild camping is prohibited and, except for the small exclave immediately east of the Motloutse crossing, the reserve is open only to guests of the Mashatu Lodge complex. Access is from the main Mashatu office near the Pont Drift cableway.

Inside the reserve is one of Botswana's most exclusive resorts, *Mashatu Main Camp* (☎ 845321), formerly called Majale Lodge. The Gin Trap, a dugout bar, overlooks a floodlit waterhole. A rustic but still luxurious alternative is the *Mashatu Tent Camp* (formerly Thakadu Tent Camp). Tents are furnished like hotel rooms with flush toilets and showers. Both camps have swimming pools. At Mashatu Main Camp, you'll pay US$249/386 for a single/double chalet, while Mashatu Tent Camp costs US$186/297. All rates include accommodation, meals, game drives and transfers from the Tuli Safari Lodge airstrip or the Pont Drift cableway. Contact Mashatu Game Reserve (☎ (011) 789 2677; fax 886 4382), Suite 4, Tulbaugh, 360 Oak Ave, Ferndale, PO Box 2575, Randburg 2125, South Africa.

## Tuli Game Reserve

The Tuli Game Reserve takes in a 7500 hectare chunk bitten out of the Mashatu Game Reserve. The beautifully situated *Tuli Safari Lodge* (☎/fax 845303), which is more down-to-earth than Mashatu, occupies a riverine oasis beside the Limpopo and is surrounded by lovely red rock country. It once sponsored Gareth Patterson, heir to George and Joy Adamson's *Born Free* legacy. Rooms at the shady main lodge cost US$176/298 per night, or US$474/784 for a three-night package. Rates include accommodation, three meals, two game drives and one game walk.

There are self-catering rondavels or tented accommodation 2km upriver for US$43 per person, including one game drive. The site is dominated by an immense mashatu tree, which has grown here for over a millennium. Guests have access to the restaurant, bar, swimming pool and other facilities at the main lodge.

Book through Tuli Safari Lodge. Landing at the private airstrip costs US$4 per seat in the plane (whether they're occupied or not), plus US$21 for customs fees.

## Limpopo Safaris Camp

The open land west of Mashatu Game Reserve is a 12,000 hectare Limpopo Safaris hunting concession, with an office at Lentswe-le-Muriti, west of the Motloutse River. Their rough and ready hunting camp, 5km north of the main road (4WD only), has very basic accommodation for US$30 per person, including game drives but no meals. Contact Gerhard Pretorius, Limpopo Safaris (☎ (011) 780 3374 or 976 3674) in Johannesburg, South Africa.

## Getting There & Away

**Air** Okavango Air (☎ 313308) has return flights between Gaborone and Tuli Safari Lodge's Pont Drift airstrip every Sunday. Flights are guaranteed with two or more passengers paying US$178 each.

**Bus** There's an occasional bus from Selebi-Phikwe to Bobonong and Molalatau, which sometimes continues on as far as Mathathane (23km from Platjanbridge). Service is erratic, so enquire at the bus terminal in Selebi-Phikwe.

**Car & Motorcycle** Some roads on the Botswana side are accessible to conventional vehicles – there's now a tarred road from Selebi-Phikwe to Lentswe-le-Muriti, for instance – but the most interesting areas, including the Motloutse River crossing, require 4WD. From Gaborone, the easiest access is via South Africa. However, when the river is too deep to be forded, you'll have to leave your vehicle in South Africa and use the Pont Drift cableway. Both the Mashatu and Tuli game lodges pick up booked guests from Pont Drift.

From the Gaborone-Francistown road, seven access routes lead into the Tuli Block: Artesia (53km north of Gaborone); Dinokwe; Mahalapye (from the north, there's a rough shortcut from Lose); 10km south or 20km north of Palapye; from Serule to Zanzibar via Selebi-Phikwe; and the good tarred road from Selebi-Phikwe to Sherwood via Sefophe.

**Hitching** Hitchers should prepare for long waits on these little-travelled byways.

## PALAPYE

Palapye began life as a humble railway station and siding serving the old Ngwato capital. The name was originally spelt Phalatswe, meaning 'many impala' in Kgalagadi or 'large impala' in Tswana. The current spelling is the result of mis-transliteration by early colonials.

When the Ngwato people shifted their capital to Serowe, 50km to the west, the town's economy shifted to agriculture, but when Botswana's largest coal reserves were discovered at Morupule in the desert west of town, mining proved more lucrative. In 1986, an immense coal-burning power plant was opened at Morupule, earning Palapye the nickname of Powerhouse of Botswana.

## Information

The commercial heart of town is the Engen shopping centre on the main highway, with a petrol station, a couple of takeaway places and the Crossroads Bookshop. Around the corner, 200m down the road towards the 'village', or town centre, is a gallery selling local arts.

## Old Phalatswe Church Ruin

The site of the Old Phalatswe Church is in the former Ngwato capital of Phalatswe, 20km east of Palapye, at the foot of the Tswapong Hills. After the Christian Ngwato Chief Khama III and his people arrived from Shoshong in 1889, Phalatswe was transformed from a stretch of desert to a settlement of 30,000.

The Gothic-style church was funded by the people and completed in 1892. When the Ngwato capital was moved to Serowe in 1902, King Khama sent a regiment to torch Phalatswe (the Palapye rail siding was left intact), but the church remained standing. Weathering has since taken its toll and bits of the church have disappeared into Serowe construction projects, but 1½ gables still stand and restoration work is underway. You can also search out the remnant poles of King Khama's kgotla and worked stones from other early Phalatswe buildings. Note that Phalatswe is a national monument and Botswana law requires that everything be left intact.

## Places to Stay & Eat

The upmarket *Cresta Botsalo* (☎ 420245; fax 420587) is frequented by weary drivers on the dreary Gaborone-Francistown route. Singles/doubles cost US$59/67. The restaurant is one of Palapye's best and the bar is predictably popular.

The friendly little *Palapye Hotel* (☎ 420277) lies opposite the railway station 5km east of the highway. It looks a bit tatty, but it's good value at US$34/43 for singles/doubles with TV and breakfast. More basic rooms start at US$23/34.

The Engen shopping centre on the main highway has two places for a quick bite: *Chicken Licken*, for chicken and chips, and *Pie City*, for tasty meat pies.

## Getting There & Away

Buses on the main Gaborone-Francistown route pass through Palapye; the fare from Gaborone is US$7. Northbound trains pass the town centre, 5km east of the main road, in the wee hours of the morning.

## MAHALAPYE

Mahalapye has little to offer but spacious skies, distant horizons and a welcome break from the highway. Drivers aim for it like a speeding bullet, past the badly written sign announcing the 'Tropic of Capricon', with the radio blaring, the pop tops open and dreams of a snack at Kaytee's – the truckies never miss this one – before facing the next stretch of open highway.

Until mis-transliteration took its toll, Mahalapye's name was Mhlatswe, which was derived from Sekgalagadi and means 'a large herd of impala'. Mahalapye is now a refuelling stop for vehicles and travellers, with lots of petrol stations, shops and takeaways. A popular place is the South African-style Shell/Whistle Stop at the north end of town.

### Shoshong

In the Shoshong Hills, 45km west of Mahalapye, are mine workings from as early as the 8th century, as well as the stone-walled ruins of an early Ngwato capital. Modern Shoshong is laid out according to the traditional Batswana plan, with both a primary and a subsidiary kgotla. You'll also see the mid-19th century remains of the Hermannsburg and LMS missions.

### Places to Stay & Eat

To reach the *Mahalapye Hotel* (☎ 410200), once affectionately called the Chase-Me-Inn, turn east at the post office, left at the roundabout and continue for about 1.5km to the hotel signpost. Singles/doubles cost US$49/55 without breakfast. Camping costs US$6 per person and a laundry service is available. Set English breakfasts cost US$6 and the dining room is good value for other meals. Marginally less expensive accommodation is available at the *Mahalapye Guest House*, 1km south of town.

Most travellers stop at *Kaytee's*, which serves up the best fare along the highway. The service is friendly and you can choose between takeaway and à la carte menus. The sign over the bar reads 'Kaytee's, the Pride of Botswana'. Other options include *Mr Rooster Golden Crisp Chicken*, the *Safari Restaurant*, the *Corner House Restaurant* and the *Chicago Takeaways Wagon*. There's also a well stocked supermarket.

### Entertainment

At Madiba, 4km west of town, is a Thursday night disco. On Friday, the Railway Club screens films, but guests must be invited by a club member. Railway Club membership (US$40 per family per year) includes use of the cinema, swimming pool and ping-pong tables as well as the basketball, tennis and squash courts and the cheapest bar in Mahalapye.

### Getting There & Away

Access to and from Mahalapye is similar to that for Palapye, but buses run more frequently to and from Gaborone (US$5).

## SEROWE

Sprawling Serowe (population 90,000), the Central District capital, is the largest village in Botswana and one of the largest in sub-Saharan Africa. Thanks to Chief Khama III, who moved the Ngwato capital from Phalatswe to Serowe in 1902, it's one of Botswana's most historically interesting villages.

South African writer Bessie Head was so taken by Serowe that she immortalised it in several of her works, including the renowned *Serowe – Village of the Rain Wind*. This book includes a chronicle of the Botswana Brigades Movement, which was established at Swaneng Hill Secondary School in 1965. This organisation has since brought vocational education to many remote areas.

### Khama III Memorial Museum

Around the mountain from The Mall is the Khama III Memorial Museum (☎ 430519). It was opened in October 1985 after a concerted effort by local citizens, including Leapeetswe Khama, who donated his home, the Red House, for the museum premises.

The museum outlines the history of the

## Sir Seretse Khama

When Ngwato chief Khama III died in 1923, he was succeeded by his son Sekgoma, who died only two years later. Because the heir to the throne, Seretse Khama, was only four years old, the job of regent went to his 21-year-old uncle, Tshekedi Khama, who left his studies in South Africa to return to Serowe.

An uproar in the Khama dynasty occurred in 1948 when Seretse Khama, heir to the Ngwato throne, met and married an Englishwoman, Ruth Williams, while studying law in London. As a royal, Seretse was expected – and required – to take a wife from a Tswana royal family. Indignant at such a breach of tribal custom, Tshekedi Khama had his nephew stripped of his inheritance. He was exiled from Serowe by the Ngwato government, and from the protectorate by the British, who assured him that he'd be better off in London than Bechuanaland.

However, Tshekedi Khama lost his regency when an overwhelming majority of the Ngwato population backed Seretse over his uncle, forcing Tshekedi Khama to gather his followers and settle elsewhere. Subsequent breakdowns in the Ngwato tribal structure prompted him to return in 1952 with a change of heart. Seretse was still being detained in the UK, however, and it wasn't until 1956, when he renounced his claim to the Ngwato throne, that he was permitted to return to Serowe with Ruth and take up residence. There, they began campaigning for Botswana's independence, which came 10 years later. As a result, Seretse Khama was knighted and became the country's first president, a post that he held until his death 14 years later.

In a final act of reconciliation, Sir Seretse Khama was buried in the royal cemetery in Serowe. Seretse's son, Ian Khama, was given the title of *Kgosi* (chief) of the Ngwato and Ian's mother, Lady Ruth Khama, now holds the title of *Mohumagadi Mma Kgosi* (honoured wife of the king and mother of the chief).

For a thorough treatment of this amazing saga, which reads like a well conceived novel, check out *A Marriage of Inconvenience – the Persecution of Seretse & Ruth Khama* by Michael Dutfield.

Sir Seretse Khama

Khama family, and includes displays on the personal effects of Chief Khama III and his descendants, as well as artefacts illustrating Serowe's history. The growing natural history section featuring a collection of African insects and snakes.

It's open Monday to Friday from 8.30 am to 12.30 pm and 2 to 4.30 pm, and on Saturdays from 11 am to 4 pm. Admission is free.

### Royal Cemetery

On Thathaganyana Hill in the village centre are the ruins of an 11th century village, which provide evidence of habitation long before the arrival of the Ngwato and the Khama dynasty in 1902. The royal graves lie atop this hill, overlooking the kgotla. The grave of Khama III is marked by a bronze duiker, the Ngwato totem. Police consider this vantage point to be sensitive, and require visitors to climb with a police escort.

## Khama Rhino Sanctuary

By the late 1980s, rhino were all but extinct in Botswana. In 1992, this drastic situation prompted Serowe residents to establish the 4300 hectare Khama Rhino Sanctuary, 20km north-west of Serowe, as a safe house for the country's few remaining rhino. Two bore holes were made at Serowe Pan and local farmers were relocated with compensation. Three white rhino have been relocated from Chobe and Moremi and five from South Africa, and there are also plans to relocate black rhino. The reserve is patrolled 24 hours a day by BDF trainees from nearby Paje village.

The reserve is open daily from 8 am to 6.30 pm. Admission is US$3 per vehicle plus US$1 per person, and camping at Mekonwa Camp is US$3 per person. Contact the Khama Rhino Sanctuary (☎/fax 430713), PO Box 10, Serowe.

## Places to Stay & Eat

The *Serowe Hotel* (☎ 430234) has bright singles/doubles with shared facilities starting at US$48/56; they're cheaper without a phone. An English/continental breakfast costs US$5/4.

The run-down *Tshwaragano Hotel* (☎ 430377), on the hillside above The Mall, has grimy singles/doubles for US$37/45. If it weren't for all the trash, it wouldn't be too bad, but only eat at the restaurant if you have sterling patience. The attached public bar is the heart of the Serowe social scene.

For meals, your best option is either the Serowe Hotel dining room or *Tshukudu* (Rhino) *Takeaways* at the Engen petrol station. You'll also find Indian and Chinese takeaway meals at the *Central Supermarket Restaurant* in The Mall.

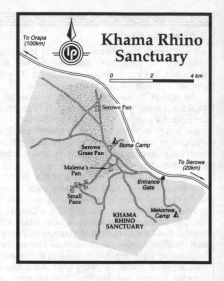

## Things to Buy

The intricate and easily recognisable Serowe woodcarving is produced at Marulamans near Serowe. You can visit either the Serowe Woodcarvers outlet near the Cash Bazaar in The Mall, or the workshop, which is a complicated trip from the centre. For directions, see the Roman Catholic mission, which sponsors the artists.

## Getting There & Away

On public transport, you'll first need to get to Palapye, where you can catch a bus for the last 46km to Serowe. Some buses continue to Orapa while others return to Palapye. Hitching from Palapye is straightforward, thanks to traffic to the Orapa diamond mine. Note that reaching Maun via Orapa requires 4WD from Rakops to the Nata-Maun road. This route isn't feasible for hitching.

# North-Eastern Botswana

With its fabulous national parks and wildlife reserves, north-eastern Botswana holds a strong appeal. Wildlife-rich Chobe National Park is one of Botswana's biggest draws and the recently amalgamated Makgadikgadi and Nxai Pan National Park offers a pristine vision of Africa.

## The Makgadikgadi Pans

Botswana's great Sua and Ntwetwe pans collectively comprise the 12,000 sq km Makgadikgadi Pans (not to be confused with the grassy national park, which includes only a corner of Ntwetwe Pan). These landscapes are like no other on earth; especially in the sizzling heat of late winter, the stark pans take on a disorienting and ethereal austerity. Heat mirages destroy all sense of space or direction, imaginary lakes shimmer and disappear, ostriches fly, and stones turn to mountains and float in mid-air.

Then, in September, herds of wildebeest, antelope and zebra move into the thirsty grasslands west of the pans to await the first rains. Although the water is short-lived, wildlife gravitates towards depressions that retain stores of water after the surface film has evaporated.

Around December, the deluge begins. The fringing grasses turn green and the herds arrive to partake of the bounty. Flamingoes, pelicans, ducks, geese and other water birds flock to the mouth of the Nata River to build shoreline nests and feed on algae and tiny crustaceans that have lain dormant in the salt during the dry period.

### Geology
The Makgadikgadi Pans are the residue of

a great lake that once covered much of northern Botswana, fed by rivers carrying salts leached from the lake's catchment area. Ancient lakeshore terraces reveal that the water depth fluctuated by as much as 33m and, at its greatest extent, the lake covered an area of 60,000 sq km. Because the basin had no outlet, the salts were concentrated in low-lying areas. Less than 10,000 years ago, climatic changes caused the lake to evaporate, leaving only salt deposits.

### Visiting the Pans
In the dry season, you can have a cursory

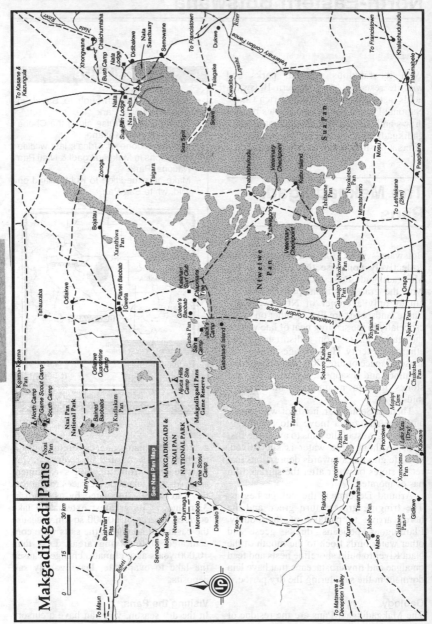

look at Sua Pan without 4WD. The easiest and quickest is in Nata Sanctuary. Another access route is via the signposted turn-off to Sua Spit.

To get deeper into the pans independently requires more of an expedition than a casual drive. The region is crisscrossed with tracks and safe routes are changeable and unreliable; always seek local advice before venturing off. Three north-south networks of tracks connect the Nata-Maun road with the Francistown-Orapa road, one on either side of the pans and one down the strip between them (which is the access for Kubu Island). For any of these, you need a 4WD, a map, compass or (preferably) GPS, lots of common sense, and confidence in your driving and directional skills (see Wild Driving in Botswana in the Botswana Getting Around chapter). You must also be self-sufficient in food, fuel, water and vehicle supplies.

Several safari companies offer organised expeditions and can save you the considerable time and expense of organising a private expedition. Phakawe Safaris (see under Maun in the next chapter) does budget mobile safaris into the wildest reaches of the pans for as little as US$60 per person per day, including meals and camping. Alternatively, you can take a short Nata Lodge tour (see under Nata) to the edge of Sua Pan for US$25 per person (with a minimum of four people). Otherwise, you may be able to share expenses and join someone else's expedition; ask around Nata Lodge or Gweta Rest Camp.

## NATA

Nata is little more than a dust hole that serves as a refuelling stop for travellers between Kasane, Francistown and Maun. If you're counting, Nata lies 190 smooth kilometres from Francistown, and 300km from both Kasane and Maun. If you have car trouble, see Peter Robson (☎ 611226 or 611227); take a left off the Francistown road immediately beyond the Nata River bridge. His shop lies 700m down this road, just over the T-junction.

## Organised Tours

For groups of up to 10 people, Nata Lodge runs Sua Pan tours and custom safaris to Makgadikgadi and Nxai Pan National Park.

## Places to Stay & Eat

The action in Nata, inasmuch as it has any, centres on Sua Pan Lodge (☎/fax 611220) with its fuel pumps, water tap, bottle store, bar, restaurant, hotel, dust-corrupted swimming pool and campground. Single or double rondavels with bath cost US$37, camping in less-than-tranquil conditions (50m from the public bar) is US$3.50 per person and a buffet breakfast costs US$6. Non-guests pay US$4 to use the pool.

The new Caltex petrol station complex includes the North Gate Restaurant & Takeaway, which specialises in meat dishes and greasy snacks.

The friendly Nata Lodge (☎ 611260; fax 611210), 10km south-east of Nata on the Francistown road, has a much nicer campground. It's set in a green oasis of monkey thorn, marula and mokolane palms, and also boasts an excellent and affordable restaurant, an outdoor bar, a Shell petrol station and a cool swimming pool. Three/four-bed chalets are US$56/72. Preset four-bed tents, which are great for groups, cost US$39 with bedding. Tent or caravan camping costs US$5 per person, including use of the pool. English/continental breakfasts cost US$7/6 and three-course dinners are US$15. Hitching from Nata isn't too difficult.

Also see Nata Sanctuary under Sua Pan in this section.

## Getting There & Away

All buses between Kasane, Francistown and Maun pass through Nata. Since the petrol station at the Sua Pan Lodge is a natural travellers' stop, it's the best place to wait for lifts. You may also arrange lifts around the bar at Nata Lodge. Mahube Express buses to Maun pass between 10 and 11 am.

## SUA PAN

Sua Pan is mostly a single sheet of salt-encrusted mud stretching across the lowest basin in north-eastern Botswana. Sua means salt in the language of the San, who once mined the pan to sell salt to the Kalanga. In wet seasons of normal rainfall, flocks of water-loving birds gather to nest at the delta where the Nata River flows into the northern end of Sua Pan. At these times, its expanses are covered with a film of water only a few centimetres deep, creating an eerie and surreal effect that reflects the sky and obliterates the horizon.

## Nata Sanctuary

The 230 sq km Nata Sanctuary is a community project designed as a refuge for the wildlife on and around Sua Pan (45% of the reserve is on the pan). The idea was first raised in 1988 by the Nata Conservation Committee and the sanctuary was realised four years later, thanks to the Kalahari Conservation Society and funding from national and international organisations. Local people voluntarily relocated 3500 cattle onto adjacent rangeland and established a network of dust roads.

Mammal species are restricted to antelope – hartebeest, kudu, reedbuck, springbok and steenbok – and springhares, jackals, foxes, monkeys and squirrels. Eland, gemsbok and zebra are being re-introduced, and current plans include engineering a permanent water hole, which will be filled with pumped water from the Nata riverbed.

However, most of the wildlife has wings and around 165 bird species – from kingfishers and bee-eaters to eagles, bustards and ostriches – have been recorded. There are also numerous savanna and woodland bird species. When the Nata River flows, this corner of Sua Pan becomes a paradise for water-loving birds from all around Africa: teals, ducks, geese, and hosts of pelicans, spoonbills and both greater and lesser flamingoes.

**Organised Tours** Nata Lodge offers good-value tours for groups.

**Getting There & Away** In the dry season,

you need a high-clearance vehicle but not necessarily 4WD. The entrance to Sua Pan lies 20km from Nata on the Francistown road. It's open from 7 am to 7 pm daily (but with special permission, you can visit earlier or later). Non-Batswana and resident non-citizens pay US$4 admission and US$4 to camp and use the braai facilities. Proceeds benefit the local community, which manages the sanctuary. At the entrance, women from surrounding villages sell hand-woven Nata baskets.

## Sua Spit

Sua Spit, about a 10 minute drive north of the Dukwe buffalo fence, is a long, slender protrusion extending into the heart of Sua Pan. It is the nexus of Botswana's lucrative soda ash industry. Security measures prevent public access to the plant, but private vehicles may proceed as far as Sua, on the pan's edge.

## Kubu Island

Near the south-western corner of Sua Pan lies Kubu Island, the original desert island. But for one tenuous finger of grass, this ancient 20m-high scrap of rock and its ghostly baobabs lie surrounded by a sea of salt. In cool weather, this bizarre sight can make visitors feel like castaways on an alien planet.

In Zulu-based languages, 'kubu' means 'hippopotamus', and as unlikely as it may seem, given the current environment, the site may have been inhabited as recently as 500 to 1500 years ago. On one shore lies an ancient crescent-shaped stone enclosure of unknown origin that has yielded numerous pot shards, stone tools and ostrich eggshell beads.

The GPS co-ordinates for Kubu Island are 20° 53' 50" S latitude and 25° 49' 41" E longitude. Note that no water is available on the island.

**Getting There & Away** Access to Kubu Island involves negotiating a maze of grassy islets and salty bays. Increased traffic has made the route considerably more obvious than it once was, but drivers still need 4WD and a compass or GPS.

Routes turn south from the Nata-Maun road at unsignposted junctions 11, 27 and 52km (at Zoroga village) west of Nata. The middle route, the most popular, crosses the old Nata-Maun road 2km from the turnoff, but keep following the crisscrossing tracks in a general southerly direction. In places, the road leads into cattle posts and appears to end but don't despair – just look in the bush beyond for tracks heading south.

After 65km, you'll reach the vaguely defined village of Thabatshukudu, which occupies an unearthly landscape on a low ridge. Villagers are used to lost visitors asking for directions to Kubu Island, and can sometimes help.

South of Thabatshukudu, the route skirts the edge of a salt pan and after 10km, passes through a veterinary checkpoint; just under 2km south of this barrier is the south-east (left) turning onto the northern route to Kubu Island (a turning to the west at Tshwagong, 5km further south, eventually leads over a corner of Ntwetwe Pan to Gweta).

Alternatively, you can approach from the south. Turn north off the Francistown-Orapa road about 20km east of Orapa (this is the road that passes between Sua and Ntwetwe pans). After 20km, you'll reach Mmatshumo village. (Approaching from Francistown, you can reach Mmatshumo via the back road from Tlalamabele via Mosu.) Mmatshumo has several exits, so make sure you get the one towards Thabatshukudu. The first 14km north of Mmatshumo is on an alternating rough and sandy track. After you cross an obvious line of trees at right angles to the road (indicating the presence of underground water), continue 6km to a veterinary checkpoint, 7.5km south of the turning to the right, which leads east to Kubu Island. The junction is marked only by a small cairn.

From either of these two turnings, you should be able to follow vehicle tracks over the salt and salt grass tussocks for 19km to Kubu Island. Before long, you'll see the island's rocky 20m summit. If you're not sure the pan is dry, stick to the roundabout route along the edge of the salt.

## NTWETWE PAN

Convoluted Ntwetwe Pan covers more area than its eastern counterpart, Sua Pan. It was once fed by the waters of the Boteti, but they were diverted at Mopipi Dam to provide water for the Orapa diamond mine and the pan is now almost permanently dry.

The western shore of Ntwetwe Pan is probably the most interesting in the Makgadikgadi area, with landscapes of rocky outcrops, dunes, islets, channels and spits.

### Green's & Chapman's Baobabs

At ephemeral Gutsa Pan, 30km due south of Gweta, rises Green's Baobab, which was inscribed by the 19th century hunter and trader Joseph Green and Ghanzi founder Hendrik van Zyl, among other characters. Fifteen km to the south-east by rough track is the enormous Chapman's Baobab, which measures 25m around and historically served as a beacon in a country of few landmarks. It's thought that it was also used as a post office by passing explorers, traders and travellers, many of whom left inscriptions on its trunk. It's frequently claimed that this is the largest tree in Africa.

### Gabatsadi Island

The enormous barchan (crescent) dune known as Gabatsadi Island may see only a handful of visitors each year, but the expansive view from the crest has managed to attract the likes of Prince Charles, who went to capture the indescribably lonely scene in watercolour. It lies west of the Gweta-Orapa track, 54km south of Gweta.

### Places to Stay

At the northern end of Ntwetwe Pan, Uncharted Africa Safaris (☎ 212277; fax 213458; <unchart@info.bw>) runs two novel camps that steep clients in retro safari luxury. *Jack's Camp*, which sits on a vast savanna surrounded by mokolane palms, is named after Jack Bousfield, an old Africa hand whose exploits carried him up and down the continent (he survived seven plane crashes before his final one in 1992). He was particularly inspired by the pans and his son Ralph set up the camp in his memory. The more remote *San Camp*, on a grassy bay at the fringe of Ntwetwe Pan, silently overlooks the sea of salt (Jack's Camp is open from 1 March to 1 January and San Camp from 15 April to 1 October).

If you can afford a splash-out, don't miss this experience, which has been described as 'a 1930s Hollywood fantasy – *Jungle Jim* or *Call Me Bwana*'. At either camp, accommodation in 1920s-style tents, full board, drinks, laundry, game drives, guides, park fees and use of ATVs (quad bikes) costs US$360/520 per day for singles/doubles, plus a US$5 community levy. Obligatory transfers from Gweta cost US$75 and air transfers from Maun are US$110 per person. Trips to Kubu Island cost US$280 per day.

For those whose means won't stretch that far, the same people have also set up the budget-oriented *Planet Baobab*, 25km from Gweta in a stand of eight giant baobabs. Here you can camp in your own tent (US$9 per day) or choose between double mud huts (US$80) with private ablutions or double San-style grass huts (US$50). Amenities include a swimming pool, laundry service, small provisions shop and communal kitchen; prepared meals are available for US$4 to US$9.

At the edge of Ntwetwe Pan, they've also established the similar *Kalahari Surf Club*, where you can camp in your own tent (US$9) or hire one of theirs (US$7 per person). It makes a good base for hiking and knowledgeable local guides may be hired to keep you oriented and to explain the complexities of the ecological system of the pan. Transfers from Gweta to either camp cost US$20 per person, with a minimum of four people.

## Ostriches

The unmistakable ostrich, the world's largest living bird, is widely distributed throughout the savanna plains of Zimbabwe, Botswana and Namibia, both inside and outside of game reserves. It's particularly common in central Botswana and on the desert plains of western Namibia.

The adult ostrich stands around 2m high and weighs up to 150kg. In breeding males, the neck and legs, which are normally bare, turn a bright red colour. The ostrich's long legs can propel it over level ground at speeds of up to 50km/h. The black, bushy plumage highlighted with white feathers in the tail and redundant wings makes the males instantly recognisable. Females are a uniform greyish brown and are slightly smaller and lighter than the males.

Ostriches are territorial and rarely live in groups of over six individuals. They feed on leaves, flowers and seeds. When feeding, the food is accumulated in the top of the neck. It then passes down to the stomach in large lumps, and it can be amusing to watch these actually sliding down the neck.

During the dry season, the male puts on quite an impressive courtship display. Having driven off any rivals, he trots up to the female with tail erect, then squats down and rocks from side to side, while alternately waving his wings in the air. The neck also gets into the action and the females are clearly impressed. Males may mate with several females, but all the eggs from a given male's mates wind up in the same nest. Therefore, nests may contain as many as 30 eggs. By day, the eggs are incubated by the head female (the first one mated with); by night, the male takes over nest duties. His other mates have nothing further to do with the eggs or chicks.

The new *Makgadikgadi Camp* offers good-value tented accommodation on Ntwetwe Pan for US$150 per person, including meals, drinks, activities and ATV transfers from Gweta. Book through Gweta Rest Camp in Gweta.

Camping is possible around the edge of the salt – indeed campers can find it a haunting experience – but unfortunately there's no fresh water.

## GWETA

The village of Gweta, 100km west of Nata, is a popular refuelling and travellers' rest stop. As with Kwe Kwe in Zimbabwe, the name is derived from the croaking sound made by of large bullfrogs (*Pyxicephalus adspersus*). This species of frog actually bury themselves in the sand until the rains provide sufficient water for them to emerge and mate.

### Organised Tours

Gweta Rest Camp organises area tours and also cooks up custom safaris further afield. Three-hour horse-riding trips cost US$12; an all-day 4WD spin through the salt pans is US$75; two-night salt pan tours on four-wheel ATVs (all-terrain vehicles) are US$149; and walking tours of Gweta village cost US$2.

### Places to Stay & Eat

The *Gweta Rest Camp* (☎/fax 612220) provides a focus of activity and an inexpensive respite along the Nata-Maun road. The popular restaurant serves up well prepared meals and snacks and the communal ablutions have some of Botswana's best showers. Single/double thatched rondavels with shared bath are US$28/34; with private bath, they're US$37/45. Camping costs US$6 per person. Fuel is sold at the co-op near the back gate.

### Getting There & Away

Gweta lies 5km south of the Nata-Maun road. You can take the Mahube Express bus from either Maun (US$5) or Francistown (US$6).

## MAKGADIKGADI & NXAI PAN NATIONAL PARK

West of Gweta, the road slices through Makgadikgadi and Nxai Pan National Park. Because of their complementary natures regarding wildlife migrations, Makgadikgadi Pans Game Reserve and Nxai Pan National Park were established concurrently in the early 1970s, in the hope of protecting the entire ecosystem. In 1992, when the tarred highway was built, Nxai Pan National Park was extended south to the road to take in Baines' Baobabs, and the two parks are now administered as one entity.

Visitors to either section must pay park and camping fees (unless you're just transiting on the Nata-Maun road) at either the Xhumaga or Nxai Pan Game scout camp.

### Makgadikgadi Pans Game Reserve Section

South of the Nata-Maun road is the Makgadikgadi Pans Game Reserve section of the park, a 3900 sq km tract of pans, grasslands and beautiful savanna country. Wildlife is plentiful but since the reserve is unfenced, animals may wander in and out at will, and you won't see the artificially high numbers found at Chobe. During the winter dry season, animals concentrate around the Boteti River, but between February and April, huge herds of zebra and wildebeest migrate north to Nxai Pan and beyond, only returning to the Boteti when the rains diminish around early May.

The range of antelope includes impala, gemsbok, hartebeest and kudu, but they only appear in large numbers during the in-migrations during May and June. Lion, hyaena and cheetah are also present and when there's water, the Boteti River supports a healthy hippo population. You'll also see a stunning array of birds, but as there are no reliable water sources, elephant and buffalo wander in only during extremely wet seasons.

**Places to Stay** The public camp site is at the *Game Scout Camp* near Xhumaga, on the park's western boundary. There's a flush

---

## Mokolane Palms

Dotted around the Makgadikgadi & Nxai Pan National Park are islands of mokolane palm (*Hyphaene petersiana*), from which comes vegetable ivory. (They're known in Zimbabwe as ilala palms and in Namibia as makalani palms.) This solid white nut carves beautifully and is used in jewellery and art, while the fronds are the main component in the beautiful Botswana baskets. The palm is also tapped for its sap, which is allowed to ferment or is distilled into a potent liquor known as palm wine. The Makgadikgadi specimens are officially protected from thirsty sap-tappers, but elsewhere, over-exploitation and increasing numbers of cattle, which nibble the young shoots, have brought the palm under serious threat.

---

toilet and a sometimes operable cold shower, but the water is quite sulphurous. Wild camping is prohibited in the park.

You'll also find two 'wild' (but legal) *camp sites* atop the two Njuca Hills, 20km from the Game Scout Camp. Each has a pit toilet, but no water is available.

Just outside the park, 6km north of Xhumaga village, lies pleasant little Xwaraga Camp (☎ 430420; fax 430992), where you can camp along a lovely stretch of the Boteti River. There are also plans to open a lodge. Camping costs US$5 per person.

The nearest food supplies are found in bush shops in Gweta and Xhumaga village.

**Getting There & Away** Access is with 4WD only. The most straightforward way is along the worn route that turns south from the Nata-Maun road, 8km east of the Phuduhudu access road. From there, it's 30km of deep sand through palm groves and savannas to the Game Scout Camp beside the Boteti.

### Nxai Pan National Park Section

After the amalgamation of Makgadikgadi and Nxai Pan national parks, the Nxai Pan region was expanded from 2100 sq km to over 4000 sq km. Nxai Pan lies on the old Mpandamatenga Trail, which connected a series of boreholes and was used until the 1960s for overland cattle drives between Ngamiland and Kazungula.

Kudiakam Pan and Nxai Pan are both part of the ancient lake bed that formed Sua and Ntwetwe pans. Kudiakam is comprised of mini salt pans, but thanks to its higher elevation, Nxai Pan escaped encrustation by leached salts.

The Nxai Pan region is specked with umbrella acacias and resembles the Serengeti (without all the safari vehicles). In the dry season, wildlife activity concentrates on one artificial water hole, just north of the Game Scout Camp, but in the February to April wet season, Nxai Pan comes alive. Your movements may be restricted by high water, but the wildlife herds in Nxai's grassy pans can be staggering; wildebeest, zebra and gemsbok appear in thousands, along with large herds of other antelope and giraffe. Bat-eared foxes emerge in force and lion, hyaena and wild dogs come to gorge on the varied menu.

From South Camp, it's 15km to the Eastern Pan Complex, which is also rich in wildlife. Nine km further on is the southern end of Kgama-Kgama Pan, where King Khama III of the Ngwato once had a cattle post.

**Baines' Baobabs** Originally known as the Sleeping Sisters, this hardy clump of baobabs was immortalised in paintings by artist and adventurer Thomas Baines on 22 May 1862. Baines, a resourceful self-taught naturalist, artist and cartographer, first came to Botswana in 1861, and travelled with trader and naturalist John Chapman from Namibia to Victoria Falls.

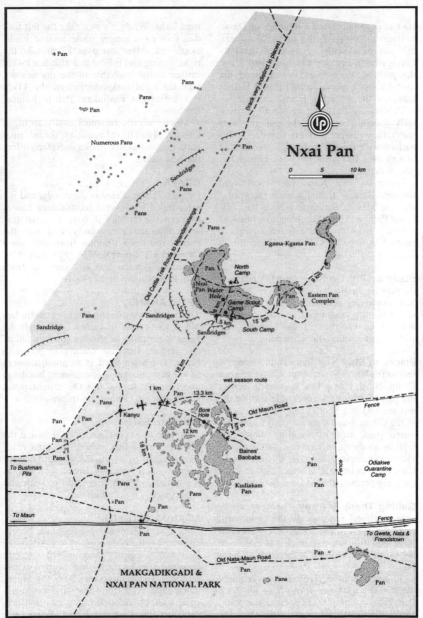

Nxai Pan

0    5    10 km

Kgama-Kgama Pan

North
Camp

Nxai
Pan Water
Hole

Game Scout
Camp

South Camp

Eastern Pan
Complex

9 km

15 km

1.5 km

Old Cattle Trek Route to Mwandamatenga

Numerous Pans

Sandridges

Sandridge

Sandridges

Sandridges

Pans

Pans

Pans

Pans

Pans

Pan

Pan

Pan

Pan

Pan

Pan

18 km

wet season route

1 km

13.3 km

Kanyu

Bore
Hole

12 km

Baines'
Baobabs

Old Maun Road

Fence

5 km

18 km

Pans

Pans

Pan

Pan

Pan

Pan

Pan

Pan

Pan

Pan

Pan

Pan

Pan

Kudiakam
Pan

Odiakwe
Quarantine
Camp

Fence

To Bushman
Pits

To Maun

Fence

To Gweta, Nata &
Francistown

Old Nata-Maun Road

Pan

Pan

Pans

Pan

MAKGADIKGADI &
NXAI PAN NATIONAL PARK

BOTSWANA

He had originally been a member of David Livingstone's expedition to the Zambezi, but was mistakenly accused of theft by Livingstone's brother and forced to leave the party. Livingstone later realised the mistake, but never admitted it and Baines remained the subject of British ridicule.

This stately cluster of trees isn't particularly special, but when the pan contains water, they present a lovely scene. A comparison with Baines' paintings reveals that in well over 100 years, only one branch has disassociated itself.

When the new Nata-Maun road went through, Baines' Baobabs were incorporated into Makgadikgadi and Nxai Pan National Park, and bush camping now requires a permit from the Game Scout Camps at either Xhumaga or Nxai Pan. There are no facilities.

**Bushman Pits** On the western boundary of the park lie the Bushman Pits. Here, ancient San people dug pits where they could hide while hunting animals that had come to drink at the waterhole. These bunkers may still be seen around the waterhole.

**Places to Stay** Nxai Pan visitors must be self-sufficient. From the Game Scout Camp, North Camp lies 8km north across the pan (it may be inaccessible during the wet season) and South Camp is 1.5km east of the Game Scout Camp. South Camp has toilets (and, most of the time, water), as well as an elevated viewing platform providing a sweeping view over the pan. North Camp has toilets and a water tap. Pay for camping permits at the Game Scout Camp.

**Getting There & Away** The very sandy approach road requires 4WD. Turn north from the Nata-Maun road 170km west of Nata and follow that track for 35km to the Game Scout Camp at the edge of Nxai Pan.

To reach Baines' Baobabs also requires 4WD. Take the same turn-off as for Nxai Pan, but drive only 18km north of the Nata-Maun road and turn right. After 1km, the road forks. When it's wet, take the left fork that follows a longer route around Kudiakam Pan. After just over 13km, take the right turning and follow that side track 4km further to the baobabs. In the dry season, take the right fork and follow the 11km shortcut across Kudiakam Pan to Baines' Baobabs.

Mobile safaris are most easily arranged through Maun travel agencies; for informal participation safaris, Phakawe Safaris offers the best value.

### ORAPA

Orapa's *raison d'être* is diamonds, and it's surrounded by several intimidating fences to keep the public at bay. To visit this self-contained community and see the mines, you need a permit from Debswana (☎ 351131; fax 352941), PO Box 329, Gaborone. Orapa has bus services from both Francistown and Palapye.

### LETHLAKANE

This aloof little diamond mining centre lies 40km south-east of Orapa. Although the Lethlakane mine is smaller than its Orapa counterpart, the gem quality is generally better. The town itself is an amalgamation of workers' housing, government buildings and petrol stations, but the mountainous heaps of mine tailings are impressive.

### Places to Eat

*The* place to eat is *Granny's Kitchen* at the Shell petrol station, where the sign reads 'Book early to avoid disappointment'. It features such typically Botswanan fare as roast beef and Yorkshire pudding with port wine sauce – by candlelight.

### MPANDAMATENGA

This minor Zimbabwe-Botswana border crossing off the Nata-Kasane road sits in the heart of sorghum and maize country between the Kazuma and Sibuyu forest reserves. The name comes from the Mpandamatenga Trail from central Botswana, a route used by colonial hunters to transport ivory to the Zambezi River. What little action there is focuses on the Shell petrol station.

There's a small border crossing to the Zimbabwean village of Pandamatenga, which is pronounced the same way. Note that you cannot visit Zimbabwe's Kazuma Pan National Park until you've checked in at the Matetsi ranger station.

# Chobe National Park

After a visit in the 1930s, Sir Charles Rey, the Resident Commissioner of Bechuanaland, proposed that Chobe be set aside as a game reserve. Nothing happened until 1960, when a small portion was placed under official protection. It wasn't until 1968, after Botswana's independence, that the present national park was created by the new government. Today, Chobe encompasses 11,000 sq km and is one of the nation's greatest tourist draws.

The riverfront strip along the northern tier of Chobe, with its perennial water supply, supports the greatest wildlife concentrations in the park, but the lovely Savuti Marshes and Mababe Depression are also prime wildlife habitats, and when they contain water they support myriad birdlife. Little-visited Ngwezumba, with its pans and mopane forests, is the park's third main region, and in Chobe's north-western corner there is the vast and magnificent Linyanti Marshes ecosystem. As yet, most of this region remains unprotected.

The northern park entrance lies 6km west of Kasane, but you need 4WD to proceed into the park. The approach from Maun is characterised by deep sand and a high-clearance 4WD is essential. Due to high water and deep mud, Savuti is normally inaccessible (and closed) from January to March. There has been discussion of building a tarred road between Maun and Kasane, but it's unlikely, as nearly everyone agrees that easy access would destroy Chobe's wild ambience.

## KASANE & KAZUNGULA
Kasane was once the capital of the Makololo, who came as refugees from the invading Ndebele. The Makololo conquered the incumbent Lozi tribe and guided David Livingstone to Victoria Falls. Modern visitors arriving from neatly manicured Victoria Falls are either charmed or appalled by its sense of African spontaneity.

Kasane sits amid a shady, riverine woodland at the meeting point of four countries – Botswana, Zambia, Namibia and Zimbabwe – and the confluence of the Chobe and Zambezi rivers. It's the Chobe District administrative centre and the gateway to Chobe National Park. As such, this small town is a focus of activity.

Six kilometres east of Kasane is tiny Kazungula, which serves as the border post between Botswana and Zimbabwe and the landing for the Kazungula Ferry between Botswana and Zambia.

### Information
Buried in a cluster of caravans east of the bank is Kasane's friendly but less-than-helpful tourist office (☎ 250327). For Chobe National Park information and rudimentary maps, visit the National Parks office 6km west of Kasane.

**Money** The Barclays Bank occupies an odd structure on the main road through town. It's open Monday, Tuesday, Wednesday and Friday from 8.15 am to 12.45 pm and on Thursday and Saturday from 8.15 to 10.45 am. At month-end, budget a few hours to wait in the queue.

**Post & Communications** The post office lies about 300m north-east of Chobe Safari Lodge. There are public telephones at the new airport, at the post office and in Kazungula village.

**Immigration** The Immigration posts for Zimbabwe, Zambia and Namibia are at Victoria Falls road, the Kazungula ferry and Ngoma Bridge, respectively. There's also a minor Namibian border post between the

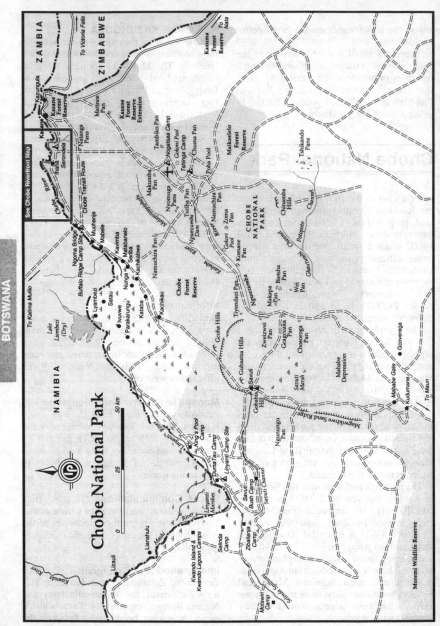

Cresta Mowana and Impalila Island lodges, which is used mainly by guests of the latter.

**Film & Photography** Film is sold at Sava's Superette and the Cresta Mowana Lodge.

**Pharmacy** After years without medication for its ills, in 1995 Kasane saw the opening of the Okavango Pharmacy (☎ 650334). It's open Monday to Friday from 8 am to 1 pm and 2 to 5 pm and on Saturday from 8 am to 1 pm.

**Vehicle Repairs** When your vehicle is protesting, see Mr Kruger at the friendly and reliable Four-Ways Motor Repairs (☎ 650117; fax 650478) in Kazungula.

**Things to See**
Visitors to Kazungula won't want to miss the two hollow baobabs at the Botswana Women's Prison; in past years, one was

actually used as a cell and the other as a prison kitchen. This is considered a strategic site and photography is prohibited.

The Chobe Reptile Park in Kazungula claims to be the proud owner of the world's largest captive crocodile (known as Nelson) and his rival, Blob, among other creatures. It's not currently open to the public but is likely to re-open soon.

Two kilometres west of Kubu Lodge, the Seep Hot Spring bubbles out above the riverbanks. The water is thought to be rich in health-promoting minerals and it's popular with local bathers.

**Activities**
The Cresta Mowana Lodge runs two-hour horse-riding trips at 6 and 9 am and 2 and 4 pm daily. The cost is US$20.

**Organised Tours**
For information on Chobe National Park

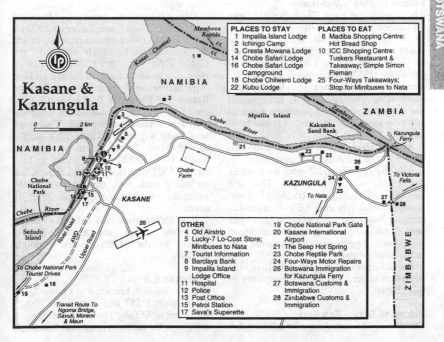

**Kasane & Kazungula**

0    1    2 km

**NAMIBIA**

**PLACES TO STAY**
1  Impalila Island Lodge
2  Ichingo Camp
3  Cresta Mowana Lodge
14 Chobe Safari Lodge
16 Chobe Safari Lodge Campground
18 Chobe Chilwero Lodge
22 Kubu Lodge

**PLACES TO EAT**
6  Madiba Shopping Centre: Hot Bread Shop
10 ICC Shopping Centre: Tuskers Restaurant & Takeaway; Simple Simon Pieman
25 Four-Ways Takeaways; Stop for Minibuses to Nata

**OTHER**
4  Old Airstrip
5  Lucky-7 Lo-Cost Store; Minibuses to Nata
7  Tourist Information
8  Barclays Bank
9  Impalila Island Lodge Office
11 Hospital
12 Police
13 Post Office
15 Petrol Station
17 Sava's Superette
19 Chobe National Park Gate
20 Kasane International Airport
21 The Seep Hot Spring
23 Chobe Reptile Park
24 Four-Ways Motor Repairs
26 Botswana Immigration for Kazungula Ferry
27 Botswana Customs & Immigration
28 Zimbabwe Customs & Immigration

Mombova Rapids
Kasai Channel
NAMIBIA
Chobe River
Mpalila Island
Kakumba Sand Bank
Zambezi River
ZAMBIA
Kazungula Ferry
To Victoria Falls
KAZUNGULA
To Nata
ZIMBABWE
Chobe Farm
KASANE
Chobe River
Sedudu Island
River Road
4WD
Upper Road
To Chobe National Park Tourist Drives
Transit Route To Ngoma Bridge, Savuti, Moremi & Maun
Chobe National Park

**BOTSWANA**

trips and tours, see River Trips and Game Drives in the next section.

## Places to Stay – Budget

The campground at *Chobe Safari Lodge* (☎ 650336; fax 650437) can get crowded and noisy, but it's the only convenient inexpensive option and it sits right on the riverbank abutting the national park. Until recently, it was popular with elephants who dropped by to dine on the tender green vegetation and thereby became a perceived threat to campers. (On a recent visit, an elephant stumbled into a vehicle where a man was sleeping, setting off the car alarm, and havoc ensued.) A fence now keeps elephants in the national park, where most Kasane residents feel they belong. Tent or caravan camping costs US$7 per person.

Camping is also available at *Kubu Lodge* in Kazungula (see below).

## Places to Stay – Mid-Range

The popular mid-range *Chobe Safari Lodge* (☎ 650336; fax 650437) overlooks the river in the heart of Kasane. Basic single or double rondavels cost US$48; chalets with en suite facilities are US$70, river-view rooms are US$78 and camping is US$7 per person. There's also a laundry service, bottle store, swimming pool, dining room and three bars of varying standards. Book in advance, especially for weekends and holidays.

*Kubu Lodge* (☎ 650312; fax 650412), 1km north of the Kasane-Kazungula road, is near the Zambia and Zimbabwe borders but a long way from Chobe. Thatched single/double chalets cost US$68/97. Basic two-bed rondavels cost US$47, riverside camping or airport transfers cost US$7 per person. An interpretive booklet available at reception will guide you along a nature trail in the hotel grounds.

For information on park activities, see Activities under Chobe Riverfront, later in this chapter.

## Places to Stay – Top End

The *Cresta Mowana Lodge* (☎ 650300; fax 650301), whose name means 'baobab', was designed by a Polish architect and is probably Botswana's most beautiful building. This lovely, delicate-looking structure makes the most of the open air and the superb view, and is designed around a large baobab, hence the name. Unique singles/doubles with river views, hand-woven rugs and porcelain washbasins cost US$164/267 with breakfast and US$198/335 with full board. For full board plus airport transfers, two Chobe activities and park fees, it's US$252/442.

The secluded *Chobe Chilwero Lodge* (☎ 650505; fax 650352; <chobe@icon.co.za>) sits on the hill about 3km from the Chobe entrance gate. The name means 'the vista' and, appropriately, its thatched bungalows afford fantastic views over the park and river. Singles/doubles cost US$405/610, including accommodation, meals, laundry, park fees, game drives and river trips.

One of Botswana's pinnacles of luxury is the tasteful *Chobe Game Lodge* (☎ 650340; fax 650223; <chobe@fast.co.za>), inside the national park, which overlooks the Chobe River and the Namibian plains. Here, you're never far from the nearest lion, elephant or hippo and in fact, Richard Burton and Elizabeth Taylor spent one of their honeymoons in a plush suite, complete with a private swimming pool. That room now costs a paltry US$480/800, single/double. More down-to-earth accommodation is US$300/520 from January to June and US$335/610 from July to September, including park fees, three lavish meals, game drives, river trips and attention to detail.

For information on Mpalila Island (Namibia) camps, see Around Katima Mulilo in the North-Eastern Namibia chapter.

## Places to Eat

A buffet English breakfast at *Chobe Safari Lodge* costs US$7 and dinners are US$15 for respectable fare. The service may seem chilly, but the coffee is hot and delicious. At

*Kubu Lodge* a buffet breakfast or lunch costs US$8 and dinners are US$16. The only other eateries are the *Simple Simon Pieman* pie shop and the *Tuskers Restaurant & Takeaway*, which does fast burgers, omelettes, sandwiches, fish and chips and other snacks. Both are in the ICC shopping centre.

Self-caterers are limited to the well stocked *Sava's Superette*, diagonally opposite the petrol station, which has a good range of freeze-dried packaged goods for bush trips. Baked goods are sold at the *Hot Bread Shop* in the Madiba shopping centre, but get there early for the best selection. If you're headed for Maun via Chobe, stock up here; in between, there's nothing but bottle shops. In Kazungula, you'll find simple snacks at the *Four-Ways Takeaways*.

### Getting There & Away

**Air** Air Botswana connects Kasane International airport to Maun (US$111), Gaborone (US$284) and Victoria Falls (US$140). On Thursday, there are flights to and from Johannesburg (US$418), via Maun.

Quicksilver Enterprises (☎ 640532; fax 650223), also called Chobe Air, runs charters around the quadruple frontier region. Single-engine five-passenger planes charter for around US$1 per kilometre; clients also pay for the plane's return to base. To Maun, the average charter rate for five passengers is US$650.

**Bus** Two daily buses run to Nata from the petrol station sometime between 9 am and 1 pm. The trip takes all day and costs US$10. From the Lucky-7 Lo-Price Store (the Gumba Shop) in Kazungula, a daily minibus leaves for Francistown at 6 am. For a pickup from elsewhere, book at Chobe Safari Lodge.

Between Kasane and Victoria Falls, UTC runs daily transfers for US$35. They leave Victoria Falls around 7.30 am; in Kasane, they pick up at the hotels between 9.30 and 10 am, then return to Victoria Falls. Under ideal conditions, the trip takes two hours, including border formalities. The border post is open daily from 7 am to 8 pm.

Buses and minibuses for Livingstone (Zambia), Victoria Falls (Zimbabwe) and Windhoek (Namibia) also serve Kasane.

**Car & Motorcycle** The Kazungula ferry crosses the Zambezi to and from Zambia from 6 am to 6 pm, but trucks must cross one at a time and drivers should queue early to minimise the wait. The trip is free for

### Sedudu Island

Travellers on the Chobe River between Kasane and the Chobe park boundary will undoubtedly notice Sedudu Island, a flat, grassy mid-river island with a look-out platform and a Botswana flag planted on it. Old German maps placed this island in Namibia, English ones had it in Botswana. During the South African occupation of Namibia, the dispute heated up and international arbitration was called in to settle the matter. The experts determined that the deeper river channel passed to the north of the island, thus placing Sedudu Island on the Botswana side.

The Namibians, on the other hand, call the island Kasikile, and they reject the ruling that it belongs to Botswana, instead maintaining that the issue 'remains in limbo'. In campaign platforms during Namibian independence elections, emotional calls were made for the repatriation of Namibia's 'stolen' territory. Even today, this issue resurfaces whenever a politician requires a common national cause to rally people together. In fact, the latest development took place on 15 February 1996, when both countries signed an agreement to take the issue to the World Court, at the cost of several million US dollars.

Botswana or Zambia-registered vehicles. Others pay US$10 for a car and US$20 for a pickup or other large vehicle. Foot passengers travel free. See also the Botswana Getting There & Away chapter.

**Hitching** For Nata or Francistown, hitching is normally more convenient than the bus. In the morning, hitchhikers have lots of company in Kazungula at the intersection of the Kasane-Francistown road. It sometimes helps to chat with drivers at the Kazungula or Chobe Safari Lodge petrol stations. If you're heading for Ngoma Bridge, ascertain whether your driver will travel via the transit route or the riverfront tourist drives. For the latter, you'll see lots of wildlife but must also pay park fees.

The cheapest way to hitch to Maun is via Nata. Hitchers trying to reach Maun through Chobe National Park must remember that most travellers on this abysmal road spend several days in Chobe and Moremi Reserve and all passengers pay park fees for each day in the parks.

**Mobile Safaris** For information on mobile

safaris between Kasane and Maun via Chobe National Park, see Maun in the Okavango & North-Western Botswana chapter.

**Getting Around**
Avis (☎ 650144; fax 650145) is at Kubu Lodge and Holiday Car Hire (☎ 650226; fax 650129) is at Chobe Safari Lodge (see the Botswana Getting Around chapter). For information on Chobe tours, see Activities under Chobe Riverfront, below.

**CHOBE RIVERFRONT**
If you're on a tight budget, a Chobe visit will probably entail a cruise or game drive along the riverfront. These trips are reasonably priced, but to the cost of the cruise you must add park fees for each day.

The riverfront landscape has been decimated by massive elephant herds, but there's a good chance of seeing lion and cheetah. By day, the water brims with hippo, which submerge at dawn and emerge at dusk; buffalo are present in their thousands; and amid the scrub live numerous giraffe, zebra, jackal, warthog, brown and spotted hyaena, baboons and wild dogs.

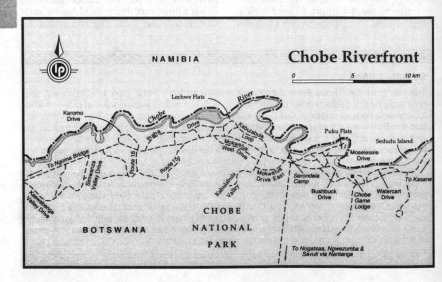

---

### Game Drives — Morning vs Evening

Morning trips are generally better if you prefer a subtle, timeless sort of experience. The sweet, dusty smell of the morning bush combined with the last stirrings of night creatures; a hazy-red sunrise; the plodding of hippo into the river; and the emergence of the daytime shift clearly demonstrate the cycles that govern the bush.

Evening drives, on the other hand, are generally more exciting. Things seem to happen on cue, and the low sun provides excellent photo opportunities. There will normally be so much wildlife (especially during the dry season) that one may soon become blasé. Big cats laze while skittish antelope keep an eye on their intentions. Immense herds of elephant gather to drink, spray and play beside the river. Hippo plod onto the shore. Hundreds of buffalo stand grazing on the dry grass and vultures pick at the remains of the unlucky while brilliantly coloured birds flit around in the late sun.

---

Most endemic antelope species – kudu, eland, roan, sable, wildebeest, tsessebe, bushbuck, impala and waterbuck – are present and you may also see the rare grysbok or oribi. The marshy river floodplain is inhabited by Chobe's two trademark antelope: the water-loving red lechwe and the rare puku, of which perhaps only 100 remain. This ruddy antelope has a face like a waterbuck, but with notched, inward-curving horns and a small, stocky build. The river is also home to crocodile and playful Cape clawless otters.

The variety and abundance of bird life ranges from flashy lilac-breasted rollers and white-fronted bee-eaters to kori bustards, korhaans, secretary birds, vultures and marabou storks. The waters support African jacanas, snakebirds, gallinules, herons, ducks and more. Along the river, listen for the screaming fish eagles overhead as they practice precision diving for fish.

### Activities

**River Trips** A great way to enjoy the riverfront is a cruise run by the Kasane-area lodges. Most enter the park and require payment of park fees. The best time is late afternoon, when the hippo amble onto dry land and the riverfront fills with elephant heading for a drink and a romp in the water.

Chobe Safari Lodge runs three-hour afternoon 'booze cruises' upriver on the pontoon *Fish Eagle*. Lodge guests (including campers) pay US$12; others pay US$15. For similar cruises, Kubu Lodge charges US$16, and also has five-seater catamaran excursions to the four-way frontier for US$10. The Cresta Mowana Lodge has afternoon booze cruises aboard *Mmadikwena* for US$16.

Chobe Game Lodge runs an afternoon cruise on the *Mosi-oa-Tunya*, a pretty good replica of the *African Queen*, for US$17. Small motorboat tours run whenever someone wants to go; non-guests pay US$25 for the two-hour trip.

Chobe Boat Charters (☎ 650415), Private Bag K-40, Kasane, organises private sunset or booze cruises for US$10 per person plus park fees. A half/full day of fishing in the river costs US$84/139 per person.

**Game Drives** Kubu Lodge and Chobe Safari Lodge ply the riverfront routes at 6.15 am and 4 pm; the trips last 2½ hours. If you take a morning game drive, you can also take an afternoon booze cruise and pay park fees for only one day. For maximum economy, you can do both game drives as well as a small boat trip at midday. The two-hour game drives cost US$14 to US$16. Cresta Mowana Lodge offers five-hour game drives with either a bush breakfast (US$30) or a champagne brunch (US$45).

BOTSWANA

## Places to Stay

*Serondela Camp*, 10km west of the park gate, is Chobe's most accessible camp site. According to game drivers, Serondela was once an inhabited village that was uprooted and shifted to Kasane when Chobe became a national park.

Serondela has toilets and cold showers. By day, campers are under constant surveillance by cheeky baboons, who understand that all the best pickings come from tents and backpacks, and the nights hum with unidentified noises that may unnerve campers. Serondela will soon be replaced by Ihaha, in a less congested area further west; when the latter opens, Serondela will be converted into a picnic site.

Chobe Game Lodge, Kubu Lodge and Chobe Safari Lodge run transfers to Serondela Camp in conjunction with morning and afternoon game drives, but as this isn't an organised tour, campers must pay park and camping fees. They'll pick you up at a pre-specified time.

At the west end of the Chobe transit route, near the Namibian border, is the new *Buffalo Ridge Camp Site*. This pleasant high-ground spot with showers, toilets and clean borehole water charges US$4 per person for camping. Day visits for picnics or showers cost US$2. A lodge and restaurant are being built across the valley.

## Getting There & Away

**Northern Entrance** The northern park entrance lies 6km west of Kasane and is accessible by conventional vehicle. However, to approach from Maun or proceed southwards across the park requires a high-clearance 4WD vehicle. Due to high water, Savuti is normally closed (and inaccessible) between January and March.

**Transit Route** The transit route across the park to the Namibian Border at Ngoma Bridge may be free of park fees, but it's not a cheap way of seeing Chobe. This wide, uninteresting swathe of new tar keeps wildlife well at bay. Look for lifts at the petrol station in Kasane.

## SAVUTI & THE MABABE DEPRESSION

As with the Makgadikgadi and Nxai pans, the Mababe Depression (no, it's not a travellers' affliction) is a remnant of the large lake that once covered much of northern Botswana. It takes in most of the southern Savuti region, which is Chobe National Park's second most popular area.

Savuti's flat, wildlife-packed expanses are an obligatory stop for overland trips between Kasane and Maun. Despite a couple of luxury lodges, this country of typically harsh African colours and vistas has a distinctly empty feeling, and it won't disappoint. The animal populations, especially from November to May, can seem overwhelming: the place teems with elephant and lion, and wild dogs and hyaena prowl through vast herds of buffalo, zebra, impala, wildebeest and other antelope.

In the past, Savuti has been well watered,

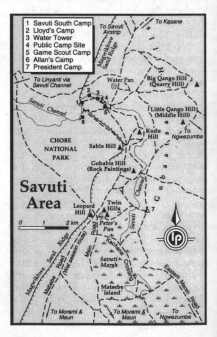

1 Savuti South Camp
2 Lloyd's Camp
3 Water Tower
4 Public Camp Site
5 Game Scout Camp
6 Allan's Camp
7 President Camp

Savuti Area

## The Savuti Channel

Northern Botswana contains a bounty of odd hydrographic phenomena – a land of mysterious channels linking the otherwise unconnected Okavango and Linyanti-Chobe river systems. For instance, the Selinda Spillway passes water back and forth between the Okavango Delta and the Linyanti Swamps. Just as odd, when the Zambezi River is particularly high, the Chobe River actually reverses its direction of flow, causing spillage into the Liambezi area. Historically, there was also a channel between the Khwai River system in the Okavango and Savuti Marsh. But the strangest of all is probably the Savuti Channel, which links Savuti Marsh with the Linyanti Marsh and – via the Selinda Spillway – with the Okavango Delta itself.

This mysterious channel, which lies within the Mababe Depression, is a 100km-long river that meanders across level ground from the Linyanti Marshes, where the Linyanti-Chobe system makes a sharp bend. Instead of carrying water to the main river, as all good tributaries should, the Savuti channels it away and dumps it in the desert. At its finish, where in good years it seeps and disappears into the sand, it waters the lovely Savuti Marshes.

Most confounding about the Savuti Channel, however, is the lack of rhyme or reason to its flow. At times it stops flowing for years at a stretch, as it did from 1888 to 1957, from 1966 to 1967 and from 1979 through to the 1990s. When it's flowing, it creates an oasis that provides water for thirsty wildlife herds and acts as a magnet for a profusion of water birds. Between flows, the end of the channel recedes from the marshes back towards the Chobe River while at other times, the Savuti Marsh floods and expands. The dead trees now standing along its bed optimistically took root during the dry years, only to be drowned when the channel reawakened.

What's more, the flow of the channel appears to be unrelated to the water level of the Linyanti-Chobe river system itself. In 1925, when the river experienced record flooding, the Savuti Channel remained dry.

According to the only feasible explanation thus far put forward, the phenomenon may be attributed to tectonics. The ongoing northward shift of the Zambezi River and the frequent low-intensity earthquakes in the region reveal that the underlying geology is tectonically unstable. The flow of the Savuti Channel must be governed by an imperceptible flexing of the surface crust. The minimum change required to open or close the channel would be at least 9m, and there's evidence that it has happened at least five times in the past century!

but has no perennial water sources, and animals lured into the area in wetter years frequently face drought conditions. Those capable of escaping to the Chobe, Linyanti and Okavango river systems do so, but others, weakened by the elements, crowd into dwindling water holes and eventually succumb to hunger and thirst. In fact, the bed of Savuti Marsh is littered with the shells of desiccated freshwater mussels. On the other hand, trees that keenly take root along intermittent watercourses during dry years may find themselves drowned or washed away during heavy flows.

### Magwikhwe Sand Ridge

From the griddle-flat plains of the Mababe Depression, the 20m Magwikhwe Sand Ridge seems a prominent feature. This 180m-wide ridge extends for over 100km across southern Chobe and is thought to have once formed a barrier beach on the western shoreline of northern Botswana's ancient great lake.

### Gubaatsa & Gcoha Hills

After years of erosion, the rocky Gubaatsa Hills have worn down to mere knobs. On their north-eastern faces, you'll see evidence of constant wave action from when the Mababe Depression was underwater. Gobabis Hill, south of Savuti gate, bears several scatters of 4000-year-old rock paintings, which are probably of San origin. Some lie near the base at the north end of the hill, but the best are halfway to the summit and face east. Visitors may leave their vehicles and walk to the paintings.

Further north of Savuti, the diminutive Gcoha Hills mark the northern extent of the Magwikhwe Sand Ridge and on this grand plain, they take on seemingly Alpine dimensions. They were formerly inhabited by the Yei people, who were displaced from the Caprivi and southern Angola by the expanding Lozi Empire. Most of Botswana's Yei now occupy the Okavango Delta area.

### Places to Stay

**Camping** Savuti is colloquially known as a 'rough camp', in reference to its frequent wildlife invasions. In the early-1990s drought, the main perpetrators were thirsty elephant who wreaked havoc on the ablutions blocks; you can imagine what happens when an elephant tries to squeeze into a toilet stall or manipulate a washbasin tap! The ruins are now being replaced by pachyderm-proof ablutions and conciliatory, elephant-friendly water points.

Also, secure your vehicle against tusky tin openers and avoid carrying oranges or other fruit. Oranges are the elephantine equivalent of chocolate bars, and once an elephant catches a citrus whiff, little can sway them.

Savuti cleanup is normally handled by clouds of perky hornbills, but at night, the site is haunted by brazen hyaena thugs who carry off anything that smells edible. Don't leave empty tins or dirty pots lying around and keep your food safely packed inside a vehicle. Baboons are also a nuisance and an unwary camper could be cleaned out the moment his or her back is turned.

**Linyanti Camp Site** The quiet Linyanti Camp Site lies beside the Linyanti River, 39km north-west of Savuti and well off the tourist routes. It offers an escape from human congestion and in the dry season, sees lots of elephant. Ablutions include flush toilets and hot showers.

**Safari Lodges** North-west of the public camp site are three private camps; all must be booked in advance.

Lloyd and June Wilmot, owners of *Lloyd's Camp* (☎/fax 660351), PO Box 246, Maun, emphasise that their camp is not a 'luxury' option. Lloyd's is known for close wildlife encounters – thanks mainly to its private water hole and viewing platform – as well as its excellent guides and exotic cuisine. (Where else could you sample sausage, raisin and spinach pizza?) Single/double high season rates are US$362/557, including accommodation, meals and activities but not park fees. Lone travellers willing to share accommodation pay US$275. No credit cards are accepted and the camp is closed from 1 December to 1 March.

Nearby *Allan's Camp*, operated by Gametrackers (☎ 660302; fax 660571), bills itself as a Botswana 'insiders' venue. Accommodation is in thatched A-frame chalets and the emphasis is on game drives, to complement Gametrackers' lodges in the Okavango Delta. Single/double rates are US$528/656, plus park fees. Its sister camp, *Savuti South* (☎ 260302), offers tented accommodation also overlooking the Savuti Channel. Rates are the same as at Allan's Camp, except in November and December, when the price drops to US$168/210, but it's accessible only to mobile operators. Air transfers from Kasane to either camp cost US$100.

### Getting There & Away

Under optimum conditions, it's a four-hour drive from the northern park entrance to Savuti. The best-travelled route leaves the national park south of Ngoma Bridge and skirts the marshy border area on a good gravel road that is passable to 2WD vehicles. However, at Kachikau, the route turns south into the Chobe Forest Reserve where parallel 4WD-only sand ruts head south towards Savuti. After a laborious 50km, the route re-enters the park and continues for a further deep and sandy 40km to Savuti.

In the dry season, an alternative would be the less popular route through Ngwezumba Pans (see later in this section), which is also passable only with a hardy 4WD vehicle. Coming from Maun, the first 100km is tarred but then the route deteriorates into intermittent sand, and some sections, especially in southern Chobe, are slow going. There's no fuel anywhere on this route.

From Maun, air transfers to Savuti start at US$100.

## NGWEZUMBA DAM & PANS

Ngwezumba, just over halfway between Serondela and Savuti by the alternative route, is marked by an artificial dam and a series of clay pans set amid mopane forest. It lacks the overwhelming numbers of animals of the riverfront or Savuti, but the geography and vegetation support herds of buffalo and elephant as well as reedbuck, gemsbok and roan. You may also see the rare oribi in its favourite Botswana habitat. This small spike-horned antelope has circular black scent glands below its ears and a sprig of black hair at the end of its tail. It lives in groups of only four or five rather than in herds.

### Places to Stay

Ngwezumba has two public camp sites. From the northern park entrance, it's 85km to the secluded and little-maintained *Nogatsaa Camp*, which has a viewing hide, cold showers and toilets – if the solar-powered pump is operational. The airstrip was built by the Botswana Defence Force for use in anti-poaching activities and has become a BDF party venue. However, it's a good distance from the camp site.

Rudimentary *Tshinga Camp* (also spelt Tjinga or Tchinga), 22km away, is little more than a bush clearing (avoid camping near the pan lest you disturb the animals' routine). Facilities are limited to a water

tank with an erratic pump that requires mechanical savvy to start; take heed and bring sufficient water.

### Getting There & Away

The clay around Ngwezumba is popularly known as 'black cotton' and when wet, it turns to molasses and defeats even 4WD vehicles. From the Chobe transit road (or Serondela Camp), the Ngwezumba route runs south past Nantanga Pans to Nogatsaa. It then passes a series of small pans to reach Ngwezumba Dam, where it turns west along the intermittent Ngwezumba River and heads for Savuti, 120km away. It takes a long day to drive this route between Kasane and Savuti. To reach Tshinga from Nogatsaa, turn south-eastwards about 5km south-west of Nogatsaa.

## LINYANTI MARSHES

The Linyanti River rises in southern Angola, where it's called the Cuando, but after crossing the Namibian border, the name is spelt Kwando. Through much of the Caprivi Strip it's called the Mashi, but when it turns sharply east and spreads into a 900 sq km flooded plain, which is reminiscent of the Okavango Delta, it becomes the Linyanti. (Further downstream, the name changes yet again – this time to the Chobe.) On the Namibian side, this well watered wildlife paradise is protected in Mudumu and Mamili national parks, but apart from 7km of frontage on Chobe National Park, Botswana's marshes are protected only by their remoteness. Thanks to poaching as well as legal hunting concessions, animals have become wary of humans.

Shallow Lake Liambezi once covered 10,000 hectares, but has been utterly dry since 1985 and much of the Namibian side has been settled by people and their herds. Even wet years have failed to refill it. It's now accepted that Lake Liambezi is gone until a dramatic flood on the Zambezi creates backwash up the Chobe (see also the North-Eastern Namibia chapter).

Similarly, the Savuti Channel – which

flows into or out of the Linyanti, depending upon the prevailing tectonic condition – hasn't watered southern Chobe since 1979 and the once-flooded Savuti Marshes are now high and dry. Another channel, the Selinda (or Magwegqana) Spillway, connects the Okavango and Linyanti river systems and overflows drain back and forth between them.

### Places to Stay

As yet, there's no easy access to this region, but several Linyanti concessionaires run luxury camps. Wilderness Safaris in South Africa (☎ (011) 884 1458; fax 883 6255) has *King's Pool Camp* and *Savuti Bush Camp*. The former occupies a magical setting on a Linyanti River oxbow. The name refers to King Gustav and Queen Silvia of Sweden, who honeymooned (and hunted) there in the mid-1970s. Air transfers from Maun are US$300. Its third camp, *DumaTau*, enjoys a wooded setting beside the vast Linyanti Marshes. Single/double accommodation at all three lodges, including meals, game drives, boat trips, guided walks and laundry, is US$475/750.

Linyanti Explorations (☎ 650505; fax 650352; <chobe@icon.co.za>) has three tented camps in the Selinda private concession. *Selinda Camp* sits at the junction of the Selinda Spillway and Linyanti River; *Zibalianja Camp* lies beside Zibalianja Lagoon in the eastern part of the Selinda Reserve; and *Motswiri Camp* sits on the Selinda Spillway at the reserve's western end. Single/double accommodation, including meals and game-viewing activities, costs US$375/550. For the same rates, they also operate well catered walking and canoeing safaris.

Photo Africa Safaris (☎ 630385; fax 650383) has *Kwando Lagoon Camp*, beside a lagoon along the Kwando River, and *Kwando Island Camp*, 35km to the south on the Kwando River floodplain. The Lagoon Camp is known for its concentration of predators, particularly lion, while the Island Camp offers lechwe and the rare and reclusive sitatunga. At either camp, tented accommodation with meals and wildlife-viewing activities costs US$225/275.

### Getting There & Away

With a 4WD vehicle, you can reach the area either along the river from Kasane or via the track along the Savuti Channel from Savuti to the turn-off from the road along the Selinda Spillway. Otherwise, air transfers from Maun or Kasane cost from US$125 to US$195 with Linyanti Explorations or up to US$300 with Wilderness Safaris.

# Okavango Delta & North-Western Botswana

The Okavango Delta sprawls like an open palm across north-western Botswana. This watery wonderland is the magnet for most of the country's visitors, and a host of lodges and tour companies scramble to package it for them, but don't be fooled. Access may be easy but it's not cheap, and recent developments have placed most of the Delta off limits to all but upper mid-range and top-end tourists.

Although they're eclipsed by the Okavango Delta, north-western Botswana's other attractions are also magical. The remote Tsodilo Hills, a wilderness art gallery of rock paintings with the country's best bushwalking, reveal unsettling cultural changes in the far deserts. Even more remote are Gcwihaba Caverns and the Aha Hills, where part of the appeal is the pervasive silence. In between lie broad spaces and scattered villages that represent Botswana at its scenic and cultural best.

## The Okavango Delta

The 1300km-long Okavango, southern Africa's third-largest river, rises near the town of Nova Lisboa in central Angola and flows south-eastwards across Namibia's Caprivi Strip, where it cascades through the Popa Falls before entering Botswana near Shakawe. There the river's annual 18.5 billion cubic metres of water begins to spread and sprawl as it's absorbed by the thirsty air and Kalahari sands. It's often described as 'the river which never finds the sea' but unlike most abortive rivers doomed to die in burning desert pans, the Okavango disappears in a maze of lagoons, channels and islands covering an area of 15,000 sq km – the size of Switzerland or the US state of Massachusetts.

---

### HIGHLIGHTS

- Travel by mokoro through the watery wonderland of the Okavango Delta
- Explore the underground world at Gcwihaba Caverns
- Hike through the Tsodilo Hills and see the 'wilderness Louvre' and the San creation site
- Take a safari through some of Africa's most beautiful wildlife country on the Moremi Tongue
- Look for lovely Ngamiland baskets in Etsha 6

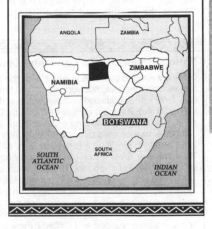

---

Once in a while you'll encounter a travel-jaded cynic who claims the Okavango Delta is overrated, but it's difficult to resist the calming spell of this watery wilderness and its extraordinary environments. The abundant water attracts great numbers and a wide variety of wildlife – elephant, zebra, buffalo, wildebeest, giraffe, hippo, kudu and myriad birds – and the remarkable landscapes of Moremi, at the eastern end of the Delta, are regarded by many people as the most scenic of any reserve in southern Africa.

On the down side, the Okavango Delta is increasingly difficult to visit on a limited budget, and even mid-range travellers have to splurge. Before you plan a visit, consider that it's impossible on a shoestring and, unless you're a real expeditionary, you're going to spend a lot of money on an outfitter – be it a wilderness camp, travel agency, tour company or even a freelance boat owner – so shop around before making any decisions.

The most popular destinations lie within Moremi Reserve, the region of wetland bordered on the west by Chiefs Island (named after the Batswana chief Moremi) and on the east by the Moremi Peninsula (often called the Moremi or Mopani Tongue). This is where the wildlife and best-protected Delta environments are located, but it's also the domain of park fees and upmarket safari camps with awe-inspiring prices – and some of the lodge offerings are downright decadent.

Also rewarding is the Inner Delta, which takes in the area west and north of Chiefs Island. Here one finds the classic Delta scenery, and accommodation ranges from camping to plush luxury lodges, but to get there, everyone must lash out on an air charter. From the least expensive camps, mokoro trips into Moremi Reserve are optional, and you're free to remain outside the reserve, where most visitors encounter at least hippo and antelope.

The Eastern Delta is accessed by a combination of 4WD vehicle, motorboat and mokoro (see the boxed text on page 534). It was once the least expensive Delta area to

---

## Natural History of the Okavango Delta

**Geology** Around two million years ago, the Okavango River probably joined the Limpopo and reached the sea, but subsequent tectonic activity eventually diverted it into the Kalahari. Until a few thousand years ago, the water flowed into a great lake which covered the Makgadikgadi Pans, Nxai Pan, the Mababe Depression and Lake Ngami. However, silting, as well as the continuous imperceptible uplifting of the land to the east, caused the lake to disappear and created the new basin which now stalls the river and seals its fate. Today, even during good flood years, only 2 to 3% of the annual in-flow finds its way into the Thamalakane River. From there, it's distributed to the Boteti which carries it towards the Makgadikgadi Pans, and the Nhabe, which takes it to Lake Ngami.

These days, the channels and boundaries of the Delta shift constantly. Think of the whole system as a garden hose left running in a very large sandbox. In a normal flood year, the river will carry two million tonnes of Angolan and Namibian real estate – sand, leached nutrients and topsoil – to deposit it along the major channels. Carried off by termites for their nests or stirred, warped and shifted by low-level tectonic activity, it alters the channels and reshapes the Delta itself.

In the 1880s, for example, the Thaoge River, which once carried water to Lake Ngami, was blocked and ceased to flow. After a series of earthquakes in 1952-53, however, the Boro River, which passes through the heart of the Delta, began flowing for the first time anyone can remember.

**Seasonal Cycles** In March or April, at the end of the rainy season along the Okavango headwaters in Angola, the river rises and rushes southwards, entering Botswana at Shakawe, and ploughing through and displacing the papyrus beds of the Okavango Panhandle. By early June, the water level has risen in the Inner Delta, drowning low islands and uprooting vegetation as it progresses south-east at about 3km per day.

visit, but a combination of local charges and exclusive private concessions has brought the prices nearly up to Inner Delta rates. However, the quality of the trips hasn't improved proportionally – for example, many polers are still unlicensed freelancers – so it's wise to seek recommendations from other travellers.

The Okavango Panhandle, the swampy finger that stretches north-westwards from the main Delta, is culturally interesting, but most of the camps cater for anglers and don't offer a classic Delta experience. The region is accessible by air or the long way around by the highway; see under North-Western Botswana later in this chapter.

The best months are normally July to September, when water levels are high and the weather dry (for other considerations, see the boxed text on the Natural History of the Okavango Delta). Bear in mind that during the rainy season, particularly January to March, some lodges close, but those that remain open – along with the rain, stifling heat, mosquitoes and humidity – will provide a unique Delta experience with few other tourists.

## MAUN

With the completion of the tarred road from Nata in the early 1990s, the former outpost of Maun became accessible to everyone and began attracting increasing numbers of tourists. What emerged was an insatiable appetite for development, with office buildings, shopping malls and tour agencies sprouting around crumbling concrete buildings and huts constructed of mud and beer cans.

The government policy of courting only

---

As it spreads out, however, it also evaporates and approximately 95% of the water that surged into the Panhandle is taken by the dry atmosphere; another 2% is lost in the sands. By July, a considerably weakened flood passes Maun, but by now, only 2 to 3% of the original inflow remains to enter the Thamalakane River and be carried on by the Boteti and Nhabe. During poor flood years – and in the following year – the Boteti rarely rises above a trickle and the Nhabe remains dry, as it has for nearly 20 years.

This means that the Okavango water levels are at their lowest during the rainy season between November and March, when channels are constricted and water access to the most interesting areas is limited. In the Panhandle the flow peaks in April and May, while Chiefs Island and the Inner Delta are at optimum levels from late May to late June but are ideal for visits until late September. The Eastern Delta has the best chance of high water from late June to late July, but the increase in flow will probably be negligible this far along, especially during poor years. The best months to visit are July to September.

**Further Reading** If you're interested in cultures, wildlife, geology and complex cycles of the Delta, the best readily available treatise is in the book *Kalahari – Life's Variety in Dune & Delta* by Michael Main. Another excellent book is *Okavango – Jewel of the Kalahari* by Karen Ross. For more on the arboreal side of things, pick up the excellent *Shell Field Guide to the Common Trees of the Okavango Delta & Moremi*, by Veronica Roodt. All three books are available in several Maun souvenir shops, and also in Gaborone bookshops.

The December 1990 edition of *National Geographic* also contains a very good article on the Okavango Delta and the issues affecting it.

Further information about the population groups living in the Delta area – the Yei, Mbukushu and Herero – may be found in the Population & People section of the Facts about Botswana chapter.

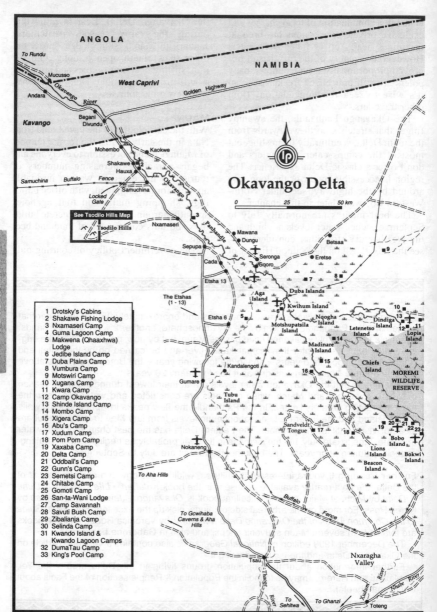

ANGOLA

NAMIBIA

West Caprivi

To Rundu

Mucusso

Andara

Kavango

Bagani

Divundu

Golden Highway

Mohembo

Kaokwe

Shakawe

Hauxa

Samuchina

Buffalo Fence

Samuchina

Locked Gate

See Tsodilo Hills Map

Tsodilo Hills

Nxamaseri

Sepupa

Cada

Etsha 13

The Etshas (1 - 13)

Etsha 6

**Okavango Delta**

0        25        50 km

Mawana

Dungu

Seronga

Gqoro

Eretse

Betsaa

Duba Islands

Aga Island

Kwihum Island

Nqogha Island

Motshupatsila Island

Madinare Island

Dindiga Island

Letenetso Island

Lopis Island

Kandalengoti

Gumare

Tubu Island

Chiefs Island

MOREMI WILDLIFE RESERVE

Sandveldt Tongue

Nokaneng

Lions Island

Beacon Island

Bobo Island

Bokwi Island

To Aha Hills

To Gcwihaba Caverns & Aha Hills

Buffalo Fence

Tsau

Nxaragha Valley

To Sehitwa

To Ghanzi

Toteng

1 Drotsky's Cabins
2 Shakawe Fishing Lodge
3 Nxamaseri Camp
4 Guma Lagoon Camp
5 Makwena (Qhaaxhwa) Lodge
6 Jedibe Island Camp
7 Duba Plains Camp
8 Vumbura Camp
9 Motswiri Camp
10 Xugana Camp
11 Kwara Camp
12 Camp Okavango
13 Shinde Island Camp
14 Mombo Camp
15 Xigera Camp
16 Abu's Camp
17 Xudum Camp
18 Pom Pom Camp
19 Xaxaba Camp
20 Delta Camp
21 Oddball's Camp
22 Gunn's Camp
23 Semetsi Camp
24 Chitabe Camp
25 Gomoti Camp
26 San-ta-wani Lodge
27 Camp Savannah
28 Savuti Bush Camp
29 Zibalianja Camp
30 Selinda Camp
31 Kwando Island & Kwando Lagoon Camps
32 DumaTau Camp
33 King's Pool Camp

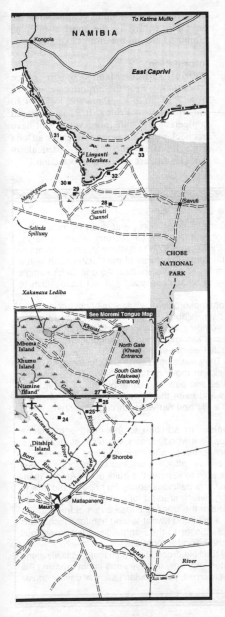

high-cost, low-volume tourism drove up prices and a bumper crop of outsiders descended to cash in on the 'Delta Scene'. Politics ran rampant; the wilderness was carved into concessions for influential bidders; and the price of paradise escalated. As a result, the rough and ready cow town of Maun has now morphed into a bastion of exclusive, high-powered tourism.

### History

Maun (which rhymes with 'down') was originally called *Maung*. This name was arrived at by adding the Tswana suffix for location to a corrupted form of the Yei word *kau*, meaning 'short reeds', thus yielding 'the place of short reeds'. The name was further slaughtered when the final 'g' was lost due to misspelling by early European settlers.

The village began in 1915 as the capital for the Tawana people. Tradition has it that at Shoshong in about 1795, King Mathiba of the Ngwato declared his son Khama I to be his successor rather than Tawana, who was the eldest son of his favourite wife and therefore, the rightful heir to the throne. Tawana objected strongly and the resulting quarrel escalated to the point of warfare and the tribe polarised into separate camps.

Feeling betrayed by his family and people, Tawana and his followers headed north-west, conquering, enslaving, assimilating and intermarrying with other groups on the way. With their numbers augmented by Yei, Mbukushu and Gologa, as well as San slaves, the Tawana settled in the Kgwebe Hills east of Lake Ngami and established themselves as the region's dominant force. Around 1824, they resettled at Toteng.

In 1883, they suffered devastating raids by Ndebele King Lobengula. His marauding warriors captured some Tawana people and drove them northwards into the Delta country, then followed confidently, poised for a decisive second attack. The Tawana, however, were familiar with the Delta and struck back with a vengeance, forcing an Ndebele retreat. Defeated, the Ndebele returned to Bulawayo and the victorious Tawana to Toteng.

In 1915, the Tawana capital was again moved, this time to Maun. The Tawana chief, Kgosi Mathiba Moremi, still presides over his people, who now share Maun with other groups, such as Herero from Namibia and a growing European population.

## Orientation

Maun is strung out for several kilometres along the tarred road that parallels the Thamalakane River. Commercial activities focus on several shopping centres, while the de facto centre is the tourism-oriented 'ambush' around the airport exit gate.

## Information

**Tourist Office** Maun's tourist office (☎ 660492), near the airport gate, is open from 7.30 am to 12.30 pm and 1.45 to 4.30 pm Monday to Friday. It varies between competent and unhelpful; you'll still have to check out the travel agencies for a Delta trip. The Matlapaneng lodges, particularly Audi Camp, are good for information.

---

### Flora & Fauna of the Okavango Delta

While the profuse flora of the Okavango Delta is magnificent and even overwhelming, unless you're wealthy enough to spend part of your Delta visit in Moremi Wildlife Reserve, the wildlife will probably seem quite elusive. It's easy enough to deduce that such an abundance of water wouldn't be overlooked by the thirsty creatures of the Kalahari; but with a swampy surfeit of hiding places, they're simply not easily spotted. As one Delta camp's brochure succinctly states: 'If you see 10% of what sees you, you will have much to remember'.

The Delta world is replete with interest. From mokoro level, visitors may get the idea that it's a papyrus-choked swamp dotted with palm islands. While that's not without some validity, the Okavango hydrography is more complex, with deeper and faster-flowing river channels and serene open areas of calmer water known as *madiba* (singular *lediba*), which are more or less permanent and remain largely free of vegetation.

The reeds and papyrus, however, are rife. They wave and clump and cluster along channels, blocking the mokoro-level view, but the slower-moving channels and even the madiba are festooned with the purple-bottomed leaves and pink and white blooms of water lilies. When roasted, their root stalks are delicious and even the flowers are edible. Polers will also tell you that one may snip the head off a lily and sip water through the stem, which acts as a natural filter against impurities.

On the palm islands, vegetation is diverse. In addition to the profuse hyphaene (mokolani) palms, you'll find savanna grasses, leadwood willows, marulas, strangler figs, acacia thorn, ebony and the whimsical sausage trees, with their long and unmistakable fruits (which yield an agent that has been proven effective against some forms of skin cancer). If you're visiting in January, you'll be able to sample the fruits of the African mangosteen and marula, while in July and August, the delicious ebony fruit ripens and falls to the ground. The beautiful mokolani palm ivory, which is used for carvings, ripens in September and is favoured by elephant, which shake the trees to cause a rain of fruit.

The waters are home to small barbel fish, a mild and sweet-tasting fish for which locals lay nets or construct elaborate weir-like traps. Closer to the Panhandle, such marvellous fish as bream and fighting tiger fish provide the basis for local diets.

The Delta's reptilian realm is dominated by the Nile crocodile, which lounges lazily along the island shorelines or lies quietly in the water, with only the eyes and snout breaking the surface. Although Okavango crocs are relatively small, you shouldn't swim at dawn or dusk.

Bookings for Moremi Reserve, Chobe National Park and the Makgadikgadi and Nxai Pan National Park are available at the Department of Wildlife and National Parks Reservations Office (☎ 661265; fax 661264), PO Box 20364, Boseja, Maun.

**Money** The Old Mall has branches of Barclays Bank and Standard Chartered Bank, and First National Bank is in the Ngami Centre. The commission to change travellers cheques ranges from US$4 to US$7 per transaction.

**Post & Communications** The post office is open from 8.15 am to 1 pm and 2.15 to 4 pm on weekdays and 8.30 to 11.30 am on Saturday. Jacana Enterprises, beside the Duck Inn, offers email services. Fax services are available from Ensign Agencies, opposite the airport entrance.

**Immigration** The immigration office is behind the Labour Office, south of the main road.

**Travel Agencies** Travel agencies and

---

Ask a knowledgeable local before plunging into the (bilharzia-free) waters at any other time. Other reptiles of note include the immense carnivorous leguaan, or water monitor, which either swims through the shallows or basks on the sand. The amphibian world is represented by the tiny frogs that inhabit the reeds – and sometimes plop into your lap as you're poled in a mokoro through reed thickets. Their resonant peeping is one of the Delta's unforgettable sounds, while the tinkle-like croaks of bell frogs and the croaking of the larger and more sonorous bullfrogs provide a lovely evening chorus.

If your Delta trip is normal, birds will probably provide the bulk of your wildlife viewing. To list but a few, you're bound to see African jacanas strutting across the lily pads while carmine bee-eaters, snakebirds, hoopoes, ibis, storks, egrets, parrots, shrikes, kingfishers, hornbills, great white herons, purple herons and greenbacked herons flit, squawk, fish, swim, dive, duck and perch along the way. Then there are the psychedelic pygmy geese (actually a well disguised duck) and the brilliantly plumed lilac-breasted roller, with its bright blue wings and green and lilac underside – and flashes of other colours which only appear in certain light. Watch also for birds of prey, like the Pel's fishing owl, goshawk, bateleur eagle and African fish eagle.

In addition to all the larger animals you'll find inside Moremi Wildlife Reserve, the northeast corner of the Delta is home to the rare and retiring sitatunga, a splay-hoofed swamp antelope which is particularly adept at manoeuvring over soft, saturated mud and soggy, mashed vegetation. When frightened, it submerges like a hippo, leaving only its tiny nostrils above the surface. In order to lure it into firing range, local hunters set fire to clumps of papyrus which soon sprout new green shoots, an irresistible sitatunga delicacy.

Another antelope of the swamps is the red lechwe, of which there are an estimated 30,000, mainly on the palm islands; it's most easily distinguished by its large rump. In the shallow and still pools of the palm islands, you'll also see reedbuck wading and grazing on water plants. The islands are also inhabited by large herds of impala.

One animal encountered throughout the Delta is the hippopotamus. Hippo go mostly unnoticed during the day as they graze happily underwater, but in the evening, they move towards shore to graze on land. Around camps, you'll also encounter troops of typically thieving baboons.

The only large cat present outside Moremi Wildlife Reserve is the leopard. It's normally nocturnal and quite shy. At the canine end of the spectrum, Moremi is home to 30% of the world's remaining Cape hunting dogs, also called the African wild dog.

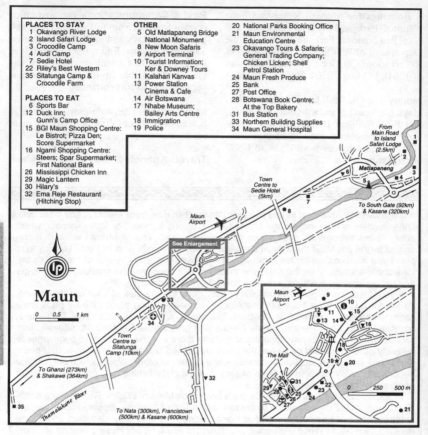

**PLACES TO STAY**
1   Okavango River Lodge
2   Island Safari Lodge
3   Crocodile Camp
4   Audi Camp
7   Sedie Hotel
22  Riley's Best Western
35  Sitatunga Camp &
    Crocodile Farm

**PLACES TO EAT**
6   Sports Bar
12  Duck Inn;
    Gunn's Camp Office
15  BGI Maun Shopping Centre:
    Le Bistrot; Pizza Den;
    Score Supermarket
16  Ngami Shopping Centre:
    Steers; Spar Supermarket;
    First National Bank
26  Mississippi Chicken Inn
29  Magic Lantern
31  Hilary's
32  Ema Reje Restaurant
    (Hitching Stop)

**OTHER**
5   Old Matlapaneng Bridge
    National Monument
8   New Moon Safaris
9   Airport Terminal
10  Tourist Information;
    Ker & Downey Tours
11  Kalahari Kanvas
13  Power Station
    Cinema & Cafe
14  Air Botswana
17  Nhabe Museum;
    Bailey Arts Centre
18  Immigration
19  Police

20  National Parks Booking Office
21  Maun Environmental
    Education Centre
23  Okavango Tours & Safaris;
    General Trading Company;
    Chicken Licken; Shell
    Petrol Station
24  Maun Fresh Produce
25  Bank
27  Post Office
28  Botswana Book Centre;
    At the Top Bakery
31  Bus Station
33  Northern Building Supplies
34  Maun General Hospital

**Maun**

safari companies are Maun's mainstay and each agency has ties with specific Delta camps, so you'll have to shop around to get the whole picture. See the boxed text overleaf for details.

**Film & Photography** Hunter's World (☎ 660924) in the Old Mall and the Photo-Vango Kodak shop in the BGI shopping centre have one-hour print and E6 slide processing.

**Bookshops** Maun now has a branch of the Botswana Book Centre (☎ 660853), in the Old Mall, where you can pick up novels, magazines and some tourist publications.

**Camping Equipment** You'll find lanterns, butane cartridges and basic camping gear at Northern Building Supplies, and the General Trading Company (☎ 660025) also sells butane cartridges. Kalahari Kanvas (☎ 660568), just west of the airport, hires camping and outdoor cooking equipment. Lightweight (3.6kg) mountaineering tents cost US$5 and sleeping bags are US$2 per day. Most Delta lodges which do mokoro trips also hire equipment on site.

## Maun Environmental Education Centre

The 2.5 sq km Maun Environmental Education Centre, on the eastern bank of the Thamalakane River, aims to provide schoolchildren with an appreciation of wildlife and the bush. From the office, visitors can pick up maps of the four walking trails and game hides where you can observe lechwe, wildebeest, impala, giraffe, zebra, warthog and other species. Non-Batswana pay US$4 admission.

Cross the Thamalakane bridge on the Nata road, turn left just east of the river, and follow that road for 2km to the Wildlife Training Centre. Be sure to carry plenty of water.

## Nhabe Museum

The Nhabe Museum (☎ 661346) outlines the natural history and culture of the Okavango area. It's housed in a historic building built by the British military in 1939 and used during WWII as a surveillance post against the German presence in Namibia. Thanks to the Generator House built to service it, this building has had electricity longer than any other structure in Maun. It boasts wildlife exhibits and cultural artefacts from around north-western Botswana. It's open Monday to Saturday from 9 am to 4.30 pm. Admission is free but donations are gratefully accepted.

The attached Bailey Arts Centre stages theatrical and cultural evenings, and sells locally produced curios and artwork. Nhabe also offers a month of Tswana courses for US$42; classes meet on Tuesday and Thursday from 5.30 to 6.30 pm.

## Okavango Swamps Crocodile Farm

The crocodile farm (☎ 660570), 12km south of Maun on the Sehitwa road, is open to visitors for US$2. There are no guided tours, but you can pick up a hand-out which provides general information on crocodile farming and the lives and loves of Nile crocodiles.

## Ostrich Farm

A new attraction in Maun is the Borobonche Ostrich Farm, 9km from town on Moremi Rd. Turn north before the Matlapaneng bridge and follow the signs. It's open Monday, Wednesday, Friday and Saturday from 10 am to 4 pm and admission is US$3. Professional consultation for would-be ostrich farmers is available for US$28 per hour.

## Matlapaneng

Matlapaneng, 8km north-east of Maun along the Chobe road, is effectively a suburb and offers several affordable accommodation options. Have a look at the Old Matlapaneng Causeway, which is now a National Monument. From Maun, you can either hitch or phone the lodges to organise a transfer.

## Shorobe

If you're in the market for fine basketry and you can't make it to Etsha 6, Shorobe makes a worthwhile day trip. This village, 40km north of Maun, is home to the Bokamoso Women's Basketry Co-operative, which is sponsored by Conservation International and consists of 70 local women who produce Ngamiland baskets in beautiful and elaborate patterns.

## Organised Tours

Numerous safari companies organise trips all around Botswana. The least expensive are participatory safaris in which clients help with cooking, washing up and erecting tents, while luxury safaris cost upwards of US$300 per day. The main players are Audi Camp, Bush Camp, Crocodile Camp, Island Safaris, New Moon and Phakawe Safaris. See the boxed text overleaf.

## Places to Stay

**In Town** The most upmarket accommodation is *Riley's Best Western* (☎ 660320; fax 660580) which is comfortable, but falls outside the luxury range. Single/double rooms cost US$80/101 and rooms in the Nhabe wing, without air-conditioning, cost

BOTSWANA

US$72/86. Its Saturday braai lunches are open to anyone.

The drab-looking *Sedie Hotel* (☎/fax 660177; <jacana@iafrica.com>), 4km north of town, charges US$53/68/76 for single/double/twin air-conditioned rooms with breakfast and transfers from town. Backpackers accommodation is US$8 per person and camping costs US$5 per person. The volleyball stands and the cool pool are welcoming and on weekends, there are outdoor braais. On Friday and Saturday nights, a disco rumbles in the public bar until 4 am.

**Matlapaneng** The most popular inexpen-

---

## Maun Tour Agents & Safari Operators

*Audi Camp Safaris*, Private Bag 28, Maun (☎ 660599; fax 660581). Audi Camp offers good value mokoro trips, and is one of few concessionaires using the Eastern Delta. Rates are US$60/90/120 per person for one/two/three days, with two people travelling together. You can also book three days in Moremi (US$300); transfers to Kasane via Moremi and Chobe (US$545); five days in the Central Kalahari (US$635); fly-in Inner Delta mokoro trips (US$185 for four days); Panhandle mokoro trips (US$75/85 for two/three days); and a 'Northern Loop' through the Okavango Panhandle, Tsodilo Hills, Mudumu & Mamili (Namibia), Chobe and Victoria Falls (US$1900). Rates are per person with a minimum of four people.

*Bathusi Travel & Safaris*, Rileys Garage, Main Rd, Private Bag 44, Maun (☎/fax 660647). Bathusi does short trips in the region and books international travel.

*Bush Camp Safaris*, Baagi House, PO Box 487, Maun (☎/fax 660847). This company runs mokoro trips in the Eastern Delta and mobile safaris to Botswana's national parks.

*Crocodile Camp Safaris*, PO Box 46, The Mall, Maun (☎/fax 660265). This friendly company does custom tours around the Okavango Delta, Moremi, Chobe, the Central Kalahari, Makgadikgadi & Nxai Pan, Mabuasehube-Gemsbok, etc, but also runs trips into Zimbabwe and Namibia. Safaris average US$227/277 per person per day in low/high season (plus a US$55 single supplement). With larger groups, the per person rate is lower.

*Desert & Delta Safaris*, Private Bag 198, Maun (☎ 661243; fax 660037). Desert & Delta runs the plush Camp Moremi and Camp Okavango, both in the Moremi area.

*Elephant Back Safaris*, Ngami Data Building, Private Bag 332, Maun (☎ 661260; fax 661005). This company runs Abu's Camp in the Okavango Delta.

*Gametrackers*, PO Box 100, Maun (☎ 660351). Gametrackers operates several Okavango Delta and Chobe lodges, including Makwena Lodge, Khwai River Lodge, Xaxaba, San-ta-Wani, Allan's Camp and Savuti South. From outside Botswana, contact the South African address: Gametrackers, Destination Africa (☎ (011) 884 2504; fax 884 3159), PO Box 786432, Sandton 2146. Plan on US$280 to US$345 per day for a participation safari.

*Game Trails Safaris*, Private Bag 62, Maun (☎ 660536; fax 660201). This informal operation books boat tours and mobile safaris, and arranges custom safaris anywhere in the Kalahari or north-western Botswana. Prices start at US$150 per day, with transport and driver; park and camping fees are extra.

*Hartley's Safaris*, Private Bag 48, Maun (☎ 661806; fax 660528). This friendly operation runs the luxury-class Xugana and Tsaro camps in Moremi Reserve. From Xugana it operates mokoro trips and from Tsaro a unique two-night walking safari along the beautiful Khwai River.

*Island Safaris*, PO Box 116, Maun (☎/fax 660300). This is the safari branch of Island Safari Lodge; it operates tailor-made mobile safaris to Botswana national parks and reserves, as well as mokoro and motorboat trips in the Okavango Delta. Island is considered a budget option, but is generally more expensive than its direct competitors. With a group of four people, plan on US$250 per person per day for catered safaris and US$150 for participation camping safaris.

*Kalahari Kavango Safaris*, Private Bag 053, Maun (☎ 661634; fax 660173). This company organises upmarket tailor-made safaris all around northern and western Botswana, including the

sive option is *Audi Camp* (☎ 660599; fax 660581), which has a bar, restaurant, swimming pool and open-air showers. There is also a novel nine-hole golf course, for which 'dust fees' are US$1, including the hire of equipment. You may encounter the occasional animal hazard, but unless it has rained, the entire course is a sand trap. Camping in your own tent costs US$5 per person; in a pre-erected dome tent, you'll pay US$13 for two people; with beds, they're US$22 for two people. A full breakfast is US$4 and dinner costs US$8. Audi Camp also arranges mobile safaris and mokoro trips (see the boxed text below).

---

Okavango Delta, Makgadikgadi Pans, Mabuasehube-Gemsbok and the Central Kalahari. Rates are US$370 per person sharing per day (the single supplement is US$258 per safari).

*Ker & Downey*, PO Box 27, Maun (☎ 660375; fax 661282; <kerdowny@abacus.global.bw>). Ker & Downey is Botswana's most exclusive and expensive luxury operator. It runs Machaba, Pom Pom and Shinde Island camps in the Okavango Delta.

*The Legendary Adventure Company*, PO Box 40, Maun (☎ 660211; fax 660379; <101754 .2427@compuserve.com>). This company runs Xudum Camp and does fully catered, luxury safaris in the Okavango Delta area: camping (US$440 per person per day); walking (US$1050/1600 for four days, with one/two people); and horseback (US$350/540 per day for one/two people).

*Merlin Services*, Private Bag 13, Maun (☎ 660635; fax 660036). Merlin isn't an operator, but acts as a booking agent for most Delta activities. It can also cobble together excursion programmes around Botswana.

*New Moon Safaris*, Private Bag 210, Maun (☎/fax 661665; <new.moon@ppl.co.at>). New Moon, which is expertly run by Tiaan Theron and Gert Felber, is one of several concessionaires operating in the Eastern Delta. A five-day all-inclusive camping tour of Maun, the Okavango Delta and Moremi Reserve costs US$475. Customised tours are available to most places in western Botswana; prices depend on the number of participants. Alternatively you can hire a vehicle and driver for US$205 per day.

*Okavango Tours & Safaris*, PO Box 39, Maun (☎ 660220; fax 660589; <okavango@global.bw>). This company's speciality is lodge-based tours in the Delta. It is also the agent for the popular budget camp Oddball's, as well as Delta Camp and Xakanaxa Camp. Five-day Oddball's camping and mokoro packages cost from US$410; six lodge-based days at Xakanaxa cost US$1220.

*Okavango Wilderness*, Private Bag 14, Maun (☎ 660086; fax 660632). This subsidiary of Wilderness Safaris arranges upmarket packages to Chitabe, Jedibe, Mombo, Duba Plains, Xigera and Vumbura camps in the Okavango, and also runs safaris in Botswana and neighbouring countries.

*Phakawe Safaris*, PO Box 20538, Maun (☎ 660567; fax 660912; <phakawe@info.bw>; Web site www.phakawe.demon.co.uk). If you're not hung up on luxury, this recommended company, run by Steve and Net Caballero, is the best value in Botswana. Delightfully informal participation safaris through Botswana's wildest regions cost from US$50 to US$65 per day, and will take you beyond even the unbeaten track to experience Botswana as few visitors have. Offerings include Mabuasehube-Gemsbok, Gcwihaba Caverns and the Aha Hills, the Tsodilo Hills, Makgadikgadi & Nxai Pan, Sua and Ntwetwe pans, Khutse Game Reserve, Chobe National Park, Moremi Wildlife Reserve, the remotest corners of the Central Kalahari and places even further afield, including hunting and gathering trips with the San of the Central Kalahari.

*Safari South*, PO Box 40, Maun (☎ 660211; fax 660379). Makes bookings for Shinde, Machaba and Pom Pom Camps.

*Sedie W-Life Adventures*, Sedie Hotel, Maun (☎/fax 660177; <jacana@iafrica.com>). Based at the Sedie Hotel, this operator is one of several with concessions for mokoro trips in the Eastern Delta.

*Travel Wild*, PO Box 236, Maun (☎ 660822; fax 660493). This friendly travel agency can make recommendations and help you organise any aspect of your trip in the Okavango Delta area.

## Wasted Waters?

From the time of the first European colonists, settlers and developers have been eyeing the Okavango Delta as a source of water to transform north-western Botswana into lush, green farmland. With more wilderness than they could handle, many early newcomers described the vast wetlands as 'wasted waters', apparently ignoring the fact that local people depended upon these wetlands for their livelihoods.

Nowadays, however, pressure from population growth, mining interests and increased tourism – particularly around Maun – are straining resources and placing the Okavango Delta at the crux of a heated debate between the Botswana government, ranchers, engineers, developers, tour operators, rural people and conservationists.

At the heart of the latest controversy is the Botswana government's Southern Okavango Integrated Water Development Project, which was laid out in 1985. It called for the dredging of 42km of the Boro River at the Delta's eastern edge. In theory, the resulting decrease in water surface area would minimise evaporation and provide enough water to fill a series of small dams at the eastern edge of the Delta. The scheme would provide a reservoir of water for Maun's growing needs, and would also be used to irrigate 10,000 hectares of planned farmland around Maun. Overflow would be diverted into the Boteti River for farmers further downstream. (Unfortunately, the sandy soil and lush environment would probably require large amounts of chemical fertilisers and pesticides before it could be coaxed into large-scale agriculture.)

However, no credible environmental impact study was conducted and it was speculated early on that beneath the emotional arguments about Maun water shortages lay a hidden agenda. Since Lake Xau (about 200km downstream, on the Boteti) dried up in the 1980s, the thirsty Debswana diamond mining operations at Orapa have had to depend upon borehole water. In the early 1990s, Orapa used five million cubic metres per year, and this figure is projected to double by the turn of the century. However, groundwater tables are dropping and at the increased usage rate, they'll be depleted by 2010.

In and around Maun, local people are divided over the plan. Safari operators don't want to see the Delta's image tainted in any way, yet people involved in other service industries realise that increased development requires more water than is currently available. In addition to the Botswana government, other major proponents of the scheme include cattle ranchers, for whom any reduction of the Delta would mean increased cattle range, and the Snowy Mountain Engineering Corporation, the engineering firm hired as consultants.

---

Next door is *Crocodile Camp* (☎ 660265; fax 660793), which was started by the renowned crocodile hunter, Bobby Wilmot. Camping in the shady campground costs US$5 per person and super quiet single/double chalets are US$50/55; for three/four people they're US$65/70. On Sunday afternoon, they hold a braai from noon to 3 pm for US$10, including drinks. In the bar, Happy Hour runs from 6 to 10 pm (where else would it last four hours?). Transfers from town cost US$12 and you can hire mekoro or canoes and paddle around the Thamalakane River for US$37 per day.

*Island Safari Lodge* (☎ 660300), 4km off the main road from the Matlapaneng Bridge, enjoys a lovely river-view setting, complete with hippo. Shady sites in the marginally maintained campground cost US$4.50 per person and chalets are US$52/62. Transfers from Maun are free to chalet guests but campers pay US$10. There's a restaurant for chalet guests; campers must pre-book meals or eat at the bar (the US$7 breakfast is available to all).

Traditional people, on the other hand, are almost universally opposed to the project. They maintain that the Delta is their livelihood, and that any threat to the water is a threat to them. Small-scale local farmers fear that dredging could disrupt the flood cycle, which brings nutrients to their land. Some of the more militant factions have even pledged to resort to armed confrontation and sabotage should the dredging actually begin.

The conservationists, for their part, advocate that the Delta be accorded World Heritage status, which would make it eligible for international funding to protect it from development. They point out that the Delta now brings in nearly US$50 million annually from tourism and any negative publicity would harm this profitable industry. (However, who could deny that tourism itself poses a threat to the Delta; Botswana's 'high-cost, low volume' policy mainly attracts tourists who require such high-impact creature comforts as laundry facilities, hot showers, flush toilets, motorised tours and supplies that must be flown in from outside.)

In reference to the Orapa connection, in 1991, Greenpeace attempted to organise an international boycott on Botswana diamonds under the slogan 'Diamonds are Death'. In addition some international consultants and aid agencies are so uneasy about being tied to the project that they've dropped it like a hot potato.

Conservationists operate on the premise that any change to the Delta's natural hydrography will irreparably destabilise the unique ecosystem and lead to its eventual destruction. However, Alec Campbell, former director of Botswana's National Museum, believes the current dredging proposals should have little effect on the Okavango Delta as a whole. The real threats, he says, will be determined by projects upstream in Angola and Namibia, where the Okavango waters originate. If proposed dams are constructed and Botswana's tap is turned off, there could be 'catastrophic effects'.

In 1991, in response to these pressures, the government halted the dredging operation and approached the International Union for the Conservation of Nature and Natural Resources to formulate guidelines for a complete environmental impact study. In the end, officials agreed to explore alternative water plans while keeping the dredging issue open as a contingency plan if no other way is found to supply water for Maun's expanding population. What will happen is anyone's guess, but it's certain the dredging plan won't just disappear.

For further information on local opinion, contact the Tshomolero Okavango Conservation Trust (☎ 660060; fax 660059), Private Bag 0013, Maun. This trust is comprised mainly of Batswana in the Maun area whose livelihoods are directly threatened by the project.

BOTSWANA

There's a laundry service and do-it-yourself laundry sinks. The shop at reception sells film, postcards and Ngamiland baskets.

The *Okavango River Lodge*, on the opposite riverbank, is mainly an overland truck stop, but also welcomes independent campers. Amenities include hot showers, volleyball, swimming pool, a games room, a bar, meals and friendly attendants. Campers pay US$3 and accommodation in pre-erected tents is US$10 per person.

**Other Camps** The secluded *Sitatunga*

*Camp* (☎/fax 660570), adjacent to the Crocodile Farm 12km south of town, charges US$5 for camping and US$40 for a single or double self-catering chalet. There's also a small shop and bottle store.

**Places to Eat**

A favourite local hang-out is *Le Bistrot* (☎ 660718) in the BGI shopping centre. As the posters say, it has 'great food, charming company and nice pictures on the wall' (The nice pictures in question are prints of the Impressionists and French masters.) The excellent meal options include a mean satay in peanut sauce (Saté Ajam Soerabaja) as well as delicious and surprisingly inexpensive dishes ranging from pasta, fish and prawns to lamb, burgers and steaks. You can wash your meal down with a range of South African wines or top it off with some creative puddings or coffee concoctions.

Next door is the basic *Pizza Den* (☎ 661391), which has small, uncomfortable tables but is mostly just a takeaway. *Mississippi Chicken Inn* (☎ 660910) serves not only chicken and chips but also monster-sized burgers. *Chicken Licken* (☎ 55127), at the Shell petrol station, has fried chicken takeaways.

An exceptional choice for lunch is *Hilary's* (☎ 661610), in the Old Mall. Hilary does wonderfully earthy meals, including home made bread, vegetarian fare, baked potatoes, soups, sandwiches, cream teas and sweets. It's open weekdays from 8 am to 4 pm and Saturdays 8 am to 2 pm.

In the shopping centre opposite Le Bistrot is *Steers* (☎ 660918), a South African fast-food chain that serves burgers, chicken, chips, steaks and ice cream. The *Power Station* complex has a small cafe, and in the Old Mall a good snack choice is the *ATT* (At the Top) bakery. For Chinese specialities, there's the *Magic Lantern*, behind the Old Mall.

The revived *Duck Inn* (☎ 660253) isn't as wild as the old Duck Inn, which flew south in the early 1990s, but it does have a bar and is open daily for lunch and dinner. On ethnic Wednesdays, the speciality may be Italian, Chinese, Mexican or seafood. The big night is Friday when, as the brochure mentions, locals gather to drink and watch the planes landing across the road.

The *Island Safari Lodge* (☎ 660300) at Matlapaneng serves pizza, chicken and chips, meat pies and other inexpensive snacks at the bar, while its dining room offers full meals. Lunches and dinners cost US$8 to US$13 while breakfast will cost you US$6. *Crocodile Camp* charges US$7 for an English breakfast and US$10/15 for lunch and dinner, respectively.

**Self-Catering** The best-stocked supermarket is *Score*, in the BGI shopping centre. If you're flying into the Delta, you're allowed 10kg of baggage, so go light on the food. In the morning, the bakery at the Spar supermarket in the Ngami Centre sells fresh hot bread and pies. The butchery in the Old Mall sells reasonably priced biltong, which is ideal for Delta trips. The greengrocer, *Maun Fresh Produce*, has a varied selection of groceries, bread and, of course, great fruit and vegetables.

### Entertainment

The *Island Safari Lodge* caters for the overland crowds with a rollicking bar scene. By 9 pm, people are dancing, drinking upside-down margaritas (don't ask, just try it) and staging climbing competitions up the roof support pole.

The airport lounge is somewhat disconcertingly called the *Tailspin Bar*. The renowned *Sports Bar* (☎ 660574), by the Boronyana Bridge, attracts expats, pilots, safari operators and tourists, with sports on wide-screen TV, dancing, drinking, pool-playing and raging, as well as pizzas and decent pub meals. The *Sedie Hotel public bar* has a more relaxed local scene; the disco is good fun and on Friday and Saturday nights, it stays open until 4 am. The same hotel also has the English-style *Cambria Arms*, with a sedate pub atmosphere.

For US$28, keen drinkers can join a 'Maun Booze Cruise', which is actually a pub crawl through six drinking dens. The price includes transport and beer and – if you can still walk at the end – a meal of pie and chips. Book at the Duck Inn.

More sophisticated entertainment is rare in Maun. The Nhabe Museum occasionally stages cultural evenings. The Power Station, the renovated ruins of an abandoned power plant, carries the industrial power-generation theme to its limit with a factory full of welded metal artwork. There are big plans for this unusual complex, but currently, it has only a cinema which screens the most recent films available.

## Getting There & Away

**Air** The airport is the heart of Maun, especially with all the tourists, freight and safari operators buzzing between Maun and the myriad Delta camps.

Air Botswana (☎ 660391) has flights each day between Maun and Gaborone (US$173); on Monday, Wednesday, Friday and Sunday, these flights continue to Francistown (US$283). On Wednesday and Sunday, you can fly to Harare via Victoria Falls. Nonstop services to Johannesburg and Windhoek run three times weekly (the Windhoek route is divided between Air Botswana and Air Namibia). Air Botswana flies to and from Kasane (US$111) three times weekly.

Short-haul routes are handled by the various air charter companies: Synergy Seating, Aer Kavango, Northern Air, Delta Air and Ngami Air. 'Flightseeing' trips and transfers to Delta camps can be organised through travel agencies. Charters also run further afield; for example, five people can visit the Tsodilo Hills for around US$800 return. For more on air charter, see the Botswana Getting Around chapter.

**Bus** The bus station is at the north-eastern corner of the Old Mall. There are two or three daily Mahube Express buses to Nata (US$6, four hours) and Francistown (US$8, 6½ hours); the first bus connects at Nata with the bus to Kasane, which leaves around 11.30 am. There are also two or three morning buses to Shakawe (US$7, 4½ hours) via Etsha 6 and Makwena.

The Sesennye bus to Mamuno (on the Namibian border) via Ghanzi departs on Mondays, Thursdays and Saturdays at 8.30 am. It leaves Mamuno for Maun on Sundays, Tuesdays and Fridays at 8.30 am.

**Hitching** Most people who've hitched to Maun have a story to tell, and many wind up in the back of an open pickup. For eastbound travellers, a good hitching spot is Ema Reje Restaurant on the Nata road.

The easiest route to Kasane is via Nata. Hitching isn't impossible on the direct Chobe route but it's wise to pre-arrange a lift from Maun. Note that you must pay park fees for each day in either Moremi or Chobe, and it may be preferable to organise a mobile safari (see the Maun Tour Agents & Safari Operators boxed text earlier in this chapter).

## Getting Around

Hitching is normally easy between the centre of Maun and Matlapaneng. Transfers to Audi Camp and Sitatunga Camp are free, but Island Safari Lodge charges US$12 per party and Crocodile Camp charges US$13, which may be divided among up to eight passengers.

Kombis run around town and to the Sedie Hotel for US$0.50 (P1.50), but they like to overcharge foreigners, so verify this rate before climbing aboard. Taxis cost a bit more and there are no meters; inquire locally for current rates.

## EASTERN DELTA

By common definition, the Eastern Delta takes in the wetlands between the southern boundary of Moremi Wildlife Reserve and the buffalo fence along the Boro and Santandadibe rivers, north of Matlapaneng.

This was once the least expensive part of the Delta, but in late 1997, a combination of politics and private concessions ended all that. Poler numbers have now been limited to 30 on the Boro and 30 on the Santandadibe at any given time. Ostensibly, these limits have been implemented to protect the environment from mass tourism, but one suspects that the real problem was that independent travellers weren't shelling out enough money for their Delta experience.

If you're short on time, however, the Eastern Delta remains a viable option. Generally, the further north you travel, the better your chances of seeing wildlife.

## Mokoro Trips

Several companies have been granted concessions to operate mokoro trips in the Eastern Delta: Island Safaris, Audi Camp, Game Trails Safaris, New Moon Safaris and

BOTSWANA

the Sedie Hotel (the Karibu and Drifters overland companies may also provide tours for their clients only).

All charge roughly the same rates. Currently, visitors pay a community fee of US$12 per day. Unlicensed/licensed polers cost US$24/34 per day (each group must include at least one licensed poler), plus US$24 per day for luggage transport. Three-day mokoro camping packages work out to around US$185/270 for one/two people. In addition, vehicle transfers from Maun cost around US$70 per person. It's also mooted that clients pay up to US$100 per day as a 'concession fee', but this has not yet been implemented.

### Motorboat Trips

If you're rushed, a motorboat trip may be your only opportunity to see the Delta. With a minimum of three people, Island Safaris does day trips by motorboat around Mporota Island for US$130 for up to six people. Bathusi Travel & Safaris organises a similar excursion for US$35 per person, including lunch.

For environmental reasons, motorboat trips aren't really encouraged. In the tranquillity of the Delta their buzzing engines sound like 747s and disturb wildlife, to say nothing of their effect on the relaxation factor. Furthermore, their wake creates ripples in the nearly still waters, disturbing and altering sand islands and delta vegetation, and there is a constant risk of engine fuel spilling into the water.

### INNER DELTA

The Inner Delta roughly takes in the area west of Chiefs Island and between Moremi Wildlife Reserve and the base of the Okavango Panhandle. It contains lodges and camps catering for several budget ranges and provides magnificent Delta scenery and experiences. This section also includes lodges and camps on the western shore of

---

## Mokoro Trips

Most Okavango visits include a journey by *mokoro* (plural *mekoro*), a shallow-draft dugout canoe that is hewn from an ebony or sausage-tree log. They may appear precarious, but are in fact amazingly stable and are ideally suited to the shallow delta waters. They're propelled by a poler who stands in the stern with a *ngashi* – a pole made from the *mogonono* tree (*Terminalia sericea*) – and accommodate three people, including the poler.

Most mokoro trips include several days with the same poler, who breaks up the journey with overnight camps and walks on palm islands. The quality of the experience depends largely upon the passengers' enthusiasm, the meshing of personalities and the skill of the poler, so the importance of finding a competent poler cannot be overstated. The keenest polers speak at least some English; recognise and identify the plants, birds and animals along the way; explain the cultures of the delta inhabitants; and perhaps even teach clients how to fish using traditional methods. What's more, your fate is largely in their hands, especially when they are negotiating labyrinthine waterways or leading you on bushwalks through wildlife country. Ask other travellers for poler recommendations and if you hear of a good one, request his services.

When organising your trip through an agency or lodge, establish beforehand whether you're expected to feed your poler and if not, whether you'll share meals (which is always more pleasant than eating separately). When meals are shared, the polers may provide a sack of mielies and cooking implements while travellers supply the relishes – tinned curry, stews and vegetables. Otherwise, the standard daily rations are 500g of mielie meal, 250g of white sugar, six tea bags and sufficient salt and powdered milk.

Chiefs Island, on the boundaries of Moremi Reserve.

## Mokoro Trips

Inner Delta mokoro trips are almost invariably arranged through the camps or lodges, each of which has its own pool of licensed (or trainee) guides/polers. The trips generally take place between the months of May and December, depending on the water level in the Delta.

Most camps and polers assume you want to enter Moremi Reserve, and you're charged the appropriate fee after your trip. To avoid park and camping fees – they're reduced to US\$9 (P30) and US\$3 (P10), respectively, because mokoro trips qualify as organised tours – inform your poler and they'll follow an alternative route. You won't see any elephant or lion, but the environment is lovely and you'll normally see antelope as well as baboon, warthog, hippo and occasionally leopard. Also, advise the poler if you'd like to break the trip with bushwalks on the palm islands.

Mekoro normally accommodate the poler, two passengers, food and camping equipment. The upmarket lodges run 'luxury' mokoro trips between established camps, in which you don't carry your own equipment. The best deals are with Oddball's and Gunn's Camp.

## Other Trips

For clients who may be uncomfortable with mokoro travel, upmarket lodges run motorboat and pontoon trips, and booze cruises (see the comments on motorboats in the Eastern Delta section). Rates vary according to the lodge; powerboat trips at the relatively inexpensive Gunn's Camp start at US\$90 per day and sunset booze cruises are US\$30.

## Camps – Budget

Both inexpensive lodges lie just across the channel from Chief's Island and Moremi Wildlife Reserve, about 70km from Maun. In theory, campers should carry food and other supplies from outside but because you're limited to 10kg of baggage, your capacity for self-catering may be strained. Most people rely on camp meals and hire equipment from the camp shops. At either camp, mokoro trips cost US\$30 per day, single or double.

*Oddball's Palm Island Luxury Lodge* (Okavango Tours & Safaris). Oddball's (☎ 660220; fax 660589), on Noga Island, is the Okavango's only real backpackers concession. As with the more upmarket lodges, it enjoys a lovely setting and a friendly and relaxed atmosphere (but the 'Luxury Lodge' bit is a facetious dig at its frightfully expensive neighbours.) Camping costs US\$40 per person, with meals, and there's a rustic bar, showers, Molly's Quickserv food shop, camping equipment rental and a couple of resident elephants (with a fondness for mokolani palms and campers' laundry). Alternatively, book the reed chalet or the unforgettable 'honeymoon suite', 5m up a jackalberry tree, for US\$120. Mokoro trips are US\$50 per day and delicious home-baked bread (ideal on mokoro trips) is US\$1.50 per loaf. Also allow days for relaxing and bushwalking around camp. Children are welcome. Air transfers from Maun cost US\$110.

*Gunn's Camp.* Gunn's Camp (☎ 660023; fax 660040; <gunnscamp@info.bw>; Web site www.africantravel.com/boj01a.html) – or *Ntswi Camp* – beside the Boro River on palm-studded Ntswi Island is a bit more upmarket than Oddball's. The campground has hot showers, flush toilets, braais, and a basic shop and bar, and costs US\$10 per person. Single/double 'luxury tents' cost US\$355/480, with meals, drinks and wildlife-viewing. Return flights from Maun cost US\$120. No-frills one-day mokoro trips are US\$50 for two people; overnight trips cost US\$145/190 per day for one/two people, with camping and food only; and three/four-day mokoro packages are US\$200/245, including air transfers from Maun, camping, park fees and two/three days in a mokoro (lone travellers pay US\$85 extra).

## Camps – Mid-Range & Top End

*Abu's Camp* (Elephant Back Safaris). Welcome to the most unique and expensive camp in the Delta. It was the brainchild of operator Randall Moore, whose book, *Back to Africa*, describes the return of three African-born, circus-trained elephants from North America to Botswana for work in the safari business. The stars are Abu,

## Rates for Delta Lodges & Camps

All Okavango Delta lodges and camps are superbly situated in scenic bush or on palm islands in lovely watery settings. Unless otherwise noted, the rates listed in this chapter include accommodation, meals and activities. These rates are for the high season, and are applicable from July to October. In the low season (from December to February), rates average about 20% lower, but some lodges close during this period. Some also have a shoulder season, which falls between early March and mid-June, and from mid-October to the end of November. Most lodges offer substantial (but unpublished) 'discounts' for regional travellers; again, foreigners pay considerably higher rates than area residents.

Single rates in this chapter have been derived by adding the single supplement to the standard per-person rate. In some cases, the supplement will be waived if a single traveller is willing to share twin accommodation with another person travelling alone, so be sure to ask when booking. To derive the single rate minus the supplement, divide the double rate by two.

To the published rates, you must also add the 10% government accommodation tax, which is normally US$7 per person per night (most lodges use US$70 as a standard accommodation rate – that is without meals, activities or other frills).

Bennie and Kathy, as well as several orphaned youngsters who follow them everywhere. Here, visitors have the novel opportunity to cruise around the bush on an African elephant. Novelty doesn't come cheap, however, and the single/double rate for a five-night stay, with meals and elephant rides, is US$7500/11,000; that's US$1500/2200 per day or US$1.04/1.52 per minute. Think about that when you're wasting time relaxing! (Also note that a clutch of new Zimbabwean lodges offer similar elephant-back programmes far cheaper.)

*Duba Plains* (Okavango Wilderness). This tented camp lies in a remote savanna and wetland region north of the Delta. All-inclusive single/double rates are US$445/690 per day, including game drives, mokoro trips and walks, but no transfers.

*Delta Camp* (Okavango Tours & Safaris). Near the southern end of Chiefs Island, Delta Camp sits in a scenic, shady spot at the end of its airstrip (complete with logs appropriately identified as the 'Domestic' and 'Transit' departure lounges). A real plus is owner Peter Sandenburgh's prohibition of motorboats, so apart from the odd plane, the silence is preserved. All-inclusive catered mokoro trips and guided walks around the island are optional. The high-season rate of US$450/720 per day includes accommodation in single/double thatched chalets, three meals, drinks and laundry. Children are welcome and transfers cost US$110.

*Jedibe Island Camp* (Okavango Wilderness). Accommodating 16 guests, Jedibe (ostrich excrement) is the Inner Delta's most remote camp and also one of its most beautiful. No motor vehicles are permitted and you're a long way from anywhere, so the peace and seclusion are nearly complete. Look for Pel's fishing owls, red lechwe and the rare sitatunga which are commonly seen in the area. Luxury mokoro trips, fishing, nature walks and pontoon cruises are available. Single/double accommodation costs US$445/690 per day. Air transfers from Maun are US$85 per person.

*Mombo Camp* (Okavango Wilderness). Off the north-west corner of Chiefs Island, Mombo Camp is excellent for wildlife viewing. Visitors have a good chance of seeing Cape hunting dogs, for which the area is known. The camp accommodates 12 guests and offers mokoro trips, motor safaris and guided bushwalks. Single/double rates are US$595/990. Mombo Camp lies within Moremi Wildlife Reserve and park fees are included.

*Pom Pom Camp* (Ker & Downey). This quite remote tented camp is accessible via air or bush track from the south-west end of the Delta. It's a particularly good area for birdwatching; other activities include game drives and short mokoro excursions. All meals and activities are included, but it's one of the more expensive Inner Delta camps at US$620/850 for a single/double, plus transfer fees.

*Semetsi Camp* (Crocodile Camp Safaris). This luxury tented camp, whose name means 'place of water', sits on a palm island opposite Chiefs Island and charges US$432/552 for single/double accommodation in dome tents, including meals, mokoro trips and wildlife-viewing activities.

*Vumbura Camp* (Okavango Wilderness). This twin camp to Duba Plains sits at the transition zone between the savannas and swamps north of the Delta and north-west of Moremi. It's one of the most remote Delta camps and the region is known for large buffalo herds. Single/double rates are US$445/690 per day.

*Xaxaba Camp*. This luxury camp beside a beautiful lagoon accommodates 24 guests and offers gourmet food, a swimming pool and bar. The name means 'island of tall trees'. Mokoro trips are available as well as booze cruises, guided walks and bird-watching. Single/double accommodation in chalets made from reeds costs US$470/590 per day. Air transfers from Maun are US$52 per person.

*Xigera Camp* (Okavango Wilderness). In a remote permanent wetland region of the Inner Delta, Xigera is known for its birdlife and the chance of seeing sitatunga antelope, as well as other wildlife. For single/double tented accommodation, meals and activities, you'll pay US$445/690 per day.

*Xudum Camp* (Legendary Adventure Co). This lovely wilderness camp at the southern end of the Delta offers single/double tented accommodation for US$500/800 per day. It's closed from 15 December to 28 February.

## MOREMI WILDLIFE RESERVE

The Moremi Wildlife Reserve, encompassing over 3000 sq km, is the bit of the Okavango Delta officially cordoned off for the preservation of wildlife. It was set aside as a reserve in the 1960s when it became apparent that overhunting was decimating wildlife.

The park has a distinctly dual personality, with large areas of dry land rising between vast wetlands; the most prominent ones include Chiefs Island, deep in the Inner Delta, and the Moremi (or Mopani) Tongue, at the north-eastern end of the

reserve. The former is best reached by mokoro from Inner Delta safari camps and the latter is accessible by 4WD. Habitats range from the mopane woodland and thorn scrub to dry savanna, riparian woodland, grassland, flood plain, marsh, and permanent waterways, lagoons and islands.

The Moremi area has a wide choice of safari lodges. The National Parks camping grounds – South Gate, Third Bridge, Xakanaxa Lediba and North Gate – provide the only lower-cost accommodation. The two entry gates are open from 6 am to 6.30 pm from March to September, and 5.30 am to 5.30 pm from October to February.

### South Gate

The more southerly of Moremi's two road entrances, aptly known as South Gate, lies 84km north of Maun. Here visitors pay park fees. Just inside the entry gate is a clean, developed camping ground with showers and a shady picnic area.

### Third Bridge

Moremi's most interesting camp site is Third Bridge, literally the third log bridge after entering the reserve at South Gate, 48km away. This rustically beautiful bridge spans a sandy tannin-coloured pool in the marshy Sekiri River. One could hardly imagine a more idyllic spot.

Camp sites are strung along the road on either end of the bridge, but there are no facilities, so use common sense when cooking and performing ablutions. Burn your rubbish, bury solid waste well away from the water, use a basin when washing up and pour waste water into the sand.

Contrary to official advice, nearly everyone swims at Third Bridge, but it's a very bad idea. If you can't be restrained, swim only in broad daylight and keep close watch in the reeds for hippo and crocs. Avoid camping on the bridge or sleeping in the open, as animals – especially lion – use the bridge as a thoroughfare.

### Mboma Island

The grassy savanna of 100 sq km Mboma

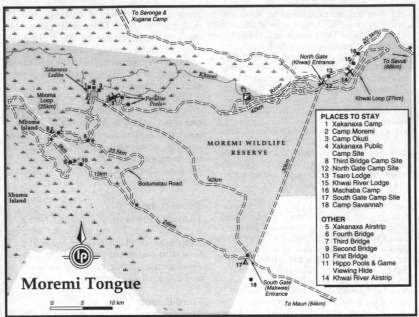

### Moremi Tongue

**PLACES TO STAY**
1 Xakanaxa Camp
2 Camp Moremi
3 Camp Okuti
4 Xakanaxa Public
   Camp Site
8 Third Bridge Camp Site
12 North Gate Camp Site
13 Tsaro Lodge
15 Khwai River Lodge
16 Machaba Camp
17 South Gate Camp Site
18 Camp Savannah

**OTHER**
5 Xakanaxa Airstrip
6 Fourth Bridge
7 Third Bridge
9 Second Bridge
10 First Bridge
11 Hippo Pools & Game
   Viewing Hide
14 Khwai River Airstrip

Island – actually just a long extension of the Moremi Tongue – contrasts sharply with surrounding landscapes. The sandy Mboma Island circuit route turns off 2km or so west of Third Bridge and makes a pleasant side trip from the standard Moremi loop.

### Xakanaxa Lediba

Around Xakanaxa Lediba are most of Moremi's private camps. The public camp site occupies a narrow strip of land surrounded by marsh and lagoon. With one of Africa's largest heronries, it's renowned as a bird-watchers' paradise. Potential sightings include marabou and saddle-bill storks; egrets; wood, sacred and glossy ibis; and seven heron species. The area also supports a large wildlife population.

### North Gate

North Gate, with a developed camp site, is the Moremi entrance for southbound traffic

from Chobe. Vehicles enter the park on a long and clattery log bridge over the Khwai River (it's tempting to suggest the obvious name for this bridge, but I'll resist). The drive between North Gate and Xakanaxa Lediba follows one of Botswana's most scenic routes. Worthwhile stops include the viewing hide at Hippo Pools, where hippo crowd along the shore, and Paradise Pools, two waterholes which are as lovely as their name would suggest.

### Moremi Camps & Lodges

This section includes top price camps and lodges within and immediately north of Moremi Wildlife Reserve.

*Camp Moremi* (Desert & Delta/The Booking Office). Camp Moremi, beside Xakanaxa Lediba, sits amid giant ebony trees and enjoys more of a savanna than a wetland environment. Activities include game drives, bird-watching trips and a sundowner cruise. Single/double occupancy costs US$800/1300 per day, including meals in a lovely elevated dining room, transfers and activities. The Chief Moremi III Suite is US$1800 double. Access is via Xakanaxa airstrip and 4WD vehicle.

*Camp Okavango* (Desert & Delta/The Booking Office). This lovely camp, set amid sausage and jackalberry trees on Nxaragha Island, was started by a Californian with elegant taste. If you want the Okavango served up with silver tea service, candelabras and fine china, this is the place to go. Singles/doubles cost US$800/1300 per day and the minimum stay is two nights. Jessie's Suite costs US$1800 per night. Rates include tented accommodation, air transfers, three gourmet meals, wildlife-viewing canoe trips and meticulous attention to detail.

*Camp Okuti.* Camp Okuti (☎/fax 660570), Private Bag 47, Maun, on Xakanaxa Lediba, accommodates 14 guests in thatch-roofed brick bungalows. The daily high season rates of US$387/507 (low season US$317/447) include meals, game drives, motorboat trips and guided walks. Park fees are US$12 and return transfers from Maun cost US$150 per person.

*Camp Savannah* (Island Safaris). This tented camp, in the Sankuyo Bayei community concession area, appropriately occupies a savanna landscape east of Moremi. Single/double tents with meals and wildlife-viewing activities cost US$320/440 per day.

*Chitabe Camp* (Okavango Wilderness). Situated on the Santandadibe River near the southern borders of Moremi, tented Chitabe Camp is technically in the Eastern Delta. The camp supports the Wild Dog Conservation Fund and there's a good chance of seeing wild dog here. Single/double rates are US$445/690 per day.

*Gomoti Camp* (Crocodile Camp Safaris). This budget tented camp on the Gomoti River, midway between Maun and Moremi Reserve, charges US$89 for single or double accommodation per day. It's readily accessible from the Maun-Moremi road.

*Khwai River Lodge.* Although Khwai River Lodge sits at the edge of the Okavango and allies itself more with dryland Moremi than the water world of the Okavango, both elephant and hippo abound. There's a swimming pool and bar. Game drives, foot safaris and guided bird-watching trips are included in the accommodation price (singles/doubles cost US$156/193 per day). One of the Delta's largest lodges, it has friendly staff and space for 24 guests in thatch-roofed brick bunga-

lows. Air transfers from Maun cost US$133 per person.

*Kwara Camp* (Island Safaris). The name of this solar-powered lodge means 'where the pelicans feed', which may seem odd, but in fact, pools fed by subterranean springs support enough fish to attract flocks of pelicans. Single/double tented accommodation beside a lagoon costs US$320/440 per day.

*Machaba Camp* (Ker & Downey). Machaba Camp sits along the Khwai River, just outside Moremi. The name comes from the local word for the sycamore fig trees which shelter the tents. The surrounding waters are an evening drinking venue for hundreds of animals, including elephant, antelope and zebra. The camp accommodates guests in luxury tents and the price includes game drives and photo safaris in Moremi. Single/double rates are US$620/850 per day. Transfers and park fees cost extra.

*San-ta-Wani Lodge.* On an island near the South Gate of Moremi Wildlife Reserve, this lodge offers gourmet meals, a bar and superb game viewing and motorboat trips. Single/double thatched bungalows cost US$470/590, plus park fees. In the off-season (November and December), it's more viable at US$168/210 per day, but access is by mobile safari only.

*Shinde Island Camp* (Ker & Downey). This camp is beside a lagoon in a remote area of Moremi Wildlife Reserve. Between the savanna and the Delta, it offers 4WD game drives and mokoro trips to the heronries and the nesting sites of numerous water birds in the remote Moremi Madiba. Mokoro trips and photographic expeditions are available. Access is by air to Shindi airstrip and then 20 minutes by vehicle. Single/double rates are US$620/850 per day (minimum stay is two nights) including accommodation, meals and activities. Air transfers cost extra.

*Tsaro Lodge* (Hartley's). Tsaro Lodge overlooks the Moremi flood plains and their diversity of wildlife, near the Khwai River. The real advantage of this camp is the two-night Tsaro Walking Trail, a wilderness camping and hiking trip that will take you on foot along the beautiful Khwai River to observe the profuse birdlife and wildlife. The single/double rates are US$450/600 per day, including meals and two game drives daily.

*Xakanaxa Camp* (Okavango Tours & Safaris). In the heart of Moremi, Xakanaxa is probably the best option if you want maximum wildlife-viewing and bird-watching. In a pleasant mix of delta and savanna, the area teems with

BOTSWANA

elephant and other wildlife. It also contains three of the Delta's largest heronries – Xakanaxa, Gadikwe and Xobega Madiba lagoons. Single/double accommodation in luxury tents costs US$400/600 per day (low season US$350/500), with meals, game drives, boat trips, fishing and bird-watching (park fees are excluded). Accommodation only costs US$160 per person per day. Flights from Maun are US$70 per person.

*Xugana Camp* (Hartley's). The Xugana Camp area was originally inhabited by San hunters, and its name means 'kneel down to drink', in reference to the welcome sight of perennial water after a long hunt. The only access to this remotest of the Moremi area camps is by air. Accommodation is in luxury tents under big shady trees, and there's a bar, gourmet dining room and swimming pool to add to the overall wilderness opulence. (Xugana Camp still gets considerable mileage out of the 1984 visit of Prince Charles.) Single/double rates are US$415/600 per day, not including transfers. For camping trips by mokoro, you'll pay US$240 per person, plus park fees. Air transfers from Maun are US$75.

### Getting There & Away

Transport for guests of the Moremi camps is normally arranged by the camps themselves, but prices vary. Otherwise, you'll need a mobile safari operator or a 4WD vehicle.

From Maun, you should take the tarred Matlapaneng road; north of Shorobe, it becomes good gravel, but, unfortunately, 10km north at the tsetse camp, it deteriorates into sand. From the signposted Moremi turn-off, it's 20km west to the South Gate entrance.

From South Gate to Third Bridge it's a two hour, 48km drive on a poor road. The upside is that the route runs through beautiful, wildlife-rich country. It's 25km from Third Bridge to Xakanaxa Lediba and from there, 60km to the northern entrance at North Gate.

Hitchers from Maun should wait at the lay-by north of the Matlapaneng roundabout. With an early start, you should reach the Moremi turnoff before dark, but finding transport from there into the park will be a matter of luck.

# North-Western Botswana

North-western Botswana is the meeting point of the Kalahari sands and the Okavango Delta. The Okavango Panhandle, which is distinct from the main body of the Delta, extends north-west to the Namibian border. Along it, people live in clusters of small fishing villages and extract their livelihoods from the rich waters. This quiet corner of Botswana is peacefully shared by the Mbukushu, Yei, Tswana, Herero, Europeans, San and refugee Angolans.

The new tarred road between Maun and Shakawe has made north-western Botswana accessible to the masses, but beyond the green Panhandle, the Kalahari sprawls west towards the Namibian border, and distances stretch out along sandy roads. This wild region has a clutch of attractions. Southwest of Maun is Lake Ngami, which merits a visit when it contains water, but alas, it has been dry for many years. More interesting is Botswana's north-western strip, which contains Gcwihaba Caverns, the Aha Hills and a landscape dotted with lovely villages.

South-west of Shakawe, the Tsodilo Hills rise from an otherwise featureless desert plain. Indigenous cultures come and go, but these lonely outcrops appear much as they did when Sir Laurens van der Post wrote *Lost World of the Kalahari* and *Heart of the Hunter*. Here, visitors may hike, climb, camp and soak in the mystery of what van der Post called 'the desert Louvre'. However, increased accessibility and tourist development mean changes are on the way.

Throughout Ngamiland, visitors will find beautiful Ngamiland baskets and in western desert villages, traditional San material arts: weapons, leatherwork, wooden and seed necklaces and beaded jewellery.

Shakawe has a petrol station permit, but as yet, you can only buy petrol from the Brigades for roughly double the price in

Maun. The only reliable petrol sources are Gumare, Etsha 6 and Divundu, 40km over the border in Namibia.

## LAKE NGAMI

The first people to see Lake Ngami and the Xautsha plain were 18th century Kwena hunters, but the area was first settled by the Tawana branch of the Ngwato in the late 18th century. In 1824, they established their tribal capital at Toteng, near the north-eastern end of the lake (see History under Maun, earlier in this chapter). The lake lacks an outflow and is filled only by over-flow from the Okavango Delta down the Nhabe River. When it's full, it lures flocks of flamingoes, ibis, pelicans, eagles, storks, terns, gulls, kingfishers, ducks and geese to feed on crustaceans (which, during dry periods, lie dormant in the lakebed awaiting moisture).

Ancient lakeshores indicate that Lake Ngami once encompassed 1800 sq km, but Dr David Livingstone, who arrived in 1849, estimated its extent at 810 sq km. At that time, it was a magnificent expanse of water, teeming with birdlife and inhabited by hippo and other water-loving creatures. It disappeared soon afterwards, reappearing briefly in the 19th century. Its next appearance, in 1962, covered only 250 sq km and lasted 20 years.

Lake Ngami may someday be worth visiting, but is currently a nondescript stretch of bush. Therefore, modern tourists should probably ignore that inviting blue swathe on Botswana maps and the tourist-brochure photos of splashing pelicans and Egyptian geese! There's no accommodation at Toteng or Sehitwa but you can camp anywhere away from the main road and villages.

### Getting There & Away

There's no public transport to Lake Ngami, but if it does refill, it will attract fishing activity from Maun. The Maun-Shakawe bus passes through nearby Sehitwa. Any track turning east from the tarred road north of Sehitwa will take you to the lake bed, but the main access route turns off the tarred

road 2km north of Sehitwa. Ignore instructions to look for a 'Fishing Camp' sign – it hasn't been there for years. Just find the first prominent track turning off north-east of Sehitwa.

## GCWIHABA CAVERNS (DROTSKY'S CAVE)

In the !Kung language, the name of this cavern system in the Gcwihaba Hills means 'hyaena's hole'. The stalagmites and stalac-tites in these caverns, which reach up to 10m in height or length, were formed by dripping water which seeped through and dissolved the dolomite rock.

The Gcwihaba Caverns were first brought to European attention in the mid-1930s when the !Kung showed them to Ghanzi farmer Martinus Drotsky, and for years they were known as Drotsky's Cave. As with many caves, Gcwihaba has an apocryphal legend of treasure; the fabu-lously wealthy founder of Ghanzi, Hendrik Matthys van Zyl, is said to have stashed a portion of his fortune here in the late 1800s.

### Visiting the Caverns

Gcwihaba has two main entrances, 300m apart, but the route through is more cir-cuitous and hence longer. However, there are no guides, lights or route markings, and no natural light filters into the cave. Visitors must carry several strong torches (and bat-teries), as well as emergency light sources such as matches and cigarette lighters.

The easiest passage through begins at the lower entrance, which is hidden halfway up the hill from the end of the road. After entering the large chamber, you'll proceed down an increasingly steep passageway. The only hairy bit is a short vertical climb down into a pit, then up the other side to a shelf, where there's a tight squeeze before you emerge in a large room.

The rest of the 1km route traverses a series of rooms and passages with lots of enticing side passages leading into the blackness. Midway through, watch for several species of bat; the most common is the large Commerson's leaf-nosed bat. As

BOTSWANA

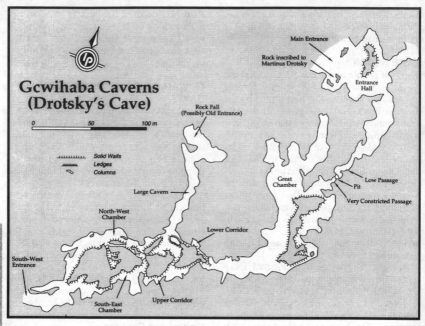

**Gcwihaba Caverns
(Drotsky's Cave)**

0        50        100 m

Solid Walls
Ledges
Columns

Main Entrance

Rock inscribed to
Martinus Drotsky

Entrance
Hall

Rock Fall
(Possibly Old Entrance)

Great
Chamber

Low Passage

Pit

Very Constricted Passage

Large Cavern

North-West
Chamber

Lower Corridor

South-West
Entrance

South-East
Chamber

Upper Corridor

you approach the other entrance, you'll see light filtering in above a steep rubbly slope. After passing through the cave, it's pleasant to climb to the hilltop and watch the sunset over the violet expanses of the Kalahari.

The caverns are utterly dry, but there are pleasant camp sites beneath the thorn trees around the entrances. Around the upper entrance, beware of the networks of aardvark burrows; vehicles get bogged and walkers may find themselves face down or buried up to their knees in sand.

### Organised Tours

Several Maun safari companies organise custom tours which include Gcwihaba Caverns and the Aha Hills. As usual, the least expensive is Phakawe, which charges US$60 per person per day.

### Getting There & Away

Gcwihaba Caverns see perhaps one vehicle in a week, so hitching is a non-starter. Your best bet is to ask around Maun or the Matlapaneng lodges; anyone with space will probably be happy to share expenses and driving. Be sure the vehicle carries sufficient water, and also take your own durable containers.

Drivers need 4WD, high clearance, long-range petrol tanks, water reserves and camping gear. Apart from the Sehitwa bottle store, there are no facilities between Maun and Gcwihaba Caverns.

The unsignposted turn-off to the caverns lies just under 2km west of Tsau. The initially clear track deteriorates as you head over dunes, ruts and deep sand. After 86km is the turning to Xhaba bore hole, which lies 27km to the south. This road leads 55km down the Gcwihabadum omuramba (fossil valley) to the caverns, which are set in the low, rocky Gcwihaba Hills. Alternatively, continue to km 144 (from Tsau), take the left turning up the Nxainxaidum fossil valley and continue 27km to the caverns.

## AHA HILLS

Straddling the Botswana-Namibia border, the 700-million-year-old limestone and dolomite Aha Hills rise 300m from the flat, thorny Kalahari scrub. They're scenic enough, but the attraction lies mostly in their end-of-the-world remoteness. The total absence of water results in an eerie dearth of animal life; there are no birds and only the occasional insect. Larger animals sometimes pass through, but the night sounds so characteristic of southern Africa are conspicuously missing, and the stillness is near perfect.

Much of this area remains unexplored and there's a lack of both water and good maps. Several large sinkholes have been discovered and major cavern systems are suspected but are not yet confirmed. If you do encounter such formations, note their location but don't attempt further exploration without proper equipment.

## Gcangwa

The friendly and charming village of Gcangwa, a difficult 25km journey north of the Aha Hills, is an agglomeration of Herero, San and Tawana communities, each with its own distinct housing and dress. In Gcangwa, research teams have conducted anthropological studies of the San culture and their work forms the basis for some of the most authoritative works on the subject.

## Organised Tours

The community development project in Nxainxai (☎ 660539 in Maun or 596285 in D'Kar) offers several organised trips with the San: four-day horseback trips to Gcwihaba Caverns (US$223); two nights camping in the Aha Hills (US$98); a three-night

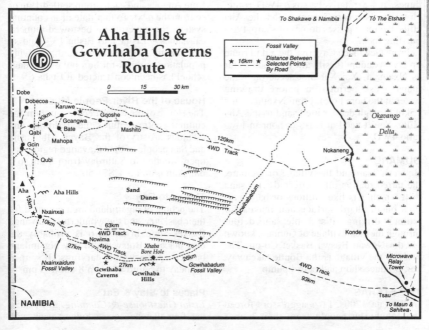

**Aha Hills & Gcwihaba Caverns Route**

Fossil Valley

★ 16km ★ Distance Between Selected Points By Road

0    15    30 km

To Shakawe & Namibia

To The Etshas

Gumare

Okavango Delta

Dobe
Dobecoa
Karuwe
30km
Gcangwa    Gqoshe
Qabi    Bate    Mashito
Gcin    Mahopa
Qubi
120km
4WD Track
Nokaneng

Aha    Aha Hills
Sand Dunes
15km
Nxainxai
10km
63km
4WD Track
Ncwima
27km    4WD Track
Xhaba Bore Hole
Nxainxaidum Fossil Valley
Gcwihaba Caverns    Gcwihaba Hills
27km
26km    Gcwihabadum Fossil Valley
4WD Track
93km

Gcwihabadum

Konde

Microwave Relay Tower

Tsau
To Maun & Sehitwa

NAMIBIA

BOTSWANA

hunting trip (US$209); and a gemsbok hunt on horseback (US$223). See also Organised Tours under Gcwihaba Caverns.

### Places to Stay & Eat

There are no facilities in the Aha Hills, but along the road are a couple of spots to pull off and camp. There's now a small community camp site at Nxainxai (for information call ☎ 660539 in Maun), which is rather steep at US$14 per person, even if water is available. Basic supplies are sold at bush shops in Nxainxai and Gcangwa.

### Getting There & Away

There are two routes to the Aha Hills. One follows the Gcwihaba Caverns route and the other turns west from the Maun-Shakawe road, north of a small bridge near Nokaneng (150km from the hills). Between Nokaneng and Gcangwa, this route is normally travelled by at least one vehicle per day, and apart from three or four deep sandy dunes, it's a relatively easy 4WD route. However, between Gcangwa and the Aha Hills, the route passes domes of sharp, tyre-bursting rock.

From Gcwihaba Caverns, the 52km route up Nxainxaidum fossil valley is good as far as Nxainxai (Xai Xai or Caecae on some maps – ask permission before drawing water at the bore hole). From Nxainxai, it's 15km through deep, rutted sand to the Aha Hills. You'll need at least an hour in low-ratio 4WD.

### GUMARE

Between Tsau and the village of Gumare, the tarred road is often covered with sand drift which acts like millions of ball bearings on the hard surface and makes for tedious driving. It's a pleasant detour through the clean village of Gumare, known for the Ngwao Boswa Basket Co-op. The heart of the village is the Bontle takeaway, bar, produce shop and petrol pump.

### THE ETSHAS

In the late 1700s, Lozi aggressors forced the Mbukushu people from their homes along the Linyanti valley of north-eastern Namibia to the banks of the Okavango in southern Angola. In turn, the Mbukushu displaced the peaceful Yei, and over the following decades their settlements spread down the Okavango River into present-day Botswana.

The Mbukushu had a reputation for skilful rainmaking, an art which originally required child sacrifice and was adopted by some neighbouring tribes. Well substantiated reports also claim that the tribal leadership was providing slaves for Portuguese traders as recently as the early 1900s.

In the late 1960s, in the early days of Angola's civil war, more Mbukushu people fled southwards and were granted refugee status in Botswana. Initially they waited in Shakawe until a new settlement, Etsha, was completed for them. In the shift to Etsha in 1969, they organised into 13 groups based on clan and social structure carried over from Angola, and each group settled 1km or so from the next. To facilitate its accounting system, the government bestowed numerical names – Etsha 1 to Etsha 13 – and so they remain. To accommodate the growing population, a multi-million pula secondary school has been constructed at Etsha 6.

### House of the River People Museum

The House of the River People museum and cultural centre features the traditions and fabulous artistry of the Bayei, Mbukushu and San people of the Okavango region. It's open Monday to Saturday from 8 am to 5 pm. Admission is US$1.50.

### Things to Buy

The people of Ngamiland are renowned for their basketry, and the wonderful Okavango Basket Shop in Etsha 6 is probably the best place in Botswana to buy Ngamiland baskets, pottery and carvings. It's open Monday to Saturday from 8 am to 5 pm.

### Places to Stay & Eat

*Etsha Guesthouse & Camping*, in Etsha 6, has four thatched guest lodges, each with

Mokoro trips are an essential part of exploring the Okavango Delta (Bot).

Red lechwe in full flight, Okavango Delta (Bot).

Chilling out in the Kalahari Desert (Bot).

two single beds, a braai stand and communal facilities. Beds cost US$9 and camping costs US$3 per person.

Tea, coffee, potato soup, sausages and the best hot chips in rural Botswana are available at *Ellen's Cafe*, beside the Shell petrol station in Etsha 6. Beside the Okavango Basket Shop is the unassuming *Mbamba Sisters' Bakery*, which sells fresh bread and serves chips, meat stew and snacks. Self-caterering supplies can be found at *Plam Fresh Produce* (the logo suggests this was probably meant to be 'Palm'), which sells limited green goodies.

### Getting There & Away

From the main highway, tarred spur routes turn off to Etsha 6 and Etsha 13. Motorists normally drop by Etsha 6 to buy fuel, which is available from 8 am to 9 pm daily, or pick up supplies at the Etsha 6 Co-operative, which opens from 8 am to 1 pm and 2.30 to 5 pm Monday to Friday, and on Saturday from 8 am to 1 pm.

The Mahube Express bus between Maun and Shakawe calls in at Etsha 6 and Makwena village.

## SHAKAWE

With the arrival of the tarred road, the desultory but picturesque village of Shakawe is no longer just a sleepy outpost on the Okavango. For travellers, it means a Botswana entry or exit stamp, the start of an Okavango Panhandle fishing expedition or a staging post for visits to the Tsodilo Hills, 40km away.

If you're heading for Namibia, exchange pula for Namibian dollars or South African rand at the Shakawe Fishing Camp or Wright's Trading Store.

### Places to Stay & Eat

Shakawe's activity centres on Wright's Trading Store, the self-service supermarket and the bottle store. In the compound opposite Wright's is *Mma Haidongo's Nice Bread Bakery*, which sells home-baked bread for US$1 per loaf. The name of the *Ema Reje Liquor Restaurant* in the centre

probably provides some clues about its specialities, but it does serve basic meals.

You'll find excellent meals at Drotsky's Cabins, 5km south of town. The Shakawe Fishing Camp also serves meals. See under the Okavango Panhandle, below.

### Getting There & Away

**Bus** The Mahube Express bus between Shakawe and Maun runs two or three times daily and takes eight hours. It leaves from Wright's Trading Store and stops at the police station.

**Car & Motorcycle** The road is now tarred to the Mohembo border post; after crossing the border, drivers must secure a Mahango Game Reserve entry permit. Transit through the park is free, but you must pay Namibian park fees to drive off the main road. At Popa Falls, north of Mahango, is a Namibian National Parks camp site (see the North-Eastern Namibia chapter).

From Divundu, north of Popa Falls, you may turn west at the T-junction towards Rundu and Windhoek, or eastwards towards Katima Mulilo, Kasane, Kazungula and Victoria Falls.

Shakawe has been granted permission for a petrol station, but as yet, petrol is available only from the Brigades for US$0.70 per litre. It's sold from drums in a military-looking compound, 5km along the river north of the secondary school.

## OKAVANGO PANHANDLE

The narrow Okavango Panhandle extends for 100km from the Namibian border south to The Etshas. It's the result of a 15km-wide geological fault which constricts the meandering river until it's released into the main Delta. The waters spread across the valley on either side to form vast reed beds and papyrus-choked lagoons. The local Mbukushu, Yei, Tswana, Herero and Angolans, whose livelihoods are largely dependent upon fishing with nets, lines and baskets, have built their villages in those places where the river meanders past dry land and forms proper riverbanks.

## Fishing

The most popular leisure activity in the Panhandle is fishing, and southern African anglers flock here to try for tigerfish, bream, pike and barbel. The tigerfish are most co-operative from September to June. Barbel are present any time from mid-September to December.

## Mokoro Trips

With the politicisation of the Eastern Delta, Audi Camp Safaris in Maun has now started fly-in mokoro trips in this little-trodden region. Two/three-day trips cost US$75/85 per person. Most area lodges also offer their own mokoro trips.

## Places to Stay

Most Panhandle camps are mid-range and cater for the sport-fishing crowd.

*Drotsky's Cabins* Drotsky's Cabins (☎ 675035; fax 675043), a lovely and welcoming camp owned by Jan and Eileen Drotsky, lies beside a channel of the Okavango River about 5km south of Shakawe. It's set amid a thick riverine forest with fabulous bird-watching and fine views across the reeds and papyrus. This is the Drotskys' home and you'll be made to feel like a family guest; imagine you're visiting good friends and you won't find better hospitality anywhere in Botswana. Single/double A-frames cost US$42/75 per day, four-person chalets are US$84 for the unit, all-inclusive packages cost US$135 and camping is US$7 per person. Meals cost from US$7 to US$14. They also rent boats and run tours: Mahango day safaris cost US$223; one/two days in the Tsodilo Hills are US$292/416; and two/three-day Tsodilo Hills/Makwena Lodge packages are US$348/471.

*Guma Lagoon Camp* (Ensign Agencies). The excellent-value Guma Lagoon Camp (☎ 660351; fax 660571) lies east of Etsha 13, on the Thaoge River. Guma profiles itself as a family resort, and long-stay family rates are available on request. The focus is tiger-fish and bream fishing. Simple half-board costs US$49 per person per day and all-inclusive accommodation, with meals, drinks, boat trips and fuel, fishing tackle and mokoro trips, is US$110. Camping costs US$5 per person. Pre-erected tents are US$12 per person. The final 11km from Etsha 13 requires a 4WD vehicle, but the lodge provides safe parking facilities and transfers from Etsha 13 for US$42.

*Nxamaseri Camp* (Okavango Horse Safaris). Nxamaseri (☎ 660822; fax 660493) provides five-star accommodation for equestrians and anglers. The highlights are bird-watching, horse-riding and fishing excursions. The camp lies midway between Shakawe and Sepupa and is accessible by 4WD from either. Single/double chalets with en suite facilities cost US$287/383 per day, with meals and fishing tackle. Three nights at the lodge plus five/10 nights on a horse tour in the bush costs US$1600/2514.

*Makwena (Qhaaxhwa) Lodge* (Drotsky's Cabins). On Qhaaxhwa (birthplace of the hippo) Lagoon, at the base of the Panhandle, Makwena Lodge (☎ 674299; fax 674302) more resembles the Inner Delta than any of the Panhandle camps. You'll often see red lechwe and even sitatunga, as well as waterbirds and raptors. Accommodation in reed chalets costs US$23 per person per day; for US$82, you also get meals, and motorboat, fishing and bird-watching excursions. The backpackers rate of US$30/45 covers accommodation only; camping is US$6 per person, mokoro trips are US$14 per day, plus US$14 per person for transfers to the mokoro area and US$1.50 per overnight – this is currently the best deal in the Delta. Transfers from nearby Etsha 13 are US$9 and meals cost from US$7 to US$12.

*Shakawe Fishing Lodge* (Travel Wild). The quirky Shakawe Fishing Lodge (☎ 660822; fax 660493) lies on the Okavango River 8km south of Shakawe. Amenities include a bar and swimming pool. Camping in the riverside campground costs US$7 per person per day. Single/double chalets cost US$62/84, and meals cost from US$10 to US$20. Airport transfers are US$21. All-inclusive packages with accommodation, meals, boating and transfers from the airstrip are US$167. For US$150 per day plus US$1 per kilometre, you can hire a vehicle to visit the Tsodilo Hills; don't laugh at the price until you've seen the road.

## TSODILO HILLS

Whether or not you believe in the spirits that gravitate towards ancient lands, the Tsodilo Hills cast a powerful spell. Like Australia's Uluru (Ayers Rock), these lonely chunks of quartzite schist rise abruptly from a rippled, ocean-like expanse of desert and are imbued with myth, legend and spiritual significance for the original Makoko and Dzucwa San inhabitants, as well as the Mbukushu newcomers. The San believe the Tsodilo Hills are the site of the first Creation and the Mbukushu claim that the gods lowered the people and their cattle onto the Female Hill (despite that, evidence suggests the Mbukushu have been here only since the early 1800s).

These four lonely chunks of rock were the 'Slippery Hills' of Sir Laurens van der Post, and it was here that his cameras inexplicably jammed, his tape recorders ceased functioning and his party was attacked by swarms of bees three mornings running. When he learned from his guide that two of his party had disturbed the Tsodilo spirits by ignoring long-established protocol and killing a warthog and a steenbok while approaching the sacred hills, van der Post buried a note of apology beneath the panel of paintings that now bears his name and it was apparently accepted.

The name 'Tsodilo' is derived from the Mbukushu word *sorile*, 'sheer'. Excavations of flaked stone tools indicate that Bantu people arrived as early as 500 AD, but layers of superimposed rock paintings and other archaeological remnants suggest that ancestors of the San have been here for up to 35,000 years. More than 3500 outline-style paintings at over 350 sites have been discovered and catalogued, and more are found every year. No date can be fixed for most of the paintings, but it's clear that some were produced after 700 AD, based on their degree of preservation and depiction of cattle (which were introduced by Iron Age Bantu pastoralists around that time). On the summit of the Female Hill are the remains of Nqoma and Divuyu, Iron Age village sites which date from between the sixth and 11th centuries.

## Orientation

The Tsodilo Hills are comprised of four chunks of rock: the Male, the Female, the Child and a hillock known as North Hill, which until recently remained nameless

(one legend recounts that it was an argumentative wife of the Male Hill, who was sent away).

The Male and Female hills are the most easily visited, and the cliffs and walls of both are streaked with vivid natural pastels – mauve, orange, yellow, turquoise and lavender. The Male Hill is the higher, rising 300m from its south-west base, while the Female Hill is an irregular series of valleys and summits, and contains the most impressive rock paintings.

The Mbukushu village, south of the hills, has flooded the countryside with its cattle, much to the dismay of the !Kung San, who hold the area sacred. Although a few !Kung San remain in the region, don't look for utopian society so esteemed by Laurens van der Post or whimsically portrayed in *The Gods Must be Crazy*. Outside influences, including tourism, have left a sadly dispossessed society that survives by selling curios, posing for photos and trading with tourists.

For further reading, see *Contested Images*, a scholarly work published by the University of Witwatersrand, Johannesburg, which contains a chapter on the Tsodilo Hills by Alec Campbell. Alternatively, see Tom Dowson's erudite *Conference Proceedings on Southern African Rock Paintings*, which may be available in South African bookshops.

## Information

Travellers must check in at the game scout camp and pay US$3 admission. As yet, there's no information centre, but the game scouts can provide basic directions.

## Rock Paintings

To modern eyes, the minimalist representations of animals, people and geometric designs that dot the Tsodilo Hills seem ingenious. While they may have been intended as little more than doodles, it's tempting to envision ancient Michelangelos straining upwards to produce masterly works on the walls of their 'Sistine Chapel'.

Most of the paintings are executed in

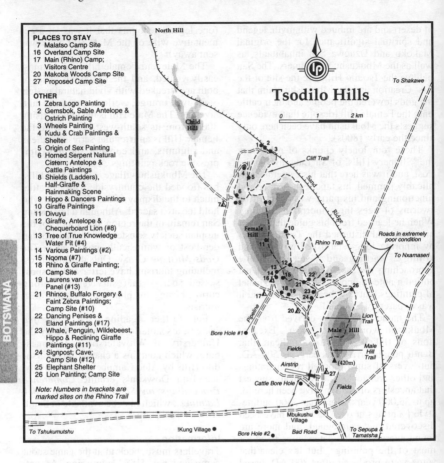

**PLACES TO STAY**
7  Malatso Camp Site
16 Overland Camp Site
17 Main (Rhino) Camp;
   Visitors Centre
20 Makoba Woods Camp Site
27 Proposed Camp Site

**OTHER**
1  Zebra Logo Painting
2  Gemsbok, Sable Antelope &
   Ostrich Painting
3  Wheels Painting
4  Kudu & Crab Paintings &
   Shelter
5  Origin of Sex Painting
6  Horned Serpent Natural
   Cistern; Antelope &
   Cattle Paintings
8  Shields (Ladders),
   Half-Giraffe &
   Rainmaking Scene
9  Hippo & Dancers Paintings
10 Giraffe Paintings
11 Divuyu
12 Giraffe, Antelope &
   Chequerboard Lion (#8)
13 Tree of True Knowledge
   Water Pit (#4)
14 Various Paintings (#2)
15 Nqoma (#7)
18 Rhino & Giraffe Painting;
   Camp Site
19 Laurens van der Post's
   Panel (#13)
21 Rhinos, Buffalo Forgery &
   Faint Zebra Paintings;
   Camp Site (#10)
22 Dancing Penises &
   Eland Paintings (#17)
23 Whale, Penguin, Wildebeest,
   Hippo & Reclining Giraffe
   Paintings (#11)
24 Signpost; Cave;
   Camp Site (#12)
25 Elephant Shelter
26 Lion Painting; Camp Site

*Note: Numbers in brackets are
marked sites on the Rhino Trail*

**Tsodilo Hills**

To Shakawe

North Hill

Child Hill

Cliff Trail

Sand Ridge

Female Hill

Rhino Trail

Roads in extremely poor condition

To Nxamaseri

Lion Trail

Male Hill

Male Hill Trail

(420m)

Bore Hole #1

Fields

Airstrip

Cattle Bore Hole

Fields

Pipeline

To Tshukumutshu

!Kung Village

Mbukushu Village

Bore Hole #2

Bad Road

To Sepupa & Tamatsha

ochres or whites using natural pigments. The older paintings, which are thought to date from the late Stone Age to the Iron Age, are generally attributed to the San people. However, it's fairly certain the most recent works were painted by 'copy-cat' Bantu artists. Interestingly, neither the San nor the Mbukushu accept responsibility for any of the works, maintaining that the paintings have been there longer than even legend can recall.

Among the most interesting paintings is the Zebra Logo on a small outcrop north of the Female Hill. This stylised equine figure is now used as the logo of Botswana National Museums & Monuments. Further south, the amazing whale and penguin paintings on the Female Hill suggest contact between the early San and the Namibian coast. However, sceptics have suggested that they're naive representations of a local bird and a fish from the shallow lake which once existed north-west of the Female Hill.

Around the corner to the west is the Rhino painting, which portrays a rhino family and a well executed giraffe. Inside the deepest hollow of the Female Hill is another rhino painting, which also includes a buffalo 'forgery' of recent origin. Directly across the valley is one of the few Tsodilo paintings containing human figures; it depicts a dancing crowd of sexually excited male figures. Alec Campbell, the foremost expert on the hills and their paintings, has dubbed it the 'Dancing Penises'.

Adept scramblers can climb up to Laurens van der Post's Panel, which overlooks the track near the south-west corner of the Female Hill. On the northern face of the Male Hill are two notable paintings: one portrays a solitary male lion and the other shows a well realised gemsbok and a rhino.

## Walks

The Tsodilo Hills development plan includes several walking circuits to lead hikers past the most interesting and renowned paintings. Most walks lead between the rock paintings around the base of the hills, but a host of other possibilities will keep you going for several days.

If it has recently rained, check the ephemeral rock pools for fairy shrimp which feed on algae and residue settling to the bottom. The eggs are laid before the water dries up but don't hatch until they are first exposed to air and then again covered by water. Watch also for the brown geckos (*Pachydactylus tsodiloensis*), which skitter around the rocks and occur nowhere else in the world.

The summit of the Male Hill is accessible in under two hours by climbing up from the hill's base near the Lion painting. The route is rough, rocky and plagued by false crests, but the summit view may well be the finest in the Kalahari.

On the Female Hill, it's a short but hazardously rocky climb to Laurens van der Post's Panel. Another route, the partially marked Cliff Trail, takes you past the unassuming site known as the Origin of Sex and around the northern end of the Female Hill and into a deep and mysterious hidden valley.

From the Overland camp site, a steep marked trail climbs past several distinctive paintings to a pit where dragonflies and butterflies flit around a slimy green puddle. Near this site is the odd tree, described to Laurens van der Post as the 'Tree of True Knowledge' by the San man who guided him to the site. According to his guide, the greatest spirit knelt beside this fetid pool on the day of creation. In the rocks beyond this pool are several 'hoofprints', which the Mbukushu believe were made by the cattle lowered onto the hill by the god Ngambe.

This marked route climbs over the crest of the hill into a bizarre grassy valley flanked by peaks, which feels a bit like an alternative universe. The route passes several kopjes and rock paintings and then descends into the prominent hollow in the eastern side of the Female Hill.

The amazing natural cistern in the rock grotto near the north-west corner of the Female Hill has held water year round for as long as anyone can remember. The San believe that this natural tank is inhabited by a great serpent with twisted horns, and that visitors should warn the occupant of their approach by tossing a small stone into the water. This impressive feature is also flanked by several rock paintings.

## Organised Tours

The cheapest way to visit the Tsodilo Hills is with Phakawe Safaris, which charges US$60 per person per day. Allow at least four days from Maun. Audi Camp Safaris offers the Tsodilo Hills as part of a 10-day Northern Loop between Maun and Victoria Falls for US$1900. Drotsky's Cabins and Makwena Lodge also offer longer tours. One/two-day trips cost US$292/416; add a stay at Makwena Lodge and two/three-day packages are US$348/471.

Several Maun travel agencies organise one-day air tours and charters starting at US$185, but they allow only three hours of sightseeing, with no time to climb and explore. You can hire a 4WD vehicle from Shakawe Fishing Camp; see Getting There & Away later in this section.

BOTSWANA

**BOTSWANA**

## Places to Stay

Visitors can camp at the Main (Rhino), Malatso or Makoba Woods campgrounds, or at wild camp sites around the base of the hills. There are no shops or services in either the San or Mbukushu village. Water is available at the Game Scouts Camp and at the bore hole several hundred metres from the airstrip (this water is intended for cattle and has a number of interesting flavours, so it's wise to purify it).

## Getting There & Away

**Car & Motorcycle** Visitors who fly to the Tsodilo Hills miss an excruciating but unforgettable drive. There are two main vehicle-access routes, one from the east that is signposted and turns off 7km south of Sepupa, and another from the north-east that turns off just south of the Samuchina Buffalo Fence; follow the fence for 7.6km and turn left at the blue sign reading I-3, which will take you right to the hills.

The first 22km of the southern route aren't bad, but at a cattle post, the road surmounts a dune and deteriorates into an excruciating 15km battle in low-ratio 4WD. The 41km northern route, however, is a contender for the Planet's Worst Drive; it's akin to spending three to four hours on a bucking bronco.

A third, little-used access route turns west near Nxamaseri, 20km north of Sepupa. For much of the way, it winds and twists through deep sand, passing abandoned villages and cattle posts, and squeezing through disconcertingly narrow gaps in the trees.

Shakawe Fishing Camp in Shakawe hires 4WD vehicles for US$150 per day plus US$1 per kilometre, including fuel, which isn't bad considering how much abuse the vehicle takes. Drivers should prepare for a challenge; if you'd rather not tackle the route yourself, a driver/guide can be provided with advance notice.

**Hitching** It's certainly not recommended, but some travellers do try to walk or hitch the 40km from the main road. The Kalahari is not to be taken lightly; let someone know where you're going and make sure most of the weight you're carrying is water. For a two days walk in the dry Kalahari heat, you need at least 8 to 10L of water per person.

## Getting Around

Once there, the best way to get around is to walk, and it's worth spending a few days exploring these magical hills. To find the best paintings, you'll probably need a guide. San guides with knowledge of the flora, fauna and local lore charge around US$5 to US$10 per group per day. Alternatively, barter with useful items: sugar, rice, shoes, T-shirts or batteries.

# The Kalahari

Stretching across seven countries – Botswana, Zambia, the Republic of South Africa, Zimbabwe, Namibia, Angola and Congo (Zaïre) – the Kalahari sands form one of Africa's most prominent geographical features. The Kalahari (or Kgalagadi in Tswana) isn't a classic desert, but rather a 1.2 million sq km deposit of sandy sediments. Unlike the Sahara, it's covered with trees and crisscrossed by ephemeral rivers and fossil watercourses, and the vast national parks and reserves that dominate western Botswana – Khutse, Central Kalahari and Mabuasehube-Gemsbok – protect fabulous, unique environments.

The magic of the Kalahari lies in its solitude, silence and vast open spaces. Botswana's aboriginal inhabitants, the San, maintain that at night, 'you can hear the stars in song'. The scant villages huddle around feeble boreholes and even the towns of Lethlakeng, Jwaneng, Kang, Ghanzi and the Kgalagadi Village Cluster would elsewhere be considered tiny outposts. However, with the newly paved Trans-Kalahari Highway between Gaborone and Windhoek, the region is opening to economic and tourist development, and dramatic changes are afoot.

### Geology
The base of the Kalahari was created in the Triassic era, when Africa was still part of the supercontinent of Gondwanaland. For 10 million years the continental rock surface was ground into the sand and sediment now called the Karoo formation. When Gondwanaland began breaking up, an outpouring of molten lava spread across the southern part of the African plate and covered the surface to depths of up to 9km. Over the next 120 million years this lava also eroded and formed the plateau that now makes up most of southern Africa.

Between 65 and two million years ago, the climate grew more arid and continuing

**HIGHLIGHTS**

- Follow the dry Nossob River through the Kalahari Gemsbok National Park
- Look for San arts and crafts in D'Kar and Ghanzi
- Travel across Botswana's empty centre to Deception Valley in the Central Kalahari Game Reserve
- Explore the Mabuasehube-Gemsbok National Park and look for gemsbok

BOTSWANA

erosion caused sandy sedimentation, which was spread over vast areas by wind, ephemeral streams and tectonic activity. Then the Great Rift formed to the north-east and Africa began to split apart, leaving a maze of faults across Zimbabwe and northern Botswana. As the land mass stretched, it left an immense, shallow basin across the southern African plateau. Uplifting around the edges diverted most of the larger rivers away from the basin and sand deposits shifted and settled into the lowest areas.

Between 25,000 and 10,000 years ago, rainfall in southern Africa was much higher than it is now and the lowest parts of the

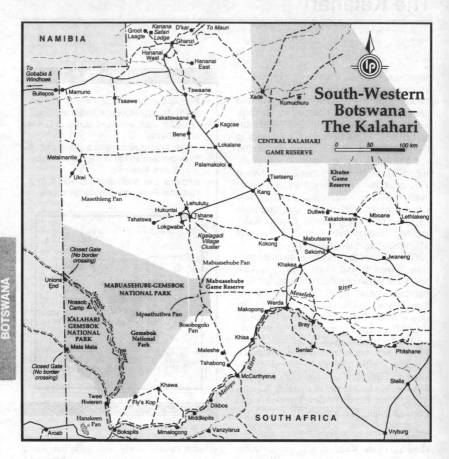

basin – the Makgadikgadi pans, the Okavango Delta, the Mababe Depression and Lake Ngami – filled with water. Due to increasing aridity and tectonic uplifting, however, only vague remnants of these great lakes are still in evidence.

## LETHLAKENG
Lethlakeng, the easternmost Kalahari outpost and the gateway to the Khutse Game Reserve, lies at the end of the tarred road, 116km from Gaborone and 124 sandy kilometres from the Khutse gate. The

Kwena name of the village means 'the place of reeds', and tradition recalls that it once bubbled with springs which attracted large numbers of elephant, rhinoceros and buffalo.

## KHUTSE GAME RESERVE
The 2600 sq km Khutse Game Reserve is a popular weekend excursion for Gaborone people. The name means 'where one kneels to drink'. Due to prolonged drought in recent years, Khutse doesn't have the concentrations of wildlife found in northern

Botswana, but the solitude of the pans and savanna scrub can be almost complete. Expect to see a variety of antelope – wildebeest, eland, duiker, steenbok, hartebeest, kudu, gemsbok and springbok – but not in large numbers. Also present are such predators as lion, leopard, brown and spotted hyaena, jackals, caracals (which the San believe to be the incarnation of the morning star) and even hunting dogs.

Around the pans, you'll also see smaller creatures – ground squirrels, bush squirrels, hares, bat-eared foxes, black-footed cats, pangolins, aardvarks, aardwolves, porcupines and warthogs. The bird life is also varied, and the reserve literature suggests that you can attract them by leaving fruit or sliced tsama melons near your camp.

### Places to Stay

Khutse has three camp sites, but only Golalabodimo Pan, near the entry gate, has running water and showers. Fourteen kilometres west from the entry gate is Khutse II Pan, with a rudimentary camp site. Much nicer is the camp site at Moreswa Pan, which lies 67km from the gate.

### Getting There & Away

Although sources claim that Khutse has been reached by conventional vehicles, 4WD is strongly recommended. Hitching is best on Friday night and Saturday morning, especially if you wait just outside Lethlakeng.

### CENTRAL KALAHARI GAME RESERVE

The 52,000 sq km Central Kalahari Game Reserve, Africa's largest protected area, sprawls across the nearly featureless heart of Botswana. It's perhaps best known for Deception (or Letiahau) Valley, the site of Mark and Delia Owens' 1974 to 1981

BOTSWANA

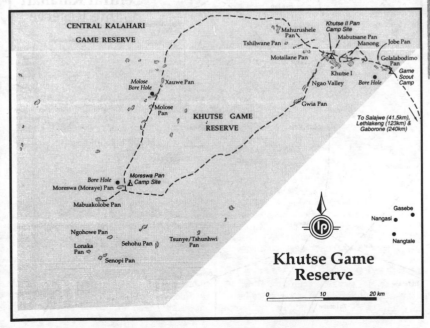

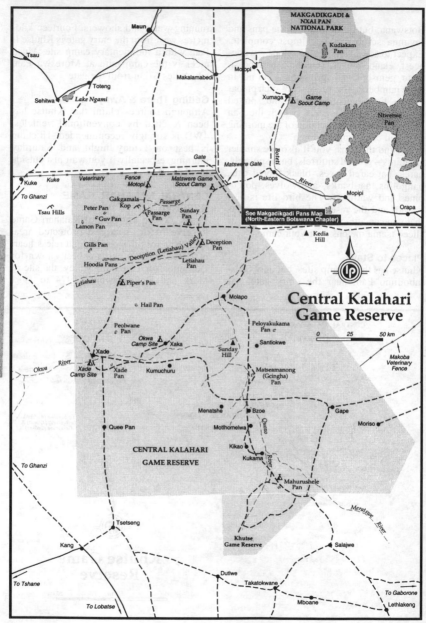

brown hyaena study, which is described in their book *Cry of the Kalahari*.

Most visitors' destination is Deception Pan, which attracts large amounts of wildlife after the rains. The brown hyaena which made the place famous emerge just after dark and you may also see lion. Three similar fossil valleys – the Okwa, the Quoxo (or Meratswe) and the Passarge – also bring topographical relief to the virtually featureless expanses, although the rivers ceased flowing more than 16,000 years ago. Other pans in the northern area of the reserve – Letiahau, Piper's, Sunday and Passarge – are artificially pumped to provide water for wildlife.

The southern part of the Central Kalahari is also home to perhaps 800 San and Bakgalakgadi, who are concentrated in small villages. Official policy has encouraged the San to opt for the relative ease of village life, ostensibly for the protection of wildlife, but more likely, to open the land to mineral exploitation and tourism. See Modern Developments in the History section of Facts about Botswana for more information.

### Information

The reserve has no shops, petrol or facilities. Entry permits are available only at the Matswere Game Scout Camp.

### Organised Tours

Most Maun operators run camping and fly-in safaris to Deception Valley (planes land at the Owens' former airstrip). A good deal is Audi Camp's five-day camping safari from Maun for US$565 per person, with four people. If you want to explore the furthest reaches of the Central Kalahari, Phakawe Safaris in Maun offers all-inclusive safaris for US$60 per person per day.

### Places to Stay

There are basic camp sites at *Deception Valley*, *Sunday Pan* and *Piper's Pan*, but they lack facilities of any kind. Deception Valley is the nicest, with some inviting acacia trees, while Piper's Pan is known for

its bizarre ghost trees (*Commiphora pyracanthoides*). There are also two other infrequently used remote camp sites, *Okwa* (also known as Xaka) and *Xade*, in the southern part of the reserve. Potable water is available only at the *Matswere Game Scout Camp*. There are no other facilities anywhere in the reserve. Bring all your firewood from outside.

### Getting There & Away

To reach the reserve, you need a high-clearance 4WD vehicle, a compass, and reserve petrol – the nearest supply is at Maun, but it's also unreliably available at Rakops.

The easiest access is from Rakops, 170km west of Orapa. From Rakops, take the 4WD track north, following the western bank of the Boteti River. After 2.5km, you'll see a turn-off to the left and a sign saying Central Kalahari Game Reserve. Turn west here and continue for 60km, until you cross a track heading north along the reserve boundary veterinary fence towards Makalamabedi (this is the approach route from Maun). Keep going straight; after 5km you'll reach the Matswere Game Scout Camp, where you can pick up an entry permit and fill up with water. From Matswere, it's 70km to Deception Pan.

From Maun, take the Maun-Nata road and turn south at Makalamabedi, 52km east of Maun. Keep going south along the sandy track following the eastern side of the veterinary fence. After 85km, you'll reach a reserve gate, but don't turn in. Keep following the fence for another 20km until you see the Matswere gate. There, turn west (right) and continue approximately 5km to the Matswere Game Scout Camp.

### JWANENG

In the late Cretaceous period – some 85 million years ago – a weakness in the earth's crust allowed molten rock in the underlying mantle to intrude into the carboniferous seams deep in the crust. These intrusions – known as kimberlite pipes – exerted enormous heat and pressure and caused the carbon to metamorphose into the diamonds which now provide 85% of Botswana's exports.

The world's largest diamond deposit was discovered at Jwaneng in 1978. By 1982, the involvement of the De Beers Botswana Mining Company Ltd (Debswana – the Botswanan subsidiary of De Beers) meant that Jwaneng had grown from just a few huts to a town of 14,000. The mine now produces nearly nine million carats annually, and in a month shifts and processes 480,000 metric tonnes of rock. Security is so tight that once a vehicle is allowed onto the mine site, it will never leave, lest it be used for smuggling diamonds.

Unlike Orapa, Jwaneng is an open town, and non-Debswana employees may settle and establish businesses. Mine tours may be arranged by appointment through Debswana (☎ 351131; fax 352941), Botsalano House, PO Box 329, Gaborone.

### Places to Stay & Eat

At the *Mokala Lodge* (☎ 380835), a cosy little place with pleasant gardens, singles/doubles cost US$55/72, with breakfast. It also has an à la carte restaurant and bar. For snacks, ice cream and soft drinks, try *KRM Takeaways* on The Mall.

### JWANENG TO GHANZI

The 650km stretch of the Trans-Kalahari Highway between Jwaneng and the cattle town of Ghanzi follows the cattle route from the Ghanzi Block freehold ranches to the BMC abattoir in Lobatse. Until recently, overland cattle drives were a regular sight on the road – however the route is now tarred and the cattle drovers have yielded to semitrailers.

At Sekoma, the road branches south to Tshabong and Bokspits. After another 170km, you enter the picturesque village of Kang, which has petrol and a friendly general store which is a good place to wait for lifts. There's also a garage and a bakery, and a welding station run by the Brigades.

Turn south at Kang for the Kgalagadi Village Cluster or Tshabong, which lies

360km away via Mabuasehube-Gemsbok National Park. Otherwise, continue northwest towards Ghanzi, which lies 270km away via the San village of Takatswaane.

### KGALAGADI VILLAGE CLUSTER

The four villages of the Kgalagadi Village Cluster – Tshane, Hukuntsi, Lokgwabe and Lehututu – make up an unlikely population centre in the remotest Kalahari. For many years, this was one of the most remote places in Botswana, but since the route from Kang has been tarred, this is bound to change. Petrol is available at the Shell petrol station in Hukuntsi.

### Hukuntsi

Hukuntsi (four compass directions) sprawls over a sandy, desolate area and has overtaken Lehututu, 12km north, as the commercial centre of the cluster. It's also the government administration centre and has the area's most reliable bore hole. Petrol is available and a bush shop sells a variety of supplies.

### Tshane

In Tshane, 12km east of Hukuntsi, take a look at the colonial police station which dates from the early 1900s. It has been targeted for renovation by the National Museum. It overlooks Tshane Pan where water shortages mean that cattle must drink from hand-dug wells around its perimeter.

### Lokgwabe

Lokgwabe (rocky pan) lies 11km southwest of Hukuntsi. Its only claim to fame is that it was settled by Nama leader Simon Kooper, who sought British protection in Bechuanaland after leading the 1904 Nama rebellion in German South West Africa (Namibia). He was pursued across the deserts by German troops and 800 camels. German detritus – including empty tins of bully beef – still litters the route.

### Lehututu

Lehututu, 10km north of Tshane, is named after the sound made by the ground hornhill. It was once a major trading place for travellers across the Kalahari, but it's now little more than a wide spot in the desert. A small shop sells basic supplies.

## Tshatswa

The San village of Tshatswa, population 277, lies about 60km south-west of Hukuntsi. Visitors should bring their own water. The village bore hole yields only about 150L of saline water daily which must be condensed and desalinated to make it potable. The extracted salt is then sold to earn a bit of money for the village.

Along the route between Hukuntsi and Tshatswa you'll pass sparkling white salt pans and, as desolate as the area seems, it supports large populations of gemsbok, ostrich and hartebeest.

## Masethleng Pan

Masethleng Pan, 90km north-west of Hukuntsi, is accessible on sand tracks developed during an oil exploration project in the late 1980s. It once teemed with both predators and prey animals, but is now known mainly for sightings of bat-eared fox and aardvark. The route from Hukuntsi is flanked by several sandy pan areas and San villages, and an incongruous camelthorn acacia bushland 10km to the west, which offers an oasis in the sand veld.

## Places to Stay & Eat

Visitors must either know someone to stay with or carry a tent; ask permission to camp from the village chief, who can direct you to suitable sites where you won't disrupt village activities. The *government hostel* in Hukuntsi is only open to the public in an emergency.

## Getting There & Away

We're talking remote here. The Kgalagadi Village Cluster lies 104km west of Kang and about 255km north of Tshabong. Although the route is tarred, there's very little traffic; if you want to try hitching, wait at the general store in Kang. Finding a lift back will be an even greater challenge.

## BOKSPITS

The picturesque frontier settlement of Bokspits sits amid ruddy sand dunes on the intermittent Molopo River in Botswana's extreme south-western corner. This centre of karakul wool production is accessible via South Africa or down the dry Molopo riverbed from McCarthysrus near Tshabong. There's no accommodation and most vehicles are merely crossing the South African border for a visit to Kalahari Gemsbok National Park.

## MABUASEHUBE-GEMSBOK NATIONAL PARK

In Botswana's remote south-west corner lies the immense Mabuasehube-Gemsbok National Park, which covers 12,800 sq km and was created in 1995 by amalgamating the former Gemsbok National Park and Mabuasehube Game Reserve. In the west, it abuts South Africa's Kalahari Gemsbok National Park; the combined areas make up one of the world's largest and most pristine wildernesses. This is the one area of Botswana where you'll see the shifting sand dunes that many mistakenly believe to be typical of the Kalahari.

### Gemsbok National Park Section

Gemsbok, after which this park is named, are best observed after the rains, between March and May. The water also attracts springbok, eland, red hartebeest and blue wildebeest. During the rest of the year, however, you may be lucky to see anything at all. The Botswana side of the park isn't accessible by road; it's reached by crossing the Nossob River from South Africa. There are no Botswana park fees.

### Mabuasehube Game Reserve Section

The Mabuasehube (or Mabuashegube – 'red earth' in Segologa) Game Reserve section covers 1800 sq km and focuses on three major pans and several minor ones. Each pan is flanked by beautiful red dunes up to 30m high on their southern and western edges. The largest pan, Mabuasehube, is used as a salt lick by itinerant herds of eland

**Mabuasehube Game Reserve Section**

0    15    30 km

.and gemsbok. At its western end are wells artificially deepened by Gologa pastoralists for their cattle. The wells often hold water even when the rest of the pan is dry.

Further south is the grassy Bosobogolo Pan, which attracts springbok as well as lion, cheetah, brown hyaena and hunting dog. There are also five other large pan complexes – Lesholoago, Malataso, Monamodi, Khiding and Mpaathutlwa – and a number of smaller ones. Vegetation highlights include several acacia species, such as *Acacia erioloba* and *Acacia lüderitzii*.

Mabuasehube is best visited in late winter and early spring when herds of eland and gemsbok migrate out from the Gemsbok National Park section. The park is open to non-campers from 6.30 am to 6.30 pm from March to September and 5.30 am to 7.30 pm from October to February. You can pick up permits and pay park fees at the Game Scout Camp at Mpaathutlwa Pan.

## Places to Stay

**Gemsbok Section** There are two big *rest camps* on the South African side of the Nossob River. The *Game Scout Camp*, on the Botswana side opposite Twee Rivieren, has cold showers and toilets. There are also three undeveloped *sites* on the Botswana bank: Rooiputs, 30km north-east of Twee Rivieren; Polentswe Pan, 60km north of Nossob; and Swart Pan, 30km south-east of Unions End. All are accessed from Kalahari Gemsbok National Park in South Africa. Campers at Polentswe and Rooiputs may pick up water and firewood at the Game Scout Camp.

**Mabuasehube Section** There are rudimentary *camp sites*, for up to two groups each, at Lesholoago Pan, Mpaathutlwa Pan (the park headquarters, with the Game Scout Camp) and Khiding Pan, as well as two sites at Mabuasehube Pan. Facilities are limited to pit latrines, and all but Khiding Pan have waterholes for wildlife-viewing. Water is reliably available only at the Game Scout Camp, but it's still wise to carry all the water you'll require.

## Getting There & Away

The Gemsbok National Park section is accessible only by crossing the Nossob River from the Kalahari Gemsbok National Park, and routes into Mabuasehube are poor and require 4WD. The shortest of the three access routes is the little-used track from the Khakea-Werda road. The west turning to Mabuasehube is just under 2km north of the Moselebe River, about 50km south of Khakea and 20km north of Werda.

You can also come in from Tshabong, which is reached via Jwaneng and Sekoma, but it's indirect unless you're coming from South Africa. The most difficult route runs via Kang and the Kgalagadi Village Cluster, and enters Mabuasehube from the north.

The nearest reliable petrol pumps are at Kang, Ghanzi and Jwaneng, while Tshabong, 100km south of the reserve, has a sporadic supply. Otherwise, cross into South Africa for fuel.

## KALAHARI GEMSBOK NATIONAL PARK (SOUTH AFRICA)

South Africa's 10,000 sq km Kalahari Gemsbok National Park is characterised by a semi-desert landscape of Kalahari dunes, camelthorn-dotted grasslands and the dry beds of the Auob and Nossob rivers. It lies in a wild and remote area of South Africa, wedged between Botswana and Namibia.

Most of the wildlife lives in the river valleys or around the pans, and because the park border is open to Botswana's Gemsbok National Park, animals aren't confined within Kalahari Gemsbok's park boundaries. Springbok and gemsbok are most common, and there's also the occasional herd of blue wildebeest. Eland inhabit the sandy dune areas and you might see red hartebeest around the northern end of the Nossob River. The park also has a full complement of predators, including lion, cheetah, leopard, wild dogs, jackal and both brown and spotted hyaena. There are also 238 bird species present; 44 of these are birds of prey.

All that's missing are the indigenous people, the San, who were displaced when the park was created in 1931; they're currently petitioning the South African government for the right to return to their traditional lifestyle within the park.

Park entry costs US$5 per car plus US$3 per person.

### Places to Stay & Eat

There are *tourist rest camps* at Twee Rivieren and Nossob, both on the Nossob River, and also at Mata Mata, where the Auob River crosses the Namibian border. Each has camp sites, caravan sites, self-catering chalets and cottages, and basic, inexpensive huts with communal cooking and ablutions facilities. Supplies are sold at all three rest camps, and Twee Rivieren has a restaurant, which is open from 6.30 am to 9 pm. Another Twee Rivieren highlight is the swimming pool for rest camp guests. Note that both the park and the rest-camp gates close at dusk.

Accommodation in Kalahari Gemsbok National Park is operated by the South African National Parks Board. *Camp sites* cost US$8 for up to six people and accommodation ranges from simple *huts* for US$20 (for up to three people) at Mata Mata and Nossob to *cottages* for US$62/45/48 at Twee Rivieren/Mata Mata/Nossob. Bookings are required on weekends, public holidays and school holidays; contact the National Parks Board (☎ (012) 343 1991; fax 343 0905), PO Box 787, Pretoria 0001, South Africa.

### Getting There & Away

From Botswana, access is via Bokspits. Cross into South Africa and follow the road northwards along the dry Nossob River. Park headquarters is at Twee Rivieren, 53km from Bokspits. From there, it's 3½ hours to Nossob Camp, and 2½ hours to Mata Mata.

From Namibia, the border crossings at Union's End and Mata Mata have been closed due to over-use of the road as a quick transit route between Namibia and South Africa – the increased traffic apparently disturbed the wildlife – but the latter should have opened by the time you read this. Otherwise, use the border crossing at Aroab/Rietfontein.

## GHANZI

The name Ghanzi is derived from the San word for a one-stringed musical instrument with a gourd soundbox, and not from the Tswana word *gantsi*, 'the flies', which would in fact be quite appropriate. The town sits atop a 500km-long limestone ridge that curves from Lake Ngami in the north-east to Windhoek, Namibia, in the west. It isn't visible from the ground, but contains great stores of artesian water which make ranching and agriculture not only feasible but also profitable.

### History

Ghanzi has quite a colourful history. Numerous traders and travellers passed through in the 19th century, but it was the ruthless Hendrik Matthys van Zyl who

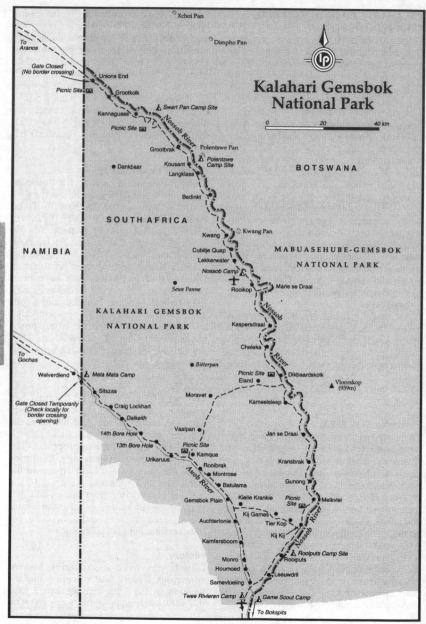

Kalahari Gemsbok
National Park

gave life to Ghanzi. In 1868, this former Transvaal MP traversed the Botswana wilderness, trading munitions, shooting elephant, killing San and earning the respect of local Bantu chiefs. In 1874 he paused at Lake Ngami and briefly usurped the leadership of dissident factions in Chief Moremi's Tawana tribe. At one stage he avenged the San murder of a Boer, William Frederick Prinsloo, by luring 33 San with tobacco and brandy and murdering them in cold blood.

In 1877, after a profitable trip to Cape Town, Van Zyl returned to Ghanzi and in his first year, shot more than 400 elephant. This yielded at least four tonnes of ivory and with the proceeds, he built a two storey mansion with stained-glass windows, filled it with imported furniture and lived like a maharajah in the wilderness. Rumours of his influence and disagreeable nature prevented Boer Dorsland Trekkers from settling around Ghanzi.

The cause of Van Zyl's death is unknown, but some incredible tales have arisen. Some have him struck down by vengeful San and others by a wily San servant in his household. Another has him angering the Damara to the point of murder, while yet another credits the Khoi-Khoi. What is known is that after his death, his wife, daughter and three sons disappeared to the Transvaal and were never heard from again.

That Ghanzi survived into the late 19th century without van Zyl is probably due to Cecil Rhodes, who saw it as a Bechuanaland foothold for the British South Africa Company. The British took over the Ghanzi Block ostensibly to thwart German aggression from Namibia, but it was almost certainly for commercial rather than strategic reasons. After Rhodes fraudulently secured land cessions from the Tawana, he diverted a contingent of Voortrekkers into Ghanzi by offering free land and equipment.

However, Rhodes' commercial ambitions were stalled by the Jameson Raid, which was an unauthorised, ill-conceived and abortive military manoeuvre intended to destabilise the Boer republics in the

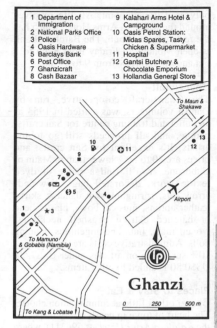

1 Department of Immigration
2 National Parks Office
3 Police
4 Oasis Hardware
5 Barclays Bank
6 Post Office
7 Ghanzicraft
8 Cash Bazaar
9 Kalahari Arms Hotel & Campground
10 Oasis Petrol Station: Midas Spares, Tasty Chicken & Supermarket
11 Hospital
12 Gantsi Butchery & Chocolate Emporium
13 Hollandia General Store

To Maun & Shakawe

Airport

To Mamuno & Gobabis (Namibia)

To Kang & Lobatse

**Ghanzi**

0    250    500 m

Transvaal and force their annexation to the Cape Colony. Rhodes was forced to resign his post as prime minister of Cape Colony, the leader Jameson was imprisoned and the Boer settlers at Ghanzi were left to fend for themselves.

Western Botswana may have been prime cattle country, but by 1908, most freehold farmers had abandoned it and Ghanzi was on the verge of becoming a ghost town. In 1913, the majority of farms were sold at auction, and over the following 50 years, land use was rationalised and the settlement grew into Botswana's most productive ranching area. The romantic days of the overland cattle drives to the Lobatse BMC abattoir may have passed, but Ghanzi's Wild West atmosphere lives on.

### Information
Despite its colourful history, Ghanzi has few attractions and most travellers use it

only as a transit point. All life revolves around the Kalahari Arms Hotel, which has the restaurant and pub. The Barclays Bank is open Monday to Friday from 8 am to 1 pm and on Saturday from 9 to 11 am.

### Ghanzicraft

The Ghanzicraft co-operative, run by Danish volunteers, was started in 1953 as an outlet and training centre for San crafts-people, and all proceeds still go to the artists. It's excellent for San crafts, and prices are 30 to 50% lower than in Maun or Gaborone. You'll find a range of dyed textile work, decorated bags, bow-and-arrow sets, springbok-skin dancing skirts, leather aprons, musical bows, plastic bead or hatched ostrich eggshell necklaces, woven mats, hats and ingenious dancing dolls. Administrative costs are covered by a 10% surcharge on articles under US$7.50; US$0.80 is added to other items.

### Places to Stay & Eat

Ghanzi offers little accommodation choice. The heart of town in nearly every respect is the *Kalahari Arms Hotel* (☎ 596311), where single/double rooms cost US$37/41 and rondavels are US$41/49. Campers pay US$4 per person, including use of the ablutions facilities and swimming pool, but watch out for the automatic sprinkler system.

Your best meal option is the forgettable but palatable fare in the Kalahari Arms dining room. When you tire of that, there's the *Tasty Chicken*, opposite the petrol station, and the *Gantsi Butchery* (note they use the Tswana 'flies' spelling!), near the airport, which also sells fabulous chocolate.

### Getting There & Away

**Air** Kalahari Air (☎ 351804; fax 312015), PO Box 41278, Gaborone, has services from Gaborone to Ghanzi on Tuesday at 9 am and Friday at 7.30 am; they return on the same days at 4 pm and 2.30 pm, respectively.

**Bus** Following the completion of the

Trans-Kalahari Highway, buses now run twice weekly in either direction between Ghanzi and Gaborone. The trip takes eight hours.

The scheduled bus between Lobatse and Ghanzi (US$17) leaves Lobatse on Monday mornings and from Ghanzi on Wednesday mornings. The scheduled bus between Maun and Mamuno passes through Ghanzi in the early afternoon on Monday, Thursday and Saturday westbound and on Sunday, Tuesday and Friday eastbound. Star Line's service to Buitepos and Gobabis, Namibia, leaves on Saturday at 8 am.

**Car & Motorcycle** Ghanzi lies on a tarred spur route off the Trans-Kalahari Highway between Windhoek (Namibia) and Gaborone. Bear in mind that the Namibian border post closes at 5 pm (during the winter months, it closes at 4 pm Namibian time). For more information, see the Botswana Getting There & Away chapter.

**Hitching** Hitchers between Maun and Namibia should plan at least one night in Ghanzi. If you're caught out at the border, the friendly officials normally allow camping. On the Namibian side, try the *East Gate Service Station & Rest Camp*, which is a desert oasis at the border post. Camping costs US$3 per person and bungalows are US$27 for three people.

Heading east, most traffic is bound for Maun. To Jwaneng and Lobatse, there's a lot of cattle traffic (except on Friday and Saturday), and patient hitchers will normally find lifts. Alternatively, ask truckers at Oasis Hardware or the petrol station.

### D'KAR

D'kar, 38km north-east of Ghanzi on the Maun road, is best known for the San-owned Kuru Development Trust, which trains the local Ncoakhoe San (the red people) in practical agriculture and animal husbandry, and sponsors leather-working and material crafts industries. At the outlet on the main road, visitors can purchase anything from leather briefcases to donkey harnesses. It's open Monday to Friday from 8 am to 5 pm and on Saturdays from 8 am to noon. Contact Kuru Crafts (☎ 596308; fax 596285), PO Box 219, Ghanzi.

At the 7500 hectare Dqãe Qare Farm, a cattle ranch 15km east of D'kar, you can learn how local people hunt and gather wild foods, and about the local uses of indigenous flora and fauna. Guided bushwalks cost US$3 per hour and in the evening, locals stage traditional dancing and storytelling sessions. Admission to the farm costs US$3 per day and camping is US$5. Basic groceries and petrol are available in D'kar. Access to the farm is by 4WD only.

## NAMIBIA AT A GLANCE

Area: 824,270 sq km
Population: 1,727,183
Population growth rate: 3.06%
Capital: Windhoek
Head of State: Sam Nujoma
Official Language: Afrikaans
Currency: Namibian dollar
Exchange Rate: US$1 = ...
Per Capita GNP: US$1,970
Time: GMT/UTC + 2 (October–April)
GMT/UTC +1 (April–October)

# Namibia

## European Exploration & Invasion

...

# Facts about Namibia

## HISTORY
### Pre-Colonial History

It's generally accepted that southern Africa's earliest inhabitants were San (Bushmen): nomadic people organised in extended family groups who could adapt to severe natural conditions. Population densities were very low and family groups moved about in search of edible wild plants and game.

These San communities probably came under pressure from Khoi-Khoi (Hottentot) groups, the ancestors of the modern Nama, with whom they share a language group. The Khoi-Khoi were organised loosely into tribes and raised livestock rather than hunting. They probably entered the area from the south, gradually displacing the San, and remained in control there until around 1500 AD. They were probably also responsible for the first pottery in the region.

Namibia is still home to descendants of the Khoi-Khoi and San (which includes most indigenous groups in southern Africa) but few indigenous people follow traditional lifestyles.

Between 2300 and 2400 years ago, the first Bantu appeared on the plateaus of south-central Africa, bringing the region's first tribal societies. The subsequent Khoisan decline may be attributed to both a retreat to the deserts and enslavement by the newcomers (a practice that continues even today).

Around 1600, the Bantu-speaking, cattle-herding Herero migrated from the Zambezi Valley to north-western Namibia, resulting in conflicts with the Khoi-Khoi, with whom they competed for grazing lands and water holes. In Kaokoland, the more aggressive Herero displaced not only Khoi-Khoi but also the remaining San and Damara (whose origins are unclear).

It's believed that the present-day Nama are descended from Khoi-Khoi groups who held out against the Herero in the violent

## NAMIBIA AT A GLANCE

**Area:** 825,418 sq km
**Population:** 1,727,183
**Population Growth Rate:** 2.94%
**Capital:** Windhoek
**Head of State:** Sam Nujoma
**Official Language:** Afrikaans
**Currency:** Namibian dollar
**Exchange Rate:** N$5.21 = US$1
**Per Capita GNP:** US$1970
**Time:** GMT/UTC +2 (October-April)
GMT/UTC +1 (April-October)

clashes from the 1840s to the 1880s. By the late 19th century, a new Bantu group, the Owambo, had settled in the north along the Okavango and Kunene rivers. The Owambo were probably descended from people who migrated from eastern Africa more than 500 years earlier.

### European Exploration & Incursion

Due to its barren, inhospitable coastline, Namibia was largely ignored by the European maritime nations until relatively recently. The first European visitors were 15th century Portuguese mariners in search of a route to the Indies. In 1486, Captain Diego Cão sailed as far south as Cape

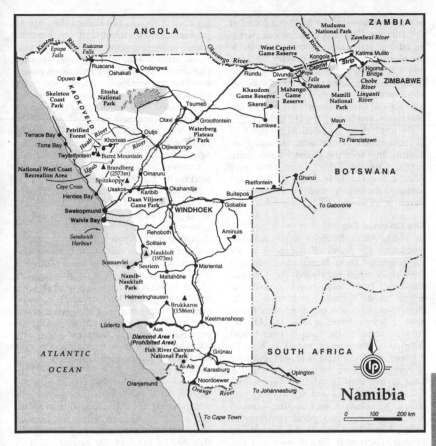

**Namibia**

0    100    200 km

Cross, where he erected a limestone *padrão* (a tribute to his royal patron, João II) to mark the big event. The cross also served as a navigational aid for subsequent explorers.

Bartolomeu Dias reached the site of present-day Lüderitz while en route to the Cape of Good Hope on Christmas Day 1487; the event is marked by another cross, on Diaz Point.

In the early 17th century, Dutch sailors from the Cape colonies explored the formidable desert coast of Namibia, but no formal settlements were established. In 1750, the Dutch elephant hunter Jacobus Coetsee became the first white to cross the Orange River into Namibia. He was followed by a series of traders, hunters and missionaries, and the Namibian interior was gradually opened up to Europeans. In 1878, the Cape Colony government put the Namibian ports of Angra Pequena and Walvis Bay under Dutch protection, fearing incursions by the British, Americans and French.

The first real European settlers, however, were missionaries, and by the early 19th century mission stations had been founded at Bethanien, Windhoek, Rehoboth, Keetmanshoop, and various other sites. In 1844, the German Rhenish Missionary Society, under Dr Hugo Hahn, began working among the Herero, but with limited success. More successful were the Finnish Lutherans who arrived in the north in 1870 and established missions among the Owambo.

By 1843, the rich coastal guano deposits of the southern Namib were attracting attention. In 1867, the guano islands were annexed by the British, who took over Walvis Bay in 1878. The British also mediated the largely inconclusive Khoisan-Herero wars during this period.

### The Colonial Era

In 1883, Adolf Lüderitz negotiated the purchase of Angra Pequena and its surroundings from Nama chief, Joseph Fredericks, then petitioned the German chancellor Otto von Bismarck to place the region under German 'protection'. The chancellor, who was occupied with European issues, preferred to leave the African colonial scene to the British, French and Belgians. 'My map of Africa is here in Europe,' he said. 'Here is Russia and here is France and here we are in the middle. That is my map of Africa.' But strong domestic lobbying – and the warning that Britain had designs on Lüderitz – forced him to concede and grant protectorate status. Years later, during the last-minute European scramble for colonies and territorial disputes between Britain and Germany, Lüderitz persuaded the chancellor to annex the entire country.

Initially, however, German interests were minimal, and between 1885 and 1890 the colonial administration amounted to three public administrators based at Otjimbingwe village, 55km south of present-day Karibib. Germany's Namibian interests were first served through a colonial company (along the lines of the British East India Company in India prior to the Raj), but this organisation couldn't maintain law and order.

In the 1880s, due to renewed fighting between the Nama and Herero, the German government dispatched Curt von François and 23 soldiers to restrict the supply of arms from British-administered Walvis Bay. However, this seemingly innocuous peacekeeping regiment evolved into the more powerful Schutztruppe, which constructed forts around the country to aid their efforts to put down opposition.

, At this stage, Namibia became a fully fledged protectorate, known as German South West Africa. The first German farmers arrived in 1892 to take up expropriated land on the Central Plateau, and were soon followed by merchants and other settlers. In the late 1890s, the Germans, the Portuguese in Angola and the British in Bechuanaland agreed on Namibia's boundaries.

Naturally, this spawned bitterness among local people, who resented the foreigners' laws, taxes and takeover of water rights and communal lands. In 1904, the Nama, under Hendrik Witbooi, launched a large-scale rebellion against the increasing colonial presence. Later that year, they were joined by the Herero – an unlikely alliance between traditional enemies, especially considering that their warring had been a catalyst for increased involvement by the colonial powers.

However, the rebellions were eventually suppressed by the Schutztruppe in conflicts which wiped out 75% of the Herero nation and a large number of Nama and German troops. By 1910, the remaining Herero had fled to the inhospitable country east of Windhoek – some as far as Botswana – where many suffered from hunger and starvation. Survivors were eventually shifted to their allocated 'homeland', the four-part Hereroland district in the barren western Kalahari.

Meanwhile, in the south, diamonds had been discovered at Grasplatz, east of Lüderitz, by a South African labourer, Zacharias Lewala. Despite the assessment of De Beers that the find probably wouldn't amount to much, prospectors flooded in to stake their claims. By 1910, the German authorities had branded the entire area between Lüderitz and the Orange River a *Sperrgebiet* (forbidden area), chucked out the prospectors and granted exclusive rights to the Deutsche Diamanten Gesellschaft.

The colonial era lasted until WWI, by which time the German Reich had dismantled the Herero tribal structures and taken over all Khoi-Khoi and Herero lands. As more colonial immigrants arrived from Europe, the best lands were parcelled into an extensive network of white farms.

The Owambo in the north were luckier and managed to avoid conquest until after the start of WWI, when they were overrun by Portuguese forces fighting on the side of the Allies. In 1914, at the beginning of WWI, Britain pressured South Africa into invading Namibia. The South Africans, under the command of Prime Minister Louis Botha and General Jan Smuts, gradually pushed northwards, forcing the outnumbered Schutztruppe to retreat. In May 1915, the Germans faced their final defeat at Khorab near Tsumeb, and a week later a South African administration was set up in Windhoek.

By 1920, many German farms had been sold to Afrikaans-speaking settlers and the German diamond-mining interests in the south were handed over to the South Africa-based Consolidated Diamond Mines (CDM), which retains the concession to the present day.

### The South African Occupation

Under the Treaty of Versailles in 1919, Germany was required to renounce all its colonial claims, and in 1921 the League of Nations granted South Africa a formal mandate to administer Namibia as part of the Union, but not to prepare it for eventual independence. However, after a brief rebellion in 1924, the mixed-race Basters at Rchoboth were granted some measure of autonomy, and the following year the territorial constitution was amended to permit the white population to set up a territorial legislature.

The mandate was renewed by the UN following WWII but South Africa was prepared to annex South West Africa as a full province in the Union and decided to scrap the terms of the mandate and rewrite the constitution. The International Court of Justice, however, determined that South Africa had overstepped its boundaries and ruled that the mandate would remain in force. The UN set up the Committee on South West Africa to enforce the original terms. In 1956, the UN decided that South African control must somehow be terminated.

Undeterred, the South African government tightened its grip on the territory, and in 1949 granted the white population parliamentary representation in Pretoria. The bulk of Namibia's viable farmland was parcelled into some 6000 farms for white settlers and the other ethnic groups were relegated to newly demarcated 'tribal homelands'. The official intent was ostensibly to 'channel economic development into predominantly poor rural areas', but it was all too obvious that it was, in fact, simply a convenient way of retaining the best lands for white settlement and agriculture.

As a result, a prominent line of demarcation appeared between the rich, predominantly white areas in the central and southern parts of the country, and the poorer tribal areas to the north. Perhaps the only positive result of this effective imposition of tribal boundaries was the prevention of territorial squabbles between previously mobile groups now forced to live under the same political entity. This arrangement was retained until Namibian independence in 1990.

### Independence

Throughout the 1950s, despite mounting pressure from the UN, South Africa refused to release its grip on Namibia. This intransigence was based on its fears of having yet another antagonistic government on its doorstep and of losing the income that it derived from the mining operations there. Namibia is rich in minerals such as uranium, copper, lead and zinc and is the

NAMIBIA

world's foremost source of gem diamonds. These were all mined by South African and western multinational companies under a generous taxation scheme that enabled them to export up to a third of their profits every year.

Forced labour had been the lot of most Namibians since the German annexation, and was one of the main factors that led to mass demonstrations and the increasingly nationalist sentiments in the late 1950s. Several political parties were formed and strikes were organised, not only among workers in Namibia but also among contract labourers working in South Africa. Among the parties was the Owamboland People's Congress, founded in Cape Town under the leadership of Shafiishuna Samuel Nujoma and Adimba Herman Toivo ja Toivo.

In 1959, the party's name was changed to the Owamboland People's Organisation and Nujoma took the issue of South African occupation to the UN in New York. By 1960, his party had gathered the support of several others and they eventually coalesced into the South West African People's Organisation, or SWAPO, with its headquarters in Dar es Salaam. Troops were sent to Egypt for military training and the organisation prepared for war.

In 1966, SWAPO took the issue of South African occupation to the International Court of Justice. The court upheld South Africa's right to govern South West Africa, but the UN General Assembly voted to terminate South Africa's mandate and replace it with a Council for South West Africa (renamed the Commission for Namibia in 1973) to administer the territory.

In response, on 26 August 1966, now called Namibia Day, SWAPO launched its campaign of guerrilla warfare at Omgulumbashe in the Owambo country. The following year, one of SWAPO's founders, Toivo ja Toivo, was convicted of terrorism and imprisoned in South Africa, where he would remain until 1984; Nujoma stayed in Tanzania. In 1972, the UN finally declared the South African occupation of South West Africa officially illegal and called for a withdrawal, and the UN secretary Kurt Waldheim proclaimed SWAPO the legitimate representative of the Namibian people.

In response, the South African government fired on demonstrators and arrested thousands of activists. While all this was going on, events were coming to a head in neighbouring Angola, culminating in its independence from Portugal in 1975, and the ascendancy of the Marxist-oriented Popular Movement for the Liberation of Angola (MPLA). This was anathema to South Africa, which, in an attempt to smash the MPLA, launched an invasion of Angola in support of the UNITA (National Union for the Total Independence of Angola) forces, which controlled southern Angola at the time. The attempt failed, and by March 1976 the troops had been withdrawn, although incursions continued well into the 1980s.

Back in Namibia, the Democratic Turnhalle Alliance (DTA, named after the site of its meetings) was officially established in 1975. Formed from a combination of ethnic parties and white political interests, it turned out to be a toothless debating

Sam Nujoma became Namibia's president after independence in 1990.

chamber that spent much of its time in litigation with the South African government over the scope of its responsibilities.

Meanwhile, in the late 1970s, the SWAPO ranks were split when two officials of the government in exile, Solomon Mifima and Andreas Shipanga, called for long overdue party elections. In response, the party's president Sam Nujoma had them imprisoned in Zambia, along with hundreds of their followers. Civil rights activists in Europe managed to have them freed, and they now head a minority party, the SWAPO-Democrats or SWAPO-D.

In 1983, after the DTA had indicated it would accommodate SWAPO, it was dissolved and replaced by yet another administration, known as the Multi-Party Conference. This turned out to be even less successful than the DTA and quickly disappeared, allowing control of Namibia to pass back to the South African-appointed administrator-general, Mr Justice Steyn, who was given the power to rule by proclamation.

The failure of these attempts to effect an internal solution did not deter South Africa, which refused to negotiate on a programme for Namibian independence supervised by the UN until the estimated 19,000 Cuban troops were removed from neighbouring Angola. In response, SWAPO intensified its guerrilla campaign. As a result, movement in the north of the country became severely restricted.

In the end, however, it may not have been the activities of SWAPO alone or international sanctions that forced the South Africans to the negotiating table. The white Namibian population itself was growing tired of the war and the economy was suffering badly. South Africa's internal problems also had a significant effect. By 1985, the war was costing some R480 million (around US$250 million) per year and conscription was widespread. Mineral exports, which once provided around 88% of the country's GDP, had plummeted to just 27% by 1984. This was due mainly to falling world demand and depressed prices, but fraud and corruption were also significant factors.

By 1988, the stage was set for negotiations on the country's future. Under the watch of the UN, the USA and the USSR, a deal struck between Cuba, Angola, South Africa and SWAPO provided for the withdrawal of Cuban troops from Angola and South African troops from Namibia. It also stipulated that the transition to Namibian independence would formally begin on 1 April 1989, and would be followed by UN-monitored elections held in November 1989 on the basis of universal suffrage. Although minor score settling and unrest among some SWAPO troops threatened to derail the whole process, the plan went ahead and in September, Nujoma returned from his 30-year exile. In the elections, SWAPO garnered a clear majority of the votes but the numbers were insufficient to give it the sole mandate to write the new constitution.

Following negotiations between the various parties and international advisers, including the USA, France, Germany and the USSR, a constitution was drafted. This provided incentive for co-operation between the executive and legislative bodies and included an impressive bill of rights, covering provisions for protection of the environment, the rights of families and children, freedom of religion, speech and the press and a host of other matters. It was adopted in February 1990 and independence was granted a month later, on 21 March, under Nujoma's presidency. His policies are based on a national reconciliation programme to heal the wounds left by 25 years of armed struggle and a reconstruction programme based on the retention of a mixed economy and partnership with the private sector.

So far, things have gone smoothly, and in the elections of December 1994, Executive President Nujoma and his SWAPO party were re-elected with a 68% landslide victory over rival Mishake Muyongo and his Democratic Turnhalle Alliance party. Hopes for the future remain high.

NAMIBIA

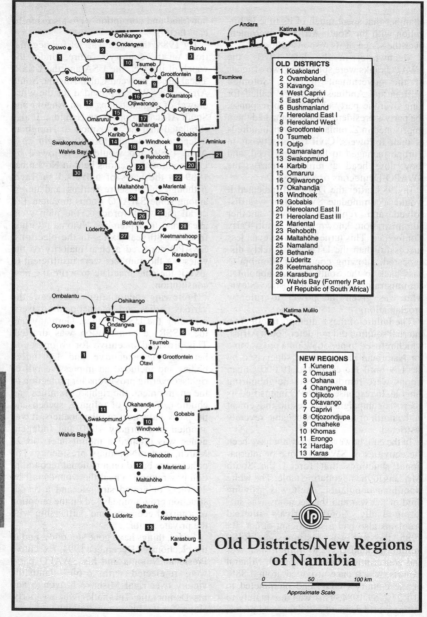

**OLD DISTRICTS**
1  Koakoland
2  Ovamboland
3  Kavango
4  West Caprivi
5  East Caprivi
6  Bushmanland
7  Hereoland East I
8  Hereoland West
9  Grootfontein
10  Tsumeb
11  Outjo
12  Damaraland
13  Swakopmund
14  Karbib
15  Omaruru
16  Otjiwarongo
17  Okahandja
18  Windhoek
19  Gobabis
20  Hereoland East II
21  Hereoland East III
22  Mariental
23  Rehoboth
24  Maltahöhe
25  Namaland
26  Bethanie
27  Lüderitz
28  Keetmanshoop
29  Karasburg
30  Walvis Bay (Formerly Part of Republic of South Africa)

**NEW REGIONS**
1  Kunene
2  Omusati
3  Oshana
4  Ohangwena
5  Otjikoto
6  Okavango
7  Caprivi
8  Otjozondjupa
9  Omaheke
10  Khomas
11  Erongo
12  Hardap
13  Karas

**Old Districts/New Regions of Namibia**

0          50          100 km
Approximate Scale

NAMIBIA

## GEOGRAPHY

Namibia is an arid country of great geographical variation. Broadly speaking, its topography can be divided into four main sections: the Namib Desert and the coastal plains; the eastward-sloping Central Plateau; the Kalahari sands along the Botswana and South African borders; and the densely wooded bushveld of the Kavango and Caprivi regions.

The Namib Desert, the world's oldest arid region, has existed for over 80 million years. It extends along the country's entire Atlantic coast and has an annual rainfall of between 15 and 100mm. The Namib owes its existence to the cold Benguela Current, which flows northwards from the Antarctic. This current brings with it cold air, which is heavier than warm air and can carry much less moisture. When this cold air meets the warmer land, the little moisture it does contain immediately condenses into a blanket of fog over the coast. This moisture sustains lichens and specialised plants that form the lowest echelons of the desert food chain and sustain the unique Namib flora and fauna that have adapted specifically to the hostile conditions.

Namib landscapes range from the mountainous red dunes in the south to the interior plains and flat-topped, steep-sided and isolated mountains – *inselbergs* – of the centre. The Skeleton Coast region in the north is known for bare scorched dunes.

Moving east, the altitude increases and the coastal dunes gradually give way to gravel plains. The width of these coastal plains varies from a few kilometres in the northern Kaokoveld to almost 300km at Lüderitz in the south. In Damaraland, the coastal plain is punctuated by dramatic mountains and inselbergs, some of volcanic origin. They're honeycombed with caves and rock shelters, which provided homes for early humans. The Brandberg and Erongo mountains north of Karibib are both well known examples.

The Namib Desert itself is scored by a number of rivers, which rise in the Central Plateau but are often dry. Some, like the ephemeral Tsauchab, once reached the sea but now end in calcrete pans. Others flow only during the summer rainy season, but at some former stage carried huge volumes of water and carved out dramatic canyons like the Fish and the Kuiseb.

East of the coastal plains, the terrain becomes more rugged and climbs steeply through rugged canyons to the savanna grasslands of the Central Plateau. This plateau is bisected by fossil river courses and is covered largely in thorn scrub. Still further east, the land slopes gently away to the sandy fossil valleys and dunes that characterise the western Kalahari.

Namibia's north-eastern strip, along the Angolan border from the Owambo country through Kavango and Caprivi, is characterised by well watered bushveld. It's bounded by the great rivers – the Kunene, Okavango, Kwando-Mashi-Linyanti-Chobe and Zambezi – which flow year-round and provide water for most of Namibia's human population.

Politically, Namibia is now divided into 13 regions, which replace the old ethnically based regions demarcated by the colonial powers. However, it will be many years before Namibians become familiar with these new regions or refer to them in common usage. For clarification, refer to the maps in this section.

## CLIMATE

Although it's predominantly a desert country, Namibia enjoys regional climatic variations corresponding to its geographical subdivisions. The most arid climate is found in the central Namib, which typically enjoys clear and windy weather. The region is cooled in the summer by cold onshore winds derived from the South Atlantic anticyclone pressure system.

The upwelling Benguela Current and onshore winds produce a steep temperature gradient between the sea and land. When the cold, moist sea breeze meets the dry desert heat, the result is instantaneous condensation and fog. In the desert, summer

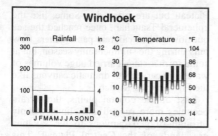

daytime temperatures climb to over 40°C, but they can fall to below freezing at night. Fog is common on the coast, generally developing during the night, and often lasts well into the morning up to 20km inland.

In the winter, the Namib region is warmed by east winds, which reach their peak between June and August. As they descend from the Central Plateau, they heat up and dry out. Especially around Swakopmund and Walvis Bay, they often create miserable conditions as they whip up clouds of swirling sand that block out the sun and penetrate everything with coarse grit.

On the Central Plateau the low humidity and gentle breeze of the winter months make for a pleasant and comfortable climate. During the summer both temperatures and humidity climb to uncomfortable levels. The area averages between 200 and 400mm of precipitation annually, all of which falls during this period. East of the Central Plateau, the rainfall decreases, and along the Botswana and South African borders one finds the near-desert conditions of the Kalahari.

Going north, however, rainfall steadily increases, reaching its maximum of over 600mm per year along the Okavango River, which enjoys a subtropical climate. The northern and interior regions experience two rainy seasons. The 'little rains' fall between October and December, while the main stormy period normally lasts from January to April.

## ECOLOGY & ENVIRONMENT

With a small human population spread over a large land area, Namibia is in better environmental shape than most African countries, but challenges remain. The Ministry of Environment and Tourism (MET) is largely a holdover from pre-independence days and, as a result, its policies strongly reflect those of its South African counterpart. Although changes are currently afoot, the country still lacks coherent environmental guidelines.

As yet, local people have seen few benefits from wildlife-oriented tourism and encroachment on protected areas continues to affect local ecosystems. Many ranchers in the southern part of the country view wildlife as a nuisance while people in the more densely populated north see wildlife reserves as potential settlement areas and wildlife itself as a food resource and a threat to crops and human life.

For further information on ecological issues in Namibia, see Useful Organisations in the Regional Facts for the Visitor chapter.

## Wildlife Concerns

Overfishing and the 1993-94 outbreak of red tide along the Skeleton Coast have decimated sea lion populations, both through starvation and commercially inspired culling (see the boxed text under Cape Cross Seal Reserve in the North-Western Namibia chapter). Also poaching of desert rhino, elephant and other species in Damaraland, which is not an officially protected area, has caused declines in the populations of these species.

Although white rhino were wiped out in Namibia prior to 1900, they've now been reintroduced into Waterberg and Etosha and are doing relatively well. Namibia was a pioneer in using dehorning to protect its rhino, but sadly dehorned female rhino in Namibia were unable to protect their young from attack by hyaena. During the drought of 1993, when other game was scarce, all calves of dehorned females were lost. The rate of rhino loss to poachers is approximately 5% annually, and growing. By the turn of the century, the desert rhino (a subspecies of the black rhino) of Damaraland may well be wiped out. The non-governmental Save the Rhino Trust (☎ (061) 222281; fax 223077), PO Box 22691, Windhoek, Namibia, has been formed to promote conservation education.

The country is also facing a dramatic decrease in its lion population. From a high of 700 animals in 1980, the number has now decreased to between 320 and 340. Of these, nearly 85% are confined to the Etosha and Khaudom reserves. One problem is that the reserve fences are penetrable to lions, and once they've escaped, it's only a matter of time before they're shot by irate ranchers to protect cattle. The good news is that Etosha's lions are free of two of the most serious causes of disease found in other parks: Feline Immunodeficiency Virus (a feline form of HIV) and Canine Distemper Virus (which has killed 30% of the lions in Tanzania's Serengeti National Park).

The stability of other species, such as the rare welwitschia plant and the Damara tern, has been compromised by human activities (including tourism and recreation) in formerly remote areas. As yet, efforts to change local attitudes have met with limited success.

### Trophy Hunting

Many foreign hunters are willing to pay handsomely for big game trophies (a leopard, for example, will fetch US$2000, while elephant provide many times that amount) and farmers and ranchers frequently complain about the ravages of wildlife on their stock. As a result, the Namibia Professional Hunting Association (NAPHA) and the MET have set up regulatory statutes on game hunting, which comprises 5% of the country's revenue from wildlife. The idea is to provide farmers with financial incentives to protect free-ranging wildlife. Management strategies include encouraging hunting of older animals, evaluating the condition of trophies and setting bag limits in accordance with population fluctuations. Because both the government and private sectors have a

stake in the success of this endeavour, it's very likely to succeed, at least as far as their economic objectives are concerned.

### Water & Power Issues

Other major environmental issues in Namibia involve projects designed to provide water and power resources for the country's growing industrial and human needs. Two major ones – which will have serious environmental impacts – are the proposed dam and hydroelectric plant on the Kunene River in the Kaokoveld (see the boxed text in the North-Western Namibia chapter) and the pipeline from the Okavango River to provide water for Windhoek (see Ecology & Environment in the Facts about Botswana chapter).

### FLORA & FAUNA

Etosha, Namibia's greatest game park, contains a variety of antelope species, as well as other African ungulates (hoofed animals), carnivores and pachyderms. Other major game parks – Khaudom, Mahango, Mudumu, Mamili and Hardap Dam – may pale by comparison, but they do present a surprising range of species and a realistic picture of Namibia's natural world before humanity crowded the wildlife into reserves.

Unprotected Damaraland, in Namibia's north-west, is home to numerous antelope and other ungulates, and also harbours desert rhino, elephant and other specially adapted sub-species. Hikers in the Naukluft mountains may catch sight of the elusive Hartmann's mountain zebra, and along the desert coasts you can see jackass penguins, flamingoes, Cape fur seals and perhaps even the legendary desert hyaena, or *Strandwolf*.

Because Namibia lies mostly within an arid zone, much of the flora is typical African dryland vegetation: scrub brush and succulents, such as euphorbia. Some floral oddities found nowhere else include the kokerboom (quiver tree), a species of aloe that grows only in southern Namibia, and the bizarre welwitschia, a slow-growing ground-hugging conifer that lives for over 1000 years. Along the coastal plain around Swakopmund lie the world's most extensive and diverse fields of lichen; when the weather is dry, they appear to be merely plant skeletons, but with the addition of water, they burst into colourful bloom.

For more on regional wildlife and vegetation zones, see under Flora & Fauna in the Facts about the Region chapter.

### National Parks & Game Reserves

Despite its harsh climate, Namibia has some of the world's most magical landscapes and boasts some of Africa's finest and most diverse national parks. The parks range from the open bush of the centre and north, where wildlife is relatively plentiful, to the barren and inhospitable coastal strip with its huge sand dunes. Even here many species have adapted to the rigours of the desert including elephant, giraffe, zebra and other large herbivores. Sadly, the lion population, which used to inhabit even coastal areas, has been wiped out by herders and poachers. In the extreme south is one of the natural wonders of the world – Fish River Canyon – which ranks as one of the most spectacular sights in Africa.

Access to most wildlife-oriented parks is limited to closed vehicles only – no bicycles or motorbikes are allowed – so visitors need a vehicle or a good lift. For most parks, 2WD is sufficient, but you need 4WD in some remote areas, such as the back roads in Namib-Naukluft Park.

Hitchhikers aren't allowed in parks containing big game unless they've found a lift beforehand. Even in parks without dangerous animals, hitching is often not viable due to sparse traffic. The only alternative if you can't muster a group and hire a vehicle is to join a tour or wait around a petrol station near the park entrance and beg for a lift.

For a rundown of Namibia's national parks and game reserves, see the boxed text.

### Visiting the Parks

National park and rest camp accommodation may be booked up to 18 months in advance through the Ministry of Environment and Tourism (MET) offices in Windhoek, Swakopmund, Lüderitz and elsewhere. However, reservations for Etosha, the Skeleton Coast Park and the Sesriem and Naukluft areas of Namib-Naukluft Park are officially handled only in Windhoek. Namib-Naukluft permits are available after hours from the Hans Kriess Garage and petrol station in Swakopmund and from the CWB petrol station in Walvis Bay. Transit permits to drive between Ugabmund and Springbokwater in the Skeleton Coast Park are available at the park gates.

In Windhoek, park permits and accommodation reservations are handled by the MET Reservations Office (☎ (061) 236975; fax 224900; <reservations@iwwn .com.na>; Web site iwwn.com.na/namtour /namtour.html), Private Bag 13267, Windhoek. The office is in the Oode Voorpost building on the corner of John Meinert Strasse and Moltke Strasse. Park entry permits (US$3 per car and US$3 per person) are payable at the park gates.

To pre-book by post, fax or email, specify the type of accommodation required, the number of adults, the ages of the children (if any) and the dates you intend to stay (along with alternative dates, if possible). The confirmation and invoice will be sent by post; fees must be paid before the due date indicated on the form or the reservation will be cancelled.

Firewood – normally split camelthorn acacia – is available for around US$2 per bundle at national park rest camps, most private camping grounds and general stores. Firewood gathering and open fires are prohibited in national parks, but even outside the parks wilderness hikers are advised to carry a fuel stove and avoid lighting open fires, which can scar the landscape and may get out of control in the typically dry conditions. If you must gather your own firewood, note that it's illegal to use anything but mopane or acacia; burning or even carrying any other sort of wood will incur a large fine, even outside national parks.

The varied faces of Namibia: San woman, Damaraland; Herero mother and child, Damaraland; Himba woman, Kaokoveld; Nama woman (Hottentot), Damaraland.

Windhoek's striking architectural styles contrast with those you will see elsewhere in Namibia.

The sandstone Waterberg Plateau looms 150m above the surrounding plain (Nam).

## NAMIBIA'S NATIONAL PARKS & GAME RESERVES

| Region | Features |
|---|---|
| **Windhoek** | |
| Daan Viljoen | This small park lies in Windhoek's backyard, and is popular with weekend visitors, who use it for picnics and camping trips. In addition to a game drive, there are several hikes that take in its wilder areas. |
| **North Central Namibia** | |
| Etosha | Namibia's best known park is Etosha, a huge area of semi-arid savanna grassland and thorn scrub surrounding a calcrete pan. Etosha Pan contains water for only a few days each year, but during this time it attracts immense herds of wildlife and flocks of flamingoes and other birds. During the May to September dry season, the water holes support huge herds of gemsbok, spring-bok, wildebeest and zebra, as well as predators and elephant. |
| Waterberg Plateau | This plateau area is used for the reintroduction of endangered wildlife. Attractions include fabulous views, a comfortable rest camp and a series of game drives and walking tracks. |
| **North-Eastern Namibia** | |
| Khaudom | This surprising park in the western Kalahari is difficult to reach, but its wildlife-viewing opportunities approach those of Etosha. The bushveld landscape is crossed by a network of *omiramba* (fossil valleys). |
| Mahango | This small park has suffered from poachers, but in the dry season it's an excellent place to see elephant. The nearby Popa Falls rest camp provides pleasant accommodation. |
| Mamili | Remote Mamili is a new national park in the vast Linyanti Marshes of the Caprivi Strip. This area is often referred to as a mini-Okavango Delta, and the wetland landscape and the wildlife-viewing opportunities certainly justify the comparison. |
| Mudumu | Mudumu takes in the alluring wetlands of the Linyanti river system and surrounding wildlife areas. It has been ravaged by poaching and has suffered damage by cattle, but is one of Namibia's loveliest landscapes and best bird-watching venues. |
| West Caprivi | Poaching and an encroaching human population have taken their toll, and except for the West Caprivi Triangle, this reserve is largely devoid of wildlife. |
| **North-Western Namibia** | |
| Skeleton Coast | The wild, foggy coastline has long been a graveyard for ships and also their crews, who were unable to survive the harsh desert |

NAMIBIA

|  | conditions. Only the stretch between the Ugab River and Terrace Bay is open to the general public. |
|---|---|
| National West Coast | The grey deserts north of Swakopmund that form this recreation area are a paradise for sea anglers. For tourists, the biggest attraction is the Cape Cross Seal Reserve, with its large colony of Cape fur seals. |

**The Central Namib** ─────────────────────────────────────────────

| Namib-Naukluft | Namibia's largest national park takes in much of the Namib Desert, as well as the surrounding gravel plains and the Naukluft Massif, a mountainous area with dramatic scenery and superb hiking trails that is also a refuge for Hartmann's mountain zebra. At Sossusvlei you can visit the archetypal Namib dunefield, where dunes rise 300m above the plains. Sandwich Harbour, south of Walvis Bay, is a well known bird sanctuary. |
|---|---|

**Southern Namibia** ─────────────────────────────────────────────

| Fish River Canyon | Claims that Fish River Canyon is second only to the USA's Grand Canyon in size are exaggerated, but it's still an impressive sight. It's also a great hiking venue, and at its southern end is the popular and relaxing hot springs resort of Ai-Ais. |
|---|---|

### Hiking

For multi-day walks at Waterberg Plateau, the Naukluft Mountains, the Ugab River, Daan Viljoen or Fish River Canyon, numbers are limited so book through MET as far in advance as possible. You need a group of at least three people and, in some cases, a doctor's certificate of fitness. As cumbersome as the booking system may seem, it's popularly defended locally and does protect the environment from unlimited tourism.

### GOVERNMENT & POLITICS

Namibia is an independent republic with three separate branches of government. The president, who has strong executive powers, is elected by popular ballot for a maximum of two five-year terms. The two-part national parliament makes up the legislative branch. One part, the National Assembly or lower house, consists of 72 members who are elected by popular vote every five years. The upper house, the 26-member National Council, is purely an advisory body and is comprised of two popularly elected representatives from each of Namibia's 13 regions, who serve six-year terms.

Any constitutional amendment requires a two-thirds majority vote of the National Assembly. In the case of an irreconcilable dispute between the executive and legislative branches, the president has the power to dismiss the entire assembly. However, in such an event, the president must also stand for re-election.

The judiciary, which is independent of the executive and legislative branches, is presided over by a chief justice.

All national government functions are centred in the national capital, Windhoek. The country is divided into 13 regions, each with its own regional government, which in turn are subdivided into municipalities.

### Politics

Since independence on 21 March 1990, Namibia has been governed by the socialist SWAPO (South West Africa People's

Organisation) party. Headed by Executive President Sam Nujoma and Prime Minister Hage Geingob, it took 57% of the vote in the first national election. In the election of December 1994, SWAPO won 76.3% of the vote and 53 seats in the National Assembly. The largest opposition group, Mishake Muyongo's conservative DTA (Democratic Turnhalle Alliance) – a coalition of 11 parties with little in common but an opposition to SWAPO's Owambo-oriented stance – took 23.7% of the vote and 15 parliamentary seats (a fall of 7% from the 1990 election). The centrist UDF (United Democratic Front) captured two parliamentary seats and the Christian conservative MAG (Monitor Action Group) and the conservative DCN (Democratic Coalition of Namibia) each won a single seat. Extremist minority parties, such as the Herstigte Nasionale Party, which advocates apartheid, do still exist but are politically powerless. However, the ACTUR (Action Front for the Retention of the Turnhalle Principles), a white-dominated party to the right of the DTA, still retains some political influence.

Despite its former Marxist affiliations, SWAPO isn't inclined towards political extremism. It takes a pragmatic view regarding the domestic economy and international relations, and has adhered to a policy of national reconciliation. However, tensions endure between the various races and tribes, and although the per capita GDP of US$3700 is high by African standards, the statistic masks the inequalities between population groups. In the end, 5% of the population controls 72% of the economy.

The government openly admits that its main problem is a lack of discipline over fiscal spending. In the past, there were attempts to encourage investment and lower personal taxes, but the 1998-99 budget has made expenditure a priority over investment. In spite of a paltry 1.4% economic growth in 1997, the overall tax burden on Namibian workers will increase from 28.9% to 30.5% of GDP. Funding for roads and welfare is being cut while spending on government personnel – a result of 'affirmative action' (growth in the public sector) and cosy retirement packages for government officials – will increase dramatically.

Other prominent issues include freedom of speech and the freedom of the press in the face of governmental corruption. The foundation of an independent agency to expose and investigate governmental corruption has been mooted. Meanwhile, Sam Nujoma is attempting to hold on to power by amending the constitution to allow him a third presidential term, and the press has been gagged by new laws prohibiting dialogue on parliamentary issues before they're discussed in parliament.

## ECONOMY

The Namibian economy is dominated by mining (diamonds and uranium), cattle and sheep-herding, tourism and fishing, as well as subsistence-level agriculture. By African standards, Namibia is already a prosperous country. It does suffer some disadvantages – water shortages, a lack of local fuel sources, vast distances and a widely scattered population – but its GDP is twice the African average and its population remains small and diverse. Currently, over 80% of the country's food and manufactured goods must be imported from South Africa, creating an unhealthy degree of economic dependence. The development of the economy rests on its ability to attract foreign investment, and develop (via education and training) its own human resources to exploit the country's vast resource potential.

### Mining

Namibia's mining income is the fourth largest in Africa and the 17th largest in the world, mainly thanks to both the world's richest diamond fields and its largest uranium mine. The diamonds are extracted mostly by strip-mining the alluvial sand and gravel of the famed Sperrgebiet (forbidden area) between Lüderitz and the Orange River. The major player is Consolidated Diamond Mines (CDM), one of Namibia's largest employers, which scours through 20

NAMIBIA

million tonnes of dirt a year, for a yield of 200kg (one million carats) of diamonds. The Rössing uranium mine, near Swakopmund, produces more than 60 million tonnes of ore annually.

Of Namibia's other mineral deposits, which include lithium, germanium, silver, vanadium, tin, copper, lead, zinc and tantalum, 70% are extracted by the Tsumeb Corporation Ltd, which operates in the phenomenally rich environs of Tsumeb, Grootfontein and Otavi in north central Namibia. Other major mining areas include Uis, with dwindling deposits of tin; Rosh Pinah, near the Orange River, which produces zinc, lead and silver; and Karibib, with quartz, lithium and beryllium.

A current source of controversy is the offshore Kudu gas field in south-western Namibia. The feasibility of development and a pipeline to the Cape region is now being assessed.

### Herding & Agriculture
Around 16% of Namibia's active labour force is involved in commercial herding, but over 70% of the people depend on agriculture to some extent. Most farmers are engaged in subsistence agriculture in the heavily populated communal areas of the north, particularly the Owambo country, Kavango and Caprivi. However, over 80% of the agricultural yield is derived from commercial herding in the central and southern parts of the country.

The industry is dominated by farmers of German or Afrikaner heritage who are involved in raising stock, especially beef cattle and sheep. This occupation is dogged by water shortages, but farms are generally well managed. The current trend is towards game-ranching and many farmers now raise gemsbok, zebra and springbok for meat and hides – as well as tourism and hunting – and there is a growing ostrich-farming industry.

In the dry southern regions, the emphasis is on karakul sheep, which resemble scraggy goats but are well suited to the conditions and produce high-quality meat

and wool. Karakul wool once formed the basis of an expanding weaving industry and the export market for luxury leather and skin goods was once dominated by karakul. However, in recent years the bottom has dropped out of the market and it remains to be seen whether a recovery is on the cards.

There is also a small amount of commercial crop farming, mainly around Otavi, Grootfontein and Tsumeb, with maize as the principal crop. Thanks to irrigation from Hardap Dam, Mariental has a growing farming base, and around Omaruru citrus is the particular speciality.

### Fishing
The Namibian coastal waters are considered some of the world's richest, mainly thanks to the cold offshore Benguela Current, which flows northwards from the Antarctic. It's exceptionally rich in plankton, which accounts for the abundance of anchovy, pilchard, mackerel and other whitefish. But the limited offshore fishing rights have caused problems, and there is resentment that such countries as Spain and Russia have legal access to offshore fish stocks. Namibia has now declared a 200-nautical-mile exclusive economic zone to make Namibian fisheries competitive.

Each year, the waters off Lüderitz yield varying numbers of crayfish (rock lobsters), most for export to Japan in the form of frozen lobster meat. The fleet, which is comprised of 20 ships, operates from the Orange River mouth north to Hottentot Bay, 75km north of Lüderitz. Strict seasons and size limits protect from overfishing. In all, the industry employs 1000 people.

The port of Lüderitz also produces and processes tinned fish, fishmeal and fish oil. However, the current decline in the fishing industry has meant that of the 11 fish-processing plants that were active in Walvis Bay and Lüderitz 20 years ago, fewer than half survive. Oysters are cultivated and marketed around Swakopmund and Walvis Bay, and a new oyster farm has opened near Lüderitz.

## Manufacturing

Currently, most manufactured goods must be imported from South Africa. Manufacturing comprises less than 5% of Namibia's gross national product, and most of this is made up of meat processing and goods and materials for the mining industry.

It is vital that Namibia develops this sector, but progress is thwarted by the high cost of raw materials, the lack of skills and training and a measure of political uncertainty. Currently, Namibia is desperately courting overseas investment for manufacturing projects, and to a large extent their success will determine the country's economic future.

## Tourism

Since independence in 1990, Namibia has gone from a war-torn backwater known only to South African hunters, anglers and holiday-makers to a popular – not to mention chic and trendy – destination for overseas visitors. Immediately following independence, the number of South African tourists dropped off sharply, then began to climb again. The country is also a big draw for German tourists, which isn't surprising since travel articles often describe the country as being 'more German than Germany'. That isn't exactly true, but in Windhoek, Swakopmund and Lüderitz, you'd be forgiven for reaching such a conclusion.

As with Botswana, the official aim is to develop a high-cost, low-volume tourist base made up primarily of wealthy Europeans, Australasians and North Americans who have grown weary of the crime and the crowded national parks of East Africa. Unlike Botswana, however, everyone pays the same national park entry fees, which, although reasonable for the majority of tourists and wealthier locals, remain out of reach for most Namibians.

## Retail

The expanding retail sector is flourishing, with a growing number of shopping venues in Windhoek and Swakopmund.

Most people, however, depend upon small market and street-trading stalls. In the Owambo areas and other parts of the north, supply and distribution of goods is handled by small *cuca* bush shops spaced intermittently along the main routes.

## POPULATION & PEOPLE

Namibia has an estimated population of 1,727,183 and one of the lowest population densities in Africa at 1.5 people per sq km. However, the annual growth rate of over 3% is one of the world's highest. Three quarters of Namibians live in rural areas but the uncontrolled drift to urban areas, particularly Windhoek, in search of work or higher wages has resulted in increased homelessness, unemployment and crime in the capital and in other cities and towns.

Namibia's population includes at least 11 major ethnic groups, ranging from pastoralists and hunter-gatherers to rural farmers and town-dwellers. Although this ethnic diversity bears a heavy colonial German and Afrikaner influence, since independence there have been efforts to emphasise the history and traditions of the individual groups.

Although it's difficult to make generalisations about people, the following descriptions briefly outline the history and distinctive characteristics of each major culture.

**Owambo** The 650,000-strong Owambo make up the largest population group and, not surprisingly, most of the ruling SWAPO party. The Owambo live mainly in the north and are subdivided into 12 distinct tribal groups. Four of these occupy the Kunene region of southern Angola, while the other eight comprise the Owambo groups in Namibia. The most numerous group is the Kwanyama, which makes up 35% of Namibia's Owambo population. The next largest groups are the Ndonga, with 30%, and the Kwambi, with 12%, while the remaining five groups each make up from 1 to 8% of the total.

Historically, each of these tribes was

headed by an all-powerful hereditary king who had below him a council of headmen. However, thanks to changes brought about by Christianity and both German and South African colonial influences, most of these tribes now operate under a council of chiefs or headmen. Other changes have included a gradual shift from a predominantly matrilineal to a patrilineal system of inheritance.

The allocation of land is handled by the appropriate chief or headman of each tribal group. Land may not be owned, sold or inherited and when a tenant dies, the authorities will decide whether it is passed on in the same family or is allotted to someone else.

In rural Owambo areas, each family has its own immaculate kraal or *eumbo*, which is very much like a small village enclosed within a stockade-like fence. Housing in these villages is in either round or square thatched huts, and there's always an area reserved for large round storage containers made of woven bark and chinked with mud. These hold mainly *mahango* or millet, which is used to make a delicious beer. In the centre of each eumbo is the family's *omulilo gwoshilongo* (sacred fire), a log of mopane that is kept burning around the clock. The eumbo is surrounded by the family lands, which are used for agriculture, including grazing cattle.

Recently, large numbers of Owambo have migrated southwards to Windhoek or to the larger towns in the north to work as labourers, craftspeople and professionals.

**Kavango** The 120,000 Kavango are divided into five distinct sub-groups – the Mbukushu, the Sambiyu, the Kwangari, the Mbunza and the Geiriku. Since the 1970s, their numbers have been swelling rapidly, thanks mainly to immigrants and refugees from warring Angola. As with other groups in northern Namibia, large numbers of Kavango, particularly young men, are migrating southwards in search of employment on farms, in mines and around urban areas.

Most rural Kavango live on the level, wooded flood plains of the north-east, south of the Okavango River, where they make a living from fishing, herding livestock and subsistence farming of millet, maize and sorghum. They're also known as highly skilled woodcarvers and create some of the finest carvings available, which are sold along the Kavango roadsides and in tourist shops around the country. Although most carvers regard their work as merely a commercial endeavour, there are several competent artists.

Kavango society is organised according to matrilineal succession, which governs inheritance, marriage, family matters and traditional religious rites. However, the tribe is governed by hereditary male chiefs, whose relatives and appointees, along with representatives from each clan, constitute the lower echelons of tribal government.

**Herero** Namibia's 100,000 Herero, who are mainly herders, occupy several regions of the country and are divided into several subgroups. The largest band includes the Tjimba and Ndamuranda groups in Kaokoland, the Maherero around Okahandja, and the Zeraua, who are centred on Omaruru. The Himba of Kaokoland are also a Herero subgroup (see the separate discussion later in this section) and the Mbandero occupy the colonially demarcated territory formerly known as Hereroland, around Gobabis in eastern Namibia.

From the early part of this century, the Herero have established various organisations, including chiefs' councils, to assert their nationalism, handle defence and oversee tribal affairs. One of these chiefs was Hosea Katjikururume Kutako, who became a national hero for his many direct petitions to the UN for help in securing Namibia's independence.

The Herero were originally part of the early Bantu migrations southwards from central Africa and their traditions assert that their origins were in the Great Rift Valley of East Africa. They arrived in present-day Namibia in the mid-16th century, and after a 200-year sojourn in Kaokoland they moved southwards to occupy the Swakop Valley and the Central Plateau. Until the colonial period, they remained as semi-nomadic pastoralists in this relatively rich grassland, herding and grazing cattle and sheep.

However, bloody clashes with the north-wards migrating Nama and German colonial troops and settlers led to violent uprisings. As a result, approximately 75% of the country's Herero population was wiped out and the remainder were dispersed around the country.

Large numbers of Herero also fled into neighbouring Botswana, where they settled down to a life of subsistence agriculture, growing grains and pulses and raising sheep, cattle and fowl. Now that Namibia is independent, many Herero would like to return to their roots, but the Botswana government has made it clear that anyone who returns to Namibia must leave behind both their herds and their money. In some cases, families have been split; some family members have gone to Namibia while others have remained behind to look after the family wealth.

For most rural Herero in Namibia today, cattle remain the most prized possessions. Tribal hierarchy divides responsibilities for inheritance between *eendag* (matrilineal) and *oruzo* (patrilineal) lines of descent, to which each person belongs. Mothers pass down material possessions, including cattle, while fathers handle religious and political instruction, rites and authority, and posses-sions that are considered sacred.

The characteristic Herero women's dress is derived from Victorian-era German mis-sionaries who took exception to what they considered a lack of modesty among local women. It consists of an immaculate crino-line of enormous proportions worn over a series of petticoats, with a horn-shaped hat or headdress.

**Himba** The distinctive Himba (or Ova-himba – 'those who ask for things') of the Kaokoveld are actually descended from a group of Herero herders who were dis-placed by Nama warriors in the 19th century. They fled to the remote north-west and continued their semi-nomadic lifestyle, raising sheep, goats and some cattle.

The Himba still eschew the modern world, and the missionary 'modesty police' never managed to persuade Himba women not to go topless. As a result, they maintain their lovely and distinctive traditional dress of multi-layered goat-leather miniskirts and ochre-and-mud-encrusted iron, leather and shell jewellery. Their skin is also smeared with a mixture of butter, ash and ochre, os-tensibly to keep it young-looking (it must work – even elderly Himba women have beautifully smooth skin), and they plaster their plaited hair with the same mixture. The effect is truly stunning.

**Damara** The Damara, who number around 100,000, share a language group, but pre-sumably no ethnic kinship, with the Nama, with whom they've historically had major conflicts.

The Damara have presented researchers with one of Africa's greatest anthropologi-cal mysteries: how did a group of hunter-gatherers of Bantu origin wind up in southern Africa speaking a Khoisan dialect? Their resemblance to some Bantu of West Africa has led some anthropologists to believe they were among the first people to migrate into Namibia from the north. However it happened, it's tempting to con-clude that the Damara have occupied the region far longer than their other Bantu neighbours, and perhaps that early trade with the Nama and San caused them to adopt Khoisan as a lingua franca. Whether such a thing ever happened, however, is still a matter of speculation, and no conclusive evidence is available.

What is known is that prior to the 1870s, the Damara occupied much of central Namibia from around the site of Rehoboth westwards to the Swakop and Kuiseb rivers and north to present-day Outjo and Khorixas. When the Herero and Nama began expanding their domains into tradi-tional Damara lands, large numbers of

Damara were displaced, killed or captured and enslaved. Between the 1870s and the early 20th century, the Rhenish Missionary Society persuaded the Herero chiefs and the colonial authorities to cede bits of territory to create a Damara homeland.

When Europeans first arrived in the region, the Damara were described as semi-nomadic gardeners, pastoralists and hunter-gatherers, who also maintained small-scale mining, smelting and trading operations. However, with colonial encouragement, they settled down to relatively sedentary subsistence herding and agriculture. In the 1960s, the South African administration purchased for the Damara over 4.5 million hectares of marginal European-owned ranchland in the desolate expanses of present-day Damaraland. Unfortunately, the soil in this region is generally poor, most of the land is communally owned and it lacks the good grazing that prevails in central and southern Namibia. Most Damara work in urban areas and on European farms, and only about a third of them actually occupy Damaraland.

**Europeans** Namibia's 85,000 Europeans are mostly of German (20,000) and Afrikaner (65,000) heritage and are concentrated in urban, central and southern Namibia.

The first Europeans, in the form of Portuguese sailors, arrived in the 15th century, but no-one settled until 1760. After 1780 came the traders, hunters and missionaries. Today, the Europeans are involved mainly in ranching, commerce, manufacturing and administration. People of mixed European and African descent, sometimes known as coloureds, number 52,000 and live mainly in Windhoek and other urban areas.

**Caprivians** In the extreme north-east, along the fertile Zambezi and Kwando riverbanks, live the 80,000 Caprivians, comprising five separate tribal groups: the Lozi, Mafwe, Subia, Yei and Mbukushu. Most Caprivians derive their livelihood

from fishing, subsistence farming and herding cattle.

Until the late 19th century, the Caprivi was under the control of the Lozi kings. Today, the lingua franca of the various Caprivian tribes is known as Rotse, which is a derivative of the Lozi language still spoken in parts of Zambia and Angola.

**San** For background information about the San, see Population & People in the Facts about Botswana chapter and the section on Bushmanland in the North-Eastern Namibia chapter.

The 37,000 San in Namibia were the region's earliest inhabitants, and still live in the north-eastern areas. They are divided into three groups: the Naro of the Gobabis area; the !Xukwe of western Bushmanland, Kavango and Caprivi; and the Ju/hoansi (a subgroup of the Qgu or !Kung) in eastern Bushmanland, particularly around the town of Tsumkwe. However, it has been over a decade since any Namibian San followed an entirely traditional lifestyle, and many now work as servants and farm hands in Kavango and Caprivi.

**Nama** Another Khoisan group is the Nama, who are variously known as the Bergdama, Oorlam, Khoi-Khoi or Hottentots (although this last designation is now out of favour). There are around 60,000 Nama in Namibia. As with the San, most Nama have a light skin colour, a slight frame and small bones, but on average they are a bit taller. They normally have high cheekbones, flattish noses and beautiful almond-shaped eyes, narrowed by an Oriental-like fold of skin on the upper eyelid.

The Nama's origins were in the southern Cape, where they were known as Hottentots. However, during the early days of European settlement in the Cape, they were either exterminated or pushed northwards by land-hungry colonial farmers. They eventually came to rest in Namaqualand, around the Orange River, where they lived as semi-nomadic pastoralists until the mid-19th century, when their leader, Jan Jonker

Afrikaner, led them to the area of present-day Windhoek.

On Namibia's Central Plateau, they came into conflict with the Herero, who already occupied that area, and the two groups fought a series of bloody wars. Eventually, the German government confined them to several separate reserves.

Today, the Nama occupy the region colonially designated as Namaland, which stretches roughly from Mariental southwards to Keetmanshoop. Many Nama have adopted western dress and Christianity, and now work in towns or on commercial farms. They're especially known for their extraordinary musical and literary abilities; their traditional music, folk tales, proverbs and praise poetry have been handed down through the generations to form a basis for their culture today.

**Topnaar** The Topnaar (or Aonin), who are technically a branch of the Nama, mainly occupy the western central Namib, in and around Walvis Bay. However, unlike the Nama, who historically had a tradition of communal land ownership, the Topnaar passed their lands down through family lines.

Today, the Topnaar are perhaps the most marginalised group in Namibia. Historically, they were utterly dependent upon the *!nara* melon, a thorny desert plant that derives its water by sending a tap root deep into the earth. This plant was the Topnaar's only source of income and the primary element in their diet, which was supplemented by hunting. Now, however, their hunting grounds are tied up in Namib-Naukluft Park – and therefore off limits to hunting – and the melon is under threat due to depleted water tables, which are being tapped to supply Walvis Bay's industrial needs.

As a result, many Topnaar have migrated into Walvis Bay and settled in the township of Narraville, from where they commute to fish-canning factories. Others live around the perimeter in cardboard boxes and make their living scrounging other groups' cast-offs. In the Topnaar community south-east of Walvis Bay, a primary school and hostel have been provided, but few students ever go on to secondary school, which would require a move into Narraville.

Those that remain in the desert eke out a living growing !nara melons and raising stock, mainly goats.

**Basters** The 35,000 Basters are descended mainly from intermixing between the Nama (Hottentots) and Dutch farmers in the Cape Colony. From early on, they strongly professed Calvinist Christianity. In the late 1860s, when they came under pressure from the Boer settlers in the Cape, they fled north of the Orange River and established the settlement of Rehoboth. Although their name is derived from 'bastards', this fiercely independent group of people still uses it proudly because it stresses their mixed heritage. Most Basters still live around Rehoboth and either follow an urban lifestyle or raise cattle, sheep and goats.

**Tswana** Namibia's 8000 Tswana make up the country's smallest ethnic group. They're related to the Tswana of South Africa and Botswana and live mainly in the eastern areas of the country, around Aminuis and Epukiro.

## EDUCATION

During the German colonial era and the South African mandate, education for the masses took a low priority on the government agenda. As a result, there was a vast disparity between the educational performance of whites, who normally paid to attend private schools, and other ethnic groups. Less than 75% of Namibian children completed five years of schooling, only 8% attended secondary school and under 1% went on to higher education or professional training. As a result, at the time of independence there was a severe shortage of qualified teachers, and furthermore they received very poor salaries. Despite government-subsidised teacher training colleges in both the Owambo areas and

Windhoek, very few black Namibians had sufficient educational background to enter teacher training.

Nowadays, education is technically compulsory for all children. SWAPO policy has designated English as the official language of instruction. (However, in some primary schools, classes may also be conducted in Afrikaans or Bantu languages, and some private schools still stick with German.) In the first four years of independence, 832 classrooms were constructed, expatriate teachers were brought in, high-quality instructional materials were purchased and enrolment increased by 21%. Between 1991 and 1993, secondary-school pass rates jumped from 38 to 51%. Nearly 75% of the population has received, or is receiving, at least a primary school education.

Another primary emphasis is on the need to 'catch up' and achieve full literacy. To that end, the government has established over 700 literacy centres around the country to provide basic reading and writing instruction for children and adults alike.

Namibia has three institutes of higher education: the University of Namibia, which began instruction in March 1993 and offers degree-level courses in arts, economics, education and medicine; the Technikon, a polytechnic school, which emphasises career-oriented courses in business, agriculture, ecology, nursing and secretarial studies; and the College for Out-of-School Training, which provides theoretical and practical courses in crafts and nursing.

Many Namibians leave the country to attend university in South Africa (at Stellenbosch, Witwatersrand or Cape Town) or study in Europe on UN or Commonwealth scholarships.

## ARTS

Namibia is still developing a literary tradition but its musical, visual and architectural arts are now established. It also enjoys a wealth of amateur material arts: carvings, basketry, tapestry, and simple but resourcefully designed toys, clothing and household implements.

## Music

Namibia's earliest musicians were the San, whose music probably emulated the sounds made by their animal neighbours and was sung to accompany dances and storytelling. The early Nama, who had a more developed musical technique, used drums, flutes and basic stringed instruments, also to accompany dances. Some of these were adopted and adapted by the later-arriving Bantu, who added marimbas, gourd rattles and animal horn trumpets to the range. Nowadays, drums, marimbas and rattles are still popular, and it isn't unusual to see dancers wearing belts of soft-drink cans filled with pebbles to provide rhythmic accompaniment to their dance steps.

A prominent European contribution to Namibian music is the choir. Early in the colonial period, missionaries established religious choral groups among the local people, and both school and church choirs still perform regularly. Namibia's most renowned ensemble is the Cantare Audire Choir, which was started by Windhoek music teacher, Ernst von Biljon. It is composed of Namibians of all races and performs both African and European religious, classical and traditional compositions for audiences around the world. Naturally, the German colonists also introduced their traditional 'oom-pah-pah' bands, which feature mainly at Karnival and other German festivals.

## Literature

Literature is fairly new to Namibia, and apart from several German colonial novels – most importantly Gustav Frenssen's *Peter Moor's Journey to Southwest Africa* (original 1905, English translation 1908) – and some Afrikaans writing, few noteworthy works emerged during the South African occupation. The best-known work from that period is Henno Martin's *The Sheltering Desert* (1956, English edition 1957), which records two years spent by the geologist author and his friend Hermann Korn in avoiding internment as prisoners of war during WWII.

Only with the independence struggle did an indigenous literature begin to take root. Unfortunately, Namibian literature isn't widely distributed either in Namibia or abroad. For the undaunted, the following suggestions may help provide an introduction to the country.

One of contemporary Namibia's most significant writers is Joseph Diescho, whose first novel *Born of the Sun* was published in 1988, when he was living in the USA. To date, this refreshingly unpretentious work remains the most renowned Namibian effort. As with most African literature, it's largely autobiographical, describing the protagonist's early life in a tribal village, his coming of age and his first contact with Christianity. It then follows his path through the South African mines and his ultimate political awakening.

Diescho's second novel, *Troubled Waters* (1993), which is a bit wooden and didactic, focuses on a white South African protagonist who is sent to Namibia on military duty and develops a political conscience.

Another significant Namibian voice is David Jasper Utley, whose first publication was a book of short stories entitled *Allsorts* (1991). These brief tales are remarkable for their incorporation of magical realism, including time travel. The stories also depart from the common African themes of gender issues and racial reconciliation. More recently, Utley has published *Ngoma* and *Click*, both Namibian detective stories.

Kapoche Victor's short *On the Run* (1994) is a political thriller set in pre-independence Namibia. Its main characters are four protesters, all A-level students, running from the South African police.

A new and increasingly apparent branch of Namibian work comes from women writers. *A New Initiation Song* (1994) is a collection of poetry and short fiction published by the Sister Namibia collective. This volume's seven sections cover memories of girlhood, body images, and heterosexual and lesbian relationships. Among the best works are those of Liz Frank and Elizabeth !Khaxas. The most

outstanding short stories include *Uerieta*, by Jane Katjavivi, which describes a white woman's coming to terms with African life, and *When the Rains Came*, by Marialena van Tonder, in which a farm couple narrowly survive a drought. One contributor, Nepeti Nicanor, along with Marjorie Orford, also edited another volume, *Coming on Strong* (1996).

Those who read German will appreciate the works of Giselher Hoffmann, which address historical and current Namibian issues. His first novel, *Im Bunde der Dritte* (Three's Company, 1984), is about poaching. *Die Erstgeboren* (The Firstborn, 1991) is told from the perspective of a San group that finds itself pitted against German settlers. Similarly, the Nama-Herero conflict of the late 19th century is described from the Nama perspective in *Die Schweigenden Feuer* (The Silent Fires, 1994). It's also concerned with the impact of western civilisation on indigenous cultures.

In addition, there are several novels set in the country written by non-Namibians. Wilbur Smith's *The Burning Shore* takes place during and after WWI. Its female protagonist is shipwrecked on the Skeleton Coast and survives by adapting to indigenous life with a San couple. Parts of Craig Thomas' *A Hooded Crow* (1992) are set in Windhoek and the Namib desert. Finally, the protagonist of Immo Vogel's intelligent German novel *Namutoni* is a young German immigrant who finds himself caught in a struggle between black freedom fighters, black workers, Afrikaners, German farmers and German racists, and has to take sides.

For further information on Namibian literature, check your local library for a copy of Dorian Haarhoff's *The Wild South-West: Frontier Myths & Metaphors in Literature Set in Namibia, 1760-1988* (1991).

## Architecture

The most obvious architectural contribution in Namibia was made by the German colonial settlers, who attempted to re-create late 19th century Germany in Namibia. In deference to the warmer African climate, however, they added such features as shaded verandas, to provide cool outdoor living space. The best examples may be seen in Lüderitz, Swakopmund and Windhoek, but German style is also evident in central and southern Namibia.

The most ornate and monumental structures, including the railway station and old prison in Swakopmund, were done in what is known as *Wilhelminischer Stil*. Art Nouveau influences are most in evidence in Lüderitz and in Windhoek's Christuskirche.

### Film

Although Namibia's bizarre desert landscapes are appearing in an increasing number of films and nearly everyone has seen foreign car, airline and insurance commercials filmed at the dunes at Sossusvlei, Namibia's own film industry is still in its infancy. The most notable Namibian film to be seen internationally is *Sophia's Homecoming*, which tells the story of an Owambo woman who, to support her family, goes to work as a domestic in Windhoek. She is away for 12 years, during which time her husband Naftali finds a job and takes up with her sister Selna. During Sophia's absence, Selna takes over the affections of not only Naftali, but also of Sophia's children. When Sophia pressures her sister to leave the family, Naftali confesses that he prefers Selna, who is pregnant with his child. Ironically, in an attempt to shift her direction, Sophia returns to Windhoek and attempts to build a new life for herself and her three children.

### Visual Arts

Most of Namibia's renowned modern painters and photographers are of European origin and concentrate largely on the country's colourful landscapes, bewitching light, native wildlife and, more recently, its diverse peoples. Well known names include François de Mecker, Axel Eriksson, Fritz Krampe and Adolph Jentsch. The well known colonial landscape artists, Carl Ossman and Ernst Vollbehr, are both exhibited in Germany.

Non-European Namibians, who have concentrated mainly on three-dimensional and material arts, have recently begun to develop their own traditions. Township art, which develops sober themes in an expressive, colourful and generally lighthearted manner, first appeared in the townships of South Africa during the apartheid years. Over the past decade, it has taken hold in Namibia and is developing into a popular art form. Names to watch for include Tembo Masala and Joseph Madisia.

## RELIGION

At least 75% of Namibians profess Christianity, and German Lutheranism is the dominant sect. As a result of early missionary activity there is also a substantial Roman Catholic population, mainly in the central areas of the country and spread through isolated areas of the north, especially Kavango. Most Portuguese-speakers are Roman Catholic.

Most non-Christian Namibians live in the north, and many people – particularly Himba, Herero and San – continue to follow old animist traditions. In general, most of these beliefs are characterised by veneration of ancestors, who aren't considered dead, but merely to have taken on a new form. It's believed that they continue to interact with mortals, and serve as messengers between their descendants and the gods.

## LANGUAGE
### Indigenous Languages

As a first language, most Namibians speak either a Bantu language – which would include Owambo, Kavango, Herero and Caprivian languages – or a Khoisan language, which may be Khoi-Khoi (Nama), Damara or a San dialect.

The Bantu language group includes eight dialects of Owambo; Kwanyama and Ndonga are the official Owambo languages. The Kavango group has four separate dialects: Kwangali, Mbunza, Sambiyu and Geiriku, of which Kwangali is the most widely used. In the Caprivi, the most widely spoken language is Rotsi (or Lozi), which originally came from Barotseland in Zambia. Herero (not surprisingly) speak Herero, which is a rolling, melodious language, rich in colourful-sounding words. Most Namibian place names beginning with an 'O' – for example, Okahandja, Omaruru and Otjiwarongo – are derived from the Herero language.

Khoisan dialects are characterised by 'click' elements, which make them difficult to learn, and only a few foreigners ever get the hang of them. Clicks are made by compressing the tongue against different parts of the mouth to produce different sounds. Names that include an exclamation mark are of Khoisan origin and should be rendered as a sideways click sound, similar to the sound one would make when encouraging a horse, but with a hollow tone (like the sound made when pulling a cork from a bottle). The other three clicks are formed by quickly drawing the tongue away from the front teeth, which is represented as /; clicking a tutting disapproval, represented as //; and a sharp pop formed by drawing the tongue from the roof of the mouth, which is represented more or less as a vertical line with two crossbars.

The first English-Ju/hoansi dictionary (Ju/hoansi is the dialect spoken by most Namibian San) was compiled in 1992 by the late Patrick Dickens and published by Florida State University in the USA.

Many native Khoisan speakers also speak at least one Bantu and one European language, normally Afrikaans. The language of the Damara, who are actually of Bantu origin, is also a Khoisan dialect.

## European Languages
When the new constitution was drawn up at the time of independence, the official language of Namibia was designated as English. Although that may seem odd when English is the native tongue of only about 2% of the population, it was decided that using English would put all ethnic groups on an equal footing. Furthermore, it was recognised that the adoption of the language

of international business would appeal to both tourists and investors.

On the other hand Afrikaans is also widely used and, although it is often dismissed as the language of apartheid, it's the first language of over 100,000 Namibians of diverse ethnic backgrounds, so it's unlikely to disappear in the near future. Most Namibian coloureds and Basters use Afrikaans as a first language; only in the Caprivi is English actually preferred over Afrikaans as a lingua franca.

When written, Afrikaans may appear intelligible to English speakers, but the guttural spoken language is another matter. Although some rural Afrikaans speakers may be reluctant (or unable) to speak any other language, visitors with English as their only tongue will have few problems.

German is also widely spoken, but is the first language of only about 2% of people. In the far north, around Rundu and Katima Mulilo, you'll also hear a lot of Portuguese.

## Afrikaans
Afrikaans pronunciation is fairly straightforward. Its Germanic roots are evident in the characteristic guttural emphasis and the rolled 'r'. The following guide is not exhaustive, but it includes the sounds most likely to trouble native English speakers.

| | |
|---|---|
| a | as the 'u' in 'pup' |
| e | as in 'ten' |
| i | as the 'e' in 'angel' |
| o | as the 'o' in fort, or 'oy' in 'boy' |
| u | as the 'e' in 'angel', but with lips pouted |
| r | rolled, as in Italian 'primo' |
| tj | as the 'ch' in 'chunk' |
| aai | as the 'y' in 'why' |
| ae | like 'ah' |
| ee | as in 'deer' |
| ei | as the 'ay' in 'play' |
| oe | as the 'oo' in 'loot' |
| oë | as the 'oe' in 'doer' |
| ooi | as 'oi', preceded by 'w' |
| oei | as the 'ooey' in 'phooey', preceded by 'w' |
| ui | as the 'ai' in 'rain' |

## Greetings & Civilities

| | |
|---|---|
| Hello. | *Hallo.* |
| Good morning, sir. | *Goeie môre, meneer.* |
| Good afternoon, madam. | *Goeie middag, mevrou.* |
| Good evening. | *Goeienaand.* |
| Good night. | *Goeie nag.* |
| Please. | *Asseblief.* |
| Thank you. | *Dankie.* |
| How are you? | *Hoegaandit?* |
| Well, thank you. | *Goed dankie.* |
| Pardon. | *Ekskuus.* |

## Useful Words & Phrases

| | |
|---|---|
| Yes. | *Ja.* |
| No. | *Nee.* |
| Maybe. | *Miskien.* |
| Sure. | *Sekerlik.* |
| What? | *Wat?* |
| How? | *Hoe?* |
| How many/ How much? | *Hoeveel?* |
| When? | *Wanneer?* |
| Where? | *Waar?* |
| Do you speak English? | *Praat u English?* |
| Do you speak Afrikaans? | *Praat u Afrikaans?* |
| I only understand a little Afrikaans. | *Ek verstaan net 'n bietjie Afrikaans.* |
| Where are you from? | *Waarvandaan kom u?* |
| From (overseas). | *Van (oorsee).* |
| Where do you live? | *Waar woon u?* |
| What is your occupation? | *Wat is jou beroep?* |

| | |
|---|---|
| daughters | *dogters* |
| sons | *seuns* |
| wife | *vrou* |
| husband | *eggenoot* |
| mother | *ma* |
| father | *pa* |
| sister | *suster* |
| brother | *broer* |

| | |
|---|---|
| bad | *sleg* |
| cheap | *goedkoop* |
| emergency | *nood* |
| expensive | *duur* |
| nice/good/pleasant | *lekker* |
| party/rage | *jol* |
| soon | *nou-nou* |

## Numbers

| | |
|---|---|
| 1 | *een* |
| 2 | *twee* |
| 3 | *drie* |
| 4 | *vier* |
| 5 | *vyf* |
| 6 | *ses* |
| 7 | *sewe* |
| 8 | *agt* |
| 9 | *nege* |
| 10 | *tien* |
| 11 | *elf* |
| 12 | *twaalf* |
| 13 | *dertien* |
| 14 | *veertien* |
| 15 | *vyftien* |
| 16 | *sestien* |
| 17 | *sewentien* |
| 18 | *agtien* |
| 19 | *negentien* |
| 20 | *twintig* |
| 21 | *een en twintig* |
| 30 | *dertig* |
| 40 | *veertig* |
| 50 | *vyftig* |
| 60 | *sestig* |
| 70 | *sewentig* |
| 80 | *tagtig* |
| 90 | *negentig* |
| 100 | *honderd* |
| 1000 | *duisend* |

## Travel Terms

| | |
|---|---|
| travel | *reis* |
| arrival | *aankoms* |
| departure | *vertrek* |
| to | *na* |
| from | *van* |

NAMIBIA

| today | vandag |
|---|---|
| tomorrow | mere |
| yesterday | gister |
| daily | daagliks |
| public holiday | openbare |
| | vakansiedag |
| single | enkel |
| return | retoer |
| ticket | kaartjie |
| am | vm |
| pm | nm |

**Days of the Week**

| Monday | Maandag, |
|---|---|
| | (abbr Ma) |
| Tuesday | Dinsdag/Di |
| Wednesday | Woensdag/Wo |
| Thursday | Donderdag/Do |
| Friday | Vrydag/Vr |
| Saturday | Saterdag/Sa |
| Sunday | Sondag/So |

**Getting Around – Town**

| art gallery | kunsgalery |
|---|---|
| avenue | laan |
| building | gebou |
| church | kerk |
| city centre | middestad |
| city | stad |
| enquiries | navrae |
| exit | uitgang |
| information | inligting |
| left/right | links/regs |
| office | kantoor |
| on the corner | op die hoek |
| pharmacy/chemist | apteek |
| priest | dominee |
| road | pad |

| rooms | kamers |
|---|---|
| station | stasie |
| street | straat |
| tourist bureau | toeristeburo |
| town | stad |

**Getting Around – Country**

| bay | baai |
|---|---|
| beach | strand |
| caravan park | woonwapark |
| field, or plain | veld |
| game reserve | wildtuin |
| hiking trail (short) | wandelpad |
| hiking trail (long) | staproete |
| marsh | vlei |
| mountain | berg |
| point | punt |
| river | rivier |
| road | pad |
| utility/pick-up | bakkie |

**Food & Drinks**

| barbecue | braaivleis or braai |
|---|---|
| bar | kroeg |
| beer | bier |
| bread | brood |
| cheese | kaas |
| cup of coffee | koppie koffie |
| dried and | biltong |
| salted meat | |
| farm sausage | boerewors |
| fish | vis |
| fruit | vrugte |
| glass of milk | glas melk |
| meat | vleis |
| vegetables | groente |
| wine | wyn |

NAMIBIA

# Facts for the Visitor

## PLANNING
### When to Go
Much of Namibia enjoys a minimum of 300 days of sunshine a year, and in the winter dry season (May to October) you can expect clear, warm and sunny days and cold, clear nights, often with temperatures below freezing. Generally, the mountainous and semi-arid Central Plateau (including Windhoek) is a bit cooler than the rest of the country. While the low-lying areas of eastern Namibia are generally hotter than the Central Plateau, and they also receive less rain.

There are two rainy seasons, the 'little rains' from October to December and the main rainy period from January to April. The latter is characterised by brief showers and occasional thunderstorms, which clean the air and soak down the dust. January temperatures in Windhoek can soar to 40°C, and from December to March, Namib-Naukluft Park and Etosha National Park become especially hot and uncomfortable. From January to March, the north-eastern rivers may flood, making some roads either impassable or tricky to negotiate.

Note that some resort areas, such as Ai-Ais Hot Springs, close in the summer. Others, such as Swakopmund, are booked solid over Christmas and Easter and during school holidays.

### Maps
Government survey topographical sheets and aerial photos are available from the Office of the Surveyor General (☎ (061) 245056), Ministry of Justice, Private Bag 13182, Windhoek. It's in the Justicia Building beside the main post office on Independence Ave, Windhoek. The 1:250,000 series maps cost US$2 each; the 1:50,000 maps are US$1.50.

The *Shell Roadmap – Namibia* is probably the best reference for remote routes and includes an excellent Windhoek city map, but it isn't clear which routes require 4WD, and the Caprivi is relegated to a small-scale inset. Shell has also published a good map of north-western Namibia entitled the *Kaokoland-Kunene Region Tourist Map*, which depicts all routes and tracks through this remote region. It's available at bookshops and tourist offices for somewhere between US$2 and US$3.

The Macmillan *Namibia Travellers' Map* at a scale of 1:2,400,000 is one of the nicest, with clear print and colour-graded altitude representation, but minor back routes aren't depicted and there are notable inaccuracies. The reverse side has decent maps of Windhoek, Swakopmund, Lüderitz, Walvis Bay, Etosha National Park and Namib-Naukluft Park.

The Ministry of Environment & Tourism (MET) produces an official *Republic of Namibia* 1:2,000,000 tourist map, which shows major routes and sites of tourist interest and will suffice for most trips around the country. It's distributed free at tourist offices, hotels and travel agencies. The reverse side has detailed maps of Windhoek and Swakopmund.

The Automobile Association Travel Service (☎ (061) 224201; fax 222446) has produced the map *Namibia* at a scale of 1:2,500,000, which does include most back roads and settlements, although the Kaokoveld and Bushmanland are largely blank. On the reverse side is a series of thumbnail town plans. The AA office is in the Carl List Building, ground floor, on the corner of Peter Müller Strasse and Independence Ave, Windhoek, but to pick up maps, you must be a member of an official Automobile Association affiliate.

## SUGGESTED ITINERARIES
### Low-Budget Tour
These suggestions are for those on a strict budget who don't have access to a vehicle. Unfortunately, travellers without a car will

miss the best of Namibia if they don't have a great deal of time to cope with the uncertainty of trying to find lifts.

The best place to look for lifts to see the dunes at Sossusvlei is Windhoek, and for Fish River Canyon at either Keetmanshoop or Grünau. However, these sites haven't been included in this itinerary. If you do get to Sossusvlei or Fish River Canyon, drop out numbers seven and eight. Note that transport time between sites isn't included in this itinerary.

1. Katima Mulilo (one day)
2. Rundu (one day)
3. Tsumeb – visit the museum and try to find a lift into Etosha National Park (one day)
4. With luck, Etosha National Park (two to four days)
5. Windhoek (three to four days)
6. Swakopmund, with a day tour to Cape Cross Seal Reserve (three days)
7. Keetmanshoop (one day)
8. Lüderitz (one day)

## Cultural & Historical Tour

This tour is for those interested in Namibia's indigenous and colonial cultures and history. For these destinations, a 2WD vehicle will suffice. If you wish to visit Bushmanland or the Kaokoveld, which are arguably Namibia's most interesting cultural areas, you'll need both more time and at least one 4WD vehicle.

1. Windhoek (two days)
2. Swakopmund (two days)
3. Damaraland – Spitzkoppe, Brandberg and Twyfelfontein (three days)
4. Etosha National Park (two days)
5. Owamboland – Ombalantu, Oshakati and Ondangwa (two days)
6. Kavango – Rundu (two days)
7. Caprivi – Katima Mulilo, Lizauli Village and Mudumu National Park (three days)

## Natural History Tours

Namibia has some of the world's most unusual flora, fauna and geology. Therefore, you'll have to pick and choose what you want to see. Generally, most visitors will want to divide the country into north-

ern and southern sections. Both of these options will require access to a car.

### Northern Namibia Best options are:
1. Windhoek, with a visit to Daan Viljoen Game Park (two days)
2. Spitzkoppe via Otjihaenamaparero Dinosaur Footprints and perhaps Ranch Ameib (two days)
3. Cape Cross Seal Reserve and Skeleton Coast Park (one day)
4. Damaraland – Twyfelfontein, Wondergat, Organ Pipes, Burnt Mountain and Petrified Forest (three days)
5. Palmwag (one day)
6. Etosha National Park (four days)
7. Tsumeb and Grootfontein – Lake Otjikoto, Hoba Meteorite and Tsumeb Mining Museum (one day)
8. Waterberg Plateau Park (two days)
9. Dordabis – Arnhem Cave (one day)

### Southern Namibia Highlights include:
1. Windhoek, with a visit to Daan Viljoen Game Park (two days)
2. Brukkaros Crater (one day)
3. Keetmanshoop – Kokerboom Forest and Giant's Playground, Singing Rocks (two days)
4. Fish River Canyon and Ai-Ais, with a day hike to the bottom of the canyon (three days)
5. Lüderitz – feral horses, Lüderitz Peninsula (two days)
6. Sesriem and Sossusvlei (two days)
7. Naukluft, with a hike around either the Waterkloof or the Olive trail (two days)
8. Namib Desert Park – Kuiseb Canyon, Homeb and Welwitschia Drive (two or three days)
9. Walvis Bay, with a day tour to Sandwich Harbour (one day)

## Wildlife Tour

If you've come to Namibia for the wildlife, you won't be disappointed. All of the following attractions will be accessible by 2WD. However, if you want to visit much of the Kaokoveld or Khaudom Game Reserve, you'll need more time and a convoy of two 4WD vehicles.

1. Windhoek, with a visit to Daan Viljoen Game Park (two days)
2. Waterberg Plateau Park (two days)
3. Etosha National Park (four days)
4. Mahango Game Reserve (two days)

NAMIBIA

## NAMIBIA HIGHLIGHTS

| Region | Feature |
| --- | --- |

### Windhoek

**Windhoek** — Namibia's big smoke is a clean, attractive capital city that occupies a lovely setting amid arid aloe-covered mountains. The central area blends turn-of-the-century German colonial buildings with bizarrely coloured, postmodernist 'birthday cake' architecture – much of it appears to be sweet and edible!

### North Central Namibia

**Etosha National Park** — Etosha National Park surrounds a vast salt pan that occasionally holds water and attracts flocks of flamingoes; the surrounding bushveld is dotted with water holes that attract wildlife. Of the three rest camps, the most striking is Namutoni, a whitewashed 'Beau Geste' German colonial fort.

**Waterberg Plateau Park** — This small park is not only a lovely place to relax and enjoy the far-ranging views, it's also a repository for endangered species such as the white rhino. You can either hike or travel through the high plateau reserve on organised game drives.

### North-Eastern Namibia

**Caprivi National Parks & Game Reserves** — The Caprivi Strip, the corridor of land stretching eastwards towards Zimbabwe and Zambia, has three small national parks and game reserves – Mudumu, Mamili and Mahango – where you can experience a more verdant side of Namibia's character.

**Khaudom Game Reserve** — This wild and hard-to-reach park in the north-east is an unexpected surprise. It's packed with every sort of wildlife found in Namibia and you're likely to have the whole place to yourself. Access is by 4WD only.

### North-Western Namibia

**The Skeleton Coast & Damaraland** — The renowned Skeleton Coast, characterised by ethereal, fog-bound coastal scenery, has long been a graveyard for ships and their stranded crews. Don't miss the herds of Cape fur seals at Cape Cross. The vast spaces of Damaraland support a variety of desert species – outside any artificially protected reserve. Natural attractions include the imposing Spitzkoppe; the Brandberg massif with its rock paintings; the rock engravings of Twyfelfontein; and the geological wonders of the Petrified Forest and Burnt Mountain.

NAMIBIA

---

**The Central Namib**

The Namib Desert — No article about Namibia is complete without a photo of the brilliant waves of red and pink dunes that characterise the desert after which the country is named. The most popular destination is the oasis of Sossusvlei, an ephemeral pan surrounded by towering dunes. The northern part of the Namib is flatter and more stony, with isolated massifs protruding from the plains.

Swakopmund — The coastal port of Swakopmund, with its long beach, provides more of a holiday atmosphere than Lüderitz. The language is German and it's packed with colonial architecture, little *Konditoreien* and beer gardens.

**Southern Namibia**

Fish River Canyon — Fish River Canyon surely ranks as one of Africa's most spectacular natural wonders. Frequently compared to the Grand Canyon, it is an immense gorge, 161km long, up to 27km wide and 550m deep. At Ai-Ais, you can have a massage or beauty treatment, or luxuriate in hot mud springs.

Lüderitz — The arid southern Namib is characterised by extraordinary pastel colours and the 'Little Bavaria' town of Lüderitz makes a good base for exploring it. Lüderitz is the northern anchor of the diamond-rich Sperrgebiet and the nearby diamond ghost town of Kolmanskop is steadily being swallowed by the dunes.

---

5. Damaraland, including Palmwag Lodge (two days)
6. Cape Cross Seal Reserve (two hours)
7. Walvis Bay – bird paradise, lagoon, salt works and a day tour to Sandwich Harbour (two days)
8. Sesriem and Sossusvlei (two days)

## HIGHLIGHTS

Namibia is a large and sparsely populated country. Superimposed on a rich diversity of African cultures is a modern and efficient infrastructure recalling the German and South African colonial legacies. The Teutonic angle adds a bizarre dimension: where else in the world could you eat *Sachertorte* on the edge of the desert, watching flamingoes flying overhead? The Namibia Highlights boxed text above has details of the top attractions.

## TOURIST OFFICES
### Local Tourist Offices

Windhoek has both city and national tourist offices – Namibia Tourism (☎ (061) 284 2111; fax 284 2364; <tourism@iwwn.com.na>) is on the ground floor of the Continental Building, 272 Independence Ave, Private Bag 13346, Windhoek.

Windhoek also has a private tourist office that will help plan your trip and make bookings. You'll also find tourist offices in municipal buildings in most towns, and there are small information bureaus in Karibib, Usakos, Omaruru, Okahandja and Gobabis, all of which are open during business hours.

Useful publications include the *Namibia Accommodation Guide for Tourists*, Engen Oil's *Guidebook – Travel in Namibia*, the

**NAMIBIA**

*Namibia Tourism Directory*, and the incredible, over-the-top production *Namibia Holiday & Travel*. They're all published annually and are available at tourist offices.

### Tourist Offices Abroad

The following Namibia Tourism addresses may be useful in planning your visit:

Germany
    *Namibia Verkehrsbüro*, Postfach 2041, 61290 Bad Homburg (☎ (06172) 406650; fax 406690; <namibia.tourism@t-online.de>)
South Africa
    *Namibia Tourism*, PO Box 78946, Sandton City, Sandton 2146 (☎ (011) 784 8024; fax 784 8340)
    Ground floor, Main Tower, Standard Bank Centre, Adderley St, PO Box 739, Cape Town 8000 (☎ (021) 419 3190; fax 215840)
UK
    *Namibia Tourism*, 6 Chandos St, London W1M 0LQ (☎ (0171) 636 2924; fax 636 2969; <namibia@globalnet.co.uk>)
USA
    *Kartagener Associates Inc*, 12 West 37th St, New York, NY 10018 (☎ (212) 465-0619; fax 868-1654)

### VISAS & DOCUMENTS
### Visas

All visitors to Namibia require a valid passport issued by their home country, valid for at least six months after their intended departure from Namibia, in addition to an onward plane, bus or train ticket. Tourists are granted an initial 90 days, which may be extended by the Ministry of Home Affairs (☎ (061) 398111) on the corner of Kasino St and Independence Ave in Windhoek. The mailing address is Private Bag 13200, Windhoek. For the best results, it's wise to be there when they open at 8 am, submit your application in the 3rd floor offices (as opposed to those on the ground floor) and make an effort to be polite.

At the time of writing, no visas were required by nationals of Australia, New Zealand, France, Germany, Austria, Italy, Spain, Portugal, the UK, Ireland, the Netherlands, Belgium, Luxembourg, Switzerland, Liechtenstein, the CIS, Canada, the USA, Brazil, South Africa, Botswana,

Zimbabwe, Zambia, Tanzania, Angola, Mozambique, Kenya, Japan, Singapore or the Scandinavian countries. All EU and Commonwealth countries should soon be excluded from visa requirements.

### EMBASSIES
### Namibian Diplomatic Missions

If you need a visa and your country doesn't have a Namibian diplomatic mission, fax or post your passport details and requested length of stay to the Ministry of Home Affairs, Private Bag X13200, Windhoek (☎ (061) 398111; fax 222567). Visas may sometimes be issued at Windhoek international airport, but never at land borders.

*Angola*
    Embassy of Namibia, 95 Rua dos Coqueiros, PO Box 953, Luanda (☎ (02) 395483; fax 333923)
*Belgium*
    Embassy of Namibia, 454 Ave de Tervueren, 1150 Brussels (☎ (02) 771 1410; fax 771 9681)
*France*
    Embassy of Namibia, 80 Ave Foch, Square de l'Avenue Foch, Paris (☎ 01 44 17 32 65; fax 01 44 17 32 73)
*Germany*
    Embassy of Namibia, Mainzerstrasse 47, 53179 Bonn (☎ (0228) 346021; fax 346025)
*South Africa*
    Tulbach Park, Eikendal Flat Suite 2, 1234 Church St, Colbyn, Pretoria, PO Box 29806, Sunnyside 0132 (☎ (012) 344 5922; fax 342 3565)
*UK*
    Namibian High Commission, 6 Chandoff St, London (☎ (0171) 636 6244; fax 637 5694)
*USA*
    Embassy of Namibia, 1605 New Hampshire Ave NW, Washington, DC 20009 (☎ (202) 986-0540; fax 986-0443)
*Zambia*
    Namibian High Commission, 6968 Kabanga Rd & Addis Ababa Drive, Rhodes Park, Lusaka (☎ (01) 252 250; fax 252 497)
*Zimbabwe*
    Namibian High Commission, 31A Lincoln Rd, Avondale, Harare (☎ (04) 304856; fax 304855)

### Foreign Embassies in Namibia

Since Namibian independence, numerous countries have established diplomatic mis-

NAMIBIA

sions. All the following addresses are in Windhoek.

*Angola*
Angola House, 3 Ausspann St, Ausspannplatz, Private Bag 12020 (☎ (061) 227535; fax 221498)

*Botswana*
101 Nelson Mandela Rd, PO Box 20359 (☎ (061) 221942; fax 236034)

*France*
1 Goethe St, PO Box 20484 (☎ (061) 229021; fax 231436)

*Germany*
6th floor, Sanlam Centre, 154 Independence Ave, PO Box 231 (☎ (061) 229217; fax 222981)

*Kenya*
5th floor, Kenya House, 134 Robert Mugabe Ave, PO Box 2889 (☎ (061) 226836; fax 221409)

*Malawi*
56 Bismarck St, Windhoek West, PO Box 23547 (☎ (061) 221391; fax 227056)

*South Africa*
RSA House, corner Jan Jonker Rd and Nelson Mandela Ave, Klein Windhoek, PO Box 23100 (☎ (061) 229765; fax 236093)

*UK*
116A Robert Mugabe Ave, PO Box 22202 (☎ (061) 223022; fax 228895)

*USA*
14 Lossen St, Ausspannplatz, Private Bag 12029 (☎ (061) 221601; fax 229792)

*Zambia*
22 Sam Nujoma Drive, corner of Republic Rd, PO Box 22882 (☎ (061) 237610; fax 228162)

*Zimbabwe*
Gamsberg Building, corner of Independence Ave and Grimm St, PO Box 23056 (☎ (061) 227738; fax 226859)

For general information on what your embassy can and can't do for you when you are travelling in a foreign country, see the Embassies section in the regional Facts for the Visitor chapter.

## CUSTOMS

Any item from elsewhere in the Southern African Customs Union – Botswana, South Africa, Lesotho or Swaziland – may be imported duty free. From elsewhere, visitors can import duty free 400 cigarettes or 250g

of tobacco, 2L of wine, 1L of spirits and 250mL of eau de Cologne. There are no limits on currency import, but entry and departure forms ask how much you intend to spend or have spent in the country.

Firearms require a temporary import permit and must be declared at the time of entry. For pets, you need a health certificate and full veterinary documentation. Bear in mind, however, that pets aren't permitted in national parks or reserves.

## MONEY
### Costs

Thanks to a favourable exchange rate, Namibia remains a relatively inexpensive country to visit. You'll probably spend considerably more than in Zimbabwe, but less than in either Botswana or South Africa.

If you're camping or staying in backpackers hostels, cooking your own meals and hitching or using local minibuses, plan on spending a minimum of US$15 per day. Unfortunately, to get around the country on this sort of budget would prove both frustrating and time consuming, since the hitching isn't great and minibus routes are limited to the main highways.

A plausible mid-range budget, including B&B or inexpensive hotel accommodation, public transport and at least one restaurant meal daily, would be around US$50 to US$80 per person per day (if accommodation costs are shared between two people).

In the upper range, the sky is the limit, but if you wish to stay at starred hotels, eat in restaurants exclusively and either take escorted tours or use 4WD, you're looking at a minimum of US$300 per person per day. It may be better value to pre-book a fly-drive or organised tour package overseas than to make arrangements on the spot.

In Namibia, the fly in the ointment is transport. To reach the most interesting parts of the country readily, you'll have to add car hire and petrol expenses. If you can muster a group of four people and share costs, you'll probably squeak by on an additional US$20 per day – that's assuming a daily average of around 200km in a 2WD

**NAMIBIA**

vehicle with the least expensive agency, including tax, insurance and unlimited mileage. If you prefer to hire a vehicle between only two people, again averaging 200km per day with unlimited mileage, double that amount.

For a 4WD vehicle shared between two people, add yet another US$50 per person. The plus side of a 4WD is that many vehicles are equipped with camping gear, which would allow you to bring down the price of accommodation.

Bear in mind, however, that if you hire the vehicle for a relatively short period – normally fewer than seven days – most agencies charge an additional US$0.20 (N$0.75) per kilometre, which must be added in.

## Currency

For three years after independence, Namibia used the South African rand, but on 15 September 1993, the country issued its own currency. The Namibian dollar equals 100 cents, and in Namibia it's valued the same as the South African rand; in South Africa, however, it fetches only about R0.70. In Namibia, the rand also remains legal tender at a rate of 1:1.

This can be confusing, given that there are three sets of coins and notes in use: old South African, new South African and Namibian. To complicate matters further, the three different coins of the same denomination are all different sizes! It takes a while to get the hang of it.

Namibian dollar notes come in denominations of N$10, 20, 50 and 100, and all bear portraits of Nama leader Hendrik Witbooi. Coins have values of 5, 10, 20 and 50 cents and N$1 and 5. South African notes are issued for R5, 10, 20, 50 and 100, and coins come in denominations of 1, 2, 5, 10, 20 and 50 cents, as well as R1 and 2. Namibia is currently hoping to phase out the 1 and 2 cent coins by encouraging rounding of prices to the nearest 5 cents.

There is no limit on the amount of currency or travellers cheques you can bring into Namibia.

## Currency Exchange

Major foreign currencies and travellers cheques may be exchanged at any bank, but the latter normally fetch a better rate. When changing money, you can opt for either South African rand or Namibian dollars; if you'll need to change any leftover currency outside Namibia, the rand is a better choice. If you're changing travellers cheques, shop around for the bank offering the lowest commission. Currently, some banks – such as the Commercial Bank – charge as much as US$6.50 per transaction.

Travellers cheques may also be exchanged for US dollars cash – if the cash is available – but the banks charge a hefty 7% commission. There is no currency black market, so beware of street changers offering unrealistic rates; they could be passing counterfeit notes or setting you up for a robbery.

## Exchange Rates

At the time of writing, the Namibian dollar had the following values against other currencies:

| Australia | A$1 | = | N$3.06 |
|---|---|---|---|
| Botswana | P1 | = | N$1.30 |
| Canada | C$1 | = | N$3.56 |
| France | 10FF | = | N$8.71 |
| Germany | DM1 | = | N$2.92 |
| Japan | ¥100 | = | N$3.70 |
| New Zealand | NZ$1 | = | N$2.59 |
| South Africa | R1 | = | N$1.00 |
| UK | UK£1 | = | N$8.52 |
| USA | US$1 | = | N$5.21 |
| Zimbabwe | Z$10 | = | N$2.90 |

## Credit Cards

Credit cards are accepted in most shops, restaurants and hotels, and credit card cash advances are available from BOB, First National Bank's automatic teller system. You'll find BOB machines in Windhoek, Gobabis, Rehoboth, Keetmanshoop, Lüderitz, Mariental, Swakopmund, Walvis Bay, Okahandja, Tsumeb, Grootfontein, Rundu, Otjiwarongo, Oranjemund, Oshakati and Ondangwa.

American Express is represented by

Woker Travel Services (☎ (061) 237946) at 6 Peter Müller Strasse, Windhoek. Nedbank will issue cash against a personal cheque, but fees are high.

## Tipping & Bargaining

Tipping is expected only in upmarket tourist establishments that don't already add a service charge as a matter of course. In any case, don't leave more than about 10% of the bill. Tipping is officially prohibited in national parks and reserves.

Bargaining is acceptable when purchasing handicrafts and arts directly from the producer or artist, such as at roadside stalls in the north. However, the prices asked are normally quite low – and do represent fair market value – so bargaining is often unnecessary. The exception is crafts imported from Zimbabwe, which are generally sold at large crafts markets for highly inflated prices; prices are always negotiable. Shop prices aren't usually negotiable, although you may be able to wrangle discounts on very expensive curios or artwork.

## Consumer Taxes

A general sales tax (GST) of 11% is applied to most purchases, including meals and accommodation. Tourists buying such luxury items as leather and jewellery for export may be exempt from this tax if they can produce a valid passport and airline tickets.

## POST & COMMUNICATIONS
## Postal Rates

Although postal rates are climbing, they're relatively good value, and for posting larger boxes overseas surface mail is a real bargain.

## Sending Mail

In major towns, post offices remain open during normal business hours; in resort areas, they open the same hours but offer limited services.

Domestic post generally moves slowly, and it can take six weeks for a letter to travel from Lüderitz to Katima Mulilo, for example. Overseas airmail is normally

better, and is limited only by the time it takes an article to reach Windhoek.

All post offices sell current issues of Namibia's lovely pictorial and commemorative stamps. Upstairs in the Windhoek main post office is a special philatelic department for stamp enthusiasts.

## Receiving Mail

Naturally, poste restante works best in Windhoek. Have correspondents print your surname clearly in block capitals, underline it and address it to you at Poste Restante, GPO, Windhoek, Namibia. As you'd expect, the further you are from Windhoek, the longer mail takes to arrive. Photo identification is required to collect mail.

American Express credit card or travellers cheque customers may have post held for them by the Windhoek American Express representative, Woker Travel Services (see under Credit Cards). Have post addressed to your name, American Express Client, PO Box 211, Windhoek, Namibia.

## Telephone

When phoning Namibia from abroad, dial the country code 264 followed by the telephone code without the leading zero, and then the desired number. To phone out of Namibia, first dial 09, then the desired country code, area code and number. You can also book reverse charge calls to Namibia or South Africa (☎ 0690) and international reverse charge calls (☎ 0920).

When making a long-distance call within Namibia, dial the first zero of the regional area code. In some cases, you must dial the code and verbally ask the exchange operator for the desired number. Note that some rural areas have a farmline (party line) code that replaces the standard regional code. Currently, many of these are being consolidated into regional codes, which will greatly simplify the system.

The Namibian telephone service is relatively efficient. There are a few telephone boxes in the streets, but you can make local or international calls from post office booths. Telecom Namibia has also

NAMIBIA

introduced phonecards, which are sold at post offices and some retail shops, but as yet cardphones are few. Currently, international calls cost US$3.50 per minute to any foreign country. Most towns now have private bureaus where you can send and receive faxes.

Cellular phones are slowly becoming more popular, but in rural areas most people who must communicate use short-wave radio. Some isolated locations use radio telephones. Radio telephone numbers use the area code 0020, but calls to these phones must be booked through an operator.

Many remote bush locations subscribe to a message service operated by Walvis Bay Radio (☎ (064) 203581); each subscriber has their own code number, and messages are passed on via radio.

There's only one slim telephone directory for the entire country, but it conveniently lists most people's private and work addresses and has a separate section for government departments. The *Yellow Pages* also covers the whole country.

## INTERNET RESOURCES

The Lonely Planet Web site (www.lonely planet.com) has several pages with information relevant to visitors to Namibia. One of the most useful Web sites, which has links to all sorts of similarly useful peripheral sites, is Horizon (www.horizon.fr /Namibia.html). It's available in both English and French, and includes addresses for tourist services as well as booking information and the latest news snippets.

The MET Web site (www.iwwn.com.na /namtour/namtour.html) provides information on booking national parks permits and accommodation.

The Namibian government Web site (www.republicofnamibia.com/) contains details on government functions, ministries and tourism promotion.

## BOOKS

Thanks to its unique history, cultures and environments, Namibia is the subject of a growing number of books in English – as well as German and Afrikaans – and nearly all Namibian bookshops have a special section dealing with Namibian and African topics. Few such books, however, are distributed in other countries; you'll have the most luck with specialist travel bookshops in the UK or the USA.

Windhoek and Swakopmund both have decent bookshops with separate sections for works in Afrikaans and German, but most books are in English. In smaller towns, there's normally a selection of pulp paperbacks in the supermarket or general store.

### History

*Namibia – the Struggle for Liberation* by Alfred T Moleah recounts SWAPO's independence struggle, telling it like it was long before success was guaranteed.

For desert survivalists, the book to read is *The Sheltering Desert* by Henno Martin, which recounts German geologists Henno Martin and Hermann Korn's two years in the Namib Desert to avoid internment by Allied forces during WWII. It contains excellent descriptions of the Namib ecology, but some passages aren't recommended for vegetarians.

For looks at colonisation and independence, see Sam Nujoma's autobiography *To Free Namibia: The Life of the First President of Namibia*; *Namibia: The Nation after Independence* by D Sparks & D Green; and *The Transition to Independence in Namibia* by L Cliffe, R Bush, J Lindsay, B Mokopakgodsi, D Pankhurst & B Tsie.

### Literature & Fiction

A literary tradition hasn't yet developed among black Namibians, but it's coming (see the Literature section in the Facts about Namibia chapter). If you'd enjoy stories set in Namibia, you're mostly limited to pulp fiction, such as Wilbur Smith's entertaining *The Burning Shore* and Craig Thomas' *A Hooded Crow*.

### Natural History Guides

*Namib Flora: Swakopmund to the Giant*

*Welwitschia via Goanikontes* by Patricia Craven and Christine Marais is excellent for plant identification around northern Namib-Naukluft Park. *The Namib – Natural History of an Ancient Desert* by Mary Seely is a useful handbook written by the director of the Desert Research Unit.

Other natural history guides that may be of interest include *Waterberg Flora – Footpaths in and around the Camp* by P Craven & C Marais; *Waterberg Plateau Park* by Ilme Schneider; *Welwitschia – Paradox of a Parched Paradise* by CH Bornman; *Animals of Etosha* by J du Preez; *The Birds of Daan Viljoen Park* and *The Birds of Etosha National Park*, both by RAC Jensen & CF Clinning; and *Etosha – Life & Death on an African Plain* by M Reardon & M Reardon.

If you're concerned with Namibian environmental issues, seek out *Namibia Environment*, which is available from the MET and some bookshops. This is one of the most amazing government publications you'll see in any country. It must have cost a bundle to produce and is loaded with facts, figures, projections, articles and fabulous colour photos.

### Travel

The *Guide to Backpacking & Wilderness Trails* covers hiking and backpacking routes in South Africa and Namibia. The *Guide to Namibian Game Parks* has the lowdown on the national parks, game reserves and other conservation areas. The *Visitors' Guide to Namibia* includes natural history and sites of interest, but practical information and cultural background are limited. All three books are by Willie & Sandra Olivier.

*Horn of Darkness – Rhinos on the Edge* by conservationists Carol Cunningham and Joel Berger describes a journey through the Namibian wilds to find and protect Namibia's remaining desert rhino.

### Souvenir Publications

For stunning photos, you won't beat *Journey Through Namibia* by Mohammed Amin, Duncan Willetts & Tahir Shah.

*Kaokoveld – the Last Wilderness* by Anthony Hall-Martin, J du P Bothma & Clive Walker is a compilation of beguiling photos that will have you making a beeline for north-western Namibia.

*This is Namibia* by Peter Joyce & Gerald Cubitt is mainly a coffee-table book with a range of lovely photos and clear, concise text presenting a wealth of background information. The photographic essay *Skeleton Coast* by Amy Schoemann is also worth a look.

### NEWSPAPERS & MAGAZINES

Six of Namibia's seven main English-language newspapers are published in Windhoek: *The Windhoek Advertiser*, which is published from Monday to Thursday and on Saturday; the biweekly *Namibia Today*; *The Times of Namibia*, published weekdays; *The Namibian*, also published weekdays; the *Windhoek Observer*, published on Saturday; and the government-owned *New Era*. *The Namib Times* is published in Walvis Bay twice weekly. German-language newspapers include the daily *Allgemeine Zeitung* and the Sunday *Namibia Nachrichten*.

The number of papers available is a direct reflection of Namibia's free press policy, which allows all views to be heard. Unfortunately, no Namibian paper is known for its coverage of international events or mastery of journalistic conventions. The readily available South African daily papers are better sources of world news, and some European newspapers, including the London dailies and various large German papers, as well as the *International Herald Tribune* and the *Washington Post*, are available in Windhoek and Swakopmund, together with a full complement of magazines such as *Der Spiegel*, *The Economist*, *Time* and *Newsweek*.

The monthly *Namibia Review* deals mostly with political, cultural and economic issues. It's available by subscription from Namibia Review (☎ (061) 222246; fax 224937), Ministry of Information & Broadcasting, Private Bag 11334, Windhoek.

Women's issues are covered in the bi-monthly magazine *Sister Namibia* (☎ (061) 230618; fax 236371; <sister@windhoek.org.na>), PO Box 40092, 163 Nelson Mandela Ave, Eros, Windhoek. Articles are written by and aimed at women across the entire Namibian social spectrum.

For travel, culture and arts-related articles and advertising, see Air Namibia's in-flight magazine, *Flamingo*. It's available by subscription from Flamingo (☎ (011) 463 3350), PO Box 98034, Sloane Park 2152, South Africa.

### RADIO & TV
The Namibian Broadcasting Corporation (NBC) operates nine radio stations, which broadcast on different wavebands in 12 languages. The national service broadcasts 24 hours a day, with news on the hour every hour between 6 am and 1 am on weekdays. On Saturday, the news is broadcast at 7, 8 and 11 am and 1, 6, 7, 9, 10 and 11 pm and midnight. On Sunday, the news broadcasts are at 8 and 11 am and 1, 7, 9, and 10 pm, and at midnight. German newscasts are also available.

NBC television broadcasts in English and Afrikaans from 5 to 11 pm Monday to Thursday and later on Friday and Saturday. On Sunday, it broadcasts Christian programming from 11 am to 1 pm, then regular programming from 3 pm. News is broadcast at 8 pm nightly. Many people, however, opt for the cable channel MNET, which features international programming.

Only the larger hotels provide TV in rooms, but at some smaller places it's an optional extra. In the big hotels, you can also tune in to CNN and MNET.

### LAUNDRY
Even the smallest hotels have some sort of laundry service and most small towns have a laundry, but self-service laundrettes are scarce outside Windhoek and Swakopmund. Washing facilities are often provided at government camp sites and resorts. Dry-cleaners are found in major towns and charge about US$2 per piece.

### HEALTH
In theory, Namibia's public health care system provides free or very inexpensive health services for all Namibian citizens. In practice, however, public clinics are drastically understaffed and underfunded and nearly everyone who can afford it opts for private health care. Visitors who'd rather avoid waiting in a queue all day to see a doctor will probably want to go the same route, especially since private care in Namibia is of a relatively high standard and is also quite affordable. The best hospital for emergencies or serious problems is probably Rhino Park in Windhoek. Pharmacies, even in the poorer areas of the far north, are generally well stocked and you'll have few problems finding any well known prescription medicine. Dental treatment is probably best handled in Windhoek, Swakopmund or Walvis Bay.

Malaria prophylaxis is recommended for travel in the Caprivi and Kavango regions, the Owambo country and the northern areas of Kunene province, particularly around Epupa Falls. Note also that schistosomiasis (bilharzia) is endemic in Namibia. For further information, see the Health section in the Regional Facts for the Visitor chapter.

### WOMEN TRAVELLERS
Solo female travellers will have few serious security problems, but common sense is still in order. By day, it's generally safe for women to walk around any Namibian town, although in recent years the number of rapes and muggings in Windhoek has increased. Don't walk through isolated areas alone at any time of day, and at night, especially in Windhoek, always take a taxi. In townships, seek local advice regarding areas to avoid.

In Windhoek and other urban areas, wearing shorts and sleeveless dresses or shirts is fine, and even in villages western dress is becoming more popular. However, if you're visiting former tribal areas or mission stations in the north, wear knee-length skirts or loose-fitting trousers. Beach wear is fine in Swakopmund or for lounging around safari lodges but isn't really appropriate elsewhere.

For women hitching, Namibia is safer than Europe and considerably safer than North America (the greatest danger is from drunken drivers). There are still risks, however, which can be lessened by taking precautions such as hitching with a male companion, or at least in pairs.

## USEFUL ORGANISATIONS
In Namibia's post-independence governmental reorganisation, the ministries for tourism and wildlife were combined into the Ministry of Environment & Tourism (MET), which now oversees national parks, game parks and most government-owned resorts. For information contact MET (☎ (061) 233875; Web site www.iwwn .com.na/namtour/namtour.html). For bookings, contact MET (☎ (061) 236975; fax 224900), Private Bag 13267, Windhoek.

For highway information, contact the Automobile Association of Namibia, 15 Carl List House, Independence Ave, PO Box 61, Windhoek 9000 (☎ (061) 224201; fax 222446).

## DANGERS & ANNOYANCES
### Theft
Theft isn't particularly rife in Namibia, but Windhoek, Swakopmund, Tsumeb and Grootfontein do have increasing problems with petty theft and muggings, so it's sensible to conceal your valuables and avoid walking alone at night.

Theft from camp sites is also a problem, particularly near urban areas. Locking up your tent may help, but anything left unattended, even in a vehicle, is still at risk.

### Wildlife
Kavango and Caprivi have lots of mosquitoes, so it's important to take antimalarial precautions. Bilharzia is present in the Kunene, Okavango and Kwando river systems, and bathing isn't recommended. The tsetse fly, present in the eastern Caprivi, is especially active at dusk. Most northern rivers also sustain hippo and crocodile populations that pose dangers to swimmers, anglers and canoeists.

### The Sperrgebiet
En route to Lüderitz from the east, keep well clear of the Sperrgebiet, the prohibited diamond area. Well armed patrols can be overly zealous and aren't interested in asking questions. The area begins immediately south of the A4 Lüderitz-Keetmanshoop road and continues to just west of Aus, where the off-limits boundary turns south towards the Orange River.

## BUSINESS HOURS
Normal business hours are Monday to Friday from 8 am to 1 pm and 2.30 to 5 pm. In early winter, when dusk begins at 3.30 pm, some shops open at 7.30 am and close around 4 pm. Lunch hour closing is almost universal, with only supermarkets in larger towns and restaurants staying open. In towns, most shops open on Saturday from 8 am to 1 pm. Generally, banks and government offices also keep these hours.

In towns, supermarkets generally stay open on weekends, and locally run convenience shops may stay open until late in the evening. Many petrol stations in cities and towns, and along well travelled highways, open 24 hours a day, but in outlying areas it may be hard to find fuel after hours or on Sundays.

## PUBLIC HOLIDAYS & SPECIAL EVENTS
### School & Public Holidays
Resort areas are busiest during both Namibian and South African school holidays. The dates vary, but Namibian holidays normally run from mid-December to mid-January, late April to early June, and the last week in August to the second week in September. School holidays in the South African province of Gauteng, which unleash half the population of Johannesburg, run from early December to mid-January, and during the last week in March and first two weeks of April, the first three weeks in July, and two weeks in the middle of October.

NAMIBIA

Holiday periods in the rest of South Africa will vary from these by about a week in either direction.

Banks and most shops are closed on the following public holidays. When a public holiday falls on a Sunday, the following day also becomes a holiday:

1 January
  *New Year's Day*
March/April
  *Good Friday, Easter Sunday, Easter Monday*
21 March
  *Independence Day*
April/May
  *Ascension Day* (occurs 40 days after Easter)
1 May
  *Workers' Day*
4 May
  *Cassinga Day*
25 May
  *Africa Day*
26 August
  *Heroes' Day*
10 December
  *Human Rights Day*
25 & 26 December
  *Christmas, Family/Boxing Day*

### Special Events

A big event to watch for is Maherero Day, towards the end of August, when the Red Flag Herero gather in traditional dress at Okahandja for a memorial service to the chiefs killed in the Khoi-Khoi and German wars. It takes place on the weekend nearest 26 August. A similar event, also at Oka-handja, is staged by the Mbanderu or Green Flag Herero on the weekend nearest 11 June. On the weekend nearest 10 October, the White Flag Herero gather in Omaruru to honour their chief Zeraua.

The Windhoek Karnival (WIKA) in late April or early May, the Küska (Küste Kar-nival) at Swakopmund in late August or early September, the Windhoek Agricultur-al Show in late September, and the Windhoek Oktoberfest in late October are all major social events, mainly among the European community.

Further information on these events is provided in individual chapters.

### ACTIVITIES

Hiking is a highlight in Namibia, but unless you're on a private guest farm (where farmers often lay out hiking routes for their guests), the best hiking trails (Daan Viljoen Game Reserve, the Naukluft, Fish River Canyon, Waterberg Plateau Park and the Ugab River) are under the control of the MET. Prospective hikers must book and pay for their hikes in advance and group sizes are limited. If you prefer organised techni-cal climbing, contact Roland Graf of the South African Mountaineering Club, Namibia Chapter (☎ (061) 228749 or 234941), in Windhoek.

The latest craze in Namibia is sand-boarding, which is as yet available commercially only in Swakopmund. In the same area, operators offer horse and camel riding, sea kayaking, quad-biking, deep-sea fishing, bird-watching, skydiving and paragliding. White-water rafting is avail-able on the Kunene River, along the Angolan border, and you can opt for either rafting or canoeing through the Orange River canyons on the South African border. See the relevant chapters for details.

### WORK

The chances of a foreigner finding work in Namibia aren't terribly good but, having said that, some people are successful. The official policy is to accept only overseas in-vestors starting up a business in the country or those who can provide skills and exper-tise not available locally. If you are offered a job, you (or better, your prospective em-ployer) must secure a temporary residence permit from the Ministry of Home Affairs (☎ (061) 398 9111; fax 223817), Private Bag 13200, Windhoek.

If you're interested in investing or start-ing a business in Namibia, direct enquiries to the Investment Centre, Ministry of Trade & Industry (☎ (061) 220241), 3rd floor, Government Offices, Private Bag 13340, Windhoek.

A number of overseas volunteer organi-sations – including VSO and the Peace Corps as well as their German, Irish, Canadian, Australian and Scandinavian counterparts – have programmes in Namibia. However, none of these organisations allows volunteers to select their own postings, so your chances of winding up in Namibia will depend on the luck of the draw.

## ACCOMMODATION

The good news is that Namibia not only offers a variety of accommodation for a range of budgets, it's also the best accommodation value in the region. Hotels and other middle and upper-range establishments are graded using a star system determined by MET inspections. Some establishments receive a T-grading, which indicates that they're geared towards foreign visitors. Hotels with restaurants also get a Y rating: YY means it only has a restaurant licence, while YYY indicates full licensing. The annual *Namibia – Accommodation Guide for Tourists* is distributed by tourist offices and agencies.

Accommodation and food are subject to 11% general sales tax, which is included in quoted rates. Some hotels have special off-season rates, so it's worth checking for possible discounts.

For advice or bookings on guest farms and safari lodges, contact the Lodge & Guest Farm Reservation Service (☎ (061) 226979; fax 226999), PO Box 21783, Windhoek, or the Namib Travel Shop (☎ (061) 226174; <nts@iwwn.com.na>), also in Windhoek. For B&B listings, contact the Budget & Home Accommodation Association (☎ (061) 251766) in Windhoek.

### Camping

Most towns have camping grounds, which provide a green spot to pitch a tent or park a caravan. Prices are normally per site, with a maximum of eight people and two vehicles per site. Some places also have bungalows or rondavels as well as a pool, restaurant and shop. There's no central reservations system, but private and municipal sites rarely fill up.

Camping in national parks is restricted to designated sites and bush camping on public land isn't allowed without special permission. The MET enforces this rule strictly and it's definitely wise to keep on the better side of this organisation. For more information, see MET National Parks Camps, Rest Camps & Resorts later in this section. Camping on private or communal land requires permission from the land owner or the nearest village, respectively.

### Backpackers Hostels

There are now several Hostelling International hostels and private backpackers hostels in Windhoek and Swakopmund, and more are planned, including a private hostel for Rundu in the near future. As with hostels anywhere, they provide dormitory accommodation and cooking facilities for very reasonable prices, ranging from US$6 to US$10 per person.

### Hotels

The Namibian hotel classification system rates everything from small guesthouses to four-star hotels.

One-star hotels must have private bathrooms or showers in at least one quarter of the rooms, and at least one communal bathroom or toilet for every eight other beds. They tend to be quite simple, but most are locally owned and managed, and do provide clean, comfortable accommodation with adequate beds and towels. Rates range from around US$20 to US$30 for a double room, with bed and breakfast. They always have a small dining room and bar, but few offer frills, such as air conditioning.

For a two-star rating, at least half the rooms must have private facilities and there must be communal facilities for every seven other rooms. There must also be a heating system, a full-time chef and 14-hour reception service. This is the most common hotel classification and takes in a wide range of establishments. Prices start at around US$35 for a double and climb to US$90 for the more elegant places.

There are only a few three-star hotels, and these must conform to the minimum

NAMIBIA

international standards: private bathrooms, heating, wall-to-wall carpets, a range of public rooms and lounges, 24-hour reception, room service and an à la carte restaurant. Double rates begin at around US$60.

Currently, there are only a couple of four-star hotels in the country, but more are planned. Essentially, to get a four-star rating, a hotel needs to be an air-conditioned palace with all the amenities of a three-star hotel plus a salon, valet service and a range of ancillary services aimed at the business and diplomatic traveller.

Any hotel whose name includes the word *garni* does not have a restaurant and is only equipped to handle simple breakfasts.

### MET National Parks Camps, Rest Camps & Resorts

The MET offers reasonable value at its rest camps and resorts. Camp sites accommodate up to eight people and cost from US$8 for an undeveloped wilderness site to US$21 in a rest camp with a pool, shop, restaurant, kiosk and well maintained ablutions blocks.

The MET also offers a range of other possibilities. All accommodation is self-catering, but most resorts have a restaurant and shop. Linen, towels and soap are normally provided, but guests must bring their own cutlery and cooking gear. National parks accommodation may be occupied from noon on the day of arrival to 10 am on the day of departure.

Prices are determined by the number of rooms and beds and the degree of luxury. For example, a four-bed flat with kitchen facilities, a toilet and a hot shower is US$45; a four-bed hut with communal facilities and a cooking area is just US$28; two/five-bed bungalows with kitchens, toilets and showers cost US$33/45; and a 10-bed dormitory room is US$16. The most expensive option is at Terrace Bay in the Skeleton Coast Park, where single/double accommodation, including all facilities and meals, costs US$90/122.

Namibian citizens receive a 50% discount on park entrance fees (but not on vehicle or accommodation fees) at all MET sites. During school holidays, visitors are limited to three nights at each camp in Etosha National Park and 10 nights at all other camps. Pets aren't permitted in any of the rest camps, but kennels are available at the gates of Daan Viljoen, Von Bach Dam, Gross Barmen, Ai-Ais and Hardap Dam.

You can pre-book accommodation at MET Reservations (☎ (061) 236975; fax 224900; <reservations@iwwn.com.na>), Private Bag 13267, Windhoek. For further details, see Visiting the Parks under Flora & Fauna in the Facts about Namibia chapter.

### Guest Farms

Thanks to recent droughts, many private farms are turning to tourism to keep afloat, and they provide insight into the rural white lifestyle in Namibia. Many have also designated blocks of land as wildlife reserves and offer excellent wildlife-viewing; many also serve as hunting reserves.

With so many guest farms springing up, it's impossible to mention them all but the most outstanding ones are described in the relevant chapters; for a complete listing see *Namibia – Accommodation Guide for Tourists*, which is free from hotels and tourist offices.

Guest farms have a rating system based on a scale of one to three stars. Generally more expensive than hotels, they seldom have more than half a dozen rooms. The emphasis is on personal service, and often there's even a measure of quaint rural luxury.

Advance bookings are essential. You may also want to ascertain whether and when hunting is permitted; some farms have a set 'hunting season' but are open for photography and wildlife-viewing at other times. It's also worth noting that many farmers keep wild animals in zoo-like enclosures, which seems curious given that most farms are attached to game ranches that could only be called vast. If enough visitors question the practice, perhaps farmers will change tack.

**Safari Lodges**

As with other accommodation sectors in Namibia, a new crop of safari lodges is sprouting up all round the country. The majority of these are set on large private ranches and offer luxurious standards of accommodation and superb international cuisine. Currently, Namibian safari lodges offer several advantages over their counterparts in Zimbabwe and Botswana. First of all, there's no multi-tier pricing, so foreigners and Namibians pay the same reasonable rates. A night in a lodge outside Etosha National Park, for example, will cost a third of what you'd pay for comparable accommodation in the Okavango Delta. What's more, prices are usually set per person, with no single supplement charges, so lone travellers aren't penalised.

## FOOD
**Traditional Cuisine**

Each ethnic group has its own pantry of preferred foods. For example, the Owambo people of the north enjoy mielie meal, which is the same cornmeal porridge enjoyed in Zimbabwe, Botswana and all around Africa. The second grain favoured by the Owambo people is *mahango* (millet), which is made into either a porridge or a soup. Both mielies and mahango are typically eaten with fish, goat, lamb or beef stew cooked in a *potjie*, a three-legged black pot. Pumpkins, peppers and onions – particularly the *omavo*, or water onion – also feature prominently in the Owambo diet.

The spiny round *!nara* melon (the exclamation mark is pronounced as a glottal click), which is a member of the cucumber family, grows on vines along watercourses, where it can tap subsurface water. It's a staple of the Nama people of the lower Kuiseb region and may be made into a naturally sweet cake, dried into flour or mashed and fermented to yield a sweet beer. The roots are said to have medicinal properties. Each year during the harvest, the Nama use donkey carts to transport the spiky fruit back to camp to be dried and pre-

pared for consumption. The seeds are removed from the rind and dried for eating. The pulp is spread on the sand to make a kind of chewy cake that preserves well. The museum in Swakopmund has a full rundown on the plant's uses.

Historically, the Herero subsisted mainly on milk products such as curds and butter. They still enjoy these staples to some extent, but nowadays the Herero diet revolves around mielies, meat and locally grown black beans.

Although the San people are now adopting the diet of other Namibians, their traditional diet depended upon their wanderings and the cycle of the seasons. It consisted mainly of various desert plants – wild fruits, nuts, berries and tubers, which ripened in turn – as well as birds' eggs (especially ostrich eggs, one of which can feed an entire clan), lizards, locusts and game hunted with small, poison-tipped arrows.

**European Cuisine**

Outside Windhoek and Swakopmund, Namibia is short of gourmet pretences. Most hotels serve three meals, but menus are almost always meat-orientated and rarely very creative.

For a great treat, try one of the German-style *Konditoreien*, where you can pig out on *Apfelstrudel*, *Sachertorte*, *Schwartzwälder Kirschtorte* and other delicious pastries and cakes. Gathemann's in Windhoek and Café Anton in Swakopmund are national institutions, and Windhoek, Swakopmund, Lüderitz and other towns also have pleasant cafés and small coffee shops. You may also want to try Afrikaner *koeksesters* and *melktart*.

Cooked breakfasts always include bacon and *boerewors* (farmer's sausage – few foreigners get through more than one of these), and don't be surprised to find something bizarre – curried kidneys, for example – alongside your eggs. Some people still eat beef for breakfast.

Small hotels normally provide a cooked breakfast with cereal and toast, and most

NAMIBIA

big hotels include a buffet breakfast in the room price. In addition to the usual English breakfast constituents, they may also include such delights as kippers (smoked kingklip), porridge and a range of German breads, cold meats, cereals and fruit. If you take full advantage of what's on offer, you may not have to eat again for the rest of the day.

One of the cheapest lunch options is a takeaway snack. Takeaway favourites include fish and chips, meat pies, and sandwiches made with a German-style bread roll known as a *Brötchen* (little bread).

Evening meals feature meat – normally beef – and carnivores will enjoy the typically high-quality cuts served in restaurants. A huge fillet steak will set you back about US$8. Fish, almost always kingklip, is best eaten in Swakopmund or Lüderitz where there's a good chance of it being fresh. Chicken is most often prepared with a fiery peri-peri sauce.

### Fruit & Vegetables

Namibia's small fruit and vegetable crops ripen during the winter season, roughly from May to September. At other times, fresh fruit and vegetables must be imported from South Africa and are quite expensive, so Namibians aren't great connoisseurs of fresh produce and vegetarianism hasn't really caught on. As a result, chips are the most popular potato incarnation and green vegetables are served sparingly and often from a tin or the deep freeze.

Among the most popular fresh vegetables are gems squash, a small and delicious green squash; pumpkin; and butternut squash, which resembles a gourd. Fruit is generally expensive, but in season the oranges are delicious. In the Kavango region, papayas are picked with a 6m pole and a basket to catch them, and are served with a squeeze of lemon or lime.

For longer road trips, you can buy fruit in bulk at Windhoek supermarkets, at the open market in Tal Strasse or at one of the wholesalers in the North Windhoek Industrial Estate. Fruit is also sold at roadside stalls in

northern Namibia and occasionally elsewhere.

### Self-Catering

All major towns have at least one supermarket selling basic necessities. Because groceries become more expensive the further you move from Windhoek, it's wise to stock up with provisions before setting out on a tour of the country. Many places also have corner shops, often Portuguese owned, which sell everything from animal feed to spit-roasted chicken.

You'll find the best variety of meat and sausage, or *wors*, at the *slagtery* (butcher shop). Biltong (dried meat in strips or shavings), either beef or *wildsbiltong* (normally gemsbok or ostrich), comes in several shapes and sizes. There is also a variety of German salami and smoked meats, as well as an utterly solid 15cm variety known as *Landjäger*. It's normally gnawed like a bone, but it's cheap, tasty and lasts a long time.

Cheese is expensive and there's little variety; Edam is the most popular type. Campers may want to buy tinned feta, which last longer than plastic-wrapped cheeses.

### DRINKS
### Nonalcoholic Drinks

Tap water is safe to drink but in some places it may emerge rather salty and unpalatable, especially around the desert areas and Etosha. Bottled water is expensive and is available in 1L containers.

Packaged fruit juices provide an alternative; the best are the locally produced Ceres juices, which are 100% natural juice. Another popular brand from South Africa is Liquifruit. Both brands offer apricot, peach, mango-pineapple and combinations. Peach juice mixed with sparkling wine makes a refreshing cocktail. The cheapest are orange and guava juice.

Every takeaway place serves coffee and tea – including an insipid herbal tea known as *rooibos* (red bush), which reputedly has therapeutic properties. Both Windhoek and

Swakopmund have several particularly fine coffee shops.

## Alcohol

You'll always find a pleasant place for a drink. All Namibian hotels have an attached bar and some larger hotels feature a beer garden with table service. Many serve food as well as drink, but some open only in the evening. The bars in smaller, inexpensive hotels, however, are less sophisticated, and away from the cities and tourist lodges, you won't find cocktails or mixed drinks. Many cafés also serve wine and beer. On Sunday outside of licensing hours, alcoholic drinks are available only at hotel bars.

Alcohol must be bought from a *drank-winkel* (bottle store); standard opening hours are weekdays from 8 am to 6 pm and Saturday from 8.30 am to 1 pm.

**Beer** Namibia's dry heat makes an ideal environment for beer drinkers and the country's greatest producer of the amber fluid is Namibia Breweries (formerly South-West Breweries). Certainly the most popular drop is Windhoek Lager, a light lager-style beer that is distinct and refreshing. It comes in standard lager strength, packaged in cans and bottles of varying sizes from a 375mL *dumpi* (equivalent to the Australian stubby) to a 'large' 500mL bottle. A dumpi costs from US$0.75 to US$1.25 in a beer garden; drankwinkels charge US$10 or so for a tray of 24 bottles. Namibia Breweries also produces the stronger and more bitter Windhoek Export, the slightly rough Windhoek Special, and Windhoek Light, which has a 1.9% alcohol content but is still quite agreeable. Guinness Extra Stout is also brewed under licence.

Windhoek's main competitor is Hansa, in Swakopmund, which produces both standard and export strength. South African beers like Lion, Castle and Black Label are also widely available.

When you're camping in the wilderness, an excellent means of cooling a beer or soft drink without refrigeration is to soak a sock in water, place the cans or bottles inside and tie it from a branch – or even your side mirrors. The contents are cooled as heat is drawn away from the liquid to provide energy for evaporation – and it really works.

**Wine** You'll also find a range of typically excellent South African wines. Most bottle stores stock everything from 750mL bottles to large 1 to 5L boxes and economy-size 1 or 2L jars. South African red wines definitely have the edge; among the best are the Cabernet and Pinot varieties grown in the Stellenbosch region of Western Cape Province. Nederberg Winery produces particularly good wines, which are available in both 250 and 750mL bottles.

**Liqueur** An excellent speciality liqueur is Amarula Cream, which is distilled in South Africa from the marula fruit. It tastes a bit like Bailey's Irish Cream – but arguably better – and is best chilled or served over ice.

**Traditional Brews** In the rural Owambo areas, people socialise in tiny makeshift bars, enjoying such inexpensive local brews as *mahango* (millet beer, which is excellent), *mataku* (watermelon wine), *tambo* or *mushokolo* (a beer made from a type of small seed), and *walende*, which is distilled from the *makalani* palm and tastes similar to vodka. All of these concoctions, except walende, are brewed in the morning and drunk the same day, and they're all dirt cheap, costing only around US$0.10 per glass.

## ENTERTAINMENT

Naturally, Namibia's entertainment capital is Windhoek, with a range of bars, discos and nightclubs to suit every taste. The capital also offers cinemas, theatre productions, concerts and sporting events. The beach resort of Swakopmund, with several discos and a light-hearted atmosphere, is a favourite with Namibia's more affluent youth.

In northern Namibia, the local social

**NAMIBIA**

scene is dominated by the hundreds of cuca shops (small bush shops selling beer), bush bars, bottle stores and roadside discos and nightclubs. At the bush bars, you can enjoy popular traditional alcoholic brews such as mahango and tambo, along with a bit of relaxation and conversation. Especially in Owambo areas, both men and women participate in these sessions.

## THINGS TO BUY

Potential souvenirs range from kitsch African curios and art on sale at the airport to superb Owambo basketry and Kavango woodcarvings. Most of the items sold along Post Street Mall in Windhoek are cheap curios imported from Zimbabwe; in Victoria Falls, you'll find the same things at a fraction of the price. Along the highway between Rundu and Grootfontein, roadside stalls sell locally produced items, from woven mats and baskets to the appealing wooden aeroplanes and helicopters that are a Kavango speciality. In Rundu and other areas of the north-east, you'll find distinctive San material arts – bows and arrows, ostrich-egg beads, leather pouches and jewellery made from seeds and nuts.

The pastel colours of the Namib provide inspiration for a number of local artists, and many galleries in Windhoek and Swakopmund specialise in local paintings and sculpture. Also, some lovely items are produced in conjunction with the karakul wool industry, such as rugs, wall hangings and textiles, which are often made to order. Windhoek is the centre of the upmarket leather industry, and there you'll find high-quality products, from belts and handbags to beautiful made-to-measure leather jackets. Beware, however, of items made from crocodile or other protected species,

and note that those comfortable shoes known as *Swakopmunders* are made from kudu leather. Several shops have now stopped selling them.

Minerals and gemstones are also popular purchases, either in the raw form or cut and polished as jewellery, sculptures or carvings. Malachite, amethyst, chalcedony, aquamarine, tourmaline, jasper and rose quartz are among the most beautiful. Chess sets and other art objects are made from marble quarried near Karibib. A good spot for an honest deal is the House of Gems near the corner of Stübel Strasse and John Meinert Strasse in Windhoek.

For something different, you may want to look for an *ekipa*, a traditional medallion historically worn by Owambo women as a sign of wealth and status. They were worn in strings hung from the waist and were originally made from ivory or hippopotamus tooth but later carved from bone, wood or vegetable ivory (the fruit of the makalani palm). Early ekipa were buried in urine-soaked earth to achieve the necessary yellowed effect, and were decorated with geometric designs. They're available in a few speciality shops in Windhoek and Swakopmund.

Buying souvenirs made from protected wild species – cheetah, leopard, elephant or (heaven forbid) rhino – isn't necessary or ethically defensible. In Windhoek and other places, you'll see lots of ivory pieces and jewellery for sale, but anything that is imported from Hong Kong is of dubious origin and should be avoided. The only legitimate stuff is clearly marked as culled ivory from Namibian national parks. Still, it's probably better to avoid ivory altogether and stop fuelling the trade that makes poaching (and culling) profitable.

# Getting There & Away

## AIR

South African Airways (SAA) operates daily flights between Johannesburg, Cape Town and Windhoek international airport, which lies about 42km east of the city.

Air Namibia has daily flights from Windhoek's in-town Eros airport to and from Alexander Bay, the airport for Oranjemund. A single fare to Johannesburg or Cape Town costs around US$175. Air Namibia also flies to Windhoek twice weekly from Harare, Lusaka, Maun and Gaborone.

## LAND
### Border Crossings

There are border control posts between Namibia and Botswana at the following locations: Ngoma Bridge (open 7 am to 6 pm), Buitepos/Mamuno (open 6 am to 6 pm), Mohembo/Mahango (6 am to 7 pm) and Mpalila Island/Kasane (7.30 am to 12.30 pm and 1.45 to 4.30 pm). The only border post between Namibia and Zambia is at Wenela/Sesheke (6 am to 7 pm), 4km north of Katima Mulilo.

Traffic between South Africa and Namibia can cross at Velloorsdrift-Onseepkans/Pofadder (open 6 am to 10 pm), Karasburg/Noenieput (open 6 am to 5 pm), Nakop/Ariamsvlei (24 hours), Hohlweg-Aroab/Rietfontein (also 24 hours), Klein Menasse-Aroab/Rietfontein (7 am to 9 pm) or Noordoewer/Vioolsdrif (24 hours). This last option is on the main tarred road between Windhoek and Cape Town. There's no public access between Alexander Bay and Oranjemund without first getting permission from the diamond company CDM; the border crossing is open from 6 am to 10 pm.

### Angola

There are three border crossings to Angola, at Ruacana/Koaleck/Concor, Oshikango/Santa Clara/Namacunda and Rundu/Calai (which is often closed due to unrest), but you need an Angolan visa permitting overland entry. See the Angolan consulate (☎ (061) 227535), Angola House, 3 Auspann Strasse, Private Bag 12020, Windhoek.

At Ruacana Falls, you can enter the falls area temporarily without a visa; just sign in at the border post. It's also often possible to cross for the day between Oshikango and Santa Clara without a visa.

### Botswana

The Trans-Kalahari Highway from Windhoek to Botswana, via Gobabis, crosses the border at Buitepos/Mamuno. A weekly Star Line bus (US$11) leaves Gobabis on Friday at 7.30 am. It arrives at the Buitepos border at 10.30 am and in Ghanzi, Botswana, at 2 pm. Between Gaborone and Windhoek, Intercape Mainliner has a bus three times weekly for US$67.

At Buitepos, on the Namibian side, the clean and friendly *East Gate Service Station & Rest Camp* has inexpensive camp sites and bungalows, and is especially handy for hitchers who've missed the 5pm border closing. The Mamuno side is little but a dusty spot at the border post where you can pitch a tent.

You can also cross between Namibia and Botswana via the Caprivi Strip at either Ngoma Bridge or Mohembo (note that neither of these crossings is open to motorcycles, as they require passing through Chobe National Park and Mahango Game Reserve, respectively). Sparse traffic makes hitching unreliable, but you'll eventually get through. The crossing between Mpalila Island and Kasane is mainly used by guests of tourist lodges on the island.

The Windhoek-Victoria Falls buses that pass through Kasane are an option for those wanting to reach northern Botswana. For more information see the Zimbabwe section later in this chapter.

## South Africa

**Bus** A luxury Intercape Mainliner (☎ (061) 227847) service from Windhoek to Capetown (US$90) or Johannesburg (US$92) runs four times weekly. In South Africa, book through the offices in Cape Town (☎ (021) 386 4400) or Johannesburg (☎ (011) 333 5231). In Windhoek, the office is on Gallilei St.

Econolux (☎ (064) 205935), in Walvis Bay, leaves for Cape Town at 7.30 am on Friday from Swakopmund (US$75) and at 12.30 pm from Windhoek (US$60). It returns on Sunday. Rates include meals. In Windhoek, book through Ritz Reisen (☎ (061) 236670).

**Train** Rail services between Namibia and South Africa have been discontinued.

**Car & Motorcycle** You can drive to Namibia along good tarred roads from South Africa, either from Cape Town in the south, crossing the border at Noordoewer, or from Johannesburg in the east, in which case the border crossing is at Nakop. An alternative route is the gravel road into south-eastern Namibia between Rietfontein and Aroab.

**Hitching** Hitching is easiest with trucks but most drivers want payment, so agree on a price before climbing aboard. After bargaining, the standard rate is around US$1.50 per 100km.

## Zambia

The only crossing between Namibia and Zambia is via the Zambezi pontoon ferry at Wenela/Sesheke, which is open from 6 am to 7 pm daily. A bridge is planned in the next few years, but don't hold your breath. (An alternative route involves crossing into Botswana at Ngoma Bridge, transiting through Chobe National Park and using the Kazungula ferry into Zambia; see Botswana, earlier in this chapter.)

From Sesheke, buses leave at around 7 am and 1 pm and travel over a horribly pot-holed road to Livingstone (US$6 to US$8), five to seven hours away. From Livingstone, buses leave at 8 am and 2 pm daily. Check whether your bus terminates at Sesheke or continues to the border.

The pontoon ferry over the Zambezi (free for pedestrians, US$15 per foreign-registered car) lies about 6km from Katima Mulilo, Namibia, and 5km from Sesheke, Zambia. When it isn't operating, passengers are carried across on canoes free of charge (paddlers are paid by the local council). The Zambian border post lies 500m from the ferry crossing and the Namibian post is 1km away; there are banks in both Sesheke and Katima Mulilo.

## Zimbabwe

There's no direct border crossing between Namibia and Zimbabwe: to get there you must take the Chobe National Park transit route from Ngoma Bridge through northern Botswana to Kasane/Kazungula, and from there to Victoria Falls.

A reliable option is the Nam-Vic Shuttle (☎ (081) 124 7297), which leaves Windhoek's Grab-a-Phone bus terminal at 6 pm on Thursday and arrives in Victoria Falls on Friday at lunchtime. From Victoria Falls, it leaves the Phumula Centre car park on Sunday at 1 pm and arrives in Windhoek on Monday at 8 pm. Book directly or through Windhoek backpackers lodges, the tourist office or Trip Travel. The fare is US$155 one-way and US$310 return.

Its competitor, Namibia-Vic Falls Travel (☎ (081) 124 9839 or (067) 234364), leaves Windhoek's Grab-a-Phone bus terminal on Tuesday at 6 pm and arrives in Victoria Falls at lunchtime on Wednesday. It leaves from Wimpy Corner in Victoria Falls on Friday at 6 pm and arrives in Windhoek/ Swakopmund on Saturday/Sunday afternoon. Between Windhoek/Swakopmund and Victoria Falls costs US$140/300.

The Central Coach Express (☎ (061) 248724) has a 5 pm Friday service from Windhoek's Grab-a-Phone terminal to Victoria Falls (US$50) and Harare (US$90).

# Getting Around

## AIR
### Domestic Air Services
Air Namibia services domestic routes mainly from Eros airport in Windhoek, although a few domestic flights use Windhoek international airport. There are flights to and from Tsumeb; Rundu and Katima Mulilo; Keetmanshoop; Lüderitz and Alexander Bay (South Africa); and Swakopmund and Oshakati.

**Air Namibia Offices** Air Namibia has the following offices:

Central Reservations, Windhoek (☎ (061) 298 2552; fax 221382)

Eros Airport, Windhoek (☎ (061) 238220; fax 236460)

Gustav Voigts Centre, Independence Ave, Windhoek (☎ (061) 229630; fax 228763)

International Airport, Windhoek (☎ (0626) 40315; fax 40367)

Katima Mulilo (☎/fax (0677) 191)

Keetmanshoop (☎ (0631) 2337; fax 292290)

Lüderitz (☎ (06331) 2850; fax 2845)

Oshakati (☎ (06751) 20284; fax 21230)

Oranjemund (☎ (06332) 2764; fax 2225)

Rundu (☎ (0671) 55854)

Swakopmund (☎ (064) 404123; fax 402196)

Tsumeb (☎ (067¹) 20520; fax 20821)

Walvis Bay (☎ (064) 203102; fax 202928)

### Air Charter
Namibia has a few air charter operations, but they tend to be expensive. Among them are Bay Air (☎ (064) 204319) in Walvis Bay; Namibia Commercial Aviation (☎ (061) 223562), Bush Pilots Namibia (☎ (061) 248316) – who even have a Tiger Moth – and Desert Air (☎ (061) 228101; fax 254345) in Windhoek; and Atlantic Air (☎ (064) 404749; fax 405832; <aviation@iml.com.na>) at 5 Roon Strasse in Swakopmund.

Return prices for up to five passengers would be about US$1650 from Eros to Victoria Falls, US$1975 from Eros to Etosha, and US$700 from Eros to Swakopmund.

## BUS
Namibia's bus services aren't extensive. Luxury services are limited to the Intercape Mainliner (☎ (061) 227847), which has scheduled services between Windhoek, Cape Town, Johannesburg, Swakopmund and Walvis Bay. You're allowed only two items of baggage, which must not exceed a total of 30kg. Fares include meals.

The rail service, Trans-Namib, has an expanding system of Star Line buses that not only replace defunct rail services, but also tie in places never connected by rail: Lüderitz, Bethanie, Gochas, Buitepos, Ghanzi (Botswana), Helmeringhausen, Outjo, Kamanjab, Opuwo, Khorixas, Henties Bay, Grootfontein, Oshakati and Rundu. There's also a route across the central Namib between Mariental and Walvis Bay.

There are also local minibuses that run up and down the B1 from Oshakati to Keetmanshoop. Minibuses depart when full and fares work out at around US$0.03 per kilometre, plus US$2 per large piece of luggage. From Windhoek, they depart for Swakopmund and Walvis Bay from the Rhino Park petrol station. Going south to Rehoboth, Mariental and Keetmanshoop, they leave from the car park north of the Wernhill Park centre. Those heading north to the Owambo areas, Kavango and Caprivi leave from the Singles' Quarters in Katutura township (for this last option, it's safer to wait on the bridge at the Independence Ave on-ramp to the Western Bypass). There are additional services from Windhoek on Friday afternoons, especially on the route north to the Owambo region; extra southbound services run on Sunday afternoons.

## TRAIN
Trans-Namib Railways operates a reasonable rail network that connects most of the major towns, but trains are slow – as one reader remarked, moving 'at the pace of an

energetic donkey cart'. In addition, passenger and freight cars are mixed on the same train, and trains tend to stop at every post.

On the other hand, rail travel isn't popular and services are rarely fully booked. Trains carry economy and business class seats but, although most services run overnight, sleepers are no longer available. Book at railway stations or through the Windhoek Booking Office (☎ (061) 2982032). Tickets must be collected before 4 pm on the day of departure. They're fully refundable up to 48 hours before departure, and 50% thereafter.

Windhoek is Namibia's rail hub, with services south to Keetmanshoop and Ariamsvlei, north to Tsumeb, west to Swakopmund and Walvis Bay and east to Gobabis. Regular fares (which are quoted in this book) are valid from Thursday to Monday; on Tuesday and Wednesday, fares are a third lower while at peak periods, such as holidays, they're a third more.

## CAR & MOTORCYCLE

The easiest way to get around Namibia is by road. An excellent system of tarred roads runs the entire length of the country from the South African border at Noordoewer to Katima Mulilo in the north-east and Ruacana in the north-west. Similarly, tarred spur roads connect the main north-south routes to Gobabis, Lüderitz, Swakopmund and Walvis Bay. Elsewhere, towns and most sites of interest are accessible on good gravel roads. Most B- and C-numbered highways are well maintained and passable to all vehicles, and D-numbered roads, although a bit rougher, are mostly (but not always) passable to 2WD vehicles. In the Kaokoveld, however, most D-numbered roads require 4WD.

As in the rest of southern Africa, vehicles keep to the left. The general speed limit of 120km/h applies on open roads, and in built-up areas it's 60km/h. Drivers and front-seat passengers must use seat belts. Petrol currently costs around US$0.50 per litre.

Theoretically, foreign drivers need an international driving licence in Namibia, but in practice a valid driving licence from your home country is usually sufficient. Note that motorbikes aren't permitted in the national parks, with the exception of the main highway routes through Namib-Naukluft Park.

### Rental

If you have a group to split the costs, car hire is probably the best way to get around. Remember to add the collision damage waiver, stamp duty and 10% general sales tax (GST) to the advertised daily rate and per kilometre charge. Because vehicles are in limited supply, book your car well in advance. Note that agencies are open only on weekdays during office hours.

To drive a Namibian hire car into a neighbouring country, you must have a police permit. To enter South Africa, Botswana or elsewhere in the Southern African Customs Union, you need a Blue Book sheet outlining the vehicle's particulars, such as the engine's serial number. If you're continuing to Zimbabwe, request proof of insurance and all the paperwork necessary to get a Zimbabwean temporary import permit.

The least expensive companies typically charge from US$55 to US$75 per day with unlimited kilometres (some have a minimum rental period) for a basic compact car. Most require a completed credit card slip or a US$225 (N$1000) cash deposit, and won't hire out to anyone under the age of 25. Note that you can't carry more than three people in the cheapest Group A car; groups of four must hire a Group B car (if you ignore this regulation and roll the car, your insurance will be void and you'll be liable for the entire value of the vehicle). Many agencies also hire out 4WD vehicles, and some can even equip your safari with all the gear you'll need.

It's normally cheaper to hire a car in South Africa and drive it to Namibia, but that requires permission from the car hire agency. Some larger agencies use travellers to return vehicles to Cape Town for just the cost of the petrol. However, you're normally limited to 24 hours for the journey.

Hiring a 4WD vehicle opens up remote parts of the country, but it can get expensive. Camping Car Hire charges US$115 per day (minimum five days hire) with unlimited kilometres. Enyandi Car Hire (probably Namibia's best car hire deal) in Otjiwarongo charges US$94 per day, including insurance, for a minimum of three days.

When hiring a vehicle, ask specifically what sort of repairs will be your responsibility, and whether or not you'll be charged

## Gravel Roads

Many main highways in Namibia are surfaced with unsealed gravel, which for drivers can be at best tricky and at worst treacherous. In fact, the high price of car hire relates directly to the number of cars rolled by foreigners who are inexperienced at driving on gravel roads. The following points may help:

- Keep your speed down to a maximum of 100km/h.
- Maximise your control by keeping both hands on the steering wheel.
- Follow ruts made by other vehicles.
- If the road is corrugated, gradually increase your speed until you find the correct speed – it'll be obvious when the rattling stops.
- Be especially careful on bends; if a curve is signposted, slow right down before attempting the turn.
- You don't meet other cars very often, but when you do, it's like dust clouds passing in the night. When a vehicle approaches from the opposite direction, reduce your speed and keep as far left as possible. On remote roads, it's customary to wave at the other driver as you pass.
- Keep your tyre pressure slightly lower than you would when driving on tarred roads.
- Try to avoid travelling at night when dust and distance may create confusing mirages.
- In rainy weather, gravel roads can turn to quagmires and desert washes may fill with water. If you're uncertain about the water depth in a wash, don't cross until it drains off.
- Be on the lookout for animals. Kudu, in particular, often bound into the road unexpectedly, resulting in an unpleasant meeting.
- Avoid swerving sharply or braking suddenly on a gravel road or you risk losing control of the vehicle. If the rear wheels begin to skid, steer gently into the direction of the skid until you regain control. If the front wheels skid, take a firm hand on the wheel and steer in the opposite direction of the skid.
- Dust permeates everything on gravel roads; wrap your food, clothing and camera equipment in dust-proof plastic or keep them in sealed containers. To minimise dust inside the vehicle, pressurise the interior by closing the windows and turning on the blower.
- In dusty conditions, switch on your headlights so you can be more easily seen. Overtaking (passing) can be extremely dangerous because your view may be obscured by flying dust kicked up by the car ahead. Try to gain the attention of the driver in front by flashing your high beams, which will indicate that you want to overtake (this isn't considered obnoxious in Namibia). If someone behind you flashes their lights, move as far to the left as possible. If you can see that it's safe for them to overtake, flash your left turn indicator. (Beware, however, that some drivers confuse their left and right, or don't fully understand the concept of signalling, so never rely on such signals from other drivers. Don't overtake until you can see the road ahead!)

NAMIBIA

for a 'valet' (cleaning the car) after the hire period. Try to limit it to just tyre punctures and window damage, as agencies may try to use your deposit for anything from wheel alignment and oil changes to cleaning dust from the back seat.

If you don't have an unlimited kilometres deal and are paying by credit card, insist on a copy of the contract so you'll know the charge for any excess kilometres. If you're paying a cash deposit and want to return the car just before you fly out, ensure that the deposit will be repaid in a currency you can use outside the country and not as a cheque for Namibian currency!

**Rental Agencies** Here's a list of most of the vehicle hire agencies in Namibia:

*Asco Car Hire*, 10 Diehl St, Southern Industrial Area, PO Box 40214, Windhoek (☎ (061) 233064; fax 232245; <asco@iafrica.com.na>)

*Auto Garage Car Hire*, PO Box 5166, Windhoek (☎ (061) 226681; fax 224718)

*Badger's Car Hire*, PO Box 544, Bismarck Strasse, Lüderitz (☎/fax (063) 202334)

*Britz Car Hire*, 4 Eros Rd, Eros, Windhoek (☎ (061) 250654; fax 250653)

*Budget*, 72 Mandume Ndemufayo Ave, PO Box 1754, Windhoek (☎ (061) 228720; fax 227665)
  Kaiser Wilhelm Strasse, Swakopmund (☎ (064) 404118; fax 404117)
  18th St, Nechville, Walvis Bay (☎ (064) 204624; fax 202931)

*Camping Car Hire*, 36 Joule St, Southern Industrial Area, PO Box 5526, Windhoek (☎ (061) 237756; fax 237757; <carhire@iwwn.com.na>)

*Caprivi Car Hire*, 8 Chopin St, PO Box 1837, Windhoek (☎ (061) 232871; fax 232374; <caprivi@iafrica.com.na>)

*Continental Self Drives*, PO Box 11115, Klein Windhoek, Windhoek (☎ (081) 124 8280; fax (061) 248280; <contisd@iafrica.com.na>; Web site www.nam.lia.net/natron/tour/rechter/cch.htm)

*Elena Car Hire*, PO Box 3127, Windhoek (☎/fax (061) 244443; <elena@iwwn.com.na>)

*Enyandi Car Hire*, PO Box 264, Otjiwarongo (☎ (0651) 303898 or (061) 232793; fax (0651) 303892; <enyandi@lianam.lia.net>; Web site www.nam.lia.net/natron/tour/enyandi/care.htm)

*Imperial Car Rental*, 43 Stübel St, Windhoek (☎ (061) 227103; fax 222721)
  Windhoek Airport (☎ (0626) 540278; fax 540046)
  Trek Service Station, 10th St, Walvis Bay (☎ (064) 207391; fax 207407)
  Shop 9, Oranjemund (☎ (06332) 2764; fax 2225)
  Travel North Namibia, Tsumeb (☎ (0671) 220728; fax 220916)

*Into Namibia Car & 4x4 Hire*, Le Pardiz Centre, 90 Sam Nujoma Drive, Klein Windhoek, PO Box 31551, Windhoek (☎ (061) 253591; fax 253593)
  1 Moltke St, Swakopmund (☎ (064) 464137; fax 464158)

*Kalahari Car Hire*, 109 Daan Bekker St, PO Box 1525, Olympia, Windhoek (☎ (061) 252690; fax 253083)

*Leopard Car & Camper Hire*, PO Box 22731, Windhoek (☎/fax (061) 236113; <leopard@nam.lia.net>; Web site www.natron.net/tour/leopard/leopard.htm)

*Leopard Travel & Tours*, PO Box 22731, Windhoek (☎/fax (061) 236113)

*Odyssey Car Hire*, 36 Joule St, Southern Industrial Area, PO Box 20938, Windhoek (☎ (061) 223269; fax 228911; <odyssey@iwwn.com.na>; Web site www.iwwn.com.na/odyssey/odyssey.html)

*Pegasus Car & Camper Hire*, Mona & Norbert Irlich, 11 Louis Raymond, PO Box 21104, Windhoek (☎ (061) 251451; fax 223423)

*Rent-a-Land-Rover*, PO Box 86, Henties Bay (☎/fax (064) 500164)

*Rent-a-Safari Automobile*, PO Box 5976, Windhoek (☎ (061) 235328; fax 233795)

*Rundu Tourism Centre*, PO Box 519, Rundu (☎ (067) 255910; fax 255909)

*Savanna Car Rental*, 57 John Meinert Strasse, PO Box 105, Windhoek (☎ (061) 227778; fax 223292; <scr@nam.lia.net>)

*Woodway Camper Hire*, Trans-Kalahari Caravan Park, PO Box 11084, Windhoek (☎ (061) 222877; fax 220335; <woodway@nam.lia.net>)

## HITCHING

Hitching opportunities in Namibia aren't bad, but hitching is illegal in national parks and there's little traffic on wide open highways, so expect long waits. On the other hand, it isn't unusual to get a lift of 1000km in the same car.

Lifts wanted and offered are advertised

daily on Windhoek radio (☎ (061) 291311) and at the Cardboard Box Backpackers in Windhoek. At the Ministry of Environment and Tourism (MET) office, also in Windhoek, there's a notice board with shared car hire and lifts offered and wanted. Truck drivers generally expect to be paid so agree on a price beforehand – the standard charge is US$1.50 per 100km. Due to light traffic, hitching through the Caprivi is especially slow.

For warnings about hitching, see the Hitching section in the Zimbabwe Getting Around chapter.

## LOCAL TRANSPORT
### To/From the Airport
A regular bus service connects Windhoek international airport with Eros airport and the Grab-a-Phone bus terminal in Windhoek city centre. Buses run to connect with both arriving and departing flights.

Taxis between the international airport and Windhoek city centre are quite expensive – approximately US$18 – and impractical when the bus is so convenient (unless you have three people to share a taxi). Taxis sometimes meet arriving flights at Eros airport; if you don't find one, you'll have to call one from the telephone box.

### Bus
In Windhoek, a network of local buses connects the city centre with outlying townships. They don't run according to a definite schedule, but you'll have the most luck in the morning and late afternoon, when people are travelling to and from work. Your best bet is to start walking towards your destination and ask locals where to find a bus stop and how frequently the buses run.

### Taxi
In Windhoek, the main taxi stand is at the Grab-a-Phone (☎ (061) 237070) bus terminal, opposite the Kalahari Sands Hotel. It's better, however, to stop a taxi on the street (difficult), pick one up at the Wernhill Park centre, or simply order one by telephone. This is especially true for anyone arriving at the Grab-a-Phone on the airport bus. The standard taxi fare within Windhoek is approximately US$0.50 to anywhere within the city, including Khomasdal and Katutura, but drivers will think up all sorts of add-on charges if they think you're an ignorant tourist. If you need a taxi in the wee hours of the night, it's best to book it beforehand.

Only in Windhoek are taxis common – no other place is big enough to warrant extensive services. To get a taxi from a provincial airport or railway station, look for business cards attached to telephone boxes.

## ORGANISED TOURS
For details of operators organising tours in Namibia, see the Organised Tours chapter earlier in the book.

# Windhoek

Namibia's Central Highlands are dominated by its small, German-influenced capital, Windhoek. Set at the geographical heart of Namibia, it serves as the road and rail crossroads and the centre of the country's business and commerce. Set among low hills at an elevation of 1660m it enjoys dry, clean air and a healthy highland climate. Its 160,000 people reflect the country's ethnic mix: on the streets, you'll see Owambo, Kavango, Herero, Damara and Caprivian people, together with Nama, San, coloureds and Europeans, all contributing to the hustle and bustle.

## History

Windhoek has existed for just over a century, but its history is as colourful as its population. The original settlement, in what is now Klein Windhoek, was called Aigams or 'fire waters' by the Nama, and Otjomuise, the 'smoky place', by the Herero. The two names refer to the hot springs that attracted early tribal attention and settlement. On a visit in 1836, British prospector Sir James Alexander took the liberty of renaming it Queen Adelaide's Bath, although it's fairly certain the monarch never did soak there. In 1840, Nama leader Jan Jonker Afrikaner and his followers arrived and again changed the name, this time to Winterhoek, after the Cape Province farm where he was born.

The modern name Windhoek, or windy corner, was corrupted from the original Winterhoek during the German colonial occupation. At that time, it became the headquarters for the German Schutztruppe, which ostensibly charged with brokering peace between the warring Herero and Nama. For over 10 years at the turn of the century, Windhoek served as the administrative capital of German South West Africa.

In 1902, a narrow-gauge railway was built to connect Windhoek to the coast at

Swakopmund, and the city experienced a sudden spurt of growth. During this period it began to evolve into the business, commercial and administrative centre of the country, although the city wasn't officially founded until 1965. Windhoek is now home to all Namibia's government offices, as well as most of the country's commercial concerns.

## Orientation

Windhoek isn't a typical African city, but could be considered interesting and even attractive. The city centre grid pattern is characterised by a blend of German colonial

618

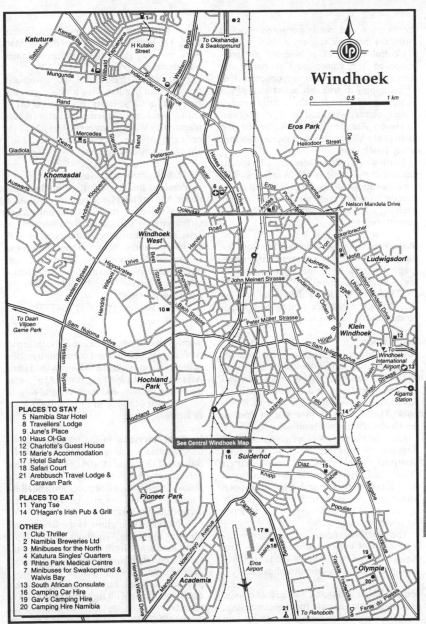

# Windhoek

0        0.5        1 km

**PLACES TO STAY**
5   Namibia Star Hotel
8   Travellers' Lodge
9   June's Place
10  Haus Ol-Ga
12  Charlotte's Guest House
15  Marie's Accommodation
17  Hotel Safari
18  Safari Court
21  Arebbusch Travel Lodge &
    Caravan Park

**PLACES TO EAT**
11  Yang Tse
14  O'Hagan's Irish Pub & Grill

**OTHER**
1   Club Thriller
2   Namibia Breweries Ltd
3   Minibuses for the North
4   Katutura Singles' Quarters
6   Rhino Park Medical Centre
7   Minibuses for Swakopmund &
    Walvis Bay
13  South African Consulate
16  Camping Car Hire
19  Gav's Camping Hire
20  Camping Hire Namibia

NAMIBIA

architecture and candy-coloured modern buildings that look vaguely edible.

Central Windhoek is bisected by Independence Ave, where most shopping and administrative functions are concentrated. The shopping district is focused on the Post St pedestrian mall and the nearby Gustav Voigts centre, Wernhill Park centre and Levinson Arcade. Zoo Park, beside the main post office, provides a green lawn and shady lunch spots.

North along Independence Ave lie the industrial expanses of North Windhoek. The suburbs sprawl across the hills which circle the city affording impressive views, but immediately beyond the city limits the wild country begins.

**Maps** Free city plans are available from the tourist offices. You can purchase topographic sheets from the map section of the Surveyor General's office (☎ (061) 2852332 or 238110), which is upstairs in the Ministry of Justice building on Independence Ave.

### Information

**Tourist Office** The friendly Windhoek Information and Publicity Office (☎ (061) 3912050; fax 3912091) on Post St Mall answers questions and distributes local advertising, including *What's On in Windhoek*. There's also an information desk at the Grab-a-Phone bus terminal.

The Ministry of Environment and Tourism (☎ (061) 236975), in the Oode Voorpost on the corner of John Meinert Strasse and Moltke Strasse, books national park accommodation and hikes. It's open Monday to Friday from 8 am to 1 pm for bookings and payment and from 2 to 3 pm for bookings only.

The *Windhoek Advertiser* provides information about current events and the Arts Association of Namibia (☎ (061) 231160) has up-to-date news on cultural events.

**Money** Major banks and bureaux de change are concentrated around Independence Ave, and all will change foreign currency into either Namibian dollars or South African rand. The bureau de change on Post St Mall does currency exchange at acceptable rates outside normal hours.

First National Bank's BOB automatic teller system handles Visa transactions, but like everyone else BOB often runs short of cash at weekends. American Express is represented by Woker Travel (☎ (061) 237946) on Peter Müller Strasse, but they don't change travellers cheques.

**Post & Communications** The recently modernised main post office on Independence Ave has telephone boxes in the lobby, and next door is the Telecommunications Office, where you can make international calls and send or receive faxes from 8.30 am to 1 pm and 1.30 to 4.30 pm Monday to Friday, and 8.30 am to 12.30 pm on Saturday. Alternatively, there's the convenient – albeit expensive – Grab-a-Phone, in the main bus terminal.

Federal Express (☎ (061) 264777) is at 1 Jeppe St.

**Immigration** For visa extensions, information on work permits and other immigration matters, check with the Ministry of Home Affairs (☎ (061) 398111; fax 222567) near the corner of Independence Ave and Kasino St. It's open Monday to Friday, from 8 am to 1 pm.

**Medical Services** In the telephone directory, doctors are listed under Medical. Dr Rabie and Dr Retief (☎ (061) 237213), near the corner of John Meinert Strasse and Stübel Strasse, have been recommended for consultations and can also provide medical certificates for hikers.

A useful private clinic is the Rhino Park Medical Centre in Windhoek North. It's a 30 minute walk from the centre. The full-service private hospital Medi-City (☎ (061) 222687), on Heliodoor St in Eros, wants payment up front, but care and service are excellent. Those with tight funds and lots of time to wait can try the Windhoek State Hospital (☎ (061) 3039111) or the government clinic on Robert Mugabe Ave, near John Meinert Strasse.

**Laundry** Windhoek has four self-service laundrettes: one near Ausspannplatz; the Rhino Park Laundrette in the Rhino Park shopping centre; Tauben Glen at Village Square; and Laundraland, near the Mini-Markt in Klein Windhoek. You'll pay around US$2 per load to wash and US$1.50 to dry.

**Dangers & Annoyances** Windhoek is generally safe by daylight, but avoid walking around at night. In the centre, pick-pocketing is a problem. One ploy used by newspaper sellers is to shove the paper in your face; while you read the headlines, your pockets are plundered by accomplices. Politeness may defuse the aggression; say something like 'no thanks, I've already read it'. Be especially wary when walking around the backstreets of Windhoek West, as there has been a spate of muggings at knifepoint; the perpetrators like to make their getaway by taxi.

Unless you have a local contact and/or a specific reason to be there, avoid the townships of Goreangab, Wanaheda, Hakahana and the southern areas of Katutura, where boredom and unemployment are rife.

Windhoek is the victim of frequent droughts, so be frugal with water; take short showers, flush toilets only when essential and don't leave taps running unnecessarily.

**Travel Agencies** Most travel agencies are clustered around the central area. The largest and most helpful is Trip Travel (☎ (061) 236880; fax 225430). Also recommended are Trans-Namib Travel (☎ (061) 2982532) in the Gustav Voigts centre and Woker Travel (☎ (061) 237946) on Peter Müller Strasse. All of these provide travel information and will book accommodation, tours and air travel.

Tourist Rendezvous (☎ (061) 221225; fax 224218), near the Shell petrol station in Klein Windhoek, provides tourist information, adventure bookings and fax services.

**Bookshops & Libraries** The Windhoek Book Den (☎ (061) 239976) just off Post St Mall is the best place for novels, European and African literature, and travel books. The best place for books on African topics is New Namibia Books (☎ (061) 235796) on Post St Mall. A limited selection of books, maps and stationery is found at the CNA bookshops in the Gustav Voigts and Wernhill Park centres. Der Bücherkeller on Peter Müller Strasse has a good selection of novels and literature in German and some in English.

For pulp reading material, see Uncle Spike's Book Exchange, on the corner of Garten Strasse and Tal Strasse.

The Windhoek Public Library (☎ (061) 224163), at 18 Lüderitz St, is open Monday to Friday, 9 am to 6 pm, and on Saturday from 9 am to noon. Visitors can apply for temporary library cards. The University of Namibia also has a library (☎ (061) 3072300).

**Film & Photography** A good range of film is available at the Express Foto Photo Lab, downstairs in the Wernhill Park centre.

**Camping Equipment** You can rent camping equipment from Gav's Camping Hire (☎/fax (061) 251526), at 21 Bevil Rudd St, Klein Windhoek; Time Out (☎ (061) 258760) in Rhino Park; or Camping Hire Namibia (☎/fax (061) 252995), 12 Louis Raymond St, Klein Windhoek. Dome tents cost from US$4 per day, sleeping bags are US$11 (up to a week), and cool boxes, jerry cans, gas cookers and eating/cooking utensils are US$1 per day.

A good place to buy quality South African camping and cycling equipment, or arrange vehicle outfitting, is Cymot (☎ (061) 234131) on Mandume Ndemufayo St. Limited camping gear is also available at Le Trip, downstairs in the Wernhill Park centre, Hike & Bike in the Gustav Voigts centre, and Trapper's Trading beside MacPie in Post St Mall. Gear for serious car camping and 4WD expeditions is available

NAMIBIA

from Safari Den (☎ (061) 231931) at 20 Bessemer St.

## Zoo Park

In Zoo Park (formerly Hendrik Verwoerd Park, which served as a zoo until 1962) is a column designed by Namibian sculptor Dörthe Berner, which commemorates a Stone Age elephant hunt that took place on the spot some 5000 years ago. In 1962, the remains of two elephants and several quartz tools used to cut up the carcasses were unearthed there. The fossils and tools were displayed *in situ* under glass, but in 1990 they were found to be decaying and were transferred to the State Museum.

The Kriegerdenkmal (war memorial), topped by a golden imperial eagle, was dedicated in 1987 to the memory of Schutztruppe soldiers who died fighting the troops of chief Hendrik Witbooi in the Nama wars of 1893-94.

## Christuskirche

Windhoek's best-recognised landmark, the German Lutheran Christuskirche, stands on a traffic island at the top of Peter Müller Strasse. This unusual building, which was constructed from local sandstone, was designed by architect Gottlieb Redecker in conflicting neo-Gothic and Art Nouveau styles. The cornerstone was laid in 1907. To see the interior, pick up the key during business hours from the nearby church office on Peter Müller Strasse.

## Alte Feste & the Owela Museum

The whitewashed ramparts of Alte Feste, Windhoek's oldest surviving building, date from 1890-92. It originally served as the headquarters of the Schutztruppe, which arrived in 1889 under the command of Major Curt von François. Minor alterations made in 1901 didn't affect the overall character. Today it houses the historical section of the State Museum, which contains memorabilia and photos from the colonial period as well as indigenous artefacts. The highlight is the superb display covering Namibia's struggle for independence.

The railway engines and coaches outside formed one of the country's first narrow-gauge trains. The bronze statue is known as the Reiterdenkmal (rider's memorial), and commemorates Schutztruppe soldiers killed during the Herero-Nama wars of 1904-8. It was unveiled in 1912 on Kaiser Wilhelm II's birthday, 27 January. The museum is open weekdays from 9 am to 6 pm and on weekends from 3 to 6 pm. Admission is free.

The other half of the State Museum, known as the Owela Museum, is on Robert Mugabe Ave. Exhibits focus on Namibia's natural and cultural history. It's open the same hours as the historical section and is also free.

Practically next door is the Windhoek Theatre, built in 1960 by the Arts Association. It's still Windhoek's major cultural centre.

## National Gallery

The National Gallery (☎ (061) 231160), on the corner of Robert Mugabe Ave and John Meinert Strasse, contains a permanent collection of works reflecting Namibia's historical and natural heritage. It also hosts visiting exhibitions.

## Tintenpalast

The road east from the Reiterdenkmal leads to the Tintenpalast, now the Parliament Building, which was designed by Gottlieb Redecker and built in 1912-13 as the administrative headquarters for German South West Africa. The name means 'ink palace', in honour of all the ink spent on the typically excessive government paperwork generated there. It has also served as the centre for all subsequent governments, including the present one. The building is remarkable mainly for its construction from indigenous materials. The surrounding gardens were laid out in the 1930s, and include an olive grove and a bowling green. Short 45-minute tours are conducted on weekdays, except when the assembly is in session; reserve by phoning ☎ (061) 229251.

## Other Historical Buildings

Near the corner of Lüderitz Strasse and Park St, take a look at the **Old Magistrates' Court**, which was built in 1897-98 as quarters for Carl Ludwig, the state architect. However, he never used the house and it was eventually drafted into service as the Magistrates' Court. The veranda on the south side provided a shady sitting area for people waiting for their cases to be called. The building now houses the Namibia Conservatorium.

Prior to the construction of Christuskirche, the 1896 building opposite the Magistrates' Court served as Windhoek's German Lutheran church. It currently houses a nursery school.

Heading down Park St from the Tintenpalast, you'll reach South West Africa House, now called the **State House**. The site was once graced by the residence of the German colonial governor, but that was razed in 1958 and replaced by the present building, which became the home of the South African administrator and, from 1977, the administrator-general. After independence, it became the official residence of the Namibian president. All that remains of the original building is part of the old garden wall.

Diagonally opposite Christuskirche on Lüderitz Strasse is the **Hauptkasse**, which was built in 1898-9 and became the revenue office of the German colonial administration. The building was extended in 1906 and 1909, and was later used as a school hostel. It now houses the Ministry of Agriculture.

A block from the Hauptkasse, on the corner of Neser Strasse and Peter Müller Strasse, is the **Ludwig von Estorff House**. It was built in 1891 as a mess for military engineers and named after the former Schutztruppe commander who lived there between campaigns from 1902 to 1910. It has also served as a residence for senior military officers, a hostel and a trade school, and now houses the Estorff Reference Library (☎ (061) 2934203).

Heading south along Robert Mugabe Ave, you'll have a good view over the city, and the road is lined with notable buildings. The first one on the right is the **Kaiserliche Realschule**, Windhoek's first German primary school, which was built in 1907-8. It opened in 1909 with 74 students, but over the next few years enrolment increased and the building had to be enlarged. The curious turret with wooden slats, which was part of the original building, was designed to provide ventilation. The building later housed Windhoek's first German high school, and after WWII an English middle school. A plaque outside will remind you that Berlin is 11,000km away.

Down the road is the **Officers' House**, built in 1905-6 by the works division of the colonial administration to provide accommodation for senior officers. It's closed to the public, but you can visit the outbuildings, which include a six-horse stable and saddle room now used as garages.

Around Werth Strasse are several interesting buildings. The **Villa Migliarina** and **Villa Lanvers**, now private homes, were designed in 1907 by Otto Busch. A cylindrical tower on the Lanvers house lends it a castle-like appearance. Both homes are surrounded by lovely gardens, but they're not open to the public. Just up the stairs is **Werth Lookout**, which affords a broad view over the city centre.

On the corner of Korner St and Robert Mugabe Ave you'll find the **Old Supreme Court**, a gabled brick structure dating from 1908. It was used as a court from 1920 to 1930, at which time the legal system was changing from the German to the South African model. Cases were heard according to whichever system seemed to be the most appropriate for the circumstances.

The **Turnhalle**, on Robert Mugabe Ave, was designed by Otto Busch and was built in 1909 as a practice hall for the Windhoek Gymnastic Club. In 1975, it was modernised and turned into a conference hall, and on 1 September of that year it was the venue for the first Constitutional Conference on Independence for South West Africa, which subsequently – and more conveniently – came to be called the Turnhalle Conference. During the 1980s, it hosted several political summits and debates on the way to Namibian independence.

Around the corner on John Meinert Strasse is a block of six **Officials' Houses**, which were built for government employees in 1908. Nearby, on the corner of John Meinert Strasse and Moltke Strasse, is the **Oode Voorpost**, a classic 1902 building that originally held the colonial surveyors' offices. Early government maps were stored in a fireproof archive. It was restored in 1988 and now houses the MET reservations office.

Southwards along Independence Ave are three colonial-era buildings, all designed by architect Willi Sander. The one furthest south was built in 1902 as the **Kronprinz Hotel**. In 1920, Heinrich Gathemann bought it and converted it into a private business, to adjoin the **Gathemann House** next door, which he had built in 1913. The furthest north of the three is the **Erkrath Building**, which dates from 1910 and was originally a private home and business.

### Monuments
On the corner of Independence Ave and John Meinert Strasse is a bronze kudu statue that honours the many kudu which succumbed to the rinderpest epidemic of 1896. Other prominent memorials are the Owambo Campaign Memorial (described in the Railway Station section below) and the Cross of Sacrifice on Robert Mugabe Ave. A statue of Windhoek's founder, Curt von François, stands outside the municipal buildings on Independence Ave.

### Railway Station
Windhoek's lovely old Cape Dutch style railway station dates from 1912 and was expanded in 1929 by the South African administration. Across the driveway from the entrance is the German steam locomotive, *Poor Old Joe*, which was shipped to Swakopmund in 1899 and reassembled for the run to Windhoek.

Upstairs is the small but worthwhile Trans-Namib Transport Museum, which outlines Namibian transport history, particularly that of the railway. It's open weekdays from 10 am to noon and 2 to 3.30 pm. Admission is US$0.50.

The Owambo Campaign Memorial at the entry to the station parking area was erected in 1919 in commemoration of the 1917 British and South African campaign against the resistant chief Mandume, of the Kwanyama Owambo. When he ran out of firepower, the chief committed suicide rather than surrender.

### St George's Anglican Cathedral
The Anglican Cathedral of St George, on Love Strasse opposite the Owela Museum, has the distinction of being the smallest cathedral in southern Africa. On the grounds of the nearby St George's Diocesan School is the oddly constructed Mansard Building, which was once a private home but now belongs to the school. It's remarkable chiefly for its mansard roof – the only one in Namibia – which is totally unsuited to the desert climate.

### Post St Mall & Gibeon Meteorite Exhibit
The throbbing heart of the Windhoek shopping district is the bizarrely colourful Post St pedestrian mall, which might have been a set in the film *Dick Tracy*. It's lined with vendors selling curios, artwork, clothing and practically anything else that may be of interest to tourists.

In the centre of the mall is a prominent display of 33 meteorites from the Gibeon meteor shower, which deposited upwards of 21 tonnes of mostly ferrous extraterrestrial boulders on the area of Gibeon, in southern Namibia (part of a Gibeon meteorite is also on display in Anchorage, Alaska!). It's rare that so many meteorites fall simultaneously, and they're thought to have been remnants of an explosion in space, which held together as they were drawn in by the earth's gravitational field.

Between 1911 and 1913, soon after their

discovery, they were brought to Windhoek for safekeeping. Over the years they've been displayed in Verwoerd Park and at Alte Feste.

### Private Castles
Near the Gobabis road are the three Windhoek 'castles' – Schwerinsburg (1913) on Schwerinsburg Strasse, Heinitzburg (1914) on Heinitzburg Strasse, and Sanderburg (1917) on Kastell Strasse. Schwerinsburg and Sanderburg are now private homes (Schwerinsburg is the Italian ambassador's residence). Heinitzburg Castle (☎ (061) 227044), which was commissioned in 1914 by Count von Schwerin for his fiancée, Margarethe von Heinitz, is now a B&B and may be visited by appointment. The European cemetery just down the hill also merits a brief look.

### South-West Brewery Building & Namibia Breweries
Until recently, the home of Windhoek Lager was the old South-West Brewery building on Tal Strasse, where the company had produced Namibia's favourite liquid since 1902. The building now houses The Warehouse Theatre, one of Windhoek's best night spots, and the brewing operation has changed its name to Namibia Breweries and moved to the northern industrial area off the Okahandja road. Tours of the modern brewery are conducted on weekdays; phone (061) 262915 for the latest times.

### Hofmeyer Walk
The Hofmeyer Walk walking track through Klein Windhoek Valley starts from Sinclair St and heads south through the bushland to finish at the point where Orban Strasse becomes Anderson Strasse.

The walk takes about an hour and affords panoramic views over the city and a close-up look at the aloes (*Aloe littoralis*) that characterise the hillside vegetation. These cactus-like plants are at their best in winter, when their bright red flowers attract tiny sunbirds, mousebirds and bulbuls.

There have been reports of robbery along this walk, so avoid walking alone or carrying valuables.

### Katutura
Unlike its South African counterparts, the black township of Katutura (Herero for 'we have no permanent place') is relatively safe by day if you stick to the northern areas or find a local who can act as a guide. Especially interesting are the colourful independence-theme murals along Independence Ave. A taxi from the centre to Katutura costs only US$0.75 (N$2.50).

### Organised Tours
The following companies provide Windhoek sightseeing tours: Otjimburu Trails (☎ (061) 234359; fax 228461); Micro Tours (☎/fax (061) 246751), which does historical and township tours; Sun Safaris (☎/fax 233485), with good rates on late bookings; The Tour Company (☎/fax (061) 241958), with city tours and day tours further afield; OC-Ventures (☎ (061) 236692), with dawn bird-watching and city tours for US$30 each; Namibia Supreme (☎/fax (061) 245792), which does city and nightlife tours; and Africa Adventure Safaris (☎ (061) 234720; fax 230001), 72 Mandume Ndemufayo St. Some companies include a trip to Daan Viljoen Game Park. The Namibian Tourist Friend (☎/fax (061) 233485; <ntf@iwwn.com.na>), at the COMAV Flying School at Eros airport, does four-hour city tours in a 'ricksha' (a tuk-tuk-style vehicle) for US$34.

For something totally different, John Branca (☎ (061) 259399) will take you for a 30 minute aerobatic spin in a Pitts Special for US$50.

### Special Events
The first big bash of the year is the Mbapira/Enjando Street Festival, which is held in March around the city centre. It features colourful gatherings of dancers, musicians and people in ethnic dress. For information, phone (061) 225411.

True to its partly Teutonic background, Windhoek stages an Oktoberfest towards

NAMIBIA

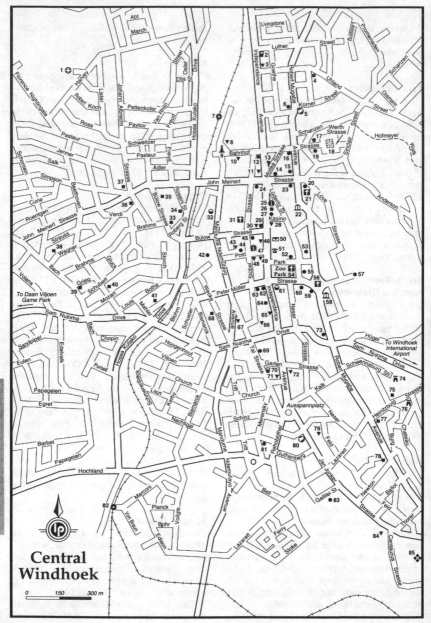

# Central Windhoek

0    150    300 m

**PLACES TO STAY**
 4  Hotel Pension Uhland
12  Thüringer Hof Hotel & Escumadeira
    Restaurant
26  Continental Hotel
33  Hotel Fürstenhof
34  Hotel Pension Handke
35  Hotel Pension Cela
36  Villa Verdi
37  Cardboard Box Backpackers
38  Chameleon Lodge
39  Backpackers Unite
40  Hotel Pension Alexander
41  Puccini International Hostel
64  Kalahari Sands Hotel
68  Hotel Pension Steiner
75  Heinitzburg Castle
77  Hotel Pension Christoph
78  Hotel Pension Moni

**PLACES TO EAT**
 3  Sports Bar & Cafe
 8  Pizza Palace
10  Steenbras
11  Nando's
13  Espresso Coffee Bar
28  Grand Canyon Spur
30  Central Cafe & King Pies
43  Restaurant Africa
46  Gathemann's; Kronprinz Hotel;
    Erkrath Building
48  Marco Polo
49  Le Bistro
65  Wecke & Voigts
66  Zum Wirt
67  Kentucky Fried Chicken
71  Sardinia
72  King Pies
79  Homestead
84  Gourmet's Inn

**OTHER**
 1  State Hospital
 2  Joe's Beer House
 5  Kenyan Embassy & Grand China
    Restaurant
 6  Old Supreme Court (Obergericht)
 7  Railway Station
 9  Owambo Campaign Memorial

14  Oode Voorpost; MET
15  Robert Mugabe Clinic
16  Turnhalle
17  Villa Migliarina
18  Werth Lookout
19  Villa Lanvers
20  Officials' Houses
21  St George's Anglican Cathedral
22  Owela (State) Museum
23  National Gallery
24  Drs Rabie & Retief
25  Namibia Tourism
27  Ministry of Home Affairs (Immigration)
29  Trip Travel; KFC
31  Roman Catholic Cathedral & Hospital
32  Minibuses for the South
42  Wernhill Park Centre
44  New Namibia Books
45  Windhoek Book Den & Levinson
    Arcade
47  Windhoek Information & Publicity
    Office
50  Main Post Office
51  Telecommunications Office
52  Old Magistrates' Court
53  South West Africa House (State
    House)
54  Old German Lutheran Church
55  Hauptkasse
56  Christuskirche (Lutheran Church)
57  Tintenpalast
58  Alte Feste (State Museum)
59  Kaiserliche Realschule
60  Ludwig von Estorff House
    (Estorff Reference Library)
61  Grab-a-Phone Bus Terminal
62  Woker Travel
63  Der Bücherkeller Bookshop
69  Namibia Crafts Centre
70  The Warehouse Theatre
73  Officers' House
74  Schwerinsburg Castle
76  Sanderburg Castle
80  Angola Embassy
81  The Weaver's Nest
82  Gammams Railway Station
83  Intercape Mainliner Office
85  Maerua Park Centre

NAMIBIA

the end of October, which beer lovers should not miss. The German-style Windhoek Karnival (or WIKA) takes place in late April and features a week of events and balls. In late September/early October, the city holds the Windhoek Agricultural, Commercial and Industrial Show, on the Jan Jonker Strasse Show Grounds.

## Frankie Fredericks

If Katutura has a favourite son, it's sprinting sensation Frankie Fredericks, who is probably the greatest role model for Namibian youth and aspiring athletes. Fredericks, who was born in 1968 in Katutura, began as a back-street football player. He was eventually offered a place on the South African professional team, the Kaizer Chiefs, but refused because he preferred track and field events.

Frankie credits his success to his mum, Riekie Fredericks, who financially supported his efforts at school and on the athletics track by working long hours as a seamstress. Her contribution was augmented by a Rössing Corporation scholarship that gave Frankie the opportunity to attend university in the USA (where he completed an MBA) and concentrate on his athletic training. Their efforts have apparently paid off, as Frankie Fredericks is now Africa's fastest sprinter, and won the silver for both the 100m and 200m sprinting events in the 1992 and 1996 Olympics in Barcelona and Atlanta. At the time of writing he was looking forward to a run for the gold at the 2000 Olympics in Sydney.

Currently, Fredericks trains in the USA for much of the year, but frequently returns to Windhoek, where a street has been named after him. He is also the patron of a charitable organisation in Katutura that promotes excellence for low-income youths. One of the secrets of his success, Fredericks claims, is that his religious convictions prevent him from touching drugs or alcohol.

## Places to Stay – Budget

**Camping** The nearest camp site to town is at *Arebbusch Travel Lodge* (☎ (061) 252255; fax 251670), PO Box 80160, Olympia, Windhoek, on the road south. Camping costs US$1 per car plus US$7 per person in a tent; caravan sites are US$12, plus US$7 per person. Double rooms are US$30; and two/five-bed chalets with bath cost US$45/53. Amenities include a bar, shop, laundrette, swimming pool and trampoline. Taxis from the centre cost US$4.

The most popular camp site is at *Daan Viljoen Game Park*, 18km from the city; sites may be pre-booked at the MET. See Around Windhoek, later in this chapter.

Other out of town options include the *Trans-Kalahari Caravan Park* (☎ (061) 222877), 22km east of town on the airport road, and the *Harmony Seminar Centre* (☎ (061) 234920), 15km south of town and 2km east on D1504.

**Backpackers Lodges** A long-established popular choice is the *Cardboard Box Backpackers* (☎ (061) 228994; fax 245587; <ahj@iafrica.com.na>), 15 minutes walk from the centre on the corner of Johann Albrecht Strasse and John Meinert Strasse. Dorm beds cost US$7, with use of the cooking facilities and swimming pool. Doubles cost US$20, but you need to pre-book for any hope of getting one. There's a notice board for lifts and it's a great place for getting groups together for car hire and trips to Sossusvlei, Etosha and elsewhere. The owners Aulden and Rachel also organise braais, *potjies*, pool parties (featuring both kinds of pool) and night club excursions.

*Chameleon Lodge* (☎ (061) 247668; <chamnam@ nam.lia.net>), 22 Wagner St, Windhoek West, is a favourite with overlanders. Here owner Jackie, her dog Crash and her meerkats create a friendly and lively atmosphere. Dorm beds cost US$7, including bedding, and private double rooms are US$19. Breakfasts, light meals and drinks are available, and guests may use the pool, dartboard, kitchen, video lounge and phone/fax.

Thanks to owners Erika and Herman,

*Backpackers Unite* (☎ (081) 1244383), at 5 Grieg St, is the quietest and most homely of Windhoek's inexpensive options. Children are welcome, but the open swimming pool makes it unsuitable for toddlers. Double rooms cost US$18, dorms are US$6 and camping is US$4. Avoid walking from the centre with all your gear; phone for a free transfer.

The *Puccini International Hostel* (☎/fax (061) 236355), 4 Puccini St, has dorm beds for US$8, and doubles with a light breakfast for US$18. Camping costs US$5 and use of the sauna is US$1.50 for 15 minutes. It's only a short walk from Wernhill Park centre, but the neighbourhood requires some vigilance, especially the Mozart St bridge. Don't walk there with all your luggage.

The *Travellers' Lodge* (☎ (061) 249089), on Andes St in Eros Park, charges 'overseas guests' US$8 (US$7 if you stay three nights), but it's mainly for local business-people. They offer free coffee, kitchen facilities, bedding and a common TV room.

**Bed & Breakfast** Away from the centre – but great value – is the friendly *Marie's Accommodation* (☎ (061) 251787; fax 252128; <brianhj@mac.alt.na>), 156 Diaz St. Large singles/doubles without bath cost US$14/23, including breakfast; rooms with shared bath and kitchen cost US$19/25; and a four-person flat is US$36. In the dry season, single/double pre-erected tents cost US$5/7. Continental breakfasts and full English or German breakfasts are also available. Guests have access to the pool, patio and barbecue, and Marie also provides information on inexpensive Budget and Home Accommodation Association places around Namibia.

Another pleasant B&B is the homely *June's Place* (☎ (061) 226054), owned by June and Hans Bunke, at 91 Nelson Mandela Dr. They have two rooms with cable TV and private facilities for US$27/41 for one/two people. Rates include breakfast served on the patio with a view of the nearby hills.

*The Guesthouse* (☎ (061) 225500) is at 29 Stein St in Klein Windhoek, near Woermann & Brock. Unpretentious single/double B&B accommodation costs US$41/50. The oddly named but friendly *Medi-City B&B* (☎ (061) 234249), 29 Heliodoor St in Eros Park, is aptly situated opposite the hospital. Singles/doubles with breakfast cost US$20/34. A comparable place is *Charlotte's Guest House* (☎ (061) 228846), at 'Awnings', 2a John Ludwig St, Klein Windhoek.

You'll find a more German atmosphere at *Haus Ol-Ga* (☎ (061) 235853), 91 Bach Strasse, Windhoek West. The name is formed from those of its owners – Gesa Oldach and Erno Gauerke. Singles/doubles cost US$23/40, including breakfast.

**Hotel** The cheapest hotel-style accommodation is the *Namibia Star Hotel* (☎ (061) 213205), 3km from the centre in Khomasdal. Singles/doubles cost US$15/20 and the quality has recently improved, but its dodgy location and reputation make it a marginal choice.

**Places to Stay – Mid-Range**
One of the least expensive mid-range places, *Hotel Pension Handke* (☎ (061) 234904; fax 225660) at 3 Rossini St, has 10 singles/doubles for US$36/52, including breakfast. Larger rooms for three or four people cost US$23 per person. This place has greatly improved in recent years.

Further upmarket is the friendly *Hotel Pension Cela* (☎ (061) 226295; fax 226246) at 82 Bülow Strasse, which charges US$45/69 for singles/doubles including breakfast. Rooms for three/four people cost US$94/116. Amenities include TVs, radios, telephones, ceiling fans, a swimming pool and fax service.

*Hotel Pension Moni* (☎ (061) 228350; fax 227124) at 7 Rieks van der Walt Strasse, south-east of the centre is a motel-style place. Bright, clean singles/doubles with telephone, radio, mini-bar and pool access cost US$42.50/60, including breakfast. The German-run *Hotel Pension Alexander*

NAMIBIA

(☎ (061) 240775), at 10 Beethoven St, has single/double B&B accommodation for US$32/44.

The *Hotel Pension Steiner* (☎ (061) 222898; fax 224234), 11 Wecke Strasse, has comfortable and spotless singles/doubles with TV and en suite facilities for US$42/61, including breakfast. Guests can use the swimming pool, braai area and lounge. A similar place is *Hotel Pension Uhland* (☎ (061) 229859; fax 220688) at 147 Uhland St, which charges US$45/55, including breakfast. There's a swimming pool and all rooms have private facilities.

The newish *Hotel Pension Cristoph* (☎ (061) 240777; fax 248560), 33 Heinitzburg Strasse, is a pleasant but large and outwardly non-descript place with a pool, just below the eastern hills. Singles/doubles with satellite TV, phone and mini-bar cost US$43/57. The restaurant decor is particularly appealing.

There are also several hotels along Independence Ave. At the very top of the middle range is the *Thüringer Hof Hotel* (☎ (061) 226031; fax 232981), which is famous for its beer garden and has singles/doubles for US$63/85. The good-value *Continental Hotel* (☎ (061) 237293; fax 231539), downhill from the main post office, is also central and offers quality accommodation. Single/double rooms with private facilities start at US$60/80 and singles with shared facilities are US$36. Rates include breakfast.

Mr Hans Vonderstein's simple but charming *Aris Hotel* (☎ (061) 236006; fax 234507), 27km south of town on the Rehoboth road, has singles/doubles with bath for US$37/57. With a shower they're US$32/50, and with bed only US$29/45. There's also a bar, beer garden, à la carte restaurant, pool and braai.

Also out of town is the refreshing *Sundown Lodge* (☎ (061) 232566; fax 232541), 25km north of town on the Okahandja road. For singles/doubles including breakfast, you'll pay US$34/48.

If you prefer to stay near the airport, the *Airport Lodge* (☎ (061) 231491; fax 236709; <airportl@nam.lia.net>), 18km

east of town, has single/double accommodation in thatched bungalows with broad vistas for US$43/59.

**Places to Stay – Top End**

On Johann Albrecht Strasse is the recommended *Villa Verdi* (☎ (061) 221994; fax 222574). This unique Mediterranean-African hybrid charges US$63/102 for singles/doubles with bath, telephone and TV. It also has a pool, bar and restaurant.

The royal B&B option is *Heinitzburg Castle* (☎ (061) 249597; fax 249598), where comfortable singles/doubles with TV, air conditioning and en suite facilities are US$75/104.

The *Hotel Fürstenhof* (☎ (061) 237380; fax 228751) may be large and impersonal, but it offers fairly good value. Single/double rooms with shower or bath cost US$66/95, including breakfast. The dining room specialises in seafood and French and German cuisine.

The immense three-star *Hotel Safari* and attached four-star *Safari Court* (☎ (061) 240240; fax 235652), near Eros airport, have leafy gardens, a shady beer garden, a large pool and a golf course next door. At the Hotel Safari, single or double rooms cost US$79, including a buffet breakfast. Budget rooms are US$66. At the Safari Court, they're US$93. It's probably the most pleasant of the top-end hotels.

In the heart of the city is the four-star *Kalahari Sands Hotel* (☎ (061) 222300; fax 222260), at 129 Independence Ave, PO Box 2254, Windhoek. It's a solid, international-standard hotel, with 187 rooms, all with TV, telephone, mini-bar and coffee machine, but note that the standard can vary. Singles/doubles start at US$99/118 and deluxe rooms at US$127/143. An English/continental breakfast costs US$7/9.

If you don't mind that it was constructed specifically for the Miss Universe pageant, the *Windhoek Country Club Resort & Casino* (☎ (061) 2055911; fax 252797), PO Box 30777, Windhoek, near Eros airport, offers a touch of Las Vegas in Windhoek. And yes, the fountains and green lawns

NAMIBIA

seem as incongruous here as they would in the deserts of Nevada. Standard single/double rooms start at US$113/135, but weekend specials are available for as little as US$57/73, including breakfast.

### Guest Farms

For the locations of these farms, see the main map in the North Central Namibia chapter.

In the Eros Mountains, 15km from town, is the German-style *Gästefarm Elisenheim* (☎/fax (061) 264429), PO Box 3016, Windhoek, owned by Andreas and Christina Werner. Singles/doubles cost US$40/63, including use of the pool and wildlife-viewing. A full breakfast costs US$7 and other meals are US$9. It's closed from 15 December to 31 January. Take the Okahandja road and get off at Brakwater; follow the D1473 until it curves north. Turn east at the first opportunity and follow this road to the farm. Transfers from Windhoek cost US$5, divided between all passengers; from the airport, they're US$40.

Another popular guest farm is the cattle and game ranch *Düsternbrook* (☎/fax (061) 232572). Single/double B&B is US$43/70 and full board is US$69/122. It has a scenic setting and offers wildlife-viewing activities, but leopards are kept in enclosures. For leopard feeding, a game drive and a light meal, day visitors pay US$44. Follow the B1 for 30km north towards Okahandja and turn west onto the D1499. From there, it's 18km to the farm.

### Places to Eat

**Fast Food & Takeaways** Some of Windhoek's best takeaways come from *Steenbras*, on Bahnhof Strasse near Independence Ave, which serves memorably delicious fish, chickenburgers and spicy chips. Another good choice is *King Pies*, with outlets on Post St Mall and Independence Ave (outside Levinson Arcade and at the corner of Garten Strasse, respectively). For lunch, a large filled meat or vegetable pie and a soft drink cost US$1. Similar is the new *MacPie*, on Post St Mall, which

does interesting combinations, including curry and vegetarian choices.

The always popular *Nando's*, on Independence Ave north of John Meinert Strasse, serves up superb Portuguese-style peri-peri chicken, spicy rice, chips and other goodies. You can also buy bottles of their delicious sauces, which come in extra hot, hot, medium and mild (which is spicy enough for most people). For something more familiar and mundane, fall back on *Kentucky Fried Chicken*, with outlets on Independence Ave and Mandume Ndemufayo St. The Maerua Park centre has a range of small eating places: a ho-hum *Wimpy*, the *Pizza Palace*, *San Francisco Coffee Roastery* and *Yogurt World*. There is also a *Pizza Palace* opposite Windhoek railway station.

**Cafes** *Le Bistro*, a bit of a fish bowl on Post St Mall, is known for its breakfasts, pizzas, salads and kebabs. They serve breakfast from 7 to 11 am; a 'health breakfast' or continental breakfast costs US$2.50 and a full English breakfast is US$3. Don't confuse it with *The Bistro*, a friendly but pricey outdoor cafe in Maerua Park centre that specialises in light meals and cocktails.

The pleasantly laid-back *Central Café*, in the Levinson Arcade, is great for meals or just coffee. It's open for lunch and dinner from Tuesday to Saturday; on Monday, it's open for lunch only, and on Sunday it opens from 8 am to midnight. Lunchtimes get extremely busy, but there's a takeaway window selling filled *Brötchen* and other fast snacks. The *Café Schneider*, in the same arcade, offers a less busy alternative.

For decent brewed coffee, cappuccino and espresso, check out the *Espresso Coffee Bar* (☎ (061) 246809), opposite the MET office. Also recommended for coffee, meals and snacks is *Wecke & Voigts* coffee bar, at the Gustav Voigts centre. The *In's Wiener Coffee Shop* in Wernhill Park centre serves up nice hot coffee and sweet treats, but with an unfortunately sour attitude.

**Lunch & Dinner** A recommended quick option is the friendly *Tim Sum* (☎ (061)

232312) in Wernhill Park centre, a coffee shop specialising in appealing vegetarian Chinese dishes. The *Zum Wirt* (☎ (061) 234503) restaurant and beer garden, on Stübel Strasse, is open for lunch daily, and serves up fine European and local cuisine.

The *Grand Canyon Spur*, on Independence Ave, has a varied menu and seating in the sun on the balcony overlooking the street. Don't miss the highlights here: the salad bar and the renowned chocolate brownies. The new *Saddles* (☎ (061) 233292) in Maerua Park centre also serves steak, but the reviews are mixed. A better Maerua-area choice is the upmarket *O'Hagan's Irish Pub & Grill* (☎ (061) 234677), at the corner of Robert Mugabe Ave and Jan Jonker Strasse, which does steak and international dishes. Also recommended is the *Buffalo Inn Restaurant & Pub* (☎ (061) 234028) at 205 Stübel St.

*Mike's Kitchen* (☎ (061) 226596), in Wernhill Park centre, is made up to look like a US family-style restaurant. It serves standard lunches and dinners – salads, steaks, chicken, burgers and chips – seven days a week, but its real forté is waffles with maple syrup and cream.

A great splash-out is *Gathemann's*, in a prominent colonial building with a sunny terrace overlooking Independence Ave. It specialises in German-style cuisine, but also offers other European fare, local specialities and Namibia's best snails in garlic butter. Expect to pay around US$15 per person. In the morning and afternoon, it does rich European-style gateaux and pastries, and downstairs there's a good sandwich takeaway.

*Sardinia* (☎ (061) 225600), on Independence Ave south of Sam Nujoma Drive, serves palatable Italian dishes and delicious *gelato*. A great Mediterranean option is *Mykonos Taverne* (☎ (061) 264459), with kebabs, shwarma and other traditional Greek and Italian specialities.

The German-style *Jägerstube* beer garden at the Thüringer Hof Hotel is great value for buffet lunches. From noon to 2 pm, you can pig out on cold cuts, cheese, salads and hot dishes. It's also open evenings from 7 to 10.30 pm. However, the beer garden attracts characters that are less than pillars of local society. The hotel also has the *Escumadeira*, which serves recommended Portuguese specialities.

Another German-Namibian specialist is the *Homestead* (☎ (061) 221958), on Feld Strasse south-east of Ausspannplatz. The menu features fresh herbs and vegetables from their own garden, served up in a pleasant outdoor setting. Vegetarians will love *Green Market Square* (☎ (061) 254849), at 160 Nelson Mandela Ave beside Eros shopping centre, which has an organic wholefood restaurant, and a health food shop, coffee shop and tea garden.

You'll find great Chinese food at *Yang Tse*, on Sam Nujoma Dr near the petrol stations in Klein Windhoek. An alternative is the *Grand China Restaurant*, near the Kenyan Embassy on Korner St. You'll find more varied Asian cuisine in the upstairs dining room at the *Windhoek Country Club* (see Places to Stay – Top End).

The fully licensed *Marco Polo* (☎ (061) 230141), on Post St Mall, serves champagne breakfasts and top-quality Italian meals and pizza, but the portions and service are variable. It's housed in the Kaiserkrone, an early hotel and social centre dating back to 1927. Also upmarket but highly recommended is *Gert's Klause*, a quiet German-style bistro in the arcade south of Post St Mall.

If you're open to new experiences, *Restaurant Africa* (☎ (061) 247178), at 3 Kosch St, between Bülow Strasse and Post St Mall, cooks up specialities from Tunisia, Nigeria, Kenya, Ethiopia, Cameroon, Angola (try camarão de coco, shrimp with coconut), Ghana, and of course Namibia. Try omaungu (mopane worms), which you can talk about for years to come. Breakfast is served at 7.30 am and features hot pepper soup, puff puff (a doughnut) with honey, and omahangu (millet porridge).

For a pretentious splash out, try the *Gourmet's Inn* (☎ (061) 232360), on Jan Jonker Strasse near Centaurus Strasse, which is a standard haunt of ambassadors, government ministers, dignitaries, VIPs and general power trippers. Reservations are essential and not easy to get – and the prices reflect the exclusivity.

The excellent restaurant at the *Hotel Fürstenhof* (☎ (061) 237380), off the beaten track near Hosea Kutako Drive, is low key, but serves elegant French cuisine with flair. You'll pay between US$10 and US$20 for a gourmet meal with wine. For more quantity than finesse, try the *Hotel Safari*'s good-value dinner buffet.

**Deliveries** If you're feeling lazy, Windhoek's remarkable *Mr Delivery* (☎ (061) 220111) service delivers orders from a range of local restaurants for a nominal charge between US$1 and US$1.75. Among the choices are Nando's, King Pies, Grand Canyon Spur, O'Hagan's Irish Pub & Grill, Mike's Kitchen and even the Pioneerspark Drankwinkel bottle store!

**Self-Catering** Self-caterers will find a grocery-shopping paradise in Windhoek. The big names are *Woolworths* in the Wernhill Park centre, the cheap and cheerful *OK Supermarket* in the Gustav Voigts centre, and the attached *Wecke & Voigts*. Wecke & Voigts is a small, expensive department store specialising in things Germanic and has an excellent food section in the basement, with a wide selection of local smoked meats and biltong. They also make good breads (especially Brötchen), cakes and deli sandwiches.

The best grocery value is at the always crowded *Model 7-Day Store* on lower Independence Ave. The *Mini-Markt* in Klein Windhoek is larger than it sounds and is open from 7 am to midnight seven days a week. On weekdays, a small market on Mandume Ndemufayo Ave sells fruit, vegetables, baskets and woodcarvings.

## Entertainment
**Pubs, Discos & Night Clubs** Windhoek has some super night spots and the best is probably *The Warehouse Theatre* (☎ (061)

225059), in the old South-West Brewery building on Tal Strasse. This delightfully integrated club is open almost every night and emphasises superb live music and theatre productions – both African and European. Many people get up and dance and it's friendly, secure and lots of fun. The cover charge varies according to which act is appearing, but it averages around US$3.

In Katutura township is the wonderful *Club Thriller*, which imposes a cover charge of US$2.50. Once you're past the weapons search at the door, the music is western and African and the atmosphere upbeat and relatively secure. Most people are there to party and have fun, and foreigners experience little hassle, but it's still not wise to carry valuables. Peripherals include a snack bar, braais and pool tables. Don't walk around Katutura at night – always take a taxi, which costs US$0.50 from town.

The large disco at *Namibia Bi-Nite* in Khomasdal has operated on and off for many years, and remains popular. It's safe inside but the neighbourhood requires some vigilance.

The *Sports Bar & Café* (formerly Roxy's and Thirty Something), features the usual sports theme. The tiny and inconsistent *Club Taj Pomodzi*, in Katutura, specialises in live Zaïrois kwasa-kwasa music and charges a US$2.75 cover charge. It's your best option for an intimate taste of Windhoek's African scene, but it's lost in the back streets and without a taxi and local help (and don't go at night without either of these) it's hard to find.

The *Casablanca* on Sam Nujoma Drive in Klein Windhoek serves up meals and basic live music in its outdoor seating area, often with a cover charge. Many people just want to play pool or attend the Windhoek Mini-Weekend on Wednesday, where the objective is to get blotto.

*Maxim's* (☎ (061) 220045), a coffee shop at 44 Rehobother St near Ausspannplatz, is open daily from 7.30 am for coffee, snacks and light meals. On Wednesday, Friday, Saturday and Sunday nights from 8 pm, it dishes up live jazz, R&B, blues, soul, swing and hip-hop with no cover charge.

Decent pubs include the *Plaza* at Maerua Park centre, with good, easy-listening music; *Joe's Beer House* (☎ (061) 232457), 440 Independence Ave, which has a large beer garden and good pub food and service (and often a cover charge); *Club Latino* in Khomasdal, a rather aggressive coloured club; and *O'Hagan's*, a chain Irish pub on Robert Mugabe Ave near Maerua Park Centre with mainstream music (the folks at Cardboard Box Backpackers – see Places to Stay – recommend bringing your cellphone and Raybans).

**Cinema & Theatre** Windhoek has a very good cinema, *Kine 300* (☎ (061) 249267), in Maerua Park centre off Robert Mugabe Ave. On Tuesdays, admission is half-price. The *Franco-Namibian Cultural Centre* (☎ (061) 225672) at 1 Mahler St, on the corner of Sam Nujoma Drive, shows French films and other international cinema productions, and also hosts visiting art and theatre exhibitions.

There are occasional theatre productions at *The New Space* (in the University of Namibia complex), and classical concerts in the *Windhoek Conservatorium*. The *Kalahari Sands Hotel* has cabaret evenings and there are productions at the *National Theatre of Namibia* on Robert Mugabe Ave. *The Warehouse Theatre* in the old South-West Brewery has jazz and light music concerts, as well as serious dramatic performances; see Pubs, Discos & Night Clubs earlier in this section.

*Sjordes* (lunchtime music and theatre productions) are sometimes held at the *Space Theatre* in the colonial maternity home, Elisabeth House, over the railway line from the centre on Storch St.

**Lectures** The State Museum in Alte Feste hosts visiting exhibitions and runs a programme of evening lectures, films and slide shows. Inquire at the desk.

**Sports** Windhoek has fine sporting facilities, including a municipal pool and mini-golf course near the corner of Jan Jonker Strasse and Centaurus Strasse. The local chapter of Hash House Harriers (☎ (061) 224550) meets on Monday at 6.30 pm.

**Things to Buy**
Windhoek is Namibia's shopping capital, and you'll find everything from camping equipment to leatherwork. Leather shops are good for inexpensive, high-quality belts and purses; locally farmed ostrich leather is quite expensive, while buffalo hide belts start at US$25 and will last forever. Handbags cost from US$110 and briefcases are double that. A good place to buy quality leather shoes is Lederwaren in the northern industrial area. Quality karakul wool products are available at The Weaver's Nest on Nachtigal St near Ausspannplatz, as well as other shops.

Windhoek also has a thriving jewellery industry, based on locally mined gold, minerals and gemstones. These are sold in specialist shops, where artisans work to order; some of the best work is with malachite and tiger-eye agates.

For raw minerals and gemstones, the best deals are from the House of Gems (☎ (061) 225202), at 131 Stübel Strasse. Owner Sid Pieters is Namibia's foremost gem expert and in 1974, along the Namib coast, he uncovered 45 crystals of jeremejevite, a sea-blue tourmaline that is the rarest gem on earth. His discovery was only the second ever; the first was in Siberia in the mid-19th century. Another of his discoveries was croccidolite pietersite, from Outjo, which is one of the most beautiful minerals imaginable – some people believe that it has special energy- and consciousness-promoting qualities.

The Namibia Crafts Centre (☎ (061) 222236) in the old South-West Brewery building at 40 Tal Strasse sells an amazing range of stuff. It's open Monday to Friday from 9 am to 5.30 pm and on Saturday from 9 am to 1 pm. If you aren't venturing into the Kalahari, check out Bushman Art at 187 Independence Ave. Even non-buyers will enjoy the variety and beauty of the wares. It also sells Himba material arts.

The city also has a full complement of curio shops selling kitsch T-shirts, mass-produced art and woodcarvings. When considering anything expensive or exotic, or that resembles an artefact, ask about its provenance, ensure that the dealer has a licenceto sell antiquities and determine whether it requires an export/import permit.

Along Post St Mall and other central streets, handicrafts brought in by the truck-load from Zimbabwe are hawked for negotiable prices. More typically Namibian are the Herero dolls sold outside the Kalahari Sands Hotel and the baskets and carvings sold around Zoo Park. Alternatively, save your money for the less expensive handicrafts that are available from artists, craftspeople and co-operative shops around the country.

If you buy anything heavy or unwieldy, most shops are happy to arrange shipping.

## Getting There & Away

**Air** Air Namibia has daily flights between Windhoek international airport, Cape Town and Johannesburg. There is also a twice-weekly service to and from London and Frankfurt; and several airlines offer services to Gaborone, Maun, Harare, Lusaka and Victoria Falls. Domestic Air Namibia flights connect Eros airport with Katima Mulilo, Keetmanshoop, Lüderitz, Oshakati, Rundu, Swakopmund and Tsumeb. Major airline offices include:

*Aeroflot*, Carl List Building, corner of Independence Ave and Peter Müller Strasse, Ausspannplatz (☎ (061) 229120)

*Air Namibia*, ground floor, Gustav Voigts Centre, 125 Independence Ave (☎ (061) 229630; fax 228763)

*British Airways/Comair*, Sanlam Centre, 154 Independence Ave (☎ (061) 248528; fax 248529)

*LTU*, 5 Macadam St (☎ (061) 238205; fax 222350)

*Lufthansa*, 3rd floor, Sanlam Centre, 154 Independence Ave (☎ (061) 226662; fax 227923)

*South African Airways*, Carl List Building, corner of Independence Ave and Peter Müller Strasse (☎ (061) 237670)

**Bus** Intercape Mainliner (☎ (061) 227847) has four weekly bus services between Windhoek and Cape Town (US$73) and Johannesburg (US$73), running via Upington (US$45). En route, they stop in: Rehoboth (US$6), Mariental (US$23), Keetmanshoop (US$34) and Grünau (US$39) – the fares given are from Windhoek. Intercape also connects Windhoek with Swakopmund and Walvis Bay four times weekly (US$14 to either).

Cheaper and more convenient are the local minibuses, which depart when full and work out at around US$0.03 per kilometre. For example, the fare to Oshakati is around US$16. For Swakopmund and Walvis Bay (US$11 to either), they leave from the Rhino Park petrol station. For the route south to Rehoboth, Mariental and Keetmanshoop, the terminal is the large car park north of the Wernhill Park centre. Those going north to the Owambo region, Kavango and Caprivi depart from the market near the Katutura Singles' Quarters. This is a pretty dodgy area, and instead of risking your luggage, you should wait at the Western Bypass on-ramp from the northern end of Independence Ave. Services are most frequent on Friday afternoons.

Namibia Contract Haulage (☎ (061) 234164) has buses to Ondangwa and Oshakati (US$10) on Tuesday and Friday at 9 am and 5 pm from the Abraham Mashego St bus terminal, in the Katutura Singles' Quarters. The northern terminals are at the BP station in Ondangwa and the market bus station in Oshakati. There's also a service running to Rundu (US$11) on Tuesday and Friday at 5 pm.

To Swakopmund or Walvis Bay, Dolphin Express (☎ (064) 204118) has convenient services departing daily from the Rhino Park petrol station for US$14.

For details on international buses, see the Namibia Getting There & Away chapter.

**Train** The railway station ticket and booking office is open from 7.30 am to 4 pm Monday to Friday. There's no longer a rail service between Namibia and South

## Budget Safaris in Namibia

If you want to see Namibia economically and you're up for a dose of adventure, try one of the following safari companies, which offer the best of Namibia for budget-friendly rates. These are all popular options, so be sure to book well in advance:

*Chameleon Safaris*, 22 Wagner St, PO Box 6017, Windhoek (☎/fax (061) 247668; <chamnam@nam.lia.net>). Chameleon does a comprehensive northern Namibia circuit, including Waterberg, Etosha, Damaraland, the Skeleton Coast and Swakopmund, and a southern Namibia circuit with Keetmanshoop, Lüderitz, Fish River Canyon, Sossusvlei and the Naukluft, for US$350 each. Transfers between Windhoek and Victoria Falls, with visits to Bushmanland, Rundu, Mahango Game Reserve, Mamili National Park and Chobe National Park (Botswana) are US$440.

*Crazy Kudu Safaris*, 15 Johann Albrecht Strasse, PO Box 86124, Windhoek (☎/fax (061) 222636; <crazykudu@hotmail.com>). Namibia's most economical safari company, run by Mike Godfrey, runs 10-day, all-inclusive adventures through Etosha, Waterberg, Damaraland, the Skeleton Coast and Sossusvlei (US$506), a six-day northern highlights tour (US$337), and a three-day Namib Desert circuit (US$169). Also, ask about the semi-annual 21-day tour that covers the best of Namibia and also strays well off the beaten track. Mike also organises great-value tailor-made safaris.

*Wild Dog Safaris*, PO Box 26188, Windhoek (☎/fax (061) 257642); <awkirby@iafrica.com.na>). This friendly operation runs a seven-day Northern Adventure to Waterberg, Etosha, Damaraland, the Skeleton Coast and Swakopmund, and a seven-day swing around Sossusvlei, Lüderitz, Fish River Canyon and Brukkaros Crater, for US$310 each. For a nine-day camping transfer from Windhoek to Victoria Falls, via Bushmanland, Popa Falls, the Okavango Delta and Katima Mulilo, you'll pay US$440 (if you want to complete the circuit back to Windhoek it will cost an additional US$50).

Africa. Trains to Keetmanshoop leave at 7 pm daily except Saturday. Weekend economy/business fares from Windhoek are: Rehoboth (US$5/7); Mariental (US$8/11); Keetmanshoop (US$9/13).

Trains run to Tsumeb (US$10/14 in economy/business) via Okahandja, Kranzberg and Otjiwarongo (where you'll find Star Line bus connections to Outjo, and onward connections to Khorixas, Kamanjab and Opuwo) on Tuesday, Thursday and Sunday. From Tsumeb to Windhoek, they operate on Monday, Wednesday and Friday.

Other services connect Windhoek with Swakopmund and Walvis Bay (US$6/9 in economy/business) via Okahandja daily except Saturday; and Windhoek with Gobabis (US$3/5 in economy/business) on Tuesday, Thursday and Sunday, on a very slow overnight run.

**Car & Motorcycle** Windhoek is literally the crossroads of Namibia – the point where the main north-south route (the B1) and east-west routes (B2 and B6) cross – and all approaches to the city are spectacularly scenic, passing over beautiful desert hills. Roads are clearly signposted and the Western Bypass avoids the town centre. For a list of car hire firms, see the Namibia Getting Around chapter.

If you'd rather leave the driving to someone else, several local drivers offer reasonable rates. A recommended driver is Desmond (☎ (0621) 502345), who does runs to Victoria Falls for US$50 per person (with at least four people). Another driver, Harry, has a commuter bus for 10 people plus luggage and will go anywhere in Namibia for US$90 per day plus petrol, tyre damage and park fees. Book either of these guys through Cardboard Box Backpackers (see Places to Stay – Budget).

**Hitching** Thanks to its location and level of traffic, hitching to or from Windhoek is easier than anywhere else in Namibia, which isn't really saying much.

### Getting Around

**The Airport** The airport shuttle (☎ (061) 263211) between Windhoek international airport, 42km from town, and the Grab-a-Phone bus terminal on Independence Ave costs US$9. Buses leave the airport one hour after international arrivals and from Grab-a-Phone two hours and 10 minutes prior to departures. Buses also stop at Eros airport and the Hotel Safari. Schedules are posted at Grab-a-Phone.

After some bargaining, taxis between the airport and the centre will cost US$18 for up to four people. Namibia Supreme Tourism (☎/fax (061) 245792) does airport transfers for US$14 per person and Ropeka Tours (☎ (061) 226119; fax 220275; <tour info@liam.lia.net>) picks up one to three people for US$34, but you must pre-book.

**Bus** City buses charge US$0.15 (N$0.50) per ride. Because Windhoek is relatively small and taxis are so cheap, few travellers bother with the buses unless they're heading for the suburbs. Timetables are perfunctorily posted at bus stops, but they usually disappear shortly thereafter.

**Car & Motorcycle** The most convenient parking is beneath Wernhill Park centre, where you'll pay less than US$1 per hour.

**Taxi** Windhoek Radio Taxis (☎ (061) 237070) has its office at 452 Independence Ave (the Grab-a-Phone bus terminal). For radio taxis, try the more basic F&P Radio Taxis (☎ (061) 211116), in Khomasdal, or White Rhino Taxis (☎ (061) 221029). You may even catch up with one of the tuk-tuk shared taxis, which have been imported from Bangkok and cost a fixed US$0.30 anywhere in the central business district.

The official fare to anywhere around Windhoek, including Khomasdal and Katutura, is US$0.75, but be warned that taxis from Grab-a-Phone often charge considerably more, and may also try to charge extra for luggage, so it's better to use the taxi ranks north of Wernhill Park centre. For long-distance taxis (eg to Daan Viljoen), try Friendly Taxis (☎ (081) 246593 or (061) 257782).

# Around Windhoek

## PENDUKA & GOREANGAB DAM

Penduka (☎ (061) 257210; <penduka@ nam.lia.net>), which means wake up, operates a women's non-profit needlework project at Goreangab Dam (Windhoek's water supply), 10km from the centre. You can purchase needlework, baskets, carvings and fabric creations for fair prices and be assured that all proceeds go to the producers. There are also live music performances and several hiking trails. It's open 8 am to 5 pm daily except Sunday.

### Places to Stay & Eat

Overlooking the dam are a lovely African restaurant and a tea room. Backpackers accommodation is US$7 and simple chalets are US$32 per person.

### Getting There & Away

Take the Western Bypass north and turn left on Monte Cristo Rd, then left on Otjomuise Rd, right on Eveline St and right again on Green Mountain Dam Rd and follow the signs to Goreangab Dam/Penduka. Unfortunately, there's no public transport, but Penduka provides lifts from town for a nominal fee.

## AVIS DAM

Avis Dam, which lies just out of town on the road to the international airport, offers rewarding bird-watching, but there's no public transport except for the airport bus.

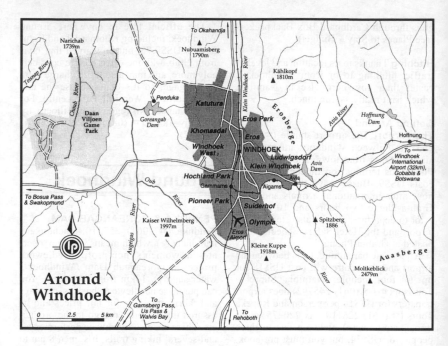

**Around Windhoek**

0    2.5    5 km

## DAAN VILJOEN GAME PARK

The beautiful Daan Viljoen Game Park sits 25km west of Windhoek in the Khomas Hochland. Because there are no dangerous animals, you can walk to your heart's content through lovely wildlife-rich desert hills and see gemsbok, kudu, mountain zebra, springbok, hartebeest and even the elusive eland. Daan Viljoen is also known for its diversity of birds, and over 200 species have been recorded, including the rare green-backed heron and pin-tailed whydah. The park office sells a bird-identification booklet. The dam is stocked with barbel, kurper and black bass; anglers need a fishing licence.

The park is open to day visitors from sunrise to 6 pm year-round; day admission is US$2.

### Hiking

Daan Viljoen's hills are covered with open thorn-scrub vegetation that allows excellent wildlife-viewing, and three walking tracks have been laid out.

The 3km Wag 'n Bietjie (Wait-a-Bit) Trail follows a dry riverbed from near the park office to Stengel Dam. The 9km Rooibos loop trail crosses hills and ridges and affords great views of Windhoek in the distance.

The two day, 34km Sweet-Thorn Trail circuits the wide and empty eastern reaches of the reserve, and if it wasn't for the distant views of the city you'd never know you were only 18km from Windhoek. One group of between three and 12 people is allowed on the trail each day and it costs US$21 per person, including accommodation in a simple shelter halfway along. Water is available at the hut, but note that the Augeigas River here is polluted and unsuitable even for filtering. Advance MET bookings are required.

NAMIBIA

## Places to Stay & Eat

The rest camp curls around one side of Augeigas Dam. Camping costs US$21 for up to eight people and two-bed rondavels are US$39/50 for one/two people, including breakfast.

The popularity of Daan Viljoen means that you're strongly advised to pre-book accommodation, camp sites and picnic sites at the MET in Windhoek. The restaurant is open from 7.30 to 9 am, noon to 2 pm and 7 to 10 pm, and there's also a kiosk which sells drinks and refreshments.

## Getting There & Away

Take the C28 west from Windhoek. Daan Viljoen is clearly signposted about 18km from the city. You're welcome to walk in the park but no motorbikes are permitted. There's no public transport to Daan Viljoen and traffic is sparse, but persistent hitchers are likely to be successful. Several companies include the park in their Windhoek tours (see the Organised Tours section earlier in this chapter).

Daan Viljoen Game Park

# North Central Namibia

For tourists, North Central Namibia is dominated by Etosha National Park, one of the world's pre-eminent wildlife areas, but the region is also replete with historical sites and lovely natural landscapes. The picturesque towns of Okahandja, Tsumeb and Grootfontein all merit a visit, and no-one will be disappointed with Waterberg Plateau Park, a lovely island in the sky, or the Erongo Mountains, which form a dramatic backdrop along the route from Windhoek to Swakopmund.

In the north, the economy is carried by two major mining districts and vast, lonely cattle ranches, while Gobabis, which is the main settlement of the Namibian Kalahari, dominates the karakul sheep-breeding area east of Windhoek.

## OKAHANDJA

Okahandja, less than an hour's drive north of Windhoek, functions mainly as a highway service centre and crossroads between the B1 and the Swakopmund road (B2). It's also the administrative centre for the Herero people, who settled in this Nama homeland in the early 19th century and thereby sparked a series of tribal wars.

### History

Okahandja (Herero for short broad river) is named after its normally dry riverbed, which the Nama originally called Gei-Keis, the broad sand. The first German visitor, missionary Heinrich Schmelen, arrived in 1827 and renamed it Schmelen's Hope, but missionary activities weren't established until 1843 by Heinrich Kleinschmidt and Carl Hahn. In 1849, Friedrich Kolbe founded a mission but, after only a few months, it was destroyed by Nama forces under their highly charged leader, Jan Jonker Afrikaner, who had been commandeering Herero cattle and objected to German interference. A subsequent mission lasted from 1870 to 1890, when it gave

## HIGHLIGHTS

- Spend a few days in Etosha National Park, one of the world's premier wildlife venues
- Climb to Mountain View on the Waterberg Plateau for a view across forever
- Gain insight into the Herero heritage in Okahandja
- Visit the Tsumeb museum and see the world's greatest diversity of minerals
- Look for dinosaurs – or at least their tracks – on Otjihaenamaparero Farm

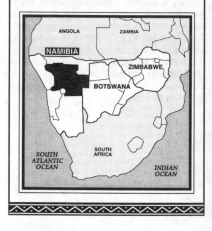

way to earnest German colonisation – and the founding of German Okahandja in 1894.

### Cemeteries

In the churchyard of the 1876 Rhenish mission church, Friedenskirche, are the graves of several historical figures, including Willem Maherero. Opposite the church are three other notable graves: Nama leader Jan Jonker Afrikaner, who died in 1861; Clemens Kapuuo, a former Democratic Turnhalle Alliance (DTA) president, who

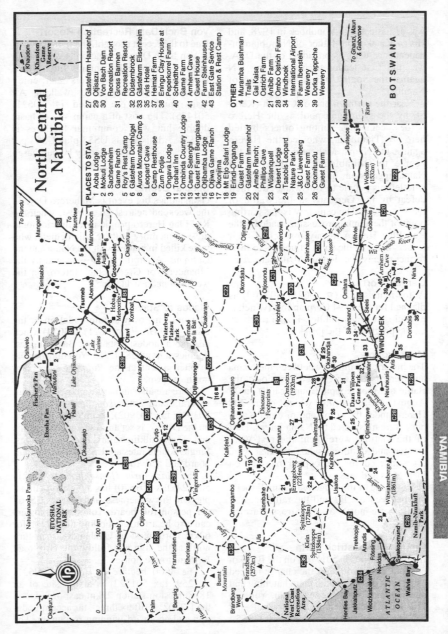

was assassinated in Windhoek in 1978; and Hosea Kutako, the father of Namibian independence who, as president of the DTA, was the first leader to petition the UN against the South African occupation of Namibia.

Near the northern end of Church (Kerk) St, by the swimming pool, is the Herero heroes' cemetery. Among others buried here are Tjamuaha, who led the Herero against the Nama; Maherero, who led the people to Otjimbingwe in the face of Nama aggression; and Samuel Maherero, who led his people to Botswana after their defeat by the Germans at the Battle of the Waterberg. The cemetery is the starting point of the annual procession made by the Red Flag Herero to pay respect to their leaders and – in the spirit of unity – to their former enemy, Jan Jonker Afrikaner.

### German Fort
A town museum (☎ (0621) 502700) is planned for the 1894 German fort (which is now closed to the public). Phone to check on the progress of the project.

### Moordkoppie
The historical animosity between the Nama and Herero had its greatest expression at the Battle of Moordkoppie (murder hill) on 23 August 1850, during which over 700 Herero under the command of chief Katjihene were massacred by Nama forces. Half of the victims were men; the rest were women and children, whose bodies were dismembered for the copper bangles on their arms and legs.

The scene of this tragedy is a small rocky hill between the B2 and the rail line, half a kilometre north of the Gross Barmen turn-off.

### Ombo Show Ostrich Farm
In Ombo (☎ (0621) 501176), on the B1 3km north of town, you have the chance to feed ostrich, sit on one, watch them hatching and dancing and, of course, eat them. You can also watch locals making Herero dolls and Kavango woodcarvings. Tours cost US$5.

### Von Bach Dam Recreation Resort
Due to the recent drought, the fishing resort at Von Bach Dam Recreation Resort, south of town on the B1, contains little water. However, even non-anglers can enjoy picnics, birdwatching or bushwalking. All visits must be pre-booked (☎ (0621) 501475). The cost of a camp site or basic double hut with communal facilities is US$21. Admission is US$3 plus US$3 per vehicle. Fishing licences may be purchased at the gate.

### Special Events
Okahandja's big event is Maherero Day, on the weekend nearest 26 August, when the Red Flag Herero people meet in traditional dress in memory of their fallen chiefs, who were killed in battles with the Nama and the Germans. A similar event is staged by the Mbanderu, or Green Flag Herero, on the weekend nearest 11 June.

### Places to Stay
The only in-town accommodation is the *Okahandja Hotel* (☎ (0621) 503024) which also has a modest restaurant. Basic singles/doubles start at US$15/23. You may be able to pitch a tent at the *Riding Centre* 2km north of town.

There are also numerous guest farms, but several stand out. *Okomitundu* (☎ (0621) 503901; fax 503902), south of Wilhelmstal on the D1967, is set amid scenic, rocky hills and offers walking safaris and game drives. Single/double rates are US$74/125 with full board and activities.

The *Gästefarm Haasenhof* (☎ (0621) 503827; fax 501870) has a German atmosphere in the wilderness, and charges US$67 per person full board. Tours and transfers can also be arranged. Follow the D2110 for 62km north-west of Okahandja, then turn north at the sign and follow the farm road for 6km to the house.

The 8000 hectare *Otjisazu* (☎ (0621) 501259; fax 501323) is at the site of an 1878 mission station 27km east of town on the D2102. It offers three-star accommodation and an award-winning restaurant. The

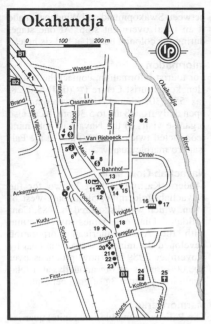

# Okahandja

0   100   200 m

friendly ambience – as well as an aquarium and reptile display – make it one of Namibia's finer guest farms. Single/double accommodation including full board costs US$132/227.

## Places to Eat
Your best casual option is the *Okahandja Bakery*, with a takeaway and pleasant little cafe. For good German cooking try the *Bürgerstübchen* (☎ (0621) 501830) which has its own butchery. The *De Solder Steakhouse & JC's Pub* is popular with travellers, and the airy *Solmar Restaurant*, in the Madeira Centre, is open daily for lunch and dinner (lunch only on Sunday). The *Riding Centre*, north of town, also has a frequently recommended restaurant and bar.

For fast snacks, try the *Pie Maker Pie Shop* on Main St or the *Fish and Chips* takeaway in the Azores supermarket. Biltong fans will love the *Namibia Biltong Factory*, which is Namibia's best. Try the delicious chilli bites – beef seasoned with peri-peri. It's currently under renovation, but should be open by the time you read this.

## Things to Buy
The two immense (and growing) craft markets – one near the junction of the B1 and B2, the other about 1km out on the B1 towards Windhoek – are great for shopping and bargaining. However, few of these articles are made in Namibia, as Zimbabwean curios can be imported very cheaply and provide greater profit margins.

## Getting There & Away
Okahandja, 70km north of Windhoek on the B1, lies on the minibus routes to both the

NAMIBIA

north and west, and on the rail line between Windhoek and Tsumeb or Swakopmund/Walvis Bay. For rail information, phone Trans-Namib (☎ (0621) 503315).

## GROSS BARMEN RECREATION RESORT

Gross Barmen, 26km south-west of Okahandja, was originally a mission station but is now Namibia's most popular hot-spring resort. It has mineral baths, tennis courts, a restaurant, and naturally heated indoor and outdoor pools. It feels like a cross between an oasis and a health farm, with lots of German-Namibians wandering around in dressing gowns.

Most people come to swim or soak, but there are also nice walks around the dam and hillsides. For birdwatchers, a path has been cut through the reedbeds, with benches where you can wait and see what flies in.

Admission is US$2 per vehicle plus US$3 per person. A session in the mineral springs or baths is an additional US$0.50.

### Places to Stay & Eat

Camp or picnic sites cost US$21 for up to eight people; even day visits must be booked in advance (☎ (0621) 501091). Self-contained double rooms are US$32, two/five-bed bungalows cost US$34/61. The site has a shop, bar, restaurant and petrol station. At the restaurant, hard-core carnivores can cash in all their hot water health chips and indulge in huge slabs of T-bone steak and inexpensive Windhoek draught beer.

### Getting There & Away

There's no public transport but, on weekends, it's not to hard to hitch from the highway turn-off south of Okahandja.

## KARIBIB

The small ranching town of Karibib, 100km west of Okahandja, began as a station on the narrow gauge Windhoek-Swakopmund line. Early rail services travelled only by day, and Karibib's position halfway between Swakopmund and Windhoek made it an ideal overnight stop. At one stage, during the colonial period, it had six hotels.

### Information

For tourist information, contact the helpful Henckert Tourist Centre (☎ (064) 550028; fax 550230; <henckert@iwwn.com.na>), open daily from 8 am to 5.30 pm. It can also organise visits to the Navachab gold mine (conducted twice monthly) and to the Palisandro marble quarry.

### Navachab Gold Mine

Modern Karibib is best known for the Navachab gold mine, 5km south-west of town, which was discovered in 1985. Consolidated Diamond Mines in consortium with the Anglo-American Corporation developed the mine. It was operational by November 1989 and now produces over 700,000 tonnes of ore annually, at a relatively low yield of 3g of gold per tonne.

### Marmorwerke

The Palisandro marble (aragonite) quarries annually yield over 1200 tonnes of the hardest, highest-quality marble in the world. The marble is processed at the *Marmorwerke* (German for marble works), west of town.

### Historical Buildings

Most buildings along Karibib's main street have historical significance. Among them are the old railway station, which dates from 1900; the Rösemann & Kronewitter Building, built in 1900 as the headquarters of an early German trading firm; the church-like Haus Woll, built of granite in the first decade of the 20th century; and the Christuskirche, built in 1910. It was the first church in Namibia to be constructed of marble.

### Places to Stay

The *Hotel Pension Erongoblick* (☎ (064) 550009; fax 550095), in the town centre, is housed in a converted boarding school but has been well refurbished and has almost completely shed its former institutional atmosphere. With a great pool and good restaurant (closed on Saturdays), it's a good mid-range option. Rooms with shared bath are US$18 per person, with breakfast. With private bath singles/doubles are US$33/44. For US$15, sundowner tours to the private Karibib game ranch can be arranged.

The cool and shady *Hotel Stroblhof* (☎ (064) 550081; fax 550240), at the eastern end of town, has air-conditioned singles/doubles for US$41/63. Amenities include a restaurant (closed Monday) and swimming pool.

### Places to Eat
In addition to the two *hotel restaurants*, there's the popular *Springbok Cafe & Steakhouse*. The *Karibib Bakery*, which is great for breakfast and real brewed coffee, was constructed in 1913 as one of Karibib's first hotels. The *Klippenburg Club* serves up steak and chips, goulash, spaghetti and other popular lunch and dinner options. Turn south at the post office.

### Things to Buy
The Wolfgang Henckert Tourist Centre specialises in beautiful Karibib tourmaline and other Namibian gems. It's also the home of Der Webervogel, a factory-shop where local women produce fine karakul weavings.

### Getting There & Away
Karibib is accessible by any bus service between Windhoek and Swakopmund. The Intercape Mainliner from Windhoek (US$19, 2½ hours) stops at the Hotel Stroblhof. Except on Sundays, trains between Windhoek and Swakopmund/Walvis Bay stop at Karibib at 2.20 am eastbound and 12.40 am westbound.

### OTJIMBINGWE
One would never suspect that the forgotten village of Otjimbingwe, 55km south of Karibib on the D1953, was once the administrative capital of German South West Africa. In Herero the name means place of refreshment, after the freshwater spring near the confluence of the Omusema and Swakop rivers. The presence of water and the fact that Otjimbingwe lay midway along the wagon route between Windhoek and Walvis Bay led Reichskommissar Heinrich Göring to declare it the colonial capital in the early 1880s.

### History
Otjimbingwe was founded by Johannes Rath in 1849 as a Rhenish mission, but the church wasn't built until 1867. After copper was discovered in the mid-1850s, the Walvis Bay Mining Company (WBM) set up operations, and the quiet mission station turned into a rollicking, Wild West-style mining town. In the early 1880s the town became the administrative seat of German South West Africa and, in 1888, the site of the country's first post office. However, when the capital was transferred to Windhoek in 1890, Otjimbingwe declined. The final blow came when it was bypassed by the Windhoek-Swakopmund railway in the early 20th century.

### Historic Buildings
Have a look at the Rhenish church; the historic WBM trading store; the wind-driven generator used to power the Hälbich wagon factory; and the 1872 powder magazine, which was intended as a first line of defence against attack by the Nama.

### Tsaobis Leopard Nature Park
The Tsaobis Leopard Nature Park occupies 35 sq km of rugged rocky country along the southern bank of the Swakop River. It was here in 1889 that Major Curt von François constructed a fortified barracks here for the Schutztruppe. In 1969, it was established as a leopard sanctuary and is now home to leopard, antelope and mountain zebra, along with wild dog, cheetah and various other enclosed animals. The scenery, hiking opportunities and accommodation are good but, without a vehicle, access is nearly impossible. The park lies 35km west of Otjimbingwe, just west of the junction of the C32 and the D1976.

NAMIBIA

## Places to Stay

The *Tsaobis Leopard Nature Park* (☎ (062252) ask for 1304; fax (061) 233690) features two-bed self-catering bungalows from US$43. Doubles with full board cost from US$33 to US$39. Meals are available.

The lovely *J&C Lievenberg Guest Farm* (☎ (062252) 3112; fax (061) 234470), on the Swakop River between Otjimbingwe and Gross Barmen, has full-board accommodation from US$85 per person; B&B is a bit cheaper. Facilities include a tennis court and a driving range.

## USAKOS

Usakos (grasp by the heel) was originally developed as a station on the narrow-gauge railway that linked the port of Walvis Bay with the mines of the Golden Triangle. Its charming architecture still makes it one of Namibia's nicest small towns. In the first decade of the 20th century, its location was deemed ideal for the country's first railway workshops and Usakos became Namibia's railway capital. It held this position until 1960, when narrow gauge was replaced by standard gauge, steam-powered locomotives gave way to diesel engines and the works yard was shifted to Windhoek.

## Information

The Namib i Tourist Information office is in the Shell petrol station.

## Locomotive No 40

In honour of Usakos' railway past, Locomotive No 40 stands proudly in front of the railway station. It was one of three Henschel heavy-duty locomotives built in 1912 by the firm of Henschel & Son in Kassel, Germany. Its counterpart, Locomotive No 41, occupies a similar position at the station in Otjiwarongo.

## Places to Stay & Eat

The only accommodation is the austere but historic *Usakos Hotel* (☎ (064) 530259; fax 530267) with rooms for US$23 per person. For snacks you're limited to *Khan Take-aways*, opposite the post office, which mainly does fish and chips.

On the fringes of the Namib, 70km south-west of town on the D1914, lies the very friendly *Wüstenquell Desert Lodge* (☎ (062242) 1312; fax (062252) 277). The name is German for desert spring. Camping costs US$5 per person (you can hire equipment) and B&B/full board is modestly priced at US$30/50 per person. Farm tours will take you through the unusual rock formations and to an abandoned 1900 colonial railway station.

## Getting There & Away

Usakos lies on the bus, minibus and railway routes between Windhoek and Swakopmund/Walvis Bay. Except on Sunday, trains stop at 12.45 am eastbound and at 1.55 am westbound.

## ERONGO MOUNTAINS

The volcanic Erongo Mountains rise as a 2320m massif north of Karibib and Usakos. After the original period of volcanism some 150 million years ago, the volcano collapsed in on its magma chamber, allowing the basin to fill with slow-cooling igneous material. The result is this hard granite-like core, which withstood the erosion that washed away the surrounding rock.

## Things to See

The Erongo range is best known for its caves and rock paintings, particularly the 50m-deep Phillips Cave on the Ameib ranch. This cave, which lies 3km off the road, contains the famous white elephant painting. Superimposed on the elephant is a large hump-backed antelope (an eland?) and around it frolic ostrich and giraffe. The Ameib paintings were brought to the world's attention in the book *Phillips Cave* by prehistorian Abbé Breuil, but his speculations about their Mediterranean origins have now been discounted. The site is open to day hikers from Ameib.

The Ameib picnic site is backed up by outcrops of stacked boulders, one of which, the notable Bull's Party, resembles a circle of gossiping bovines. Another formation that is much-photographed resembles a Herero woman in traditional dress, standing with two children. Day permits for Ameib Ranch cost US$5.

### Places to Stay
*Ameib Ranch* (☎ (062242) 1111), whose name means green hill, sits at the base of the Erongo foothills. It began in 1864 as a Rhenish mission station and now operates as a luxurious guest farm and camp site. In fact, a stay can be a bit like stepping into German Namibian history. Unfortunately, the attached wildlife sanctuary is little more than a zoo, with unappealing cages.

Accommodation in the historic farmhouse is US$70 per person with full board and use of the pool. Camp sites cost US$8 per person and double pre-erected tents are US$20. No caravans are allowed. Breakfast costs US$6, lunch is US$10 and substantial dinners are US$12. Booked guests are picked up from Usakos, but campers pay US$10 per trip.

### Getting There & Away
North of Ameib, the D1935 skirts the Erongo Mountains before heading north into Damaraland. Alternatively, you can head east towards Omaruru on the D1937. This route virtually encircles the Erongo massif, and provides access to minor 4WD roads into the heart of the mountains. These roads will take you to some of the range's best wild bushwalking.

## OMARURU
Omaruru's dry and dusty setting beside the shady Omaruru riverbed lends it a real outback feel. Its name means bitter, thick milk in Herero and refers to the milk produced by cattle which have grazed on bitterbush (*Pechuelloeschae leubnitziae*). In dry periods, this hardy plant remains green and tasty long after other vegetation has become insipid.

### History
Omaruru began as a trading post and Rhenish mission station in 1870, and it was here that the New Testament and the liturgies were first translated into Herero, thanks to the zeal of missionary Gottlieb Veihe.

As with so many Central Namibian towns, the colonial occupation brought with it a German garrison and, consequently, local resistance. In January 1904, Omaruru was attacked by Herero forces under chief Manassa. German captain Victor Franke, who had been engaged in suppressing an uprising in southern Namibia, petitioned Governor Leutwein for permission to march north and relieve the besieged town. After a 20 day, 900km march, he arrived in Omaruru and led the cavalry charge that defeated the Herero attack.

For his efforts Franke received the highest German military honours and, in 1908, the grateful German residents of Omaruru erected the Franke Tower in his honour.

### Information
The Omaruru tourist office (☎ (064) 570277) is on the main street. Opening hours are Monday to Friday, from 8 am to 1 pm and 2.15 to 5 pm.

### Franke Tower
Captain Franke's tower, which was declared a national monument in 1963, holds a historical plaque and affords a view over the town. It's normally locked; if you want to climb it, pick up a key at either the Central Hotel or the Hotel Staebe.

### Rhenish Mission Museum
The Rhenish mission station, which was constructed in 1872 by missionary Gottlieb Viehe, now houses the town museum. Displays include 19th century household and farming implements, an old drinks dispenser, and lots of historical photographs. Opposite is the cemetery where Herero chief Wilhelm Zeraua and several early German residents are buried. Admission is free; pick up the museum keys from the tourist office.

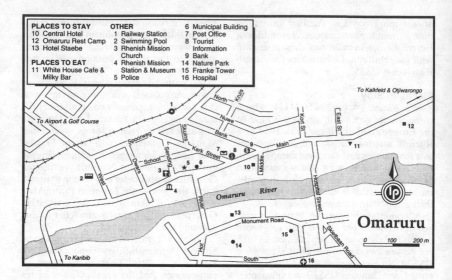

| PLACES TO STAY | OTHER | 6 Municipal Building |
|---|---|---|
| 10 Central Hotel | 1 Railway Station | 7 Post Office |
| 12 Omaruru Rest Camp | 2 Swimming Pool | 8 Tourist |
| 13 Hotel Staebe | 3 Rhenish Mission | Information |
| | Church | 9 Bank |
| PLACES TO EAT | 4 Rhenish Mission | 14 Nature Park |
| 11 White House Cafe & | Station & Museum | 15 Franke Tower |
| Milky Bar | 5 Police | 16 Hospital |

## Anibib Farm

Anibib farm (☎ (062232) 1711 or (064) 571711), off the D2315, has one of Namibia's largest collections of ancient rock paintings. This gallery is known for depictions of humans and animals, whose positions represent various activities. Farmer Lamie Drotskie runs two guided tours daily for groups. Pre-booking for these is essential.

## Festivals

Each year on the weekend nearest 10 October, the White Flag Herero people hold a procession from the Ozonde suburb to the graveyard, opposite the mission house, where their chief Wilhelm Zeraua was buried after his defeat in the German-Herero wars.

## Places to Stay

The leafy *Omaruru Rest Camp* (☎/fax (064) 570516) charges US$5 per person for camping or overnight stays in birdwatching huts. Basic two/three-bed bungalows cost US$20 and self-catering chalets are US$30 for four people.

The German-run *Hotel Staebe* (☎ (064) 570035; fax 570450) occupies a pleasant green setting across the river from town and charges US$35/50 for single/double rooms, including breakfast. The smaller, more spartan *Central Hotel* (☎ (064) 570030; fax 570353) singles/doubles cost US$25/30.

On the Omaruru River, 16km east of town, is the new *Omaruru Game Lodge* (☎ (064) 570044; fax 570134). It offers a taste of the bush on a scenic, well-watered game farm with a wide variety of antelope and other animals. Singles/doubles with breakfast cost US$79/140.

Omaruru lies in the heart of guest-farm country, and there are a couple of options. The hospitable *Erindi-Onganga Guest Farm* (☎ (06532) 1202) lies 6km off the D2351, 75km north-west of Omaruru. Singles/doubles with bath and full board cost around US$55/75.

The *Gästefarm Immenhof* (☎/fax (067) 290177; <colourgem@iafrica.com>), run by Friedhelm and Ria von Seydlitz, offers farmhouse accommodation for birdwatchers and rockhounds amid lonely hills. Single/double rooms with breakfast cost

US$58/99; with full board they're US$81/143. Note that this is also a hunting farm.

### Places to Eat
The cosy *White House Cafe & Milky Bar* on the main street is housed in a historic building dating from 1907. In addition to German baked goods, they do 'farmhouse' breakfasts, lunch and snacks. It's open daily from 8 am to 7 pm. For takeaways, fresh bread and ice cream, see the *Mini-Markt*, also on the main street.

Both hotels have restaurants attached; the wholesome German-style meals at the *Hotel Staebe* are recommended.

Omaruru is in a major fruit-growing area and people sell citrus at roadside stalls from July to September.

### Getting There & Away
Omaruru lies 280km from Windhoek, but there's no public transport. With your own vehicle, the well maintained C33, which passes through Omaruru, provides the quickest route between Swakopmund and Etosha.

All rail services travelling to or from Tsumeb from Walvis Bay or Windhoek call in at Omaruru. The weekday economy/sleeper class fare from Windhoek is US$4.20/12; on weekends, it's US$8.50/25. For rail information, phone Trans-Namib (☎ (064) 570006).

### KALKFELD
Around 200 million years ago Namibia was covered in a shallow sea, which gradually filled in with wind-blown sand and eroded silt. Near the tiny town of Kalkfeld, these sandstone layers bear the evidence of a 25m dinosaur stroll which took place 170 million years ago. The prints were made in what was then soft clay by a three-toed dinosaur that walked on its hind legs – probably a forerunner of modern birds.

The tracks lie 29km from Kalkfeld on Otjihaenamaparero farm, just off route D2414. The site was declared a national monument in 1951, but visits are still subject to the farmer's permission.

### Places to Stay
There's no accommodation in Kalkfeld, but nearby is the luxurious *Mt Etjo Safari Lodge* (☎ (0651) 304464; fax 304035), PO Box 81, Kalkfeld. It's set in the heart of the private nature reserve owned by conservationist Jan Oelofse. The name Etjo means place of refuge, and its place in history was sealed in April 1989 when the Mt Etjo Peace Agreement was signed, ending the bush war and setting the stage for Namibian independence the following March. Singles/doubles with en suite facilities start at US$75/137, including full board and game drives. Transfers are extra.

### OUTJO
Bougainvillea-decked Outjo was established in 1880 by trader Tom Lambert. It was rather a latecomer by local standards and, unlike many other local towns, it never served as a mission station. In the mid-1890s it did a stint as a German garrison town, but it didn't see enough trouble to earn itself a place in history.

Today, Outjo's environs boast citrus groves and, as with most of central Namibia, the economy concentrates heavily on cattle-ranching. For visitors, it serves as a jumping-off point for trips into the Okaukuejo area of Etosha National Park.

### Information
Information and fax/email services are available at the Camp Setenghi information office (☎/fax (0654) 313445; <setenghi@iafrica.com.na>) behind the Caltex petrol station.

### Naulila Monument
This monument commemorates the 19 October 1914 massacre of German soldiers and officials by the Portuguese near Fort Naulila on the Kunene River in Angola. It also commemorates soldiers killed on 18 December 1914, under Major Franke, who was sent to avenge the earlier losses.

### Franke House Museum
The Franke House, originally called the

NAMIBIA

Kliphuis or stone house, is one of Outjo's earliest buildings, constructed in 1899 by order of Major von Estorff as a residence for himself and subsequent German commanders. It was later occupied by Major (formerly Captain) Victor Franke, who gave it his name. It now houses the Outjo Museum, with exhibits on political and natural history.

The museum is open Monday to Friday from 10 am to 12.30 pm and 3 to 5 pm. At other times, pick up a key from the tourist office on the main road. Admission is free.

### Windmill Tower
On the C39, east of Outjo, the old stone windmill tower rises 9.5m beside the Etosha Garten Hotel. It was constructed in 1900 to provide fresh water for German soldiers and their horses, as well as for the hospital.

### Places to Stay & Eat
Outjo's top hotel, the *Hotel Onduri* (☎ (0654) 313014; fax 313166), has singles/doubles with private facilities for US$32/45. It caters for tourists en route to Etosha, and has a restaurant, bar, pool table, swimming pool, and a beer garden set amid fragrant citrus trees. The smaller *Etosha Garten Hotel* (☎ (0654) 313130; fax 313419), on the Otavi road, charges US$31 per person with breakfast.

The jacaranda-studded *Ombinda Country Lodge* (☎ (0654) 313181; fax 313478) is 1km south of town. The single/double reed-and-thatch chalets cost US$50/70 with breakfast; double pre-erected tents are US$15; and camp sites cost US$5 per person.

The beautifully situated *Camp Setenghi* (☎/fax (0654) 313445; <setenghi@iafrica.com.na>), run by Wayne and Ilvia MacAdam, lies on the slopes of the Ugab Terrace, 4km down the Kalkfeld turnoff (which is 4km south of town). It offers highly acclaimed tented or natural stone bungalow accommodation for US$50 per person with breakfast. Camping costs US$6 per person and horse rides start at US$23.

The *Guest Farm Bergplaas* (☎ (06548) ask for 1802; fax (0654) 313000) is a lovely 12,000 hectare German-oriented spread in the Great Paresis mountains, 20km south of Outjo on the D63. B&B costs US$32 per person and half/full board is US$39/43.

### Places to Eat
The restaurants and bars at both in-town hotels serve meals and snacks; Etosha Garten's *Jacaranda* is especially nice. The super little *Outjo Café-Bäckerei* (☎ (0654) 313055), diagonally opposite the tourist office, serves chicken, Wiener schnitzel and burgers, and the bread and sweet treats are famous throughout the region.

### Getting There & Away
A Star Line bus between Outjo and Otjiwarongo (US$3, one hour) leaves Outjo on Monday and Thursday afternoons and departs Otjiwarongo on the same days at 7 am. On Monday, there are connections to Khorixas, Kamanjab and Opuwo; and on Thursday, to Khorixas, Henties Bay, Swakopmund and Walvis Bay. Hitchers see Outjo as a logical jumping-off point for Etosha's Andersson Gate, which lies 105km away on the C38.

## OTJIWARONGO
At the agricultural and ranching centre of Otjiwarongo (Herero for the pleasant place), the roads between Windhoek, Swakopmund, Outjo/Etosha and the Golden Triangle (Otavi, Tsumeb and Grootfontein) converge. In September and October, the town explodes with the vivid colours of blooming jacaranda and bougainvillea. On the B1 into town from the south, watch west of the road for the twin Omatako peaks – the name is Herero for buttocks.

After an 1891 treaty between German missionaries and the Herero chief Kambazembi, a Rhenish mission station was established and a German military garrison arrived in 1904. The town was officially founded in 1906 with the arrival of the narrow-gauge railway from Swakopmund to the mines at Otavi and Tsumeb.

## Information

Tourist information is available from the Hamburger Hof Hotel.

## Locomotive No 41

At the railway station stands Locomotive No 41, which was manufactured in 1912 by the Henschel company of Kassel, Germany, and was brought to Namibia to haul ore between the Tsumeb mines and the port at Swakopmund. It was retired from service in 1960 when the 0.6m narrow gauge was replaced with a 1.067m gauge.

## Crocodile Ranch

One unusual attraction is Namibia's first crocodile ranch (☎ (0651) 302121), which produces skins for export to Asia. It's open weekdays from 9 am to 4 pm and weekends from 11 am to 2 pm. A cafe serves snacks and light meals. Admission costs US$2. The ranch is on the corner of Zingel St and Hospital St, next to the Caravan Park.

## Places to Stay

The *Otjiwarongo Caravan Park* (☎ (0651) 302231; fax 302098) is conveniently located beside the crocodile ranch, allowing campers to take advantage of the cafe. Camping costs US$7 per site plus US$1 per person. However, be warned that security is poor and we have had several reports of violent robbery here.

Karen Falk's friendly *B&B Otjiwarongo* (☎/fax (0651) 302616) at 21 Industria Ave is a welcome mid-range option, and bird-lovers will appreciate the colourful aviary. Singles/doubles with en suite facilities are US$23/41. The similar *Out of Africa B&B* (☎ (0651) 303397), near the corner of Tuin (Garden) St and Oosweg, at the southern end of town, has a simple, homely atmosphere. Singles/doubles with TV, air conditioning and private facilities cost US$22/35.

The recently renovated *Rent-a-Room* (☎ (0651) 302517; fax 303005) has sparkling singles/doubles with shared facilities and breakfast for US$32/40. With bath and air conditioning, they're US$36/44.

The air-conditioned *Hamburger Hof* (☎ (0651) 302520; fax 303607) is not, as it's name may suggest, any sort of fast-food outlet. Budget singles/doubles cost US$35/40; rooms with TV and private bath are US$43/66. Breakfast is extra.

**Out of Town** The rather low-key *Otjibamba Lodge* (☎ (0651) 303133; fax 303206) lies 3km south and 1km west of Otjiwarongo. Cute little single/double chalets cost US$37/46, with breakfast, and there's a restaurant, bar, pool and nine-hole golf course.

The *Otjiwa Game Ranch Rest Camp* (☎ (0651) 302665; fax 302668), 30km south of town on the B1, has bungalows for one/three people for US$29/40 and an eight-bed bungalow for US$65. Meals are available for an extra charge. The main attraction of this private ranch is the wildlife viewing.

The renowned *Okonjima* (☎ (0651) 304563; fax 304565), the 'place of baboons', is technically a guest farm but more resembles a safari lodge. Run by the Hansen family, it's one of Namibia's most pleasant and unique lodges. Single/double bungalows cost US$190/330 in high season and US$165/280 from late February to early June. This includes three home-cooked meals a day, game walks, game drives, Bushman and Bantu trails and bird-watching. There are over 200 speciesto be seen locally, including the Damara rock-runner, Monteiro's hornbill and Hartlaub's francolin.

The big attraction, however, is the cats. The owners have established a unique cheetah and leopard rehabilitation centre, where problem cats are taught not to ravage cattle, but their organisation, Africat, protects all endangered native cats. In addition to their rehab cases, they keep two tame pet cheetahs, Caesar and Chinga, who behave like overgrown kitties and get on well with guests. There's also a baboon called Elvis, a warthog named Scratch and even a house-trained caracal. As a result, no children under 12 are allowed. For information on

NAMIBIA

their efforts, contact Africat (☎ (0651) 304563; fax 304565), PO Box 793, Otjiwarongo.

To reach the farm, follow the B1 for 49km south of Otjiwarongo and turn west onto the D2515. Follow this road for 15km and turn left onto the farm road for the last 10km.

### Places to Eat
The in-town hotels have bars and restaurants serving meals and snacks, and the crocodile ranch also serves light meals. On the main street through Otjiwarongo you can find the usual range of takeaway facilities. *Carstensen's* is an excellent bakery in the centre of town.

### Getting There & Away
**Bus** Minibuses between Windhoek and the Owambo country pass through Otjiwarongo and stop at the Engen petrol station. There's also an occasional minibus to Okakarara. Star Line (☎ (0651) 5202) has buses to Outjo (US$3, one hour) on Monday and Thursday mornings. These services return in the afternoon on the same days.

On Monday and Thursday, there are connections to Khorixas, Kamanjab and Opuwo, and on Thursday they also run to Henties Bay, Swakopmund and Walvis Bay. The 7 am Wednesday bus to Okakarara passes within 21km of Waterberg Plateau Park.

**Train** The rail services which run between Windhoek or Walvis Bay and Tsumeb call at Otjiwarongo. For information, phone Trans-Namib (☎ (0651) 5202).

### WATERBERG PLATEAU PARK
The Waterberg Plateau Park takes in a 50km-long, 16km-wide sandstone plateau, which looms 150m above the plain. As its name suggests, this sheer-sided plateau has an abundance of freshwater springs. Rainwater is absorbed by sandstone layers and percolates through the strata until it reaches the south-west tilting mudstone, forming an aquifer that emerges in springs at the cliff

base. The resulting lush mosaic of trees and scrub savanna supports a profusion of wildlife.

The park is also known as a repository for rare and threatened species, including sable and roan antelope and both white and black rhino. You may also see wild dog, tsessebe, buffalo, leopard, cheetah and lesser bushbabies, among other species. Waterberg also has more than 200 bird species including the black eagle, the rare Ruppell's parrot, rockrunners and both Bradfield's and Monteiro's hornbills.

### History
In 1873, a Rhenish mission station was established at Waterberg, but it was destroyed in 1880 during the Herero-Nama wars. In 1904, it was the site of the decisive Battle of the Waterberg between the German colonial forces and the Herero resistance. Due to superior communications, the Germans prevailed.

Every year, on the weekend nearest 11 August, the local Herero, the Scouts, the MOTH, and the Alte Kamaraden (the German legion) commemorate the confrontation. The ceremony takes place at the memorial in the cemetery near the resort office. If you wish to attend, sober dress is appropriate.

### Information
The warden's office at the Bernabé de la Bat Rest Camp can help with tourist inquiries. The camp is open year round from 8 am to 1 pm and from 2 pm to sunset. Park admission is US$3 per person plus US$3 per vehicle.

For useful information, see the booklet *Waterberg Flora: Footpaths In and Around the Camp* by Craven & Marais, which costs US$8 at the camp shop, or pick up *Waterberg Plateau Park* by Ilme Schneider, which is sold in bookshops and rest camps around the country.

### Bernabé de la Bat Walking Tracks
Around the pink sandstone rest camp are nine short walking tracks, including one up

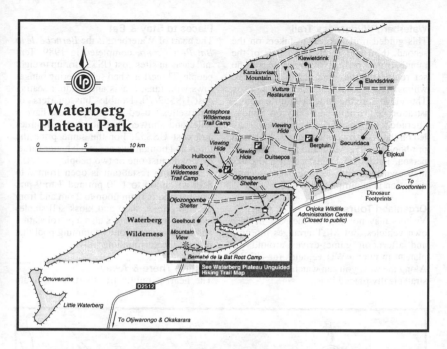

## Waterberg Plateau Park

0   5   10 km

to the plateau rim at Mountain View. The tracks are good for a pleasant day of easy walking, but watch for snakes, which sun themselves on rocks and even on the tracks themselves. No reservations are required for these walks.

### Okarukuvisa Vulture Sanctuary

In the Okarukuvisa Mountains, on the plateau's northern edge, is Namibia's only Cape vulture sanctuary. Vultures were nearly wiped out after insecticides were sprayed on surrounding farms in the 1950s. MET now hopes to increase their numbers by establishing a 'vulture restaurant' on the plateau, which provides a regular menu of kudu and gemsbok carcasses. Visitors can watch the vultures chomping away every Wednesday morning.

### Unguided Hiking Trail

The four day, 42km unguided hike around a figure-eight track in the southern area of the park begins at 9 am on Wednesday between 1 April and 30 November. You need a group of between three and 10 people and must pre-book through MET in Windhoek (☎ (061) 233875).

The first day begins at Mountain View and follows the escarpment for 13km to Otjozongombe shelter. The second day's walk to Otjomapenda shelter is just a three hour, 7km walk. The third day comprises an 8km route that loops back to Otjomapenda for the third night. The fourth and final day is a six hour, 14km return to Bernabé de la Bat. Both shelters have drinking water, and you'll need to drink 3 to 4L per day, especially in April, May, October and November.

The hike costs US$21 per person and the minimum age for taking part is 12. Accommodation is in basic shelters, and hikers must be self-sufficient.

NAMIBIA

### Waterberg Wilderness Trail

This guided trail is open to hikers on the second, third and fourth weekends of the month, from April to November. There's no set route and the itinerary is left to the whims of the guide. Walks begin at 4 pm on Thursdays from the Onjoka wildlife administration centre and end early on Sunday afternoon. Groups of six to eight people are led on the walk by armed guides. You must pre-book through MET and pay US$45 per person. Participants must be fit and carry their own food and sleeping bags. Accommodation is in simple huts en route.

### Organised Tours

Visitors may not explore the park in their own vehicles, but MET arranges morning and afternoon game drives around the plateau in open 4WD vehicles for US$12. Along the way, you can watch wildlife from strategically placed hides.

### Places to Stay & Eat

The heart of Waterberg is the *Bernabé de la Bat Rest Camp*, completed in 1989. Tent and caravan sites cost US$21 for up to eight people. Three/four-bed self-catering bungalows with fans, braais and outdoor seating cost US$52/70. Double 'bus quarters' or 'tourisettes', used by group tours, have a toilet and showers but no other amenities and cost US$52. For the same price the three-bed bungalows are much better value, even with just one or two people.

The camp restaurant is open from 7 to 8.30 am, noon to 1.30 pm and 7 to 9 pm. The bar opens from noon to 2 pm and from 6 to 10 pm. A shop and kiosk sell staples and snacks, and there's also a petrol station and a russet sandstone swimming pool that reflects the surrounding hills.

### Getting There & Away

The nearest public transport is the 7 am

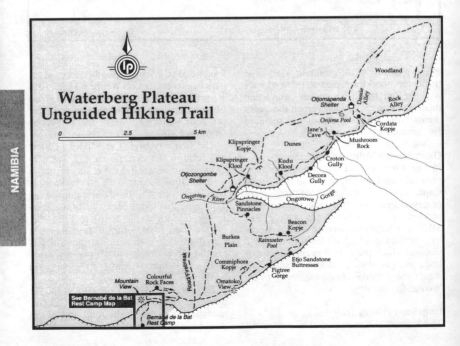

Waterberg Plateau Unguided Hiking Trail

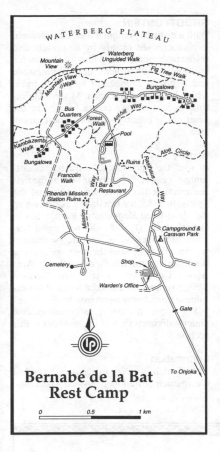

WATERBERG PLATEAU

Mountain View

Waterberg Unguided Walk

Fig Tree Walk

Mountain View Walk

Bungalows

Bus Quarters

Forest Walk

Anthill Way

Kambazembi Walk

Pool

Bungalows

Aloe Circle

Ruins

Rasthaus Way

Francolin Walk

Rhenish Mission Station Ruins

Bar & Restaurant

Mission Way

Campground & Caravan Park

Cemetery

Shop

Warden's Office

Gate

To Onjoka

**Bernabé de la Bat Rest Camp**

0        0.5        1 km

Wednesday bus from Otjiwarongo to Okakarara on the C22, which passes within 21km of Bernabé de la Bat. Most travellers attempt to hitch from the C22 to the camp, or you can take a taxi for around US$25. Note that bicycles and motorbikes aren't permitted in the park. If you have a good vehicle, you can travel the particularly scenic D2512 between Waterberg and Grootfontein.

## OTAVI

Between Otjiwarongo and Tsumeb the B1 passes Otavi, 'the place of water', near the mountains of the same name. The town was originally a German garrison whose natural springs were used to irrigate the surrounding land to cultivate wheat. Otavi grew after the railway was established in 1906 and became a major copper-mining centre, linked to Swakopmund via a narrow-gauge railway.

The Khorab Memorial, 2km north of Otavi, was erected in 1920 to commemorate the German troops who surrendered to the South African army under General Louis Botha on 9 July 1915. To get there, follow the road past the Otavi Gardens Hotel, cross the railway line and turn right along the signposted track.

In recent history, Otavi is best known as the site of the 'Otavi ape' discovery. In 1991, French and US palaeontologists uncovered the jawbone of a prehistoric ape-like creature (*Otavipithecus namibiensis*), which may shed some light on the prehistoric 'missing link'.

The tourist office is in the municipal buildings beside the Lions Caravan Park.

### Places to Stay & Eat
Otavi's basic *Lions Caravan Park* has 10 grassy camp sites for US$4 per site plus US$1 per person, and six self-catering four-bed bungalows for US$10 per person.

The *Otavi Gardens Hotel* (☎ (067) 234333; fax 234336) has 11 singles/doubles for US$40/54, with breakfast. For meals, you can choose between the attached bar and restaurant or the *Total Takeaway*.

On the highway between Otavi and Tsumeb is the *Camp Resthouse Zum Potjie* (☎ (067) 221454; fax 234300), which is set in a nice hilly area. It offers a restaurant and basic single/double bungalows for US$40/57. Camping is also available.

### Getting There & Away
All minibuses between Windhoek and Tsumeb or Oshakati pass through Otavi.

### HOBA METEORITE
The Hoba meteorite is the world's largest

NAMIBIA

and was discovered in 1920 by hunter Jacobus Brits on the Hoba Farm, 25km west of Grootfontein. No-one knows when it fell to earth (it's thought to have been around 80,000 years ago) but it weighs in at around 54,000kg and must have made a hell of a thump. Its rare cuboid shape suggests it broke up on impact and that more pieces await discovery. Analysis reveals that it's composed of 82% iron, 16% nickel, and 0.8% cobalt, with traces of other metals.

In 1955, after souvenir hunters began hacking off bits to take home, the site was declared a national monument, and a conservation project was launched with funds from the Rössing Foundation. There's now a visitors information board and a short nature trail, as well as a shady picnic area and camp site (US$2 per person). Admission is US$2.

### Getting There & Away

From Grootfontein, follow the C72 toward Tsumeb. After 4km, turn west on the D2859 and continue for about 18km to the Hoba Farm, then follow the 'Meteoriet' signs. To visit the abandoned mines at nearby Ghaub, turn north off the B8 at Kombat onto the D2863, signposted Ghaub. There's no public transport to either Hoba or Ghaub, but taxis from Otavi or Grootfontein cost around US$15.

## GROOTFONTEIN

With a distinctly colonial feel, Grootfontein is characterised mainly by an upright and respectable ambience. Many of the town's buildings are constructed of local limestone and it boasts avenues of jacaranda trees, which bloom in September. Modern Grootfontein is a market centre located in the heart of the country's major cattle-farming area.

### History

It was the spring that attracted Grootfontein's earliest visitors, as well as the first European settlers who arrived around the 1880s. In 1885, the Dorsland trekkers set up the short-lived Republic of Upingtonia in Grootfontein. By 1887 the settlement was gone but, because of the area's mineral wealth, six years later the town became the headquarters for the German South West Africa Company. In 1896 the German Schutztruppe constructed a fort and Grootfontein turned into a garrison town.

For more historical information, see under individual sites of interest later in this section.

### Information

Grootfontein's tourist office is at the end of the municipal building, just off Okavango Road.

---

## The Red Line

Between Grootfontein and Rundu, and between Tsumeb and Ondangwa, the B8 and B1 cross the Red Line, a veterinary control fence separating the commercial cattle ranches of the south from the communal subsistence lands to the north. This fence bars the north-south movement of animals as a precaution against foot-and-mouth disease and rinderpest, and animals bred north of this line may not be sold to the south or exported to overseas markets.

As a result, the Red Line also marks the effective boundary between the First and Third Worlds. The landscape south of the line is characterised by a dry scrubby bushveld of vast ranches which are home to nothing but cattle and a few scattered ranchers. However, north of the Animal Disease Control Checkpoint, travellers enter a landscape of dense bush, baobab trees, mopane scrub and small kraals, where people and animals wander along the road and the air is filled with smoke from cooking fires and bush-clearing operations.

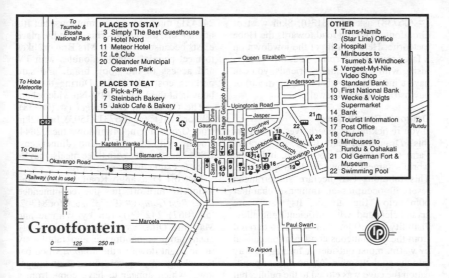

## Grootfontein

```
0    125    250 m
```

PLACES TO STAY
3 Simply The Best Guesthouse
9 Hotel Nord
11 Meteor Hotel
12 Le Club
20 Oleander Municipal
   Caravan Park

PLACES TO EAT
6 Pick-a-Pie
7 Steinbach Bakery
15 Jakob Cafe & Bakery

OTHER
1 Trans-Namib
  (Star Line) Office
2 Hospital
4 Minibuses to
  Tsumeb & Windhoek
5 Vergeet-Myt-Nie
  Video Shop
8 Standard Bank
10 First National Bank
13 Wecke & Voigts
   Supermarket
14 Bank
16 Tourist Information
17 Post Office
18 Church
19 Minibuses to
   Rundu & Oshakati
21 Old German Fort &
   Museum
22 Swimming Pool

### Grootfontein Spring

The Herero knew this area as *Otjiwanda tjongue*, or leopard's crest, but the current name, Afrikaans for large spring, parallels the Nama name *Geiaus*, which means the same thing. This reliable source of water has attracted both people and wildlife for thousands of years, and also became a halt for European hunters as early as the 1860s.

Later, the water attracted the area's first European settlers. In 1885, 40 families of Dorsland (thirstland) trekkers arrived from Angola to settle this land, which had been purchased by their leader, Will Jordan, from the Owambo chief Kambonde.

The spring after which the town is named and the adjacent Tree Park, which was planted by the South West Africa Company, can be seen near the swimming pool at the north end of town.

### German Fort & Museum

In 1896, a contingent of Schutztruppe soldiers were posted to Grootfontein and, using local labour, they constructed a fort between Upingtonia Rd and Eriksson St. It was enlarged several times in the early 20th century and, in 1922, a large limestone extension was added. Later, it served as a boarding school, but in 1968 it fell into disuse. It was only a last minute public appeal that saved the building from demolition, and in 1974 it was restored to house the municipal museum. Displays outline the area's mineral wealth, early industries and colonial history, and there are collections of minerals, domestic items, old cameras and typewriters, and a restored carpentry and blacksmith's shop.

It's open on Tuesday and Friday from 4 to 6 pm and on Wednesday from 9 to 11 am. At other times, phone (☎ (067) 242351 or 243584) to have it unlocked. Admission is free.

### Cemetery

In the town cemetery, off Okavango Road, are the graves of several Schutztruppe soldiers who died around the turn of the century.

### Gai Kaisa Ostrich Farm

If you're fascinated with big dumb birds, you should visit Tekla and Udo Unkel

(☎ (06738) ask for 83130), 8km west of Grootfontein on the road towards the Hoba meteorite. Here you'll get the lowdown on a fast-growing enterprise and, after fraternising with some feathery friends, you can have a meal (guess what's on the menu) or buy ostrich eggshell jewellery.

### Dragon's Breath Cave

If you're ticking off superlatives, how about this? Dragon's Breath Cave, on Harasab Farm 46km from Grootfontein, holds the world's largest known underground lake. This fabulous two hectare subterranean reservoir occupies an immense chamber 60m below the surface. Its waters are crystal clear and, with sufficient light, allow visibility for 100m. The name is derived from the spontaneous condensation caused by warm, moist outside air forcing its way into the cool chamber. At the time of publication the cave was closed to the public, but organised caving expeditions may be granted permission to explore it. For details, ask at the tourist office in Grootfontein.

### Places to Stay

The *Oleander Municipal Caravan Park* (☎ (067) 243101), beside the swimming pool, costs US$5 per camp site plus US$2 per car and US$1 per person. Four-bed chalets cost US$23, plus US$4 for bedding. For a luxury self-catering chalet, you'll pay US$44/52 for a single/double, and US$61/69 for three/four people. Security has improved greatly, but it's still advisable to watch your gear and valuables closely. The pool is open from 1 September to 30 April.

The friendly *Meteor Hotel* (☎ (067) 242078; fax 243072) has singles/doubles for US$34/59, including breakfast. The integrated bar is fun and offers a pleasant whiff of fresh air. The more spartan *Hotel Nord* (☎/fax (067) 242049), on Kaiser Wilhelm St, has 11 rooms and charges US$18 per person. *Le Club* (☎ (067) 242414) has single/double en suite rooms with breakfast for US$33/50.

To call a place *Simply the Best Guesthouse* (☎ (067) 242772 or 243315; fax 242431) may seem presumptuous, but it's not far off the mark. This friendly place exists because the owner Mrs Brandt 'likes to meet people'. Singles/doubles with TV and access to the pool, braai, and safe parking cost US$21/32. During the day, book in at the Vergeet-Myt-Nie video shop.

The *Gästefarm Dornhügel* (☎ (06738), ask for 81611; fax (06731) 3503), lies 42km from Grootfontein, 24km down the D2844. Rooms with breakfast and dinner cost US$42 per person; with three meals, they're US$46. Game drives cost extra.

Just off Okavango Road, opposite the Tsumkwe turn-off, lies the recommended *Roy's Rest Camp* (☎ (06738), ask for 81302; fax (067) 242409), run by Wimpie and Marietjie Otto. Everything in this lovely bush camp is handmade and fabulously rustic, right down to the *tamboti* wood bar furnishings. Two-level, four-person bungalows, which appear to have come from a fairy tale illustration, cost US$45 for the first person and US$25 for each additional person, with breakfast. Camp sites cost US$5 per person. Breakfast and dinner are US$5 to US$7 and there's a nice pool. The Ottos also run tours of their working cattle ranch.

### Places to Eat

Meat can't be ignored here in cattle country, and the steakhouse *Die Kraal*, 7km out on the road to Rundu, specialises in just that. It's the town's finest dining. The *Meteor Hotel* restaurant, on the other hand, is strong on seafood. For coffee, sweet treats and light meals, try *Steinbach* bakery and coffee shop, which is open from 7 am to 6 pm or the *Jakob Cafe & Bakery*. The *Pick-a-Pie* shop on Bismarck Strasse is open in the daytime from Monday to Saturday.

The bar and restaurant *Le Club* specialises in pizza and steak, and serves pub lunches on weekdays. Takeaway meals are available at the Shell petrol station and Wecke & Voigts supermarket.

### Getting There & Away

Despite its size and importance, Grootfontein no longer lies on the passenger rail line or the Intercape Mainliner route. Star Line (☎ (0671) 242628) runs buses to Tsumkwe on Monday with returns on Friday (US$8, 6½ hours); to Rundu on Tuesday and Wednesday, with return services on Wednesday and Thursday; and to Oshakati on Thursday (the return requires an overnight stop in Tsumeb). Minibuses for Tsumeb, Windhoek, Rundu and Oshakati leave when full from the main road near the appropriate end of town.

### Getting Around

Grootfontein has only a limited local taxi service. The Meteor Hotel is the local agent for Imperial Car Hire.

### TSUMEB

Tsumeb lies at the apex of the Golden Triangle of roads linking it with Otavi and Grootfontein. The name is derived from the melding of the San word *tsoumsoub* (to dig in loose ground) and the Herero word *otjisume* (place of frogs). To fathom the latter derivation, however, requires some imagination. Tsumeb isn't really known for its frog population; it's just that the red, brown, green and grey streaks created by minerals looked like dried scum (in Afrikaans, *paddaslyk* or frog spawn) that had been scooped out of a water hole and splattered on the rocks. As a result, both the frogs and the digging equipment appear on the town crest.

The prosperity of this mining town is based on copper ore and a phenomenal range of other metals and minerals (lead, silver, germanium and cadmium) brought to the surface in a volcanic pipe. It's also the home of Africa's most productive lead mine, which is the fifth-largest in the world., and of the 184 minerals found here, 10 are unique to this area. Mineral collectors justifiably rank Tsumeb as one of the greatest natural wonders on earth, and specimens have found their way into museum collections around the globe. The most complete collection is displayed in the Smithsonian Natural History Museum in Washington, DC, but you'll also see a fine assembly of minerals and historical data at Tsumeb's small town museum.

### History

Numerous prehistoric sites demonstrate that Tsumeb's mining history dates back to the Iron Age. The first European to recognise its riches was Sir Francis Galton, who passed through in 1851, but it was over 40 years before Europeans took serious interest. On 12 January 1893, Matthew Rogers, a British surveyor working for the South West Africa Company of London, saw the extraordinarily colourful volcanic pipe. In his report he exclaimed: 'In the whole of my experience, I have never seen such a sight as was presented before my view at Tsumeb, and I doubt ... that I shall ever see such another ...'.

As a result, exploration began in earnest in 1900. Early on, the German company Otavi Minen und Eisenbahn Gesellschaft (OMEG) determined that the extent of the deposits merited a railway, and in November 1903 they signed a contract with the South West Africa Company to construct the 560km narrow-gauge railway to the coast at Swakopmund. Despite the interruption caused by the German-Herero wars, construction of the railroad was completed in August 1906.

Mining operations commenced in 1907 and, after seven years, they were producing 75,000 tonnes of ore annually. WWI halted production, but it resumed in 1921, and by 1930 the annual output peaked at 236,000 tonnes. Operations were again interrupted by WWII and, after Germany lost the war, OMEG was put up for sale by the 'custodian of enemy property'. The Tsumeb Corporation, a consortium of South African, US and British interests, was formed to purchase the operation at a cost of one million pounds sterling. A new flotation plant was built to separate zinc from copper and lead, and in 1948 production resumed. By the mid-1960s, the Tsumeb mining operation was recording a yield of over one million tonnes of ore every year.

NAMIBIA

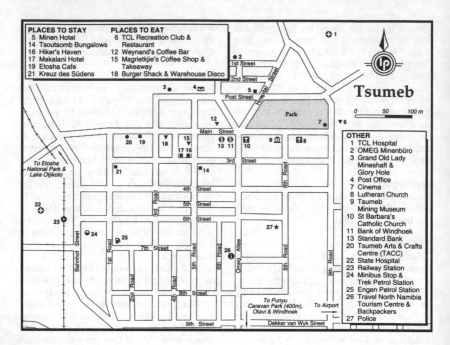

## Information

**Tourist Office** The excellent Travel North Namibia (☎ (067) 220728; fax 220916; <travelnn@tsumeb.nam.lia.net>) is the best tourist office in the country, and also the friendliest. Anita and Leon Pearson offer nationwide information, accommodation and transport bookings, airline ticketing and charters, car hire, fax and Internet services, safe-storage facilities, Etosha bookings, and a range of other services; they really go the extra mile. They also sell lovely hand-made San and Herero arts and crafts.

**Vehicle Repairs** An honest and recommended mechanic is Mr Kalish, whose Motor and General Repairs shop is behind the Engen Petrol Station.

## Tsumeb Mining Museum

Tsumeb's history is told in this museum, housed in the old German private school,

which dates from 1915. The building served two brief periods as a school and also did a stint as a hospital for German troops. In addition to outstanding mineral displays (I guarantee you'll never have seen anything like psitticinite!), mining machinery, stuffed birds and Himba and Herero artefacts, the museum holds lots of militaria, including weapons recovered from Lake Otjikoto. This was part of a dump of military materials, including German and South African field guns, cannons and vehicles, which was abandoned by German troops prior to their surrender to the South Africans in 1915. Entry costs US$1 and it's open from 9 am to noon and from 3 to 6 pm weekdays and 9 am to noon Saturday.

## Tsumeb Arts & Crafts Centre

This place is a real highlight. Run by Mr Martin Aiff, who is committed to promoting local culture, it provides stalls where artists and artisans can sell their work. There's woodwork from Caprivi, San arts, Owambo basketry and information on their distinctive styles. It's open weekdays from 8.30 am to 1 pm and 2.30 to 5.30 pm.

### Grand Old Lady Mineshaft

Visitors can now see the Grand Old Lady mineshaft and the Glory Hole where Tsumeb's modern mining history began. The worthwhile one hour tour costs US$7. Book through Travel North Namibia.

### St Barbara's Church

Tsumeb's distinctive Roman Catholic church was consecrated in 1914 and dedicated to St Barbara, the patron saint of mineworkers. It contains some fine colonial murals and an odd tower, which makes it look less like a church than a municipal building in some small German town.

### OMEG Minenbüro

Thanks to its soaring spire, the ultramodern Otavi Minen und Eisenbahn Gesellschaft Minenbüro building on First St is frequently mistaken for a church (in fact, it looks more like a church than St Barbara's!). It's probably Tsumeb's most imposing building – and you'd never guess that it dates back to 1907!

### Organised Tours

Muramba Bushman Trails (☎ (06738) ask for 6222; fax (067) 220916; <natron@lianam.lia.net>) operates day tours on the Omuramba Owambo farm, west of Tsumeb, where owner Reinhard Friederich conducts cultural walks with local Heikum San people. Participants learn about traditional lifestyles, bushcraft and the collecting of useful wild plants and herbs. You can also stay overnight, either in traditional beehive huts or thatched chalets.

### Places to Stay – Budget

The *Punyu Caravan Park* (☎ (067) 221056; fax 221464), about 1km from the town centre along the lonely double-lane entry into town, costs US$5/7 for tent/caravan sites plus US$1 per adult. Picnics cost US$5 and showers are US$3. It's now protected by an electrified fence, but it still pays to keep watch over your belongings.

In response to Tsumeb's popularity with backpackers, the Makalani Hotel opened the *Hiker's Haven* (☎ (067) 220420; fax 221575). Dorm beds and use of kitchen facilities cost US$12/9 with/without sheets. If you arrive between 2 and 5.30 pm, check in at the Makalani Hotel reception. The Travel North Namibia tourist office also intends to open a backpackers lodge and rent rooms; it should be operating by the time you read this and, as with everything else this office does, it's bound to be superb.

For clean, inexpensive accommodation, try the friendly *Etosha Cafe* (☎ (067) 221207), which has singles/doubles with shared bath for US$16/27. The small and recommended *Kreuz des Südens* (☎ (067) 221005; fax 221067), owned by Manfred and Erika Steinicke at 500 Third St, has rooms with a shower for US$16 per person; breakfast is US$4.

If you have a group, the basic but convenient *Tsoustomb* (☎ (067) 220404; fax 220592) self-catering bungalows, in the town centre, offer good value. For a self-contained six/eight-bed bungalow, you'll pay US$63/86.

### Places to Stay – Mid-Range

The *Makalani Hotel* (☎ (067) 221051; fax 221575) in the centre is quite a nice option at US$44/65 for singles/doubles with breakfast, TV and phone. The restaurant does good European-style lunches and dinners for US$9/12. There are two bars: the lively Golden Nugget Bar and the more subdued Pierre's Pub.

At the *Minen Hotel* (☎ (067) 221071; fax 221750), air-conditioned single/double courtyard rooms cost US$44/66. The hotel's greatest asset is probably its nice green setting, near the end of a lovely avenue of jacaranda trees.

### Places to Stay – Out of Town

The *Sachsenheim Game Ranch* (☎ (067)

NAMIBIA

230011; fax (0678) 13521), owned by Gerd and Babi Sachse, lies off the B1, 80km north-west of Tsumeb and 30km from Etosha's Von Lindequist Gate. You can choose between rooms for US$30 per person with breakfast, or camping for US$5 per person plus US$1 per site.

### Places to Eat

The homely and friendly *Etosha Cafe* (☎ (067) 221207) is a cosy spot for coffee, a light meal or a drink among tropical flowers in the leafy beer garden.

A decent place for quick meals, and especially pizza, is *Burger Shack & Warehouse Disco* (☎ (067) 220075), which opens from 8.30 am to 2 pm and 6 to 11 pm Monday to Saturday. The disco portion rages on Friday and Saturday nights.

A good inexpensive cafeteria is the *TCL Recreation Club* opposite the cinema. It's for members only, but visitors can pick up a temporary membership card from the tourist office. The *B&B Club*, on Third Rd just off Main St, has a popular bar and cafe.

Smaller and quicker places include *Weynand's Coffee Bar*, near the park on Main St, *Magrietkjie's Coffee Shop & Takeaway*, near Hiker's Haven, and the various petrol station takeaways.

### Things to Buy

Tsumeb has several shops specialising in minerals and ores (such as azurite) for collectors. They also deal in carvings, curios and jewellery made from local minerals. The shop in the tourist office is very good value.

### Getting There & Away

**Air** Air Namibia flies to Tsumeb on Tuesday, Wednesday and Saturday from Eros Airport in Windhoek (US$80).

**Bus** Minibuses to and from Windhoek and Oshakati stop at the Trek petrol station (look for the fibreglass zebra); most pass around midday. Star Line (☎ (067) 220358) connects Tsumeb with Oshakati (US$7, four hours) on Monday, Thursday, Friday

and Saturday. To Rundu (US$7, four hours), services run on Wednesday, and from Rundu on Wednesday and Thursday, all via Grootfontein. An additional service comes from Grootfontein (US$1, 45 minutes) on Thursday.

**Train** On Tuesday, Thursday and Sunday, there's a rail service from Walvis Bay at 5 pm and from Windhoek at 5.30 pm. From Tsumeb, the Windhoek and Walvis Bay train leaves on Monday, Wednesday and Friday at 11 am. Trains are split and combined at Kranzberg. For rail information, contact Trans-Namib on ☎ (067) 220358.

**Hitching** As the main jumping-off point for Namutoni in Etosha National Park, Tsumeb sees lots of hopeful hitchers. However, hitching can be slow, it's forbidden in the park, and you must have park reservations from MET in Windhoek.

### Getting Around

Travel North Namibia, the local agent for Imperial Car Hire (☎ (067) 220157; fax 220916), has special deals on Windhoek-Tsumeb transfers and special Etosha rates.

## AROUND TSUMEB
### Lake Otjikoto

Lake Otjikoto (Herero for deep hole) lies 24km north-west of Tsumeb on the B1. In May 1851, explorers Charles Andersson and Francis Galton stumbled across this unusual lake, which fills a limestone sinkhole measuring 100m by 150m. Galton measured the depth of the lake at 55m. Interestingly, Lake Otjikoto and nearby Lake Guinas are the only natural lakes in Namibia. They're also the only known habitats of the unusual mouth-breeding cichlid fish (*Pseudocrenilabrus philander*). These are coloured anything from dark green to bright red, yellow and blue; biologists believe the absence of predators made camouflage unnecessary. It's thought that these fish have evolved from tilapia (bream) washed into the lake by ancient floods.

In 1915 the retreating German army dumped weaponry and ammunition into the lake to prevent it falling into South African hands. It's rumoured that they jettisoned five cannons, 10 cannon bases, three Gatling guns and between 300 and 400 wagonloads of ammunition. Some of this stuff was recovered and salvaged in 1916 at great cost and effort by the South African Army, the Tsumeb Corporation and the Windhoek State Museum. In 1970, divers discovered a Krupp ammunition wagon 41m below the surface; it's now on display at the State Museum in Windhoek. In 1977 and 1983, two more ammunition carriers were salvaged and a cannon, which was captured from the South Africans early in the 20th century, has been restored and is on display in the Tsumeb Mining Museum. Qualified divers who'd like to see what's still down there can contact Theo Schoeman of the Windhoek Underwater Club (☎ (061) 238320).

An enterprising local has fenced the lake and installed toilets and a curio shop. The lake itself lies beyond a bizarre assemblage of clutter, but it's worth a stop, if only to read the sign painted on the curio shop. The site closes at 6.30 pm in the summer and 5.30 pm in winter. Admission is US$1.50.

### Lake Guinas

South-west of Lake Otjikoto lies the geologically similar Lake Guinas, which is used to irrigate surrounding farmland. It's smaller than its counterpart but is also less touristy and twice as deep. It's also less accessible. Drive 27km north-west of Tsumeb on the B1 and turn south-west on the D3043. After 20km, turn south-east onto the D3031. The lake is 5km further along.

### Auros Mountain Camp & Leopard Cave

The Auros Mountain Camp sits on a ridge in the Otavi Mountains, and has a spectacular mountain view. It's a great inexpensive getaway and offers a 4WD trail and a network of hiking trails, including a route up 2148m-high Mt Umenaub. The nearby

Leopard Cave, which can be explored with a torch, has abundant stalagmites, stalactites and other cave decorations. For a two-bed A-frame bungalow with a kitchen and bath, you'll pay US$68 for four people plus US$17 for each additional person. Cave visits cost US$7. Access is by 4WD only. Book through Travel North Namibia in Tsumeb.

### Tamboti Nature Park

The Tamboti Nature Park (☎ (067) 220140; fax 221718), a private game farm 22km north-west of Tsumeb and 11km off the B1, has a good range of wildlife and makes a viable base for Etosha trips. Accommodation is in railway carriages for US$27 per person or in thatched lodges for US$84, both with breakfast and one game drive. Camping is US$6, and hikers will enjoy the three walking tracks.

# Etosha National Park

Etosha National Park is undoubtedly one of the world's greatest wildlife-viewing venues. Its name, which means great white place of dry water, is taken from the vast white and greenish-coloured Etosha Pan, but it's the surrounding woods and grasslands which provide habitat for Etosha's diverse wildlife. This vast park takes in over 20,000 sq km and protects 114 mammal species, as well as 340 bird species, 16 reptiles and amphibians, one fish species and countless varieties of insects.

### Geology

Etosha Pan is an immense, flat, saline desert covering over 5000 sq km which originated 12 million years ago as a shallow lake fed by the waters of the Kunene River. Over the intervening period, climatic and tectonic changes have lowered the water level and created a salt pan, which only occasionally holds water. In good rainfall years, this vast shallow depression is fed by incoming channels: either *oshanas* – dry river channels – or *omiramba* (*omuramba* in the singular) – fossil river valleys which may flow underground. These include the oshanas Ekuma and Oshigambo in the north and the omuramba Owambo in the east. For a few days each year, Etosha Pan becomes a shallow lagoon teeming with flamingos and white pelicans.

### History

Although indigenous peoples knew of this wildlife-rich place for centuries, the first Europeans to see Etosha were traders Charles Andersson and Francis Galton, who travelled by wagon to Namutoni in 1851. They were followed in 1876 by an American trader, G McKeirnan, who observed: 'All the menageries in the world turned loose would not compare to the sight I saw that day.'

However, Etosha didn't attract the interest of tourists or conservationists until after the turn of the century, when the governor of German South West Africa, Dr F von Lindequist, became concerned over diminishing animal numbers and founded a 99,526 sq km reserve which included Etosha Pan. At the time, the land was still unfenced and animals could follow their normal migration routes. In subsequent years, the park boundaries were altered several times, and by 1970 Etosha had been pared down to its present 23,175 sq km.

### Orientation & Information

Only the eastern two-thirds of Etosha is open to the general public; the western third is reserved exclusively for tour operators. Each of the three rest camps has an information centre, and the staff at either of the main gates can sell maps and provide basic information.

**Post & Communications** Namutoni has both a coin phone and a card phone. At Okaukuejo, you can book calls at the post office. There's no post office at either Halali or Namutoni.

### Flora & Fauna

Etosha's most widespread vegetation type is mopane woodland, which fringes the pan and constitutes about 80% of the vegetation. The park also contains umbrella-thorn acacias (*Acacia torilis*) and other trees favoured by browsing animals and from December to March, this sparse bush country bears a pleasant green hue.

The area dubbed the Haunted Forest, west of Okaukuejo, is so named for its bizarre baobab-like *moringa* trees (*Moringa ovalifolia*). San legend recounts that after God had found a home for all the plants and animals on earth, he discovered a bundle of leftover moringa trees. He flung them into the air and they fell to earth with their roots pointing skywards – and so they remain. Lately, this forest has suffered a good measure of elephant damage.

Depending on the season, visitors may observe elephant, giraffe, Burchell's zebra, springbok, red hartebeest, blue wildebeest, gemsbok, eland, kudu, roan, ostrich, jackals, hyaena, lion, and even cheetah and leopard. Among the endangered animal species are the black-faced impala and the black rhinoceros.

The park's wildlife densities vary with the local ecology. As its name would suggest, Oliphantsbad (near Okaukuejo), is attractive to elephant, but for rhino, you couldn't do better than the floodlit water hole at Okaukuejo. In general, the further east you go in the park, the more wildebeest, kudu and impala join the springbok and gemsbok. The area around Namutoni, which averages 443mm of precipitation annually (compared with 412mm at Okaukuejo), is the best place to see the black-faced impala and the Damara dik-dik, Africa's smallest antelope. Etosha is also home to many smaller creatures, including both yellow and slender mongooses, honey badgers and leguaans.

Birdlife is also profuse. Yellow-billed hornbills are common, and on the ground you should look for the huge kori bustard, which weighs 15kg and seldom flies. You may also observe ostrich, korhaans,

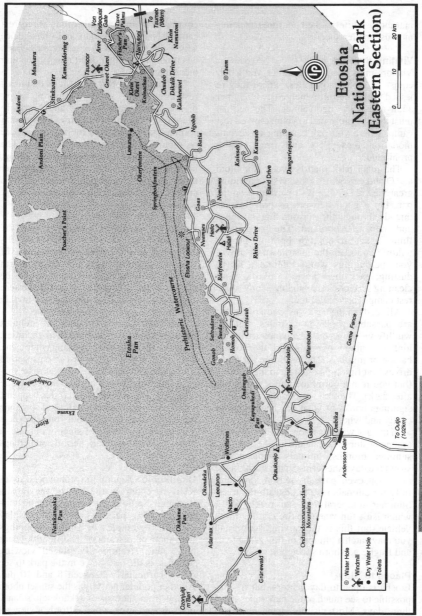

Etosha National Park (Eastern Section)

0   10   20 km

Legend:
⊚ Water Hole
✳ Windmill
● Dry Water Hole
⊕ Toilets

NAMIBIA

marabou, white-backed vultures and numerous smaller species.

### Visiting the Park

Visitors must check in at either Von Lindequist or Andersson gates, where they're issued with a permit which costs US$7 per adult and US$3 per vehicle. The permits must then be presented at your reserved rest camp, where you pay camping or accommodation fees. Pets and firearms are prohibited.

The main park road between Namutoni and Okaukuejo skirts Etosha Pan, providing great views. Driving isn't permitted on the pan, but a good network of gravel roads threads through the surrounding savannas and mopane woodland. The park speed limit is set at 60km/h both to protect wildlife and keep the dust down. If any of your belongings won't tolerate a heavy dusting, pack them away in plastic. Car-cleaning services are available at any of the rest camps for a small fee.

All roads in the eastern section of Etosha are passable to 2WD vehicles, but for wildlife viewing you'll be happier with the higher vantage point in a Land Rover, bakkie or minibus. The best time for game drives is at first light and late in the evening (but you're not permitted out of the camps after dark). The three rest camps each have sightings books of what has been seen recently and where.

In the dry winter season, wildlife clusters around water holes, while in the hot, wet summer months, animals disperse and spend the days sheltering in the bush. In the afternoon, even in the dry season, look carefully for animals resting beneath the trees. Summer temperatures can reach 44°C, which isn't fun when you're confined in a vehicle, but this is the calving season and you may catch a glimpse of tiny zebra foals and fragile newborn springbok.

### Places to Stay

Etosha is open to day visitors, but it's impossible to see much of the park in less than three days. Most visitors spend at least a couple of nights at one of its three rest camps (Namutoni, Halali and Okaukuejo) which are spaced at 70km intervals. Each has its own character, so it's worth visiting more than one.

Each camp is open year round and has a restaurant, bar, shop, swimming pool, picnic sites, petrol station and kiosk. In March 1998 the Namutoni restaurant complex was destroyed by fire, but should be rebuilt by the time you read this. The restaurants serve meals from 7 to 8.30 am, noon to 1.30 pm and 6 to 8.30 pm. At other times, the kiosks are open. The prices given are per unit, rather than per person, except where specified.

**Camping & Self-Catering** Inside the park, you have a choice of camping or self-catering. Camp sites at all three camps cost US$30 for up to eight people. A fourth camp will eventually be constructed at the Galton (Otjovasandu) Gate in the western end of the park but, as yet, it serves mainly as a conservation researchers' camp.

Self-catering accommodation includes linen, towels, soap and kitchen facilities, but you'll need to bring cooking equipment. You must arrive in the rest camps before sunset and can only leave after sunrise; specific times are posted on the gates. Anyone returning later is locked out; if this happens, a blast on your car horn will send someone running to open the gate, but you can expect a lecture on the evils of staying out late, a black mark on your park permit and perhaps even a fine.

**Okaukuejo** Okaukuejo (pronounced o-ka-KUI-yo) Camp is the site of the Etosha Research Station; the visitors centre outlines ongoing park research (one display identifies examples of animal droppings with their perpetrators). The floodlit water hole, with strategically placed viewing benches, is the best place in the park to see rhino, particularly between 8 and 10 pm. Another popular activity is the sunset photo frenzy from the top of Okaukuejo's landmark stone tower, which affords a view all

the way to the distant Ondundozonananandana Mountains; try saying that after three
pints of Windhoek lager (or even before)!

The campground is a bit of a dust hole,
but the self-catering accommodation may
be the nicest in the park. The bungalows
accommodate two/three/four people for
US$50/63/72. All have a kitchen, braai pit,
and bathroom and toilet facilities. 'Luxury'
bungalows with four beds are US$81 and
double 'bus quarters', rooms with a bath
but no kitchen, cost US$63.

**Halali** The middle camp, Halali, lies in a
unique area with several incongruous
dolomite outcrops. It takes its name from a
German term for the ritual blowing of a
horn to signal the end of a hunt, and a horn
now serves as Halali's motif. The short
Tsumasa hiking track leads up Tsumasa
Kopje, the hill nearest the rest camp. A
floodlit water hole extends wildlife viewing
into the night, and allows observation of
nocturnal creatures.

Halali has similar facilities to Okaukuejo
but the self-catering accommodation, which
shelters beneath mopane trees, is slightly
cheaper. Self-contained four-bed bungalows cost from US$68 to US$71 and double
bus quarters are US$61.

**Namutoni** The most popular and best-kept
of the camps is Namutoni, with its landmark whitewashed German fort. Namutoni
originally served as an outpost for German
troops, and in 1899 the German cavalry
built a fort from which to control Owambo
uprisings. In the battle of Namutoni, on 28
January 1904, seven German soldiers un-
successfully defended the fort against 500
Owambo warriors. Two years later, the
damaged structure was renovated and
pressed into service as a police station. In
1956, it was restored to its original specifications and two years later was opened as
tourist accommodation.

The tower and ramparts provide a great
view, and every evening, a crowd gathers to
watch the sunset; you have to arrive early to
stake out a decent spot. Each night, the flag

is lowered and a ceremonial bugle call
signals sundown and in the morning, a
similar ritual drags you out of your bed or
sleeping bag.

Beside the fort is a lovely freshwater
limestone spring and the floodlit King
Nehale water hole, which is filled with
reedbeds and some extremely vociferous
frogs. The viewing benches are nice for
lunch or watching the pleasant riverbank
scene, but the spot attracts surprisingly few
thirsty animals.

The campground is home to quite a few
nuisance jackals, some rabid, so keep your
distance and pack edibles safely away in
your vehicle.

Namutoni's accommodation offerings
include two-bed rooms in the walls of the
fort. With private/communal facilities,
they're US$43/63. Doubles with bath and
kitchen facilities are US$63 and two-room,
four-bed flats are US$61. Namutoni also
has four-bed self-catering bungalows for
US$72.

**Safari Lodges** The luxurious *Mokuti
Lodge* (☎ (067) 229084; fax 229091), 2km
south of the Von Lindequist gate, is an
alternative for those who consider the rest
camps too spartan. Although it suffered a
devastating fire in April 1997, it's now back
on line. With 100 rooms and its own private
game reserve, it's certainly impressive, but
the low-profile buildings create an illusion
of intimacy. And don't miss the resident
snake collection and the daily serpentine
demonstrations; all the participants were
captured around Mokuti. (Now that's a
comforting thought!) Single/double rates
start at US$90/120 with half board. The
restaurant has a very favourable reputation.

The friendly *Aoba Lodge* (☎ (067)
229100; fax 229101), PO Box 469,
Tsumeb, set on a 70 sq km private ranch,
caters for up to 20 people in comfortable
thatched bungalows. Single/double rates are
US$106/144, including dinner, bed and
breakfast. Etosha game drives cost US$75.

The very affordable *Toshari Inn* (☎/fax
(06548) 3702), 27km south of Andersson

Gate, is a modestly priced safari-style place with 16 rooms. Rates start at US$35/48 for singles/doubles including breakfast. For full board, they're US$52/90.

The upmarket *Ongava Lodge* (☎ (061) 226174; fax 239455) occupies its own wild-life reserve, at Andersson Gate beside the Ondundozonananandana Mountains. Its Herero name means black rhino. You can choose between the luxurious stone and thatch main lodge or the rustic tented bush camp. Either costs US$220 per person, in-cluding meals and wildlife-viewing activ-ities. Horseback trips cost an extra US$33.

### Places to Eat
For meals, you're limited to the safari lodges (guests only) or the rest camp restau-rants, kiosks, shops and bars.

### Getting There & Away
From Windhoek, Air Namibia flies to the Mokuti Lodge airstrip, just outside the Von Lindequist gate, on Tuesday, Wednesday, Friday and Saturday for US$80.

The two main entry gates to Etosha are Von Lindequist (Namutoni), west of Tsumeb, and Andersson (Okaukuejo), north of Outjo. Tsumeb has the nearest commer-cial airport to Etosha, and is also the nearest bus and rail depot. From there, you'll have to either join a tour or hire a car as there is no scheduled public transport into the park. Imperial Rent-a-Car has a branch in Tsumeb (see Getting Around in the Tsumeb section for details), but book well in advance.

You may not hitch within Etosha, but it is possible to hitch to the park. However, hitchers may well create problems for the driver they ride in with, because when the latter try to leave the park, some of their original party will appear to have vanished! When entering, explain that you need a sep-arate entry permit for your own records. However, it's probably unwise to reveal that you're hitchhiking.

### Getting Around
Pedestrians, bicycles, motorbikes and hitch-ing are prohibited in Etosha, and open bakkies must be screened off. Outside the rest camps, visitors must stay in their vehi-cles (except at toilet stops, which are marked on the map in this book). Although hitching is prohibited from Okaukuejo or Namutoni, you may be able to find lifts with delivery or maintenance workers who reg-ularly travel between the camps.

# East of Windhoek

## DORDABIS
The area between Gobabis and Dordabis is the heart of Namibia's karakul country, and there are a number of farms raising the sheep and also several weaveries. The most visited weavery is Farm Ibenstein, 4km down the C15 from Dordabis. Here, visitors learn about spinning, dyeing and weaving – and may purchase the finished products. It's open Monday to Friday from 8 am to 12.30 pm and 2.30 to 5.30 pm, and on Saturday from 8 am to noon. You can also visit the two other weaveries, Dorka Teppiche, on Peperkorrel Farm, and Kiripotib (☎ (0628) ask for Nouas 4303). Both are within a few kilometres of Dordabis.

### Places to Stay
Volker and Stefanie Hümmer's appealing *Eningu Clay House Lodge at Peperkorrel Farm* (☎ (0628) 1402) lies 63km out on the C51, south of the Windhoek-Gobabis road (turn off 3km east of Windhoek Interna-tional Airport). The sun-dried adobe lodges create an odd sort of African-Amerindian architectural cross. There's a swimming pool and activities such as hiking; wildlife-viewing on the ranch; archery; and tours of the attached Dorka Teppiche and other arts enterprises.

At Rainer and Marianne Seifart's friend-ly farm, *Heimat* (☎ (0628) ask for Nina 3622), PO Box 11186, Klein Windhoek, at Nina, you'll gain a perspective on Namib-ian ranch life. Camping costs US$4 and rooms with home-cooked meals cost US$39 per person. Day visits, including a meal, are US$23. From the international airport, turn south on the D1808; at the T-junction 58km further on, turn left and continue 37km to Nina. Return transfers to Windhoek cost US$50.

The lovely 7400 hectare *Scheidthof Game Farm* (☎ (0628) 1422) offers a full complement of activities, but the highlights are a 32km hiking trail and two 4WD tracks (which may also be used for hiking). Camping costs US$5 per person and farmhouse B&B is US$40. Turn south on the M51, east of the international airport, and turn east on the DR1506. The farm lies 6km down this road.

### Getting There & Away
Head east from Windhoek on the B6 and turn right onto the C23, 20km east of town. Dordabis lies 66km down this road. At 7.30 am on Fridays, Star Line runs a bus from Windhoek to Dordabis (US$3). It returns at 4.45 pm the same day.

### ARNHEM CAVE
Arnhem Cave, at 2800m the longest cave system in Namibia, was discovered by farmer DN Bekker in 1930 and was originally used as a source of bat guano. It was formed in a layer of limestone and dolomite, sandwiched between quartzite and shale, in the rippled series of synclines and anticlines known as the Arnhem Hills. The dryness of the cave means that there are few stalagmites or stalactites, but it is home to five species of bat: the giant leaf-nosed bat (*Hipposideros commersoni*), leaf-nosed bat (*Hipposideros caffer*), long-fingered bat (*Miniopterus schrelbersi*), horseshoe bat (*Rhinolophus denti*) and Egyptian slit-faced bat (*Nycteris thebalca*). The cave is also inhabited by a variety of insects, worms, shrews and shrimps.

Admission costs US$8 and hire of helmets and torches is US$3 (there's no artificial lighting). Contact the Bekkers (☎ (0628) ask for 1430; fax (061) 243413), PO Box 11354, Windhoek.

### Places to Stay & Eat
Camping costs US$5 and braai facilities are available. There are also four thatched double bungalows for US$35 each. The recommended meals may be booked in advance.

### Getting There & Away
The cave lies on the private farm of Mr J Bekker, south of the international airport. To get there, turn south just east of the airport on the D1458, towards Nina. After 66km, turn north-east on the D1506 and continue for 11km to the T-junction. There, turn south on the D1808 and continue 6km to the farm.

### GOBABIS
Gobabis, with 11,000 people, lies 120km from the Botswana border at Buitepos. The name is Khoi-Khoi for the place of strife, but a slight misspelling (Goabbis) would render it place of elephants, which locals seem to prefer (despite its lack of elephants). It's the main service centre for over 800 surrounding cattle and sheep ranches and is likely to gain prominence as traffic increases on the Trans-Kalahari route.

However, there isn't much to look at. It's said there was once a traffic light, but when it turned green, the cows ate it. (Don't believe it – in a good rainy season, the area turns relatively lush.) The only historic building is the old military hospital, the Lazarett, which once served as a town museum. It's not officially open, but you can pick up a key at the library.

### History
Gobabis came into existence in 1856, when a Rhenish mission station was established on the site. In 1865, an attempt by the head missionary to broker a peace agreement between the squabbling Damara and the Khoi-Khoi resulted in his expulsion from the area and the temporary fall of the mission. Missionary work was reactivated in 1876, only to be shut down again by a renewal of hostilities. When they tired of fighting each other, the two groups turned

around and started a rebellion against the German occupation. Things got so out of hand that in 1895, Major Leutwein ordered German troops to quell the disturbances; this resulted in the construction of a fort which was later destroyed.

### Information

For basic tourist information contact Kalahari i (☎ (061) 562551; fax 563012).

### Places to Stay & Eat

The *Gobabis Hotel* (☎ (061) 562568; fax 562641), on Mark St, has single/double rooms for US$24/33 and family rooms for US$46. The swimming pool, bar, beer garden, restaurant and weekend disco amount to at least 80% of Gobabis' action.

The *Central Hotel* (☎ (061) 562094; fax 562092) on Voortrekker St is less appealing but cheaper at US$19/25. It has a bar and restaurant.

The amenable *Welkom Rest Camp* (☎ (0688) 12213; fax (061) 562909) has five four-bed bungalows for US$15 per person. Camping costs US$3 per vehicle, US$3 per site and US$3 per person. It's 18km from Gobabis, north of the highway east of town.

The *Farm Steinhausen* (☎ (06202) 3240; fax (061) 561419), north-west of Gobabis, charges US$35/70 for single/double rooms including breakfast. To reach it from town, head 3km back towards Windhoek on the B6 and turn north on the C30. It's then 117km to Steinhausen.

---

### Karakul Sheep

Around the southern and eastern borders of Namibia, you'll undoubtedly notice the karakul sheep, scraggy and uninspiring goat-like creatures which have come to be known as Namibia's 'black gold'. This hardy sheep, which was first bred for its pelt in Central Asia, is able to survive in harsh arid conditions.

The first karakul sheep – two rams and 10 ewes – were imported to German South West Africa in 1907, and two years later a further 22 rams and 252 ewes arrived. By the start of WWI, their success at breeding in the new country was well illustrated by sheer numbers: the country had a total of 350 rams and nearly 850 ewes, as well as over 20,000 mixed breed sheep. After the war, a breeding and experimental station was established and it was found that the presence of karakul sheep actually improved land quality. Their grazing habits stimulate the growth of new plants, and other plant material trodden into the ground by their hooves helps to prevent surface erosion of the soil.

By the early 1990s, 2500 breeders were producing five million pelts annually and the national breeding herd numbered well over a million purebreds. However, numbers are unstable due to intermittent drought conditions, which cause herd sizes to diminish drastically. During the dry spell of the past several years, the numbers have plummeted.

Most karakul sheep are black, but there are also grey, white, brown and spotted individuals. Today the industry is centred on Keetmanshoop, Maltehöhe and Dordabis. The wool is the basis for Namibia's thriving textile industry, but it's the karakul pelts which are renowned. Unlike other wool, which is sheared from the sheep, karakul wool is taken from newborn lambs in the form of pelts, which of course requires the lambs to be slaughtered. When pelt prices are low, the lambs are sold for mutton.

Although the Central Asian republics and Afghanistan produce larger quantities, the quality of the Namibian pelts is considered the world's finest and they fetch good prices at the triennial pelt auctions held in Frankfurt. Karakul also forms the basis for Namibia's luxury leather-goods exports and is marketed under the name Swakara (South West African Karakul).

## Getting There & Away

The B6 is well tarred from Windhoek to the border with Botswana, but many D-numbered roads in Hereroland require the use of a 4WD vehicle. Slow overnight trains run from Windhoek on Tuesdays, Thursdays and Sundays at 10 pm and return from Gobabis on Mondays, Wednesdays and Fridays at 7 pm. Economy/business class costs US$3/5.

The Star Line (☎ (061) 562416) bus to Buitepos and Ghanzi (Botswana) leaves on Friday at 7.30 am and arrives in Ghanzi at 2 pm. It leaves Ghanzi at 8 am Saturday and arrives in Gobabis at 4 pm.

## BUITEPOS

Buitepos, a wide spot in the desert at the Namibia/Botswana border (open 6 am to 6 pm Namibian time), is little more than a petrol station and customs and immigration post.

## Places to Stay

On the Namibian side of the border, the *East Gate Service Station & Rest Camp* rises from the desert like a mirage – and the toilets are more than remarkable. Camping costs US$3 per person and a bungalow for three people is US$30. It's a particularly handy option for hitchhikers between Namibia and Botswana.

## Getting There & Away

To get there, follow the B6 east of Gobabis. Star Line's Windhoek-Ghanzi bus stops at Buitepos. From Mamuno, just over the border in Botswana, a bus leaves for Ghanzi and Maun at 8.30 am on Sunday, Tuesday and Friday.

# North-Eastern Namibia

Windhoek may be Namibia's capital, but north-eastern Namibia, with the country's highest population density, is its cultural heartland. Known as the Land of Rivers, this culturally varied region is bounded by the Kunene and Okavango rivers along the Angolan border, and in the east by the Zambezi and the Linyanti/Chobe systems.

North-eastern Namibia has the country's highest rainfall and is geographically distinct from the rest of Namibia. Most people live in small settlements on the plains of the Owambo region, or on or near the Okavango River, which flows eastwards and feeds Botswana's Okavango Delta.

The eastern part of the Otjozondjupa region, formerly known as Bushmanland, is a wild and sparsely populated expanse of scrub acacia forest and scattered San villages at the northern fringes of the Kalahari. This is one of Namibia's most fascinating areas, and to date remains little-affected by tourism.

## The Owambo Country

The regions of Omusati, Oshana, Ohangwena and most of Otjikoto, which make up the former district of Owamboland, comprise the homeland of the Owambo people, Namibia's largest population group. Most members of the eight Owambo clans pursue subsistence agricultural lifestyles, growing their own crops and raising cattle and goats. Visitors will be impressed by the clean and well-kept nature of this rural area, which gives the overall impression of a healthy and prosperous African society.

The Owambo landscape is characterised by flat, sandy plains dotted with *makalani* palms, patches of savanna and *mopane* forest. Its semidesert climate is characterised by cool nights and hot days, and

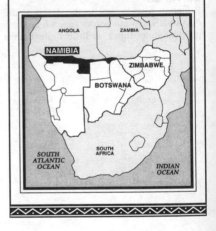

summer daytime temperatures can climb to over 40°C.

During the war for independence, Owamboland served as a base and primary support area for SWAPO. The villages of Ombalantu, Oshakati and Ondangwa were converted into bases and supply centres for the occupying army. After the South Africans left, these new commercial centres attracted growing numbers of entrepreneurial people who set up small businesses. Currently, the government is providing resources for housing projects, electricity

672

lines, roads, irrigation, agriculture, health care, schools, telephone services and other projects.

Most of the Owambo people live in Oshana country, which is named after the web of *oshanas* (ephemeral watercourses) of the Culevai drainage system. The oshanas are filled during the *efundja* (periods of heavy rainfall) but because they're underlain by solid rock, they hold underground water throughout the year. Some kraals and villages depend on bore holes, but the main supply runs through the Ogongo canal/aqueduct along the C46.

The Owambo country is known for its high-quality basketry and canework, which is sold at roadside stalls or artisans' homes for a fraction of what you'd pay in Windhoek. Favourites include rounded baskets with lids in every size up to 1m in diameter, and shallow woven plates and bowls. Designs are simple and graceful, usually in-

corporating a brown geometric pattern woven into the pale yellow reed.

## OSHAKATI

Oshakati, the Owambo capital, may be a friendly, bustling hive of activity, but the uninspiring commercial centre is little more than a strip of development along the highway. It lacks specific attractions, but you'll enjoy an hour wandering around the large covered market, which produces a range of mostly unpleasant smells. Here you'll find everything from clothing and baskets to *mopane* worms and glasses of freshly brewed *tambo*. At the front of the market stands an odd monument: a dour Afrikaner type standing with a crashed plane. No-one in town seems able to make a positive identification.

### Information

Your best source for information is the

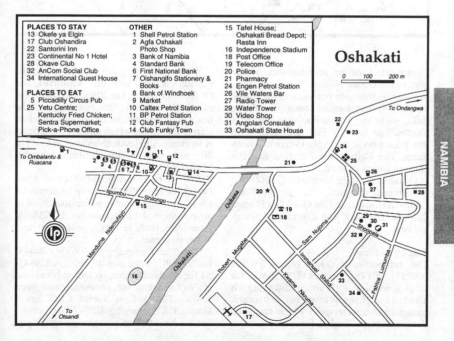

PLACES TO STAY
13 Okefe ya Elgin
17 Club Oshandira
22 Santorini Inn
23 Continental No 1 Hotel
28 Okave Club
32 AnCom Social Club
34 International Guest House

PLACES TO EAT
5 Piccadilly Circus Pub
25 Yetu Centre;
   Kentucky Fried Chicken;
   Sentra Supermarket;
   Pick-a-Phone Office

OTHER
1 Shell Petrol Station
2 Agfa Oshakati
   Photo Shop
3 Bank of Namibia
4 Standard Bank
6 First National Bank
7 Oishangifo Stationery &
   Books
8 Bank of Windhoek
9 Market
10 Caltex Petrol Station
11 BP Petrol Station
12 Club Fantasy Pub
14 Club Funky Town

15 Tafel House;
   Oshakati Bread Depot;
   Rasta Inn
16 Independence Stadium
18 Post Office
19 Telecom Office
20 Police
21 Pharmacy
24 Engen Petrol Station
26 Vile Waters Bar
27 Radio Tower
29 Water Tower
30 Video Shop
31 Angolan Consulate
33 Oshakati State House

**Oshakati**

0    100    200 m

To Ondangwa

To Ombalantu &
Ruacana

To Otsandi

NAMIBIA

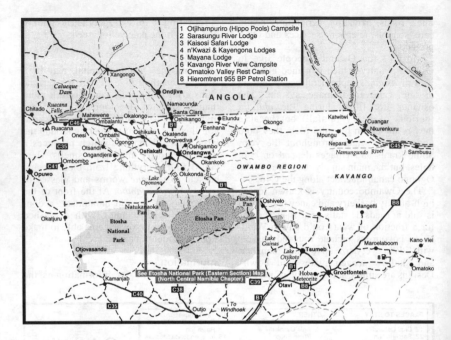

1 Otjihampuriro (Hippo Pools) Campsite
2 Sarasungu River Lodge
3 Kaisosi Safari Lodge
4 n'Kwazi & Kayengona Lodges
5 Mayana Lodge
6 Kavango River View Campsite
7 Omatoko Valley Rest Camp
8 Hieromtrent 955 BP Petrol Station

Engen petrol station at the corner of the highway and Sam Nujoma Rd. For changing money, there are branches of all major banks in the commercial centre. For phone calls, go to the Pick-a-Phone at the Yetu Centre. You can buy Fuji and Agfa slide and print film at the Agfa Oshakati Photo Shop. The Caltex petrol station has the cleanest toilets in town.

Oshakati has three hospitals: the 800-bed government hospital, the Onandjokwe Lutheran Hospital and the Oshikuku Roman Catholic Hospital. The church-run places are best.

**Places to Stay**

The *International Guest House* (☎/fax (06751) 20175) charges US$50/61 for singles/doubles with air-conditioning. It also has a pool, tennis court, bar, restaurant, gardens and a waterspout which has been described as an 'English fountain'.

Want to feel like you've died and gone to Florida? Check out the *Santorini Inn* (☎ (06751) 20457; fax 20506), on the main road north of town. This motel-style place has a pool, bar, restaurant, and an attached refrigeration shop which ensures the air-con is working. Singles/doubles start at US$50/70; with self-catering facilities, they're US$65/89.

The Afrikaner-oriented *Okave Club* (☎/fax (06751) 20892), in a quiet corner of town, has single/double accommodation in air-conditioned bungalows for US$35/65. Amenities include a bar, restaurant and swimming pool.

The *Club Oshandira* (☎ (06751) 20443; fax 21189), by the airport, charges US$45/54 for singles/doubles, including breakfast. It also has a pool, bar, restaurant, and green lawns. The *AnCom Social Club* has a simple B&B charging US$17 per person, but it's hard to find someone to check you

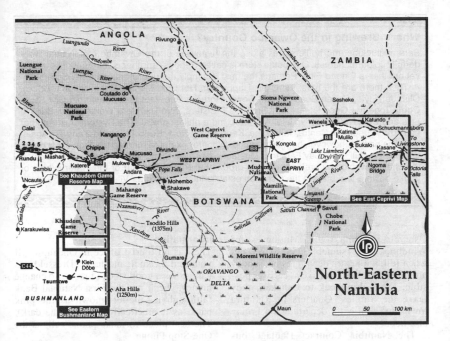

**North-Eastern Namibia**

in. Your cheapest option is *Okefe ya Elgin* guesthouse and restaurant, which is attached to a church. Basic rooms cost US$12 per person.

The *Continental No 1 Hotel* (☎ (06751) 20701), on the main road resembles a furniture outlet, but it isn't bad and has a bright patio, bar, bottle store and restaurant. Singles/doubles cost US$33/39. Reception is around the back.

**Places to Eat**

Your best meal options are the *Piccadilly Circus Pub* or the lodges, particularly *Club Oshandira*, *Okave Club* and *Santorini Inn* (their ads recommend the 'pig's trotters with sour cabbage, mashed potatoes and much more'). There's also a new *Kentucky Fried Chicken* in the Yetu centre, as well as the *Yetu Sentra Supermarket*. For unpretentious baked goods, try the *Oshakati Bread Depot & Rasta Inn*.

**Entertainment**

Oshakati enjoys a lively local entertainment scene, and lots of small clubs feature live bands. The most popular bar is *Club Fantasy*, near the market, which has a disco on Wednesdays and weekend evenings. The smaller *Tafel House* bar has a weekend disco. A bit wilder is *Club Funky Town*, on the main street.

**Getting There & Away**

For flight information, see under Ondangwa, later in this section. The C46 and B1 through the Owambo region are tarred and in good condition, but off these routes maintenance is poor and 4WD is required in places, especially after rain. Fuel is available at Ombalantu, Oshakati, Ondangwa and Oshikango.

From the Oshakati market bus terminal, white minibuses leave for Ondangwa frequently, and also serve other towns on the

## What's Brewing in the Owambo Country?

Bars, nightclubs and bottle stores along the highways of the Owambo region bear wonderfully colourful names. One bottle store is called Serious, another is the Fruit of Love and yet another is Fine to Fine. Perhaps the best is simply the unpretentious Botol Stor.

Then there are the bars: the Clinic Happy Bar, Hot Box, Melody Shop, Salon for Sure, Club Jet Style, Seven Seas Up and Down, Sorry to See, Hot Line, California City Style, Come Together Good Life, Happy Brothers & Sisters, Join Us, Hard Workers Bar, Bar We Like and USA No Money No Life. A few are more philosophical: The System, Just Another Life, The Agreement Centre, Take Time, Keep Trying No 1, Keep Trying No 2 and Try Again.

Some names, however, boggle the mind. Who, for example, named the Sign of Mr Hans, We Push & Pull, Club Say Father of Mustache or Three Sister in Beer Garden? And given the choice, would you prefer to down a drop in the Peace Full Bar or the Water is Life, or choke down a foul brew in the Oshakati establishment known as Vile Waters?

Oshivelo-Ruacana route. Minibuses for Windhoek via Tsumeb (US$16) set out when full, with extra departures on Sunday afternoon. It's best to arrive as early as possible. From Windhoek to Oshakati, they leave the Singles' Quarters in Katutura township, with extra departures on Friday afternoon.

The Namibia Contract Haulage bus between Windhoek and Oshakati leaves the bus terminal in Katutura on Fridays at 7.30 am and 5 pm and departs from the market in Oshakati twice on Sundays. The fare is just US$10. It's advisable to book a seat as early as possible.

The comfy Star Line bus service connects Oshakati with Tsumeb (US$7, four hours) daily except Sunday and Wednesday. Note that on Tuesday the service only runs southbound and on Thursday it runs northbound only. On Tuesday/Thursday there are connections to/from Grootfontein.

## ONDANGWA

Ondangwa is the second largest town in the Owambo country. It's a commercial centre and is known for its huge warehouses, which supply *cuca* shops. There are more than 6000 of these shops serving the Owambo region. (The word cuca is taken from the name of a once-popular Angolan beer.)

### Information

There is no tourist office in Ondangwa. If you need a vehicle mechanic, Dressel Haus garage has a good stock of parts. To change money, check out the First National Bank (although it's better known as the pink bank, as it practically glows in the dark). The best place to make phone calls is the One-Stop Phone.

### Olukonda National Monument

Among the makalani palms and mahango fields 13km down the D3606 lies the collection of historic Finnish Mission buildings which now comprise Olukonda National Monument ($\pi$ (06756) 884622 or 40241; fax 40472).

Nakambale House, the first mission house and northern Namibia's oldest structure, was built in the late 1870s by Finnish missionary Martti Rautanen (1845-1926), known locally as Nakambale. In 1889, Reverend Rautanen also built the area's first church.

When a new church was constructed in 1972, the old building began to deteriorate and wasn't renovated until 1991, with funds and expertise from the Finnish government. Martti Rautanen, his family and the local chief Ellifas are buried in the churchyard. At the attached Ndonga Homestead, visitors can see a traditional Owambo kraal, learn about local life, sample local foods, and camp or sleep in a rural hut.

The museum is open on Monday, Tuesday, Thursday and Friday from 8 am to 1 pm and 2 to 5 pm, on Saturday from 8 am to 1 pm and on Sunday from noon to 5 pm. Admission to the museum is US$0.25 and to the Ndonga Homestead it's US$1. Guided tours of the site cost US$1. For accommodation information, see Places to Stay later in this section.

### Lake Oponono
Lost in a maze of routes and tracks 27km south of Ondangwa is Lake Oponono, a large wetland fed by the Culevai oshanas. After rains, it attracts an amazing variety of birdlife, including such species as the saddlebill stork, crowned crane, flamingo and pelican.

### Places to Stay & Eat
The standard choice for business travellers is the dingy *Punyu International Hotel* (☎/fax (06756) 40660), 300m north of the Shell petrol station. Singles/doubles including breakfast and shower cost US$30/41. You may also find a dorm bed at the *Lutheran Mission*, several kilometres south of town; turn at the Shell petrol station. They charge about US$10, including breakfast.

The clean but cluttered *Ondangwa Rest Camp* (☎ (06756) 40310) surrounds a fetid pond between the pink bank and the purple primary school (if there's no-one around, check in at the Ondangwa Total service station). Camping costs US$5 per person. The attached cafe sells Coke, chips and basic meals, but otherwise your choices are limited; try *Tony's Takeaway* at the BP petrol station or the *Viva Supermarket*, in the pink building with the First National Bank.

The *ABC Trading Centre* (☎ (06756) 40121) in the Oluno suburb sells everything from A to Z, and also has a bar, restaurant and cheap accommodation. An interesting option is the traditional accommodation at *Olukonda National Monument* (☎ (06756)

884622). Admission to the rest camp costs US$3; tent/caravan sites are US$2/3; and accommodation in traditional Owambo huts costs US$3, plus US$3 to use the kitchen. The affiliated *Elcin Guesthouse* (☎ (06756) 40241; fax 40472) in Oniipa, 8km east of town, offers friendly, good-value accommodation.

### Things to Buy
For a typical and useful souvenir, check out the household goods market in front of the Desert Inn Pub near the eastern end of town. You'll find a range of useful items from wooden kitchen utensils to some amazing wire mousetraps.

### Getting There & Away
Air Namibia (☎ (06751) 20284; fax 21230) has services to and from Windhoek Eros on Friday and Sunday, and to and from Windhoek International on Thursday. All minibus and Star Line services between Oshakati, Tsumeb and Windhoek stop at the BP petrol station in Ondangwa. Punyu Wholesalers hires out cars and 4WD vehicles at a good rate.

The Oshikango border crossing to Santa Clara in Angola, 60km north of Ondangwa, is now open and carries frequent cross-border truck traffic. It's open from 6 am to 5 pm, and you should be able to hop across for a quick look around. To stay overnight or travel further north, however, you'll need an Angolan visa from either Windhoek or Oshakati.

## OMBALANTU
Dusty Ombalantu is one of Namibia's most typically African commercial towns, and makes a nice brief stop. It now has a First National Bank, a Total petrol station, the Onawa supermarket and the Super Foods Takeaway.

### The Omukwa Baobab
Ombalantu's main attraction is the old South African army base, which is dominated by an enormous baobab tree. This tree, known locally as *Omukwa*, was once

NAMIBIA

used to shelter cattle from invaders, and later used as a turret from which to ambush invading tribes. It didn't work with the South African army, however, which invaded and used the tree for everything from a chapel to a coffee shop (a sign on the wall reads *Die Koffiekamer Koelte*, The Coffee Chamber Cult), a post office, a storage shed and an interrogation chamber for prisoners of war. The site is now loosely described as the Omusati Region Museum, and includes a nearby bomb shelter and a lookout tower dating from the South African days.

The base entrance is at the police station, about 350m from the petrol station. If there's anyone around in uniform, respectfully ask permission to enter.

### Ongulumbashe

Ongulumbashe (originally Omugulug-weembashe, the forest of giraffes) is the birthplace of modern Namibia. It was here on 26 August 1966 that the first shots of the war for Namibian independence were fired, and the People's Liberation Army of Namibia was victorious over the South African troops which had been stationed in the area to root out and quell potential guerrilla activities.

The area is less than inspiring – just typically flat Owambo country scrubland – but you can see some reconstructed bunkers and the 'needle' monument that marks the great event. See the reverse for the etching of a *Ppsha* (*pistolet-pulemyot shpagina*), the Russian-made automatic rifle that played a major role. The event is commemorated each year on 26 August.

From Ombalantu, turn south on the D3612 to the pleasant village of Otsandi (Tsandi); Ongulumbashe lies 20km down an unnumbered track which turns west from the eastern end of the village.

### Ongandjera

Ongandjera, President Sam Nujoma's birthplace, has recently become an informal national shrine. The rose-coloured kraal that was his boyhood home is distinguished from its neighbours by a prominent SWAPO flag hung in a tree. It's fine to look from a distance, but it remains a private home and isn't open to the public.

Ongandjera lies on the D3612, 52km south-east of Ombalantu, just a few hundred metres outside the large village of Okahao. It's also accessible via the C41 from Oshakati.

## RUACANA

Tiny Ruacana takes its name from the Herero *orua hakahana* (the rapids). Here, the Kunene River splits into several channels before plunging over a staircase of escarpments and through a 2km-long gorge of its own making.

Ruacana was originally built as a company town to provide housing and services for workers on the 320-megawatt underground Ruacana hydro-electric project, which now supplies over half of Namibia's power. It has a more ordered feel than other Owambo population centres and, during the bush war, it also served as a base for the South African Defence Forces.

In 1926, a German-Portuguese boundary dispute was settled when the upper Kunene was given to Angola, and it was decided that below the falls the boundary would follow the main channel to the Atlantic Ocean.

### Ruacana Falls

The 85m Ruacana Falls were once a natural wonder, but that changed with the construction of Angola's Calueque Dam, 20km upstream. The flow is controlled by an intake weir 1km above the falls, which ushers water through the hydroelectric plant. As a result, the falls are only worth seeing in the wettest seasons, when water is released over the spillway. Try in March or April.

The falls lie 15km west of town along the river road. To visit the gorge, visitors must temporarily exit Namibia by signing the immigration register. From the office, you can descend the 488 steps to the old power station.

## Places to Stay & Eat

Beside an oxbow lagoon at the mouth of the Ruacana Gorge is the *Otjihampuriro Camp Site* (☎ (06758) ask for 16) – formerly called Hippo Pools – which charges US$3 per person. It's certainly Namibia's worst camp site; the taps don't work, the toilets don't flush (and never have, from the looks of it), goats and cattle graze on the site and there's trash everywhere. Lest prospective campers take one look and retreat in disgust, the 'attendants' now collect the fees as you enter at the gate.

In town, the *Waterfalls Guest House* (☎ (06758) ask for 26), in an old Namibia Development Corporation house 250m off the Ruacana Loop, has four double rooms with fans and communal facilities for US$25 each. Camping costs US$5 per person (or US$5 per car plus US$1 per person). Meals are available on request.

The best accommodation is the *NAMPOWER Guesthouse* (☎ (06758) ask for 31), on the main Oshakati road, 500m from the petrol station. It has a pool, tennis courts and colourful tropical gardens, and the dining room does breakfast, snacks and dinner (US$11), but you need to pre-book. Rooms cost US$41 per person, including breakfast.

The corporate-sounding *Ruacana No 2 Supermarket*, opposite the petrol station, stocks a good range of supplies.

## Getting There & Away

Ruacana lies at a minor crossroads between Opuwo, the Owambo country and the torturous river route to Epupa Falls (see the North-Western Namibia chapter). For westbound travellers, the 24-hour BP petrol station is the last before the Atlantic. The petrol station is the terminal for the afternoon minibuses to and from Oshakati and Ondangwa. Occasionally, the Opuwo route is also served by local minibuses.

Note that the Angolan border post is now open. Visas are sometimes available at the border for an arbitrary fee, but it's wiser to pick one up at the consulates in Windhoek or Oshakati.

# Kavango

The heavily wooded and gently rolling Kavango region is dominated by the Okavango River and its broad floodplains. There's little wildlife these days, but the water does attract millions of butterflies, many as yet unclassified, as well as a large crocodile population.

The Kavango people cultivate maize, sorghum, millet and green vegetables along the banks of the river, and supplement their diet with fish caught in woven funnel-shaped fish traps. The men also practise spearfishing from the riverbanks or from dugout canoes known as *watu* or *mekoro* (singular *mokoro*). The region is also home to the Mbarakweno San people, who remain largely subservient to local Mbukushu, Sambiyu and other Caprivi tribal groups, and whose services are 'inherited' within families.

In colonial days, Kavango was a focus of operations for German Roman Catholic missionaries, and the church still sponsors missions, hospitals and clinics in Nyangana, Sambiu and Andara. Several of the mission stations and hospitals along the Okavango River welcome travellers. The one at Andara has an especially interesting statue of Christ.

## RUNDU

Rundu occupies a lovely setting on the bluffs above the Okavango River. It's a great spot for fishing and birdwatching along the river, but don't expect round the clock excitement.

### Things to See

It's worth visiting the Mbangura Woodcarvers' Co operative, which is part of a government development scheme marketing traditional drums and lovely handmade furniture. There are plans for a Kavango museum (the building has already been constructed); check for progress at the Tourism Centre. At Sambiu, 30km east of

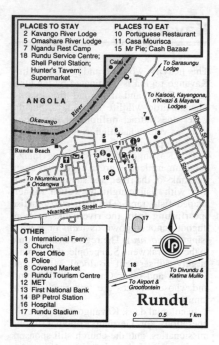

**PLACES TO STAY**
2 Kavango River Lodge
5 Omashare River Lodge
7 Ngandu Rest Camp
18 Rundu Service Centre;
   Shell Petrol Station;
   Hunter's Tavern;
   Supermarket

**PLACES TO EAT**
10 Portuguese Restaurant
11 Casa Mourisca
15 Mr Pie; Cash Bazaar

**OTHER**
1 International Ferry
3 Church
4 Post Office
6 Police
8 Covered Market
9 Rundu Tourism Centre
12 MET
13 First National Bank
14 BP Petrol Station
16 Hospital
17 Rundu Stadium

**Rundu**

0    0.5    1 km

Rundu, is a Roman Catholic mission museum (☎ (0672) 1111), which exhibits crafts and woodcarvings from Angola and Kavango. Phone to arrange a visit.

### Information

Rundu's privately run Tourism Centre (☎ (067) 255910; fax 255909) distributes brochures, answers queries and books hotels and safaris. It's open weekdays from 8 am to 5 pm and Saturdays from 8 am to 1 pm. They also sell Kavango curios and offer car hire, phone, fax and photocopy services, as well as overnight vehicle lock-up. Rundu also has a useful pharmacy one block east of the Tourism Centre.

### Organised Tours

The Tourism Centre runs Happy Hippo Sundowner Cruises on the Okavango River, costing US$34 for up to 12 people. Book before 1 pm on the day you want to go.

### Places to Stay

The *Rundu Service Centre* (☎ (067) 255787), beside the Hunter's Tavern at the Shell petrol station, has uninspiring rooms with fan/air-conditioning for US$41/45 for up to four people. The *Omashare River Lodge* (☎/fax (067) 255753; fax 256111), overlooking the river, has single or double rooms with fans – essential in this climate – for US$61.

*Kavango River Lodge* (☎ (067) 255244; fax 255013), with Rundu's best sunset view, perches above the river 1km west of the centre. Basic single/double self-catering bungalows, with air-con, TV and breakfast supplies, start at US$43/66; ask for one with a veranda. Four-bed family units cost US$70. All guests may use the tennis courts.

The large and central *Ngandu Rest Camp* (☎ (067) 256723; fax 256726), 150m down the Sarasungu road, has basic doubles for US$28, and air-conditioned self-catering single/double bungalows for US$34/52. Dorms are US$16 and camping costs US$5.

Friendly German/Portuguese-run *Sarasungu River Lodge* (☎ (067) 255161; fax 256238) occupies a shady riverside setting 4km from the centre. For single/double bungalows nationals of the region pay US$41/57, but for foreigners they're overpriced at US$62/72. Campers pay US$6, regardless of nationality. Amenities include hot showers, a great restaurant specialising in pizza, a cool veranda and a swimming pool. Phone to be picked up from the Shell petrol station. Canoes for pottering around on the river cost US$7 per hour.

The next place downstream is *Kaisosi Safari Lodge* (☎/fax (067) 255265). This stark riverside camp has single/double bungalows for US$45/57; camping costs US$6. You can arrange river raft cruises for under US$10 per person per hour and transfers from the town/airport cost US$8.50/14.

Valerie and Wynand Peypers' *n'Kwazi Lodge* (☎ (067) 242054; fax 242058; <n'kwazi@iafric.co.na>) offers a peaceful riverside retreat with great Afrikaner-style meals and a warm friendly atmosphere;

guests are treated more like family than strangers. For single/double bungalows with breakfast, you'll pay US$65/104, which is excellent given the level of standards and service. Camping is US$6 per person. Boat trips and water-skiing on the river cost US$18 per hour for up to four people, horse-riding is US$12 per hour and mokoro trips cost only a gratuity for the poler. The attached *Kayengona Lodge*, named after a local chief, 'the man without front teeth', is used for overland truck groups. Bungalows with en suite facilities are US$34 per person; two- or four-bed bungalows with shared facilities cost US$18 per person, dormitories are US$30 per group and campers pay US$6. Transfers from town are free.

*Mayana Lodge* (☎ (067) 255888), 21km from Rundu, served as a police camp during the war for independence. It's set in a leafy grove beside the Okavango and affords excellent sunrise views. Four-bed huts with communal ablutions cost US$18/27; with private facilities, they're US$27/36. The à la carte restaurant is recommended.

The *Kavango River View Camp Site* lies 100km east of Rundu and 5km off the main road, opposite the Khaudom turn-off.

### Places to Eat

An unexpectedly good place to eat is the *Casa Mourisca*, which serves Portuguese specialities, pizza and even snails. It's open Mondays, Wednesdays, Thursdays and Fridays from 10 am to 2 pm and 5 pm to midnight; on Saturdays from 5 pm to midnight; and Sundays from 10 am to 2 pm and 5 to 10 pm. There's also the *Portuguese Restaurant* and, in the Cash Bazaar shopping centre, the *Mr Pie* takeaway. For a real treat, get down to *Sarasungu River Lodge* for a pizza – the delicious *Pizza alla Diavola* is as devilish as its name suggests.

The *Hunter's Tavern* at the Shell petrol station on the B8 at the turn-off to Rundu centre, serves breakfast, lunch and dinner seven days a week. At the *ROC Club*, near the Kavango River Lodge, you'll get decent burgers or fish and chips.

Self-caterers can get supplies from the well-stocked supermarket in the centre and the supermarket at the Shell petrol station. For provisions, go to the large covered market at the north-eastern end of town; from July to September, they sell sweet papaya straight from the trees.

### Entertainment

Rundu's most popular night spot is the pleasantly integrated Sauyema Night Club, beside a tree sporting coloured lights in the Sauyema suburb, south-west of town. On weekends, it rocks all night.

### Things to Buy

Thanks to their woodlands, the Kavango people have developed woodcarving skills and arguably produce Namibia's finest wood work. Animal figures, masks, wooden mugs for beer, walking sticks and boxes are carved in the light *dolfhout* (wild teak) hardwood and make excellent souvenirs. The best carvings are elusive, but you'll find nice pieces at stands along the B8 towards Grootfontein. Some of the stands specialise in toy trucks, aeroplanes and helicopters.

The San people also sell craft work – mainly bows, arrows, quivers and ostrich-eggshell necklaces – and can often be found near the Shell petrol station. For a casual tropical look, you could try a palm-leaf hat – a cross between a coolie and a Panama.

### Getting There & Away

**Air** At the time of writing, Air Namibia flights to Rundu had been suspended. However, it's best to check, as this situation is likely to change.

**Bus** Minibuses from Windhoek, Grootfontein and Katima Mulilo stop at the Shell petrol station. Star Line runs a bus from Rundu to Tsumeb (US$7, four hours), via Grootfontein, on Wednesday and Thursday at 7 am. From Grootfontein to Rundu (US$7, three hours), it leaves at 1 pm on Tuesday and Wednesday. All bus services between Windhoek and Victoria Falls, and

Livingstone and Harare also pass through Rundu. See the Namibia Getting There & Away chapter.

**Car & Motorcycle** The road from Grootfontein is excellent, but extra care must be taken north of the Red Line, due to the many pedestrians and animals on the road. Heading east, you can choose between the monotonous Golden Highway or the more scenic and leisurely river road. The routes merge 48km east of Mashari.

**Hitching** The B8 doesn't carry much traffic, but hitching between Grootfontein and Rundu isn't overly difficult. The road running east to Katima Mulilo is a bit more challenging.

**Boat** The Rundu-Calai international ferry service has been suspended until the border reopens.

## KHAUDOM GAME RESERVE
The wild and undeveloped 384,000 hectare Khaudom Game Reserve, which borders on Bushmanland, is like nowhere else in Africa. Meandering sand tracks lure you through pristine bush where you'll see roan, wild dogs, elephant, zebra and many other species in an unspoilt and untouristed setting.

The park is crossed by a series of *omiramba* (fossil river valleys), which run parallel to the east-west-oriented Kalahari dunes. The poor roads will hamper visits in the summer, when the birdlife is best; the easiest time to go is during the drier winter.

### Places to Stay
Khaudom has two main camps, Khaudom and Sikereti (yes, it means cigarette). Basic four-bed huts at either camp cost US$23 and camp sites for up to eight people are US$18. Accommodation must be pre-booked at the MET offices in Windhoek, Rundu or Katima Mulilo.

### Getting There & Away
Access may be difficult – in the dry, the

deep sand roads are excruciating and during the rainy season, they deteriorate into mud-slicks – but you're unlikely to regret the effort. MET requires drivers to travel in a convoy of at least two self-sufficient 4WD vehicles, equipped with food and water for at least three days. Note that caravans, trailers and motorbikes are prohibited from entering the reserve.

From the north, you can enter Khaudom on the sandy track from Katere on the B8 (signposted 'Khaudom') about 120km east of Rundu. After 45km, you'll reach the Cwibadum omuramba, where you should turn east (left) into the park.

Alternatively, it's possible to enter from the south, via Tsumkwe and Sikereti. From Tsumkwe, it's 20km to Groote Döbe and another 15km from there to the Dorslandboom turn-off (see the Eastern Bushmanland map later in this chapter). From here, it's 25km north to Sikereti Camp.

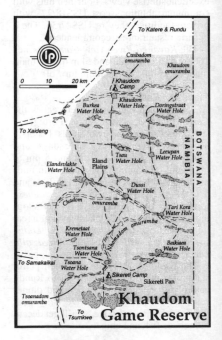

# The Caprivi

Namibia's spindly north-eastern appendage, the Caprivi Strip, is a largely unexceptional landscape typified by expanses of forest – mainly mopane and terminalia broadleaf. In fact, the land is so flat that the difference between the highest and lowest points in the Caprivi Strip, which measures nearly 500km in length, is a trifling 39m. Throughout the Caprivi are traces of the *shonas*, parallel dunes which are remnants of a drier climate and now characterise the Kalahari sands.

The region's original inhabitants were subsistence farmers who cultivated the banks of the Zambezi and Kwando rivers. It has also long been home to substantial San populations, but none still follow their original nomadic hunter-gatherer lifestyles. Most modern inhabitants of the Caprivi are concentrated along the Okavango, Zambezi and Kwando/Mashi/Linyanti/Chobe river systems.

Minor roads are in poor condition and apart from a handful of roadside cuca shops, there are no facilities along the Golden Highway between Divundu and Kongola. Petrol is available only at Rundu, Divundu, Kongola, Linyanti and Katima Mulilo.

For many travellers, the Caprivi is the easiest access route between Victoria Falls, Chobe and the main body of Namibia. However, visitors with time, cash and patience will find such hidden gems as Mudumu and Mamili national parks, the Mahango Game Reserve, the Lizauli Traditional Village, the West Caprivi Triangle and the town of Katima Mulilo.

## History

Until the late 19th century, the Caprivi area was known as Itenge and was under the rule of the Lozi (or Barotse) kings. Although modern Caprivians belong mainly to the Mafwe, Subia, Bayei and Mbukushu tribes, Lozi remains the regional lingua franca and is used as a medium of instruction in primary schools.

The Caprivi's notably odd shape is a story in itself. In the late 19th century, the Caprivi Strip was administered by the British Bechuanaland protectorate. In 1890, Germany laid claim to British-administered Zanzibar. Britain naturally objected and in July 1890, the Berlin Conference was called to settle the dispute. In the end, Queen Victoria acquired Zanzibar, and a strip along the eastern boundary of German South West Africa was appended to Bechuanaland. Germany was granted the North Sea island of Heligoland and the strip which was subsequently named the Caprivi Strip, after German chancellor General Count Georg Leo von Caprivi di Caprara di Monte cuccoli.

Germany's motivation behind the swap was to acquire access to the Zambezi River, and provide a link with Tanganyika and, ultimately, the Indian Ocean. Unfortunately, the British colonisation of Rhodesia stopped them well upstream of Victoria Falls, which proved a considerable barrier to navigation on the Zambezi.

The absorption of the Caprivi Strip into German South West Africa didn't exactly make world news, however, and it was nearly 20 years before some of its population realised they were under German control. In fact, not until October 1908 did the government dispatch an Imperial Resident, Herr Hauptmann Streitwolf, to oversee local administration.

The local Lozi people reacted by rounding up all the cattle they could muster – including those which belonged to rival tribes – and driving them out of the area. The cattle were eventually returned to their rightful owners, but the Lozi chose to remain in Zambia and Angola rather than submit to German rule.

On 4 August 1914, Britain declared war on Germany and, just over a month later, the German administrative seat at Schuckmannsburg was attacked by the British from their base at Sesheke and seized by the police. An apocryphal tale recounts that

German governor von Frankenburg was having tea with the English resident administrator across the river in Northern Rhodesia (now Zambia) when a servant arrived with a message from British authorities in Livingstone. After reading it, the British official declared his guest a prisoner of war, and Schuckmannsburg had fallen. Whatever the case, the seizure of Schuckmannsburg was the first Allied occupation of enemy territory of WWI.

During the British occupation, the Caprivi was again governed as part of Bechuanaland but it received little attention and was known as a lawless frontier area. When its administration was handed over to South Africa in 1935, the British moved their headquarters to Katima Mulilo, Seventh-Day Adventist missionaries set up a mission and mercantile activities commenced. In 1939, the rather idiosyncratic magistrate, Major Lyle French W Trollope, was posted to Katima Mulilo and remained long enough to be regarded as local royalty.

### Dangers & Annoyances

UN travel restrictions were lifted several years ago, but due to the on-and-off war in Angola, travel still carries a slight risk. However, most cross-border raids are inspired more by robbery than politics. There's no call for paranoia but it's wise to keep informed.

### THE WESTERN CAPRIVI STRIP

Although it technically belongs to the Kavango Region, the attractive area immediately west of the Okavango River lies in the Caprivi Strip. Attractions include Popa Falls and the wildlife-rich Mahango Game Reserve.

### Mahango Game Reserve

This small (25,400 hectare) but diverse park occupies a broad flood plain north of the Botswana border and west of the Okavango River. In the dry it attracts huge concentrations of thirsty elephant. Mahango is the only wildlife park in Namibia where visitors may walk on their own; winter is the

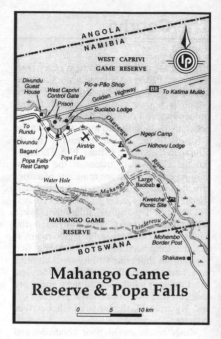

**Mahango Game Reserve & Popa Falls**

best time to see wildlife and stay safely visible.

With a 2WD vehicle, you can either zip through on the Mahango transit route or follow the scenic loop drive past Kwetche picnic site, east of the main road. With 4WD, you can also explore the 20km Circular Drive loop, which follows the omiramba Thinderevu and Mahango to the best wildlife-viewing. It's particularly nice to stop beside the river in the afternoon and watch the elephant swimming and drinking among hippos and crocodiles.

The nearest MET accommodation is at Popa Falls, 15km north of Mahango.

### Divundu

Divundu, with two (nominally) 24-hour petrol stations, is merely a product of the road junction; the real population centres are neighbouring Mukwe, Andara and Bagani. On the road south lie Popa Falls, the Mahango Game Reserve and several riverside lodges.

## Popa Falls
Near Bagani, the Okavango River plunges down a broad series of cascades misleadingly known as Popa Falls. They're nothing to get too excited about, although low water may expose a drop of 4m. Birdwatchers will be especially impressed by the variety and number of birds to be seen locally.

Day entry (sunrise to sunset) is US$3 per person and US$3 per vehicle (also valid for Mahango). The nearby Rest Camp has camp sites accommodating eight people for US$18, and four-bed huts for US$41. A small on-site shop sells the essentials: tinned food, beer, candles and mosquito coils.

## Places to Stay & Eat
From the people who brought you Audi Camp in Maun comes *Ngepi Camp*, 4km off the road near Mahango Game Reserve. The name is Mbukushu for 'how are you' and people who stay here are just fine. Camp sites cost US$4 per person, domed tents are US$11 and bedded tents are US$18. Organised activities include Mahango game drives and canoe or mokoro trips on the Okavango River (US$12/14 for one/two people) or in the Okavango Panhandle (US$75/85 per person for two/three days).

On a bluff behind the Bagani Malaria Control Research Centre, below Popa Falls, lies the German-run *Suclabo Lodge* (☎ (067) 556222. Camping costs US$5, single/double bungalows without bath are US$21/39, including breakfast; with bath, they're US$44/63. The lodge also runs river trips (US$7). The view is superb, but non-Germans may feel disoriented.

A good choice is Roy and Lynne Vincent's *Ndhovu Lodge* (☎ (064) 203581, ask for 436), a homely tented camp beside the wide Okavango. Comfortable single/double accommodation costs US$55/95, including breakfast. Other meals are served in the large restaurant/bar. Wildlife-viewing by boat and Mahango game drives cost

from US$10 to US$20. Their Windhoek agent is Ondese (☎ (061) 220876; fax 239700).

Bueno Mununga's basic *Divundu Guest House* (☎ (067) 256572 or 217116) offers meals and accommodation in a friendly environment near the Shell petrol station. Rooms cost US$21 per person.

## Getting There & Away
Transit traffic through Mahango doesn't require a permit, but to take either of the loop drives costs US$3 per vehicle plus US$3 per person. The same permit is valid for Popa Falls.

## WEST CAPRIVI GAME RESERVE
The Golden Highway between Rundu and Katima Mulilo traverses the West Caprivi Game Reserve. This is now almost devoid of wildlife and there has been talk of turning much of it into an official resettlement area, but the sections immediately west of the Kwando River and east of the Okavango River will probably retain protected status. Travellers must pass through MET control points at Divundu and Kongola.

### West Caprivi Triangle
The West Caprivi Triangle, the wedge bounded on the north by Angola, the south by Botswana and the east by the Kwando River, is actually the Caprivi Strip's richest wildlife area, but hunting, bush clearing, burning and human settlement are placing stress on the environment. Access is via the road along the western bank of the Kwando River, near Kongola. However, the best wildlife viewing is north of the main road, towards Angola.

### Places to Stay
The only camp site is at Nambwa, 23km south of Kongola in the West Caprivi Triangle, but it lacks any sort of facilities. Book through MET in Katima Mulilo, Rundu or Windhoek. To get there, follow the 4WD track south along the western bank of the Kwando River. When you

arrive, pick up your permit at the Susuwe ranger station, north of the highway on the west bank of the river.

*Mazambala Island Lodge* (☎ (061) 229075; fax 263224), PO Box 1935, Ngweze, Katima Mulilo, sits in a lovely clump of large trees near the marshy Kwando banks. It's run by the friendly and intrepid Ms Salome Visser, who arranged this concession through local chiefs and ensures that her operation benefits the community. Camping costs US$7 per person, accommodation in pre-erected single/double tents is US$22/34 including breakfast, and reed and thatch bungalows are US$41/68. Meals are available. Activities include day-long game drives in the West Caprivi Triangle (US$23 per person, with a minimum of two people), boat trips or short drives to Hippo Pool (US$6) and fishing trips (US$16). The lodge lies 5km south of the Golden Highway, near Kongola; with 2WD, access is possible but challenging.

## KATIMA MULILO
Sultry Katima Mulilo, Namibia's most remote outpost, sits out on a limb at the end of the Caprivi Strip. This is as far from Windhoek as you can get in Namibia – over 1200km away – and it feels more like Zambia (OK, Zambia *is* only half a kilometre away). The Lozi name means 'to quench the fire', probably a reference to the burning embers carried by travellers, which were often extinguished by the river crossing at Mbova Rapids.

At one time, elephant had the right of way, but now they've all gone. Still, the river vegetation, the huge lush trees, the tropical birds, monkeys, and lolling hippos and crocs make for pleasant walks along the riverbanks.

## Information
**Tourist Information** MET, on the Ngoma Bridge road east of town, can provide information and camping permits for Mudumu and Mamili national parks, and the West Caprivi Game Reserve. For informal tourist information, contact Katie Sharp

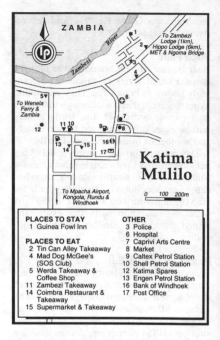

### Katima Mulilo

**PLACES TO STAY**
1  Guinea Fowl Inn

**PLACES TO EAT**
2  Tin Can Alley Takeaway
4  Mad Dog McGee's (SOS Club)
5  Werda Takeaway & Coffee Shop
11  Zambezi Takeaway
14  Coimbra Restaurant & Takeaway
15  Supermarket & Takeaway

**OTHER**
3  Police
6  Hospital
7  Caprivi Arts Centre
8  Market
9  Caltex Petrol Station
10  Shell Petrol Station
12  Katima Spares
13  Engen Petrol Station
16  Bank of Windhoek
17  Post Office

(☎ (0677) 3453), whose office is 6km out of town on the Wenela road.

**Money** The Bank of Windhoek, near the post office, changes cash and travellers cheques at a typically tropical speed; they rarely have South African rand. It's open weekdays from 9 am to 12.45 pm and 2 to 3.30 pm.

**Post & Communications** The post office is open Monday to Friday from 8 am to 1 pm and 2 to 5 pm, except on the second and third Wednesday of the month, when it opens at 9 am. The public telephone is near the post office in the main square.

**Medical Services** Katima Mulilo has a well equipped hospital as well as several VSO doctors and a chemist.

**Vehicle Repairs** A good honest place for

vehicle repairs and parts is the friendly Katima Spares.

## Caprivi Arts Centre

The Caprivi Arts Centre, run by the artists' self-help group CACA (the Caprivi Art & Cultural Association), is a good place to look for curios and material arts, such as wood carvings of elephants and hippos, baskets, bowls, weavings, kitchen implements, knives, traditional weapons, and so on. There's a good range and some work is pleasantly original. It's open daily, 8 am to 5.30 pm.

## Special Events

The Caprivi Cultural Festival is held in late September.

## Places to Stay

The relaxed *Hippo Lodge* (☎/fax (0677) 3684), 6km downstream from town, has camping for US$5 per person and single/double rooms for US$41/59. However, the service isn't memorable and meals and drinks are overpriced. Redeeming factors include the sunset over the river and a riveting frog chorus after dark.

The pre-fab *Guinea Fowl Inn* (☎ (0677) 3349; fax 3835), near the police station – follow the guinea fowl signs – charges US$5 per person for riverside camping and US$25/32 for singles/doubles with shared facilities. With bath and toilet, they're US$34/41. There's also a restaurant and takeaway.

The *Zambezi Lodge* (☎ (0677) 3203; fax 3631) has single/double self-catering bungalows for US$54/63, including breakfast. Four-person family rooms are US$78 and camping in tents/caravans is US$3/4 per person and US$2 per car. Amenities include a pool, restaurant, floating bar, and a nine-hole golf course, and the reception desk keeps guests oriented with signs designating Arrivals and Departures.

The affiliated *King's Den*, opposite Kasikile (Sedudu) Island, offers full board accommodation for US$122 per day, including birdwatching, nature walks, village visits, fishing, and cruises on the *Zambezi Queen* riverboat.

*Kalizo Lodge* (☎ (06778) ask for 1403; fax (0677) 3453), PO Box 1854, Ngweze, Katima Mulilo, 40km downstream, is known for its excellent fishing, birdwatching and mokoro trips, but is accessible only by 4WD. Camping costs US$6 per person and thatched reed chalets cost US$62/102, including full board and return transfers from Katima Mulilo or Mpacha. They have a new self-catering chalet. Transfers for campers from Katima Mulilo cost US$44. Fishing tackle rents for US$7 per day.

## Places to Eat

Your best meal choice is *Mad Dog McGee's*, also known as the SOS Club. It's a popular hangout for NGO staff, foreign tourists and ex-pats of all sorts, but be warned – it's a vegetable-free zone. The waiter told us the vegetables always wound up in the bin and they decided to save the money! Specialities include pizzas, burgers, seafood, chicken and alcohol. The more formal *Zambezi Lodge* serves decent hot lunches and its evening meals are recommended.

The *Coimbra Restaurant & Takeaway*, near the square, specialises in Portuguese-African food and the lager goes down well on hot, sticky afternoons. Near the military base on the Ngoma road, look out for *Tin Can Alley Takeaway*, in an enormous beer can, which is popular with local workers. The restaurant and takeaway at the *Guinea Fowl Inn* specialises in pizza and the *Zambezi Takeaway* at the Shell petrol station sells sandwiches, pies and chicken. *Werda Takeaway & Coffee Shop* near the river does typical takeaway snacks.

There are two supermarkets in the main square and a thriving open-air market near the Caprivi Arts Centre.

## Things to Buy

Your best bet for curios is the Caprivi Art Centre, but along the Kongola road you'll pass stands selling the Caprivi's famous wood and soapstone elephant carvings.

NAMIBIA

## Getting There & Away

**Air** The airport is at Mpacha, signposted as an army base, 18km south-west of town and there are no taxis. The Air Namibia (☎ (0677) 3191) office is in the main square. There are services to Windhoek International airport every day except Tuesday. All except the Wednesday flight make a stop at Etosha (Mokuti Lodge). Flights from Windhoek International are on the same days and all call at Etosha except the Sunday service, which connects via Victoria Falls. There are flights to and from Victoria Falls daily except Thursday. The Victoria Falls flight affords great views and the pilots often oblige passengers with a free 'Flight of the Angels' on the way.

Charter flights to outlying lodges, such as Lianshulu, are available from COMAV (☎ (061) 235821; fax 249864).

**Bus** Minibuses stop at the Engen petrol station, which can provide schedule information. Local buses between Katima Mulilo and Ngoma Bridge (US$3, 1½ hours) depart from the main square; they run according to no fixed schedule. Buses

between Windhoek and Victoria Falls, Harare and Livingstone all pass through Katima Mulilo; see Zimbabwe and Zambia in the Namibia Getting There & Away chapter.

**Car & Motorcycle** Now that the Golden Highway is tarred between Rundu and Kongola, Katima Mulilo is readily accessible from the rest of the country. Minor untarred roads in the region are typically in very poor condition and some become impassable in the rainy season. Before exiting Namibia, drivers of Namibian-registered vehicles must pick up an export permit from the police station.

**Hitching** Although lots of people do it, hitching from Rundu can entail long waits, especially on the lonesome stretch between Divundu and Kongola. In either of these places, it's best to wait at the petrol stations or the West Caprivi control gates.

**To Botswana & Zambia** The Zambezi River pontoon ferry (free for passengers, but US$15 for foreign-registered vehicles),

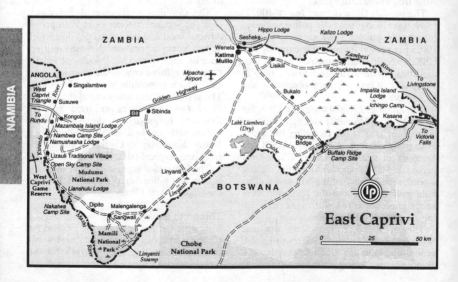

6km from Katima Mulilo, connects Wenela with the Zambian market town of Sesheke. There it's easy to hitch or find public transport to Livingstone (US$8, five hours on a horrid road) and beyond; buses leave at around 7 am and 1 pm daily.

The relatively well-used Ngoma Bridge border with Botswana, open daily from 6 am to 7 pm, provides access to Victoria Falls, and most drivers and hitchers manage it in one day. If you avoid the Chobe riverfront, you're excused from Botswana park fees.

## AROUND KATIMA MULILO
### Schuckmannsburg

Schuckmannsburg, on the Zambezi 50km east of Katima Mulilo, was named after an early governor of German South West Africa. It was founded in 1909 as the administrative capital of the Caprivi by Imperial Resident Herr Hauptmann Streitwolf and at the outbreak of WWI, it was the first enemy territory to be taken by the Allies (see History at the beginning of this Caprivi section).

When South Africa took over Namibia in 1935, the administration was shifted to Katima Mulilo and Schuckmannsburg languished; all that remains is a clinic, a police post and a handful of scattered huts. Follow the Ngoma Bridge road to Bukalo, 30km south-east of Katima Mulilo, and turn north-east on the D3509. From the junction, Schuckmannsburg is a rough 47km by 4WD.

### Mpalila Island

Mpalila Island, driven like a wedge between Botswana and Zambia, sits at Namibia's outer limits, and the Kakumba sandbank, at its eastern end, actually reaches out and touches the western point of Zimbabwe. On an area map, it resembles Michelangelo's *Creation of Adam* on the ceiling of the Sistine Chapel (really – check it out!). In addition to that gratuitous distinction, it's home to a couple of safari lodges which lie within easy reach of Victoria Falls and Botswana's Chobe National

Park. Kasane/Mpalila border hours are 7.30 am to 12.30 pm and 1.45 to 4.30 pm.

**Places to Stay** The *Impalila Island Lodge* (☎/fax (27-11) 706 7207; <impalila@icon .co.za>), PO Box 70378, Bryanston 2021, South Africa, overlooking the impressive Mombova rapids, makes an excellent upmarket getaway. The single/double rate of US$277/427 includes accommodation, full board, transfers and game walks, drives and cruises. For a five-night package, you'll pay US$1266/1928. Access is usually by boat from Kasane, Botswana; in Kasane, phone (☎ (267) 650795).

Also on Mpalila Island is the tented *Ichingo Camp* (☎ (267) 650143; fax 650223), PO Box 206, Kasane, Botswana. Guests arrive by boat from Kasane in Botswana, or by air charter to the Mpalila Island airstrip from Maun in Botswana, or Victoria Falls in Zimbabwe. Single/double rates are US$190/260, including accommodation, meals and activities: Chobe river cruises, game drives in Botswana's Chobe National Park and fishing in the Chobe and Zambezi rivers. You'd never guess you were in Namibia!

### Lake Liambezi

As recently as 1958, Lake Liambezi was just a low-lying plain. However, in that year the water in the Zambezi rose to record levels and the backwash up the Chobe River poured over the higher ground between Ngoma Bridge and Katima Mulilo, in the process creating a new lake which acted as a magnet for waterbirds.

In 1985, however, low rainfall restricted the backflow and the lake dried up and disappeared. For two years, fires ravaged the dry reeds and turned the lake into a blackened dust hole. It's thought that the process was catalysed by overhunting of hippos; without the hippos to flatten tracks through the reeds, river channels became choked with vegetation, which restricted inflow from the Chobe. Access is along tracks from the Ngoma Bridge road, best negotiated with 4WD.

NAMIBIA

## MUDUMU NATIONAL PARK

Mudumu National Park was once Namibia's richest wildlife habitat, teeming with elephant, rhino, giraffe, zebra, buffalo, hippo, crocodiles, Cape clawless otters, waterbuck, eland, roan, wildebeest, impala, tsessebe, sable, lechwe, sitatunga and the rare puku, as well as such predators as lion, cheetah, leopard, wild dog and hyaena. By the late 1980s, however, the park had become a hunting concession gone mad. The wildlife was decimated by trophy hunters, while the native Caprivians, who believed that fires would ensure good rains, set the bush alight and turned it to scorched earth.

In 1989, in a last-ditch effort to rescue the area from total devastation, MET designated Mudumu and nearby Mamili as national parks. Under such protection, some of Mudumu's wildlife has begun to return, but it will take years of wise policy-making and

community awareness before it approaches its former glory.

### Lizauli Traditional Village

As Mudumu's wildlife population grows, so does the number of conflicts between wildlife and humans: elephant raid crops, hippos injure people and lion and crocodiles take cattle and other stock. Locals naturally question the motives of those who would protect wildlife at their expense. The environment falls victim to the bitterness of disgruntled communities for which national parks, wildlife and tourism are a nuisance, and no-one wins.

In the hope of linking conservation, sustainable use of natural resources and local economic development, Grant Burton and Marie Holstensen of Lianshulu Lodge – along with MET, the private sector and the Linyanti Tribal Authority – helped the Lizauli community set up the Lizauli tradi-

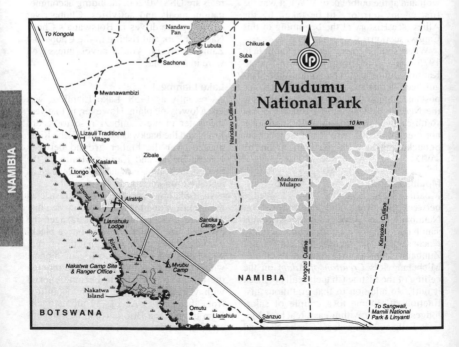

tional village. Here, visitors learn about traditional Caprivian lifestyles and gain insight into the local diet, fishing and farming methods, village politics, music, games, traditional medicine, basket and tool-making and so on. Mudumu game scouts are now recruited from Lizauli and other villages, and given responsibility for community conservation and anti-poaching education.

Tours cost US$6 and afterwards, visitors can buy good value local handicrafts without sales pressure (I picked up a hippo caller – an ingenious device used to prevent hippos raiding the crops!). This is one of the best-run local efforts in Africa. It's worth the side trip – and supporting it is an effective way to improve the local economy and restore some of Mudumu's former splendour. Lizauli lies 38km down the D3511, south of Kongola.

## Places to Stay

One of Namibia's most beautifully situated lodges is *Lianshulu Lodge* (☎ (064) 207290, ask for 1277; fax 207497, mark 'attn: 1277'), PO Box 142, Katima Mulilo, a private concession inside Mudumu National Park. Meals are strong on chicken, fish and vegetarian dishes. At lunch, leguaans beg for leftovers; at night hippos emerge to graze on the lawn and diners are serenaded by an enchanting wetland chorus of insects and the haunting *tink-tink* of bell frogs.

Single/double accommodation in comfortable bungalows costs US$300/400 with meals, activities and transfers from Katima Mulilo (try for chalet No 9). If you book inside Namibia, you'll pay US$81/110 for single/double accommodation, with full board. With nature drives, walks and cruises included, the price is US$250/300. River cruises in the pontoon *Jacana* take you to nesting colonies of carmine bee-eaters, as well as 400 other bird species and more wildlife than you'd ever expect to find in this recovering area.

To get there follow the D3511 52km south of Kongola and turn west on the sign-posted Lianshulu track. Road/air transfers from Katima Mulilo are US$41/157.

Between Mudumu and Kongola is *Namushasha Lodge* (☎/fax (061) 240375), PO Box 21182, Windhoek, on a bluff above the Kwando River, lies outside Mudumu National Park, and is accessible by boat or vehicle. The lodge is popular with Namibian tourists and enjoys a faithful weekend clientele from Katima Mulilo, but doesn't really cater for international guests. Half-board accommodation with a short game drive and boat trip is US$76 per person. Accommodation alone costs US$44.

The *Open Sky* camp site (☎/fax (0677) 2029), 26km south of Kongola, is a basic camp site on the banks of the Kwando. It's a good spot for birdwatching and lies within striking distance of Mudumu. Camp sites cost US$8 per person or US$12 for a pre-erected tent plus US$8 per person. A bar, restaurant and self-catering and braai facilities are available.

Mudumu's only camp site is *Nakatwa*, 7km south-east of Lianshulu Lodge, which is little more than a tent site overlooking extensive wetlands. It lacks facilities of any kind and at last notice, camping was free. The *Santika* (*Sitwe*) and *Mvubu* camps, formerly run by Touch Africa Safaris, are currently defunct but may be resurrected in the future.

## MAMILI NATIONAL PARK

Wild and little-visited, Mamili National Park is Namibia's equivalent of the Okavango Delta, a watery wonderland of wildlife-rich islands, river channels and delightful wetlands. The largely forested islands brim with sycamore figs, jackalberry, leadwood and sausage trees, and are fringed by reed and papyrus marshes and open vleis. As with the Okavango Delta, the dry season is actually the period when the water levels are at their highest, so the best time to visit is between September and early November.

Although poaching has taken a toll, Mamili's wildlife – mainly semi-aquatic species like hippo, crocodiles, puku, red

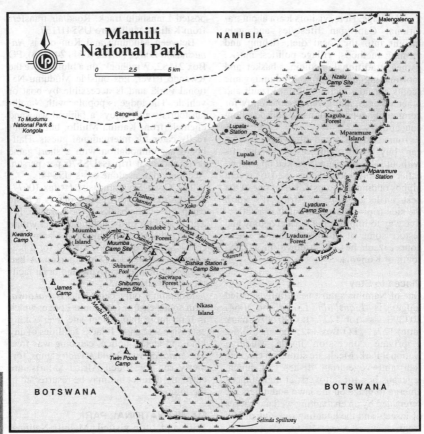

**Mamili National Park**

0    2.5    5 km

NAMIBIA

To Mudumu
National Park &
Kongola

Sangwali

Malengalenga

Nzalu
Camp Site

Kaguba
Forest

Lupala
Station

Casitu
Channel

Mparamure
Island

Lupala
Island

Mparamure
Station

Nzabara
Channel

Xoko Channel

Lyadura
Camp Site

Chorombe Channel

Muumba
Island

Rudobe
Forest

Muumba
Channel

Muanabiyi
Channel

Lyadura
Forest

Liadura-Iuongo River

Kwando
Camp

Muumba
Camp Site

Shibumu
Pool

Sishika Station &
Camp Site

Linyanti

Shibumu
Camp Site

Sacwapa
Forest

James
Camp

Nkasa
Island

Twin Pools
Camp

Malili River

BOTSWANA

BOTSWANA

Selinda Spillway

lechwe, sitatunga and otters – will still impress. You'll also see elephant, buffalo, warthog, giraffe and predators, concentrated on Lupala and Nkasa islands. Mamili's crowning glory, however, is its 430 bird species.

**Places to Stay**

Accommodation is limited to five undeveloped wilderness camp sites: in the eastern area are *Lyadura* and *Nzalu*, and in the west, *Muumba*, *Shibumu* and *Sishika*. Camping permits are available from MET in Katima

Mulilo or Windhoek. For accommodation on the Botswana side, see under Linyanti Marshes in the North-Eastern Botswana chapter.

**Getting There & Away**

Access to the park is by 4WD track from Malengalenga, north-east of the park, or from Sangwali village, which is due north.

For information on tour operators, see the Organised Tours chapter earlier in this book or the Budget Safaris in Namibia boxed text in the Windhoek chapter.

# Bushmanland

Thanks to increased interest in traditional Kalahari cultures, the eastern reaches of the Otjozondjupa region – better known as Bushmanland – are opening up to visitors. This lovely and remote area is the home of the Ju/hoansi San, who constitute a sub-group of the !Kung. Although westerners may perceive the San as a self-sufficient hunting and gathering society, it has been well over a decade since any Namibian groups have followed an entirely tradition-al lifestyle.

### History
For thousands of years, the San pursued a traditional hunter-gatherer lifestyle in their harsh Kalahari home with little outside in-fluence. In the present century, however, they – along with the rest of the world – have seen plenty of changes.

From 1970, Bushmanland was estab-lished as a San homeland, but with Namibian independence in 1990, the San territory shrank from 33,300 sq km to 9700 sq km and 11 of their 15 bore holes were expropriated by other interests. As a result, the Ju/hoansi were left without sufficient land to maintain their traditional lifestyle. This forced many to abandon their *n!oresi* (homelands or 'lands where one's heart is') to work as farm labourers or migrate to Tsumkwe or other towns, where they met with western influences. These shifts re-sulted in disease, prostitution, alcoholism, domestic violence, malnutrition, and other social ills associ- ated with poverty and dis-possession.

During the war for Namibian indepen-dence, many remaining n!oresi were commandeered as South African military bases and 150 San men were attracted by high wages into the South African and ter-ritorial defence forces. They formed a Bushman battalion, known as Battalion 31, to fight the SWAPO rebels in northern Namibia and Angola. As a result, the

western concept of a salaried wage was in-troduced into a non-cash economy. A peace-loving people, who had historically preferred to move on rather than face con-flicts, were thus exposed to war and all its attendant horrors. Having said that, some of their ancestors had seen plenty of horrors, as the San were historically pressed into service as executioners in the kraals of Owambo chiefs.

In 1980, US filmmaker John Marshall and his British colleague, Claire Marshall, arrived in Namibia and over the next 10 years they drilled bore holes, established 35 villages and formed the Ju/hoansi Bushmen Development Foundation, which encour-aged the San to return to their traditional lands and take up farming of dry-land crops and raising cattle. This fostered the creation of the Nyae Nyae Farmers' Co-operative Organisation to oversee production and assist in decisions which affect the farmers' interests.

Unfortunately, the development founda-tion has recently suffered ideological conflicts among its expatriate staff. Points of contention include the introduction of cattle (an original cornerstone of the devel-opment foundation) and tourism. Many purists feel that both are big trouble, while pragmatists believe both can better the lot of this forgotten people.

### EASTERN BUSHMANLAND
The largely flat landscape of eastern Bush-manland is characterised by scrubby vegetation, but areas which receive more water, such as the meandering omiramba, also support baobabs and stands of camelthorn, red umbrella thorn and black-thorn acacia.

Despite official reassurances that cattle, agriculture and traditional gathering would be accommodated, attempts to create a game reserve in eastern Bushmanland have met with local resistance. However, even without official protection, the region sup-ports a rich natural ecosystem. In the dry season, elephant, antelope and other wildlife congregate around the Panveld;

NAMIBIA

## Traditional San Life

We know a great deal about the traditional life of the San because they are one of the most heavily studied peoples in the history of anthropology. An important stimulus for this research was the idea that they were one of the world's last original hunter-gatherer societies. Scholars treated them as if they had lived in complete isolation, and this belief soon took hold among the general public. In fact, however, they have interacted and traded with other peoples for centuries.

Historically, the San have generally lived as hunter-gatherers or foragers. The women were skilled at finding the fruits, nuts and roots which provided most of the daily diet. The meat which was hunted by the men – mostly various species of antelope – was a treat and was the most valued food. Some researches have suggested that the San lived in a state of 'primitive affluence'. That is, they had to work only a short time each day to satisfy all their basic needs. At certain times and locations this might have been true, but during some seasons and conditions life could be harsh, for their desert environment was above all very unpredictable.

Mostly, the San lived in nomadic groups of between 25 and 35 people. Each group comprised several families. They had their own land division system; groups had well-defined territories which could measure up to 1000 sq km. During part of the year, the whole group camped together at a water hole; then in the wet season they'd scatter over the country. They had no political hierarchy or chiefs, and decisions were reached by group consensus; both men and women had a say.

However, not all the San lived by hunting and gathering alone. In the early 19th century, the San were responsible for one of the most extensive pre-colonial trade networks which extended across the Kalahari.

The San people today are, by modern standards, unequivocally impoverished. However, some are finding new lifestyles such as learning to farm or keeping small numbers of cattle and goats on what land remains for them. Nevertheless, many still hunt when they have the opportunity. A group of such farmers in Namibia have joined together to form the Nyae Nyae Farmers' Co-operative (NNFC), which is supported by the Ju/hoansi Bushmen Development Foundation in Namibia.

In 1991, at the Namibian National Land Conference, the Minister for Land stated that the San system of land-holding would be recognised by the government.

In the past, the flexibility of their society helped the San people to evade conquest and control. But, at the same time, it made it exceedingly difficult for them to organise themselves to form pressure groups and claim and defend their rights. However, through organisations such as NNFC in Namibia and The First People of the Kalahari in Botswana, some things, at least, are improving. The first signs of hope were the two regional conferences on Development for Africa's San Peoples (in 1992 and 1993), in which San delegations from both Namibia and Botswana were present and made their needs known.

**Survival International, UK**

when the rains come, they disperse to the west and north-west.

A note to visitors: this region of Namibia is one of the most fragile in Africa and tourism has been very limited. When visiting San villages, visitors are expected to trade for beadwork, walking sticks, ostrich shell necklaces, bow and arrow sets, and so on. Locally prized items include T-shirts, shoes, trousers, baseball caps and other useful items. People will also ask for sugar and tobacco; you'll have to decide whether

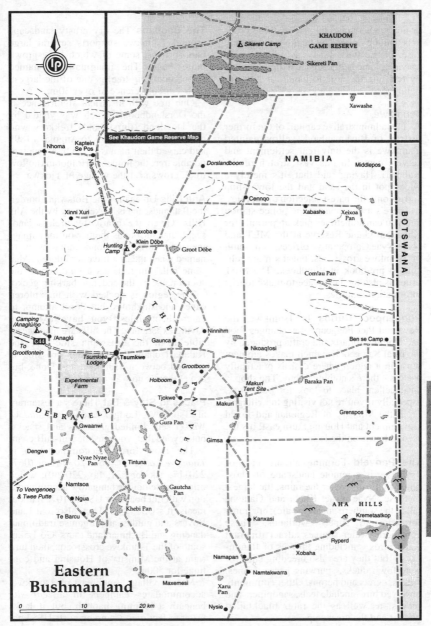

KHAUDOM GAME RESERVE

Sikereti Camp

Sikereti Pan

Xawashe

See Khaudom Game Reserve Map

NAMIBIA

Nhoma

Kaptein Se Pos

Dorslandboom

Middlepos

BOTSWANA

Xinni Xuri

Cennqo

Xabashe

Xeixoa Pan

Xaxoba

Klein Döbe

Groot Döbe

Hunting Camp

T H E

Com!au Pan

Camping /Anaglú/oo

/Anaglú

Ninnihm

C44

Gaunca

To Grootfontein

Tsumkwe Lodge

Tsumkwe

Nkoaq!osi

Ben se Camp

Experimental Farm

Grootboom

Holboom

P A N V E L D

Makuri Tent Site

Baraka Pan

Tjokwe

Makuri

D E B R A V E L D

Grenspos

Gwaanwi

Gura Pan

Gimsa

Dengwe

Nyae Nyae Pan

Tintuna

To Veergenoeg & Twee Putte

Namtsoa

Ngua

Gautcha Pan

AHA HILLS

Te Barcu

Khebi Pan

Kanxasi

Kremetaatkop

Ryperd

Namapan

Xobaha

Namtakwarra

Eastern Bushmanland

Maxemesi

Xaru Pan

Nysie

0    10    20 km

or not to encourage the use of these products and their attendant health risks. In any case, please trade fairly, avoid excessive 'payment' and help keep local dignity intact by resisting the urge to hand out gifts for nothing!

### Tsumkwe

As the 'administrative capital' of the former district of Bushmanland, yellow-painted Tsumkwe is the only real settlement and service centre in this vast stretch of the Kalahari. Having said that, it's merely a wide spot in the sand and the town shop carries only the barest selection of supplies.

There's a telephone at the police station and you can sometimes pick up permits for Khaudom Game Reserve at the MET and Nyae Nyae Co-operative offices, 1km south of Tsumkwe crossroads, but it's more reliable to pre-book in Windhoek. The MET office is also the best place to make tourist information inquiries.

**Poggenpool Curios** In Tsumkwe, the Reverend Piet Poggenpool exchanges food and clothing for arts and crafts produced by the rural San people, which makes eminent sense in a region where cash is practically useless – there's nothing to buy. The shop is an excellent place to look for San work, especially if you're not visiting the villages. From the Ministry of Regional and Local Government and Housing, turn east; it's the second house on the left.

**The Panveld** Forming an arc east of Tsumkwe is a remote landscape of phosphate-rich pans. After the rains, the largest of these, Nyae Nyae, Khebi and Gautcha (all at the southern end of the arc), are transformed into superb wetlands. These ephemeral water sources attract itinerant water birds – including throngs of flamingoes – but they are also breeding sites for waterfowl: ducks, spurwing geese, cranes, crakes, egrets and herons. Other commonly observed birds include teals, sandpipers and reeves, as well as the rarer blacktailed godwit and the great snipe.

**The Baobabs** The dry crusty landscape around Tsumkwe supports several large baobab trees, some of which have grown quite huge. The imaginatively named Grootboom (big tree) is one of the largest, with a circumference of over 30m.

One tree with historical significance is the Dorslandboom, which was visited by the Dorsland (thirst land) trekkers who camped here on their trek to Angola in 1891 and carved their names in the tree. Another notable tree, the immense Holboom (hollow tree), grows near the village of Tjokwe.

**Aha Hills** Up against the Botswana border, the flat landscape is broken only by the Aha Hills. Given the nearly featureless landscape that surrounds them, you may imagine these low limestone outcrops were named when the first traveller uttered 'Aha, some hills'. In fact, it's a rendition of the sound made by the endemic barking gecko.

The region is pocked with unexplored caves and sinkholes, but don't attempt to enter them unless you have extensive caving experience. The hills are also accessible from the Botswana side (see the Kalahari chapter). A border crossing is planned between Tsumkwe and Dobe, but as yet there's no way across.

**Places to Stay & Eat** There's a restaurant at Tsumkwe Lodge, and the *Tsumkwe Winkel* sells limited groceries and snacks, but beyond that, you must be self-sufficient.

The most formal accommodation is *Tsumkwe Lodge* (☎ (064) 203581 or (067) 220117, ask for 531; fax 220060), which offers single/double bungalow accommodation with full board for US$64/107. Without meals, it's US$42/62. They also rent Land Rovers and guides, and organise traditional dancing and Bushmanland tours. Go 1.5km south of the Tsumkwe crossroads, then turn right at the Ministry of Housing and continue for 500m.

Makuri village, south-east of Tsumkwe, accommodates campers in a *tent site* beneath a looming baobab, but it lacks water or facilities. Camping costs US$3 per person. Activities include walks with the village folk to seek out bush tucker, and singing, dancing and clapping evenings around the campfire. These cost US$3 per bush guide (up to 10 guides – don't pay for more) or singer/dancer (again, up to 10). See Mr Kageshe/Kashe in Makuri.

The *Camping /Anaglú/oo*, in Anaglú village, has a nice little camp site with picnic areas, trash barrels, firewood, water, a toilet and showers. Camping costs US$2 per person. It lies 11km west of Tsumkwe on the C44, then 1km north.

The more elaborate *Omatako Valley Rest Camp*, lies 11km south-west of the Kano Vlei veterinary gate at the D3306 junction. It's a scenic location, set deep in the Omatoko omuramba and has solar power, a water pump, hot showers and a caretaker. Camping costs US$3 in your own tent or a thatched camping shelter, and four-bed bungalows are US$5 per person. Various activities are available, from birdwatching to horse-riding and village visits.

**Getting There & Away** Star Line runs a bus service from Grootfontein to Tsumkwe (US$8, 6½ hours) on Monday and Thursday at 11.30 am; it returns on Tuesday and Friday at 9 am. The Tsumkwe road is negotiable by 2WD vehicles, but it's a long, tedious gravelled route that still gets rough in places. The petrol station in Tsumkwe has now closed, which means that the only petrol in the area is at the 'Hieromtrent 995 BP', which lies 12km south of the C44 on the D2893, then 2km west on a ranch road. Unless you have reserves, don't miss it or you won't have enough fuel to get to Tsumkwe and back.

**Getting Around** Most visitors swing through en route from Central Namibia to the Caprivi strip via Khaudom Game Reserve. There are no tarred roads and only the C44 is good gravel; other routes are little more than tracks, some very sandy. In remote areas, it's wise to travel in a convoy of two or more vehicles.

# North-Western Namibia

For most armchair travellers, the classic – and largely accurate – image of the Skeleton Coast is one of a formidable desert coastline littered with shipwrecks and engulfed by icy breakers and sinister fog. As one moves inland, the dank fogs give way to the wondrous desert wilderness of Damaraland and the Kaokoveld, where the predominant cultures include the mysterious and hardy Damara and Himba, and classic African wildlife has adapted to unimaginably harsh conditions.

Access has recently improved and tourism has increased, but only major routes are maintained and the best of the region lies on little-travelled 4WD routes. Petrol is available at Henties Bay, Uis, Sesfontein, Khorixas, Palmwag, Kamanjab, Opuwo and sometimes at Aba-Huab.

# Damaraland

In the northern Namib, dispersed springs and ephemeral rivers – the Hoanib, Uniab, Huab, Ugab, Omaruru etc – provide streaks of greenery and moisture for wildlife, people and livestock. Moving inland from the dunes and plains of the bleak Skeleton Coast, the terrain gradually rises through wild desert mountains toward the scrubby plateaus of central Namibia.

Damaraland, which occupies much of this transition zone, is named after the Damara people who make up much of its sparse population. These broad spaces are one of Africa's last 'unofficial' wildlife areas, and you can still see zebra, giraffe, antelope, elephant and even black rhino ranging outside national parks or protected reserves. It also has many natural attractions, including the Brandberg massif, which culminates in Namibia's highest peak – the 2573m Königstein. The Brandberg,

along with Twyfelfontein and Spitzkoppe, has some of Namibia's finest prehistoric rock paintings and engravings.

## THE SPITZKOPPE

The 1728m Spitzkoppe (sharp head), one of Namibia's most recognisable landmarks, rises mirage-like above the dusty pro-Namib plains of southern Damaraland. Its shape has inspired its nickname, the Matterhorn of Africa, but similarities between this granite inselberg and the glaciated Swiss alp begin and end with its sharp peak. The Spitzkoppe is actually the remnant of

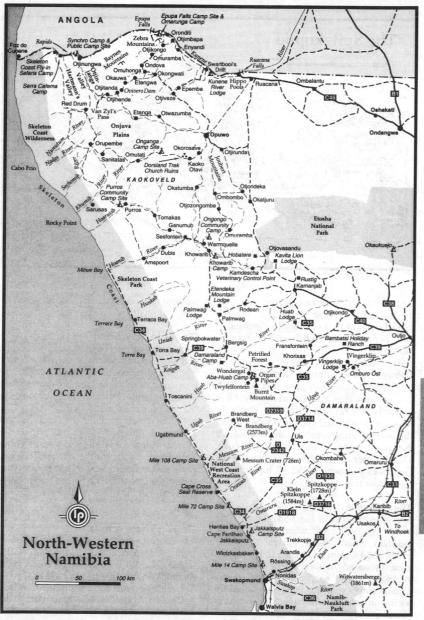

ANGOLA

Foz do Cubene
Rapids
Epupa Falls
Synchro Camp & Public Camp Site
Skeleton Coast Safaris Camp
Serra Cafema Camp
Zebra Mountains
Baynes Mountains
Epupa Falls Camp Site & Omarunga Camp
Oronditi
Otjimbapa
Enyandi
Otjikongo
Omuramba
Ondova
Okongwati
Swartbooi's Drift
Ruacana Falls
Otjinungwa
Omuhonga
Etengwa
Epembe
Kunene River Lodge
Kunene Hippo Pools
Ruacana
River
Ombalantu
Okauwa
Otjitanda
Oovivero Dam
Otjiveze
Red Drum
Otjihende
Ohakati
Ondangwa
B1
Van Zyl's Pass
Etanga
Otwazumba
C46
Onjuva Plains
Opuwo
Skeleton Coast Wilderness
Onganga Camp Site
Okorosave
Otjirunda
Orupembe
Omutati
Sanitatas
Dorsland Trek Church Ruins
Kaoko Otavi
Joubert Mountains
KAOKOVELD
Cabo Frio
Purros Community Camp Site
Okatumba
Otjozongombe
Ombombo
Otjondeka
Okatjuru
Etosha National Park
Sarusas
Purros
Tomakas
Ganumub
Ongongo Community Camp
Omuramha
Rocky Point
Sesfontein
Warmquelle
Okaukuejo
Dubis
Khowarib
Hobatere
Otjovasandu
Kavita Lion Lodge
Amspoort
Khowarib Camp
Kamdescha Veterinary Control Point
Rustig
Kamanjab
Möwe Bay
Skeleton Coast Park
Etendeka Mountain Lodge
Rodean
Huab Lodge
Otjikondo
C38
Palmwag Lodge
Palmwag
C35
C40
Outjo
Terrace Bay
C34
Uniab
Springbokwater
Bergsig
Fransfontein
Bambatsi Holiday Ranch
C39
Torra Bay
C39
Damaraland Camp
Petrified Forest
Khorixas
Vingerklip
Vingerklip Lodge
Torra Bay
Koigab
Wondergat Aba-Huab Camp
Organ Pipes
C35
Omburo Ost
ATLANTIC OCEAN
Toscanini
Huab
Twyfelfontein
Burnt Mountain
Ugab River
DAMARALAND
Ugabmund
Brandberg West
Brandberg (2573m)
D2359
D3714
Uis
Mile 108 Camp Site
National West Coast Recreation Area
Messum Crater (726m)
D 2342
Okombahe
Omaruru
C33
Cape Cross Seal Reserve
C35
Klein Spitzkoppe (1584m)
Spitzkoppe (1728m)
D1930
D3716
Mile 72 Camp Site
C34
Omaruru
D1918
Karibib
B2
Henties Bay
Cape Farilhao
Jakkalsputz
Jakkalsputz Camp Site
Trekkopje
B2
To Windhoek
Wlotzkasbaken
Arandis
Usakos
Rössing
Khan
Mile 14 Camp Site
Nonidas
Witwatersberge (1861m)
North-Western Namibia
Swakopmund
Swakop River
Namib-Naukluft Park
C36
0    50    100 km
Walvis Bay

NAMIBIA

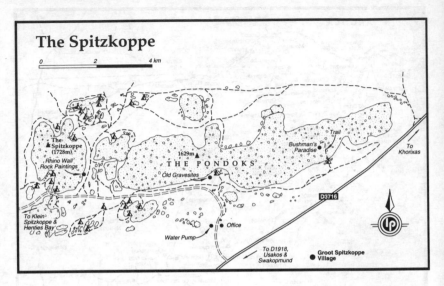

# The Spitzkoppe

an ancient volcano, formed in the same way as the nearby Brandberg and Erongo massifs. It was first climbed in 1946 and is now popular with both local and foreign mountaineers.

The Spitzkoppe was transferred from the Damara Administration to the MET in 1986, and it's currently protected as a MET conservation area, which is necessary if it is to survive the ravages of tourism. One only hopes that increased visitation won't affect the overpowering sense of lonely wonder it currently inspires. Day admission costs US$1.50 per car and US$1.50 per person. Guides cost around US$2.50 for a two to three hour tour.

## The Pondoks

Immediately east of the Spitzkoppe is the lower Pondok massif where, in 1896, the German South West Africa Company established a farm and a dam to provide irrigation water. At the eastern end of this rocky jumble a wire cable leads up the granite slopes to a vegetated hollow known as Bushman's Paradise where an overhang shelters a vandalised panel of ancient rhino

paintings (much of the damage is caused by a coat of shellac).

## Places to Stay & Eat

Dotted around the base of the Spitzkoppe and surrounding outcrops are a number of designated *camp sites*. Most are set in magical rock hollows and provide a sense of real isolation. Facilities at the entrance to the camping area include a reception office, ablutions, braai stands and a small bar and *restaurant*. Proceeds from this project are shared with the adjoining village of Gross Spitzkoppe. Water for the village is trucked in by tanker, so it's best to bring your own. Camp sites cost US$2.50 per person plus US$1.50 per car. There's also a small craft shop.

## Getting There & Away

The nearest you'll get to the Spitzkoppe on public transport is the junction of the B2 and D1918, 30km away, which is accessible on any Windhoek-Swakopmund bus.

Under normal dry conditions, 2WD is sufficient to reach the mountain. Turn north-west off the B2 onto the D1918 toward Henties Bay; after 15km, turn north onto the D3116, which passes the mountain 15km farther on. Coming from Uis, take the D1930 south and after 90km (with great views of the mountain all the way) turn right on the D3116, which takes you the final few kilometres.

For day trips, see Organised Tours under Swakopmund in the Central Namib chapter.

## THE BRANDBERG

The Brandberg, the 'fire mountain', is named after the effect created by the setting sun on its western face, which causes this granite massif to resemble a burning slag heap glowing red. Its summit, Königstein, is Namibia's highest peak at 2573m. Plenty of technical climbs are available, but the climb to the peak requires only the agility and patience to clamber over the huge boulders and rock faces that block the Tsisab and Numas ravines.

### Tsisab Ravine

The Brandberg's main attraction is the gallery of rock paintings in the Tsisab (leopard) Ravine, first discovered in 1918 by the German surveyor Dr Reinhard Maack on a descent from Königstein.

The best-known site, Maack's Shelter, contains the famous painting, the *White Lady of the Brandberg*. The figure, which isn't necessarily a lady, stands about 40cm high. In one hand, it carries what appears to be a wine glass (South Africa's Sinnya Valley winery recognised this and uses the figure on its label) and in the other, a bow and several arrows. Its hair is straight and light-coloured – distinctly un-African – and the body is painted white from the chest down. It appears to be a central figure in a bizarre hunting procession which includes several women, one of whom has skewered a small animal – an antelope with gemsbok horns and striped legs. Another figure, who may be a shaman, is holding a bunch of carrots in his left hand and in his right hand, a stick with which he's prodding the white figure.

The first assessment of the painting was in 1948, when Abbé Henri Breuil speculated on Egyptian or Cretan origins for the work, based on similar ancient art he'd seen around the Mediterranean. However, this fanciful idea has now been discounted and it's generally accepted that the painting is of indigenous origin. The *White Lady* hasn't been reliably dated, but may be 16,000 years old.

From the car park, it's a 45 minute walk up a scenic track to Maack's Shelter. Along the way, watch for baboon, klipspringer and mountain zebra, and carry plenty of water. Further up the ravine are several other shelters and overhangs containing ancient paintings. As you climb higher, the terrain grows more difficult and, in places, the route becomes a harrowing scramble over house-sized boulders.

From Uis, head 15km north on the D2369 and turn west on the D2359, which leads 26km to the Tsisab car park. An attendant will guard your vehicle for a tip.

### Numas Ravine

Numas Ravine, slicing through the western face of the Brandberg, is another treasure house of ancient paintings. Without a guide, however, your hunt for ancient art may wind up as more of a pleasant stroll through a dramatic ravine. Most people try to find the rock facing the southern bank of the riverbed, which bears paintings of a snake, a giraffe and an antelope. It lies about 30 minutes walk up the ravine. After another half hour, you'll reach an oasis-like freshwater spring and several more paintings in the immediate surroundings.

From the westward turning 14km south of Uis, follow the D2342 for 55km, where you'll see a rough track turning eastward. After about 10km, you'll reach a fork; the 4WD track on the right leads to the Numas Ravine car park.

### Places to Stay

There are unofficial *camp sites* near the mouth of both the Numas and Tsisab ravines, but neither has water or facilities. Despite the barrel at the parking area, there

NAMIBIA

isn't any rubbish collection, so please burn your leftovers or carry them away.

## MESSUM CRATER

One of Damaraland's most remote natural attractions is the highly mysterious-looking Messum Crater, a secluded volcanic feature in the Gobobose Mountains south-west of the Brandberg. The crater measures more than 20km in diameter, creating a vast lost world which visitors are likely to have to themselves.

### Getting There & Away

Messum is best accessed from the D2342 west of the Brandberg, but you'll need the relevant topographic sheets (available from the Surveyor General in Windhoek). Follow the 4WD track leading west along the Messum River for about 30km, where you enter the crater through a gap in the rim. The track then turns south and leads towards a kopje in the heart of the crater, with several possible camp sites. From here you must decide whether to return the same way or head south to the coast through the National West Coast Recreation Area. On the latter route, stick to the track to avoid damage to the fragile lichens which carpet the plains.

## UIS

The company town of Uis (Khoi Khoi for bad water) sprang up in 1958 when the South African ISCOR corporation bought out the small-scale tin mining operations that had gone on since 1911. The mine closed in 1991 due to low world tin prices and although private operations still eke out a meagre living, Uis appears to be a ghost town in the making. Services include a convenience supermarket, a bakery and a petrol station that's open daily from dawn to dusk (except Sunday, when it closes earlier).

### Places to Stay & Eat

The *Brandberg Rest Camp* (☎/fax (064) 504038; <brandbrg@iml-net.com.na>) has an unobstructed view of a heap of tin-mine tailings. Area tours are available and there's

not only a restaurant, swimming pool and tennis court, but also a nine-hole golf course. Camping costs US$5 per person; singles/doubles are US$27/45; a four-bed flat is US$68; and six/eight-bed bungalows cost US$68/90. Also in the village is the popular *Welkom Bakery*.

## KHORIXAS

As the administrative capital of Damaraland, the decrepit town of Khorixas might seem a good choice as a base for exploration. However the atmosphere is less than welcoming, and as a result most travellers stop only long enough to refuel at the petrol station. In May, the town holds an arts festival, but at other times there's little to detain you, and if you don't require creature comforts you'll probably be happier elsewhere.

### Information

Tourist information is available from the municipal buildings. The bank opens only on weekday mornings.

### Places to Stay & Eat

The convenient *Khorixas Rest Camp* (☎ (065712) 196; fax 388) lies off the Torra Bay road, 3km north-west of town. Camping costs US$6 per vehicle plus US$6.25 per person. There are also 40 fully furnished single/double bungalows for US$43/75. Luxury stone chalets with four beds, and a bath, shower and lounge cost US$188. Amenities include a restaurant, braai area, swimming pool and general shop.

Unless you count the petrol station takeaways, your only choice for meals is the rest camp restaurant. The *Makro Shop* ostensibly sells groceries, but the pickings get quite slim. One Lonely Planet reader found nothing on offer but Marmite and pitted olives.

### Things to Buy

The Khorixas Community Craft Centre is a self-help co-operative that provides a sales outlet for local artists and craftspeople.

## Getting There & Away

Star Line buses run between Otjiwarongo and Walvis Bay via Outjo, Khorixas and Henties Bay. From Otjiwarongo (US$7, 4½ hours), they leave on Thursday at 7 am and from Walvis Bay (US$11, 7½ hours), on Friday at 1 pm. There's also a Monday bus from Otjiwarongo at 7 am; it leaves Khorixas at noon to return to Otjiwarongo.

The natural wonders of Khorixas' hinterland are reached only by private vehicle or undependable hitching. Note that the trouble-ridden petrol station may be without petrol for several days.

## PETRIFIED FOREST

The Petrified Forest is an area of open veld scattered with petrified tree trunks up to 34m long and 6m around. These chunks are estimated to be around 260 million years old. The original trees belonged to an ancient group of cone-bearing plants known as *Gymnospermae*, which includes such modern plants as conifers, cycads and welwitschias. Because of the lack of root or branch remnants, it's thought that the fossilised trunks were transported to the site in a flood.

About 50 individual trees are visible, some half buried in sandstone. In some cases they're so perfectly petrified in silica – complete with bark and tree rings – that it's difficult to believe they're fossilised. In 1950, after souvenir hunters had already begun to take their toll on the Petrified Forest, the site was declared a national monument. It's now strictly forbidden to carry off even the smallest scrap of petrified wood.

There's no admission charge (although they may attempt to collect something anyway), but you may be expected to take a guide. Plan on a tip of US$1.25 per group for the 500m tour. There's a large thatched picnic shelter and a small curio shop selling mainly palm ivory pendants, wood carvings, local crystals and gems.

## Getting There & Away

The Petrified Forest, signposted as Ver-steende Woud, lies 40km west of Khorixas on the C39. En route from Khorixas, watch for the prominent sandstone formation known as The Ship, which is visible just south of the C39, 52km west of Khorixas.

## TWYFELFONTEIN

The main attraction at Twyfelfontein (doubtful spring) is its large gallery of rock art, one of the most extensive in Africa. The original name of this water source in the Huab Valley was Uri-Ais, or 'surrounded by rocks', but in 1947 it was renamed by European settler Mr D Levin, who deemed its daily output of one cubic metre of water insufficient in this harsh environment.

## Rock Engravings

The 6000-year-old Twyfelfontein works aren't paintings but petroglyphs, engravings made by cutting through the hard patina covering the local sandstone. In time, this skin reformed over the engravings, thus protecting them from erosion. Most of them date back at least 6000 years to the Early Stone Age and are probably the work of San hunters. From differentiations in colour and weathering, researchers have identified at least six distinct phases, but some are clearly the work of copy-cat artists and may have been done as recently as the 19th century.

Animals, animal tracks and geometric designs are well-represented but there are surprisingly few human figures. Many depict animals which are no longer found in the area – elephant, rhino, giraffe and lion – and a sea lion engraving indicates contact with the coast more than 100km away. Another portrays a lion with pawprints in place of feet and an oddly angular tail.

The farm became a national monument in 1952 but had no formal protection until 1986, when MET designated it a natural reserve. In the interim, many petroglyphs were damaged by vandals and some were removed altogether.

Twyfelfontein has over 2500 engravings but the loop trail leads past only the most striking sites. Admission is US$1.25 per

NAMIBIA

vehicle and US$1.25 per person. Guides (which are technically compulsory) are available, but the route isn't difficult to follow and if you prefer not to feel rushed you can normally arrange to walk alone. Note that some guides attempt to speed up tours by surreptitiously omitting the first part of the circuit; make sure you see the spring, the pump and the clawlike Wave Rock. A reasonable tip for good service would be US$1.25 per group.

### Wondergat

Wondergat is an enormous sinkhole affording daunting views into the subterranean world. Turn west off the D3254 4km north of the D2612 junction. It's about 500m to Wondergat.

### Burnt Mountain & Organ Pipes

South-east of Twyfelfontein rises a barren 12km-long volcanic ridge, and at its foot lies the hill known as Burnt Mountain, an expanse of volcanic clinker which appears to have been literally exposed to fire. Virtually nothing grows in this eerie panorama of desolation, but over the road from the entrance is an incongruous quartz field, which glistens in the sun.

The Burnt Mountain parking area lies off the D3254, 3km south of the Twyfelfontein turn-off. Over the road, you can follow an obvious path into the small gorge which contains a 100m stretch of unusual 4m-high dolerite (coarse-grained basalt) columns known as the Organ Pipes.

### Places to Stay

*Aba-Huab Camp* (☎/fax (065712) 104), self-described as 'simple, rustic and natural', charges US$0.50 entry and US$5 to camp. Thanks to the expert management of Mr Elias 'Aro Xoagub, many travellers rate it among Namibia's finest camp sites. Camping is in tents or comfortable thatched A-frame shelters. Hot open-air showers, cold drinks, basic supplies and sporadic petrol are available, and you can also order meals. It lies beside the Huab riverbed, immediately north of the Twyfelfontein fork.

### Getting There & Away

There's no public transport in the area and very little traffic. Turn off the C39 73km west of Khorixas, turn south on the D3254 and continue 15km to a right turning signposted Twyfelfontein. It's 5km to the site.

### KAMANJAB

The unspectacular town of Kamanjab sits amid some lovely remote countryside, and functions as a minor service centre for northern Damaraland and the southern Kaokoveld. Heading north, it has the last supplies and petrol before Opuwo or Sesfontein. The bank is open sporadically for foreign exchange.

The good gravel road north to Hobatere and Ruacana is open to 2WD vehicles. About 10km north of Hobatere, it crosses the Red Line veterinary cordon fence, where commercial ranching gives way to subsistence herding. Here, the vegetation has suffered the ravages of millions of munching goats, and erosion has already begun to take its toll on the semi-denuded landscape.

### Rock Engravings

In the Peets Alberts Kopjes on Kamanjab farm, 10km along the Outjo road, is a superior rock engraving site. You can visit with permission from the farmer.

### Places to Stay & Eat

At the *Oase Guest House* (☎ (06552) 32) half board accommodation costs US$40 per person. For meals, you're limited to the bakery and takeaway.

On the borders of Etosha National Park, 37km out on the Ruacana road, is the friendly *Kavita Lion Lodge* (☎ (06552) 1430), run by Uwe and Tammy Hoth. Single/double half board rates are US$75/85. Camping in thatched A-frame shelters costs US$7 per person. Customised day tours are available.

Heidi and Jörgen Göthje's 6000 hectare farm *Rustig* (☎ (06552) ask for 1903) has rewarding wildlife-viewing and offers good country cooking. Full board singles/doubles

The ungainly appearance of the wildebeest makes it instantly recognisable (Nam).

In the dry season, the water holes of Etosha NP act as magnets for thirsty animals (Nam).

The dunes of the Namib Desert are continually sculpted by the wind.

cost US$72/117. Camping costs US$8. Game drives are US$7. Turn north on the D2763 8km north-west of Kamanjab, and 14km later turn right on the D2695. The farm lies 20km along this road.

Over the park fence from Etosha's proposed Otjovasandu Camp is *Hobatere* (☎ (06552) 2022; fax (061) 234342), a private game lodge operated by Steve and Louise Braine. The name means 'you'll find it here' and – depending what 'it' is – that seems to hold a lot of promise. This vast ranch, which is a palette of stunning desert scenery, has been compared to Kenya's Great Rift Valley. It's a great habitat for mountain zebra, black-faced impala and Damara dik-dik. Full board single/double accommodation in dispersed cottages costs US$60/75. Activities include game drives, game walks and forays into Etosha's western reaches. Follow the Ruacana road 70km north of Kamanjab and turn west at the Hobatere gate. From there, it's 16km to the lodge.

Amid dramatic granite kopjes lies *Huab Lodge* (☎ (06542) ask for 4931), 55km from Kamanjab on the Khorixas road, then 35km west on the D2670 from the Monte Carlo turnoff. Its fabulous setting on the banks of the normally dry Huab River also attracts wildlife, including elephant, kudu, mountain zebra, klipspringer, gemsbok and 140 bird species. For US$150 per person, you get accommodation, full board, drinks, game walks and drives, laundry services, a swimming pool and a natural hot spring.

### Getting There & Away
Star Line has a bus from Otjiwarongo to Opuwo, via Outjo and Kamanjab, on Monday and Thursday at 7 am. From Opuwo, it returns at 10 am Tuesday and 7 am Friday. From Kamanjab to Opuwo takes five hours and costs US$9; to Otjiwarongo it's four hours and US$7.

## VINGERKLIP
The 35m-high Vingerklip (finger rock), also known as Kalk-Kegel (limestone pillar), rises above the Bertram farm, 75km east of Khorixas. It's an erosional remnant of a limestone plateau that was formed over 15 million years ago and a large cave in its rubbly base makes it appear even more precariously balanced. It was first climbed in 1970 by American Tom Choate.

### Organised Tours
The folk at Omburo Öst Farm (☎ (06532) ask for Epupa 3311 or (0654) 313498) run two-hour tours to the Hei-//Om rock paintings, 5km from Vingerklip.

### Places to Stay
The *Bambatsi Holiday Ranch* (☎ (06542) 1104), with nine rooms, a pool and a tennis court, lies near the junction of the C39 and the D2743, 54km east of Khorixas and 21km north of Vingerklip. Full board accommodation costs US$48 per person. The surrounding wild landscapes are characterised by mopane forests.

If you can stay at only one lodge in north-western Namibia, *Vingerklip Lodge* (☎/fax (0651) 302063) would be a good choice. It enjoys a commanding setting and the panorama from the bar compares with the famous scenes of Monument Valley in old John Ford westerns. Comfortable single/double bungalows cost US$113/155, with full board. However, the solar heating system may mean hot water shortages.

### Getting There & Away
From Khorixas, follow the C39 east for 54km and turn south on the D2743. The Bertram farm lies 21km south on this road and Vingerklip – which should be obvious at this stage – rises 1km west of the farm entrance.

## PALMWAG
The stark red hills and broad plains of Damaraland can boggle the mind, especially those areas covered with an evenly distributed layer of uniformly sized stones. How this came about is anyone's guess, but at Palmwag, all this wildness is punctuated by an inviting green oasis. The region includes two wildlife concessions: Palmwag

~~~~~~~~~~~~~~~~~~~~~~~~~~~~~~~~~~~~~~~~~~~~~~~~~~~~~~~~~~~~~~~~~~~

### Euphorbia Euphoria

The several species of the prominent cactus-like euphorbia grow all over southern Africa, from the highlands of Zimbabwe where they reach tree-size (*Euphorbia ingens*) to the gravel plains of Damaraland, Namibia, where there's a variety known as melkbos, or milk-bush (*Euphorbia damarana*), after its milky sap. Although euphorbia are poisonous to humans, they're regularly eaten by monkeys and baboons, and for black rhinos they're a real treat. In fact, they've been dubbed 'black rhino's ice cream'.

Euphorbia have also been useful to humans. The ancient San boiled them down and used them in their rock paintings, and locals still use them for fishing. When placed in the water, the sticky substance clogs the gills of fish and suffocates them.

~~~~~~~~~~~~~~~~~~~~~~~~~~~~~~~~~~~~~~~~~~~~~~~~~~~~~~~~~~~~~~~~~~~

Lodge in the south and west and Etendeka Mountain Lodge in the north and east. Either can arrange excellent game drives through their respective concessions.

### Places to Stay

The lovely but aloof *Palmwag Lodge* is run by Desert Adventure Safaris (☎ (064) 404459; fax 402434), PO Box 339, Swakopmund. It nuzzles up to an unexpectedly green marsh and the air is so clear you'll swear it has never seen a carbon monoxide molecule. There are several excellent hiking routes and the human watering hole has a front row view of its elephantine counterpart, fringed by makalani palms. Even black rhino have been known to drop by. Full board single/double accommodation in reed bungalows costs US$68/113 and camping is US$8 per person. For guests there's a restaurant, bar, swimming pool, shop and laundry service, and the petrol station can repair punctures. Bookings are essential, even for campers.

To explore the concession independently, ask at the reception for a permit and directions. Otherwise, Desert Adventure Safaris tours cost US$39 per hour for up to five people, or US$270 for a full day. The most popular destination is the fabulous wildlife-rich Aub Canyon and Van Zylsgat Gorge, on the Uniab River. Self-drive to these places costs US$5 per vehicle and US$2 per person.

The *Etendeka Mountain Lodge* (☎ (061) 226979; fax (061) 226999) tented camp, run by environmental activists Barbara and Dennis Liebenberg, lies east of Palmwag, beneath the foothills of the truncated Grootberg mountains. As a host of the Black Rhino Trust, this lodge actively supports black rhino conservation and thus deserves international patronage. A highlight is the three-day, four-night hike, with overnight stops in trail camps. Full board accommodation with walks and drives costs US$170 per person. Drivers are met at the entrance and shuttled to the camp.

Wilderness Safaris run the solar-powered *Damaraland Camp* (☎ (061) 226174; fax 239455), a desert outpost with distant views of stark truncated hills, which offers an oasis of luxury in one of the wildest settings imaginable. All-inclusive half/full board tented accommodation costs US$63/96. (Rack rates are US$300/400 for singles/doubles with full board; that's what you pay if you book outside Namibia.) The novel pool occupies a rocky canyon behind the camp. Activities include game drives and walks, as well as guided hikes of up to a week. The camp lies 13km down a rough track west of the Palmwag-Sesfontein road.

### Things to Buy

A great way to support initiative in this region of almost total unemployment is to buy a pendant made from *uinidi* or vegetable ivory, the nut of the makalani palm. Nuts are carved with animal designs, mounted on a thong and sold by local teens for less than US$4.

## Getting There & Away
Palmwag lies just off the D3706, 157km north-west of Khorixas and 105km south of Sesfontein. Coming from the south, you'll cross the Red Line 1km south of the lodge.

## SESFONTEIN
The dusty and threadbare town of Sesfontein (six springs), Damaraland's most northerly outpost, is almost entirely encircled by the Kaokoveld. After an 1896 rinderpest outbreak, the German colonial government established a military post here. A barracks was added in 1901 and four years later, a fort was constructed to control cattle disease, arms smuggling and poaching. This arrangement lasted until 1909 when the military appeared to be redundant and it was requisitioned by the police, who used it until the outbreak of WWI. In 1987, the fort was restored by the Damara Administration. It deteriorated badly in the following years, but has now been converted into a comfortable lodge.

### Things to See
Modern Sesfontein is unique in Namibia, and is often compared to the Tamanrasset oasis in the Algerian Sahara. Don't miss the historic graveyard or the views of the town and surrounding ranges from the shale and limestone hills behind the fort.

### Warmquelle
Warmquelle (warm springs) is administratively part of the Kaokoveld, but is more closely affiliated with Damaraland. It was named after the warm springs on the Hoanib River, which seep out of the artesian system 1km east of the D3706. The springs were purchased in 1900 by Dr C Schletwein, as part of a vegetable farm which supplied the German troops at Sesfontein. In the early 1920s, the property was sold to the government as a reserve for the Topnaar Khoi-Khoi people. Visitors can swim in the springs, but are bound to attract lots of attention; turn east at the primary school turnoff and follow the road around to the left for 600m. It's also worth a brief stop at the Okonjou Herero Traditional Village (admission US$3), just south of Warmquelle.

### Organised Tours
Fort Sesfontein runs day tours to Himba and Damara villages, the Hoanib River, rock paintings, Ongongo and Khowarib. Half/full-day tours for up to four people cost US$135/248.

### Places to Stay & Eat
The renovated *Fort Sesfontein* (☎ (061) 228257 or (064) 203581 ask for 401); fax (061) 220103) is now a unique rest camp. Singles/doubles in the fort cost US$84/111 and camping is US$6 per person. The only remaining bit of the original fort houses a campers' bar and braai area. The town also has a Trek petrol station and several shops selling staples. For meals, your only choice is the rest camp *restaurant* (lunch costs US$7 and dinner US$12).

The *Ongongo Community Camp* (appropriately meaning 'beautiful little place') lies 6km up the Italian-built irrigation aqueduct from Warmquelle. Along with Khowarib Camp (see later in this section), it was established by the MET, Save the Rhino Trust and the Natal Branch of the Wildlife Society of Southern Africa. It's now run by the local community, which benefits from the proceeds. This lovely desert oasis features the paradisiacal Blinkwater falls and rock pool, created by a natural tufa formation. Look for the turtles living in the pool. Camping in your own tent or a basic hut costs US$3. Bring a good sleeping bag and ground cover – the days may swelter, but it's cold at night.

On a bluff above the Hoanib River, 3km east of Khowarib on the D3706 lies *Khowarib Camp*, run by Mr Eliu Ganuseb. Group camping at enigmatically named sites – Laughing Dove Camp or Waterfall Camp – costs from US$6 to US$14 per site plus US$3 per person. You can also choose

NAMIBIA

from rustic double A-frame shelters, beehive-shaped chalets or two-bed chalets for US$6. Facilities include long-drop toilets and hot bucket showers. Guided hiking/donkey-cart rides cost US$3/14 per day and a small curio shop sells generally unremarkable craft items.

The third community camp site, *Hoanib River*, about 20km west of Sesfontein, is the wildest of the three and offers birdwatching, hiking trails, guided tracking of desert rhino and elephant and some lovely desert mountains to climb. Camping costs US$5 per person.

Khowarib, Ongongo and Hoanib River lack restaurants, but Khowarib village does have a small bush shop.

### Getting There & Away
The road north from Palmwag has been improved in recent years, but one hill climbs at a 30% grade and may be unsuitable for some vehicles. The good gravel road from Sesfontein to Opuwo is accessible to all vehicles. Petrol is available in Sesfontein.

# The Kaokoveld

You'll often hear Namibia's north-western corner, the Kaokoveld, described as Africa's last great wilderness. Even if that isn't exactly accurate, the area certainly is wild and represents Namibia at its most primeval. This vast repository of desert mountains and indigenous cultures is crossed only by untarred tracks and remains refreshingly short of tourist facilities. Although the Kaokoveld technically includes parts of Damaraland as well as the colonially demarcated region of Kaokoland, for the purpose of this discussion, Kaokoveld and Kaokoland are used interchangeably.

Even the Kaokoveld wildlife has adapted to the arid conditions. The desert elephant, of which only about 35 remain, has survived in harsh conditions that would be devastating to other elephant. This adapta-

### Language Basics
When travelling around the Kaokoveld, the following words of Oshaherero may prove useful:

| | |
|---|---|
| Hello. | *Moro.* |
| How are you? | *Muwepe nduka?* |
| Fine, thanks. | *Nawa.* |
| Yes. | *Eh.* |
| No. | *Eee.* |
| Goodbye. | *Kana ranawa.* |

tion, along with its especially long legs, has led taxonomists to consider it a separate sub-species. In addition, small numbers of black rhino remain, as well as gemsbok, kudu, springbok, ostrich, giraffe and mountain zebra.

### Travelling in the Kaokoveld
Although the Kunene dam project has opened up Epupa Falls and the Sesfontein-Opuwo road to 2WD vehicles, access to the furthermost corners of the western Kaokoveld is via a network of rugged 4WD tracks laid down by the South African army during the bush war. The only maintenance these tracks receive is from the wheels of passing vehicles.

Travel isn't straightforward. Off the main tourist route between Sesfontein, Opuwo and Epupa Falls, there's little traffic and the scattered villages lack services of any kind. Before contemplating an independent trip, consider that the region west of Opuwo has no hotels, shops, showers, hospitals or vehicle spares or repairs. If that makes you uncomfortable, you may want to consider a going with a tour operator.

If you're undaunted, then careful preparation is in order. For any trip off the Ruacana-Opuwo-Epupa Falls route or off the Sesfontein-Opuwo road, you need a robust 4WD vehicle, plenty of time, and supplies to see you through the entire journey. This includes water, as there are few bore holes and natural supplies are unreliable. It would also be useful to take a guide who knows the region and travel in a convoy of at least two vehicles. Carry spare tyres for each vehicle, a tyre iron, a good puncture repair kit and a range of vehicle spares, as well as twice as much petrol as the distances would suggest. For navigation, use a compass, or preferably a Global Positioning System, and the *Kaokoland-Kunene Region Tourist Map*, produced by Shell, as well as the 1:500,000 *Opuwo 1711* topo sheet.

Poor conditions on some tracks may limit your progress to 5km/h, but after rains, streams and mud can stop a vehicle in its tracks. Allow a full day to travel between Opuwo and Epupa Falls, and several days for the return circuit from Opuwo to Hartmann's Valley or Marienflüss (note that Van Zyl's pass may be crossed only from east to west).

## OPUWO

Although it's the Kaokoveld 'capital', Opuwo is little more than a dusty collection of concrete commercial buildings ringed by traditional rondavels and Himba huts. In fact, in Herero, Opuwo means The End. You'll see lots of Himba and Herero people here, but many tourists have passed this way and locals no longer appreciate having cameras waved in their faces (and who would?). The going rate for a 'people shot' is around US$0.50. Please respect local wishes and either pay or put the camera away.

### Information

Guests of the Ohakane Lodge will find reliable information at the front desk, but

## Visiting a Fragile Environment

Camping in the Kaokoveld requires a special awareness of the environment and people. Avoid camping in riverbeds, however shady and inviting they may appear as large animals often use them as thoroughfares and even when there's not a cloud in the sky, flash floods can roar down them with alarming strength and speed. In the interest of the delicate landscape and flora, keep to obvious vehicle tracks; in this dry climate, damage caused by off-road driving may be visible for hundreds of years to come.

Because natural water sources are vital to local people, stock and wildlife, please don't use clear streams, springs or water holes for washing yourself or your gear. Similarly, avoid camping near springs or water holes lest you frighten the animals and inadvertently prevent them drinking.

Visitors should ask permission before entering or camping near a settlement or camp, particularly as you may inadvertently violate a sacred fire or cross a ritual burial line. Also, be sure to ask before taking photos. Most rural Himba people, especially those who've had little contact with tourists, will be willing models. Some, however, may ask for payment, generally in the form of sweets, tobacco, sugar, mielies or soft drinks. In the interest of protecting teeth that may never meet a dentist, it's probably best to stick with mielies. Alternatively, you could offer some fruit, which is hard to come by locally.

Few visitors would want to turn traditional Kaokoveld cultures into 'fishbowl' tourist curiosities, but as tourism increases and the modern western world encroaches ever further into the region, things are bound to change. Along main routes, tourists will encounter traditionally dressed Himba people who wave down vehicles and ask for tips to model for photos. Whether you accept is naturally up to you, but bear in mind that encouraging this trade draws people away from their herds and their semi-nomadic lifestyle and towards a cash economy which undermines long-standing values and community co-operation.

others are out of luck. The post and telephone office is hidden behind the bakery; it's open weekdays from 8.30 am to 4.30 pm and Saturday from 8 am to noon. For vehicle repairs, the BP station poses the least risk, but don't break down here if you can possibly avoid it.

### Organised Tours
Ohakane Lodge runs culturally sensitive half-day visits to Himba villages (US$57), day tours to Epupa Falls (US$450) and Epupa Falls transfers (US$337 for up to five people). For all tours, book at least one week in advance.

### Places to Stay
The *Ohakane Lodge* (☎ (06562) 31; fax 25), behind the BP station, charges US$68/90 for air conditioned singles/doubles with nice chunky furniture and en suite facilities. There's also a swimming pool and a bar and restaurant (guests only). In the evening they put on a *boma* braai.

The *Opuwo Guesthouse* backpackers lodge has pleasantly cool dorms for US$12 and camping on the green lawn costs US$6. Guests may use the kitchen facilities. Turn at the BP petrol station then take the next right. Past the old hospital, turn left. It's several houses down on the right, beside a mobile home.

The amenable *Kunene Village Rest Camp* occupies a lovely green spot in a natural amphitheatre. Camp sites with braais cost US$6 and bungalows cost US$32 per person. Go 3km toward Sesfontein, turn right along an open sewer and through a scrap yard to a clump of trees. Turn right again and follow the dust road to the camp.

### Places to Eat
The Opuwo equivalent of culinary delights are available at the *bakery* beside the BP station; you'll find doughnuts, pastries, yoghurt, beer, bread and delicious sausage rolls. Behind it is the *Opuwo Fish and Chips Takeaway* which rarely has fish and chips, but you might find goat and chips. The only meals you'll get at the *Opuwo*

*Recreation Club Restaurant* are liquid and alcoholic.

The best-stocked supermarket is the *Power Save* and the *drankwinkel* next door sells soft drinks and alcohol. The *Opuwo Supermarket* beside the curio shop stocks only basics.

### Things to Buy
Opuwo's main attraction is the brightly painted self-help curio shop (☎ (06562) 106), which was started by a Christian group and now sells local arts and crafts on consignment. With a few exceptions, all items are used locally. You'll find all sorts of Himba adornments smeared with ochre: conch-shell pendants, wrist bands, chest pieces and even headdresses worn by Himba brides. There's also a range of original jewellery, appliquéd pillowslips, Himba and Herero dolls, drums and wooden carvings. It's open Monday to Friday from 8.30 am to 12.30 pm and 2.30 to 5.30 pm, and on Saturday from 8.30 am to 12.30 pm.

### Getting There & Away
Star Line runs a bus from Otjiwarongo to Opuwo (US$15, 9½ hours) on Monday and Thursday at 7 am. From Opuwo, it leaves at 10 am on Tuesday and 7 am on Friday.

Hitching is a difficult option, but it's generally better from Ruacana than from the south.

## SWARTBOOI'S DRIFT
From Ruacana, a rough 4WD track heads west along the Kunene River (the name means 'the right hand') toward Swartbooi's Drift, where a monument commemorates the Dorsland Trekkers who passed here en route to their future homesteads in Angola.

The Namibia Blue Sodalite mine, 5km south of Swartbooi's Drift on the Otjiveze/Epembe road, describes its product as 'stone from the desert, blue like the sea'. Sodalites, which are coloured by volcanic intrusions, are used for tiles, wall decoration, ornamental columns and lovely sculpture. Only guests of Kunene River

Lodge may visit the mine, but you'll sometimes find sodalites along the roadside.

## Organised Tours

The Kunene River Lodge and Whitewater Eco Tours (☎ (081) 1220014; fax (061) 228259; <wet@is.com.na>) runs five-day rafting and camping trips on the Kunene from the class IV Ondarusu rapids (upstream from Swartbooi's Drift) to Epupa Falls. Other options run from one to four days and cost US$45 per day.

South Africa's Felix Unite (☎ (021) 683 6433; fax 683 6488); <bookings@felix. co.za>), at 1 Griegmar House, Main Rd, PO Box 96, Kenilworth 7745, Cape Town, South Africa, has 10-day Kunene rafting trips for US$888, plus US$113 for return transport from Cape Town.

## Places to Stay

The friendly *Kunene River Lodge* (☎ (064) 207290, ask for 3256; fax 207497, mark 'attn: 3256'; <pharon@iafrica.com.na>), 5km east of Swartbooi's Drift, makes an idyllic riverside stop. Camping costs US$5 and single/double accommodation in bungalows costs US$32/36. Guests may hire canoes or motorboats for US$5 per person per hour and meals are available.

The basic *Okapupa Camp* (☎ (067) 222131; fax 222133), on the Ruacana road near the Okapupa Rapids 21km east of Swartbooi's Drift, is used by rafting tours, but is also open to the public. Accommodation in pre-erected tents costs US$6 and camping is US$5 per person. There's also a small shop selling staples.

## Getting There & Away

From Swartbooi's Drift, it's 93km to Epupa Falls via the river road. This is the Namibian Riviera and it's among the loveliest places in Africa, but the route is challenging even with 4WD and can take up to 12 hours. The easier but less scenic 2WD route to Epupa Falls goes via Otjiveze/Epembe.

## OPUWO TO EPUPA FALLS

It's now possible to drive from Opuwo to Epupa Falls with 2WD, but the route is still very rough and slow-going. At Otjikeze/ Epembe, 73km north-west of Opuwo, an eastward turning onto the D3701 leads toward Swartbooi's Drift, 50km away. At the ramshackle village of Okongwati, 31km further along the road to Epupa Falls, there's a basic bottle store. Another 12km will take you to Omuhonga village, where locals have established a 'traditional Himba kraal' for the benefit of tourists. Admission costs US$1.25. Avoid walking between the holy fire and the cattle kraal or the door of the main hut as it is believed this would bring misfortune to the village. Further north, watch for the unusual Zebra Mountains; you'll have no doubt how they got their name!

## EPUPA FALLS

The dynamic series of falls and cascades known as Epupa Falls (Herero for falling waters) defies description. Here, the Kunene fans out and is ushered through a 500m wide series of parallel channels, dropping a total of 60m over 1.5km. The greatest single drop – 37m – is commonly identified as *the* Epupa Falls. It tumbles into a dark, narrow cleft like a miniature Victoria Falls. The best time to visit is in April and May, when the river is in peak flow.

The pools above the falls make fabulous natural Jacuzzis, and you're safe from crocodiles in the eddies and rapids, but hang onto the rocks and keep away from the lip of the falls; once you're caught by the current, there's no way to prevent being swept over (as at least two people have learned too late). Swimming here isn't suitable for small children.

There's excellent hiking along the river west of the falls and plenty of mountains to climb which afford panoramic views along the river and far into Angola.

## Places to Stay & Eat

The public *camp site* at Epupa Falls gets extremely crowded, but there are flush toilets and showers which are maintained by the local community. Enclosed group sites with braais cost US$5 per person; roughly marked sites are US$4 per person.

Just upstream is Ermo Safaris German-run *Omarunga Camp* (☎/fax (061) 257123 or ☎ (06552) ask for 1312), which operates through a concession granted by the local chief. Tented accommodation costs US$109 per person, with meals, airstrip transfers and activities (visits to Himba villages and sundowner hikes) included. Camping in the adjoining compound costs US$5. If you pre-book, breakfast/dinner are available for US$5/10.

*Epupa Camp* (☎ (061) 232740; fax 249876), 800m upstream, was originally used by hydro project consultants and has now been converted into a luxury tourist camp. Tented accommodation with meals, drinks and activities (Himba visits, sundowner hikes, scenic river drives and trips to rock engravings) costs US$131 per person.

---

### A Dam in Himba Country

If you want to see Epupa Falls as nature created it, go now, as it may soon be forever altered by a hydroelectric scheme on the Kunene. In addition to supplying Namibia's power requirements, it would produce power for export to neighbouring countries.

In 1995, the NamAng Consortium was awarded the contract to undertake a technical feasibility study of the proposed Epupa Hydropower Scheme. NamAng's able environmental consultants set about finding suitable dam sites on the lower Kunene between the Zebra Mountains and Foz do Kunene. After preliminary studies, four possible sites – named A, B, C and E – were chosen for further environmental impact assessments, which determined that the most suitable sites were B and E.

The B and E proposals are in two different types of landscape. Dam site E (also called the Baynes site) would rise 200m above the river 40km downstream of Epupa Falls and would flood 45 sq km, almost up to the foot of Epupa Falls. It would produce an estimated 300 to 450 megawatts. Dam site B would require a 150m high dam approximately 6km downstream of Epupa Falls, would flood between 200 and 330 sq km upstream, and would destroy the falls. This dam would also generate a capacity of 300 to 450 megawatts, but its larger surface area would increase the evaporation factor.

Both sites present other pros and cons. Approaching it from an environmental perspective, site B supports greater diversity (239 vertebrate species recorded at site B, as opposed to 189 at site E), and habitats at site B would be more impacted than at site E. There are also fewer red-data (threatened or endangered) species at site B than site E (12 as opposed to 15). A dam at site E would also drown less area than at site B, and would be less costly to build.

Due to the nomadic nature of the Himba, it would be difficult to say how many people would be displaced by the dam. According to one study, site B has 113 households, totalling 1479 people, within the headship of Mr Hikuminwe Kapika. Most of these people are opposed to the dam, particularly the site B proposal.

The question of whether or not the dam will be built will be determined by two main groups: the pro-dam lobby and the locals on both the Namibian and Angolan sides of the river. The pro-dam lobby, including the unemployed potential workers, stand to lose nothing if the dam is built, and they believe the project will give them access to the western wage-labour-based market economy. The locals in the project area, however, see no tangible benefits for themselves, but rather the loss of control over their lands and resources, and the erosion of the socio-economic structures which have sustained them for generations.

**Dr Daniel O Okeyo, University of Namibia**

## Getting There & Away

**Car & Motorcycle** Epupa Falls is now accessible by 2WD, but the route is still very rough and you'd be happiest with a high clearance vehicle. Ohakane Lodge in Opuwo runs transfers to Epupa Falls for US$337 for up to five people, but you must book a week in advance.

**Walking** Keen hikers can manage the 120km route through enchanting riverine scenery from Ruacana to Epupa Falls in six days. You're never far from water, but there are lots of crocodiles and, even in the winter, the heat can be oppressive and draining. Some hikers go by the full moon and walk at least part of the way at night. Carry extra supplies, since you may have to wait for lifts back to Opuwo or Ruacana.

## THE NORTH-WEST CORNER

West of Epupa Falls lies the Kaokoveld of travellers' dreams: stark, rugged desert peaks, vast landscapes, sparse scrubby vegetation, drought-resistant wildlife and nomadic bands of Himba people and their tiny settlements of beehive huts. This region, which is contiguous with the Skeleton Coast Park & Wilderness, is currently being considered for protection as the Kaokoland Conservation Area.

### Otjinjange (Marienflüss) & Hartmann's Valleys

Allow plenty of time to explore the wild and magical Otjinjange (the upper part of this valley is called Marienflüss) and Hartmann's valleys, which lead to the Kunene River. The former ends at Kaokohimba Safaris Synchro Camp on the Kunene. The Hartmann's track ends at Skeleton Coast Fly-In Safaris Camp, which is open only to their safari participants.

**Places to Stay** The only public *camp site* lies at the end of the road at the mouth of the Otjinjange valley; camping costs US$5 and travellers must be self sufficient. Facilities are limited to long-drop toilets. Synchro Camp, at the same place, is open to clients

of Kaokohimba Safaris. Desert Adventure Safaris in Swakopmund operates Serra Cafema Camp at the mouth of Hartmann's Valley, which is named after the striking mountain range across the Kunene River in Angola. Access is limited to clients of Desert Adventure Safaris. Note that no camping is permitted upstream in the Hartmann's or Otjinjange valleys.

### Onganga & Kaoko Otavi

To return to Opuwo, you can choose between the eastern and western routes to Orupembe. There's a village *camp site* at Onganga, from which it's 186km east to Opuwo via Kaoko Otavi, where there's a ruin of a church built by the Dorsland Trekkers who were searching for their 'Beulah Land' in the late 1870s. The ruin was declared a national monument in 1951, but is little more than a heap of rubble.

### Purros

To foster sustainable tourism in the western Kaokoveld, a joint project by MET, the Integrated Rural Development and the World Wildlife Fund (WWF) has established the *Ngatutunge Pamwe camp site*, near the confluence of the Hoarusib and Gamadommi riverbeds in Purros. Campers may join guided nature hikes, donkey cart tours to Himba and Herero villages and game drives to observe desert-adapted wildlife and learn about the natural pharmacopoeia. Facilities include showers and flush toilets. Camping costs US$5 per person.

### Organised Tours

Skeleton Coast Fly-In Safaris runs tours to Hartmann's Valley and the upper Hoarusib Valley. Five-day, fly-in trips taking in the lower Skeleton Coast, the Kunene River, Hartmann's Valley and Etosha cost US$2050 all inclusive. A four day tour to the Skeleton Coast and the Kunene area is US$1860.

Desert Adventure Safaris in Swakopmund offers fly-in or wild 4WD tours between Palmwag Lodge in Damaraland and the delightful Serra Cafema Camp on the Kunene. The 4WD option is a gruelling passage across 400km of Namibia's wildest country, but you'll get a good feel for the harshness of the terrain.

For contact details see the Organised Tours chapter earlier in this book.

### Getting There & Away

Currently, the easiest way to visit this region is with an organised camping safari. These aren't cheap, but some mid-range companies offer participation safaris in which the operator provides transport, drivers, guides and equipment: clients erect their own tents, prepare meals and help with packing and loading. Some overland companies also enter the Kaokoveld and may accept additional passengers in Opuwo.

Otherwise, wait around the petrol stations in Ruacana or Opuwo and talk with passing expeditions. If you're a cook, vehicle mechanic or a doctor you have the best chances of convincing someone you're indispensable.

From Okongwati, the westward route crosses the dramatic and treacherously steep Van Zyl's Pass into the Otjinjange Valley. This is a one-way road which may only be crossed from east to west.

# The Skeleton Coast

The term Skeleton Coast is derived from the treacherous coastline, which has long been a graveyard for unwary ships and their crews (see the boxed text on page 718). Early Portuguese sailors called it *As Areias do Inferno* (the sands of hell) as once a ship had washed ashore the survival of the crew was out of the question. This region is still imbued with a mys- terious air, perhaps due to the almost perpetual fogs that hang over the shore.

The term Skeleton Coast properly applies to the coastline between the mouths of the Ugab and Kunene rivers, but is often used as a blanket term for the entire desert coast

of Namibia, even as far south as the Orange River. For the purposes of this discussion, it covers the National West Coast Recreation Area and the Skeleton Coast Parks, which stretch from just north of Swakopmund to the Kunene River. The Skeleton Coast parks take in nearly two million hectares of gravel plains and sand dunes to form one of the world's most inhospitable waterless areas.

### NATIONAL WEST COAST RECREATION AREA

The National West Coast Recreation Area, a 200km-long and 25km-wide strip from Swakopmund to the Ugab River, makes up the southern end of the Skeleton Coast. No permits are required and the salt road from Swakopmund is easily passable with 2WD.

This stretch is extremely popular with sea anglers, who flock here from Zimbabwe and South Africa to tackle such salt-water species as galjoen, steenbras, kabeljou and blacktail. Between Swakopmund and the Ugab River are hundreds of concrete buildings, spaced at intervals of about 200m. These aren't coastal bunkers guarding against offshore attack, but merely toilet blocks for coastal anglers and campers.

On the roadsides, you may spot clusters of broad-leafed plants, which may seem incongruous in such a desert. Chances are they're wild tobacco, which is native to the Americas. No-one knows how they arrived on this desolate coast, but it's speculated that the seeds were transported along with hay for the horses during the German-Khoi-Khoi wars. Botanists are currently removing the wild tobacco to learn what effect it has had on indigenous species.

### Henties Bay

The relatively reliable Omaruru River issues into the Atlantic at Henties Bay, 80km north of Swakopmund. Because it's a rich feeding ground for offshore fish, this village serves as a fishing resort for anglers from around southern Africa. It was named after Hentie van der Merwe, who visited its spring in 1929. Nowadays, it's comprised

## Lichen Fields

Neither plants nor animals, lichens actually consist of two components – an alga and a fungus – and perhaps provide nature's most perfect example of symbiosis between two living things. The fungus portion absorbs moisture from the air, while the alga contains chlorophyll which produces sugar and starch to provide carbohydrate energy. Both algae and fungi are cryptogams, which mean that they lack the sex organs necessary to produce flowers and seeds, and are therefore unable to reproduce as plants do.

Lichens come in many varieties. Perhaps the most familiar are the *crustose* varieties that form orange, black, brown or pale green ring patterns on rocks, but there are also *foliose* lichen, which are free-standing. The gravel plains of the Namib support the world's most extensive fields of these foliose lichen, which provide stability for the loose soil in this land of little vegetation. These fields are composed mostly of stationary grey lichen (*Parmelia hypomelaena*) and free-standing black lichen (*Xanthomaculina convoluta*), but there's also a rarer orange variety (*Teleschistes capensis*), an especially bushy lichen which grows up to 10cm high.

By day, the lichen fields very much resemble thickets of dead shrivelled shrubs, but with the addition of water the magic appears. On nights of heavy fog, the dull grey and black fields uncurl and burst into blue, green and orange 'bloom'. It's the fungus component that provides the lichen's root system and physical rigidity, absorbs the water droplets and draws limited nutrients from the soil. At the first light of dawn, however, before the sun burns off the fog and sucks out the moisture, the alga kicks in with its contribution: using the water droplets, light and carbon dioxide to photosynthesise carbohydrates for both itself and the fungus.

Lichens are incredibly fragile and slow-growing, and the slightest disturbance can crush them. Once that happens, it may take 40 or 50 years before any regeneration is apparent. Most of the damage is now caused by thoughtless off-road driving.

The best places to observe the Namib lichens are south-west of Messum Crater, in scattered areas along the salt road between Swakopmund and Terrace Bay, and near the start of the Welwitschia Drive.

---

mainly of holiday homes, but also provides refuelling and provisioning for anglers headed up the coast.

**Information** A map of the best fishing spots is provided in the tourist publication *Henties Bay – Beauty Beyond Description*, available at the tourist office in Swakopmund. Most services are available at Henties Bay, including police (☎ (064) 500201) and ambulances (☎ (064) 500020). The Bank of Windhoek is open six days a week. For photo services, see the 3R Bookshop.

**Places to Stay & Eat** You'll find supplies in Henties Bay, which also has several places to stay. The primary one is *De Duine* (☎ (064) 500001; fax 500724), PO Box 1, Henties Bay. Singles/doubles with bath cost US$36/50. The basic *Die Oord Cottages* (☎/fax (064) 500239), PO Box 82, Henties Bay, has self-catering cottages for three/five/six people for US$25/30/35. Bring towels. The *Eagle Flats* (☎ (064) 500032; fax 500299) has four-bed self-catering flats with TV for US$50.

The *Eagle Steak Ranch & Mile 50 Bar* (☎ (064) 500543), on the salt road, rustles up beef and other hearty meals and drinks. The best restaurant is the *Spitzkoppe Restaurant & Beer Garden* (☎ (064) 500394), which has Namibia's longest bar. It specialises in seafood (what else?) and the disco, pool tables and slot machines will keep anyone busy until the wee hours. It once boasted a painstakingly collected display of rare bottles, but this was destroyed in a fire in the mid-1990s. It's on Duine Rd, one block west of the salt road.

The *Jacomien Takeaway & Market* is a nice clean establishment offering good-value breakfast, lunch and dinner options. It's open daily from 6 am to 10 pm.

**Getting There & Away** Non-anglers can choose between the C35, which turns inland through Damaraland towards Uis and Khorixas or the coastal salt road, which continues north to the Cape Cross Seal Reserve.

The Star Line bus between Otjiwarongo and Walvis Bay passes through Henties Bay. It leaves Otjiwarongo (US$13, nine

hours) on Thursday at 7 am and from Walvis Bay (US$3, 2½ hours) on Friday at 1 pm.

**Cape Cross Seal Reserve**
Cape Cross is known mainly as a breeding reserve for thousands of Cape fur seals (see the boxed text below). In 1486, Portuguese explorer Diego Cão, the first European to set foot in Namibia, planted a 2m-high, 360kg *padrão* (a tribute to João II) at Cape Cross in honour of King John I of Portugal. In 1893, however, a German sailor, Captain Becker of the boat *Falke*, removed the cross and hauled it off to Germany. In 1894, Kaiser Wilhelm II ordered that a replica made with the original inscriptions in Latin and Portuguese, as well as a commemorative inscription in German. There's also a second cross, made of dolerite, which was

---

### Cape Fur Seals

Cape Cross has the best known breeding colony of Cape fur seals (*Arctocephalus pusillus*) along the Namib Coast. This appealing species isn't a true seal at all, but an eared seal, which is actually a species of sea lion. Fur seals have a thick layer of short fur beneath the coarser guard hairs which remain dry and trap air for insulation, so the animals can maintain an internal body temperature of 37°C and spend long periods in cold waters. At Cape Cross, a large colony of these seals take advantage of the rich concentrations of fish in the cold Benguela Current.

Male Cape fur seals average less than 200kg, but during the breeding season they take on a particularly thick accumulation of blubber and balloon up to 360kg or more. Females are smaller, averaging 75kg, and give birth to a single, blue-eyed pup in late November or early December. About 90% of the colony's pups are born within just over a month.

Pups begin to suckle less than an hour after birth, but are soon left in communal nurseries while their mothers leave to forage for food. When mothers return to the colony, they identify their own pup by a combination of scent and call.

The pups moult at four to five months of age, turning from a dark grey to olive brown. Mortality rates in the colony are high, and up to a quarter of the pups fail to survive their first year, with the bulk of deaths occurring during the first week after birth. The main predators are the brown hyaena (*Hyaena brunnea*) and black-backed jackal (*Canis mesomelas*), which account for 25% of the pup deaths. Those which do survive may remain with their mother for up to a year.

Cape fur seals eat about 8% of their body weight each day and the colonies along the western coast of southern Africa consume more than a million tonnes of fish and other marine life (mainly shoaling fish, such as pilchards, and cephalopods, like squid and octapi) each year. That's about 300,000 tonnes more than is taken by the fishing industries of

erected in 1980 on the site of Cão's original cross.

There is also a pattern of concrete circles containing information on the area's history. It's laid out in the shape of the Southern Cross, the constellation which guided Diego Cão's original expedition.

The reserve is open daily from 10 am to 5 pm, year-round. Admission costs US$3 per person plus US$3 per vehicle. There's no accommodation but beside the seal slaughterhouse, there's a basic snack bar with public toilets. No pets or motorbikes are permitted and visitors may not cross the barrier between the viewing area and the rocks where the colony lounges.

### Places to Stay & Eat

Besides the accommodation in Henties Bay, along the salt road in the National West

Coast Recreation Area are several bleak beach camp sites used mainly by sea anglers: *Mile 4* (see under Swakopmund in The Central Namib chapter), *Mile 14*, *Jakkalsputz*, *Mile 72* and *Mile 108*. Basic camp sites at Mile 14 or Jakkalsputz are US$18, while Mile 72 and Mile 108 cost US$14, with hot showers for US$0.20. Mile 72 and Mile 108 each have a petrol station which is open until 6 pm, and during Namibian school holidays they have kiosks selling snacks. At other times, you can buy fish from anglers along the beach, but you should still be self-sufficient. Water sells for US$0.05 per litre.

### SKELETON COAST PARK

At Ugabmund, 110km along the salt road north of Cape Cross, the road passes the entry gate to the Skeleton Coast Park. (UK

Namibia and South Africa put together. Naturally, this has been a source of conflict between seals, anglers and commercial fishing enterprises.

The inevitable knee-jerk reaction to this has been artificial reduction of the seal populations. Historically, the seal slaughter was a free for all, but in recent years, management programmes have been implemented to prevent the colony from growing. However, because marine predators other than seals also compete with humans for the same fish, a reduction in the seal population causes a proliferation of these predators and the number of fish available to the fishing industry remains the same.

Still, the culling continues and every morning during the season – 1 April to 15 November – men take to the beach with butcher knives to kill nearly 200 seals. Currently, the programme is run by a private company, Sea Lion Products, which operates a slaughterhouse beside the snack bar. Here, the genitals are removed for export to the aphrodisiac markets in Asia (this lucrative market is the major reason for the culls), the pelts are turned into high-quality skins for the European market, the meat goes to Taiwan and the rest is ground into a sort of protein sludge to be used as cattle feed. Sea Lion Products is understandably quite sensitive about its position here and although you're welcome to have a look around (if your stomach can take it) photography is forbidden.

Nature has also taken its toll on the colony. As recently as 1993, the Cape fur seals at Cape Cross numbered 250,000, but an outbreak of red tide (an algae whose growth is spurred by high levels of toxins and/or low oxygen levels in the water) in 1994, which caused the shoals of fish to remain further out to sea, has had a drastic effect on the seal population. In mid-1994, the Skeleton Coast was littered with the bodies of both pups and adults that had succumbed to starvation and it was estimated that the population had decreased to less than 25,000. The red tide appears to run on a 30-year cycle; the fish have been returning, and in recent years seal populations have increased steadily and are now approaching their previous level.

## Skeletons on the Coast

Despite the many postcard images of rusting ships embedded in the hostile sands of the Skeleton Coast, the most famous have either long disappeared or remain remote and inaccessible to the average visitor. Little more than traces remain of the countless ships which must have been swept ashore on this barren coast during the sailing era. Of the more recent wrecks, few could be more remote than the *Dunedin Star* which was deliberately run aground just south of the Angolan border after hitting offshore rocks. She was en route from Britain around the Cape of Good Hope to the

Middle East war zone, and was carrying more than 100 passengers and a military crew and cargo.

Fifty of the passengers and crew were ferried ashore through heavy surf in a lifeboat. A wave slammed the *Dunedin Star* onto the beach and stranded the rest of the people on board. When help arrived two days later, getting the castaways off the beach proved an almost impossible task. Some people were hauled back onto the wreck by a line through the surf and more were taken off the beach in another lifeboat (before it too was damaged by the surf). Meanwhile, one of the rescue ships had also been wrecked and a rescue aircraft had managed to land on the beach but bogged down in the sand. They were evacuated by an overland truck convoy which took two weeks of hard slog to cross 1000km of desert, but eventually all the passengers were rescued. Today, the *Dunedin Star* is little but scattered wreckage.

Further south – and nearly as difficult to reach – are several more intact wrecks. The *Eduard Bohlen* ran aground south of Walvis Bay in 1909 while carrying equipment to the diamond fields in the far south. The shoreline has since changed so much that she now lies beached in a dune nearly 1km from the shore. On picturesque Spencer Bay, 200km further south and just north of the abandoned mining town of Saddle Hill, lies the dramatic wreck of the *Otavi*. This cargo ship was wrecked in 1945 and lies mainly intact on Dolphin's Head (the highest point on the coast between Cape Town's Table Mountain and the Angolan border), although the bow has broken off. In 1972, Spencer Bay also claimed the Korean ship *Tong Taw*.

journalist Nigel Tisdall wrote in the *Daily Telegraph* 'If hell has a coat of arms, it probably looks like the entrance to Namibia's Skeleton Coast Park'.)

Only the southern zone of the park (that is, south of the Hoanib River) is open to individual travellers, but everyone needs a permit. These cost US$5 per person plus US$5 per vehicle and require you to stay at either Terrace Bay or Torra Bay (the latter is open only in December and January). To

stay in either camp, you must pass Ugabmund before 3 pm and/or Springbokwater before 5 pm.

No day visits are allowed, but permits allowing you to transit on the Ugabmund-Springbokwater road cost US$5 per person and US$5 per vehicle and can be bought at the MET offices or either checkpoint. You must enter through one gate before 1 pm and exit through the other before 3 pm the same day. Transit permits aren't valid for

Torra Bay or Terrace Bay, but in December and January, transit travellers may refuel in Torra Bay.

## Ugab River Hiking Route

The 50km Ugab River guided hiking route is open to groups of between six and eight people on the second and fourth Tuesday of each month. Hikes begin at 9 am from Ugabmund and end on Thursday afternoon. Most participants stay Monday night at Mile 108 (40km south of Ugabmund), which allows you to arrive at Ugabmund by 9 am. Hiking costs US$45 per person and must be booked through MET in Windhoek. Hikers must provide and carry their own food and camping equipment.

The route begins by crossing the coastal plain, then climbs into the hills and follows a double loop through lichen fields and past caves, natural springs and unusual geological formations. Watch for lion, hyaena, and gemsbok and other antelope.

## Torra Bay

Torra Bay is open only during December and January, to coincide with Namibian school holidays. In the backdrop rises a textbook field of barchan dunes, the southernmost extension of the incredible dunefield which stretches all the way to the Curoca River in Angola.

Camp sites cost US$21 for up to eight people plus one tent or caravan. Petrol, water, firewood and basic supplies are available only in December and January. Campers may use the restaurant at Terrace Bay.

## Terrace Bay

Terrace Bay, 49km north of Torra Bay, is more luxurious than its counterpart and is open year-round. As with all the Skeleton Coast sites it caters mainly to surf anglers and there's little of interest but the sparse coastal vegetation and a line of dunes to the north. Wildlife this near to the coast is limited to black-backed jackal and brown hyaena.

Singles/doubles at Terrace Bay cost US$90/122, with hot showers, three meals and – of course – freezer space for the day's catch. The site has a restaurant, shop and petrol station.

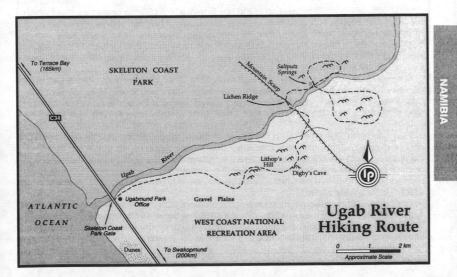

**Ugab River Hiking Route**

## Getting There & Away

The National West Coast Recreation Area and the southern half of the Skeleton Coast Park are accessed via the salt road which begins in Swakopmund and ends 70km north of Terrace Bay. Distances are measured in miles from Swakopmund. The park is also accessible via the C39 gravel road which runs between Khorixas and Torra Bay. Note that no motorbikes are permitted in the Skeleton Coast Park. Hitchhikers may be discouraged by the bleak landscape, cold sea winds, fog, sandstorms and sparse traffic.

Skeleton Coast Fly-In Safaris operates tours in the area (see the Organised Tours chapter earlier in this book).

## SKELETON COAST WILDERNESS

The Skeleton Coast Wilderness, between the Hoanib and Kunene rivers, makes up the northern two-thirds of the Skeleton Coast Park and is what the Skeleton Coast is all about. Seemingly endless stretches of foggy beach are punctuated by eerie, rusting shipwrecks, dolphins jump offshore, and the beach rings with the cries of kelp gulls and gannets. It's amazing that this desolate landscape can support life but, in fact, 64 bird species have been counted, one-quarter of which are migratory waders from the northern hemisphere, including sandpipers, turnstones and plovers.

In order to protect the unique desert-adapted species of the region, MET has considered extending the protected area by creating a Kaokoland Conservation Area, which would incorporate the western half of the Kaokoveld and double north-western Namibia's protected areas.

A lone park ranger lives at Möwe Bay and radios daily weather reports to Swakopmund. He also maintains a small museum of shipwreck detritus and newspaper clippings recounting the stories of Skeleton Coast shipwreck survivors.

### A Tern for the Worse

Around 90% of the world population of the tiny Damara tern (*Sterna balaenarum*), of which there are just 2000 breeding pairs worldwide, breed along the open shores and sandy bays of the Namib coast from South Africa to Angola. Adult Damara terns, which have a grey back and wings, a black head and white breast, measure just 22cm long and more closely resemble swallows than they do other tern species, and are also considerably more agile. In their natural environment they feed offshore in small groups on shrimp and larval fishes.

Damara terns nest on gravelly flats well away from other more prominently marked birds lest they attract the attentions of jackals, hyaenas or other predators. They usually hatch only a single chick each year. However, because of their small size the terns cannot carry food to predator-free islands to feed their chick. Instead, they must remain near their food source.

When alarmed they try to divert the threat by flying off screaming; their nest and egg or chick are usually sufficiently well-camouflaged to escape detection. However, if their breeding place is in any way disturbed, the parent tern abandons the nest and sacrifices the egg or chick to the elements. The following year, it seeks out a new nesting site, but more often than not, it discovers that potential alternatives are already overpopulated by other species, which it instinctively spurns.

Over the past few seasons, this has been a problem along the Namib coast, due mainly to the proliferation of off-road driving along the shoreline between Swakopmund and Terrace Bay. For several years now, the terns have failed to breed successfully and if the current situation continues they'll probably be extinct within 20 years.

## History

In the early 1960s, Windhoek lawyer Louw Schoemann began bringing business clients to this region and became involved in a consortium to construct a harbour at Möwe Bay, at the southern end of the present-day Skeleton Coast Wilderness. However, in 1969 the South African government dropped the project, and in 1971 declared the region a protected reserve. Five years later, when the government decided to permit limited tourism, the concession was put up for bid and Schoemann's was the only tender. He set up Skeleton Coast Fly-In Safaris and for the next 18 years led small group tours and practised eco-tourism long before it became a buzzword.

In 1993, however, the concession was revoked and transferred to the German company Olympia Reisen. After a hotly contested series of court cases, the Schoemanns lost access to the region. Sadly,

Louw Schoemann passed away during the dispute but the family has since altered their itineraries to include the main Skeleton Coast Park, the Kunene region and areas further inland.

## Things to See

The most visited sites lie around Sarusas (which has historically been a commercial source of amethyst-bearing geodes), and include the coastal dunes, the Cabo Frio seal colony, the Clay Castles in Hoarusib Canyon and the Roaring Sands, which are named after the 'string bass' sound made when millions of sand grains roll down the dune faces.

## Getting There & Away

The Skeleton Coast Wilderness is closed to individual travellers and access is only with organised fly-in safaris operated by the official concessionaire.

NAMIBIA

# The Central Namib

Unlike the relatively well-vegetated Kalahari, most of the Namib Desert gives an impression of utter barrenness. Stretching over 2000km along the coast from the Oliphants River in South Africa to San Nicolau in southern Angola, its attractions are numerous and diverse. Its Nama name, which also inspired the name of the entire country of Namibia, rather prosaically means 'vast dry plain'; but nowhere else on earth do such desolate landscapes reflect so many moods and characters. Around every bend is another grand vista and you won't tire of the surprises this region has to offer.

Numerous watercourses, like linear oases, slice through the gravel and sands to the sea. Some flow regularly, but others contain water only during exceptionally rainy periods. However, these riverbeds conduct sufficient subsurface water to support stands of green trees along their courses.

Much of the Namib's surface is covered by enormous linear dunes, which roll back from the sea towards the inland gravel plains. In the north, the dunes stop abruptly at the Kuiseb River, where they give way to flat, arid gravel plains interrupted by isolated ranges and hills known as *inselbergs*. The dunes may seem lifeless but they actually support a complex ecosystem capable of extracting moisture from the frequent fogs. These are caused by condensation when cold, moist onshore winds, influenced mainly by the South Atlantic's Benguela Current, meet with the dry heat rising from the desert sands. They build up overnight and normally burn off during the heat of the day. Underwater, the nitrogen-rich Benguela current supports a rich soup of plankton, a dietary staple for fish, which in turn attracts birds and marine mammals.

On the gravel plains live ostrich, zebra, gemsbok, springbok, mongoose, ground squirrels and small numbers of other animals, such as black-backed jackal, bat-

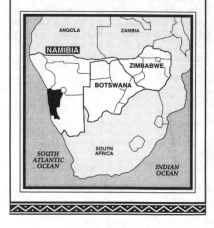

## HIGHLIGHTS

- Look for Africa's greatest flocks of flamingoes in Walvis Bay lagoon
- Spend a day sandboarding down the dunes at Swakopmund
- Explore Namibia's German heritage in the architecture and sweet treats of Swakopmund
- Hike the Waterkloof and Olive trails in the Naukluft
- Climb the dunes at the amazing oasis of Sossusvlei

eared fox, caracal and aardwolf. After good rains, seeds germinate and the seemingly barren gravel is transformed into a meadow of waist-high grass teeming with wildlife.

Much of the Namib harbours ancient archaeological sites, providing evidence and artefacts of the hunting and gathering people who've lived here for as many as 750,000 years. The coastline is dotted with middens of shells and fishbones which belonged to what the locals call the *strand-lopers* (beach walkers), who were probably early Khoi-Khoi or San people. Inland,

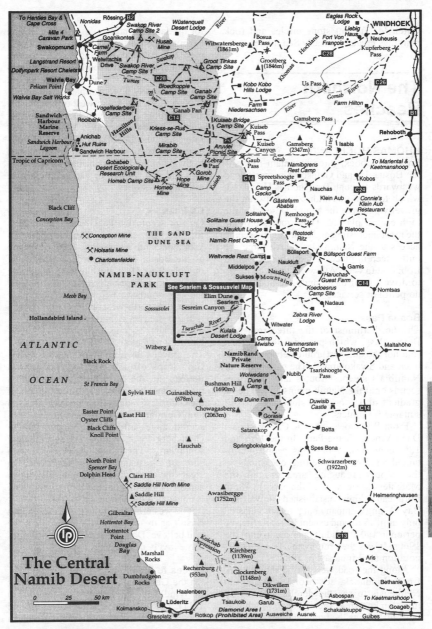

The Central Namib Desert

watch for ancient stone circles and rock paintings created by early San hunters.

# The Northern Reaches

## KHOMAS HOCHLAND

From Windhoek, three mountain routes – the Bosua, Us and Gamsberg passes – lead westwards through the Khomas Hochland, which forms a transition zone between the gravelly plains of the Namib Desert and the high central plateau. These routes provide the most interesting and dramatically scenic access to the Namib Desert. All three are quite steep in places and are best travelled from east to west. Allow six to seven hours to drive any of them, and note that there's no petrol or services.

## Bosua Pass

The northernmost of the three routes is Bosua Pass, which provides the shortest (but not the quickest) route between Windhoek and Swakopmund. The pass is one of Namibia's steepest routes and, as it descends onto the Namib plains, it reaches a gradient of 1:5 or 20% slope and it isn't suitable for trailers.

From Windhoek, take the C28 west past Daan Viljoen Game Park. In the 17th and 18th centuries, indigenous people maintained small-scale smelting operations in the copper-producing area around the Matchless Mine, west of the park. In 1856, European colonists established the Walfisch Bay Mining Company but production lasted only until 1860, and except for a brief active period in 1902, it didn't open again until the 1960s. It was then run by the Tsumeb Corporation until it closed in 1983.

Along the road westwards, about 40km from Windhoek, it's worth stopping at Neuheusis to see the derelict two-storey mansion known as Liebig Haus, which was built in 1908 as the home and headquarters for the farm manager of an Anglo-German Farming Consortium. When it was occupied, this colonial dwelling was the picture of opulence, and even sported a lavish fountain in the salon. It's now dilapidated but may eventually be reincarnated as a hotel.

Near Karanab, 15km west of Neuheusis, are the ruins of Fort von François and its stables. It was named after Major Curt von François, who established a series of military posts to guard the road from Windhoek to Swakopmund. This one had an ignominious end as a drying-out station for German military alcoholics.

## Us Pass

On the scenic Us Pass route, the D1982 follows the shortest distance between Windhoek and Walvis Bay. It isn't as steep as the Bosua Pass, reaching a gradient of only 1:10 or 10%, but the road condition can be poor, especially after rain. Follow the C26 south-west from Windhoek; after 38km, turn north-west on the D1982, which is signposted 'Walvis Bay via Us Pass'.

## Gamsberg Pass

The gravel C36 from Windhoek to Walvis Bay drops off the edge of the Central Plateau at the Gamsberg Pass, which reaches an altitude of 2334m at the top of the Gamsberg range. The name is a Khoisan and German construction meaning 'obscured range', after the flat-topped, 2347m Gamsberg Peak, which blocks the view southwards. The mountain is capped with an erosion-resistant layer of sandstone. On clear days, it affords wonderful views across the Namib, but more often, the vista is concealed by dust.

The western side of the pass is steep, but it isn't as treacherous as some would have you believe. Don't be put off or you'll miss some lovely countryside.

## Places to Stay

On the Gamsberg Route, 65km south-west of Windhoek, is *Farm Hilton* (☎ (0628) 1111), a basic camp which revolves around horse-riding. Excursions range from an afternoon on the farm to three to five-day horseback camping safaris. Die-hard equestrians can opt for a 10 day ride from the highlands to the sea at Swakopmund. This isn't cheap at nearly US$1700, but is normally booked months in advance. Transfers are available from Windhoek.

On the Us Pass Route, 72km east of its junction with the C14, is *Farm Niedersachsen* (☎ (0628) ask for Hochland 1102; fax (061) 225820), PO Box 3636, Windhoek, run by Barbara and Klaus Ahlert. Although it's registered as a hunting farm, it also welcomes non-hunting guests. Have a look at one of the desert hideouts used by Henno Martin and Hermann Korn during WWII. Single/double full-board accommodation costs US$85/100 per day. They also organise desert 4WD excursions.

*Kobo Kobo Hills Lodge* (☎/fax (064) 204711), run by Gert and Caroline Behrens, lies 8km east of the D1985, north of the Us Pass route (the D1982). The name means 'black eagle', and the farm has its own breeding pair of these birds, as well as lot of other watchable feathered wildlife. Larger groups pay US$113 per person for full-board accommodation in thatched cottages, including drinks and game drives. The granite peaks offer excellent hiking.

North of the Bosua Route on the D1958 lies *Eagles Rock Lodge* (☎ (061) 234542; fax 257122; <eaglerok@iafrica.com.na>), which occupies a pleasant garden-like setting in the highlands. It's a very nice wilderness spot, just 38km from Windhoek. The owners can arrange horse-riding and trips to ancient rock paintings. Single/double bungalows with Italian-oriented full board cost US$76/124. B&B is US$55/86.

## SWAKOPMUND

With palm-lined streets, seaside promenades and some fine hotels, Swakopmund is Namibia's most popular holiday destination. Its pleasant summer climate and decent beaches attract surfers, anglers and beach lovers from all over southern Africa.

Swakopmund bills itself as Namibia's beachfront paradise, and perhaps that's why the tourist office rarely discloses the origin of its name. In German, it's simply 'mouth of the Swakop', but when you get to the bottom of the matter, *swakop* is a variation on the Nama words *tsoa xoub*, or 'bottom excrement'. It was inspired by the appearance of the sea around the river mouth during high water.

For better or worse, Swakopmund feels overwhelmingly German – indeed, it has been described as more German than Germany. There are plenty of flower gardens, half-timbered houses and colonial-era structures, and if not for the wind-blown sand and the palm trees, it wouldn't look out of place on the North Sea coast of Germany. Many German-Namibians own holiday homes here, and the town draws throngs of overseas German-speaking tourists, who feel right at home. This Teutonic atmosphere contributes to the town's pervasive *Gemütlichkeit*, a distinctively German appreciation of comfort and hospitality.

Swakopmund gets busy around Namibian school holidays in December and January, when temperatures average 25°C, but in the cooler winter months, the mercury hovers around 15°C and there are few tourists. Thanks to the mild temperatures and negligible rainfall, it enjoys a statistically superb climate, but there's a bit of grit in the oyster. When an easterly wind blows, the town gets a good sand-blasting, and the cold winter sea fogs often create an incessant drizzle and an unimaginably dreary atmosphere. This fog rolls up to 50km inland and provides moisture for desert plants, animals and 80 species of lichen.

### History

Small bands of Nama people have lived in the area from time immemorial but the first permanent settlers were Germans who arrived in Swakopmund in early 1892. Because nearby Walvis Bay had been annexed by the British-controlled Cape Colony in 1878, Swakopmund remained German South West Africa's only harbour,

NAMIBIA

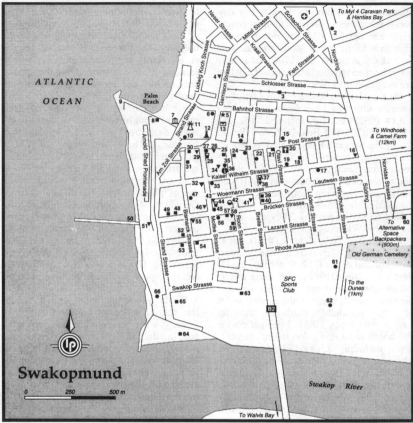

ATLANTIC
OCEAN

Palm
Beach

Swakopmund

0    250    500 m

Swakop River

To Walvis Bay

NAMIBIA

and as a result, it rose to greater prominence than its poor harbour conditions would have otherwise warranted. Early passengers were landed in small dories, but after the pier was constructed, they were winched over from the ships in basket-like cages (an example of one of these unusual contraptions is on display in the Swakopmund Museum).

Construction began on the first building, the Alte Kaserne (the old barracks), in September 1892. By the following year, it housed 120 Schutztruppe soldiers and ordi-

nary settlers arrived to put down roots. The first civilian homes were prefabricated in Germany and transported by ship and by 1909, it had become a municipality.

The port eventually became the leading trade funnel for all of German South West Africa, and attracted government agencies and transport companies. During WWI, however, when South West Africa was taken over by South Africa, the harbour was allowed to silt up (Walvis Bay had a much better harbour) and Swakopmund transformed into a holiday resort. As a result, it's

**PLACES TO STAY**
3 Swakopmund Hotel & Entertainment Centre (Historic Railway Station)
8 Strand Hotel
18 Deutsches Haus
21 Karen's Attic
24 Atlanta Hotel & Fagin's Pub
25 Hansa Hotel
30 Hotel-Pension Schweizerhaus & Cafe Anton
31 Hotel-Pension Rapmund
39 Hotel Grüner-Kranz
40 Hotel Schutze
48 Jay Jay's
49 Dig-by-See (Digby's)
52 Hotel Europa Hof
53 Pension Princessin Rupprecht-Heim
54 Youth Hostel
57 Hotel-Pension d'Avignon
59 Thimbi-Thimbi Backpackers' Lodge
60 Sam's Giardino House
63 Swakopmund Rest Camp
64 Alte Brücke Holiday Resort
65 Hotel Garni Adler

**PLACES TO EAT**
4 Bayern Stubchen
16 Papa's
26 Erichs
29 Swakopmund Bistro
34 Swakopmund Brauhaus
38 La Paloma Takeaways
41 Napolitana Pizzeria & Mediterranean Restaurant
43 Frontiers
44 Kücki's Pub
46 Piccolo Pizzeria
51 The Tug

55 African 'T' Kitchen
58 Original China Tong Hua Restaurant

**OTHER**
1 Hospital
2 Alte Gefängis (Old Prison)
5 Police
6 Altes Amtsgericht (Old Magistrate's Court)
7 Swakopmund Museum
9 The Mole
10 Kaiserliches Bezirksgericht (State House)
11 Lighthouse
12 Marine Memorial
13 Post Office
14 Old Franciscan Hospital
15 Old German School
17 OMEG Haus & Otavi Bahnhof
19 Villa Wille
20 German Evangelical Lutheran Church
22 The Muschel Book & Art Shop
23 Litfass-Saule
27 Altona Haus & Ludwig Schröder Haus
28 O'Kelly's
32 MET
33 Former Hotel Kaiserhof
35 CNA Bookshop
36 Namib i Tourist Office & Air Namibia
37 Hans Kriess Garage
42 Long Distance Bus Terminal
45 Peter's Antiques
47 Woermannhaus; Public Library
50 The Jetty
56 Hohenzollern Building
61 Stables & Okakambe Tours
62 Swakop River Angoras
66 National Marine Aquarium

now generally more pleasant on the eye than the industrial-looking Walvis Bay.

Despite the weather – which you must see to believe – tourism remains a major earner. Another notable source of employment is the immense Rössing Corporation mine east of town, which includes the world's largest open-cast uranium mine.

### Information
**Tourist Office** The Namib i tourist office (☎ (064) 404827 or 402224; after hours 462194; fax 405101), on Kaiser Wilhelm Strasse, is open Monday to Friday from 8 am to 1 pm and 2 to 5 pm and on Saturday from 9 am to noon. The friendly and helpful MET office (☎ (064) 404576 or 405513), on Bismarck Strasse, books permits and camp sites for Namib-Naukluft Park. It's open Monday to Friday from 7.30 am to 1 pm and 2 to 4.30 pm. After hours and on weekends, pick up entry permits from Hans Kriess Garage, at Kaiser Wilhelm Strasse and Breite Strasse.

**Money** The branches of all major banks,

NAMIBIA

including Standard, First National and Swabank can be found on Kaiser Wilhelm Strasse. They're all open Monday to Friday from 9 am to 3.30 pm and on Saturday from 8 to 11 am.

**Post & Communications** The main post office, on Garnison Strasse, has a public telephone for international calls. You can send or receive faxes at the public fax office (☎ (064) 402720) in the post office. For fax services, Photographic Enterprises (☎ (064) 405872; fax 405874), 55 Kaiser Wilhelm Strasse, charges US$0.50 per page, plus phone charges. It's open weekdays from 8.30 am to 1 pm and 2 to 5 pm and on Saturday from 9 am to 1 pm.

**Bookshops & Libraries** Swakopmund has a couple of good bookshops, probably thanks to its reputation as a holiday town. The new CNA on Roon Strasse, near the tourist office, sells popular paperbacks and tourist publications. For more serious literature and local titles, as well as novels in German and English, see the Swakopmunder Büchhandlung on Kaiser Wilhelm Strasse. You'll find more esoteric art and local history books at The Muschel Book & Art Shop at 32 Breite Strasse. On the corner of Moltke Strasse and Brücken Strasse is a second-hand shop which has a back room full of used books in English, German and Afrikaans for less than US$1 each.

Researchers working on Namibian or African topics can hole up in The Sam Cohen Library (☎ (064) 402695), near the old Otavi Bahnhof building. It houses the town archives, including newspapers dating from 1898, as well as 6000 books, a third of which deal with African topics. The public library is in Woermannhaus and travellers who stay a while may get a library card.

**Laundry** The Swakopmund Laundrette (☎ (064) 402135) is at 15 Swakop Strasse, opposite Hansa Brewery by the Swakopmund Rest Camp. The Le Club Casino & Joy World upstairs have plenty of diversions to keep you occupied.

**Emergency Services** Swakopmund uses the following emergency numbers: police (☎ 10111), hospital or ambulance (☎ (064) 405731) and fire brigade (☎ (064) 402411; after hours pager (064) 461503).

**Firewood** You can buy firewood for US$2.25 per 15kg bundle at the Swakopmund Laundrette. It's also sold at the Woermann & Brock supermarket and the Vineta Shell petrol station (towards Myl 4 Caravan Park). After hours, try Hans Kriess Garage, on the corner of Kaiser Wilhelm Strasse and Breite Strasse.

### Historic Buildings & Structures

Swakopmund brims with historic buildings and is especially interesting for fans of traditional German architecture. To learn more about the town's colonial history and sites, pick up *Swakopmund – A Chronicle of the Town's People, Places and Progress*, which is sold at the museum and in local bookshops.

**The Jetty** In 1905, the need for a good cargo and passenger-landing site led Swakopmund's founders to construct the original wooden pier. Over the years, however, it was damaged by woodworm and battered by the high seas, and in 1911 construction began on a 500m iron jetty. However, when the South African forces occupied Swakopmund, the port became redundant. The old wooden pier was removed in 1916 and the unfinished new pier, still less than 300m long, was left to the elements. In 1985, it was closed for safety purposes, but a year later, a public appeal raised a quarter of a million rand to restore the structure. It's now open to the public, but is again suffering from neglect.

**The Mole** The seawall, designed by architect FW Ortloff in 1899, was intended to enhance Swakopmund's poor harbour and create a mooring place for large cargo vessels. Unfortunately, Mr Ortloff was unfamiliar with the Benguela Current, which sweeps northwards along the coast, carrying with it a great load of sand from the southern deserts. Within 4½ years, the harbour entrance had been closed off by a sand bank and two years later, the harbour itself had been invaded by sand to create what is now known as Palm Beach. The Mole is now used as a mooring for pleasure boats.

**Lighthouse** The lighthouse, an endearing Swakopmund landmark, was constructed in 1902. It was originally built 11m high, but an additional 10m was added in 1910.

**Alte Kaserne** This imposing fort-like Alte Kaserne (old barracks) was designed and built in 1906 by the railway company. It was used as a school and hostel for many years, and now serves as the HI hostel.

**Marine Memorial** Often known by its German name, Marine Denkmal, this memorial was commissioned in 1907 by the Marine Infantry in Kiel, Germany, and was designed by Berlin sculptor AM Wolff. It commemorates the German First Marine Expedition Corps, which helped beat back the Herero uprisings of 1904. As a national historical monument, it will continue to stand, but one wonders how long it will be before the Herero erect a memorial of their own.

**Kaiserliches Bezirksgericht (State House)** This imposing building, designed by Carl Schmidt in 1901, was constructed in 1902 and originally served as the District Magistrate's Court. It was extended in 1905 and again in 1945, when a tower was added. After WWI, it was converted into the official holiday home of the territorial administrator. In keeping with that tradition, it's now the official Swakopmund residence of the executive president.

**Altes Amtsgericht** Designed by Otto Ertl, this gabled building was constructed in 1908 as a private school. However, when the funds ran out, the government took over the project and requisitioned it as a magis-

trate's court. In the 1960s, it functioned as a school dormitory, and now houses municipal offices. Just so no-one can doubt its identity, the words *Altes Amtsgericht* are painted across the front.

**Railway Station (Bahnhof)** The ornate Bahnhof (railway station) was built in 1901 as the terminal for the Kaiserliche Eisenbahn Verwaltung (Imperial Railway Authority) railway, which connected Swakopmund with Windhoek. In 1910, when the railway closed down, the building assumed the role as main station for the narrowgauge mine railway between Swakopmund and Otavi. It was declared a national monument in 1972 and now houses a hotel and casino.

**Franciscan Hospital** The 1907 Franciscan hospital on Post Strasse, one block east of the old post office, was designed by colonial architect Otto Ertl. It was originally called the St Antonius Gebaude and functioned as a hospital until 1987.

**Litfass-Saule** In 1855, the Berlin printer Litfass came up with the notion of erecting advertising pillars on German street corners. For the citizens of early Swakopmund, they became a common source of information and advertising. The only remaining example sits on the corner of Post Strasse and Breite Strasse.

**Hohenzollern Building** The Baroquestyle Hohenzollern Building has stood on the corner of Moltke Strasse and Brücken Strasse since 1906. It's fairly obvious that this imposing structure was originally intended as a hotel. Its rather outlandish decor is crowned by a fibreglass cast of Atlas supporting the world, which replaced the precarious cement version which graced the roof prior to renovations in 1988.

**German Evangelical Lutheran Church** In 1906, Dr Heinrich Vedder organised a Lutheran congregation for which the neoBaroque Evangelical Lutheran Church was

designed by architect Otto Ertl and constructed on Otavi Strasse between 1910 and
1911. It was consecrated on 7 January 1912.

**Old German School** Opposite the Lutheran Church is the building which houses
the former government and municipal secondary schools. The Baroque-style design
of the building is the result of a 1912 competition which was won by Emil Krause.
The building was completed in 1913.

**Deutsche-Afrika Bank Building** This
handsome neo-Classical building near the
corner of Woermann Strasse and Moltke
Strasse has served as a bank since 1909,
when it opened as the branch office of the
Deutsche-Afrika Bank.

**Hotel Kaiserhof** The former Hotel Kaiserhof, on the corner of Kaiser Wilhelm
Strasse and Moltke Strasse, was built in
1905. It originally had two storeys but was
destroyed in a fire nine years later and was
rebuilt as a single-storey building.

**Prinzessin Rupprecht Heim** This single-
storey Prinzessin Rupprecht Heim, one of
Swakopmund's earliest buildings, was constructed in 1902 and was first used as the
Lazarett (military hospital). In 1914 it was
transferred to the Bavarian Womens Red
Cross, which named it for their patron,
Princess Rupprecht, wife of the Bavarian
Crown Prince. The idea was to expose con-
valescents to the healthy effects of the sea
breeze. Until recently, one wing was used as
a maternity ward (the tourist literature
claims it was closed due to a storks' strike).
It's now a private guesthouse.

**Woermannhaus** When seen from the
shore, the delightfully German-style Woermannhaus stands out above surrounding
buildings; you'd be forgiven for assuming
it's the town hall. In fact, it was designed by
Friedrich Höft and built in 1905 as the main
offices of the Damara & Namaqua Trading
Company but in 1909 it was taken over by
the Woermann & Brock Trading Company,

which supplied the current name. In the
1920s, it was used as a school dormitory
and later did a stint as a merchant sailors
hostel. It eventually fell into disrepair, but
was declared a national monument and
restored in 1976.

For years, the prominent Damara tower
(formerly a water tower) provided a landmark for ships at sea and for traders arriving
by ox-wagon from the interior. It now
affords a splendid panorama and houses the
Swakopmund Military Museum and a
gallery of historic paintings. The tower and
museum are open the same hours as the
library, also housed here, where you can
pay a nominal amount and pick up a key to
both.

**Old German Homes** On the corner of
Otavi Strasse and Kaiser Wilhelm Strasse is
Villa Wille, the 1911 home of the early
colonial builder Karl Hermann Wille. The
two-storey design comes complete with an
ornamental tower. A block north, on the
corner of Post Strasse and Otavi Strasse, is
the 1910 home and surgery of Dr Schwiet-
ering, who was the town's doctor. The nice
colonial home next door on Post Strasse is
also worth a look.

Along Bismarck Strasse, south of
Brücken Strasse, is a line of simple and
unimposing colonial homes and flats, including the MC Human Flats, which date
back to 1902.

At the western end of Post Strasse is the
old Lüdwig Schröder Haus, which was constructed in 1903 for an employee of the
Woermann Shipping Lines as an extension
of the Woermann Lines headquarters. The
next year, architect Friedrich Höft designed
the Altona House around the corner on
Moltke Strasse. It would also serve as aux-
iliary company offices.

**Alte Gefängnis (Old Prison)** The impressive 1909 Alte Gefängnis was designed by
architect Heinrich Bause, and if you didn't
know it was a prison, you'd swear it was
either an early East German railway station
or a health-spa hotel. In fact, the main

building was used only for staff housing while the prisoners were relegated to less opulent quarters on one side. Note that it still serves as a prison and is considered a sensitive structure, so photography is not permitted.

**OMEG Haus** Thanks to the narrow-gauge railway to the coast, the colonial company Otavi Minen und Eisenbahn Gesellschaft (OMEG), which oversaw the rich Otavi and Tsumeb mines, also maintained an office in Swakopmund. Until 1910, the OMEG Haus on Kaiser Wilhelm Strasse served as a warehouse. Next door is the Otavi Bahnhof, the railway station for the narrow-gauge Tsumeb line; there are plans to turn it into a transport museum.

### Living Desert Snake Park

The Living Desert Snake Park (☎ (064) 405100) is at 15 Kaiser Wilhelm Strasse. The owner knows everything you'd want to know – or would rather not know – about snakes, scorpions, spiders and other widely misunderstood creatures. She feeds them daily at 4 pm. Admission is US$2.

### National Marine Aquarium

The National Marine Aquarium, on the waterfront south of The Tug restaurant, provides a superb introduction to the cold offshore world in the South Atlantic. Most impressive is the tunnel through the largest aquarium, which allows close-up views of graceful rays, toothy sharks (you can literally count the teeth!) and other marine beasties found on seafood platters around the country. It's open Tuesday to Saturday from 10 am to 6 pm and on Sunday from 11 am to 5 pm. It's closed on Monday unless there's a public holiday. Admission is US$1.50 for adults; pensioners pay half price. The fish are fed daily at 3 pm, which makes for an interesting spectacle.

### Beaches

Swakopmund is *the* beach resort in Namibia, but don't expect too much. Even in the summer, the seas are cold and the air

temperature rarely climbs above 22°C, making it more like the Isle of Wight or northern California than the Kenya coast. The most popular bathing beach is near the lighthouse. North of town, however, you can stroll along miles of deserted beaches stretching towards the Skeleton Coast. In the lagoon at the mouth of the Swakop River, you can watch ducks, flamingoes, pelicans, cormorants, gulls, waders and other birds.

In town, seaside amenities include a formal promenade, a pier, tropical gardens, mini golf and a heated swimming pool (open from 8 to 10 am and 2.30 to 7 pm).

### Dunes

Across the Swakop River sprawls a large field of sand dunes which are accessible on foot from the town centre and make a nice excursion for a couple of hours. In early 1996, however, Caledonia Mining Corporation announced plans to mine heavy metals in the sands, and was given the green light by MET. The project is expected to create 800 jobs, but no-one really knows what the environmental impact will be.

### Swakopmund Museum

If an ill wind blows, don't worry about it. The Swakopmund Museum at the foot of the lighthouse is a great place to hole up. It occupies the site of the old harbour warehouse which was destroyed in 1914 by a 'lucky' shot from a British warship.

Displays include exhibits on Namibia's history and ethnology, including information on local flora and fauna. Especially good is the display on the !nara melon, which was vital to the early Khoi-Khoi people of the Namib region. It also harbours a reconstructed colonial home interior, Emil Kiewittand's apothecary shop and an informative display on the Rössing Mine. Military buffs will be impressed by the stifling uniforms worn by the Camel Corps and the room of Shell furniture (so called because it was homemade from petrol and paraffin tins during the 1930s depression).

It's open daily from 10 am to 12.30 pm

and from 3 to 5.30 pm; admission is US$1.50 (students pay half-price).

## Hansa Brewery

Beer fans who think that German-style lager is the bee's knees will certainly want to visit the Hansa Brewery (☎ (064) 405021) at 9 Rhode Allee, which is the source of Swakopmund's favourite amber nectar. Free tours – with ample opportunity to sample the product – run on Tuesday and Thursday, but must be pre-booked.

## Historical Cemeteries

It's worth a quick stroll past the historical cemeteries beside the Swakop River bed. The neatly manicured German cemetery dates from colonial times and the stones, which are maintained by the families, tell hundreds of stories. The adjoining African cemetery makes an equally intriguing cultural statement, and has plenty of stories of its own.

## Activities

Swimming in the sea is best done in the lee of the Mole sea wall, although even in summer, the water is never warmer than 20°C. You'll probably be happier at the municipal swimming pool, which is open Monday to Friday from 8 to 10 am and 5 to 7 pm, Saturday from 8 am to noon and 5 to 7 pm; and Sunday from 5 to 7 pm. The best surfing is at Nordstrand or 'Thick Lip' near Vineta Point.

The Rössmund Golf Club (☎/fax (064) 405644) accommodates anyone hankering after 18 holes of desert golf. This par 72 course lies 5km east of Swakopmund. You can hire equipment, it's open daily and one green fee is good all day.

Swakopmund is trying hard to become a waterless Victoria Falls and has got the ball rolling with sandboarding, quad-biking, parachuting and other adrenaline boosters. Sandboarding with Chris and Beth at Alter Action (☎/fax (064) 402737 or (081) 1282737; <alteraxn@iafrica.com.na>) is certain to increase your heart rate. For US$20, you get a new sandboard, gloves,

goggles, transport to the dunes and enough sandboard polish to ensure an adrenaline high. The highlight is a 60km/hour schuss down a 120m sand mountain. The catch is there aren't any lifts, so you need to be fit and healthy (which isn't a bad idea anyway) to slog up the dunes. The less adventurous can opt for bird-watching tours to the salt pans, sewage works and Nonidas wetlands.

Jeff at Desert Explorers (☎ (064) 408098 or (081) 1292380; fax (064) 405649) leads ecologically sensitive quad-biking tours on the dunes, which include instruction, helmets, goggles and lunch and cost US$55 per day. Venues range from a sundowner on the dunes to the Khan River, the Swakop River Bed, the Moon Landscape and Goanikontes.

For more stomach-churning thrills, the parachute club (☎ (064) 462125 or (061) 402841) runs internationally recognised weekend parachuting courses for US$90, including instruction, one jump and a logbook. Each additional jump costs US$30. On request, they'll do accelerated free-fall jumps for US$160. Contact Craig Milne (☎ (064) 462125).

The Crazy Camel (☎ (081) 1282670), PO Box 2146, Swakopmund, runs 'mind-blowing' climbing and abseiling trips to the Spitzkoppe. You can choose between day and overnight expeditions.

Okakambe Trails (☎ (064) 402799) runs overnight wilderness horseback trips along the Swakop River to Goanikontes oasis. A two hour US$17 ride takes you down the Swakop River, through a dune field and back to town on the beach. Full-day river rides from Goanikontes to town cost US$41, with lunch at the golf club. Return trips from Swakopmund to Goanikontes, with a night camping at the oasis, are US$68, with meals.

## Special Events

Swakopmund stages several events with a German orientation, including a Reitturnier (gymkhana) in January and the Swakopmund Karnival in August. At the latter, the festivities are sustained by copious consumption of Hansa, Swakopmund's own German brew. Events include a parade of whimsically decorated floats and a traditional masked ball.

## Organised Tours

Numerous operators run day-long sightseeing and overnight tours. The most popular include Charly's Desert Tours, Namibia Photo Tours, Rhino Tours, Namib Wilderness Safaris, Anton's Day Tours, Eagle's Nest Tours, Afro Ventures, Desert Adventure Safaris and the German-oriented Abenteuer Afrika. If a booked tour isn't running, the companies often share clients to make up the requisite numbers, so you have a good chance of finding a tour when you want to go. For any of these companies' contact details, see the Organised Tours chapter earlier in this book.

Half-day options (rates are per person) include Cape Cross (US$41); Rössing Mine gem tours (US$34); and Welwitschia Drive (US$31). All-day trips run to the Spitzkoppe (US$44); the Kuiseb Delta, Walvis Bay Lagoon and a Nama settlement (US$52); a geology and botany tour (US$52); Welwitschia Drive (US$41); Swakopmund city tours (US$14); and Walvis Bay sightseeing (US$23). Namibia Photo Tours runs sundowner tours on the dunes or at sea (US$22), beach braais (US$29) and shark fishing (US$60); Namib Wilderness has champagne and oyster sundowners at Walvis Bay Lagoon (US$25); Rhino Tours visits the Brandberg (US$55); and Abenteuer Afrika has star-gazing tours (US$17). Trips to Sandwich Harbour (US$63) may or may not run, as increased siltation has caused severe ecological changes and there are few birds to see there.

Namibia's ethereal landscapes take on a new perspective from the air. Charter 'flightseeing' trips with Pleasure Flights, on Kaiser Wilhelm Strasse, will take you over the salt works, Sandwich Harbour, Welwitschia Drive, the Brandberg, Namib dunes, the Skeleton Coast and beyond. An hour-long flight between Swakopmund and Sandwich Harbour costs US$44 per person

and day tours to Fish River Canyon and the Sperrgebiet are US$320 per person, with at least five passengers.

Westcoast Angling Tours organises deepsea fishing trips for snoek and yellowtail, as well as rock and surf angling from the beach. From November to May, the main game is the copper shark, which weighs up to 180kg. Tours start at US$55 per day, with equipment. Blue Marlin (☎ (064) 404134) charges US$54 for a few hours in quest of kob, steenbras, galjoen and shark and US$66 for snoek, yellowtail and larger game fish. Whale-watching and photography cruises are US$34.

Desert Explorers or run various quadbiking tours on the dunes (see the Activities section above for details).

Finally, for an idiosyncratic tour through historic Swakopmund (alas, for Germanspeakers only), telephone Ms A Flamm-Schneeweiss (☎ (064) 461647) or contact her through the Namib i tourist office. She also runs amateur photo bird-watching trips to the salt works for US$10.

For further contact details, see the Organised Tours chapter earlier in this book. For activity tours, see under Activities, earlier in this section.

## Places to Stay

During the school holidays from October to March (and especially December and January) Swakopmund accommodation books up well in advance, so either come prepared to camp or make accommodation bookings as early as possible.

### Places to Stay – Budget

The bleak *Myl 4 Caravan Park* (☎ 461781; fax 462901), on the beach 4km along the salt road towards Henties Bay, has 400 camp sites for US$3 per tent plus US$2 per person and a one-time fee of US$3 per vehicle. It's exposed to the wind, sand and drizzle – and security can be a problem – but it's one of the most unusual camp sites you'll ever see. Electric hook-ups are available. Small bungalows cost US$11, and a self-catering cottage costs US$41. Either must be booked three months in advance, except for December, which must be booked a year in advance. There's no restaurant or shop, but during December school holidays, the itinerant Grub Tub stand sets up and serves snack meals.

Travellers love the atmosphere at *Alternative Space* (☎ (061) 404027; <thespace@iafrica.com.na>; Web site www.users.iafrica.com/t/th/thespace), on the desert fringe at 46 Dr Alfons Weber Strasse. It's run by Frenus, Sybille and Rafael Rorich and their able assistant Johnny; the catch is that only 'Friends of Frenus' are welcome, but not to worry – he makes friends easily. Dorm beds cost US$5, including cooking facilities and use of a bizarre turret toilet. Highlights include the castle-like architecture, an industrial-waste-recycling theme, saturation artwork and the always friendly welcome. Town transfers are free upon request. It's just a 15 minute walk to a great sunset view from the dunes. There's no safe vehicle parking, but they do provide shuttles to the guarded car park at the Entertainment Centre.

Karsten and Annaliese's *Thimbi-Thimbi Backpackers Lodge* (☎ (064) 404634) is also friendly and quite central. The two eight-bed dorms cost US$8 per bed and the bizarre 'honeymoon suite' in a derelict VW kombi is US$18 for two people.

Another good backpackers choice is *Karen's Attic* (☎ (064) 403057 or (081) 1246997; fax (064) 405679), run by a former mayor of Windhoek at the corner of Otavi and Post Strasse. With superior kitchen facilities and a comfortable TV lounge, it's one of Namibia's plusher budget accommodation options. Beds in two, three or six-bed dorms cost US$8.

The *Swakopmund Rest Camp* (☎ (061) 402807; fax (064) 402076), Private Bag 5017, Swakopmund, near the southern edge of town, is so entangled in security barbed wire that it has been dubbed 'Stalag 13'. You can choose between six-bed A-frame chalets (US$44 per chalet), four-bed 'luxury flats' (US$51), basic two/four-bed 'fishermen's shacks' (US$15/24), and four-

bed 'fishermen's flats' (US$33). A six-bed 'VIP bungalow' with a TV, kitchen and bath costs US$59. All guests may use the braai facilities. Advance booking is advised for weekends and holidays, and no animals or motorbikes are allowed.

The ambience at the *HI Hostel* (☎ (064) 404164), in the Alte Kaserne (Old Barracks) on Lazarett Strasse, is appropriately military and mature adults may feel cramped. Dorm rates are US$5; private doubles cost US$11. Kitchen and laundry facilities are available. Note the old German paintings that adorn the walls, including the crests of the German Federal States which existed during the colonial era.

An inexpensive option near the beach is *Jay Jay's* (☎ (064) 402909), on Brücken Strasse, which has simple singles/doubles with bath for US$9/16, without bath for US$7/13 and dorm beds for US$5. It's clean and well located just half a block from the sea. There's a basic restaurant and bar downstairs; the latter sometimes gets lively.

Next up the scale in price – but not as clean – is the stark *Hotel Schutze* (☎/fax (064) 402718), which charges US$14 for a single with communal facilities and US$17/30 for a single/double with private facilities. The purpose of this establishment appears to be linked to its relationship with the attached Ho-Yin's Pub, so women on their own may want to stay clear. Still the restaurant does serve excellent German-style meals; look for the menu written on a blackboard outside.

*Mrs Viviane Scholz-Valkoff* (☎ (064) 461683) runs a very friendly and inexpensive B&B at 81 Seeadler St, Vineta, PO Box 3182, Swakopmund. She charges US$12/18 for a single/double in a self-contained flat. It's highly recommended.

More unusual is *Villa Anna* (☎ (064) 402371), which is housed in the cloisters of an old convent at 1 Breite Strasse. It's run by Mrs Joost and charges US$10/15 for a single/double.

### Places to Stay – Mid-Range
The pleasant *Pension Dig-by-See* (☎ (064)

404130; fax 404170) – or just Digby's – at 4 Brücken Strasse, PO Box 1580, Swakopmund, has singles/doubles for US$26/37 including a large and varied breakfast. Rooms for three/four people are US$18 per person, with breakfast. Self-catering holiday flats cost US$80 per night. All rooms have a bath, shower, toilet and TV.

The *Pension Prinzessin-Rupprecht-Heim* (☎ (064) 402231; fax 402019), in the former colonial hospital, has a lovely garden and charges US$32/54 for singles/doubles with bath. Smaller single rooms with shared facilities are US$16 and family flats cost US$50 for two, plus US$14 for each extra person up to four people. All rates include breakfast.

Moving up in price, a very friendly option is *Hotel-Pension Rapmund* (☎ (064) 402035; fax 404524), PO Box 425, Swakopmund, near the lighthouse. It costs US$30/34 for a single/double room in the back and US$52/57 for one with a sea view. All rooms include breakfast and you probably won't feel more welcome at any other mid-range place in Swakopmund.

As its name suggests, the *Deutsches Haus* (☎ (064) 404896; fax 404861), 13 Lüderitz Strasse, PO Box 13, Swakopmund, oozes with meticulously clean German atmosphere, but the ambience falls short of warm and cosy. Singles/doubles cost US$34/50, with breakfast. A three-bed room is US$63. To use a TV or park in the garage costs US$3 each per day.

The *Hotel-Pension d'Avignon* (☎ (064) 405821; fax 405542), on Brücken Strasse, is politely accommodating. It caters mainly for German tourists and others may feel a bit out of place. For singles/doubles with bath it charges US$27/44, with breakfast.

Also adequate is the central *Atlanta Hotel* (☎ (064) 402360; fax 405649), at 6 Roon Strasse. Singles/doubles cost US$25/36, with breakfast. All rooms have private bath and telephones; TVs cost US$3 per day.

In a similar range is *Hotel Grüner-Kranz* (☎ (064) 402039; fax 405016; <lyonr@iml-net.com.na>). For a single or double room with television and bath, it charges US$34.

Breakfast is an additional US$4. You can party in the rollicking 1st floor disco or retire to the video lounge to relax.

If you like a European atmosphere, a good value choice is the *Hotel Europa Hof* (☎ (064) 405061), which resembles a Bavarian chalet, complete with colourful flower boxes, aloof service, marginal showers and European flags flying from the 1st floor windows. Singles/doubles are US$45/69.

Also nicely located is the homely *Hotel Garni Adler* (☎ (064) 405045; fax 404206) at 3 Strand Strasse, but the building itself resembles a modern house lost somewhere in German suburbia. Standard single rooms with breakfast cost from US$50 to US$65; doubles are US$72. Singles/doubles with a sea view cost US$59/81. Studio flats are US$88/135. Garage parking or TV use is US$3 and saunas cost US$6.

The *Hotel Schweizerhaus* (☎ (064) 402419; fax 405058), a popular spot near the sea with a good view of the lighthouse, is best known as the hotel attached to Cafe Anton. Standard single/double accommodation costs US$43/77, while rooms with sea view are US$53/84 and deluxe suites cost US$88/112.

If you prefer to restrict your noise to sea sounds, go to *Alte Brücke Holiday Resort* (☎/fax (064) 404918), near the river mouth, south of town. Single/double self-catering bungalows cost US$41/63. With three/four adults sharing, they're US$70/85. Family units for two adults and two children cost US$65.

A recommended private B&B is *Brigadoon* (☎ (064) 406064; fax 464195), 16 Ludwig Koch Strasse, run by Bruce and Bubble Burns. They have three Victorian cottages opposite Palm Beach costing US$34/59 for single/double occupancy, including breakfast and airport transfers.

*K & E Wojtas* (☎ (064) 402402; fax 405387) at 4 Windhoeker Strasse have one self-catering flat for US$35 for two people and US$10 for each additional occupant and another for US$15/23 with one/two people. Other mid-range home-stay options

NAMIBIA

include *Huis Johann* (☎ (064) 404825; fax 405679), at the corner of Otavi and Post Sts and *Huis Veronica* (same phone as Huis Johann), at 5 Dolphin St. Both charge US$23 for a double.

*Sam's Giardino House* (☎ (064) 403210; <samsart@iafrica.com.na>; Web site www .eia.com.na/dune/accom/sgiardino.htm), 89 Lazarett St, is a slice of central Europe in the desert. Run by Samuel Egger from Lausanne, Switzerland, it emphasises wine-tasting, cigar-smoking, and relaxing in the rose garden beside the fish pond, all backed up by strains of hotel-style muzak. You can even choose from 32 channels of satellite TV! Single/double economy rooms with breakfast cost US$30/37. More elaborate rooms start at US$40 for a double. There is a charge of US$9 each for animals.

### Places to Stay – Top End
The *Hansa Hotel* (☎ (064) 400311; fax 402732; <hansa@iml-net.com.na>), which bills itself as 'luxury in the desert', makes much of the fact that it has hosted the likes of Aristotle Onassis, Sir Laurens van der Post, Eartha Kitt, Oliver Reed and Ernest Borgnine. Standard singles/doubles start at US$54/72, each individually decorated. Rooms with a balcony and garden view cost US$66/88.

The *Swakopmund Hotel & Entertainment Centre* (☎ (064) 400800; fax 400801), in the historic railway station, underwent renovation to house a four-star hotel, the Mermaid casino, two cinemas, a large pool and a conference centre. Singles/doubles are US$81/117 (if you book in Namibia, special rates of US$70/86 are available in most seasons). Luxury singles/doubles cost US$92/138.

On the main beach behind the Mole is the two-star *Strand Hotel* (☎ (064) 400315; fax 404942), which isn't the most prepossessing of buildings, but it does enjoy a fine sea view. Singles/doubles with a large breakfast cost US$63/84.

### Places to Eat
As befits a seaside resort, Swakopmund has restaurants serving everything from take-away fare right up to four-star gourmet meals. For tasty, inexpensive takeaways, there's the well-established *La Paloma* (☎ (064) 404700), on Breite Strasse south of Kaiser Wilhelm Strasse. Near the corner of Moltke Strasse and Woermann Strasse is the recommended German takeaway, *Wurst Bude*. Less exciting is the *Bridge Inn Takeaways* on Brucken Strasse or *Kentucky Fried Chicken* (☎ (064) 405687), at 13 Roon Strasse, which stays open until 10 pm.

A good funky place with lots of tasteful art is the *African 'T' Kitchen* (☎ (064) 461060), at the corner of Brücken Strasse and Bismarck Strasse. The breakfasts are Swakopmund's most original; for lunch and dinner, the emphasis is on sandwiches, steak, salad, seafood and burgers. It's open every day from 8 am to 3 pm; on Friday, Saturday and Sunday, it also serves dinner from 6 pm until late.

An atmospheric no-frills option is the locally popular *Fagin's* (☎ (064) 402360), an inexpensive pub and bistro. It's reminiscent of a US truckies' stop, complete with jocular staff and a faithful clientele. *Kücki's Pub* (☎ (064) 402407) does the best pub meals; if your budget permits, don't miss the amazing seafood platter. Just down the block is the *Frontiers*, which serves up laudable steaks. Its popular dinner buffet is good value at US$8.

The *Western Saloon* (☎ (064) 405395), a cowboy-theme place at 8 Moltke Strasse, is known for its steaks and seafood. Glitches do occur, but the fish is normally served fresh from the sea. It's open Monday to Saturday from 5.30 to 9.30 pm and on Sunday from 6 to 9 pm.

Pizza is also big, and most locals reckon the best comes from *Papa's* (☎ (064) 404747), in the Shop-Rite Centre. Delivery service (US$1) is available Tuesday to Sunday from 6.30 to 9.30 pm. Another favourite is the superb and inexpensive *Napolitana Pizzeria & Mediterranean Restaurant* (☎ (064) 402773) at 33 Breite Strasse. It's open Monday to Sunday from 10 am to 2 pm and 5.30 to 10 pm. Don't

On the road in the Kaokoveld (Nam).

Storage basket in an Owambo kraal (Nam).

The magnificent cascades at Epupa Falls (Nam).

Cape fur seals lounging on the Namib coast.

The bleak expanses of the Namib Desert.

MITCH REARDON

The diamond-mining ghost town of Kolmanskop is slowly being engulfed by the dunes (Nam).

DAVID WALL

Fish River Canyon has excellent hiking (Nam).

DEANNA SWANEY

Stained glass in Felsenkirche, Lüderitz (Nam).

miss the icy German-style draught lager. Pizza deliveries are available until 9.30 pm for US$1 to anywhere in town or for US$1.10 to Vineta, including Myl 4 Caravan Park. The popular *Piccolo Pizzeria* on Moltke Strasse has nice outdoor seating. An ethnic alternative is the *Original China Tong Hua Restaurant* (☎ (064) 402081), at the corner of Brücken and Roon Strasse, which also serves pizza.

For breakfast, the very hungry should try the *Strand Hotel* (☎ (064) 400315), which is also recommended for its German cuisine accompanied by draught Hansa lager. The rest of the day, it's good for vegetarian options. The *Swakopmund Bistro* (☎ (064) 402333) does excellent and imaginative breakfasts, lunches and dinners: salads, vegetarian specialities, crepes, gyros, game dishes, steaks and seafood specials. It's open daily from 8 am to 10 pm. A place for one of Swakopmund's most sought-after commodities is the *Swakopmund Brauhaus* (☎ (064) 402214), a restaurant and boutique brewery at 22 Kaiser Wilhelm Strasse (behind the Namib i tourist office).

Seafood figures prominently. Perhaps the most prestigious option for fish is *Admiral's*, on the beach near the Strand Hotel. The upmarket *Erichs* (☎ (064) 405141), on Post Strasse, specialises in fish and steak dishes, and does a mean Tiroler knödelsuppe. Another good choice for fish is *The Tug* (☎ (064) 402356), which is housed in the beached tugboat *Danie Hugo* near the jetty. The *Seaview Pub & Restaurant* (☎ (064) 402164), on Strand Strasse at the Mole, also does recommended seafood, steak and pasta specialities. For steak, seafood and barbecued ribs, the upmarket *De Kelder* (☎ (064) 402433), at 10 Moltke Strasse, is open daily except Monday for lunch and dinner.

For German specialities (this is Swakopmund, after all), try the mid-range *Bayern Stubchen* on Garnison Strasse. The down-to-earth restaurant at *Jay Jay's*, on Brücken Strasse, serves hearty, inexpensive boerekos (Afrikaner fare).

The admired but pretentious *Cafe Anton* (☎ (064) 402419; fax 405850), in the Hotel Schweizerhaus, has legendary (albeit expensive and skimpy) coffee, Apfelstrüdel, Kugelhopf, Mohnkuchen, Linzertorte and a host of other German delights. It's great for an afternoon snack in the sun. Other German-style Konditoreien include the *Seebad Cafe* on Kaiser Wilhelm Strasse and the *Hansa Bäckerei & Cafe Treff*, on the same street. It opens at 7 am and serves a large, good value English breakfast.

The Woermann & Brock Supermarket, at the corner of Moltke Strasse and Kaiser Wilhelm Strasse, sells groceries and the coffee bar does snacks, even on Sunday mornings.

## Entertainment

*O'Kelly's*, which emphasises local music and disco dancing, has been described as the place where you go when you're too drunk to care and don't want to go home. It's open from 8 pm until 4 am nightly. The *Kalabash Sports Bar* above the Swakopmund Bistro is the local hangout for rugger and footie fanatics.

The bar at *Jay-Jay's*, with its locally popular pool table, stays open until the wee hours. Another favourite and down-to-earth watering hole for locals and visitors alike is *Fagin's Pub*, near the Atlanta Hotel on Roon Strasse. *Bacchus Taverna* is a rather pedestrian pub in the row of historic flats opposite the Europa Hof Hotel.

Young people go for *The Stage Night Club & Disco*, upstairs in the Hotel Grüner Kranz. There's also a quiet private bar on the opposite side of the hotel. The more highbrow *Tavern Pub* in the Swakopmund Hotel & Entertainment Centre is open Monday to Saturday until late, and sometimes stages live music performances.

Now that the historic Atlanta Cinema has closed, filmgoers are limited to the two screens at the *Swakopmund Hotel & Entertainment Centre*.

## Things to Buy

At Swakop River Angoras, you can learn about spinning, dyeing and weaving processes and buy quality clothing made of angora rabbit hair. It's open daily from 10 am to 5 pm.

The NDC Craft Centre (formerly Karakulia), on Knobloch St, produces and sells hand-woven rugs, carpets and wall-hangings made of karakul wool and offers tours of the spinning, dyeing and weaving processes. The Muschel Bookshop has lovely local art and the shop at the Hotel-Pension Rapmund sells light-hearted paintings. African art, handicrafts and curios are sold on the street below Cafe Anton.

Swakopmund is known for its hard-wearing kudu leather *veldskoene* shoes called 'Swakopmunders' which sell for US$18 to US$25 at the Swakopmund Tannery (☎ (064) 402633; fax 404205), 7 Leutwein Strasse. You'll also find hand-bags, sandals, belts and other leather goods at excellent prices.

There are a number of shops and small art galleries which specialise in prints and paintings, ranging from classic water-colours to modern surrealistic African art. The small Reflections Gallery near Cafe Anton often has exhibits of local artists' work. A number of African souvenir and curio shops and several expensive jewellers sell local gems and semiprecious stones. Pieces may be commissioned and you can often watch the goldsmith at work. Tusk T-Shirts in Brücken Strasse prints and sells its own unique designs.

You'll also want to check out the Ali Baba's cave of treasures at the phenomenal Peter's Antiques (☎/fax (064) 405624), at 24 Moltke Strasse. This unique place spe-cialises in colonial relics, historic literature, politically incorrect German paraphernalia and genuine African art and religious arte-facts from around the continent. It's a highlight, not to be missed.

## Getting There & Away

**Air** Air Namibia flies from Windhoek's Eros Airport to Swakopmund four times weekly. You can also fly to or from Lüderitz, Oranjemund and Cape Town four

times weekly. Its office is at the Namib i tourist office.

**Bus** The long-distance bus terminal is on Roon Strasse between Woermann Strasse and Brücken Strasse. Dolphin Express (☎ (064) 204118) runs daily between Swakopmund/Walvis Bay and Windhoek, and other minibuses run when full. Star Line bus services between Walvis Bay and Otjiwarongo also call in at Swakopmund. The more luxurious Intercape Mainliner departs from Windhoek/Swakopmund on Monday, Wednesday, Friday and Saturday at 6 am/12.15 pm (US$22, 4¼ hours). Book any of these buses through Trip Travel (☎ (064) 404013; fax 402114) at 11 Post Strasse.

**Train** The overnight rail service from Windhoek (US$13/9 in business/economy class) departs at 8 pm daily except Saturday and arrives in Swakopmund at 5 am, then continues to Walvis Bay. In the opposite direction, it leaves Walvis Bay at 7 pm Sunday to Friday, stops in Swakopmund at 8.35 pm, and continues on to Windhoek, arriving at 6.50 am the next day. On Tuesday, Thursday and Sunday northbound and Monday, Wednesday and Friday south-bound, this train splits at Kranzberg to provide connections to and from Tsumeb (US$12/9 in business/economy class). For more rail information, phone Trans-Namib (☎ (064) 463538).

**Hitching** Hitching isn't difficult to Wind-hoek or Walvis Bay, but hitchhikers risk heat stroke, sandblasting and hypothermia – sometimes all in the same day! Come pre-pared. Hitching to Sossusvlei and other Namib Desert locales is considerably more challenging.

## Getting Around

Taxis run to and from the airport but other-wise, you can walk just about anywhere in town. Most Namibian car-hire agencies have branches in Swakopmund; see the Namibia Getting Around chapter.

You can hire bicycles from the Cycle Clinic (☎ (064) 402530), at 10 Roon Strasse, for US$3/13 per hour/day.

## AROUND SWAKOPMUND
### The *Martin Luther*
In the desert 4km east of Swakopmund, you'll pass a lonely and forlorn little steam locomotive. In 1896, the 14,000kg machine was imported to Namibia from Halberstadt, Germany, by 1st Lieutenant Edmund Troost of the Imperial Schutztruppe, to replace the ox-wagons which until that time carried freight between Swakopmund and the interior. Unfortunately, the loco exceeded the unloading capacity at Swakopmund and had to be taken to Walvis Bay. However, its inauguration into service was delayed by four months when the good lieutenant was called away by the outbreak of the Nama-Herero wars. Meanwhile, the locomotive engineer who was contracted to reveal its secrets had returned to Germany when his five-month contract expired.

A US prospector eventually got the engine running, but it consumed enormous quantities of water, which simply weren't available. In fact, it took three months just to move it from Walvis Bay to Swakopmund. The engine survived just a couple of short trips inland before grinding to a halt within sight of Swakopmund. When it became apparent that this particular technology wasn't making life any easier for anyone, it was abandoned where it stood and dubbed the *Martin Luther*, in reference to the great reformer's words to the Diet of Reichstag, in Worms, in 1521: 'Here I stand. May God help me, I cannot do otherwise.' It was restored in 1975 and declared a national monument.

### Burg Hotel Nonidas
The former Burg Hotel Nonidas lies on the main road about 10km east of Swakopmund and, as its German name would imply, is built in the form of a castle. The current structure was built over the top of an early 1890s customs and police post. All that remains of the original building is the bar area, which is full of historical photos and artefacts. However, it hasn't operated as a hotel since 1993, and now appears to be abandoned.

### Camel Farm
Want to play Lawrence of Arabia in the Namib Desert? Visit the Camel Farm (☎ (064) 400363), 15km east of Swakopmund on the B2. Camel rides cost US$7 for 40 minutes. It's open from 3 to 5 pm. To book a camel and arrange transport from town, ring and ask for Ms Elke Elb.

### Rössing Mine
Rössing Uranium Mine (☎ (064) 402046), 55km east of Swakopmund, is the world's largest open-cast uranium mine. Uranium was first discovered in the 1920s by Peter Louw, but his attempts at development failed. In 1965, the concession was transferred to Rio Tinto Zinc and comprehensive surveys determined that the formation measured 3km long and 1km wide. Ore extraction came on line in 1970 but didn't reach capacity for another eight years. The current scale of operations is staggering; at full capacity the mine produces one million tonnes of ore per week.

Rössing (an affiliate of Rio Tinto Zinc), with 2500 employees, is currently the major player in Swakopmund's economy. The affiliated Rössing Foundation provides an educational and training centre in Arandis, north-east of the mine, as well as medical facilities and housing for its Swakopmund-based workers. It has promised that the eventual decommissioning of the site will entail a massive clean-up, but you may want to temper your enthusiasm about its environmental commitments until something is actually forthcoming.

Mine tours, which last 4½ hours, leave from Cafe Anton on Friday at 8 am and cost US$3, including transport. Proceeds go to the museum. Book tours before Thursday afternoon at the museum.

### Trekkopje
The military cemetery at Trekkopje lies

about 112km east of Swakopmund and 1km north of the B2. In January 1915, after Swakopmund was occupied by South African forces, the Germans retreated and cut off supplies to the city by damaging the Otavi and State railway lines. However, the South Africans had already begun to replace the narrow-gauge track with a standard gauge, and at Trekkopje, their crew met the German forces. When the Germans attacked their camp on 26 April 1915, the South Africans defended themselves with guns mounted on armoured vehicles and easily prevailed. All fatalities of this battle are interred in the Trekkopje cemetery, which lies immediately north of the railway line, near the old railway station.

### Welwitschia Drive

The Welwitschia Drive, which turns off the Bosua Pass route east of Swakopmund, lies inside the Namib-Naukluft Park, but is most often visited as a day trip from Swakopmund. At the MET or Namib i offices, you can pick up entry permits and leaflets describing the drive, with numbered references to 'beacons' or points of interest along the route. The drive takes about four hours.

A highlight is the fields of grey and black lichen (1 and 4 on the map), which almost appear to be small dead bushes. In the BBC production *The Private Life of Plants*, it was here that David Attenborough saw these delightful examples of plant-animal symbiosis (see the boxed text 'Lichen Fields' in the North-Western Namibia chapter), which burst into 'bloom' with the addition of fog droplets. If you're not visiting during a fog, sprinkle a few drops of water on them and watch the magic.

Another interesting stop is the Baaiweg (3), the ox-wagon track which was historically used to move supplies between the coast and central Namibia. The tracks remain visible because the lichen that were destroyed when it was built have grown back at a rate of only one mm per year, and the ruts aren't yet obscured. Later in the main loop is further evidence of human impact in the form of a camp site (7) used by South African troops for a few days in 1915. They were clearly *not* minimum-impact campers!

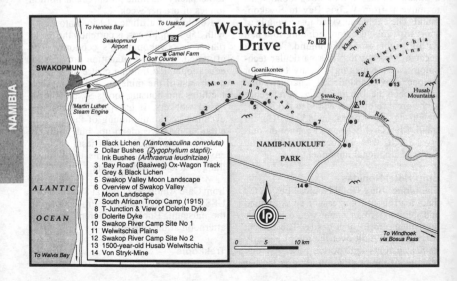

## Welwitschias

Among Namibia's many botanical curiosities, the extraordinary *Welwitschia mirabilis*, which exists only on the gravel plains of the northern Namib Desert from the Kuiseb River to southern Angola, is probably the strangest of all. It was first noted in 1859, when Austrian botanist and medical doctor Friedrich Welwitsch stumbled upon a large specimen east of Swakopmund. He suggested it be named *tumboa*, which was one of the local names for the plant, but the discovery was considered to be so important that it was named after him instead. More recently, the Afrikaners have dubbed it *tweeblaarkanniedood* or 'two-leaf can't die'.

Welwitschias reach their greatest concentrations on the Welwitschia Plains east of Swakopmund, near the confluence of the Khan and Swakop rivers, where they're the dominant plant species. Although these plants are the ugly ducklings of the vegetable world, they've adapted well to their harsh habitat. It was once thought that the plant had a tap root down through clay pipes to access the water table 100m or more beneath the surface. In fact, the root is never more than 3m long and it's now generally accepted that, although the plant gets some water from underground sources, most of its moisture is derived from condensed fog. Pores in the leaves trap moisture and longer leaves actually water the plant's own roots by channelling droplets onto the surrounding sand.

Despite their dishevelled appearance, welwitschias actually have only two long and leathery leaves, which grow from opposite sides of the corklike stem. Over the years, these leaves are darkened in the sun and torn by the wind into tattered strips, causing the plant to resemble a giant wilted lettuce.

Strangely, welwitschias are considered to be trees and are related to conifers, specifically pines, but they also share some characteristics of flowering plants and club mosses. Females bear the larger greenish-yellow to brown cones, which contain the plant's seeds, while the males have more cones, but they're smaller and salmon-coloured. They're a dioecious species, meaning that male and female plants are distinct, but their exact method of pollination remains in question. It's thought that the large sticky pollen grains are carried by insects, specifically wasps.

Welwitschias have a slow rate of growth, and it's believed that the largest ones, whose tangled masses of leaf strips can measure up to 2m across, may have been growing for up to 2000 years. However, most mid-sized plants are less than 1000 years old. The plants don't even flower until they've been growing for at least 20 years. This longevity is probably only possible because they contain some compounds which are unpalatable to grazing animals, although black rhinos have been known to enjoy the odd plant. The plants' most prominent inhabitant is the yellow and black pyrrhocorid bug (*Probergrothius sexpunctatis*), which lives by sucking sap from the plant. It's commonly called the push-me-pull-you bug, due to its almost continuous back-to-back mating.

Further east is the Moon Landscape (6), a vista across eroded hills and valleys carved by the Swakop River. Here you may want to take a quick 12km return side trip north to the farm and oasis of Goanikontes, which dates from 1848. It lies beside the Swakop River amid fabulous desert mountains and makes a nice picnic site. There are also several shady camp sites and basic bungalows are available for reasonable prices.

A few kilometres beyond the South African Troop Camp, the route turns north. Shortly thereafter, you'll approach a prominent black dolerite dyke (9) splitting a ridgetop. This was created when molten igneous material forced its way up through a crack in the overlying granite and cooled.

On a short side trip from the main loop lie the Welwitschia Plains (11), where you'll find several ancient welwitschia plants (see the boxed text on the previous page). These unique plants are recognisable by their two long and leathery leaves which are normally torn into a tangle of wind-blown strips. Some welwitschias have lived for up to 2000 years. They grow in several locations on the gravel plains of the Namib Desert. Most sites are kept quiet to prevent vandalism, but the superb specimens on the Welwitschia Plains are open to visitors. The large plant known as the Husab welwitschia (13) is estimated to be at least 1500 years old.

**Places to Stay**  The National Parks camp site, at the Swakop River crossing on the Welwitschia Plains detour, is available to one party of up to eight people at a time. It must be prebooked through MET in Wind-hoek or Swakopmund.

### Salt Works

Originally, the site of the salt works, north of Myl 4 Caravan Park, was one of many low salty depressions along the desert coast, but in 1933, the Klein family began extracting salt here. When it ran out 20 years later, they excavated a series of shallow evaporation pans to concentrate and extract the minerals. Now, water is pumped into the pans directly from the sea and the onshore breeze provides an ideal catalyst for evaporation.

Water is moved through the several pans over a period of 12 to 18 months. The water-borne minerals are concentrated by evaporation and eventually crystals of sodium chloride and other salts develop. Thanks to the variety of algae in the mineral soup that's created at the various stages of desalination, each pond takes on a different brilliant colour – purple, red, orange, yellow and even greenish hues. From aloft, it takes on the appearance of a colourful stained-glass window.

Thanks to the sheltered environment, the ponds provide habitat for small fish, and for the flamingoes, avocets, sandpipers, teals, grebes, gulls, cormorants, terns and other birds that feed on them. The Kleins have now registered the site as a private nature reserve, and they've also erected a large wooden platform – an artificial island – which is used by cormorants as a breeding site. After the breeding season, scrapers are sent onto the platform to collect the guano deposits. Another peripheral enterprise is the Richwater Oyster Company, which was established in 1985 when 500,000 oysters were brought from the island of Guernsey in the English Channel. It now occupies the first pan reached by the seawater.

The 1½ hour tours of the salt works and the oyster farm run daily from Monday to Friday. To book, either visit or phone the salt-works offices (☎ (064) 402611) in Swakopmund during business hours. After hours, phone (☎ (064) 404015). You can also arrange guided bird-watching tours.

### WALVIS BAY

Walvis Bay (pronounced *VAHL-fis*) is the only decent port between Lüderitz and Luanda and until recently, its main claim to fame was a clutch of fish canneries. Its superb natural harbour is created by the sandspit Pelican Point which forms a natural breakwater. The town itself may be architecturally uninspiring, but it exudes a sort of otherworldly charm which still may elude some visitors.

Now a busy port with 40,000 people, modern Walvis Bay boasts a tanker berth, a dry dock and facilities to load and unload container ships. It also supports a salt works and a fish-processing industry. Due to de-clining fish stocks, the late 1980s saw numerous factory closures and high unem-ployment but strict controls have now stabilised the industry and it appears to be on the upswing. In an effort to diversify the economy, a waterfront tourism develop-ment project is currently planned.

### History

Portuguese navigator Bartolomeu Dias sailed into Walvis Bay in the *São Cristóvão* on 8 December 1487 and named it Bahia de Santa Maria da Conceição, but later, it came to be known as Bahia das Baleias, the 'Bay of Whales'. However, a lack of fresh water meant that this excellent natural harbour lay forgotten for the next 300 years.

From 1784, American whalers began operating in the area, calling it simply Whale Bay. Word got out that rich pickings were to be had and on 23 January 1793 the Dutch vessel *Meermin* arrived from the Cape to annex the bay and translate its name into Dutch: Walvisbaai. This sparked off a 200-year game of political football with the 1124 sq km enclave.

In 1795, when the Cape Colony was taken over by the British, Captain Alexander of the British fleet went north and claimed Walvis Bay for Britain. He hoped to ensure safe passage for vessels around the Cape.

Around the mid-1840s, Nama leader Jan Jonker Afrikaner constructed a trail to transport Matchless Mine copper to the port in Walvis Bay. By 1878, after it was realised that Germany had its eye on Walvis Bay, the port was formally annexed by Britain and six years later, attached to the Cape Colony. In 1910, it became part of the Union of South Africa. When the Germans were defeated after WWI, South Africa was given the United Nations mandate to administer all of German South West Africa and the Walvis Bay enclave was transferred to the mandate. This stood until 1977, when South Africa unilaterally decided to return it to the Cape Province. The United Nations wasn't impressed by this unauthorised act and insisted that the enclave be returned to the mandate immediately, but South Africa refused to bow.

When Namibia achieved its independence in 1990, its new constitution included Walvis Bay as part of its territory, but the South Africans stubbornly held their grip. Given the strategic value of the natural harbour, plus the salt works (which produced 40,000 tonnes annually – 90% of South Africa's salt), the offshore guano platforms and the rich fishery, control over Walvis Bay became a matter of great importance for Namibia.

In 1992, after it had became apparent that white rule in South Africa was ending, the two countries agreed that South Africa would remove its border posts and that both countries would jointly administer the enclave. Finally, facing growing domestic troubles and its first democratic elections, South Africa gave in and at midnight on 28 February 1994, the South African flag was lowered for the last time, and the Namibian flag was raised.

## Orientation

Walvis Bay is laid out in a grid pattern. The streets, from First to Fifteenth, run northeast to south-west. The roads, from First to Eighteenth, run north-west to south-east. At times this does get confusing.

## Information

**Tourist Office** The helpful tourist office (☎ (064) 205981; fax 204528) is on the main floor of the monumental Civic Centre. It's open weekdays from 8 am to 1 pm and 2 to 5 pm, 4.30 pm on Friday. Ask to see the carved wooden panels on the wall in the next room. Namib-Naukluft Park permits are available at the CWB petrol station.

**Money** Along Seventh Rd are several banks offering foreign exchange, and also a BOB automatic teller.

**Post & Communications** The post office on Seventh St also has public telephone boxes and fax services.

**Emergency Services** Emergency services include the police (☎ 10111), ambulance service (☎ (064) 205443), hospital (☎ (064) 203441), fire brigade (☎ (064) 203117) and sea-rescue service (☎ (064) 202064).

**Bookshop** The Viggo-Lund Booksellers & Stationers on Seventh St is the only bookshop around, but don't expect much.

**Laundry** The Super Laundrette (☎ (064)

NAMIBIA

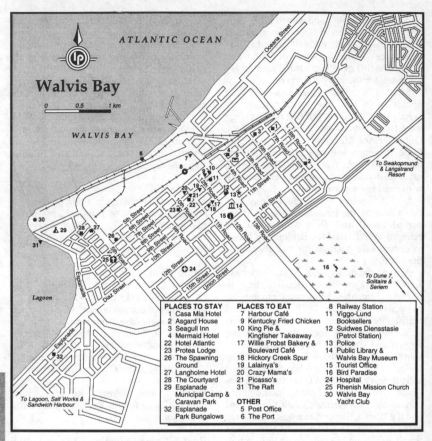

ATLANTIC OCEAN

**Walvis Bay**

0    0.5    1 km

WALVIS BAY

To Swakopmund
& Langstrand
Resort

To Dune 7,
Solitaire &
Seriem

Lagoon

To Lagoon, Salt Works &
Sandwich Harbour

| PLACES TO STAY | PLACES TO EAT | |
|---|---|---|
| 1 Casa Mia Hotel | 7 Harbour Café | 8 Railway Station |
| 2 Asgard House | 9 Kentucky Fried Chicken | 11 Viggo-Lund |
| 3 Seagull Inn | 10 King Pie & | Booksellers |
| 4 Mermaid Hotel | Kingfisher Takeaway | 12 Suidwes Diensstasie |
| 22 Hotel Atlantic | 17 Willie Probst Bakery & | (Petrol Station) |
| 23 Protea Lodge | Boulevard Café | 13 Police |
| 26 The Spawning | 18 Hickory Creek Spur | 14 Public Library & |
| Ground | 19 Lalainya's | Walvis Bay Museum |
| 27 Langholme Hotel | 20 Crazy Mama's | 15 Tourist Office |
| 28 The Courtyard | 21 Picasso's | 16 Bird Paradise |
| 29 Esplanade | 31 The Raft | 24 Hospital |
| Municipal Camp & | | 25 Rhenish Mission Church |
| Caravan Park | **OTHER** | 30 Walvis Bay |
| 32 Esplanade | 5 Post Office | Yacht Club |
| Park Bungalows | 6 The Port | |

203425), which is next to the CWB petrol station on Seventh St, is open every day from 8 am to 8 pm.

### Walvis Bay Museum
The town museum in the library concentrates on the history and maritime background of Walvis Bay, but also has archaeological exhibits, a mineral collection and natural history displays on the Namib Desert and the Atlantic Coast. It's open weekdays from 9 am to 12.30 pm and 3 to 4.30 pm. Admission is free.

### Rhenish Mission Church
Walvis Bay's oldest remaining building, the Rhenish Mission Church on Fifth Rd, was prefabricated in Hamburg, Germany, and reconstructed beside the harbour in 1880. Services were first held the following year. Because of machinery sprawl in the harbour area, it was relocated to its present site earlier this century. It functioned as a church until 1966.

### Bird Island
Along the Swakopmund road, 10km north

NAMIBIA

of Walvis Bay, take a look at the offshore wooden platform known as Bird Island. It was built to provide a roo_ and nesting site for seabirds and a source of guano for use as fertiliser. The annual yield is around 1000 tonnes and the smell from the island is memorable.

## The Railway

During the winter, rail services between Swakopmund and Walvis Bay are often plagued by windblown sand which covers the tracks and undermines the track bed and sleepers. This isn't a new problem – 5km east of town on the C14, notice the embankment which has interred a section of narrow-gauge track from the last century. In front of the railway station are the remains of the *Hope*, an old locomotive which once ran on the original narrow-gauge railway. Both were abandoned after the line was repeatedly buried beneath 10m sand drifts. The *Hope* is now a national monument and stands on Sixth St in front of the railway station.

## The Port

With permission from the Public Relations Officer of the Portnet (☎ (064) 208320; fax 208390) or from the Railway Police at the end of Thirteenth Rd, you can visit the fishing harbour and commercial port and see the heavy machinery that keeps Namibia's import-export business ticking. It's actually more interesting than it sounds. Take your passport.

## Dune 7

Dune 7, in the bleak expanse just off the C14 8km east of town, is popular with locals as a slope for sandboarding and skiing. The picnic site, which is now being engulfed by sand, has several shady palm trees tucked away in the lee of the dune. Water is sometimes available.

## Nature Reserves

Three diverse wetland areas – the lagoon, the Bird Paradise at the sewage works and the salt works – together form Southern Africa's single most important coastal

---

## Flamingoes

Flamingoes flock in large numbers around the salt pans of Botswana and Namibia, and in pools along the Namibian coast, particularly around Walvis Bay and Lüderitz. They're especially attracted by the proliferation of algae and crustaceans which thrive in the intermittent lakes of the Nata Delta in Botswana and Etosha Pan in Namibia. Flamingoes are excellent fliers and have been known to cover up to 500km overnight.

Flamingoes have a complicated and sophisticated system for filtering the foodstuffs from highly alkaline – and toxic – soda lakes, seawater and brackish pans. The lesser flamingo filters algae and diatoms from the water by sucking in and vigorously expelling water from its bill – which is held upside down in the water – several times per second. The minute particles are caught on fine hair-like protrusions which line the inside of the mandibles. The suction is created by the thick fleshy tongue which rests in a groove in the lower mandible and pumps back and forth like a piston. It has been estimated that a million lesser flamingoes can consume over 180 tonnes of algae and diatoms daily.

While lesser flamingoes obtain food by filtration, the greater flamingo supplements its algae diet with small molluscs, crustaceans and other organic particles from the mud. When feeding, it will rotate in a circle stamping its feet, apparently to scare out potential meals.

The greater and lesser flamingoes are best distinguished by their colouration. Greater flamingoes are white to light pink, and their beaks are whitish with a black tip. Lesser flamingoes are a deeper pink – often reddish – colour and have dark red beaks.

NAMIBIA

wetland for migratory birds. Up to 150,000 transient avian visitors stop by annually.

**Lagoon** The shallow and sheltered 45,000 hectare lagoon, south-west of town and west of the Kuiseb Mouth, attracts a range of coastal water birds and supports half the flamingo population of southern Africa. You may also see chestnut banded plovers and curlew sandpipers, as well as other migrants and waders. It's also a permanent home of the rare Damara tern.

**Salt Works** South-west of the lagoon is the Walvis Bay salt works (☎ (064) 202376). As with the one in Swakopmund, these pans concentrate salt from seawater with the aid of evaporation. The 3500 hectare salt-pan complex currently supplies over 90% of South Africa's salt. Phone to arrange a tour.

**Bird Paradise** Immediately east of town at the municipal sewage purification works is the bird sanctuary known as Bird Paradise, which consists of a series of shallow artificial pools, fringed by reeds. An observation tower and a short nature walk afford excellent birdwatching. It lies 500m east of town, off the C14 towards Rooikop airport.

**Rooibank**
Rooibank, at the south-eastern corner of the former Walvis Bay enclave, is named after a cluster of red granite outcrops on the northern bank of the Kuiseb River. This area is best known as the site of one of Namibia's few Topnaar Khoi-Khoi settlements. Notice the unusual vegetation, which includes the fleshy succulent dollar bush (*Zygophyllum stapffii*) and the !nara bush (*Acanthosicyos horrida*), a leafless plant that bears the spiky !nara melons which are still a food staple for the Topnaar Khoi-Khoi people. The !nara bush grows a long tap root to derive moisture from underground sources and thereby monitors underground water tables: when the plants are healthy, so is the water supply.

To the east of Rooibank, 1.5km upstream towards Scheppmansdorp, is a marked 3km walking track which will take you along the sandy riverbed to some picturesque dunes. At Scheppmansdorp itself is a monument marking the site of an old church built by the missionary Scheppman in 1846.

**Organised Tours**
Contact details for the following companies are found in the Organised Tours chapter earlier in this book. Inshore Safaris does half/full-day tours of the town and Welwitschia Drive for US$30/35, with a minimum of four people. Half-day 4WD tours to Sandwich Harbour (if they're running – see under Namib-Naukluft Park in the following section for times) cost US$44. The water-oriented Mola-Mola Safaris runs half-day dolphin-watching trips for US$34, seabird-watching trips for US$45 and all-day cruises to Bird Island, Pelican Point and Sandwich Harbour for US$68. Trips depart from the yacht club. Levo Tours, which is affiliated with the Levo Guest House, does a range of fishing trips, and sightseeing, seal and dolphin-watching cruises. Most sea-oriented trips from all companies feature champagne and Walvis Bay oysters.

In addition to fishing trips (US$50 per day), Afri-Fishing & Safaris runs day and overnight tours into the Namib Desert Park, including visits to the Kuiseb Delta area (US$40), Vogelfederberg (US$45), Welwitschia Drive (US$44), Bloedkoppie (US$66) and a camping tour of the highlights in the northern part of the park (US$77).

A particularly rewarding experience is a visit to the Kuiseb River Topnaar community. Four-hour 4WD tours, run by Rudolph Dauseb (☎ (064) 207208), cost US$80. Mr Dauseb is a Topnaar community leader and provides insights into the culture, cuisine and natural environment of this fascinating group.

A new hit in Walvis Bay is bird-watching and dolphin-viewing by sea kayak on the lagoon with Jeanne Mientjes' Eco-Marine Kayak Tours; you can choose from trips to shipwrecks, Pelican Point, Bird Island, seal and dolphin-watching, and the oyster farm.

## !Nara Melons

Historically, human existence in the Namib has been made possible by an unusual spiny plant, the !nara melon (*Acanthosicyos horrida*). It was first described taxonomically by the same Friedrich Welwitsch who gave his name to the welwitschia plant.

Although the !nara bush lives and grows in the desert – and lacks leaves to prevent water loss through transpiration – it is not a desert plant as its moisture is taken from the ground-water table via a long tap root. Its lack of leaves also protects it from grazing animals, although ostrich do nip off its tender growing shoots.

Like the welwitschia, the male and female sex organs in the !nara melon exist in separate plants. Male plants flower throughout the year, but it's the female plant which each summer produces the 15cm melon that provides a favourite meal for jackals, insects and humans. Indeed, it remains a primary food of the Topnaar Khoi-Khoi people and has also become a local commercial enterprise. Each year at harvest time, the Topnaar erect camps around the Kuiseb Delta to collect the fruits. Although melons can be eaten raw, most people prefer to dry them for later use, or prepare, package and ship them to urban markets.

Trips last from three to five hours and cost from US$14 to US$36.

### Special Events
During the annual Walvis Bay Arts & Crafts Festival (WAC), from mid- to late December, you can learn silk-painting, glass-etching, porcelain-painting, dyeing, batik and make pottery and stained glass, among other things. Competitions include sand-castle construction (appropriate in Walvis Bay), chess, mural-painting and pavement art.

### Places to Stay – Budget
The Walvis Bay area has two campgrounds. The friendly *Esplanade Municipal Camp & Caravan Park* (☎ (064) 206145; fax 204528), near the Esplanade, charges US$6 per site plus US$2 per person. There are several special backpackers camp sites, complete with a kitchen area for self-catering. Campers may also use the tennis courts.

Namibia's most oddly named accommodation is *The Spawning Ground* (☎ (064) 205121), and no, it's not a brothel, but a very agreeable backpackers lodge. This lively place adds a welcome bright splash of colour in an otherwise drab part of town. Beds cost US$7 and camping costs US$5.

The other-worldly *Langstrand Resort* (☎ (064) 203134) lies 15km north of town and looks like a desert mirage, especially in a fog or sandstorm. Campers pay US$9 per site plus US$1 per person and two/four-bed bungalows cost US$27/39. The restaurant has a good reputation and you can poke around tide pools and swim in the pool or from the jetty. Also in Langstrand is the mid-range *Guesthouse Levo* (☎/fax (064) 207555), owned by Ottmar and Merrilyn Lieppert.

The cheap but seedy *Mermaid Hotel* (☎ (064) 206212; fax 206656), on Sixth St, charges US$21/25 for a single/double for the entire night, but they'd happily rent it for two hours. Ask for the quietest and safest room available.

### Places to Stay – Mid-Range
The motel-style *Seagull Inn* (☎ (064) 202775; fax 202455) – formerly the Golden Fish – has simple single/double rooms for US$23/32. Self-catering rooms cost US$32/36 and four/six-bed rooms are US$41/50. Homely *Asgard House* (☎ (064) 209595; fax 209596) is a little family-run guest

NAMIBIA

house at 72 Seventeenth Rd, at the eastern end of town. Single/double accommodation costs US$30/41.

*The Courtyard* (☎ (064) 206252; fax 207271), at 16 Third Rd, near Second St, has single/double accommodation for US$32/45, with breakfast. It's spotlessly clean and has a pool, a sauna and a bright spacious garden. Nearby is the equally white, bright and airy *Langholme Hotel* (☎ (064) 207666; fax 209430; <lang holm@iafrica.com.na>), which charges US$37/62 for singles/doubles with TV. Suites cost from US$56 to US$90.

The *Esplanade Park Bungalows* (☎ (064) 206145) has five/seven-bed self-catering bungalows for US$42/53 in the holiday season and slightly less off season. It's near the sea wall, west of the town centre. The *Lagoon Chalets* (☎ (064) 207151; fax 207469), south-west of town, has six-bed one/two-bedroom chalets for US$38/43 and eight-bed three-bedroom chalets for US$49. All units are self-catering.

The self-catering *Dolfynpark Beach Chalets* (☎ (064) 204343), 12km north of town, has a swimming pool and water park. Four/six-bed self-catering chalets cost US$39/46. You couldn't imagine a structure more alien to its setting than this. Kids will love the pool and 'hydro-slide'.

The good-value *Hotel Atlantic* (☎ (064) 203811; fax 205063), on Seventh St between Tenth and Eleventh Rds, charges US$43/66 for singles/doubles with break-fast. The plush and central *Walvis Bay Protea Lodge* (☎ (064) 209560; fax 204097) has double standard rooms for US$65. Smaller doubles are US$52. The attached Waldorf Restaurant is open daily for three meals.

The friendly *Casa Mia Hotel* (☎ (064) 205975; fax 209565) charges US$56/68 for singles/doubles, with breakfast. Single/double suites are US$85/100. It's one of the most comfortable options in town, and the bar and restaurant are both worthwhile.

## Places to Eat

*Crazy Mama's* (☎ (064) 207364) is reason enough to visit Walvis Bay. The service and atmosphere are great, prices are right and it serves fabulous pizzas, salads and vegetarian options, among other things.

The popular *Raft* (☎ (064) 204877), which sits on stilts offshore and looks more like a porcupine than a raft, serves indescribably fine fare; highly recommended are the hunters' venison (ostrich and oryx stir-fry), the Greek salad and the vegetable skewer (kebab). You'll also have a great front-row view of the ducks, pelicans and flamingoes that inhabit the lagoon.

Equally fabulous is the *Waterfront Express & Amigo's Bar* (☎ (064) 207009); it's housed in three railcars stranded between the dunes and the sea on a barren stretch of beach, just north of Langstrand. The prices are good and it's known for outstanding seafood, burgers, salads and sweets. The last category includes famous waffles, hot brown pudding and lemon mousse.

*The Bushbaby* (☎ (064) 205490) serves tasty food – steaks, fish, crayfish and Walvis Bay oysters – at excellent prices. It also does fabulous bar lunches which are popular with the local office crowd. The competing *Hickory Creek Spur* (☎ (064) 207990), of the ubiquitous South African chain, has a recommended salad bar. It's open daily from 11 am to 2 am. The posh *Lalainya's* (☎ (064) 202574) on Seventh St serves upmarket dinners, including an excellent seafood platter.

You'll also enjoy the recommended *Willie Probst Takeaway & Boulevard Café*, which is always crowded at lunch hour, and the down-to-earth *Harbour Café*. For a takeaway treat, see *King Pie & Kingfisher Takeaways* (☎ (064) 203477), on Seventh St, or for something more ordinary, *Kentucky Fried Chicken*. *Picasso's* serves lunch and coffee until 5 pm.

For fresh fish, try the *Sea Pride Food Services* (☎ (064) 207661). It sells the catch of the day, as well as Lüderitz lobster tails, Alaskan smoked salmon and other frozen or processed seafood products through its wholesale shop on the corner of Thirteenth

Rd and Sixth St. It's open Monday to Friday from 8.30 am to 1 pm and 2 to 5.30 pm, and on Saturday from 8 am to 1 pm.

## Entertainment

When you first see Walvis Bay, you'll probably wonder whether entertainment is even feasible; people seem too lethargic to care one way or another. Surprisingly, however, there actually are a couple of things to do at night – and that's in addition to uncorking a bottle of booze or downing a six-pack of lager in one sitting.

The *Plaza Cinema* not only shows films, but also has a lively bar and dance floor. For more rollicking local entertainment and dancing, visit the *Palace disco* in the Narraville township, east of the town centre. The *Casa Mia Hotel* has two bars: the Nautilus Karaoke Bar and the more intimate Captain Simon's.

## Getting There & Away

**Air** The airport for Walvis Bay is at Rooikop (red hill), 10km east of town on the C14. The airport shuttle (☎ (064) 209113; after hours (064) 202481) stops opposite the Hickory Creek Spur. The fare is US$17. Air Namibia (☎ (064) 203102) has three flights a week between Walvis Bay and Windhoek. Twice weekly, you can fly direct to or from Cape Town.

**Bus** The Intercape Mainliner bus runs four times weekly between Windhoek and Walvis Bay (US$23, five hours). The terminal is the Omega petrol station at the corner of Seventh St and Fifteenth Rd. Dolphin Express (☎ (064) 204118) has daily services between Windhoek and Walvis Bay for US$15. Star Line buses connect Walvis Bay with Mariental (US$16, 12 hours), via Büllsport, Maltahöhe and various farms and bush shops along the way. They leave Mariental on Monday at 7.30 am and Walvis Bay on Tuesday at 8.30 am. Book at the railway station.

**Train** The overnight rail service to Walvis Bay from Windhoek (US$13/9 in business/economy class) leaves at 8 pm daily except Saturday and from Walvis Bay at 7 pm daily except Saturday. On Tuesday, Thursday and Sunday northbound and Monday, Wednesday and Friday southbound, the train splits at Kranzberg for connections to/from Tsumeb (US$12/9 in business/economy class). For rail information, phone Trans-Namib (☎ (064) 208504).

## Getting Around

Dolphin Express minibuses operate around town and to other parts of the former Walvis Bay enclave. For car-hire suggestions, see the Namibia Getting Around chapter.

# Namib-Naukluft Park

The present boundaries of Namib-Naukluft Park, one of the world's largest national parks, were established in 1978 by merging the Namib Desert Park and the Naukluft Mountain Zebra Park with parts of Diamond Area 1 and bits of surrounding government land. Today, it takes in over 23,000 sq km of desert and semi-desert, including the diverse habitats of the Namib Desert Park between the Kuiseb and Swakop rivers, the Naukluft (formerly the Naukluft Mountain Zebra Park), the high dunefield at Sossusvlei and the bird lagoon at Sandwich Harbour.

The Namib Desert is one of the oldest and driest deserts in the world. As with the Atacama in northern Chile, it is the result of a cold current – in this case, the Benguela Current – sweeping north from Antarctica, which captures and condenses humid air which would otherwise be blown ashore. Its western strip is a sea of sand comprised mainly of apricot-coloured dunes interspersed with dry pans, of which Sossusvlei is the best known. This normally dusty pan is surrounded by 300m dunes, but on the rare occasions when the Tsauchab River flows, Sossusvlei fills with water and will attract gemsbok, springbok, ostrich and aquatic birds.

Heading north, the dunes end abruptly at the Kuiseb River and the Namib takes on an entirely different character: a landscape of endless grey-white gravel plains specked with isolated kopjes. It supports gemsbok, springbok and mountain zebra as well as the bizarre welwitschia plants whose only source of moisture is dew and fog. Historically, the region was also home to desert elephant and black rhino, but these are now gone and attempts to reintroduce them have met with failure. The park's eastern extreme

## The Dune Community

Despite their barren appearance, the Namib dunes actually support a unique ecosystem. Nowhere else on earth does life exist in such harsh conditions, but here it manages, thanks mainly to grass seed and bits of plant matter deposited by the wind and the moisture carried in by fog.

The sand provides shelter for a range of small creatures and even a short walk on the dunes will reveal traces of this well-adapted community. By day, the surface temperatures may reach 70°C, but below, the spaces between sand particles are considerable and therefore, air circulates freely below the surface, providing a cool shelter. In the chill of a desert night, the sand retains some of the warmth absorbed during the day and provides a warm place to burrow. When alarmed, most creatures can also use the sand as an effective hiding place.

The best places to observe dune life are Sossusvlei and the dunes south of Homeb, on the Kuiseb River. Early in the morning, look at the tracks to see what has transpired during the night; it's easy to distinguish the trails of various dune-dwelling beetles, lizards, snakes, spiders and scorpions.

Much of the dune community is comprised of beetles, which are attracted by the vegetable material on the dune slipfaces, and the Namib supports 200 species of the tenebrionid family alone. However, they're only visible when the dune surface is warm. At other times, they take shelter beneath the surface by 'swimming' into the sand.

The fog-basking tenebrionid beetle (*Onomachris unguicularis*), which is locally known as a *toktokkie*, has a particularly interesting way of drinking. By day, these beetles scuttle over the dunes, surviving on the plant detritus on the slipfaces, but at night, they bury themselves in the sand. They derive moisture by condensing fog on their bodies. On foggy mornings, toktokkies line up on the dunes, lower their heads, raise their posteriors in the air, and slide the water droplets down the carapace into the mouth. They can consume up to 40% of their body weight in water in a single morning.

The large dancing spider known as the 'White Lady of the Namib' (*Orchestrella longpipes* – it could be a character in a children's novel) lives in tunnels constructed beneath the dune surface. To prevent the tunnels from collapsing, they are lined with spider silk as they are excavated. This enormous spider can easily make a meal of creatures as large as palmato geckos.

The dunes are also home to the loveable golden mole (*Eremitalpa granti*), a yellowish-coloured carnivore which spends most of its day buried in the dune. It was first discovered in 1837, but wasn't again sighted until 1963. The golden mole, which lacks both eyes and ears, doesn't burrow like other moles, but simply swims through the sand. Although it's rarely spotted, look carefully around tufts of grass or hummocks for the large rounded snout, which often protrudes above the surface. At night, it emerges and roams hundreds of metres over the dune faces foraging for beetle larvae and other insects.

culminates in the dramatic Naukluft Massif, which is characterised by a high plateau bounded by gorges, caves and springs cut deeply from dolomite formations.

Most of the main park roads are open to 2WD, but minor roads are in poor condition and services are few. You don't need a permit to transit on the main routes – the C28, the C14, the D1982 or the D1998 – but to turn off onto minor roads or visit picnic sites or sights of interest, you need a park permit. These are available for US$3 per vehicle and US$3 per person at MET offices in Windhoek or Swakopmund, at

---

The shovel-snouted lizard (*Aporosaura anchitae*) uses a unique method of regulating its body temperature while tearing across the scorching sand. This lizard can tolerate body temperatures of up to 44°C, but surface temperatures on the dunes can climb as high as 70°C. To prevent overheating, the lizard does a 'thermal dance', raising its tail and two legs at a time off the hot surface of the sand. When threatened, the lizard submerges itself in the sand.

Another unique creature is the rather appealing little palmato gecko (*Palmatogecko rangei*), also known as the web-footed gecko after its unusual feet, which act as scoops for burrowing in the sand. This translucent nocturnal gecko has a pinkish-brown colouration on its back and a white belly. It grows to a length of 10cm and has enormous eyes, which aid hunting at night. It's often photographed using its long tongue to clear its eyes of dust and sand. The tongue is also used to collect condensed fog droplets from the head and snout. Other gecko species present in the dunes include the barking gecko (*Ptenopus garrulus*) and the large-headed gecko (*Chondrodactylus anguilifer*).

Another dune lizard is the bizarre and fearsome looking Namaqua chameleon (*Chamaeleo namaquensis*), which grows up to 25cm in length, and is unmistakable due to the fringe of brownish bumps along its spine. When alarmed, it emits an ominous hiss and exposes its enormous yellow-coloured mouth and sticky tongue, which can spell the end for up to 200 large beetles every day. Like all chameleons, its eyes operate independently in their cone-shaped sockets, allowing the chameleon to look in several directions at once.

The small, buff-coloured Namib sidewinding adder (*Bitis peringueyi*) is perfectly camouflaged on the dune surface. It grows to a length of just 25cm and navigates by gracefully moving sideways through the shifting sands. Because the eyes are on top of the head, the snake can bury itself almost completely in the sand and still see what's happening above the surface. When its unsuspecting prey happens along – normally a gecko or lizard – the adder uses its venom to immobilise the creature before devouring it. Although it is also poisonous to humans, the venom is so mild that it rarely causes more than an irritation.

The three species of Namib sand snakes (*Psammophis* sp.) are longer, slinkier and faster-moving than the adders, but hunt the same prey. These 1m-long back-fanged snakes grab the prey and chew on it until it's immobilised by venom, then swallow it whole. As with the adders, they're well camouflaged for life in the sand, ranging from off-white to pale grey in colour. The back is marked with pale stripes or a pattern of dots.

Several varieties of Namib skinks (*Typhlosaurus* sp.) are commonly mistaken for snakes. Because they propel themselves by swimming in the sand, their limbs are either small and vestigial or missing altogether, and their eyes, ears and nostrils are tiny and therefore well-protected from sand particles. At the tip of their nose is a 'rostral scale', which acts like a bulldozer blade to clear the sand ahead and allow the skink to progress. Skinks spend most of their time burrowing beneath the surface, but at night, emerge on the dune slipfaces to forage. In the morning, you'll often see their telltale tracks.

Sesriem or several after-hours petrol stations in Swakopmund and Walvis Bay.

Camp sites (US$16 per site for the Namib Desert Park camps, US$30 for Sesriem and US$18 for Naukluft) must be prebooked through the MET offices in Windhoek or Swakopmund. Camping fees are payable when the park permit is issued. Note that permits for entry and hikes in the Sesriem/Sossusvlei and Naukluft areas must be booked in Windhoek.

## SANDWICH HARBOUR

Sandwich Harbour, 50km south of Walvis Bay, historically served as a commercial fishing and trading port, and indeed, the name may well be derived from an English whaler, the *Sandwich*, which operated in the mid-1780s. It's thought that the captain of this ship produced the first map of this coastline. (However, the name may also be a corruption of the German word *Sand-fische*, a type of shark often found here.)

Although it's now a total wilderness, Sandwich Harbour has historically hosted various enterprises, from fish processing and shark-oil extraction to sealing and guano collection. In the late 1800s, the southern end of the lagoon even supported an extensive abattoir, which was set up by some enlightened soul who'd taken up the notion of driving cattle over the dunes to the harbour for slaughter and export. All that remains of these enterprises is an early to

mid-1900s hut used for guano collection, a rusting barge, a graveyard and some wooden beams from the abattoir.

Over the years, as the inlet silted up, commercial activities ceased, but until the mid-1990s, the marshy northern end of the lagoon supported an ideal environment for a quite extraordinary range of birdlife. However, continued siltation has rendered it unappealing for the enormous flocks it once attracted and today, it may not be worth the considerable effort required to get there. The site is open daily between 6 am and 8 pm; however, there are no facilities for visitors.

### The Wetlands

Anichab, at the northern end of the reserve, lies 3.5km south of the angling concession car park. This area is characterised by a series of increasingly silty and sandy wetland pools filled from both the sea and the Anichab freshwater springs (created by water percolating through the dunefield from the Kuiseb River, 40km to the north). The name Anichab is derived from the Nama word for 'spring water' and under normal conditions, the Anichab springs reduce the salinity of the wetland area and make it amenable to salt-tolerant freshwater bird species. In the past, these reed-filled pools provided sustenance and nesting sites for an astonishing variety of waterbirds – 100 species in all and numbers up to 150,000.

Over the past decade, however, the sand has encroached on the southern part of the lagoon, causing the sandspit which protects the wetlands to recede. This in turn has widened the area open to the sea, and the increased wave action has built a beach along the eastern shore of the lagoon. With more sediment pouring in, the lagoon has become shallower and saltier, and the northern sandspit sheltering the lagoon has moved inland. As a result, the reed pools are silting up and many of the terrestrial birds and wading birds have gone. It's speculated that over the next several decades, the lagoon may disappear.

~~~~~~~~~~~~~~~~~~~~~~~~~~~~~~

### Sandwiched Treasure

Local legend has it that over 200 years ago, a ship carrying a cargo of gold, precious stones and ivory intended as a gift from Lord Clive to the Moghul emperor was stranded at Sandwich Harbour en route to India. It's believed that the cargo, which was valued at UK£6 million, lies somewhere beneath the towering dunes. However, not a trace of it has yet been found – and not for a lack of searching.

~~~~~~~~~~~~~~~~~~~~~~~~~~~~~~

## Getting There & Away

Thanks to the increasing sand infiltration, few Swakopmund or Walvis Bay tour companies run their advertised Sandwich Harbour tours. If you're intent on getting there, make sure your group is large enough to persuade them to go!

Otherwise, Sandwich Harbour is accessible only with a sturdy high-clearance 4WD vehicle. Take the left fork 5km south of Walvis Bay and when the road splits at the salt works, bear left again and continue across the marshy Kuiseb Delta. After 15km, you must show your park permit to enter the Namib-Naukluft Park.

For the final 20km, you can either continue straight along the sandy beach (time your journey for low tide) or bear left past the control post and follow the tracks further inland. However, dune shifts may present tedious stretches of deep sand or alter the route entirely. Bring a shovel, tow rope and a couple of planks for unbogging. Vehicles aren't permitted beyond the car park at the southern limit of the angling concession, which lies 3.5km north of MET's Anichab hut.

## NAMIB DESERT PARK

The relatively accessible Namib Desert Park lies between the canyons of the Kuiseb River in the south and the Swakop River in the north. Although it does include a small area of linear dunes, it's characterised mostly by broad gravel plains punctuated by abrupt and imposing ranges of hills, many of which appear to have been moulded from chocolate or caramel.

Although this region doesn't support an abundance of large mammals, there is wildlife about. Along the road, you may see families of chacma baboons, or dassies, which like to bask on the kopjes. The Kuiseb Canyon, on the Gamsberg Route between Windhoek and Walvis Bay, is also home to klipspringer and even leopard. Spotted hyaena are often heard at night and jackal make a good living from the herds of springbok on the plains.

For information on Welwitschia Drive, which is inside the park but is most often visited as a day trip from Swakopmund, see the Around Swakopmund section earlier in this chapter.

## Kuiseb Canyon

The dramatic Kuiseb Canyon lies on the Gamsberg Route west of the Khomas Hochland. For much of the year, the ephemeral Kuiseb River is little more than a broad sandy riverbed. It may flow for two or three weeks a year, it only ever gets as far as Gobabeb and seeps into the sand before reaching the sea. At Rooibank, drinking water for Walvis Bay is pumped from this subterranean supply.

It was here that geologists Henno Martin and Hermann Korn went into hiding for three years during WWII, as recounted in Henno Martin's book *The Sheltering Desert*. The canyon's upper reaches are uninhabited, but where the valley broadens out, scattered Topnaar Khoi-Khoi villages occupy the north bank.

## Desert Ecological Research Unit

Gobabeb, the 'place of figs', west of Homeb, is the site of the Desert Ecological Research Unit of the Desert Research Foundation of Namibia. This complex of laboratories, research facilities and a weather station was established in 1963 by South African researcher Dr Charles Koch and appropriately sits at the transition between the Namib's three ecosystems: the gravel plains, the dune sea and the Kuiseb Valley.

The centre isn't normally open to the public, but it does hold one or two 'open days' each year, which feature self-guided nature trails, lectures and field demonstrations, as well as educational demonstrations by the local Topnaar community. For specific dates or other information, contact the Director, Desert Ecological Research Unit, PO Box 1592, Swakopmund, or the Friends of Gobabeb Society, Desert Research Foundation, PO Box 37, Windhoek. If you wish to visit for scientific research purposes, contact Dr Hu Berry on the radio phone

NAMIBIA

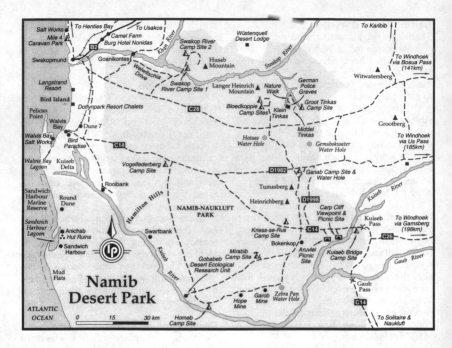

from the MET offices in Windhoek or Swakopmund.

## Hamilton Mountains

The range of limestone hills known as the Hamilton Mountains, south of Vogelfederberg, rises 600m above the surrounding desert plains. It provides lovely desert hikes and the fog-borne moisture supports an amazing range of succulents and other botanical wonders.

## Places to Stay

The central Namib has eight exclusive *camps* (some of which have multiple but widely spaced sites) which cost US$16 and accommodate one party at a time: Kuiseb Bridge, Mirabib, Kriess-se-Rus, Vogelfederberg, Bloedkoppie, Groot Tinkas, Ganab and Homeb. These sites may also be used as picnic areas with a day-use permit. Sites have tables, toilets and braais, but no

washing facilities. Brackish water is available for cooking and washing but not drinking, so bring all you need. All sites must be pre-booked through MET in Windhoek or Swakopmund. Fees are payable when your park permit is issued.

**Kuiseb Bridge** This shady double site, at the Kuiseb River crossing along the C14, is merely a convenient place to break up a trip between Windhoek and Walvis Bay. The location is scenic enough, but the dust and noise from passing vehicles makes it less appealing than other sites in the park. There are pleasant short walks into the canyon, but after rains, keep close tabs on the weather, as flash flooding can be a problem.

**Kriess-se-Rus** This shaded site, 107km east of Walvis Bay on the Gamsberg route, lies amid the camelthorn acacias beside a streambed on the gravel plains. It's not the park's most scenic site, but makes a convenient stop between Windhoek and Walvis Bay.

**Mirabib** Mirabib, with two very pleasant camp sites, is comfortably placed beneath rock overhangs in a large granite inselberg. There's evidence that these shelters were used by nomadic peoples as many as 9000 years ago, and also by pastoralists in the 4th or 5th century AD.

**Vogelfederberg** This small inselberg about 2km south of the C14 makes a convenient overnight camp within easy striking distance of Walvis Bay, 51km away, but it's more popular as a picnic site or a place for a short walk. It's worth having a look at the intermittent pools on the top, which are home to *triops*, a species of brine shrimp whose eggs hatch only when the pools are filled with rainwater. The only shade is provided by a small overhang with two picnic tables and braai pits.

**Bloedkoppie** The beautiful camp sites at the large inselberg, Bloedkoppie, or 'blood hill', are among the most popular sites in the park. If you're coming from Swakopmund, they lie 55km north of the C28, along a signposted track. The northern sites are readily accessible to 2WD vehicles, but they're often plagued by the worst sort of yobs, who drink themselves silly and make life miserable for other campers. The southern sites are quieter and more secluded, but can be reached only by 4WD. The surrounding area offers pleasant walking, and at Klein Tinkas, about 5km east of Bloedkoppie, you'll see the ruins of a colonial police station and the graves of two German police officers dating back to 1895.

**Groot Tinkas** Groot Tinkas, 15km east of Bloedkoppie, must be accessed with 4WD and rarely sees much traffic, so if you want a secluded camp site, it's a good choice. It enjoys a lovely setting beneath ebony trees and the surroundings are superb for nature walks. During rainy periods, the brackish water in the nearby dam attracts varied birdlife.

**Ganab** The dusty and exposed camp site at Ganab (Nama for camelthorn acacias) sits beside a shallow streambed on the gravel plains. It's shaded by hardy acacia trees and a nearby windmill-powered bore hole provides water for antelope, zebra, hyaena, aardwolf, fox and caracal.

**Homeb** The scenic camp site at Homeb, which accommodates several parties, lies just upstream from the most accessible set of dunes in the Namib Desert Park. Residents of the nearby Topnaar Khoi-Khoi village dig wells in the riverbed to access water flowing beneath the surface, and one of their dietary staples is the !nara melon, which takes its moisture through a long tap root which reaches the water table. This hidden water also supports a good stand of trees, including camelthorn acacia, ebony and figs, along the banks of the riverbed.

**Swakop River** The shady Swakop River camp sites lie – not surprisingly – on the banks of the Swakop River, in the far northern reaches of the park. The southern site accommodates five parties and is the more preferable of the two, featuring lots of greenery – camelthorn, anaboom and tamarisk trees – while the northern one, beside a plain of welwitschias, is utterly flat and treeless. The only shade is beneath an odd sunken picnic site. The sites are accessible via Welwitschia Drive (see Around Swakopmund, earlier in this chapter).

### Getting There & Away
The only public transport through the Namib Desert Park is the weekly Star Line bus between Mariental and Walvis Bay, via Maltahöhe and Solitaire. The westbound trip is on Monday and the eastbound on Tuesday.

### KLEIN AUB
The small village of Klein Aub, 94km west of Rehoboth on the C47, has a petrol station

and *Connie's Restaurant* (☎ (0627) 525440), which provides meals, snacks and coffee from 7 am to 6 pm daily.

## NAUKLUFT MOUNTAINS

The Naukluft Massif, which rises steeply from the gravel plains of the central Namib, is mainly a high-plateau area cut around the edges by a complex of steep gorges. Indeed, the park's name is German for narrow gorge. The Tsondab, Tsams and Tsauchab rivers all rise in the massif and the relative abundance of water creates an ideal habitat for mountain zebra, kudu, leopard, springbok and klipspringer.

### History

In the early 1890s, the Naukluft was the site of heated battle between the German colonial forces and the Witbooi Namas. The Nama resistance to German rule was led by the gifted military strategist Hendrik Witbooi, who refused to bow to colonial rule. In January 1893, a contingent of Schutztruppe soldiers under Major Curt von François was posted near Oniab, north of the Naukluft, and managed to force Witbooi and his followers to flee their settlement at Hoornkrans. Von François was transferred in March 1894 and replaced by Major Theodore Leutwein, who launched a campaign against the Nama forces in the Naukluft Mountains. At the end of that month, German cavalryman Richard Kramers was killed in a skirmish near what is now the Hiker's Haven hut in the Naukluft Valley (his grave is still visible).

The Germans had estimated they could defeat the Nama within three days, but their unfamiliarity with the territory and lack of experience in guerrilla warfare slowed them down. In late August, they'd captured the Nama camp at Oniab, and Witbooi and his forces retreated into the mountains. The Germans chased the Nama across the plateau with their cannon and other firepower (portions of the old cannon route remain visible).

After heavy losses, Witbooi approached the Germans with a conditional surrender, which stipulated that he would accept German sovereignty over the country and permit them to set up a military post at Gibeon if he could retain his chieftaincy and the Nama could hang onto their lands and weapons. Leutwein accepted and the Battle of the Naukluft was over.

### Hiking Routes

Most Naukluft visitors come to hike either the Waterkloof or Olive Trails. These hikes are open to day visitors, but most hikers want to camp at Koedoesrus, which must be booked as far in advance as possible. There are also four-day and eight-day loops, which have more restrictions attached. Thanks to stifling summer temperatures and potentially heavy rains, they're only open from 1 March to the third Friday in October on Tuesday, Thursday and Saturday of the first three weeks of each month. The price of US$21 per person includes accommodation at the Hikers Haven hut on the day before and after the hike, as well as camping at trailside shelters and the Ubusis Canyon Hut. Groups must be comprised of three to 12 people.

**Waterkloof Trail** This lovely 17km anticlockwise loop takes about seven hours to complete. Hikers need to carry two to three litres of water per person. The trail begins at Koedoesrus camp site, 2km west of the park headquarters and it climbs the Naukluft River past a frog-infested weir and a series of pools which offer cool and refreshing drinking and swimming. About 1km beyond the last pool, the trail turns west, away from the Naukluft River and up a tributary. From there to the half-way point, the route traverses increasingly open plateau country.

Shortly after the half-way mark, the trail climbs steeply to a broad 1910m ridge, which is the highest point on the route. Here you'll have fabulous desert views before you begin a long, steep descent into the Gororosib Valley. Along the way, you'll pass several inviting pools full of reeds and tadpoles, and climb down an especially

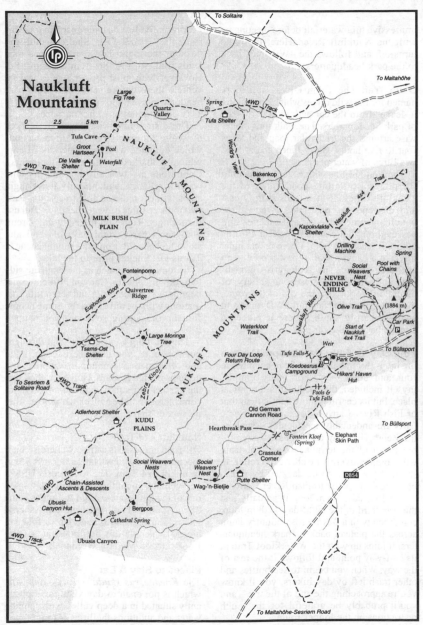

**Naukluft Mountains**

0    2.5    5 km

To Solitaire

To Maltahöhe

Large Fig Tree

Quartz Valley

Spring

4WD Track

Tufa Shelter

Tufa Cave

NAUKLUFT

Groot Hartseer

Pool

Die Valle Shelter

Waterfall

4WD Track

World's View

Bakenkop

MOUNTAINS

MILK BUSH PLAIN

Naukluft 4x4 Trail

Kapokvlakte Shelter

Drilling Machine

Spring

Fonteinpomp

Social Weavers' Nest

Pool with Chains

Euphorbia Kloof

Quivertree Ridge

NEVER ENDING HILLS

(1884 m)

Olive Trail

Car Park

NAUKLUFT MOUNTAINS

Large Moringa Tree

Waterkloof Trail

Naukluft River

Start of Naukluft 4x4 Trail

Tsams-Ost Shelter

Four Day Loop Return Route

Weir

To Büllsport

Zebra Kloof

Tufa Falls

Park Office

To Sesriem & Solitaire Road

4WD Track

Koedoesrus Campground

Hikers' Haven Hut

Adlerhorst Shelter

KUDU PLAINS

Old German Cannon Road

Pools & Tufa Falls

Heartbreak Pass

Fontein Kloof (Spring)

Elephant Skin Path

To Büllsport

Social Weavers' Nests

Social Weavers' Nest

Crassula Corner

D854

Chain-Assisted Ascents & Descents

Wag-'n-Bietjie

Putte Shelter

4WD Track

Ubusis Canyon Hut

Bergpos

Cathedral Spring

Ubusis Canyon

4WD Track

To Maltahöhe-Sesriem Road

NAMIBIA

impressive tufa waterfall before meeting up with the Naukluft River. Here, the route turns left and follows the 4WD track back to the park headquarters.

**Olive Trail** The 11km Olive Trail loop, named for the wild olives which grow along it, leaves from the car park 4km north-east of park headquarters. The walk runs clockwise around the triangular loop and takes four to five hours. Carry lunch and at least two litres of water per person.

The route begins with a steep climb onto the plateau, affording good views of the Naukluft Valley. It then turns sharply east and descends a constricted river valley, which becomes deeper and steeper and passes through a couple of perfect U-turns before it reaches a point where hikers must traverse a canyon wall – past a pool – on anchored chains. The geology is astonishing, and the rocks present a gallery of natural artwork. Near the end of the route, the trail strikes the Naukluft 4WD route and swings sharply south, where it makes a beeline back to the car park.

**Four-Day & Eight-Day Loops** The two big loops through the massif can be hiked in four and eight days. For many people, myself included, the Naukluft is a magical place, but its charm is more subtle than that of Fish River Canyon, for example. Some parts are undeniably spectacular – such as the Zebra Highway and Ubusis Canyon – but much of the terrain is desert plateau, with comparatively little change in relief. In short, if you want to be dazzled by mind-blowing scenery, go to Fish River Canyon.

The four-day, 60km loop is actually just the first third of the eight-day 120km loop, combined with a 22km cross-country jaunt across the plateau back to park headquarters. It joins up with the Waterkloof Trail at its half-way point and follows it the rest of the way. When you begin to see bottles and other trash left by day hikers, you'll know you're approaching the end of the trip – and you'll probably be grateful for the tough restrictions on the longer route.

Alternatively, you can finish the four-day route at Tsams-Ost Shelter, mid-way through the eight-day loop, where a road leads out to the Sesriem-Solitaire Rd. However, you must pre-arrange to leave a vehicle there before setting off from park headquarters. Hikers may not begin from Tsams-Ost under any circumstances.

These straightforward hikes are marked by white footprints (except those sections which coincide with the Waterkloof Loop, which is marked with yellow footprints). Conditions are typically hot and dry, and water is reliably available only at overnight stops. Hikers must be able to carry at least two to three litres of water per day – and use it sparingly. Those on the eight-day circuit who can't carry eight days of food and stove fuel should drop off a supply cache at Tsams-Ost Shelter prior to the hike.

In some places, such as the requisite side trip down Ubusis Canyon, hikers must negotiate dry waterfalls and steep tufa formations with the aid of chains. Some people find this off-putting, so be sure you're up to it.

This isn't big game country, but throughout the route, you may see baboon, kudu and Hartmann's mountain zebra, and perhaps even a leopard. However, the most dangerous creature you're likely to come across will be a black mamba or other poisonous snake.

### Naukluft 4x4 Trail
Off-road enthusiasts can now exercise their machines on the new National Parks 73km Naukluft 4x4 Trail. The route costs US$45 per vehicle, including accommodation in one of the four stone-walled A-frames at the 28km point. Facilities include shared toilets, showers and braais. Up to four vehicles/16 people are permitted at a time. Book through MET in Windhoek.

### Places to Stay & Eat
The *Koedoesrus* (*kudu's rest*) *camp site*, which is not open to day visitors, is pleasantly situated in a deep valley with running water and ablutions facilities. At night, you

can wander up the riverbed with a torch to see the incredible frog life that inhabits the river pools. Sites cost US$18 for up to eight people, but it books up quickly and the maximum stay is three nights. Firewood is sold at the park entrance ranger office.

The nearest accommodation is at *Büllsport Guest Farm* (☎ (06638) ask for 3302; fax (061) 235453), Private Bag 1003, Maltahöhe, run by Ernst and Johanna Sauber. There's a charm in this austere setting below the Naukluft Massif, and its attractions may be reached on foot or on a 4WD excursion. There's a ruined colonial police station, the Bogenfels arch and several mountain pools. Singles/doubles cost US$100/160, with full board. There's also a shop and petrol station.

In a particularly beautiful setting amid the Tsaris Mountains is the friendly *Zebra River Lodge* (☎ (063) 293265; fax 293266). It's run by Rob and Marianne Field, who bought their own Grand Canyon and set up this lodge to share it with visitors. The area is a real wonderland of desert mountains, plateaus, valleys and natural springs which are accessible on a network of hiking tracks. Single or double lodges with three excellent meals cost US$82 and a cottage, 4km from the main lodge, is US$77. You'll need high clearance to drive into the lodge; if your vehicle falls short, they'll pick up booked guests at the gate.

Wolfgang and Milena Sauber's *Haruchas Guest Farm* (☎ (0668) ask for 4202; fax (061) 251682; <haruchas@nam.lia.net>) occupies a 20,000 hectare farm on the D855 south of Büllsport near the Naukluft Massif. Full board single/double accommodation costs US$66/108. If you're staying a week or longer, transfers are free from Windhoek. Guided group trips to Naukluft/Sossulvlei cost US$146/214.

### Getting There & Away

The Naukluft is most easily accessed via the C24 from Rehoboth and the C14 north from Gamis (or the less travelled short-cut along the D1206 from Rietoog). From Sesriem, 103km away, the nearest access is via the dip-ridden D854. The Star Line Mariental-Walvis Bay bus passes Büllsport and puts you within reasonable hitching distance of the Naukluft park entrance.

## SESRIEM & SOSSUSVLEI

Welcome to Namibia's number one attraction! The name Sesriem means 'six thongs', which was the number of joined leather ox-wagon thongs necessary to draw water from the bottom of the gorge. Both Sesriem Canyon and Sossusvlei are open year-round between sunrise and sunset. If you want to witness the sunrise over Sossusvlei – as most people do – you must stay at Sesriem. Otherwise, you can't get through the gate early enough to reach Sossusvlei before sunrise.

### Sesriem

At Sesriem are the park headquarters, a small food shop and the Karos Lodge. All visitors headed for Sossusvlei must check in at the park office and secure an entry permit.

### Sesriem Canyon

The 30m deep Sesriem Canyon is 4km south of the Sesriem headquarters. Here the Tsauchab River has carved a 1km-long gorge through the 15-million-year-old deposits of sand and gravel conglomerate. There are two pleasant walks: You can hike upstream to the brackish pool at its head or 2.5km downstream to its lower end. Note the bizarre sphinx-like formation on the northern flank near the mouth of the canyon.

### Elim Dune

This oft-visited red dune, 5km from the Sesriem camp site, can be reached with 2WD, but also makes a pleasant morning or afternoon walk. It lies on the former Elim Farm, which is now included in the Namib-Naukluft Park.

### Dune 45

The most accessible of the large red dunes found along the route between Sesriem and

NAMIBIA

Sossusvlei is Dune 45, so called because it's 45km from Sesriem. It rises over 150m above the surrounding plains and is flanked by several scraggly but picturesque trees, which will provide your photos with foreground interest.

### Sossusvlei

Sossusvlei is a huge ephemeral pan set amid red sand dunes which tower up to 200m above the valley floor and over 300m over the underlying strata. Wildlife includes sand-loving gemsbok and ostrich, but in the summer months, the pan may contain water (as it did throughout 1997). This happens only when the Tsauchab River has gathered enough volume and momentum to push beyond the thirsty plains to the sand sea. When it does, it creates an ethereal vision of red dunes reflected in a still pool, attended by aquatic birdlife.

If you experience a sense of *déjà vu*, don't be too concerned. Sossusvlei has appeared in many films and advertisements worldwide, and every story ever written about Namibia features a photo of it. This is the most accessible part of the 300km-long

and 150km-wide sand sea that covers over 32,000 sq km of western Namibia. This vast sandy desert stretches from the Khoichab River in the south to the Kuiseb River in the north, and contains some of the world's highest and most picturesque dunes. The best way to get the measure of this sandy sprawl is to climb a dune.

This sand probably originated in the Kalahari between three and five million years ago. It was washed down the Orange River and out to sea, where it was swept northwards with the Benguela Current to be deposited along the coast.

Currently, there are plans to tar the road to the 2x4 Car Park. Bear in mind that only 50 vehicles are permitted at one time, with four 'sessions' per day. A shuttle is also planned.

### Hidden Vlei

The 4km walk from the 2x4 Car Park to Hidden Vlei makes a rewarding excursion for anyone who remains energetic after seeing Sossusvlei. The route, which is marked by white-painted posts, leads to an intriguing and unearthly dry vlei amid

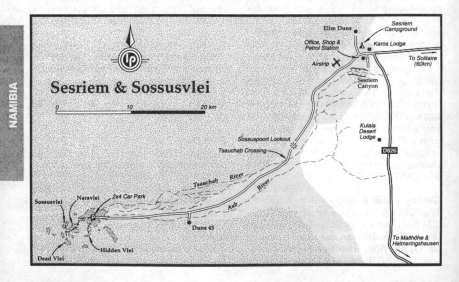

lonely dunes, and you're unlikely to see another person.

## Dead Vlei

The rugged 6km return walk from Sossusvlei to Dead Vlei is popular with those who think the former is getting a bit over-touristed. Despite the name, it's a lovely spot and is nearly as impressive as its more popular neighbour.

## Organised Tours

Most Namib area lodges and guesthouses run day tours to Sossusvlei, and prices are generally proportional to the amount you're paying for accommodation. See Places to Stay later in this discussion. A good-value option is offered by the Maltahöhe Hotel in Maltahöhe. See the Southern Namibia chapter.

## Places to Stay

**Sesriem** Sesriem is the most convenient *camp site* for Sossusvlei. Sites must be booked in Windhoek and cost US$30, but arrive before sunset or they'll re-assign your site on a stand-by basis; anyone who was unable to book a site in Windhoek may get in on this nightly lottery. Failing that, you'll be relegated to the unappealing overflow camp outside the gates.

The once pristine camp site now has an upmarket backdrop in the form of a luxury hotel, *Karos Lodge* (☎ (27-11) 643 8052 or (0638) ask for 4322; fax (27-11) 643 4343). This curious place bears a strong resemblance to what happens when fighting children topple a stack of coloured blocks. While there's a call for a tourist-class hotel at Sesriem, it could be a bit further from the campground. Single/double accommodation in the cuboid tent/bungalows costs US$135/172 with half board. In Namibia, contact Trip Travel (☎ (061) 236880; fax 225430).

**Around Sesriem** If you're not camping, an inexpensive and convenient option is the ultra-friendly *Solitaire Guest House* (☎ (0638) 3230), Private Bag 1009, Mal-

tahöhe, at the petrol station in Solitaire, 65km north of Sesriem. This pleasant place, named after the dead tree that has become its renowned motif, has recently been used in a Toyota Camry advert. In earlier times, it might have provided the inspiration for the film *Baghdad Café*, but its popularity with overland trucks has affected its unique ambience. Nevertheless, it remains a warm, friendly spot in the desert. Dusty camp sites cost US$3 per vehicle and US$4 per person. Double aluminium rondavels are US$34. At the shop, the freshly baked bread can't be beaten and the food at the attached restaurant is consistently good Lunch costs US$3 to US$4 and dinners are US$8. There's also a small aviary and a snake terrarium; a new development is an abused-equine sanctuary – real *Horse Whisperer* stuff.

About 20km south on the D826 is the small and refreshingly unobtrusive Belgian-run *Kulala Desert Lodge* (☎ (063) 293234; fax 293235). From a distance, it actually resembles a Bedouin camp. This is *the* luxury accommodation around Sossusvlei. Single/double adobe/canvas rooms with en suite facilities and private verandas cost US$135/158. Sossusvlei tours cost US$57 and hot-air ballooning is US$223.

Willie and Zanne Swarts' simple *Weltevrede Rest Camp* (☎ (063) ask for 3221), 30km south of Solitaire, offers full-board bungalow accommodation in a stark desert setting for US$43 per person. Double self-catering bungalows are US$36 and camping costs US$14 per group of up to four, plus US$4 for each extra person.

The *Namib Rest Camp* (☎ (063) 293211), PO Box 1075, Swakopmund, run by Pieter and Ella Vosges, lies west of the C36 on the Dieprivier Farm, 16km south of Solitaire. Single/double accommodation in two/four-bed self-catering bungalows costs US$57/40 per person. Camping costs US$9 per person. They also run excursions to Sesriem and Sossusvlei. An interesting attraction on the farm is the unusual violet-coloured Tsondab sandstone formation, an exposed section of an active dunefield that was solidified by moisture some 20 million years ago. This formation underlies most of the Namib sand sea.

Just to the north is the upmarket *Namib-Naukluft Lodge* (☎ (06632) 3203), PO Box 22028, Windhoek. Single/double accommodation costs US$101/158 with full board. In self-catering bungalows, it's US$75 per person with breakfast. Road or air transfers from Windhoek cost extra. For bookings, contact African Extravaganza (☎ (061) 263082; fax 215356; <afex@iwwn.com.na>).

The *Gästefarm Ababis* (☎ (0668) ask for Solitaire 3340; fax (061) 220275), PO Box 1004, Maltahöhe, run by Meike and Klaus Würriehausen, lies just south of the C14, 15km south-east of Solitaire. This working farm raises mainly cattle, sheep and ostrich, but there's also a fair amount of wildlife on the property and the farmers run game drives and organise vulture-feeding sessions. Full board single/double accommodation costs US$79/133.

The *Rostock Ritz* (☎ (064) 404030; fax

---

## The Namib Dunes

The magnificent Namib dunefields, which take on mythical proportions in tourist literature, stretch from the Orange River to the Kuiseb River in the south (this area is known as the dune sea) and from Torra Bay in Skeleton Coast Park to Angola's Curoca River in the north. They're composed of colourful quartz sand, and come in hues which vary from cream to orange, red and violet.

Unlike the Kalahari dunes, those of the Namib are dynamic. Over time, the wind shifts them and even sculpts them into a variety of distinctive shapes. The top portion of the dune which faces the direction of migration is known as a slipface. Here the sand spills from the crest and slips down. Various bits of plant and animal detritus also collect here and provide a meagre food source for dune-dwelling creatures. It's here that the majority of dune life is concentrated.

Along the eastern area of the dune sea, including around Sossusvlei, the dunes are classified as parabolic or multi-cyclic and are the result of variable wind patterns. These are the most stable dunes in the Namib and, therefore, are also the most vegetated.

Near the coast south of Walvis Bay, the formations are known as transverse dunes, which are long linear dunes lying perpendicular to the prevailing southwesterly winds. Therefore, their slipfaces are oriented towards the north and north-east.

Between these two types of dunes – for example around Homeb in the Central Namib –

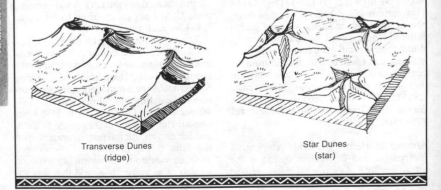

Transverse Dunes
(ridge)

Star Dunes
(star)

402797; <bushtrack@iafrica.com.na>), east of the C14 just south of the C26 junction, has been established by Kücki of Kücki's Pub in Swakopmund. Dome-shaped single/double chalets cost US$63/108.

An excellent option – and an attraction in its own right – is the *Namibgrens Rest Camp* (☎ (0628) ask for Namibgrens 1322; fax (061) 234345), PO Box 21587, Windhoek, which is run by Mr JJ Rabie. This beautiful game farm, which is known for its hiking trails, occupies a scenic position on the Spreetshoogte Pass (Namibia's steepest road, with a hair-raising 1:4 slope – that's a 25% gradient!) north-east of Solitaire. The one to three hiking routes form a ragged figure eight; accommodation is in basic huts where the loops cross. Hikers can fill their water bottles in boreholes along the way, while earth dams provide water for wildlife. Hiking costs US$7 per day, while non-hikers can take the soft option and tour the farm by vehicle for US$12. Single/double accommodation in the spacious old farm-

---

are the prominent linear or *seif* dunes, which are enormous north-west/south-east oriented sand ripples. They reach heights of 100m and are spaced about 1km apart and show up plainly on satellite photographs of the area. They're formed by seasonal winds; during the prevailing southerly winds of summer, the slipfaces lie on the north-eastern face. In the winter, the wind blows in the opposite direction and slipfaces build up on the south-western dune faces.

In areas where individual dunes are exposed to winds from all directions, a formation known as a star dune appears. These dunes have multiple ridges and when seen from above may appear to have a star shape. Considerably smaller are the tiny hump dunes, which build up around vegetation – mainly near water sources – and are only between 2m and 3m in height.

Around the southern portion of the Skeleton Coast Park and south of Lüderitz, barchan dunes prevail. These are the most highly mobile dunes of all, and are created by unidirectional winds. As they shift, these dunes take on a crescent shape, with the horns of the crescent aimed in the direction of migration. It is barchan dunes which are slowly devouring the ghost town of Kolkmanskop near Lüderitz. They're also the so-called 'roaring dunes', named after the rumbling sound they make as sand grains spill over the slipface. On particularly large dunes, or in especially warm weather, the roar is at its loudest.

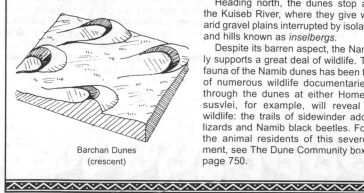

Barchan Dunes
(crescent)

Heading north, the dunes stop abruptly at the Kuiseb River, where they give way to flat, arid gravel plains interrupted by isolated ranges and hills known as *inselbergs*.

Despite its barren aspect, the Namib actually supports a great deal of wildlife. The unique fauna of the Namib dunes has been the subject of numerous wildlife documentaries. A walk through the dunes at either Homeb or Sossusvlei, for example, will reveal traces of wildlife: the trails of sidewinder adders, dune lizards and Namib black beetles. For more on the animal residents of this severe environment, see The Dune Community boxed text on page 750.

house costs US$25/45, with breakfast and use of kitchen facilities. With half board, it's US$36/68.

The pleasantly located *Camp Gecko* (☎/fax (061) 222266; <toctrvl@nam.lia .net>), to the west, also lies on the Spreetshoogte Pass (D1275). Activities include desert drives, farm drives, photographic tours and hiking trails. Tented accommodation costs US$23 per person and half board is US$41. All safaris cost US$0.50 per kilometre.

South of Sesriem and west of the Maltahöhe road is the 140,000 hectare *Namib Rand Nature Reserve* (☎ (06632) 5230), the largest privately owned property in southern Africa. Accommodation ranges from basic camp sites to fully catered packages at Mwisho luxury tented camp. Most people come for the unique early-morning balloon flights over the dune sea, which cost US$246; full board accommodation and activities, with a balloon flight, costs US$341. A night at the Wolwedans Dune Camp, including meals and scenic drives, is US$134 per person. Three-day packages with fullboard, 'Dunehopper' charter flights from Windhoek and a flight over Sossusvlei cost US$1078 per person double occupancy. Walking trips on Die Duine Farm cost US$68/40 per night for foreigners/locals. Book through the Namib Travel Shop (☎ (061) 236720; fax 220102), PO Box 5048, Windhoek. Also on Die Duine Farm in the NamibRand Nature Reserve is Mark and Elinor Dürr's *Tok-Tokkie Guest House* (☎/fax (06638) ask for 5230), which offers inexpensive accommodation, one to four-day hikes and desert activities.

The delightfully quirky *Nubib Adventures* (☎ (06638) ask for 5713; fax (061) 240818), is run by a couple of oddballs nicknamed Sakki and Boesman (Beandré and Gideon). This budget option occupies a most intriguing setting 80km south of Sesriem on the horrid D826. Camping costs US$5; half board accommodation is US$45 per person; dorm beds are US$7, with breakfast; and a nine-bed farmhouse costs US$68. There's a bar, and meals or self-catering facilities are available. Activities include walking and guided desert and Nubib mountain hikes (US$100 for up to 12 people), donkey cart rides (US$7) and unique tours to Sossusvlei (US$75 takes you to the Witberg, where no other tour goes, but fitness is requisite).

For more options, see Maltahöhe in the Southern Namibia chapter.

### Places to Eat
Apart from the various accommodation options and the shop/restaurant at Solitaire, your only option is the small shop at the Sesriem office, which sells little more than crisps and cold drinks.

### Getting There & Away
You reach Sesriem via a signposted turn-off from the Maltahöhe-Solitaire road (C36). The 65km road south-west from Sesriem is good gravel (it's currently being tarred – with a special pink tar, believe it or not!) to within 4km of Sossusvlei, where it enters deep sand and requires 4WD. Visitors with lesser vehicles park at the 2x4 Car Park and walk the remaining distance, which takes about 1½ hours. There's petrol at Solitaire, Sesriem and a bush BP station 93km south of Sesriem on the D826.

# Southern Namibia

Southern Namibia takes in the vast expanses from Rehoboth south to the Orange River (which forms the South African border), east to the Botswana border and west to the diamond coast, encompassing everything from the rich cattle country of Namaland and the semi-desert of the Kalahari borders to the forbidden wilderness of the southern Namib and sensational Fish River Canyon. Other major attractions include Hardap Dam Recreation Resort and Game Park, Duwisib Castle, the Kokerboom forests, Brukkaros Crater and the bizarre Bavarian-style town of Lüderitz, which brims with colonial architecture.

## The Central Plateau

Namibia's Central Plateau is characterised by wide open country, and the region's widely spaced and typically uninspiring towns function mainly as commercial market centres. This is the country's richest karakul sheep and cattle ranching area, and around Mariental a growing range of citrus fruit and market vegetables is being cultivated under irrigation.

The region is bisected by Namibia's main north-south route, the B1, which stretches from Windhoek southwards towards the South African border. For most drivers, this excellent road is little more than a mesmerising broken white line stretching towards a receding horizon – a paradise for leadfoot drivers and cruise-control potatoes. Indeed, most of the Central Plateau's attractions lie off the main route and visitors with time and a vehicle will find plenty of intriguing and unspoilt possibilities.

### REHOBOTH
Rehoboth, the first town on the B1 south of Windhoek, lies just a stone's throw north of

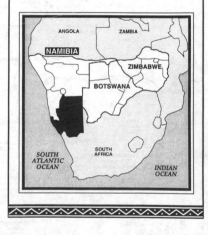

the Tropic of Capricorn. There's little to lure visitors, but it's generally more lively than other Namibian towns south of the Red Line, and the streets are normally thronged with people and activity.

### History
In the mid-19th century, the incumbent Nama were displaced by the Herero from the north. Rehoboth first developed around a Rhenish mission station founded in 1844

NAMIBIA

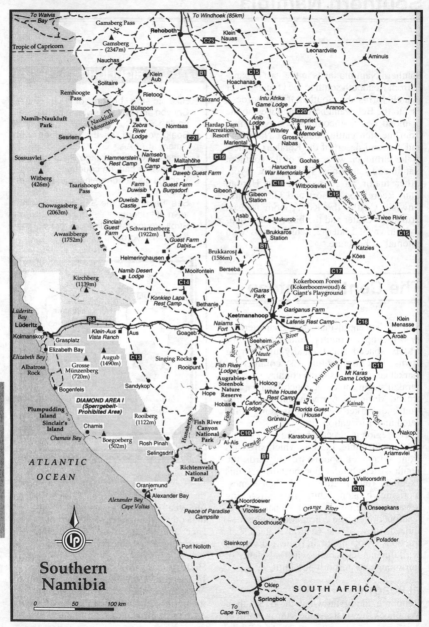

# Southern Namibia

by Heinrich Kleinschmidt, who named it after the biblical place of wide open spaces. Kleinschmidt and his mission were displaced in an 1864 attack by Jan Jonker Afrikaner; the missionary fled with his family to the German mission at Otjimbingwe, where he promptly died.

The Rehoboth mission was revived in the early 1870s by the Basters, an ethnic group of mixed Khoi-Khoi and Afrikaner origin, who had migrated north from the Cape under their leader Hermanus van Wyk. Their original plan had been to settle at the Orange River, but when the Cape government demanded proof of land ownership in the mid-1860s, they pushed north and set down stakes in Rehoboth. Permission to settle was given in exchange for an annual tribute of one horse each to the Nama, Afrikaners and Herero groups.

The Rehoboth Basters remain proud of both their heritage and their name, which literally means bastards. Never mind that the word is used as an insult elsewhere; to this independent, western-oriented group, it emphasises a proud ancestry. Recent attempts by the Basters to control traditional communal lands within a 10km radius of Rehoboth have met with defeat in the Supreme Court.

### Rehoboth Museum

The Rehoboth Museum (☎ (0627) 2954), beside the post office, is housed in the 1903 residence of the settlement's first colonial postmaster. The museum outlines the area's natural and cultural history and features a photographic exhibition of the mission station from 1893 to 1896, which was rebuilt by the Basters under Hermanus van Wyk.

Outside is a garden of local plants and examples of historic homes and transport. The museum is open Monday to Friday from 10 am to noon and 2 to 4 pm, and on Saturday to noon. Admission to the garden is US$2.

There's also an archaeological annexe at an Iron Age site, 10km from town, which can be visited by prior arrangement.

### Reho Spa

The Reho Spa complex surrounds a thermal spring and an elaborate spa complex complete with a 39°C thermal pool, bungalows and a camp site (see Places to Stay). The early Nama knew it as *aris* (smoke) after the steam which rose from the hot spring. Accommodation must be prebooked, but the spa is open to day visitors without bookings from 7 am to 6 pm. Admission costs US$3 plus US$0.50 to use the hot baths. Note that security isn't optimum; watch your valuables.

### Oanob Dam

The 2.7 sq km Oanob Dam, 10km west of Rehoboth, was completed in 1990 to provide the district's water supply. A lookout presents an impressive view of the dam and you'll find a picnic site and small exhibition outlining its history and construction. Several short walking tracks have also been laid out. The big attraction for locals is the entertainment complex, which features a casino, and the range of watersports available. Speedboats, water skis, jetskis, pedalos, canoes and inner tubes are available for hire. Picnic sites cost US$6 and there's a bar, restaurant and campground. The route is well signposted from the B1.

### Places to Stay

The *Reho Spa Recreation Resort* (☎ (0627) 2774) lies down a gravel road less than 1km off the main street; turn off near the church. You can choose between six-bed bungalows for US$57 or four/five-bed models for US$39/43. All units are self-catering. Camp sites for up to eight people cost US$18. Facilities include a cafeteria, swimming pool and thermal bath.

The nicer campground at *Oanob Dam* (☎ (0627) 522370; fax 522165; <oanob@nam.lia.net>) has sites for US$5 per vehicle and US$1 per person. On-site caravans for up to six people cost from US$9 to US$12, plus US$5 per person. Chalets are US$79 for up to four people, plus US$12 for each extra adult.

NAMIBIA

The basic *Rio Monte Hotel* (☎ (0627) 2161), near the railway station, has minimal facilities and charges US$18/21 for singles/doubles.

### Places to Eat
The *Reho Spa Restaurant* serves cheap and adequate food. In the town centre are *Sigi's à la Carte Restaurant* and the basic but locally popular *Dolphin Fish and Chips*.

### Getting There & Away
The Intercape Mainliner between Windhoek and South Africa stops at Rehoboth, as does the train between Windhoek and Keetmanshoop. Taxis south from Windhoek town centre to a good hitching spot cost around US$3.50. Alternatively, minibuses to Rehoboth leave about every 20 minutes from the Wernhill Park bus stop and cost US$2.

## MARIENTAL
Mariental is a small administrative and commercial centre and supports several economic endeavours, including ranching, an ostrich abattoir and large-scale irrigated farming (thanks to the Fish River and Hardap Dam). Crops include cotton, wheat, lucerne (alfalfa), maize, grapes, tomatoes and garden vegetables.

Mariental also remains a stronghold of the Nama people, who are mainly of Khoi-Khoi descent. It's a convenient place to refuel or take an overnight break, but don't expect any action; this is one of the most lethargic and lifeless places you'll ever see.

### History
Mariental's original Nama name was *Zaragaebia* (dusty). The current name, 'Maria's Valley', was that of the farm belonging to the area's first white farmer, Hermann Brandt. He'd purchased the land from Nama chief Hendrik Witbooi in 1890 and named it in honour of his wife, Anna Maria Mahler.

From 1903 to 1907, this area saw a great deal of action as the colonial and Nama forces engaged in battle after battle and

quite a few German civilians died in guerrilla raids. After the railway came through in 1912, Mariental residents petitioned for village status, but their hopes were dashed by the German surrender to the South African Defence Force in 1915. It wasn't until the construction of Namibia's first Dutch Reformed church in 1920 that Mariental was granted official status.

### Information
Believe it or not, Mariental has a tourist office. It's in the town hall, off Michael van Niekerk St, 1km from the town centre.

### Places to Stay
The nearest camp site is at Hardap Dam (see later in this section). The *Sandberg Hotel* (☎/fax (063) 242291), near the northern turn-off from the B1, has basic singles/doubles for US$23/32. The hotel also has a restaurant and bar. This place receives mixed reviews, but I've found it fairly friendly and helpful.

A block down Main St is the new *Mariental Hotel* (☎ (063) 242466; fax 242493), which presents a more plush option. Single/double accommodation here costs US$42/66.

The nicest choice is the tasteful and respectable *Guglhupf Cafe* (☎ (063) 240718; fax 242525) which charges US$25/36 for singles/doubles. It has a swimming pool, and the attached café serves excellent steaks and beef dishes.

Further out of town is the posh *Intu Afrika Game Lodge* (☎ (061) 248741; fax 226535). It lies on the Onze Rust Game Ranch, along the D1268, 44km north of the C20. Singles/doubles cost US$103/168 and chalets are US$114 per person, including full board and game drives. However, there is some controversy over their use of a !Kung San village as an attraction, especially considering what they charge for village visits and instruction on traditional lifestyles. Use your own judgement.

### Places to Eat
Apart from the hotel and guesthouse restau-

rants, there's little choice of eateries. Locals seem to love the *Wimpy* bar at the Engen petrol station on the Keetmanshoop side of town. The other Engen near the Sandberg Hotel has *Bambi's Takeaways* and the *Corducal Takeaways & Entertainment Centre* is somewhat of a local mainstay. The *Mariental Bakery* is next to the Caltex petrol station.

### Getting There & Away
**Bus** Buses stop at the Engen petrol station at the Keetmanshoop end of town. Intercape Mainliner has bus services four times weekly between South Africa and Windhoek. Minibuses run several times daily between Windhoek and Keetmanshoop, via Mariental.

The Star Line bus between Mariental and Walvis Bay (US$16, 12 hours) runs westbound on Monday at 7.30 am and eastbound on Tuesday at 8.30 am. It drops off supplies at various farms and calls in at Maltahöhe, Büllsport, Solitaire and Rostock.

**Train** Windhoek-Keetmanshoop rail services pass Mariental daily except Sunday at 1.18 am. Northbound, a train passes at 11.23 pm daily except Saturday. The business/economy class fare to Windhoek is US$10/7; to Keetmanshoop, it's US$9/6.

### HARDAP DAM RECREATION RESORT & GAME PARK
If there's one reason to visit Mariental, it's Hardap Dam, 15km north of town. The idea of siting a dam on the upper Fish River was first discussed in 1897 by German geologist Theodore Rehbock, but it was 63 years before a 39m dam wall was constructed to hold back a 25 sq km reservoir. The name is Nama for 'nipple', after the conical hills topped by dolerite knobs which dot the area.

Most holiday-makers come for the blue lake, which breaks up the arid plateau landscape and provides anglers with carp, barbel, mudfish and blue karpers. Entry permits cost US$3 per car and US$3 per person, entitling you to use the splendid swimming pool. Swimming in the lake isn't permitted.

### Visitor Centre
An appealing and unobtrusive visitor centre sits perched on a crag overlooking the dam and the surrounding landscape of sparse vegetation and sombre colours. The park office is open from sunrise to 1 pm and 2 pm to sunset. There's an information centre and an aquarium full of bored, anonymous fish from the lake. There's also a research establishment where MET studies the feasibility of fish breeding and commercial exploitation. Fishing licences are available here.

### Hardap Dam Game Park
The 80km of gravel roads west of the dam lead through the 25,000 hectare Hardap Dam Game Park, which harbours antelope, zebra, birds and small animals. There are few dangerous animals, so you may walk wherever you like. In the northern end of the reserve is a 15km loop walk with a short-cut across the middle which makes it into a 9km loop. It's not well-marked, so pay close attention to where you're going.

The vegetation is a combination of flat shrub savanna plains with stands of camelthorn, wild green-hair trees and buffalo thorn. You're bound to see kudu, gemsbok, springbok, ostrich and mountain zebra, and might even see an eland or red

---

#### Cheetahs Never Win
The Hardap Dam terrain is ideal for cheetah, and indeed, it once supported a large number of these big cats, but the rich game pickings caused a population explosion. The antelope numbers just couldn't take the strain and MET moved all the cheetah to other parks, which really does seem a bit drastic; they could have left a few!

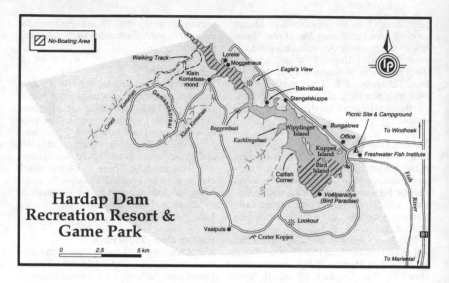

Hardap Dam Recreation Resort & Game Park

No-Boating Area

Walking Track

Lorelei
Moggelneus
Eagle's View
Klein Komatsas-mond
Bakvisbaai
Stengelskuppe
Boggembaai
Wipplinger Island
Bungalows
Office
Kuchlingsbaai
Kupper Island
Bird Island
Catfish Corner
Voëlparadys (Bird Paradise)
Vaalputs
Lookout
Crater Kopjes
Picnic Site & Campground
To Windhoek
Freshwater Fish Institute
Fish River
B1
To Mariental

Gross Komatsas
Gemsbokgraai
Klein Komatsas

0    2.5    5 km

hartebeest. The rocky kopjes support dassies and klipspringer and at the northern end of the park are three black rhino translocated from Damaraland in 1990.

The reserve and reservoir areas provide habitat for over 260 bird species, particularly water-loving birds: flamingoes, fish eagles, pelicans, spoonbills, Goliath herons and many varieties of migrants and bush dwellers. However, you may want to ignore the sign reading 'Voëlparadys' (Bird Paradise), which indicates a stand of dead camelthorn trees where a colony of white-breasted cormorants took up residence immediately after the dam filled up in 1963. When the water levels receded, the birds lost interest and went off in search of a new paradise.

### Places to Stay & Eat
Camp sites cost US$21 and two/five-bed bungalows are US$32/59. Other amenities include a shop, restaurant, kiosk, swimming pool and petrol station. The restaurant and pool both enjoy wonderful cliff-top views over the lake.

There are picnic sites, costing US$21 per

group, at the rest camp at Lorelei, near the north-western end of the lake, and at Crater Hills, near the southern boundary of the reserve.

### Getting There & Away
There's no public transport, but the entrance is only 6km from the B1 and there are no restrictions on walking. Just carry plenty of water. From sunrise to sunset, you can walk anywhere in the reserve, but camping is permitted only at the rest camp.

## STAMPRIET & GOCHAS
Thanks to lush artesian springs, the small settlement of Stampriet enjoys ideal conditions for growing fruit and vegetables. The water also attracts an inordinate amount of birdlife to this otherwise desert area. At the Gross Nabas farm, 25km south of Stampriet on the C15, a monument commemorates the battle fought from 2 to 4 January 1905, when colonial forces led by Lieutenant von Burgsdorff were defeated by Hendrik Witbooi's Nama resistance.

Gochas, whose Nama name means 'many candle-thorn trees', lies beside the

Auob River 53km south-east of Stampriet. On the C18 south-west of the village, towards Witbooisvlei, are war memorials commemorating battles on 3 and 5 January 1905, which took place on the Haruchas farm (☎ (06662) 1121) between the German troops of General Stuhlmann and the Nama under Simon Kooper. Phone in advance for an appointment to visit. A cemetery in the village bears graves of numerous German soldiers killed in these and other turn-of-the-century battles with the Nama resistance.

### Places to Stay & Eat

The only accommodation is the basic *Gochas Hotel* (☎ (06662) 44), which has an equally basic restaurant – and of course a bar. Singles/doubles cost US$20/37.

Midway between Mariental and Stampriet, 3km north of the C20, is *Anib Lodge* (☎ (063) 240529; fax 240516), PO Box 800, Mariental, run by Anka and Claus Schultz. This guest farm, which bills itself as 'your nest on the edge of the Kalahari', offers comfortable accommodation with private facilities, a swimming pool and good bird-watching opportunities in a secluded setting. For full board, they charge US$101/158.

The simple but comfortable *Auob Lodge* (☎/fax (06662) 39), amid the fossil Kalahari dunes 6km from Gochas, lies on an 8000 hectare farm on the banks of the Auob River. Single/double accommodation costs US$57/70.

### Getting There & Away

Star Line has return buses from Mariental to Gochas (US$5, three hours) on Tuesday and Wednesday mornings and to Stampriet (US$3, 1½ hours) on Monday, Thursday and Friday mornings.

### GIBEON

The former Rhenish mission station of Gibeon, 91km south of Mariental and 9km west of the B1, was founded by missionary Knauer beside the Gorego-re-abes spring (where zebras drink) in 1863. The mission

was named after the biblical character mentioned in the Old Testament book of Joshua.

In 1894, a German garrison was established on orders from Major Theodore Leutwein. While a fort was under construction, the troops were housed in the mission church. A kimberlite pipe was discovered here in the late 19th century, but brief attempts at diamond exploration were abandoned in the early 1900s.

As a result of the fierce battle of 27 April 1915, Gibeon's name will forever be associated with Germany's loss of Southern Namibia to the South African Defence Forces. The results are visible in the graveyard beside the Gibeon railway station, beyond the B1, 10km east of town.

Nowadays, Gibeon is best known for the meteorites which grace Windhoek's Post Street Mall. These 33 fragments of space rock – along with at least 44 more found within a 2500 sq km area around Gibeon – fell to earth in a single meteor shower sometime in the dim and distant past. Those discovered contain at least 90% iron.

### Getting There & Away

Star Line runs return buses from Mariental to Gibeon (US$3, two hours) on Wednesday and Friday at 2.30 pm.

### MUKUROB

The Mukurob, which was once a dramatically balanced stone pinnacle, collapsed on 8 December 1988 when seismic waves from the Armenian earthquake of 7 December reached Namibia. All that remains is a 1.5m-wide neck of rock on a pedestal, while bits of the 12m, 500-tonne rock-head lie scattered about.

The Mukurob was actually a remnant of the Weissrand sandstone formation which was shot through with vertical intrusions of softer rock material. When that material eroded, most of the remaining sandstone blocks collapsed, but this one remained balanced there for at least 50,000 years. The Nama name means 'look at the neck', probably in reference to the spindly pedestal on which it once rested. Afrikaners called it the

NAMIBIA

Vingerklip, or Finger Rock, and Anglo-Namibians knew it as the Finger of God. When the rock crashed down, white Namibians interpreted the event as a sign of divine discontent with the notion of Namibian independence. Blacks countered with the speculation that God had in fact held up a single finger *until* the prospect of Namibian independence!

### Getting There & Away

Turn east onto the D1066 from the B1 about 2km south of Asab; after 12km, turn right onto the D620 and continue 10km to the site.

## BRUKKAROS

The 2km-wide crater of the extinct volcano Brukkaros is plainly visible from the B1 between Mariental and Keetmanshoop. The name combines the Afrikaans words *broek* (trousers) and *karos* (leather apron), in deference to Brukkaros' Nama name, Geit-sigubeb, a traditional article of clothing worn by Nama women.

### History

Brukkaros was formed some 80 million years ago when a magma pipe came in contact with groundwater about 1km below the earth's surface. The superheated water vaporised and expanded, causing the surface to swell into a bulge 10km across and 500m high. This left space for more magma to intrude, which in turn heated more water and caused further swelling. It reached the point where something had to give – and something did. The resulting explosion caused the surface material and all the water to collapse into the magma pipe, setting off further explosions which ejected material from deep in the earth and deposited it around the gaping crater, forming a rim.

Before long, hot springs appeared in the crater, created a lake and deposited quartz and other minerals. Over the following millions of years, erosion removed all the surrounding material, leaving the 650m erosion-resistant plug we see today.

### Hiking

In the 1930s, a track was constructed to provide access to the Smithsonian Institute's sunspot-research post on the crater's western rim. This site was chosen for its preponderance of sunshine and phenomenally clear air. From the modern car park (accessible by 4WD), it's a 3.5km hike to the crater's southern entrance. Along the way, watch for the remarkable crystal formations embedded in the rock. As you approach the crater entrance, the trail traverses the wall of the crater's outflow canyon, high above an intermittent waterfall.

From the crater entrance, you can either head for the kokerbooms and crystal fields on the crater floor or follow the route, which turns sharply left and climbs to the abandoned research station on the rim. You'll still see bits of rubbish left behind when the station was abandoned. The walk takes at least 2½ hours each way. As usual, be sure to carry plenty of water.

### Places to Stay

The clear night skies make camping at Brukkaros a magical experience. There are several bare camp sites at the car park and along the road up to it, but in fact, camping is permitted anywhere in or around the crater. There's no water, so bring all you'll need.

### Getting There & Away

Brukkaros rises 35km west of Brukkaros Station on the B1. Follow the C98 west for 40km and turn north on the D3904 about 1km east of Berseba. It's then 18km to the car park.

## BERSEBA

The tiny Nama settlement of Berseba dates back to 1850 and now has around 1800 people. This is as lonely and forlorn a place as you could imagine, but it's worth a brief side trip from Brukkaros to see the proud church, the graveyard and the corrugated iron dome dwellings which appear to be unique in Namibia. No petrol is available.

## KEETMANSHOOP

Keetmanshoop, with 15,000 people, is the main crossroads of southern Namibia and a centre for the karakul wool industry. It has more petrol stations per capita than any other town in Namibia, which may hint at its main function for travellers.

### History

The original Keetmanshoop was a Nama settlement evocatively called Nugaoes (Nama for black mud), on the banks of the Swartmodder River (Afrikaans for black mud). A mission station was established in April 1866 by Reverend Johann Schröder of the Rhenish Mission Society at the behest of Nama people, who'd undergone a conversion to Christianity. When Reverend Schröder founded the town, it was named after the German industrialist and philanthropist Johann Keetmann, who funded the mission.

Schröder's successor, Reverend Thomas Fenchel, constructed the first mission station and church, then stayed on for 33 years. The church was swept away in an 1890 flood of black mud. Five years later, a new church was constructed and served the Christian community until 1930, when it was abandoned. Over the following years, it became a hang-out for squatters and suffered serious vandalism until 1960, when it was renovated. In 1978, it was declared a National Monument and now houses the town museum.

### Information

The Southern Tourist Forum office (☎ (063) 223316; fax 223813) in the municipal building is open Monday to Friday from 7.30 am to 12.30 pm and 2 to 5 pm and on Saturday from 9 to 11 am. It also sells a selection of Keetmanshoop postcards which will someday be collectors items.

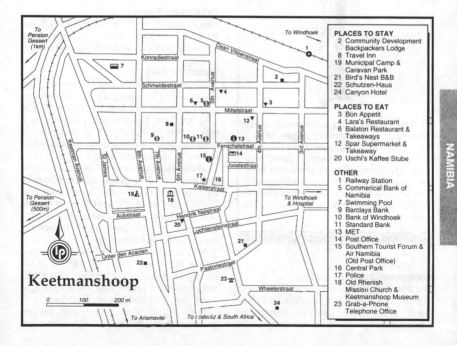

PLACES TO STAY
2  Community Development Backpackers Lodge
8  Travel Inn
19  Municipal Camp & Caravan Park
21  Bird's Nest B&B
22  Schutzen-Haus
24  Canyon Hotel

PLACES TO EAT
3  Bon Appetit
4  Lara's Restaurant
6  Balaton Restaurant & Takeaways
12  Spar Supermarket & Takeaway
20  Uschi's Kaffee Stube

OTHER
1  Railway Station
5  Commerical Bank of Namibia
7  Swimming Pool
9  Barclays Bank
10  Bank of Windhoek
11  Standard Bank
13  MET
14  Post Office
15  Southern Tourist Forum & Air Namibia (Old Post Office)
16  Central Park
17  Police
18  Old Rhenish Mission Church & Keetmanshoop Museum
23  Grab-a-Phone Telephone Office

Keetmanshoop

0    100    200 m

To Pension Gessert (1km)

To Windhoek

To Pension Gessert (500m)

To Windhoek & Hospital

To Ariamsvlei

To Lüderitz & South Africa

NAMIBIA

## Kokerbooms

Kokerbooms (*Aloe dichotoma*), or quiver trees, are widespread throughout southern Namibia and north-western South Africa. They are in fact aloes and can grow to heights of 8m. The name is derived from the lightweight branches, which were formerly used as quivers by San hunters. They removed the branches' fibrous heart, leaving a strong, hollow tube.

The slow-growing kokerbooms occur mainly on rocky plains or slopes, storing water in their succulent leaves and fibrous trunk and branches. Water loss through transpiration is prevented by a waxy coating on the leaves and branches. In June and July, their yellow blooms appear, lending bright spots of colour to the desert.

### Keetmanshoop Museum
The museum, which is housed in the 1895 Rhenish mission church, merits a look. Displays concentrate on the history of Keetmanshoop and there are lots of old photos and examples of early farming implements, an old wagon and a model of a traditional Nama home. The garden outside contains a variety of interesting local plants. It's open Monday to Friday from 7.30 am to 12.30 pm and 2 to 5 pm; and on Saturday from 9 to 11 am. Entry is free.

### Old Post Office
Keetmanshoop has several fine examples of colonial architecture. The most prominent is the Kaiserliches Postamt (the Imperial Post Office), on the corner of Fifth Laan and Fenchelstraat. It was designed by the architect Gottlieb Redecker and built in 1910 for the newly established post and telegraph services. The prominent gable on the front supported the telegraph mast and the remainder of the building housed postal officials, who still made deliveries by camel. It now houses Air Namibia and the Southern Tourist Forum tourist office.

### Organised Tours
Gondwana Tours (☎/fax (063) 223892), run by Mr Lothar Gessert, also organises more upmarket tours around southern Namibia.

### Places to Stay
The bougainvillea-decked *Municipal Camp & Caravan Park* charges US$3 per vehicle, US$3 per site and US$3 per person. The coin-operated laundry will probably be a welcome sight, but reports are that you still need old South African coins (this is bound to change in the near future).

The plush *Lafenis Rest Camp*, 5km south along the road to South Africa, has fully equipped two/four-bed bungalows for US$32/50. Camping costs US$3 per vehicle and US$3 per person. Guests may use the laundry and swimming pool, or opt for horse-riding and mini-golf.

You can also stay at the Kokerboomwoud on the *Gariganus Farm* (☎ (063) 222835) run by Coenie Nolte. Camping costs US$3 per person and simple single/double bungalows cost US$30/52, with breakfast. With full board, they're US$50 per person. *//Garas Park* (☎ (063) 223217) also has camp sites for US$3 per person, plus a US$1.50 entrance fee (for more on both options, see Around Keetmanshoop).

Another inexpensive option is the *Community Development Backpackers Lodge* (☎ (063) 223454), Gate 12, Schmeidestraat. Dormitory beds cost US$6 and rooms are US$14 per person. Meals are available for good rates. The friendly and recommended *Pension Gessert* (☎ (063) 228832 or 223892), at 138 Thirteenth Ave, 1km west of the town centre, has six singles/doubles for US$43/52, with breakfast.

The excellent value *Bird's Nest B&B* (☎ (063) 222906; fax 222261), 16 Pastoriestraat, has singles/doubles with private facilities, TV and phone for US$30/57, with breakfast. This is probably the best value in town, especially for Intercape Mainliner passengers, who arrive just around the corner.

There are also two hotels. The adequate *Travel Inn* (☎ (063) 223344; fax (064) 222138) on Sixth Ave has single/double aircon rooms for US$42/58, with breakfast and a carwash. Budget single rooms cost US$35 and family rooms for up to four people are US$85. Among the amenities are a restaurant, laundry, fax and a very quiet beer garden. Note that the pool is empty, most rooms lack air-con, and the colours on the 'colour' TVs are limited to black, white and grey.

The *Canyon Hotel* (☎ (063) 223361; fax 223714), which is a bit nicer and more popular, has rooms from US$54/84. The affiliated Gondwana Tours organises day trips to the Kokerboomwoud, Lüderitz and Fish River Canyon.

The *Schutzen-Haus*, 200m south of the Municipal Camp & Caravan Park, has simple double rooms with shower and toilet for US$30.

### Places to Eat

The popular *Lara's Restaurant*, on the corner of Fifth Ave and Schmeidestraat, may have strange decor and equally strange music, but the meals are recommended. You'll also find basic meals at the *Schutzen-Haus*, a German-style pub and restaurant 200m south of the municipal camp site. The bar boasts an unusual billiard table and there's also informal accommodation.

Another good option is the Hungarian-oriented *Balaton Restaurant & Takeaways* (☎ (063) 222539), which is open for breakfast, lunch and dinner. *Uschi's Kaffee Stube* (☎ (063) 222445), at the corner of Fifth Ave and Hendrik Nelstraat, serves breakfast, lunch, coffee, tea and afternoon snacks.

For coffee or snacks, the *Canyon Hotel* coffee shop is open 9 am to 7 pm. The hotel restaurant is open daily from 6.30 to 9 am, 12.30 to 2 pm and 7 to 10 pm. The Travel Inn restaurant is more expensive but not any better.

The *Spar supermarket* on the corner of Fourth Ave and Mittelstraat is open until late, and diagonally opposite is the *Bon Appetit* restaurant.

### Entertainment

Keetmanshoop doesn't rock around the clock, but what action there is focuses on Rosy's Inn, Bottle Store & Disco. There's also a 50m swimming pool on Konradiestraat at the north-west end of town. It's open weekdays from 10 am to 7 pm.

### Getting There & Away

**Air** Keetmanshoop's JG van der Wath Airport lies north-west of town on the D609. Air Namibia's thrice-weekly flights between Windhoek to Cape Town call in at Keetmanshoop en route. The one-way fare between Keetmanshoop and Windhoek is US$149.

**Bus** Intercape Mainliner buses between Windhoek and Cape Town pass the Du Toit BP petrol station in Keetmanshoop at 10 pm on Monday, Tuesday, Thursday and Saturday southbound and 12.45 am on Monday, Wednesday, Friday and Saturday northbound. The fare to or from Windhoek or Cape Town is US$39 and US$57, respectively.

Star Line (☎ (063) 292202) bus services to Lüderitz (US$9, 4¾ hours) depart daily

NAMIBIA

at 8 am, then leave Lüderitz for Keetman-shoop at 1 pm, returning to Berseba (US$3, two hours) on Monday, and to Bethanie (US$7, 3½ hours) and Helmeringhausen (US$8, six hours) on Tuesday and Friday.

**Train** Overnight trains run daily except Saturday between Windhoek and Keetman-shoop. The trip takes 11 hours and costs US$13/9 in business/economy. On Wednes-day and Saturday mornings, these trains continue to Ariamsvlei. For further infor-mation, phone Trans-Namib (☎ (0631) 292202).

**Hitching** Hitching is fairly easy on the B1 between Keetmanshoop and Windhoek or Grünau but there's less traffic between Keetmanshoop and Lüderitz. Hitchers to Fish River Canyon normally have the more luck getting to Ai-Ais via Grünau than to Hobas via Seeheim.

## AROUND KEETMANSHOOP
### Kokerboom Forest & Giant's Playground

Namibia's largest stand of kokerbooms or quivertrees (*Aloe dichotoma*; see the boxed text on page 774) lies at Kokerboomwoud, on the Gariganus Farm, 14km north-east of town. Day admission and access to the picnic facilities is US$3 per vehicle plus US$1.50 per person.

Visitors also have access to the Giant's Playground, a bizarre natural rock garden 5km away. The odd black formations were created by igneous intrusions into overlying sediments around 170 million years ago. When the surrounding sediments eroded away, all that remained was the more resis-tant *ysterklip* or 'iron rock' (which contains no iron – only basalt).

Camping and accommodation are avail-able; for details see Places to Stay under Keetmanshoop.

### //Garas Park

The small //Garas Park natural site is another place to stroll through the bush and see stands of kokerbooms and other aloes,

as well as intriguing rock formations. Ad-mission is US$1.50. It lies 22km north of Keetmanshoop, then 1km west. There are also camp sites; see Places to Stay under Keetmanshoop.

### Naute Dam

This large dam on the Löwen River, sur-rounded by low truncated hills, attracts large numbers of water birds and is mooted as a new recreation area and wildlife reserve. As yet, it's used mainly as a picnic site, although informal camping is permit-ted on the southern shore. Drive 30km west of Keetmanshoop on the B4 and turn south on the D545. After about 25km, you'll reach the dam. If the gate is locked, pick up a key from the attendant at the water plant, 1km from the dam.

### Naiams Fort

About 13km west of Seeheim (on the B4) is the Naiams farm, where a signpost indicates a 15 minute walk to the remains of a German fort built in 1906. The purpose of the fort was to prevent Nama attacks on travellers and freight using the Lüderitz route.

## GOAGEB

This dying little place has little to offer but petrol, which is very handy indeed if you're heading for Lüderitz from Fish River Canyon. Otherwise, there's nothing to detain you except a food market selling tinned pilchards (and nothing else!) and a bottle shop that's fortunately locked up most of the time.

## BETHANIE

Bethanie, one of Namibia's oldest settle-ments, was first called Klipfontein (rock spring in Afrikaans), but was later renamed Bethanien (this was eventually Anglicised to Bethanie), after the Jerusalem suburb. It was founded in 1814 by the London Mis-sionary Society, but oddly, the first missionary, Reverend Heinrich Schmelen, wasn't English but German. London had experienced a staffing crisis and recruited missionaries trained in Berlin. After seven years, the mission was abandoned due to tribal squabbling and although Schmelen attempted to revive it several times, he was thwarted by drought and in 1828 he left. Twelve years later, Bethanie was handed over to the Rhenish Missionary Society.

### Things to See

Schmelen's original 1814 mission station, now known as Schmelenhaus, occupied a one-storey cottage. It was burned when he left Bethanie in 1828, but was rebuilt in 1842 by the first Rhenish missionary, Reverend Hans Knudsen. The building now sits on the grounds of the Evangelical Lutheran Church and houses a museum that outlines the history of the mission using old photographs. If the building is locked, a notice on the door will tell you where to pick up a key.

Other historical buildings include an 1859 church, built by missionary Hermann Kreft. It once had two towers, but they started to collapse and were removed. It used to serve as a school, but is now dilapidated. It's currently scheduled to be restored, towers and all.

Also, have a look at the 1883 home of Captain Joseph Fredericks, the Nama chief who signed a treaty with the representatives of Adolf Lüderitz on 1 May 1883 for the sale of Angra Pequena, which is now Lüderitz. In this house in October of the following year, Captain Fredericks and the German Consul General, Dr Friedrich Nachtigal, signed a treaty of German protection over the entire territory.

### Places to Stay & Eat

The basic *Bethanie Hotel* (☎ (06362) 13) has six rooms and charges US$25/35. There's also a dining room. Barring that, try the enigmatically named *Bethanie Outfitters & Motors* (☎ (06362) 7, after hours (06362) 2; fax 87), where groups of up to seven people can camp for US$7. Room accommodation costs US$17/21 for a single/double, with breakfast.

Beside the Konkiep River, 35km from Bethanie on the C14, is the simple and inexpensive *Konkiep Lapa Rest Camp* (☎ (06362) ask for 1121), which has simple log cabins and camp sites with a kitchen, pool and braai facilities.

### Getting There & Away

The Bethanie turnoff is signposted on the B4, 140km west of Keetmanshoop. On Tuesday and Friday, a Star Line bus runs from Keetmanshoop (US$7, 3½ hours) at 7.30 am and returns at 4 pm. The daily Keetmanshoop-Lüderitz bus also calls in at Bethanie.

### DUWISIB CASTLE

Duwisib Castle, a curious baroque structure 70km south-west of Maltahöhe, was built in 1909 by Baron Captain Hans-Heinrich von Wolf, who came from Dresden and was descended from Saxon nobility. After the German-Nama war, he went home and married Jayta Humphries, the step-daughter of the US consul in Dresden. Upon their return to German South West Africa, the couple commissioned architect Willie Sander to design a home that would reflect von Wolf's commitment to the German military cause and closely resemble the Schutztruppe forts of Namutoni, Gibeon and Windhoek.

Although the stone was quarried nearby, much of the raw material for the home was imported from Germany, and it required 20 ox-wagons to transport it across the 640km of desert from Lüderitz. Artisans and masons were hired from as far away as Ireland, Denmark, Sweden and Italy. The result was a U-shaped castle with 22 rooms, suitably fortified and decorated with family portraits and military paraphernalia. Rather than windows, most rooms have only embrasures, emphasising von Wolf's apparent obsession with security.

In August 1914, the von Wolfs set sail for England in search of stud horses for their stables, but WWI broke out and their ship was diverted to Rio de Janeiro. Jayta (still a US citizen) found a passage on a Dutch ship to Holland, but von Wolf had to travel as a

NAMIBIA

stowaway. Eventually, they reached Germany, where von Wolf rejoined the army. In 1916, however, he was killed at the Battle of the Somme in France. Jayta settled in Switzerland and in 1920, sold the castle to a Swedish family, who in turn sold it in 1937 to the Duwisib Pty Ltd.

Duwisib Castle and the surrounding 50 hectares were transferred to the state in the late 1970s. It was opened to the public in 1991 and now houses an impressive collection of 18th and 19th century antiques and armour. It's open 8 am to 1 pm and 2 to 5 pm daily. Admission is US$3, with official guided tours.

### Places to Stay

The *MET camp sites* in the castle grounds cost US$18 per site and accommodate up to eight people. An adjoining kiosk sells refreshments, including snacks, coffee and cool drinks.

The friendly *Farm Duwisib* (☎ (06638) ask for 5304; fax (061) 220275), 300m from the castle, has self-catering rooms accommodating two/four people for US$14 to US$18 per person. Meals are available on request. Have a look at the old blacksmith shop, which will eventually become a restaurant.

### Getting There & Away

There's no public transport to Duwisib Castle. Coming from Helmeringhausen, head north on the C14 for 62km and turn north-west onto the D831. Continue for 27km, then turn west onto the D826 and it's a further for 15km to the castle.

### MALTAHÖHE

Maltahöhe, in the heart of a karakul ranching area, has little to recommend it apart from an excellent hotel. It's name means 'Malta's heights', in honour of Malta von Burgsdorff, who was the wife of Lieutenant von Burgsdorff. The lieutenant was made commander of the Gibeon district after the German-Nama war. Thanks to its convenient location on the back route between Lüderitz and Sossusvlei, the region supports a growing number of camps and guest farms.

### Things to See

The main sites of interest are historic graveyards. The one just east of town contains graves of Schutztruppe soldiers killed in the wars between the colonial forces and Nama leader Hendrik Witbooi. At the Nomtsas farm, 55km north of Maltahöhe, are the graves of the family and neighbours of Ernst Hermann, who were killed in 1904 by Hendrik Witbooi's rebels.

### Places to Stay & Eat

Maltahöhe's run-down and unguarded *camp site* should be used only in an emergency. The comfortable *Hotel Maltahöhe* (☎ (063) 293013; fax 293133), PO Box 20, Maltahöhe, run by Manfred and Gerda Schreiner, has single/double accommodation for US$25/41. The restaurant and bar are open in the evening, and the owner organises inexpensive day trips to Sossusvlei. It has repeatedly won Namibia's Hotel of the Year award.

On the C14 2km south of Maltahöhe you'll find the pleasant *Daweb Guest Farm* (☎/fax (0668) 3088 or (063) 293088), run by Rolf and Rosemarie Kirsten; the Nama name means tamarisk. Singles/doubles in the lovely Cape Dutch-style farmhouse cost US$62/101 with full board. Guests can learn about Namibian cattle-ranching or participate in guided walking and 4WD expeditions through the surrounding countryside.

More unusual is the *Namseb Rest Camp* (☎ (063) 293166; fax 293157), PO Box 76, Maltahöhe, in a spectacular setting on a private game ranch run by ostrich farmers Jan and Piens Bruwer. It lies at the edge of the Schwarzrand Range, on a back road about 5km north-west of Maltahöhe. The boxy and oddly conceived accommodation is set on a rise. Self-catering six-bed chalets cost US$106 and singles/doubles with full board cost US$40/60. Meals are available in the restaurant and yes, they do serve ostrich.

Midway between Maltahöhe and Sesriem, 1km east of the C36, is the *Hammerstein Rest Camp* (☎ (0633) 295111; <colourgem@iafrica.com>), run by Anton and Gerty Porteus. It has five self-catering bungalows and 10 double rooms for US$62 per person. With full board, they're US$85 per person.

### Getting There & Away
Star Line's bus between Mariental (US$4, four hours) and Walvis Bay (US$12, eight hours) passes Maltahöhe on Monday at 11.30 am heading west, and on Tuesday at 5.30 pm heading east. There's also a service from Mariental at 8 am on Wednesday and Friday, which returns at noon the same day.

## HELMERINGHAUSEN
Tiny Helmeringhausen is little more than a homestead, hotel and petrol station, which has been the property of the Hester family since 1919.

### Agricultural Museum
The village highlight is the idiosyncratic Agricultural Museum, which was established in 1984 by the Helmeringhausen Farming Association. It may appear to be a pile of discarded junk, but on closer inspection, you'll find all sorts of interesting old furniture and farm implements – wagons, machinery and tools collected from farms around the area. There's also an antique fire engine from Lüderitz. It's open daily and admission is free. Pick up a key from the hotel next door.

### Mooifontein
At the end of the 19th century, Mooifontein (beautiful spring – one of hundreds in southern Africa), 21km south-east of Helmeringhausen, was the site of a German garrison. The current farmhouse is a rebuilt version of the original barracks, which was prefabricated in Germany in 1899 and transferred to this site beside the Konkiep River. You can also visit the semi-circular cemetery for German soldiers who died

during the German-Nama war, which lasted from 1903 to 1907.

### Places to Stay
The friendly *Helmeringhausen Hotel* (☎ (06362) ask for 7; fax (061) 242934; <natron@icafe.com.na>), PO Box 21, Helmeringhausen, run by Heinz and Altna Vollertson, has B&B/full-board for US$21/30 per person. The food is excellent, the beer is always cold and they keep a well stocked cellar. However, even those who like game meat may feel uncomfortable in the restaurant, which is full of accusing stuffed animal heads. They also run day tours to the graveyard at Mooifontein and nearby rock paintings.

The two-star *Sinclair Guest Farm* (☎ (06362) 6503; fax (061) 226999), run by Gunther and Hannelore Hoffmann, lies 65km west of Helmeringhausen on the D407. The property was originally purchased from a Nama chief by two Scottish settlers in the 1870s to gain access to the historic copper mines. Legend has it that the price was two wheelbarrows of brandy. Later, they set up a farm and sold it to the grandparents of the present owner. Guests can now enjoy organised walks, drives and excursions to the ancient copper workings 3km from the farmhouse. The five rooms cost a very reasonable US$79 per person, with full board.

North-west of town, 7km off the C14, is the *Guest Farm Dabis* (☎ (06362) 6820; fax (061) 249937), on a karakul farm run by Jo and Heidi Gaugler. Single/double accommodation in comfortable rooms costs US$79/110 with meals and activities. Meals include bread, eggs, meat and vegetables produced on the farm. Activities feature hiking, wildlife-viewing, sunset drives and instruction on karakul farming.

### Getting There & Away
Star Line runs a bus between Keetmanshoop to Helmeringhausen, via Bethanie, on Thursday at 6.30 am. It leaves Helmeringhausen for the return journey at 2.30 pm the same day.

# The South Coast

The South Coast area includes the town of Lüderitz, which is rich in colonial architecture, the Sperrgebiet (forbidden Diamond Area) and the southern end of the Namib-Naukluft Park.

## AUS

Tranquil Aus, whose curious name means 'out' in German, lies 125km east of Lüderitz on the B4. After the Germans surrendered to the South African forces at Otavi on 9 July 1915, Aus became one of two internment camps for German military personnel. Military police and officers were sent to Okanjanje in the north and the non-commissioned officers went to Aus.

Soon, 1552 prisoners and 600 South African guards were housed in tents and exposed to poor conditions and extreme temperatures. However, these resourceful inmates turned to brickmaking and constructed houses, then sold the excess bricks to the guards for 10 shillings per 1000. The houses weren't opulent – roofs were tiled with unrolled food tins – but they did provide protection from the elements. The prisoners also built several wood stoves and eventually sunk bore holes to provide water and built barracks for the guards.

After the Treaty of Versailles, the camp was dismantled and by May 1919, it was closed. Virtually nothing remains, but some attempt has been made to reconstruct one of the brick houses. It lies 4km east of the village, down a gravel road, then to the right; there's now a national commemorative plaque.

If you understand Afrikaans, see the book *Aus 1915-1919*, which contains a map and covers the historical background. It's sold at the bookshop in Lüderitz.

### The Aus-Lüderitz Road

If you've come as far as Aus, chances are you're headed for Lüderitz. West of Aus, the southern Namib landscape is quite distinct from the flat gravel plains to the north. The pastel-coloured Awasib and Uri-Hauchab ranges rise from a greenish-grey plain though a mist of wind-blown sand and dust, and the effect is split between mesmerising and ethereal. About 10km out of Aus, start watching for feral desert horses (see the boxed text), which are possibly descended from the stud animals bred by Baron von Wolf of Duwisib Castle in the early 1900s.

### Places to Stay & Eat

Part of the appeal of rustic-looking Aus is the friendly and quaint *Bahnhof Hotel* (☎ (063332) 82), where musty but comfortable singles/doubles cost US$21/27. Larger rooms with bath are US$27/36. There's also an acceptable bar and restaurant.

The *petrol station* (☎ (063332) 29) has a small grocery, takeaway and coffee shop. It also oversees a four-bed self-catering flat, which rents for US$12 per person, and the *campground* over the road, which costs US$4 per person.

*Klein-Aus Vista Ranch* (☎ (063332) ask for 1103; fax (061) 272828), a few kilometres west of Aus, is an attraction in its own right. The big draws are hiking and horse-riding through astounding desert scenery. Accommodation on the 34km of trails is in mountain huts, but you've never seen mountain huts like these. With fridges, stoves, hot showers and design integrity, there's no roughing it. Six-person camp sites, with access to showers, braais, and laundry and kitchen facilities, cost US$9 plus US$1.50 per person. Hiking, with hut accommodation, is US$10 per person; self-catering accommodation is US$13; and with breakfast/half board (even out on the trail!), you'll pay US$18/25. With a traditional braai and potjie at the mountain huts, it's US$20. Klein-Aus also runs tours to the internment camp and graveyard in Aus.

In the desolate Tirasberge north of Aus is *Namib Desert Lodge* (☎ (06362) 6640; fax (061) 233597), PO Box 19, Aus, a German-oriented guest farm run by Renate and Walter Theile. Singles/doubles with full

## Feral Desert Horses

On the desert plains west of Aus live the world's only wild desert-dwelling horses. There are several theories about the origins of these eccentric equines. Some theorise that they are descended from German Schutztruppe cavalry horses abandoned during the South African invasion in 1915. Others claim that they were brought in by Nama raiders moving north from beyond the Orange River. Another tale asserts that they're descended from a load of shipwrecked horses en route from Europe to Australia. Others maintain they're descended from the stud stock of Baron Captain Hans-Heinrich von Wolf, the owner of Duwisib Castle, who set off for Germany in search of more horses but was killed in battle in France and never returned to Namibia.

These horses, whose bony and scruffy appearance belies their probable high-bred ancestry and apparent adaptation to the harsh conditions, are protected inside Diamond Area One and in years of good rains, they grow fat and their numbers increase. At present, the population fluctuates between 150 and 160, but there have never been more than 280 individuals. Their only source of water is Garub Pan, which is fed by an artificial bore hole.

If not for the efforts of Consolidated Diamond Mines (CDM) security officer Jan Coetzer, they would probably have been wiped out long ago. He recognised that they were clearly horses of high breeding and managed to secure funding to install the bore hole at Garub. At one stage, MET considered taming the horses for use on patrols in Etosha National Park, but nothing ever came of it. There have also been calls to exterminate them, by individuals citing possible damage to the desert environment or disruptions of gemsbok herds. So far, however, their potential for tourism has swept aside all counter-arguments and in Europe, various wildlife organisations have organised fund-raising drives to benefit the horses so, at the moment anyway, their future appears to be secure.

The horses may also be valuable for scientific purposes. The region is so dry that the horses are relatively free of diseases and parasites, and having been isolated for so long, they're unlikely to have any immunity to disease, making them ideal for immunity studies. Because they urinate less and are smaller than their supposed ancestors, they're able to go without water for up to five days. These adaptations may be valuable in helping scientists understand how animals cope with changing climatic conditions.

There's now a hide and a water hole where people can view the horses, as well as a small informative display. It lies 100km east of Lüderitz about 1.5km north of the highway.

board cost US$60 per person. Take the C13 north for 55km, then turn west on the D707 and continue for 60km to the farm.

### Getting There & Away

Star Line buses between Keetmanshoop and Lüderitz stop in Aus.

### LÜDERITZ

Lüderitz is a surreal colonial relic huddling against the barren, windswept Namib Desert coast. Scarcely touched by the 20th century, this remote town is what you might expect of a Bavarian *Dörfchen* (small village), with *Konditoreien*, coffee shops, half-timbered houses and a Lutheran church rising above the lesser buildings.

Here, the icy but clean South Atlantic supports seals, penguins and other marine life and the desolate beaches are also home to flamingoes and ostrich. The picturesque port supports a fleet of crayfish (rock lobster) boats, which are active during the season from November to April. Other industries include the harvest of seaweed and seagrass, which are mainly exported to Japan, and experimental oyster, mussel and prawn farms.

NAMIBIA

## History
Although artefacts have revealed that early Khoi-Khoi people passed by here, it's unlikely that they lived permanently in such an inhospitable spot.

On Christmas Day in 1487, Portuguese navigator Bartolomeu Dias and his fleet of three ships sailed down the coast he called the Areias do Inferno (sands of hell) into Lüderitz Bay, which he named Angra das Voltas (bay of the turnabouts), because he could only enter the bay by tacking cautiously into the wind. (Later, the bay came to be known – somewhat less creatively – as Angra Pequena, or little bay.) Here Dias sheltered from the weather for five days, and in July 1488, returned north from the Cape of Good Hope and, in keeping with Portuguese seafaring custom, erected a stone cross at Diaz Point near the entrance to the bay.

Apart from a brief 1677 attempt by Cornelius Wobma of the Dutch East India Company to trade with the Nama, it was over 300 years before Europeans returned to Lüderitz. In 1793, however, faced with possible rival interests, the Dutch governor of the Cape sent Captain Duminy in his ship *Meermin* to annex Angra Pequena and its surrounding islands.

Over the next half century, Dutch whalers operated there and the offshore islands became a rich source of guano. Between 1844 and 1848, hundreds of thousands of tonnes of guano were scraped off the most productive islands. The rich pickings attracted more guano collectors than the islands could support and inevitably, clashes occurred. There are reports that initially, the various groups lobbed penguin eggs at each other to prevent perceived infringements of collection rights. When they graduated to firearms, a British warship was dispatched to restore order and shortly thereafter, the British administration in the Cape sent Captain Alexander in his ship, the *Star*, to annex Angra Pequena and all the guano islands for Britain's Cape Colony.

On 9 April 1883, Heinrich Vogelsang, under orders of Bremen merchant Adolf Lüderitz, entered into a treaty with Nama chief Joseph Fredericks. It granted Vogelsang rights to lands within a five-mile radius of Angra Pequena in exchange for £100 sterling and 60 rifles; for a further £500 and another 60 rifles, he also purchased a 20-mile-wide coastal strip from the Orange River to the 26th parallel.

Later that year, Adolf Lüderitz himself made an appearance and on 24 April 1884, on his recommendation, the German chancellor Otto von Bismarck designated South West Africa a protectorate of the German Empire. In October 1886, on the verge of bankruptcy, Adolf Lüderitz sailed south to the Orange River in search of business prospects, but on the way back, he went missing at sea and was never seen again.

In 1904, during the German-Nama war, Lüderitz was used as a prisoner of war camp and two years later, the railway line was completed to Keetmanshoop. On 1 November 1909, after the discovery of diamonds in the desert (see the boxed text) had brought growth and prosperity to the remote outpost, Lüderitz was officially granted town status.

## Information
**Tourist Office** The Lüderitz Foundation tourist office (☎ (063) 202532), in the Karaman Weavery at the top of Bismarck Strasse, does an excellent job. It's open from 8.30 am to noon and 2 to 4 pm weekdays, and until noon on Saturday. The very helpful MET office is open weekdays from 8 am to 1 pm and to 2 to 5 pm, and on Saturday from 8 am to noon.

**Money** Several major banks have branches in Bismarck Strasse.

**Post & Communications** The post office on Bismarck Strasse has facilities for international calls.

**Bookshops** The Lüderitzbuchter Boekwinkel sells newspapers, jewellery and even a few books. The Tailings Shop in town sells used paperbacks and the Kolmanskop Cafeteria in Kolmanskop (see Around Lüderitz later in this section) has a selection of historic German novels and modern German pulp fiction.

**Laundry** At Lüderitz Laundry, washing and folding costs US$2 per kg. Add ironing and it's US$3.50. It's on Wagenbauer St, one block west of the southern end of Bismarck St.

## Diamond Dementia in the Desert

Although diamonds were discovered along the Orange River in South Africa as early as 1866, and had also turned up on guano workings taken from offshore islands around Lüderitz, it didn't seem to occur to anyone that the desert sands around Lüderitz might also harbour a bit of crystal carbon.

In May 1908, however, railway worker Zacharias Lewala found a shiny stone along the railway line near Grasplatz and took it to his employer August Stauch, who knew exactly what it was. Stauch took immediate interest and to his elation, the state geologist Dr Range confirmed that it was indeed a diamond. Stauch applied for a prospecting licence from the Deutsche Koloniale Gesellschaft and set up his own mining concern, the Deutsche Diamanten Gesellschaft, to begin exploiting the presumed wealth.

This sparked off a diamond frenzy, and hordes of prospectors descended upon Lüderitz in hopes of exploiting the fabulous wealth that lay buried in the sands, awaiting to be uncovered. As a result, Lüderitz was soon rolling in money, and service facilities sprang up to accommodate the growing population. In September 1908, after the diamond mania had got well and truly out of control, the German government intervened and proclaimed the Sperrgebiet. This 'forbidden area' extended from 26°S latitude southward to the Orange River mouth, and stretched inland for 100km. Future independent prospecting was prohibited and those who'd already staked their claims were forced to form mining companies. In February 1909, a Diamond Board was formed to broker all diamond sales.

After WWI, the world diamond market was so depressed that in 1920, Ernst Oppenheimer of the Anglo-American Corporation was able to purchase Stauch's company, along with eight other companies which were still producing, and combined them to form the Consolidated Diamond Mines, or CDM.

During WWI, however, Lüderitz was occupied by South African forces and all white residents were hauled off to POW camps in South Africa. They were later permitted to return, but during their absence, the town had been ransacked. After the war, all diamond interests in the former German territory were taken over by a new CDM, a subsidiary of De Beers South Africa, which set up its headquarters at Kolmanskop. In 1928, however, rich diamond fields were discovered around the mouth of the Orange River and, in 1944, the CDM headquarters was transferred south to the purpose-built company town of Oranjemund. Kolmanskop's last inhabitants – including some transport staff and hospital personnel – finally left in 1956 and the dunes have been encroaching ever since.

As a footnote, in 1994 competition presented itself to CDM in the form of a small British-Canadian company, the Namibian Minerals Corporation (NAMCO). The Namibian government awarded NAMCO offshore diamond-mining concessions at Lüderitz and Hottentots Bay, which were estimated to hold a total of 27 million carats at a value of US$4 billion. The diamonds are recovered by vacuuming the diamondiferous sands beneath the sea bed. It remains to be seen whether the yield will stand up to the projections but if so, De Beers may lose its stranglehold on the market and it will have a significant effect on both the diamond market and prices.

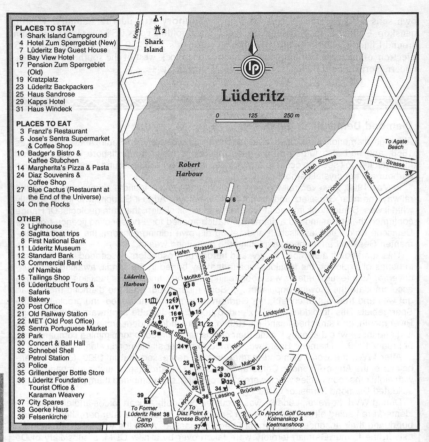

**PLACES TO STAY**
1 Shark Island Campground
4 Hotel Zum Sperrgebiet (New)
7 Lüderitz Bay Guest House
9 Bay View Hotel
17 Pension Zum Sperrgebiet (Old)
19 Kratzplatz
23 Lüderitz Backpackers
25 Haus Sandrose
29 Kapps Hotel
31 Haus Windeck

**PLACES TO EAT**
3 Franzl's Restaurant
5 Jose's Sentra Supermarket & Coffee Shop
10 Badger's Bistro & Kaffee Stubchen
14 Margherita's Pizza & Pasta
24 Diaz Souvenirs & Coffee Shop
27 Blue Cactus (Restaurant at the End of the Universe)
34 On the Rocks

**OTHER**
2 Lighthouse
6 Sagitta boat trips
8 First National Bank
11 Lüderitz Museum
12 Standard Bank
13 Commercial Bank of Namibia
15 Tailings Shop
16 Lüderitzbucht Tours & Safaris
18 Bakery
20 Post Office
21 Old Railway Station
22 MET (Old Post Office)
26 Sentra Portuguese Market
28 Park
30 Concert & Ball Hall
32 Schnebel Shell Petrol Station
33 Police
35 Grillenberger Bottle Store
36 Lüderitz Foundation Tourist Office & Karaman Weavery
37 City Spares
38 Goerke Haus
39 Felsenkirche

**Lüderitz**

0   125   250 m

**Vehicle Repairs** Your best bet for spares and repairs is City Spares, at the top of Bismarck Strasse.

**Dangers & Annoyances** Be sure to stay well clear of the Diamond Area 1 or Sperrgebiet (which is German for forbidden area). The northern boundary of this region is formed by the B4 and extends nearly as far east as Aus. The boundary of the Sperrgebiet is patrolled by some fairly ruthless characters and trespassers will definitely be prosecuted.

**Felsenkirche**
The prominent Evangelical Lutheran church, Felsenkirche, dominates Lüderitz from high on Diamond Hill. Lüderitz first petitioned for a church as early as 1906, and due to the German-Nama war, the railway and the discovery of diamonds, by 1909 the population was sufficient to bear the costs. The building was designed by Albert Bause, who implemented the Victorian influences he'd seen in the Cape. With assistance from private donors in Germany, construction began in late 1911 and was

completed the following year. The brilliant stained-glass panel over the altar was donated by Kaiser Wilhelm II himself and the Bible was a gift from his wife.

You can visit Felsenkirche on Monday to Saturday from 6 to 7 pm (from 5 to 6 pm in winter). This is the best time to see the late sun shining through the extraordinary stained-glass work over the altar and every evening a long and hearty spiel on the history of the church and the town is delivered in German to a large audience. You can arrange to visit at other times by phoning Mr Schröder (☎ (063) 202381).

### Lüderitz Museum
The Lüderitz Museum (☎ (063) 202582) on Diaz Strasse contains information on the town's history, including displays on natural history, local indigenous groups, Bartolomeu Dias and the diamond-mining industry. It's open weekdays from 3.30 to 5 pm in the winter and 4.30 to 6 pm in the summer, or at other times by phoning (☎ (063) 202312). Admission is US$1.

### Colonial Architecture
Lüderitz is chock-a-block with colonial buildings and every view reveals something interesting. The curiously intriguing architecture, which mixes German Imperial and Art-Nouveau styles (check out the odd little Concert & Ball Hall), makes this bizarre little town appear even more other-worldly.

### Goerke Haus
Lieutenant Hans Goerke arrived in Swakopmund with the Schutztruppe in 1904 and was later posted to Lüderitz, where he served as a diamond company manager. His home, which was designed by architect Otto Ertl and constructed in 1910 on Diamond Hill, was one of the town's most extravagant.

Goerke left for Germany in 1912 and eight years later, his home was purchased by the newly formed Consolidated Diamond Mines (CDM) to house their chief engineer. When the CDM headquarters was transferred to Oranjemund in 1944, the house was sold to the government and

occupied by the resident Lüderitz magistrate. In 1981, however, the magistrate was shifted to Keetmanshoop and the house so desperately needed repair that it was sold back to CDM for a token sum of R10 on condition that it be renovated.

They did an admirable job and now this amazing blend of Art Nouveau elements and period furnishings is open to the public as a window into the more garish side of the town's past. The house is open weekdays from 2 to 3 pm and on weekends from 4 to 5 pm. Admission is US$1.50.

### Old Railway Station
The imposing Lüderitz railway station sits on the corner of Bahnhof and Bismarck Strasse. The original building was completed in 1907 – along with the railway line itself, but with the discovery of diamonds, the facilities became swamped and a new station was commissioned in 1912 to handle the increased traffic. It was designed by state architect Lohse and completed two years later.

### Old Post Office
The old post office was originally designed by railway commissioner Oswald Reinhardt, but before the building was constructed his successor added a first floor and a tower. Construction was completed in 1908; it now houses the MET.

### Activities
A most unusual activity is to dig for the lovely crystals of calcium sulphate and gypsum known as sand roses, which develop when moisture seeps into the sand and causes it to adhere and crystallise into flowery shapes. MET issues US$3 digging permits which are valid for a two hour dig and good for up to three sand roses or a total weight of 1.5kg. You can't use any hard tools lest you damage other buried specimens. Diggers must be accompanied by an MET official.

Believe it or not, there's a golf course 5km outside the town, near the airport. However, it isn't exactly green and there is no shortage of sand traps. It's open daily for golf, but the clubhouse opens only on Wednesday and Friday evenings after 6 pm, and all day on Saturday.

### Organised Tours

Sailing trips on the single-masted yacht *Sagitta* (☎ (063) 202170) to the Cape fur-seal sanctuary at Diaz Point leave the harbour jetty daily, weather permitting. The trips last two to three hours and cost US$17. If the seas are calm, you can also include the penguin sanctuary on Halifax Island for an additional US$6. Take warm gear.

Town tours and trips to Agate Beach, Diaz Point and the Sperrgebiet are offered by Lüderitzbucht Safaris & Tours (☎ (063) 202719; fax 202863). In addition to Kolmanskop, you can visit Elizabeth Bay, the Cape fur-seal colony at Atlas Bay and the Bogenfels. Because CDM permits are required, you must book at least 24 hours in advance through its office near the old Pension Zum Sperrgebiet.

### Places to Stay

The town's beautifully situated camp site, *Shark Island*, is also one of the world's windiest and most exposed. The island is connected to the mainland by a causeway 1km north of town. Camping costs US$14 for up to eight people.

Kirsten and Toya's *Lüderitz Backpackers* (☎ (063) 203632; fax 202000), at 7 Schinz Strasse, has dorm beds for US$8. The dorm is a real novelty, as you have to enter through the bathroom! Double rooms cost US$18 and laundry is US$6 per load. It's friendly and highly recommended.

Mrs van Bach's rustic *Haus Windeck* (☎ (063) 203370; fax 203306), at 6 Mabel Strasse, has simple self-catering accommodation for US$17 per person. Kristina Looser's *Haus Sandrose* costs the same. The informal *Kratzplatz* (☎/fax (063) 202458), run by Monica Kratz at 5 Nachtigal Strasse, charges US$21/32 for single/double rooms.

The friendly *Lüderitz Bay Guest House* (☎ (063) 203347), housed in a colonial building near the harbour, has homey German-style singles/doubles with shared facilities starting at US$27/41, with use of kitchen facilities. The self-catering flat costs US$20 per person, with a minimum of three people.

The old *Pension Zum Sperrgebiet* (☎ (063) 202856; fax 202976) has recently expanded and lost a bit of its charm, but it enjoys a central location and a measure of old German-style luxury. Singles/doubles cost US$36/68 with breakfast. The new *Hotel Zum Sperrgebiet* (☎ (063) 203411; fax 203414), at the corner of Woermann Strasse and Göring Strasse (now here's a street name that's ripe for changing!), charges US$49/90. It boasts a swimming pool, terraces and even a banana tree, and is a natural favourite with German visitors.

The two main hotels in Lüderitz are still owned by descendants of the original Lüderitz family. The *Bay View* (☎ (063) 202288; fax 202402) complex has 30 rooms opening from shady courtyards; there's also a pool. Cool and airy singles/doubles cost US$43/73. Nearby is the affiliated *Kapps Hotel* (☎ (063) 202345; fax 202402), which charges US$37/61 for a single/double room. This is the town's oldest hotel.

### Places to Eat

If the sea has been bountiful, the *Bay View* and *Kapps* hotels serve up the catch of the day; specialities include crayfish, local oysters and kingklip. If the luck hasn't been running, you get frozen fish. The Bay View has two eateries: *Ray's Cafe* on the ground floor and the *Bahnhof Ocean View Bar/ Restaurant* upstairs.

A great place for lunch is *Badger's Bistro* which serves great burgers, toasted sandwiches, seafood specials, soup, salad and other light meals. It's open weekdays from 9 am to midnight and Saturday from 9 am to 2 pm and 6 pm to midnight. The *Kaffee Stubchen* coffee shop upstairs serves coffee and sweet snacks. The nearby *Margherita's Pizza & Pasta* provides a recommended Italian option.

The *Diaz Souvenirs & Coffee Shop* serves excellent toasted sandwiches, light meals, coffee and cakes. It's open weekdays from 7.30 am to 5 pm, Saturday from 7.30 am to 1 pm and 3 to 5 pm and on Sunday from 3 to 5 pm.

The funky *Blue Cactus Pub & Grill*, alias 'Restaurant at the End of the Universe', serves up alcohol, steak and seafood, including a four-lobster tail special for US$27. The food and atmosphere are very agreeable.

*On the Rocks* (☎ (063) 203110), next to the Shell petrol station, specialises in seafood and beef dishes, and serves the cheapest and best crayfish in town. It's open daily except Wednesday from 7 pm. At the stark north end of town is the good-value *Franzl's Restaurant* (☎ (063) 202292), which is popular with local patrons; it specialises in seafood and Bavarian cuisine, but also does lamb and game from the owners' farm near Bethanie. Don't miss the milkshakes!

For self-catering, there's a *Spar Market*, and also the *Sentra Portuguese Market* near the top of Bismarck Strasse. In good Portuguese tradition, the latter closes from 1.30 to 4 pm. The friendliest place to buy alcohol is Mr Crispin Clay's *Grillenberger Bottle Store*.

### Entertainment
The Hotel Kapps skittle alley remains bizarrely segregated. It's open to women on Monday evenings and to men on Tuesday and Thursday.

### Things to Buy
The Karaman Weavery (☎ (063) 202272), at 25 Bismarck Strasse, is certainly worth visiting. It produces high-quality rugs and garments, which are woven in desert pastel colours with Namibian flora and fauna as favoured designs. It also specialises in glasswork and other crafts. It accepts special orders and posts them worldwide. Visitors are welcome Monday to Friday from 8 am to 1 pm and 2 to 7 pm, and on weekends by arrangement.

Diaz Souvenirs in the town centre has a range of kitsch curios and T-shirts.

### Getting There & Away
**Air** Air Namibia flies four times weekly between Windhoek, Swakopmund and Lüderitz. It also flies four times weekly from Windhoek to Cape Town, via Lüderitz and Alexander Bay (South Africa).

**Bus** The Star Line (☎ (063) 312875) bus from Keetmanshoop (US$9, 4¾ hours) departs daily at 8 am. It returns from Lüderitz daily at 1 pm.

**Car & Motorcycle** Lüderitz is worth the 300km trip from Keetmanshoop, via the B4, which is all tarred. Between Aus and the coast, the road crosses the desolate southern Namib; to the south lies the forbidden Diamond Area 1. When the wind blows – which is most of the time – the final 10km into Lüderitz may be blocked by the barchan dunefield which seems bent upon crossing the road. The drifts pile quite high before the road crews clean them off and conditions do get hazardous, especially if it's foggy.

If you're considering a dune buggy trip from Lüderitz through the Namib Desert to Sossusvlei, note that a permit to do so takes at least 1½ years to process and you need a very good reason to want one. So far, the only people allowed through have been tourist office film crews making promotional videos to be shown abroad. (Is it just me or does it seem odd to promote tourism in Namibia with scenes of places off-limits to tourists?)

### Getting Around
There's a limited taxi service between the airport and the town centre.

### AROUND LÜDERITZ
#### Kolmanskop
A popular excursion from Lüderitz is to the ghost town of the former diamond-mining centre of Kolmanskop, which was named after an early Afrikaner trekker, Jani Kolman, whose ox-wagon became bogged in the sand there. Kolmanskop once boasted a casino, skittle alley and theatre with fine

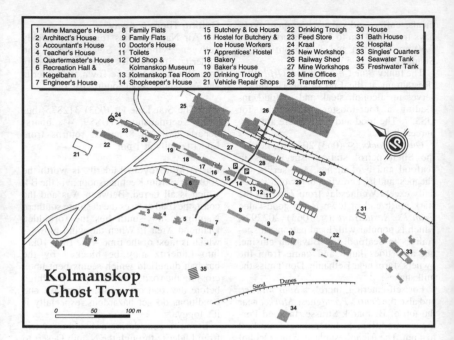

| | | | |
|---|---|---|---|
| 1 Mine Manager's House | 8 Family Flats | 15 Butchery & Ice House | 22 Drinking Trough | 30 House |
| 2 Architect's House | 9 Family Flats | 16 Hostel for Butchery & | 23 Feed Store | 31 Bath House |
| 3 Accountant's House | 10 Doctor's House | Ice House Workers | 24 Kraal | 32 Hospital |
| 4 Teacher's House | 11 Toilets | 17 Apprentices' Hostel | 25 New Workshop | 33 Singles' Quarters |
| 5 Quartermaster's House | 12 Old Shop & | 18 Bakery | 26 Railway Shed | 34 Seawater Tank |
| 6 Recreation Hall & | Kolmanskop Museum | 19 Baker's House | 27 Mine Workshops | 35 Freshwater Tank |
| Kegelbahn | 13 Kolmanskop Tea Room | 20 Drinking Trough | 28 Mine Offices | |
| 7 Engineer's House | 14 Shopkeeper's House | 21 Vehicle Repair Shops | 29 Transformer | |

## Kolmanskop Ghost Town

acoustics, but the slump in diamond sales after WWI and the discovery of richer deposits at Oranjemund ended its heyday and it was deserted by 1956. Some buildings have been restored, but many have already been invaded by the dunes and the ghost-town atmosphere remains.

**Information** Permits to visit Kolmanskop are sold for US$4 from Lüderitzbucht Tours & Safaris (☎ (063) 202719) in Lüderitz. Tours are conducted in English and German from Monday to Saturday at 9.30 and 10.45 am, and on Sunday at 10 am. During the high season, there may be additional tours at 2 pm. Visitors must provide their own transport from town. To photograph the town at other times of day, you can purchase a special 'sunrise to sunset' permit for US$6.

Before and after your tour, you're welcome to visit the impressive museum,

which contains relics and information on the history of diamond-mining in Namibia. Also impressive is the display on Oranjemund, the boom town to the south that supplanted Kolmanskop as the CDM headquarters and turned it into a ghost town.

The tea room in Kolmanskop serves unimpressive cakes and chicory coffee (which seems unfathomable for a German-Namibian enterprise) until noon.

### Elizabeth Bay

In 1986, CDM again began prospecting in the northern Sperrgebiet and found heavy diamond concentrations around Elizabeth Bay, 30km south of Kolmanskop. Although the suspected 2.5 million carat diamond deposits weren't expected to last more than 10 years, CDM installed a full-scale operation. However, because it was so near Lüderitz, the company opted not to build on-site housing, but rather to provide daily worker transport from town.

Half-day tours to Elizabeth Bay are available from Lüderitzbucht Tours & Safaris. Prices start at US$23 and also take in Kolmanskop and the Atlas Bay Cape fur seal colony.

### Bogenfels

A third of the way down the Forbidden Coast between Lüderitz and Oranjemund is the 55m natural sea arch known as Bogenfels (bow rock), which has only recently been opened to the public. The only access to this amazing spot is with Lüderitzbucht Tours & Safaris. Bogenfels tours also take in the mining ghost town of Pomona, the Maerchental Valley, the Bogenfels ghost town and a large cave near the arch itself. Tours cost US$68, with lunch and permits.

### Radford Bay

Radford Bay was named after David Radford, the first European settler to live there. As there was no water, he survived by collecting the dews created by the heavy

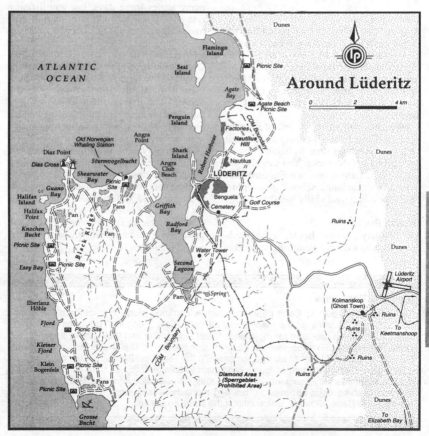

coastal fog. The oyster farm in Radford Bay is open Monday to Friday from 10 am to noon.

## Sturmvogelbucht

This picturesque and relatively calm bay has a lovely beach and is viable for swimming, but the water temperature would only be amenable to a polar bear. The 1914 Norwegian whaling station is little more than a rusty ruin but the salty pan just inland, which appears to be iced over, merits a quick stop. It's also a pleasant spot for a braai.

## Diaz Point

At Diaz Point, 22km by road from Lüderitz, is a lovely classic lighthouse and a replica of a cross erected in July 1488 by Portuguese navigator Bartolomeu Dias on his return voyage from the Cape of Good Hope. Portions of the original cross have been dispersed as far as Lisbon, Berlin and Cape Town.

From the point, there's a view of a nearby sea-lion (Cape fur seal) colony and jackass penguins are often seen frolicking, diving and surfing off the rocks. You can also see cormorants, flamingoes, wading birds and even the occasional school of dolphin. Dress for windy and chilly weather.

## Grosse Bucht

The 'big bay', Grosse Bucht, at the southern end of the Lüderitz Peninsula, is another wild and scenic beach. This normally cold, windy spot is favoured by flocks of flamingoes, which feed in the tidal pools. It's also the site of a small but picturesque shipwreck on the beach. Just a few kilometres up the coast is Klein Bogenfels, a small rock arch beside the sea. When the wind isn't blowing a gale, it makes a pleasant picnic spot.

## Agate Bay

North of Lüderitz, there is the wonderful beach at Agate Bay, which is made of tailings from diamond workings. There aren't many agates these days, but you'll find a fine sand consisting partially of tiny grey mica chips.

## ORANJEMUND

Oranjemund, in the Sperrgebiet at the mouth of the Orange River, owes its existence to diamonds. So great was its wealth that in 1944, it supplanted Kolmanskop as the Consolidated Diamond Mines headquarters. With a population of 8000, it's now an archetypal company town, with 100% employment, subsidised housing and medical care for workers and their families. Despite its desert location, the company maintains a golf course and large areas of green parkland. In fact, CDM now accounts for 90% of the Namibian government's tax revenue, which explains why CDM is still protected from competition and the Sperrgebiet continues to exist.

---

## Jackass Penguins

The jackass penguin or Cape penguin, which is common along the southern Namibian coast, lives in colonies on the many rocky offshore islets. Penguins' wings have evolved into flippers which are used for rapid underwater locomotion and their stocky appearance belies their ability to manoeuvre gracefully through the water. The skin is insulated against the cold water by a layer of air trapped beneath the feathers. Penguins also have supraorbital glands which excrete salts, allowing them to take their liquids from salt water.

Like Australia's fairy penguins, jackass penguins breed twice annually. They produce an average of three eggs per season, but egg mortality is fairly high. The penguins' main enemies are Cape fur seals, which inhabit the same coastline.

All Oranjemund visitors must have a permit from CDM and as yet, there's no real tourism. Applications must be made at least a month in advance of your intended visit and should be accompanied by a police affidavit stating that you've never been convicted of a serious crime. Normally, permits are issued only to those who have business in the town.

Security is so strict that broken-down equipment used in the mining operations may never leave the site, lest it be used to smuggle diamonds outside the fence. Despite all this, a fair number of stolen diamonds manage to reach the illicit market. Thieves come up with some ingenious methods of smuggling the diamonds over the security fence, including carrier pigeons, discarded rubbish and even tunnels.

### Sperrgebiet Museum
If you do have reason to visit, don't miss the Sperrgebiet Museum (☎ (063332) 2183), which contains exhibits and relics from Sperrgebiet ghost towns, as well as background on natural history – particularly fossils, diamonds and minerals.

### Getting There & Away
Oranjemund's airport is across the river in Alexander Bay, South Africa. The town's only road access is also via Alexander Bay. Air Namibia has four flights weekly to and from Lüderitz, Swakopmund, Windhoek and Cape Town.

# The Far South

Set in the angle between South Africa's two most remote quarters, Namaqualand and the Kalahari, Namibia's bleak southern tip exudes a sense of isolation from whichever direction you approach. Travelling along the highway, the seemingly endless desert plains stretch to the horizon in all directions. You can imagine how surprising it is

to suddenly encounter the startling and spellbinding Fish River Canyon, which forms an enormous gash across the desert landscape.

## GRÜNAU
For most travellers, Grünau is either the first petrol station north of the South African border or a place to await a lift to Ai-Ais, Fish River Canyon or points beyond.

Grünau is a stop that time has passed. There was a hand-cranked phone in my hotel room, the dinner was whatever delicious thing the cook decided to cook, the street was unpaved and the rooms were amazingly good value ...

**Wayne Lidlehoover, USA**

### Augrabies-Steenbok Nature Reserve
This forgotten nature reserve north-west of Grünau was created to protect not only steenbok, but also Hartmann's mountain zebra, gemsbok and klipspringer. Camping is allowed, but the only facilities are some basic toilets.

To get there, follow the C12 for 59km north-west of Grünau, then turn west and continue for another 10km to the reserve. Admission is free.

### Places to Stay
The inexpensive *Hotel Grünau* (☎ (06342) 26201), down a side road about 1km from the petrol station, is just about acceptable. Singles/doubles cost US$16/23. The petrol station on the main road has a shop, snack bar and takeaway.

The *White House Ruskamp* (☎ (06342) ask for Grünau 1520), 11km towards Windhoek then 1km east, has safe, quiet, self-catering accommodation for US$16 per person, plus US$5/7 for breakfast/dinner. Gerrit and Retha Viviers' *Florida B&B* (☎ (06342) ask for Grünau 1111) has self-catering bungalows for US$17, including breakfast. It lies 33km north of Grünau, then 1km off the main road. The good-value *Vastrap Guest House* (☎ (06342) 1340), run by the Steenkamp family, lies 5km east of

Grünau on the B3, and is highly recommended.

For other options, see under Hobas, later in this chapter.

## FISH RIVER CANYON NATIONAL PARK

Nowhere else in Africa is there anything like Fish River Canyon. The Fish River, which joins the Orange River 70km south of the canyon, has been gouging out this gorge for aeons, with stunning results. Although the typically breathless Namibian tourist literature claims that it's the world's second largest canyon (after Arizona's Grand Canyon), it's in fact well down the list, but that makes it no less awe-inspiring. The chasm now measures 160km in length and up to 27km in width, and the dramatic inner canyon reaches a depth of 550m.

The Fish River typically flows between March and April. Early in the tourist season, from April to June, it normally diminishes to a mere trickle, and later in the winter, to just a chain of remnant pools along the canyon floor.

The main access points are Hobas, near the northern end of the park, and Ai-Ais Hot Springs resort, in the south. Both are administered by MET, and all accommodation should be prebooked in Windhoek.

### History

The early San had a legend that the wildly twisting Fish River Canyon was gouged out by a frantically scrambling snake named Koutein Kooru as he was pursued into the desert by hunters.

The geological story is only a bit different. Fish River Canyon is actually two canyons, one inside the other, which were formed in entirely different ways. It's thought that the original sedimentary layers of shale, sandstone and loose igneous material around Fish River Canyon were laid down nearly two billion years ago and were later metamorphosed by heat and pressure into more solid materials, such as gneiss. Just under a billion years ago, cracks in the formation admitted intrusions of igneous material, which cooled to form the dolerite dykes (which are now exposed and readily visible in the inner canyon).

The surface was then eroded into a basin and covered by a shallow sea, which eventually filled with sediment – sandstone, conglomerate, quartzite, limestone and shale – washed down from surrounding exposed lands. Around 500 million years ago, a period of tectonic activity along crustal faults caused these layers to rift and to tilt at a 45° angle. These forces opened up a wide gap in the earth's crust and formed a large canyon. This was what we now regard as the outer canyon, the bottom of which was the first level of terraces we see approximately 170m below the east rim and 380m below the west rim. This newly created valley naturally became a watercourse (the Fish River, in fact) which began eroding a meandering path along the valley floor and eventually gouged out what is now the 270m-deep inner canyon.

### Hobas

The Hobas Information Centre, at the northern end of the park, is open daily from 7.30 am to noon and 2 to 5 pm. It's also the check-in point for the five-day canyon hike. Packaged snacks and cool drinks are available, but little else.

From Hobas, it's 10km on a gravel road to Hikers Viewpoint, a picnic site with tables, braai pits and toilets. Here is the start of the walking track to Ai-Ais and just around the corner is a good overview of the northern part of the canyon. Main Viewpoint, a few kilometres further south, is probably the best – and most photographed – overall canyon view. Both these viewpoints take in the sharp river bend known as Hell's Corner.

Admission costs US$3 per person and US$3 per vehicle. This permit is also valid for Ai-Ais.

**Places to Stay & Eat** Camp sites cost US$21 at the pleasant, well shaded *Hobas campground*, 10km from the main viewpoints near the northern end of the canyon.

NAMIBIA

Facilities are clean and there's also a kiosk and swimming pool. There's no restaurant or petrol.

Riëtte and Louis Fourie's friendly *Fish River Lodge* (☎ (063) 223762; fax 223222), about 60km north of Hobas, lies on a ranch cradled in the confluence of the Löwen and Fish River Canyons amid some of the most fascinating geology you'll ever see. Don't miss a trip into the canyon to swim in the river pools and see the bizarre petroglyphs in the rippled and phenomenally hard black rock. There's also a 60km five-day hiking trail with camp sites. Backpackers rooms are US$17 per person; dorms are US$9; and doubles/family rooms cost US$68/101. Transfers from Keetmanshoop cost US$34 per person with a group of four people. Ask about backpackers specials. All rates include breakfast.

One of Namibia's most interesting lodges is the remarkable *Cañon Lodge* (☎ (06342) ask for Grünau 3631; fax (061) 251863), 7km south of Hobas. It consists of 20 bungalows which are integrated into the red rock backdrop and the restaurant is housed in a restored 1910 farmhouse. B&B accommodation is excellent value at US$58/89. Camping costs US$5 to US$12 per person and meals are US$9 to US$11.

### Fish River Hiking Trail

The four to five-day hike from Hobas to Ai-Ais is Namibia's most popular long-distance walk – and with good reason. The magical 85km route, which follows the sandy riverbed (in May and June, water does actually), begins at Hikers Viewpoint and ends at the hot-spring resort of Ai-Ais.

Due to summer heat and potential flash floods, the route is only open from 1 May to 30 September. Permits for groups of three to 40 people cost US$21 per person but you must arrange your own transport and accommodation in Hobas and Ai-Ais. Hikers must sign an indemnity form releasing MET from any responsibility.

Thanks to the typically warm, clear weather, you probably won't need a tent, but you must carry a sleeping bag and food.

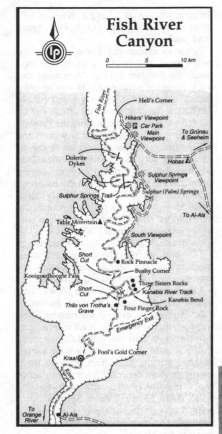

In Hobas, check on water availability in the canyon. In August and September, the last 15km of the walk can be completely dry and hikers will need several 2L water bottles to manage this hot, sandy stretch. Large plastic soft-drink bottles normally work just fine.

**The Route** From Hobas, it's 10km to Hikers Viewpoint, which is the start of the trail. Hikers must find their own transport there. The steep and scenic section at the beginning takes you from the canyon rim to the river where you'll have a choice of fabulous sandy camp sites beside cool, green river pools.

After an exhausting 13km through the rough sand and boulders along the east bank, the Sulphur Springs Viewpoint day track joins the main route. If you're completely exhausted at this stage and simply can't hack the conditions, this route can be used as an emergency exit from the canyon. If it's any encouragement, however, the going does get easier as you move downstream, so why not head a further 2km downstream to Sulphur Springs, set up camp and see how you feel in the morning.

Sulphur Springs – more commonly called Palm Springs – is an excellent camp site with thermal sulphur pools (a touch of paradise) to soothe your aching muscles. The springs, which have a stable temperature of 57°C, gush up from the underworld at an amazing 30L per second and contain not only sulphur but also chloride and fluoride.

Legend has it that during WWI, two escaped German prisoners of war hid out at Palm Springs to escape internment. One was apparently suffering from asthma and the other from skin cancer, but thanks to the spring's healing powers, both were cured. It's said that the palm trees growing there sprang up from date pits discarded by these two. This site is also accessible on day walks down from the Palm Springs viewpoint. Unfortunately it's normally crowded and fouled by the picnic trash left behind by careless day hikers.

The next segment consists mostly of deep sand, pebbles and gravel. The most direct route through the inside river bends requires hikers to cross the river several times. The Table Mountain formation lies 15km beyond Palm Springs and a further 15km on is the first short cut, which omits the area of dense thorn scrub known as Bushy Corner. Around the next river bend, just upstream from the Three Sisters formation, is a longer short cut past Kanebis Bend up to Kooigoedhoogte Pass. At the top, you'll have a superb view of Four Finger Rock, an impressive rock tower consisting of four

thick pinnacles that more closely resemble a cow's udder than fingers. If you see a sign reading 'Cold Drinks 7km', you're not hallucinating; read on.

After descending to the river, you'll cross to the west bank and start climbing over yet another short-cut (although you can also follow the river bend). At the southern end of this pass, on the west bank of the river, lies the grave of Lieutenant Thilo von Trotha, who was killed on this spot during a 1905 confrontation between the Germans and the Nama.

The final 25km to Ai-Ais, which can be completed in a long day, follows an easy but sandy and rocky route. South of the soldier's grave, the canyon widens out and becomes drier, with fewer bends, and river pools are less frequent. At the end of the winter, the final 15km are normally completely dry, so carry sufficient water. The lemonade and hot dog stand advertised at Four Finger Rock is 5km south of Von Trotha's grave. It's not 100% reliable, but when it's open, few hikers pass it by.

**Day Walks** If the entire Fish River route seems too daunting, you can begin at either the Sulphur Springs or Hikers Viewpoints and descend 500m to the canyon floor for a picnic and a swim before returning the same way. Alternatively, follow the bottom of the canyon between the two viewpoints. This requires a good early start and unless you have two vehicles, you may have to walk the 10km back to Hobas from your finishing point. Note also that these options require a 500m ascent out of the canyon during the hottest part of the day.

### Ai-Ais Hot Spring Resort

For many travellers, Ai-Ais (Nama for scalding hot) serves as both the starting and finishing point for their canyon hike. This pleasant hot-spring oasis lies beneath towering peaks at the southern end of Fish River Canyon and is popular with Namibians and South Africans who come to soak up the natural thermal baths which originate beneath the riverbed.

Although the 60°C springs have probably been known to the San for thousands of years, the legend goes that they were 'discovered' by a nomadic Nama shepherd rounding up stray sheep. They're rich in chloride, fluoride and sulphur, and are reputedly salubrious for sufferers from rheumatism or nervous disorders. The hot water is now piped to a series of baths, Jacuzzis and an outdoor swimming pool.

A pleasant diversion is the short, rocky hike to the peak which rises above the opposite bank. It affords a superb view of Ai-Ais itself and you'll even see the four pinnacles of Four Finger Rock rising far to the north. The return trip takes two hours.

Due to the flooding risk, Ai-Ais is closed from 31 October to the second Friday in March. In fact, in early 1972, a year after the resort opened, the entire complex (save one building which sat on higher ground) was utterly destroyed by the Fish River's worst flood in recorded history. In early 1988, it was again flooded and required a three month clean-up.

The site is geared mainly towards Namibian and South African holidaymakers, so foreigners may feel a bit out of place, but the setting is pleasant enough. Admission costs US$3 per person and US$3 per vehicle. This permit is also valid at Hobas. Day visitors are welcome between sunrise and 11 pm.

**Places to Stay & Eat** Amenities at Ai-Ais include a shop, restaurant, petrol station, tennis courts, post office and, of course, a swimming pool, spa and mineral bath facilities (US$0.50 per session). Camping costs US$21 for up to eight people, with ablutions blocks, braai pits and use of resort facilities. Four-bed huts with shared bath cost US$41, four-bed flats are US$59 and two-bed 'luxury' flats are US$63. All flats have private baths and basic self-catering facilities. Accommodation should be pre-booked through MET in Windhoek. The restaurant is open from 7 to 8.30 am, noon to 1.30 pm and 6 to 8.30 pm and the attached shop sells basic groceries.

## Getting There & Away

There's no public transport to either Hobas or Ai-Ais; hitchers should have the most luck between mid-March and 31 October. The best-travelled routes to Ai-Ais are via the turn-off 20km north of Noordoewer and the one 30km south of Grünau. From Ai-Ais, most holiday-makers head for the northern viewpoints, which means that hitching is possible. From Seeheim, on the Keetmanshoop-Lüderitz road, the C12 turns south, passes the Augrabies Steenbok Nature Reserve and after 87km, reaches Holoog, where the D601 turns south-west. After 31km is the west turning to Hobas, 18km away. However, this route is relatively little-travelled and hitchers report waiting up to four days for a lift from Seeheim.

## ORANGE RIVER

The Orange River has its headwaters in the Drakensberg Mountains of Natal, South Africa, and forms much of the boundary between Namibia and South Africa. It was named not for its muddy colour, but for Prince William V of Orange, who was the Dutch monarch in the late 1770s. The 4WD route from Noordoewer to Rosh Pinah makes a spectacular desert adventure.

Most people visit this region for river trips, but for the adventurous traveller, Mr Kobus Jansen of Fish River Paddle & Saddle (☎ (063342) ask for 251 or (0631) 24415), on a farm near the mouth of the Fish River, runs worthwhile multi-day horse-riding, canoeing and camping trips between Ai-Ais and the Orange River. An excellent excursion includes a four-day horseback tour from Ai-Ais to the Orange River plus two days canoeing for US$170. If you can't reach Mr Jansen at home, try Kallie Le Roux (☎ (063342) ask for 170 or 91), PO Box 195, Rosh Pinah. Alternatively, track him down through the Ai-Ais Hot Springs Resort.

## River Trips

Several South African companies offer Orange River canoeing and easy rafting trips from Noordoewer to Selingsdrif (spelt

NAMIBIA

Sendelingsdrif on some maps). Part of the route follows the river boundary between Namibia's Fish River Canyon National Park and South Africa's Richtersveld National Park. Trips are normally done in stages and last from three to six days, although two-day weekend trips can be arranged. These aren't treacherous trips – the white-water never exceeds class II – and the appeal lies in the experience of this wild canyon country.

The stages include Noordoewer to Aussenkehr; Aussenkehr to the Fish River mouth; Fish River mouth to Nama Canyon; and Nama Canyon to Selingsdrif. Some companies also do a five day stage from Pella Mission to Goodhouse, further upstream. Generally, canoe trips are slightly more expensive than raft trips. For some idea of prices, a four/six-day canoe trip costs US$190/250, while the raft trips are around US$165/220. The following operators currently run trips:

*Adventure Runners*, 31 De Korte St, PO Box 31117, Braamfontein, South Africa (☎ (011) 403 2512; fax 339 4042). This company runs four-day 75km canoe/camel trips from near Blouputs, South Africa, to Warmbad, costing from US$213.

*Felix Unite*, 1 Griegmar House, Main Rd, PO Box 96, Kenilworth 7745, South Africa (☎ (021) 683 6423; fax 683 6488; <book ings@felix.co.za>). Offers a range of canoe trips on the Orange River, as well as on other South African rivers, and also hires canoes. Four/six-day standard trips cost US$197/242, plus US$45 for return transport from Cape Town. You can also organise your own canoe trip and hire a two-person canoe package – canoes, paddles, life vests and cool boxes – for US$28 per day. A guide costs an additional US$39 per day.

*Namibian River Adventures*, PO Box 3, Noordoewer (☎ (0637) 7161 or (0637) 7283). This is one of few Namibian offices offering canoe trips on the Orange River.

*Orange River Adventures*, 48A Strand St, Cape Town, South Africa (☎/fax (021) 419 1705). This company offers five-day canoe trips between Noordoewer and Fish River mouth. Four/six-day tours cost US$187/224 per person.

*The River Rafters*, 35 Kendal Rd, Diep River 7856, South Africa (☎ (021) 725094; fax 725241). This informal rafting operation runs four, five and six-day raft trips year-round. They're the least expensive available at US$120 for a self-catered six-day trip. Add meals and it's US$180.

*River Runners*, PO Box 583, Constantia 7848, South Africa (☎ (021) 762 2350; fax 761 1373). This friendly company runs both canoeing and rafting trips on the Orange River. It comes highly recommended.

*Southern Africa Adventure Centre*, 48a Strand St, Cape Town, South Africa (☎ (021) 419 1704; fax 419 1703). This isn't an operator, but rather an adventure-travel agency selling a range of thrill-oriented trips, including Orange River runs in both South Africa and Namibia.

*South African River Adventures*, PO Box 4722, Cape Town 8000, South Africa (☎/fax (021) 685 1569). This company runs raft trips on the Orange and other South African rivers, and is one of the least expensive.

### Places to Stay

The *Camel Lodge* (☎ (0637) 7171; fax 7143) in Noordoewer has singles/doubles for US$24/38. Four-bed rooms cost US$45. On the South African side, 12km downstream from Vioolsdrif, is the relaxing *Peace of Paradise Campsite*. Grassy sites with access to ablutions facilities cost US$6 per person and meals are available. Turn west on the gravel road near the police post and continue for 12km, then turn north at the four palm trees and go 1km to the riverbank.

## KARASBURG

Although it's Southern Namibia's third largest town, Karasburg is little more than a service centre along the main route between Namibia and Johannesburg. The name means 'rocky mountains', after the nearby Karas Mountain range. The Nama people, however, still call it Kalkfontein (limestone springs) Suid. It has a good supermarket, a bank, several petrol stations and two hotels.

### Warmbad

The main site of interest is the historic mission, fort and spa village of Warmbad (German for warm bath), 36km south of town. Warmbad, Namibia's first mission station, was founded in 1805 by missionary Edward Cook. The ruins of the old spa building are currently being restored as a national monument and a museum is planned for the portals and gatehouse of the old fort (now the police station).

## Places to Stay & Eat

Both of Karasburg's hotels, the *Kalkfontein Hotel* (☎/fax (0634) 270172) and the *Van Riebeeck* (☎/fax (0634) 270023), are under the same management. The former has a restaurant and charges US$30/42 for a single/double air-conditioned room. The latter costs US$27/39.

Near the junction of the C26 and the D259, 119km north of Karasburg, lies the basic *Mt Karas Game Lodge* (☎ (06352) 3212; fax (0631) 23222), owned by David and Anna Fourie. It enjoys views of the Karas Mountains and lies within easy reach of several historical sites, including the Stansvlakte monument; the Baron von Schauroth castle; graves from the German-Nama war; and numerous ancient San paintings. Amenities include an 11km hiking trail.

# Glossary

**ANC** – African National Congress

**apartheid** – 'separate development of the races'; political system in which people are officially segregated according to race

**assegais** – Ndebele spears

**ATV** – all terrain vehicle

**bakkie** – utility or pick-up truck

**barchan dunes** – migrating crescent-shaped sand dunes

**Basarwa** – *Batswana* name for the San people

**Batswana** – the citizens of Botswana

**BDF** – Botswana Defence Forces

**bilharzia** – disease caused by blood flukes (parasitic flatworms) that are passed on by freshwater snails

**biltong** – normally anonymous dried meat that can be anything from beef to kudu or ostrich; it's usually delicious and makes a great snack

**BMC** – Botswana Meat Corporation

**boerewors** – spicy Afrikaner sausage

**bogobe** – sorghum porridge, a staple food in Botswana

**bojalwa** – sorghum beer drunk in Botswana; brewed commercially as *Chibuku*

**boloko** – a mixture of termite mound soil and cow dung used in the construction of traditional Tswana homes

**boomslang** – a dangerous snake that measures up to 2m and likes to hang out in trees

**braai** – a barbecue that normally includes lots of meat grilled on a special stand or in a pit

**BSAC** – British South Africa Company

**CDM** – Consolidated Diamond Mines

**Chibuku** – the 'beer of good cheer'. The alcoholic drink of the Zimbabwean masses. It's also drunk in Botswana and parts of Namibia.

**chikuva** – small platforms placed behind Shona huts for offerings to ancestral spirits

**cuca shops** – small bush shops of north-ern Namibia; named after a brand of Angolan beer normally sold there

**daga hut** – in Zimbabwe, a traditional African round house

**difaqane** – forced migration; see *mfecane*

**dikgotla** – traditional *Batswana* town council

**dipolwane** – bricks made from soil taken from termite mounds, used in the construction of traditional homes

**dolfhout** – Afrikaans name for wild teak

**drankwinkel** – literally 'drink shop'; Namibian or South African off-licence

**drift** – a river ford

**dumpi** – a 375mL beer; Namibian equivalent of an Australian stubby

**dwala** – bald, knob-like domes of slickrock

**efundja** – period of heavy rainfall in northern Namibia

**ekipa** – a traditional medallion historically worn by Owambo women as a sign of wealth and status

**ESAP** – Economic Structural Adjustment Programme

**eumbo** – immaculate Owambo *kraal*; very much like a small village enclosed within a pale fence

**euphorbia** – several species of cactus-like succulents that are found in southern Africa

**Frelimo** – Frente pela Liberacão de Moçambique, or Mozambique Liberation Front

**Gemütlichkeit** – a distinctively German atmosphere of comfort and hospitality

**gudza** – tree bark used by the Shona for making blankets, mats and clothing; it's made soft and pliable by chewing on it

**guti** – drizzly mists that occur in Zimbabwe's Eastern Highlands

**ilala** – Zimbabwean name for the palm *Hyphaene petersiana*. It's a source of thatching material, vegetable ivory and palm wine.

**induna** – early Ndebele military captain; also translated as 'chief'

**inselbergs** – isolated ranges and hills; common in the Namib Desert

**jesse** – dense, thorny scrub, normally impenetrable to humans

**kapenta** – *Limnothrissa mioda*, an anchovy-like fish caught in Lake Kariba and favoured by Zimbabweans

**karakul** – variety of Central Asian sheep that produces high-grade wool and pelts; raised in Namibia and parts of Botswana

**kgotla** – traditionally constructed *Batswana* community affairs hall, used for meetings of the *dikgotla*

**Khoisan** – language grouping taking in all southern African indigenous languages, including San and Khoi-Khoi (or Nama), as well as the language of the Damara (a Bantu people who speak a Khoi-Khoi dialect)

**kimberlite pipe** – geological term for a type of igneous intrusion, in which extreme heat and pressure have turned coal into diamonds

**kloof** – a ravine or small valley

**kokerboom** – quiver tree; grows mainly in southern Namibia

**Konditorei** – a German pastry shop, as found in larger Namibian towns

**kopje** – small hill, often just a pile of boulders on an otherwise flat plain

**kraal** – either an enclosure for livestock or a fortified village of *daga huts*

**LMS** – London Missionary Society

**location** – Namibian name for *township*

**mabele** – Tswana for sorghum; used to make *bogobe*

**madiba** – serene open areas of still water in the Okavango Delta; singular lediba

**mahango** – millet; a staple of the Owambo diet and used for brewing a favourite alcoholic beverage of the same name

**makalani** – Owambo name for the palm *Hyphaene petersiana*; see *ilala*

**mambo** – Shona king

**maotwana** – roof poles used in the construction of traditional Tswana homes

**marimba** – African xylophone, made from strips of resonant wood with various-sized gourds for sound boxes

**mbanje** – Zimbabwean name for cannabis

**mbira** – thumb piano; it consists of 22 to 24 narrow iron keys mounted in rows on a wooden sound board. The player plucks the ends of the keys with the thumbs.

**MET** – the Ministry of Environment & Tourism in Namibia

**mfecane** – an exodus or forced migration by several southern African tribes in the face of Zulu aggression

**mhondoro** – literally lion; a Shona spirit that can influence natural conditions and bring fortune or disaster on a community. When a problem such as a plague or drought strikes, these are the spirits that must be consulted.

**midzimu** – spirits of Shona ancestors

**mielie pap** – Afrikaans name for maize meal porridge, known in Zimbabwe as *sadza*

**miombo** – dry open woodland, comprised mostly of acacia and/or mopane or similar bushveld vegetation

**mokolane** – *Batswana* name for the palm *Hyphaene petersiana*; see *ilala*

**mokoro** – dugout canoe used in the Okavango Delta, propelled by a poler who stands in the stern; plural mekoro

**mombo** – a powerful chief or king in pre-colonial Zimbabwe

**morgen** – unit of land measurement used by early Boer farmers, equal to about 1.25 hectares

**motshikiri** – thatching grass used in the construction of traditional Tswana homes

**mujejeje** – stone bells; natural rock formations, caused by exfoliation, that produce melodic tones when struck

**mukwa** – a rich-grained wood used in Zimbabwean carvings and other crafts

**musika** – Shona township market and bus terminal

**mutasa** – a Manyika dynastic title established in the 16th century

**Mwari** – supreme being in traditional Shona religion

**nagana** – Zimbabwean name for *trypanosomiasis*

**n'anga** (also spelt nyanga or nganga) – a shaman

**!nara** – a type of melon that grows in the Namib Desert; a dietary staple of the Topnaar Khoi-Khoi people

**n!oresi** – traditional San lands; 'lands where one's heart is'

**ntlo** – pole and *daga rondavels* in a Tswana village

**nxum** – San 'life force'

**omaeru** – soured milk; a dietary staple of the Herero people

**omiramba** – fossil river channels in northern Namibia and north-western Botswana; singular omuramba

**omulilo gwoshilongo** – 'sacred fire' that serves as a shrine in each Owambo *eumbo*; a log of mopane that is kept burning round the clock

**oshana** – dry river channel in northern Namibia and north-western Botswana

**padrão** – tribute to a royal patron, erected by early Portuguese navigators along the African coast

**photographic safari** – type of safari where the participants carry cameras rather than guns

**pondo** – pound, occasionally used in Botswana to refer to two *pula*

**pula** – rain in Tswana; the Botswana unit of currency

**pungwe** – 'from darkness to light'; during the Second Chimurenga, all-night celebrations of nationalistic unity between villagers and guerrillas. Now, any sort of event that begins in the evening and carries on through the night.

**Renamo** – Resistência Nacional de Moçambique, or Mozambique National Resistance (MNR)

**renkini** – Ndebele township market and bus terminal

**rondavel** – a round, often thatched hut

**rooibos** – literally 'red bush' in Afrikaans; an insipid herbal tea that reputedly has therapeutic qualities

**sadza** – Zimbabwean name for maize meal porridge

**sefala huts** – traditional *Batswana* granaries

**seif dunes** – prominent linear sand dunes, as found in the central Namib Desert

**shebeen** – an illegal drinking establishment-cum-brothel

**skokiaan** – a dangerous and illegal grain-based swill spiked with whatever's lying around. It's no longer popular.

**Sperrgebiet** – forbidden area; alluvial diamond region of south-western Namibia

**Swakara** – South West African Karakul; name used in the marketing of Namibian karakul products

**SWAPO** – South West Africa People's Organisation; Namibia's liberation army and the currently ruling political party

**tenebrionid** – a collection of beetle species that inhabit the Namib Desert

**toktokkie** – Afrikaans name for the fog-basking *tenebrionid* beetle, *Onomachris unguicularis*

**township** – high-density black residential area outside a central city or town

**trypanosomiasis** – sleeping sickness; disease passed on by the bite of the tsetse fly; known in Zimbabwe as *nagana*

**tsama** – a bitter desert melon historically eaten by the San people; also eaten by livestock

**tsotsis** – thieves

**UDI** – Unilateral Declaration of Independence (of Rhodesia from the UK)

**UNITA** – União pela Independência Total de Angola

**UTC** – Universal Time Co-ordinate (formerly GMT)

**veld** – open grassland, normally in plateau regions. One variation, bushveld, has thorn scrub instead of grassland.

**vetkoek** – literally fat cake; a type of doughnut eaten in Botswana and other places with Afrikaner influences
**vlei** – any low open landscape, sometimes marshy

**wag 'n bietjie** – Afrikaans name for the buffalo thorn tree; literally wait-a-bit
**watu** – Kavango dugout canoe, used on rivers and in wetlands of north-eastern Namibia
**welwitschia** – *Welwitschia mirabilis*, an unusual plant that grows in the Namib Desert. It is thought to be related to coniferous trees.

**ZANLA** – Zimbabwe African National Liberation Army
**ZANU** – Zimbabwe African National Union
**ZAPU** – Zimbabwe African Peoples' Union
**zhii** – 'vengeful annihilation of the enemy'; cry of solidarity among black Zimbabweans against colonial power in the late 1950s
**ZIPRA** – Zimbabwe Peoples' Revolutionary Army
**ZUM** – Zimbabwe Unity Movement

# Index

## ABBREVIATIONS

## MAPS

## TEXT

Map references are in **bold** type.
Safari Guide references are in ***bold italic*** type.

---

## NATIONAL PARK & WILDLIFE RESERVES

## Boxed Text

814

**Thanks**

Many thanks to the travellers who used the last edition and wrote to us with helpful hints, useful advice and interesting anecdotes. Writers to whom thanks must go include:

Marc Adams, Guy Alexander, Julie Alexander, Keira Armstrong, Mike Arron, Lisa Arthur, Laurie & Jeremy Baig, Claire Barnes, Tiffany Barry, Liz Bayley, Claudine Beers, Susan Beney, Mario Biagioni, Gavin Biggs, Steve Bolnick, M Boonekamp, Carolyn Brewer, A & S Broughton, Stephanie Brownbridge, NK Bryant, Cristiano Burmester, Rev R Butler, Richard Carr, Miguel & Monica Casviner, Yvonne Chaddendale, Betty Chen, Mike Clark, Fiona Clarkson, Jeanette Clayton, Ilan Cohen, Juan Colmenar Rueda, Andrea Condiescu, Barb Connellan, Mal Cooper, Phillipe Cornelis, Dr Donald Cramer, Wendy Crawford, Andrew Cripps, Jennifer Cullins, Gareth Dart, Walter DeBoeck, Paul & Val de Montille, Richard Desomme, Dr Alexander J de Voogt, C Dieffenbacher, Valerie Donald, Tamsen Douglass-Love, Ben Druss, Rick Duchscher, Annemiek Duijvesteijn, Wendy Easen, Birgit & Gerd Eggert, Magnus Eriksen, Steven & Tanja Faber, Carol Faulkes, Peter Faulkner, Victor Fiorillo, Robert Foitzik, Carla Foolen, Stephen Foster, Brian Freestone, Ingmar Frei, Isobel Frisken, Tanja Frohlich, Fern Fromey, Dr Ruth Gasser, Matthew Gavin MD, Penny & Malcolm Gee, Peter Ginn, Ulrich Gisser, Richard & Belinda Gordon, Kevin Green, Martha & Doug Guerrant, Ruth Harvey, Sue Haskins, Patricia & Phillip Haupt, Michael Hauser, Chris Hayward, Ruth Hayward, Ted Hearn, Angela Heidrich, Joan Henderson, Lutz Hensel, Richard Hipstroff, Joan Hoff, William Hofmeyr, M Hofstetter, Judith Holbrook, Peter Holmes, Christine Holtschoppen, FC Hubbard, Amber Hughes, John Hurst, Mette Jacobsgaard, Rebecca James, Lenka Janecek, Derek & Leanne Janzen, Tim Jenkins, Ian Johnson, Peter Johnson, Jacqui Kadey, Steffi Kahl, Dirk Kascher, Leanne Kaufman, Eileen Kawola, John & Kathleen Kay, Peter Kelly, Christopher Kessel, Philip Kestelman, Francis Kint & friends, Maria Klambauer, Petter Konig, Vera Kotz, Ewan & Geeske Kouwenhoven, David Krieser, Philippe Kulig, Anne Kusttenhill-Lowe, Wiebke Laasch, Eileen Lacey, AR Lalloo, Elizabeth Lamond, Matthias Lang, Pia Larque, Mr & Mrs M Levy, Michele Lischi, Lawrie Little, Sarah Lloyd, E Lotz, Harris Lucas, L Lurvink, Iain Mackay, Michael Magee, Algars Manor, David & Sally Martin, Paul Matthys, Trevor McDonald, EE McKinney, JF McLaren, Monica McLean, Colin McVey, Enrico Meeuwsen, Lisa Menke, Lorenzo & Maria Micheletta, Anna Michielsen, Edith Millan, Simon Miller-Cranko, Greg Minns, Jess Moore, Declan Moran, Larry Moulton, Christo Muller, Russell & Elaine Murdoch, Berhard Niebaum, Jurgen Nijs, Teresa Nolan, Anna Nylund, Felicitas Ochotta, MJ Orenland, Owen Parnell, MH & JM Parton, Jeffrey Pestrak, Corinna Peters, Sue Phillip, Ges Pierrot, Vittorio & Monica Pietri, Guy & Janet Pinneo, Huibert Poot, Mr & Mrs J Prince, Peter Puttemans, PA Reavley, Geoff Renner, Yvonne Richards, Matthias Ripp, Sally Robinson, Florian Roser, Norberto Rosetti, Sandy Roth, Lyn Rowley, Andrea Russell, GB & JM Ryan, Karen & Donncha Ryder, M Sabatier, Andreas Sandler, W Sawyer, Don Schenck, Lisa Schipper, Frank Schmidt, Sebastian Schmitz, Frederic Schneider, Fran & Wade Schroeder, Holger Schulze, Sebastian Schwertner, Dr PR Scott, Maartje Sevenster, David Seymour-Smith, Shetal Shah, Trish Shalloe, Julie Sheard, Mary Shellene, Latham Shinder, Andrew Silk, Tom Silverside, Katie Sim, Oliver Simon, Barry & Rowena Simpson, Fred-Arne Sivertsen, Kristian Skjerning Kyed, Chris Smaje, Russell Smith, D Smith, Anne & Peter Smith, Mary Smith, E Spanjaard, Marilyn Staib, Pascal Stauble, Annick Stenman, Colin Stevenson, Helen Steward, Willemke Stilma, Elise Stray, Mr MF Tang, Peter Taylor, Ruth Taylor, Bas Tensen, Huw Thomas, N Thompson, Jessima Timberlake, Arjen vande Merve, Reijco vande Pol, K van Dorenmalen, JDR Vernon, Jose Verweij-Hoogendijk, Trine Viken Sumstad, Tomaz Vizintin, Martin von Knorre, Margaret & Martin Wakalin, D & E Wakefreed, Charles Wale, Graham & Jane Walker, AC Ward, M Janink Wegeneeys, Clare White, Welby Whiting, Sally Wilde, Hugh Wilkins, Edward Willem Spiegel, Grant Williams, Grant & Barbara Williams, Samantha Williamson, David Willis, John Wilmut, Alexander Winter, Sara Wright, Dianne Young, Barry Zeve, and Paula & David Zilbart.

# LONELY PLANET PHRASEBOOKS

Building bridges,
Breaking barriers,
Beyond babble-on

**Nepali** phrasebook

Listen for the gems

**Ethiopian** Amharic phrasebook

Speak your own words

**Latin American Spanish** phrasebook

Ask your own questions

**Ukrainian** phrasebook

Master of your own image

**Greek** phrasebook

**Vietnamese** phrasebook

- handy pocket-sized books
- easy to understand Pronunciation chapter
- clear and comprehensive Grammar chapter
- romanisation alongside script to allow ease of pronunciation
- script throughout so users can point to phrases
- extensive vocabulary sections, words and phrases for every situation
- full of cultural information and tips for the traveller

'...vital for a real DIY spirit and attitude in language learning' – Backpacker

'the phrasebooks have good cultural backgrounders and offer solid advice for challenging situations in remote locations' – San Francisco Examiner

'...they are unbeatable for their coverage of the world's more obscure languages' – The Geographical Magazine

---

Arabic (Egyptian)
Arabic (Moroccan)
Australia
   *Australian English, Aboriginal and
   Torres Strait languages*
Baltic States
   *Estonian, Latvian, Lithuanian*
Bengali
Brazilian
Burmese
Cantonese
Central Asia
Central Europe
   *Czech, French, German, Hungarian,
   Italian and Slovak*
Eastern Europe
   *Bulgarian, Czech, Hungarian, Polish,
   Romanian and Slovak*
Ethiopian (Amharic)
Fijian
French
German
Greek

Hindi/Urdu
Indonesian
Italian
Japanese
Korean
Lao
Latin American Spanish
Malay
Mandarin
Mediterranean Europe
   *Albanian, Croatian, Greek,
   Italian, Macedonian, Maltese,
   Serbian and Slovene*
Mongolian
Nepali
Papua New Guinea
Pilipino (Tagalog)
Quechua
Russian
Scandinavian Europe
   *Danish, Finnish, Icelandic, Norwegian
   and Swedish*

South-East Asia
   *Burmese, Indonesian, Khmer, Lao,
   Malay, Tagalog (Pilipino), Thai and
   Vietnamese*
Spanish (Castilian)
   *Basque, Catalan and Galician*
Sri Lanka
Swahili
Thai
Thai Hill Tribes
Tibetan
Turkish
Ukrainian
USA
   *US English, Vernacular,
   Native American languages and
   Hawaiian*
Vietnamese
Western Europe
   *Basque, Catalan, Dutch, French,
   German, Irish, Italian, Portuguese,
   Scottish Gaelic, Spanish (Castilian)
   and Welsh*

# LONELY PLANET JOURNEYS

JOURNEYS is a unique collection of travel writing – published by the company that understands travel better than anyone else. It is a series for anyone who has ever experienced – or dreamed of – the magical moment when they encountered a strange culture or saw a place for the first time. They are tales to read while you're planning a trip, while you're on the road or while you're in an armchair, in front of a fire.

JOURNEYS books catch the spirit of a place, illuminate a culture, recount a crazy adventure, or introduce a fascinating way of life. They always entertain, and always enrich the experience of travel.

---

## THE RAINBIRD
### A Central African Journey
### *Jan Brokken*
#### *translated by Sam Garrett*

*The Rainbird* is a classic travel story. Following in the footsteps of famous Europeans such as Albert Schweitzer and H.M. Stanley, Jan Brokken journeyed to Gabon in central Africa. A kaleidoscope of adventures and anecdotes, *The Rainbird* brilliantly chronicles the encounter between Africa and Europe as it was acted out on a side-street of history. It is also the compelling, immensely readable account of the author's own travels in one of the most remote and mysterious regions of Africa.

*Jan Brokken* is one of Holland's best known writers. In addition to travel narratives and literary journalism, he has published several novels and short stories. Many of his works are set in Africa, where he has travelled widely.

---

## SONGS TO AN AFRICAN SUNSET
### A Zimbabwean Story
### *Sekai Nzenza-Shand*

*Songs to an African Sunset* braids vividly personal stories into an intimate picture of contemporary Zimbabwe. Returning to her family's village after many years in the West, Sekai Nzenza-Shand discovers a world where ancestor worship, polygamy and witchcraft still govern the rhythms of daily life – and where drought, deforestation and AIDS have wrought devastating changes. With insight and affection, she explores a culture torn between respect for the old ways and the irresistible pull of the new.

*Sekai Nzenza-Shand* was born in Zimbabwe and has lived in England and Australia. Her first novel, *Zimbabwean Woman: My Own Story*, was published in London in 1988 and her fiction has been included in the short story collections *Daughters of Africa* and *Images of the West*. Sekai currently lives in Zimbabwe.

*This project has been assisted by the Commonwealth Government through the Australia Council, its arts funding and advisory body.*

# LONELY PLANET TRAVEL ATLASES

Lonely Planet has long been famous for the number and quality of its guidebook maps. Now we've gone one step further and produced a handy companion series: Lonely Planet travel atlases – maps of a country produced in book form.

Unlike other maps, which look good but lead travellers astray, our travel atlases have been researched on the road by Lonely Planet's experienced team of writers. All details are carefully checked to ensure the atlas corresponds with the equivalent Lonely Planet guidebook.

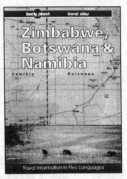

The handy atlas format means no holes, wrinkles, torn sections or constant folding and unfolding. These atlases can survive long periods on the road, unlike cumbersome fold-out maps. The comprehensive index ensures easy reference.

- full-colour throughout
- maps researched and checked by Lonely Planet authors
- place names correspond with Lonely Planet guidebooks
  – no confusing spelling differences
- legend and travelling information in English, French, German, Japanese and Spanish
- size: 230 x 160 mm

**Available now:**
Chile & Easter Island • Egypt • India & Bangladesh • Israel & the Palestinian Territories •Jordan, Syria & Lebanon • Kenya • Laos • Portugal • South Africa, Lesotho & Swaziland • Thailand • Turkey • Vietnam • Zimbabwe, Botswana & Namibia

---

# LONELY PLANET TV SERIES & VIDEOS

Lonely Planet travel guides have been brought to life on television screens around the world. Like our guides, the programmes are based on the joy of independent travel, and look honestly at some of the most exciting, picturesque and frustrating places in the world. Each show is presented by one of three travellers from Australia, England or the USA and combines an innovative mixture of video, Super-8 film, atmospheric soundscapes and original music.

Videos of each episode – containing additional footage not shown on television – are available from good book and video shops, but the availability of individual videos varies with regional screening schedules.

**Video destinations include:** Alaska • American Rockies • Australia – The South-East • Baja California & the Copper Canyon • Brazil • Central Asia • Chile & Easter Island • Corsica, Sicily & Sardinia – The Mediterranean Islands • East Africa (Tanzania & Zanzibar) • Ecuador & the Galapagos Islands • Greenland & Iceland • Indonesia • Israel & the Sinai Desert • Jamaica • Japan • La Ruta Maya • Morocco • New York • North India • Pacific Islands (Fiji, Solomon Islands & Vanuatu) • South India • South West China • Turkey • Vietnam • West Africa • Zimbabwe, Botswana & Namibia

*The Lonely Planet TV series is produced by:*
**Pilot Productions**
The Old Studio
18 Middle Row
London W10 5AT UK

**For video availability and ordering information contact your nearest Lonely Planet office.**

*Music from the TV series is available on CD & cassette.*

# PLANET TALK

*Lonely Planet's FREE quarterly newsletter*

We love hearing from you and think you'd like to hear from us.

*When*...is the right time to see reindeer in Finland?
*Where*...can you hear the best palm-wine music in Ghana?
*How*...do you get from Asunción to Areguá by steam train?
*What*...is the best way to see India?

*For the answer to these and many other questions read PLANET TALK.*

Every issue is packed with up-to-date travel news and advice including:

- a letter from Lonely Planet co-founders Tony and Maureen Wheeler
- go behind the scenes on the road with a Lonely Planet author
- feature article on an important and topical travel issue
- a selection of recent letters from travellers
- details on forthcoming Lonely Planet promotions
- complete list of Lonely Planet products

*To join our mailing list contact any Lonely Planet office.*

*Also available: Lonely Planet T-shirts. 100% heavyweight cotton.*

---

# LONELY PLANET ONLINE

*Get the latest travel information before you leave or while you're on the road*

Whether you've just begun planning your next trip, or you're chasing down specific info on currency regulations or visa requirements, check out Lonely Planet Online for up-to-the minute travel information.

As well as travel profiles of your favourite destinations (including maps and photos), you'll find current reports from our researchers and other travellers, updates on health and visas, travel advisories, and discussion of the ecological and political issues you need to be aware of as you travel.

There's also an online travellers' forum where you can share your experience of life on the road, meet travel companions and ask other travellers for their recommendations and advice. We also have plenty of links to other online sites useful to independent travellers.

And of course we have a complete and up-to-date list of all Lonely Planet travel products including guides, phrasebooks, atlases, Journeys and videos and a simple online ordering facility if you can't find the book you want elsewhere.

**www.lonelyplanet.com**
**or**
**AOL keyword: lp**

# ELY PLANET PRODUCTS

ly Planet is known worldwide for publishing practical, reliable and no-nonsense travel mation in our guides and on our web site. The Lonely Planet list covers just about every accessible part of the world. Currently there are nine series: *travel guides, shoestring guides, walking guides, city guides, phrasebooks, audio packs, travel atlases, Journeys – a unique collection of travel writing and Pisces Books - diving and snorkeling guides.*

## EUROPE

Amsterdam • Andalucia • Austria • Baltic States phrasebook • Berlin • Britain • Canary Islands • Central Europe on a shoestring • Central Europe phrasebook • Czech & Slovak Republics • Denmark • Dublin • Eastern Europe on a shoestring • Eastern Europe phrasebook • Estonia, Latvia & Lithuania • Finland • France • French phrasebook • Germany • German phrasebook • Greece • Greek phrasebook • Hungary • Iceland, Greenland & the Faroe Islands • Ireland • Italian phrasebook • Italy • Lisbon • London • Mediterranean Europe on a shoestring • Mediterranean Europe phrasebook • Paris • Poland • Portugal • Portugal travel atlas • Prague • Romania & Moldova • Russia, Ukraine & Belarus • Russian phrasebook • Scandinavian & Baltic Europe on a shoestring • Scandinavian Europe phrasebook • Slovenia • Spain • Spanish phrasebook • St Petersburg • Switzerland • Trekking in Spain • Ukrainian phrasebook • Vienna • Walking in Britain • Walking in Italy • Walking in Switzerland • Western Europe on a shoestring • Western Europe phrasebook

*Travel Literature:* The Olive Grove: Travels in Greece

## NORTH AMERICA

Alaska • Backpacking in Alaska • Baja California • California & Nevada • Canada • Chicago • Deep South • Florida • Hawaii • Honolulu • Los Angeles • Mexico • Mexico City • Miami • New England • New Orleans • New York City • New York, New Jersey & Pennsylvania • Pacific Northwest USA • Rocky Mountain States • San Francisco • Seattle • Southwest USA • USA phrasebook • Washington, DC & the Capital Region

*Travel Literature:* Drive thru America

## CENTRAL AMERICA & THE CARIBBEAN

• Bahamas and Turks & Caicos • Bermuda • Central America on a shoestring • Costa Rica • Cuba • Eastern Caribbean • Guatemala, Belize & Yucatán: La Ruta Maya • Jamaica

*Travel Literature* Green Dreams: Travels in Central America

## SOUTH AMERICA

Argentina, Uruguay & Paraguay • Bolivia • Brazil • Brazilian phrasebook • Buenos Aires • Chile & Easter Island • Chile & Easter Island travel atlas • Colombia  Ecuador & the Galápagos Islands • Latin American Spanish phrasebook • Peru • Quechua phrasebook • Rio de Janeiro • South America on a shoestring • Trekking in the Patagonian Andes • Venezuela

*Travel Literature:* Full Circle: A South American Journey

## ISLANDS OF THE INDIAN OCEAN

Madagascar & Comoros • Maldives • Mauritius, Réunion & Seychelles

## AFRICA

Africa - the South • Africa on a shoestring • Arabic (Moroccan) phrasebook • Cairo • Cape Town • Central Africa • East Africa • Egypt • Egypt travel atlas • Ethiopian (Amharic) phrasebook • The Gambia & Senegal • Kenya • Kenya travel atlas • Malawi, Mozambique & Zambia • Morocco • North Africa • South Africa, Lesotho & Swaziland • South Africa, Lesotho & Swaziland travel atlas • Swahili phrasebook • Tunisia • Trekking in East Africa • West Africa • Zimbabwe, Botswana & Namibia • Zimbabwe, Botswana & Namibia travel atlas

*Travel Literature:* Mali Blues • The Rainbird: A Central African Journey • Songs to an African Sunset: A Zimbabwean Story

# MAIL ORDER

Lonely Planet products are distributed worldwide. They are also available by mail order from Lonely Planet, so if you have difficulty finding a title please write to us. North American and South American residents should write to 150 Linden St, Oakland CA 94607, USA; European and African residents should write to 10a Spring Place, London NW5 3BH; and residents of other countries to PO Box 617, Hawthorn, Victoria 3122, Australia.

## NORTH-EAST ASIA

Beijing • Cantonese phrasebook • China • Hong Kong • Hong Kong, Macau & Guangzhou • Japan • Japanese phrasebook • Japanese audio pack • Korea • Korean phrasebook • Kyoto • Mandarin phrasebook • Mongolia • Mongolian phrasebook • North-East Asia on a shoestring • Seoul • Taiwan • Tibet • Tibet phrasebook • Tokyo
*Travel Literature*: Lost Japan

## MIDDLE EAST & CENTRAL ASIA

Arab Gulf States • Arabic (Egyptian) phrasebook • Central Asia • Central Asia phrasebook • Iran • Israel & the Palestinian Territories • Israel & the Palestinian Territories travel atlas • Istanbul • Jerusalem • Jordan & Syria • Jordan, Syria & Lebanon travel atlas • Lebanon • Middle East • Turkey • Turkish phrasebook • Turkey travel atlas • Yemen
*Travel Literature:* The Gates of Damascus • Kingdom of the Film Stars: Journey into Jordan

## ALSO AVAILABLE:

Brief Encounters • Travel with Children • Traveller's Tales • Not the Only Planet

## INDIAN SUBCONTINENT

Bangladesh • Bengali phrasebook • Bhutan • Delhi • Goa • Hindi/Urdu phrasebook • India • India & Bangladesh travel atlas • Indian Himalaya • Karakoram Highway • Nepal • Nepali phrasebook • Pakistan • Rajasthan • South India • Sri Lanka • Sri Lanka phrasebook • Trekking in the Indian Himalaya • Trekking in the Karakoram & Hindukush • Trekking in the Nepal Himalaya
*Travel Literature:* In Rajasthan • Shopping for Buddhas

## SOUTH-EAST ASIA

Bali & Lombok • Bangkok • Burmese phrasebook • Cambodia • Ho Chi Minh City • Indonesia • Indonesian phrasebook • Indonesian audio pack • Indonesia's Eastern Islands • Jakarta • Java • Laos • Lao phrasebook • Laos travel atlas • Malay phrasebook • Malaysia, Singapore & Brunei • Myanmar (Burma) • Philippines • Pilipino phrasebook • Singapore • South-East Asia on a shoestring • South-East Asia phrasebook • South-West China • Thailand • Thailand's Islands & Beaches • Thailand travel atlas • Thai phrasebook • Thai audio pack • Thai Hill Tribes phrasebook • Vietnam • Vietnamese phrasebook • Vietnam travel atlas

## AUSTRALIA & THE PACIFIC

Australia • Australian phrasebook • Bushwalking in Australia • Bushwalking in Papua New Guinea • Fiji • Fijian phrasebook • Islands of Australia's Great Barrier Reef • Melbourne • Micronesia • New Caledonia • New South Wales • New Zealand • Northern Territory • Outback Australia • Papua New Guinea • Papua New Guinea phrasebook • Queensland • Rarotonga & the Cook Islands • Samoa • Solomon Islands • South Australia • Sydney • Tahiti & French Polynesia • Tasmania • Tonga • Tramping in New Zealand • Vanuatu • Victoria • Western Australia
*Travel Literature:* Islands in the Clouds • Sean & David's Long Drive

## ANTARCTICA

Antarctica

# THE LONELY PLANET STORY

Lonely Planet published its first book in 1973 in response to the numerous 'How did you do it?' questions Maureen and Tony Wheeler were asked after driving, busing, hitching, sailing and railing their way from England to Australia.

Written at a kitchen table and hand collated, trimmed and stapled, *Across Asia on the Cheap* became an instant local bestseller, inspiring thoughts of another book.

Eighteen months in South-East Asia resulted in their second guide, *South-East Asia on a shoestring*, which they put together in a backstreet Chinese hotel in Singapore in 1975. The 'yellow bible', as it quickly became known to backpackers around the world, soon became *the* guide to the region. It has sold well over half a million copies and is now in its 9th edition, still retaining its familiar yellow cover.

Today there are over 350 titles, including travel guides, walking guides, language kits & phrasebooks, travel atlases and travel literature. The company is the largest independent travel publisher in the world. Although Lonely Planet initially specialised in guides to Asia, today there are few corners of the globe that have not been covered.

The emphasis continues to be on travel for independent travellers. Tony and Maureen still travel for several months of each year and play an active part in the writing, updating and quality control of Lonely Planet's guides.

They have been joined by over 80 authors and 200 staff at our offices in Melbourne (Australia), Oakland (USA), London (UK) and Paris (France). Travellers themselves also make a valuable contribution to the guides through the feedback we receive in thousands of letters each year and on our web site.

The people at Lonely Planet strongly believe that travellers can make a positive contribution to the countries they visit, both through their appreciation of the countries' culture, wildlife and natural features, and through the money they spend. In addition, the company makes a direct contribution to the countries and regions it covers. Since 1986 a percentage of the income from each book has been donated to ventures such as famine relief in Africa; aid projects in India; agricultural projects in Central America; Greenpeace's efforts to halt French nuclear testing in the Pacific; and Amnesty International.

*'I hope we send people out with the right attitude about travel. You realise when you travel that there are so many different perspectives about the world, so we hope these books will make people more interested in what they see. Guidebooks can't really guide people. All you can do is point them in the right direction.'*

– Tony Wheeler

## lonely planet

## LONELY PLANET PUBLICATIONS

**Australia**
PO Box 617, Hawthorn 3122, Victoria
tel: (03) 9819 1877  fax: (03) 9819 6459
e-mail: talk2us@lonelyplanet.com.au

**USA**
150 Linden St
Oakland, CA 94607
tel: (510) 893 8555 TOLL FREE: 800 275-8555
fax: (510) 893 8572
e-mail: info@lonelyplanet.com

**UK**
10a Spring Place,
London NW5 3BH
tel: (0171) 428 4800  fax: (0171) 428 4828
e-mail: go@lonelyplanet.co.uk

**France:**
1 rue du Dahomey, 75011 Paris
tel: 01 55 25 33 00  fax: 01 55 25 33 01
e-mail: bip@lonelyplanet.fr

**World Wide Web: http://www.lonelyplanet.com**
**or AOL keyword: lp**